COMPUTER SUPPORT FOR COLLABORATIVE LEARNING: FOUNDATIONS FOR A CSCL COMMUNITY

Proceedings of CSCL 2002
Boulder, Colorado, USA
January 7 – 11, 2002

edited by Gerry Stahl

Routledge
Taylor & Francis Group
LONDON AND NEW YORK

First published 2002 by Lawrence Erlbaum Associates, Inc.

Published 2019 by Routledge
2 Park Square, Milton Park, Abingdon, Oxon OX14 4RN
52 Vanderbilt Avenue, New York, NY 10017

Routledge is an imprint of the Taylor & Francis Group, an informa business

ISBN 13: 978-0-8058-4443-6 (pbk)

INTRODUCTION: FOUNDATIONS FOR A CSCL COMMUNITY

A NEW ERA OF LEARNING

Learning takes place in communities, facilitated by artifacts, which in turn sustain the communities that generate them. A series of CSCL conferences – archived in proceedings artifacts like this one – have been foundational events for a growing CSCL community that has an important role to play in a rapidly, painfully self-transforming global culture.

The CSCL community addresses complex and urgent social issues associated with learning in the information era. Despite its healthy growth curve, this research community is still searching for its foundations; to date, there is little consensus on theory, pedagogy, technology or methodology – even less in the broader world of learning stakeholders.

Learning has become a central force of production. Traditional theories and institutions that rose to meet the needs of reproducing knowledge in an industrial world have become fetters on progress: The focus on individual learners obscures the group as the locus of knowledge building and ignores the global interdependence of learning. Fixation on facts distorts the nature of problem-solving inquiry. Modes of thought deriving from the age of rationality and machinery fail to grasp the subtlety of interaction in hyper-networked environments.

CSCL instinctively aims beyond yesterday's concepts. *Collaborative Learning* does not just mean that individual learning is enhanced by participation in small groups; it means that it is the groups themselves that learn. Knowledge is a product of the collaboration process: it arises through interaction of different perspectives, heats up in the cauldron of public discourse, is gradually refined through negotiation, and is codified and preserved in cultural or scientific artifacts. Knowledge is not static and other-worldly: it lives, situated – both locally and historically – in groups, teams, organizations, tribes, social networks and cultural flash points.

Computer Support does not just mean automating the delivery and testing of facts; it means supporting forms of collaboration and knowledge building that could not otherwise take place without networked communication media and software tools for developing group understandings. Computers can manage the complexity of many-to-many discussions, allowing multiple perspectives to interact without hierarchical structuring. They can overcome the limitations of human short-term memories and of paper-based aides to generating or sharing drafts of documents. CSCL should enable more powerful group cognition, which can synthesize complex interactions of ideas at different scales of collaboration, from small classroom project teams to global open source efforts.

A NEW PARADIGM OF LEARNING RESEARCH

The keynote talks for CSCL 2002 propose a new paradigm for a distinctive form of educational research. Timothy Koschmann focuses on the micro-level practices that need to be studied, while Yrjö Engeström considers the larger social contexts in which groups interact with other groups to produce learning. Koschmann offers this definition for the CSCL domain:

> CSCL is a field of study centrally concerned with meaning and the practices of meaning-making in the context of joint activity, and the ways in which these practices are mediated through designed artifacts.

It is clear that "meaning and the practices of meaning-making" are here intended as public, observable, socially shared phenomena. This has foundational implications for CSCL research. It does not entail a rejection of quantitative studies of learning outcomes under controlled conditions. However, while these provide important information and ensure empirical grounding, they can in principle never provide the complete story. CSCL is a human science, concerned with its subjects' own interpretations of their ideas and behaviors. Therefore, CSCL also requires qualitative studies of learning practices – such as thick descriptions that incorporate and explore the understanding of the participants in collaborative learning. As public phenomena, the meanings (learning) generated in collaboration processes can be studied directly, particularly with the help of computer logs and digitized video recordings, rather than just being inferred from post-tests.

As already suggested, the description of CSCL as concerning "the practices of meaning-making in the context of joint activity" does not so much entail looking at *individuals'* practices in social settings, as it focuses on the essentially *social* practices of joint meaning-making. Even when conducted by an individual in isolation, meaning-making is a social act, based on culturally defined linguistic artifacts and oriented toward a potential public audience. An adequate theoretical foundation for CSCL must explain how individual practices are social without forgetting that the social is grounded in individual activities; concepts of *praxis*, *activity*, *social reproduction*, *structuration* and *enactment* begin to address this dialectic.

Koschmann's definition of CSCL includes the study of "the ways in which these [meaning-making] practices are mediated through designed artifacts." He refers here to CSCL technology as mediational artifacts, as software objects designed to support collaborative learning. But this formulation can be taken more generally as raising the question of how meaning-making is mediated by artifacts. This is an extraordinarily broad issue, since all human activity is meaning-making and everything in our physical, intellectual and cultural world can be considered an artifact: physical tools, linguistic symbols, cultural entities, cognitive mechanisms, social rules, . . . It is striking that such a fundamental issue has been so little explored. How do different classes of artifact mediate the creation, sharing, teaching and preserving of meaning? A clearer understanding of the functioning of non-digital artifacts might help us understand how to design software to more effectively foster and convey collaborative meaning-making.

A NEW CSCL COMMUNITY

The new era of learning and the new research paradigm call for a community that can integrate results from philosophy, social theory, ethnography, experimentation and pedagogy. More than this, it must be able to carry out research that integrates the foundations of these disciplines into a coherent and productive field of inquiry. As its conceptual framework and software products mature, the CSCL community must broaden to incorporate educational practitioners, teachers, trainers, lifelong learners and students around the world.

The CSCL 2002 conference aims to incrementally build the foundations for such a CSCL community. The call for papers elicited over 300 submissions, of impressive quality and reflective of an energetic international community. Many leaders of this community participated on the Program Committee, joined by even more who served as additional reviewers in an exemplary peer-review process.

The long papers in this Proceedings will be presented in thematic panels at the conference. The papers represented here by abstracts will be presented during interactive poster sessions. All of these papers passed an extremely competitive peer review, which unfortunately had to reject many excellent submissions due to space and time constraints.

In addition to the papers, the conference will include keynote discussions (featuring Timothy Koschmann, Yrjö Engeström and a few outstanding papers on foundational themes), an extensive program of interactive events (organized by Daniel Suthers), workshops (organized by Tamara Sumner and Paul Mulholland), tutorials (organized by Anders Mørch) and a doctoral consortium (organized by Michael Eisenberg and Amy Bruckman). An active Steering Committee (chaired by Gerhard Fischer) handled the many other aspects of preparing the conference. My colleagues at Fraunhofer-FIT, Germany, (formerly GMD-FIT) have been very supportive of my work on the conference. Carla Valle compiled the papers in these Proceedings.

Financial support for CSCL 2002 came from CSCL 1999 (Stanford and SRI), Euro-CSCL 2001 (Maastricht), the National Science Foundation, the Coleman Family Fund, Microsoft, Apple and IBM. The conference is hosted by the Center for LifeLong Learning and Design, the Institute of Cognitive Science, the Department of Computer Science and the Engineering School of the University of Colorado at Boulder.

I believe that this collaborative artifact – the conference *pre*ceedings – reflects the current state of CSCL research, particularly in North America and Western Europe. It documents an extremely heterogeneous, productive phase of inquiry with broad social consequences. I hope that the conference will contribute to the foundations of a vibrant CSCL community and that it will stimulate you as a member of that community.

Gerry Stahl

CSCL 2002 Program Chair

TABLE OF CONTENTS

PROGRAM COMMITTEE

Cecilia Baranauskas	Unicamp, SP, Brazil
Lecia Barker	University of Colorado
Philip Bell	University of Washington
John Bransford	Vanderbilt University
Alain Breuleux	McGill University
Amy Bruckman	Georgia Inst. of Technology
Tom Calvert	Simon Fraser U., Canada
Tak-Wai Chan	National Central U., Taiwan
Andy Cockburn	U. Canterbury, New Zealand
Alan Collins	Northwestern University
Bob Craig	University of Colorado
Chris di Giano	SRI, Inc.
Pierre Dillenbourg	University of Geneva
Tom Duffy	University of Indiana
Mike Eisenberg	University of Colorado
Skip Ellis	University of Colorado
Yrjö Engeström	UCSD & Helsinki
Barry Fischman	Michigan University
Geri Gay	Cornell University
Ricki Goldman-Segall	New Jersey Inst. of Tech.
Louis Gomez	Northwestern University
Mark Guzdial	Georgia Inst. of Technology
Jorg Haake	Fraunhofer—IPSI, Germany
Kai Hakkarainen	University of Helsinki
Thomas Herrmann	University of Dortmund
Randy Hinrichs	Microsoft
Christopher Hoadley	SRI, Inc. & Stanford
Ulrich Hoppe	University of Duisburg
Michele Jackson	University of Colorado
Tim Koschmann	U. of Southern Illinois
Kari Kuutti	Ohlu University, Finland
Curtis LeBaron	Brigham Young University
Erno Lehtinen	U. of Turku, Finland
Mike Lightner	University of Colorado
Jose Rafael Lopez Islas	Monterrey Tech., Mexico
Mary Marlino	UCAR, Boulder
Bob McLean	U. of Toronto
Marcelo Milrad	Vaxyo U., Sweden
Michele Minnis	University of New Mexico
Naomi Miyake	Chukyo U., Japan
Anders Mørch	University of Oslo
Paul Mulholland	Open University, UK
Som Naidu	University of Melbourne
Mitch Nathan	University of Colorado
Hiroaki Ogata	U. of Tokushima, Japan
Leysia Palen	University of Colorado
Roy Pea	SRI, Inc.
Wolfgang Prinz	Fraunhofer—FIT, Germany
Margaret Riel	U. of C., Irvine
Jeremy Roschelle	SRI, Inc.
Mark Schlager	SRI, Inc.
Jim Slotta	U. of C., Berkeley
Gerry Stahl	Fraunhofer—FIT, Germany
Reed Stevens	University of Washington
Masanori Sugimoto	University of Tokyo
Tammy Sumner	University of Colorado
Dan Suthers	University of Hawaii
JosieTaylor	Open University, UK
Loren Terveen	AT&T
Earl Woodruff	University of Toronto
Volker Wulf	Fraunhofer—FIT, Germany

ADDITIONAL REVIEWERS

Junghyun An	U. Ill., Urbana-Champaign
Ken Anderson	Intel
Hans Christian Arnseth	University of Oslo
Nelson Baloian	Universida de Chile
Wolf-Gideon Bleek	University of Hamburg
Britte Cheng	UC Berkeley
Michael Chorost	SRI, Inc.
María de los Angeles Constantino-González	ITESM-Campus Laguna
Hal Eden	University of Colorado
Markus Eisenhauer	Fraunhofer—FIT
Jason Ellis	Georgia Institute of Tech
Ola Erstad	University of Oslo
Kurt Fendt	MIT
Alejandro Fernández	Fraunhofer—IPSI
Cathy Fett	UC Irvine
Mercedes Fisher	UC Irvine
Annita Fjuk	Telenor, Norway
Carl Frederiksen	McGill University
Hugo Fuks	PUC-Rio, Brazil
Judi Fusco	SRI, Inc.
Kathy Garvin-Doxas	University of Colorado
Bernie Gifford	UC Berkeley
Andy Gorman	University of Colorado
Judith Green	UC Santa Barbara
Irene Greif	Lotus
Mark Gross	University of Washington
Frode Guribye	University of Bergen
Roger Hadgraft	Monash U., Australia
Victoria Hand	Stanford University
Bruce Havlock	University of Washington
Elke Hinrichs	Fraunhofer—FIT
Cindy Hmelo-Silver	Rutgers University
Shirley Holst	Fraunhofer—IPSI
Jim Hudson	Georgia Institute of Tech
Mitsuru Ikeda	Osaka University
Akiko Inaba	Osaka University
Michael Janneck	University of Hamburg
Toshinobu Kasai	Okayama University
Sandra Katz	University of Pittsburgh
Michelle Kazmer	U. Ill., Urbana-Champaign
Constance Kim	EDC Center for Children
Ralf Klamma	RWTH Aachen
Melissa Koch	SRI, Inc.
Elizabeth Lenell	University of Colorado
Bern Lindstrom	Goteborg University
Sten Ludvigsen	University of Oslo
Peter Mambrey	Fraunhofer—FIT
Martin Mühlenbrock	U. of Duisburg, Germany
Hans-Rüdiger Pfister	Knowledge Media, Germany
Volkmar Pipek	U. of Bonn, Germany
Rolf Plötzner	Knowledge Media, Germany
Marjaana Rahikainen	University of Helsinki
Jason Ravitz	SRI, Inc.
David Redmiles	UC Irvine
Jochen Rick	Georgia Institute of Tech
Margaret Riel	UC Irvine
Roger Saljo	Goteborg University
Gerardo Ayala San Martin	U. de las Ameicas Puebla
Flavia Santoro	Fed. U. of Rio de Janeiro
Alena Sanusi	University of Colorado
Rebecca Scheckler	Indiana University
Ulrik Schroeder	Ludwigsburg University
Amy Soller	University of Pittsburgh
Elsebeth Sorensen	Aalborg University
Marcus Specht	Fraunhofer—FIT
Mia Stern	Lotus Corporation
Denise Stockley	Queen's University
Daniel Tietze	Fraunhofer—IPSI
Jennifer Turns	University of Washington
Michael Twidale	U. Ill. Urbana-Champaign
Phil Vahey	SRI, Inc.
Carla Valle	Fraunhofer—FIT
Martin Wessner	Fraunhofer—IPSI
Matthias Will	Deutsche Telekom
Mike Williams	consultant
Tim Wright	University of Canterbury
Yunwen Ye	University of Colorado

CONFERENCE STEERING COMMITTEE

Conference Chair	Gerhard Fischer	University of Colorado
Program Chair	Gerry Stahl	Fraunhofer—FIT
Consultant	Tim Koschmann	University of Southern Illinois
Interactive Events	Dan Suthers	University of Hawaii
Workshops	Tammy Sumner	University of Colorado
	Paul Mulholland	Open University
Tutorials	Anders Mørch	University of Oslo
Doctoral Consortium	Mike Eisenberg	University of Colorado
	Amy Bruckman	Georgia Institute of Technology
Teacher Participation	Mary Lamon	University of Toronto
	Linda Polin	Pepperdine University
Community Memory	Bruce Henderson	University of Colorado
	Curtis LeBaron	Brigham Young University
	Reed Stevens	University of Washington
Student Community	Leysia Palen	University of Colorado
	Rogerio de Paula	University of Colorado
	Gabe Johnson	University of Colorado
Student Paper	Mark Dubin	University of Colorado
International Relations	Masanori Sugimoto	University of Tokyo
	Som Naidu	University of Melbourne
	Kai Hakkarainen	University of Helsinki
General Manager	Donna Caccamise	University of Colorado
Publicity	Chris diGiano	SRI, Inc.
	Marilyn Salzman	Genomica
Industry Relations	Shana Lourie	University of Colorado
Technology	Andy Gorman	University of Colorado
Fund Raising	Hal Eden	University of Colorado

KEYNOTE DISCUSSIONS

Both keynote speakers have played remarkable roles in the establishment of theoretical foundations for CSCL and in the building of a CSCL community.

Timothy Koschmann has been centrally involved in producing the defining books and conferences of our field. His Introduction to the first CSCL book (*CSCL: Theory and Practice of an Emerging Paradigm*, 1996) attempted to define a distinctive paradigm for this field – in his keynote here he continues to redefine that paradigm. He has been intimately involved in the organizing of each of the CSCL conferences: 1995 in Bloomington, 1997 in Toronto, 1999 in Stanford, 2001 in Maastricht, 2002 in Boulder, and no doubt 2003 in Bergen as well. With academic training in philosophy and computer science and research experience studying the Southern Illinois Medical School's PBL curriculum, he has been well situated to investigate foundational issues in the interdisciplinary domain of CSCL. At CSCL 2002, he is bringing out a new edited volume that is likely to be as influential as his original collection: *CSCL 2: Carrying Forward the Conversation.*

Yrjö Engeström has had an impact in Europe, particularly in the Nordic region, that is hard to over-estimate. As a result, CSCL is extraordinarily active there, where it has a distinctive flavor. Internationally, Engeström – who spends half his year at UC San Diego and half at his large research lab in Helsinki – is widely acknowledged as the leading contemporary exponent of Activity Theory, a major basis for the theoretical foundations of CSCL. Building on the radical departure of Vygotsky and his followers, Engeström has proposed a notion of "expansive learning" that locates learning in its broader social context.

As the Proceedings go to press, Engeström is working on a new statement (unfortunately not yet ready for publication) about expansive learning in the commercial world, a paradigm of learning that not only goes beyond the individual psychological model of learning but even beyond the model of a single homogeneous learning community to include interactions among communities. It thus provides a vital complement to Koschmann's keynote that centers on the micro-analysis of meaning-making.

The two talks raise methodological issues of qualitative research methods that move away from traditional experimental design and statistical analysis, and explore discourse analytic and ethnographic approaches. They set the stage for a conference that can begin to articulate an important paradigm shift in the CSCL research community -- a shift that differentiates this work from traditional educational mainstream research and emphasizes a socio-cultural perspective.

Of course, not everyone at the conference will agree with the proposed new paradigms or accept their methodological implications. That's Ok. Controversy is a precondition for scientific progress. Discussion of the keynote presentations will be initiated by critical remarks from the Conference and Program Chairs of CSCL '99 and Euro-CSCL.

In place of a third keynote talk, several plenary speakers have been selected from the CSCL community through the peer review process. These are authors of papers that received top review ratings and that address foundational issues in innovative ways:

- "Epistemological Foundations for CSCL" reviews three models of knowledge-building communities that have been particularly influential in the CSCL research community. This paper provides a thoughtful reflection on past sources of thinking about foundations for our work.
- "Instructional Artifacts" adopts a qualitative research approach to exploring the nature of artifacts. It looks at the discourse, work practices and shared artifacts within an empirical setting. It draws out implications for broadening and sharpening the concept of artifact.
- "Social Information Sharing in a CSCL Community" takes a quantitative, statistical approach to understanding the role of social networks in computer-mediated communication. It thereby provides a glimpse into how the social structure of groups affects the learning that takes place by the group, and simultaneously demonstrates one way of rigorously determining social network structure.
- "A Walk on the WILD Side" looks to the future of CSCL as affected by changing hardware technologies. It ponders how collaborative learning may change with the advent of smaller, cheaper, more flexible, more specialized computational devices. In particular, the paper proposes ways in which these practical changes will affect the theoretical foundations of CSCL.

Dewey's Contribution to the Foundations of CSCL Research

Timothy Koschmann

Southern Illinois University School of Medicine

tkoschmann@siumed.edu

ABSTRACT

In this paper, I review two studies (Roschelle, 1996; Baker, Hansen, Joiner, & Traum, 1999) which I believe to represent paradigmatic examples of CSCL research. I offer a critique of these studies based on the theory of inquiry developed by the American pragmatist philosopher John Dewey. Inquiry, for Dewey, represented an exceedingly broad category of activity of which joint problem solving is a special case. I conclude by proposing a description of what I think research in CSCL is, or at least should be, about. This description can be used to distinguish what is done in this field from traditional research in education on learning outcomes, research based on classical information processing theory, and conventional research on social interaction.

Keywords

Deweyan inquiry, conceptual change, common ground, social interaction, theories of meaning

INTRODUCTION

When asked to prepare this keynote presentation, I was informed that the chosen theme for this conference would be "Foundations of the CSCL Community." My charge, therefore, would be to write something that spoke to where we came from as a research community and where we might be going. After deliberating on this matter for some weeks, I have decided to proceed in the following fashion.

First, I have selected two examples of what I, at least, consider to be paradigmatic CSCL research. I will briefly describe each of these studies and then provide a critique, not of the research *per se*, but rather of the theoretical framings within which the research was conducted. I will base my critique on a reading (mine) of certain works by the American pragmatist philosopher and educator, John Dewey. I will conclude by offering a description of what I believe to be the distinguishing features of research in CSCL.

TWO STUDIES OF LEARNING IN COLLABORATIVE SETTINGS

The first paradigmatic example of CSCL research can be found in a chapter written by Jeremy Roschelle (1996). It describes a longitudinal case study of two high school students (Carol and Dana) and their use of a program that graphically simulates the trajectories of Newtonian particles. In analyzing the interaction of these two students, Roschelle drew on two quite different research traditions. On the one hand, he employed ideas from the literature on conceptual change in cognitive science. He defined conceptual change as "learning to register deep features of situations" and "restructuring systems of physical metaphors" (p. 210). At the same time, he drew on the literature of Conversation Analysis which, he argued, has established that meaning is "constructed, monitored, and repaired" through "conventional structures of face-to-face interaction" (p. 210).

Blending these two traditions together, Roschelle conjectured that "conversational interaction provides a means for students to construct increasingly sophisticated approximations to scientific concepts collaboratively, through gradual refinement of ambiguous, figurative, partial meanings" (p. 210). This hypothesized process, he reasoned, has four features: "(a) the construction of a deep-featured situation at an intermediate level of abstraction from the literal features of the world, (b) the interplay of metaphors in relation to each other and to the constructed situation, (c) an iterative cycle of displaying, confirming, and repairing situated actions, and (d) the applications of progressively higher standards of evidence for convergence" (p. 211). How convergent conceptual change is possible using "only figurative, ambiguous, and imprecise language and physical interactions" (p. 212) is the puzzle that motivated his study.

Roschelle's data consisted of videotapes of the two students working in front of a computer monitor over two one-hour sessions in which the students worked their way through a series of pre-defined "challenges." He also recorded interviews with the participants after the sessions. His analysis focused on five brief exchanges from the computer sessions. For each exchange he describes the "conversational action" capturing not only the lexical components, but also timing, prosodic features, and affiliated gestures; the "conceptual change" evidenced in the exchange; and, finally, the displayed "shared knowledge."

The second study that I will discuss can be found in a chapter authored by Baker, Hansen, Joiner, and Traum (1999) and published in a collection edited by Dillenbourg (1999). Unlike Roschelle's study, this study involved pairs of students communicating through a program that structured their interactions. Rather than communicating face-to-face, they were required to perform a shared task while communicating through a designed interface. The interface provided a graphics tool kit that allowed the students to construct graphs collaboratively. They could also send messages to each other. One group of subjects was provided with a chat-like facility; the other group was given a selection of buttons that could be used to generate messages of the type typically needed to complete the task. The task involved jointly producing a graph to represent energy transfer in a simple electric circuit.

Like Roschelle, Baker et al. sought to bridge two different research traditions in framing their analysis. From the tradition of Cultural-Historical Activity Theory (CHAT), they derived the notion of *learning as appropriation*. Appropriation, as they describe it, involves learners' use of culturally-provided tools, both "material tools, such as pens and computers, and semiotic tools, such as sign-systems" (p. 31). They specify, "Appropriation ... takes sign-mediated assistance from other members of the culture, who scaffold children's first attempts with the cultural object in such a way that they gradually move from being able to use tools under guidance to being able to use them on their own, and in their own way" (pp. 31-32). The second theoretical influence for their analysis came from work in psycholinguistics on common ground and grounding. Baker et al. wrote:

> A *common ground* of mutual understanding, knowledge, beliefs, assumptions, pre-suppositions, and so on, has been claimed to be necessary for many aspects of communication and collaboration. *Grounding* is the process by which agents augment and maintain such a common ground. (p. 33)

The purpose of their study was to "understand how these processes—grounding and appropriation—that operate on quite different timescales, lead to collaborative learning" (p. 32).

Later in the chapter, Baker et al. make a distinction between *pragmatic* and *semantic* grounding. They explained:

> Pragmatic-level grounding is part of *learning to collaborate*: one learns to understand generally what the other will be trying to tell us. Semantic-level grounding ... relates to attaining mutual understanding of what is meant by certain terms and expressions; it thus relates more closely to learning in a specific knowledge domain by means of interpersonal interaction. (pp. 45-46)

Based on this distinction, the authors offer the following conjecture: "collaborative learning will be associated with a gradual transition from the use of language as a medium for grounding communication (pragmatic) to grounding on the level of the medium itself (semantic), leading to appropriation of the medium" (p. 46). The authors provide two transcripts, one involving students using the chat interface and another involving students using the structured interface. Both transcripts are rather sparse, however, and the analysis fails to address the authors' conjecture with regard to transitions from pragmatic to semantic grounding and appropriations of the medium.

The Roschelle and Baker et al. chapters have certain similarities. Both display a concern with the practices of learning rather than focusing on learning outcomes, as is more typically the case in educational research. There is also a common theme of intersubjectivity that runs through both studies—the Baker et al. chapter is explicitly about grounding procedures, while the Roschelle chapter involves assessing "evidence for convergence" (p. 211). They are useful examples for discussion here because each has connections to currently active areas of research in CSCL. The topic of common ground, for example, has received considerable attention in recent publications (Arnseth, Ludvigsen, Wasson, & Mørch, 2001; Dillenbourg & Traum, 1999; Mäkitalo, Salo, Häkkinen, & Järvelä, 2001). In the ways that Roschelle's subjects formulate theories and test predictions, his study has connections to ongoing research on scientific argumentation (Bell, 2002; Felton & Kuhn, 2002). Similarly, the use of structured conversation tools in the Baker et al. study has connections to a time-honored issue in CSCL research, namely that of procedural facilitation (see Koschmann, 2002). It is an issue that continues to have significance for current research (cf., Bell, 2002; Guzdial & Kehoe, 1998; Suthers, Toth, & Weiner, 1997). Finally, because the Baker et al. study involves communication through a designed interface, it has relevance to recent discussions of reflexive awareness in computer- and video-mediated environments (Kato et al., 2002; Smith, 2002). As a result, they are both important papers worthy of our careful scrutiny. I have certain misgivings, however, about how both papers were framed theoretically.

Roschelle's study defines learning as cognitive change.[1] By positing the existence of conceptual structures and treating learning as a process of changing these representations, an implicit form of dualism creeps into his analysis. For example, Roschelle observed at one point in his analysis, "Carol's response to Dana (#2) therefore marks the first appearance of *a*

---

[1] Before launching into a critique of Roschelle's chapter, it is perhaps worth noting that the chapter was a reprint of an article that was previously published in 1992 (Roschelle, 1992a) which in turn was based on his dissertation work completed in 1991 (Roschelle, 1991). To fully appreciate the novelty of this piece of work, therefore, it is important to evaluate it as a historically-situated contribution.

new conceptual structure" (p. 219, italics added). In documenting a subsequent episode he added, "This wrong proposal is an indication that Carol's conceptual structure was not yet complete" (p. 229). But, where do these structures reside and how are we to know them? Furthermore, through references to "*the* scientific meaning of acceleration" (p. 212, italics added) and to the students' need to "construct increasingly sophisticated approximations to scientific concepts" (p. 210) we are left with the impression that there is one and only one canonical representation shared by the scientifically literate. An analysis of conceptual change, therefore, not only assumes that everyone possesses a conceptual structure but also that this representation is either right or wrong (i.e., "scientific" or misconceived). The problem this poses for the analyst, however, is that the subjects' conceptual structures are mental abstractions, not available to inspection. To his credit, Roschelle never claims to have privileged knowledge of Dana and Carol's conceptual structures, but he does advance theories about them that he then attempts to support empirically. My concern, therefore, is not with the analysis itself, which I find exemplary, but rather with how the analysis was framed theoretically.

When we turn to the Baker et al. chapter, a different set of problems arise. The goal of this study was to show how grounding leads to appropriation. But to do so, we need an adequate model of how grounding works in the first place. Traditional models of "reference repair" (e.g., Clark & Marshall, 1981) provide a less than satisfactory account of how people negotiate mutual understanding in concrete settings (cf., Koschmann, Goodwin, LeBaron, & Feltovich, 2001). Perhaps the problem lies with the underlying notion of common ground itself, which presupposes more than we can ever hope to demonstrate empirically.

I will argue in the section that follows that the weaknesses I have identified in these theoretical framings could be overcome by employing a different kind of framework. The framework I have in mind is derived from the writings of the American pragmatist philosopher and educator John Dewey. I will attempt to show that Dewey, in his description of the processes of inquiry, laid the groundwork for a distinctive vision of learning and human problem solving.

DEWEY'S THEORY OF INQUIRY

When one speaks of Dewey's contributions, it is important to note which Dewey we are drawing upon. Dewey was a prolific author and wrote for a variety of audiences. In education, we tend to focus on that middle period in his career when he was most directly involved in education and educational research. Regrettably, less interest has been taken in his later writings after he left the University of Chicago and directed his attention more exclusively to philosophical questions.

In his later writing, Dewey proposed a novel form of logic based on what he described as the "theory of inquiry" (Burke, 1994; Dewey, 1938/1991; Hickman, 1998).[2] Though Dewey began to grapple with the problems of logical theory in some of his earliest work, his biggest contributions appeared in a book entitled *Logic: The Theory of Inquiry*, published late in his career. Dewey (1938/1991) defined inquiry as follows: "*Inquiry is the controlled or directed transformation of an indeterminate situation into one that is so determinate in its constituent distinctions and relations as to convert the elements of the original situation into a unified whole*" (p. 108). When Dewey speaks of an "indeterminate situation" he uses the term *situation* in a technical sense. He wrote:

> What is designated by the word 'situation' is *not* a single object or event or set of objects and events. For we never experience nor form judgments about objects or events in isolation, but only in connection with a contextual whole. The latter is what is called a 'situation'. (p. 72)

A situation is not just a context for problem solving, however, but an "indeterminate" or disrupted setting for action. Burke (1994) wrote, "Situations, occurring in the ongoing activities of some given organism/environment system, are instances or episodes (or 'fields') of disequilibrium, instability, imbalance, disintegration, disturbance, dysfunction, breakdown, etc." (p. 22). When the indeterminate situation is transformed through the processes of inquiry "into a unified whole" the aspects of the original situation that were initially experienced as problematic, what Dewey sometimes refers to as the "subject-matter" of inquiry, are reabsorbed into the background of experience. Inquiry, for Dewey, represented an exceedingly broad category of activity, ranging from the struggles of a one-celled organism to find sustenance to the most sophisticated forms of scientific research. The forms of joint problem solving that we study in CSCL are a species or special case of Deweyan inquiry.

Dewey was critical of (and struggled to break free of) notions of knowledge as a substantive. These notions remain prevalent today and underlie the commonly accepted metaphors of learning as acquisition and instruction as a process of delivery or inscription. Dewey (1938/1991) wrote, "that which satisfactorily terminates inquiry is, by definition, knowledge; it is knowledge because it *is* the appropriate close of inquiry" (p. 15). "But," Dewey went on, "[that] statement may be supposed, and has been supposed, to enunciate something significant instead of a tautology" (p. 15). In his

---

[2] I would like to acknowledge Jeremy Roschelle's role in bringing to my attention the importance of Dewey's theory of inquiry to research on collaboration and learning (cf., Roschelle, 1992b).

discussions on logic, Dewey preferred the use of the term "warranted assertion" (p. 16) in place of 'knowledge.' In later writing (Dewey & Bentley, 1949/1991), Dewey abandoned the use of the term entirely in favor of "knowings and knowns" (p. 47). As described by Burke (1994), knowings are instances of inquiry, i.e. "specific instances of the application of one's dispositions, aptitudes, and habits to solving given problems" (p. 256). Dewey (1939/1991, as quoted by Burke) wrote, "the denotative reference of 'mind' and 'intelligence' is to funding of meanings and significances, a funding which is both a product of past inquiries or knowings and the means of enriching and controlling the subject-matters of subsequent experiences" (pp. 520-521).

One might submit that what we discuss as 'learning' is also closely related to this "funding of meaning and significances," since it is through its ability to enrich and control future inquiry that learning derives it's benefit. This view of learning provides the basis for the critique that is being developed here both of learning as conceptual change and of common ground as a repository of shared knowledge.

In some places Roschelle's discussion of conceptual change might seem to be consistent with a Deweyan model of inquiry. He proposed, "the process of conversational interaction affords opportunities for co-participants to negotiate the meanings of metaphors-in-situation. In a case of scientific conceptual change, these meanings are in the relationship between deep-featured situations and theory-constitutive metaphors" (p. 216). This would seem to resonate with Dewey's (1938/1991) assertion that:

> [T]he meanings that a conventional symbol has is not itself conventional. For the meaning is established by agreements of different persons in existensial activities having reference to existensial consequences. ... For agreements and disagreements are determined by the consequences of conjoint activities. (p. 53)

Dewey espoused a constitutive rather than a denotative theory of meaning. When Roschelle, in his analysis, speaks of co-participants negotiating meanings, he operates with a theory of meaning consistent with Dewey's. When Roschelle lapses into discussions of "conceptual structures," however, he is vulnerable to Dewey's critique of knowledge treated as a substantive. For Dewey there could be no fixed conceptual structure corresponding to 'acceleration' or 'velocity.' The meaning of these constructs must be constantly created anew in practical activity.

The discussion of grounding in the Baker et al. chapter, like Roschelle's discussion of negotiated meaning, would also seem to parallel Dewey's theory of learning as constitutive. Here as well, however, the framing of the analysis takes a direction that may be at odds with Dewey's theories of inquiry and experience. To speak of mutual knowledge and common ground is to suggest that two or more knowers are having the same experience. But, as we know, my experience of a situation can never in any literal sense be the same as yours. Yet, in many circumstances we must go on, trusting that our understandings are sufficiently in alignment for joint activity to proceed. When this assumption becomes problematic, some negotiation in meaning is called for. One might model this negotiation as reference repair as Clark and Marshall (1981) did, and such a model seems to be assumed when we speak of processes of grounding. Such a model assumes that meaning is fixed and, in a simple sense, denotative. Looking at meaning negotiation from the perspective of Deweyan inquiry, on the other hand, leads to the development of a very different sort of model. Diagnosing discrepancies in understanding, by this view, does not require the introduction of special mechanisms, such as grounding or reference repair. Instead, meaning construction is simply treated as a recursive aspect of the process of inquiry itself. In such a model, meaning is never fixed and settled but is instead continuously open to re-negotiation and re-specification. This does not in itself preclude the construction of computational models of meaning negotiation, as discussed in the Baker et al. chapter, but would likely require a very different form of underlying logic.[3]

TOWARD A SCIENCE OF MEANING-MAKING PRACTICE

Despite the critical analysis presented in the previous section, I consider both the Roschelle and Baker et al. chapters to be paradigmatic examples of CSCL research in the Kuhnian sense (cf., Koschmann, 2001a). That is to say, I think they serve as examples of what makes CSCL research distinctively different from other forms of research currently practiced in instructional technology. To make explicit in what ways these studies differ from other forms of research, I would like to propose a definition of what I, at least, believe to constitute CSCL research. I would offer the following definition: *CSCL is a field of study centrally concerned with meaning and the practices of meaning-making in the context of joint activity and the ways in which these practices are mediated through designed artifacts.* There are several implications that follow from this.

For example, the assertion that we are "centrally concerned with meaning and the practices of meaning-making" sharply distinguishes what we do from more traditional research in education. To study meaning and meaning-making practices in

[3] See Burke's (1994) discussion of some of the implications of Dewey's logic in the concluding chapter of his book.

the way suggested by Dewey will require documentation of how learners *do* learning (to borrow a phrase from Jordan and Henderson, 1985). This is quite different from researching learning outcomes isolated from situations of use.

It might be noted here in passing that research on " meaning and the practices of meaning-making" is not, at least not methodologically, at odds with what is frequently termed "cognitive task analysis." Classic information processing theory (cf., Newell & Simon, 1972) was also centrally concerned with documenting meaning in applied settings. By examining meaning-making "in the context of joint activity," however, we do part ways with traditional methods of protocol analysis. As Stahl (2002) wrote:

> The point is that for two or more people to collaborate on learning, they must display to each other enough that everyone can judge where there are agreements and disagreements, conflicts or misunderstandings, confusions and insights. In collaborating, people typically establish conventional dialogic patterns of proposing, questioning, augmenting, mutually completing, repairing, and confirming each other's expressions of knowledge. Knowledge here is not so much the ownership by individuals of mental representations in their heads as it is the ability to engage in appropriate displays within the social world. (p. 177)

In traditional forms of task analysis, talk-aloud protocols are used to infer the expert's representation of a problem space. We on the other hand, treat meaning, not as something inferred from action, but rather as an observable and accountable form of meaning in its own right.

Our focus, in CSCL research, on "the ways in which these practices are mediated through designed artifacts" is what separates us from traditional research on language and social interaction. Ours is not a purely descriptive enterprise— we actively participate in the design and implementation of technologies for collaboration and learning.

In this presentation I have argued that we might find some clues in the writings of John Dewey for how we might theorize some of our work in different ways. In other recent talks and papers, I have suggested that additional clues might be found in the writings of Bakhtin (Koschmann, 1999) and Wittgenstein (Koschmann, 2001b). You need to be forewarned, however, that in all cases, suggestions are all that you will find in these recommended sources, not pre-formulated solutions. Much work remains to transform these proffered hints into a viable program of research.

REFERENCES

Arnseth, H., Ludvigsen, S., Wasson, B., & Mørch, A. (2001). Collaboration and problem solving in distributed collaborative learning. In P. Dillenbourg, A. Eurelings, & K. Hakkarainen (Eds.), *European perspectives on computer-supported collaborative learning* (pp. 75-82). Mahwah, NJ: Lawrence Erlbaum Associates.

Baker, M., Hansen, T., Joiner, R., & Traum, D. (1999). The role of grounding in collaborative learning tasks. In P. Dillenbourg (Ed.), *Collaborative learning: Cognitive and computational approaches* (pp. 31-63). Oxford, U.K.: Pergamon.

Bell, P. (2002). Using argument map representations to make thinking visible for individuals and groups. In T. Koschmann, R. Hall, & N. Miyake (Eds.), *CSCL 2: Carrying forward the conversation* (pp. 449-486). Mahwah, NJ: Lawrence Erlbaum Associates.

Burke, T. (1994). *Dewey's new logic: A reply to Russell.* Chicago: Univ. of Chicago Press.

Clark, H., & Marshall, C. (1981). Definite reference and mutual knowledge. In A. K. Joshi, B. Weber, & I. A. Sag (Eds.), *Elements of discourse understanding* (pp. 10-63). NY: Cambridge University Press.

Dewey, J. (1938/1991). Logic: The theory of inquiry. In J. A. Boydston (Ed.), *John Dewey: The Later Works, 1925–1953, Vol. 12* (pp. 1-5). Carbondale, IL: SIU Press. [Originally published in 1938]

Dewey, J. (1939/1991). Experience, knowledge, and value: A rejoinder. In J. A. Boydston (Ed.), *John Dewey: The later works, 1939–1941, Vol. 14* (pp. 3-90). Carbondale, IL: SIU Press. [Originally published in 1939]

Dewey, J., & Bentley, A. (1949/1991). Knowing and the known. In J. A. Boydston (Ed.), *John Dewey: The later works, 1949–1952, Vol. 16* (pp. 1-5). Carbondale, IL: SIU Press. [Originally published in 1949]

Dillenbourg, P. (Ed.). (1999). *Collaborative learning: Cognitive and computational approaches.* Oxford, U.K.: Pergamon.

Dillenbourg, P., & Traum, D. (1999). Toward a dialogic theory of learning: Bakhtin's contribution to understanding learning in settings of collaboration. In C. Hoadley & J. Roschelle (Eds.), *Computer Support for Collaborative Learning* (pp. 127–135). Mahwah, NJ: Lawrence Erlbaum Associates.

Felton, M. & Kuhn, D. (2002). Science as argument. In T. Koschmann, R. Hall, & N. Miyake (Eds.), *CSCL 2: Carrying forward the conversation* (pp. 493-498). Mahwah, NJ: Lawrence Erlbaum Associates.

Guzdial, M., & Kehoe, C. (1998). Apprentice-based learning environments: A principled approach to providing software-realized scaffolding through hypermedia. *Journal of Interactive Learning Research, 9*(3/4).

Hickman, L. (1998). Dewey's theory of inquiry. In L. Hickman (Ed.), *Reading Dewey: Interpretations for a postmodern generation* (pp. 166–186). Bloomington, IN: Indiana University Press.

Jordan, B., & Henderson, A. (1995). Interaction analysis: Foundations and practice. *Journal of the Learning Sciences, 4*, 39–104.

Kato, H., Yamazaki, K., Suzuki, H., Kuzuoka, H., Miki, H., & Yamazaki, A. (2002). Designing a video-mediated collaboration system based on a body metaphor. In T. Koschmann, R. Hall, & N. Miyake (Eds.), *CSCL 2: Carrying forward the conversation* (pp. 409-424). Mahwah, NJ: Lawrence Erlbaum Associates.

Koschmann, T. (1999). Toward a dialogic theory of learning: Bakhtin's contribution to understanding learning in settings of collaboration. In C. Hoadley & J. Roschelle (Eds.), *Computer Support for Collaborative Learning* (pp. 308– 313). Mahwah, NJ: Lawrence Erlbaum Associates.

Koschmann, T. (2001a, December). Revisiting the paradigms of instructional technology [Keynote Address]. Annual Conference of the Australasian Society for Computers in Tertiary Education, Melbourne, Australia.

Koschmann, T. (2001b, September). Wittgenstein's contribution to a science of collaboration and learning [Keynote Address]. ITU-Konferansen 2001, Oslo, Norway.

Koschmann, T. (2002). Becoming more articulate about the theories that motivate our work. In T. Koschmann, R. Hall, & N. Miyake (Eds.), *CSCL 2: Carrying forward the conversation* (pp. 347-356). Mahwah, NJ: Lawrence Erlbaum Associates.

Koschmann, T., LeBaron, C., Goodwin, C., & Feltovich, P. (2001). Dissecting common ground: Examining an instance of reference repair. In J. D. Moore & K. Stenning (Eds.), *Proceedings of the Twenty-Third Annual Conference of the Cognitive Science Society* (pp. 516–521). Mahwah, NJ: Lawrence Erlbaum Associates.

Mäkitalo, K., Salo, P., Häkkinen, P., & Järvelä, S. (2001). Analyzing the mechanism of common ground in collaborative web-based interaction. In P. Dillenbourg, A. Eurelings, & K. Hakkarainen (Eds.), *European perspectives on computer-supported collaborative learning* (pp. 445-453). Mahwah, NJ: Lawrence Erlbaum Associates.

Newell, A., & Simon, H. (1972). *Human problem solving*. Englewood Cliffs, NJ: Prentice-Hall.

Roschelle, J. (1991). *Students' construction of qualitative physics knowledge: Learning about velocity and acceleration in a computer microworld.* Unpublished doctoral dissertation, University of California, Berkeley.

Roschelle, J. (1992a). Learning by collaboration: Convergent conceptual change. *Journal of the Learning Sciences, 2*, 235-276.

Roschelle, J. (1992b). What should collaborative technology be? A perspective from Dewey and situated learning. *ACM SIGCUE Outlook, 21*(3), 39–42. Retrieved October 3, 2000, from http://www.cica.indiana.edu/cscl95/outlook/39_roschelle.html

Roschelle, J. (1996). Learning by collaboration: Convergent conceptual change. In T. Koschmann (Ed.), *CSCL: Theory and practice of an emerging paradigm* (pp. 209-248). Mahwah, NJ: Lawrence Erlbaum Associates.

Smith, R. (2002). Awareness in video-mediated communication. In T. Koschmann, R. Hall, & N. Miyake (Eds.), *CSCL 2: Carrying forward the conversation* (pp. 425-432). Mahwah, NJ: Lawrence Erlbaum Associates.

Stahl, G. (2002). Rediscovering CSCL. In T. Koschmann, R. Hall, & N. Miyake (Eds.), *CSCL 2: Carrying forward the conversation* (pp. 169-181). Mahwah, NJ: Lawrence Erlbaum Associates.

Suthers, D., Toth, E., & Weiner, A. (1997). An integrated approach to implementing collaborative inquiry in the classroom. In R. Hall, N. Miyake & N. Enyedy (Eds.), *Proceedings of CSCL '97* (pp. 272-279). Mahwah, NJ: Lawrence Erlbaum Associates.

New Forms of Expansive Learning at Work: The Landscape of Co-Configuration

Yrjö Engeström

Center for Activity Theory and Developmental Work Research
P.O.Box 47, 00014 University of Helsinki, Finland
& Laboratory of Comparative Human Cognition
University of California, San Diego, CA 92093 USA
yrjo.engestrom@helsinki.fi

A viable theory of work-related learning needs to be founded on an analysis of the historical development of work. A new landscape of learning emerges as work in industrialized countries is transformed from mass production and mass customization to co-configuration of customer-intelligent products and services with long life cycles. Co-configuration work takes place in divided multi-organizational terrains. It requires continuous re-configuration of the shared object between the multiple producers, the customer or user, and the product or service itself. In such a landscape, learning takes on three characteristics. First, it is transformative learning, focused on expanding the objects of work. Secondly, it is horizontal learning, focused on dialogue, boundary crossing and 'knotworking' between the different activity systems involved. Thirdly, it is subterranean learning, focused on blazing inconspiucous cognitive trails across the terrain.

I will examine and concretize the theoretical ideas sketched above by analyzing data from an ongoing longitudinal study in the care of chronic patiens with multiple illnesses in Helsinki. The study follows three methodological principles: (1) following the trajectory of the object, (2) giving the object a voice, and (3) re-mediating the participants' realtionship to the object by constructing and implementing shared reflective tools.

A. (THEORY TRACK): FEATURED FOUNDATIONAL PAPERS

Epistemological Foundations for CSCL: A Comparison of Three Models of Innovative Knowledge Communities

Sami Paavola, Lasse Lipponen, Kai Hakkarainen

Centre for Research on Networked Learning and Knowledge Building, Department of Psychology, University of Helsinki

Sami.Paavola@helsinki.fi

ABSTRACT

CSCL is based on the idea that computer applications can scaffold and implement advanced socio-cognitive processes for knowledge sharing and knowledge building. But do we really understand these processes that are supposed to be implemented? This paper will focus on the "epistemological infrastructure" of CSCL. We will analyze three models of innovative knowledge communities in order to better understand basic epistemological processes of knowledge advancement: i.e., Nonaka and Takeuchi's model of knowledge-creation, Yrjö Engeström's expansive learning model, and Carl Bereiter's theory of knowledge building. It is argued that these models provide a way of overcoming the dichotomy of the acquisition and participation metaphors of learning by providing a third metaphor of learning as a process of knowledge creation. In order to facilitate educational change through CSCL also certain kind of larger social infrastructure is needed that supports these epistemological processes.

Keywords: knowledge-creation metaphor; epistemological infrastructure, knowledge building, innovative knowledge community

INTRODUCTION: KNOWLEDGE-CREATION METAPHOR OF LEARNING

Processes of innovation and discovery are not easy subjects to analyze. In philosophy of science it has been customary to separate the context of discovery and the context of justification (see e.g., Nickles 1980) and to claim that only the latter is subject to conceptual analysis. There have been some very significant exceptions -- e.g., N.R. Hanson (see 1972) -- but the general view has been that the processes of discovery are something that cannot be captured with conceptual means. Nowadays this clear-cut distinction is often challenged in philosophy of science. There are some notable models that try to conceptualize processes of discovery (see e.g., Hintikka 1985), but still the idea often is, that discovery in genuine sense is something that is not susceptible to conceptual analysis.

The need to understand innovative learning and innovative knowledge advancement is felt in various fields, especially in education, cognitive science, and in business sciences (Nonaka & Takeuchi, 1995; Bereuter, in press). The purpose of the present article is to examine models of innovative knowledge communities that address the problem of explaining how knowledge advancement takes place. All of these models are focused on examining knowledge advancement at a communal level and provide potential models for implementing practices of CSCL in education. Simultaneously, the models challenge our notions of what learning and knowledge are all about. It can be maintained that in these models learning is understood through, what we call, a knowledge-creation or knowledge advancement metaphor. *The knowledge-creation metaphor* of learning means that learning is seen as analogous to processes of inquiry, especially to *innovative* processes of inquiry where something new is created and the initial knowledge is either substantially enriched or significantly transformed during the process.

Anna Sfard (1998) has distinguished two metaphors of learning, *the acquisition metaphor* and *the participation metaphor*. The former represents a traditional view according to which learning is mainly a process of acquiring desired pieces of knowledge. The acquisition metaphor appears to rely on a 'folk theory' of mind according to which the mind is a container of knowledge, and learning is a process that fills the container, implanting knowledge there. Or in other terms, learning is a matter of individual construction, acquisition, and such outcomes, which are realized in the process of transfer; it consists in a person's capability to use and apply knowledge in new situations. Knowledge is a property and possession of an individual mind.

An alternative model, according to Sfard, is the participation metaphor of learning that examines learning as a process of participating in various cultural practices and shared learning activities. According to it, the focus is on activities, i.e., on "knowing", and not so much on outcomes or products, i.e., on "knowledge" in the traditional sense. Knowledge does not exist either in a world of its own or in individual minds but is an aspect of participation in cultural practices (Brown, Collins, & Duguid, 1989; Lave, 1988; Lave & Wenger, 1991). Cognition and knowing are distributed over both individuals and their environments, and learning is "located" in these relations and networks of distributed activities of participation. Within the participation metaphor, learning is a matter of participation in a social process of knowledge construction (Greeno, 1997; Vygotsky, 1978), "enculturation" (Brown, Collins, & Duguid, 1989), or legitimate peripheral participation (Lave & Wenger, 1991). If one reads through the recent papers published in CSCL research (e.g., Dillenbourg, Eurelings, & Hakkarainen, 2001; Hoadley, 1999) most of them appear to rely on the wide sociocultural framework.

The notion of learning through participation was, however, originally used to characterize educational practices in certain aboriginal (e.g., midwives at Yucatan or tailors of Ivory Coast, Lave & Wenger, 1991) or traditional cultures that appear, however, to be relatively stable. It is typical for those using the many variations of the participation metaphor to examine how knowledge is transmitted from one generation to another without substantial and deliberate changes or cultural transformations. Many researchers argue, however, that one simply cannot understand the fundamental changes in modern knowledge society, such as emergence of work focused on deliberate knowledge advancement, by examining how people grow up from peripheral to full participation or how novices learn gradually to master experts' knowledge and skills (see Ahonen, Engeström, & Virkkunen, 2000; Bereiter, in press). In modern knowledge communities, it is argued, there are not such clear-cut roles for newcomers and old-timers (only old-timers having access to the most valuable knowledge and skills) because everyone has to function as a newcomer in a sense of continuously surpassing his or her earlier achievements, and because sometimes new generations develop competencies that are very difficult for older generations to attain (see Bereiter & Scardamalia, 1993).

The distinction between the acquisition metaphor and the participation metaphor has its roots in a debate between cognitive and situated (or situative) perspectives of learning (see Anderson, Reder & Simon 1996, 1997; Greeno 1997). Cognitive approaches emphasize computational models of mind, and the aim is to simulate the way the individual mind operates with knowledge. Situated approaches emphasize situatedness of human cognition, and participation in interactive, social processes as basic processes in learning. A cognitive perspective emphasizes *knowledge*, whereas a situated approach emphasizes participation in social *practices* and *actions* (Anderson, Reder & Simon 1997).

In order to develop a framework that would help one to understand innovative knowledge communities that are emerging in the knowledge society, it appears to be necessary to go beyond the acquisition and participation dichotomy. The present investigation explores the knowledge creation metaphor of learning that appears to help to overcome the separation of the cognitive (the acquisition metaphor) and the situative (the participation metaphor) perspectives. Knowledge creation means that knowledge is emphasized (as in the acquisition metaphor), but not as such but according to the processual point of view. In the participation metaphor "the permanence of *having* gives way to the constant flux of *doing*" (Sfard 1998, 6). But in the knowledge creation metaphor it is not just the situatedness of action, and participation on social interaction that is emphasized but rather the process of developing and creating *knowledge*.

We analyze and compare three models of innovative knowledge communities, i.e. the model of knowledge creation by Ikujiro Nonaka & Hirotaka Takeuchi, the model of expansive learning by Yrjö Engeström, and the model of knowledge building by Carl Bereiter. At the outset, these models appear *not* to have much in common. Nonaka and Takeuchi's framework concerns especially the area of knowledge management and how to organize firms to operate in an innovative way. Engeström's model is strongly rooted in the tradition of cultural-historical activity theory, which seeks to analyze and change practices of learning and working-life. Bereiter's theory is a way of understanding what is important in education based on the criticism of the folk theory of mind and knowledge. Thus, it could be argued that these models are meant to apply to communities showing very great differences with one another. At the outset, we acknowledge that there are many differences in these frameworks, and a comparison cannot capture all aspects of these models. Yet a comparison based on some of the more salient features can bring out intriguing aspects of innovative knowledge communities and knowledge creation (see also Engeström 1999, Bereiter, in press).

These models represent attempts to determine how epistemic communities should be organized in order to facilitate knowledge advancement and creation. The models appear to provide valuable guidance for restructuring school according to innovative knowledge communities through helping teachers and students work deliberately for advancing their knowledge, and supporting them in reflecting on and transforming of their communities. Bielaczyc (2001) has argued that in order to facilitate educational change through CSCL it is not enough to implement CSCL tools but one also needs an appropriate *social infrastructure*, i.e., social structures and practices that support desired interaction between the participants. We will argue that besides technical and social infrastructure, educators and educational psychologists should also consider the epistemological foundations of CSCL. These involve theories or models that help to understand the role of different agents (e.g., individuals, communities, networks) in knowledge creation, mechanisms of knowledge advancement (e.g., resolving epistemic contradictions or explicating implications of existing knowledge), nature of knowledge (to what extent knowledge is "in the head" or "in the world"), and processes of inquiry (the role of questions and theories) involved. By comparing models of innovative knowledge communities, our aim is to better understand the *"epistemological infrastructure"* of CSCL and collaborative learning in general. Epistemological infrastructure refers to individual and collective practices of working with knowledge and engaging in inquiries for advancing knowledge that are important in knowledge work.

THREE MODELS OF INNOVATIVE KNOWLEDGE COMMUNITIES

Ikujiro Nonaka and Hirotaka Takeuchi have presented a very famous and influential model of the innovation processes in their book, *The Knowledge-Creating Company* (1995). The basis of their model is an epistemological distinction between two sorts of knowledge, i.e., tacit and explicit. Explicit knowledge means knowledge that is easy to articulate and express formally and in clear terms. Tacit knowledge, which is more important in innovation, means "personal knowledge embedded in individual experience and involves intangible factors such as personal belief, perspective, and the value system" (viii). Another starting point in their model is an "ontological" distinction between different levels of "entities" that operate in knowledge creation, i.e., individual, group, organizational and inter-organizational level. According to Nonaka and Takeuchi knowledge is created and transformed "spirally" from individual level to organizational level and finally between organizations.

The dynamics of this model comes from the interaction between tacit knowledge and explicit knowledge. A "knowledge spiral" is based on four alternative types of knowledge conversion, i.e., a) from tacit knowledge to tacit knowledge, which Nonaka and Takeuchi call *socialization*, b) from tacit to explicit knowledge, i.e., *externalization*, c) from explicit to explicit knowledge, i.e., *combination*, and d) from explicit to tacit knowledge, i.e. *internalization*. The knowledge creation spiral can be understood so that it starts from *socialization*, when tacit knowledge and experiences are shared at the group level. This means a close interaction and collaboration within a group. This socialization creates common understanding and trust within the group. The next phase, *externalization*, is the central phase in knowledge creation. It means that tacit knowledge is explicated and conceptualized by using metaphors, analogies and concepts. In Nonaka and Takeuchi's model, tacit knowledge is the basic source of innovation, but it must be explicated in order to be transformed to knowledge that is useful at a group level and to the whole organization. *Combination* means that already existing explicit knowledge is combined and exchanged. Finally, *internalization* means that explicit knowledge at the group or organizational level must be internalized into individuals' tacit knowledge and into action in order to have real effects in organization. After internalization a new round in the knowledge spiral can start again.

Yrjö Engeström has analyzed Nonaka and Takeuchi's model and presented the theory of expansive learning as an alternative and a more extensive model for innovative learning (Engeström 1999). He has studied innovative learning cycles in work teams using cultural- historical activity theory, and the theory of expansive learning as a framework for his analysis (see also Engeström 1987). Engeström's model is based on a learning cycle with seven stages in its ideal form (383-384; cf. Engeström 1987, 188-191, 321-336). The cycle starts by 1) individual subjects *questioning* and criticizing of some accepted practices, by certain individuals; which is followed by 2) *analyzing* the situation, i.e., analysis of those (historical) causes and empirical inner relations that are involved in the activity system in question. Then participants engage in 3) *modeling* of a new solution to the problematic situation. They often are 4) *examining the new model* by experimenting and seeing how it works, and what potentialities and limitations it has. Participants undertake 5) *implementing the new model* to practical action and applications, and then, 6) *reflecting* on and evaluating the process. Finally, participants engage in 7) *consolidating the new practice* into some new form of practice. Innovative learning cycles do not follow any fixed order. The model should be understood more as an ideal or heuristic for analyzing elements in the expansive learning cycle. Engeström makes no claim that these steps universally follow one another in just this particular order.

According to Engeström, the central problem with Nonaka and Takeuchi's model is that it does not take into account the first two phases in the expansive cycle, i.e., questioning and analyzing the situation. Their model is based too much on the idea of sharing tacit knowledge in the socialization phase and does not take into account the importance of controversies and conflicts in knowledge creation. These phases are, according to Engeström, excluded, and the problems are taken as given or treated as defined by the management (without analyzing how they originate) in Nonaka and Takeuchi's model.

Carl Bereiter has also criticized Nonaka and Takeuchi's model on the grounds that it is still rooted in mentalistic "folk epistemology". Nonaka and Takeuchi's model is based on the externalization of tacit knowledge and appears to rely on a mentalistic assumption that knowledge resides and is created in an individual's head. What is missing from this model is knowledge "in the world" that Bereiter considers as "conceptual artifacts". He proposes that the development of a knowledge society has given rise to dealing with knowledge as a thing that can systematically be produced and shared between members of a community. Due to mentalistic assumptions, Nonaka and Takeuchi's model is unable to capture essential features in knowledge work, i.e., how knowledge is created, understood, and used in collaborative knowledge building. The concept of knowledge building refers to collective work for the advancement and elaboration of conceptual artifacts, such as theories, ideas, and models, the entities of Popper's World 3 (i.e., the world of cultural knowledge). Popper emphasized that besides physical and material reality (World 1) and reality that concerns mental states (World 2), there is third realm (World 3) which includes conceptual things such as theories and ideas. This World 3 is especially important for humans because human beings do not operate only in the mental realm but can understand and develop objects belonging to this third realm. Although World 3 is dependent on World 2 and World 1, it is still quite autonomous. Bereiter has criticized theories of learning that do not take into account World 3 and so are based on the *mind-as-a-container metaphor*; i.e., an idea that learning relies on accumulation of a ready-made information to the human mind, and mind is understood as a kind of a container or an archive. Table 1 presents a schematic representation of the relations between the innovative communities as depicted in the three models examined here.

Table 1. Three frameworks for Understanding Innovative Knowledge Communities

	Nonaka & Takeuchi	Engeström	Bereiter
The role of individual expertise	Black box, individuals create knowledge	Socially embedded	Theory of expertise
Main focus	Externalization of tacit knowledge (insighting)	Knowledge embedded in practices (acting)	Knowledge objects (conceptualizing)
Type of processes focused	Emphasize bodily processes, personal experience	Emphasize material object-oriented activities	Emphasize solving of knowledge problems
Source of innovation	Transforming tacit knowledge to explicit knowledge	Overcoming tensions, disturbances, and ambiguities by expansive learning	Working deliberately for extending and creating new knowledge objects
Scope of framework	Different ontological levels (individual, innovative team, organization, and inter-organization level)	Activity systems and networks of activity systems	Knowledge-building communities
Educational application	Knowledge-creating schools	Expansive learning school	Schools as knowledge-building communities

An important aspect of Bereiter's (in press) theory is to make a conceptual distinction between *learning* (which operates in the realm of mental states, i.e. in Popper's World 2) and *knowledge building* (which operates in Popper's World 3). In modern enterprises and science, knowledge is considered to consist of objects (e.g., product plans, business strategies, marketing plans) that can be systematically produced and developed. Correspondingly, scientific research groups are typically working with theories and models that may be understood as shared knowledge objects rather than as representing mental states. Naturally, learning also does occur in the business world and scientific research, but it is not the main focus of these domains of activity. The primary goal of members of an innovative expert community is not merely to learn something (i.e., change, or simply add to, their own mental states), but to solve problems, originate new thoughts, and advance communal knowledge. But in knowledge building knowledge work is seen as a collaborative achievement, where people develop, create, understand, and criticize various conceptual artifacts, not just "learn" something. Bereiter's theory diverges from the other two models in the sense that he emphasizes more strongly a conscious effort to advance knowledge and a commitment go beyond existing knowledge and understanding, an effort to solve knowledge problems through collaboration in innovative communities within a knowledge society.

COMMON ASPECTS IN THE THREE MODELS OF INNOVATIVE COMMUNITIES

In spite of differences in Nonaka and Takeuchi's, Engeström's, and Bereiter's models, they have many features that are in common. In this chapter we delineate six such features.

First of all, they can be seen as instances of the knowledge creation metaphor, instantiations that have many similarities. The focus of Nonaka and Takeuchi's book is "on knowledge *creation*, not on knowledge per se" (Nonaka & Takeuchi 1995, 6). Engeström's model concentrates on expansive, qualitative changes in activity systems (Engeström 1987). Bereiter's model is based on dynamic expertise and progressive problem solving where the goal always is to surpass previous achievements (Bereiter & Scardamalia 1993). It is no coincidence that this kind of innovative learning is characterized with some sort of a spiral or a cycle (see Engeström 1999, 383-384; Nonaka & Takeuchi 1995, 70-73). The processes of knowledge creation usually take a lot of time. They are iterative and recursive processes which are not correctly described by traditional narratives of heroic individuals making ingenious discoveries through sudden moments of insight. These processes are not linear, either (Engeström 1987, 214). Knowledge creation is more based on ambiguity and "creative chaos" (Nonaka & Takeuchi 1995, 78-80). Creative chaos involves, unlike destructive chaos, the sense of progress.

Secondly, all of the three frameworks challenge attempts to restrict our understanding of knowledge exclusively to conceptual or propositional knowledge. Propositional knowledge is one important form of knowledge but it is only one form of knowledge. The models emphasize knowledge which can be called *know-how* and *tacit knowledge*. Bereiter and Scardamalia (1993, 43-47) have described a distinction between three basic areas of knowledge: 1) declarative knowledge which means "formal" or propositional knowledge, 2) procedural knowledge or know-how (Gilbert Ryle's term) which means knowledge embedded in skills, and 3) "hidden knowledge" or "tacit knowledge" (Michael Polanyi's term), which is based on such things as impressions and a "sense" of things. These models of innovative learning criticize the traditional view according to which human cognition is a symbolic system that mainly relies on explicit propositional knowledge and functions according to explicitly formed production rules. The emphasis on explicit knowledge can lead to so-called "paralysis by analysis" syndrome (Nonaka & Takeuchi 1995, 198). Rylean know-how is based on the idea that our activities and skills are not guided by explicit rules and propositional knowledge; rather, rule-like behavior emerges as an outcome of knowledgeable action (summarized in Bereiter, in press).

Besides declarative and procedural knowledge, there is the third area of knowledge, i.e., tacit knowledge, which is important also in Bereiter's model of expertise. Skills and know-how are things that manifest themselves in performance, but tacit knowledge is much harder to recognize directly. Still, creative expertise is very much based on tacit knowledge concerning promising ideas (Bereiter & Scardamalia 1993, 133- 152). Based on experience of solving problems concerning their own field, creative experts have some sort of sense of what is promising in their field and how to solve new problems. And creative experts are also all the time consciously trying to find out new and more promising ways of doing things in their field. There is always venturesome and risky effort, but this uncertainty is part of innovative processes. Similarly Nonaka and Takeuchi emphasize tacit knowledge in their model. According to them tacit knowledge includes subjective insights, intuitions, hunches, and ideals, which are the crucial basis for innovative processes (Nonaka & Takeuchi 1995, 8-10).

Thirdly, although these models of innovative learning criticize propositional and conceptual knowledge when it is seen as the only form of knowledge, they still emphasize the role of *conceptualization* in innovative processes. Bereiter's model is based on the idea of conceptual artifacts and of solving problems of understanding. In Nonaka and Takeuchi's model, one key process is the externalization of tacit knowledge. And in Engeström model an important phase in an expansive learning cycle is *modeling*, i.e., constructing an explicit model that offers a new solution to the situation in question. So it appears that an important point in these models of innovative learning is the "dialectical" interaction between different forms of knowledge.

Fourthly, all these models try to avoid mentalism and Cartesian dualism. It can be argued that this is done by bringing some mediating element to the process of knowledge creation (although in Nonaka and Takeuchi's model this is not so obvious). Bereiter emphasizes objects in World 3 that are neither part of the material realm (World 1) nor part of the subjective, mental realm (World 2). Engeström emphasizes the element of "thirdness" in his model in order to avoid mentalism (Engeström 1987, 221-222, 302-304). The concepts of activity and dialectics operate as mediating factors that bring dynamics to the model (140, 310). Nonaka and Takeuchi try to avoid the "Cartesian split" between subject and object (which is, according to them, typical of Western thought) by referring to the Japanese way of thinking. Japanese tradition does not do separate humanity and nature, body and mind, nor self and others so sharply as the Cartesian tradition has done (Nonaka & Takeuchi 1995, 20-32). The Japanese way of thinking as depicted here may sound a little bit mysterious, but the idea is that knowledge and rationality is not so clearly separated from things such as emotions, figurative speech, actions, and so on; in the processes of innovation these vague and even chaotic elements are the fuel for something new.

From Bereiter's viewpoint, Nonaka's model is still rooted in the folk psychological theory of mind because the latter so strongly emphasizes embodied and tacit knowledge that appears to be contained within an individual human mind, and does not seem to take into account the idea of knowledge building in Popper's World 3. This is one basic difference in Bereiter's and Nonaka and Takeuchi's model, because in Nonaka and Takeuchi's model there is no explicit room for *conceptual artifacts*. But the difference between these models may not actually be so large. Bereiter himself acknowledges that Nonaka and Takeuchi's model goes as far as is possible in the folk psychological way of thinking about knowledge creation. It is important to notice the knowledge spiral in Nonaka and Takeuchi's model; that knowledge is produced collaboratively (and not only in individual minds); and that the explication of knowledge to group and organizational level is focal.

Questions and problems also have a mediating role in these models. In Bereiter's model, questions, and problems of understanding are the moving force for progressive knowledge building (Bereiter 1993, 210- 211). In Engeström's model the questioning and criticism of accepted practices is the basis for the expansive learning cycle (Engeström 1999, 383). Engeström, as already stated, criticizes Nonaka and Takeuchi's model that it does not take into account phases of formulating and debating a problem, or takes these phases more or less as given (ibid., 380). One reason for this difference might be that Engeström has analyzed knowledge creation in *western* organizations whereas Nonaka and Takeuchi worked especially in *Japanese* organizations. In Japanese culture, harmony and group thinking are much more strongly emphasized than in western culture, where the meaning of individual differences and also conflicts are more easily taken as a starting point (see Nonaka & Takeuchi 1995, 31, 63). But it appears that both of these aspects, the creation of mutual trust and understanding by strong socialization, and the opportunity and acceptance for criticism and questioning, are needed in knowledge innovation. As a matter of fact, although Nonaka and Takeuchi do not emphasize conflicts or questions in their model, these topics are not totally left out either. Socialization in their model involves dialogue and discussion, and "[t]his dialogue can involve considerable conflict and disagreement, but it is precisely such conflict that pushes employees to question existing premises and to make sense of their experience in a new way" (1995, 13-14).

Fifthly, All of the frameworks agree that knowledge creation is a fundamentally social process in nature. They appear to share with Naomi Miyake the view according to which social interaction provides cognitive resources for human cognitive accomplishment (Miyake 1986). According to Miyake's analysis, understanding is iterative in nature, i.e., it emerges through a series of attempts to explain and understand processes and mechanisms being investigated. In a shared problem-solving process, agents who have partial but different information about the problem in question appear collectively to improve their understanding through social interaction. Accordingly, new ideas and innovations emerge among rather than within people.

Sixthly, although innovation processes are fundamentally social in nature, individual activity is also emphasized; not individuals separately, but individuals acting as a part of social stream of activities. In Engeström's model, although individual activities are embedded to their cultural-historical background, it is *individual* subjects questioning the accepted practices, which is the starting point for the expansive learning (Engeström 1999, 383; 1987, 322). Nonaka and Takeuchi emphasize that new knowledge always starts with an individual (Nonaka & Takeuchi 1995, 13, 59). In their model the role of individuals seems to be more central than in Engeström's or Bereiter's model. But also in this model, it is individual initiative embedded in group and organizational activities. Nonaka and Takeuchi criticize Western tradition, arguing that it is too much focused on the individual subject and largely abandoned the social interaction. Knowledge conversion is, in a fundamental way, a social process and "not confined *within* an individual" (Nonaka & Takeuchi 1995, 61; see also 31-32, 226). However, individuals appear to be taken as given in Nonaka and Takeuchi's framework; they talk a great deal about individual heroes that pursue processes of innovation but remain, to a large extent, unanalyzed black boxes. The idea of individual transformation through collective activity is much stronger in Bereiter's and Engeström's frameworks.

CSCL AND MODELS OF INNOVATIVE KNOWLEDGE COMMUNITIES

Fjuk and Ludvigsen (2001) argued that the educational implications of CSCL can be understood only by extending the unit of analysis from technology and pedagogy to those social contexts in which CSCL is used. They argued that it is important to investigate how real-life situations in which people are using CSCL develop across extended periods of time rather than just focus on short courses. Traditional approaches to CSCL -- including sometimes our own approaches -- have suffered from a too narrow theoretical and methodological orientation that has guided researchers to look at individual classrooms and courses rather than consider larger social structures and how they may constrain participation in CSCL. Success of CSCL experiments has, however, usually been constrained by various organizational (i.e., content of the curriculum, boundaries between classrooms as well as between domains of knowledge), pedagogical (prevailing practices of learning and instruction), and epistemological (fact-centered educational epistemology and knowledge-delivery orientation) factors (e.g., Hakkarainen, Lipponen & Järvelä, in press). Only gradually have we started to understand that the unit of our analyses has been too small, and it is more and more clear that in order to succeed, one needs to better understand how school communities function and find innovative ways transforming whole educational communities.

The present investigation arises from an attempt to explore models that may guide CSCL researchers in developing more innovative communities of inquirers within an educational system through CSCL. Each of the present models provides its distinct perspective on educational communities and organizations. The models indicate that innovation or intelligence arise from systemic features of whole community or an organization rather than from characteristics of individuals or their work. Knowledge creation is not primarily a matter of creative individuals but requires fundamental reorganization of functioning of a whole epistemic community. The knowledge-creation metaphor appears to have contact with the participation metaphor by emphasizing importance of taking part in certain kind of social practices of working for advancing knowledge. The models of innovative educational communities to be examined below indicate that the epistemological infrastructure of CSCL requires a kind of social infrastructure; mere epistemology is not enough without supporting social practices, and *vice versa*.

Schools as knowledge-building communities

Bereiter and Scardamalia's model of knowledge building school is both historically and conceptually very closely associated with CSCL research. Their seminal work for developing networked environments for computer-supported learning has profoundly affected the formation of our field of inquiry. The present researchers have pursued, over several years, models of facilitating progressive inquiry at school, by relying on Carl Bereiter's theory of knowledge building and Jaakko Hintikka's interrogative approach to inquiry (Hakkarainen, 1998; Hakkarainen & Sintonen, in press). Scardamalia and Bereiter (1994) argued that there are no compelling reasons why school education should not have the dynamic character of scientific inquiry. They proposed (1994) that scientific thinking could be facilitated in schools by organizing schools to function like scientific research communities and guiding students to participate in practices of progressive scientific discourse. Although students are learning already-existing knowledge, they may be engaged in the same kind of extended processes of question-driven inquiry as scientists and scholars. They also proposed that there is a close relation between the processes of scientific discovery and learning scientific knowledge. The argument was that it is essential to cultivate reasoned "processes of invention" that characterize scientific inquiry, to involve students with same kind of extended process of problem solving through which scientists articulate new knowledge.

Simultaneously, however, the theoretical foundations of the knowledge-building approach have profoundly changed from theories of intentional learning and expertise to the theory of collaborative efforts in building knowledge objects, and conceptual artifacts, and solving knowledge problems. One of the best examples of knowledge-building projects in Finland is the Citizen Memory project. Upper elementary school students have been participating in collaboration with local communities in a project that focuses on collecting information about local history. The project aimed at searching for information about how people used to live in the area and how it had changed. The students were guided to interview their grandparents and other elderly people in order to examine how they had been living during earlier periods of time. These interviews were transcribed from audiotapes and posted on the web, together with digitized photographs, so that there emerged a continuously growing body of local knowledge. In so doing, the students engaged in knowledge-building, rather than just learning (i.e. learning as it is understood in the theory of knowledge building). They constructed a very rich, organized database that can be used, reorganized and analyzed by other students, researchers or teachers; therefore, their activity went beyond the boundaries of mere learning. Innovative collaborative technology enriches conventional learning situations by a shared space that allows the users to work together for advancement of their knowledge. Educational implications of the Bereiterian line of mature knowledge-building inquiry are, however, just starting to be explicated.

Knowledge-creating schools

Discussion of the concept of intelligent organizations emerging from Nonaka and Takeuchi's work is approaching the educational domain. For instance, David Hargreaves (1999) talked about the "knowledge- creating school." His argument is that in order to answer the challenges of knowledge society, schools and especially teachers and headmasters need themselves to become creators of professional knowledge. This means a deliberate effort to articulate teachers' professional experiences into shareable knowledge within and between schools. In order to help students to develop skills and competencies needed in knowledge creations, teachers should themselves have personal experience of building their professional knowledge. Hargreaves' makes a very good case for the challenge of teachers' professional development. He does not, however, have anything to say about how to guide students to develop corresponding competencies (see also Engeström, Engeström, & Suntio, in press). Our own efforts to implement practices of knowledge-building at school have been constrained by the fact that we have often worked just with a few teachers rather than with teachers' pedagogical communities. It is easy to understand at the conceptual level that in order to guide students' knowledge-building processes, teachers should have personal experiences of knowledge creation. Yet we have just started to implement corresponding practices.

Expansive Learning at Schools

While traditional theories of learning focused only on individual learning and addressed acquisition of some relatively well-defined knowledge or skills, activity theory focuses on examining transformations in an activity system. It appears to provide tools that help to examine relations within networks of activity systems as well as address larger processes of socio-cultural transformation in the context of CSCL (Fjuk & Ludvigsen, 2001). Engeström, Engeström, and Suntio (in press) carried out an eleven-week change- laboratory intervention with a teacher community of a middle school. They pointed out that there are several factors that make transformation of school very difficult, such as social, spatial, and temporal structures embedded in classroom-based studies (study of autonomous texts for exams and grading) and teachers' tradition of working as individual professionals. These fundamental constraints make it very difficult for participants to collectively reflect on their practices and engage in sustained expansive learning. Expansive learning is a process of systematically exploring possibilities of transformation through asking questions, generating models and artifacts, and testing and experimenting with new practices.

The change laboratory focused on making constraints visible to the participants and helping them to surpass those challenges. The intervention focused on identifying developmental challenges of the activity system of the school, collectively constructing a vision of the school's future, and implementing a series of practical changes. Toward this end, the researchers videotaped classroom lessons and interviewed teachers, students, and parents. These recordings provided a "mirror" that helped the teacher community to collective discuss their current practices in relation to its historical formation and trajectories of future development. Researchers thus helped a teacher community to reflect of its current practices, determine the basic tensions and contradiction in it, and identify a collective zone of proximal development. One of the issues that arose in change-laboratory meetings was the integration of different domains of knowledge in constructing of students "final project" just before they left the school. The final project appeared to function as a boundary object that helped to transform a traditional school learning task into a more meaningful one, go beyond requirements of school work and curricular requirements, and simultaneously improve one's school grades. Expansive possibilities opened up also because more positive talk about students was associated with teachers' discussion of the final projects. Through exploring various ways of conducting the final work, the students appeared themselves to be active participants in the process of transforming their practices of schooling, and they engaged in expanding their own and their fellow students' perspectives.

The above examples do not, as such, represent CSCL but it would be natural to utilize CSCL environments both for helping teachers to share and reflect on their experiences, coach students and carry out various kinds of individual and collaborative projects. A number of CSCL studies are either relying on ideas of knowledge-building or utilizing activity-theoretical frameworks. It appears to us that it is important to focus more attention of the CSCL community of investigators on these broader socio-cultural processes, develop corresponding new methods and theoretical frameworks, and pursue corresponding lines of empirical inquiry. In order to use CSCL to increase the quality of learning, we should take school communities into the center rather than periphery of our discussion. The above discussion indicates that the three innovation models explored open up interesting and promising lines of inquiry that are likely to help us to bring about revolutionary changes in schools.

CONCLUSION

We have delineated epistemological foundations (or "epistemological infrastructure") for collaborative and innovative learning by comparing three influential models of innovative epistemic communities. We have argued that in these models learning and knowledge advancement are understood through a knowledge-creation metaphor that emphasizes the importance of going beyond information given. All of them are trying to answer to the challenge of the "learning paradox" by focusing on processes of innovation. The learning paradox (or the "Meno paradox") is the classical problem of explaining how something conceptually more complex is created using existing knowledge (see Bereiter 1985). These three models of innovation take the learning paradox to be a basic epistemological question by highlighting the importance of explaining how something new is created.

There are many similarities in how these models try to avoid the learning paradox. First of all, they concentrate on explaining dynamic processes of knowledge transformation. This is not self-evident. Often models of learning are based on the acquisition metaphor of learning where knowledge is taken more or less as such, and not from the point of view of knowledge *creation*. Or alternatively, the emphasis is on the participation in social interaction but not so much in *knowledge* creation. Secondly, there are many similarities in how these models understand knowledge. They avoid mentalism and a too individualistic approach by criticizing the classical conception of knowledge, as propositional knowledge only. Within the three models, knowledge is seen as a part of dynamic processes of innovation embedded in various skills, emotions, and hunches of the people involved. Thirdly, these newer models emphasize the elements of *mediation* in knowledge creation. They avoid the Cartesian dualism of mind and matter by bringing in conceptual artifacts, theories, activities, questions, problems, metaphors, dialectics, as mediating factors to epistemological processes. Fourthly, these models try to avoid a dichotomy of individual and social levels by concentrating on analyzing how individuals act as participants in innovative processes of knowledge creation.

Although the present paper emphasize similarities between the three models, there are also fundamental differences in philosophical and epistemological foundations of the models that make them even more interesting. One difference is with respect to the fundamental target or object of innovation. In Nonaka and Takeuchi's model, the focus is on *ideas* and *insights* related to new products that are developed in firms. In Engeström's model, *activities* and *practices* are the main focus. Bereiter, however, emphasizes the meaning of *conceptual artifacts* and objects in world 3 in knowledge work. In epistemological domain, however, the three models appear to be close to each other because they address the same kinds of questions concerning how new knowledge is created by innovative communities. In collaborative knowledge advancement it is important to expansively transform both ideas, practices, and conceptual artifacts. In this sense the three models complement each other.

REFERENCES

Ahonen, H., Engeström, Y., & Virkkunen, J. (2000) Knowledge management – the second generation: Creating competencies within and between work communities in the competence laboratory. To appear in Y. Malhotra (Ed.). *Knowledge management and virtual organization*. Hershey, PA: Idea Group Publishing.

Anderson, J. R., Reder, L. M. & Simon, H.A. (1996) Situated Learning and Education. *Educational Researcher*, **25**, 4, 5-11.

Anderson, J. R., Reder, L. M. & Simon, H.A. (1997) Situative Versus Cognitive Perspectives: Form Versus Substance. *Educational Researcher*, **26**, 1, 18-21.

Bereiter, C. (1985) Towards a Solution of the Learning Paradox. *Review of Educational Research*, **55**, 2, 201-226.

Bereiter, C. (in press) *Education and mind in the knowledge age*. Hillsdale, NJ: Erlbaum.

Bereiter, C. & Scardamalia, M. (1993) *Surpassing ourselves*. Open Court, Chicago.

Bielaczyc, K. (2001) Designing social infrastructure: The challenge of building computer-supported learning communities. In P. Dillenbourg, A. Eurelings, & K. Hakkarainen (Eds.), *European perspectives on computer-supported collaborative learning. The proceedings of the First European Conference on Computer-Supported Collaborative Learning* (pp.106-114). University of Maastricht.

Brown, J. S., Collins, A. & Duquid, P. (1989). Situated cognition and the culture of learning. *Educational Researcher*, **18**, 32-42.

Engeström, Y. (1987) *Learning by expanding*. Orienta-Konsultit Oy, Helsinki.

Engeström, Y. (1999) Innovative learning in work teams: Analyzing cycles of knowledge creation in practice. In Y. Engeström, R. Miettinen & R.-L-. Punamäki (Eds.), *Perspectives on activity theory*, (pp. 377-404). Cambridge: Cambridge University Press,.

Engeström, Y, Engeström, R., & Suntio, A. (in press) Can a school community learn to master its own future? An activity theoretical study of expansive learning among middle school teachers. Available: *http://www2.ucsc.edu/people/gwells/CHATbook/Engetal.html*

Fjuk, A., Ludvigsen, S. (2001) The complexity of distributed collaborative learning: Unit of Analysis. In P. Dillenbourg, A. Eurelings, & K. Hakkarainen, (Eds.), *European perspectives on Computer-supported collaborative learning: Proceedings of the First European Conference of Computer-supported Collaborative Learning (Euro-CSCL)* (pp. 237-244), Maastricht, The Netherlands, March 22-24, 2001.

Greeno, J. G. (1997) On Claims That Answer the Wrong Questions. *Educational Researcher*, **26**, 1, 5-17.

Hakkarainen, K. (1998) *Epistemology of inquiry and Computer-supported collaborative Learning*. Unpublished Ph.D. thesis. University of Toronto.

Hakkarainen, K., Lipponen, L. & Järvelä, S. (in press) Epistemology of inquiry and computer-supported collaborative learning. An article to appear in T. Koschmann, N. Miyake, & R. Hall (Eds.), *CSCL2: Carrying Forward the Conversation*. Mahwah, NJ: Erlbaum.

Hakkarainen, K. & Sintonen, M. (in press) Interrogative approach on inquiry and computer-supported collaborative learning. *Science & Education*.

Hanson, N. R. (1972) *Patterns of Discovery*. Cambridge: Cambridge University Press, , first printed 1958.

Hargreaves, D. H. (1999) The knowledge-creating school. *British Journal of Educational Studies*, **47**, 122-144.

Hintikka, J. (1985) True and false logic of scientific discovery. *Communication & Cognition*, **18**, 1/2, 3-14.

Lave, J. & Wenger, E. (1991). *Situated learning: Legitimate peripheral participation*. Cambridge: Cambridge University Press.

Miyake, N. (1986) Constructive interaction and the iterative process of understanding. *Cognitive Science*, **10**, 151-177.

Nickles, T. (ed.) (1980) *Scientific Discovery, Logic, and Rationality*. Dordrecht: Reidel.

Nonaka, I. & Takeuchi, H. (1995) *The Knowledge-Creating Company: How Japanese Companies Create the Dynamics of Innovation*. New York: Oxford University Press,.

Scardamalia, M., & Bereiter, C. (1994). Computer support for knowledge-building communities. *The Journal of the Learning Sciences*, **3**, 265-283.

Sfard, A. (1998) On two metaphors for learning and the dangers of choosing just one. *Educational Researcher*, **27**, 4–13.

Instructional Artifacts

Berthel Sutter

Blekinge Institute of Technology, Sweden

berthel.sutter@bth.se

ABSTRACT

This paper addresses the question of attribution of agency to artifacts. Taking an activity-theoretical perspective, I argue that artifacts are used to guide actions. In other words, I claim that artifacts have instructional impact. The introductory part of the paper is an account of how three kinds of artifacts - physical artifacts, linguistic representations, and graphic representations – are instructionally used in coronary diagnostic work. The main part of the paper is an empirical exploration of how a forth kind of artifact, organization of work, is instructionally used. The empirical case analyzed involves clinical diagnostic work conducted as a video-mediated conference between two collaborating diagnostic sub-teams, one of which had made the coronary investigation by means of coronary angiography, while the other was to take actions in the form of by-pass surgery or balloon dilatation. In the concluding sections, I discuss in what way it makes sense to say that organization of work and other artifacts have instructional properties.

Keywords

Instruction, artifact, collaborative work, coronary diagnostics, activity-theoretical approach

INTRODUCTION

The role of artifacts, material and ideal, the role of the body as a source of knowledge, and the role of the "situatedness" of action and learning has met a growing interest in research approaches dealing with the new information and communication technologies (ICT). The reason is probably that the material of ICT, a "material without characteristics" (Löwgren & Stolterman 1998) forces us to sharpen our attention for matter, bodies, and local circumstances. Whatever the reasons, at least within some research fields and approaches, there is now a new attention to those phenomena. My paper also addresses the phenomena by exploring possible instructive properties of artifacts.

In my opinion, instruction, in diverse forms, is an aspect of collaborative work. Instruction, I claim, like all kinds of activity, has two forms of existence, the artifacts and the activity of the subject (Enerstvedt, 1982, p. 179). Another way to put it is to say that there are live praxis and inert artifacts (Sartre 1960), or that human activity has a "live" (subjective) side and a "frozen" (objective) side (Lektorsky 1982; Popper 1972), or that there is a duality of participation and reification (Wenger 1998). In my opinion, all these formulations can be read as attempts to grasp the basis of human activity ("Gegenständliche Tätigkeit").

As said, I will approach the distinction of the inert and the live aspects of activity from the perspective of instruction and collaborative work. In earlier studies on clinical diagnostic work (Sutter 2000a, b), I have come to the conclusion that the representational aspects of artifacts, which Wartofsky (1979) calls "secondary artifacts," can be described as artifact-bound instruction. To "represent" means to "instruct." Artifacts are instructive. I have discerned three kinds of artifact-bound instruction - physical-artifact representations, linguistic representations, and graphic representations. I will illustrate them in turn. An example of a linguistic artifact used in coronary diagnostics is a "coding scheme" (category and event relevant for a group of professionals) (Goodwin 1994). One such coding scheme can be called "Fifty percent," a shorthand for a risk criterion based on experience. It refers to a coronary artery where the diameter of a stenosed part of a blood-vessel is measured to 50% or less of the normal artery. If the criterion is met, the physicians are expected to take measures or explain in view of the circumstances why they do not. The coding scheme "Fifty Percent" is a linguistic artifact used in oral and written forms in this community of diagnostic practice to say "we take measure when the stenosis is 50% or more."

We can take an artifact associated to the "Fifty Percent" coding scheme to illustrate a graphic representation. A standard graphic representation that is used in the heart conference is a schematized drawing of each patient's coronary arteries. If there are stenosed or blocked parts, they are marked with a line and a number that indicates the percentage of the stenosis. Thus, the graphic representation gives a comprehensive picture of the patient's heart and instructively points out what parts to inspect and how they are to be evaluated as a single condition. (For a detailed study of the production and use of the angio graphic, see Sutter 2001.)

I am sure the reader can imagine many physical artifacts that are used in this clinical diagnostic work. One is a special device that the radiologist is maneuvering when presenting and commenting on the angio video at the heart conference. With the help of the special device the radiologist controls a video display pointer in the form of an arrow, with which he can pinpoint details and comment on them. The special device has instructive affordances offering how it should be handled.

To sum up, I operate with a conception of mutual dependency of inert artifacts and live actions, or in other words, of artifact-bound instruction by means of physical-artifact representations (e.g. affordances), linguistic representations, graphic representations, and corresponding instructional praxis when the artifacts are put into use. Based on my empirical investigations I have come to realize that there also are "organizational representations." It is the specific purpose of this paper to consider what organizational representation may mean.

Artifacts are often imagined as sustainable and robust. "Technology is society made durable", to use Latour's expression (Latour 1991). But of course artifacts also can be fragile, unstable, transitory – before they are abandoned or transformed into more durable artifacts. The organizational artifact that I present here is fragile, and it was abandoned as part of organizing the thorax clinic at Karlskrona. Nevertheless, it is an example that displays how an organizational artifact may function before it has been stabilized and turned into "infrastructure" (Bowker and Star 1999) or part of the organizational base ("division of labor," "community," and "rules" in Engeström's model of an activity system). The taken-for-grantedness of the artifact is not yet established and, thus, the artifact has not turned invisible.(1)

The overall aim of this paper is to argue that instruction is built into artifacts, and that this built-in property is used in collaborative work. The more specific aim is to explore how one kind of artifact, organization of work, is used as a heuristic device in a work setting of collaborative clinical diagnoses. More specifically, I claim that organizations have an instructional impact on work.

Background

The specific case I will discuss is the organization of coronary diagnostic work as it has been developed at Blekinge hospital in Karlskrona, Sweden. Only lately coronary diagnostic work has become an issue to be dealt with locally in Karlskrona. During the 1980's and up to 1993, patients suspected to suffer from coronary illness were sent from the regional hospital to the University Clinic at Lund, some hundred kilometers away. In 1993, primarily of economic reasons, the Karlskrona hospital decided to conduct the coronary angiography on patients from the county (and a neighboring county) and then let the cardiologist and radiologist from Karlskrona take part in the heart conferences that were held weekly in Lund, at the thorax clinic. At the same time, technological deployment made it possible, first, to test, and later on to conduct regularly heart conferences between the Karlskrona team and the Lund team by means of a video conference facility equipped with a special video within the video conference. This special video made it possible for the two sub-teams simultaneously to watch and discuss the X-ray videotape of the patient coronary, which always was presented by a Karlskrona radiologist.

Such was the background to the appearance of a uniquely organized coronary diagnostic activity. For a short period of three years, 1993-1996, special circumstances concerning coronary diagnostics and surgery in the south of Sweden led to the emergence of a distributed clinical heart conference. (For details, see Kehler et al. 1996, and Sutter 1999.) At the clinical heart conference a number of patient cases were presented to and discussed among surgeons, radiologists, and cardiologists, with the aim to make a joint diagnosis for future treatment. A central input in the heart conference was the video-taped coronary angiography of the patient, i.e. a short video sequence of the X-rayed coronary in action. It is aspects of this distributed and telemediated clinical diagnostic work that I discuss in this paper.

For the sake of comprehensiveness, I need to mention that the next step in the development of the local coronary diagnostic work was the establishment of a thorax clinic at the Karlskrona hospital. In December 1996 the unique telemedicine project that had been launched for full three years came to an end. The telemediated and distributed heart conference was replaced by a regular one, locally organized within the thorax clinic.

The organizational forms of the heart conferences corresponding to the phases in the development of coronary diagnostic work at the Karlskrona hospital of course varied. However, the organizations displayed one feature in common, namely that the organizational form had an instructional impact on the collaborative work practice. In another paper I have tried to show how it works in the thorax clinic (Sutter 2001). In this paper I will restrict my detailed account to the organization of work that the video-mediated heart conference made both necessary and possible.

The coronary diagnostic work I have been studying is saturated with computer support for collaborative learning, but the CS and CL parts are so embedded in the work activity that they may go unnoticed. Some decades ago, when computer use was not so frequent, CSCL was established as a special field of research and artifact innovations (Koschmann 1996). Now when computers are ubiquitous we do not primarily need specially designed gadgets ("computer support") to promote learning; to a great extent they are already available. What we need, in my opinion, is to research how collaborative learning is carried through and how artifacts of all kinds interweave in productive work and learning activities. This is how I see the context of my study.

---

(1) In Sutter (2001) I have described two organizational artifacts – a cardiologist-radiologist dyad and an afternoon mini heart conference – which have been made more durable at the radiology unit of the thorax clinic.

ORGANIZING WORK – THREE EMPIRICAL EXAMPLES

The empirical part of the paper will address the organizing and use of a patient queue in distributed clinical diagnostic work. The queue of the patient-cases stems from the fact that only one patient case can be discussed at a time, and that about 10-15 cases have to be presented at each heart conference. The imposed order is a way of coordinating the actions of the physicians, and particularly the actions between the two sub-teams, the cardiologist and radiologist in Karlskrona, and the surgeon and the radiologist in Lund. It might be the case that the imposed order is just a casual order, but most often this is not the case. Instead, the ordering takes into account that a radiologist in Lund needs to be present at the patient cases where balloon dilatation or "PTCA" (an acronym the members themselves most often use in their internal talk) is the expected outcome of the diagnosis. At the time of the study the radiologists were the specialists that made the PTCA interventions, and therefore the possible PTCA patient cases (normally) were placed first among the patient cases that were to be presented. The rational of this "queuing procedure" is that when the PTCA candidates have been presented the radiologists could leave the heart conference and continue with their other duties.

My method in this study is to pick out three video-documented weekly held heart conferences (out of 17 that I have recorded from March 1995 to August 1996). In these three cases the use of the queue-organization or the presentation order of the patients is obvious also for me as an observer because such usage was expressly stated by the members themselves. The first reason why I have picked out these cases is that they show that the organization works as an instructive artifact. The second reason is that they throw light on the relation between inert artifacts and live actions, and thus problemitize my idea that artifacts are instructive. The heart conferences from which I will use data here were held in January, February, and August 1996.

I will present data from the conference, first, by giving the structure of the three conferences, and then by discussing some details of special interest for the concern of this paper.

Let us start with a first glance at Table 1. It shows that the number of patients (P) that have been discussed at the selected heart conferences is between 10 and 17. It is possible to discern a pattern in each of the conferences: In the site in Lund there are, at the start of the conference, other physicians present in addition to the surgeon. These physicians (in the examples, a radiologist and, in two of the cases, also a cardiologist) leave the conference before it is finished. In the February conference it happens after the first patient has been discussed, in the January conference after Patient 7, and in the August conference after Patient 4. *Before their leave*, the decisions made of what action to take are (with few exceptions that I will discuss in a moment) PTCA or balloon dilatation. This is what happened in 6 of 7 cases in the January conference, 1 of 1 case in the February conference, and 4 of 4 cases in the August conference. *After their leave*, the decision pattern displays a similar uniformity in favor of surgery (7 of 10 in January, 10 of 13 in February, and 4 of 6 in August). The "few exceptions" I just mentioned comprise Patient 1 (January), where the decision was to make a new investigation; 4 patients that had "normal coronaries" according to the Karlskrona team, assessments that were accepted from their words by the team at Lund (i.e. no video film was presented); Patient 8 (February) who was "already presented," namely at a demonstration of the videoconferencing technology some days before, and finally, there is a PTCA decision at each conference breaking the rule (P10, P9, and P7, respectively). These latter exceptions are of special interest in this study, and I will discuss them in detail below.

Heart conference January 1996	**Heart conference February 1996**	**Heart conference August 1996**
Present at Lund: Surgeon, radiologist	Present at Lund: Surgeon, radiologist, cardiologist	Present at Lund: Surgeon, radiologist, cardiologist
P1: a combined heart- and kidney case. Decision: Make an angiography	P1: PTCA? Check at Lund	P1: PTCA
	Radiologist and cardiologist leave	
P2: PTCA	P2: OP	P2: PTCA
P3: PTCA	P3: OP	P3: PTCA
P4: PTCA	P4: OP	P4: PTCA
		Radiologist and cardiologist leave
P5: PTCA	P5: OP	P5: OP
P6: PTCA	P6: OP	P6: OP
P7: PTCA? Check at Lund	P7: "normal coronaries"	P7: PTCA
Radiologist		

leaves		
P8: OP	P8: "already presented"	P8: OP
P9: "normal coronaries"	P9: PTCA	P9: "normal coronaries"
P10: PTCA	P10: OP	P10: OP
P11: OP	P11: OP	
P12: "normal coronaries"	P12: OP	
P13: OP	P13: OP	
P14: OP	P14: OP	
P15: OP		
P16: OP		
P17: OP		

Table 1. Organization of a patient queue in three heart conferences: "expected outcome" and real outcome of the collaborative decisions. (*Legend*: P1= patient case 1, OP=surgery, PTCA=balloon dilatation, PTCA?=postponed decision (the team in Lund will check the case more thoroughly later), "normal coronaries" = what the coronary angiography investigation showed according to the Karlskrona team, an assessment that was accepted by Lund on their words, the video film was not presented.)

So far I have given an account of the overall pattern of organization of work and which decisions were made that can be seen in Table 1: There is an organization of the patient order to be presented. This order at the same time contains a "hypothesis" of the Karlskrona team, a hypothesis of which patients will get balloon dilatation as a recommended move and which will have surgery. In my opinion, instruction is taking place here, and it can be stated: "Take into consideration our preliminary decisions!" or "Let us discuss our suggestions!" or "Mind the indications favoring PTCA!"

When I talk about instruction, I have in mind instruction as *actions* or strings of actions as well as instruction as a specific *activity*. One sort of instruction as activity is school teaching (at least in its best forms), where the grown up generations teach the new generation what they hold important (and which is not learned "spontaneously"). Thus, school instruction has as its objective "learning the given new" ("new" for the children, and "given" for the culture at issue) (e.g. Engeström 1987). Another kind of activity of instruction is, I believe, the kind of mutual coaching that colleagues are doing when supporting each other in collaborative work. I call this kind of instruction "co-coaching." Instruction here is connected to development of the work activity, and to learning of what is new in the society. Nobody has an a priory position as "instructor" or "learner," the positions change depending on circumstance. It is about mutual instruction-*and*-learning, or "co-coaching." In other words, instruction is a specific activity with the motive to assist a (collective or individual) subject's self-organized activity to change its way of working, and it can take the form of, for example, school instruction or co-coaching at work.

It is common today to say that learning occurs whenever one is taking part of a community of practice or is active within a learning environment. In a way, I agree. Learning actions are part of every activity. Not only learning actions, but also instructional actions are involved. Instruction and learning go together. Therefore, instructional actions and learning as actions are inseparable from human activity. Instruction as a general activity has nicely been described by ethnomethodology. Instruction in that sense is what ethnomethodology calls members' methods of "making instructably observable" (Garfinkel 1996). When interacting, people point out aspect of the world they pay attention to and want others to pay attention to. Thus, whenever there is interaction, "making instructably observable" is an aspect of the interaction. I summarize my activity approach to instruction and learning in Figure 2.

	INSTRUCTION	LEARNING
GENERAL ACTIVITY	Members' method: "making instructably observable" (Garfinkel 1996)	Side effects of every activity
SPECIFIC ACTIVITY	e.g. school instruction; or co-coaching at coronary diagnostic work	Learning activity (a subject's – collective or individual – self-organized activity to change its way of working)

Figure 2. Instruction and learning as general and specific activity.

Now, let us continue and look more in detail on the three heart conferences that I have chosen as empirical material. In Table 1 there are two features addressed in this paper. The first feature is organization of work, on a low level so to say(2), the arrangement of the order the patients are to be presented. There was a "list" order of patients, an order that is rearranged before or in the beginning of the heart conference. The arrangements take into account two factors: (1) patients that according to the preliminary decision of the Karlskrona team may be treated by means of balloon dilatation (PTCA), and (2) the time interval during the fixed heart conference meeting time when radiologist(s), and often also cardiologist(s), are able to attend (most often in the beginning of the conference). The outcomes of three of these rearrangements can be inspected in Table 1. What we can see is thus an arrangement of things, the building of an organizational artifact, which is expected to support the work practice. The second feature which is addressed in the paper is the strings of actions that make up the collaborative decision, and where the decision at the same time "deviate from the plan." It is, in other words, the open nature of actions and the collaborative diagnostic work that are made visible here.

Now we move to a more detailed analyses in which I focus on the two features of work that are being dealt with in this paper, work organization as an instructional artifact, and the relation between inert artifacts and live actions as part of an ongoing activity. I do so by giving an account of the interactions of relevance for the local organizing of work, and for the "unexpected decisions" (at least for the Karlskrona team) that were the result of the collaborative diagnostic work. The presentation will start with the February conference, followed by the August conference, and finally the January conference. The reason for this order is that the January conference is rather complex, and is easier to understand if we have looked at the other two conferences first.

Heart conference, February 1996

The first patient is a possible PTCA candidate. "It is number four on the list," explains the Karlskrona cardiologist who presents the patient history, by way of helping the Lund colleagues to find the patient journal in the paper stack in front of them. The list mentioned by the cardiologist is the patients ordered in the order they underwent angiography in Karlskrona. Now the order is rearranged in such a way that patients that possibly may have balloon dilatation are discussed first. In this case, there is only one PTCA candidate. "Then I think we only have old jalopies," said the radiologist, meaning that the patients were so sick that only surgery was an alternative. After that, two persons, the cardiologist and the radiologist, leave the studio at Lund. The presenting cardiologist in Karlskrona continues: "Then we start from the beginning [of the list] – with the 'old jalopies' if one says so." As expected the following patients all got a surgery decision, except in one case, patient 9, for whom PTCA was recommended. It was a decision that was suggested by the surgeon, and it is obvious that it was surprising for Karlskrona team, although they quickly did adapt to the surgeon's proposal:

Surgeon	Yes, should one make PTCA on that LAD?
Radiologist	Yes, that you could do of course. *(Intonation and his voice indicate that the radiologist is surprised.)*
	And then let … then leave the marginal as it is yes … sure
Surgeon	I think so
Radiologist	We do that then

(2) Organization of work is a sort of classification and standardization (Bowker and Star 1999) with consequence for people's handling and thinking. The organization of work is instructional in a sense that may be regarded as trivial. Trivial or not, what I intend to do is to see how organization of work is *used* as part of activity of work. On higher level of organizations of work this can be difficult to show at the same time as it is trivially evident that division of labor, compartmentalization, and other kinds of groupings are of great importance.

Cardiologist	Yes *(The cardiologist also approves)*
Surgeon	We do that then

Commentary: The case is clear-cut The decision suggested of the surgeon for Patient 9 is totally unexpected for the Karlskrona team. However, they have no objections, on the contrary, they quickly accept the proposal of the surgeon. Despite the efforts to plan the work activity, unforeseen things pop up. From the planning view, this is a disturbance, but from the activity perspective, a good complexity. The surgeon's suggestion was "better" in that it quickly got matter-of-fact approval from the Karlskrona team.

Heart conference, August 1996

Surgeon	Let us start with those acute PTCA cases. *(Patient 1-3 got a PTCA decision)*
Radiologist	We have one patient left, so if you have time to stay *(addressed to the radiologist and the cardiologist in the studio at Lund)*
	Also this patient, Patient 4, got a PTCA decision. After that the radiologist and the cardiologist in at Lund leave, "Have a nice weekend!" Patients 5 and 6 got a decision of surgery.
Surgeon	(He points out that the patient has a thin main stem of the coronary artery, and the cardiologist in Karlskrona agrees.) Isn't it possible to make a PTCA on the circumflex only, and wait with the others? He *(the patient)* has, as we know, nothing on scint anteriot. *(The meaning is that the scint measurement shows that it is not life threatening for the patient to neglect "the other" stenosed arteries for the moment)*
Cardiologist	No, nothing, it is inferiot, posteriot with central spreading."
Surgeon	We can show them *(the radiologists at Lund)* the film. It is pretty tiny to make a surgery on in my opinion." *(The cardiologist also approves)*
Cardiologist	But it was the fact that he had so many different parts (*stenosed*) that I thought they (*the radiologists at Lund*) wouldn't accept PTCA. But, sure, if you take that aspect into account and see how he is doing, he is doing rather well now.

Commentary: It seems that the unexpected decision for Patient 7 stems from the fact that the surgeon and the Karlskrona team stress different principles in their (first) assessment. There are two general principles guiding physicians, and consequently also the decisions in the heart conferences. Conditions that are immediately life threatening should be treated immediately, and conditions that are severely debilitating to a person, too. To judge from what the Karlskrona cardiologist said in his last quoted utterance, he (and his team) initially seems to put forward the "many" significantly blocked parts of the coronary arteries. They can be a threat against the patient's life, so action has to be taken. But, the surgeon brings into the overall picture indications from another measure, the scint, which shows that there is sufficient delivery of oxygen to the heart muscles. The patient's life is not at stake, but his well being can be improved by making PTCA on the artery called Circumflex. When the surgeon suggests this possibility, the Karlskrona team changes their initial assessment in favor of the alternative launched by the surgeon.

Heart conference, January 1996

In the preparatory talk in the Karlskrona studio the radiologist that is going to present the angio videos says to his colleagues before the Lund people are connected: "We have, I will look ... one, two, three, I think four PTCA candidates."

Cardiologist	*(When Patient 1 has been finished.)* Then we jump directly to a possible PTCA candidate *(Patient 2, 3 and 4 got a PTCA decision.)*
Surgeon	That was that. Do you have more PTCA cases?
Cardiologist	We have one more, yes. *(Patient 5 got PTCA.*

	Also Patient 6 got a PTCA.)
Surgeon	How many are there on the PTCA side?
Cardiologist & radiologist	*(They speak simultaneously, stuttering. It is not possible to hear what they are saying)*
Radiologist	It is *(name of patient 7)*, shall we take him? *(addressed to the cardiologist)*
Cardiologist	I do not remember it, but *(name of patient 7)* ... I did not mark him *(as a PTCA candidate).*
Radiologist	But when I look at ... two stenoses, it ought to work.
Cardiologist	It is difficult to find it here now *(He browsed through the stack.)* It is before *(name of a patient 8)*
Radiologist	Yes, before *(name of patient 8)* *(Patient 7 was an unclear case. It was decided that they check him later in Lund.)*
Surgeon:	Send it *(the film)* and we will take a closer look at it and roll it back and forth. *(After that the radiologist at Lund leave the meeting with a 'Have a nice weekend!')*
Cardiologist	And then we continue. Now we start from the beginning *(of the list)* *Patient 8 got OP.* *Patient 9 was "skipped" because he according to the cardiologist had "normal arteries."*
Surgeon	*(Patient 10 is presented.)* PTCA?
Radiologist	Yes, you could do that
Surgeon	Peter *(name of the radiologist at Lund that left some minutes ago)* ought to have seen it
Radiologist	Yes he probably should
Cardiologist	Shall we ask for PTCA?
Surgeon	I write that and you send the film
Cardiologist	Then we do that
Surgeon	And then I leave it to Peter *(the radiologist)*
Cardiologist	Now we go to *(name of patient 11)* and I don't think we can do anything for her, with PTCA in any case

Commentary: Here it is obvious that the ordering of the queue by placing possible PTCA patients in the former part, is not an organizing that take place once and for all as in the other cases. This can be inferred from the radiologist's words just before the conference started ("We have /.../ three, I think four PTCA candidates") and the cardiologist's answer to the surgeon's question (after Patient 4), if there were more PTCA candidates ("We have one more, yes").

DISCUSSION

In what way does it make sense to say that organizing of work and other artifacts are instructive? This is the question this paper tries to answer. Here I will discuss some themes that compose an answer.

To "make instructably observable." The ordering of the patient cases by putting the PTCA candidates first on the list before the by-pass candidates, presupposes diagnostic work made by the angiography team in Karlskrona. It also includes a pre-assessment of what treatment to recommend, which, of course, is of a preliminary nature. The organizing is thus a hypothesis of the decision, or a "proffered truth" (Wartofsky 1979, p. xviii) of what is the patient's problem and its proper treatment. The standard procedure in the heart conference is that the Karlskrona angiography team conducts the coronary angiographies and assesses partial conditions of the coronaries. Measurements of critical states of the coronary are recorded on a patient form that is attached to the patient journal. This journal is at hand for each of the participants at the heart conference. If the Karlskrona team has an opinion about what kind of overall decision is appropriate for the patient, this is not expressed in their preparatory work handed over to the surgeons and radiologists in Lund. However, when they rearrange the patient queue with the additional verbal comments that they first want to present a number of potential PTCA patients, they effectively express their pre-decision of the patient cases. The team's rearrangement of the patient list is a way of "making instructably observable" to the colleagues in Lund of their hypotheses of the cases. It is a pre-evaluation they have made based on the indicators they have available.[3]. This is the reason why this work situation is suitable to study if one is interested in how organization of work can be used as an instructive artifact.

---

(3) They are fully aware that the final decision of treatment will be made at the heart conference It may happen that the final decision is further postponed and delegated to the team in Lund. It may also happen that a decision made at the heart conference will be changed later at Lund because of unforeseen events.

Instruction - potential and realized. It may be correct to claim that past activities are "resting" in artifacts and used in later activity, but it is only one side of the matter. The other side is that the "use" of the artifact in an activity does not follow an instruction inherent in the artifact. The artifact-bound instruction is only a suggestion, a potential instruction, which is turned into a real instruction when the agent/subject accepts the suggestion and makes it his/her/their own.

Therefore, how to make sense of the interaction between the inert (or static) artifact-instruction and live actions in the situation is the problem. If the potential artifact-bound instruction is used as a resource and in that way is turned into a real instruction is dependent on the situation as a whole, and not only on the artifact. There is an interplay between artifacts as potential instructions and actions, which are situated and thus open until they are accomplished. After the fact it can be stated if the potential instruction was turned into a real instruction or if other potential resources in the situation were transformed into real resources.

Artifacts are "structured." It is a fact (in my opinion) that artifacts are potentially instructive and that this potentiality is realized, under certain circumstances, in human activity. The potential intentions/instructions are meritoriously recognized by Actor Network Theory (although the step to interpret the potentiality as an actant-capacity of the artifact is, for me, to go too far).

But how to understand the instructive potentiality of artifacts and its realization? I will try a line of argumentation that artifacts are (potentially) instructive, taking as a starting point the two famous thought experiments of Karl Popper (1972, pp. 107-108) and Lektorsky's critique of them. Popper's thought experiments both have a common pre-condition, namely that "All our machines and tools are destroyed and all our subjective learning, including our subjective knowledge of machines and tools, and how to use them." In Experiment 1 the libraries and our capacity to learn from books survive, but in Experiment 2, this is not the case. The outcome of Popper's thought experiments is that the "objective knowledge" that is inherent in the texts matters. In Experiment 1 our civilization will recover within reasonable time, but not in Experiment 2, where the evolutionary process has to start over again. Against Popper's argumentation Lektorsky (1984, p. 237f) raises the objection:

> Assume that a civilisation is dead and no one knows the language once spoken by its subjects. Although the books written in that extinct language survive, no one is capable of decoding them and the connection is thus lost between the defunct culture and the actual social-cultural process, including the cognitive one. And that means that the books preserved no longer contain any knowledge. Properly speaking, they are not even books but simply objects with strange strokes in them.

Although I generally agree with Lektorsky's critique of Poppers epistemology, I do not in this case. In my interpretation Popper says that artifacts ("World 3 objects") have something to tell, there are in them inherent properties that we can use and have to count with. So far I think Popper is correct. I will argue that artifacts are men's offspring, and in them humans recognize themselves and their activities. There is a "grammar" or structure of human activity, a structure that is built into the artifacts, and make it possible for humans (with their activity and its structure) to "see" that there is a structure in the artifact. The "objects with strange strokes on them" that Lektorsky is talking about, are, in my view, man-made objects and they are discernable as such. There is a structure in them, which make them possible to decode, at least in principle. This fundamental condition makes archeology possible, and, I am convinced, gives the possibility to decode codes and extinct languages. Artifacts speak, and in an ongoing practice, their voices are made instructive.

"The riddle of things." Men are not only single individuals thinking with their brains, and things are not only dead artifacts. These are insights nowadays spreading in not so few circles. We can talk of "The return of the artifact" (a title of collection of Latour papers published as a book in Swedish 1996) referring to Latour's (1993) idea that "we have never been modern" because we thought we could be totally separated from things and thus modern, but we did not succeed, and now they are back again, the artifacts, in the networks that, together with us, make up the world. So, if things are not only things, what are they? A riddle. How can they be explained? In the article "The riddle of things" Miettinen (1999) makes an attempt at a serious answer on several points. Two of them are similar to what I have found. First, the interplay between artifact with its potential instruction and the use of the artifact-bound instruction (thus making it realized) cannot be solved theoretically (When is a potential instruction realized?). It depends on thousands of details. If there is a solution of this conflict, it will be found in the situation, or, in Miettinens words, in an "object-oriented, culturally and socially mediated local activity" (p. 190). In my case: When is a local work organization created for instructive purposes? The other point where my answer is close to Miettinen's concerns the future-orientedness of what Wartofsky calls "tertiary artifacts" (artifacts used for imaging future possibilities to state it shortly). How to imagine future coronary diagnostics? In the paper I have not dealt with this issue, albeit it is touched upon, again and again, by the physicians (What criteria is fitting when doing interventions? How to combine PTCA and OP?). Obviously the object of their work have a regulating role on their actions.

Artifact-bound instruction. Two of the kind of artifact-bound instruction mentioned in Figure 1 above are more "reflective," the linguistic and graphic ones. They are what Wartofsky calls "secondary," that is, they constitute "*reflexive* embodiments of forms of action or praxis" (...) "created for the purpose of *preserving* and *transmitting* skills" (1979, p. 201: italics in original). The other two, the physical-material and the organizational, are not that reflective, but they nevertheless have a reflective quality, i.e. they represent aspects of human activity. In this paper I have attempted to show, in some detail, (1) how organization of work also represent human activity, and thus is instructive for how to accomplish work; and (2) that instruction as an activity emerges out of an interplay between artifacts and their uses (artifact-bound instruction does not work alone, and neither do unmediated instructional actions).

By way of introduction I discerned four kinds of artifact-bound instruction. This does not mean there only are those four. Lucy Suchman (1987; among others) has studied the use of linguistic artifacts ("manuals" and plans), Charles Goodwin (1994; among others) has studied how graphic artifacts are used in work practice, Donald Norman (1993, among others) has studied how affordances give directions for actions, and I have in this paper made an attempt to demonstrate how organization of work can be used as an artifact with instructional properties. I do not say these four kinds of artifact are all that are. It only means that these are the ones I have observed in my studies of coronary diagnostic work. I see no reason to imagine there are limits to what artifacts can be representational. On the contrary, I believe, to put it in Wartofsky's vocabulary, that "Anything (in the strongest and most unqualified sense of 'anything') can be a representation of anything else" (1979, p. xx). If this is trustworthy, we will surely find representational usage of other kinds of artifacts, and we will surely find the uses of a great variety of instructional artifacts in human activity. But we have to find it out, by close studies of work practices.

Conclusions

Organizational artifacts have instructional properties, and as with all artifacts, they have "humanized" properties. They bear evidence of having been structured by human activity. The structure of the artifacts can be used to re-represent human activity, and its intentionality to direct one's own actions. The bridging of the past to the present of work activity, here accounted for in terms of instructional artifacts and their uses, needs to be complemented by a future-orientation offered by the object of work. Therefore, "situated actions" are determined/informed by a "situatedness" that includes potential artifact-bound instruction as well as the comprehensiveness and future-orientation that are rendered by the object of the work activity.

REFERENCES

Bowker, G. and Star, S. L. (1999). *Sorting things out. Classification and its consequences.* Cambridge, Massachusetts: The MIT Press.

Engeström, Y. (1987). *Learning by expanding. An activity-theoretical approach to developmental research.* Helsinki: Orienta-Konsultit.

Enerstvedt, R. (1982). *Mennesket som virksomhet.* Oslo: Tiden. (Man as activity)

Garfinkel, H. (1996). Ethnomethodology's program. *Social Psychology Quarterly,* 1966, *59*, 5-21.

Goodwin, C. (1994). Professional vision. *American Anthropologist, 96* (3), 606-633.

Kehler, M, P.O. Bengtsson, M. Freitag, B. Lindström, and J. Medin (1996). "Radiological teleconferencing in Sweden." *Journal of Telemedicine and Telecare.* 1996 (2):166-164.

Koschmann, Timothy (1996). CSCL – Theory and prctice of an emerging paradigm. Mahwah, N.J.: Erlbaum

Latour, Bruno. (1991). "Technology is society made durable." In: J.Law. Ed., *A sociology of monsters. Essays on power, technology and domination.* London: Routledge.

Latour, B. (1993). *We have never been modern.* Cambridge, Massachusetts: Harvard University Press.

Latour, B. (1998). *Artefaktens återkomst.* Stockholm: Nerenius & Santérus Förlag.

Lektorsky, V. (1984). *Subject, object, cognition.* Moscow: Progress Publishers.

Löwgren, J. and Stolterman, E. (1998). *Design of informationsteknik – materialet utan egenskaper.* Lund: Studentlitteratur.

Miettinen, R. (1999). The riddle of things: Activity theory and Actor-Network Theory as approaces to studying innovations. *Mind, Culture, and Activity*, 1999, *6*, 170-195.

Norman, D. (1993). *Things that make us smart.* Reading, Massachusetts: Addison-Wesley.

Popper, K. (1972). *Objective knowledge.* An evolutionary approach. Oxford: Oxford University Press.

Sartre, J-P (1968/1960). *Search for a method.* New York: Vintage Books.

Suchman, L. (1987). *Plans and situated actions. The problem of human-machine communication.* Cambridge: Cambridge University Press.

Sutter, B. (1999). Instruction and learning in the development of telemediated coronary work Researching Work and Learning. A First International Conference. Conference proceedings. University of Leeds, UK, 11-12 September 1999.

Sutter, B. (2000a). Instructions at work: A case f coronary diagnostics. *In Proceedings of the Fourth International Conference of the Learning Sciences* (ICLS 2000), ((Eds, B.J. Fishman & S.F.O'Connor-Divelbiss), University of Michigan, Ann Arbor, Mahwah, NJ: Lawrence Erlbaum.

Sutter, B. (2000b). Co-coaching at work. Instruction and collaboration in coronary diagnostics, *Occasional Papers from the Work Practice Laboratory*, Vol. 1, No. 3:2000, Department of Human Work Science, Blekinge Institute of Technology, Ronneby, Sweden.

Sutter, B. (2001). A graphic artifact at work – the "angio" in coronary diagnostics. Unpublished manuscript.

Wartofsky, M. (1979). *Models. Representation and the scientific understanding*. Boston: Reidel.

Wenger, Etienne (1998). *Communities of practice. Learning, meaning, and identity*. Cambridge: Cambridge University Press.

Social Information Sharing in a CSCL Community

Hichang Cho, Michael Stefanone, Geri Gay
Human Computer Interaction (HCI) Group
Cornell University
hc71[mas223; gkg1]@cornell.edu

ABSTRACT

This study is designed to clarify important features of social network analysis for analyzing community-based activities in a CSCL setting. The theoretical and methodological background is social/communication network analysis, which is employed to identify and understand students' communication and interaction patterns when collaborating through wireless computer networking tools. Thirty-two students were given high-end laptops with access to the wireless Internet, and their use of and communicative patterns via these systems were gathered through a proxy server. Findings show that social influences, in the form of network prestige effects, strongly affected the likelihood and the extent to which information posted in the CSCL environment was shared by peers in this learning community.

Keywords
Network Prestige Effects, Wireless Computing, Computer-Mediated Communication (CMC), Social Network Analysis

INTRODUCTION

Studies in collaborative learning have called for greater research focus on the communicative processes involved in successful (and unsuccessful) peer interactions rather than just on learning outcomes. This approach differs from traditional perspectives on leaning that typically view learning as acquisition of knowledge by isolated individuals and focus on the development of techniques, and technologies for more efficient school practices. In the perspective of Situated Learning theory (Lave and Wenger, 1991), for example, it is critical that the theoretical focus not be on learning itself. Instead, their theoretical starting point is learning situated in the practices of communities, with learning viewed as a feature of social participation in a community of practice.

So what is a community? What impact does community structure, formed both online and offline, have on information searching and sharing behavior? How do we analyze the complex community structures and social dynamics within these systems? Although cooperative learning and other kinds of computer supported collaborative learning (CSCL) are flourishing in classrooms, researchers are just beginning to identify and understand the social dynamics that influence learning in these settings (Webb, 1989).

The purpose of this study is to describe the utility of social network theory in analyzing students' interaction and learning in community-based groups, especially those based on CMC, and to clarify some aspects that have not been tested previously. More specifically, we are attempting to refine a technique through which to assess the communication dynamics of a computer-mediated communication system, such as a computer-supported collaborative learning (CSCL) environment. Such a methodology will give researchers the ability to identify central, influential actors in a group or class. Central, prominent or prestigious actors, defined by specific structural attributes in the communication network, have consistent characteristics that could theoretically aide implementation and maintenance of CSCL systems. Central actors have a strong influence on adoption patterns, as well as perceptions of utility of a given technology, for example.

LITERATURE REVIEW

Social navigation

Affiliation with community has benefits that extend beyond that of knowledge building. People located in social networks offer guidance with regard to information seeking, as well. Numerous strategies are available for information seeking on-line. The hyper-linked nature of the World Wide Web promotes aimless wandering, or browsing strategy, which lacks utility when seeking specific information. Relying on meta-data for navigation through information spaces greatly reduces chances for successful landfall (Lynch, 1997). The ocean of information accessible through the Internet, and the dynamic nature of content fuel each other, creating a rather unfriendly information-searching environment. The community around an individual can be a valuable resource by helping to guide information seeking.

Having a standardized format for text and multimedia documents has lead to the exponential growth of Internet web pages, which can be located only by knowledge of the specific URL. Users are faced with the option of trudging through cyberspace without sound navigation aids to a specific local, or, better yet, to follow a suggested URL originating from someone in a social network. Social navigation, collaborative filtering, and recommendation systems are tools with the potential to increase learning efficiency regarding information seeking behavior within and outside class boundaries.

Traditionally, much of the literature on the relationship between peer interaction and learning focuses on the value of information shared through social exchanges. Because the opportunity to share resources and knowledge is one of the most commonly cited advantages of community-based learning, a number or studies have investigated factors influencing the extent to which information or knowledge is shared within a given learning community. In general, researchers hold that whether peer interactions will ultimately lead to their learning efficacy primarily depends on several variables. To be effective for learning, for instance, knowledge or information must be timely, relevant, of sufficient elaboration, understood by recipient, and applied by the recipient to the problem at hand (Vedder, 1985; Webb, 1989).

While these studies identified factors influencing learning outcomes and efficiency, scholars in CSCL argue that past research failed to look at how collaboration and communication tools in a CSCL setting interact with processes involved in peer interactions (Haythornthwaite, 1999). In this regard, many emphasized that studies should look at processes of the social mechanisms rather than outcomes of learning. Peer-interactions and information sharing influenced by learners' positions in a given learning community network may be one of the many social mechanisms that have not fully investigated previously.

Social network analysis

Collaborative learning requires interaction and exchange among learners as they share experiences and solve problems cooperatively. In computer-supported learning classes it is often difficult to know to what extent individuals are interacting and communicating with other class members, and how much these communicative behaviors influence various types of community-based learning activities (Haythornthwaite, 1999). We propose social network analysis as a methodology to analyze the processes involved in successful (and perhaps more importantly, unsuccessful) peer interactions that influence collaborative learning behaviors and outcomes.

The idea of examining the structure of social networks has been adopted by a wide variety of researchers. Sociologists use network analysis techniques to examine the migration to urban environments on the composition and resources resident within social networks (Wellman, 1990). Other research explores the relationship between network structure and diffusion of innovations including pharmaceutical drugs (Coleman, Katz, & Menzel, 1957).

Based in part on Systems theory (Buckely, 1967), social network analysis provides a vocabulary to identify and measure network communication flow (Monge & Contractor, 1987). The greatest benefit of network research is that it considers how the communication network structure of a group shapes participant behavior and cognition. For example, Anderson and Jay (1985) examined the adoption pattern of a computerized information system by physicians. The results suggest that network variables are better predictors of adoption of the system by physicians than individual attribute variables.

There are differing levels of analysis in network methodology. At the individual level, key communicators hold the potential to shape behavior and perceptions of others in the network (Marsden, 1986). Key communicators can be identified by several measures. Their prominence in a network is observable via the range of their network (overall size of the network) and their centrality within the system being analyzed (Tichy, 1981). For our study, we focus on the role of "key communicators" who occupy a central position in a given social/communication network, and test how those key actors influence others' behaviors in the form of social navigation. Individuals differ in the degree to which they are prominent in a given communication or social network. There are several network metrics that attempt to represent this characteristic. The simplest definition of actor centrality is "degree centrality." By definition, it refers to the number of ties (connections) that an actor holds in a given social network. It is assumed that central actors must be the most active in the sense that they have the most ties to other actors in the network or graph (Wasserman & Faust, 1994). An actor with a high centrality level, as measured by its in-and out- degree, is "where the action is" in the network. Thus, this measure focuses on the most visible actors in the network. An actor with a large degree is in direct contact or is adjacent to many other actors. This actor should then begin to be recognized by others as a major channel of relational information, indeed, a crucial cog in the network, occupying a central location (Wasserman & Faust, 1994). In contrast, actors with low degrees are clearly peripheral in the network. Such actors are not active in the relational process.

There is considerable research support for the role of central communicators in the use of new communication technologies. For instance, Papa and Tracy (1988) report that highly connected individuals in an organization's communication network were also the most productive with the technology, and reported the most positive experience. Other studies show that central actors in social networks exert powerful influences in diffusion of innovations (Albrecht & Hall, 1991) or shaping employee perceptions in organizations (Ibarra & Andrews, 1993). More relevant to this study, researchers have found that network prominence, reputation, and perceptual processes (e.g., network proximity) may influence the recognition and evaluation of the relevance and quality of an individual's expertise for a given subject matter (Cicourle, 1990; Walsh & Ungson, 1991) when collaborating on decision-making or information sharing.

More recently, the social network approach has been applied in educational context by several authors. For instance, Haythornthwaite (1999) found that a learner's centrality was positively associated with sense of belongingness in a learning community. Similarly, Baldwin, Bedell, and Johnson (1997) found that centrality measure was positively correlated with satisfaction with a team-based learning program. With regard to information exchange among peers, proximity and the strength of ties between peers lead to the exchange of more kinds of information and the use of more media (Hauthornthwaite & Wellman, 1998)

In sum, the above literature review suggests that peer interactions in a CSCL setting, more particularly social navigation practices in this study, should be influenced by actors' positions and proximities in a given learning network/community.

Hence,

- RQ1: With regard to social navigation, do URL's recommended by central actors in the email and discussion board networks generate a higher peer-response than URL's recommended by actors on the periphery of the communication networks?
- H1a: The number of page views to a referred URL is positively associated with the centrality/prestige of an actor who posted the URL.
- H1b: The number of unique visitors to a referred URL is positively associated with the centrality/prestige of an actor who posted the URL.

  In addition to the research question and hypothesis, we are also interested in evaluating the effectiveness of communication/collaboration tools employed in the current study. More specifically, we ask whether or not there would be any significant differences between two communication channels (the class listserv vs. discussion board) used for social navigation practices.

Hence,

- RQ2: Is there any significant difference between the class listserv and discussion board in terms of generating more peer-response?
- H2a: There is significant difference in the number of page views between the class listserv and discussion board.
- H2b: There is significant difference in the number of unique visitors between the class listserv and discussion board.

METHODS

Sample and data collection

The current study is based on data about thirty-two students and their mobile computing usage patterns, who enrolled in a Communication course at a major research university. Participants of this study were given high-end laptop computers with access to newly installed campus wireless modem network for the duration of a semester. Students' Web browsing and email exchanges using these laptops were set to pass through proxy servers, and network protocol breakdowns and statistics were gathered daily. For instance, Web browsing patterns on these laptops (including: URLs, dates, IP addresses, and times) were recorded 24 hours/day, 7 days/week in a log file by a proxy server during most of the semester (about 15 weeks). Similarly, under strict rules assuring anonymity, participants' email log files were collected, providing information about who sent emails to whom and when. All participants were required to sign a consent form informing them of their responsibilities and the scope of data collection. Among thirty-two students, 24 students (75%) were undergraduate level and 8 students (25%) were graduate level. Gender-wise, 22 students (68.7%) were male and 10 (31.3%) female. Over 44 percent (n=14) of the class was comprised of communication students.

Class description

In this study a physical community of students meeting in a classroom on campus was supplemented by mobile computers and CMC tools in an attempt to foster a parallel virtual community. The community focus of the class design, and the implementation of CSCL tools throughout the semester encouraged participants to practice cooperative learning and other kinds of community-based group instruction. For instance, the class web site functioned as a portal where students could post contributions which would be available to teaching staff, as well as the rest of the student body. Asynchronous tools included a semi-moderated class listserv and a web-based class discussion board. Two students were selected each week and asked to post questions associated with class readings to these on-line forums. This activity was required throughout the duration of the semester, and discussion threads allowed users to retrace topics in dialog form. The class portal included web folders for students and groups to store and share information. These folders provided user space on the class server, designed to provide a central location for students to leave and share documents/objects.

Relevant to this study, students utilized both a web-based discussion board and a class listserv for email message exchange to practice social navigation as a means of recommending useful websites and other information to other class members. Students were encouraged to engage in open discussion. Topics comprised of issues related to theoretical approaches to CMC, as well as issues garnering attention in popular media (see for example, http://www.wired.com/wired/archive/8.04/joy.html). Aside from the weekly class meeting, students were divided between two lab sessions, which met once weekly.

Measure and analysis

The unit of analysis in this study is URLs (n=50) recommended by students in the class. Explicit recommendations of URLs posted by students were identified by examining discussion board threads and the class listserv. For each URL recommended, the total number of page views (measured by the number of Web pages opened) by other class members and the number of unique visitors to the URL were quantified using the proxy server log file.

Hypothesis 1a and 1b predict that the number of page views and unique visitors to a referred URL will be positively associated with the centrality of an actor who posted the URL. To test these hypotheses, two different sets of network matrices were created using the above-described data, and centrality measure for each individual actor was computed using UCINET 5.0 (Version 1.0; Borgatti, Everett, & Freeman, 1999). The discussion board network (n=32) consists of communication linkages in the online discussion board. The "in- and out-degree centrality" was measured by counting the number of interaction partners per each individual in the form of discussion threads. For instance, if person X responded to messages posted by three different persons, then the out-degree centrality for the actor was "3." In contrast, if five persons responded to messages posted by the actor X, then the in-degree centrality for him/her was "5."

In a similar vein an email network matrix (n=31) and centrality measures were computed using email log file data. One student who participated in the discussion board network refused to use a proxy server for email, so the network size for email dropped to thirty-one. The in- and out- degree centrality measures for the email matrix refer to the number of class members who sent email to an actor X (in-degree) or the number of email recipients to whom an actor X sent emails (out-degree).

The second centrality measure, Bonacich's power, more directly reflects prominence an actor based on network graph theory. If one's influence domain is full of prestigious actors, one's prestige should also be high. If, however, an actor's domain contains only peripheral, or marginally important actors, then the status of this actor should be low. To quantify this idea, Bonacich's power reflects the degree to which an actor's prestige is a function of the prestige of the actors to whom the actor is connected (mathematical details, and examples of the use of this measure can be found in Bonacich (1987)). This measure is also computed based on the discussion board and email matrices using UCINET 5. 0 (Borgatti, Everett, & Freeman, 1999).

To test Hypothesis I and II, product-moment correlation and t-tests were conducted, respectively. While multiple regression analysis using dummy variable for communication channel would be a good alternative in order to test both the hypotheses at once, this approach was avoided due to high intercorrelations (and therefore a multicollinearity problem) among the network measures (see Table 1).

RESULTS AND DISCUSSIONS

At the outset of the semester, students used the set of communication tools frequently. The discussion board and listserv functioned well for 'umbrella' type communication, conveying content of interest tot the entire class. Throughout the semester, students and staff members posted fifty URLs on the class listerserv (n=28) and the discussion board (n=22). The phenomenon of social navigation was evident, indicating strong community participation. When comparing the number of URLs hit before and after recommendation, a significant difference was found ($\underline{M}$=50.55, $\underline{t}$=2.59, $\underline{p} \leq .01$). More than 95% of page views and unique visitors occurred within one or two weeks after the URLs posted. This is clear evidence that when students posted a URL of interest to either the discussion board or listserv, other students in the social network of the class followed and explored the referred URL.

The social/communication network structures captured by email and discussion board networks resemble each other. Figure 1 and 2 visually represents communication structures in the two networks. In these sociograms, nodes represent social actors and lines between them show the communication linkages. The lines are weighted, meaning that thicker lines represent stronger ties (more frequent interactions between dyads). As shown in the figure some actors held strongly central and prestigious positions, and others located in peripheral positions. It is interesting to note that there are three social isolates in the discussion board network ("i, s, ff" in the figure), whereas in the email network every actor is connected to at least one social tie. On average, members in both networks contain similar number of network partners (email = 5, discussion board =4.8) and interaction frequencies (email = 12.97, discussion board = 7.3), although they used the email slightly more frequently than the discussion. Network densities (measured by the total number of existing linkages divided by the total number of possible ties) of the email and discussion board networks are 0.167 and 0.085, respectively. It indicates that actors in the email networks are more densely connected than those in the discussion board network.

Figure 1. Class Email Communication Network Structure (n=31)

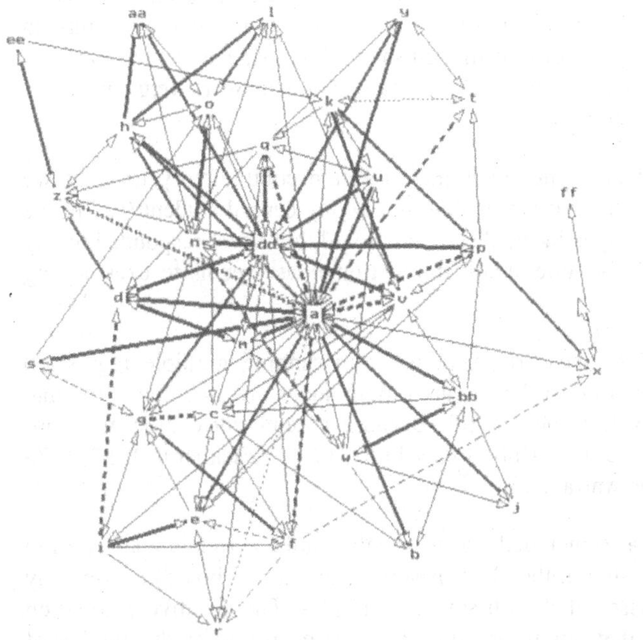

Figure 2. Class Discussion Board Communication Network Structure (n=32)

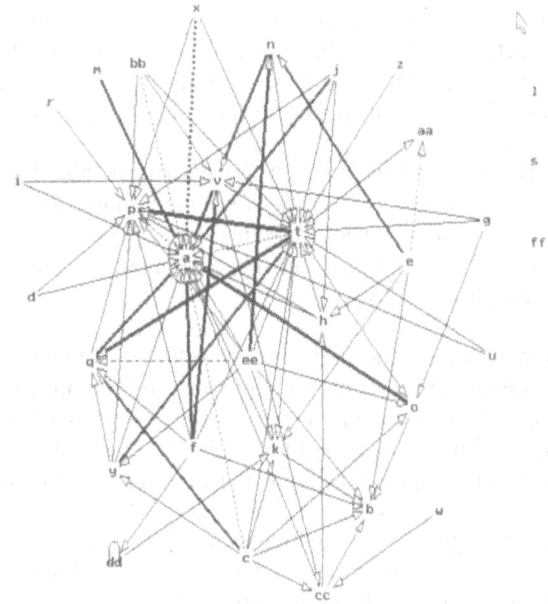

To test Hypothesis 1a and 1b, we conducted bi-variate product-moment correlation tests. Variables like "pageviews" and "unique viewers" were correlated with "degree-centrality (in- and out- degree)" and "Bonacich's power" both in the email and discussion board networks. The results are shown in Table 1.

Table 1. Product-Moment Correlation Test Results

	1	2	3	4	5	6	7	8	9
1. Pageview	-	-	-	-	-	-	-	-	-
2. Unique visitors	.754**	-	-	-	-	-	-	-	-
3. Email_Outdegree	.475**	.531*	-	-	-	-	-	-	-
4. Email_Indegree	.501**	.639**	.971**	-	-	-	-	-	-
5. Email_power	.488**	.582**	.996**	.989**	-	-	-	-	-
6. Discussion_Indegree	.439**	.629**	.780**	.863**	.818**	-	-	-	-
7. Discussion_Outdegree	-.403*	-.373	-.627**	-.694**	-.657**	-.712**	-	-	-
8. Disuccsion_power	.495**	.656**	.944**	.981**	.965**	.921**	-.617**	-	-
9. Time_Week	-.296*	-.209	-.411*	-.452*	-.430*	-.297	.206	-.392*	-

* $\underline{p} \leq .05$, ** $\underline{p} \leq .01$

Note that the number of URLs decreased to forty-two for this correlation analysis. In order to allow social network variables (e.g., degree centrality of actors) to influence actors' behavior and cognition, we limited the analysis of URLs posted two weeks after the beginning of the course. We assumed that centrality (prominence) of an actor would likely become visible (and influential) to other social network members only after a period of time had passed. The results were compared to those with the original fifty URLs, and no notable difference was found.

Hypothesis 1a and 1b are supported by the test results. As predicted, both the number of pageviews and unique visitors to recommended URLs are positively associated with all centrality measures, except for the "out-degree" in the discussion board network. The results indicate that network participants in this CSCL community were more likely to follow social recommendations made by highly central/prestigious actors than those by peripheral actors. Note that the unit of analysis in this analysis is URLs, therefore the fact that central actors tended to post more URLs did not affect the results of this correlational analysis, because each URL was treated equally. This finding is consistent with previous social network studies in which researchers find that prominence, reputation, and perceptual processes (e.g., network proximity) may influence the recognition and evaluation of the relevance and quality of an individual's expertise for a given subject matter (Cicourle, 1990; Walsh & Ungson, 1991). While timeliness, usability, relevance, and sufficiency of information may be crucial factors determining the degree to which students learn something out of these social navigation practices (Webb, 1999), social influences, in the form of network prestige effects, strongly affected the extent to which information posted in CSCL tools was actually shared by peers in this learning community. In other words, the likelihood of information exchanges between peer members (i.e., unique visitors) and the amount of information shared (i.e., pageviews) were at least partially determined by quantifiable characteristics of actors in a given social/communication network (e.g., position, prestige, range), regardless of the content type or value of information.

The negative associations between the discussion board out-degree and other measures are contradictory to what we hypothesized. Upon reviewing dataset carefully, however, we found that it was due to a highly central student ("a" in the figure) who sent and received many emails and posted many messages in the discussion board, but never responded to any messages posted by other class members. Since the sample size is quite small, this extreme case seems to exert strong effects on statistical analyses.

As mentioned before, the high inter-correlations among network measures kept us from running multiple regression analyses, although this approach might reveal a more in-depth picture of the research topic under investigation. Note that high intercorrelations among network measures are statistically less meaningful. Because of auto-correlation and non-independence of observation problems inherent in network measures (see Hubert & Schultz, 1976; Krackhardt, 1987, 1988 for reviews), careful interpretation on these associations should be warranted.

In addition to the previously mentioned variables of interest, we also included a time variable in the correlation analyses in order to test if time (measured by weeks when an URLs were posted in the class listserv or discussion board) exerted any mediating influence. As shown in Table 1, time is negatively associated with several variables. The negative correlation between "time" and "pageviews" ($r = -.296$, $p = .057$) indicates that less information (at least measured by the number of Web pages opened) was processed/consumed by other class members as the semester progressed. Also, it is interesting to note that the time variable is negatively associated with all the centrality measures in the email network, and Bonacich's power in the discussion board network. This indicates that less central/prestigious actors were more likely to post URLs later on in the semester, suggesting that peripheral actors require time to "catch on to" community-based practices. In addition, while central actors in the community enjoy network prestige effects by generating higher peer interactions and responses, more peripheral actors are less successful in generating rich peer responses.

This finding relates to the concept of legitimate peripherality in Situated Learning theory (Lave & Wenger, 1991). Recognizing the role of socialization in learning, the theory holds that the learner gradually moves from legitimate peripheral participation towards full participation in the community of practice, and that participation in the community is the real curriculum. Access for newcomers to the community of practice and all that the membership entails is the critical force behind the movement from legitimate peripherality to full participation. To become a full member of a community of practice requires access to a wide range of ongoing activities, veteran members, other members of the community, information, resources, opportunities for participation, and the artifacts (Lave & Wenger, 1991; p. 100-101). The finding that peripheral actors not only tend to be late in participation, but also ignored by other community members, underscores the importance of the role of socialization in designing a virtual online community of learning. From a practical point of view, this finding suggests that teaching staff should employ early interventions like identifying peripheral members in a learning community as soon as possible to help them become more active members in community-based practices. Social network analysis, as described in the current study, may be a valuable tool to monitor as well as evaluate such intervention.

Hypothesis 2a and 2b were tested by t-tests. The original fifty URLs were categorized by two communication tools where those URLs were posted (listserv=28, discussion board=22). On average, URLs posted on the class listserv generated significantly more pageviews ($\underline{M} = 38.50$) than those on the discussion board ($\underline{M} = 4.9$, $\underline{t}=2.864$ $\underline{p} \leq .01$). Similarly, significantly more students visited URLs posted on the class listserv ($M = 4.44$) than those on the discussion board ($\underline{M} = 1.42$, $\underline{t} = 2.10$, $\underline{p} = .051$). The most plausible interpretation of this finding would be that the class listserv is a "push technology." That is, any messages posted on the listserv were delivered to every student in the class. In contrast, messages on the discussion board were accessible only to those who accessed the class website and opened the discussion board. While both the technologies are surely interactive media in that users make decisions whether or not to consume contents delivered to them, at least some "push" might be necessary to have learners be fully involved in community-based activities as illustrated in this case.

CONCLUSION AND FUTURE DIRECTIONS

This study claims that learners' social and communicative relationships should be considered, along with instruction design, technology implementation, and individual aptitude, for the successful design of a CSCL class. To empirically support this claim, this study analyzed how structural positions (e.g., central and peripheral actors) and relations emerged in a CSCL class, and how these structural properties mediated learners' perceptions and behaviors related to community-based information sharing practice.

Overall, findings in the current study reveal that social network analysis can be a valuable tool for analyzing the complex processes involved in successful (and perhaps more importantly, unsuccessful) peer interactions that shape collaborative learning behaviors and outcomes. More specifically, an actor's structural properties such as degree centrality and Bonacich's power were significantly correlated with variables measuring the frequency and the amount of peer responses (i.e., unique visitors and pageviews, respectively) to the actor's social recommendation. The results indicate that participants in a social network—even a virtual one—are more inclined to follow the lead of the network's central actors than of the network's peripheral actors. The emergence of such statistically significant results suggests that quantitative characteristics of social network members—even prior to examining the content or value of information—can be useful predictors of meaningful behavioral outcomes. In other words, the current research shows the nature of peer interaction and the resultant social networks in an educational context can significantly influence what and how information is shared and exchanged in a CSCL setting.

While the current study presents interesting findings and implications for both theoretical and methodological reasons, there are a number of limitations that warrant directions for future research. First, the hypothesis testing was based on correlation tests, which prevents us from determining the causal direction of many of the relationships identified here. This is a problem when trying to determine the extent to which network prestige effects influence students' social navigation practices. Our finding of positive associations between network centrality and information sharing and seeking is generally consistent with other social network studies. However, we also believe that an alternative interpretation for this finding is plausible in that URLs posted by central actors actually contain more valuable or interesting information, and therefore generated a higher level of responses (follow-ups) from other members. Future research might analyze the actual contents of URLs analyzed in this study, and control for those effects. A similar problem exists in interpreting the differences between the two communication tools (email vs. discussion board). The significant differences between the two tools may be due to unknown factors other than communication channel effects.

The second limitation is related to the first one. Sample size for the current study is relatively small (thirty-two subjects and fifty/forty-two URLs). Due to this problem, we were unable to conduct a more complex test, adding more variables to control for exogenous effects.

Finally, since both network measures and Web browsing patterns are longitudinal data, the causal direction of relationships would have been specified if time-series analyses had been applied. Again, due to relatively small sample size and high-intercorrelations among measures, this approach was not attempted for the current study. Ultimately, future research in this kind would benefit from time-series analyses.

ACKNOWLEDGMENTS

This material is based upon work supported by the National Science Foundation under Grant No. CDA-97-03470. Any opinions, findings, and conclusions or recommendations expressed in this material are those of authors and do not necessarily reflect the views of the National Science Foundation.

REFERENCES

Albrecht, T. L. & Hall, B. (1991). Relational and content differences between elites and outsiders in innovation networks, *Human Communication Research,* 17(4): 535-561.

Anderson, J. & Jay, S. (1985). Computers and Clinical Judgment: The Role of Physician Networks. *Social Science and Medicine*, 20(10): 969-979.

Baldwin, T. T., Bedell, M. D., & Johnson, J. L. (1997). The social fabric of a team-based M.B.A. program: Network effects on student satisfaction and performance, *Academy of Management Journal*, 40(6): 1369-1397.

Bonacich, P. (1987). Power and centrality. *American Journal of Sociology,* 92, 1170-1182.

Borgatti, S. P., Everett, M. G. & Freeman, L. C. (1999). *UCINET 5 for Windows*. Harvard, MA: Analytic Technologies.

Buckley, W. (1967). *Sociology and Modern Systems Theory.* NY: Prentice-Hall.

Cicourel, A. V. (1990). The integration of distributed knowledge in collaborative medical diagnosis. In J. Galegher, R. E. Kraut, & C. Egido (Eds.), *Intellectual Teamwork: Social and Technical Foundations of Cooperative Work:* 214-242: Hillsdale, NJ: Lawrence Erlbaum Associates.

Coleman, B. S., Katz, E. & Menzel, H. (1957). The Diffusion of an Innovation Among Physicians. *Sociometry*, 20: 253-270.

Haythornthwaite, C. (1999). Networks of information sharing among computer-supported distance learners, In *Proceedings of the Computer-Support for Collaborative Learning (CSCL) 1999 Conference,* C. Hoadley & Roschelle (Eds.), Dec. 12-15, Stanford University, Palo Alto, California, Mahwah, NJ: Lawrence Erlbaum Associates.

Haythornthwaite, C. & Wellman, B. (1998). Work, friendship and media use for information exchange in a networked organization. *Journal of the American Society for Information Science*, 46(12), 1101-1114.

Hubert, L. & Schultz, J. (1976). Quadratic Assignment as a general Data Analysis Strategy. *British Journal of Mathematical Statistical Psychology*, 29: 190-241.

Ibarra, H., Andrews, S. B. (1993). Power, social influence, and sense making: Effects of network centrality and proximity on employee perception, *Administrative Science Quarterly,* 38: 277-303.

Krackhardt, D. (1987). QAP Partialling as a Test of Spuriousness. *Social Networks*, 9: 171-186.

Krackhardt, D. (1988). Predicting with Networks: Nonparametric Multiple Regression Analysis of Dyadic Data. *Social Networks*, 10: 359-381.

Lave, J. & Wenger, E. (1991): *Situated Learning. Legitimate Peripheral Participation.* Cambridge University Press. Cambridge. 1991.

Lynch, C. (1997). Searching the Internet: Organizing Material on the Internet. Scientific American, 276, 52-56.

Marsden, P. (1986). Heterogeneity and Tie Strength: An Analysis of Second Order Association. Unpublished Manuscript.

Monge, P. R., & Contractor, N. (1988). Communication networks: Measurement techniques. In C.H. Tardy (Ed.), *A handbook for the study of human communication:* 107-138. Norwood, NJ: Ablex.

Papa, M. J. & Tracy, K. (1988). Communicative indices of employee performance with new technology. *Communication Research*, 15(5), 524-544.

Tichy, N. M. (1981). Networks in Organizations. In P.C. Nystrom & W. H. Starbuck (Eds.), *Handbook of Organizational Design*. New York: Oxford University Press.

Vedder, P. (1985). *Cooperative learning: A study on processes and effects of cooperation between primary school children,* Westernhaven Croningen, Netherlands: Rijkuniversiteit Groningen.

Walsh, J. P. & Ungson, G. R. (1991). Organizational memory. *Academy of Management Review*, 16: 57-91.

Wasserman, S. & Faust, K. (1992). *Social Network Analysis: Methods and Applications*. Cambridge, UK: Cambridge University Press.

Webb, N. M. (1989). Peer interaction and learning in small groups. *International Journal of Educational Research*, 13, 21-39.

Wellman, (1990). The Place of Kinfolk in Personal Community Networks. *Marriage and Family Review*, 15: 195-228.

A Walk on the WILD Side: How Wireless Handhelds May Change CSCL

Jeremy Roschelle, Roy Pea

SRI International, Center for Technology in Learning

jeremy.roschelle@sri.com and roy.pea@sri.com

ABSTRACT

Designs for CSCL applications usually presume a desktop/laptop computer. Yet future classrooms are likely to be organized around Wireless Internet Learning Devices (WILD) that resemble graphing calculators or Palm handhelds, connected by short-range wireless networking. WILD learning will have physical affordances that are different from today's computer lab, and different from classrooms with 5 students per computer. These differing affordances may lead to learning activities that deviate significantly from today's images of K-12 CSCL activities. Drawing upon research across a range of recent handheld projects, we suggest application-level affordances around which WILD-based CSCL has begun to organize: (a) augmenting physical space, (b) leveraging topological space, (c) aggregating coherently across all students, (d) conducting the class, and (e) act becomes artifact. We speculate on how CSCL research may consequently evolve towards a focus on kinds of systemic coupling in an augmented activity space.

Keywords

Handhelds, design, wireless networking, collaborative learning architectures, CSCL controversies, WILD (Wireless Internet Learning Devices), shared knowledge, augmentation frameworks, classroom workflow, data mining.

INTRODUCTION

Handheld computers will become an increasingly compelling choice of technology for K-12 classrooms because they will enable a transition from *occasional, supplemental* use to *frequent, integral* use (Soloway et al., 2001; Tinker, 1997). This transition is driven partly by the relationship between cost and the student-computer ratio. With desktop technology, cost is high, and computer resources must be shared. Today the typical student-computer ratio is 5:1, with computers in schools most often located in special computer labs rather than the ordinary classroom (Cattagni & Ferris, 2001). A teacher must schedule lab use and move the class there (Becker, 1999). This practice guarantees occasional, supplemental computer use at best, a challenge to integrating it with other learning materials and activities in the classroom. Further, this limits the possible overall impact of computing in education: if an instructional resource is used infrequently, it is unlikely to have a large effect.

By comparison, handhelds are more affordable, making a 1:1 student-computer ratio and ready-at-hand computing feasible. Today many math classes either purchase a classroom set of graphing calculators, or require every student to purchase their own unit, enabling frequent, integral use. Some reform-oriented mathematics texts require handheld technology (whereas almost no widely-sold curricula require desktop computers, because of their limited availability). In the near term, Wireless Internet Learning Devices (WILDs) will likely become available in the same price range as today's Palm devices or advanced graphing calculators, and include short-range wireless networking. WILDs will be at least as powerful as early Macintosh computers, and far more powerful than Apple IIs—allowing a range of powerful learning software. And WILDs will be portable, so students can take them into the field for scientific data gathering (Rieger & Gay, 1997; Soloway et al., 1999; Staudt & Hsi, 1999), to their study hall, on the bus, to a museum (Bannasch, 1999), or anywhere learning happens. The 1400 applicants to the Palm Education Pioneers grant program (administered by SRI's Center for Technology in Learning) illustrate that Palm-sized computers are attractive to teachers and schools. Already, companies are directing attention to creating and supporting WILD classrooms, such as Texas Instruments, Palm, Symbol Technologies, Mindsurf, Classroom Connect, and Scholastic.

Given the continuing emphasis on collaborative and communicative processes in subject matter standards, many WILD classrooms will also be CSCL classrooms. Students will work towards shared understanding in groups. Students will build joint representations of their knowledge. To enhance understanding, students will point to, annotate, and use external representations in diverse sense-making and discourse practices (Pea & Gomez, 1992). And teachers will have a strong role in managing a learning process that involves many active, communicating learners. Yet, because of the differences in WILD classrooms vs. computer labs, we conjecture that CSCL applications may have to radically change, and that new research questions will surface.

Like conventional computer labs, WILD classrooms will support computational media with cognitively-empowering representations (e.g., simulations, manipulable mathematical notations, modeling tools, diagramming tools). And like recent computer labs, WILD classrooms will support network communication both among local peers and to distant servers. But unlike desktops, WILD classrooms will likely feature relatively small screens. Battery life and heat dissipation issues will prevent intensive use of streaming media or broadband networks for years (Ledbetter, 2001). And the basic functional characteristics (screen size, processing power, network speed) of handhelds are not rapidly increasing with Moore's Law; improvements have been slight over the last 3 years.

Perhaps even more importantly, WILD classrooms will have affordances not available today that are ripe for new CSCL uses. One of the more intriguing is the capability of directed communication (infrared beaming) to a specific person via a physical gesture, instead of selecting a logical name or typing it in. Moreover, WILD classrooms will naturally support peer-to-peer and multicast network topologies, beyond today's predominant client-server computing style. Peer-to-peer communication is naturally supported by beaming, and as Napster makes clear, can have very different collective characteristics and emergent phenomena than client-server communication. Multicast will be supported because radio-based wireless is naturally multicast in a classroom-sized space.

Further, although CSCL research brought to light theories of distributed intelligence (Pea, 1993) or distributed cognition (Hutchins, 1996), that knowledge was only visible in two kinds of places in typical CSCL activities: a student's head or a computer display. In a WILD classroom, there may arise more differentiated places for information and knowledge, and highly differentiated "things that make us smart" (Norman, 1994): devices with different characteristics may proliferate (some larger screens, some with more computational power, some with more colors, or special graphics co-processors) and special purpose information appliances may emerge (e.g., "SmartProbes" that can store data, Lego MindStorms™ robots, printers driven by IR beaming). Students are more likely to be choosing appropriate assemblages of devices for their knowledge work than in conventional desktop-based CSCL, highlighting a growing need for the development and deployment of meta-tool knowledge. In this paper, we consider how these changing affordances may change CSCL applications.

Our article kicks off surveying several early WILD applications, in order to abstract some application-level affordances of WILD (as compared to the physical-level capabilities we discussed above). We then suggest some of the differences these application-level affordances may bring to CSCL, and highlight how WILD is likely to create a new application type, along the lines of augmented activity spaces. Beyond thinking about possible application types, we may speculate about the fault lines that might organize future CSCL research.

A LOOK AT WILD IN THE WILD

Although classroom research using handheld computers has been going on for years, and spawned some large research grants recently, there are no formal surveys of WILD applications. We forego assembling a complete survey here, instead describing a handful of WILD application types involved in one or more projects at SRI, or that have been described at past CSCL meetings. The SRI projects include *CILT*—the Center for Innovative Learning Technologies (http://cilt.org, a distributed center with broad-based participation from hundreds of organizations in collaborative projects on themes including "Ubiquitous Computing"), the *Palm Education Pioneers* program (awarding competitive grants of free handheld computers to every student and teacher in over one hundred classrooms), *SimCalc* (a mathematics project that has investigated handheld learning for 4 years), and a U.S. Department of Education grant that developed a handheld assessment tool. We only include application types that: (a) have been used by multiple researcher/developers in building WILD prototypes, and (b) have some early evidence that the prototypes yield interesting classroom experiences.

We will consider the systems in the following list:

- *ClassTalk* is a networked classroom communication system in which any of five question types (multiple choice, numeric, short and long text, algebraic expressions) can be provided by a teacher to students, so that when their answers are submitted, a histogram of their aggregate work is displayed to the students and the teacher so as to guide subsequent classroom discourse (Dufresne et al., 1996; Abrahamson et al., 2000).

- *ImageMap* is an assessment feedback system for supporting media-rich learning conversations that we are developing at SRI International. An image (e.g., graph, map, photo) is distributed to each student with a handheld networked device, a question is asked about the representation, and each student annotates the image with a response. A server receives these responses from the pool of students, aggregates their responses by superimposing their annotations in some manner on the image that was distributed, and projects them on a public display, allowing students and teachers to see the distribution pattern of different answers.

- *Probeware* describes the use of probes and sensors connected to computers (whether handheld or desktop) to collect and display real-time measurements of environmental parameters such as temperature, light, motion, force, sound and electrical power (Tinker & Krajcik, 2001). Thornton (1997) demonstrated that high school students' intuitive ideas about motion, velocity, acceleration, and force become more accurate when using probeware than using any other instructional strategy, including lectures, problems, or traditional labs.

- Mobile computing can enhance field study (such as botanical species identification) using digital imagery (Rieger & Gay, 1997).

- *Participatory Simulations* is a paradigm for using small wearable computer 'badges' or handheld computers to create life-size simulation activities in which participants can represent conceptual entities in a complex system so as to simulate, for example, the spread of viruses, or cars in traffic (e.g., Colella et al., 1998). After experiencing a simulation, participants work together to analyze data, create hypotheses, and conduct experiments to infer underlying rules for their simulation.
- Building on the work of the SimCalc project on the *"Hubcalc"* concept of connecting many handheld devices to the teacher's computer, Texas Instruments developed a wireless classroom communication system that connects handheld graphing calculators so that programmed tasks can be sent within a classroom to calculators for students to work on. Wilensky and Stroup (2000) developed such a task, where students each control a traffic light on a projected traffic grid and the class as a whole has the goal of setting up rules for smooth traffic flow. Additionally, a NSF-funded project is investigating classroom wireless networks of handheld computing versions of SimCalc environments for learning the mathematics of change and variation.
- In one CILT project, the Exploratorium is exploring use of a wireless network and handheld computers to provide information and scaffolding for museum visitors as they virtually explore an outdoor setting. Visitors walk through the landscape with a handheld networked device, linked to a wealth of information and media related to their direct experience of the ecosystem. The online information is navigated through a visual representation of the trails and of the wetlands at large; at the same time, sensors in the environment read the movements of the visitor, enabling the delivery of information specific to that location (http://www.exploratorium.edu/lagoon; also see Bannasch, 1999).

In addition to this list, there are many functional WILD uses in classrooms that are not particularly collaborative: organizer, attendance, and student record keeping. Here we maintain the emphasis on inquiry processes, social constructivist analyses, and distributed cognition designs that are characteristic of CSCL (Koschmann, 1996).

ANALYSIS OF WILD APPLICATION-LEVEL AFFORDANCES

In this section, we will generalize across the list of WILD applications above, and describe application-level affordances that seem characteristic of this emerging technology.

1. Augmenting physical space with information exchanges

Perhaps the most striking characteristic of almost all the WILD applications is that they augment or amplify an existing physical space with information exchanges (Engelbart, 1962); the space the students are engaged in during their activity includes the devices, but is not limited to the space within the screen. Participatory Simulation activities illustrate this robustly; the badges or devices overlay information exchanges on the physical movements of the students, and the information and students' memory of their movements are the focus of inquiry. Probeware and the museum scenarios share this characteristic, but it is less prominent in the HubCalc, NetCalc and ClassTalk scenarios, although the activity space is still very much a physical classroom space (the "moves" enacted by the teacher and students are significantly moves in the classroom discourse space, which is augmented by information exchanges). In contrast, archetypal CSCL most often concentrates attention on spaces that are wholly contained within the bounds of the computer screen.

This potential power of augmentation may be understood by analogy to microworlds. Piaget, the intellectual spirit behind Papert's concept of microworlds, theorized that facility with abstract representations, which are more advanced than concrete representations, arrives later developmentally. Developers of microworlds invert this theory with the design principle that transforming abstract ideas into a manipulable, exploratory concrete form makes the abstraction more learnable. But microworlds only took the abstractions as far back as concretely realized sign systems. Participatory Simulations and Probeware reconnect abstractions with embodied, physical, spatial explorations that precede concrete sign systems. This may make the learners' experience of abstract concepts yet more visceral and meaningful (Colella et al., 1998; Colella, 2000).

2. Leveraging topological space, of two distinct kinds

Lemke (1999) makes a striking distinction between typological and topological representations, suggesting the interplay of language-based, taxonomic, categorical representations ("typological") and spatially based, visual, continuously varying representations ("topological"). Lemke argues that much of the history of mathematics revolves around the fruitful interplay of these representations.

The WILD applications noticeably leverage topological space, capturing information based on spatial proximity and preserving for reflection that which is simultaneously topological and typological. For example, the ImageMap assessment represents degrees of student understanding through a direct spatial mapping of individual contributions to an aggregate representation. Even the more rudimentary ClassTalk—in the first instance a multiple-choice/typological system—emphasizes topological representations by presenting: (a) results as an easily interpreted histogram, rather than tables of numeric data, and (b) students with stimuli that are choices among multiple visual representations. Likewise, Participatory Simulations exchange information based on inter-student proximity in the virus role-play to examine the dynamics of disease transmission. SimCalc representations are editable graphs that are topological in nature, and in Probeware, the placement of a probe in a data source (a spatial act) results primarily in a graph (a spatial representation). The museum scenarios focus on image capture and proximity to an exhibit (or outdoor landscape element) as key drivers of the information exchange.

This emphasis on computer use to bring more topological representations into the classroom continues an overall trend to balance topological (e.g., graphs) and typological (e.g., algebra) that has been an important part of past CSCL research. But beyond that, WILD classrooms have new affordances that make topological representations even more powerful, and typological representations less so. The *stylus* used with handheld computers as a pointing and inscriptional device makes it especially easy to correlate user control with spatial representations, even more so than with a mouse. Further, directional beaming and probe placement connects information exchanges to simple physical gestures, whereas most conventional CSCL exchanges must use icons or labels to represent logical destinations and sources of information flows. Conversely, it is intriguing that Palm OS devices, the trendsetter in user interfaces for handhelds, have dramatically simplified their design vis-à-vis desktop computers in part by simplifying typological representations from hierarchies to flat categorical lists: on a Palm OS handheld, one cannot organize folders of folders of folders of files; only a single level of categorization is allowed. And although a portable keyboard makes writing easier, Palm OS devices are not good for reading or writing large amounts of text.

We make an important distinction between two kinds of topological representations that we designate as "*geo*spatial" and "*semio*spatial." Geospatial representations (geo = "of the world") are defined by formally specifiable mapping functions from measurable spatial parameters of the physical world (distance and direction, as in terms of height, depth, width) and their representational system counterparts (i.e., inscriptions: such as 2D and 3D maps, drawings, pictures). In contrast, semiospatial representations are those in which the spatial attributes of the topological representation are *not* mappable to spatial attributes of the physical world (except to those of the inscription itself). Semiospatial representations include graphs, concept maps, flowcharts, and non-geo-gridded information visualizations generally. More technically, semiospatial representations are those for which, if one were to ask a geospatial question about aspects of a specific representation—such as "*How many meters away is the concept 'President' from 'Vice President' in an organizational chart for the U.S. government?"—one would be committing what Gilbert Ryle (1949) would have called a "category mistake," from which various logical fallacies and conceptual conundrums may follow. Semiospatial representations are useful for supporting reasoning, argumentation, and deictic functions that are important for establishing co-reference and attentional alignment in collaborative learning.

The following scenario illustrates the power of topological features of semiospatial representations for learning. A teacher creates a diagram on a whiteboard, captures it with a digital camera, and then distributes it to the students' handheld computers in the classroom. These handhelds allow pointing with a stylus to spaces on that diagram so as to answer her question: "Which link in this concept map did you find most difficult?" An instructional discourse then ensues when the class and teacher see the aggregated results of their link selections depicted on the computer-projected display of the diagram with data superimposed. The semiospatial representation provided by this technological augmentation of the physical whiteboard space, in the diagram's depiction on each student's handheld display, provides the common spatial framework for CSCL.

Lemke's typological/topological distinction and our geospatial/semiospatial distinction can be viewed as part of an overall educational technology interest in understanding the cognitive value and educational use of multiple representations (Kaput, 1992; Kozma et al., 1996; Shafrir, 1999). For handhelds, such multiple representations are likely to be distributed across multiple devices. In NetCalc classrooms, we observed students aligning multiple devices so they could compare multiple representations. In the Datagotchi scenarios developed as a CILT seed project (http://www.cilt.org/images/DataGotchi.pdf), we suggested that students would naturally line up their WILD handhelds to form larger spaces along which representations could be compared (in the manner of Rekimoto, 1998).

3. Aggregating coherently across all students participating individually

Another interesting characteristic of three of the WILD applications is that they aggregate information generated by *all* the *individual* students in the classroom. This is most salient in the ClassTalk and ImageMap applications, where each student contributes an answer, and all answers are rapidly aggregated into a single representation. In planned extensions to the ImageMap, we take this strategy further so that an exploration can occur simultaneously with all students participating. The idea is that an unknown shape (perhaps a phase plot of a chaotic motion) can be generated by having many students each exploring different portions of the parameter space. As the plot fills in with different contributions, students can start to see regions that haven't been explored, and ones where something interesting might be happening. This intermediate representation can then direct their continued exploration, as they see what they are building together (Pea, 1994). Aggregation across everyone also features prominently in Participatory Simulations. Many NetCalc/HubCalc scenarios involve students contributing individual mathematical objects to an overall aggregate representation that includes the whole class. Not only are all the students' responses aggregated, but they are also aggregated in a coherent representation that can be read and understood as a whole fairly easily. They are thus akin at a within-classroom level to the aggregate scientific visualizations in student-scientist partnership projects such as GLOBE, Global Lab, and KidsNet, in which students from disparate sites collect local data defined by scientific protocols that are then aggregated at a remote server and reflected back for interpretative discussions at local sites (Cohen, 1997). In contrast, in archetypal CSCL it is far more common for only 2 or 3 students to contribute to a shared representation (e.g., Single Display GroupWare). Or in cases with large numbers of contributors (e.g., Knowledge Forum), the aggregation emerges slowly and asynchronously and may not produce a cohesively readable overall representation.

Aggregating coherently across all students is particularly important because it enables quick formative assessments that can allow the teacher to "take the pulse" of learning progress for the classroom as a whole. Further, because all students have individual devices, the teacher can ensure that all students are participating individually. And because every student has a role in the aggregate representation, they may take a more active role in discussions; they are literally *represented in* the information structure that supports the instructional discourse, rather than *outside of it* as an information consumer. By contrast, in conventional CSCL, with multiple students crowded around one machine, freeloading is a common phenomenon and the teacher must visit each group of students to track progress.

4. Conducting classroom performances

It has become fairly common to describe the change in the teacher's role brought about by CSCL as a move from "sage-on-the-stage" to "guide-by-the-side." The move to "guide-by-the-side," however, is at least partially an artifact of desktop technology; there is literally nowhere else for the teacher to go when 2 to 4 students are crowded around a single monitor. In a WILD classroom, this physical constraint does not apply, and it is not at all clear from our examples that the teacher will only be a "guide-by-the-side," as more interesting and powerful roles are possible. What then will be the apt metaphor for the role of the teacher in a WILD classroom?

The WILD applications above have in common a teacher role much more like the "conductor-of-performances" for an orchestra: students in a WILD classroom are contributing to an overall performance. In the ImageMap application (and especially the extended version described above), they generate an overall aggregate representation, with a coherent visual gestalt. In Participatory Simulations, they participate in a simulation run (like an emergently-choreographed performance). In SimCalc/NetCalc, they contribute to an overall animation. For all three cases, students contribute to a joint performance, verbally and with input technology. The teacher attends primarily to group performance, not to each individual student. Moreover, the teacher, like the conductor, has responsibility for choosing and sequencing the material to be performed (the curricular activities), interpreting the performance, and guiding it toward its desired forms. As in rehearsal, the conductor might direct groups of students to practice something alone, or in small groups. During performance, the teacher will work to ensure that all parts are heard, that everyone gives their best performance—directing attention towards the students who need the most encouragement while keeping the overall performance moving forward.

WILD technology is radical and revolutionary because (unlike personal desktop computers) it creates the communication and computational conditions that make collective performance with representations both possible and meaningful in the aggregate. In some ways, such collective performances share key elements of the sage-on-the-stage, but are more dialogic by design. Full group participation contexts will be featured more fully, and teacher-led discussion around the contributions of an individual or group will become more prominent. But unlike sage-on-the-stage, the teacher need not bear primary responsibility for filling in the turns of the representational and conversational space. WILD technology will readily facilitate contributions from students and groups that can create transformative learning conversations as the norm (Pea, 1994; Polman & Pea, in press), rather than those of information transmission. Moreover, like the conductor, the WILD paradigm puts the teacher naturally in a position to notice whether and how much each participant is contributing, and thus can help the teacher work on having all the students continuously working towards the classroom performance.

5. Act becomes artifact

The final application affordance we draw attention to is that WILD applications have the potential to *instrument the learning space* to collect summaries of messaging patterns and messaging content over longer timespans and over multiple sets of classroom participants to enable multi-level analyses of patterns of interactions and outcomes. Instant messaging (also called "texting" or SMS) is hugely popular among teens in countries where SMS is universally available on cell phones. We expect that messaging of text, representations, and data will become much more frequent in WILD learning spaces, and that the overall patterns of messaging, as well as message contents might be productively analyzed. Of our sample applications, this potential is most clear in the Exploratorium/museum examples; by giving individual visitors devices for interacting with exhibits, interesting use histories can be collected across a large set of visitors. Each visitor's exhibit inter*act*ion becomes a captured artifact; the database of interactions can be data-mined, analyzed, and reflected upon. A teacher will be able to request an aggregate data set on what her students did with a particular exhibit. The class could then reflect back in the classroom on different phenomena they noticed in the exhibit. Researchers and designers may reflect on these results (with appropriate permissions concerning privacy of data), looking at the history of when the exhibit was used, how it was used, and what different classes of visitors did with it.

This possibility to mine the data generated in the "act becomes artifact" cycle is nascent in the other sample WILD applications. But it will become more prominent as classrooms become "persistently WILD." Since classrooms will spend much more time with personal, ready-at-hand WILD applications than they currently do with computers in labs, far more of the students' interactions will be captured on devices (and servers that aggregate the information). Further, the classroom communications networks can be instrumented to track information exchanges, so that patterns of exchanges can be examined. All electronically-mediated or "e-interactions" could be tagged with values for a broad range of parameters, including facts like time-stamp, user identity, institutional demographics, and response characteristics, but also user profile characteristics explicitly defined or tacitly inferred. The value of those "e-transactions" can be mined as to their properties in context and concomitant results. Once the WILD conversational acts are captured and indexed in the flow of networked message transactions, the teacher and learners themselves may reflect on the patterns of their interactions.

Finally, the actual "workflows" required by a CSCL activity, such as a jigsaw classroom, can be directly enacted on the devices, so that the topology of the network and devices matches the conceptual topology of problem-solving roles and knowledge exchanges (thus an artifact, the curriculum, becomes more directly en*act*able).

These "act becomes artifact" possibilities will create tremendous CSCL research opportunities, analogous to bio-informatics (Witten & Frank, 2000). With conventional textbook curricula, researchers make a distinction between the bought curriculum (textbook), the teacher's planned curriculum, the taught curriculum (what is enacted in the classroom), and the learned curriculum. It is now very hard to get statistical data on more than the bought curricula, because of the difficulty of tracking what actually happens in the classroom; it is even harder to track what students learn in a fine-grained way. If WILD applications make CSCL activities more directly enactable in an instrumented networked classroom, it will become much more possible to track the taught curriculum. Further, if ClassTalk/ImageMap formative assessment techniques are easy to give as quick, take-the-pulse quizzes, information will be generated about the learned curriculum. Mining the correlations among the bought, planned, taught, and learned curriculum could create a very powerful research process for curriculum improvement. Yet these prospects have "big brother" like overtones of continuous surveillance. Much nuanced work will be necessary on privacy and security policies and safeguards so mining of the act-becomes-artifact cycle is devoted to services that help learners.

AUGMENTED ACTIVITY SPACES EMERGE

We have suggested five WILD application affordances already illustrated by early handheld CSCL applications: (1) augmenting physical space; (2) leveraging topological space, of two distinct kinds; (3) aggregating coherently across all students' individual contributions; (4) conducting classroom performances; and (5) "act becomes artifact." Looking for the larger pattern in these directions, we see WILD-based CSCL leading to considerably different CSCL application types than those of the desktop: those more grounded in physical space, about spatial relationships, simultaneously engaging whole classrooms, and encouraging a "conductor" metaphor for teaching more than one of "guide-on-the-side." Overall WILD-based CSCL seems headed towards augmented activity spaces.

These are early impressions, of course, and as WILD applications develop, new directions may become evident. In any event, the major point of our argument holds—the differing physical capabilities of personal, palm-sized computers and wireless ad-hoc networks create differing application-level affordances, which creates quite different potentials for CSCL. Moreover, given how compelling handhelds are likely to be in the next few years, compared to bulky, expensive, complex desktop computers, we can expect that these differing application affordances will become very significant for the majority of innovators exploring K-12 learning situations. Today's archetypal CSCL applications include:

- *Distance Learning*: participation in a shared, possibly immersive, virtual space that mimics some characteristics of real learning spaces, e.g., a virtual campus and offices for teacher professional development organizations and participants using MOO technology (TAPPED IN: Schank et al.,1999).
- *Single Display GroupWare*: Side by side use of a shared, large display by a group of 2-4 students and (intermittently) a teacher (e.g., Dynagrams: Pea, 1992; Stewart et al., 1998).
- *Knowledge Spaces:* contribution to a shared conceptual space that organizes individual knowledge elements, such as OISE's CSILE (Scardamalia & Bereiter, 1994).
- *Messaging*: writing notes or messages to a partner or discussion forum (e.g., Honey et al., 1994).

Distance learning will still be a significant issue for universities seeking to broaden their audience to students who cannot readily come to class. But for the largely local and classroom-based K-12 audiences, "virtual spaces" inside tiny palmtop screens will not be compelling compared to the augmented physical spaces they will inhabit. Distance learning will still be interesting in the "act becomes artifact" sense, emphasizing comparative analyses across data from different sites, but not in the "communicating with a distant partner" sense.

However, assuming these devices spread popular instant messaging capabilities, and that these capabilities are active on the devices when students are on the bus, in the café, or at home, a new kind of "distance learning" may emerge. After they leave class, teams of students may be able to coordinate ongoing groupwork more closely: they may engage in coordinating schedules, sending each other updated information, asking spontaneous questions of each other, all from various locations in their neighborhood. A common story from European countries is of groups of teenagers talking about messages coming in on cell phones as they sit in a café together. New and interesting patterns of CSCL may emerge where "groupwork" engages additional outsiders as a school-based group member is messaged while sitting among a non-school-based group. Thus, we speculate that analyses of messaging patterns, uses, and practices (presently a smallish specialty within CSCL) may grow in interest and importance.

The CSCL thread that studies shared knowledge generated around shared screens (e.g., Dillenbourg & Traum, 1999) will change with WILD. Large shared screens will be less common than small personal screens, though a few large, public displays (such as in the ClassTalk application) will likely be very important. Suthers (2001) highlights the problem of following the "same" conceptual object as it moves around different displays. This problem will, we expect, become more prominent: how will students track "their" contribution as it gets beamed around to different displays, with differing representational characteristics, and amid derivative works? Further, among CSCL issues, it may be that the maintenance of *shared attention* will be more problematic with smaller screens, while the problems of negotiating control of a single mouse may be less problematic. In general, CSCL issues concerning how shared knowledge arises in a classroom with multiple representational devices with different technical characteristics and different user capabilities are likely to be rich.

Finally, we believe the creation of "knowledge spaces" within and across classrooms will have a very distinctive flavor with WILD classrooms. WILD lends itself more to creating knowledge spaces through peer-to-peer and multicast "synchronization" of contributions to the same semantic category than it does to client-server "construction" of contributions in complex, integrated, server-based systems. Frankly, we do not yet know about what peer to peer knowledge sharing systems for CSCL will be like, but chances are they will be more ad hoc, more diverse, more fragmentary, and more decentralized than today's client-server knowledge spaces. Creating appropriate synchronization capabilities among handhelds for classrooms (which we at SRI term "ClassSync" in contrast to the PalmOS "HotSync"), such that knowledge spaces thrive, will be an interesting research area.

SPECULATIONS ON NEW RESEARCH DIRECTIONS

In closing, we envision research directions for CSCL in a future WILD age. Koschmann (1996) notes that educational technologies have evolved through the paradigms of CAI, ITS, Logo-as-Latin, and CSCL. The paradigms can be organized as two dialectic pairs of forces. Early debates focused on the relationship of student to computer: computer-controlling-student (CAI) vs. student-controlling-computer (Logo). This split was recast as the choice of computer as tutor (CAI), tutee (Logo), or tool (Taylor, 1980). Later, the debate split on the role of cognitive representations in educational technology (Lajoie & Derry, 1993) with an ITS camp emphasizing *information-processing-model-based interventions* to trace student cognition and compare it to normative models, another emphasizing computer-based models and their representations as a *semiotic intervention* mediating CSCL discourse among students and teachers, emphasizing contributions of sociocultural theories of learning (e.g., Vygotsky, Leont'ev, and Rogoff).

We find that the *control* (tutor, tutee, tool) and *representational issues* (modeling the learner vs. mediating learner conversations) are insufficiently rich to organize the interesting R&D debates. We speculate that an interesting debate will form around the kinds of *system couplings* (Morrison & Goldberg, 1996) among the information in different distributed devices, and critical theory discourse around power relationships in schooling contexts (Apple, 1992; Segal, 1996). Overly tight coupling, where every information exchange among personal devices is centrally controllable and tracked, may be too close to Orwellian scenarios. Overly loose coupling, where each Palm is an information island, will not lead to interesting shared knowledge spaces and activity artifacts. The kinds of coupling needed may also diversify with different pedagogical strategies and activity designs. Some CSCL researchers have been turning to Activity Theory as fertile ground for design theory (e.g., Gifford & Enyedy, 1999), an approach that has attracted attention for CHI design generally (Bodker, 1991; Nardi, 1996). In an activity theoretic perspective, activity occurs within the framework of an objective and a community of other users, in which rules and roles affect participants' behaviors, and in which the outcome can become another activity or artifact. While not necessarily committing to the different aspects of the social theory that guides such work, we find it useful for articulating different kinds of systemic coupling that may become important for CSCL. Activity Theory is a methodological framework with a core representation being the diagram displayed here (adapted from Nardi, 1996).

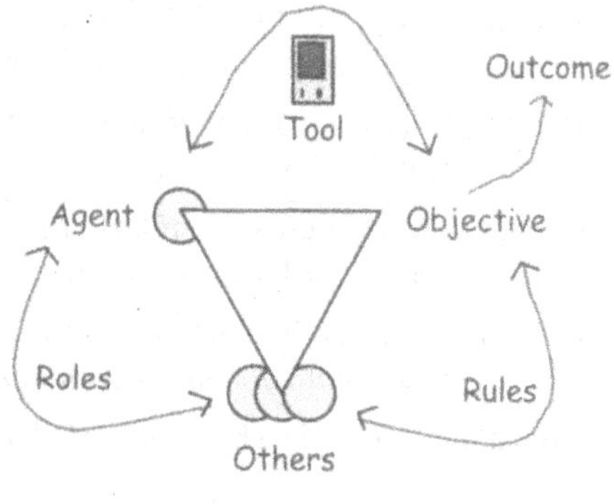

The tutor, tutee, tool debate, as well as the representation debate, have largely focused on the topmost agent-tool-objective relationship of the diagram.

Tutor: Computer is the agent, student problem-solving behavior is the objective (goal), model tracing is the tool

Tutee: Student is the agent, a computer program written by the student is the objective, microworlds are the tools

Tool: Student is the agent, computer is the semiotic tool, shared knowledge is the object

With WILD, other parts of the framework become important system couplings. For example, "rules" and "roles" become important categories of coupling in the distributed system, especially rules that protect privacy, but also privilege-like rules about "roles" that define capabilities one is enabled to have with one's device in specific situations, such as rules about who can make or take what kind of contribution to or from a knowledge synchronization system. This generative nesting is fertile for inventing new pedagogical activities in WILD settings; the coupling of the output of one activity to the next sequential activity, or within a hierarchical framework of activity becomes interesting. Further, "division of labor" becomes an interesting category of coupling, as students may choose to divide up multiple representations among multiple devices, to provide a larger overall screen space. Thus rules and roles interact.

In the past, debates focused on the *control issue* (tutor, tool, or tutee) or the *representation issue* (model tracing inventions vs. semiotic inventions). Whereas these clashes may continue in educational technology now, as far as WILD classrooms go, only the tool and semiotic perspectives make a good fit. We see little evidence that students want to be "tutored" by their personal devices, and while they may tweak parameters in simulations, or do constructionist activities with them, it is unlikely that Logo-as-Latin will be the primary paradigm, with students spending most of their time WILD programming. Moreover, while there will be many interesting uses of intelligent modeling in the data mining/act-becomes-artifact sense, the low power of palmtops makes embedded intelligent model tracing unlikely. WILD is a much better fit for semiotic intervention with new forms of modeling and representation.

Going beyond these historical clashes over control and uses of representation, WILD will differ from traditional CSCL applications by creating a more distributed systems peer-to-peer network topology. The kinds of coupling and regulation of those couplings in such a system should be fertile ground for future innovation and controversy. Finally, Lemke's distinction between topological/typological representational systems will find new purchase in WILD activities, and there is much to explore in the prospects of geospatial and semiospatial representational systems for augmenting the physical spaces in which learning, teaching, and communication more broadly occur.

ACKNOWLEDGMENTS

Thanks to the many contributors from the WILD and SimCalc teams: John Brecht, Mark Chung, Tristan de Frondeville, Chris DiGiano, Jim Kaput, Sarah Lewis, Judy Li, Charlie Patton, Deborah Tatar, Phil Vahey, and Wenming Ye. We gratefully acknowledge support from the National Science Foundation, SRI International, Palm Inc., and Texas Instruments.

REFERENCES

Abrahamson, L., Davidian, A., & Lippai A. (2000). *Wireless calculator networks: Why they work, where they came from, and where they're going*. Presented at the 13th Annual International Conference on Technology in Collegiate Mathematics, Atlanta, Georgia, November 16-19, 2000.

Apple, M. (1992). Computers in schools: Salvation or social disease? *The Education Digest. 57*(2). 47-52.

Bannasch, S. (2000, Fall). Beam Me Up, Scottie! Handheld computers extend the range of wireless communication in schools. *Concord Consortium Newsletter*, *4*(3). (http://www.concord.org/library/2000fall/beam.html)

Bannasch, S. (1999, Fall). The electronic curator: Using a handheld computer at the Exploratorium. Concord *Consortium Newsletter.* (http://www.concord.org/library/1999fall/electronic-curator.html)

Bannasch, S. (2001, Spring). Wireless Computers and Probeware Support a New Science Curriculum: Using iPAQ Pocket PCs to study science fundamentals. *Concord Consortium Newsletter, 5*(1). (http://www.concord.org/library/2001spring/newscience.html)

Becker, H., & Reil, M. (1999). Teacher and teacher-directed student use of computers and software. Irvine, CA: Center for Research on Information Technology and Organizations, University of California.

Bødker, S. (1991). *Through the interface: A human activity approach to user interface design.* Hillsdale, NJ, Lawrence Erlbaum Associates.

Cattagni, A., & Ferris, E. (2001, May). *Internet Access in U.S. Public Schools and Classrooms: 1994 – 2000.* National Center for Education Statistics (NCES 2001-07).

CILT [Center for Innovative Learning Technologies] (1998). *Datagotchi deep dive: Imagineering a low-cost handheld mathematical tool for collaborative learning.* (http://www.cilt.org/images/DataGotchi.pdf)

Cohen, K. C. (1997). (Ed.). *Internet links for science education* (pp. 189-220). New York, NY: Plenum Press.

Colella, V., Borovoy, R., & Resnick, M. (1998). Participatory Simulations: Using computational objects to learn about dynamic systems. In *Proceedings of CHI '98*, Summary, pp. 9-10, (Los Angeles CA, April 1998).

Colella, V. (2000). Participatory Simulations: Building Collaborative Understanding through Immersive Dynamic Modeling. *Journal of the Learning Sciences, 9(4),* 471-500.

Crawford, K., & Staudt, C. (1999, Fall). A computer in the palm of their hands. *Concord Consortium Newsletter* (http://www.concord.org/library/1999fall/palm-computer.html).

Dillenbourg, P. J. & Traum, D. (1999). Does a shared screen make a shared solution. In C. M. Hoadley & J. Roschelle (Eds.), *Proceedings of the Computer Support for Collaborative Learning (CSCL) 1999 Conference (pp. 127-135).* Palo Alto, CA: Stanford University [Available from Erlbaum Associates, Mahwah, NJ].

Dufresne, R.J., Gerace, W.J., et al. (1996). Classtalk: A classroom communication system for active learning, *J. Comput. in Higher Education, 7*, 3-47.

Engelbart, D.C. (1962, October). *Augmenting human intellect: A conceptual framework* (Summary Report, AFOSR-3233). Menlo Park, CA: SRI International.

Gifford, B.R. & Enyedy, N.D. (1999). Activity-centered design: Towards a Theoretical Framework for CSCL. In C. M. Hoadley and J. Roschelle (Eds.), *Proceedings of the Computer Support for Collaborative Learning (CSCL) 1999 Conference (pp. 189-196).* Palo Alto, CA: Stanford University [Available from Erlbaum Associates, Mahwah, NJ].

Honey, M., Bennett, D., Hupert, N., Kanze, B., Meade, T., Panush, E.M., Powell, K., Spielvogel, R., Dubitzky, B., Cohen, M., Melnick, H., & Peterson, L. (1994). The mathematics learning forum online: Using telecommunications as a tool for reflective practice. *Machine-Mediated Learning*, 4(2&3), 163-176.

Hutchins, E. (1996). *Cognition in the wild.* Cambridge, MA: MIT Press.

Kaput, J. (1992). Technology and mathematics education. In D. Grouws, Ed., *Handbook of research on mathematics teaching and learning (pp. 515-556).* New York: Macmillan Co.

Koschmann, T. (1996). Paradigm shifts and instructional technology: An introduction. In T. Koschmann (Ed.), *CSCL: Theory and practice of an emerging paradigm (pp. 1-23).* Mahwah, NJ: Lawrence Erlbaum Associates.

Kozma, R.B., Russell, J., Jones, T., Marx, N., & Davis, J. (1996). The use of multiple, linked representations to facilitate science understanding. In S. Vosniadou, R. Glaser, E. De Corte, & H. Mandel (Eds.). *International perspective on the psychological foundations of technology-based learning environments (pp. 41-60).* Hillsdale, NJ: Erlbaum.

Ledbetter, J. (2001, June 17). Wireless secrets and lies. *The Industry Standard* (http://www.thestandard.com/article/0,1902,27206,00.html?nl=int)

Lajoie, S.P. & Derry, S.J. (1993). *Computers as cognitive tools.* Hillsdale, NJ: Erlbaum Associates.

Lemke, J. (1999). Typological and Topological Meaning in Diagnostic Discourse. *Discourse Processes, 27(2),* 173-185.

Morrison, D. & Goldberg, B. (1996). New actors, new connections: The role of local information infrastructures in school reform. In T. Koschmann (Ed.), *CSCL: Theory and practice of an emerging paradigm (pp. 125-145).* Mahwah, NJ: Lawrence Erlbaum Associates.

Nardi, B., (1996). (Ed.). *Context and Consciousness: Activity Theory and Human-Computer Interaction.* Cambridge, MA, MIT Press.

Norman, D. A. (1994). *Things that make us smart: Defending human attributes in the age of the machine.* Perseus Press.

Pea, R. D. (1992). Augmenting the discourse of learning with computer-based learning environments. In E. de Corte, M. Linn, & L. Verschaffel (Eds.), *Computer-based learning environments and problem-solving* (NATO Series, subseries F: Computer and System Sciences). New York: Springer-Verlag GmbH (pp. 313-343).

Pea, R. D. (1993). Practices of distributed intelligence and designs for education. In G. Salomon (Ed.). *Distributed cognitions.* New York: Cambridge University Press, pp. 47-87.

Pea, R. D. (1994). Seeing what we build together: Distributed multimedia learning environments for transformative communications. *Journal of the Learning Sciences*, *3*(3), 283-298.

Pea, R. D., & Gomez, L. (1992). Distributed multimedia learning environments: Why and how? *Interactive Learning Environments*, 2(2), 73-109.

Polman, J. L., & Pea, R. D. (in press). Transformative communication as a cultural tool for guiding inquiry science. *Science Education.*

Rekimoto, J. (1998). A multiple device approach for supporting whiteboard-based interactions. In *Proceedings SIGCHI'98: Human Factors in Computing Systems (pp. 344-351).* Los Angeles, CA.

Rieger, R. & Gay, G. (1997, December). Using Mobile Computing to Enhance Field Study. In *Proceedings of CSCL '97* (pp. 215-223). Toronto, Ontario: Ontario Institute for Studies in Education.

Ryle, G. (1949). *The concept of mind.* Oxford: Basil Blackwell.

Scardamalia, M., & Bereiter, C. (1994). Computer support for knowledge-building communities. *Journal of the Learning Sciences*, *3*(3), 265-283.

Schank, P., Fenton, J., Schlager, M., & Fusco, J. (1999). From MOO to MEOW: Domesticating technology for online communities. In C. M. Hoadley and J. Roschelle (Eds.), *Proceedings of the Computer Support for Collaborative Learning (CSCL) 1999 Conference (pp. 518-526).* Palo Alto, CA: Stanford University [Available from Lawrence Erlbaum Associates, Mahwah, NJ].

Segal, H.P. (1996). The American ideology of technological progress: Historical perspectives. In S, T. Kerr (Ed.), *Technology and the future of schools.* Chicago: The National Society for the Study of Education, pp. 28-48.

Shafrir, U. (1999). Representational Competence. In I. E. Sigel (Ed.), *Theoretical Perspecitives in the Development of Representational Thought.* New Jersey: Lawrence Erlbaum Associates.

Soloway, E., Norris, C., Blumenfeld, P., Fishman, B., Krajcik, J. & Marx, R. (2001, June). Log On Education: Handheld Devices are Ready-at-Hand. *Communications of the ACM*, *44*(6), 15-20.

Soloway E., Grant W., Tinker R., Roschelle J., Mills, M., Resnick M., Berg R. and Eisenberg M. (1999). Science in the Palms of Their Hands. *Communications of the ACM*, *42*(8), 1999, 21-27.

Staudt, C. (1999, Fall). Probing untested ground: Young children learn to use handheld computers. *Concord Consortium Newsletter* (http://www.concord.org/library/1999fall/untested-ground.html)

Staudt, C. & Hsi, S. (1999, Spring). Synergy projects and pocket computers. *Concord Consortium Newsletter.* (http://www.concord.org/library/1999spring/synergyproj.html).

Stewart, J., et al. (1998). When two Hands are better than one: Enhancing collaboration using single display Groupware. In *Adjunct Proceedings of SIGCHI'98: Human Factors in Computer Systems (pp. 287-288).* Los Angeles, CA.

Suthers, D. D. (2001, to appear). Towards a systematic study of representational guidance for collaborative learning discourse. *J. Universal Computer Science*, *7*(3). (http://lilt.ics.hawaii.edu/lilt/papers/2001/)

Taylor, R. (1980) Introduction. In R. Taylor (Ed.) *The computer in the school: Tutor, tool, and tutee* (pp. 1–11). New York: Teachers College Press.

Thornton, R.K. (1997). Learning physics concepts in the introductory course: microcomputer-based labs and interactive lecture demonstrations. In J. Wilson (Ed.), *Conference of the Introductory Physics Course* (pp. 69-86). NewYork: Wiley & Sons.

Tinker, R. (1997, July 7). *The whole world in their hands.* Concord Consortium (http://www.concord.org/library/pdf/future.pdf).

Tinker, R. & Krajcik, J. (2001). (Eds.), *Portable technologies: Science learning in context.* New York: Kluwer Academic/Plenum Publishers.

Wilensky, U., & Stroup, W.M. (2000, June 14-17). Networked Gridlock: Students Enacting Complex Dynamic Phenomena with the HubNet Architecture. In B. Fishman & S. O'Connor-Divelbiss (Eds.), *Fourth International Conference of the Learning Sciences (pp. 282-289).* Mahwah, NJ: Lawrence Erlbaum Associates.

Witten, I. & Frank, E. (2000). *Data Mining.* New York: Morgan Kaufman.

LONG PAPERS

These 50 papers ranked exceptionally highly in the peer review process. To a surprising extent, they fall into thematic groups, representing topics of current interest in active CSCL research. These groupings will be presented at the conference as panels, including the paper presenters and discussants from research and teaching practice. The panels are grouped into parallel tracks on theory, methodology, pedagogy and technology.

B. (THEORY TRACK): THE ROLE OF ARTIFACTS IN COLLABORATIVE LEARNING

Contributions to a Theoretical Framework for CSCL

Gerry Stahl
Fraunhofer Institute for Applied Information Technology – FIT, Germany
& University of Colorado at Boulder, USA
Gerry.Stahl@fit.fraunhofer.de
http://orgwis.gmd.de/~gerry

ABSTRACT

Looking at computer supported collaborative learning (CSCL) in terms of (a) collaborative knowledge building, (b) group and individual perspectives, (c) mediation by artifacts and (d) micro-analysis of conversation provides a rich, multi-dimensional starting point for conceptualizing and studying a specific variant of CSCL.

These four contributions to CSCL are inter-related. The notion of collaborative knowledge building defines a useful paradigm for conceptualizing learning as social practice. The social interactions and knowledge management activities in which shared knowledge is constructed can be analyzed as the result of interweaving group and personal conversational perspectives. In general, collaborative interaction is mediated by artifacts: sometimes only by transitory artifacts like spoken words or gestures, but increasingly by physical or digital artifacts and media. Empirical studies of collaborative knowledge building employing micro-ethnographic analysis of speech, gesture, artifacts and media can make the details of these collaboration interactions visible, highlighting the interplay of perspectives and artifacts in the trans-personal construction of knowledge.

A theoretical framework incorporating models of knowledge building, perspectives and artifacts – and grounded in empirical analysis of collaborative interaction – can guide the design of computer-based artifacts and media as support for collaborative learning with appropriate, elaborated and unified conceptualizations.

Keywords

Collaborative knowledge building, perspectives, artifacts, conversation analysis, computer support, theory, CSCL

INTRODUCTION

I would here like to introduce four themes that play major roles in the papers for CSCL 2002 (this volume). I have come to be convinced in my own work that these particular notions are important for thinking about computer supported collaborative learning (CSCL) and can contribute to a theoretical foundation for advancing the field:

- Collaborative knowledge building
- Group and individual perspectives
- Mediation by artifacts
- Interaction analysis

These themes have been developed in distinct academic literatures (e.g., education, psychology, activity theory and conversation analysis, respectively), but I believe they should be brought together for the kind of theoretical and methodological framework required by the complex and profoundly interdisciplinary field of CSCL.

I will present these themes in terms of four proposals – that would have to be investigated further in the future:

1. The term "knowledge building" is more concrete and descriptive than "learning" when we are interested in collaboration. It may also help to avoid the baggage of individualistic epistemology in favor of a social practice view.
2. Collaborative knowledge building is structured by the intertwining of group and personal perspectives. One should neither ignore nor fixate upon the role of individual minds, but see them in interaction with group understandings.
3. The construction of knowledge proceeds on the basis of artifacts already at hand – including linguistic, cognitive, cultural, physical and digital artifacts – and creates new artifacts to formulate, embody, preserve and communicate new knowledge.

4. Naturally occurring and carefully captured examples of collaborative knowledge building – such as video recordings of classroom interactions – can be rigorously analyzed to make visible the knowledge building activities at work, the intertwining of perspectives and the mediating role of artifacts.

To some extent, these four themes each fly in the face of conventional pedagogical wisdom – oriented toward mental contents of individual students – although they all have their respected advocates as well. Within the limited confines of this paper, I cannot defend them against all contenders while also demonstrating their relevance and importance to CSCL. I shall just try to motivate how they could help to clarify the domain of CSCL and define a specific approach within the field.

It should be noted at the outset that these are not intended as four independent theoretical claims; rather they contribute in a tightly interwoven way to a single framework or paradigm for thinking about CSCL. Collaborative knowledge building (theme a) moves away from approaches to learning focused on individual minds in two ways: first, by focusing on group activities, which necessarily include roles for individuals within the groups (theme b), and secondly by noting the importance of artifacts in the world, such as spoken, written or published texts that capture newly constructed knowledge (theme c). The evidence for these views can be found primarily in the kinds of micro-ethnographic studies of learning interactions that have recently become possible with the methods of conversation analysis using digital video (theme d). Conversely, when applied to CSCL such interaction analysis should be guided by (a) an interest in knowledge building activities, (b) an awareness of contrasting perspectives and (c) a focus on artifacts – without such guidance detracting from the intersubjective rigor of the analytic methodology. So the four contributions shed light on one another and together represent an integral contribution to theory.

One final point should perhaps be mentioned up front, rather than tacked onto the end as if in apology. That is, that the view of CSCL projected here is a visionary one. Collaborative knowledge building may be a way of life on the leading edge of scientific research, but it has proven devilishly hard to foster in contemporary school classrooms. The idea that new technologies will transform learning practices has not yet led to the collaborative ideal. The task of designing effective computer support along with appropriate pedagogy and social practices is simply much more complex than imagined. An explicit, elaborated, adopted and actualized theoretical framework is needed to (a) clarify the nature of collaborative knowledge building as a desired goal, (b) indicate how people can participate in it with concrete curricular approaches, (c) design tools to support it effectively in various contexts and (d) develop methods for observing and assessing it in practice.

Let us look a bit closer at each of the four proposed contributions to CSCL theory.

A. COLLABORATIVE KNOWLEDGE BUILDING

There are two troubling problems with the term "learning" if one wants to develop a theoretical framework for CSCL:

- Learning is everywhere; whenever someone engages in conscious activity, one can say that learning took place in someone's mind. In fact, even non-conscious activity can reinforce tacit competences.
- Learning is never seen; only the consequences of learning can be observed, and they generally turn out to be statistically insignificant when one tries to be rigorous about this (Russell, 1999). This approach to evaluating learning is a hold-over from behaviorist measurement of changes due to operant conditioning (drill and practice).

In contrast, the notion of "collaborative knowledge building" seems more tangible:

- It cannot simply be applied everywhere, but refers to specific, identifiable occurrences. Cases in which new knowledge is actually constructed by groups – rather than reified facts being recycled – are actually relatively rare in classrooms.
- With care and practice, one can directly and empirically observe the knowledge being built, because it necessarily takes place in observable media, like talk. Moreover, it produces knowledge objects or artifacts, which provide lasting traces and a basis for evaluating the knowledge building.

The term "knowledge building" is attributable to Scardamalia and Bereiter (1991), who have long advocated the restructuring of classrooms into knowledge building communities and who have spearheaded the development and testing of computer support for such communities (1996).

Their concept borrows explicitly from dominant forms of research in today's scientific communities, where theories are progressively developed through professional discourse and inscription (Latour & Woolgar, 1979) – involving, for instance, peer review and critique of papers published in conference proceedings. Here, a scientific community learns about its subject matter by collaboratively building knowledge in the form of documents that gradually define a path of inquiry and successively elaborate theory while also raising issues for future deeper investigation. Conflicting theoretical perspectives are essential to the process, as are the roles of specific participants. Discourse activities – such as questioning, proposing, arguing, critiquing, clarifying, negotiating, accusing, repairing, agreeing – are as important as the artifacts around which, through which and into which the discourse moves.

Not all important learning is collaborative knowledge building. Bereiter (2002) defines the latter in terms of the development of knowledge objects such as scientific concepts and theories. This does not include the learning of passed down facts, of practical or social skills, or of techniques of learning itself. However, social discourse about ideas – the core of knowledge building – can certainly motivate and exercise skills like reading, writing and thinking as a side effect.

The thrust of collaborative knowledge building is to emphasize the construction and further development of a knowledge object that is shared by the group or "learning community." The focus is not on personal learning by the participants – who, it is assumed, retain some of what the group discovered, deepen their collaboration skills and enjoy positive experiences of inquiry and intellectual engagement – but on the growth of communal understanding as reflected in increasingly elaborate artifacts.[4]

Many models of curriculum design are compatible with collaborative knowledge building, and the elaboration of appropriate pedagogical practices remains an important area of active research. Progressive inquiry, for instance, dates back to analyses of problem solving by Dewey and Pierce. This has led us to an interrogative model of inquiry (Hakkarainen & Sintonen, 2001) based on an analysis of types of questioning according to the philosophy of science (e.g., Popper, Kuhn, Hintikka). A systematic approach to having groups of students pursue the posing and investigation of knowledge building questions is offered by problem-based learning, or PBL (Barrows, 1994). This approach tries to cover the breadth of a domain (such as medical education) – in addition to the depth gained through explorative inquiry – by providing a carefully designed set of cases as problems to be pursued consecutively.

PBL is thus a form of the case-based method (Collins & Stevens, 1983), but one which requires the student group to become self-reliant investigators, with the teacher or tutor only facilitating the small-group process. More generally, PBL is a specific approach to project-based learning (Blumenfeld et al., 1991), in which a group of students conducts a project. A potential issue with project-based activities that do not adhere to a model like PBL is that tasks often get divided up so that participants cooperate (as opposed to collaborate) on the over-all project but do not collaborate on the knowledge building; they may subsequently share their individual expertise through jig-sawing (Brown & Campione, 1994), but the basic knowledge building takes place outside the group interaction.

For a theoretically grounded approach to CSCL, we may want to focus on pedagogical approaches – like PBL – that center on group discussion as the core activity in inquiry. This discussion may take place verbally in face-to-face meetings. However, for the sake of providing computer support (e.g., searching capabilities or customizable displays) as well as to maintain persistence of the discourse for subsequent review and reflection, significant parts of the discussions should be captured textually on the computer network – as typed minutes, chat streams or discussion threads.

Because collaborative knowledge building necessarily involves the use in discourse of concepts whose meaning is continually changing and growing, a trained observer can (given the time and tools) observe how knowledge was built up step by step. Evidence exists in the interpretation of words, gestures and documents used. Because the knowledge was built by more than one participant, the changing understandings of the participants had to be shared with one another and may therefore be available to an outside observer as well. Roschelle (1996), for example, has provided an exemplary demonstration of this for a pair of collaborating high school physics students (see below).

The characteristics of collaborative knowledge building just reviewed – that it is typical in modern science, that it is rarely achieved in classrooms, that it can effectively motivate other forms of learning and that it can be observed in practice – suggest that it might provide a useful pedagogical focus for CSCL. Of course, the main attraction of the notion of collaborative knowledge building is the hope that computer support can significantly increase the ability of groups of students to build concepts, ideas, theories and understandings together.

B. GROUP AND PERSONAL PERSPECTIVES

After more than 2,500 years of knowledge building discourse about the nature of ideas and the meaning of meaning – dating back at least to the forum of Athens – we still find the concept of knowledge to be paradoxical and bewildering. However, two things seem clear:

- Wherever meaningful symbols, representations and artifacts may be found, they are only meaningful for individual minds. Interpretation is required, and that is necessarily carried out by individuals within the horizons of their personal perspectives (Gadamer, 1960/1988).
- Isolated from social interaction, physical artifacts and historical cultures, human brains are poor thinkers and could never have developed into powerful minds (Donald, 1991). In fact, it can be argued that modern minds are simply

[4] Koschmann, in his keynote address (this volume), would no doubt prefer the term "meaning-making" to "knowledge-building" because "knowledge" carries mentalistic connotations. But so does "meaning" – or any terms in which learning has been conceptualized in mainstream modern Western thought. Bereiter's (2002) focus on knowledge objects underlines their intersubjective, publicly accessible character. His unfortunate reliance on Popperian ontology is best replaced by an analysis of artifacts as physical objects embodying meaning.

> collections of cognitive artifacts internalized from inter-personal interactions (Vygotsky, 1930/1978). The mental is primordially a social or group phenomenon.

This means that anything like a theory of knowledge building must pay due regard to essential roles of both collaborative groups and their individual members.

The social basis of knowledge is deeply rooted. It is not just a matter of artifacts in the world extending the limited short-term memory of individual minds, like notes scattered about as external memory traces (Hutchins, 1996; Norman, 1993). Meaning arises in the historically given, social world. We are from the start situated in the shared, meaningful world into which we are born and with which we are engaged (Heidegger, 1927/1996). From the infant's first inkling of intentionality in the mother's gesture (Vygotsky, 1930/1978), to the moment of mutual human recognition (Hegel, 1807/1967; Mead, 1934/1962), to the world-transforming paradigm shifts of expansive learning (Engeström, 1999), meaning springs from inter-personal interaction.[5]

The dilemma between personal and group perspectives plays itself out on the theoretical plane as a dialectic of hermeneutic and social-cultural approaches. Hermeneutics, as the philosophy of interpretation, is concerned with how one can interpret the text of a distant author here and now. Heidegger's foundational analysis of human existence as an interpretive enterprise carried out on the basis of tacit, situated pre-understanding (1927/1996) appears at first sight to give priority to the individual as grantor of meaning. However, a critical closer reading shows that the individual is always essentially engaged in a shared world and that the network of meanings that define the individual's situation are historically, culturally, socially defined. Thus, in his influential explication of Heideggerian hermeneutic philosophy, Gadamer (1960/1988) argues that the possibility of understanding a distant text depends upon the author and interpreter sharing an historical horizon – one that includes the historical reception of the text itself within the cultural milieu that links author and reader.

The analysis that Gadamer applies to communication across the centuries is relevant to face-to-face conversation as well. Ethnomethodology (Garfinkel, 1967) stresses that the meaning of a communicative context is established interactively and is achieved by the participants creating a social order "on the fly." That is, the meaning of individual utterances is not given by some preconceived ideas represented in the speaker's mind or from her personal perspective, which are then expressed and conveyed in verbal symbols. Rather, the meaning of the utterances is negotiated by the speaking and responding parties; it exists only in the group perspective that is formed by the intertwining of personal perspectives in the communicative interaction itself. The meaning of a specific utterance may be defined and affected by subsequent utterances, responses, gestures, pauses, repairs, etc. (Sacks, 1992). That is, the meaning of statements made by individuals is constructed or achieved in the discourse of the group and forms the interpretive horizon in which knowledge is shared during the moment of interaction – regardless of whether or not we choose to attribute individual learning to the participants in the long run.

Discourse is the traditional medium of knowledge building. New ideas – and their interpretation by speakers and hearers – arise in the discourse in ways that transcend any individual's role:

> The mark of a really successful design or problem-solving meeting is that something brilliant comes out of it that cannot be attributed to an individual or to a combination of individual contributions. It is an emergent, which means that if you look at a transcript of the meeting you can see the conceptual object taking shape but you cannot find it in the bits and pieces making up the discourse. (Bereiter, 2002)

Clearly, each word in the discourse can trivially be attributed to an individual speaker. However, the meaning of that word is defined by its position in the discourse context, that is, by its relationship to arbitrarily many other words (by other individuals as well as by the word's speaker) and to the Gestalt meaning of the discourse as a whole, which is the group's, as we shall see in the next section.

In Roschelle's (1996) analysis of the physics students, for instance, their collaborative knowledge building coalesced in the phrase, "It pulls it." Roschelle was able to show that the students understood this to mean that the fat arrow (representing acceleration in their computer simulation) caused a specific kind of change to the other arrow (representing velocity). Within the context of their computer model of Newtonian mechanics this change had a predictable effect upon the movement of a particle – and the students understood this. The statement "It pulls it" is an elliptical, indexical statement that has little meaning on its own as an isolated sentence. In the context in which the students were collaborating, however, it amounted to the discovery of the physics principle that acceleration is "the derivative of velocity with respect to time." This latter way of stating it would not have made sense to these students, but only has meaning within the context of

[5] The inter-personal nature of learning is established in the relationship of a young child with his or her parents. The social can be very personal. Throughout the duration of my relationship with my parents, they motivated my attitude toward the generation of knowledge as social praxis. I wrote the Introduction to these Proceedings on November 19, 2001, the final day of my parents' living relationship to me, and in my mind this publication is dedicated to their memory.

Newton's theories of motion and calculus. The students' statement made sense to them in terms of the components in their computer simulation, their experience with the simulation, their previous discussion and their general world-knowledge of pulling.

When I analyzed a discourse among five middle school students and a teacher (Stahl & Sanusi, 2001), I was at first mystified by the cryptic interchanges in the transcript of a particularly intense and consequent collaborative moment. Within a matter of 30 seconds, the students exchanged 24 turns at speech, mostly consisting of sentence fragments or single words indicating disagreement or assent. It was clear that the students were intently engaged and shared a common understanding of what was taking place in the discourse: the resolution of a knotty problem for their collaborative inquiry and the achievement of a hard-fought consensus. But my retrospective interpretation of the transcript – which I developed in collaboration with experienced conversation analysts and others – required a careful reconstruction of the argumentation back several minutes as well as an understanding of the details of artifacts active in the knowledge building context. The meaning of a given utterance was not a simple function of the words used, the propositional content, the isolated speech act or even a conversational pair of utterances. Meaning was a shared, collaborative, interactive achievement. It was an ephemeral, rapidly evolving group perspective.

Of course, in this analysis I was also able to track the personal perspective and personality of each participant. The flow of discussion as well as the individual conversational moves derived from the individuals in some sense as well. With different participants contributing from different personal perspectives, the discourse would have been completely different. And yet, the actual knowledge building that took place had "a mind of its own." The group perspective, which unfolded and prevailed probably had more to do with the conceptual issues that were brought to the fore by the curriculum and by the artifacts which set the shared context and posed the problems to be discussed than with pre-existing ideas, intellectual orientations or personal values of the individual participants. So, while personal perspectives certainly contributed to the discourse and left observable traces there, the interaction achieved a group perspective that determined the meaning of individual contributions and within which knowledge was collaboratively built and comprehended.

C. MEDIATION BY ARTIFACTS

Knowledge building is mediated by artifacts. The interaction and interweaving of personal and group perspectives is mediated by artifacts. What does this mean? What is mediation and what are artifacts?

"Mediation" means that something happens by means of, or through the involvement of, a mediating object. For instance, when a student uses a technical term to construct knowledge or when a class of students uses a software collaboration system to discuss a theme, that term or that system is mediating the activity: It is providing a medium or middle ground through which the students interact with their ideas. The specific form of the mediation generally affects the nature of the activity profoundly, often determining the nature of the task itself, that is, the choice of medium can define the ends or goal as well as the possible means. In Roschelle's example, the metaphor of pulling mediated the students' knowledge building and allowed them to formulate a theory, to share their understanding of how the simulation worked, to bring their bodily skills to bear, and to solve some but not all of the challenges posed by the teacher.

An artifact is a meaningful object created by people for specific uses. The term "pull" – as elaborated metaphorically by the students and as operationalized by them in manipulating the computer simulation of accelerating forces – functioned as a knowledge building artifact on several levels: It was a pre-understood concept that they could build upon, it provided a tool that they could use for collaborative thinking about the simulated phenomena and it resulted in a knowledge object that incorporated their new shared understanding.

The concept of artifact is perhaps most familiar in anthropology, where it refers to discovered objects that were made by ancient people and that still display traces of their intended function or symbolic import. Hegel (1807/1967) spoke of artifacts as objects on which meaningful form had been imposed and he situated the primordial act of artifact creation in the interpersonal interaction in which people recognize each other and themselves as self-conscious actors. Marx (1844/1967; 1867/1976) took the analysis of artifacts another step to argue that their character was largely determined by prevailing socio-economic relations, so that in our age most artifacts are produced as commodities for monetary exchange. For Hegel, artifacts retain the externalized subjectivity in physical form, and for Marx they retain both concrete human labor that went into producing them and the abstract value of the labor time they required.

These classic analyses of mediation and artifacts are relevant to a contemporary CSCL theory. While theory is now a trans-disciplinary undertaking drawing upon multiple traditions in the social, human and natural sciences, the concepts of mediation and artifact can be traced back to the philosophy of Hegel, whose dialectical analyses revealed the mediated and historical dynamic everywhere. Marx critiqued idealist and subjectivist aspects of Hegel's thought and grounded the mediations in concrete analyses of historically-specific social relationships. Contemporary theories prevalent in CSCL can be traced back to their roots in Hegel and Marx or later developments based on Vygotsky (e.g., activity theory), Heidegger (e.g., situated theory) or Dewey (e.g., inquiry theory).

Vygotsky (1930/1978; 1934/1986) wanted to supplement Marx's social theory with a psychology of mediated cognition (a perspective on the individual as intertwined with the group perspective). He extended the notion of physical artifact (tool) to encompass linguistic artifacts (symbols) as well. The individual's activity was then seen to be mediated by both varieties of artifact. The human ability to use physical and linguistic artifacts is a cultural development that allowed mankind to evolve beyond its biological basis.

Vygotsky argued – on the basis of empirical psychology experiments – that the meaning of artifacts and our understanding of that meaning are first created in inter-personal contexts, such as mother and child or teacher and student, and subsequently may be appropriated and internalized in an individual mind. The discussion of learning in a student's "zone of proximal development," scaffolded by a teacher, is based on this. We can call the internalized result of this process a "cognitive artifact." For instance, a work group might develop a list of tasks or a diagram of a work flow on a white board and a member of the group might then internalize and later mentally recall that list or diagram in order to monitor future work. The internal mental representation is then a cognitive artifact that resulted from group knowledge building and that may mediate subsequent knowledge building by the individual or the group. In this analysis, the mental representation is a result of collaborative activities and did not first arise subjectively to then be expressed externally. (The deconstruction of artifacts often shows that things developed in the opposite order from how they now appear – that is characteristic of the reification of meaning in an artifact.)

A complete working out of Vygotsky's approach could portray the human mind as nothing but a growing set of cognitive artifacts, appropriated and internalized by each of us in our personal development from our interactions with those around us and our embeddedness in our cultural world. Vygotsky and others who investigate infant development have suggested how even the most basic senses of intentionality, meaning and intersubjectivity may arise in interpersonal interaction – as sketched by Hegel theoretically. The folk theories of mind – roundly criticized by Bereiter (2002), Dennett (1991) and others – can be viewed as metaphors (mind as a container of ideas, a theater of experiences, a homunculus mind within the mind) which may have served their purpose but have now outlived their usefulness. Minksy (1986), for instance, has proposed an alternative "society of mind" metaphor to capture the computational structure of mind as a decentralized set of cognitive artifacts.

If we adopt a Vygotskian view of mediation by artifacts, then the knowledge building process can be conceptualized as the construction of knowledge artifacts, involving physical and symbolic artifacts as starting point, as medium and as product. The process proceeds collaboratively and intersubjectively, within a socio-cultural context. The final knowledge artifact may be internalized by one or more of the participants. While the internalized learning outcomes may be problematic to assess, the shared understanding within the collaborative knowledge building is experienced by the participants and may be subject to reconstruction from traces left in various artifacts, including video recordings and their transcripts.

The task of education in this approach is to revive meanings that have been captured and preserved in artifacts. This is the problem of cultural transmission. Culture can be conceptualized as a body of cognitive and other artifacts. In literate society, for instance, culture includes systems of numbers and written language. Schooling is largely the attempt to help young students to internalize the vast repertoire of meaning that has been associated with these artifacts. Although it is often possible for individuals who have mastered certain skills (cognitive artifacts) to develop related knowledge artifacts on their own, it is at other times useful to recreate the intersubjective conditions of knowledge creation in carefully structured contexts of collaboration with well-designed mediational artifacts to scaffold further learning. Within CSCL efforts, this would mean designing software to support the right kinds of interpersonal interaction, of mediation by artifacts and of knowledge artifact construction.

One does not have to buy Vygotsky's whole approach as sketched out here in order to recognize the importance of an analysis of mediation and of artifacts for a theoretical framework for CSCL. Such an understanding of artifacts as humanly meaningful physical objects can, for instance, overcome Bereiter's (2002) dependence upon Popper's questionable "third world" ontology of knowledge objects. Perhaps the most urgent undertaking at this time is further empirical investigation of how artifacts and their understanding actually function in concrete instances of collaborative knowledge building. For this we need a methodology of interaction analysis.

D. INTERACTION ANALYSIS

Roschelle presented his analysis of two students working with a physics micro-world simulation as an instance of student learning as conceptual change, facilitated by collaborative use of a computer artifact. One could reconceptualize his analysis as an attempt by the students to rediscover the meaning or affordances that were designed into the software artifact as a model of physics. The term "pull" which they interpreted and developed in this connection was a linguistic artifact that they collaboratively constructed as a knowledge object and then individually internalized as an expression of their group learning. Roschelle used conversation analysis of video tapes as well as interviews of the students to conduct his study of the collaborative knowledge building and the internalized conceptual change.

The question of how people rediscover meaning in artifacts is an important and difficult problem. When artifacts are created, their meaning is shared and relatively accessible. The artifact functions importantly to capture, formulate and encapsulate that meaning. But the meaning does not remain simply available on the surface of the artifact. As a note in the discussion database from my seminar on artifacts put it,

> *Thoughts on meaning in artifacts* by Bob Craig on Dec. 12, 2000
>
> Do artifacts "embody meaning" or do they embody meaningful traces of human activity? … Meaning is not "in" the artifact; rather it is "in" the total situation that includes artifacts, minds and social practices.

The meaningful traces transform, reify, distort and hide the meanings that originally existed in the live human interactions. New minds who encounter the artifacts must recreate the appropriate social practices, reconstruct the cultural contexts and rediscover the meaning within their own personal and group perspectives.

To investigate how people disclose the meaning of artifacts that they do not understand, I undertook an analysis of a specific computational cognitive artifact. I looked at how the five middle school students referred to in Section B above struggled to uncover the structures designed into a rocket simulation. I started by trying to follow the students' knowledge building discussion in a transcript of their discourse. But the most interesting and intense collaborative discussion was particularly hard to interpret. The student utterances did not assume the explicit form of scientific propositions of articulate arguments. Nor could the conversational turns be coded as coherent speech acts (Searle, 1969).

Here is the transcript of the pivotal moment of the three-hour long project with the rocket simulation:

1:22:05	Brent	This one's different
1:22:06	Jamie	Yeah, but it has same no…
1:22:07		(1.0 second pause)
1:22:08	Chuck	… Pointy nose cone
1:22:09	Steven	Oh, yeah
1:22:10	Chuck	But it's not the same engine
1:22:11	Jamie	Yeah it is …
1:22:12	Brent	… Yes it is
1:22:13	Jamie	[Compare two 'n' one
1:22:13	Brent	[Number two
1:22:14	Chuck	I know
1:22:15	Jamie	Are the same
1:22:16	Chuck	Oh

These one-second utterances make little sense on their own. They are elliptical and indexical – like Rochelle's "It pulls it." By "elliptical" I mean that these are primarily sentence fragments, phrases that may complete or be completed by another student's utterance, but do not stand on their own. They are fragments of a discussion that is only meaningful at the group level. By "indexical" or "deictic" I mean that they point to or intend something without explicitly stating their referent ("it," "this one"). They index important elements of the shared situation that it would be redundant or superfluous to name. Where words and phrases are repeated, the repetitions play important roles of indicating agreement and shared understanding, which is also signified by the way utterances tend to complete each other.

The discourse is only meaningful on the group level, where the meaning spans individual utterances of individuals and even conversational pairs. The meaning is integrally situated in the temporally unfolding group activity, centered on the simulation artifact (Vikkunen & Kuutti, 2000).

Figure 1. Students discuss a computer simulation artifact.

To understand what took place in this ten seconds, one must reconstruct the argument that reaches its climax here but that was set up in the previous ten minutes. (A theoretical foundation for this is given by Bakhtin (1986), who argues that an utterance is only meaningful in terms of its references back to preceding utterances to which it responds and forward to anticipated responses of a projected audience, and by Heidegger (1927/1996), who situates meanings within the extended dimensions of human temporality.) One must also understand the task of the three-hour project and analyze the affordances of the software artifacts that the students are working with. (Activity theory, as formulated by Engeström (1999), proposes general structures of the broader effective context, including societal dimensions as well as the goals and tools of group activities.) In addition, it is necessary to observe closely the bodily orientations, gaze and gestures of the students.

In Fig. 1, Brent (circled) thrusts his body forward and shifts the group's focus to a rocket description on the monitor, about which he says "This one's different." The ensuing discussion debates what is the same and what is different about this rocket. The rocket to which "this one" is compared actually shifts here ("compare two 'n' one"), and that shift enlightens Chuck, who has resisted the teacher and the peer group, and has long tried to promote his personal perspective. Now, his "Oh" acknowledges a new-found acceptance of the group perspective.

A detailed analysis of this transcript would make visible the knowledge building process that took place, in which the students displayed for each other verbally and non-verbally their shifting understandings and interactively achieved the creation of shared meaning. This meaning was partially encapsulated in terms like "same" and "different," that took on specific functions in their collaboration.

More generally, the elements of this kind of interaction analysis have been developed on a rigorous methodological basis by the theory of ethnomethodology (Garfinkel, 1967) and the science of conversation analysis (CA) (Sacks, 1992). With the availability of digital video to capture and facilitate detailed analysis of naturally occurring interpersonal interaction, the CA approach has been combined with the study of gesture, gaze, bodily orientation, etc. into techniques for interpreting detailed behavior known as micro-ethnography (LeBaron & Streeck, 2000; Streeck, 1983). Most communication analysis in this tradition has studied pairs or small groups in face-to-face situations without technological mediation, although studies of telephone conversations played a major role in the early years of CA (Hopper, 1992; Sacks, 1992). However, the foregoing observations on the rocket simulation discourse suggest that such methods can be applied to CSCL situations as well – with appropriate adaptation. If this is done, attention must be paid to the central mediational role of digital as well as linguistic artifacts. Also, in cases of collaborative knowledge building the unit of analysis for meanings should take into account the intertwining of personal and group perspectives by interpreting individual utterances as elements of the larger discourse and activity.

CSCL FOUNDATIONS AND APPLICATIONS

A theory for CSCL should help us to think about collaborative learning, to structure pedagogy, to design software media and to study actual occurrences of knowledge building inside and outside of classrooms. I think the four foundational themes discussed here start to address these needs. The notion of knowledge building focuses us on activities associated with knowledge management and the further development of theories. A concern with the intertwining of personal and group perspectives suggests curricular approaches and classroom practices that integrate individual and team efforts. The analysis of artifacts conceptualizes the roles of CSCL systems and their databases as mediators and preservers within processes of creating knowledge objects. Finally, interaction analysis allows one to view and assess the knowledge building activities, the intertwining of perspectives and the mediation by artifacts.

The need for these four theoretical contributions arose for me in my work designing and deploying a CSCL software system named `WebGuide` (Stahl, 2001). This system prototyped knowledge creation and knowledge management functions that extended a conventional discussion forum. `WebGuide` investigated methods for intertwining notes in personal and group perspectives, that provided interlinked organizations of shared ideas. The effort to reflect upon the nature of the `WebGuide` software I was designing led me to a view of it as a mediating artifact. Rather than trying to analyze the complex interactions of a class using `WebGuide`, I started by looking at how students learned about a simpler digital artifact, `SimRocket` (Stahl & Sanusi, 2001) – and that led me to a growing fascination with conversation analysis and micro-ethnography. I believe that the theoretical framework that emerged from my work on `WebGuide` will prove valuable in designing and deploying the next system I will be working on, `BSCL` (Leinonen et al., 2001). Perhaps it can help others as well.

ACKNOWLEDGEMENTS

The ideas in this paper grew out of collaborative knowledge building mediated by `WebGuide` in a series of seminars on CSCL at the University of Colorado. I would particularly like to thank participants Alena Sanusi, Curt LeBaron and Bob Craig from the Communication Department as well as the teachers and students at Platt Middle School in Boulder who were involved with `SimRocket`. The paper was written during my transition from L^{3}D in USA to the GMD and the ITCOLE Project in Europe, and therefore owes much to my long-time colleagues in Colorado.

REFERENCES

Bakhtin, M. (1986) *Speech Genres and Other Late Essays,* (V. McGee, Trans.), University of Texas Press, Austin, TX.

Barrows, H. (1994) *Practice-based Learning: Problem-Based Learning Applied to Medical Education,* SIU School of Medicine, Springfield, IL.

Bereiter, C. (2002) *Education and Mind in the Knowledge Age,* Lawrence Erlbaum Associates, Hillsdale, NJ.

Blumenfeld, P., Soloway, E., Marx, R., Krajcik, J., Guzdial, M., & Palincsar, A. (1991) Motivating project-based learning: Sustaining the doing, supporting the learning, *Educational Psychologist,* 26 , pp. 369-398.

Brown, A. & Campione, J. (1994) Guided discovery in a community of learners. In K. McGilly (Ed.) *Classroom Lessons: Integrating Cognitive Theory and Classroom Practice,* MIT Press, Cambridge, MA, pp. 229-270.

Collins, A. & Stevens, A. R. (1983) Goals and strategies of inquiry teachers. In R. Glaser (Ed.) *Advances in Instructional Psychology,* Lawrence Erlbaum Associates, Hillsdale, NJ.

Dennett, D. C. (1991) *Consciousness Explained,* Little Brown and Company, Boston, MA.

Donald, M. (1991) *Origins of the Modern Mind: Three Stages in the Evolution of Culture and Cognition,* Harvard University Press, Cambridge, MA.

Engeström, Y. (1999) Activity theory and individual and social transformation. In Y. Engeström, R. Miettinen, & R.-L. Punamäki (Eds.), *Perspectives on Activity Theory,* Cambridge University Press, Cambridge, UK, pp. 19-38.

Gadamer, H.-G. (1960/1988) *Truth and Method,* Crossroads, New York, NY.

Garfinkel, H. (1967) *Studies in Ethnomethodology,* Prentice-Hall, Englewood Cliffs, NJ.

Hakkarainen, K. & Sintonen, M. (2001) The interrogative model of inquiry and computer-supported collaborative learning, *Science & Education,* in press .

Hegel, G. W. F. (1807/1967) *Phenomenology of Spirit,* (J. B. Baillie, Trans.), Harper & Row, New York, NY.

Heidegger, M. (1927/1996) *Being and Time: A Translation of Sein und Zeit,* (J. Stambaugh, Trans.), SUNY Press, Albany, NY.

Hopper, R. (1992) *Telephone Conversation,* Indiana University Press, Bloomington, IN.

Hutchins, E. (1996) *Cognition in the Wild,* MIT Press, Cambridge, MA.

Latour, B. & Woolgar, S. (1979) *Laboratory Life,* Sage Publications, Thousand Oaks, CA.

LeBaron, C. & Streeck, J. (2000) Gesture, knowledge and the world. In D. McNeill (Ed.) *Language and Gesture,* Cambridge University Press, Cambridge, UK.

Leinonen, T., Hakkarainen, K., Appelt, W., Dean, P., Gómez-Skarmetav, A., Ligorio, B., Lipponen, L., Merisaari, L., Mielonen, S., Pontecorvo, C., Sligte, H., & Vosniadou, S. (2001) ITCOLE Project: Designing innovative technology for collaborative learning and knowledge building, In: Proceedings of *Ed-Media 2001: World Conference on Educational Multimedia, Hypermedia and Telecommunications*, Tampere, Finland.

Marx, K. (1844/1967) Alienated labor. In L. G. K. Easton (Ed.) *Writings of the Young Marx on Philosophy and Society,* Doubleday, New York, NY, pp. 287-300.

Marx, K. (1867/1976) *Capital, Volume I,* (B. Fowkes, Trans.), Vintage, New York, NY. Available at: http://www.marxists.org/archive/marx/works/1867-c1/index.htm.

Mead, G. H. (1934/1962) *Mind, Self and Society,* University of Chicago Press, Chicago, IL.

Minsky, M. (1986) *Society of Mind,* Simon & Shuster, New York, NY.

Norman, D. A. (1993) *Things That Make Us Smart,* Addison-Wesley Publishing Company, Reading, MA.

Roschelle, J. (1996) Learning by collaborating: Convergent conceptual change. In T. Koschmann (Ed.) *CSCL: Theory and Practice of an Emerging Paradigm,* Lawrence Erlbaum Associates, Hillsdale, NJ, pp. 209-248.

Russell, T. (Ed.) (1999) *The No Significant Difference Phenomenon,* Mindspring Press. Available at: http://cuda.teleeducation.nb.ca/nosignificantdifference/.

Sacks, H. (1992) *Lectures on Conversation,* Blackwell, Oxford, UK.

Scardamalia, M. & Bereiter, C. (1991) Higher levels of agency in knowledge building: A challenge for the design of new knowledge media, *Journal of the Learning Sciences,* 1 , pp. 37-68.

Scardamalia, M. & Bereiter, C. (1996) Computer support for knowledge-building communities. In T. Koschmann (Ed.) *CSCL: Theory and Practice of an Emerging Paradigm,* Lawrence Erlbaum Associates, Hillsdale, NJ, pp. 249-268.

Searle, J. (1969) *Speech Acts: An Essay in the Philosophy of Language,* Cambridge University Press, Cambridge, UK.

Stahl, G. (2001) WebGuide: Guiding collaborative learning on the Web with perspectives, *Journal of Interactive Media in Education,* 2001 (1). Available at: www-jime.open.ac.uk/2001/1 and http://orgwis.gmd.de/~gerry/publications/journals/jime2001/webguide.pdf.

Stahl, G. & Sanusi, A. (2001) Multi-layered perspectives on collaborative learning activities in a middle school rocket simulation project, In: Proceedings of *22nd Annual Ethnography in Education Research Forum*, Philadelphia, PA. Available at: http://orgwis.gmd.de/~gerry/publications/conferences/2001/ethnography2001/ethnography.pdf.

Streeck, J. (1983) *Social Order in Child Communication: A Study in Microethnography,* Benjamins, Amsterdam, NL.

Vikkunen, J. & Kuutti, K. (2000) Understanding organizational learning by focusing on "activity systems", *Accounting, Management and Information Technologies,* 10 , pp. 291-319.

Vygotsky, L. (1930/1978) *Mind in Society,* Harvard University Press, Cambridge, MA.

Vygotsky, L. (1934/1986) *Thought and Language,* MIT Press, Cambridge, MA.

Exploring Foundations for Computer-Supported Collaborative Learning

Lasse Lipponen
Department of Psychology, University of Helsinki
P.O. Box 1300014 University of Helsinki, Finland
Lasse.Lipponen@Helsinki.Fi
Tel. +358-9-19123772 fax: +358-9-19123443

ABSTRACT
In 1996 Koschmann (1996) suggested computer-supported collaborative learning (CSCL) as an emerging paradigm of educational technology. After six years, how has the field developed? What does research say about CSCL to date? What is the state of the art? The aim of the present paper is to explore the foundations for CSCL, and in doing so, to contribute to the theoretical as well as empirical understanding and development of CSCL research.

Keywords:
Collaboration, collaborative technology, learning theories

INTRODUCTION: WHAT IS COMPUTER-SUPPORTED COLLABORATIVE LEARNING (CSCL)?

In 1996 Koschmann (1996) recognized computer-supported collaborative learning (CSCL) as an emerging paradigm of educational technology. According to Koschmann (1996), CSCL research is grounded on a very different concept of learning, pedagogy, research methodology, and research questions than its antecedents, CAI (Computer Assisted Instruction), ITS (Intelligent Tutoring Systems), and, Logo-as-Latin did. But now after six years, how has the field developed? What does research say about CSCL to date? What is the state of the art?

Throughout history, our conceptions about human cognition and learning have been related and shaped by the development of technology (Bolter, 1984). This parallelism between our psychological understanding and the technologies available is clear in the field of computer-supported collaborative learning, where technology meets psychology, philosophy and pedagogy. Instructional designers and software developers, educational psychologists, learning theorists, computer scientists, and even sociologists are interested in this rather new area of research.

It is hard to say when CSCL emerged as a separate field of study, or as an emerging paradigm of educational technology. The first CSCL workshop took place in 1990 (Koschmann, 1994), and the first international CSCL conference was held 1995 in Bloomington, Indiana. However, O'Malley and Scanlon already used the term computer-supported collaborative learning in 1989 (O'Malley & Scanlon, 1989). Partly, the inspiration for CSCL arose from the research on Computer-Supported Cooperative Work (CSCW). This research has revealed issues about the collaborative nature of work supported by groupware (Galegher, Kraut, & Egido, 1990; Greenberg, 1991) Thus, in a sense, CSCL is the younger sibling of CSCW.

How should one define computer-supported collaborative learning? Put briefly, CSCL is focused on how collaborative learning supported by technology can enhance peer interaction and work in groups, and how collaboration and technology facilitate sharing and distributing of knowledge and expertise among community members. Whilst talking about computer-supported collaborative learning one typically refers to the acronym CSCL, and does not speculate about the latter "C" word (the first stands for 'computer') and what it might stand for. The short history of CSCL shows, however, that there have been different interpretations and suggestions for the "C" word such as, collective (Pea, 1996), coordinated, cooperative and collaborative (see Koschmann, 1994). There have been even different interpretations of the meaning of the whole acronym. The latest, computer support for collaboration and learning, pointed out by Koschmann (1999), suggests that we should link research on learning and working more closely to each other, as well as the research on the CSCL and CSCW. Despite the different interpretations of the "C" word and the acronym, most researchers appear to use them nowadays as already suggested by Koschmann in 1994. He proposed "the best policy might be to simply use the acronym, allowing individual interpretation of what the letters might be (1994, p.220).

At first glance, the speculation about the meaning of the "C" word and the acronym might look somewhat meaningless. This conversation is, however, related to the central questions concerning CSCL such as, What is collaboration, What are we studying when we are studying collaboration supported by technology, and, What should we be studying?

Concepts and Theories underlying CSCL research

Concepts of collaboration

When referring to collaboration, about what is one actually speaking? To put it simply, in the public conversation the term 'collaboration' appears to refer to any activities that a pair of individuals, or a group of people perform together. Among researchers, however, including those in academic fields, the term 'collaboration' is understood rather differently. Within learning sciences, common to the different definitions of collaboration is that they stress the idea of co construction of knowledge and mutual engagement of participants. In this sense, collaboration can be considered as a *special form of interaction*. Rochelle and Teasley (1995) for instance, stressed the role of shared understanding, and wrote that collaboration is "a coordinated, synchronous activity that is the result of a continued attempt to construct and maintain a shared conception of a problem" (p. 70). Or consider Crook (1994) who offers an intriguing perspective on collaboration. He holds that there is a developmental line from children's secondary intersubjectivity and symbolic play to sophisticated reciprocal understanding and shared knowledge. In children's symbolic play, the material world plays a crucial role in coordination of play activities and in creating a shared framework for collaboration. Most theories or approaches to collaboration neglect the impact and possibilities of the material world for facilitating mutual understanding and shared goals. However, the management of the material world offers rich referential anchors for monitoring grounding and mutual understanding. Computers, especially, can offer a rich repertoire of referential anchors, and points of shared reference (e.g. simulation on a screen). According to Crook (1998), there are three features of interaction that are central to successful collaboration: intimacy among participants, rich supply of external resources, such as computers, and histories of joint activity of those interacting. Further, Engeström (1992) has elaborated a three-level notion of developmental forms of interaction; coordination, cooperation, and reflective communication. On the level of coordination each actor concentrates and performs his or her own role and actions, which are scripted or predetermined. In 'cooperative' interactions, says Engeström, actors focus on a shared problem, trying to find mutually acceptable ways to conceptualize it. This level corresponds to the definition of collaboration (although Engeström uses the concept, 'cooperation'), just given, above, from Roschelle and Teasley (1995). The third form of interaction elaborated by Engeström is reflective communication, in which the actors focus on reconceptualizing their own interaction system in relation to their shared objects of activity; both, the objects and the scripts are reconceptualized. Only through this expansive cycle, is the interaction system transformed, and new motives and objects for collaborative activity created. The advance of this model is that it tries to explain how new forms of collaborative activities are created. According to Engeström (1992), these three phases are a natural cycle of any genuine learning activity.

There exist also broader definitions of collaboration than those referring to a special type of interaction, such as stressing the mutual engagement of the parties (in fact, Engeström's third definition, reflective communication, could also be considered as "participating in activity system", and thus, representing broader definition of collaboration than just stressing the mutual engagement). Collaboration can be defined as a *process of participating in knowledge communities*. As pointed out by Brufee (1993, p.3) collaboration is "a reculturative process that helps students become members of knowledge communities whose common property is different from the common property of the knowledge communities they already belong to". Scardamalia and Bereiter (1994) speak about knowledge-building communities. Knowledge building is a special form of collaborative activity oriented towards the development of conceptual artifacts, and towards the development of collective understanding. In a community of learners, as proposed by Brown and Campione (1994), the core activity is participation in collaborative process of sharing and distributing expertise. As stated by Brown (1994, p. 10), "Learning and teaching depend on creating, sustaining, and expanding a community of research practice. Members of the community are critically dependent on each other. No one is an island; no one knows it all; collaborative learning is not just nice, it is necessary for survival". The idea that collaboration is a basic form of human activity, essential for cultural development, is stressed intensively by many writers throughout the history of psychology (Bruner; 1996; Engeström, 1987; Hutchins, 1995; Mead, 1934; Tomasello, 1999; Vygotsky, 1962; 1978; Wundt, 1921).

In sum, even this very short look to the definitions of collaboration has shown how difficult it is to find a total consensus in this issue, although both approaches, collaboration as a special form of interaction, and collaboration as a process of participation in collective activities ("working together"), include the idea of achieving shared goals. One may ask whether we even need an agreed interpretation of collaboration, or should we just accept the diversity, and let the future determine which definitions will survive. It appears that we can--that perhaps we must--analyze collaborative activities on both micro and macro levels, and, as proposed by Dillenbourg (1999), concern ourselves with aspects such as situation, interactions, processes, and effects.

Theories of collaboration

Whether one considers collaboration as a special form of interaction or as a process of participation, traces back to the conversation of two metaphors of learning, acquisition and participation, or on the debate between the cognitive perspective and the situative perspective of learning (Anderson, Greeno, Reder, & Simon, 2000; Sfard, 1998).Within acquisition metaphor learning is a matter of construction, acquisition, and outcomes, which are realized in the process of transfer. Within the participation metaphor cognition and knowledge are distributed over both individuals and their environments, and learning is "located" in these relations and networks of distributed activities of participation. Learning and collaboration are not only a matter of epistemology but also a matter of ontology. Knowledge is not all that is constructed but also humans and their identities are constructions; learning is also a matter of personal and social transformation (Packer & Goicoechea, 2000). This ontological line of research should be considered also more in the CSCL research .

Whether relying on the acquisition or participation metaphor of learning, there exist two main theoretical perspectives for a mechanism promoting learning in a CSCL setting. These perspectives, which seem to be agreed among researchers, trace back to the thinking of Piaget and Vygotsky. The first mechanism that is seen to promote learning in the context of CSCL is Piagetian socio-cognitive conflict. Children on different levels of cognitive development, or children on the same level of cognitive development with differing perspectives, can engage in social interaction that leads to a cognitive conflict. This "shock of our thought coming into contact with others" (Piaget, 1928, p. 204) may create a state of disequilibrium within participants, resulting to construction of new conceptual structures and understanding. According to this view, new knowledge is not so much a product of co-construction or shared understanding but is rather understood as taking place in the individual minds. This new understanding can then be brought back to the level of social interaction, and collaborative activities. Another interpretation of Piaget's theory stresses more the idea of co-construction of knowledge and mutual understanding. The co-construction of knowledge takes place through one's increasing ability to take account of other peoples' perspectives. This ability develops through five, distinct, developmental stages; from an undifferentiated and egocentric social perspective to in-depth and societal-symbolic perspective taking (Selman, 1980; Järvelä & Häkkinen, in press).

The second well-known mechanism for promoting learning in context of social interaction is formulated on the basis of Vygotsky's ideas. There are two basic interpretations of Vygotsky's thought. The first, and the more traditional view, assumes that because of engagement in collaborative activities, individuals can master something they could not do before the collaboration. People gain knowledge and practice some new competencies as a result of internalization in collaborative learning. In other words, collaboration is interpreted as a facilitator of individual cognitive development. The other interpretation of Vygotsky's ideas emphasizes the role of mutual engagement and co-construction of knowledge. According to this perspective, learning is more as a matter of participation in a social process of knowledge construction than an individual endeavor. Knowledge emerges through the network of interactions and is distributed and mediated among those (humans and tools) interacting (Cole and Wertsch, 1996).

Influenced by Piaget and Vygotsky, a great variety of research goes under the label of CSCL covering many, even very different instructional and theoretical approaches, that aim to support individual and group learning with technology. In many cases the theories of Piaget and Vygotsky are seen to represent opposite explanations of human development and learning. In the future, a fruitful approach might be to attempt to reconcile these two perspectives (Hickey & McCaslin, in press; Packer & Goicoechea, 2000).

Empirical research on CSCL

Whilst the antecedents educational technology paradigms relied strongly on experimental research design, CSCL adopts a variety of methods from the fields of anthropology, communication science, and linguistic research, just to mention a few. Typical methods for analysis are ethnographical methods and discourse analysis with descriptive, observational, and non-experimental data. Stress is put on the ecological validity of the research. In contrast to its predecessors that studied human cognition with experimental design and in laboratories, CSCL research is conducted also in "real world contexts", for instance, at schools.

What then should researchers study in the context of CSCL? Some researchers propose that we should study very specific interactions of mutual engagement and intimacy. Dillenbourg (1999) suggested that one should not talk about the effects of collaborative learning in general but more specifically about the effects of particular categories of interactions. One should, for example, analyze a posteriori which interactions did actually take place during collaboration (Dillenbourg, 1999, pp. 16-17), for instance, to study the sequences of improvement and refinement of ideas, and focus not so much on individual statements in discourse (Stahl, in press). In other words, one should in collaborative interactions zoom in more intensively on the micro level.

If one studies only interactions of mutual engagement one can then ask, what is the relevance of CSCL research at schools, or in workplaces in general. The dilemma is this: if collaboration is understood as "a coordinated, synchronous activity that is the result of a continued attempt to construct and maintain a shared conception of a problem" (Roschelle & Teasley, 1995, p. 70), it refers to a form of interaction that can be, strictly speaking, maintained only among a small number of people, and perhaps, only in face-to-face situations. An approach to collaboration solely in terms of face to face encounters among small groups appears, however, to be very limited approach to CSCL, for it is very common to speak about collaboration and learning communities in the same context, and related to networked learning environments. As pointed out earlier, collaboration can also considered as a process of participating in practices of a community.

How then, should one speak about and analyze collaboration at the collective (macro) level? One idea would be to think about communities as interaction networks, and interactions representing strong and weak links among participants. Links among community members that frequently meet each other are usually strong, and conversely (see Granovetter, 1973). We may assume that strong links and intensive interaction among community members also represent intensive and productive collaboration. Thus, as pointed out by Wellman and others (Wellman, Salaff, Dimitrova, Garton, Gulia, & Haythornthwaite, 2000), we could speak about computer-supported social networks. Or the unit of analysis could be an activity system, as proposed by Engeström (1987). To date, there is no consensus about the unit of analysis, whether it should be individuals, dyads, groups, communities, or as argued by Bereiter (in press), collaboratively produced knowledge objects or conceptual artifacts. All these units of analysis have been, individually, used in the studies that go under the label CSCL, the unit of analysis depending on the theoretical background and definitions of 'collaboration' used.

It is a challenging task to compare empirical studies conducted under the label CSCL, because they differ from each other in several significant aspects. First of all, there is no agreement whether one should study *effects of* or *effects with* CSCL. In 1991, Salomon, Perkins, and Globerson made educators aware of two ways of thinking about learning and technology. According to them, one should look at *effects of technology*, this is, what one has learned and can transfer from those situation working with computer. Yet one should also look at the *effects with* technology; what one could achieve in synergy with a computer. In the same sense one can speak about *effects of CSCL*; that is, as a result of interacting with others and computers, persons individually practice new competencies and gain knowledge that can be transfer to new situations. Or, by contrast, one may speak of *effects with CSCL*, referring to processes people and computers achieve in synergy.

Secondly, there is a variation in research procedures; in length of the study, in number of students participating, in students' age, and whether students worked individually, in pairs, or in small groups. Whilst analyzing learning in CSCL settings, researchers have used different learning tasks, and have studied how special concepts are learned (Roschelle, 1992). They have analyzed sociocognitive effects of CSCL (Järvelä, Hakkarainen, Lehtinen, & Lipponen, 2000), complex reasoning and levels of argumentation (Hoadley & Linn, 2000), explored science learning and inquiry processes (Edelson, Gordin, & Pea, 1999; Lipponen & Hakkarainen, 1997; Hakkarainen, Lipponen, & Järvelä, in press), collaborative knowledge building (Lipponen, 2000; Scardamalia, Bereiter, & Lamon, 1994), studied cognitive and metacognitive understanding (Brown, Ellery & Campione, 1998), design processes (Seitamaa-Hakkarainen, Raami, Muukkonen, & Hakkarainen, in press), and motivational aspects in CSCL (Hakkarainen, Lipponen, Järvelä, & Niemivirta, 1999). Lately, stress is also put on issues of participation (Guzdial & Turns, 2000; Lipponen, Rahikainen, Hakkarainen, & Palonen, 2001). These are just few of the research topics that have emerged in the context of CSCL.

Thirdly, what makes the comparison even more difficult among different studies is that there exists a great variety in the technologies used; also in the purposes sought, and how some particular applications were used: Is students' collaboration supported around the computer (for instance, with simulation programs), or is it supported with networked learning environments, and is technology used for structuring the collaboration or to mediate collaboration (see, Hall, Miyake, & Enyedy, 1997; Hoadley, 1999; Dillenbourg, Eurelings, & Hakkarainen, 2001). There has already been mention of the differences in methodologies and units of analysis applied

The boundless enthusiasm towards technology has made us researchers mainly focus on the potentials of CSCL. In some respects, this has blinded us, and made us to consider the potentials of technology and collaboration as empirical evidence for the actual benefits of CSCL. It is true, that some very intensive studies have had success in promoting high-quality learning supported with computer networks (Hakkarainen, 1998; Scardamalia, et al., 1994). But, on a large scale, there is no solid evidence that collaboration through networks leads to excellent learning results. Stahl (in press) has even proposed that CSCL environments are mainly used for exchange of personal opinions, and for delivering surface knowledge, not for collaborative knowledge building. In addition, we can also speculate whether some of these results achieved in the CSCL studies would have been achieved without any networked computer support. Among other constraints on the dominant research in CSCL is that there exists little research on how students participate in networked mediated collaboration, and on the consequences of different types of participation patterns, and how are these related to other aspects of CSCL, such as quality of students' discourse (but see Lipponen et al., 2001). As a consequence of the ambiguity (or richness if you will) of the empirical studies in the CSCL research, it is difficult to integrate the empirical studies and findings or to make any solid conclusions that some particular approach, instructional method, or application would give better results than some others. One does not know exactly the circumstances in which one set of results can be extended to another context.

Challenges and Advantages of CSCL

Collaboration can be supported with very different instructional ideas and computer applications. Crook (1994), for instance, has proposed four kinds of interaction in which computers play a part: 1) interactions at the computers, 2) interactions around computers, 3) interactions related to computer applications, and 4) interactions through computers. In the following paragraphs, I concentrate on the fourth issue, interaction and collaboration through computers.

The first three aspects proposed by Crook are face-to-face interaction situations where meanings are mediated through spoken language, faces, and gestures. In these situations, computers can act as a referential anchor, and mediate the coordination of attention and collaborative actions (Järvelä, Bonk, Lehtinen, & Lehti, 1999; Roschelle, 1992). By contrast, collaboration through networked learning environments is still mainly based on written language. Thus, interaction taking place through computer networks lacks certain basic features of face-to-face collaboration: social cues such as faces, gestures and intonations of speech. It also lacks the rich referential field of the material world that is present in face-to-face interactions. The lack of referential anchors is quite pronounced in written communication. This means that explicating referential relations in a written message is important because, in written language, such explications of a message create context and grounding; in contrast these referents are usually known by participants or are easily checked in face-to-face discourse. Building a common ground is considered an essential part of coordinating collaborative activities and knowledge sharing (Clark & Brennan, 1991).

The idea of collaboration as mutual engagement appears to imply synchronous activity or even a situation of face-to-face interaction. Hence, one may ask, how is this prerequisite for collaboration, mutual and reciprocal engagement, created through networked learning environments, or is it possible at all? There are some initial attempts to analyze this phenomenon in asynchronous CSCL environments (see Järvelä & Häkkinen, in press) but there is still a lack of evidence whether asynchronous computer-mediated collaboration is possible at all, and if it were, what expressions or communicative acts would be indicators of reciprocal interaction and understanding. From this perspective one can presume that collaboration is a form of activity that seldom manifests in students' interactions in networked learning environments.

There are other challenges of CSCL: knowledge management problems with large databases, fact-oriented knowledge construction, short discussion threads with divergence topics, and unequal participation patterns (Guzdial & Turns, 2000; Lipponen et. al., 2001; Lipponen, Rahikainen, Lallimo, & Hakkarainen, 2001). According to Stahl (1999), the clearest failures related to computer-supported collaborative learning environments are that for different personal and cultural reasons, students and teachers are hesitant to use them. Further, if the technology itself is put intensively into use, there still might be considerable difficulties in bringing about genuine collaboration and knowledge construction.

Why has CSCL been so slowly adopted? As proposed by Kling (1991) in the context of CSCW, it might be that the meanings attached to collaboration are too positively loaded, or the collaborative settings are interpreted too narrowly referring only to positive phenomenon. This may restrict one from seeing that collaborative situations are also full of contradictions, competition, and conflicts. A realistic picture of collaboration should also take these issues in to consideration. Only recently has the interest in overcoming the existing barriers of computer-supported collaborative learning grown (Lipponen, 1999; Stahl, 1999).

On the other hand, technology offers the kind of potentials for learning which are very different from those available in other contexts. A wave of empirical research has revealed a long list of the promises and reported benefits of computer networks for collaboration (see Lehtinen, Hakkarainen, Lipponen, Rahikainen, & Muukkonen, 1999, for a review). One self-evident benefit is, that computer networks break down the physical and temporal barriers of schooling by removing time and space constraints. The delay of asynchronous communication allows time for reflection in interaction. Making thinking visible by writing should help students to reflect on their own and others' ideas and share their expertise. Shared discourse spaces and distributed interaction can offer multiple perspectives and zones of proximal development (ZPD) for students with varying knowledge and competencies. CSCL environments can also offer greater opportunities to share and solicit knowledge. Further, the database can function as a collective memory for a learning community, storing the history of knowledge construction processes for revisions and future use.

Technology for collaboration

At present, the current understanding appears to be that collaboration is a synonym for good learning and good educational technology; almost any web-based application is labeled as 'collaborative.' This loose usage is also because there is no established way to classify the variety of tools that might be considered as collaborative, and moreover, because almost any technological application, could, in some way, be used in support of collaboration, i.e., by people working together on something.

Hence, it might be meaningful to make a distinction between *collaborative use of technology* and *collaborative technology*. Imagine a pair of students working at the computer running a simulation program in physics. The simulations on the screen can help the students to collaborate, by creating a referential anchor, a point of shared reference (Crook, 1994). This referential anchor can function as a "concrete" shared representation, can support the negotiation of meanings, and mediate students' communication activities in their development of reciprocal understanding (Hakkarainen, et al., 1998; Järvelä, et. al., 1999). In this case, the technology, the software developed for the individual user, is utilized in creating and establishing

collaborative activities.

On the other hand, collaboration can be supported through computer networks, but not (without special efforts) those most well-known on the Internet. As stated by Roschelle and Pea (1999), most of the Internet tools and discussion forums available are not robust and simple enough for use in average classrooms, or do not translate to the classroom setting. Typical Internet chat or bulletin board systems or e-mail do not organize conversations well for learning. These applications are not, in the first place, designed for pedagogical purposes of building collaborative knowledge. However, with advanced pedagogical practices, these applications can also be utilized for collaborative learning.

The most pure and original applications of CSCL and collaborative technology are, perhaps, networked learning environments (or 'groupware'), such as CSILE (Computer Supported Intentional Learning Environment, see Scardamalia & Bereiter, 1994), which are designed especially for educational use and for collaborative knowledge building. A common feature of advanced network applications designed for educational purposes is that they support users' cognitive activities by providing advanced socio-cognitive scaffolding, by offering many ways to structure discussion to create collaborative representations and by including community-building tools. "These tools all scaffold learning by prestructuring the kinds of contributions learners can make, supporting meaningful relationships among those contributions, and guiding students' browsing on the basis of socio-cognitive principle" (Pea, Tinker, Linn, Means, Brandsford, Roschelle, Hsi, Brophy, & Songer 1999, p. 33). Even if there exists a body of research with respect to CSCL applications, there is one crucial thing to remember. With respect to learning results, it is very hard to find solid evidence that some particular CSCL application is better than some other or better than some traditional classroom uses of computers.

Technology itself does not solve the challenges of learning and collaboration. For collaborative technology can, of course, be used for other purposes than for supporting collaboration; it can easily be applied in transmitting and delivering knowledge. An important part of the use of collaborative technology is how the technology is implemented, for instance, in school setting. Among the issues for which there is still a lack of good research data are the following: Is it possible to implement CSCL without already having a deep understanding of collaborative learning and collaborative technology? Or is it possible to introduce new ideas of learning and human cognition with new technology? These are among the most important questions to respond if CSCL if going to work on a large scale.

IMPLEMENTATION OF CSCL: FROM TECHNICAL INFRASTRUCTURE TO SOCIAL INFRASTRUCTURE

One of the major challenges of CSCL, or educational technology in general, is scaling-up; how to expand and implement the good practices that researcher and teachers have found and developed. In other words, what is needed in successful implementation of technology? Although technology, in some cases, may act as a "Trojan Mouse" (Papert, 1993) and serve as a catalyst for change, nowadays it seems very clear that technology itself does not necessarily make any deep changes in learning activities in school. Whilst creating new learning environments or learning communities, it is not just a matter of implementing and putting into use new technology but in many cases, also applying simultaneously new practices of learning and instruction.

In 1999 I proposed (Lipponen, 1999) that we should pay more attention to the factors that inhibit or support the implementation and use of CSCL at schools. To successfully implement and use CSCL in natural settings, one has to resolve technical, organizational, and pedagogical challenges. Bielaczyc (2001) has presented a parallel idea. According to her, one of the key factors in successful implementation of CSCL is to build an appropriate social infrastructure around the technical infrastructure. She proposed three levels of social infrastructure important for successful implementation and use of CSCL. These three include, cultural level (the philosophy and norms established among educators and students), activity level (practices), and tool level (technology). Thus, instead of focusing extensively on the technology, one should turn towards thinking about the social settings that support the implementation and use of technology.

Bielaczyc is right on the mark, but only partly. Namely, her model still appears to be slightly technology driven for it implies that the social infrastructure should be built around the technology; implicitly, the technological infrastructure appears to be the primary structure that is supported by some special social activities. I propose that we have two other advanced possibilities to think about this issue. First, one could explore and find the advanced and innovative pedagogical practices (or needs) that already exist in the particular context that aims to take technology in use. While these practices and activities are found, technology could be implemented to support and extend these already existing, good practices. In this case, the social infrastructure is primary to the technical infrastructure. An even more advanced idea would be to find the zone of proximal development of the particular community and to implement technology that has the potential to help to transform the community towards more advanced learning activities through an expansive learning cycle (Engeström, 1987). The third alternative is that technological and social infrastructure co-evolve. This is what happens, of course, in the two previous alternatives too. But what I propose, is that the idea of co-evolution should be the starting point for thinking about implementing technology and new forms of learning activities. This approach is very much pedagogy and activity driven. It implies that technology should be very flexible and tailorable. Learners are not the same as the everyday people or experts, but need software designed especially for the learners. As far as I can see, the concept of social infrastructure has the potential to help us to think about the problems of implementing technology and building learning communities, and should be carefully studied in the future. There is one more thing to consider concerning infrastructures. Perhaps, as stated by Crook (1994), classrooms are still too neatly resourced for successful collaboration, and the material world is too often underestimated in building collaboration; material objects offer points of shared reference for developing genuine collaborative interactions.

CONCLUSIONS

In sum, even if the stress in CSCL research is on socially-oriented theories of learning, descriptive, observational, and non-experimental data, and methods from the fields of anthropology, communication science, and linguistic research, there is still no unifying and established theoretical framework, no agreed objects of study, no methodological consensus, or agreement about the concept of collaboration, or unit of analysis. Positively considered, this ambiguity can be seen as reflecting the richness or diversity of the field. Negatively interpreted, it seems that the field is proceeding along more and more divergent lines. If we concur that in an established scientific paradigm, the theories and methods as well as objects of study are agreed, it is not an exaggeration to say that CSCL is an emerging educational technology paradigm. Perhaps, as suggested by Hall (2001), researchers in the learning sciences should pay more attention to characterizing their work practices (their theory and method), that is, how to do this kind of research. According to Hall (2001), such efforts are important, for such efforts would help clarify how they theorize and investigate cognition, learning, and teaching, and teach newcomers how to do research.

I share the idea that appears on the homepage of the CSCL 2002 conference (http://www.cscl2002.org/intro.html): " ... further progress is needed to provide a solid foundation for CSCL as a robust, effective research field. We [CSCL researchers] need to start to coalesce and strengthen a set of coherent foundations --without imposing a narrow approach or stifling the healthy interchange of conflicting interdisciplinary perspectives". This task is absolutely worthwhile of striving for. But as my exploration showed, it will also be a very demanding task, it might be even a mission impossible.

REFERENCES

Anderson, J. R. Greeno, J. G., Reder, L. M., & Simon, H. (2000). Perspectives on Learning, Thinking, and Activity. *Educational Researcher, 29,* 11-13.

Bereiter, B. (in press). *Education and mind in the knowledge age.* Lawrence Erlbaum Associates.

Bielaczyc, K. (2001). Designing social infrastructure: The challenge of building computer-supported learning communities. In P. Dillenbourg, A. Eurelings, & K. Hakkarainen (Eds.), *European perspectives on computer-supported collaborative learning. The proceedings of the First European Conference on Computer-Supported Collaborative Learning* (pp.106-114). University of Maastricht.

Bolter, J. D. (1984). *Turing's man: western culture in the computer age.* Chapel Hill: The University of North Carolina Press.

Brown, A. L. (1994). The advancement of learning. *Educational Researcher, 23,* 4-12.

Brown, A. L. & Campione, J. C. (1994). Guided discovery in a community of learners. In K. McGilly (Ed.), *Classroom lessons: Integrating cognitive theory and classroom practice* (pp. 229-270). Cambridge, MA: MIT Press.

Brown, A. L., Ellery, S., & Campione, J. C. (1998). Creating zones of proximal development electronically. In J. G. Greeno & S. V. Goldman (Eds.), *Thinking practices in mathematics and science learning* (pp.341-367). Mahwah, NJ: Lawrence Erlbaum Associates.

Brufee, K. (1993). *Collaborative learning.* Baltimore: Johns Hopkins University Press.

Bruner, J.S. (1996). *Culture of education.* Cambridge, MA: Harvard University Press.

Clark, H. H., & Brennan, S. E. (1991). Grounding in communication. In L. B. Resnick, J. M. Levine & S. D. Teasley (Eds.), *Perspectives on socially shared cognition* (pp. 127-149). Washington, DC: American Psychological Association.

Cole, M., & Wertsch, J. V. (1996). Beyond the individual-social antinomy in discussions of Piaget and Vygotsky. *Human Development, 39,* 250-256.

Crook, C. (1994). *Computers and the collaborative experience of learning.* London: Routledge.

Crook, C. (1998). Children as computer users: the case of collaborative learning. *Computers and Education, 30,* 237- 247.

Dillenbourg, P. (1999). Introduction: What do you mean by "collaborative learning"? In P. Dillenbourg (Ed.), *Collaborative Learning: Cognitive and computational approaches* (pp. 1-19) Amsterdam: Pergamon, Elsevier Science.

Dillenbourg, P., Eurelings, A., & Hakkarainen, K. (Eds.). (2001). *European perspectives on computer-supported collaborative learning. The proceedings of the First European Conference on Computer-Supported Collaborative Learning.* University of Maastricht.

Doise, W., & Mugny, G. (1984). *The social development of the intellect.* Oxford, England: Pergamon.

Edelson, D. C., Gordin, D. N., & Pea, R. D. (1999). Addressing the challenges of inquiry-based learning through technology and curriculum design. *Journal of the Learning Sciences, 8,* 391-450.

Engeström, Y. (1987). *Learning by expanding. An activity-theoretical approach to developmental research.* Helsinki: Orienta-Konsultit Oy.

Engeström, Y. (1992). *Interactive expertise. Studies in distributed working intelligence.* Research bulletin 83, department of education, University of Helsinki.

Galegher, J. & R. Kraut, E. & Egido, C. (Eds.) (1990), *Intellectual teamwork: Social and technological foundations of cooperative work* (pp. 1-20). Hilsdale, NJ: Lawrence Erlbaum Associates.

Greenberg, S. (Ed.). (1991). *Computer-supported cooperative work and Groupware.* New York: Academic Press.

Guzdial, M., & Turns, J. (2000). Effective Discussion Through a Computer-Mediated Anchored Forum. *Journal of the Learning Sciences, 9,* 437- 469.

Granovetter, M. (1973). The Strength of Weak Ties. *American Journal of Sociology, 78,* 1360-1380.

Hakkarainen (1998). *Epistemology of scientific inquiry in computer-supported collaborative learning.* Unpublished doctoral dissertation, University of Toronto.

Hakkarainen, K., Järvelä, S., Lipponen, L., & Lehtinen, E. (1998). Culture of collaboration in computer-supported learning: Finnish perspectives. *Journal of Interactive Learning Research, 9, 271-287.*

Hakkarainen, K., Lipponen, L., & Järvelä, S. (in press). Epistemology of inquiry and computer-supported collaborative learning. In T. Koschmann, R. Hall, & N. Miyake (Eds.), *CSCL2: Carrying Forward the Conversation.* Mahwah, NJ: Lawrence Erlbaum Associates

Hakkarainen, K., Lipponen, L., Järvelä, S., & Niemivirta, M. (1999). The interaction of motivational orientation and knowledge-seeking inquiry in computer-supported collaborative learning. *Journal of Educational Computing Research, 3,* 261-279.

Hall, R. (2001). Schedules of practical work for the analysis of case studies of learning and development. *Journal of the Learning Sciences 10,* 203–222.

Hall, R., Miyake, N., & Enyedy, N. (Ed.). (1997). *Proceedings of CSCL '97: The Second International Conference on Computer Support for Collaborative Learning.* Mahwah, NJ: Lawrence Erlbaum Associates

Hickey, D. T., & McCaslin, M. (in press). A comparative, sociocultural analysis of context and motivation. In S. Volet and S. Järvelä (Eds.), *Motivation in learning contexts: Theoretical and Methodological implications.* A volume in the EARLI/Pergamon "Advances in Learning and Instruction" series.

Hoadley, C. (Ed.). (1999). *Proceedings of CSCL '99: The Third International Conference on Computer Support for Collaborative Learning.* Mahwah, NJ: Erlbaum.

Hoadley, C., & Linn, M. (2000). Teaching science through online, peer discussions: SpeakEasy in the Knowledge Intergration Environment. *Journal of Science Teaching, 22,* 839-857.

Järvelä, S., Bonk, C.J., Lehtinen, E. & Lehti, S. (1999). A theoretical analysis of social interactions in computer-based learning environments: Evidence for reciprocal understandings. *Journal of Educational Computing Research, 21,* 359-384.

Järvelä, S., Hakkarainen, K., Lehtinen, E. & Lipponen, L. (2000). Creating Computer-supported Collaborative Learning (CSCL) Culture in Finnish Schools: Research Perspectives on Sociocognitive *Effects. International Journal of Continuing Engineering Education and Life-Long Learning, 10, 1-10.*

Järvelä, S., & Häkkinen, P. (in press). The levels of web-based discussions using perspective-taking theory as an analysis tool. In H. van Oostendorp (Ed.), *Cognition in a digital world.* Lawrence Erlbaum Associates.

Kling, R. (1991). Cooperation, coordination and control in computer-supported work. *Communications of the ACM, 34,* 12, 83-88.

Koschman, T. (1994). Toward a theory of computer support for collaborative learning. *Journal of the learning sciences, 3,* 219-225.

Koschmann, T. (1996). Paradigm shifts and instructional technology: An introduction. In T. Koschmann, (Ed.), *CSCL: Theory and practice of an emerging paradigm,* (pp. 1-23). Mahwah, NJ: Lawrence Erlbaum Associates.

Koschmann, T. (1999). Computer support for collaboration and learning. *Journal of the learning sciences, 8,* 495-497.

Lehtinen, E., Hakkarainen, K., Lipponen, L., Rahikainen, M., & Muukkonen, H. (1999). *Computer-supported collaborative learning: A review of research and development* (The J.H.G.I Giesbers Reports on Education, 10). Netherlands: University of Nijmegen, Department of Educational Sciences.

Lipponen, L. (1999). Challenges for computer-supported collaborative learning in elementary and secondary level: Finnish perspective. In C. Hoadley (Ed*.), Proceedings of CSCL '99: The Third International Conference on Computer Support for Collaborative Learning* (pp. 368-375). Mahwah, NJ: Lawrence Erlbaum Associates.

Lipponen, L. (2000). Towards knowledge building discourse: From facts to explanations in primary students' computer mediated discourse. *Learning Environments Research, 3,* 179-199.

Lipponen, L., & Hakkarainen, K. (1997). Developing culture of inquiry in computer-supported collaborative learning. In R. Hall, N. Miyake, & N. Enyedy (Ed.), *Proceedings of CSCL '97: The Second International Conference on Computer Support for Collaborative Learning* (pp. 164-168). Mahwah, NJ: Lawrence Erlbaum Associates.

Lipponen, L., Rahikainen, M., Hakkarainen, K., & Palonen, T. (2001). *Effective participation and discourse through a computer network:Investigating elementary students' computer-supported interaction.* Manuscript submitted for publication.

Lipponen, L., Rahikainen, M., Lallimo, J., & Hakkarainen, K. (2001). Analyzing patterns of participation and discourse in elementary students' online science discussion. In P. Dillenbourg, A. Eurelings, & K. Hakkarainen (Eds.), *European perspectives on computer-supported collaborative learning. The proceedings of the First European Conference on Computer-Supported Collaborative Learning* (pp. 421-428). University of Maastricht.

Mead, G. H. (1934). *Mind, self, and society.* Chicago: University Chicago Press.

O'Malley, C. & Scanlon, E. (1989). *Computer-supported collaborative learning: Problem solving and distance education.* Centre for Information Technology in Education. Report No. 75. Open University, Great Britain.

Packer, M. J., & Goicoechea, J. (2000). Sociocultural and constructivist theories of learning: Ontology, not just epistemology. *Educational Psychologist, 35,* 227-241.

Papert, S. (1993). *The children's machine: rethinking school in the age of the Computer.* New York: Basic Books.

Pea, R. D. (1996). Seeing what we build together. Distributed multimedia learning environments for transformative learning. In T. Koschmann, (Ed.), *CSCL: Theory and practice of an emerging paradigm* (pp.171-186) Mahwah, NJ: Lawrence Erlbaum Associates.

Pea, R., Tinker, R., Linn, M., Means, Brandsford, J. Roschelle, J., Hsi, S., Brophy, S., & Songer, N. (1999). Toward a learning technologies knowledge network. *Educational Technology Research and Development, 47,* 19-38.

Piaget, J. (1928). *The judgement and reasoning in children.* London: Routledge and Kegan.

Roschelle, J. (1992). Learning by collaborating: convergent conceptual change. *The Journal of the Learning Sciences, 2,* 235-276.

Roschelle, J., & Pea, R. (1999). Trajectories from today's WWW to a powerful educational infrastructure. *Educational Researcher, 43,* 22-25.

Salomon, G., Perkins, D., & Globerson, T. (1991). Partners in cognition: Extending human intelligence with intelligent technologies, *Educational Researcher, 20,* 9-20.

Scardamalia, M., & Bereiter, C. (1994). Computer support for knowledge-building communities. *The Journal of the Learning Sciences, 3,* 265-283.

Scardamalia, M., Bereiter, C. & Lamon, M. (1994). The CSILE project: Trying to bring the classroom into World 3. In K. McGilly (Ed.), *Classroom lessons; Integrating cognitive theory & classroom practice* (pp. 201-228). Cambridge, MA: MIT Press.

Seitamaa-Hakkarainen, P., Raami, A., Muukkonen, H., & Hakkarainen, K. (in press). Computer-support for collaborative designing. *International Journal of Technology and Design Education.*

Selman, R. L. (1980). *The growth of interpersonal understanding.* New York: Academic Press.

Sfard, A. (1998). On two metaphors for learning and the dangers of choosing just one. *Educational Researcher, 27,* 4–13.

Stahl, G. (1999). Reflections on WebGuide. Seven issues for the next generation of collaborative knowledge-building environments. In C. Hoadley (Ed.), *Proceedings of CSCL '99: The Third International Conference on Computer Support for Collaborative Learning* (pp. 600-610). Mahwah, NJ: Lawrence Erlbaum Associates.

Stahl, G. (in press). Rediscovering CSCL. In T. Koschmann, R. Hall, & N. Miyake (Eds.), *CSCL2: Carrying forward the conversation.* Mahwah, NJ: Lawrence Erlbaum Associates.

Tomasello, M. (1999). *The cultural origins of human cognition.* Cambridge, MA: Harvard University Press.

Vygotsky, L. S. (1962). *Thought and language*. Cambridge, MA: MIT Press.

Vygotsky, L.S. (1978). *Mind in Society: The Development of Higher Psychological Processes.* Cambridge, MA: Harvard University Press.

Wellman, B., Salaff, J., Dimitrova, D., Garton, L., Gulia, M., & Haythornthwaite, C. (2000). Computer networks as social networks: Collaborative work, telework, and virtual community. In E. L. Lesser, M. A. Fontaine, & J. A. Slusher (Eds.), *Knowledge and Communities* (pp. 179-207). Boston: Butterworth-Heinemann.

Wundt, W. (1921). *Elements of folk psychology*. London: Allen and Unwin.

Describing Construction of Knowledge through Identification of Collaboration Patterns in 3D Learning Environments

Ingeborg Krange
InterMedia, University of Oslo
and Telenor R&D
ingeborg.krange@intermedia.uio.no

Annita Fjuk
Telenor R&D
and InterMedia, University of Oslo
annita.fjuk@telenor.com

Anniken Larsen
Telenor R&D
anniken.larsen@telenor.com

Sten Ludvigsen
InterMedia, University of Oslo
sten.ludvigsen@intermedia.uio.no

ABSTRACT
Recent research has to a limited extent explored the nature of collaborative knowledge construction in 3D environments. In this paper we describe this issue by identifying two collaboration patterns that are manifested in the students' dialogues and actions in a particular 3D learning environment. The theoretical framework is found within socio-cultural perspectives that view learning as socially and culturally constructed and of whichartefacts are considered as inseparable from human activity. In agreement with the intellectual heritage, the collaboration patterns are identified through analyses of various extracts of dialogues and actions taken place between the students and how these extracts are operationalised by available artefacts. Interaction analysis constitutes the analytic tool.

Keywords
3D environments, collaboration patterns, joint construction of knowledge, dialog analyses.

INTRODUCTION
The aim of the paper is to describe how students construct knowledge collaboratively in 3D learning environments. We approach this issue by identifying collaboration patterns specific to such environments. Collaboration patterns are understood in terms of how students (actors) act in dialogues and in the usage of artefacts in a particular 3D learning environment. These kinds of environment "evoke a feeling of immersion, a perceptual and psychological sense of being in the digital environment presented to the sense" (McLellan 1996: 457). This means that interactivity is of vital importance; seeing as it includes the feeling of touch, sense orientation and position in space (Gorman et al. 1999). As such, 3D environments provide ways to experience and view information that are dynamic and interactive. In addition, they are proclaimed to be appropriate for model building and problem solving (McLellan 1996).

Technological advances have unquestionably been the driving force behind most designs and developments associated with 3D environments. Also, Hoffman & Vu (1997) point to the fact that there is a substantial gap between the technologies available today and the technology that is needed for realising the expectations for 3D technologies as tools for knowledge construction. Most of the educationaluses of 3D environments have been developed for professional training in technical fields such as medical education and military training (Ludvigsen & Fjuk, in press). There exist recent and limited insights into the nature of human actions in a 3D environment, and more precisely, how these activities evolve with respect to learning. To achieve a deeper insight into this area of learning, empirical analysis is necessary.

To study the area of learning or construction of knowledge (Mercer & Wegrif 1999) we thoroughly identify collaboration patterns in a particular 3D learning environment: Corpus Callosum. This environment is developed for the purpose of constructing a simulated learning environment for collaborative activities. The 15-year-old students are located geographically separated in such a way that their collaboration only takes place in networks and through real-time communication. The environment represents a planet that is threatened by an ecological disaster. The students aim to create a joint environment for task-oriented conversations and problem solving associated with various forms of disasters (flooding, drought and erosion). In this strongly visual 3D environment, all actions are operationalised by various 3D-based artefacts. The students canmanipulate different kinds of available 3D-based artefacts alone or together, and their movements and actions become visible both to themselves and the others during social interaction and oral conversation. Figure 1 illustrates a situation in which the students (represented by avatars) operationalise an action by manipulating different pieces of the aqueduct.

Figure 1: Students collaborating in Corpus Callosum solving the aqueduct task.

We analyze extracts of dialogues and actions taking place between the students, with interaction analysis as the analytic tool (Jordan & Henderson 1995), and with socio-cultural theory as the framework for discussion (Vygotsky 1978; Engeström 1987).

3D LEARNING ENVIRONMENTS: A REVIEW OF THE LITERATURE IN SCIENCE EDUCATION FOR STUDENTS

3D learning environments that are designed and organised for undergraduate students and in K-12 are very few. In the literature we find two such environments particularly interesting, and which have been the subject of research into learning situations. The content in both cases is science education.

Barab et al. (in press) focus on how learning processes in 3D learning environments evolve among 14-15 year-old youth. The environment developed is aimed at stimulating student-centred learning, in the domain of astronomy. The students are meant to collaborate "around the computer" rather than through computer networks. The students are exposed to tasks where they have to transform artefacts. This approach is coloured by their use of activity theory as an analytical tool. Barab et al. (in press) focus on two basic contradictions during their analysis of classroom activities. One is between *learning astronomy* and *building 3D models*. Another is between *teacher directed instruction* and the *emergent student directed learning*. Both contradictions lose their validity when studying how learning processes in 3D learning environments evolve. Concerning the former, the authors claim that learning and building models are parts of the same processes. When it comes to the latter, thetasks are directed towards the construction of new artefacts, which imply that the tasks have the possibilities to create learning trajectories which go beyond the distinction between instruction based or student centred learning environments (Barab et al., in press).

Roussos et al.'s (1999) focal point has been to explore 3D learning environments within the context of primary education. The designed environment is aimed at giving the students opportunities to explore the life cycle of a garden. The students should solve tasks for better understanding of various biological processes. They were meant to collaborate through computer networks. Roussos et al. (1999) embrace a constructivist, collaborative and narrative approach to learning. Their study shows some interesting results related to technical, orientation, affective, cognitive, pedagogical and collaborative aspects. Here we would like to stress two aspects related to what they have identified as pedagogy and collaboration. Concerning the former the authors underline that spreading the lessons over multiple "virtual-reality sessions" appears to be more effective than covering many topics in a single session. Concerning the latter Roussos et al. (1999) emphasize that the teachers' role mainly was to keep order and to stimulate the students to focus on the task.

THEORETICAL FRAMEWORK

Socio-cultural theories represent a distinct perspective for understanding human activity. The *relationship* between the social, collective level and how actors think, reason and act is at the core of the theories. As such, the theories are powerful for understanding and analysing the situated relationships between actors, activities and artefacts. In the study presented in this paper, these concepts are used to describe construction of knowledge through identifying collaboration patterns in 3D learning environments.

We use socio-cultural theories in a broad sense and aspects from activity theory more specifically (Vygotsky 1978; Cole 1996; Wertsch 1998; Leontiev 1978, 1983; Engeström 1987). The core argument for using these theories is the emphasis on the *social and cultural basis of human development* and the rich approach of understanding the *integrated role of artefacts*. The human development is dependent on various kinds of tools. In this respect, language has an essential role for individuals' learning and for collaboration in a learning community and between various communities (Edwards & Mercer 1987; Bowker & Star 1999; Mercer 2000). Language is thus considered as a socialmode of thinking. Moreover, how artefacts are developed and used is dependent on the object of the activity since they serve as a means to acquire, construct and retrieve different kinds of knowledge and performance (Vygotsky 1978; Leontiev 1983). Artefacts are mediators of both the *interactional* and the *operational* aspect of human actions. The former aspect is the way knowledge is constructed – individually and collaboratively. The latter aspect of the same action is mediated by the chosen tools. This implies that the artefacts become both *means for knowledge construction* and *tools*.

According to socio-cultural theories the context is essential for understanding how knowledge is constructed and for identifying how collaboration patterns evolve within learning communities. Collective aspects such as *rules of communication* and *division of work* are emphasised (Engeström 1987). These aspects mediate the students' activities in such a way that they are not isolated, but part of a *learning community*. The artefacts used, the learning community the student belongs to, and the explicitly or implicitly expressed rules and the division of work/task within that community therefore affect the individual's actions.

In the design of the learning environment, Corpus Callosum, we stressed the organisation of mutual relations between actors, actions and artefacts. In that way, this environment differs from most 3D environments because it is arranged especially for learning. Outlined from narrow studies of the students' learning activities in Corpus Callosum containing a set of various artefacts, three main situational relations were identified (Fjuk & Krange 1999). First, the actor-actor relationship makes the students able to talk through a real-time communication system. Second, the actor-object relationship makes it possible for the students to operate and manipulate artefacts by clicking, lifting and moving them, and makes premises on how they can act according to socio-material possibilities and constraints in the learningenvironment. Third, the object-object relationship concerns how manipulation of one artefact affects another artefact in the learning environment. This relation can be initiated by an actor where the result is a kind of domino effect between artefacts andit can be subscribed by how characteristics of one artefact seen in relation to another artefact can give significant information to the student. To construct joint knowledge about how to solve a task in this specific learning environment, the students have to interact and collaborate (actor-actor); they must individually or collaboratively construct knowledge about the relation between artefacts (object-object); they must individually or collaboratively manipulate certain objects and coordinate themselvesaccording to the possibilities and constraints in the learning environment (actor-object). In other words, the way in which language, dialogues and talks are supported and mediated by artefacts in 3D learning environments becomes a complex area of study,which is grounded in how the actors relate themselves to other actors, but also to the material environment they are a part of.

METHODOLOGY

The socio-cultural perspectives offer a rich set of possible units of analysis and levels of descriptions. This provides the analysts with tools that, e.g., make it possible to vary from broad descriptions of activities, to more detailed levels of actions and operations. To study learning processes in Corpus Callosum, we have analysed extracts of dialogues and the individuals' actions by using interaction analysis as an analytical tool (Jordan & Henderson 1995). Data gathered from *video recordings* of the students' activities in the virtual environment constitute the basis in this study. It is straightforward to have one of the networked clients act as a recorder, allowing the entire session in the 3D learning environment to be played back during later analysis. We used the teacher client as a recorder. The teachers' position provided an overview of all the activities in the 3D environment. This approach provides us with possibilities to focus on the temporal organisation of dialogues and actions, but also on how the technical artefacts are used to operationalise certain actions. Another important aspect is that the experiences of the students become visible and documented in the "temporal orderliness and project ability of the events they construct" (Jordan & Henderson 1995: 61). The temporal dimensions are important, but we also want to emphasize the socio-spatial aspects.By socio-spatial aspects we mean how the students oriented themselves in the environment. This becomes especially important when the students move with avatars in Corpus Callosum.

To explore how students construct knowledge in 3D learning environments by studies of how collaboration patterns evolve, three extracts of dialogues associated with the students' work with the aqueduct task were chosen. The rationale of the task was that the students had to pick up and place the aqueduct pieces in the remaining aqueduct-foundation (the H's). The aqueduct pieces have different colours, and by placing the pieces correctly, the colours formed a colour spectrum from red to blue. The task was constructed so that the students themselves found what objects to use and how to place them as well as forming the correct colour spectrum. In the empirical analysis we studied all the dialogues and actions performed by the students. The extracts are chosen to show major differences in how the students relate to each other and to the artefacts in the environment. The aqueduct task was rather complex in the sense that it required integration of other tasks as well as reasoning and negotiation.

The transcriptions of the data are conducted in the following way: When the students only talked together, we transcribed the dialogue as it unfolded. Short pauses and overlaps are indicated in the text. When students both talked and performed actions we transcribed the utterances as they unfolded, but also made an indication of what the students were doing. Such an approach creates a high level of transparency so that the reader can follow the argumentation.

EMPIRICAL ANALYSIS: CONSTRUCTION OF KNOWLEDGE BY IDENTIFYING COLLABORATION PATTERNS IN A 3D LEARNING ENVIRONMENT

Joint construction of knowledge is described by identifying two main collaboration patterns. These patterns are characterised by either sequentially or dynamically oriented activities. By sequentially oriented we indicate that the students perform the actions one after the other, and that they neither reflect upon them nor the specific character of the learning environment they are a part of. Dynamically oriented actions have a more cyclic character. When an actor tries something out, they will return to these actions and have some kind of reflection about the actions performed. This implies that the students' activities differ according to how they relate to each other, and how they manipulate and share their experiences connected to the artefacts.

It is important to note that the identification of collaboration patterns should be understood as analytical constructions, based on the data in itself, and the theoretical lenses used. We argue that there is no direct mapping from data to theory – or vice versa – a direct mapping from data to the analysis performed. Our empirical analysis is rather described as a bottom-up approach where the concepts are developed through our work with the data. These concepts arethen used as part of the analysis where the theoretical framework is used. In the next passages, we exemplify this by studies of some extracts of dialogues and related actions.

Collaboration pattern one: Sequential

There are two main subcategories of collaboration patterns according to the sequentially oriented actions. These are either based on actions characterised by hypotheses testing or on actions typified by trial and error.

Collaboration based on hypotheses testing

The dialogue that follows is selected from a setting where some students are about to start solving the aqueduct task. They have chosen to locate in the same area of the planet, while listening to the exercise.

Teacher	What shall we do then?
	(2)
Student 1	Yesterday, when I was moving around, I saw a lot of pieces around the mountains, that I didn't really know what was.
Student 2	Maybe it's the purple ones?
Student 1	Yes. Or they were a kind of long sticks with a sort of ... They were grey and red.
	(2)
Student 2	Mmm
	(1)
Student 2	Some of the things I saw were similar.
Student 3	I saw them as well.
Teacher	Shall we assume that those are the right ones, and begin to collect them?
Student 3	Yes. But where shall we put them ... to build those things?
Student 4	On that island?
Student 3	Yes
Student 2	Do you think that we can manage to bring them with us alone, or do you think that we have to get together two and two?
Student 4	We must try. Try alone first.
Student 2	Yes.
Student 4	Can't we?
Student 1	Shall we start walking, or ...?

Student 3	We'll go around searching, and then we will see what we find.
Teacher	Yes. Okay. Great. Go on ...

This extract of dialogue shows three different negotiation sequences. First (sentence 1-8) the students are negotiating about *what* kind of objects that can be used for building the aqueduct. Further, (sentences 9-11) they negotiate about *where* they shall bring the objects. Finally, (sentence 12-15) they discuss *how* they can manage to bring the objects to the island. Through these negotiation sequences the students are making several hypotheses that they will try out in their further work. The extract also gives us important information about the students' and teachers' actions during communication while one of the students asks if they shall start to walk (sentences 16-18). This indicates an interesting issue, namely that the students have not moved their avatars during the conversation. This interpretation is confirmed if we look at the video recordings of the pupils' interactions: The group does not split up until they have set out detailed hypotheses on how they are going to solve the task. Another interesting aspect is the teacher's role in the students' collaborative processes. The teacher takes the initiative related to the activities the students should perform (sentence 1), summarizes and stimulates to a turn in the students' discussion (sentence 8) and confirms that the students can start to act (sentence 18).

The analysis of this extract of dialogue indicates that the students mainly collaborate through *hypotheses testing* and *sequentially* oriented actions. The *actors* make a scenario associated with their expectation of what *artefacts* they are going to use and what *actions* they must perform in order to solve the task. During their collaboration it became evident that they were strictly loyal to the hypotheses they had made. They did not change their hypotheses for action in their meeting with the artefacts. They act as if they had total knowledge of the environment. In this way they exclude the probability of including unforeseen artefacts and different action possibilities. Further, their collaboration pattern is also characterised by a low level of division of work, and their activities are guided by collectivistic norms (Engeström 1987). This observation indicates that the students principally relate to the activities and the artefacts as representations and not as parts of their collaborative praxis.

According to the sequentially oriented collaboration the students are able to construct joint knowledge of the development of the action expiration, but they do not attain such knowledge striving to solve the task. This becomes evident because they are first able to solve the task when the teacher gives them a specific and directional hint. In other words, the sequentially oriented pattern, dominated by hypotheses testing collaboration, does not stimulate joint construction of knowledge that is relevant for solving the problem.

Collaboration based on trial and error

The conversation below is gathered from a situation where some students have worked with the aqueduct exercise for a while. One of the aqueduct pieces has already been placed at the foundation. The students move around with different aqueduct pieces. One of the students is just looking and does not participate in the dialogue that follows.

Student 1	Now I placed it somewhere. *(He has an aqueduct piece in his hands and gets rid of it up in the air.)*
Student 2	Yes, it's there. *(We can see the aqueduct piece hanging in the air.)*
Student 3	Where?
Student 2	I'm nearly standing on it. *(He fetches Student 1's aqueduct piece.)*
Student 1	No, shit.
Student 3	Now you fetched it. Yes. Then it is okay. *(He tries to place an aqueduct piece without succeeding.)*
Student 1	One of the iron things landed in the air, but when you get closer to it, it suddenly disappears.
Teacher	Can you see any differences in the various aqueduct elements?
Student 3	Maybe some of them are a little bit smaller than the others? *(They move around with objects while talking.)*
	(1)
Student 1	I would like to use that one.
Student 3	The one Thala has looks quite small.
Student 1	They look small when you hold them, I think. When you place them they look a lot bigger.
	(3)
Student 3	Yes. Thala succeeded in placing one. *(The aqueduct piece increases while it is placed on the foundation and is placed next to the piece that is already there.)*

(1)

Student 1	Did they fit together? There are different colours on each of them. At least these two. *(The students get rid of the objects and look at the aqueduct pieces together.)*
Student 2	Yes, but then …
Student 3	Maybe it's going to be …
Student 1	It doesn't look like they really fit together. *(They are hanging around and are looking to see if the aqueduct pieces fit together.)*
Student 3	Maybe it should be rr …
Student 1	And – the one Thala placed is kind of vertical on the end.

This extract of dialogue consists of two sequences. In the first (sentences 1-7), we see that the students are discussing *where* and *how* to place the aqueduct pieces. Moreover, we observe that they struggle to put the different objects in the intended places. They are confused about what is happening and it seems obvious that they do not really understand the functionality of the system. They do not manage to share each other's experiences. It is not until the second sequence that they manage to build on each other's knowledge and their work process seems to turn into a new phase (sentences 8-19). It is important to mention that this seems to be a result of the teacher's intervention (sentence 8). The teacher gives them an essential hint that leads to a breakthrough in the collaboration.The students start to discuss the difference between the aqueduct pieces, about the size and why it varies (sentence 10). Thereafter it is the shape of the objects that is in focus: first the colours (sentences 14-18) then the construction of each element (sentence 19).

The dialogue between the students indicates that this collaboration process can be characterized as *trial and error oriented.* Unlike group one, group two starts to act prior to setting out hypotheses on how to relate to the artefacts and which activities that must be completed to solve the task. Further, it is primarily after the teacher's involvement that it is possible to register something that resembles hypotheses testing activities. In the first sequence it is quite obvious that there is no common strategy for their activities. In the second sequence (8-19) there is a slight change. The students are still acting prior to reflection, but now they are at least discussing the outcome of their actions after words. The collaboration can also be characterised as rather *sequentially* oriented, but in the opposite way of the first extract of dialogue: They act prior to sharing the information from individual experiences.

This means that the actors do not make any action expirations. They have an opposite collaboration pattern to that of the students in the first extract of dialogue. At best we see *actors* discussing the outcome of their *actions* and the use of different *artefacts* together. The primary basis for *action* is the *artefacts*. Their collaboration patterns are characterised by a high division of labour, and individualistic norms describe their activities (Engeström 1987). We maintain that the *actors* in the second group primarily relate to their *actions* and the *artefacts* in the 3D learning environment on an individual basis and that the problem solving therefore never really becomes a part of collaborative praxis.

According to the sequentially oriented collaboration the students are not able to construct joint knowledge on their own. Only after the teacher's intervention do they manage to construct such knowledge in such a way that they are able to solve the task. In other words, the sequentially oriented pattern, dominated by trial and error collaboration, does not stimulate to joint construction of knowledge that is relevant for solving the problem.

These two groups of students have in one sense distinct ways of collaboration represented by the concepts of being hypotheses testing and trial and error oriented. Nevertheless, their collaboration patterns indicate an important sign of equation, namely the sequentially divided work pattern and the lack of joint construction of knowledge related to problem solving. None of them seem to have gained consistent knowledge of how the 3D learning environment actually works. This implies that the students are not able to utilise the functionality of the 3D learning environment in a way that it is transparent for them and their problem-solving activities. The relation between actors, actions and artefactsbecomes sequential.

Collaboration pattern two: Dynamic

There is one main dynamically oriented collaboration pattern. The following conversation is between some students when they are about to start off the aqueduct task. They are moving around in the 3D learning environment.

Student 1	Okay, then I think we just pick up some pieces and place them in the H's … those iron things.
Student 2	Now I picked up an aqueduct.
Student 3	Okay, shall we get the ones which are placed around?
Student 4	Yes, the ones that look like they can conduct water.
Student 2	The aqueduct has been picked up.

Student 1	It's not … there are many …
Student 3	Shall they … do they like, live in the H's? *(Bringing in an aqueduct piece, and putting it on the foundation.)*
Student 2	I think they should lie in the H's *(Moves towards the aqueduct base.)*
	(3)
Student 1	Okay, I'll try that. I'm not sure about it.
Student 2	Okay, Student 1 is on his way with an object. *(All four of them are gathering around the aqueduct.)*
Student 1	Yes. *(He is coming towards the island with an aqueduct object.)*
Student 2	We also have to ensure that they fit smoothly into each other.
Student 3	They will do that automatically for sure.
Student 1	Like this. I placed one. I don't know how it looks. Lets see …
Student 4	That turned out well, I think.
Student 1	Oh yeah. It's beautiful.

The extract of dialogue contains two sequences. In the first sequence (sentences 1-8), the students are discussing *what* objects they shall collect, what they look like, and *where*they shall place them. They manage to develop a common platform for understanding *how* to solve the task. It is striking how the students make use of figurative descriptions to give information to the others, which utterances like "look like they can conduct water" (sentence 2) and "the H's" (sentences 3 and 4) are examples of. It is also important to note that the students in this sequence change between moving their avatars in different areas of the learning environment executing different activities and being co-located around the aqueduct. In the second sequence (sentences 9-16), their discussion becomes even more specific while they in collaboration try out different strategies for rebuilding the aqueduct and evaluate how it looks afterwards. The students are co-located around the aqueduct while talking. The students start to move around and act immediately. At the same time, they try to convince each other that the choices they are making are the correct ones. It is also worth mentioning that the teacher in this sequence does not intervene in the students' collaboration processes. Instead it seems that Student 1 takes a kind of moderator-role. He starts out by suggesting *what to do* (sentence 1), after a while he *summarises* the discussion (sentence 9) and lastly he *concludes* the outcome (sentence 16). In this way, he seems to gather the students both socially and thematically, and stimulate the progression in the problem solving process.

The students' collaboration is characterized by continuous shifts between *trial and error oriented* activities and *hypotheses testing* activities. This observation indicates a more *dynamic* collaboration pattern. This implies that the students interact in a specific manner with each other as well as with the artefacts at the "same time". This way of collaboration enables the students to reform and correct their original hypotheses during their collaboration processes, and further, the flexibility seems to be crucial for their joint construction of knowledge.

This entails that the *actors* are making a kind of action expiration together at the same time as they are inter*acting* with the *artefacts*. This makes it likely to include unforeseen artefacts and different action possibilities concurrently as these are the focus of their conversational problem solving. This group is able to optimise the learning opportunities, because they both explore the environment and reflect on their actions. They learn how to use the contingencies and constraints of the environment (Greeno 1995). This group, opposed to the two previous groups, has found a balance in their activities. Their collaboration patterns are characterised by a combination of a high and a low degree of division of work, and their norms provide opportunities for the individual actor to perform specific actions, but these actions have to be reported back to the other students, a form of collectivistic individualism (Engeström 1987). We thus claim that the *actors* relate to their *actions* and the *artefacts* in the 3D learning environment at a collective basis and that the problem solving therefore really becomes a part of their collaborative praxis.

According to their dynamically oriented collaboration the students are able to construct joint knowledge while solving the task. In opposition to the sequentially oriented patterns, the students are able to gain consistent knowledge of how the 3D learning environment actually works. This implies that the students manage to utilise the functionality of the 3D learning environment in such a way that it is transparent to them during the problem solving process. The relation between actors, actions and artefacts becomes dynamic.

CONCLUDING REMARKS AND FURTHER WORK

This paper is a contribution to understanding collaboration patterns in 3D environments and how the embedded actions evolve with respect to learning. The aim has been to identifyvarious collaboration patterns to describe collaborative knowledge construction in a specific 3D learning environment. The patterns are identified through analysis of the interrelations between actors, actions and artefacts. Interaction analysis has constituted the analytical tool.

We have identified two main collaboration patterns that are characterised as either sequentially or dynamically oriented actions. These have been discussed in the light of two subordinated aspects. These are actions characterised by hypotheses testing or trial and error. These aspects operate separately in the sequentially oriented pattern, and flexibly in the one that is dynamically oriented. The main conclusion is that the students who work sequentially oriented have problemsconstructing joint knowledge associated with problem solving, while those who work more dynamically oriented are more successful when working with the task. One important aspect of their success is their movement in different areas of the environment and how they relate these actions to each other. When talking to each other and trying out different aspects of the environment, they use the spatial affordences more creatively than the two other groups. In other words, the dynamically oriented group is able to utilise the functionality of the 3D learning environment in a way that becomes transparent to them during their problem solving process, while the former does not.

The findings in this paper point out two important issues. One is related to the design of the 3D learning environment and to what extent it is adequate in supporting and mediating different learning activities, and the other is related to the teachers' role shaping and how this is related to the students' collaborative processes. According tothe former, our analysis indicates that it is just the students whose collaboration is characterised as dynamically oriented that are able to construct joint knowledge that is relevant for problem solving. This in spite of the fact that all of them actually manage to solve the task. This implies that the design of the 3D learning environment makes is possible to solve the task - at one level - without achieving a shared understanding of the tasks and the specific functionality of the environment.

Corpus Callosum is a "closed" community, which implies that the learning activities are performed 'on demand' and synchronously amongst the students. Concerning a more demanding and complex knowledge domain the assumption that all learning activities should be operationalised in the 3D learning environment is arguably too simplistic. We know from learning research that the quality of the learning processes is highly dependent on the learners' previous knowledge, the complexity of the knowledge domain, the learners'ability to regulate the learning processes, and the situated character of knowledge acquired (Brandsford et al. 2000). These processes raise the question of complexity related to the way in which different aspects will influence the learning environment over a period of time. Moreover, Roussos et al. (1999) and Dede et al. (1996) argue for instance that spreading the lessons over multiple 3D sessions appears to be more effective than covering many topics in a single session. If we make a normative turn in argumentation, this implies that other types of learning resources should be part of a new design, and further, that the 3D learning environment should be included in a more comprehensive curriculum. The students' work could be organized in larger projects. This may support a more adequate learning trajectory for the students, simultaneously with the 3D learning environment becoming an important part of the students' learning processes.

The latter essential feature concerns how the teachers shape their role in this specific learning environment. The teacher plays an ambiguous role, also in learning activities that take place in 3D learning environments. Concerning how the students performed in Corpus Callosum, neither of the students that acted sequentially oriented were able to construct joint knowledge related to task solving. As a result, the teacher had to intervene to generate a more adequate work progress. This issue is similar to Roussos et al.'s (1999) findings where the teacher had to intervene to keep the students on the task. These are immediately problematic findings because the teacher's directional role probably never really gives the students the opportunities to form their own agenda. Moreover, neither the students nor the teacher manage to interact with artefacts in an adequate way for problem solving. This issue constitutes an interesting scope for further work.

Concerning the students that acted more dynamically oriented, they were able to use the artefacts constructively in their collaborative processes. Whether this could be explained by the more passive role of the teacher is an open question. Barab et al. (in press) claim that neither the teacher nor the pupils are directing the activities, but artefacts are. This claim is concerned with the process of learning from and with artefacts. In Corpus Callosum it is possible to give feedback to actors by help of artefacts. This feedback can in principle give procedural direction, or on the other hand, give learning possibilities for activities with a cyclic character. But without a collective effort among the students, the feedback cannot be transformed to process where knowledge is co-constructed. Since few complex concepts could be learned based on a procedure and within a short time frame and hardly in one teaching session, the design process should make dynamic and cyclic oriented actions and activities more transparent, both inside and outside a 3D environment. This direction of design can break the dichotomy between students or teacher centred learning environment, because the focus would be on the use and construction of artefacts. If so, the students and the teacher must focus on production of knowledge and new artefacts in different situations rather than how the student-teacher relationships should be regulated. This does not eliminate the problem of the teacher-student relationships, but provides insight into how to design a learning environment where the production of artefacts is in focus.

ACKNOWLEDGMENTS

The 3D learning environment is part of the EduAction project (see: http://www.telenor.no/fou/program/nomadiske/eduaction.shtml) and is developed by using the DOVRE API (Hagen 1999). Several papers and reports are being published during the project period. Most of these are design-oriented (Krange & Fjuk 1999; Fjuk & Krange 1999; Krange et al. 2000), but some have also focused on characteristics of knowledge construction (Larsen & Krange 2001). We want to thank Telenor Research and Development and the Network for IT-Research and Competence in Education for funding our research project, EduAction. Corpus Callosum was developed together with Simen Hagen, Ragnhild Halvorsrud, Nina Khalayli, Ivar Kjellmo, Lars Nilsson, Heidi Rognskog, Ola Ødegård, and the teachers and students at Ringstabekk secondary school. We are grateful to them all. We also want to thank teachers and students at Nordberg and Ringstabekk secondary schools for participating in the field trial. Finally, we want to thank Rich Ling for fruitful discussions related to the labelling of the collaboration patterns.

REFERENCES

Barab, S., A., Barnett, M., Yamagata-Lynch, L., Squire, K., & Keating, T. (in press). "Using activity theory to understand the contradictions characterizing a technology-rich introductory astronomy course." To appear in *Mind, Culture, and Activity*. At http://inkido.indiana.edu/research/onlinemanu/papers/acttheory.pdf

Bowker, G.C. & Star, S.L. 1999: *Sorting Things Out*. Cambridge, Mass: MIT Pres.

Brandsford, J., Brown, A.L. & Coocking, R. 2000. *How People Learn*. Washington DC: National Academy Press.

Dede, C., Salzmann, M. C. & Loftin, R. B. 1996. "ScienceSpace: Virtual realities for learning complex and abstract scientific concepts." In *Proceedings of the IEEE 1996 Virtual Reality Annual International Symposium*. CA, Los Alamitos: IEEE Computer Society Press.

Cole, M. 1996. *Cultural Psychology. A once and future discipline*. Cambridge Mass: Harvard University Press.

Edwards, D & Mercer, N. 1987. *Common Knowledge: The Development of Understanding in the Classroom*. London: Methuen.

Engeström, Y. 1987. *Learning by expanding: An activity-theoretical approach to developmental research*. Helsinki: Orienta-Konsultit.

Fjuk, A. & Krange, I. 1999. "The situated effects of awareness in distributed collaborative learning: Interactive 3D an example." In Hoadley, C. & Roschelle, J. (eds.) *Proceedings for: Computer Support for Collaborative Learning. Designing New Media for a New Millenium: Collaborative technology for learning. Educating and Training. Stanford University*.

Gorman, Meier & Krummel, 1999. "Simulation and Virtual Reality in Surgical Education." In *Archives of Surgery*. Vol. 134. No. 11. (http://archsurg.ama-assn.org/issues/v134n11/full/ssa9016.html)

Greeno, J.G. 1995. "Understanding Concepts in Activity." In Weaver, C., Fletcher, C.R, & Mannes, S. (eds.) *Discourse comprehension: Essays in honor of Walter Kintsch*. N.J. Hillsdale: Lawrence Erlbaum.

Hagen, S. 1999. "DOVRE white paper." *Internal report. Telenor R&D*.

Hoffman, H. & Vu, D. 1997. "Virtual Reality: Teaching Tool of the Twenty-first Century?" In *Academic Medicine*. Vol. 72. No 12. Pp: 1076-1081.

Jordan, B. & Henderson, A. 1995. "Interaction Analysis: Foundations and Practice." In *The Journal of the Learning Sciences*. Vol. 4. Nr. 1. Pp: 39-103.

Krange, I. & Fjuk, A. 1999. "Designing collaborative learning system through distributed interactive 3D: A Culture-Historical Perspective." In *Proceedings at the 19th World Conference on Open Learning and Distance Education*. ICDE. Vienna 20th – 24th June 1999.

Krange, I., Kristiansen, T., Helljesen, L., Ødegård, O. & Fjuk, A. 2000. "Collaborative learning in schools by distributed use of interactive 3D technology." *Telenor R&D report 18/2000*.

Larsen, A. & Krange, I. 2000. "Analysing learning and collaboration in distributed 3D learning environments." *E-CSCL 2001: Poster presentation*.

Leontiev, N. 1978. *Activity, Consciousness, Personality*. Englewood Cliffs, Prentice Hall. New York.

Leontiev, N. 1983. *Virksomhed, bevidsthed og Personlighed*. Köbenhavn: Forlaget Progress.

Ludvigsen, S. & Fjuk, A. (in press). "Tools in Social Practice: Learning, Medical Education and 3D Environments." To appear in *Outlines*.

McLellan, H. 1996. "Virtual Realities." In Jonassen, D.J. (Ed.) *Handbook of Research for Educational Communications and Technology*. New York: Macmillian.

Mercer, N. 2000. *Words and Minds: How we use language to think together*. London: Routlegde.

Mercer, N. & Wegrif. R. 1999. "Is 'exploratory talk' productive talk?" In Littleton, K. & Light, P. (eds.). 1999. *Learning with computers. Analyzing productive interaction*. New York: Routledge.

Roussos, M., Johnson, A., Moher, T., Leigh, J., Vasilakis, C. & Barnes, C. 1999. "Learning and Building Together in an Immersive Virtual World." *Presence*. Vol. 8. No. 3. Pp: 247-263.

Vygotsky, L.S 1978. *Mind in Society*. Cambridge: Harvard University Press

Wertsch, J.V. 1998: *Mind as Action*. New York: Oxford University Press.

OCAF: An Object-oriented Model of Analysis of Collaborative Problem Solving

N.M. Avouris[1], A. Dimitracopoulou[2], V. Komis[1], C. Fidas[1]

[1]University of Patras, Patras, Greece

[2]University of the Aegean, Rhodes, Greece

N.Avouris@ee.upatras.gr, adimitr@rhodes.aegean.gr, komis@upatras.gr, fidas@ee.upatras.gr

ABSTRACT

Computer-supported collaborative problem solving requires new methodological approaches of interaction and problem solving analysis. Usually analysis of collaborative problem solving situations is done through discourse analysis or interaction analysis, where in the center of attention are the actors involved (students, tutors etc.). An alternative framework, called "Object-oriented Collaboration Analysis Framework (OCAF)" is presented here, according to which the objects of the collaboratively developed solution become the center of attention and are studied as entities that carry their own history. This approach produces a view of the process, according to which the solution is made of structural components that are 'owned' by actors who have contributed in various degrees to their development. OCAF is based on both actions and dialogues of actors, providing qualitative as well as quantitative indicators of collaboration and solution quality. The paper presents first the framework notation. Examples of its use in analysis of distance groups and face-to-face collaborative activities are provided next, followed by the dimensions of the framework supported analysis for teachers and researchers. Web-based tools supporting the OCAF approach are also presented.

Keywords

Collaborative problem solving analysis, face-to-face collaboration analysis, dialogue-action analysis, web-based analysis tools

INTRODUCTION

The methodological issues of collaboration analysis are important to the effectiveness of the collaborative learning process, the designation of appropriate learning activities and settings, as well as the design of collaborative technology-based learning environments. Analysis of collaborative problem-solving situations is usually done through discourse analysis (Baker *et al.*, 1999), task analysis interaction analysis, or even a combination of methods (Komis, Avouris & Fidas, 2001), with the objective to evaluate the situation, the learning process and often the tools used. A number of different approaches have been developed for the analysis of collaborative activities in different mediums and environments. Some of them are focused on problem solving strategies or on plan recognition (Hoppe & Ploetzner, 1999), others on the evaluation of partners' involvement (Simmof, 1999), or on the process of mutual understanding and the learning effects (Baker *et al.*, 1999). There are approaches of analysis implemented after the interaction and others that are applicable during the evolution of the collaborative process, thus providing assistance tools that are able to evaluate personal contribution and visualise collaboration patterns (Simmof, 1999).

It seems that in this research field, collaboration analysis is mainly based on analysis of naturally occurring dialogue, due to a remaining dominant psychological interest in answering general questions related to understanding collaborative learning. It is interesting to examine the main analysis approaches, in the specific category of technology-based collaborative problem solving systems related to 'diagrammatic solutions', a category where the actions of collaborative partners are of main importance. This is due to the fact that these actions reveal information on the quality of involved concepts and strategies of pupils in a learning process. In this category, representative research and analysis approaches are: The networked collaborative concept mapping system produced by CRESST (Chung *et al.*, 1999), the CardDalis prototype (Muehlenbrock & Hoppe, 1999) interesting in terms of group action-driven interaction analysis, the research related to the C-CHENE system (Baker *et al.*, 1999), designed to support dyads of students collaborating in the construction of diagrams of energy chains, and the BELVEDERE v.2, a networked software system, allowing students to collaborate during scientific inquiries (Suthers, 1999). Dominant approach of analysis in relevant experimentations, is the dialogue-oriented one. Even if in some cases, like the COLER system experimentations (Suthers & Hundhausen, 2001), common transcripts of dialogues and actions are reported, a well coordinated analysis related to the components of the reported solutions is not included. Moreover, in all these analysis techniques the center of attention are usually the actors (students, teachers etc.) and the dialogues, while the developed objects often enter the scene only as items on which operations are effected and as subjects of discussion.

An alternative and complementary framework of analysis is presented here, according to which the objects of the solution, that is the objects that exist in the 'micro world', become the center of attention and are studied as entities that carry their own history and are acted upon by their owners. This perspective produces a new view of the process, according to which the solution is made up of structural components that are "owned" by actors who have contributed in various degrees to the produced solution. This view of the world, which is a reversed view of the one we usually build of the problem solving process, can be useful, as it reveals the contribution of the various actors in parts of the solution, identifies areas of intense collaboration in relation to the final solution and can relate easily to other analysis frameworks like interaction analysis.

According to this view an operational framework of analysis and evaluation of collaborative problem solving has been defined called 'Object-oriented Collaboration Analysis Framework" (OCAF), also described in Avouris *et al.* (2001). OCAF's corresponding analytic model identifies patterns of interaction and relates them to objects of the shared solution. The model provides a new way of representing collaborative problem solving activity, taking into account both actions and dialogues of partners and supports qualitative and quantitative representations that can be used as meta-analysis and evaluation tools. The framework has been used for the analysis of various kinds of collaborative problem solving environments based on jointly developed diagrammatic 'solutions', made of well distinguished objects, such as concept maps, entity-relationship diagrams, diagrams of specific modeling formalisms, architectural diagrams, etc. It is shown that this approach can be applied both in synchronous distance-collaboration environments (dialogue via written messages) and in co-located group collaboration when a more oral-dialogue oriented collaboration occurs.

The proposed analysis framework proposes a model that can be generated and further processed by adequate tools, attached to a collaboration support environment. These tools could be used not only by researchers but also by teachers managing on-line distance collaborative problem solving or by students, in an appropriate form, as a meta-cognitive or collaboration meta-analysis tool, helping them self-regulate their actions and their involvement.

Most of the existing collaboration systems present limitations when used by young students in real school settings. Some of the limitations are attributed to the fact that the teacher who is in charge of several students, fails to interpret the enormous number of complex interactions that can take place simultaneously. Acknowledging this limitation, researchers have started to work on addressing this problem. Systems that aggregate the interaction data of logfiles into a set of high-level indicators and present them to the participants or the teacher have been proposed. From these systems, we could distinguish three main categories: (a) Systems that present or visualize indicators concerning exchanged patterns in a discussion. The system proposed by Simmof (1999) visualizes in an innovative way discussion threads with nested boxes exploiting quantitative information on participation rates in exchanged messages. In MarCo, a dialogue oriented system (Tedesco & Self 2000), a mechanism detects disagreements and conflicts between users' beliefs or intentions, on the basis of selected dialogue acts. (b) Tools based on qualitative analysis of members actions, deriving higher order descriptions of group activities, such as the CardDalis system (Muehlenbrock & Hoppe 1999) were applied in the low level conceptual task of puzzle resolution. FACT (More & Moriyon 2001) is another framework that produces tree-like histories, related to actions. (c) Systems that analyse messages and actions such as the system under development by Jermann et al. (2001) that displays separate indicators of participation rates on messages and others on actions. Other systems, such as EPSILON (Soller & Lesgold, 2000) and COLER (Constantino-Consalez & Suthers, 2001), analyse data from actions and messages and monitor directly group members by appropriate messages, without presenting the derived information to users (students or teachers).

In order to develop effective analysis frameworks and tools for collaborative problem solving, the research community needs to investigate some key questions:

How to coordinate the analysis of actions and dialogues?

How to inter-relate collaboration features with problem solving content and process?

How to go beyond simple quantitative indicators (e.g. participation rates) to more sophisticated ones, such as role distribution that involve analysis of semantic aspects of interaction?

- How to provide a rich variety of analysis output, to assist facilitators or experienced learners?

This paper makes an attempt to explore some of the above issues. First the OCAF framework and its model in textual and diagrammatic form are presented. Subsequently, some analysis examples are presented, through two different case studies, involving a synchronous distance-collaboration environment and a co-located group collaboration. The analysis dimensions of these cases are discussed in view of OCAF applicability and usefulness in research and teaching issues. The main functionality of a tool supporting the OCAF framework is also presented.

THE OCAF FRAMEWORK

The proposed framework is based on two basic considerations, one related to the *object oriented view* of collaborating actors' roles and contributions and the other to the *unified analysis of dialogues and actions on objects*.

a) The diagrammatic solution of the problem is a representation of the shared effort of the involved partners as well as of their shared memory. In OCAF we shift the center of attention on these objects of the solution. That implies that these objects, constitutive of the solution, are studied as entities that carry their own history and are acted upon by their owners (the actors involved in their conception, creation, modification and inter-relation in the specific diagrammatic solution built by them). This perspective produces a new view of the process, according to which the solution is made up from structural components that are "owned" by actors who have contributed in various degrees to the produced solution. This "object oriented view" focuses on the ownership of the constitutive objects of the solution, covering also parts of the solution that have not been completed or have been rejected in the process.

b) Previous research has shown (Baker *et al.*, 1999) that mutual understanding among the collaborative agents takes place via a combination of perception of graphical action and communication. Furthermore, depending on the provided tools facilitating dialogue, the collaboration mode can vary from a more action-dominant mode to a more discussion-based mode. For these reasons, it is argued that there is a need to apply a unified analysis and interpretation of both dialogue and actions related to the solution objects, in order to analyze and evaluate collaborative activities in diagrammatic problem solution.

From the resulting framework of analysis, a model M of the solution is defined, conceived in this context, as a formal model, that can be used to analyze or reconstruct certain aspects of both actions and dialogues occurring in the problem-solving group. This model of ownership of the solution is based on the notion of ownership of the components of the diagrammatic solution. Such a diagram in many cases is made of objects (entities) that are shown in the diagram in abstract or pictorial form. These can be related through relationships often shown or implied in the solution. The entities have attributes or properties that are associated to them. The entity/relationship/attribute constructs could be the basic objects that make a diagrammatic solution according to the proposed notation of the framework. The proposed model according to OCAF has been formalized in textual and diagrammatic form as follows:

Let a given Solution S of a problem X be: $S(X) = \{ E_i , R_j, A_m, \}$, Where E represent the node entities of the solution, (i=1, …, k) R the relationships connecting them (j=1,…,l) and A the attributes of the entities (m=1, …, n) that participate in the solution.

The model of the solution can be:

$$M(S)= \{ E_i \ * \tau i /P_i f_j, P_k f_l, \dots R_j \ * \tau i / P_i f_j, P_k f_l, \dots, \ A_m \ * \tau i / P_i f_j, P_k f_l, \dots;$$

$$-E_i \ * \tau i / P_i f_j, P_k f_l, \dots, -R_j \ * \tau i / P_i f_j, P_k f_l, \dots, -A_m \ * \tau i / P_i f_j, P_k f_l, \dots \}$$

Where: E, R, A, are the entities, relations and attributes that are part of the final solution, while with –E, -R, -A the items discussed during the problem solving process, but not appearing in the final solution, are shown. τ_i is an index of the item, as implied by its initial action of insertion or by its discussion in the timeline of the problem solving process.

To each item a sequence of P_i f_j is associated. Each P_i f_j represents the human agent Pi (e.g. a student, teacher or facilitator) participating in a direct or indirect way in the problem solving process and his/her functional role f_j related to the particular part of the solution.

The different functional roles f used in OCAF are described in Table 1. It should be noticed that two functional roles concern the initial proposition to insert the item (by action (I) or by dialogue (P)), while the others express the discussion on each item. Also testing of the proposed solution is done through argumentation (A) in the case of static-diagrammatic solutions, while testing can involve use of alternative representations and provided testing tools in case of development of dynamic models of the solution (T).

So for example: [E (Storehouse)]=A_P B_M A_I indicates that the entity Storehouse has been produced from interaction of Agents A and B. Agent A made the initial proposal (A_P), which was modified subsequently by Agent B (B_M), finally Agent A inserted the object in the shared Activity space (A_I), accepting the final solution.

It has to be noticed that the actors' functions in interaction have been defined as 'functional roles' of 'communicative acts'. Initially, the 'functional role', was a term used in dialogue analysis in linguistics (Moeschler, 1992), transferred in educational research (Sabah *et al.*, 1999) in the context of verbal dialogues. A 'communicative act' (Bunt, 1989; Baker & Lund, 1997; Burtin, Brna & Pilgington, 2000) was a term referred on both oral and written communication. In our context, the term of 'communicative act' refers not only on messages (written dialogues during collaboration by distance), and oral utterances (during face to face collaboration), but also on actions of collaborative agents, given that during a synchronous collaborative activity these actions have a strong communicative value. Consequently, in our context of computer-based collaborative problem solving, a functional role reports the purpose of a 'communicative act', from the point of view of its 'actor' or 'interlocutor', thus constituting an interpretation of the actors/interlocutors intention in communication.

ID	Functional Role	Derived from :	Example
I =	Insertion of the item in the shared space	*action analysis*	*Action:* 'Insertion' of Entity "Velo"
P=	Proposal of an item or proposal of a state of an item	*dialogue analysis*	*Message:* "I believe that one entity is the firm 'ABC'" or "let us put the value of entity flow to state *locked*"
C=	Contestation of the proposal	*dialogue analysis*	*Message: I think that this should be linked to the entity B by the "analogue to" relation*
R=	Rejection / refutation of the proposal	*action and/or dialogue analysis*	*Message:* "What their attributes will be ? I don't agree". Or *Action:* 'Delete' Entity "Velo"
X=	Acknowledgement/ acceptance of the proposal	*Action and / or dialogue analysis*	*Message:* "That's right" *or* *Action: Insertion of* a proposed enitity
M=	Modification of the initial proposal	*action & dialogue analyses*	*Message:* I suggest we put the state to "unlock" *Action:* "Modify"
A=	Argumentation on proposal	*dialogue analysis*	*Message:* "I believe that I am right because this is …"
T=	Test/Verify using tools or other means of an object or a construct (model)	*actions & dialogue analyses*	*Message:* Let us run this model to observe this part of the model behavior *Action:* Activate 'Graph Tool' , or 'Barchart Tool''

Table 1. Unified "functional roles" definitions

An alternative, diagrammatic representation of the model involves association of the solution items to their history as shown in the figures of next section. The advantage of the textual representation is that it can be produced and processed by an adequate tool, while the diagrammatic representation is easier for the human to study. The two representations of the model are equivalent.

CASE STUDIES OF OCAF APPLICATION

In this section application of the OCAF framework is presented in two different collaborative problem solving settings. In the following typical extracts of analysis are included. Subsequently, a discussion on the analysis dimensions is provided.

Case A : Collaborative distance problem solving

The first case study involves use of Representation V.2. (Komis, Avouris & Fidas, 2001), a system for synchronous collaborative problem solving, expressed through semantic diagrams. The system supports the simultaneous development of these diagrams by partners situated at a distance, through the use of a shared 'Activity Space'.

The case study, discussed more extensively by Komis, Avouris & Fidas (2001), is taken place in the context of a University undergraduate course. The problem solving task involved the collaborative building of a data model of the activities of an imaginary goods transport company (ABC) that supplies the stores of a supermarket chain (VELO), transporting goods from a number of storehouses owned by the supermarket company to the supermarket stores. The purpose of this model is to be used in the design of a database to support the companies involved in scheduling their trucks and delivery of supplies. The students had to express the model as an entity-relationship (ER) diagram, a representation often used in data modeling.

The main objective of the experimentation was to study the degree of collaboration and the development of problem solving strategies. Main sources of data for our analysis have been the log files, which contain details of inter-group communication acts (chat messages) and shared activity space actions, as well as the produced ER diagrams of the students. An extract of a log file, as well as its interpretation in terms of OCAF functional roles is shown in Table 2.

Partner E (Actions & Messages)	*Partner F (Actions & Messages)*	***Functional roles***	τ_i
E: ... about the entities, strong entities are ABC and VELO		ABC : E_P VELO: E_P	1 2
	F: Yes and also TRUCKS, STOREHOUSES and STORES	ABC : F_A VELO: F_A TRUCK : F_P STOREHOUSE : F_P STORES : F_P	 3 4 5
E: Attributes of (supermarket) VELO are the STOREHOUSES and the STORES		VELO.STOREHOUSE : E_P VELO. STORES : E_P	6 7
	F: and attributes of ABC the TRUCKS	ABC.TRUCK : F_P	8
Added rectangle object			
	F: No they are not attributes they are weak entities	VELO.STOREHOUSE : F_C VELO. STORES : F_C STOREHOUSE : F_A STORES : F_A	
E: ...and for ABC the TRUCKS (are attributes) and we need to show the JOURNEYS somehow		ABC.TRUCK : E_A	
The rectangle object is named VELO		VELO : E_I	
	F: I cannot see what you are doing	(Control statement)	
Added object- named object ABC		ABC : E_I	
	Could you pass me the action key please?	(Control statement)	

Table 2. Extract of interaction between partners E and F, in case study A [τ_i = index of solution items]

An example of analysis of collaborative solution is presented here. The problem solving team studied in this section is made of students E-F. The produced solution by this group is modeled, according to the OCAF framework, as shown in Figure 1. The last five items of M_{EF} concern objects discussed during problem solving process but not reported in the final solution due to conflicts between collaborating agents or not completed negotiation. The same model is shown in diagrammatic form in the same figure

An*alysis supported by the model* : From this descriptive model, firstly, a qualitative analysis on the content of solution may concern the appropriateness and completeness of the proposed solution. So, regarding the 'objects' of the solution, a researcher or teacher, can identify that for instance the object 'relation *Storehouse owns Trucks'* is not correct, since such ownership is not included in the problem description: the correct relationship could have been *Trucks are loaded at Storehouses*. In parallel, regarding the 'object' history related to collaboration, one can observe that this relationship has not been subject of strong collaboration. Another important aspect to study in a solution process, is the parts of the solution that lead to conflicts and did not take part in the final solution. For instance Actor E proposed Store as an attribute of entity VELO that was abandoned in favor of inserting Store as a separate entity, a solution that is more appropriate for the specific problem.

The model, can also, support a global quantitative analysis orientated to the solution items: Number of items in the model = 20, Number of items discussed and not included in the final model = 5, Number of items of unresolved conflicts =4.

Concerning the collaborative history of the produced solution, we could firstly, examine the history of each object of the solution. A quantitative analysis oriented to interaction patterns can identify (10) different interaction patterns in the model. The items produced per interaction pattern are:F_I = 5 (item inserted by F implicitly accepted by E), F_{IM} = 4 (item inserted by F, subsequently modified by same actor), F_{PI} = 3 (item proposed by F and subsequently inserted by the same actor), E_P F_I = 2 (proposed by E and inserted by F), F_P E_C F_A F_I = 2 (item proposed by F, contested by E, acknowledged argument by F and finally inserted by F), E_P F_R = 2, E_P F_C = 2 (item proposed by E and proposal rejected or contested by F with no further discussion) while five more patterns occurred once.

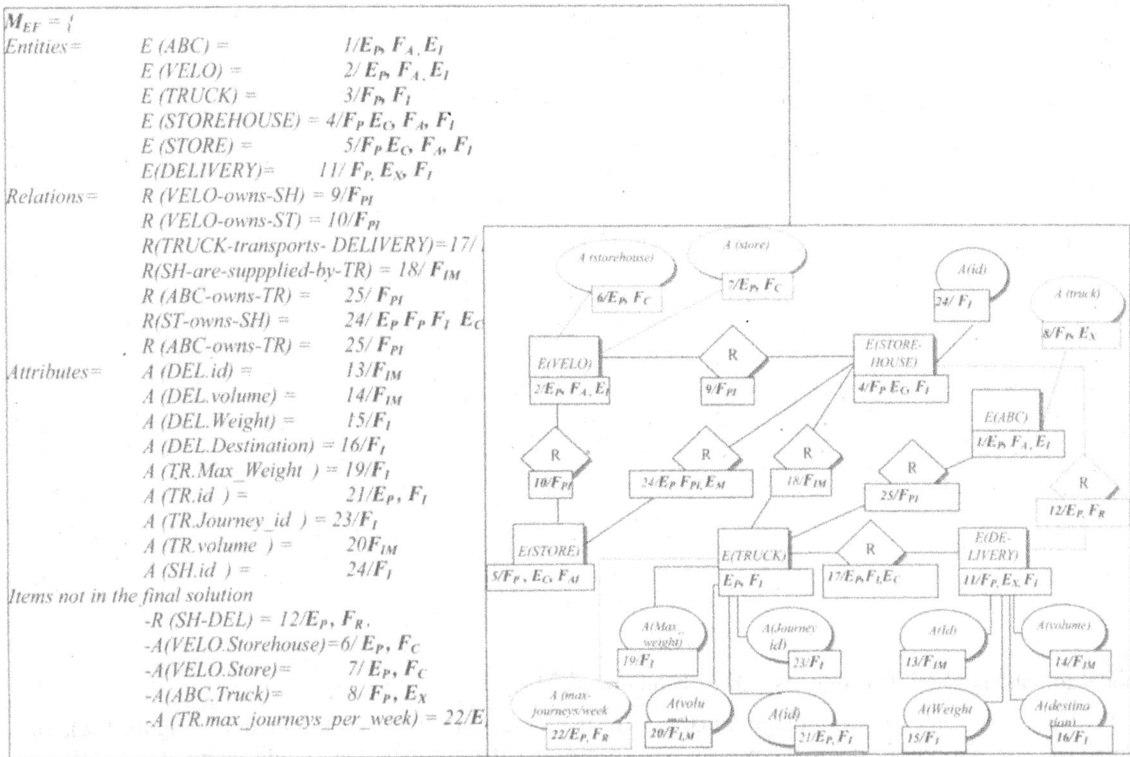

Figure 1. The solution expressed as OCAF model in (a)textual and (b) diagrammatic form

In relation to the *contributors* (in this example students E and F), one can determine that in this collaborating team, 25 items have been discussed, of which 12 have one owner and 13 two owners. The distribution of items proposals among the agents involved is: E=4 (20%), F=16 (80%), while 4 more items proposed by E and 1 proposed by F did not take part in the final solution. Such a distribution provides a strong indication of ownership and involvement.

Regarding the functional roles of each member, we can observe that member 'F' takes stronger action roles (e.g. I, M), while the observer (F) takes stronger verbal roles (e.g. P, C). Taking into account that the possession of the action-enabling key (permitting actions on the shared workspace to its owner) was 40% of the time for E and 60 % for F, one can infer the collaborative mode adopted by the group.

If the analysis is orientated towards examination of the '*subject*' of collaboration (where the group has focused), we could examine for instance the items of the solution in relation to ownership. In the presented example it is observed that the most important items of the developed solution (i.e. entities and relationships) are 8 of dual ownership (67%) and 4 of single ownership. In other words there has been stronger interaction in the process of creation of the backbone parts of the solution than the secondary parts (i.e. attributes).

Case B: Face to face collaborative problem solving

This case study involves a group of two 15 years old pupils (A and B) working as a group, in the presence of a facilitator F (a teacher-researcher). The experimentation took place in a laboratory. The students were asked to study a simple situation where a barrel can be filled by the water of a tap and build a model of the relations involved using MODELSCREATOR, a learning environment allowing creation and testing of models using pre-defined objects (Dimitracopoulou *et al.* 1999, Komis *et al.* 2001). The environment is a single-user tool, so one of the pupils is the operator of the tool, while the second pupil and the facilitator are observers. In order to build a solution, the pupils have to determine the relevant entities, their properties and the relations between them.

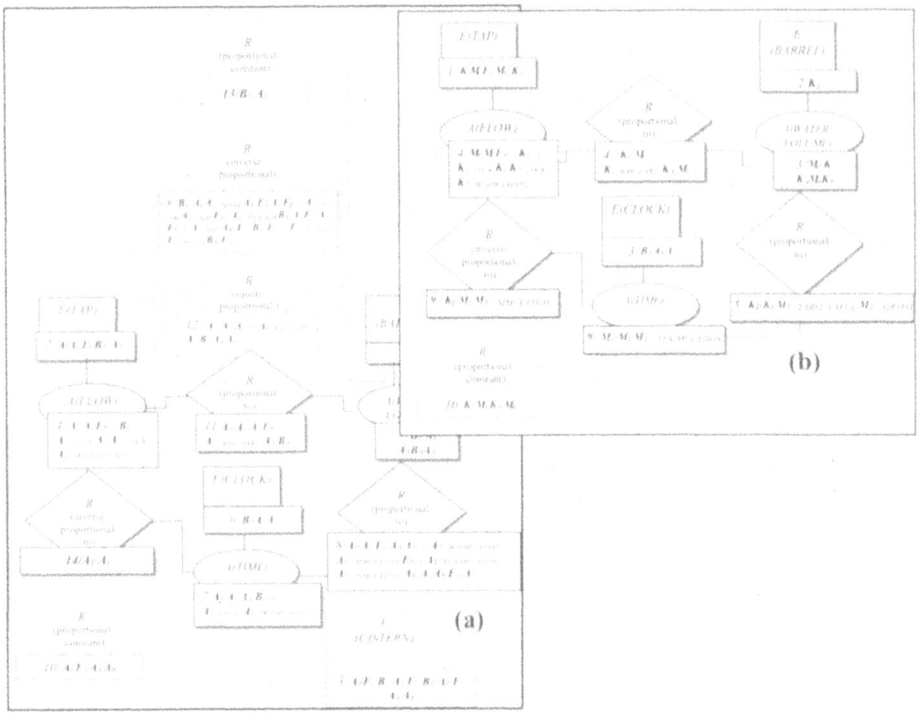

Figure 2, OCAF model for case study B. (a) students A,B, (b) students K,M

Typical models of this study are represented in diagrammatic form in figures 2a, 2b. From the model of figure (2a), an initial qualitative analysis, concerning the items themselves, can determine the appropriateness and completeness of the proposed solution. In order to interpret the conceptual difficulties of students or their mental models about implicated concepts, it is useful to consider a time dimension in the problem solving process, exploiting information derived from the order/index of items discussion (variable τ_i in OCAF model). For instance, the central entity CLOCK (τ_i=6) is inserted with some delay, due perhaps to the abstract nature of the concept of time. Additionally, it can be examined in which phases of the problem solving process the presence of facilitator (teacher) appears decisive. Examining the index of items discussion, in the presented example could be observed that the presence of F (facilitator) appears decisive in early stages (e.g. items 3, 8, 9), while the rejection of incorrect parts of the solution at a later stage (e.g. items 12 and 13) is done by the pupils themselves with no intervention of the facilitator.

Qualitative analysis oriented to the collaboration can be derived examining the history of collaboration of each solution 'object'. Observing the OCAF model, one can see that a number of solution items have been the subject of very strong exchanges. Additionally, a global quantitative analysis identifies, a wide variety of interaction patterns, with multiple exchanges. The rich interaction that took place is eventually due to the co-location of actors, the presence of the facilitator, and the existence of multiple tools that were used to validate alternative solutions.

If the analysis is oriented more specifically to each contributor (A, B and F), one can determine that in this collaborating team, 14 items have been discussed, of which 2 (14%) had one owner, 7 had two owners (50%) and 5 three owners (36%). From the objects of multiple ownership most of them have been assigned long interaction patterns, indication of strong interaction about the concepts involved.

Regarding the functional roles of each member contribution, we can account the distribution of items proposals among the agents participating that provides an indication of ownership and involvement. In this example, it was as following: A=10 (71%), B=4 (29%), F=0, ratio=2,5. It infers that actor A was mainly the operator ('Insertions' from A=15 and 'Insertions' from B=0, so this non-uniform distribution of ownership reflects these roles. Examining closer other 'roles', we can distinguish some problem solving strategies concerning the evaluation process of the produced solution: for instance, it can be observed that the pupils have tested parts of the solution (e.g. the relations) by using mostly manual simulation (Tool: M-SIMULATION) and did not validate the overall model (absence of tool 'RUN'), due perhaps to the simple structure of the developed model. Examining the indices of T(est) role, we have observed that only some of the available alternative representations (graphs, Bar charts, tables of values), have been used, and this in a limited degree.

From this analysis, one can deduce that most collaborative activity concerns the relationships (R). The objects themselves are inserted without many objections and therefore they do not become objects of discussion. Another observation on the density of collaboration is that there is a lot of interaction on objects not inserted in the model (e.g. relationship inverse-proportional between water-volume and tap-flow and on entity Cistern, see figure 2a).

The above analysis is focused on the exploitation of OCAF model's information related to a specific solution. Researchers and teachers can also derive significant information comparing two or more models of the same problem solutions provided by different groups. For instance, comparing the diagrammatic model of the solution of group AB (see figure 2a) with this corresponding of group KM, shown in figure 2b, one can distinguish differences in objects involved in each solution, in conflict points, identify items of intense collaboration in one group and low collaboration in the other group and so on.

TOOLS TO SUPPORT OCAF

An attempt has been made to support the OCAF Framework through a logging data storing and presentation tool. The tool has been implemented in the case of an environment of distance collaboration, where interaction was based on exchange of text messages and actions in the common activity space. The events are serialized and stored in a database. Actions are categorized according to the functional roles of Table 1. Classification of text messages is left to the researcher, since no structured dialogue tool has been used in this case. A web-based interface has been built, through which inspection of these log files and grouping of information is achieved. Views of interaction as presented by this tool are shown in figure 3.

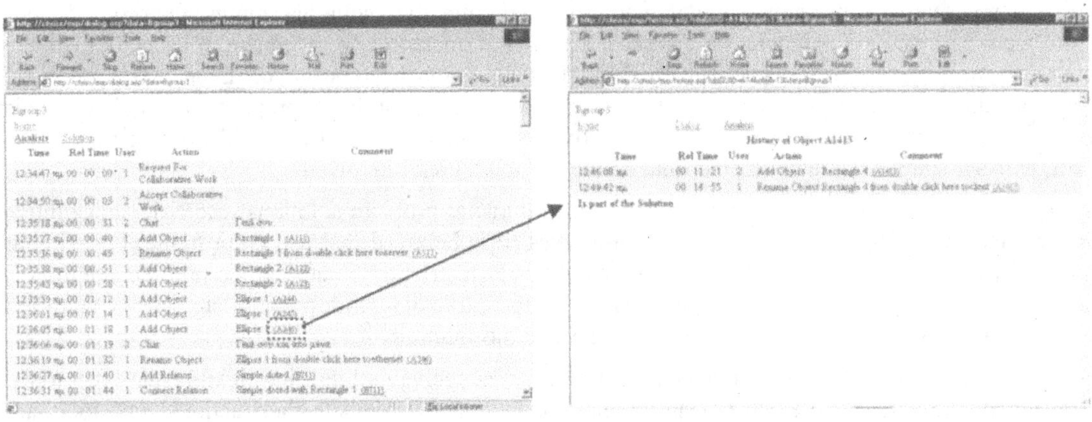

Figure 3. OCAF tool for log file visualization

In figure 3(a) interactions are presented according to the time dimension. Every time a new object is inserted in the activity space, a hyperlink is built to it, which allows the researcher to see the object view of this particular item, as shown in figure 3(b). Alternative views are also created according to actors, items of the solution, structure of the solution, etc. An interesting aspect is that these views are created automatically; since the information is built in a database and the web interfaces shown in figures 3 are created dynamically through queries to the database. The tool was proven useful to the analysis described in the previous section, while new functionality is planned to be built relating to the run-time use of the log files. Complementary tools are planned to be developed enabling an automated production of diagrammatic models of OCAF framework.

DISCUSSION

Collaboration is a phenomenon for which we lack adequate analytic models. It is not claimed that the complex phenomena of social interaction and particularly of collaborative learning can be comprehensively reconstructed by analytic models. These models are bound to be partial, capturing only specific facets of actions or interactions in groups. The value of an analytic model like OCAF, is related to its capacity to bring up interesting points of view and thus provide information to researchers relating to some of the following issues:

A) *The quality of the solution*: firstly it can identify solution items that take part of the solution. Further information that can help to interpret the solution and infer mental models of students are: (a) Items discussed and rejected and items that were abandoned due to a conflict. (b) The collaborative history of objects, for instance non appropriate solution items that have been derived from low collaboration, (c) The order of each item discussion (τ). Information on the problem solving strategy can be extracted by the study of some 'functional roles' of objects' solution history related to testing approaches and tools used (see analysis of Case study B)

B) *Collaboration modes and quality of collaboration,*: Information that can be derived can concern among others the following: (a) Degree of participation of group members, based on indicators such as distribution of solution items per member, (b) Contribution of group members to the developed solution, (c) Determination of roles of group members, and

the degree of their involvement, (d) Existence of some functional roles (e.g. argumentation or test) (d) Density of interaction; (e) Identification of interaction patterns per item of solution.
Some of the above points are related to quantitative aspects of interaction, and appear often in studies of collaborative distance learning environments, while others relate to a more cognitive and meta-cognitive view, as for instance is the case of solution validation strategies. These questions have been effectively tackled using OCAF, as demonstrated in the presented case studies.

A second point relates to the diagrammatic form of the OCAF model. This contributes in a supplementary way to the analysis, providing a perceptual view. A teacher that examines and compares two diagrammatic OCAF models of solutions, can directly distinguish, for instance, solution objects that are not appropriate and were not discussed in a group, or others that were discussed a lot and revised. Such information can support teachers to propose intra-group collaboration in order to discuss specific issues.
The teachers can identify conflict points, not appropriate approaches and give advice on topics of the debriefing session internal to the group and recognize semantically significant differences between approaches on problem solving and advice further intra-group discussions.

Related to the diagrammatic form, one can consider this view as an attempt to relate the time dimension (predominant in interaction analysis) to the space dimension (predominant in diagrammatic solution representation). Various transformations of this view can make it suitable for different users. For instance, by adequate color-coding of the participants and their roles, the association of ownership to solution items could become vivid,. Even if the presented abstract form of this diagram may be useful to researcher or teachers, may not be appropriate to students. This representation can increase their cognitive load. In this case, alternative representations can be used, like the diagram of the produced solution itself, with associations to the history of interaction to each 'object' involved.

The framework was applied in two cases both of them involving diagrammatic problem solutions where the constitutive items of the solution were entities, relations and attributes or properties. It is believed that using the framework, similar models can be produced containing various kinds of solution items, the only restriction being that the problem solution is made of independent items. So many diagrammatic or object-based solutions, like diagrams, puzzles, etc., can be analyzed In contrary, this framework cannot easily be applied in text-based or algebraic solutions.

In conclusion the presented work is part of a research agenda that seeks to conceive and develop flexible and open tools, able to assist users of collaborative learning environments to monitor and/or self-regulate their actions. The tools are designed to be open in order to allow a substantial adaptation of participants' *functional roles*, and are designed to be linked with different kinds of systems, based on various dialogue interfaces among collaborators.

ACKNOWLEDGMENTS

Financial support has been provided by the Représentation Project, Educational Multimedia - Task Force (project 1045) and IST2000-25385 *ModelingSpace* Project of the EU and Programs Seirines and Pinelopi of the Greek Ministry of Education.

REFERENCES

Avouris N.M., Dimitracopoulou A., Komis V., (2001, Submitted). On analysis of collaborative problem solving: An object-oriented approach, *Int. J. of Interactive Learning Research.*

Baker M., Hansen T., Joiner R., & Traum D. (1999). The role of grounding in collaborative problem solving tasks. In P. Dillenbourg (Ed) *Collaborative-learning: Cognitive and Computational Approaches*. pp. 31-64, Pergamon, Elsevier.

Baker M., Lund K., (1997). Promoting reflective interactions in a computer-supported collaborative learning environment, *Journal of Computer Assisted Learning*, 13 (3), 175-193.

Bunt H.C. (1989). Information dialogues as communicative action in relation to partner modelling and information processing, in (Eds) MM. Taylor, et al., *The Structure of Multimodal Dialogue*, pp. 47-74. Elsevier Sciences Publishers, North-Holland.

Constantino-Conzalez M.A. & Suthers D.(2001) Coaching Collaboration by Comparing Solutions and Trackning Participation, in *Proc. of European Conference on CSCL,* Maastricht, NL, March 2001. pp.173-180.

Chung W.-T., O'Neil H.F., & Herl H.E. (1999). The use of computer-based collaborative knowledge mapping to measure team processes and team outcomes. *Computer in Human Behavior*, 15, pp. 463-493.

Dillenbourg P. (1999). What do you mean by collaborative learning ? In P. Dillenbourg (Ed) *Collaborative-learning: Cognitive and Computational Approaches,* pp. 1-20, Pergamon, Elsevier.

Dimitracopoulou A., Komis V. Apostolopoulos P. & Politis P. (1999). Design Principles of a New Modelling Environment Supporting Various Types of Reasoning and Interdisciplinary Approaches, *Proc. of 9th Int. Conference of Artificial Intelligence in Education*, IOS Press, Ohmsha, pp. 109-120.

Hoppe U. & Ploetzner R. (1999). Can Analytic Models Support Learning in Groups? In P. Dillenbourg (Ed) Collaborative-learning: Cognitive and Computational Approaches., pp. 147-169, *Advances in Learning and Instruction series*, Pergamon, Elsevier.

Jerman P., Soller A. & Muhlenbrock M. (2001). From Mirroring to Guiding: A Review of State of the Art Technology for Supporting Collaborative Learning, *Proc. of EuroCSCL*, Maastricht, NL, pp.324-331.

Komis V., Avouris N, & Fidas C. (submitted, 2001). Computer Supported Collaborative Problem Solving: Interaction through diagrammatic and free-text communication, *Computers and Education*.

Komis V., Dimitracopoulou A., Politis P., & Avouris N. (2001). Expérimentations exploratoires sur l'utilisation d'un environnement informatique de modélisation par petits groupes d'élèves, *Sciences et Techniques Educatives*,. 8, (1-2), Avril 2001, pp.75-86 (in French).

Mora M.A. & Moriyon R. (2001). Guided Tutoring Through Learning History Analysis: the FACT Framework. *Proc. of European Conference on CSCL*, Maastricht, The Netherlands, March 2001. pp.680-681

Muhlenbrock M. & Hoppe U. (1999). Computer Supported Interaction Analysis of Group Problem Solving. In C. Hoadley & J. Rochelle (Eds). *Proceedings of 3rd Conference on CSCL*, December 12-15, 1999.

Ploetzner R., Hoppe H.U., Fehse E., Nolte C., Tewissen F. (1996). Model-based Design of Activity Spaces for Collaborative Problem Solving and Learning. *Proc. European Conf. on AI in Education*, pp. 372-378, Lisbon: Colibri.

Simmof S. (1999). Monitoring and Evaluation in Collaborative Learning Environments. In C. Hoadley & J. Rochelle (Eds). *Proc. 3rd Conference on CSCL*, Stanford, December 12-15, 1999.

Soller A. & Lesgold A. (2000) Knowledge acquisition for adaptive collaborative learning environments. *Proceedings of the AAAI Fall Symposium: Learning How to Do Things*, Cape Cod, MA.

Suthers D., & Hundhausen (2001). Learning by constructing collaborative representations: An empirical comparison of three alternatives. *Proc. of EuroCSCL*, Maastricht, The Netherlands, March 2001. pp.577-584

Suthers D., (1999). Effects of Alternate Representations of Evidential Relations on Collaborative Learning Discourse In C. Hoaley & J. Rochelle (Eds). *Proc. 3rd Conference on CSCL*,, Stanford, December 12-15, 1999.

C. (THEORY TRACK): FOUNDATIONAL ISSUES OF CSCL

Making Sense of Shared Knowledge

Hans Christian Arnseth, Ivar Solheim
Department of Educational Research, University of Oslo, Norway
h.c.arnseth@ped.uio.no
Department of Educational Research, University of Oslo and Norwegian Computing Centre[1]
ivar.solheim@nr.no

ABSTRACT
In this paper we explore issues to do with *intersubjectivity* and *shared knowledge* in human activity. We discuss these issues by contrasting two different views of language and communication, one being a model developed by Clark and Brennan, the other being a situated action approach. Clark and Brennan's model has gained substantial popularity in CSCL research. We develop our argument by presenting illustrative analyses of two data extracts concerned with the development of shared knowledge, the negotiation of goals and the conditional relevance of technological tools. We conclude that Clark and Brennan's model retains a communication-as-transfer view of language and communication, and that a situated action approach is more suitable for grasping the complex dynamics of joint activity.

Keywords
Shared Knowledge, Intersubjectivity, Computer-Supported Collaborative Learning, Language and Communication, Situated Action.

INTRODUCTION
An important issue in sociocultural approaches to human action and learning, such as situated action, situated cognition, situated learning and activity theory, and one lately emerging also in the Computer-Supported Collaborative Learning community, concerns how *shared knowledge* is developed and sustained in human activity (Baker et al, 1999, Dillenbourg, 1999). The possibility of developing abstract theoretical models of the communicative processes involved, as a guide for technological systems design, has also been keenly discussed in the CSCL and CSCW (Computer Supported Cooperative Work) communities (Nardi, 1996, Dourish & Button, 1998, Arias et al., 2000). The emphasis on shared knowledge, goals and concepts is also concurrent with the growing concern regarding how culture and context mediate cognitive activity (Cole, 1996). Shared conceptions of artefacts and tasks, and of the joint activity itself, are obviously important in collaborative activities. Any theoretical disagreement is concerned rather with how we, as analysts, should describe the attainment of shared knowledge and the processes that sustain it. According to Matusov (1996) the research on the role of intersubjectivity in joint activity is still characterized by a view of shared knowledge as overlapping subjectivities. According to him this leads to an overemphasis on agreement in joint activity, and a disregard of disagreement as well as more rhetorical features of talk.

In this paper we want to discuss the issue of shared knowledge, or *pragmatic intersubjectivity* (Edwards, 1997), which is the term we prefer to employ. The reason for choosing this term is that we want to emphasize the procedural and action oriented features of 'shared knowledge': what people treat as shared, how this is accomplished in discourse, and in what ways it is tied to local practices and activities.

To examine this topic we choose a *situated action* approach (Edwards and Potter, 1992, Edwards, 1997, Suchman, 1987) as our analytical point of departure[2]. This entails that topics such as problem solving, reasoning, educational goals and the role of artefacts are approached as sociocultural phenomena constituted in the experienced, lived-in world of different social actors. These topics are part and parcel of pragmatic intersubjectivity. In alignment with this approach, we will try to

---

[1] In the academic year 2001/2002 Ivar Solheim is visiting researcher at the Center for Lifelong Learning and Design, Department of Computer Science, University of Colorado at Boulder.

[2] A clarification of the term situated action is perhaps in order. Situated action is not a theory in the traditional sense of the word. It would be more appropriate to describe it as a loosely defined research program with certain analytical commitments. Much situated action research, and especially discursive psychology, has been heavily influenced by ethnomethodology and conversation analysis. Another distinct feature is the emphasis on the situated production of meaning as well as on the constructive nature of language use.

demonstrate how the development of shared knowledge is due to active work by participants in joint activity. Popular dichotomies such as distributed and co-located communication, or online and offline communication are thus subsumed under this more general issue, that is to say, it is reformulated as an issue that has to do with the resources available to people in different social practices. We develop our arguments by contrasting this approach with Clark and Brennan's (1991) model of communication. The final section is devoted to a discussion of the issues that were originally defined, where they are considered in relation to important topics concerned with how goals are negotiated in the course of interaction, and with how technological tools are incorporated and made relevant in joint activity.

THEORETICAL APPROACH

Intersubjectivity is not a new topic in the social and behavioral sciences. Theories of learning and communication are in one way or another expected to account for the fact that people are able to understand each other and solve problems jointly. To put it crudely one could say that the theoretical accounts differ according to whether they emphasize shared knowledge as founded on structural features of the mind, or on features of an objective reality. Philosophically, these positions are generally labelled rationalism and empiricism respectively. Common features, however, are a conception of language as a paradigmatic and syntagmatic system of signs and referents and of communication as transfer of meaning, or to put it differently, of language as a container of meaning and of communication as transfer of information bits

In recent cognitive models of the mind, knowledge is often conceived in terms of cognitive scripts and schemata.[7] The objective is to develop general models of how meaning is organised, processed and communicated. Scripts and schematas act as selection mechanisms that specify how certain elements of knowledge relate to one another, and these scripts or specific parts of them are invoked in context. Nevertheless, a problem with these approaches is that language-in-use is still conceived as epiphenomenal and idiosyncratic realizations of basic structural properties of thinking and communication, and the impact of diverse factors in pragmatic contexts is accounted for by putting them under experimental control in order to describe their effects.

A situated action approach contrasts with the previous account in at least two important respects. First, it is maintained that the development of shared knowledge is a practical accomplishment by social actors using different kinds of tools that were developed through complex interrelations between culture, individuals and collectives. In this sense, knowledge is reconstructed through human practice, and the issue at stake, for analysts, is to describe how this is accomplished in different kinds of activities and contexts. Second, the emphasis on action enables us to transcend the mind – matter dualism that characterizes empiricism and rationalism.

We will pursue this line of thinking further, by outlining an analytical perspective on intersubjectivity, where the unit of analysis is discursive actions in context. To provide a test bed for our approach we will compare this view to Clark and Brennan's (1991) model of language use. They stress the importance of shared knowledge as well as *grounding*, which is the designated term for the achievement and development of this *common ground*. Common ground is a prerequisite for the development and sustainability of meaningful communication. Attempts to fuse this model with cultural-historical activity theory (CHAT) have recently been made by Baker et al. (1999). They describe how grounding and common ground are prerequisites for the long-term appropriation of cultural tools and signs. An obvious rationale for fusing a theory of learning with a theory of language use is to provide analytical tools for making more detailed descriptions of how collaborative learning actually in takes place in practical situations. According to Baker et al.: "Language sciences provide fine-grained cognitive models of the grounding process, collaboration, and how the two relate, within the short timescale of verbal interactions" (1999:32).

Our analytical departure is as already mentioned a situated view of action (Atkinson & Heritage, 1984, Garfinkel, 1967, Heritage, 1984, Suchman, 1987). To be more specific we utilise analytical insights and commitments developed within the approach termed discursive psychology (Edwards and Potter, 1992, Edwards, 1997), where the interactive and constructive nature of communication is emphasized. Regarding the foundations of shared knowledge, this approach differs from Clark and Brennan's. The analytical starting point is social practice, and cognition is conceived as inextricably linked to observable and accountable actions. According to Edwards and Potter, the construction of meaning through language is an inter-active accomplishment by participants in communication. Meaning is tied to a specific context and dependent on the sequential order of interaction. This does not imply that individuals are the sole self-determining creators of meaning, on

[3] According to Cole (1996:124-128) *schema theory and script theory*, such as neopiagetian approaches and Schank and Abelson's theory, introduce the domain specificity of reasoning and thinking. In this sense these theories imply a step forward from a view that understands thinking to be a general faculty of the mind. Cole argues that this perspective introduces the context specificity of thinking. However, context is nevertheless understood as external to thinking. This contrasts with the more dialogical and dynamic view of thinking and communication that we are putting forward in this paper.

the contrary, they are very much accountable for their actions, even though they might have different agendas and master different resources.

Communication and social interaction

According to the sociological theory of ethnomethodology, an important characteristic of human action is a fundamental reliance on procedures of contextual determination (e.g. Heritage, 1984, Garfinkel, 1967). However, people are not "cultural dopes" whose actions are constrained by structures beyond their control. On the contrary, people mindfully try to make sense of situations by taking advantage of available resources, and if this understanding breaks down in some way or another, they try to repair it in various ways. This does not imply that actions are idiosyncratic, rather, human interaction is an ordered and structured phenomenon. However, the structures of this interaction have a complex relation to situated human action, that is to say, social structure is produced in and through people's actions.

In this sense, activities are not just educational because they are conducted in an organised school environment, but they are made educational in and through teachers' and students' actions. For expository purposes one could say that the practice of decontextualization is a typical feature of educational discourse, a feature that contrasts with the taken-for-granted context of everyday use of language and tools. This tension between different practices find its' expression in the practical problem of contextualizing utterances and actions (Gustavsson, 1988). In our view student's misconceptions or lack of appropriate problem-solving strategies, can just as well be attributed to tensions between different communicative practices, as to their individual reasoning abilities. These practices of decontextualization, or perhaps the term recontextualization would be more appropriate, which nevertheless are shaped by a particular context, could be expected to be an important reason for breakdowns in processes of meaningful communication, and hence for the trajectories of learning and development.

The regularity of social interaction, which we only alluded to above, implies that different actions set up different expectations of what are conceived as relevant actions from others. If actions do not conform to these patterns of interaction, i.e. that questions are regularly followed by answers, the participants will perceive the action as being just that even so. Even if it is not a direct answer, it is understood to be a comment on the question in one way or another. There is no escape from the fact that participants will orientate to what others say or do. Therefore, the meaning of a particular utterance in talk will depend on how it is responded to by others. Analytically it is therefore difficult to categorize one utterance as a question without taking the sequential unfolding of the talk into account.

Utterances are oriented to and contextually shaped by previous talk, and they provide context for further contributions. This context is continually established and redefined and meaning is as such negotiated and never pre given or finally settled. Whether a question is to be characterized as a proper question depends on the collaborative accomplishment of the acts of questioning and answering. If the utterance is to be classified as a question we, as analysts, have to examine the sequence in order to see how the other part responds. Then it is possible to categorize it as the speech act of questioning. This dynamic and dialogical nature of talk also works in reverse. The answer to an utterance may recast the meaning of the utterance to which it responds. As such, to respond to a question with an acknowledgement is to try to make the first part a request. To answer the question "have you cleaned your room?" with "yes, I have cleaned my room" would make it into a proper question. To say, *"it's not my turn"*, would turn it into an accusation and so on. This illustrates the finely tuned context-dependent and context-renewing nature of social interaction (e.g. Antaki, 1994). Before we develop these arguments further it is necessary to give a short account of Clark and Brennan's theory.

LANGUAGE IN USE

According to Clark and Brennan (1991), all collective actions are founded on common ground and its accumulation. Common ground is the knowledge that two or more participants in communication have in common or assume they have in common, and this common ground is continuously updated and developed through the process of *grounding*.

> Grounding is essential to communication. Once we have formulated a message, we must do more than just send it off. We need to assure ourselves that it has been understood as we intended it to be. Otherwise, we have little assurance that the discourse we are taking part in will proceed in an orderly way (Clark and Brennan, 1991:147).

There are two important factors that shape grounding, the first being the intentional purpose of the activity, that is to say, what the interactants are actually trying to accomplish. The second is the medium of communication, or the techniques available within each medium as well as the costs involved.

Obviously, there is never complete symmetry in understanding among different individuals, and the necessary shared knowledge is dependent on the activity being performed. Clark and Brennan describe this as *the grounding criterion*, which means that common ground is relative to the common understanding necessary for performing successful communication and action. This criterion is established by the participants, and tends to be guided by what Clark and Brennan describe as the principle of least collaborative effort. This means that participants take the trouble that is necessary to get their meaning across to the other interlocutors and thereby, in the course of the interaction, contribute to the solving of different tasks.

On a micro-analytic level Clark and Brennan make a distinction between two phases in communication. These are the presentation phase and the acceptance phase, which are intimately related in the sense that the acceptance phase provides evidence of the fact that your interlocutor has understood or perhaps misunderstood what you were trying to convey. To put it differently, one could say that the answer supports or undermines your reading of the other participants mind, which, because you are able to communicate, already contain a certain amount of commonly shared cultural knowledge. Participants always look for positive evidence of mutual understanding, and the establishment of common ground is due to active work by the different parties in conversation, in the sense that you actively have to display your intentions as well as read your interlocutors intentions. Participants must continuously pay attention to the others' contributions and acknowledge their utterances, as well as seek the others' acknowledgement. Further, there is a need to monitor the conversational flow and respond with the relevant information at the relevant point in the conversation.

While Clark and Brennan's model to a large extent focuses on cognition and how individual intentional knowledge is synchronized and developed in discourse, the situated or discursive action approach focuses on action. Cognitive issues such as remembering, reasoning, attributing and so on are reformulated as belonging to a social world of interdependent relationships. Operationally, cognition become reports, descriptions, accounts, formulations, arguments, explanations and so on, and the inferences they make available. Such matters are situated in activities and are closely intertwined with other matters of concern. To provide some structure we will emphasize three points: *action, fact and interest, and accountability.*

The first point is that cognitive phenomena are recasted as actions. "Discursive psychology generally is concerned with people's practices: communication, interaction, argument; and the organization of those practices in different kinds of settings." (Edwards & Potter, 1992:156). The concern is with how people carry out reasoning and problem solving as part of their practical activities. Analytically we, as researchers, should be careful with applying analytical categories to do with phenomena such as degrees of shared knowledge, depth of understanding and impact of technology on discourse, and instead be sensitive to what social actors actually do through talk and text.

The second point highlights how discourse is always produced from a position, which is to say that it has a rhetorical organization. It is people situated in space and time, with different interests, stakes and concerns, who produce actions. Actions are therefore never neutral in any simple sense; they are produced with specific goals in mind. These, however, are features of the content and organization of discourse, not of people's individual motivations or thoughts. This means that people treat each other as competent knowledgeable members with motivations, abilities and interests, and that these concerns are displayed in their discourse. An important objective in discourse analysis is to analyse the organization of these actions, as well as identify the devices that the participants rely on to accomplish this in different settings.

The last point concerns accountability, that is to say, speakers routinely deal with issues of agency and responsibility when giving accounts or descriptions of events and other phenomena. How teachers orient to accountability when providing assessments of pupils, would be an interesting topic to pursue further. When pupils fail to accomplish a task, is this attributed to bad teaching or to the pupils' lack of reasoning ability? These are common concerns in teacher-pupil interaction. In this regard educational discourse is about social relationships, where issues related to pupils learning and abilities, are practical concerns for the teacher, and do no refer merely to what the pupil actually know. In this regard the pupils' "thinking" is interlinked with a matrix of social relationships and concerns.

To sum up, the focus of this approach is not on cognition conceived as psychological entities located "under the skull", but on discourse and its sequential organization grounded in people's activities and social practices. We, as analysts, are interested in how specific formulations are deployed, and how they are related to the particular context in which they appear. This context is established in activities that are pragmatically organized.

Therefore, instead of considering cognition, problem solving and remembering as merely psychological phenomena, they enter into this model as discursive resources which teachers and pupils use to do specific interactional work. People think together and engage in collaborative activities by continuously trying to understand each other's motives, understanding and ideas.

COMPARISON OF THE TWO APPROACHES

We have argued for an understanding of shared knowledge as something that is actively constructed and used for various pragmatic purposes in discourse, and as such, it is not a category that actually describes the knowledge people have in common. We as analysts should never ask, "what is the exact content of the shared knowledge in this particular activity?" This is a question that cannot be answered from a discursive action point of view. Intersubjectivity is first and foremost a concern for the participants in discourse, and it is our job as analysts to conceive how they achieve this joint understanding and what kind of local, situational and pragmatic work it involves. That some context is jointly held can be observed, however, in interaction. By subsuming the notion of shared knowledge under what we have termed 'pragmatic intersubjectivity' (Edwards, 1997), it is treated as something that is at stake for participants in the communication, it is what they treat as shared and how this is related to the local and pragmatic context of the discourse.

Our main criticism of Clark and Brennan's model is that it retains a communication-as-transfer-between-minds view of language[4]. Secondly that it treats intentions and goals as pre-existing psychological entities that are later somehow formulated in language. This gives rise to conceptual and methodological problems, which largely can be avoided by reformulating the issue as dealing with pragmatic intersubjectivity. As mentioned above, meaning can be packed and described in variable ways, and what meanings different words take on, depend on where the word is located and how it is taken up in discourse. We have already said that doing questioning is an interactive and dialogical accomplishment, not something that pre-exists as an intention, which is then put into words. Analysing intersubjectivity as a practical concern of the participants, tied to social action instead of cognition, has methodological advantages, even if these are bought at the expense of simplicity. From the communicational model point of view, the explanatory burden is placed on an unobservable and private domain of the mind, while in the latter discursive action approach; the phenomena of interest are arguably present in the discourse. Treating discourse as a window on cognition contrasts with the indexical nature of meaning, a notion that is so central in the situated action approach. According to this view there is a loose fit between words and their referents, something which makes language into a flexible resource that can be tailored to fit different pragmatic concerns.

THE PRACTICAL MANAGEMENT OF INTERSUBJECTIVITY IN EDUCATIONAL DISCOURSE

In the following section we discuss the notion of intersubjectivity in the context of educational discourse. We use material from our own research on the educational use of multimedia in schools. We focus on a central aspect of intersubjectivity: the situated production of educational goals and the role of technology in this connection.

The following scene is quite common to many pupils and students trying to use the Internet for educational purposes, and it illustrates difficulties with finding appropriate information on the Internet. Before this particular dialogue occurred, three 14-year-old girls had spent a couple of hours searching the Internet for material about the situation of women in Africa. They were supposed to use a video about women in Burkina Faso to define themes and "research questions" for their project work. Before this sequence they had already defined and formulated their themes of study.

The class was divided into groups of 3-4 pupils each, which worked in separate rooms. The teacher rotated between groups to see how they were getting on, but this group did not summon her. The dialogue starts as the teacher enters the room.

Excerpt 1

1. Teacher: How are things going here?

2. Monica: No, we think it is difficult. We cannot find much material

3. Anne: What we found was a legal bill concerning polygamy in Uganda, but we cannot enter that website.

4..Teacher:But how do you define the basic themes of your study?

5. Monica: How much do African mothers decide over their son's family.

6. Anne: Or to what extent they have the right to decide.

7. Cathrine: How much they decide, that's it.

8. Teacher: There may be something wrong with your themes of study, if you can't find any material on it. Because it is evident that a lot of this is unwritten laws and rules so that...may be you should add two or three more questions.

9. Cathrine: But what else is the video about?

10.Teacher: It has to do with women's rights.

This extract is in many ways representative of instructional discourse, and, as such, it is interesting to relate it to important findings in the literature on teacher-learner interaction. A robust finding is that this kind of discourse is characterized by

---

[4] We are not denying that transfer of meaning takes place. What we want to highlight is that a model, which emphasizes transfer, is methodologically and conceptually problematic and misleading, basically because it neglects or overlooks the fundamental insight of the situated and constructive character of learning and meaning.

asymmetric interactional patterns controlled by the teacher (Edwards & Mercer, 1987, Mehan, 1979, Nystrand, 1997, Wertsch, 1998).

This relationship is articulated in several ways, i.e. in the teacher's right to ask questions and the pupils' obligation to answer, and in the more basic social asymmetry between 'those who know' and 'those who do not know'. It seems obvious that this asymmetric pattern is an important feature of intersubjectivity. The crucial question is however how we should approach this phenomenon in a fruitful manner. Or to put in a more precise way related to our topic: how do we study "teaching goals" and the ways participants "understand" and relate to these goals?

First, the above dialogue can be approached as a situated speech exchange *producing pragmatic intersubjectivity, i.e intersubjctivity as the participants practical concern.* The pupils approached their problem as a *search-and-seek problem* when they found a reference to an important text, but could not find this on the World Wide Web (line 3). The teacher expressed the view that the pupils probably would not succeed in finding material unless they redefined their searching criteria as well as their basic way of stating and formulating the problem. These different perspectives on goals, task and problem solving procedures, are only meaningful in this particular context, and are also produced, developed and changed throughout. According to Baker et al. (1999:51) it is theoretically assumed in most CSCL research that the goals do not undergo any change in collaborative learning situations. Baker attributes this flaw to the short timescale of the activity considered in many studies. We agree with Baker et al's main argument. Our example indicates not only that there are changes in goals, but also that goals are part of the situated production of intersubjectivity. However, in contrast to Baker et al., we believe that this change in goals is even apparent on a 'limited' timescale, such as in the activity reported above.

Second, there is as mentioned a striking asymmetry in the dialogue, reflecting not only that the participants have different goals and views concerning how to continue the work, but also that social roles and power relations are produced and reproduced. From our perspective we do not take this power structure for granted as pre-defined "common ground", but will instead focus on its production and realization in situated practices. We learn from the literature that there is often some asymmetry present, but "asymmetry" is a very abstract notion that contributes less to an understanding of the actual production and reproduction of social relations. Applying a discursive approach, we observe that the teacher did not directly respond to the student's diagnosis of the problem, but instead introduced a completely different issue, the basic work of formulating and defining the goal of the project work, i.e. their themes of study. Rather than saying that the goals are negotiated in this discourse (which is a fairly common phrase in the literature on goals in social settings), it seems more appropriate to characterize the teacher's utterance in line 4 as a kind of *rhetorical conversational device* aimed at redefining the foundation of the dialogue. It seems reasonable to see the teacher' rhetoric intervention as a kind of *prolepsis* which Michael Cole (1996) describes as a possible instructional strategy in which the teacher, centered in the present tense of an activity, is both "looking backward, looking forward" (p. 185). The teacher's intervention focuses on a matter that the teacher presumes the students will have to address in order to solve the task. This rhetoric device is shown to have a concrete interactional function. The teachers wants (line 9) the themes of study to be defined more focused on womens' rights.

Third, it may be disputed that this dialogue led to identifiable "common ground" in terms of clearly detectable goals as "rules" governing the social and discursive process. Rather, the concept of "goal" should be understood as a part of an ongoing interactive process, which is defined and redefined throughout. The students' diagnosis of the problem is not met with any kind of detailed counter-arguments explaining `why their approach may be wrong. Rather than explicitly relate to the students' formulation of their problem, the teacher, in an ostensibly un-socratic and rhetoric way, (Billig, 1987) started to talk about something else – the pupils' way of presenting and formulating their problem. This is what prolepsis is about, without being explicit, the teacher asks a question that makes the students work in new, specific directions. The pupils are expected to exhibit their themes of study, and they demonstrated that they were not quite sure what these formulations were. There is no doubt that there is an important development in this extract regarding fundamental goals, but it is less meaningful to characterize this as "grounding" in the sense that the participants are getting closer to some kind of mutual understanding of the goals. It seems more appropriate to say that the students adopted the teacher's basic notion of what should be considered a proper goal.

At this point our analysis also resonates with Matusov (1996) who argues that traditional definitions of intersubjectivity overemphasize agreement and consensus and de-emphasize disagreement among participants in joint activity. With Matusov (1996) and Billig (1987), We consider disagreements and contradictions in communication to be fundamental in the study of social interaction and intersubjectivity. But, in contrast to Matusov, we do not consider disagreement as a general, inherent feature of communication. Rather, we consider it to be interesting only if it plays a significant part in discourse – as a topic in the participant's collaborative construction of meaning.

Fourth, the excerpt is part of a larger project undertaken by this class over a period of one week. It is important to note that this very dialogue, and especially due to the teacher's intervention, was an important milestone in the group's work because it led to a shift of focus and redefinition of their work, which proved productive from an educational point of view in the sense that the group accomplished what was expected from them. The group redefined their themes of study and changed their focus in a way, which among other things, caused them to successfully redefine their criteria for search on the internet. The redefinition of the overall goals led them to formulate searching criteria that were relevant to their problem solving. But the change of goals was not due to any identifiable change in some out-of-context or decontextualized mutual understanding; It was specifically related to the fact that the teacher told them to redefine the goals.

Reflections on "a computational model for grounding".

This process of goal setting and goal production seems to be locally produced, and it can be argued that it can hardly be generalized and "theorized" in a traditional way because the phenomenon itself is said to be inherently situated and would almost by definition avoid any kind of abstraction and theorizing. Interestingly, this kind of theorizing is an important goal for Baker et al. when they argue that it is relevant to develop:

> ...a computational model of grounding...In this model, utterances are seen as the performance of particular kinds of speech acts (such as initiate, continue, repair and acknowledge) that change the state of groundedness of some information. The model allows one to form a precise theory (which may still turn out to be incorrect) of what is grounded and what actions need to be performed to achieve grounding at any point in the conversation. (Baker et al 1999:38)

This kind of theorizing is based on the fundamental premise that "common ground" is actual, objective and identifiable as bits of information available for out-of-context computational formalization. What this notion of actual, shared knowledge does not take into account is how all these things (shared knowledge, experiences, linguistic evidence etc) are potentially capable of being described in several ways.

With a parallel to the lively discussion regarding the closely related concept of internalisation (e.g. Wertsch, 1993, Wertsch et al., 1995, Säljö, 2000), it could be maintained that grounding, in the sense Baker et al. and Clark define it, is problematic because it encourages us in a search for internal concepts, rules and other mental entities. The very idea of grounding presupposes that some kind of cognitive agreement is provided by the assumption that the actors share a system of culturally established symbols and meanings. Different definitions of situations may occur, of course, but these are handled as conflicting subcultural traditions or idiosyncratic deviations from the (culturally established) cognitive consensus.

In contrast, we agree with Garfinkel (1967) and Wittgenstein (1953) that the order and stability of the social world is not a consequence of a "cognitive consensus", some objective "common ground" or due to an "underlying structure". It is rather a result of situated actions that create and sustain shared understandings on specific occasions in interaction. Shared knowledge should therefore be considered an emergent product of situated action, rather than as its foundation.

MAKING SENSE OF TECHNOLOGICAL TOOLS

The context and participants of the next excerpt is the same as for the first, but it occurred later in the project. In this particular activity the pupils used a particular software tool called Syncrolink, a tool designed to support the construction of multimedia presentations. How the pupils made sense of the technology is shown to be a relevant clue pointing towards the issue of practical management of intersubjectivity.

Excerpt 2.

1. Monica: OK, then we start. Let's play *(the video)* now.

2. *Video starts.*

3. Cathrine: Where shall we insert a link? *(in the video)*

4. Monica: Perhaps after it is said that "The mother has decided". Then we write that this is a "typical example of the power of the mother-in-law."

6. Cathrine: *(writes)* "The mother-in-law" is in power.

7. Monica: No, don't stop, just push PLAY

8. Monica: Here it is "Do as I say, obey".

9. Carhrine: Then we know that, it is 42160, write it down .

10. *Monica writes the number for an exact location of the link to the video.*

11. Cathrine:Then we exit this *(The multimedia tool)* and enter *(enters the editing tool)*

"Front page"

12. Monica: (writes) "This is a typical example of the power of the mother-in-law in the home"

The video presented a filmed dramatization focusing on the important role and power of the mother-in-law in Burkina Faso. The initial pedagogical idea for this project work was that the pupils should learn more about other cultures and races in general, and the situation for African women in particular. In this context the intentional role of the technological tool was to support the pupils in their activity.

The technology was quite complex and the pupils had to use and navigate between different types of technologies (the multimedia tool, writing on paper, an editing and writing tool and file management). The crucial task in this excerpt was "linking", which meant that the pupils were supposed to use the multimedia tool to edit and comment the video by inserting relevant links at appropriate places. A "link" would typically be an additional and supplementary text. The excerpt shows that the pupils' main *practical* goal was to use the multimedia tool to insert link*s* in the video (see lines 1, 2 and 3). Immediately after the start of the video, one pupil asked, "Where shall we insert a link?" The others did not dispute this question, a question that also implicated an establishment of a goal in the joint activity. On the contrary, its relevance was confirmed by the next reply, which proposed precisely (line 9) where a link could be inserted. In this way the technology became both the means and the goal in the pedagogical process. Of course, the central question is how to account for this focus on a technologically derived goal that was different from the goal defined by the teacher. It is a consequence of the ways the pupils themselves made sense of the multimedia tool, a tool that was developed and dedicated to the production of links.

The production of goals as well as intersubjectivity is here shown to be practical accomplishments by the participants. Taking the pedagogical situation and the technological environments into account, the pupils tried to make sense of the whole process of project work. In this regard, if we accept the principle of least collaborative effort, which implies that the participants will try to minimize their collaborative effort (Clark & Wilkes-Gibbs, 1986), the concentration on the insertion of video links is perfectly understandable. *Not* to focus on the production of links was certainly possible and was encouraged by the teacher, but our data indicate that the *rationale* for the whole learning environment was dedicated to the production of links. But this rationale is not something objective, out-of-context, or pre-defined, rather, it is produced, situated and subjective – as a result of accountable human action interplaying with a technology with particular features and constraints..

CONCLUDING REMARKS

In the CSCL community due attention has been devoted to Clark and Brennan's conceptual framework, and several authors have developed it further (i.e. Baker et al., 1999, Dillenbourg, 1999). In the paper we have outlined and argued for an alternative understanding of communication and language-use, emphasizing the situated and pragmatic character of sense-making practices. By subsuming the issue of shared knowledge under what we have termed pragmatic intersubjectivity, we are better enabled to grasp the complexity and indeterminacy of joint activity. This is due to the fact that we do not have to look beyond social practice, to mental entities and the like, to describe the phenomena of interest. The phenomena are arguably there in the discourse. In our first analytic example we demonstrated how the consensual understanding between teacher and pupil's were produced and locally tied to specific pragmatic concerns related to the establishment of criteria for information seeking on the Internet. In the second we illustrated how pupils made sense of a multimedia software tool in a practical pedagogical setting, and how the use of the software was tied to pragmatic concerns connected to the solution of a particular task.

In the introduction we pointed out that the development of models of shared knowledge to guide systems design, have been keenly discussed in the CSCL-community. Even though we do not take up this issue in the paper, we believe the general argument can throw light on this contentious discussion. We have already argued against ideas of computational models and formalizations of "grounding", which seem to be based on a notion of shared knowledge as an objective and identifiable prerequisite for human communication. If such ideas gain momentum in the CSCL community, it would certainly pave the way for more abstract and theory driven systems design. It is not our view that general models are analytical dead ends in CSCL-research. Prescriptively they can function as heuristic artefacts that support the design of new tools in diverse ways. However, our concern is that such models can become reified descriptions of actual human practice. In our view there is nothing to bear out an assertion of that kind.

In several respects our approach resonate with Suchman's criticism of Winograd and Flores' technological implementation of a speech act model of language use (Suchman, 1994). Winograd and Flores' argument is that theoretically driven design not only will produce ordered technology that is easily implemented, but also that the field of human practice has to adapt to this coherent structure of action. Suchman, however, emphasizes that the success of such applications just as well can be attributed to how it is tailored to fit the situations where it is used. According to this line of argument one should be cautious with theoretically derived and abstractly organized structures of social interaction, which are implemented as predefined categories in technologies. To view the use of such applications as if the field of human practice has to adapt to this abstract logic, contrasts with peoples' skillful ways of applying technologies to fit practical situations of use.

ACKNOWLEDGMENTS

Support for this work was provided by the University of Oslo, Faculty of Education and the Norwegian Research Council (grant nr. 130654/520). We would like to thank Roger Säljö, University of Gothenburg, Svein Østerud and Sten Ludvigsen

University of Oslo, Klaus Bruhn Jensen, Copenhagen University, and Frode Guribye, University of Bergen for valuable criticism and helpful suggestions on earlier draft of the paper.

REFERENCES:

Antaki, C. (1994) *Explaining and Arguing. The Social Organization of Accounts.* London: Sage.

Arias, E., Eden, H., Gorman, A., & Scharff, E. (2000): Transcending the Individual Human Mind - Creating Shared Understanding through Collaborative Design. *ACM Transaction on Computer-Human Interaction (TOCHI)* Vol.7, No. 1, 84 - 113.

Atkinson, J. M. & Heritage, J. (1984). *Structures of social action*. Cambridge: Cambridge University press.

Baker, M., Hansen, T., Joiner, R. & Traum, D. (1999): The Role of Grounding in Collaborative Learning Tasks. In Dillenbourg, P. (Ed.): *Collaborative Learning: Cognitive and Computational Approaches*. Amsterdam: Pergamon.

Billig, M. (1987) *Arguing and thinking. A rhetorical approach to social psychology.* Cambridge: Cambridge University Press.

Button, G., Coulter, J., Lee, J. R. E. & Sharrock, W. (1995): *Computers, Mind and Conduct.* Cambridge: Polity Press.

Clark, H. H. & Brennan, S. E. (1991): Grounding in Communication. In Resnick, L., Levine, J. M. & Teasley, S. (Eds): *Perspectives on socially shared cognition.* Washington: American Psychological Association.

Clark, H. H. and Wilkes-Gibbs, D. (1986): Referring as a collaborative process. *Cognition,* **22**. 1-39.

Cole, M. (1996): *Cultural Psychology. A Once and Future Discipline.* Cambridge MA & London: The Belknap Press of Harvard University Press.

Dillenbourg, P. (1999): What do you mean by collaborative learning? In Dillenbourg, P. (Ed): *Collaborative learning: Cognitive and Computational Approaches.* Oxford: Pergamon.

Dourish, P. & Button, G. (1998): On "Technomethodology": Foundational Relationships between Ethnomethodology and System Design. *Human-Computer Interaction*, Vol. **13**, 395-432.

Edwards, D. (1997): *Discourse and cognition*. London: Sage.

Edwards, D. & Mercer, N. (1987): *Common Knowledge. The Development of Understanding in the Classroom.* London: Methuen.

Edwards, D. & Potter, J. (1992): *Discursive psychology.* London: Sage.

Garfinkel, H. (1967): *Studies in Ethnomethodology.* New Jersey: Prentice-Hall Inc.

Gustavson, L. (1988): *Language Taught and Language Used. Dialogue processes in dyadic lessons of Swedish as a second language compared with non-didactic conversations.* Linköping Studies in Arts and Sciences. No. **18**.

Heritage, J. (1984): *Garfinkel and Ethnomethodology.* Cambridge: Polity Press.

Matusov, E. (1996): Intersubjectivity Without Agreement. *Mind, Culture and Activity.* Vol 3, No. **1**. 25-45.

Mehan, H. (1979): *Learning Lessons. Social Organization in the Classroom.* Cambridge, MA. & London: Harvard University Press.

Nardi, B. (1996): *Context and Consciousness. Activity Theory and Human Computer Interaction.* London: MIT Press.

Nystrand. M. (1997): *Opening Dialogue. Understanding the dynamics of Language and Learning in the English Classroom.* New York: Teachers College Press, Columbia University.

Säljö, R. (2000): *Lärande i praktiken. Ett sociokulturelt perspektiv.* (Learning in practice. A sociocultural perspective) Stockholm: Bokförlaget Prisma.

Suchman, L. (1987): *Plans and Situated Actions. The Problem of Human Machine Communication.* Cambridge: Cambridge University Press.

Suchman, L. (1994): Do Categories Have Politics? The language/action perspective reconsidered. *Computer Supported Collaborative Work,* 2, 177-190.

Wertsch, J. V., (1993): *Voices of the Mind. A Sociocultural Approach to Mediated Action.* Cambridge, Mass.: Harvard University Press.

Wertsch, J. V., del Rio, P. & Alvarez, A. (1995) *Sociocultural Studies of Mind.* Cambridge: Cambridge University Press.

Wertsch, J. V., (1998): *Mind as Action.* New York: Oxford University Press.

Wittgenstein, L. (1953): *Philosophical Investigations*. Oxford: Basil Blackwell

CSCL for Schools that Learn

James M. Laffey, Dale R. Musser, Linda Espinosa, Herbert Remidez Jr., Joshua S. Gottdenker, Ran-Young Hong, Chris Amelung
Center for Technology Innovations in Education
University of Missouri-Columbia
LaffeyJ@missouri.edu

ABSTRACT
Learning communities and organizations are being recognized both as a mechanism for bringing learning about and as an explanation of what learning takes place. Systems that support learning in context and collaborative learning are increasingly being used to support performance and learning for school reform and business productivity. Similarly, many of the performance and learning outcomes that we care the most about, e.g., higher order thinking, problem solving, communication competencies, are understood as developing in the authentic activity of a community, such as a profession, a trade, or an academic discipline. Computer Supported Collaborative Learning (CSCL) is a method for bringing the power of technology to support collaborative and contextual learning. This article argues that CSCL can be a framework for school reform, not just as a method of curriculum implementation, but also as a framework for enterprise-wide, process change. The article will also illustrate how cscl-type systems can facilitate schools becoming learning organizations, not just organizations that support learning.

Keywords
Learning communities, CSCL, school reform, learning systems

INTRODUCTION
The work of Lave and Wenger (1991) provided leadership in showing how professions and disciplines have communities of practice wherein learning takes place through experience and induction takes place through apprenticeship. They argue that learning is not a type of activity, but rather is an aspect of all activity. Wertsch (1998) and others taking a socio-cultural approach have shown that the "intelligence" of actions is only meaningfully understood in the context of knowledge about the cultural tools invoked. Similarly, Donald Norman's book, Things That Make Us Smart (Norman, 1993), shows how technology does not simply improve the way we do things, but actually changes what we do. Multiplying with a calculator is a different mental and physical task then is multiplying with paper and pencil. These works have helped frame a view of cognition as distributed and a stance toward facilitating learning that calls for situated and social practice.

Scardamalia and Bereiter (1994) concur with the movement to view learning as a social practice, but argue that situating learning in communities of professional practice does not serve school-based learners. Scardamalia and Bereiter developed a framework of a knowledge-building community that emphasizes intentional learning of curriculum objectives as the product of the educational community of practice. Their vision for how computers could support the collaborative learning of school curriculum has provided a foundation for the development and implementation of CSCL for school reform.

Along with new curriculum models, such as situated and collaborative learning, advances in digital media and network technologies provide opportunities and expectations for school reform. To that end the U.S. Department of Education states as a primary goal that, "Digital content and networked applications will transform teaching and learning" (Office of Educational Technology, 2000). These expectations for transformation and improvement in teaching and learning are fueled by (1) dramatic increases in the levels of access to technology in our nation's schools (e.g., the percent of schools with Internet access increased from 35% in 1994 to 95% in 1999. (Williams, 2000)), and (2) the experience, common to almost all citizens, of change through information technology in so many aspects of life (business, entertainment, medicine, etc.).

Hope for improvement, however, is tempered by the recognition that even with substantial increases in access to technology the impact on public education has been limited. After a yearlong process of review and hearings, the Web-based Education Commission summarized the impact of Internet-based technology on education as: "Across America, people told us that the Internet offers one of the most promising opportunities in education ever. And yet they were troubled by their inability to harness its potential advantages" (Web-based Education Commission, 2000). Referring to an earlier wave of technology and its expectations for school reform, Larry Cuban provided a one-line synopsis: computers meet classroom; classroom wins. This epithet of computer assisted instruction indicates that even with substantial investment and great efforts at reform the role of computer assisted instruction was at best marginal and did not change the ways that teachers and students worked in classrooms. Current investments in wiring schools and bringing Internet access to teachers and students face the same challenge of actually making a difference in the ways that schools work, teachers teach, and students learn.

In The Fifth Discipline (Senge, 1990), one of the seminal management books of the last 75 years, Peter Senge described new ways of working and communicating that enable an organization to thrive in challenging and changing times and achieve a sustainable competitive advantage. The term "learning organization" was coined to emphasize the need for organizations to get smarter about their work by learning from experience. Just as we know that individuals get smarter (becoming better at understanding conditions, solving problems, and judging solutions) through experience, feedback and discipline (ways of thinking about their experiences and feedback), so to do organizations. Senge's book described five disciplines (ways of thinking) that facilitate organizational learning. The five disciplines are:

- Personal Mastery - personal empowerment through the identification and realization of a personal vision
- Mental Models - processes of reflection and inquiry that make tacit knowledge visible and shared.
- Shared Vision - establishing and nourishing a common purpose
- Team Learning - enabling teams to think, learn, and mobilize for change (motivated by a commitment to a shared vision)
- Systems Thinking - ways of thinking in which understanding interdependency and "change processes" lead to appropriate solutions to complex problems.

In some ways all communities are learning communities or they would cease to exist, but high performing learning communities can be defined as enterprises that place a high value on developing the capacity to learn, see learning as the outcome of the authentic activities of that community, use the outcomes of learning as scaffolding for future activity, and enable activities as social practices (e.g., not bound by arbitrary isolation of individuals, such as individual seat work in school). These same principles that have been applied in the service of business productivity and improvement can also be applied to improving the school as a system and organization.

COMPUTER SUPPORT FOR LEARNING ORGANIZATIONS

Nearly 40 years ago Douglas Engelbart working from early experiences with communication technologies and a vision of the future with new and advancing technologies formulated a framework for "augmenting" the human intellect and improving human productivity that fits well with a model of distributed cognition and situated learning. By augmenting he meant "increasing the capability of a man to approach a complex problem situation, to gain comprehension to suit his particular needs, and to derive solutions to the problem." (Engelbart, 1962, p. 1). Considering the worker, the learner, and the work situation as an integrated whole with conditions that negate or facilitate "increasing capability." was fundamental to Engelbart's framework and links his work to distributed cognition and to Senge's model of a learning organization.

Engelbart's work was a seed for later efforts at computer-supported collaborative work (CSCW), electronic performance support systems (EPSS), and most recently a set of knowledge management systems with names, such as, ERP (enterprise resource planning), CRM (customer relationship planning) and SCM (supply chain management), etc. Von Krogh, Ichijo, and Nonaka (2000) stress that improved business practices come from implementing knowledge management systems in a "knowledge creating" company. They stress that "knowledge creation" calls for new roles and responsibilities for everyone in the organization so that innovation can be nurtured and new knowledge can be created, shared, and used for sustained advantage and productivity. The work of seeing organizations as knowledge creation enterprises takes the learning organization framework provided by Senge and maps it to the power and potential of information technology and knowledge management systems.

Similar to the substantial investment to place technology in schools and the apparent limited return on this investment, business investment in information technology experienced a "productivity paradox" from the 1960's into the 1990's. Critics claimed and had ample evidence in support of their case that huge investments in technology had not led to increased business productivity. In a comment that parallels the line from Larry Cuban about computers in schools, the Nobel Laureate Economist Robert Solow characterized the results of technology in industry: "we see productivity everywhere except in the productivity statistics." More recent analyses of productivity show that in the late 1990s technology is substantially contributing to productivity. Brynjolfsson and Hitt (1998) summarized the recent research by declaring that "computers are pulling their weight." They suggest that the question is no longer "Does technology payoff?" but rather, "How can we best use technology?" The research shows, however, that just investing in technology does not bring improved productivity. Some firms with high investments in technology have shown gains and others with equal investments have failed to show gains. A study funded by IBM (IBM Business Consulting, 2001) with collaborators from academia and business publishing associated the contributions of technology to productivity gains with a focus (1) on customers, (2) business process transformation, and (3) organizational learning.

The lessons learned about deriving productivity gains from technology investments learned in industry and summarized in the IBM report are a guide for thinking about systems design and implementation in schools. Many of the technology implementations we see in schools today are beneficial, but substantial school improvement will not occur because of one teacher in an elementary school who uses technology, or a few projects done in the middle schools, or even an entire, but single school, in a district with advanced uses of technology. Similar to ERP (enterprise resource planning), CRM (customer relationship planning) and SCM (supply chain management) systems in business, schools need enterprise wide, networked systems that implement school processes in ways that contribute to student learning outcomes. As educators and developers our understanding and ability to develop these systems are still quite primitive, but new network-based learning systems are coming into use that offer the possibility of integrating curriculum experiences and student information systems. These new systems can help change the metaphor of the Internet from library to workspace and the metaphor of student information from report card to feedback in a systems model. We will call these integrating and process oriented systems Networked Learning Systems (NLS). An NLS is defined as a program or set of programs designed to operate over a network and support users as they undertake tasks or participate in processes related to learning. One framework for these systems for K-12 is to build out the student information system into a web-based tracking system. These systems, PowerSchool by Apple Computer is a strong example, offer great advantages for school management and administration and assist the instructional process as well as providing new linkages between parents and school teachers and administrators. Another model is to build-out the cscl-type systems that are emerging in schools to support teaching and learning so as to include information management systems that foster collaboration and new roles in the educational enterprise for all participants, students, teachers, administrators, and parents. This paper argues for using a CSCL framework that places student work as the design center of the system. Focusing on the work of teaching and learning is analogous to the focus on customers found to be associated with productivity gains in the IBM study. However, this agenda will also be advanced by building the student information-type systems so as to be web-based environments for student work, not just environments "about" student work.

A key educational implication of situated learning and the socio-cultural approach to understanding teaching and learning actions has been to set a goal of providing students with participation in the authentic work of communities of practice. Lessons learned from the research on business productivity suggests that we need to also consider the school as a community of practice for doing "school." Schooling can be improved by understanding the practices of its participants and creating environments and systems to help the school be a learning organization.

SCHOOLS AS LEARNING ORGANIZATION

In Senge's most recent book, Schools That Learn (Senge et al., 2001), the five disciplines are applied against the challenges and problems of schools. This approach allows educators and policy makers to see the school as a learning community, not just in the traditional framework of students learning the school curriculum, but in the sense of an organization or community that needs to get smarter about how it works, takes on challenges and mobilizes for school improvement. Schools That Learn references the role that technology (e.g., email or conferencing) can play in facilitating the actions of communication and sharing. However, Senge focuses upon institutional innovation, and fails to show how technology can be used to change ways of thinking and ways of working. Donald Norman's book, Things That Make Us Smart (Norman, 1993), shows how technology does not simply improve the way we do things, but actually changes what we do. Multiplying with a calculator is a different mental and physical task then is multiplying with paper and pencil. Having a door that is designed in a way that indicates that you should push when actually you should pull will lead to lots of less than dumb actions. This insight allows designers and developers to create systems that allow people to act as they are able and amplify, transform, and extend their work to new or additional outcomes. Efforts to build knowledge management systems so that information collected in one part of an organization can be used to make decisions in another part of the organization (over time or distance) has been a powerful tool in organizational improvement. Brown and Duguid (2000) argue that information-driven technologies lead to a tunnel vision, and that the implementation of technology needs to be grounded in the social life of the institution rather than in the information space. This argument recognizes that learning and knowledge are the result of multiple and intertwining forces of content, context, and community, and that similar to Senge, these authors see the need to harness the richness and diversity found in the community members of the organization.

USING CSCL TO SUPPORT THE SCHOOL AS A LEARNING ORGANIZATION

How can schools change the way they work and realize productivity gains of similar magnitude as those being realized by businesses? We believe that Senge's five disciplines can serve as guide for schools as they attempt to answer this question, and that recent advances in networked technologies empower schools to implement the five disciplines of learning communities in ways that have not been possible heretofore. The remainder of this article illustrates how one such systems, Shadow netWorkspace™ (SNS) (Laffey, Musser, and Espinosa, 2000), supports ways of working that enact the five disciplines.

SNS is a web-based work environment designed and developed specifically to support K-12 schools. Much like a personal computer's desktop SNS provides a personal workspace for organizing, storing and accessing files and an environment for running applications. Figure 1 shows the personal desktop view of the SNS interface. The desktop has a navigation dock to the left side, an information bar along the top of the window, and an application space that in this view shows the personal desktop of the user. The desktop provides access to data storage, groups and specialized tools. The top of the dock shows a set of locations always available to the user. The middle of the dock shows the applications that are currently active but not in the application view for easy movement between applications, such as the address book, message board and chat currently shown. The bottom of the dock shows session control options. The bar shown in the figure indicates to the user when they are running out of system rersources on the server and need to close down some active applications. Other options available to the user include choosing the language (English, Spanish. Korean, etc.) of the interface or choosing the theme (screen configuration, color scheme, etc.) that would be most appropriate for the current computing environment. For example, an experienced user on a computer with a small monitor may choose to collapse the dock into a set of icons leaving more space for the application window.

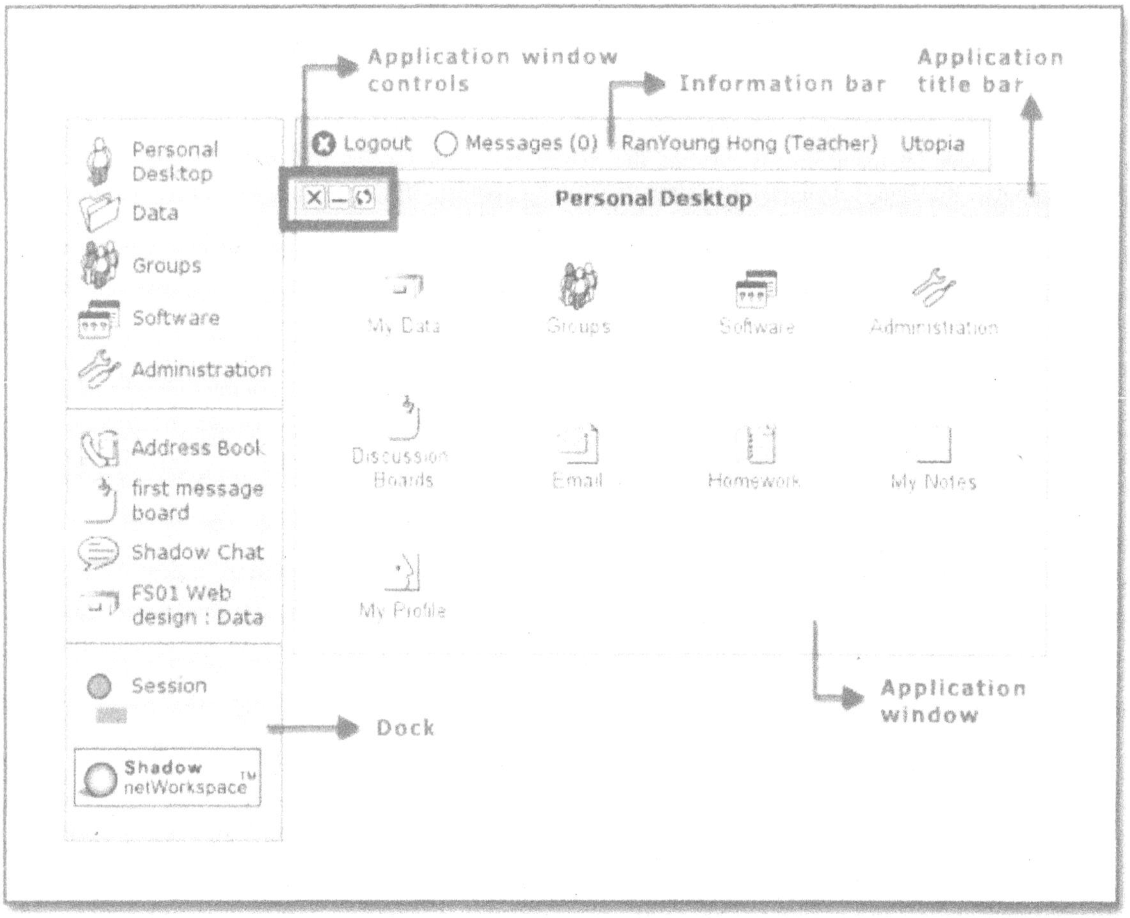

Figure 1. SNS Personal Desktop

SNS provides the ability to create groups and for each group to have a "group desktop" analogous to the personal desktop shown in figure 1 for file sharing, communication and collaboration. Because it is Web-based, teachers and students can access their workspaces from any computer that can access the World Wide Web, and partners (parents or mentors), who are unable to participate in schools because of time or distance, can participate in the internet-based workspace. SNS is freely available to all users, designed to be installed at individual school locations, and comes with an open source (GNU Public License) and Application Programming Interface (API) so others can develop applications for it and participate in enhancing and supporting it.

SNS is both an information space for organizing, storing and accessing files, and a social space in that SNS users have roles (e.g., teachers, students, parents, etc.) that structure the system interaction as well as groups for sharing, communicating and collaborating. The next sections illustrate the ways in which SNS supports activities that instantiate the five disciplines and build a learning community.

Personal Mastery.

Community members must have a personal identity that both empowers them to achieve to a high level of personal satisfaction and represent themselves in the community in a way that is coherent with their own self image. For example, programmers in the open source community are empowered with tools (licenses, source code, web-based information and sharing) and invest their time and resources to create interesting and powerful programs. These programmers want to share their work freely with others who could benefit or learn from it. If the programs were made available anonymously there would be far less drive to mastery, creation and sharing. SNS provides each member of the community with an identity and an extensive section for presenting a profile. SNS also provides substantial customizability for the desktop and organization of files. Users in all roles can create groups, invite members to participate, invoke chat or other communication tools, and share their work in multiple ways. The name "netWorkspace" signifies that core to the design of SNS is a work environment, a place to accomplish a variety of types of work, and one which is resourced, connected and customizable. The workspace facilitates students having a personally meaningful identity in school that is associated with their accomplishments, so that they will see themselves as a part of the school community.

Mental Models.

Mental models are guides to behavior. Much like the set of expectations we have for going to a restaurant causes us to take a seat, order food, and pay for it before leaving. Our expectations and models for how the world works and how we will work within it guide our actions and the sense we make of the actions of others. Senge argues that we need to have a clear understanding (or visible representation) of our mental models as well as the mental models of those with whom we work. Reflecting on our own models is how we will change them or adjust them to best fit the situation. Inquiring into the models of others is how we come to understand their actions as goals and intentions, not simply behaviors. Central to the processes of reflection and inquiry are ways of making these assumptions visible, so that they can be examined and communicated. A way of thinking about this idea that especially fits schools is to think of making learning visible. Making learning visible challenges the learner to represent what they know and enables the teacher or learning partner to not only see an answer but to see the underpinnings and mechanisms that generate that answer. Much like asking a student in mathematics to show their work of calculating an answer we want students to show their work in all forms of learning.

SNS supports making learning visible by: (1) providing online tools for creating multimedia content, providing a special viewer application for examining media, and facilitating the sharing of most document types, (2) allowing users to organize and store documents so that iterative steps toward a final production can be maintained and shared, and (3) supporting multiple reviewer types (including teachers, other students, parents, mentors from in and outside of the local community) so that the teacher does not have to be the only source of review and feedback. One of the key barriers to examining mental models or making learning visible is the lack of time and the pressure to cover subject matter. Since the student's workspace is available wherever they have an Internet computer or appliance, teachers can create teaching materials for asynchronous teaching and learning. It may be unreasonable to expect many teachers to create many materials, but teachers and other members of the extended school community could collaborate to develop instructional materials and have a common and easily accessible platform for implementation.

Shared Vision.

The articulation and sharing of mental models provide individuals with the opportunity to discover other individuals with similar mental models and personal visions. This discovery can lead to the aggregation of individuals into groups and the identification and shaping of a shared vision. This shared vision serves to motivate individuals and foster commitment to learning and action (Team Learning). Key to building a shared vision is participation and inclusion of all the stakeholders in the learning community. By providing a social context for participation (members have roles with appropriate rights and authority), easily available grouping techniques, and an easy to use interface, SNS supports the participation of all appropriate members and facilitates their interaction and sharing.

Team Learning.

How can members of a community interact and mobilize to achieve common goals so that the collective effort is greater than what could be accomplished by isolated individuals? SNS makes it easy for schools to setup classes with teachers, but also allows any member to create workgroups or review groups. Each type of group provides different rights and privileges for the members of the group. For example, in a class group students cannot throw a document created by the teacher into the trash, whereas in workgroups all members have equal rights and responsibilities regarding the managing and editing of files. Workgroups can be setup for the purpose of a group of students working on a team project, teachers collaborating on curriculum development, or students forming a chess club. Review groups allow an individual to organize a set of work for review by others. Review groups could be setup for the purpose of an electronic portfolio, a science fair exhibit, or having a teacher, student, guidance counselor, truant officer, and parent collaboratively review a students work over time. To date, SNS provides the three group types described above, but other group types could be developed based upon new definitions of roles and rights.

Being in a group of a certain type provides affordances and constraints for what the member can do, and what can be done with documents. Within a group, members can invoke discussion boards or chat sessions whenever appropriate. The user experience is that of easy and flexible group formation, various communication tools, and file sharing and security. Just as the name "netWorkspace" communicates an environment for personal mastery, it represents customizable work environments for teams and groups. The groups and types of groups in a learning community can change as the need for new types of social interaction emerge over time.

The review panel, as an example, illustrates how the feature set of SNS can be used to support the type of process transformation that can be valuable to schools and has been associated with productivity gains in the IBM study. Feedback and evaluation of student work is one of the most important processes of schooling. Typically feedback is only provided by the primary teacher and only on the current work effort. Portfolios are recognized as mechanisms that allow students to aggregate work into meaningful chunks and provide for more extensive review. In practice, however, portfolios have many problems. Physical portfolios are cumbersome and it is difficult to mange the review process for more than a very small number of students. Electronic portfolios usually call for technical skills on the part of the producer or reviewer that often yield weak approximations of the goal of appropriate and extensive feedback to important work by the student. The Review Panel Group of SNS facilitates both the work of the portfolio producer and reviewer. An example desktop for a review panel group is shown in Figure 2. In this case the group is being used by the member, Jim Laffey, for a review called "Interface Design Review." The desktop provides a file storage space called Portfolio. In this space the owner can place any documents (including word processing, spreadsheets, graphics, or video) that are to be reviewed. The owner can arrange these documents in folders, and thus has a great deal of presentation flexibility. The owner can provide instructions for reviewers, as well as an introduction to him or herself and to the work to be reviewed. Communication tools such as discussion boards or the ability to leave notes are available. The owner can use the Member Editor tool to invite reviewers to the portfolio. If the reviewer is a member of the SNS community, the Review Panel will show up in that members Groups. If the reviewer is not a member of the SNS community, for example a college admissions officer, then the invitation process creates an email or letter to be sent to the non-member reviewer with a specialized password that will admit the reviewer to this panel but not to other areas of the SNS community. For students using SNS to carry out their regular school work the creation of a portfolio is an easy process of copying files from their personal workspace or other group space to their new portfolio space. Reviewers have easy access to the files and communication tools for collaborating with other reviewers or interacting with the student. If specialized scoring or grading is required new applications could be developed and added to the desktop. This review panel example illustrates how the key steps and transactions of an important process of schooling can be facilitated in a networked learning system.

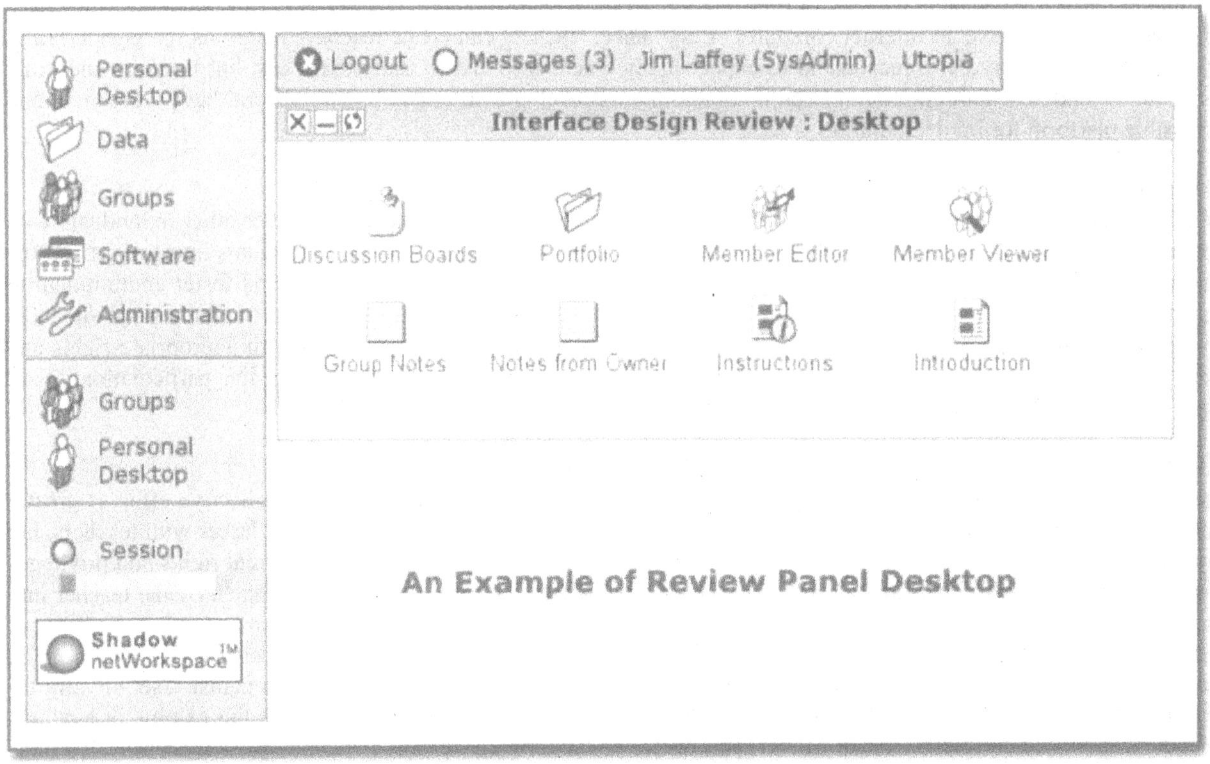

Figure 2. Desktop of Review Panel Group

Systems Thinking.

Senge calls systems thinking the fifth discipline of learning organizations, and entitled his seminal book, The Fifth Discipline, to highlight how important systems thinking is to bringing the benefits of the other disciplines to bear on knowledge creation and learning. While there is much to be understood about systems thinking, the practice of systems thinking starts with a simple concept called "feedback." Feedback provides the information needed to recognize causality, to see patterns, and to understand the interrelationship of phenomena. If NLS become places where much of the important work of schools is done or represented, then representations of this work can be viewed, reviewed, and monitored for patterns and relationships. While it is certainly possible to build NLS that represent unimportant or non-critical aspects of the work of schools, and build elaborate systems models that will lead to no substantial improvement in schools; the hard and creative work of systems thinking is drilling down to the essentials and core focus of the enterprise. The report from IBM suggests that information systems in business must be clearly tied to the effect of work on customers, and its is likely that in schools NLS must focus on students and student work. Neither SNS nor any other NLS that we have examined claims much progress in providing the core feedback needed for school improvement. One of the goals of NLS developers who have created open source licenses for their work is to build communities of users so that the shared experience of the school communities can provide feedback to the NLS development, which in turn can lead to systems that improve over time and experience.

SUMMARY

Networked Learning Systems hold great potential and promise for school improvement. The rapid deployment of technology into schools and the relentless advancement of technology for digital representation and network services for information and work, call for "ways of thinking" that will turn schools into learning organizations in the fullest sense of the term. Although substantial investments and deployment efforts are being made in schools, the scope of this work is miniscule when compared to the experience and lessons learned over the past 40 years of bringing information technology to bear on business productivity. Lessons from this work may not be directly translatable into school practices, but they point us towards a focus on student work, enterprise wide systems, and mapping technology use to process improvement in the organization. Further the work undertaken in the business community focuses our attention on turning schools into learning organizations that not only work to support student learning, but also work to improve their ways of working. NLS can be a substantial contributor to helping schools become learning organizations.

Systems like Shadow netWorkspace are early and somewhat primitive instances of the environments we envision for schools as learning organizations. These systems must advance through evolutionary and learning processes of their own. Schools must adopt NLS and begin the process of fundamental change to management, organizational structures and human resource allocation that these systems will enable. NLS as a vision in schools has been impeded by limitations in access to technology (not every child and/or parent has a computer and computers are not in all the places we want them to be) and limitations in bandwidth (some things just are not worth doing over a 28.8 modem connection). However, we are already seeing instances of schools where every child has a laptop and it is not hard to imagine a future where in many schools every child has some form of PDA. Similarly, wireless connections and Internet2 connections into schools foreshadow ubiquitous high bandwidth. Our implementations of NLS and our ways of thinking about schools need to advance, so that as ubiquitous access becomes a reality, we will have schools that can learn to bring these new network services to bear on improved teaching and learning.

The foundational work of scholars such as Scardamalia and Bereiter for using computers to support collaborative learning can be a basis for enterprise wide systems that focus on the total process of teaching and learning. If we do not find creative ways to make the work of student learning the design center for knowledge management systems, we will end up with knowledge management systems for schools that fail to represent the real work of schools, and we will have failed to learn from the lessons of the "productivity paradox" in business.

REFERENCES

Brown, J. S. & Duguid, P. (2000). The Social Life of Information. Boston, MA: Harvard Business School Press

Brynjolfsson, E. & Hitt, L. (1998). Beyond the productivity paradox. *Communications of the ACM* ***41***, 8, 49-55.

Engelbart, D. (1962). Augmenting Human Intellect: A conceptual framework, summary report, SRI International. On Contract AF 49(638) 1024.

IBM Business Consulting. (2001). Beyond the productivity paradox: New views on the value of information technology. www.ibm.com/services/whitepapers/productivity.html

Laffey, J., Musser, D. & Espinosa, L. (2000) Shadow netWorkspace Learning Systems Project. *Proceedings of the International Workshop on Advanced Learning Technologies*. (Palmerstown North, New Zealand), IEEE Computer Society. pp. 188-189.

Lave, J. & Wenger, E., (1991) Situated learning: Legitimate peripheral participation. Cambridge, U.K.: Cambridge University Press.

Norman, D. (1993). Things that make us smart : defending human attributes in the age of the machine. Reading, MA: Addison-Wesley.

Office of Educational Technology. (2000). e-Learning: Putting a world-class education at the fingertips of all children. Washington, DC: U.S. Department of Education.

Scardamalia, M., & Bereiter, C. (1993-1994). Computer support for knowledge-building communities. *The Journal of the Learning Sciences*, 3, 265-283.

Senge, P. *The fifth discipline.* Doubleday, New York, NY, 1990.

Senge, P., Cambron-McCabe, N., Lucas, T., Smith, B., Dutton, J., & Kleiner, A. Schools that learn. Doubleday, New York, NY, 2001.

Von Krogh, G., Ichijo, K. and Nonaka, I. (2000). Enabling Knowledge Creation. Oxford, Oxford University Press.

Web-based Education Commission. (2000) The power of the Internet for learning: Moving from promise to practice (Report). Washington, DC: U.S. Department of Education.

Wertsch, J. (1998). Mind as Action. Oxford, Oxford University Press.

Williams, C. (2000). Internet access in public schools: 1994-1999 (NCES 2000-086). U. S. Department of Education. Washington, D. C.: National Center for Educational Statistics.

D. (METHODOLOGY TRACK): QUANTITATIVE ANALYSIS OF SOCIAL STRUCTURES

Gender and Programming Achievement in a CSCL Environment

Amy Bruckman, Carlos Jensen
Georgia Institute of Technology
{asb,carlosj}@cc.gatech.edu

Austina DeBonte
Microsoft
austinad@microsoft.com

ABSTRACT
In this study, we analyzed 3.4 GB of log file data from the participation of 475 children in a CSCL environment over a period of five years. Using scripts to divide the children's commands typed into categories, we found that girls spend significantly more time than boys communicating with others in the CSCL environment. Analyzing the children's level of programming achievement, we found that gender does not affect programming performance. Regression analysis shows that performance is correlated with prior programming experience and time on task. Boys are more likely than girls to have prior programming experience, and spend more time programming on average. We contrast these quantitative findings with our qualitative observations, and conclude that quantitative analysis has an important role to play in CSCL research. These results suggest that educators wishing to increase gender equity in technical skill should focus on strategies for fostering interest among girls.

Keywords
Gender, programming, learning, CSCL

A GENDER GAP?
Since the earliest days of the personal computer (and perhaps earlier), researchers have been asking questions about gender equity in computer use. "If males and females participate differentially in computer learning environments, this could lead to differences in cognitive attainments and career access," wrote Marcia Linn in 1985 (Linn, 1985). Linn studied organized middle-school programming classes, and found that girls and boys have similar levels of programming achievement once they enroll in classes, but that girls are less likely to enroll. In the following decade a number of researchers have studied gender differences in how children learn and use computers both in schools and at home (for overviews see Bannert 96 and Giacquinta 93) and the reasons behind these differences (Turkle 86). A number of studies have shown that girls tend to have less exposure to computers. Studies have shown a strong positive relationship between prior experience and both attitudes towards computers and achievement (Kersteen 88, Shashaani 94). When gender role identity and previous experience are accounted for, boys and girls perform equally well (Colley 94).

Since Marcia Linn did her first study, much has changed about computers, access to technology, and how computers are used at home as well as schools. However, the basic facts of gender and computing for kids have not changed: our results replicate Linn's early findings. Most of the work to date has been done using surveys and attitudinal inventories. In this study, we use quantitative log file analysis as well as qualitative observations and interviewing to study student programmers in a mixed school and free-time use environment. While boys develop significantly more programming expertise than girls (25% difference, p=.004), regression analysis shows that in fact this difference is attributable to the fact that boys chose to spend more time programming in the environment, and are more likely to have prior programming experience. Boys are more likely to chose to program both before and during their exposure to our programming environment, and time on task predicts level of achievement.

BACKGROUND: MOOSE CROSSING
In the spring of 1992, Amy Bruckman presented a paper on the fluidity of identity in text-based virtual worlds (or "MUDs") to a student reading group at the MIT Media Lab. A few days later, Mitchel Resnick, then a graduate student but about to join the faculty, posed a question to Bruckman: would it make sense to create a MUD based on the *Babysitter's Club* series of books to encourage elementary and middle-school girls to be interested in computers? This was the beginning of the MOOSE Crossing project.

A new programming language ("MOOSE") and programming environment ("MacMOOSE") were developed to make it easier for children to learn to program (Bruckman, 1997; Bruckman & Edwards, 1999). (A Windows version of the programming environment, "WinMOOSE," was developed a few years later.) The *Babysitter* series theme was abandoned in favor of a more open-ended, gender-neutral theme. Rather than create an environment for girls, we decided to create an environment we hoped would appeal to both genders, so that we could compare girls' and boys' activities there. However, gender was soon relegated to a lower research priority, because there was simply so much fundamental work to do on the basic nature of learning in this new kind of CSCL environment (Bruckman, 2000; Bruckman, Edwards, Elliott, & Jensen, 2000).

Children began to use MOOSE Crossing in the fall of 1995. Everything typed on MOOSE Crossing is recorded, with written informed consent from parents and assent from children. In January 1996, then undergraduate Austina De Bonte joined the MOOSE Crossing development team as part of MIT's Undergraduate Research Opportunities (UROP) program. DeBonte (then Austina Vainius) wrote a series of Perl scripts to break down children's commands typed on MOOSE Crossing into categories (see Table 1).

- Movement in the virtual world
- Communication with others
- Consulting the help system
- Looking at people and objects
- Creation objects
- Seeking information about others
- Scripting
- Manipulating object properties
- Looking at object properties
- Using the in-world mail

DeBonte analyzed 700MB of MOOSE log file data from the first use by kids in September 1995 until April 1997. A total of 160 children participated during this time. Comparing girls and boys use of each of these categories of commands, she found no significant differences. Girls spent more time communicating with others online, and boys had a slightly higher percentage of their commands typed in other categories; however, none of these differences were significant. At the time, we were disappointed in this result—it seemed uninteresting. It is discussed in a few pages of Bruckman's PhD thesis (Bruckman, 1997), but was not published elsewhere.

Five years later, we looked back at this result, and saw it in a new light. No significant differences is not a lack of results—it is in fact an interesting finding. Consequently, Carlos Jensen dusted off DeBonte's Perl scripts, and repeated the analysis on our greatly enlarged data set. Additionally, new scripts have been written to analyze children's level of programming achievement.

DATA ANALYSIS

Categorizing Activity

Through November 2000, 457 children have now participated in MOOSE Crossing. Of those, some children continue to participate for many years, while others try the environment once and never return (see Table 2). This nearly 3-fold increase in experimental subjects has led to a nearly 5-fold increase in the amount of log file data. As of November 2000, we have 3.4 GB of data (compared to 0.7 GB in 1997).

	BOYS	GIRLS	ALL
Mean	4036.8	4914.9	4444.2
Standard Deviation	8906.2	17642.7	13662.5
Median	580	459	516
Minimum	2	5	2
Maximum	55709	177680	177680

Table 2: Time on Task (Commands Typed) By Gender

In total, 46% of MOOSE users are girls, and 54% are boys. This is little changed from 1997, when 43% were girls. It is also similar to the gender distribution on the Internet as a whole. While men dominated the Internet in the mid-90s, men and women were roughly equally represented online by the turn of the century (Abernathy, 2000).

Participation on MOOSE Crossing is measured by counting the total number of commands typed by a member (see Table 2). Since a user might leave a connection window open without actually being present at the computer, connect time is not a useful metric. Total commands typed is a better measure of degree of participation. Differences in time on task by gender are not statistically significant. A few girls have extremely high participation rates (see Figure 4), leading to the mean commands typed being higher for girls while the median is higher for boys. Given the highly variable nature of participation rates, median values are more indicative than means.

A typical entry in our log files looks like this:

```
16:05:38 #218 #78 >>>> say hi
16:05:40 #78 << You say 'hi'
16:05:40 #99 << Amy says, 'hi'
```

Data is stored in files for each day. Each line of input from the user consists of a timestamp, the unique identifier of the room in which the user is located, the user's object number, and ">>>>", followed by what the user typed. Each line of output presented to a user is proceeded by a timestamp, the user's object number, and then "<<", followed by what the user saw. In the above log, Amy (player #99) is in Ginny's Little Cottage (room #218), and says hi. Ginny (#99) hears her.

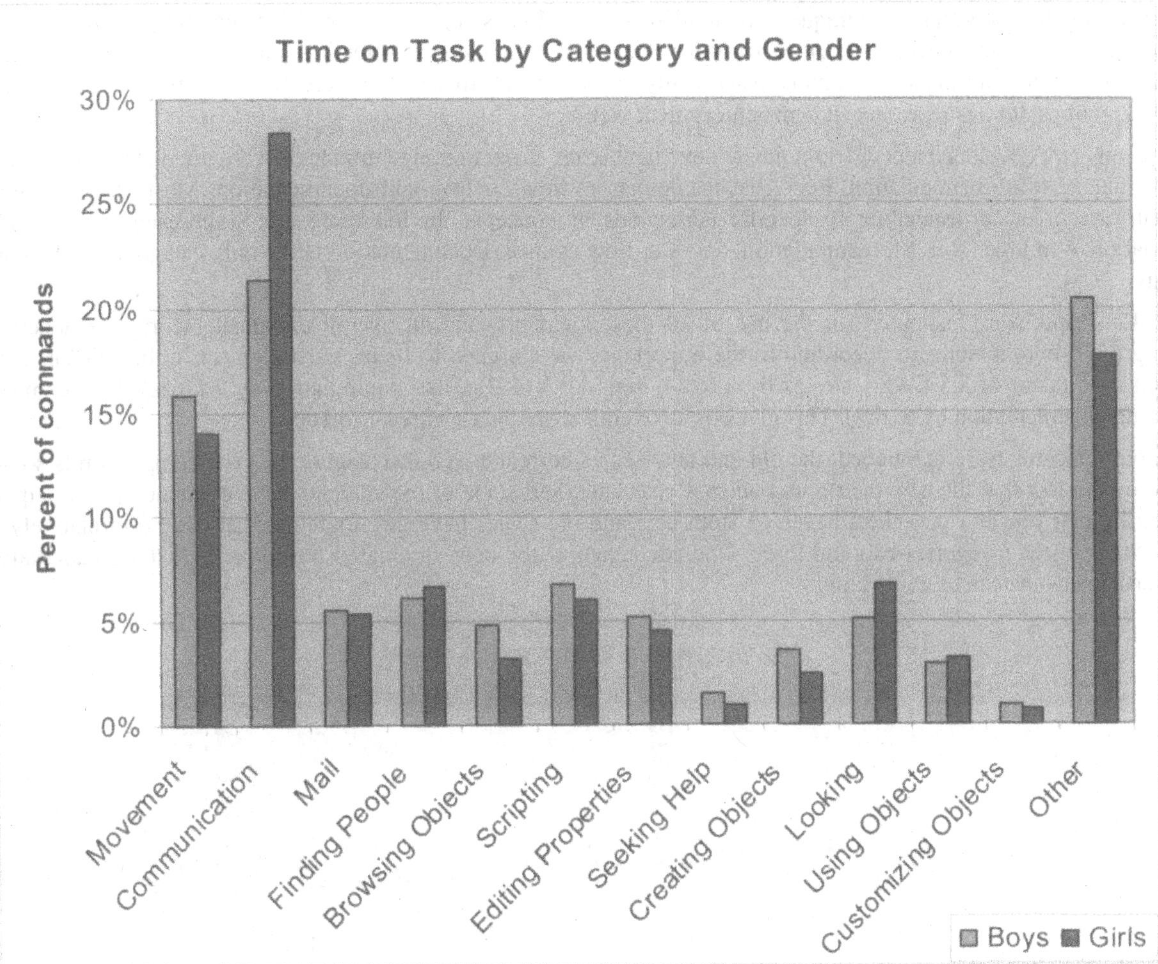

Figure 1

All transactions between client and server are also recorded, allowing us to see when the user looked at a particular object, script, help message, etc. Simple regular expression matching enables us to sort more than 80% of commands typed into categories (see Figure 1).

Only one gender difference in this chart approaches statistical significance: girls spend more time (as a percentage of total commands typed) communicating with others compared to what boys do (marginal significance: $p=.082$). This trend was also observed in the 1997 data analysis, but at the time was less significant. Time on task as measured by proportion of total commands typed is a zero-sum game. While none of the other differences are significant, the fact that girls are spending more time communicating means they are spending slightly less time than boys in almost all other categories.

We might infer from this that girls appreciate the social nature of the CSCL environment. It is unclear, however, what impact if any this has on girls' learning. Conversation might or might not be contributing to their intellectual growth. We have not analyzed what percent of the communication is "on task" (about programming or writing), versus being purely social. Furthermore, even when communication is purely social, it is not clear to what extent this contributes to the development of writing skills. Thus, this finding is intriguing but difficult to interpret.

Scoring of Student Achievement

In 2000, we used portfolio scoring techniques to analyze students' programming achievement on MOOSE Crossing according to the following scale:

0: Wrote no scripts
1: Demonstrated understanding of basic input/output
2: Used variables and properties
3: Performed list manipulation and flow control
4: Demonstrated mastery of all aspects of the system

These ratings were produced by two human raters. In cases where the raters disagreed, a third person rated the student's level of accomplishment. This technique was applied to a random sample of 50 participants (Bruckman et al., 2000). Subsequently, we became concerned that perhaps our categories were poorly designed. What if kids are learning commands in an unusual order, learning some commands typically classified as "advanced" before others we think of as elementary? Does this set of categories represent student achievement well?

Consequently, we developed a new 100-point achievement scale. Programming commands were divided up into categories: input & output, string manipulation, logic, list manipulation, flow control, and documentation. Most of these categories have sub-categories corresponding to specific commands or concepts. In I/O there are 8 sub-categories, 3 in string manipulation, 4 in logic, 8 in list manipulation, and 8 in flow control. Documentation is the only category that had no sub-elements.

Each kid's scripts were examined for the use of all these elements, and an overall composite score was generated by weighing the different elements according to the importance we assigned to them. Each element in the I/O category was weighted by a factor of 3.5 (28%), strings by 2 (6%), logic by 3 (12%), list manipulation by 2 (16%), flow control by 4 (32%), and documentation by 6 (6%). This gives us an overall score on a scale of 1 to 100.

In fact, our concerns were unfounded: the old and new scores correlate well (see Figure 2). (The comparison is somewhat strained by the fact that the new metric was taken a year later, and some of the students have continued to participate and learn during that year but the others haven't.) Both new and old scales have the limitation that there are relatively subtle differences between categories two and three. One advantage of the new automated technique is that we can analyze all study participants instead of a sub-sample.

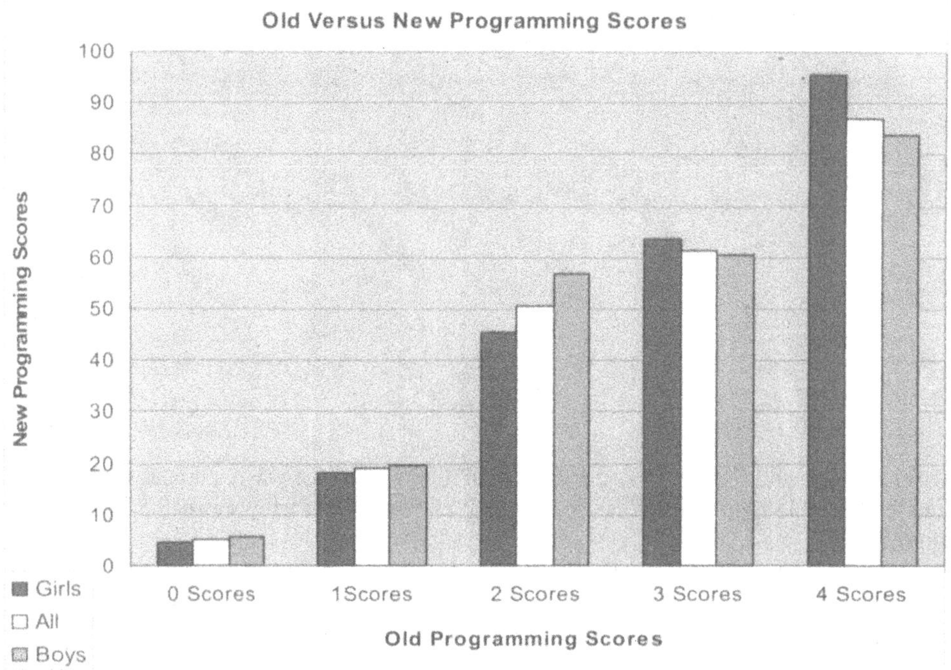

Figure 2

On registering for MOOSE Crossing, all participants are asked if they have previous programming experience. Prior experience is self reported, and generously interpreted. If a student reported any kind of programming experience (for example, having authored HTML), this was counted as an affirmative response. Students with previous experience have significantly higher levels of programming achievement (p=.001) (see Figure 3). The error bars show the extremely large degree of variability in students' achievement. However, despite this variability, the large size of the data set means that the effect is highly significant.

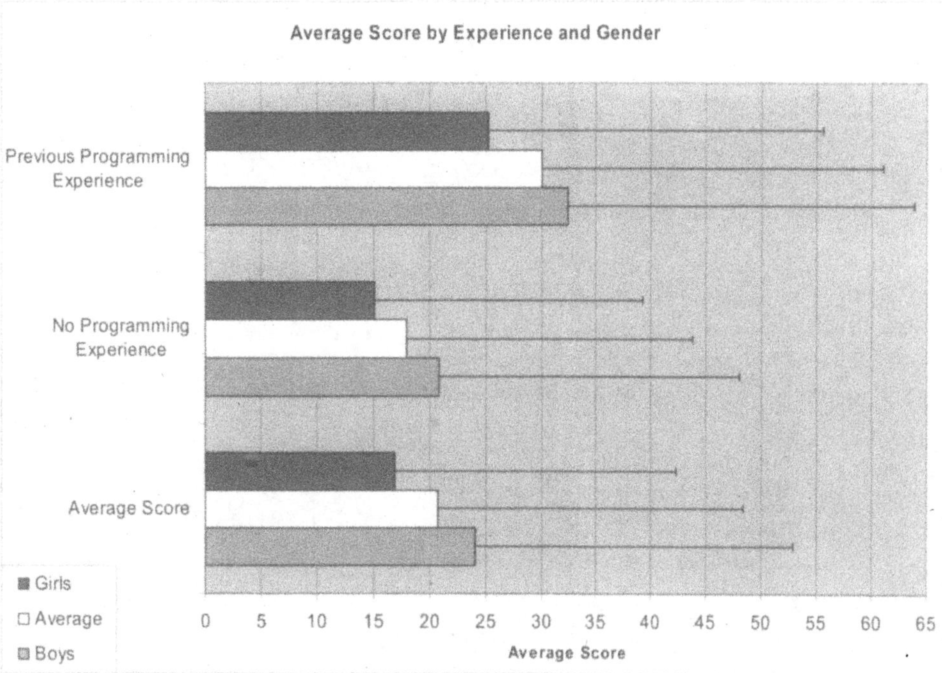

Figure 3

At first glance, boys have a higher level of programming achievement than girls (p=.004). However, regression analysis shows that the difference is explained by prior programming experience (see Figure 3).

Regression analysis is a statistical tool for evaluating the relationship of a set of independent variables to a single dependent variable. This method is particularly useful in situations such as this, where we cannot control the independent variables, yet need to determine their individual effects. Regression analysis seeks to take a set of data-points and find the mathematical equation which best and most reliably describes the given data set. The resulting equation serves as a predictor for the "weight," or "importance" of the different independent variables in relation to the dependent variable, and to each other. In this case, we used a Least Square estimation method, excluding outliers (kids with more than 60,000 commands typed, kids who first used computers after the age of 13, kids who first started using MOOSE after the age of 16, or who spent more than 20% of their total time-on-task programming). Looking at Programming Score, the resulting equation was:

Programming Score = 5.595
+ 3.589 * (if the subject has previous programming experience)
- 0.007 * (time talking to others)
+ $2.93 * 10^{-7}$ * $(\text{time talking to others})^2$
+ 0.006 * (time on task)
- $1.03 * 10^{-7}$ * $(\text{time on task})^2$
+ 0.009 * (time spent scripting)

(Adjusted $R^2 = 0.76$, S.E.=12.8, $p<0.01$ for all except Previous Programming Experience, $p<0.05$).

In other words, programming scores were positively related to time on task, time spent programming (effort), and previous programming experience. Time on Task has a decreasing marginal return (its positive effect plateaus). Programming scores were negatively related to the time they spent talking to others, or engaging in any activity other than programming. (time on task is a zero-sum game). The negative marginal effect of time talking to others is lower the more they talk (it plateaus as it becomes a predictor for continued membership). Gender, environment of use (home, school or other) proved not to be statistically significant.

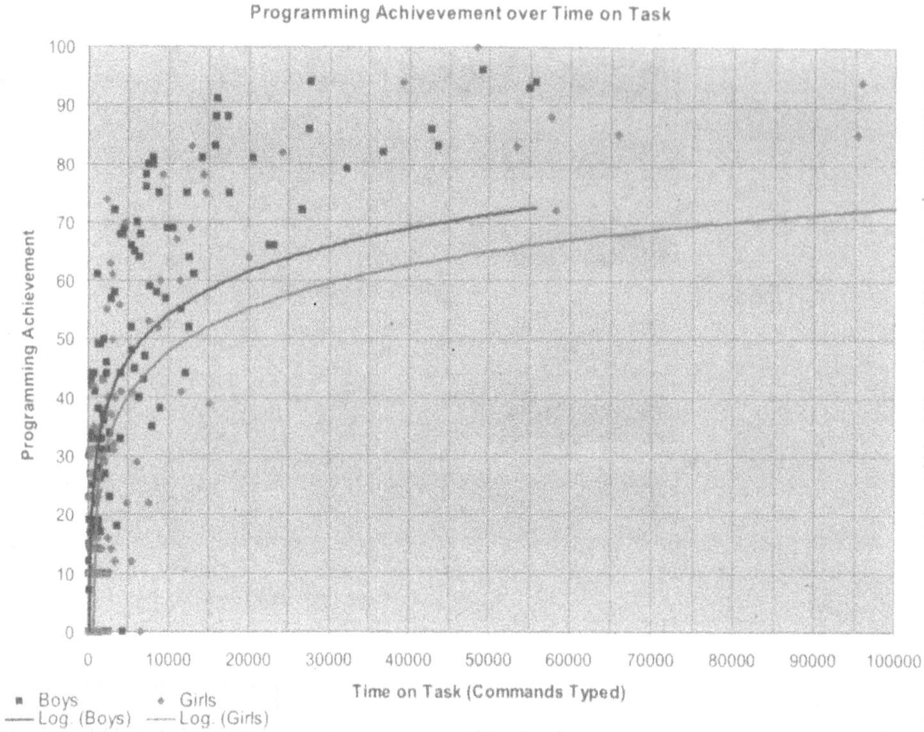

Figure 4

Programming achievement seems most directly related to the time spent in MOOSE as a whole, and more specifically on programming within MOOSE. We therefore chose to look at the factors that determine how much effort the kids put into programming on MOOSE. This resulted in the following equation:

Time spent scripting = 66.42
+ 48.19 (if the subject is a boy)
+ 0.141 * (time talking to others)
- $5.153 * 10^{-6}$ * (time talking to others)^2
+ 3.33 * (help commands)
- 0.003 * (help commands)^2
(Adjusted R^2=0.61, S.E.=233.57, p<0.05 for all)

In other words, gender has an effect on the amount of time spent scripting. Interestingly, we find strong evidence for the social nature of MOOSE Crossing and the community support for learning. This can be seen by the fact that communicating with others is a strong indicator for time spent on scripting. The positive marginal effect of time talking to others is lower the higher the level (i.e. at some point communication is not supporting learning, but rather purely social). We also see that consulting the built-in help system has a positive, but marginally decreasing effect (again, the difference between looking up something and randomly accessing help functions). All other factors proved to be statistically insignificant.

Self-Selected Versus Mandatory Use

Home users of MOOSE Crossing are self-selected. On the other hand, school users generally have no choice: they are assigned to participate. It's not surprising, then, that home users have a higher average level of achievement — they have chosen to participate of their own free will, and hence have higher motivation. (This difference is not statistically significant, but the apparent trend is suggestive.) Interestingly, this difference is greater in girls than boys. Boys working from home score on average 1.54 points higher (6.5% higher) than those working from school; girls working from home score on average 4.98 points higher (35% higher) than girls working from school. (These figures are suggestive but not significant.)

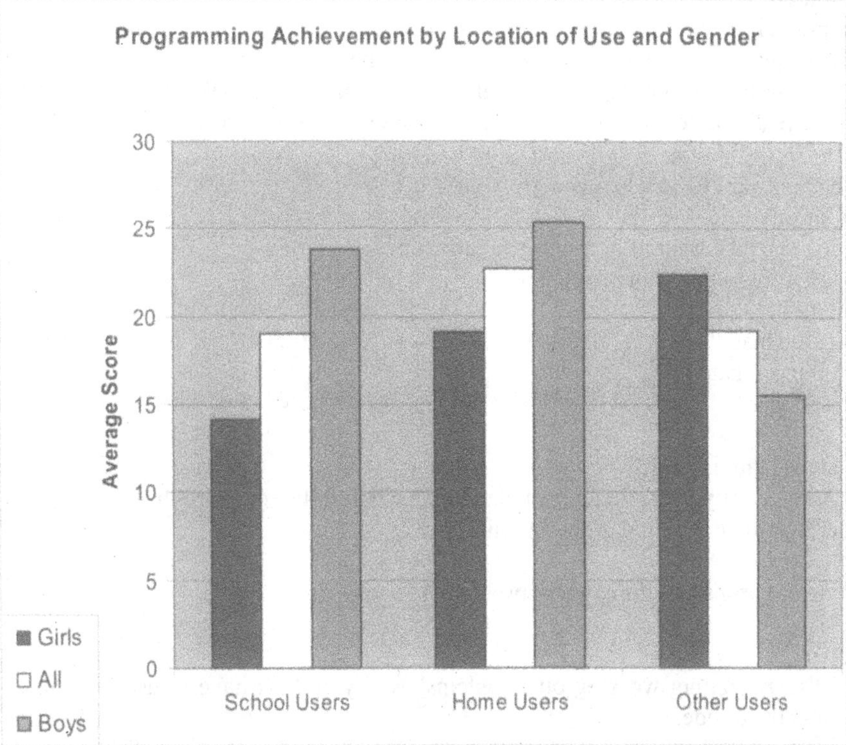

Figure 5

This apparent trend is consistent with our other findings. Overall, girls tend to be less interested in programming than boys. Those girls who self-select to participate are those who happen to be interested. Among the school-use population, girls are less likely to be sincerely interested in the activity. Performance correlates with interest.

Comparison of Quantitative Findings and Informal Observations

Much research in CSCL relies on qualitative data. Sometimes this data is detailed and systematic in its collection; sometimes it is anecdotal. Log file data is easy to collect but difficult to interpret. For example, versions of the Logo programming language generate "dribble files," but few studies have ever made sense of the data in them.

Since 1995, roughly a dozen administrators have spent hundreds of hours each, working with children on MOOSE Crossing. Through those interactions, we necessarily develop informal impressions of the comparative achievement of girls and boys in the environment. The consensus of these impressions is that the achievement of the girls is particularly remarkable, and exceeds that of boys. These impressions turn out to be incorrect. As Figure 4 indicates, the top five participants in terms of total commands typed are girls. A disproportionate amount of our interactions with users are with these dedicated regulars, and this skews our impressions. Quantitative analysis forms a clearer picture. Quantitative analysis is particularly valuable when working with the subject of gender, because opinions about gender are so susceptible to ideology (Popper, 1971). CSCL researchers in general are vulnerable, as we were, to forming impressions based on the behavior of their most active users. Quantitative analysis is a useful partner to qualitative for understanding CSCL systems.

CONCLUSION

We initially designed the MOOSE Crossing environment with the goal of encouraging girls to become interested in technology. Evidence suggests that we have been partly successful in that endeavor. Mouse[1] (girl, age 9) says that she hates math, but loves to write programs on MOOSE Crossing. The following interview took place during an after-school program:

Amy: What's your favorite subject in school?
Mouse: Writing.
Amy: What kinds of things do you like to write in school?
Mouse: Stories about imaginary people.
Amy: Have you done any writing on MOOSE Crossing?
Mouse: Yes.

[1] All real and screen names of research subjects have been changed to protect their privacy.

Amy: What kinds of things do you write on MOOSE Crossing
Mouse: Programs, and....
Amy: How is writing a program different from writing a story?
Mouse: Programming it everything has to be right, so the thing you're making can work. But in stories it doesn't have to be really perfect-- It doesn't have to be so every word is correct.
[...]
Amy: What do you want to be when you grow up?
Mouse: I don't know
Amy: What do you NOT want to be when you grow up?
Mouse: I do NOT want to be... a mathematician!
Amy: How come?
Mouse: Cause I hate math?
Amy: How come you hate math?
Mouse: Cause... it's hard
[...]
Amy: "How come math is hard?
Mouse: I don't know.... If you're a mathematician you have to figure out hard problems.
Amy: But isn't figuring out a hard problem fun?
Mouse: No. It takes forever.
Amy: Is writing programs like doing math problems?
Mouse: No.
Amy: How come?
Mouse: Cause, it's *writing*, not working out problems! And you don't have to use the plus and minus.... and the equals, and the divide.
Amy: Now wait a second! You were just using a greater-than in your program. That's a math symbol!
Mouse: That's not a plus, a minus, a times, a divide, or an equals!
Amy: <laughs>
Mouse: It doesn't count
Amy: It doesn't count, OK.
Mouse: Go talk to somebody else!
Amy: Oh... OK....
Mouse: I'm working on something interesting!

While Mouse sees math as something she has no talent for or interest in, she is proud of her writing ability. In this environment, she sees programming as a form of writing. For at least this one child (and presumably some others), this environment has made computer programming more appealing than it likely otherwise would be. But if differences in achievement persist even in this environment, what is their source? Data analysis presented in this paper suggest that educators wishing to increase girls' level of technical achievement should explore strategies for increasing girls' interest in technical subjects. In both the BASIC programming environment Marcia Linn studied in the early to mid-1980s and in the CSCL environment we designed and studied from the mid 1990s to the present, girls program equally well as boys when they devote equal time to the activity.

ACKNOWLEDGMENTS

The authors would like to thank everyone who has contributed to the MOOSE Crossing project over the years, especially Mitchel Resnick, Elizabeth Edwards, Will Scott, Adam Skwersky, Trevor Stricker, and Steve Tamm. Current MOOSE administrators include Alisa Bandlow and Tysen Perszyk. Jason Elliott and Jon Orwant provided help with Perl scripts. Christian Jensen assisted with statistics. Special thanks to the kids, teachers, and parents who have participated in MOOSE Crossing. Research in the Electronic Learning Communities Group (http://www.cc.gatech.edu/elc/) at Georgia Tech is supported by IBM, Intel, Microsoft, Neometron, Ricoh, and the National Science Foundation.

REFERENCES

Abernathy, D. J. (2000). "How Men and Women Use the Internet Differently." *Career Journal.*

Bannert, M., & Arbinger, P., R. (1996) "Gender-Related Differences in Exposure to And Use of Computers: Results of a Survey of Secondary School Students" *European Journal of Psychology of Education 11*(3), 269-282.

Bruckman, A. (1997). *MOOSE Crossing: Construction, Community, and Learning in a Networked Virtual World for Kids.* Unpublished PhD, MIT.

Bruckman, A. (2000). "Situated Support for Learning: Storm's Weekend with Rachael." *Journal of the Learning Sciences, 9*(3), 329-372.

Bruckman, A., & Edwards, E. (1999). *Should We Leverage Natural-Language Knowledge?* Paper presented at the CHI, Pittsburgh, PA.

Bruckman, A., Edwards, E., Elliott, J., & Jensen, C. (2000, June). *Uneven Achievement in a Constructionist Learning Environment.* Paper presented at the International Conference on the Learning Sciences, Ann Arbor, MI.

Colley, A., M., Gale, M., T., & Harris, T., A. (1994) "Effects of Gender Role Identity and Experience on Computer Attitude Components." *Journal of Educational Computing Research 10*(2), 129-137.

Giacquinta, J. B., Bauer. J., A., & Levin, J., E. (1993). "Beyond Technology's Promise." Cambridge England: Cambridge University Press.

Kersteen, Z., A., Linn, M., C., Clancy, M., & Hardyck, C. (1988) "Previous Experience And The Learning of Computer Programming: The Computer Helps Those Who Help Themselves." *Journal of Educational Computing Research 4*(3), 321-333.

Linn, M. C. (1985). "Fostering Equitable Consequences from Computer Learning Environments." *Sex Roles, 13*(3/4), 229-240.

Popper, K. (1971). *The Open Society and Its Enemies* (5th ed.). Princeton: Princeton University Press.

A Machine Learning Approach to Assessing Knowledge Sharing During Collaborative Learning Activities

Amy Soller, Janyce Wiebe, Alan Lesgold

University of Pittsburgh
Pittsburgh, PA 15260
soller@pitt.edu, wiebe@cs.pitt.edu, al@pitt.edu

ABSTRACT

Students bring to a collaborative learning situation a great deal of specialized knowledge and experiences that undoubtedly shape the collaboration and learning processes. How effectively this unique knowledge is shared and assimilated by the group affects both the process and the product of the collaboration. In this paper, we describe a machine learning approach, Hidden Markov Modeling, to analyzing and assessing on-line knowledge sharing conversations. We show that this approach can determine the effectiveness of knowledge sharing episodes with 93% accuracy, performing 43% over the baseline. Understanding how members of collaborative learning groups share, assimilate, and build knowledge together may help us identify situations in which facilitation may increase the effectiveness of the group interaction.

Keywords

Assessing collaborative learning, interaction analysis, knowledge sharing, dialog coding, machine learning

INTRODUCTION

A group of students gather around a table to solve a problem, and begin to exchange the knowledge each brings to bear on the problem. Each group member brings to the table a unique pool of knowledge, grounded in his or her individual experiences. The combination of these experiences, and the group members' personalities and behaviors will determine how the collaboration proceeds, and whether or not the group members will effectively learn from and with each other (Brown and Palincsar, 1989; Dillenbourg, 1999; Webb & Palincsar, 1996).

If we take a closer look at the interaction in this group, we might see that the way in which a student shares new knowledge with the group, and the way in which the group responds, determines to a large extent how well this new knowledge is assimilated into the group, and whether or not the group members learn the new concept. It is reasonable to assume that, in effective knowledge sharing conversation, the presentation (sharing) of new concepts and ideas would initiate questioning, explaining, and critical discussion. Studying the interaction that provokes and follows knowledge sharing events may help us assess the ability of the group to assimilate new information that group members naturally bring to bear on the problem.

In this paper, we describe a machine learning approach, Hidden Markov Modeling, to identifying, analyzing, and assessing on-line knowledge sharing conversations. We begin by discussing work related to analyzing knowledge sharing conversations, and then describe how Hidden Markov Modeling was used to assess these conversations. The fourth section reports on the results of an experiment in which this technique was successfully used to classify instances of effective and ineffective knowledge sharing interaction. We conclude by discussing the implications of this research, and pointing to a few open-ended questions.

KNOWLEDGE SHARING

We define a *knowledge sharing episode* as a series of conversational contributions (utterances) and actions (e.g. on a shared workspace) that begins when one group member introduces new knowledge into the group conversation, and ends when discussion of the new knowledge ceases. New knowledge is defined as knowledge that is unknown to at least one group member other than the knowledge sharer. In general, analyzing knowledge sharing episodes involves the following three steps:

1. Determining which student played the role of knowledge sharer, and which the role(s) of receiver
2. Analyzing how well the knowledge sharer explained the new knowledge
3. Observing and evaluating how the knowledge receivers assimilated the new knowledge

The use of Hidden Markov Models to accomplish step (1) above is described in (Soller and Lesgold, in press). In this paper, we describe their application to steps (2) and (3). Studying the effectiveness of knowledge sharing involved collecting sequences of interaction in which students shared new knowledge with their peers, and relating these sequences to the group members' performance on pre and post tests. The tests targeted the specific knowledge elements we expected the students to share and learn during the experiment. To ensure that high-quality knowledge sharing opportunities exist, each group member was provided with a unique piece of knowledge that the team needed to solve the problem. This *knowledge element* was designed to mirror the sort of unique knowledge that students might naturally bring to the problem from their own experiences. By artificially constructing situations in which students are expected to share knowledge, we single out interesting episodes to study, and more concretely define situations that can be compared and assessed.

In order for a knowledge element to be shared "effectively", three requirements must be satisfied (F. Linton, personal communication, May 8, 2001):

the individual sharing the new knowledge (the "sharer") must show that she understands it by correctly answering the corresponding pre and post test questions

the concept must come up during the conversation, and

at least one group member who did not know the concept before the collaborative session started (as shown by his pre-test) must show that he learned it during the session by correctly answering the corresponding post-test question.

In this paper, we focus on situations in which criteria (1) and (2) are satisfied, since these criteria are necessary for studying how new knowledge is assimilated by collaborative learning groups. Other research has addressed how students acquire new knowledge (criteria 1, Gott & Lesgold, 2000), and how to motivate students to share their ideas (criteria 2, Webb & Palincsar, 1996).

Experiments designed to study how new knowledge is assimilated by group members are not new to social psychologists. *Hidden Profile* studies (Lavery, Franz, Winquist, and Larson, 1999; Mennecke, 1997), designed to evaluate the effect of knowledge sharing on group performance, require that the knowledge needed to perform the task be divided among group members such that each member's knowledge is incomplete before the group session begins. The group task is designed such that it cannot be successfully completed until all members share their unique knowledge. Group performance is typically measured by counting the number of individual knowledge elements that surface during group discussion, and evaluating the group's solution, which is dependent on these elements.

Surprisingly, studying the process of knowledge sharing has been much more difficult than one might imagine. Stasser (1999) and Lavery et al. (1999) have consistently shown that group members are not likely to discover their teammates' hidden profiles. They explain that group members tend to focus on discussing information that they share in common, and tend not to share and discuss information they uniquely possess. Moreover, it has been shown that when group members do share information, the quality of the group decision does not improve (Lavery et al., 1999; Mennecke, 1997). There are several explanations for this. First, group members tend to rely on common knowledge for their final decisions, even though other knowledge may have surfaced during the conversation. Second, "if subjects do not cognitively process the information they surface, even groups that have superior information sharing performance will not make superior decisions (Mennecke, 1997)." Team members must be motivated to understand and apply the new knowledge.

At least one study (Winquist and Larson, 1998) confirms that the amount of unique information shared by group members is a significant predictor of the quality of the group decision. More research is necessary to determine exactly what factors influence effective group knowledge sharing. One important factor may be the complexity of the task. Mennecke (1997) and Lavery et al.'s (1999) tasks were straightforward, short-term tasks that subjects may have perceived as artificial. Tasks that require subjects to cognitively process the knowledge that their teammates bring to bear may reveal the importance of effective knowledge sharing in group activities. In the next section, we describe one such task.

EXPERIMENTAL METHOD

In our experiment, five groups of three were each asked to solve one Object-Oriented Analysis and Design problem using a specialized shared workspace, while communicating through a structured, sentence opener interface. The communication interface, shown on the bottom half of Figure 1, contains sets of sentence openers (e.g. "I think", "I agree because") organized in intuitive categories (such as Inform or Discuss). To contribute to the group conversation, a student first selects a sentence opener. The selected phrase appears in the text box below the group dialog window, where the student may type in the rest of the sentence. Each sentence opener is associated with a particular conversational intention, given by a subskill and attribute. For example, the opener, "I think" corresponds to the subskill (or category) "Inform", and the more specific attribute, "Suggest".

Sentence openers provide a natural way for users to identify the intention of their conversational contribution without fully understanding the significance of the underlying communicative acts (Baker & Lund, 1997, McManus & Aiken, 1995). The categories and corresponding phrases on the interface represent the conversation acts most often exhibited during collaborative learning and problem solving in a previous study (Soller et al, 2001). Further details about the functionality of the communication interface can be found at http://lesgold42.lrdc.pitt.edu/EPSILON/Epsilon_software.html.

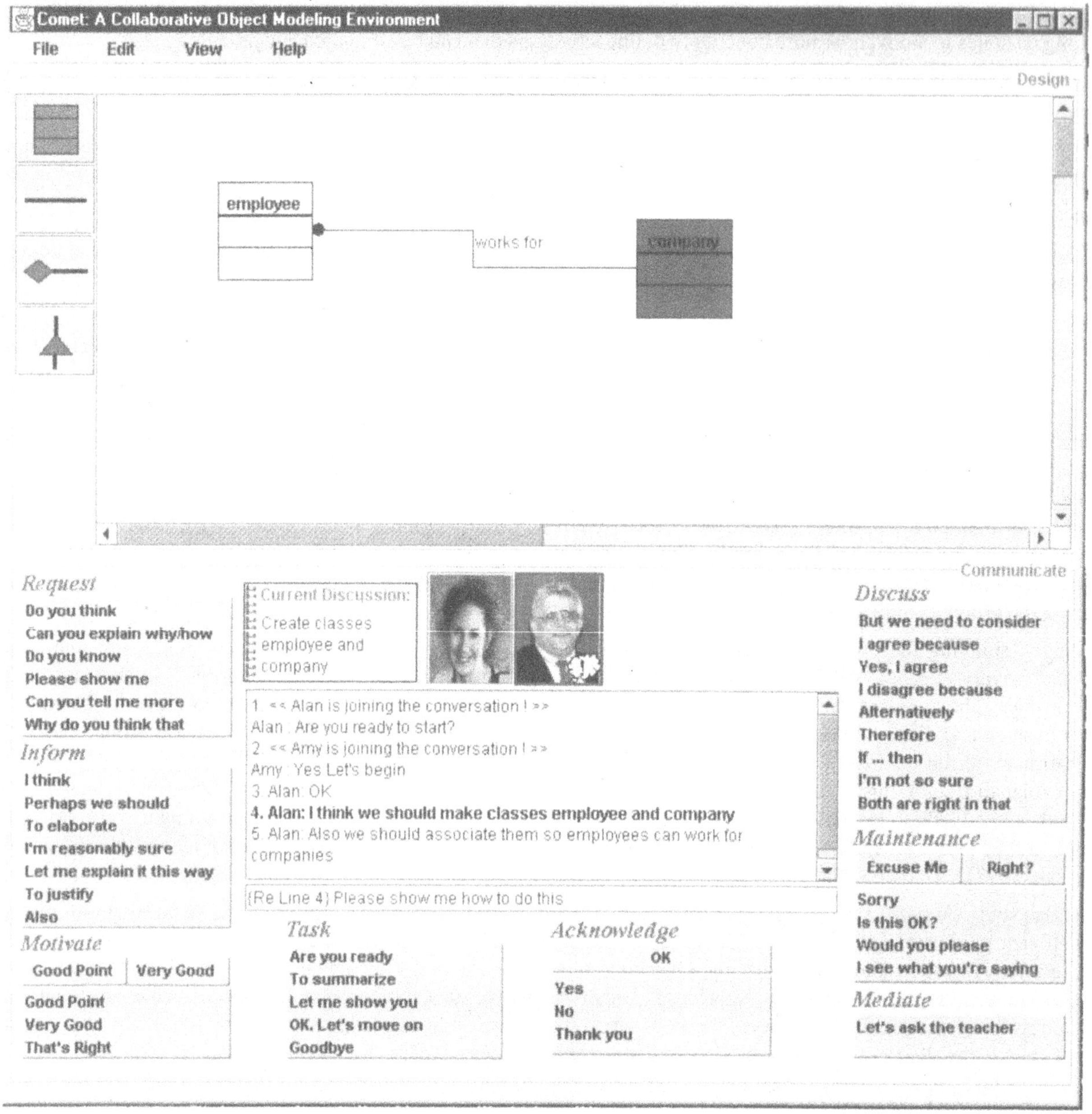

Figure 1. The shared OMT workspace (top), and sentence opener interface (bottom)

The specialized shared workspace is shown on the top half of Figure 1. The workspace allows students to collaboratively solve object-oriented design problems using Object Modeling Technique (OMT) (Rumbaugh, Blaha, Premerlani, Eddy, and Lorensen, 1991), an object-oriented analysis and design methodology. Software engineers use methodologies such as OMT to construct graphical models for optimizing their designs before implementation, and to communicate design decisions. These models are also useful for preparing documentation, or designing databases. Object-oriented analysis and design was chosen because it is an open-ended domain usually done in industry by teams of engineers with various expertise, so it is also an inherently collaborative domain. An example of an OMT design problem is shown below.

Exercise: Prepare a class diagram using the Object Modeling Technique (OMT) showing relationships among the following object classes: school, playground, classroom, book, cafeteria, desk, chair, ruler, student, teacher, door, swing. Show multiplicity balls in your diagram.

The shared OMT workspace provides a palette of buttons down the left-hand side of the window that students use to construct objects, and link objects in different ways depending on how they are related. Objects on the shared workspace can be selected, dragged, and modified, and changes are reflected on the workspaces of all group members.

Subjects. Five groups of three students each participated in the study. The subjects were undergraduates or first-year graduate students majoring in the physical sciences or engineering, none of which had prior knowledge of Object Modeling Technique. The subjects received pizza halfway through the four hour study, and were paid at the completion of the study.

Procedure. The five groups were run separately. The subjects in each group were asked to introduce themselves to their teammates by answering a few personal questions. Each experiment began with a half hour interactive lecture on OMT basic concepts and notation, during which the subjects practiced solving a realistic problem. The subjects then participated in a half hour hands-on software tutorial. During the tutorial, the subjects were introduced to all 36 sentence openers on the interface. The subjects were then assigned to separate rooms, received their individual knowledge elements, and took a pre-test. Individual knowledge elements addressed key OMT concepts, for example, "Attach attributes common to a group of subclasses to a superclass." Each knowledge element was explained on a separate sheet of paper with a worked-out example. The pre-test included one problem for each of the three knowledge elements. It was expected that the student given knowledge element #1 would get only pre-test question #1 right, the student given knowledge element #2 would get only pre-test question #2 right, and likewise for the third student. To ensure that each student understood his or her unique knowledge element, an experimenter reviewed the pre-test problem pertaining to the student's knowledge element before the group began the main exercise. Students who missed the pre-test problem on their knowledge element were asked to reread their knowledge element sheet and rework the missed pre-test problem, while explaining their work out loud (Chi et al., 1989).

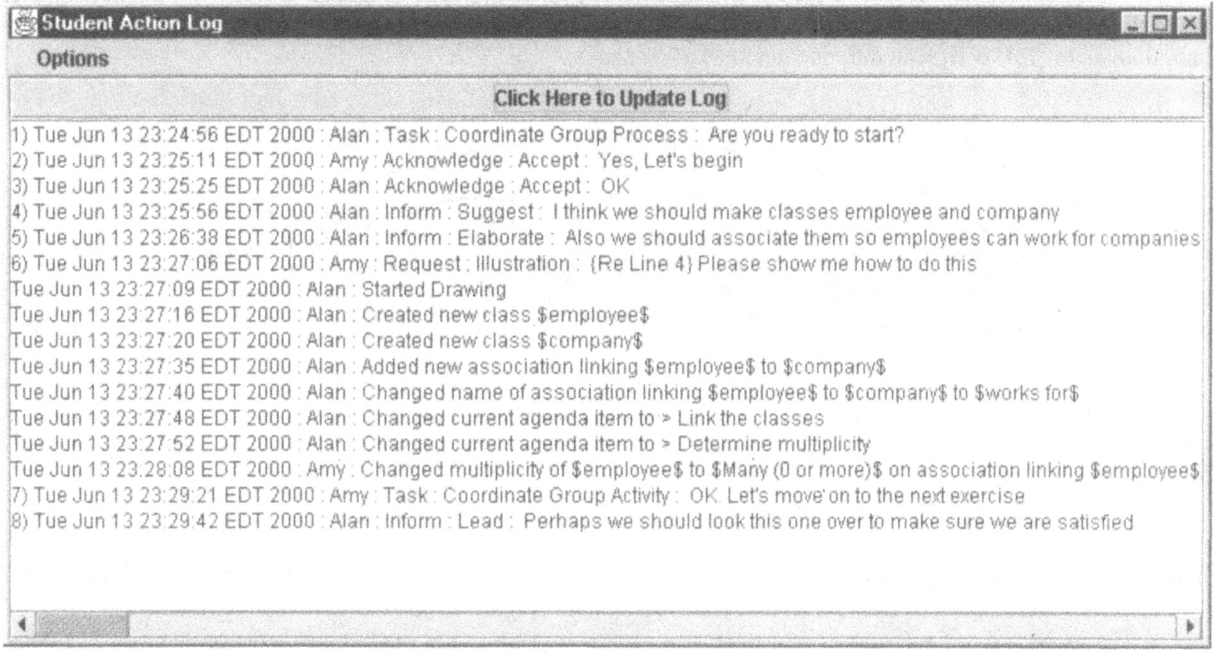

Figure 2. The student action log dynamically records all student actions and conversation

The subjects were not specifically told that they hold different knowledge elements, however they were reminded that their teammates may have different backgrounds and knowledge, and that sharing and explaining ideas, and listening to others' ideas is important in group learning. All groups completed the OMT exercise on-line within about an hour and fifteen minutes. During the on-line session, the software automatically logged the students' conversation and actions (see Figure 2). After the problem solving session, the subjects completed a post-test, and filled out a questionnaire. The post-test, like the pre-test, addressed the three knowledge elements. It was expected that the members of effective knowledge sharing groups would perform well on all post-test questions.

The next section describes the findings from this study, gives a brief introduction to the analysis method, Hidden Markov Models, and discusses how we used them to train a computer to recognize instances of effective and ineffective knowledge sharing.

RESULTS

Four of the five groups showed both instances of effective knowledge sharing and instances of ineffective knowledge sharing. Recall from the section on knowledge sharing that in order for a knowledge element to be effectively shared, three requirements must be satisfied: (1) the individual sharing the new knowledge (the "sharer") must show that she understands it by correctly answering the corresponding pre and post test questions, (2) the concept must come up during the conversation, and (3) at least one group member who did not know the concept before the collaborative session started (as shown by his pre-test) must show that he learned it during the session by correctly answering the corresponding post-test question (F. Linton, personal communication, May 8, 2001).

Since there were 15 subjects, there were a maximum of 30 possible opportunities for effective knowledge sharing: 2 opportunities for each student to learn the other 2 students' elements. Ten of these were effective (i.e. they met all 3 criteria), and two students did not meet criteria (1), eliminating 4 opportunities. We are now in the process of determining why the students did not take advantage of the other 16 opportunities.

The student action logs (e.g. Figure 2) from the five experiments were parsed by hand to extract the dialog segments in which the students shared their unique knowledge elements. Fourteen of these *knowledge sharing episodes* were identified, and tagged as either effective or ineffective (this process is described later in this section). These sequences do not directly correspond to the 30 opportunities in the previous paragraph, since one episode may result in 2 students learning, or one student may learn across several episodes. The knowledge sharing episodes were used to train a system to analyze and classify new instances of knowledge sharing. We now describe the training algorithm, and how it was applied.

A Brief Introduction to Hidden Markov Models

Hidden Markov Models (HMMs) were used to model the sequences of interaction present in the knowledge sharing episodes from the experiment. HMMs were chosen because of their flexibility in evaluating sequences of indefinite length, their ability to deal with a limited amount of training data, and their recent success in speech recognition tasks. We begin our introduction to HMMs with an introduction to Markov chains.

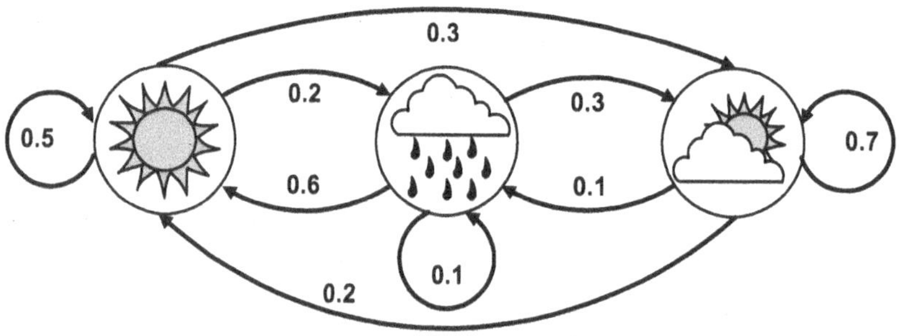

Figure 3. A Markov chain describing the probability of various weather patterns

Markov chains are essentially probabilistic finite state machines, used to model processes that move stochastically through a series of predefined states. For example, a model of the weather might include the states sunny, rainy, and overcast (see Figure 3). The probability of entering a rainy state after visiting a sunny state might be 0.2, the probability of entering an overcast state 0.3, and the probability of another sunny state 0.5. In other words, if today is sunny, there is a 20% chance that tomorrow will be rainy, a 30% chance that tomorrow will be overcast, and a 50% chance that it will be sunny again. In Markov chains, the arcs describe the probability of moving between states. The probability of a sequence of states is the product of the probabilities along the arcs. So, if today is sunny, then the probability that tomorrow will be rainy, and the next day overcast $(0.2)(0.3) = 0.06$.

Hidden Markov Models generalize Markov Chains in that they allow several different paths through the model to produce the same output. Consequently, it is not possible to determine the state the model is in simply by observing the output (it is "hidden"). Markov models observe the Markov assumption, which states that the probability of the next state is dependent *only* upon the previous state. This assumption seems limiting, however efficient algorithms have been developed that perform remarkably well on problems similar to that described here. Hidden Markov Models allow us to ask questions such as, "How well does a new (test) sequence match a given model?", or, "How can we optimize a model's parameters to best describe a given observation (training) sequence?" (Rabiner, 1989). Answering the first question involves computing the most likely path through the model for a given output sequence; this can be efficiently computed by the Viterbi (1967) algorithm. Answering the second question requires training an HMM given sets of example data. This involves estimating the (initially guessed) parameters of an arbitrary model repetitively, until the most likely parameters for the training examples are discovered. The explanation provided here should suffice for understanding the analysis in the next section. For further details on HMMs, see Rabiner (1989) or Charniak (1993).

Coding the Interaction

The fourteen knowledge sharing episodes varied in length from 5 to 62 contributions, and contained both conversational elements and action events. The top part of Figure 4 shows an example of one such sequence. The sentence openers, which indicate the system-coded subskills and attributes, are italicized. The bottom part of Figure 4 shows the actual sequence that is used to train the HMM to recognize similar knowledge sharing sequences.

Student	Subskill	Attribute	Actual Contribution (Not seen by HMM)
A	Request	Opinion	*Do you think* we need a discriminator for the car ownership
C	Discuss	Doubt	*I'm not so sure*
B	Request	Elaboration	*Can you tell me more* about what a discriminator is
C	Discuss	Agree	*Yes, I agree* because I myself am not so sure as to what its function is
A	Inform	Explain/Clarify	*Let me explain it this way* - A car can be owned by a person , a company or a bank. I think ownership type is the discrinator.
A	Maintenance	Apologize	*Sorry* I mean discriminator.

Actual HMM Training Sequence
A-Request-Opinion
C-Discuss-Doubt
B-Request-Elaboration
C-Discuss-Agree
A-Inform-Explain
A-Maintenance-Apologize
Sequence-Termination

Figure 4. An actual logged knowledge sharing episode (above), showing system coded subskills and attributes, and its corresponding HMM training sequence (below)

Some of the extracted sequences included actions that students took on the workspace. These actions were matched to a list of predetermined "productive" actions – those that were expected to lead students to a model solution. Productive actions were labeled as such, and included in the sequence with the name of the student who took the action (e.g. A-Productive-Action).

The system codes were obtained directly from the sentence openers that students choose to begin their contributions, and may not accurately reflect the intention of the contribution. For example, a student might choose the opener, "I think", and then add, "I disagree with you". Each sentence opener is associated with one subskill and attribute pair that most closely matches the expected use of the phrase; however even having gone through sentence opener training (described in the previous section), students may not always use the openers as expected. In order to determine to what degree the students used the openers as they were intended, 2 researchers recoded 3 of the 5 dialogs (selected at random). Tables 1 and 2 show the agreement between the 2 coders (A and B) and between each of the coders and the system, averaged over all 3 dialogs. As shown by the tables, agreement between the raters and the system was high for the subskill case, and reasonable for the attribute case (Carletta et al., 1997).

Table 1. Agreement statistics for subskill codes codes

Coder 1	Coder 2	% Agreement	κ
A	B	87.0	.85
A	System	90.1	.88
B	System	86.4	.84
Average of A & B	System	88.25	.86

Table 2. Agreement statistics for attribute

Coder 1	Coder 2	% Agreement	κ
A	B	71.2	.71
A	System	85.5	.73
B	System	71.5	.60
Average of A & B	System	78.49	.66

The next section describes the results of training Hidden Markov Models to assess the effectiveness of the 14 knowledge sharing episodes. This analysis was done using the system codes (those based on the sentence openers that the students selected), however similar results were obtained when the recoded dialogs were substituted as test sequences.

Assessing the Effectiveness of Knowledge Sharing Episodes

Two 6 state Hidden Markov Models were trained[1]. The first was trained using only sequences of effective knowledge sharing interaction (we call this the effective HMM), and the second using only sequences of ineffective knowledge sharing (the ineffective HMM). Testing the models involved running a new knowledge sharing sequence – one that is not used for training – through both models. The output from the effective HMM described the probability that the new test sequence is effective, and the output from the ineffective HMM described the probability that the new test sequence is ineffective. The test sequence was then classified as effective if has a higher path probability through the effective HMM, or ineffective if its path probability through the ineffective HMM was higher. Since the probabilities in these models can be quite small, we usually take the log of the path probability, which results in a negative number. The largest path probability is then given by the smallest absolute value.

Since HMMs "learn" by generalizing sets of examples, training the HMMs to model effective and ineffective knowledge sharing meant collecting sequences of interaction indicative of effective and ineffective interaction. The transcripts from the experiment described earlier were parsed, and 14 situations were identified in which the students discussed the unique knowledge elements each learned before the problem solving session began. These 14 sequences were tagged as being either effective or ineffective. A sequence is considered effective if at least one of the students receiving the new knowledge did not know it before the session (as shown by his pre-test) and demonstrated that he learned it during the session (as shown by his post-test). Recall that the pre and post tests directly target the three knowledge elements that the students are expected to share during the group problem solving session (see section entitled, "Experimental Method"). A sequence is considered ineffective if a knowledge element was discussed during the episode, but none of the receiving students demonstrated mastery of the concept on the post test.

Of the 14 knowledge sharing sequences identified, 7 were found to be effective and 7 were found to be ineffective. Because of the small dataset, we used a 14-fold cross validation approach, in which we tested each of the 14 examples against the other 13 examples (as training sets), and averaged the results. Figure 5 shows the path probabilities of each test sequence through both the effective and ineffective HMMs. The y-value shows the log of the Viterbi path probability (Rabiner, 1989). This value is highly dependent on the length of the test sequence (longer sequences will produce smaller probabilities), and so will vary for each sequence. Notice that the path probabilities of the 7 effective test sequences (labeled E1 through E7) were higher through the effective HMM, and the path probabilities for 6 of the 7 ineffective test sequences (labeled I8 through I14) were higher through the ineffective HMM, resulting in an overall 92.9% accuracy. The baseline comparison is chance, or 50%, since there is a 1/2 chance of arbitrarily classifying a given test sequence as effective or ineffective. The HMM approach successfully performed at almost 43% above the baseline.

[1] Before choosing the 6 node HMM, we experimented with 3, 4, and 5 node HMMs, obtaining similar (but not optimal) results. Performance seemed to decline with 7 or more states.

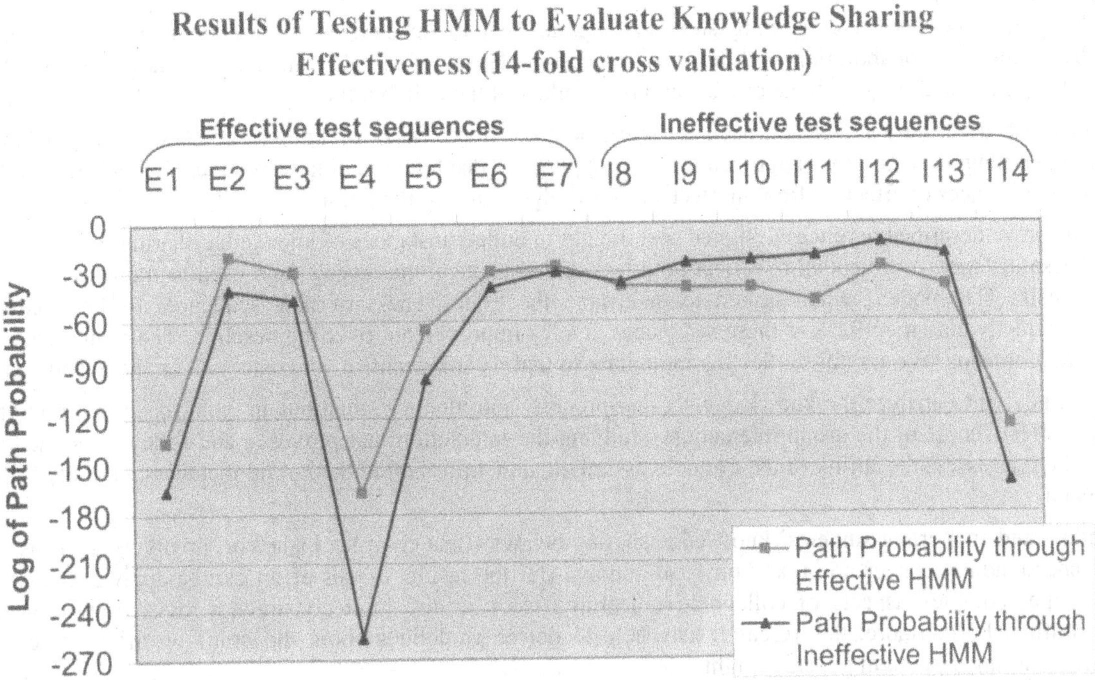

Figure 5. Viterbi path probabilities of each test sequence through both the effective and ineffective HMMs

The analysis in this section shows that artificial intelligence models of collaborative interaction may be useful for identifying when students are effectively sharing the new knowledge they bring to bear on the problem. Once we have discovered a situation in which students are not effectively interacting, we can formulate hypotheses about the various facilitation methods that might help the students collaborate more effectively.

DISCUSSION AND FUTURE WORK

Determining from a sequence of coded interaction, such as that shown in Figure 4, how well new knowledge is assimilated by the group is a very difficult task. Other researchers have explored a number of different methods, including finite state machines (McManus & Aiken, 1995), fuzzy inferencing (Barros & Verdejo, 1999), decision trees (Constantino-Gonzalez & Suthers, 2000; Goodman, Hitzeman, Linton, & Ross, 2001), rule learning (Katz, Aronis, & Creitz, 1999), and plan recognition (Muehlenbrock & Hoppe, 1999), for analyzing collaborative learning interaction (see Jermann, Soller, and Muehlenbrock, 2001, for a review of different approaches). Why does the HMM approach work so well? The models are trained to represent the possible ways that a student might share new knowledge with his teammates, and the possible ways that his teammates might react. The HMM, in this case, is therefore a sort of compiled conversational model. This means that, for example, the effective model includes a compilation of the conversational patterns students use when knowledge is effectively built by the group members. Our next step is to take a closer look at the differences between the effective and ineffective sequences in order understand the qualitative differences. For example, we might expect to see more questioning and critical discussion in effective knowledge sharing episodes, and more acknowledgement in less effective episodes (Soller, 2001).

The long-term goal of this project is to support learning groups on-line by mediating situations in which new knowledge is not effectively assimilated by the group. Understanding *why* a knowledge sharing episode is ineffective is critical to selecting a proper mediation strategy. A knowledge sharer may need help in formulating sufficiently elaborated explanations using, for example, analogies or multiple representations. Or, a knowledge receiver may need encouragement to speak up and articulate why he does not understand a new knowledge element. Research is now underway to develop a generalized model of ineffective knowledge sharing that includes models in which new knowledge is not effectively conveyed by the sharer, and models in which new knowledge is not effectively assimilated by the receivers. A system that can differentiate between these cases may be able to better recommend strategies for supporting the process of knowledge sharing during collaborative learning activities.

CONCLUSION

Students bring to a collaborative learning situation a great deal of specialized knowledge and experiences that will undoubtedly shape the collaboration and learning processes. How effectively this unique knowledge is shared and assimilated by the group affects both the process and the product of the collaboration.

In this paper, we describe a novel approach to assessing the effectiveness of knowledge sharing conversation during collaborative learning activities. Our approach involves applying a machine learning technique, Hidden Markov Modeling, to differentiate instances of effective from ineffective knowledge sharing interaction.

The experiment we described here was designed specifically to collect instances of knowledge sharing during collaborative learning. These instances were coded to reflect both task and conversational events, and used to train two 6 state Hidden Markov Models. The models, when tasked to determine the effectiveness of new sequences of knowledge sharing interaction, correctly classified 92% of these sequences, a 42% improvement over the baseline. The preliminary results of this study are promising. We are now collecting more data so that we may confirm and elaborate on these findings

Our research goal is to analyze the knowledge sharing process, and identify situations in which facilitation might help to increase the effectiveness of the group interaction. Studying the interaction that provokes and follows knowledge sharing events may help us assess the ability of the group to assimilate new information that group members naturally bring to bear on the problem.

Understanding and supporting students' knowledge sharing behavior is a complex endeavor, involving analysis of student learning, understanding, conversation, and physical actions. But the results of this effort can be applied to analyzing and supporting other complex aspects of collaborative learning, such as the joint construction of shared knowledge, and cognitive conflict. Furthermore, this research may help to define guidelines about the limits on the kinds of support a collaborative learning system, in general, might offer.

ACKNOWLEDGEMENTS

The Kappa statistics presented here would not have been possible without the partnership and dedication of Tricia Chirumbole. Thanks also to Kwang-Su Cho and Patrick Jermann for helping to run the experiment, and for their suggestions and insights. This research was supported by the U.S Department of Education, grant R303A980192, and an Andrew Mellon Predoctoral Fellowship.

REFERENCES

Baker, M., and Lund, K. (1997). Promoting reflective interactions in a computer-supported collaborative learning environment. *Journal of Computer Assisted Learning*, 13, 175-193.

Barros, B., and Verdejo, M.F. (1999). An approach to analyse collaboration when shared structured workspaces are used for carrying out group learning processes. *Proceedings of the Ninth International Conference on Artificial Intelligence in Education*, 449-456.

Brown, A. and Palincsar, A. (1989). Guided, cooperative learning and individual knowledge acquisition. In L. Resnick (Ed.), *Knowledge, Learning and Instruction* (pp. 307-336), Lawrence Erlbaum Associates.

Carletta, J., Isard, A., Isard, S., Kowtko, J., Doherty-Sneddon, G., and Anderson, A. (1997). The reliability of a dialogue structure coding scheme. *Computational Linguistics*, 23, 13-32.

Charniak, E. (1993). *Statistical Language Learning*. Cambridge, MA: MIT Press.

Chi, M. T. H., Bassok, M., Lewis, M. W., Reinmann, P., and Glaser, R. (1989). Self-Explanations: How students study and use examples in learning to solve problems. *Cognitive Science*, 13, 145-182.

Constantino-Gonzalez, M., and Suthers, D. (2000). A coached collaborative learning environment for Entity-Relationship modeling. *Proceedings of the 5th International Conference on Intelligent Tutoring Systems*, Montreal, Canada, 324-333.

Dillenbourg, P. (1999). What do you mean by "Collaborative Learning". In P. Dillenbourg (Ed.) *Collaborative Learning: Cognitive and Computational Approaches* (pp.1-19). Amsterdam: Elsevier Science.

Goodman, B., Hitzeman, J., Linton, F., and Ross, H. (2001). Intelligent agents for collaborative learning: Predicting the roles of dialogue participants. Manuscript in preparation.

Gott, S., and Lesgold, A. (2000). Competence in the workplace: How cognitive performance models and situated instruction can accelerate skill acquisition. In R. Glaser (Ed.) *Advances in Instructional Psychology: Vol. 5. Educational Design and Cognitive Science* (pp. 239-327). Mahwah, NJ: Lawrence Erlbaum Associates.

Jermann, P., Soller, A., & Muehlenbrock, M. (2001). From mirroring to guiding: A review of state of the art technology for supporting collaborative learning. *Proceedings of the First European Conference on Computer-Supported Collaborative Learning*, Maastricht, The Netherlands, 324-331.

Katz, S., Aronis, J., and Creitz, C. (1999). Modelling pedagogical interactions with machine learning. *Proceedings of the Ninth International Conference on Artificial Intelligence in Education*, LeMans, France, 543-550.

Lavery, T., Franz, T., Winquist, J., Larson, J. (1999). The role of information exchange in predicting group accuracy on a multiple judgment task. *Basic and Applied Social Psychology*, 2(4), 281-289.

McManus, M. and Aiken, R. (1995). Monitoring computer-based problem solving. *Journal of Artificial Intelligence in Education*, 6(4), 307-336.

Mennecke, B. (1997). Using group support systems to discover hidden profiles: An examination of the influence of group size and meeting structures on information sharing and decision quality. *International Journal of Human-Computer Studies*, 47, 387-405.

Muehlenbrock, M., and Hoppe, U. (1999). Computer-supported interaction analysis of group problem solving. *Proceedings of the Third International Conference on Computer Support for Collaborative Learning (CSCL '99)*, Stanford, California, 398-405.

Rumbaugh, J., Blaha, M., Premerlani, W., Eddy, F., and Lorensen, W. (1991). *Object-Oriented modeling and design.* Englewood Cliffs, NJ: Prentice Hall.

Rabiner, L. (1989). A tutorial on Hidden Markov Models and selected applications in speech recognition. *Proceedings of the IEEE*, 77(2), 257-286.

Soller, A. (2001) Supporting social interaction in an intelligent collaborative learning system. *International Journal of Artificial Intelligence in Education*, 12, in press.

Soller, A., and Lesgold, A. (in press). Modeling the process of knowledge sharing. In U. Hoppe & M. Ikeda (Eds.) *New Technologies for Collaborative Learning.* Kluwer Academic Publishers.

Stasser, G. (1999). The uncertain role of unshared information in collective choice. In L. Thompson, J. Levine, and D. Messick (Eds.) *Shared Knowledge in Organizations* (pp 49-69). Hillsdale, NJ: Erlbaum.

Viterbi, A. (1967). Error bounds for convolutional codes and an asymptotically optimal decoding algorithm. *IEEE Transactions on Information Theory*, 13, 260-269.

Webb, N., & Palincsar, A. S. (1996). Group processes in the classroom. In D. Berlmer & R. Calfee (Eds.), *Handbook of Educational Psychology* (pp. 841-873). New York: Simon & Schuster Macmillan.

Emergent Leadership in Small Groups Using Computer-Mediated Communication

Ryoko Yamaguchi, Nathan Bos, Judy Olson
University of Michigan
{ryokoy, serp, jsolson} @umich.edu

ABSTRACT

When small groups meet online, the communication channel they use may affect the emergent leadership styles that individuals attempt. We studied 66 three-person groups playing a social dilemma game and communicating via one of four channels: face-to-face, videoconference, audio conference, or Internet chatroom. We found that the narrower the channel, the less likely groups were to use relationship-focused leadership styles. We also found that for mixed-gender groups, lower levels of relationship-focused leadership led to poorer group performance on the cooperation task. The more autocratic task-focused leadership style was not inhibited by communication channel. Additional results are also given linking gender composition to choice of leadership style. The statistical technique used in this research, Hierarchical Linear Modeling is particularly useful for studying group work, and so is explained in some detail.

Keywords Computer-mediated communications, CMC, emergent leadership, collaborative learning, small group work, trust, social dilemma

In the future, it may be common for virtual teams of learners to work together at a distance, and interact exclusively using computer-mediated communications (CMC). This will happen increasingly as distance education, commuter-friendly education, inter-school collaborations, and various other forms of e-learning are explored. Research on computer-supported collaborative learning has identified effective models for using CMC in conjunction with face-to-face classroom interaction (Koschmann, 1996; Hewitt, Scardamalia & Bereiter, 1997). However, new challenges may arise when groups rely on CMC for all communications.

Small groups are very often asked to take on ambiguous tasks without any pre-assigned roles, with often no designated group leader. This is true in both educational and workplace settings (Hackman, 1987). These groups are more effective when leadership functions are performed by one or more members-- that is, when they experience emergent leadership (Morris & Hackman, 1969; Borg, 1957; Bormann, 1990).

Emergent leadership can take several forms. For example, a single dominant individual can emerge to take over the group process. Or, groups can take on a more democratic character, with equitable contribution of ideas and consensus-building processes. Leadership is accomplished in either of these cases, but the styles are quite different. One often-used way of characterizing emergent leadership styles is to contrast 'task-focused' and 'relationship-focused' leadership (Fiedler, 1967; Stodgill and Coons, 1957). Briefly, task-focused leadership refers to focusing exclusively on the task at hand, while relationship-related leadership refers to improving group cohesion. Task-focused leadership is often associated with dominance behavior, such as initiating structure, while relationship-focused leadership is associated with affiliative behavior, such as democratic decision-making (Fiedler, 1967).

Previous research shows that students, even at a young age, may prefer a relationship-focused leadership style. French and Stright (1991) studied fourth and sixth graders engaging in a group picture-rating task. Although one might expect such young students to confuse dominance with leadership, in fact, the behaviors most associated with peer- and teacher-reported leadership were soliciting opinions from others, facilitating the task, and recording outcomes. Level of participation was only weakly correlated with leadership, showing that even young students can distinguish between what we would call task-focused leadership (dominance) and relationship-focused leadership.

The two types of leadership are highly gendered (Eagly & Karau, 1991; Karau & Eagly, 1999; Kolb, 1999). Males tend to emerge as task-focused leaders, while women tend more toward relationship-focused leadership (Eagly & Karau, 1991; Karau & Eagly, 1999). To complicate matters, researchers have found that it may not gender per se, but gender group composition that influences emergent leadership. Specifically, male-majority groups show more task-focused behaviors while female-majority groups show more social and communal behaviors (Berdahl, 1996, 1998).

Regardless of the style, some form of emergent leadership may be necessary for small group effectiveness (Borg, 1957; Hardy, 1971, 1972, 1976; Pryer, Flint, & Bass, 1962). One foundational study by Borg (1957) found that teams of Air Force officer candidates, working on situational problems such as escaping from a simulated prison compound, performed better when a leader emerge. Similarly, Bormann (1990) found that the emergence of leadership improved undergraduate discussion groups.

In online settings, there may be an even greater need for emergent leadership. Jarvenpaa's 1998 study of international project teams documents both difficulties and success stories, and leadership functions were strongly associated with success. In this study, 29 teams of 4-6 undergraduates were grouped together in such a way that no two students were from the same country. They were assigned to complete an online research project using only email and some chat sessions for group coordination. Based on case studies of high and low-performing groups, Jarvenpaa identified leadership as an important characteristic of the successful groups. These leaders were sometimes single members and sometimes multiple members, but they tended to share these characteristics: leaders took initiative early on in the task, leaders maintained a positive outlook, and group members could count on receiving timely and predictable responses to communications from group leaders. The less-successful groups, in contrast, had no leadership or negative (complaining) leadership, lack of individual initiative, and unpredictable communications between members. Email records from these less-successful efforts portray directionless groups where email questions go unanswered, important process questions are never addressed, and other leadership functions are unfulfilled.

Given the considerable challenges associated with managing group work online, research is needed on how emergent leadership functions tend to occur in different telecommunications conditions. Beyond purely descriptive work, research is needed on what management strategies or teaching interventions are likely to be effective in virtual teams. The study reported here compares emergent leadership in four communication conditions, differentiates between relationship-focused and task-focused leadership styles, and identifies characteristics that may lead to success in these new settings.

RESEARCH QUESTIONS

Our data supports examination of these three questions:

Research Question 1: How do communication media influence emergent leadership?

Research Question 2: How does group gender composition influence emergent leadership?

Research Questions 3: How does emergent leadership influence cooperation in group work?

METHODS

Experimental task

Sixty-six groups of three volunteers played an online social dilemma game called 'Daytrader'. These groups were allowed to discuss the ongoing game periodically using one of four communication conditions: face-to-face meeting, a high-quality videoconference, a standard phone conference, and an Internet chatroom.

The Daytrader game is a social dilemma devised for this research, adapted from previous research by Rocco (1998). Social dilemmas are useful for studying cooperation and trust-building in groups. In Daytrader, participants must decide every round how to divide a 30 token investment between individual and group investment. Giving to the group investment pays a higher overall rate (3x), but entails some risk, because it is dependent on the actions of others. The proceeds of the group investment are divided equally among participants, so that individuals who contribute to the group risk being exploited by those who contribute little or nothing. The alternative to investing with the group is investing as an individual, which pays a guaranteed lower rate (2x) that is not dependent on others. Maximum cooperation (and maximum payoff) are achieved when all three participants contribute all of their funds to the group. Groups differ on whether, and how quickly they are able to reach the maximum cooperation level. The differences in group payoff are therefore a good measure of cooperation, and correlate highly with post-test measures of trust in group members.

As reported in a previous paper (Bos, Gergle, Olson, & Olson, 2001), the communication media does affect groups' cooperation and self-reported trust. Face-to-face groups were the most cooperative, followed by video, audio, and text chat. The three technology mediated conditions all showed slower-developing trust and more frequent opportunistic betrayals among group members.

As part of the experimental post-test, participants reported on their own emergent leadership behavior during group discussions. This data provides a context for studying how emergent leadership arises across the four communications conditions, and examining whether leadership style had an effect on group performance.

Participants

Participants were 197 people recruited through a paid subject list at a large university in the Midwest. There were 49% female participants and the mean age was 23.

Group Gender Composition

Participants were randomly assigned to the following gender group composition: female only (11%), majority female (39%), male only (15%), and majority male (35%).

Group Condition

Groups were randomly assigned to one of the following communication mediums: face-to-face (24%), video conferencing (26%), audio conferencing (26%), and chat (24%).

Measures

The leadership scales, task and relationship-focused leadership, were adapted from Stogdill's Leadership Behavior Descriptor Questionnaire (Stogdill, 1948, 1969; Stogdill & Coons, 1957). One scale measured task-focused leadership (5-item scale, alpha=.84) with items such as "I took charge of what the group should do during the game" and "I gave directions to the other players on how we should play the game." Relationship-focused leadership items focused on individuals' actions promoting group cohesion (4-item scale, alpha=.87) with items including "In the discussions I suggested how we could all work together" and "I made sure that everyone in my group was listening to one another." These items measured subjects' self-perceptions of leadership behaviors. Self-perceptions are used because they best measure the intentions of the actors, rather than observable behaviors or external impressions. Future analysis of this data will examine the degree to which these intentions resulted in observable leadership behaviors.

Cooperation is measured by looking at the total group payoff in the Daytrader game, after discarding the first five rounds before any communication occurred. The more quickly and consistently groups cooperated in the game, the higher the total group payoffs. This measure was used in other research on this data, and correlates highly with self-reports of trust within the group.

Analysis

Because the data for this study has multiple levels (student and group level), hierarchical linear modeling (HLM) is used to answer how emergent leadership is associated with communication media, gender group composition, and cooperation. HLM is a statistical (maximum likelihood) procedure that was developed by Bryk and Raudenbush (1992) to address the unit of analysis problem in multi-level analysis. HLM is a series of regression-like equations that takes into account the interdependence, or nestedness, of the data (Bryk & Raudenbush, 1992; Pollack, 1998).

HLM is a good statistical technique for analyzing small group data because this data is 'nested'—that is, data from individual participants cannot be considered independent of all others, but rather are partly dependent on their small groups. One other way that such group data is sometimes handled is by using only group averages, but this discards much useful information. HLM makes it possible to analyze all the data at hand.

RESULTS

Task-focused Leadership

There were no significant differences in task-focused leadership across the communication mediums. In gender group composition, female-only groups had lower levels of task-focused leadership, as compared to male-only groups (β =-0.696, $\underline{t}$ = -3.713, $\underline{p}$<.001).

Effects of Task-focused Leadership on Cooperation

While task-focused leadership was not directly related to cooperation, it improved cooperation in certain communication mediums. Specifically, in the audio condition, task-focused leadership positively influenced cooperation (β =34.015, $\underline{t}$ = 2.058, $\underline{p}$<.05) (See Figure 1).

Figure 1: Task-Focused Leadership in the Audio Condition

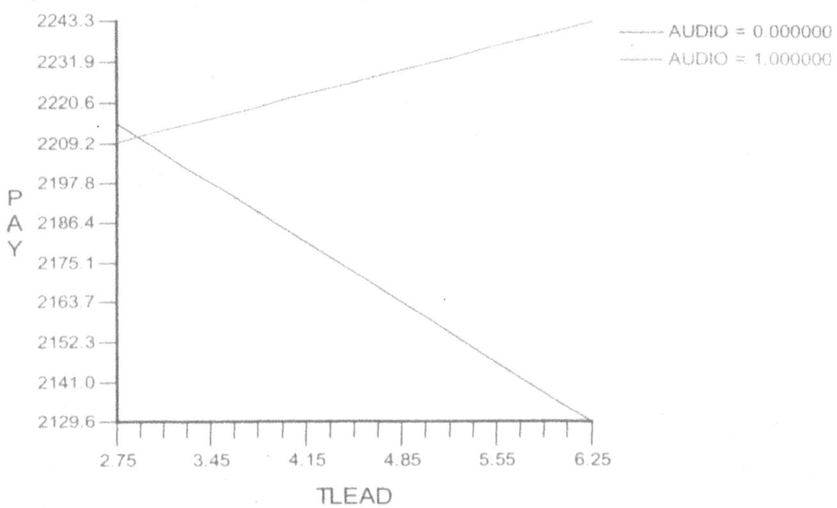

Relationship-focused Leadership

There were significant differences in relationship-focused leadership across communication media and gender group composition. In communication mediums, the chat condition had the lowest levels of relationship-focused leadership (β =-

0.530, t =-2.715, p<.01). The β value for relationship-focused leadership was -.453 (t = -2.567, p<.05) in the audio condition, and -.344 (t = -1.924, p<.10) in the video condition. Hence, perceptions of relationship-focused leadership became progressively lower as the communication medium went from fuller to narrower.

In group gender composition, female-majority groups had lower relationship-focused leadership (β = -.42, t= -2.10, p<.05), and were even lower in female-only groups (β = -.51, t= -1.91, p<.10).

Effects of Relationship-focused Leadership on Cooperation

While relationship-focused leadership was not directly related to cooperation, it had significant effects in cooperation depending on the gender group composition and the communication medium. Specifically, in female-majority groups, relationship-focused leadership was positively related to cooperation (β = 91.548, t = 2.733, p<.05). In male-majority groups, relationship-focused leadership was also positively related to cooperation (β =67.514, t = 1.784, p<.10).

In the communication medium, relationship-focused leadership negatively influenced cooperation in the chat condition (β =-131.909, t = -3.152, p<.01) (See Figure 2).

Figure 2: Relationship-focused Leadership in the Chat Condition as compared to other conditions

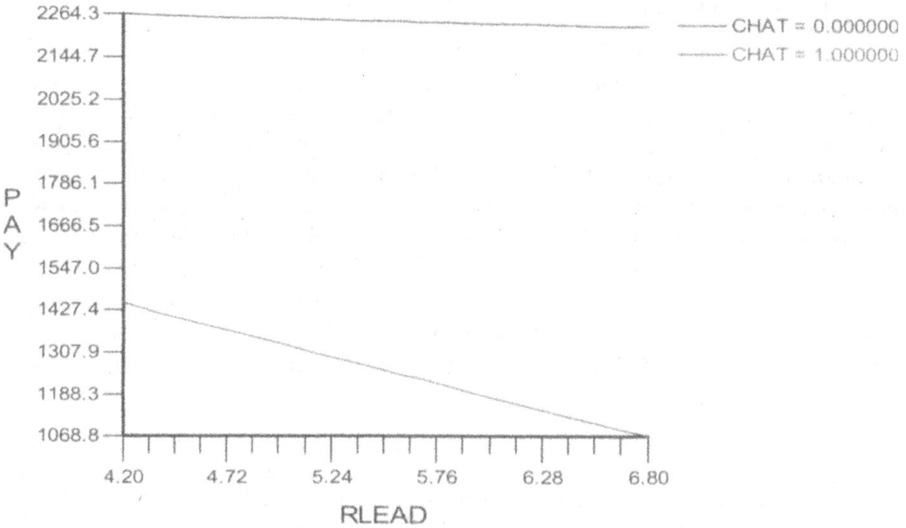

DISCUSSION

How does communication medium influence emergent leadership?

Task-focused leadership did not change much across the different communications conditions. Apparently, narrowed communication channels did not hinder this kind of emergent leadership. Relationship-focused leadership was affected by media, however. Levels of relationship-focused leadership were progressively lower as the communication channel narrowed from face-to-face to video, to audio, and to on-line chat. As was previously found with trust, (Bos, et. al. 2001), it seems that this leadership style is inhibited by mediated channels. Why might this be? It could be that participants attempted relationship-focused strategies but found them to be less effective in mediated conditions, and therefore abandoned them early in the task. Or, it could be that because of the feeling of social distance afforded by this technology (Siegel, Dubrovsky, Kiesler, and McGuire, 1986) participants did not even attempt to build up a sense of group cohesion. In either case, this presents an interesting challenge for computer-supported group work settings where instructors would like to foster relationship focused leadership skills.

How does group gender composition influence emergent leadership?

Female-only groups had lower levels of both task-focused and relationship-focused leadership, and female-majority groups also had lower levels of relationship-focused leadership. The first part of this finding (lower task-focused leadership) is consistent with past research on gender differences in emergent leadership. Female-majority groups usually report less task-focused leadership than male-majority groups (Karau & Eagly, 1999; Kolb, 1999). But the second part of this finding, that female-majority and all-female groups showed lower relationship-focused leadership, is unexpected and harder to interpret within our theoretical framework. Female-majority groups did not have lower overall cooperation levels, so if there was less leadership it did greatly inhibit overall team performance. Perhaps the combination of a distancing media and a competitive task dissuaded female-majority groups from using what would have been their preferred leadership styles.

This finding is especially interesting in light of research which shows that female students are less inhibited in computer-mediated conversations and participate on a more equal footing males (Hsi & Hoadley, 1997). Could it be that the same technology which encourages individual female students to speak up also tends to inhibit female-majority groups from forming strong group relationships?

There is one other possible interpretation. Perhaps women only rated their relationship-focused strategies as lower because the measures used were self-reports, and women have a tendency to under-rate themselves in leadership (Owen, 1986). Analyses of the conversation transcripts currently underway should help decide which of the above interpretations is more accurate.

How does emergent leadership influence cooperation in group work?

Was emergent leadership necessary for effective small group interaction in these experiments? In the Daytrader game, there were no overall effects on cooperation success from either leadership style. But there were some interactions with media and gender composition, indicating that emergent leadership did affect success for some types of small groups.

Relationship-focused leadership seemed to benefit both sets of the mixed-gender groups, female-majority and male majority, but failed to have significant impact in the female-only or male-only groups. This could mean that when groups are mixed-gender, there is a greater need for these groups to create and maintain positive group relationships, and greater harm to cooperation if there is no relationship-focused leadership.

Looking at communication conditions, we found that relationship-focused leadership seemed to harm the performance in one media channel, the chat condition. We had already reported that chat led to less relationship-focused leadership; this new finding goes even further, saying that when relationship-focused strategies were attempted in chat they actually backfired, resulting in slightly worse cooperation. There is one alternate explanation, which is that relationship-focused strategies were only attempted after other attempts to cooperate had already failed, and thus were only used when group cooperation was already well below average. Obviously the implications of these two interpretations are very different—one argues that relationship-focused leadership should not even be attempted via text chat, while the other is not prescriptive. The first interpretation seems less consistent with other research, which has found relationship-focused leadership to be beneficial or, at worst, a neutral influence. It is also inconsistent with previous research on chat (Zheng, Bos, Olson and Olson, 2001) which shows that trust can be built via chat communication. The issue of when chat groups attempted relationship-building (before or after cooperation had gone sour) may be settled by further discourse analysis of the current data.

As for task-focused leadership, it was significantly related to cooperation only in the audio condition. Specifically, task-focused leadership improved cooperation in the audio condition. This may indicate that because audio conferencing involves real-time interactions without visual cues, task-focused leadership is critical to the success of these groups.

CONCLUSION

The most important finding of this research is that narrower computer-mediated channels seem to inhibit relationship-focused leadership. Since these authors, and we suspect most educators, prefer relationship-focused leadership as a desirable strategy for learning groups, this finding presents a pedagogical challenge. We do not, however, consider that this challenge is insurmountable. There are many interventions we can imagine that might help virtual teams develop relationship-focused self-management techniques, including team-building exercises, direct instruction on effective leadership. It may also be a good idea for newly-formed groups to get to know each other use a richer communication channels such as videoconferencing for the purpose of relationship-building. Even chatrooms might be useful for this if meeting time is explicitly set aside for socialization. Pre-task chatroom meetings were found to improve trust in Zheng, et al. 2001. Perhaps there are similar, relatively simple interventions that can overcome the leadership-style tendencies described in this paper. Future research should focus both on clarifying why communication channels may affect emergent leadership, and also help identify effective strategies for promoting positive leadership.

ACKNOWLEDGMENTS

This research was funded by National Science Foundation grant IIS 9977923 to Judy and Gary Olson

REFERENCES

Berdahl, J. L. (1996). Gender and leadership in work groups: Six alternative models. Leadership Quarterly: Special Issue: Leadership and diversity: I., 7(1), 21-40.

Berdahl, J. L. (1998). The dynamics of composition and socialization in small groups: Insights gained from developing a computational model. Composition: Research on managing groups and teams, 1, 209-227.

Borg, W. R. (1957). The behavior of emergent and designated leaders in situational tasks. *Sociometry, 20*(2), 95-104.

Bormann, E. G. (1990). *Small Group Communication: Theory and Practice* (Third ed.). New York: Harper and Row.

Bos, N.D., Gergle, D., Olson, J.S., & Olson, G.M. (2001) Trust without touch: video is (almost) as good as being there. Proceedings of CHI 2001. New York: ACM. [on-line] http://intel.si.umich.edu/crew/technical_reports.htm

Bryk, A. S., & Raudenbush, S. W. (1992). Hierarchical Linear Models: Applications and Data Analysis Methods. Newbury Park: Sage Publications.

Eagly, A. H., & Karau, S. J. (1991). Gender and the emergence of leaders: A meta-analysis. Journal of Personality and Social Psychology, 60(5), 685-710.

Fiedler, F. E. (1967). *A Theory of Leadership Effectiveness*. New York: McGraw-Hill.

French, D. C., & Stright, A. L. (1991). Emergent leadership in children's small groups. Small Group Research, 22(2), 187-199.

Hackman, J.R. (1987). The design of work teams. In J. W. Lorsch (Ed.), Handbook of Organizational Behavior (pp. 315-341). Englewood Cliffs, NJ: Prentice-Hall).

Hardy, R. C. (1971). Effect of leadership style on the performance of small classroom groups: A test of the contingency model. *Journal of Personality and Social Psychology, 19*(3), 367-374.

Hardy, R. C. (1972). A developmental study of relationships between birth order and leadership style for two distinctly different American groups. *Journal of Social Psychology, 87*(1), 147-148.

Hardy, R. C. (1976). A test of the poor leader-member relation cells of the contingency model on elementary school children. *Child Development, 46*(4), 958-964.

Hewitt, J. (1997). Beyond threaded discourse. Paper presented at *WebNet 97*. [on-line] http://csile.oise.ca.edu

Hsi, S. & Hoadley, C. (1997). Productive discussion in science: gender equity through electronic discourse. *Journal of Science Education and Technology 6* (1), 23-36.

Jarvenpaa, S.L., Leidner, D.E. (1998). Communication and trust in global virtual teams. Journal of Computer-Mediated Communications 3 (4). [on-line] http://www.ascusc.org/jcmc/vol3/issue4/jarvenpaa.html

Karau, S. J., & Eagly, A. H. (1999). Invited Reaction: Gender, social roles, and the emergence of leaders. Human Resource Development Quarterly, 10(4), 321-327.

Kolb, J. A. (1992). Leadership of creative teams. Journal of Creative Behavior, 26(1), 1-9.

Kolb, J. A. (1999). The effect of gender role, attitude toward leadership and self-confidence on leader emergence: Implications for leadership development. Human Resource Development Quarterly, 10(4), 305-320.

Koschmann, T (1996) *CSCL: Theory and practice of an emerging paradigm*. Mahwah, NJ: Erlbaum.

Morris, C. G., & Hackman, J. R. (1969). Behavioral Correlates of Perceived Leadership. *Journal of Personality and Social Psychology, 13*(4), 350-361.

Owen, W. F. (1986). Rhetorical themes of emergent female leaders. Small Group Behavior, 17(4), 375-486.

Pollack, B. N. (1998). Hierarchical linear modeling and the "unit of analysis" problem: A solution for analyzing responses of intact group members. Group Dynamics: Theory, Research, and Practice, 2(4), 299-312.

Pryer, M. W., Flint, A. W., & Bass, B. M. (1962). Group effectiveness and consistency of leadership. *Sociometry, 25*(4), 391-397.Rocco, E. Trust breaks down in electronic contexts but can be repaired by some initial face-to-face contact, *Conference proceedings on human factors in computing systems*, 1998, pp496-502.

Rothaus, P., Davis, R. T., & Banker, C. A. (1969). Participants in adolescent autonomous groups. *Journal of Genetic Psychology, 114*(1), 135-142.

Siegel, J., Dubrovsky, V., Kiesler, S., & McGuire, T. (1986). Group processes in computer-mediated communication. Organizational behavior and human decision processes 37, 157-187.

Stogdill, R. M. (1948). Personal factors associated with leadership: A survey of the literature. *Journal of Psychology, 25*, 35-71.

Stogdill, R. M., & Coons, A. E. (Eds.). (1957). Leader Behavior: Its Description and Measurement. Columbus, OH: Ohio State University, Bureau of Business Research.

Stogdill, R. M. (1969). Validity of leader behavior descriptions. Personnel Psychology, 22(2), 153-158.

Webb, N. M., Nemer, K. M., Chizhik, A. W., & Sugrue, B. (1998). Equity issues in collaborative group assessment: Group composition and performance. American Educational Research Journal, 35(4), 607-651.

Golem, from Prague to Cyberspace: The Use of CSCL in Cultural Education for Diasporas

Zvi Bekerman, Gabriel Horenczyk

Melton Center, School of Education, The Hebrew University of Jerusalem

mszviman@mscc.huji.ac.il; gabriel@vms.huji.ac.il

ABSTRACT

In this paper we present, and provide the theoretical basis of, a computer supported and mediated educational research project which encourages cultural production and sustainability. We first describe the CD-Golem project which was developed in light of the perceived needs of a Diaspora community's attempts to impart its youth with a sense of belonging and continuity. Next, we characterize Cultural Education and discuss the theoretical rationale of our approach in the context of current theories of identity and cultural construction, multicultural education and computer-supported collaborative learning. We conclude by briefly reviewing and critically evaluating some of the lessons we have learned in our first years of activity.

Keywords:

Computer-Supported Collaborative Learning, Multicultural Education, Cultural Education, Diaspora, Technology and education, Ethnic Identity, Cultural Identity, Jewish Education.

INTRODUCTION

Given the enthusiastic use of computers to confront a variety of cognitive and pedagogical challenges in education (CTGV, 1993; Jonassen, 1994) we asked ourselves how these technologies could be employed in order to help minority cultural groups develop and sustain a sense of pride in their cultural heritage.

In this paper we describe and theorize about a computer supported and mediated educational research project which encourages cultural production and sustainability. We begin with a brief description of the CD-Golem project (Cultural Dimension Golem; http://cdgolem.huji.ac.il) that was developed in light of the perceived needs of a Diaspora community's attempts to impart its youth with a sense of belonging and continuity under less than optimal conditions. Next we discuss the theoretical rationale of our approach in the context of current theories of identity and cultural construction, multicultural education and computer-supported collaborative learning. We conclude by briefly reviewing some of the lessons we have learned in our first years of activity, and presenting some preliminary impressions gained from our ongoing monitoring and critical evaluation.

THE CD-GOLEM PROJECT

In an attempt to usher Cultural education into the world of computer-based learning, the CD-Golem was developed as an innovative educational and recreational website which serves Jewish schools worldwide. A combination of practical and theoretical concerns shaped our goals in designing the site. Practically speaking, we wanted to create activities in which children and youth would enjoy participating. We were confronted with the need to merge what we perceived to be the possible interests of Jewish schools and their students with our own ideas of educational efficacy in the realm of culture and identity. Theoretically, we wanted to create activities which would offer opportunities for ongoing communication on issues of culture and identity, along the lines of constructivist approaches grounded in Piagetian perspectives on reflective abstraction (Piaget, 1926) and Vygotskyan (Vygotsky, 1978) understandings of thought as the outcome of dialogical activity.

The CD-Golem site offers participants, 8-15 years of age, a variety of activities divided into four sections: "World of Writing", "Roots and Traditions"," World of Communities" and "Golem Challenges You". The "World of Writing" offers participants a wide range of opportunities to share with others their ideas related primarily to culture and identity. For example, they can engage in journalism through writing for the "Golem Gazette", author their own stories based on suggested themes (or on themes raised by the participants themselves) and offer interpretations of pictures related to a variety of socio-political issues. In the section on "Roots and Traditions", the participants are given the opportunity to build their own genealogical tree, by interviewing parents and gathering stories from relatives, and also to confront some dilemmas related to their communities' historical and religious traditions. The "World of Communities" allows participants to choose their own way to introduce themselves, their families, and their communities to the other members of the Golem worldwide community. Finally, "Golem Challenges You" is a section in which participants are afforded the opportunity to take part in dramatized court cases, stimulating collaboration and argumentation towards cultural and ethical problem solving.

Participants in CD-Golem connect with one another through the Golem Communication Center which links students to bulletin boards, moderated discussion and chat groups, their personal e-mail, and 'ICQ-like' options. The site is facilitated and mediated by the Golem, a mythical polyglot cyber-persona, who functions as an 'educational agent or manager', navigating, supporting, motivating and challenging the participants throughout the program to think through and better elaborate their views regarding the ethical and value-laden issues raised in the diverse activities. The Golem can be thought of as one of the 'partners' in the Vygotskyan "Zone of Proximal Development" (Cole, 1996; Wertsch, 1985), encouraging and assisting participants in their evolving performance.

CD-Golem functions on a rather modest software of the type used by academic institutions for long-distance learning (i.e. WebCT) and clearly does not compete with the commercial sites developed for children activities and play. The site is loosely structured and its not presented as a curricular program. CD-Golem is suggested for use in Jewish schools and other informal educational settings, and it is only through these institutions that participants can join. The hope is that the site will encourage curricular integration by getting teachers involved in a variety of disciplines to collaborate in developing, together with the children, different aspects of an activity (i.e. teachers of history, social studies and Judaic studies may choose to collaborate on a global community activity). It is expected that peer interaction will further the co-construction of knowledge, while affording rewards that are intrinsic to the activity, thereby avoiding the problems of extrinsic rewards that dominate school activity. For example, participants have been encouraged to respond individually and cooperatively to current socio-political dilemmas such as the destruction of the Buddha statues by the Taliban or the anti-Semitic propaganda of Holocaust denial websites. Lastly, we hope for teachers in general and Jewish areas of study to recognize the potential of using a system which, in addition to its contents, offers intrinsic textual, computational, and linguistic literacy for students. The lingua franca of the system is English, although children can write in any language using Latin characters, and recently a Hebrew option has been also added.

In the three years of CD-Golem's operation approximately fifty schools in five continents and over 15 countries have steadily or periodically participated in the project. At this point there are 25 schools enrolled and participating at different levels of involvement.

CULTURAL EDUCATION

The CD-Golem project was envisioned as a cooperative community-university project: The community of Jews in Israel and the Diaspora, and the Hebrew University of Jerusalem. CD-Golem was shaped for the benefit of both parties: the educational web environment was expected to offer valuable educational activities relevant to the realities of school life, and at the same time to provide rich data for educational research. All in all we wanted to attempt to bridge the gap between the practice of Cultural Education, theoretical advancements in the field of cultural and identity development, and the new educational technologies.

By Cultural Education (CE) we mean the educational efforts invested by minority groups who want to sustain what they perceive to be their socio-historical heritage [when confronted with the globalizing assimilatory power of an hegemonic West (Castells, 1997; Featherstone, 1995). Ethnic, religious, cultural or political minorities are not necessarily to be understood only in terms of relative numbers within a nation-state. Thus in Israel, where Jews are a numerical majority, current western globalizing trends can create a sense of minority for some Jewish groups present (Bekerman & Silverman, 1999; Kimmerling, 1993; Smooha, 1998).

Both concepts -- "Culture" and "Education" -- have histories, which for the most part have been forgotten. The terms have become independent, reified nouns in contrast to their processual, developmental, historicized meanings (Elias, 1998; Watt, 1997; Williams, 1961). This process of reification and fixation is part of the problem we are seeking to ameliorate. We find that the restoration of the developmental process embodied in these historically re-contextualized concepts constitutes a partial solution towards these same problems, as well as an educational model (Bekerman, in press-a).

Traditionally the basic humanities curriculum puts a great emphasis on classical philosophical inquiry, mostly from an idealistic perspective concerned with the nature of reality and problems of virtue in political educational contexts. It also envisions traditional textual literacy as the heart of cultural (in our case Jewish) production and maintenance. Finally, humanities curricula suggest a strong connection between traditional views of 'universal' humanism and traditional particularistic cultural worldviews. Textual learning in these settings has been presented in a dislocated and mostly de-historicized way, unsuccessfully engaging learners in interpretative practices that might make these texts relevant to their present contexts.

Cultural Education is geared to cultivate in members of culturally, economically, or politically oppressed groups a critical consciousness (McLaren, 1997; Nichols & Brown, 1996) of their situation as the foundation of their libratory praxis while recognizing that their greatest enemy is the fatalistic belief in the inevitability and necessity of existing beliefs and structures.

The classic humanities curriculum implicitly (and partially explicitly) assumes certain modern understandings of concepts such as culture, identity, and education, which are associated with individual, cognitive, and autonomous activities. In the last decades, theoretical developments within the 'new' humanities and social sciences have led to a reexamination of cultural production and maintenance and the related issues of identity development, and educational theory and strategies (Giddens, 1991; Harre & Gillett, 1994; Holzman, 1997).

Thus our understanding of culture, identity and education (and related concepts such as language, power and memory) has undergone a shift from de-contextualized, ideal models to historicized, dialogically produced and transformed ones. Our focus has therefore shifted from the individual to the social arena and from the intra-psychological to the inter-psychological (Schwandt, 1998). The theoretical relocation into the social interactional sphere where historically situated participants calibrate their positions according to complex socio-cultural relations, has the potential to promote a re-thinking of educational aims and strategies (Bekerman, in press-b).

It is the curricular organization towards these aims and its resulting practices, which we call Cultural Education (CE). CE is geared towards the joint production of agents aware of historical processes, the interdependence of social phenomena, and the participation of a multiplicity of powers and interests in the shaping of present meanings. This awareness should allow agents to devise the strategies necessary for change (if change is indeed their goal), and to consider the feasibility of their implementation in the multiple arenas in which interested powers struggle for domination (educational institutions, media channels, political arenas, etc.). These are not uniquely Jewish educational challenges. They are salient for a multitude of other cultural groups which have suffered from western social, cultural, political, and or economic colonizing tendencies in the modern era.

CD-Golem reflects this educational approach in its activities which are constructed under the premise that culture has little to do with the habits we train people to adopt and has everything to do with the environments we build for people to inhabit (Varenne & McDermott, 1998). Culture and identity are approached as contexts. Not the ones into which one is placed, but context as a behavioral arena of which one is part. In short CD-Golem proposes that social interaction continuously produces culture and identity. CD-Golem approaches education as a social enterprise in which all individuals have an opportunity to contribute and to which all feel a responsibility (Lave & Wenger, 1991; Wenger, 1998).

CULTURAL EDUCATION, MULTICULTURAL EDUCATION AND CSCL

Cultural Education departs from multicultural education in that it is particularistically bounded and aligns with it in that it wishes to strengthen tolerance and recognition towards multiple cultural forms enabling them to interact on equal bases in the public arena. Like multicultural approaches, Cultural Education is supportive of introducing to educational practice concepts related to content integration, knowledge construction and prejudice reduction (Banks, 1995).

Computer-Supported Collaborative Learning (CSCL) suits our aims to assist youth from a minority culture Diaspora to both achieve cultural sustainability and strengthen multicultural sensitivities. Our approach shares with CSCL constructivist perspectives, which emphasize an understanding of problem-based apprenticeship, situatedness, and distributive cognition (Duffy & Cunningham, 1996). The use of computers and the location of the project in the World Wide Web made it possible to render choices available for the content and directions of learning, to support collaborative learning between student peers and teachers, and to offer activities which would allow for different patterns in the organization of learning as well as afford widely dispersed Diaspora groups to sustain consistent synchronic and a-synchronic communication. The technology implemented promotes, by its mere existence, the boundedness of what was until now for the most part an "imagined community" (Anderson, 1991). We would like to suggest that CD-Golem is doing CSCCE (Computer-Supported Collaborative Cultural Education).

LESSONS LEARNED

The main goal of CD-Golem is to search for new and creative ways to develop a sense of belonging within an evolving cultural sphere while both sustaining a polisemic and multivalent perspective and promoting multicultural understanding and awareness (Ridley, Mendoza, & Kanitz, 1994).

When considering that from the start our aim was to implement the project not in a particular school or network of schools in a city but on a variety of educational institutions around the world it will surprise no one if we state that developing the project has been both challenging and frustrating. We had assumed that private schools would be technologically well-equipped, that the teachers of a Diaspora nation, with a powerful rhetorical tradition of unity, would welcome the opportunity to easily connect and sustain communication, and that private and public benefactors would readily support the introduction of new technologies in an educational setting they identified as an ideological imperative for the further evolution of their community. Soon we discovered these assumptions to be unrealistically optimistic. Although most schools that joined the program had computer equipment, the equipment was mostly used to introduce students to computer literacy and was rarely integrated into other curricular areas. When integrated, computers played a role in high-status curricular tracks (mathematics, language, business), while Jewish educational areas, traditionally perceived as secondary in terms of expected academic achievements, were segregated from the general studies and particularly from computer support.

One of our first surprises came from the types of teachers who expressed an interest in participating in the project. They can be classified into three categories. In Israel and some non-English speaking Diaspora communities, the first to join were those teaching English as a second language. For them, CD-Golem became an opportunity to teach the language, not in the abstraction of a detached class, but in a context in which its use served real communicational purposes (i.e. pen pal correspondence or communicating with the Golem character). It became a welcomed opportunity to integrate cherished cultural activities into their language discipline without impeding ??? upon language development. The second category included computer lab teachers who welcomed the Golem as a project which offered the opportunity to add some substance to the rather bland technical learning they usually conducted in their computer literacy lessons. Last came the few Jewish educators who, aside from their work in a disciplinary area, were young computer 'freaks'. Many of these teachers proved to be short-term participants who found it difficult, in spite of their early enthusiasm, to relate to the educational issues raised and the educational approaches and learning perspectives offered by CD-Golem.

It was clear from the start that reaching what we had thought to be our first target, Jewish educators at large, would be no easy task. It soon became apparent from those who did join, that they had little familiarity with either the technologies or the theoretical approaches which supported the project. The on-line support system we had build for them soon proved to be of no help. It was clear that teachers unfamiliar with the technology could not and would not use that same tool to overcome their handicap. Ultimately we 'regressed' to the supposedly obsolete long distance telephone calls and, wherever possible, on-site visits became the central tools of training and support. Overcoming this obstacle was not enough. The learning approach and the theoretical perspectives regarding the constructive and dialogical aspects of culture and identity, on which CD-Golem is grounded, proved difficult to grasp for our school partners. In many instances we had reports of teachers downloading activities from the site to use them, transformed into hard copies, in regular classes, derailing our efforts to encourage synchronic or a-synchronic communicational activity. For the most part, teachers used CD-Golem in class in ways which did not encourage collaborative work. They preferred activities which could be done individually, i.e. writing to Golem, answering a quiz.

Most of the problems mentioned above have been well documented in recent research (CTGV, 1996; Harris, 1995; Siegel, 1995; Witmer, 1998). We are forced to recognize that in spite of the two decades or more since the introduction of technologies into school life, the new technologies are still difficult to adapt to traditional educational paradigms. The situation is more acute in 'low status' educational fields such as, in our case, Jewish education.

We have encountered other challenges to our project. Some are ideological and others of a more technical nature. Though the CD-Golem is offered as a tool which can potentially strengthen ties between the Jewish community worldwide, present ideological perspectives, which emphasize the centrality of Israel for the Jewish world (Cohen, 1991) seem to prevent teachers from experimenting with the Golem system to create ties between schools within a Diaspora community or among Diaspora communities themselves (for example, to create a local network among the schools presently participating in Mexico City, or to attempt communication between schools in England and Argentina).

Global Jewish dispersion also brings about serious scheduling problems which schools find difficult to overcome. Indeed, communicating between Los Angeles and Israel could mean having children in Los Angeles working at eight o'clock in the morning and those in Israel at six o'clock in the afternoon -- a time when schools are regularly closed. True, the technology is not school dependent and it could be possible to create the connection between students working from home. However, this would depend upon participating students owning relevant equipment, and a coordinated school effort to generate student commitment to the program outside of school hours. At present we are struggling to find creative solutions to these problems.

The students, for their part, seem to participate in activities mostly when encouraged to do so by their teachers. There has been little participation by students outside of school activity in the privacy of their homes though they each hold a personal password which would allow them to access the system from anywhere. Reviewing the activity logs, it becomes apparent that the participants prefer activities which directly relate to their own experiences rather than engaging in activities dealing with issues of a social or political nature. Thus an activity which called upon students to choose an animal they would enjoy becoming for a day and to render an explanation for their choice, produced a rather large amount of responses (a total of 70 messages, over a month), while discussion activities around issues such us 'Should the Israeli Defense Forces retreat from Lebanon?' or 'Can the Taliban be justified for destroying the Buddha statues?' attracted very little participation (ten to fifteen responses each). The animal activity included a second stage in which students were asked to suggest which animal would better represent the Jewish people; this stage of the activity also produced few responses.

CD-Golem offers an opportunity to contact other children around the world. Corresponding with participants through personalized e-mail accounts offered by the system is one way of achieving this aim. This correspondence reinforces the ideological discourse of Jewish education that cherishes the strengthening of a worldwide Jewish community. Yet pen pal activities have not been easy to develop. They have primarily succeeded on the 'school in Diaspora' to 'school in Israel' track. As of yet, no contacts between different schools in Diaspora or between schools in Israel have developed. The contacts are usually initiated by teachers who were personally interested in encouraging the students and asked us to establish the necessary connections to support the correspondence. Once the connections were established, they produced a rather large amount of e-mail exchanges (over 100 and over 70 in two separate occasions during the span of three months of activity). Still, the contents of the exchange between students were limited to short biographical statements with little follow-up activity.

One of the dilemma activities offered dealt with the need to decide who, out of two critically ill, hospitalized patients who are in urgent need of a very rare blood type transfusion will receive the only blood portion which Adam can offer. One belongs to Adam's community, whereas the other is a stranger. Participants in this activity were happy to express their views and react to Golem's messages challenging their statements (over forty messages were exchanged with the students in one of the participating classes). However, students have yet to engage in research to further substantiate their positions, even though links to knowledge-enriching sites are made available.

There was a fair amount of participation in activities related to festivals and traditions (six schools participated on different occasions), and the information submitted was relatively richer in content than other activity responses, due to the overlap between the activity's content and the contents taught in regular classroom sessions.

Apparently the activities undertaken by teachers and students mostly reflect the present, traditional assumptions of what constitutes Jewish education. Festival-related work and networking with Israeli Jewish youth are teacher-preferred activities because they fall within the boundaries of traditional perceptions of Jewish education. Political and social issues, on the other hand, seem less attractive since they do not fit traditional conceptions of what constitutes the purview of Jewish educators. Students choose to become involved mostly with issues which engage them on a personal, experiential level, but even then only within the limits of school activities. The students' limited type of involvement also reflects current compartmentalizing conceptions of Jewish education. Readily engaging in festival and root-type activities, students will make no apparent effort to engage in socio-political issues which might not be perceived as belonging to the field of Jewish study, nor will they invest in widening their present scope of knowledge by voluntarily accessing outside resources.

In spite of the rather gloomy picture, we remain enthusiastic. In the last three years, both the amount of participants and the levels of participation have steadily grown. From a modest start with six schools and one hundred and fifty participants, we are now working with twenty-five schools and almost one thousand registered members.

We have learned much in the few years of the project's operation, and much more has yet to be understood for CD-Golem to achieve its aim. It becomes more and more apparent that for technology to foster collaborative learning and cross-disciplinary critical exploration, we may have to help more actively educators and students rethink their paradigms regarding relevant educational contents and applications, in light of communal needs and the expanding temporal and spatial boundaries of Cultural Education perspectives, while also looking for new ways to assess student and teachers performance (Means & Olson, 1994). New technologies may not, all by themselves, have the power to help minorities overcome the basic cultural and educational premises which control them. When uncritically used, they might even help the process of social reproduction. For new technologies to become liberating educational tools they are in need of accounting for the wider interpretative contexts within which they function. Anderson (1991) highlighted the interrelationship between systems of cultural production, productive relations, and communicational technologies when trying to better understand the processes of nation development. The use of new technologies in education in general, and our specific interest in the use of these technologies to benefit minorities interested in sustaining their socio-historical heritage, call for serious research efforts along these lines.

ACKNOWLEDGMENTS

We wish to express our deep appreciation to Michael Cole from University of California, San Diego and the Fifth Dimension Project that served as inspiration to our work. We are also thankful to Gaby Fachler, Debi Katz, and Keri Warshawsky from the Hebrew University of Jerusalem for their ongoing commitment and support.

REFERENCES

Anderson, B. (1991). Imagined Communities: Reflections on the Origins and Spread of Nationalism. London: Verso.

Banks, J. A. (1995). Multicultural education; historical development, dimensions, and practice. In J. A. Banks & C. A. M. Banks (Eds.), Handbook of research on multicultural education (pp. 3-24). New York: Macmillan.

Bekerman, Z. (in press-a). Constructivist Perspectives on Language, Identity and Culture: Implications for Jewish Identity and the Education of Jews. Religious Educacion.

Bekerman, Z. (in press-b). Towards the re-enchantment of Ethnic-Cultural education. .

Bekerman, Z., & Silverman, M. (1999). Slaves of tradition - Slaves of freedom: Social constructivist perspectives on the 'culture' of Israeli traditionalists and liberals. Israel Studies, 4(2), 90-120.

Castells, M. (1997). The power of identity. Oxford: Blackwell.

Cohen, S. M. (1991). Israel in the Jewish identity of American Jews: A study in duality and contrasts. In D. M. Gordis & Y. Ben-Horin (Eds.), Jewish identity in America (pp. 119-135). Lon Angeles: Wilstein Institute.

Cole, M. (1996). Cultural Psychology: A once and future discipline. Cambridge: Belknap Press of Harvard University Press.

CTGV, C. a. T. G. a. V. (1993). Designing learning environments that support thinking. In T. M. Duffy, J. Lowyck, & D. H. Jonnassen (Eds.), Designing environments for constructivist learning (pp. 9-36). New York: Springer.

CTGV, C. a. T. G. a. V. (1996). Looking at technology in context: A framework for understanding technology and education research. In D. C. Berliner & R. C. Calfee (Eds.), Handbook of Educational Psychology (pp. 807-840). New York: Mcmillan Library Reference USA.

Duffy, T. M., & Cunningham, D. J. (1996). Constructivism: Implications for the design and delivery of instruction. In D. H. Jonassen (Ed.), Handbook of research for educational communications and technology (pp. 170-198). New York: Macmillan Library Reference USA.

Elias, N. (1998). Civilization, culture, identity: ' "Civilization" and "Culture": Nationalism and Nation State Formation': an extract from the Germans. In J. Rundell & S. Mennell (Eds.), Classical Readings in Culture and Civilization . New York: Routledge.

Featherstone, M. (1995). Undoing culture: Globalization, postmodernism and identity. London: SAGE.

Giddens, A. (1991). Modernity and self identity. Stanford CA: Stanford University Press.

Harre, R., & Gillett, G. (1994). The discursive mind. London: Sage.

Harris, J. (1995). Teaching teachers to use telecomputing tools. ERIC Review, 4(1), 2-6.

Holzman, L. (1997). Schools for growth: Radical alternatives to current educational models. Mahwah, New Jersey: Lawrence Erlbaum Associates, Publishers.

Jonassen, D. H. (1994). Sometimes media influences learning. Educational Technology Research and Development, 42(2), 309-321.

Kimmerling, B. (1993). Civil society relations in Israel. In A. Ram (Ed.), Israel society: Critical perspectives (pp. 118-146 (Hebrew)): Breirot.

Lave, J., & Wenger, E. (1991). Situated learning: Legitimate peripheral participation. New York: Cambridge University Press.

McLaren, P. (1997). Revolutionary multiculturalism: Pedagogies of dissent for the new millennium. USA: Westview Press.

Means, M., & Olson, K. (1994). The link between technology and authentic learning. Educational Leadership, 51(7), 15-18.

Nichols, R. G., & Brown, V. A. (1996). Critical theory and educational technology. In D. H. Jonassen (Ed.), Handbook of research for educational communication and technology (pp. 226-252). New York: Macmillan Library Reference USA.

Piaget, J. (1926). The mechanism of perception (G N Seagrim, Trans.). London: Routledge and Kegan Paul Ltd.

Ridley, C. R., Mendoza, D. W., & Kanitz, B. E. (1994). Multicultural training: Reexamination, operationalization, and integration. The Counseling Psychologist, 22(2), 227-289.

Schwandt, T. A. (1998). Constructivist, interpretativist approaches to human inquiry. In N. K. Denzin & Y. S. Lincoln (Eds.), The Landscape of Qualitative Research (pp. 221-259). London: Sage Publication.

Siegel, J. (1995). The state of teacher training. Electronic Learning, 14(8), 43-53.

Smooha, S. (1998). The implications of the transition to peace for Israeli society. Annals of the American Academy of Political and Social Sciences, 555, 26-45.

Varenne, H., & McDermott, R. (1998). Successful Failure: The Schools America Builds. Colorado: Westview Press.

Vygotsky, L. S. (1978). Mind in Society. Cambridge: Harvard University Press.

Watt, I. (1997). Myths of Modern Individualism: Faust, Don Quixote, Don Juan, Robinson Crusoe. Cambridge: Cambridge University PressW.

Wenger, E. (1998). Communities of Practice: Learning, Meaning, and Identity. Cambridge: Cambridge University Press.

Wertsch, J. W. (1985). The social formation of mind: A Vygotskian approach. Cambridge: Cambridge University Press.

Williams, R. (1961). Culture and society, 1780-1950. Hardmondsworth: Penguin Books.

Witmer, D. F. (1998). Introduction to computer-mediated communication: A master syllabus for teaching communication technology. Communication Education, 47, 162-182.

E. (METHODOLOGY TRACK): QUALITATIVE STUDIES AND THEIR IMPLICATIONS FOR CSCL

The Development of Deep Learning During a Synchronous Collaborative On-line Course

Gillian Armitt, Frances Slack, Sharon Green, Martin Beer

Departments of Computer Science & Allied Health Professions, University of Liverpool

School of Computing & Management Sciences, Sheffield Hallam University

gillian@csc.liv.ac.uk, f.slack@shu.ac.uk, sgreen@liv.ac.uk & m.beer@shu.ac.uk

ABSTRACT

As Internet bandwidth improves and connections become more reliable, on-line course designers will be encouraged to make more structured use of synchronous communications. Little work has so far been reported on how to make the best use of synchronous communications to support a problem solving approach. The OTIS pilot course made extensive use of synchronous communication to support learning through case studies in occupational therapy. The transcripts of communication sessions have been analysed using the SOLO taxonomy, to study the development of deep learning week by week. Results show that synchronous peer-to-peer working meetings have an important role to play in the development of deep learning.

Keywords

Synchronous communications, SOLO taxonomy, deep learning, collaboration, role of tutors, occupational therapy, assistive technology

INTRODUCTION

Synchronous communication is little-used in on-line courses at present, owing to real-time communications not being sufficiently reliable and the greater bandwidth requirement compared with email-based courses such as those based on FirstClass or Blackboard.com. When Internet Chat facilities are available, they are simple add-ons and are not integrated into the course structure. However, future improvements in communications will make it possible for courses to use synchronous communications systematically. It is recognised that synchronous communications promote motivation and group cohesion, as well as providing good feedback, supporting consensus and decision making, and assisting pacing - encouraging people to keep up to date and providing discipline (Mason, 1998). However, it is more difficult to schedule group meetings, and synchronous tutorials are relatively more expensive as the optimum group size is so much smaller. Synchronous working meetings follow face-to-face groups in typically having less than ten participants, compared with asynchronous groups of twenty or more. Given these disadvantages, it is important to establish what aspects of synchronous courses lead to the effective development of deep learning, and the factors that promote a successful outcome. The Occupational Therapy Internet School (OTIS) pilot course has provided an opportunity to study the development of deep learning in a ten-week course with a substantial degree of synchronous communication.

Synchronous communication was a key requirement for the OTIS pilot course, entitled *"High level assistive technology in European occupational therapy"* (Armitt et al., 2001). The course was collaboratively developed and run by four higher education institutions in Liverpool (UK), Amsterdam (Netherlands), Kortrijk (Belgium) and Linköping (Sweden) during January - March 2001. Students were divided into four tutorial groups of mixed nationalities, each group solving a different case study. The course was designed to promote specialist skills in occupational therapy, while also developing generic core skills. Embedded within this latter skill set is the essential ability to communicate effectively and collaborate with a wide range of clients and allied professionals. In the case of OTIS, the course sought to stimulate synchronous communication and collaboration within international student groups, and also with 'patients' (tutors role-playing patients) and experts such as health care specialists or representatives of companies marketing assistive technology devices.

Transcripts of communication sessions showed that in-depth discussions about possible solutions to the case studies were taking place, as well as revealing a variety of tutor styles. The SOLO taxonomy (Biggs & Collis, 1982, 1989) was used to undertake a more detailed analysis of the transcripts.

THE SOLO TAXONOMY

The SOLO taxonomy (Structure of the Observed Learning Outcome) is a well-established technique for establishing the presence of deep learning, and is becoming widely used in education, including:

1. allocating a cognitive level to individual course objectives (Australian National University, 2000)
2. helping students analyse their own work and see how to improve it (University of Alberta, 2001; University of Bradford, 2001)
3. explanation of assignment grades (University of Sydney, 2001)
4. assessment (Hoddinott, 1998)
5. predictor of potential (Crowley & Tall, 2001)
6. research into education (Anderson & Walker, 1997)

The SOLO taxonomy identifies the complexity of thought processes in the statements, based upon a classification into prestructural, unistructural, multistructural, relational and extended abstract, the stages being derived from the work of Piaget and his stages of cognitive development. Statements are expected to show a continuum of learning from initial recognition to reflection and complex understanding (Hewson & Hughes, 1998). As with Piaget's stages, once a student has reached a particular level in SOLO regarding a concept, s/he is now capable of continuing to operate at that level with regard to that concept. However, a student may not always show evidence of being at that level consistently, since SOLO levels are used to "describe a particular performance at a particular time" (Biggs & Collis, 1982; p.23) and not to indicate a student's ability.

DEEP LEARNING

It is important for all health care professionals to experience deep learning in their professional training programmes. This not only ensures quality learning but is also a safeguard for the future, in that such health care professionals will display a holistic approach to their clients, with emphasis on quality of care. Clinical education has been shown to be effective in facilitating deep learning (Coles, 1989, 1990) and for students in the academic environment realistic case studies explored via a stimulating problem-solving approach, can form a close approximation to learning from real life.

Educators suggest that students who are personally involved in learning from real life situations are the ones who are most likely to experience deep learning. McAllister et al (1997) suggest that "deep approaches to learning are found in students who are affectively involved in searching for personal meaning and understanding (their own personal practical knowledge), seeing the whole picture or person - not just the isolated features or disembodied problems - drawing on their personal experience to make sense of new ideas and experiences and relating evidence to conclusions. These deep learning approaches are in marked contrast to surface approaches exhibited by students who seek only to memorise and reproduce information or skills, see only the discrete "bits", expect the educator to be in control of their learning, and are largely motivated by the external imperative to pass an assignment or gain their qualification."

The stimulation of reflection is essential for deep learning, as the reflective process includes synthesis of knowledge through re-evaluation of the experience by undertaking association, integration, validation and appropriation (Boud et al., 1985). Reflection may be facilitated through interaction with peers or tutors, or alone through writing (Lincoln et al., 1997). Synchronous on-line courses must answer the question of whether real-time communication with peers and tutors is effective in promoting reflection.

THE PILOT COURSE

The OTIS course concerned the application of high-level assistive technologies (e.g. computer applications, intelligent monitoring of homes) to patient need. The course employed a problem-solving approach, in which students tackled one of four case studies in collaborative international groups of three to six undergraduate and post-graduate occupational therapy students. Although the case studies were in different areas of occupational therapy (e.g. partial paralysis, speech difficulties), all four case studies required students to follow the same general approach of (1) analysing the patient's circumstances, (2) identifying the patient's needs and expressing those needs as characteristics of assistive technology devices, and (3) selecting appropriate technologies to match those needs.

The eighteen students who completed the course were divided into four tutorial groups, such that the different student nationalities were spread as evenly as possible between the groups. The language of the course was English, and all students spoke and wrote English well, even though English was a second language for the Dutch and Swedish students and a third language for the Belgians. The course timetable provided for tutorial sessions of 1 - 1.5 hours in most weeks, plus occasional synchronous sessions with 'patients' and experts such as health care specialists and company representatives. These sessions were based on the OTIS system's Talk and Page facilities, a form of Internet Chat hosted on the OTIS server (Armitt et al., 2001). Students solved the case study in weeks 2 - 7, and undertook a peer review of a different group's completed case studies in weeks 8 & 9, week 10 being devoted to completion of a reflective personal account of the course.

Liverpool provided two tutors, and Amsterdam and Kortrijk provided one each. Although much time was spent in advance of the course in discussion of the philosophy and concepts of problem based learning, no detailed guidance was given to tutors and differences emerged in the way in which each group was managed.

METHOD

The Data:

Since the problem-solving approach requires synchronous communication it was appropriate to evaluate evidence of deep learning using the students' own utterances in the communication sessions. The OTIS software allowed logging of all user activities, including all communications using the 'Talk' and 'Page' Internet Chat facilities. 'Talk' allows a user to broadcast to everyone present in the same 'meeting room', and 'Page' enables a user to make a private comment to one or more selected users. When registering to use the OTIS system, all users gave their written consent to their personal data being used anonymously for research purposes, including establishing patterns of activity. There was no specific intention until after the course had finished of using primary data from transcripts for evaluation of the course, so the behaviour of participants is unlikely to have been affected by the data collection.

Initial data extraction:

The transcripts provided several hundred pages of data, concerning not only the solution of the case study, but also the process of preparing the assignments, social interactions and discussion of how to use the OTIS system and various technical problems. A decision was made to focus on the following published learning outcome for the OTIS course:

Upon successful completion of this course participants who have reached the required educational level will have:

displayed expertise in following a problem-solving process to match technology to individual client need.

A preliminary extraction was performed, in which all utterances in which students discuss the solution of the case study were extracted, plus intermediate 'linking' utterances required to understand the flow of the conversation. Throughout this study, an utterance has been defined as a sentence or group of sentences that the student sends or broadcasts as a unit (utterances from tutors, clients and experts were ignored). At this stage it was established that the client and expert session data largely consisted of students questioning the clients and experts. Such data was largely excluded from the following analysis, except where the students were actively discussing the case solution.

The SOLO Taxonomy:

Analysis of the transcript data from the preliminary extraction was carried out using the SOLO taxonomy, focusing solely on the utterances directly concerned with the learning outcome. The first step was to specify the meaning of each level in the SOLO taxonomy in terms of the selected OTIS learning outcome on matching technology to client need. This method allows the learning outcome to be evaluated in a qualitative way by describing the student's points of learning in a specific task. The levels from 'unistructural' to 'relational' are seen to be the "target mode" (Biggs & Collis, 1989; p.152) of the learning outcome, whereas 'prestructural' indicates that the student has not yet achieved the target mode and 'extended abstract' shows that the target mode has been overshot.

To illustrate the use of this technique with the learning outcome defined above; Figure 1 defines each level in the SOLO taxonomy and gives an example from the OTIS transcripts.

The SOLO taxonomy was then applied to the preliminary extraction. Some of the utterances in the preliminary extraction could not be used for SOLO. A problem was encountered whereby most of the students' utterances were very short. This is a feature of synchronous communication, because students wished to make their point in a conversation quickly before the thread of the topic moved away. These short utterances made the SOLO classification more difficult to interpret and not all utterances could be classified. Also, linking utterances and other utterances not directly relevant to the selected learning outcome were abandoned at this stage.

Figure 1: Structural levels in learning. Examples are from the 'Esther' case study, concerning a teenage girl with learning and speech disabilities.

SOLO Level	Example
Prestructural	The utterance ignores the client, the client's need and the technology.
Unistructural	The utterance focuses on one relevant aspect: the client, the need or the technology. e.g. "that is the problem; we don't really know what the [Esther's] cognitive level is"

Multistructural	The utterance identifies more than one aspect about the client, the need or the technology, but does not integrate them. e.g. "f.e. [for example] (i think) Tellus [an assistive technology aid], you can put it instead of the wheelchair table, so you can eat, write,... on it, and if you want to communicate, you put the raster on it"
Relational	The utterance makes a coherent link between the issues related to the client, their need and technology. e.g. "the thing is that her coputerized [computerised] comm. [communication] aid has to be rather small and not wheigh [weigh] too much and be easy to handle for Esther, but maybe it's possible with a very small laptop to combine her speech and education."
Extended abstract	The utterance explores issues relating to the client's needs and technologies in general, beyond the scope of the case studies. e.g. "i guess every centre has got several aid[s], so more than one kid can use the computer with an other aid, you just have to change the aid when an other kid uses the pc." (based on the student's experience of adapting an aid to Esther's circumstances)

RESULTS

Initial Data Extraction:

The simple procedure of performing an initial data extraction of all material concerning the solution of the case study proved a powerful tool in evaluating the course. This showed examples of students interacting with each other as they engaged in reflection and synthesis of knowledge (Figure 2).

Figure 2: example of student interaction (names changed) **Week 5, tutorial group B**
Ingrid asks "there are some amazing things you can do to adapt the pc, for example running it with infrared light so you just have to be able to move your head slightly etc, have you tried that?" Dirk says, "i did once" Gerhard asks, "me neither, is it easy to do so regarding to Esthers problem?" Ingrid says "I don't hink the infrared is a solution for Esther since she might have some problems in focusing and keep the balance with her head, maybe scanning would be something for her, or pointng as she do now" Dirk says, "that is why i asked to mr vandyk [Esther's father] how she can use her head, he answerd that it s difficult when she is tyred, and i don't know if that is very good for the spastic patern " Dirk says, "i agree with that ingrid"

The initial data extraction revealed marked differences between the tutorial groups, concerning:

1. the relative amount of time spent discussing the solution to the case study (the "content"), compared with establishing administrative/mechanical details (what to do and when to do it, the "process").
2. when discussion of the case study takes place (in tutorials or in peer group meetings).

Figure 3 shows the pattern of extracted data by week of the course and tutorial group during weeks 2-7 when the case study was solved. Tutorial group A spent much more time than the other groups in discussing case study solutions during tutorials. In the other groups, most of the tutorial time was spent on the process rather than the content. Even in group A, the amount of time spent discussing the process during tutorials increased as the course proceeded. However, group A was the only group not to meet outside the tutorial session to discuss the case solution. The other groups undertook the majority of their discussion of content in the peer booked meetings, peer ad-hoc meetings being predominantly social.

Figure 3: occurrences of data concerning content (number of relevant student utterances in brackets)				
Week	**Tutorial Group A**	**Tutorial Group B**	**Tutorial Group C**	**Tutorial Group D**
Number of students	6	3	5	4
Week 2	After tutorial (37)	Tutorial (4) Extra tutorial (4)	-	-
Week 3	Before tutorial (26) Tutorial (84) After tutorial (18) Peer ad-hoc meeting (19)	Client session (32) Tutorial (15)	Peer ad-hoc meeting (6) Peer ad-hoc meeting (9)	-
Week 4	Before client session (13)	-	-	-
Week 5	Before tutorial (6) Tutorial (24)	Client session (25) After tutorial (12) Peer booked meeting (90)	Peer booked meeting (56)	Peer booked meeting (40)
Week 6	Expert session (70)	Peer booked meeting (69)	Tutorial (4) Peer booked meeting (69)	Expert session (8)
Week 7	Tutorial (30)	Expert session (10)	-	Peer ad-hoc meeting (16)

Further to this transcript data, the role of the tutor and the pattern of social exchange (discussing personal matters outside the course or their impressions and feelings about the course) within the groups were examined. This established that:

- Tutor A held "text book" problem-based learning sessions in the early weeks, and did not believe in being proscriptive in directing the students' learning. The fervent hope was that students would collaborate outside the tutorials, but in practice this did not happen except in the peri-tutorial period, when either the tutor arrived to start the session, then 'disappeared' for a period, or after the tutorial (weeks 2 & 3). In week 5, the tutor advised students to send each other emails if they did not meet on-line.

- Tutor B strongly encouraged students (weeks 2 & 3) in general terms to meet each other without the tutor being present. They met socially for 64 and 55 minutes in each of weeks 4 & 5, before the working sessions in weeks 5 & 6 recorded above as "peer booked meetings". This student group also used email extensively from week 5, to pass round information acquired on assistive technology devices.

- Tutor C strongly encouraged students during the week 5 tutorial to meet to discuss the case study, following a more general comment in week 3: "It is good to show collaboration throughout, rather than just as a conclusion". The group booked working sessions in weeks 5 & 6. Up to this point, they had had little interaction outside the tutorials.

- Tutor D strongly encouraged students to share their findings by email (tutor utterances in weeks 2, 3 & 5). The email data is not available to the research team. The students booked a peer group meeting in week 5, in which they mostly exchanged information about their individual approaches to the case study (listing references or websites), rather than discussing the outcome of the case study.

Application of the SOLO Taxonomy:

Figure 4 shows the results of applying the SOLO taxonomy to the utterances concerning the selected course outcome, by group and week, for the weeks during which the case study was 'solved' (weeks 2-7). Utterances were only included if there was sufficient information relevant to the learning outcome for them to be categorised to the appropriate SOLO level.

Figure 4: breakdown of raw data by group and week

Tutorial Group A:

SOLO Level	Week 2	Week 3	Week 4	Week 5	Week 6	Week 7
Prestructural						
Unistructural	4	24			1	
Multistructural	3	13	1	1	2	
Relational		4		1	1	
Extended abstract						

Tutorial Group B:

Prestructural						
Unistructural	4	7		13		1
Multistructural		5		7	8	1
Relational		6		24	5	1
Extended abstract				2	1	2

Tutorial Group C:

Prestructural						
Unistructural		3		10	3	
Multistructural		1		3	6	
Relational		1			17	
Extended abstract						

Tutorial Group D:

Prestructural						
Unistructural				11		
Multistructural				1	2	2
Relational				2	1	6
Extended abstract						

Looking at all the groups, the SOLO results offer the following indications:

- the lack of prestructural utterances shows that students were aware of the problem domain and were already working in the appropriate mode of the learning cycle.
- the decreasing number of unistructural utterances show that students were, in the early weeks, establishing the ground for their task. This is borne out by the fact that many of the unistructural utterances were in the form of a question.
- the highest number of multistructural utterances were found in the middle weeks of the course and show that students were exploring more than one aspect of the task, but not yet making links.
- most relational utterances were also found in the middle weeks of the course when students were linking together the issues of the learning outcome; i.e. the client, the client's need and the assistive technology.
- extended abstracts emerged from week 5 onwards. This shows that students were taking the issues of the learning outcome, abstracting and generalising them beyond the confines of the case study.

ANALYSIS/DISCUSSION

Application of the SOLO Taxonomy

This study has offered a unique opportunity to use the SOLO taxonomy on transcripts derived from synchronous communications. We believe that this method has not been reported before. Since the method used here is a qualitative approach to the analysis of a case study, the results cannot be generalised to other studies. However, some of the issues identified in this work may be extrapolated into other similar studies.

There have been limitations in the application of SOLO. Firstly, synchronous communications favour relatively short utterances so that the sender can avoid the conversational thread being diverted by other participants. This means that a thought may be transmitted as two or more utterances, which while connected in the sender's mind, would score relatively lowly under SOLO. Also, when established groups communicated, they sometimes did so in a type of 'shorthand' that had an underlying assumption that the others knew what they meant. A question late in the course "What about using Tellus?" (an assistive technology device) actually meant in the context of the discussion, "What about using Tellus for Esther? We've all agreed on Esther's needs and capabilities, and Tellus seems to have the right features to match her need. Do you agree?" (relational). The same question early in the course would be information-seeking (unistructural). This meant that SOLO was particularly difficult to apply to utterances late in the course, when students were working at a higher conceptual level. This may partially account for the relatively low number of classified utterances later in the course.

Nevertheless, SOLO provides a good indicator of the relative levels attained within the different collaborating groups through the weeks. The low number of relational utterances for tutorial group B in week 6 appeared anomalous. Revisiting the transcript showed that this seemed to arise from problems applying SOLO - the group was brainstorming at a highly relational level in a many threaded 'shorthand', which was difficult to analyse.

Synchronous Communication and Reflection

The results from the initial extraction show that high quality synchronous discussions such as that shown in Figure 2 do occur, though collaborative consideration of the course content generally did not happen as often as the course organisers would have liked. A feature of such discussions is that students develop a theme as they reflect on the information and thoughts put forward by other students as well as themselves. In such conversations, the whole is better than the sum of the parts - in other words, synthesis of knowledge is taking place as a direct result of the interaction. Through discussion, students are making cognitive connections between different themes.

It has been generally accepted that synchronous communication is inferior to asynchronous in stimulating reflection, as the student does not have as long to compose a reply (Mason, 1998). We suggest that both types of media are potentially valuable, and this is consistent with Lincoln et al.'s conclusion (1997) that reflection can be stimulated either through interaction with other people (peers, tutors) or alone through personal reading and writing. Students who are used to working in groups, such as health care students undertaking problem-based learning, are used to taking advantage of both means of reflection. For such students, the complementary approaches of synchronous and asynchronous activities mirror their complementary approaches to reflection.

Taken in conjunction with the quoted advantages of synchronous learning - motivation, group cohesion - and the enjoyment of other people's company, synchronous communications can potentially enrich on-line courses greatly. Synchronous discussion should have the advantage of allowing restructuring, reflection, synthesis, and challenging of ideas in a more dynamic and responsive way than email. One of the criticisms of forum-type discussion groups in wholly asynchronous courses (Chambers, 2000, Cox et al., 2000) is that students can be overwhelmed by emails as a discussion develops. This can lead to shallow reading and a 'cut and paste' approach. Synchronous discussions, by comparison, allow immediate clarification and development of thoughts.

Development of Deep Learning During the Course

Although the amount of SOLO data on each individual group is quite small, it does demonstrate very different patterns of learning in the four groups. Apart from group A, where there is insufficient data after week 3, all groups showed the expected advancement from unistructural to relational levels as the course proceeded. There seemed to be an improvement of approximately one SOLO level in each week *in which relevant utterances were identified.* There seemed to be no such improvement in weeks without relevant utterances, even though students may be assumed to be working on their own, or may be collaborating by email. This is seen particularly clearly in groups C & D. This suggests that a synchronous element in on-line courses does indeed assist in promoting deep learning.

The point at which relational utterances exceeded other types of utterances varied considerably (group A: not at all, group B: week 5, group C: week 6, group D: week 7). It appears that the sooner the group starts to make relevant utterances, the sooner it reaches the relational level. Many of the higher-level SOLO utterances arose during long peer group meetings in weeks 5 & 6. In this course, peer group meetings had great value in stimulating reflection, and peer groups that held more frequent working meetings had a clear developmental advantage over other groups. Given the high cost of tutoring in a synchronous environment, it seems that courses would gain most educational benefit from using this environment mainly for reflective peer group discussions. The peer group meetings seemed also to help with time management, encouraging students to work more evenly through the course, rather than leaving everything to the last minute.

Stimulation of Peer-to-Peer Collaboration

This course confirms earlier work, which shows that students who have never met each other do not spontaneously collaborate in peer groups (Chambers, 2000). This study showed that tutors needed to make their expectations for collaboration known. The tutors for groups B & C actively encouraged their students to set up peer group meetings, which subsequently took place. The tutor for group A hoped that students would set up working meetings, but this did not happen. The tutor for group D encouraged the group to collaborate primarily by email, and this was what happened.

This is consistent with the necessity for groups to pass through the third stage of Salmon's Five Stage Model for induction into CMC systems (Salmon & Giles, 1999; Salmon, 2000):

1.Gaining access to the system, logging in, getting started, 'netiquette'

2.Becoming familiar with the on-line environment, finding others with whom to interact

3.Encouragement to seek and give information to each other

4.Interacting in group discussions

5.Looking for other benefits from the system to achieve personal goals

This study also supports earlier work (Wegerif, 1998; Cox et al., 2000) that shows that prior social interaction and bonding is important in groups becoming effective educationally. Group B, which had long social conversations early on, achieved the relational level in SOLO quicker than other groups. The tutor for group B had strongly encouraged students during weeks 2 & 3 to meet informally, and this may have been a factor in the faster development of this group.

CONCLUSIONS

We have found that the SOLO taxonomy can be useful in the initial analysis of transcript data. Extraction of transcript data relevant to a particular learning outcome provides immediate pointers to the successes and failures of a course, and these pointers can be confirmed using SOLO, despite difficulties in applying SOLO to short utterances in synchronous communications.

Results for the OTIS pilot course show that development of deep learning in synchronous groups does not happen spontaneously throughout the course, and is promoted by on-line discussion of the course content. Groups which interact more effectively develop cognitively more quickly than other groups as the course proceeds. Where in depth on-line discussions take place, SOLO has shown an immediate benefit in terms of the depth of learning achieved. It is significant that many of these discussions were peer-to-peer in the absence of the tutor, at later stages in the course when the students are becoming autonomous learners within the subject area. While wholly synchronous courses are probably not financially viable owing to the tutoring costs for small groups, this study shows that a synchronous peer-to-peer element can be beneficial in promoting active reflection. We propose that the most cost-effective and educationally advantageous way to deploy synchronous communications is for peer-to-peer meetings later in the course, within courses primarily tutored asynchronously.

Groups do not spontaneously coalesce to undertake effective in-depth synchronous discussions. This study demonstrates the importance of tutors ensuring at an early stage in the course that students understand their expectations regarding when and how to collaborate. More work is needed into the changing balance of the activities of the student and tutor at different points in the course, taking into account the promotion of the social and collaborative development of the group and the group's developing capabilities as a community of autonomous learners.

ACKNOWLEDGEMENTS

The OTIS project is funded by the European Union through the TEN Telecom programme. The pilot course was realised by Andrew Sixsmith, Martin Beer, Sharon Green & Gillian Armitt (University of Liverpool, UK), Hanneke van Bruggen & Ramon Daniels (Hogeschool van Amsterdam, Netherlands), Ludo Ghyselen (Hogeschool West-Vlaanderen, Belgium) and Jan Sandqvist (Linköpings Universitet, Linköping, Sweden) and their students.

REFERENCES

Anderson, D. & Walker, R. (1997) Quality of learning outcomes amongst teacher education students, *Refereed Proceedings of the 27th Annual Conference of the Australian Teacher Education Association (ATEA)*, Yeppoon, Queensland, Australia, July 1997 [on-line] http://atea.cqu.edu.au/content/soc_base/anderson.html

Armitt, G., Green, S. & Beer, M. (2001) Building a European Internet School!: Developing the OTIS Learning Environment, *European Perspectives on Computer-Supported Collaborative Learning, Proceedings of the First European Conference on Computer-Supported Collaborative Learning, March 2001, Maastricht, Netherlands*, 67-74, Maastricht McLuhan Institute.

Australian National University, Department of Computer Science (2000) COMP3100: Software Engineering Group Project [on-line] http://cs.anu.edu.au/Student/2001/COMP3100/

Biggs, J.B. and Collis, K.F. (1982) *Evaluating the quality of learning: the SOLO taxonomy*, Academic Press.

Biggs, J.B. and Collis, K.F. (1989) Towards a model of school-based curriculum development and assessment: using the SOLO taxonomy, *Australian Journal of Education, 33*(2), 151-163.

Boud, D., Keogh, R. & Walker, D. (1985) Promoting reflection in learning: A model. In D. Boud, R. Keogh & D. Walker (eds), *Reflection: Turning experience into learning,* 18-40, London, Kogan Page.

Chambers, E. (2000) Contextualizing the CEFES project: A selective review of the computer conferencing literature. In Baumeister, H-P., Williams, J. & Wilson, K. (eds) *Teaching Across Frontiers: A Handbook for International Online Seminars*, Deutsches Institut für Fernstudienforschung an der Universität Tübingen, 153-166.

Coles, C. (1989) The role of context in elaborated learning. In Balla, J., Gibson, M. & Chang, A. (eds.) *Learning in medical school: A model for the clinical professions.* Hong Kong University Press, Hong Kong.

Coles, C. (1990) Elaborated learning in undergraduate medical education, *Medical Education*, 24, 14-22.

Cox, E.S., Clark, W., Heath, H. & Plumpton, B. (2000) Key Facilitation Skills for Effective On-Line Discussion Groups: Herding Cats through Piccadilly Circus, '*Distance Education: an open question?' Conference Proceedings*, Adelaide, Australia, Sept. 2000 [on-line]

http://www.com.unisa.edu.au/cccc/papers/refereed/paper11/Paper11-1.htm

Crowley, L. & Tall, D. (2001) Attainment and Potential: Procedures, Cognitive Kit-Bags and Cognitive Units, submitted to PME25, July 2001 [on-line] http://www.uky.edu/LCC/MATH/Crowley/papers/PME25.pdf

Hewson, L. and Hughes, C. (1998) Templates for online teaching, *ASCILITE'98*, 329-338 [on-line] http://cedir.uow.edu.au/ASCILITE98/asc98-pdf/hewsonhughes.pdf

Hoddinott, J. (1998) Constructive alignment: A pedagogical model applied to a plant physiological ecology subject delivered over the world wide web, *ASCILITE'98 Proceedings Supplement* 21-22 [on-line] http://cedir.uow.edu.au/ASCILITE98/abw_09c.html

Lincoln, M., Stockhausen, L. & Maloney, D. (1997) Learning Processes in Clinical Education. In McAllister, L., Lincoln, M., McLeod, S. & Maloney, D. (eds), *Facilitating Learning in Clinical Settings*, 99-129, Stanley Thornes, Cheltenham

McAllister, L., Lincoln, M., McLeod, S. & Maloney, D. (eds) (1997) *Facilitating Learning in Clinical Settings*, Stanley Thornes, Cheltenham.

Mason, R. (1998) *Globalising Education: Trends and Applications*, Routledge [on-line]

http://iet.open.ac.uk/pp/r.d.mason/globalbook/syncasync.html

Salmon, G. & Giles, K. (1999) Creating and Implementing Successful On-Line Learning Environments: A Practitioner's Perspective. *European Open and Distance Learning Journal* [on-line] http://kurs.nks.no/eurodl/eurodlen/index.html

Salmon, G. (2000) *E-Moderating: The Key to Teaching and Learning On-Line*, Kogan Page, London

University of Alberta, Department of Biology (2001) Botany 431 - Physiological Plant Ecology. Teaching, Learning and the Development of Student Thinking [on-line]

http://www.biology.ualberta.ca/courses.hp/bot431.hp/thinking.html

University of Bradford, Department of Civil and Environmental Engineering (2001) Communication Skills - First Class Answer [on-line] http://www.brad.ac.uk/acad/civeng/studsupp/fca.htm

University of Sydney (2001) BACH5186 Graduate Skills for Professional Development, Grades Table, Explanation of Assignment Grade [on-line] http://www.cchs.usyd.edu.au/bach/5186/grades_table.htm

Wegerif, R. (1998) The social dimension of asynchronous learning networks, *Journal of Asynchronous Learning Networks vol. 2 no. 1*, 34-49 [on-line] http://www.aln.org/alnweb/journal/vol2_issue1/wegerif.htm

Cracking the Code: Learning to Collaborate and Collaborating to Learn in a Networked Environment

Vic Lally[1], Maarten de Laat[2]

University of Sheffield[1] University of Nijmegen[2]

v.lally@sheffield.ac.uk m.delaat@ped.kun.nl

ABSTRACT

This paper is based on the central idea that networked teaching may best be improved by those engaged in it. Systematic enquiry into educational interactions can yield understandings and insights about one of the fundamental relationships of all educational endeavours: between teaching and learning. The paper explores this relationship through analyses of teaching and learning in a networked collaborative learning environment using two new content analysis schemas. The first of these probes the social co-construction of knowledge in a collaborative online event by analysing the social, cognitive and metacognitive contributions to an online learning event. In the second schema the presence of teacher processes is investigated. Computer assisted qualitative data analysis is used for this. In conclusion, consideration is given to the prospects for this type of approach as a means of enriching understandings of the complexity of the relationship between teaching and learning in networked collaborative learning environments.

Keywords

Social constructivism, content analysis, collaborative teaching and learning, on-line tutoring

INTRODUCTION

The central idea in this paper is that networked teaching may best be improved by those engaged in it. This is based upon the premise that systematic enquiry into educational interactions can yield understandings and insights about one of the central relationships of all educational endeavours: between teaching and learning. Unless teachers make rich links between their teaching 'acts' and students' learning it is difficult for them to improve their own teaching in order to improve learning. This is not a new idea. It is self-evident in some senses: teachers will naturally claim responsibility if their students are successful in examinations. In their attribution, their teaching acts have brought about learning in their students - as measured by the output, examination performance. This may be a rather bold and unhelpful assertion. Firstly it is a very general one; it offers no detailed insight into what 'worked' and what 'didn't'. Therefore, it provides no local evidence base on which the individual teacher can act about the details of her teaching. Nor does it provide any systematic basis for communicating the effective and efficient aspects of practice to others. Secondly it takes no pro-active account of the different needs of students; it gives no insight into what it was about the teaching that produced 'good' measurable learning outcomes in some of the students, nor what happened to students who didn't demonstrate these outcomes. Thirdly it equates learning with assessable outcomes, in a way that limits the understanding of learning to the data provided by the output measurement instrument. Learning as an ongoing set of processes, happening in time and space, within an individual and groups, does not feature in detail in this general analysis. Fourthly it makes no connection with learning theories or, if it does it, it is with personal and usually tacit understandings about learning held by the individual teacher. In summary, the main problem with this self evident linking of teaching and learning is that it is un-evidenced, overlooks the diversity of students' learning needs and processes, and generates relatively little localised insight into what works and what doesn't. Sotto (Sotto, 1996) has argued this point very cogently: that good teaching in higher education is far from self-evident, and that its connection to students' learning is complex, both in terms of learning outcomes at the end of a teaching and learning event (lecture seminar or whatever) and learning processes occurring during that event.

ANALYSING NETWORKED TEACHING AND LEARNING

The networked environment provides the teacher with some new opportunities to understand the nature of teaching and its many and complex links with learning. As the text remains available to the teacher and the students, after the primary interactions between them have moved on, it is a resource that can be used as part of an attempt by the teacher or the students to understand the nature of the teaching and learning that have taken place. The challenge, when looking back at messages exchanged between students and teachers in a networked collaborative learning environment, is to understand what Popping (Popping, 2000) has called the world of 'meanings, values and norms' which are 'invisible' to a casual observer. In a teaching and learning context, then, it's more than trying to understand what was said about whatever subject was under discussion between the learners and the teacher. It is about trying to understand the social and cognitive processes of knowledge and meaning construction occurring between and within individuals and the group. An important educational aim of attempting content analysis in order to develop these understandings is broadly the same as for Action Research in any context: to help improve the quality of the situation, in this case the learners' learning and the teacher's teaching. In the case of this type of content analysis, the understandings created about the social and cognitive processes occurring can be used: for the immediate benefit of present learners in the context, that is, to use specific understandings to make immediate (and probably relatively small scale) improvements to some aspects of the situation; for the benefit of future learners in the context, by making more general improvements to aspects of the situation (perhaps structural).

The major challenge facing the teacher is how to attempt an analysis of messages, to understand the implications of this analysis for teaching and learning, and then to act upon the situation in order to improve it for the learners, as well as for her or himself. Tools for analysing communication patterns have been developed in several disciplines, (for example applied linguistics), but are generally based upon analysis of large bodies of text (corpora) and involve relatively cumbersome methods. They are not designed for Action Research use in the immediacy of particular teaching and learning situations. Furthermore, they are not designed to analyse dynamic, ongoing social situations where knowledge is actively being co-constructed by the participants. In the next section we will describe our coding schemas and the rationale for our choice. This is followed by a description of the educational context on which we have drawn for the analyses presented here.

THEORETICAL BASIS OF LEARNING, TEACHING AND CONTENT ANALYSIS

In previous work (Barrett and Lally, 1999; De Laat, De Jong and Ter Huurne, 2000; De Laat, De Jong and Simons, 2001; Lally, 2001; Lally and Barrett, 1999) we have explored a range of aspects of collaborative learning and begun to develop analytical frameworks in order to understand the complex teaching and learning processes that are occurring. In the analysis presented in this paper we are interested in gaining insight into collaborative knowledge construction and teacher presence in a collaborative learning environment through the use of two compatible coding schemas. The students featured here were following a Master's Programme in Networked Collaborative Learning (see below for details). Our analysis is based upon work conducted by students and a tutor in the first workshop of this programme. Here we were particularly interested to explore the relationship between knowledge construction and teacher presence as these evolved over time within the workshop. Previously we have used Henri's approach to content analysis (Henri, 1989; 1992) using categories that focus on the social activity and the interactivity of individuals in a group at the same time as giving a picture of the cognitive and meta-cognitive processes of those individuals. However, one of its major limitations is that it gives us no impression of the social co-construction of knowledge by the group of individuals as a group, in a discussion or a seminar. We have also attempted to address this limitation using a schema proposed by Gunawardena et al. (1997), with some success. Influenced principally by the work of Vygotsky (1962; 1978) (although see Gillen, 2000 for a critique of the fashionableness of this process) many authors (for example: Goldstein, 1999; Lave, 1988; Lave, 1996; Lave & Wenger, 1991; Salomon & Perkins, 1998), in attempting to define cognition in groups (group mediated cognition or gmc), have suggested that, in a group meeting, the situation itself may exert a strong mediating effect on individual cognitive and conceptual processes. The thinking of individuals is influenced by the group in which they are working. The merger of intellectual and social processes may be a fundamental feature of group mediated cognition. A second key feature is the tension between the conceptual structure or understanding (of the problem or ideas under discussion) of the group and that of the individuals within it. These individual understandings may vary from each other as well as the group. This tension is the driving force for the collective processing of the group. So, for example, when an individual member of the group expresses her opinion in relation to the shared public understanding of the group, this will be based on an attempt to synthesise her own understanding with the public one. The other members of the group will compare this new synthesis with their own understandings of the group-accepted version and their own disagreements with it. Depending on the outcome of this process there may be further interaction and negotiation until a new meaning or understanding is accepted by the group. In this process interaction between individuals, as well as their shared and individual cognitions, are the key aspects of co-construction of knowledge, meaning and understanding.

We have premised our present analysis on this 'social-constructivist' view of learning: learners linking new knowledge to their prior knowledge- i.e. learning as a cumulative process: learners constructing new internal representations of the information being presented (Boekaerts & Simons, 1995). Learning is a process by which the learner personalizes new information by giving meaning to it, based upon earlier experiences. Meaning is seen as rooted in, and indexed by experience (Brown, et al., 1989). Each experience with an idea, and the environment of which that idea is part, becomes part of the meaning of that idea (Duffy & Jonassen, 1992). Learning is therefore understood as situated in the activity in which it takes place (Brown, et al. 1989; Lave & Wenger, 1991). Whereas the social-constructivist perspectives makes a distinction between the individual cognitive activities and the environment in which the individual is present, the socio-cultural perspective regards the individual as being part of that environment. They point out that learning cannot be understood as a process that is solely in the mind of the learner (Van Boxtel, 2000). Knowledge is constructed in settings of joint activity (Koschmann, 2000). Learning is a process of participating in cultural practices a process that structures and shapes cognitive activity (Lave & Wenger, 1991). The socio-cultural perspective gives prominence to the aspect of mutuality of the relations between members and emphasizes the dialectic nature of the learning interaction (Sfard, 1998). Construction of knowledge takes place in a social context, such as might be found in collaborative activities of the MEd in Networked Collaborative Learning featured in this paper (see McConnell, 2000 for a much more detailed exploration of collaborative learning). In addition, Lethinen et al. (1999) argues that conceptual understanding is fostered through explaining a problem to other students. Therefore, in collaborative learning it is necessary to formulate learning objectives, to make learning plans, to share information, to negotiate about knowledge and to take decisions (Veldhuis-Diermanse & Biemans, 2000). In a setting of collaborative learning, students can criticize their own and other students' contributions, they can ask for explanations, they can give counter arguments and, in this way, they will stimulate themselves and the other students. Additionally, they can motivate and help each other to finish the task. Social-constructivist collaborative learning is a powerful educational method to realise academic goals. In the MEd programme the tutor acts as in three important ways: to design the curriculum and the environment, in outline; to facilitate discourse among participants, and to provide some direct instruction related to the topics under discussion. However, it is important to acknowledge that these roles may also be undertaken by the students in this course environment. In networked learning settings we see that learners become tutors and that tutors become learners (Gartner & Riessman, 2000). Their roles interact and change over time. The original role of the teacher moves from a central position towards a guide on the side, fostering an online learning culture in which participants take charge of their own learning (Collison, 2000).

In order to probe collaborative knowledge construction and teacher presence in this learning environment we used two new coding schemas. The first, modified from Veldhuis-Diermanse and Biemans (2000) was used to investigate group knowledge construction. This included four main categories. The first is cognitive activities (thinking activities) students use to process the learning content and to attain their learning goals. The category 'cognitive activities' consists of three subcategories: (1) debating, (2) using external information and experiences and (3) linking or repeating internal information. The second category is metacognitive activities: metacognition refers to metacognitive knowledge as well as to metacognitive skills. Metacognitive knowledge can be defined as knowledge concerning one's own cognitive processes and products or anything related to them. Metacognitive skills concern the extent to which students can regulate their cognitive activities and, therefore, their own learning process. These skills are essential to successful learning because they enable individuals to manage their cognitive skills, and to determine problems that can be solved by applying other cognitive skills. The third category is affective activities. These are used to cope with feelings occurring during learning and can lead to a state of mind influencing the learning process positively, negatively or neutrally (Vermunt, 1992). The final category, miscellaneous, was used to score all other units. This category includes social talk as well as units that can not be coded according to one of the other categories. The second schema, adapted from Anderson and Rourke et al. (2000), is used to probe teacher presence. This includes three main sub-categories. The first, design and organization, refers to the construction of the processes, structures, evaluation and interaction components of the course. The second, facilitating discourse, refers to the maintenance of interest, motivation and engagement of students in active learning. The term discourse is used, rather than discussion, to highlight the focused and sustained deliberation that marks learning in a community of inquiry (Lipman, 1991) or as Scardamalia and Bereiter (1994) refer to it, the knowledge-building community. The third sub-category is direct instruction. This refers to the teacher's provision of intellectual and scholarly leadership and the sharing of subject matter knowledge with students. Davie (1989) describes this as the ability to set and communicate the intellectual climate of the course or seminar, and model the qualities of a scholar. The teacher communicates content knowledge that is enhanced by the teacher's personal interest, excitement and in-depth understanding of the content. The cognitive apprenticeship model espoused by Collins & Brown (1991), Rogoff's (1995) model of apprenticeship in thinking or Vygotsky's (1978) scaffolding analogies illustrate an assistive role for teachers in providing instructional support to students from their position of greater content knowledge.

COMPUTER ASSISTANCE FOR CONTENT ANALYSIS

In the process of analysing teaching and learning situations in a networked collaborative learning environment, messages from a learning event need to be coded and analysed. The central purpose of coding is to extract, generalise and abstract from the complexity of the original data in order to find significant themes and develop theories about the situation that illuminate it. This is a delicate balance between oversimplification, resulting in the loss of subtlety and insight into complex processes, and over-coding where the themes and trends are still obscured by too many sub-categories. Bearing these dangers in mind, we decided to use computer assisted data analysis software (CAQDAS). The main advantages of such an approach include: partial automation of the coding process, with increased speed of coding; a wider range of ways to search, recode and interrogate the coded data (in this case messages), including visual coding and more sophisticated coding at 'nodes' - this allows instantaneous access to all the text coded for a particular category; the possibility to code creatively, that is, to develop new codes, and re-code, in response to the patterns in the coded data as they emerge (a grounded approach). A helpful account of some of the issues around the use of CAQDAS have been provided by Barry (Barry, 1998). One powerful package which we have found suitable for coding networked collaborative learning interactions is QSR NUD*IST Vivo (NVivo) (Qualitative Solutions and Research, 1999). This package offers powerful tools for coding and interpretation of coded conferences and events from on-line situations. The messages can easily be imported directly into NVivo for coding, and nodes created from any categories used for coding. A very useful overview of the use of NVivo in this type of work is provided by Richards (Richards, 1999).

THE MASTER'S PROGRAMME IN NETWORKED COLLABORATIVE LEARNING

The MEd in Networked Collaborative Learning by action research is an advanced part-time programme designed to provide participants with a comprehensive grounding in the theory and application of networked teaching and learning. The programme focuses on learning about information and communication technologies; designing online learning; developing learning communities; and working with online groups of collaborative learners. The MEd programme is suitable for a wide variety of professional people who wish to develop their understanding of, and expertise in, this form of learning. Current participants include: professional trainers and developers, self employed or in public and private sector organizations; teachers and lecturers in Further, Higher and Open Education; adult continuing educators; people working in libraries and resource centers; open and distance learning educators and developers. The programme is based upon the establishment of a research learning community among the participants and tutors. In this community activities are undertaken around five workshops over a two year period. In brief, the workshop structure is:

Year One

Workshop One (4 months online): An Introduction to Online Learning

Workshop Two (4 months online): Networked Learning and Computer Supported Cooperative Work

Workshop Three (4 months on-line): The Internet as a Learning Environment

Year Two

Workshop Four (3 months on-line): Designing for Research and Evaluation

Workshop Five (9 months online): Research Dissertation

RESULTS

Figures 1 to 4 show the results of coding three samples from one learning set of workshop one of the MEd. In this analysis we have attempted to reveal the social co-construction of knowledge in a set of threaded discussions undertaken by a sophisticated group of adult learners. At the same time, we have also tried to reveal the teaching processes that may be supporting this co-construction. In attempting to make sense of this analysis it is important to understand the pedagogical context of their work. The participants collaborated for approximately 10 weeks in order to construct a group project around an aspect of networked learning. It is this collaboration that forms the focus of the analysis presented here. The overall structure of the activity was predetermined by the course tutor team, and published in the WebCT group space well in advance of the commencement of the activity. The group had previously spent approximately one month together in the online space, engaged in a set of activities designed to support the establishment and development of the research learning community. The project work followed on from this process. Each learning 'set' or sub-community was assigned a tutor. The three tutors shared a common approach, with an agreement to some variation according to the tutor's own views and style of working. The approach consisted of supporting and facilitating the group's work, and providing some knowledge input when appropriate, according to the tutor's own expertise and interests. In many respects the tutor undertook to behave as a participant in the group, rather than as a leader or more traditional instructor. Therefore, there is little evidence of direct instruction by either the tutor, or other participants, in any of the discussions featured in this analysis. This is typical of the 'style' of teaching espoused by the course tutor team for the course as a whole. In all cases we coded units of meaning with either the appropriate subcategory of the learning schema or the teaching schema. These were used exclusively. The collaborative project of this set consisted of approximately 1000 messages. Our sample, at the beginning, middle and end of this discussion consists of approximately 10 per cent of that total.

Figure One. Early Phase of Discussions (x axis = days; y axis = percentage of all coded units of meaning)

Learning (After Veldhuis-Diermanse & Biemans, 2000)

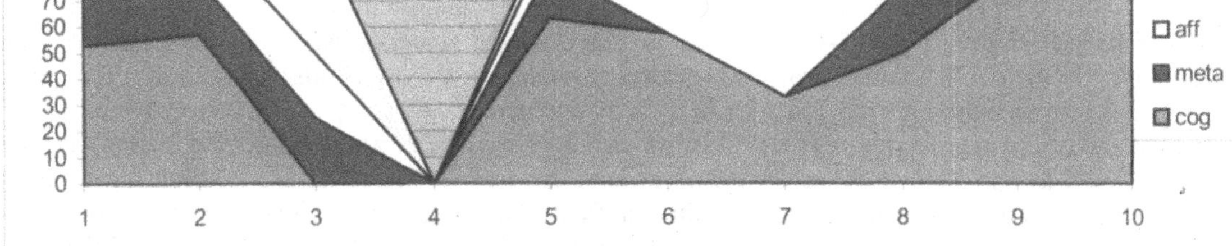

Teaching (After Anderson, et al.,2000)

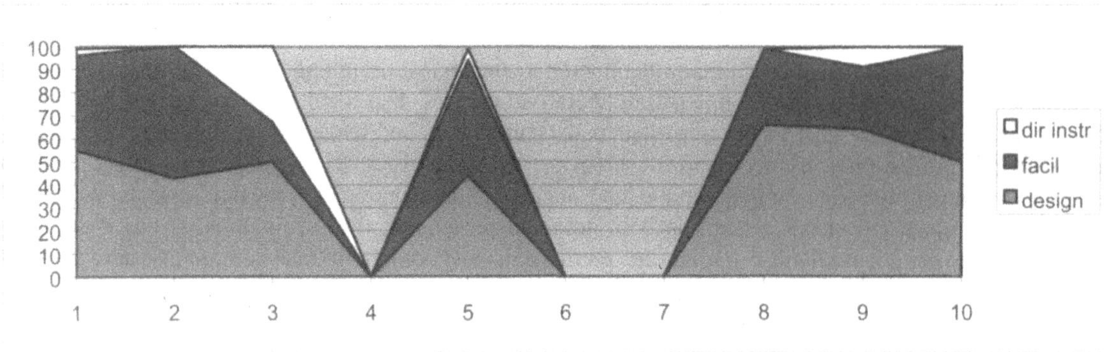

The first sample of discussion threads occurs in the early phase of the group collaborative project (figure 1 and 30-10 to 9-11 in figure 4). At this point the students were formulating their project, with the aid of the tutor, and agreeing procedures to facilitate their work together. The main features of this phase of group activities include a high level of cognitive activity, as indicated using the learning schema to code the interactions. This activity is in a ratio of approximately 3.3:1 with metacognitive activity. There are two discernible peaks in learning activity. These coincide with peaks in teaching activity. Much of the teaching has been coded as design and organization discussion, together with facilitation. The simultaneous peaking of the teaching and learning discussion within the group indicates a strong linkage between these two types of processes. There is little direct instruction taking place in the group's deliberations.

Figure Two. Middle Phase of Discussions (x axis = days; y axis = percentage of all coded units of meaning)

Learning (After Veldhuis-Diermanse &Biemans, 2000)

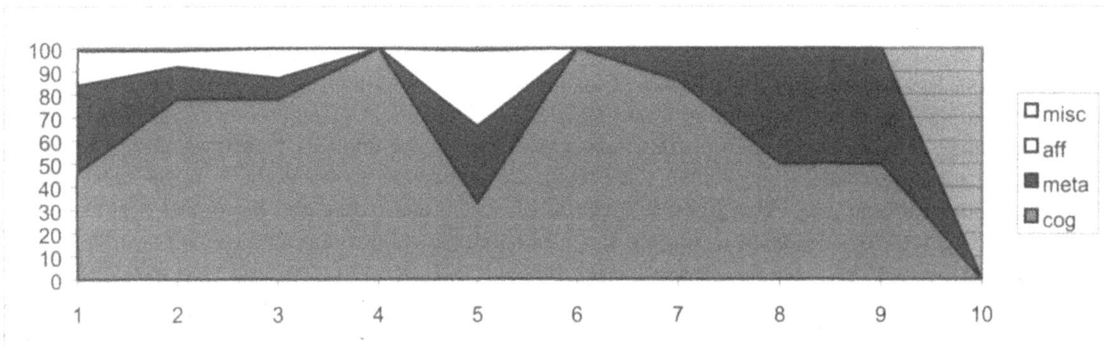

Teaching *(After Anderson, et al.,2000)*

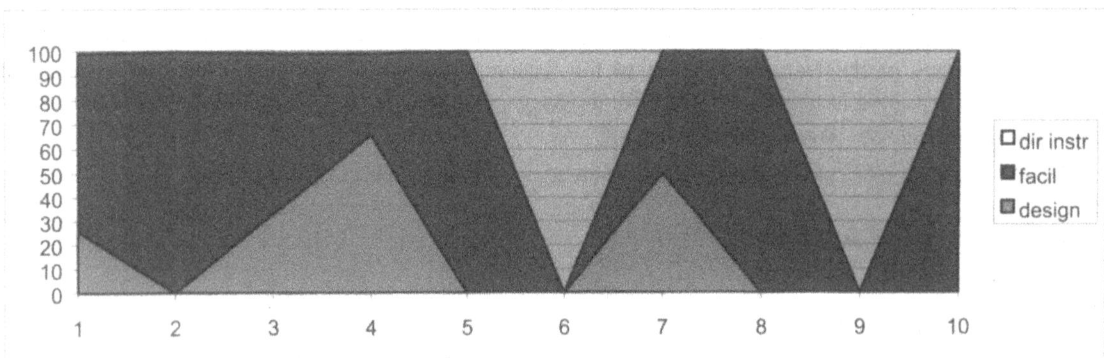

In the second sample of threads (figure 2 and 5-12 to 11-12 in figure 4) the students were well advanced with the development and compilation of their collaborative project. The level of cognitive activity is raised further as a proportion of all learning sub-categories, compared to the early threads (70 per cent compared to 60 per cent in the early threads). This corresponds to a relative reduction in affective activity from 16 per cent to 10 per cent, suggesting that social and motivational comments offered to one another by group members have reduced as their working relationship becomes established and they focus more on the task in hand. Metacognitive activity shows little change overall (18 per cent in the early phase and 20 per cent in the middle phase) and its ratio to cognitive activity stays quite constant at 3.5:1. It is interesting to note that within teaching activity there has been a major shift of emphasis. In the early phase 50 per cent of the teaching activity was coded as design and organization, and 35 per cent was facilitation. In the middle phase the design and organisation has decreased to 25 per cent and facilitation to 75 per cent. This is compatible with the notion that much of the organizational arrangements have been made for the project, and the students and tutor are now helping each other to discuss and explore the project as they work. There is one large peak of learning activity, occurring early in this phase (around 6-12). Once again we see this peak at the same time as the peak in teaching activity, as with the early phase thread sample. This underscores the linkage in time already identified between learning and teaching aspects of the discussions observed in the early phase.

Figure Three. Concluding Phase of Discussions (x axis = days; y axis = percentage of all coded units of meaning)

Learning (After Veldhuise-Diermanse & Biemans, 2000)

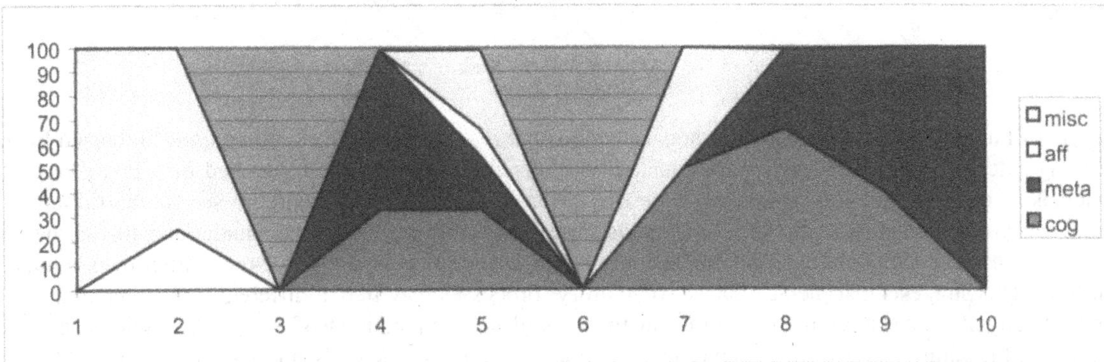

Teaching (After Anderson, et al., 2000)

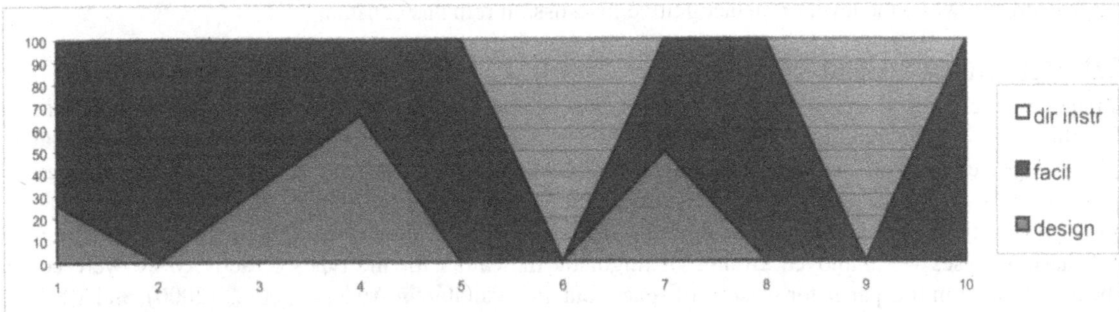

In the third (concluding) sample of threads (figure 3 and 29-12 to 14-1 of figure 4) the project work is drawing to a close and students, together with their tutor, are reflecting on the process and discussing their preparations for the presentation of their work to the other groups. Within the learning discussions, the balance between cognitive and metacognitive activity has shifted to a ratio of 1.9:1 (42 per cent of cognitive activity and 22 percent of metacognitive activity), as a result of an overall decrease in cognitive discussion. At the same time, the level of metacognitive discussion has stayed almost constant. Affective discussion is at a similar level to the middle phase (10 per cent), with miscellaneous discussion activity appearing in this phase to replace, to some extent, the cognitive discussions. Within the teaching activity there is still a strong emphasis on facilitation (65 per cent). However, this has reduced from the middle phase, with a concomitant small increase in design and organization as the students think about their presentation to the other groups. Once again we see an alignment, in time, between the learning and teaching activity within the group, but with some notable differences. There are three peaks of activity (3-1, 9-1 and 13-1). All of the learning peaks are aligned, in time, with peaks for teaching. One noticeable difference in the learning peaks, when compared to earlier patterns, is that in the first peak the maximum cognitive and metacognitive levels coincide. However, in the second smaller peak the raised level of metacognitive activity precedes the cognitive activity. In the third learning peak there is raised cognitive activity, but this is not associated with a rise in metacognitive discussion.

In our view, some clear patterns have emerged from our analysis. Using two coding schemas, for teaching and learning, and coding contributions to the discussion over time, has enabled us to interrogate the complex relationship between these processes within a group. The most striking feature of the discussions in the group is that, within the discernible peaks of discussion activity, high levels of learning and teaching are co-incident in time. This is a clear pattern that can be seen throughout the samples of the three phases of activity. While it is not possible to describe this relationship as causal, the analysis does indicate a strong linkage of these two types of activity within the group as a whole. At this level the analysis does not enable us to identify whether some individuals are acting in a teacherly way while others are learning. This will be probed in future analyses. However, the pattern is consistent and deserves further attention to attempt to understand the nature and significance of the interaction in more detail. Further patterns are identifiable. The levels of cognitive activity throughout the discussions are in the order of two to three times higher than for metacognitive activity.

Figure Four. Learning and teaching interaction (x axis = days; y axis = percentage of all coded units of meaning)

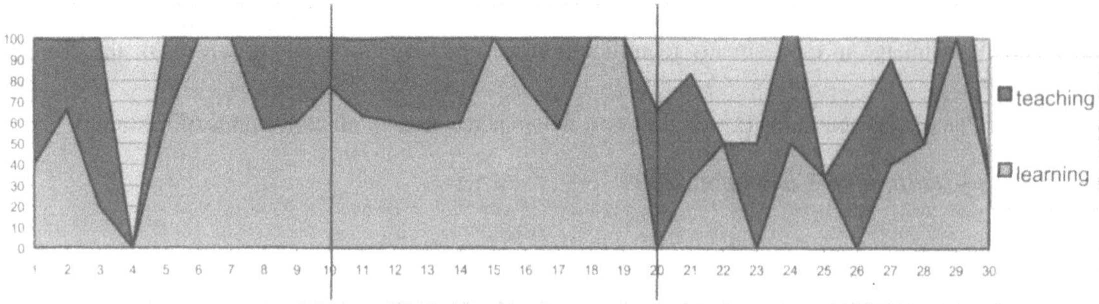

Yet peaks in both types of activity occur together. This suggests to us that regulative activities, of the types indicated by the metacognitive learning categories we have used, are associated with discussions about the topic, and may be a necessary part of increased levels of cognitive activity associated with this. Once again, it is not possible to see the partitioning of these functions between group members at the level of analysis we have employed. We shall undertake this as part of further work. In one case, in the concluding phase, the metacognitive peak precedes the cognitive one, rather than being co-incident with it in time. This suggests that metacognitive 'regulatory' processes may play a different role in relation to the more 'subject-focused' cognitive discussions, depending on the overall stage or context of the work being undertaken. Furthermore, the nature of teaching activity changes within the group over time. In the early phase of discussions there is a relatively high level of design and organisation as the group prepares for the task. As the task proceeds this is replaced by facilitation of discussion that continues for the remainder of the work. At the same time, as the task is concluded the levels of cognitive activity decrease, while the level of metacognitive discsussion remains constant.

DISCUSSION AND CONCLUSIONS

The aim of this paper is to explore the relationship between teaching and learning in a networked collaborative learning environment. For this purpose we used two new content analysis schemas. The first of these probes the social co-construction of knowledge (learning) in a collaborative online event by analysing the affective, cognitive and metacognitive contributions to the event. In the second schema, the presence of teacher processes (teaching) is revealed and discriminated using sub-categories for design and organisation, facilitation of discussion, and direct instruction (after Anderson et. al., 2000). In each of these analyses we employed a range of linguistic indicators for the types of activity we were coding. These have not been presented in this paper for reasons of space, but are available in Anderson et. al. (2000), and Veldhuis-Diermanse and Biemans (2000).

These analyses begin to reveal the detail of the processes occurring as a group works to construct new knowledge and understanding over time. Furthermore they indicate that high levels of teacher functions are occurring as this construction proceeds, and seem to be interacting with it in regular, discernible but complex ways. Regulation of cognitive activity is revealed to be an ongoing process, often but not always co-incident with it, indicating the possibility of more than one mode of interaction between cognitive and metacognitive processes. All of these functions are undertaken by many of the participants in the group. There is no strong indication that the tutor is initiating these processes within this discussion. However, further and more detailed analysis will be required to explore the precise nature of the tutor's role as a participant within the group. The triggering mechanisms for peaks of activity remain to be identified, as does the process by which these become magnified within the group into high levels of learning and teaching.

These analyses, using two compatible coding schemas and allied to a computer assisted approach to coding, have enabled us to characterise a substantial collaborative learning and teaching event within the MEd. in Networked Collaborative Learning. However, many questions still remain to be answered. We have not looked in detail at the correlations between learning and teaching processes and learning outcomes. The group featured in this analysis was a high functioning group that created a substantial report of high quality. There was good participation by all members of the group. In this sense the processes illuminated in this paper represent those of a high achieving group collaborating on an extended project. The group members were contributing both learning and teaching activity to the group processes. Our analysis does not feature the nature of individual processes within the group. It is not possible, therefore, to elucidate the interactions between the individual as a learning entity and the group as another learning entity. This will have to wait for future analysis, and is part of our ongoing project to fully analyse the nature of all of the learning and teaching interactions occurring within a collaborating group. A further limitation of our analysis is that it is based only on those processes that are articulated by group members. Processes that are not articulated may be having an effect on the explicit processes, but they are hidden from direct analysis. In order to understand these processes we shall, in future investigations, use stimulated recall by participants at significant points in the development of the expressed processes. With this data it may then be possible to relate the hidden processes in the event to those that we can see expressed on the screen.

The title of this paper reflects our concern to 'crack the code' of learning and teaching processes occurring in real, complex events in collaborative online education. Our analysis reveals a complexity and time-related development of these processes that can be correlated with the structure of the educational task and the skills required by group members to address it successfully. We are optimistic that the approach we have described and used here will enable us to probe a range of different events and understand the processes revealed in ways that can yield insights that may be of value to online educators in many contexts. We shall report this work in further papers in due course.

REFERENCES

Anderson, T., Rourke, L., Garrison, D. R. and Archer, W. (2000). Assessing Teaching Presence in a Computer Conferencing Context. http://www.atl.ualberta.ca/cmc/publications.html [27/3/2001]

Barrett, E., & Lally, V. (1999). Gender differences in an on-line learning environment. *Journal of Computer Assisted Learning, 15*(1), 48-60.

Barry, C. A. (1998). Choosing Qualitative Data Analysis Software: Atlas/ti and Nudist Compared. *Sociological Research Online, 3*(3), 1-17.

Boekaerts, M. & Simons, P.R.J. (1995). Leren en instructie: psychologie van de leerling en het leerproces [Learning and instruction: psychology of the learner and his learning process]. Assen: Dekker & Van de Vegt.

Brown, J. S., Collins, A., & Duguid, P. (1989). Situated cognition and the culture of learning. *Educational Researcher, 18*(1), 32-42.

Collins A. & Brown J. S. (1991). Cognitive apprenticeship: Making things visible. American Educator 15(3) 38-46.

Collison, G., Elbaum, B., Haavind, S., & Tinker, R. (2000). Facilitating online learning: Effective strategies for moderators. Madison: Atwood.

Davie, L. (1989). Facilitation techniques for the on-line tutor, In R. Mason and A. Kaye (Eds.), Mindweave: Communication, computers and distance education (pp. 74-85). Oxford: Pergamon Press,.

De Laat, M., De Jong, F., and Ter Huurne, J. (2000). Supporting a Community of Practice: The Role of Workers as Learners. Paper presented at Ed-Media, Montreal, Canada June 26 2000.

De Laat, M., De Jong, F., and Simons, R-J. (2001). Supporting Self Regulation of Learning Activities in Online Communities of Practice. Poster paper presented at the First European Conference on Computer Supported Collaborative Learning, Maastricht, Netherlands, March 2001.

Duffy, T. M., & Jonassen, D. H. (1992). Constructivism: new implications for instructional technology. In T. M. Duffy & D. H. Jonassen (Eds.), *Constructivism and the technology of instruction: a conversation.* New Jersey: Lawrence Erlbaum associates.

Gartner, A., & Riessman, F. (2000). Peer-tutoring: Toward a new model. *http://www.educationplanet.com.*

Gillen, J. (2000). Versions of Vygotsky. *British Journal of Educational Studies, 48*(2), 183-198.

Goldstein, L. S. (1999). The relational zone: The role of caring relationships in the co-construction of mind. *American Educational Research Journal, 36*(3), 647-673.

Gunawardena, C. N., Lowe, C. A., & Anderson, T. (1997). Analysis of a Global Online Debate and the Development of an Interaction Analysis Model for Examining Social Construction of Knowledge in Computer Conferencing. *Journal of Educational Computing Research, 17*(4), 397-431.

Henri, F. (1989). La Téléconference assistée par ordinateur dans une activité de formation à distance. Unpublished Thèse de doctorat, Concordia University, Montreal.

Henri, F. (1992). Computer Conferencing and Content Analysis. In A. R. Kaye (Ed.), *Collaborative Learning Through Computer Conferencing: The Najaden Papers* (pp. 117-136). London: Springer-Verlag.

Koschmann, T. (1999). *Toward a dialogic theory of learning: Bakhtin's contribution to understanding learning in settings of collaboration.* Paper presented at the CSCL'99, Palo Alto.

Lally, V. (2001). Analysing Teaching and Learning in a Networked Collaborative Learning Environment: Issues and Work in Progress. In Day, C. W. and van Veen, D. (Eds.), *Educational Research in Europe Yearbook 2001* (pp. 219-237). Leuven: Garant/EERA.

Lally, V. E., & Barrett, E. (1999). Building a Learning Community On-Line: towards socio-academic interaction. *Research Papers in Education, 14*(2), 147-163.

Lave, J. (1988). *Cognition in Practice*. Cambridge: Cambridge University Press.

Lave, J. (1996). Teaching as Learning, in Practice. *Mind, Culture and Activity, 3*(3), 149-164.

Lave, J., & Wenger, E. (1991). *Situated Learning: legitimate peripheral participation*. Cambridge: Cambridge University Press.

Lethinen, E., Hakkarainen, K., Lipponen, L. Rahikainen, M. & Muukkonen, H. (1999). *Computer supported collaborative learning: A review*. CL-Net Project. Available: http://www.kas.utu.fi/clnet/clnetreport.html [1999, August 17].

Lipman, M. Thinking in education. Cambridge: Cambridge University Press, 1991.

McConnell, D. (2000). *Implementing Computer Supported Co-operative Learning*. London: Kogan Page.

Popping, R. (2000). *Computer Assisted Text Analysis*. London: Sage.

Qualitative Solutions and Research. (1999). QSR NUD*IST Vivo (NVivo) (Version 1.1). London: Sage.

Richards, L. (1999). *Using NVivo in Qualitative Research*. Bundoora, Victoria, Australia: Qualitative Solutions and Research.

Rogoff, B. (1995). Apprenticeship in thinking. New York: Cambridge University Press.

Salomon, G., & Perkins. D. N. (1998). Individual and Social Aspects of Learning. *Review of Research in Education*, 23, 1-24.

Scardamalia, M., & Bereiter, C. (1994). Computer support for knowledge-building communities. Journal of the Learning Sciences, 3(3), 265-283,.

Sfard, A. (1998). On two metaphors for learning and the dangers of choosing just one. *Educational researcher, 27*(2), 4-13.

Sotto, E. (1996). The Self-evident Nature of Teaching. *Innovations in Education and Training International, 33*(3), 203-209.

Van Boxtel, C. (2000). *Collaborative Concept Learning: collaborative learning tasks, student interaction and the learning of physics concepts.*, Universiteit Utrecht

Veldhuis-Diermanse, A. E. and Biemans, H. J. A. (2000). Is CSCL an adequate tool to reach a deep level of academic learning? Submitted to *Learning and Instruction*

Vygotsky, L. S. (1962). *Thought and Language* (E. Hanfmann and G. Vakar, Trans.). Cambridge, MA: MIT Press.

Vygotsky, L. S. (1978). *Mind in Society: the development of higher psychological processes* (M. Cole, V. John-Steiner, S. Scribner and E. Souberman, Trans.). Cambridge MA: Harvard University Press.

Taking The 'No' Out of Lotus Notes: Activity Theory, Groupware, and Student Groupwork

John Halloran, Yvonne Rogers, Mike Scaife

Interact Lab, School of Cognitive and Computing Sciences, University of Sussex, UK

{johnhall,yvonner,mikesc}@cogs.susx.ac.uk

ABSTRACT

This paper describes a study that examined why groupware that was tailored to support collaborative student learning (Lotus Notes) was unsuccessful. In particular, it examines why the tutors' aspirations of helping the students to collaborate were not met. It was found that students tended not to use the groupware, preferring other, self-developed support tools. Our study shows that the failure was multidetermined: there was a complex interacting set of factors including software use problems, systems integration issues, conflicting tutor/student perceptions of the value of using the groupware, and conflicts in each group's view of how best to complete the course. There has been interest in using Activity Theory to approach multidimensional analysis in CSCL, but existing Activity Theory-based frameworks can be difficult to apply to instances of collaborative learning marked by conflict. To address this need, we use an Activity Theory-based analytic tool called the Activity Space. The tool is also used to show how multiple changes could be made to improve the potential for groupware to be used as intended.

Keywords

Student Groupwork, Groupware, Lotus Notes, Activity Theory, Activity System, Activity Space

INTRODUCTION

In this paper, we discuss a study of how students worked together on an undergraduate computer science course. On this course, students, working in groups, had to design and program a computer game. The course had two main objectives: first, to give collaborating students experience of dealing with a complex, distributed software development task; and second, to help them develop group management, coordination and communication skills - regarded as valuable preparation for postgraduate employment. Tutors were concerned to support both these objectives through the use of Lotus Notes, which was configured accordingly. However, despite Lotus Notes being apparently suited to students' and tutors' needs, the students avoided using it.

Resistance to use of Lotus Notes for collaborative work is not a new finding. Orlikowski (1992) discusses the non-uptake of Lotus Notes in an organization, elucidating the issues surrounding rejection. These are 'cognitive' - the absence of appropriate understanding of the software ('weak technological frames'), but also 'structural': the organization was hierarchically organized with competition for promotion, such that the collaborative, knowledge-sharing principles Lotus Notes represents were 'counter-cultural'. Thus, there was no incentive for staff to learn Lotus Notes. The implication here is that cognitive and structural factors need to be consistent with the purposes of groupware if there is to be genuine incentive, and the groupware is to be adopted. What is perhaps surprising about the rejection of Lotus Notes in our study is that the conditions for adoption appear to have been in place. Students did not have major problems understanding what sort of application Lotus Notes was and how it functions (appropriate technological frames existed); and the organization in which they work, a computer science department, is geared towards supporting learning through collaboration. Students are used to working together in groups, and need to do so to progress in their academic careers. Thus, there seems to have been ample incentive.

Our study, then, examines a persistent problem (non-uptake of Lotus Notes) in a new context (CSCL) with apparently different reasons. What were these reasons, and what are the general implications for supporting collaborative learning with groupware? Our study shows that the failure of Lotus Notes was determined by multiple, interacting factors such that is difficult to explain this failure in terms of a mismatch between the organizational ethos and the purposes of the groupware, or in terms of inadequate student understanding of the application. The reasons seem more elusive. On top of this, however, in common with Orlikowski's study (and other studies of groupware adoption problems, for example Grudin [1988]), there appears to have been conflict surrounding the use of the application. There was conflict in the perceptions of tutors and students on what the essential work necessary to complete the course was, conflict on the use of the tool as an aid to assessment, and conflict concerning the real value of the groupware for the groupwork.

To understand the failure of Lotus Notes to be used as intended on the course, and to address general problems of groupware adoption in student groupwork, we propose that a multidimensional analysis is needed. Within CSCL, there has been interest in multidimensional analysis and Activity Theory has been recognized as having potential for doing this (see, for example, Gifford and Enyedy, 1999). However, where tensions and contradictions are identified between the parties to collaborative learning, existing Activity Theory-based frameworks can be difficult to apply. In this paper, we use a new

Activity Theory-based framework, called the Activity Space. This allows us to deal with the issue of conflict while preserving the distinctive interactionism of Activity Theory. We use the Activity Space framework first as an analytic tool to identify, and specify the interactions between, the factors involved; and second, as a means of generating recommendations, in terms of groupware, to better support collaborative learning.

THE STUDY

Background and Method

The course that Lotus Notes was used for is a ten-week first-year undergraduate computer science course in software design and evaluation. Students, typically working in groups of four, have, first, to develop one of three pieces of software which, when put together, compose a game. Next, the group acquires the two other modules from other groups, and integrates these with their own. A group term paper is submitted documenting the whole process.

The introduction of Lotus Notes (chosen over alternatives because the University has a site licence and knowledgeable administrators) was intended to make collaboration easier for students, through provision of shared space for storage and editing; messaging facilities for everyday communications, including threading by topic; and space for writing minutes of meetings. In addition, supporting and assessing students' groupwork skills (management, coordination, communication) had previously presented difficulties for tutors as these processes tended to be invisible (assessment was done through evaluating students' *post-hoc* self-report in their term paper). Lotus Notes was intended to provide a solution: students were made aware that material they put onto their Lotus Notes group accounts would be tutor-viewable, and that the reason for this was that tutors could comment on, and assist with, group processes as they unfolded. Some material, notably minutes of meetings, would contribute to tutors' formal evaluation of students' group management skills, an assessable component of the course. What tutors hoped for, then, was full use of Lotus Notes not only for students to support themselves but also to provide rich data enabling tutor involvement in the group process.

Over the ten weeks of the course, we shadowed selected groups of students using ethnographic techniques including video observations (researcher-present or non-present); non-video observations (researcher-present), notetaking, informal interviews, inspection of students' written materials and course instructions. Students' Lotus Notes accounts were also available for us to inspect. We found that the use of the groupware differed a good deal from what tutors had intended.

Findings

At the very beginning of the course (in the first week), students used Lotus Notes to make contact, to begin to communicate about what they needed to do, to organize meeting times, and as a space to store early versions of their software designs. However, a major finding across all groups was that, as the course went on, postings to Lotus Notes became infrequent and highly formulaic, consisting mainly of minutes of meetings organized according to a standard template with sparse entries, apparently quickly produced. As a messaging system, Lotus Notes was also neglected: students did not use it for formatting and organizing day-to-day communications. This was done through students' standard e-mail accounts, held on the UNIX teaching network, even though this meant that specific communications about the groupwork on the course would appear in inboxes unsorted. There was little or no use of Lotus Notes as a shared storage or editing space – as had been planned by the tutors.

Interestingly, while students did not use Lotus Notes as planned, they appeared to appreciate its functionality enough to try to recreate some of it elsewhere. Several groups of students made shared spaces on the UNIX network including functionality like code storage and message archiving – functions Lotus Notes already offered. This is surprising because it carried a work overhead, one of the reasons both Grudin and Orlikowski give for non-adoption of groupware. To create the UNIX space, an individual student needed to create a directory on his/her UNIX account. Student accounts are protected; there is no permission for others to access them. Therefore, the students creating the spaces had to approach support staff at the University to get the permissions changed for the relevant group of students. Postings to the shared space also needed to carry read/write permissions for the group. On top of this extra work, some of the functionality of the UNIX alternative seemed impoverished compared with Lotus Notes. One example is that there were no facilities for discussion threads: students needed to keep track of course-related communications as they came through with general e-mail, and needed to save important ones through their own efforts. Another is that the spaces did not function well as awareness tools or as an immediately available resource centre, having to be specially accessed, while Lotus Notes could remain available permanently on desktops by keeping a browser open. However, in some ways the UNIX shared spaces worked better than Lotus Notes. There were difficulties in integrating Lotus Notes with UNIX. This had an impact on programming. Code stored in Lotus Notes could not be run there, but needed to be re-exported to UNIX, and the only form of communication between the two systems was via cut and paste. To move large amounts of code either way was troublesome.

These general findings concerning the students' avoidance of Lotus Notes to communicate and share, and instead a preference for a more basic support structure which they had to set up themselves, are puzzling. Why was this? One reason is that what we may regard as positive aspects of Lotus Notes - for example ease of producing minutes of meetings - were not seen as such by students. During one non-researcher present video observation, a group of students realized they needed, for assessable purposes, evidence of a 'standards committee meeting', a meeting in which standards for software development are agreed between different groups who will later trade software. However, they had not had such a meeting. So they organized a meeting with other groups involved to construct this evidence retrospectively. This meant tutors sometimes got rushed or even invented material not particularly representative of the actual collaborative practices that may have obtained and which they wished to be able to support. Equally, during another meeting where there was no researcher present, one student, from this same group, observed 'we had better put this stuff on Lotus Notes', adding that the system was 'a bloody nuisance'. This seems to reflect a widespread attitude. In other words, Lotus Notes represented work students might not have wished to do. However, again, this is problematic, since this work had to be done in order for the students to be successful.

Other reasons for students' avoidance of using Lotus Notes might be attributed to usability problems with some of the Lotus Notes interfaces. For example, Lotus Notes featured a pulldown menu of categories for postings (Figure 1a). There were four categories: 'agendas', 'meetings', 'general discussion', and 'other'. Some groups used the default, 'agendas', for all postings. Others used categories indiscriminately; for example, meeting minutes appeared under 'agendas', 'meetings', and 'general discussion'. There is also a messaging problem. To enter a posting from the front screen (not shown) the icon 'New Main Topic' must be clicked. This creates the top level of a thread - we are inside a message within such a thread in Figure 1b. To respond to a posting within the thread, the Lotus Notes user must be inside a posting (as shown) and then click 'New Response'. This continues the thread. However, an option near this is 'Close', which takes users back to the front screen. Using 'New Response' was only done in a few cases. Students tended to hit 'Close', return to the front screen, and use 'New Main Topic' to enter a posting. Thus, threading tended not to happen. Even if the posting was intended to be a response to a message inside a thread, it looked like the beginning of a new one. The implication is that the behaviour of the interface may have limited students' ability to organize material by topic. However, this limitation seems to be only part of the picture.

Figure 1a: Category Pulldown

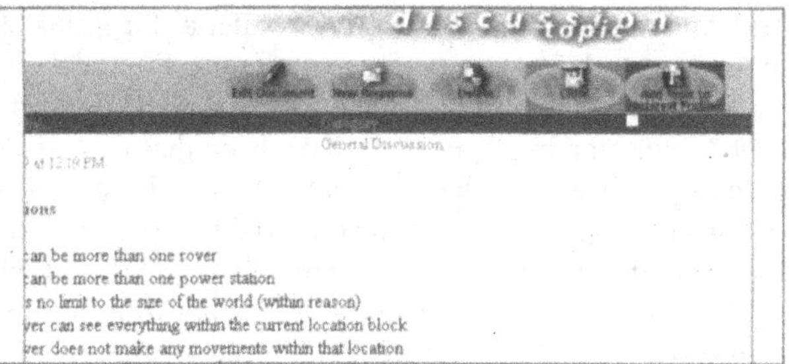
Figure 1b: Responding to a Message

Our findings, in contrast to those of Orlikowski, do not give a clear picture of why Lotus Notes was not used. There seems to have been ample incentive for students to use it, and students appear to have understood the system and realized its usefulness. Despite this, they preferred to avoid the system - but paradoxically created alternatives which reproduced some of Lotus Notes' functionality. In not using Lotus Notes they also potentially risked loss of marks (by, for example, not keeping up with tutor-viewable minutes of meetings – and, more generally, not providing tutors with assessable materials). These findings seem to go counter to students' own interests and motivations, and, at least on the face of it, are difficult to analyze in such a way that we might arrive at better groupware solutions in such a context: they present an analytic challenge.

THE ANALYTIC CHALLENGE

Problems in Analyzing the Failure of Lotus Notes

Why did students say 'No' to Lotus Notes, despite the apparent suitability of the groupware for their purposes? In this section, we will show that there was an interacting set of factors which we will address in sequence: software, systems, 'cognitive', and 'structural'.

First, we will consider the software level. By this, we mean usability issues to do with the Lotus Notes interface. One approach to explaining such issues is to take an 'artefact perspective' (Bødker, 1996). When a software interface stops users fulfilling their purposes, Bødker calls this a 'breakdown'. Breakdowns can be identified by 'focus shifts' - where users look around for solutions - and by frustration and confusion. Breakdowns are evidence that the software needs improvements. If there were breakdowns in students' use of Lotus Notes, this could explain their avoidance. In terms of the category pulldown menu, it is not immediately obvious, as Lotus Notes has its own design protocol for a pulldown, that any category *other* than 'agendas' is available. However, there was little if any evidence of focus shifting, frustration or confusion in students' use of the pulldown, whether or not it was realized to be a pulldown. Equally, those students who did categorize appropriately, simply found the functionality through exploratory clicking (since the pulldown is represented by a button with a down arrow), and no breakdown appeared to have occurred. Those who posted to inappropriate categories did not seem concerned about this – implying that categorization issues were not just to do with the pulldown.

As we saw, to respond to a posting inside a thread, the Lotus Notes user must first access the message and then click on 'New Response' inside that message. Use of the 'Close' option means a message is exited. The continuation of the thread is lost when 'New Main Topic' is used. However, again, this did not appear to be a source of frustration and was not associated with focus shifts, suggesting that students were simply not highly concerned to organize messaging as threads.

This discussion suggests that there may be issues other than, or additional to, those identifiable at the software level that are responsible for the avoidance of Lotus Notes. Our next level of analysis is the systems level. This refers to applications rather than application features (the software level), as well as integration of different applications. Two issues we have already seen are learning overheads, and UNIX/Lotus Notes integration problems. We might observe that because students already knew how to use UNIX, they simply wished to avoid the work overheads represented by Lotus Notes. This would explain why shared spaces were created on UNIX. However, work avoidance because of difficult-to-use systems seems to be contradicted by the fact that the creation of shared spaces on UNIX also carried significant work overheads. A possible way of accounting for this is the poor integration of Lotus Notes with UNIX. Students use UNIX for their day-to-day work, especially programming and e-mail. Posting evidence of collaborative work to Lotus Notes involved cutting and pasting. Students were especially concerned to produce working code, but if this was posted to Lotus Notes it needed to be immediately transferred back to UNIX to be run. Thus it may have been easier for students to simply mail code with any comments directly across UNIX, bypassing Lotus Notes. However, in itself, this does not explain why students avoided Lotus Notes, which offered other, direct functions like messaging and writing minutes which could be displayed on the desktop alongside UNIX windows.

Our next level of analysis considers issues to do with student perceptions of Lotus Notes – a cognitive level of analysis. By 'cognitive' is meant not just understanding of systems (Orlikowski's 'technological frames') but also beliefs and attitudes. The student who regarded the production of material for Lotus Notes as 'a bloody nuisance' (without dissent from others in the group) appears to have done so for two reasons. First, doing messaging and writing minutes at all appears to have been something perceived as extraneous to the issue of producing software – this work was not done on the UNIX shared spaces. The students' understanding appears to have been that this was not a valuable thing to do. There was also a public/private issue. Students had been told that material posted to Lotus Notes, notably minutes of meetings, would be tutor-accessible. However, students appeared to feel uncomfortable with this – that they were being 'checked up on' without their consent. Thus, students preferred to go private, explaining why, faced with other functionality problems, they were happy to make use of UNIX-based private shared spaces. However, this still does not explain why students appeared to regard the tutor- and groupware-supported development of group management, coordination, and communications skills as something inessential which *could* be avoided, especially as this was assessable.

The three levels of analysis we have looked at – software, systems, and cognitive – have not provided us with clear answers as to what really was responsible for the avoidance of using Lotus Notes. Another possible answer might lie at the 'structural' level of analysis. After Orlikowski, this refers to the organizational context, e.g. the priorities of the different people working in the organization, and their interactions. There were two parties to the collaborative learning – tutors and students. Collaboration was not only intended to be between students; but also between tutors and students, reflected in tutors' introduction of Lotus Notes into the course. However, tutors and students are different sets of people with different experiences and concerns. Tutors appear interested in process: teaching the skills, transferable to professional settings, that lead to successful product development. In contrast, students seem product- rather than process-oriented: they were more interested in getting the software working by any means rather than developing group management strategies. This suggests that the avoidance of Lotus Notes was, in fact, to do with the way students define their work, with the use of Lotus Notes being seen as extraneous to this. Thus, in Orlikowski's terms, Lotus Notes could be seen as, for students, 'counter-cultural' – and if so, it should be expected to fail. However, this explanation is still problematic: it is unclear why students might neglect an assessable component of the course, which results in marks and so should have been strongly motivated. We might expect Lotus Notes use to have been pro-cultural not counter-cultural.

Developing an Analytic Tool

There are two basic issues which need to be addressed when analyzing the problems of using Lotus Notes for supporting students. The first is that there are contributory factors at different levels of analysis, none of which appears, on its own, to explain the failure of Lotus Notes. The second, related, issue is conflict that can arise between the parties to the collaborative learning – tutors and students. On the course, there were conflictual attitudes between what each party saw as necessary to complete it, including different perceptions of the level of salience of some work, and differences between attitudes toward inspectability. Thus we need an account of how and why conflict arose and persisted.

To try to answer the need for an analytic tool capable of coordinating and integrating findings at different levels of analysis, and to elucidate types of conflict, we have developed a framework called the Activity Space (Halloran, 2000). This is based on Activity Theory (Kuutti, 1994; Leont'ev, 1982; Nardi, 1996; Vygotsky, 1978). There has been interest in Activity

Theory for CSCL, and use of Activity Theory-based frameworks, notably Engeström's Activity System (1990: see, for example, Bellamy, 1996; McAteer *et al*, 2000; Mwanza, 2001). Why not just use this? One reason is that the Activity System approach focuses on the interactions that enable an activity to be stable and functional, rather than on conflictual activities. A diagram of the Activity System appears as Figure 2:

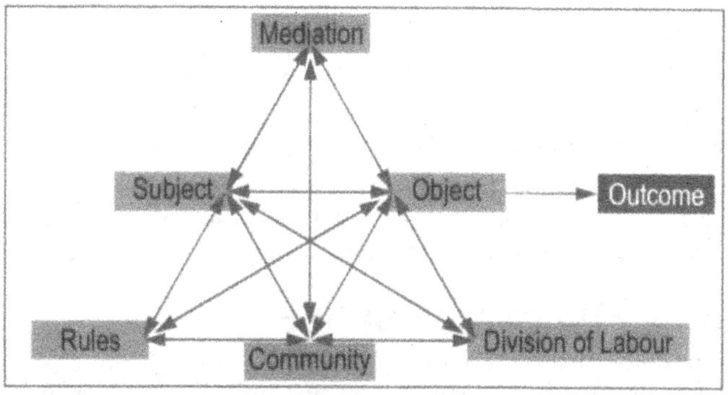

Figure 2: Activity System

In an activity system, the 'object' is what is driving the activity, for example, to provide educational services. Where this is a group activity, this object is 'common': everyone, regardless of what their specific job is, is working towards the same thing. There is also a 'collective subject' – the parties to the activity are all united in wishing to achieve the common object. 'Mediation' means the tools used to complete the activity. These can include what we commonly regard as tools (computers, filing cabinets, phones, fax machines) but there also cognitive tools (beliefs, attitudes, skills, concepts, etc.). These are well coordinated. The other nodes are 'rules', 'community', and 'division of labour', all responsible for the coordination of the system – these nodes can be seen as relating to Orlikowski's 'structural' level. The interaction of the nodes in the activity leads to the outcome, i.e. the product of the activity.

There are problems in using the Activity System framework to analyze conflict between different groups of people within the same activity. Because nodes do not feature internal conflicts, for example those which occurred between student and tutor perceptions of Lotus Notes, we need to conceive of two different activity systems with each group as the subject of that system. We then need to describe the 'contradictions' between those two systems. This seems counter-intuitive as the activity is just one – in our study, specifically the software design and evaluation course – and we would like to be able to represent this. A second problem is that it is difficult to conceptualize what the 'rules', 'community' and 'division of labour' would be on the course, as all of these things are ambiguous given the conflicts between tutors and students in terms of their perceptions, attitudes, and actions. In other words, there is not a strong 'structure' in Orlikowski's sense. Rather, there seems to have been two different groups (tutors and students) which, although they might, to greater or lesser degrees, have rules, community, and a division of labour within themselves, do not have an overall set governing and uniting both groups.

The Activity Space is another extension of Activity Theory designed to show, in contrast to the Activity System, how it is that an activity becomes conflictual through problematic interactions. The Activity Space is shown in Figure 3:

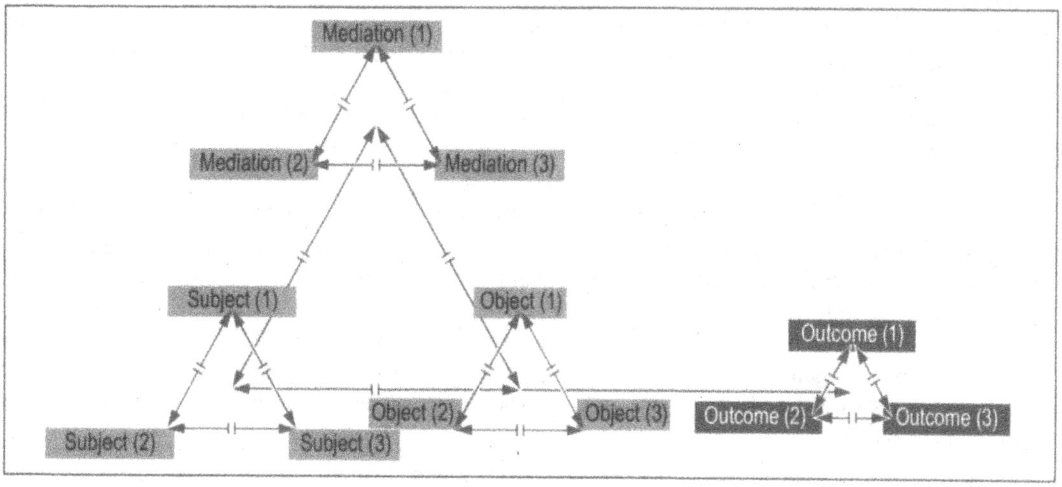

Figure 3: Activity Space

The Activity Space consists of a base triangle with three main nodes: subject, object, and mediation. Because of the difficulties of conceptualizing 'rules', 'community' and 'division of labour', these nodes are omitted. Between each of these nodes, there can be conflicts, represented as parallel lines ('='). In the diagram, each node is exploded into a number of sub-nodes. This enables us to conceptualize different subjects, objects, and mediation within the same main node, and, again, there can be conflicts. In addition, the outcome of the activity can be conflictual. In this particular diagram, there are three sub-nodes to each main node, but this number is arbitrary. The number could vary according to the activity we were looking at, the diagram changed accordingly.

The Activity Space predicts that conflicts at one node will propagate to the others and vice versa, implying that they are co-determining (they all affect each other). This means we cannot explain conflicts at a particular node, for example between tutor and student views of the significance of Lotus Notes, without reference to the other nodes. Thus, the representation enables a multidimensional analysis, offering a systematic way of examining relations between the different levels of analysis. These include groupware features, integration of applications and systems, cognitive and structural factors. The implication is that none of these levels of analysis is sufficient on its own.

STUDENT GROUPWORK AS AN ACTIVITY SPACE

The main findings identified in our study of the use of Lotus Notes by students are represented as an Activity Space in Figure 4. In this diagram, there are only two subject sub-nodes, two object sub-nodes, and two outcome sub-nodes. The other sub-nodes, which have no significance in this context, are greyed out.

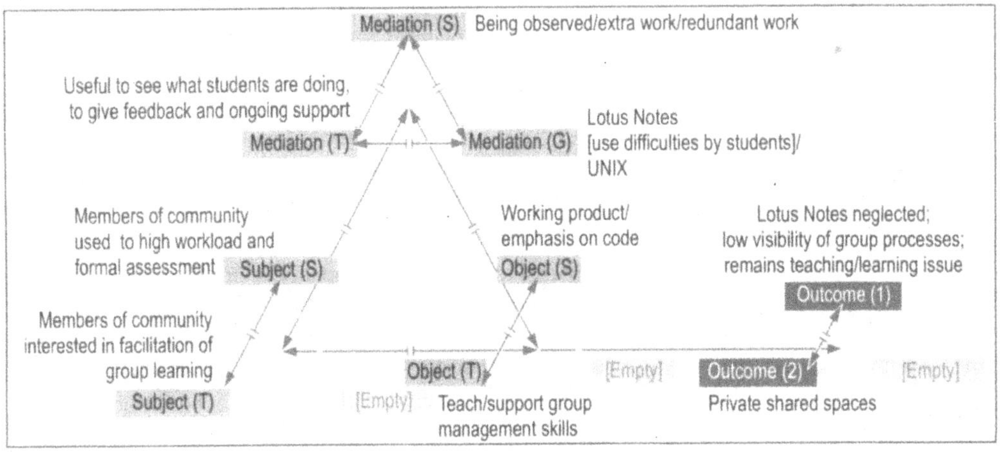

Figure 4: The course as an activity space

We saw that there were issues with the use of mediation in the shape of Lotus Notes on the course. There are cognitive conflicts between tutors/students in terms of beliefs concerning the value and significance of using Lotus Notes. At the Mediation (S) node (S for 'Students'), students believe they are being observed, and are uncomfortable with this – possibly because group processes felt to be 'messy' rather than well-organized might not be positively assessed. On the other hand, tutors (Mediation (T)) wish to be able to see exactly these sorts of process so that they can support group coordination and communication. Equally, students appear to believe that the work represented by using Lotus Notes is redundant, which contradicts the tutor view. There are also software/cognitive conflicts, in two senses. First, students did not make use of Lotus Notes functions by virtue of their belief about the use of the groupware; but also the cognition required to master these functions was not particularly exercised. This reveals that the functions of Lotus Notes as a piece of software in isolation are not necessarily problematic; but become so because of the tool's position in an activity where it is seen as representing something undesirable.

As we have noted, students made shared spaces on UNIX. This software mediation is consistent with their beliefs about Lotus Notes. The two forms of software mediation are in conflict (Mediation (G) [G for 'Groupware']). However, the conflict between these systems is not just a function of their design, but also relates to cognition. Students believed that UNIX was private, limited to work they themselves saw as valuable, while Lotus Notes was public in a non-desirable way, involving redundant work. The belief about UNIX meant that students were prepared to undergo the learning overheads in creating shared spaces on UNIX and the difficulties of use. Therefore, the coordination of these systems was not something students particularly attempted. Again, we cannot say that the avoidance of Lotus Notes was due to other functionality issues like difficulty of access from UNIX. In other words, having only two levels of analysis - the software and systems levels of analysis – is inadequate.

At the mediation node, we can see there are several interacting types of conflict. But where do the mediation conflicts come from? At the subject node in Figure 4, there are conflicts between the two groups, students and tutors. These are different sets of people with different experiences and concerns – they have different 'subject characteristics'. As we suggested in our initial analysis, students tend to be product-oriented, while tutors are interested not only in product but also in process. This goes further, reflecting affiliations to different models of learning (Rogoff, forthcoming). Implicit in the tutors' idea of using Lotus Notes is a 'participant' model of collaborative learning, where parties work together non-hierarchically to solve a problem. The tutor acts as a facilitator. This implies that in collaborative learning, tutors are an active party. However students seem to interpret what they are doing in terms of an 'acquisition' model: that is, they are left to acquire a solution (a product) through their own efforts, which will then be assessed. Lotus Notes was there to help support the process. The students' model of learning had an impact at the Mediation (S) node both in terms of beliefs about Lotus Notes and attempts to use it. It was seen as an assessment tool. Students were uncomfortable with the extra assessment it appeared to entail. Thus, the belief concerning observation as assessment is reinforced by this group's subject characteristics. This conflicts with the belief held by tutors (Mediation (T)): their observation is important to help students develop essential process skills. This belief led to the introduction of the groupware. Here, then, we see how cognitive factors to do with the tutors' and students' different subject characteristics can help explain the students' avoidance of Lotus Notes despite the tutors' view that it would be a useful support tool.

According to Activity Theory, the driver of any activity is its object. An object is what the party or parties to an activity wish to achieve. On the course, objects are in conflict. Tutors wanted to be able to support students in learning how to work together and this was their purpose in introducing Lotus Notes. Being able to see the details of their meetings would help tutors to address issues as they came up. Thus, the tutor object in relation to Lotus Notes was 'help students collaborate' by teaching/supporting group management skills (Object (T)). Being able to look at Lotus Notes entries served this object. However, for students, the object was 'avoid creating assessable materials except where this is absolutely essential. Instead, concentrate on the most important assessable components, i.e. working product' (Object (S)). Thus, the two objects are in contradiction. Again, we can begin to relate these nodes to others. The objects proceed from beliefs at the mediation level, beliefs concerning the meaning of making group processes public. However, each group's subject characteristics, which derive from its cultural affiliations and social position within education, are also conflictual.

Thus, the Activity System helps us to conceptualize how nodes (which can be seen as effects at particular levels of analysis) are co-determining. For example, the subject characteristics of each group are related to their beliefs and attitudes at the mediation node; and to their objects. However, at the same time, the objects reinforce the mediation, and, indeed, the subject characteristics – especially when there is an apparently satisfactory outcome (students managed to get through the course). In parallel, tutors still saw facilitation of group process as a live issue – in fact, more urgent than before. Their own objects, mediation, and subject characteristics also persisted, reinforcing each other. The factors leading to students' avoidance of Lotus Notes, then, appear to be self-perpetuating.

DISCUSSION

What use can be made of such an analysis in terms of better supporting collaborative learning with groupware? The analysis suggests that supporting collaborative learning involves more than changing software functions of groupware (for example, improving interfaces). In addition to these, other kinds changes to the course are needed.

We can conceptualize conflicts at each node of an activity space as being *artifacts* of conflicts at the others – artifacts in the sense that these conflicts are undesirable and would not necessarily exist without determination by those other nodes. However, because there is interaction, changes at single nodes might not work. Although changes at particular nodes to reduce conflict might have positive effects at others, we might simultaneously need to concentrate on changes at those other nodes. In this section we describe two scenarios whereby the Activity Space framework can be used to conceptualize change. These are derived from our study, but are intended to have general relevance.

Scenario 1: 'Heavyweight' Change

The first scenario for change involves improving the functionality of groupware and dropping any inspectability requirement. These changes, and the effects on the activity space, are shown in Figure 5:

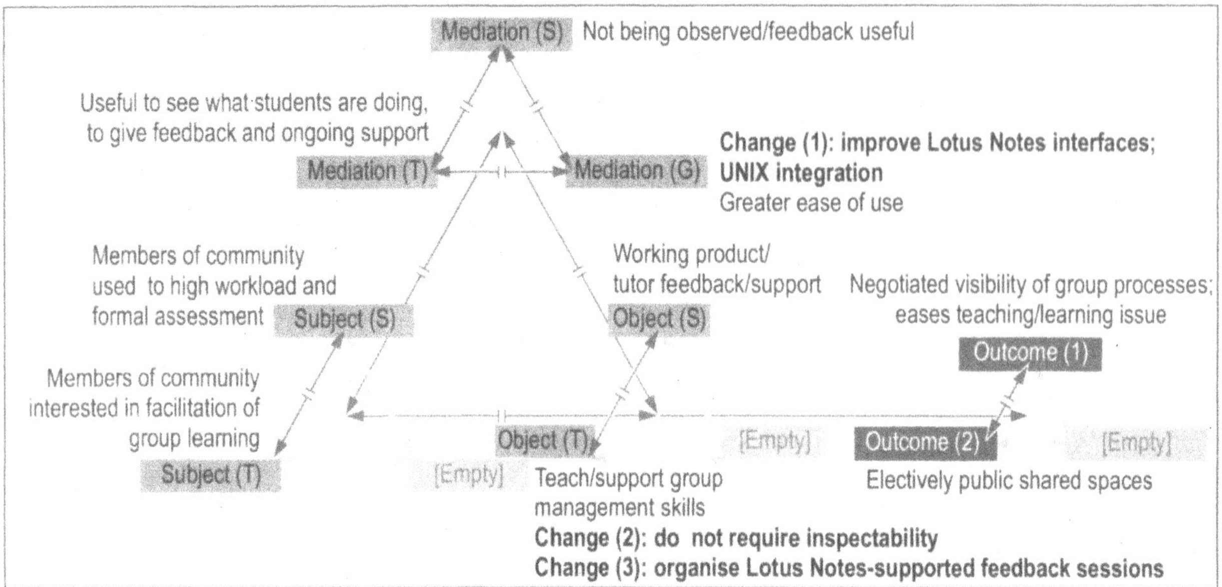

Figure 5: Using the Activity Space framework to approach heavyweight change

In this proposal, three 'active' changes (shown in bold) would be made. First, the groupware interface functionality is improved, together with integration with other systems (Change (1)). In terms of the software design and evaluation course, this could be achieved, for example, by changing the pulldown menu to radio buttons; and to adding a warning to the 'Close' button when inside a message. Integration with UNIX could be assisted through creating weblinking facilities under Lotus Notes. Second, tutors could drop the inspectability requirement; that is, they could choose not to require that Lotus Notes postings are viewable remotely (Change (2)). Third, they introduce feedback sessions for groups at which groupware, and other materials, could be used, depending on the choices of students (Change (3)).

These active changes can be hypothesized to produce 'referred' change; that is, to affect other nodes. Changes both active and referred feed back and reinforce each other. This means that not every node need necessarily be subjected to active change. The way the scenario would work is by raising the salience of group processes in a way which reduces the students' notion of redundancy and obviates their fears concerning visibility. Thus, compared with Figure 4 (the unchanged activity), we see that student beliefs about being observed might change (Mediation (S)) without there being any active change needed at this node. This would have effects in terms of mediation and objects coming more closely into line for each group, not to mention outcomes. At the same time, subject characteristics might start to change a little with each group coming to recognize the other's position and motivations.

The changes proposed are quite significant. There would need to be a fair amount of work done on the systems (interface improvements to Lotus Notes; integration of Lotus Notes with UNIX). In addition, tutors would need to free up time to create the feedback sessions which would effectively replace the remote access practice. This may not be realistic. Our second scenario features changes which are more lightweight.

Scenario 2: 'Lightweight' Change

Scenario 2 is shown in Figure 6. In this scenario, there would be no changes to the groupware. Students would be required, as part of the course, to produce assessable coursework on group processes (management, coordination, communications) (Change (1)). Again, tutors would not require access to the groupware (Change (2)), but would, during the lecture series, include material on group management which could be made use of as students produced the required coursework (Change (3)). This proposal suggests that existing time (both tutors' and students') would be re-used (lecture topic change/coursework change), so the changes are less demanding of time/resources than in Scenario 1. Again, we could expect these active changes to produce referred change (for example, students learn to work around Lotus Notes interface issues) with feedback effects. The importance of group processes would be raised by both the need to produce assessed work, and by having been lectured on this topic. This would drive the use of groupware, and this interaction would in turn raise the salience of group processes and provide motivation to address the issue.

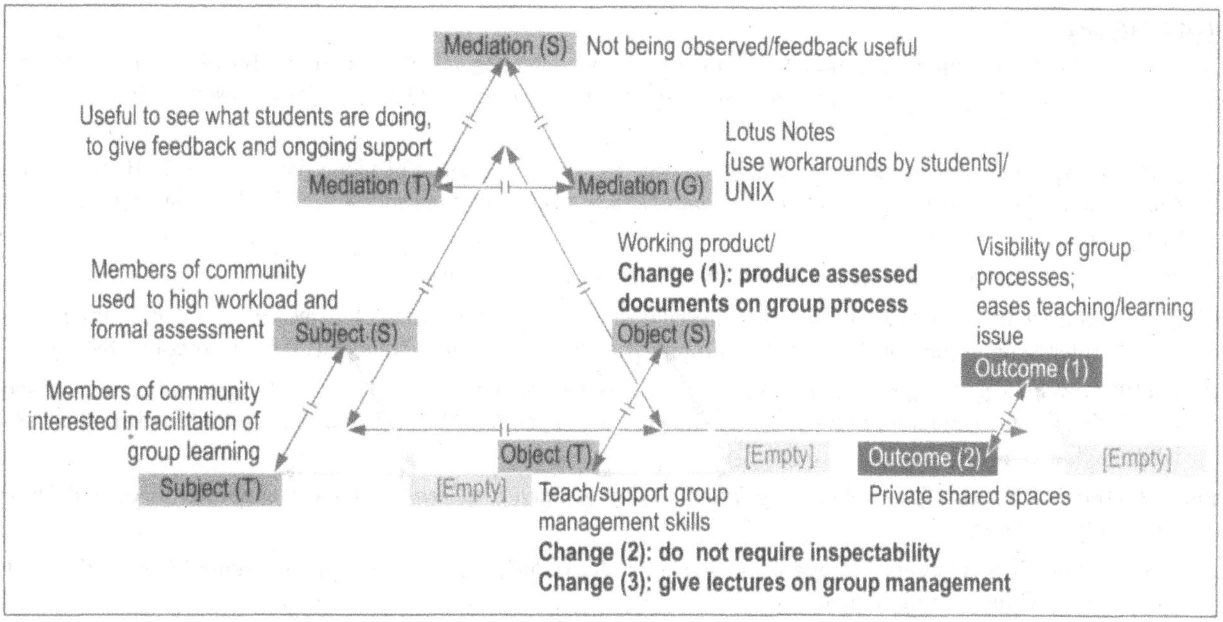

Figure 6: Using the Activity Space framework to approach lightweight change

The referred changes might differ somewhat, and possibly be more superficial, that those resulting from the heavyweight changes suggested in Scenario 1. The hope is, here, that the students' belief that using the groupware was not a priority, would come to be overridden by a real need to use it. However, if this need was interpreted solely in the interests of assessment, there is some doubt about its real use to students, or in terms of tutors' aspirations to teach group processes as valuable skills in themselves. Thus, problematic beliefs at the mediation node might persist, as could students' subject characteristics. There might be negative feedback effects on the active changes in that students might not like being 'forced' to use Lotus Notes. On the other hand, the scenario is designed to produce an increase in student perception of the value of using groupware beyond assessment purposes.

CONCLUSION

We began our paper with an empirical problem: the failure of Lotus Notes to support collaborative learning on a software design course as expected/intended by tutors. As we saw, groupware adoption problems are familiar: it is a persistent problem. In the CSCW literature, failure can be traced to conflict between what the groupware stands for, and the way the organization actually works. These can be inconsistent. However, we focus on a different context: a CSCL context where groupware is intended to support student groupwork. A major issue is that it is difficult to determine why groupware fails in this context, too. Organizational and groupware aims seem consistent. The failure, then, is harder to analyze, and appears multidetermined by a complex set of interacting factors including conflicting systems, perceptions, and cultural affiliations.

In CSCL, there is interest in multidimensional analysis which relates groupware to social context. Activity Theory has been used to do this. However, existing frameworks can be difficult to apply to instances of collaborative learning marked by conflict. The purpose of our framework - the Activity Space - is to produce a practical analytic tool which preserves the distinctive interactionism of Activity Theory, but which can deal more easily with conflict. Here, we show how an Activity Theory-based framework can act as a tool for systematically organizing and relating observations at different levels of analysis in such a way as to produce a detailed account of groupware roles and functions in collaborative learning contexts. It provides a way of treating these roles and functions as the outcomes of many interacting factors. It allows us to hypothesize how change could occur in an activity space, both 'active', and 'referred'. It also shows what the scope and desirability of that change would be. The Activity Space framework needs further research involving implementing the scenarios and assessing it in light of the results to see how well it works as a predictive tool. As it stands, its main value is to show that in thinking about how to support collaborative learning, we need to go beyond groupware features *per se* to analysis of a range of interacting factors. These include perceptions, attitudes, the different roles of tutors and students in educational establishments, and their different cultural affiliations.

ACKNOWLEDGMENTS

The research this study is based on was supported by an ESRC/CASE DPhil studentship with British Telecom. Thanks go to Dr Michael Gardner of BT. Thanks also go to Dr Rose Luckin of Sussex University for giving permission to observe the student groupwork described in the study.

REFERENCES

Bellamy, R. E. (1996) Designing educational technology: computer-mediated change. In B. Nardi, (Ed). *Context and Consciousness: Activity Theory and Human-Computer Interaction.* Cambridge, Massachusetts: MIT Press, 123-146.

Bødker, S. (1996) Applying activity theory to video analysis: How to make sense of video data in HCI. In B. Nardi, (Ed). *Context and Consciousness: Activity Theory and Human-Computer Interaction.* Cambridge, Massachusetts: MIT Press, 69-102.

Engeström, Y. (1990) *Learning, Working and Imagining.* Helsinki: Orienta-Konsultit.

Gifford, B. R., and Enyedy, N. D. (1999) Activity centered design: towards a theoretical framework for CSCL. Proceedings of Computer Support for Collaborative Learning, CSCL 99 (Palo Alto, December 1999), unext.com, 189-196.

Grudin, J. (1988) Why CSCW applications fail: problems in the design and evaluation of organizational interfaces. Proceedings of the Conference on Computer-Supported Cooperative Work. September 26-28, 1988, Portland, OR USA.

Halloran, J. (2000) *The Activity Space: Analyzing Intentionality in Open Cooperative Work.* Unpublished Doctoral Thesis, University of Sussex.

Kuutti, K. (1994) *Information Systems, Cooperative Work and Active Subjects: The Activity Theoretical Perspective.* Oulu: University of Oulu Printing Center.

Leont'ev, A. N. (1982) *Problems of the Development of the Mind.* Moscow: Progress.

McAteer, E., Tolmie, A., Crook, C., and Macleod, H. (2000). Grounding communication skills development in practice and play. European Conference on Educational Research (ECER 2000), Edinburgh.

Mwanza, D. (2001). Changing tools changing attitudes: effects of introducing a computer system to promote learning at work. Proceedings of the First European International Conference on Computer-Supported Collaborative Learning, Euro-CSCL 01, March 22-24, 2001, University of Maastricht, the Netherlands.

Nardi, B. (Ed) (1996). *Context and Consciousness: Activity Theory and Human-Computer Interaction.* Cambridge, Massachusetts: MIT Press.

Orlikowski, W. (1992) Learning from Notes: organizational issues in groupware implementation. Proceedings of the ACM 1992 Conference on Computer-Supported Cooperative Work. October 31-Novermber 4, 1992, Toronto, Canada.

Rogoff, B. (forthcoming) *The Cultural Nature of Human Development.* New York: Oxford University Press.

Re-contextualization of Teaching and Learning in Videoconference-based Environments: An Empirical Study

Ulf Hedestig, Victor Kaptelinin

Umea University, Sweden

uhstig@informatik.umu.se, vklinin@informatik.umu.se

ABSTRACT

The paper reports an empirical study of the use of videoconferences in decentralized university education. The study focuses on breakdowns that occur during the transition of educational practices from regular classrooms to videoconference-based environments. It was found that the main cause of breakdowns was discoordinations of teaching and learning resulting from physical and organizational distribution of decentralized education. The paper concludes that implementation of educational activities in new types of learning environments requires both downwards contextualization, an adaptation to the limitations and affordances of the environment, and upwards contextualization, locating the activity in a larger-scale context.

Keywords

Decentralized education, learning environments, videoconference settings, breakdowns, activity theory

INTRODUCTION

One of the main ideas behind the current trend towards "virtual universities" (Cunningham et al., 1998) is a possibility to make a better use of educational expertise of university teachers. It is assumed that information and communication technologies (ICT) allow for extending educational activities of a university to include students who cannot participate in traditional on-campus education. Such an extension, which takes various forms (Lau, 2000), presents a challenge to CSCL research. Traditional university education has been shaped by centuries of historical development. Moving from traditional classrooms to "new communication environments" (Mantovani, 1996) cannot be accomplished by a direct translation of existing educational practices into a new setting. Instead, it requires a *re-contextualization* of teaching and learning and development of new social organization within the setting. This notion, which is widely accepted in the field of CSCL (Koschmann, 1996), has, unfortunately, not influenced much of practical developments in distance education, web-based learning, and so forth.

The study presented in this paper addresses the problem of re-contextualization of teaching and learning in ICT-based environments by focusing on coordination breakdowns of educational activities under new conditions and the emerging practices of coping with such breakdowns in everyday educational use of technology. The object of our study was decentralized education at a Swedish university (thereafter, "the University"). More specifically, we were interested in the use of videoconferences within decentralized courses delivered by the University to students living in other towns. The reason behind choosing this specific form of technology-based education was that videoconferences could be considered the closest match to traditional classroom settings. One of the reasons behind the widespread use of videoconferences at the University has been an assumption that practically any teacher can successfully use his or her experience with delivering traditional courses in a videoconference setting. In a pilot study by Esbjörnsson (1997) it was shown that this assumption was not correct. Successful teaching and learning in a videoconference setting was found to be associated with special types of arrangements and expertise, which could be rather complex and difficult to accomplish. The lack of such arrangements and expertise resulted in various problems and breakdowns. In the present study we specifically focus on breakdowns in videoconference settings to identify potential problems related to attempts to deliver traditional courses in the new environment.

The rest of the paper is organized as follows. Immediately follows a brief overview of conceptual frameworks that can be used in studies of coordination breakdowns and the reasons why activity theory has been selected as the main theoretical approach employed in the study. Then a background information about the University is provided, as well as a description of videoconference-based learning environments analyzed in the paper. After that the method and the findings of the study are presented. Finally, implications of the findings for analysis and design of ICT-based learning environments are discussed.

POTENTIAL CONCEPTUAL FRAMEWORKS FOR STUDYING COORDINATION BREAKDOWNS

A variety of approaches seem to be plausible frameworks for studying coordination breakdowns in videoconference-based learning environments. They include, among others, coordination theory, distributed cognition, situated actions, and activity theory. Each of these approaches, from out point of view, has its strengths and weaknesses.

Coordination theory (Malone and Crowston, 1992, 1994; Crowston and Osborn, 1998) focuses on various types of dependencies between actors and activities within one coherent system. It provides powerful generalized representations that can be used for capturing and re-designing a wide range of processes, such as business processes. In case of videoconference-based learning environments the main problem is, however, not to optimize and streamline dependencies between activities but rather to discover what these activities are and what they could be. Coordination theory appears to be a useful analytical tool at a later stage of analysis, when the basic components and structures of teaching and learning in the setting are identified and understood.

Distributed cognition can be characterized in a similar way, despite all the differences between this approach and coordination theory. The distributed cognition framework makes it possible to create detailed and insightful representations of how people and artifacts are coordinated within a coherent system. According to Hutchins, "One important aspect of the social distribution [...] is that the knowledge required to carry out the coordinating actions is not discretely contained inside the various individuals. Rather, much of the knowledge is intersubjectively shared among the members of the team" (Hutchins, 1995, p. 219) Such sharing can only be possible if a common ground for intersubjectivity has been established through evolutionary development of a settings. It is often not the case when it comes to videoconference-based learning environments. In fact, in our earlier work we found a very different phenomenon. Successful functioning of a videoconference as a setting critically depended on the expertise of one concrete individual, the facilitator. Ironically, the importance of this "invisible" expertise was not recognized by the managers responsible for the setting (Hedestig, 2000).

The situated actions approach (Suchman, 1987), which is partly based on conversation analysis, provides a number of useful insights into coordination mechanisms necessary to make videoconference environments work. In particular, it emphasizes that communication is "not so much as alternating series of actions and reactions between individuals as it is a joint action accomplished through the participants' continuous engagement in speaking and listening." (Suchman, 1987, p. 71) Therefore, flexibility, coherence, and resources necessary to remedy communicative troubles should be important concerns in design of learning environments. However, the potential of situated actions as a guiding approach in addressing the above issues appears to be limited. Even though the importance of communicative resources can be clearly identified, the ways to provide such resources given the constraints of a specific setting may remain an open issue. Besides, the notion of plans as a weak resource of an action (Suchman, 1987) is hardly applicable to many learning environments, since actions in environments of this kind are often strictly determined by a number of plans, such as course schedules.

Finally, activity theory that focuses on hierarchically organized, mediated, and developing individual and collective activities can help formulate some key questions and provide conceptual tools helping to address these questions (Kaptelinin, 1996)*. Formulating key issues for a systematic empirical analysis, based on activity theory, appears to be a promising starting point for understanding the differences between traditional on-campus courses and their videoconference-based versions. Representations of these two types of learning as activities can help identify goals specific for each setting, as well as essentially common goals, that are being accomplished in different settings through different operations. A useful concept that can be utilized in the above analysis is the notion of mutual transformations between individual and collective activities (Kaptelinin, Cole, 1997). The main limitation of activity theory is that this approach is rather abstract and needs to be made more concrete by developing concepts and representations specific for a domain in question (cf. Kaptelinin, Nardi, Macaulay, 1999).

Therefore, even though a theoretical framework that can be directly used for analysis of coordination and re-coordination in videoconference-based learning environments does not exist yet, a number of frameworks can provide useful insights (c.f. Nardi, 1996). In our study we relied mostly on activity theory. Following the principles of this approach, we focused on actors participating in the setting, their goals and sub-goals, with special attention to conflicts between various goals, mediating artifacts, and developmental transformations of individual and collective activities.

THE USE OF VIDEOCONFERENCES AT THE UNIVERSITY: A SETTING IN A CONTEXT

The University has a strong history of distance and decentralized education. Decentralized education, which combines traditional classroom activities with distance learning, has become the main form of off-campus education at the University. Over 5000 students located outside the University campus (the distance is ranging from 100 km to 700 km) are currently

* Space limitations do not allow for an extensive discussion of activity theory in this paper. A detailed exposition of this approach can be found elsewhere (e.g., Leontiev, 1978).

participating in various courses and programs. The University is the major educational and research center in Northern Sweden, and to meet current demands it is more and more involved in decentralized education, gradually transforming itself into a "virtual" university. The gradual character of the transition is important, because it provides a possibility for the University to try various forms of decentralization without radical changes of the whole system and to capitalize upon existing expertise of the teachers. As mentioned above, that was one of the main reasons why videoconferences have been so widely used at the University.

Videoconference-based learning settings at the University are composed of two main types of components: (a) the *teacher's site*, or video studio, located on campus, and (b) the *students' site* (or sites), a videoconference classroom at a so-called "study center" located off campus. A typical arrangement of these sites is shown in Figure 1.

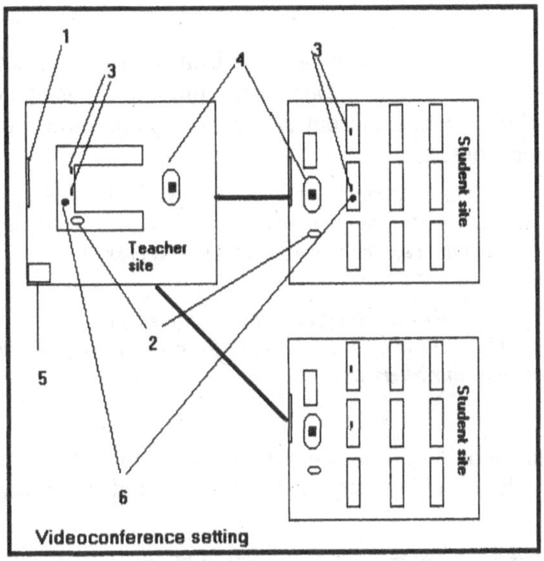

Figure 1. **A typical structure of a videoconference setting. At the teacher's site the teacher can use a whiteboard or an electronic whiteboard (1); at all sites there are document cameras for slides (2), two or more stationary microphones (3), TV-monitor(s), a video recorder and camera (4), and remote controls (6). At the teacher's site there is also a computer connected to the videoconference system (5).**

The teacher's site. When teachers use videoconference settings at the university they follow the same teaching styles as in traditional classroom teaching, that is, traditional lectures, seminars, and tutoring sessions (Hedestig, Kaptelinin, 2001). The studios are relatively small but include seating arrangements for groups up to 10-15 persons. The equipment consists of a document camera, an electronic whiteboard, a computer, a projector, TV-monitors, and hands-free microphones. The most common types of activity at video studios are lectures delivered by teachers to one or more student sites.

The students' site. The videoconference equipment at the students' site is usually installed in a traditional classroom at a local study center, that is, a room with rows of tables and chairs. Such an arrangement directs students' attention towards the monitor, that is, towards the teacher. Devices, such as cameras and microphones, can vary depending on how much a study center can afford to invest in equipment. Most study centers provide a camera, a document camera, a TV-monitor for incoming and outgoing images and one or two microphones (see Figure 1). Usually there is a student at the students' site, who is responsible for the remote control connected to the equipment. At students' sites there are usually no technicians or facilitators to provide support during sessions.

VIDEOCONFERENCE-BASED LEARNING – A WEB OF POTENTIAL BREAKDOWNS

The findings reported in this section are based on (a) field observation of videoconference sessions (about 100 hours in total), (b) interviews with teachers, students, and technicians/facilitators, and (c) a one-year ethnographic study of the work of a videoconference facilitator. The field observations have been conducted both at students' sites and teacher's sites. During these sessions we also recorded certain events, such as turn taking and breakdowns. The interviews were both unstructured and semi-structured. Most of unstructured interviews were first interviews with new informants. Semi-structured interviews were based on the Activity Checklist (Kaptelinin, Nardi, Macaulay, 1999). In the ethnographic study of facilitator's work one of us had been closely observing the facilitator almost every day for over a year and interviewing him both before and after each session.

In our field observations we have identified different types of coordination breakdowns. It should be noted that this paper does not deal with technical breakdowns, which are left beyond the scope of the present study (analysis of them can be found in, e.g., Dallat et al, 1992; Abbot et al, 1993; Rosengren 1993). Our findings, which are presented below, are divided into two main groups. When dealing with coordination breakdowns identified in the study the first and the most basic distinction was between (a) breakdowns caused by certain aspects of the settings and (b) breakdowns caused by factors existing in the larger context, outside the videoconference setting. These groups of breakdowns can be interpreted as indicators of two types of contextualization of activities, introduced by Engeström (1990): downward contextualization, that is, an adaptation of activities to the limitations and affordances of the environment, and upwards contextualization, that is, locating activities in a larger-scale organizational and inter-organizational context.

Downwards contextualization: Breakdowns originating from within the setting

Coordination breakdowns at students' sites

Most of the students' sites had the traditional classroom arrangement with few cameras and microphones. At sites where each student had an opportunity to control the camera and audio there were more spontaneous questions than at sites where students had to share a microphone and a remote control (see Table 1). Students from sites with only one camera and one or two microphones often commented on the difficulty of asking questions:

> *"It's impossible to ask spontaneous or short questions during a video session. It takes too much time. First I have to ask someone to give me the microphone. Then I have to ask the student who has the remote control to push the mute-button, so the teacher can hear me. At the same time the student also has to direct the camera towards me. This process takes too much time, and many of us do not bother to even think of asking a question"*

> *"Since it is necessary for us to push the mute-button at our site, it takes too long time to ask the teacher a question. Instead many of us so to speak seat back and watch the 'show'. We see it more as a TV-broadcast program, and a TV-program that you never interrupt! If there is something unclear we prefer to ask questions afterwards, if at all."*

Interactions are further complicated by the fact that students are looking at the same direction, so they do not face each other and cannot use nonverbal cues. Instead of talking to each other they mostly address the student(s) who has the microphone and the remote control.

A way of handling the coordinated use of equipment by the students was to move the student in charge of the technology in front of the room so that he or she could face the group. A common problem with this type of seating arrangement was a role conflict experienced by the student in charge of technology. The student had to choose whether to pay attention to the teacher and take notes or watch for any cues from the students and work with the cameras and microphones.

The role of a technician seldom shifted from student to student. A student who was a "designated technician" in the beginning of a course usually remained in this role during the rest of the course. The result was that the whole class became very dependent on this student, and when he or she was absent (for instance, due to illness) there were problems with finding a replacement. Typically nobody wanted to volunteer and someone was forced to take the responsibility. This person often lacked the skills of using the equipment, which affected the quality of interaction.

Coordination breakdowns at the teacher's site

In face-to-face classrooms instructors develop skills of coordinating and delivering a lecture with the use of familiar artifacts. In a videoconference studio these skills are often not applicable. Teachers have to change their practices to adjust them to a different context featuring different kinds of technical artifacts. Empirical data obtained in our study allow to differentiate between three types of coordination activities in a video session: (1) coordination related to course content, (2) coordination related to teacher's presentation (the outgoing image), and (3) coordination related to students' activities (the incoming image) (Hedestig, Kaptelinin, 2001).

Coordination related to course content. Teachers had to prepare to videoconference sessions much more carefully than to traditional classes. Most of the teachers we interviewed were aware that videoconference-based teaching is much more intensive and it was impossible to just copy a two-hour face-to-face lecture to a two-hour videoconference session. In their preparation teachers produced special materials suitable for the media: slides of different style, handouts to be distributed in advance, time schedules, storyboards, etc. Teachers' preparation phase was based on a very structured plan of a session. During a session teachers would often realize that their plans did not take into consideration the complexity and heterogeneity in the setting. Videoconference sessions are very situated because the frequency of technological breakdowns is still rather high and time schedule is rarely followed. It is not unusual that starting time and estimated breaks were delayed by 5-20 minutes (see Table 1). For a teacher the consequence of those delays could imply significant changes of the original plan of a lecture.

Video-session	Planned starting time	Real starting time	Planned break, min	Real break, min	Difference, min
1	10.15	10.23	15	21	+14 (8+6)
2	9.00	9.11	15	22	+18 (11+7)
3	13.15	13.20	10	18	+13 (5+8)
4	8.15	8.16	15	25	+11 (1+10)
5	10.00	10.10	15	19	+14 (10+4)
6	10.15	10.25	-	-	+10

Table 1. Examples of differences between planned and actual timing of videoconference sessions

Coordination of the outgoing image. When teachers act according to pre-planned content they have to concentrate on monitor(s) showing the outgoing image. Since the setting requires high concentration of both students and teachers it is common that the view is being changed from time to time, so that students do not look at slides only during the whole session. Actions involved in this sequence include zooming documents or images on document camera, showing slides or computer applications, showing the teacher or an area of the whiteboard, etc. These actions take place rather often, up to once in every second minute (see Tables 2 and 3). Usually technicians are responsible for those actions, but sometimes the responsibility lies solely on the teacher.

Descrption	S1	S2	S3	S4	S5
Lecture time (min)	56	83	84	69	91
Change video source	0	0	0	0	0
Zooming	5	10	8	5	10
Camera movements	10	34	55	51	67
Audio adjustments	2	0	0	2	2

Table 2. Examples of sessions (S1-S5) when the teacher uses a regular whiteboard

Description	S1	S2	S3	S4	S5	S6
Lecture time (min)	73	45	44	47	47	103
Change video source	43	29	26	23	13	80
Zooming	2	0	0	0	4	11
Camera movements	0	0	0	0	0	1
Audio adjustments	0	1	1	1	2	9

Table 3. Example of sessions (S1-S6) when the teacher uses slides on the document camera

Coordination of the incoming image. Sessions become even more difficult to coordinate when the teacher has to concentrate on reactions and responses of the students. The teacher has to discover verbal and non-verbal cues from students by viewing the monitor for the incoming image, which often resulted in communication breakdowns (see Table 4).

User-User breakdown	S1	S2	S3	S4	S5	S6	S7	S8	S9	S10
Turntaking breakdowns	0	3	2	12	6	7	4	2	3	18
Lack of feedback	17	2	2	0	0	6	1	5	4	0
Understanding problems	1	4	1	1	0	1	1	0	2	3

Table 4. Examples of sessions (S1-S10) with communication breakdowns.

A consequence of the above problems was that coordination of a session became very complicated, especially in cases of "multipoint" sessions, when more than two studios were involved. It was not uncommon that teachers focused exclusively on the content, paying no attention to the audience and leaving most of coordination to the facilitator.

Coordination among actors at teacher's sites: interaction between the teacher and the facilitator

Teachers were usually helped by a technician/facilitator, whose role greatly depended on the format of a session. In situations when lectures was delivered from a video studio*, the goal of the facilitator was to help the teacher and control incoming and outgoing images. Actions carried out by the facilitator included changing camera angles, zooming, switching between different sources, and adjustment of the audio.

Most interactions between the teacher and the facilitator were based on non-verbal cues, such as eye contact, gestures, and other kinds of signs. The facilitator had also an eye on the students' site and could give signals to the teacher if something would go wrong. In fact, the facilitator became more of a teacher assistant by sharing the responsibility of coordinating activities among the participants. This support was especially important for the teachers because for many of them teaching in a videoconference environment was a new experience and they had to develop new work practices (Hedestig, 2000).

Upwards contextualization: Breakdowns originating from outside the setting

Activities within a videoconference session could also be affected by external factors. In our study we have focussed on some interdependencies between videoconference settings and the broader context, which affected teaching and learning in the setting.

Coordination breakdowns across intra-organizational boundaries

A three-year program at the University can consist of up to 15-20 courses involving departments across different faculties. Different departments have different work practices, different competencies in technology use, and different organizational

* Lectures typically fell into one of the following categories: (a) lectures based on the use of the whiteboard, (b) lectures based on PowerPoint slides, and (c) "technology intensive" lectures, in which the whole range of available technology was used, including electronic whiteboards and various computer applications.

structures, which are difficult to integrate. Coordination of these organizational units of the University is often problematic, which can be illustrated by following examples:

1. *Teacher X planned a videoconference session to take place two weeks after his course started. The day before the session students contacted him and informed that it was impossible for them to participate in the session because another teacher (Y), who taught the previous course, scheduled an examination on the same day. Teacher X called the department in charge of the previous course but none there could help him. Teacher X got the name of teacher Y from the students and tried to contact him, but teacher X was out of town. The video session had to be cancelled.*
2. *A teacher was planning a discussion seminar during a video session. He asked the course administrator (who was also a webmaster) to put a list of questions on the web, so that students could prepare for the discussion. The administrator made a mistake and placed the questions to the 'Exercises", not the "Discussions" section. The students misinterpreted the aim of the session and when the teacher tried to initiate a discussion they refused to participate, claiming they were unprepared. The teacher had to cancel the discussion and deliver a lecture instead.*

Decentralized education courses at the University are usually conducted by teacher teams working with both on-campus and distant students. For many departments functioning of teacher teams is associated with serious coordination problems since participating teachers are always on the road. They become a "virtual team" and have difficulties in coordinating their activities within the group, as well. Constantly traveling to off-campus sites teachers cannot easily meet and keep each other updated on a day-to-day basis. Besides, they experience coordination problems with students. For instance, they have difficulties with answering students' questions when these questions refer to lectures given by other teachers.

Coordination breakdowns across inter-organizational boundaries

Distance and decentralized education usually involve several organizations, which often have different structures, cultures, communication patterns etc. Collaboration and communication between those actors can be easily disrupted by actors who do not share the same common ground or perspectives. The complicated nature of coordination required to solve the most trivial problems when an inter-organizational cooperation is involved, can be illustrated with a simple example of room reservation. When teachers planned a videoconference session, they had to make reservation for a room/studio both in a study center and on campus. This reservation procedure could take days to accomplish. The problem was caused by the need to coordinate several organizational actors, each working with its own reservation system. Reservation systems were not integrated with each other and nobody had a full control over the status of all video studios. If a site were occupied during the time a teacher planned to use it, a negotiation procedure would occur were either the teacher or administrative personal would try to find a solution. Coordination breakdowns resulted from this included the following ones:

- *Students occasionally did not turn up because they were not notified of changes. Also, students would arrive to a site when the videoconference classroom was closed because study center personnel were not informed about the reservation.*
- *Sometimes teachers made reservations with "wrong" people, that is, those who were not actually responsible for reservations. At some study center reservations was made by an administrator, at others by a technician. In our interviews with teachers it turned out that some of them made reservations with technicians and these reservations were later on cancelled by administrators, who did not even inform the teachers on the grounds that the teachers did not follow the correct procedure.*
- *When teachers made room reservations they did not know exactly what equipment was available in the room. Sometimes they would discover that crucial equipment did not exist there and it was impossible to conduct a lecture as planned.*
- *Study center personnel could not make any reservation for an external organization wanting to rent a video studio (which could potentially be very profitable for the center) because teachers always made reservations in short notice.*

A distinctive feature of decentralized education in our study was a complicated system of dependencies between different organizations: the University with its faculties and departments, local authorities, and companies running local educational facilities.

This lack of coordination between the above stakeholders was a major source of actual and potential breakdowns. Videoconference settings for decentralized education can be considered boundary objects that create new challenges for all institutional actors. In particular, they make especially evident the obstacles to coordination that still exist in organizations. For instance, most information and decision support systems at the University had been developed and implemented within the University, which means that external actors cannot access this information. To make inter-organizational cooperation work, new informal ways of coordination and communication between organizations have emerged, and these new communication patterns evolved on an operational level and often exist without being noticed by those working on strategic levels. The complex interactions between various "players", which compose organizational context influencing teaching and learning in videoconference settings at the University, are summarized in Figure 2.

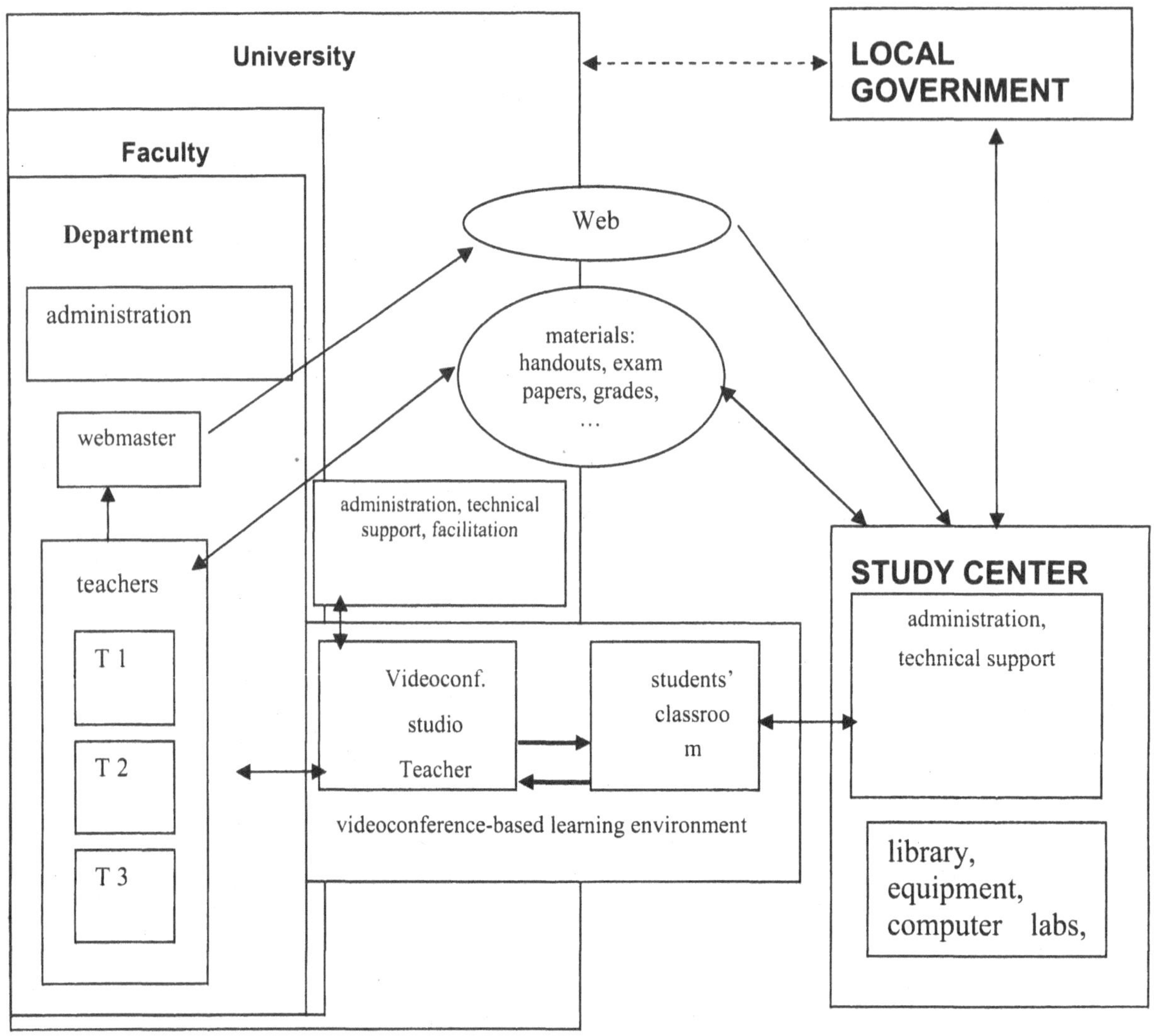

Figure 2. A simplified model of the organizational context of videoconference-based learning environment at the University

GENERAL DISCUSSION

Traditional classroom education is a well-established genre with a long history that goes back for centuries. The evolution of this genre has resulted in strategies, tools, and environments that provide a basis for smooth functioning of the system as a whole. Decentralized education implemented through videoconferences is a relatively new genre. As a result, the participants may have conflicting expectations, such as teachers considering it as something very similar to regular classrooms and students seeing it as a type of TV-broadcast.

Strategies and methods developed within traditional education are not necessarily applicable to videoconference settings. While in regular classrooms teachers can draw students' attention to key contents by using subtle cues, perhaps even without being aware of that, in videoconference settings teachers and facilitators should carry out special, sometimes complex actions to direct students' attention to relevant information. In a way, teachers should acquire competences similar to those of film directors. Interaction with students is also quite different in videoconference settings; it requires new communication skills. Besides, in videoconference settings teachers have more limited possibilities to monitor the audience and they have to develop the ability to use available cues for getting appropriate feedback. Finally, the possibility to monitor the outgoing image (that is, to observe himself or herself "from the outside"), time management, and the need to coordinate activities in the setting with the technician/facilitator also present new challenges to the teacher.

Success or failure of videoconference sessions critically depend on appropriate infrastructure, that is whether the students are informed about the schedule and assignments, whether a room and equipment are available, etc. During a videoconference session the teacher and students may look like being together in a "virtual classroom" but in fact they are separated not only by physical distance but by institutional boundaries, as well. Facilities used by the teacher and the students are often provided and maintained by different organizations. An extensive coordination work carried out by various actors from different organizations (such as teachers, managers, technical support people, webmasters, secretaries, etc.) is needed to combine the above facilities into integrated learning environments. In decentralized education teachers and students have to deal with multiple and not always compatible organizational policies, routines, and requirements. Therefore, educational practices need to be contextualized in a larger organizational and inter-organizational context.

To sum up, coordination mechanisms and structures developed at various levels of traditional education often fail in new learning environments. Spatial and organizational boundaries cause communication breakdowns both in information exchange between the sites and inter-organizational cooperation necessary to create and maintain a setting. There is a need for "re-contextualization", that is, development and implementation of new coordination structures and mechanisms appropriate for new learning environments.

The study reported in this paper was primarily informed by activity theory. Following the basic principles of this approach, we focused on actors and their goals, conflicts, mediation, and development. This approach provided support in discovering breakdowns in activities we observed, and it can be concluded that activity theory can be a fruitful approach at an early exploratory phase for identifying key issues and concerns. In our future research we plan to use activity theory for developing more detailed representations of actual activities in videoconference settings. Representations of that kind could help take a next step in our analysis and provide a basis for understanding emerging practices that deal with the breakdowns described in this paper. Besides, such representations can potentially reveal new and advanced uses of technology that go beyond traditional education and allow accomplishing new goals.

Finally, even though in this paper we do not discuss design implications of our findings, we believe the findings do have direct implications for design of videoconference-based environments. This issue, however, requires a special treatment. In our view, there is a need to go beyond tool-centered perspective to a practice/activity-centered perspective not only in analysis but in design, as well. *System design* should be embedded into and subordinated to *interaction design*, which, in turn, should be embedded into *design of educational activities* mediated by technology. Such an arrangement could provide a meta-framework for interdisciplinary cooperation between, respectively, software engineering, Human-Computer Interaction, and Computer Support for Collaborative Learning, and assure the most efficient use of social science insights in supporting education with new tools, systems, and environments.

ACKNOWLEDGEMENTS

The study reported in this paper has been conducted within a research project funded by The Bank of Sweden Tercentenary Foundation.

REFERENCES

Abbot, L., Dallat, J., Livingston, R., Robinson, A. (1993) *Videoconferencing and Distance Learning*. Faculty of Education and Department of Adult and Continuing Education, University of Ulster.

Cunningham S et al. (1998) *New media and Borderless Education: A review of the Convergence between Global Media Networks and Higher Education Provision,* Australian Government, Department of Employment, Education, training and Youth Affairs, Evaluations and Investigations Program, Higher Education Division. (http://www. deetya.gov.au/highered/eippubs/eip97-22/eip9722.pdf

Crowston, K., Osborn C. (1998) *A coordination theory approach to process description and redesign.* CCS wp No 204, Center for Coordination Science, MIT.

Dallat, J., Fraser, G., Livingston, R., Robinson, A. (1992). *Videoconferencing and the Adult Learner.* Faculty of Education and Department of Adult and Continuing Education, University of Ulster.

Esbjörnsson, M. (1997). *Förutsättningar för den distribuerade utbildningen.* Den fysiska och virtuella miljöns påverkan på inlärningsprocessen. Department of Informatics, No 97.14, Umea University.

Hedestig, U., Kaptelinin, V (2001*). Teachers work practice in videoconference settings - Implications for design of virtual learning environments.* In *Proceedings of 20th World Conference on Open and Distance Education*, ICDE, Dusseldorf, Germany.

Hedestig, U. (2000). *Facilitators dolda expertis i videokonferens - Konsekvenser för design av virtuella lärmiljöer.* Department of Informatics, Umeå University, Sweden.

Hutchins, E. (1995) *Cognition in the wild.* Massachusetts: The MIT Press.

Kaptelinin, V., Cole, M (1997). Individual and collective activities in educational computer game playing. In: *Proceedings of the International CSCL'97 Conference on Computer Support for Collaborative Learning* Toronto, Canada.

Kaptelinin, V., Nardi, B., Macaulay, C. (1999). Structuring the "space" of context: The Activity Checklist. *interactions,* vol. VI.4, July/August 1999.

Kaptelinin, V. (1996) Computer-mediated activity: Functional organs in social and developmental contexts. In: Nardi, B. (ed.) *Context and Consciousness: Activity Theory and Human-Computer Interaction.* Cambridge, Mass.: The MIT Press.

Koschmann, T. (1996) (ed.) *CSCL: Theory and practice of an emerging paradigm.* New Jersey: Lawrence Erlbaum Associates, Publishers, Mahwah.

Lau, Linda (2000). *Distance Learning Technologies: Issues, Trends and Opportunities.* Idea group Publishing Hershey, US.

Leontiev, A. N. (1978) *Activity. Consciousness. Personality.* Englewood Cliffs, NJ: Prentice Hall.

Malone, T., Crowston, K. (1992): What is coordination theory and how can it help design cooperative work systems? In R Baecker (ed): *Groupware and Computer Supported Cooperative Work.* California: Morgan Kaufman.

Malone, T., Crowston, K. (1994) The Interdisciplinary Study of Coordination. In *ACM Computing Surveys*, 26, (1).

Mantovani, G. (1996). *New Communication Environments. From Everyday to Virtual.* Taylor & Francis Publishers. London.

Nardi, B (1996) Studying Context: A Comparison of Activity Theory, Situated Action Models, and Distributed Cognition. In B. Nardi (ed*) Context and Consciousness.* Cambridge: The MIT Press.

Rosengren, B. (1993*) När- och distansutbildning med dubbelriktad bild- och ljudkommunkation - en fallbeskrivning.* Department of Computer and System Sciences, report No 93-012-DSC, Royal Institute of Technology, Stockholm.

CML – The ClassSync Modeling Language

John Brecht, Mark Chung, Roy Pea

The Center for Technology in Learning, SRI International

john.brecht@sri.com mark.chung@sri.com roy.pea@sri.com

ABSTRACT

The ClassSync Modeling Language (CML) addresses the problem of creating a controlling overlay to classroom learning activities, or e-learning workflows. Our aim is to allow authors and teachers to generate a mapping from activity design to its implementation in a wirelessly networked classroom with ubiquitous use of handheld computers for information exchange. CML models e-learning workflows with three major components: actors, data objects, and interaction networks. Actors are the diverse performers of actions, data objects are the semantically typed information units that are made available for exchange. Interaction networks are virtual networks constructed on top of whatever network ClassSync is running on, and dictate how information may flow through the ClassSync system (from actor to actor). Activities are the processes performed via these three components, in which actors create and consume data objects and exchange them over an interaction network. The benefits of this approach for students, curriculum designers, teachers, publishers and learning sciences researchers are highlighted.

Keywords

EML (Education Modeling Language), handheld devices, wireless networking, instructional discourse, classroom workflow

NEED

The design and performance of instructional activities is a fundamental problem for research in interactive learning environments. These issues are particularly problematic for the teacher wishing to implement various CSCL scenarios such as small group learning, although more common patterns of classroom interaction, such as the familiar whole-class IRE pattern (Initiation-Response-Evaluation, as in Mehan, 1978), can also be demanding. In non-computer based collaborative patterns of instruction, teachers assemble plans for assigning students to groups, distribute written or oral instructions for their work, including assignment of specific roles to students and constraints on their work in terms of time, document access, and work products required to result from their activity. Teachers collect work, annotate it with scores or comments, and re-distribute it to students to further their learning. Dozens of learning activity cycles like these a day define the work of the classroom.

Designing, implementing, and monitoring these learning activities is a workflow challenge, as research in teacher cognition, planning, and learning has highlighted (e.g., Borko & Putnam, 1996; Cohen et al., 1993; Hammond & Sykes, 2001; Little & McLaughlin, 1993). Teachers currently plan and manage these efforts using a broad array of documents and physical resources, including class lists, publishers' teacher activity guides, seat-based distribution of textbook instructions or photocopied materials, physical separation of groups in the classroom space, worksheets to be completed, informal observations of equitable participation by students in discussions, and the like. In the case of small-group learning, tracking group progress and individual students' participation is important, given well-known problems in group work such as the "free rider" phenomenon (Salomon & Globerson, 1989), and the likelihood that student work in groups can be beset with collaboration breakdowns (Barron, 2000) and unproductive inquiries if interim project milestones are not required (Polman, 1999).

These classroom activity structures and affiliated workflow patterns have become yet more complex with the introduction of computer technologies in classrooms, in which individual use of shared resources such as desktop computers, printers, computer projectors for displaying work, data collection probes and sensors, and other devices need to be integrated with non-computer facilitated classroom activity components.

Furthermore, much of the effort required to set up such arrangements of learners, documents, and task structures, much less to learn from the outcomes of such designs in ways that could lead to improvements, does not result in searchable records and re-usable activity structures. We call this the 'act becomes artifact' problem—and opportunity for innovation and research. With increasing teacher accountability for promoting student learning, it will become increasingly important to provide support for ongoing formative assessment to help diagnose student difficulties and determine productive strategies for overcoming them. Semantic tagging of the actors, data objects, and interaction networks has significant promise for "informating" (rather than "automating": Zuboff, 1988) classroom workflow by turning normally transient instructional (and learner) acts into artifacts for data mining.

Traditional desktop-based Instructional Learning Systems (ILSs), that pre-define activity and response frameworks for individuals are not up to meeting the challenges of learning workflow needs for diverse activity structures among teachers and students (Roschelle et al., 2001). Schwartz et al. (1999) and Barron et al. (1998) highlight the importance for learning environments of flexibly adaptive instruction and formative assessment, in which the teacher deals contingently with the emerging needs of learners and groups to provide constructive learning opportunities.

We envision an extremely low cost system with a wireless network, individual handheld computers, minimal maintenance during school, and with low-threshold user interface for teacher and student use to handle the major proportion of instructional workflow. Real value needs to be added to the paper now primarily used for these purposes. Such a system needs to handle access permissions, distribution of tasks and instructional resources, and collection of activity results from students without requiring teachers to become network system administrators. HotSyncing (in the manner of Palm OS synchronization of desktop and palmtop computer contents) does not logistically meet our needs because the model of coordinating desktop and handheld devices does not support the just-in-time quality that classroom workflow requires.

APPROACH

CML, the ClassSync Modeling Language, is a language for generating a mapping from activity design to implementation of the activity on a network of handheld computers. CML has three components: actors, data objects, and interaction networks. *Actors* are the performers of action in the system, including people (students or teachers, coupled with their devices), groups of actors (where each actor has a well-defined group role), and computer agents called "bots" which help manage the system. *Data objects* are the information units in the ClassSync system and include artifacts such as media, messages, records, and processes (which may control tools for creating or modifying such artifacts or refer to them). Each data object may be classified in terms of one or more semantic types. *Interaction networks* are virtual networks constructed on top of whatever network ClassSync is running on. Interaction networks dictate ways in which information (data objects) may flow through the ClassSync system (from actor to actor). Activities are the processes performed via these three components. An activity will be a process in which actors consume and create data objects and exchange them over some interaction network.

CML is a modeling language that will allow authors and teachers to construct activities by creating assemblages of these component elements. Once such an activity has been modeled in this way, it is up to the ClassSync system to implement an activity at runtime. It is our intent that the CML description will allow for a wide range of implementations, on a wide range of technical platforms. Our goal is that CML will become useable in real time for assembling new activities "on the fly" as new learning and teaching opportunities emerge, as well as a means of preparing activities ahead of time by the teacher or other educational agents.

A CML SCENARIO

To introduce CML, we first present a usage scenario and later explore CML components in more detail.

A User Interface for Flexible Activities "At the Board"

Imagine a user interface for the teacher supporting activities "at the board," in which one or more students are called upon to solve a problem in view of the class. This interface uses a theatrical metaphor. The theater has a stage, an audience, a script, and a backstage area where the props are stored. The script is a list of scenes specifying the cast (group definition of actors), situation (activity), and props (data objects). The teacher acts as director and calls actors, represented by icons, onstage from the audience. Once onstage, the actors have control of the props. The audience has a view of the action on stage. (The stage and actors model will be familiar from Programming by Rehearsal (Finzer & Gould, 1984), Stagecast (Smith & Cypher, 1998), and other Xerox PARC-influenced approaches to developing a computer program. We find the metaphor apt but not our point.)

Running the Show – IRE (Initiation-Response-Evaluation)

Mehan (1978) defined a now well-recognized classroom discourse structure in the Initiation-Response-Evaluation sequence, which characterizes many instructional scenarios as: a teacher initiates an instructional sequence by asking a question, a student responds, and the teacher evaluates that response. So, let's follow the production of a CSCL variant of an IRE scene in our theater. Suppose our classroom is about to participate in GLOBE, a worldwide program for primary and secondary school students to collect, analyze, and report earth science data (GLOBE, 2001; Means & Coleman, 2000). The students have been instructed that they will be working together in groups to collect and analyze data. In order to ensure that the students understand this process well, the teacher will call upon some students to perform a measurement and analysis activity in front of the classroom. Collectively, they will measure the air temperature, pressure, and humidity and compare those values with similar measurements from another classroom across the country, and a set made at the same school in the previous semester.

First, the teacher initiates the scene by clicking "casting call" on it in the script. The Casting bot asks everyone who is to be invited to "try out" (in this case the entire class) by sending a message to the class group manager, which relays the message to every member of the class. The content of this message is a solicitation with the scene description ("You will work with a group of students to collect and analyze data…") and a list of the roles that may be volunteered for ("Analyst,

Temperature Measurer, Pressure Measurer, etc…"). The Casting bot passes responses back to the teacher. The teacher's GUI highlights the icons for the students who volunteered ("raised their hands"). (Some equity-related statistics may pop up as well, such as the time since the student last raised their hand or the total number of times the student has raised their hand on that day and overall.)

Next, the teacher picks students to participate in the scene by dragging their actor icons onstage to the positions corresponding to the roles they should play. When the selection is complete the teacher clicks "positions." The Casting bot then adds the selected students to the "cast" group for the scene. A Stage Director bot moves props from backstage (the teacher's repository) to front stage (the class group repository), according to the script. The cast group manager notifies students as they are added to the cast group, tells them where the props are and how to control them and tells them what their role is in the group. In this case, the "prop" the analyst receives is a spreadsheet containing the data to which the new data are to be compared. The other students in the activity get physical props—probes to attach to their handhelds.

The teacher now clicks "lights," a command giving the class group view permission on the props and on the cast group manager itself, and allowing each member of the class group to see the cast group manager's member list. The GUI on the students' devices then provides each student with a view of the props, and a list of the cast—the illuminated stage. Having a "view" of a prop means that the prop can be viewed but not controlled by the viewer. For instance, the entire class could look at the data in the analyst's spreadsheet, but could not change it or add to it.

Finally, the teacher clicks "Action", which gives the cast group control of the props (and thus permission to modify them). Then the cast may begin to perform the scene by controlling the props and communicating with each other. As they do so, the audience's views are updated appropriately. So, in our GLOBE scenario, the action begins with the three measurers making their measurements. As each one performs the specified steps for these subactivities within the overall activity, the other students will have a view of what is going on in the measurers' devices. One by one, they transmit their measurements to the analyst who plots the data. When they complete these tasks, the group members prepare a summary by editing a shared summary document viewable by the class.

The teacher may end the scene by dismissing the actors (casting bot removes them from the cast group) and dropping the lights (view permission taken away from the class group.) Before the lights are dropped, of course, it is likely that the teacher will want to take the stage and discuss the final state of the props of the class, or even modify them further. Likewise, the teacher may, at any time, add him or herself to the group onstage, and manipulate the props in some manner with them. For example, the GLOBE teacher may review and annotate the summary document before the class, or jump in during the analysis phase to demonstrate the procedure for generating a scatter plot in the spreadsheet application.

ACTIVITIES IN CML

Definition

At a modeling level of description, classroom activity can be defined as an information processing function having an input, an output, and a process by which the output is to be generated from the input This functional definition of an activity can be used to model activities ranging from IRE sequences, to role-playing activities (such as participatory simulations), to small group project-based work, to seatwork or homework exercises.

Linked collections of activities

To achieve this versatility we allow for activities to be chained, networked, and nested. We call such a group of activities a *linked* activity. In the case of a chained activity, the output of one activity process becomes the input of another. For instance, one step in a sequence of a scientific activity might be to do data collection and a next step of the activity might be to do analysis of the data. So the output of the first step, the parameters and values of the collected data, becomes the input of the second step, whose output, in turn, could be a report of the analysis.

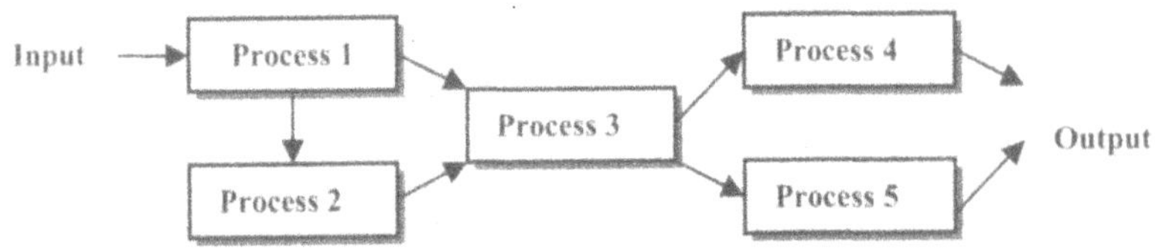

Figure 1: A networked activity

A networked activity (Figure 1) is a more general case of a chained activity, but now there are branches in the chain. At a branching point, the next process is chosen based on the outcome of the current activity. Note that Process 4 and Process 5 both produce the same output. How is it that two different processes can lead to the same output? When activities are defined in CML, they are defined as having one or more specifiable semantic types of input and one or more specifiable semantic types of output. The specific value for the input does not necessarily have to be chosen until the activity is assigned. For instance, imagine the input of the activity diagrammed in Figure 1 is defined as *triangle* and the output is defined as *area*. This means that when the problem is assigned to a student, a specific triangle must be supplied, and a value representing an area will be the output that is ultimately produced by the activity (regardless of the path through the network). Inputs and outputs are data objects. We will discuss data objects and their associated semantic types in greater depth below.

Nesting activities provide a means by which a chained or networked activity is encapsulated in one activity, which in turn forms a part of another linked activity. So long as the linked activity has one input and one output it can be treated in CML just as an ordinary "one step" activity for the purposes of networking. By allowing activities to be nested in this way we make it easy to reuse activities and allow for designers to work on many levels of granularity.

Activity Lifecycles

The simplest lifecycle for an activity to have is to be transitory. The activity is assigned, the student immediately begins work on the process, and the activity ends when they generate the output. However, networks of activities can take on a more dynamic character. Consider the networked activity portrayed in Figure 1. Now, rather than one student making their way through the network, imagine instead that each activity in the network has been assigned to a different student. Further, rather than each activity in the network being performed once, instead imagine that an assigned activity *lingers*. In this situation, each activity is performed whenever the student to which it has been assigned receives the input associated with the activity.

In addition to activities lingering, ClassSync allows for *simultaneity* in the system. By this, we mean that there may be multiple data objects moving through the system simultaneously. In fact, ClassSync allows more than one input to be "processed" by an activity simultaneously. Imagine the class is engaged in a role-playing exercise in which they play the parts of legislators passing laws. It might be interesting in this exercise for a legislator to have more than one bill on their desk at a time. A simpler example might be a common situation where individual students do basic research on some set of topics, and then as a group, they bring their reports together to generate an overall report based on all the individual reports.

The third dynamic quality of ClassSync is *contingency*. Contingency has already shown up implicitly in our networked activity with branching. By contingency we simply mean that activities are not necessarily performed. Rather, they are only performed if the appropriate input data object is sent to the actor to whom the activity has been assigned.

Authors specify when activities end, and can do so in a number of ways (with the teacher having the option to override the end condition). One way is similar to our transitory activity. As soon as the activity produces its final output, the activity ends. Of course, the author may intend that the students perform the activity process a few times, generating multiple outputs. In this case, there are a number of options. There can be an explicit time limit, at the end of which any existing intermediary or final output is collected. Another end condition is that the activity ends after all the required inputs have been supplied, and an output has been generated for each input.

COMPONENTS OF CML

Before we can continue to discuss how activities are created and used in practice, we must digress to introduce the components of CML—actors, data objects, and interaction networks.

Actors

While activities are the processes performed in the ClassSync system, actors are the entities in the system that either perform these processes or that facilitate their performance. CML includes three kinds of actors: *person, group manager,* and *bot*. A person is one individual and his or her associated device. A teacher is a special case of a Person. The teacher is the "superuser" of the ClassSync system. A group manager is the hub of an interacting group of actors (persons or other groups), primarily characterized by the interaction topology it enables amongst the members of the group. A bot is a computer agent, capable of performing specific tasks and of communicating its capabilities. Actors have three categories of properties associated with them: descriptors (metadata), data, and one or more transient states. These properties are summarized in Table 1 below. (All actors have the properties listed in the first row.)

Table 1: Properties of CML Actors

Actor	Descriptors	Data	Transient states
All	• ID, address repository	• List of associated data objects	• Transfer Queue[1] • Linkage[2]
Person	• e.g., gender • e.g., academic level	• List of group affiliations as ordered pairs: (group ID, role(s) played in group) • List of activities	• Activity progress
Group Manager	• Interaction topology • Purpose/type	*As per Person, plus* List of members as ordered pairs: (actor, role)	• Activity progress
Bot	• Description of capabilities[3]	• Schedule	• Current task

Data Objects

Data in ClassSync system are encapsulated as data objects, as described by the Model-View-Controller architecture pioneered by Smalltalk-80™. A data object has a set of semantic types and parent/child relationships associated with it. The semantic types serve to identify in what ways the data object can be used in activities. Parent/child relationships are used to create collections of related objects. Data objects may be shared (simultaneously viewed or edited) by multiple actors in a group, as well as transferred from actor to actor.

Interaction Topologies

Actors may be members of various groups, but they may not interact (perform data object transfers, including messaging) with them until they are linked to the members of the group and/or its manager. The first step in beginning group interaction is to open a link to the group manager. What happens next depends on the topology of the group's network. Regardless of network topology, it should be possible for an actor to send a data object to every member of the group in one step (mass mailing.) Likewise, once linked to the group manager, it should also be possible to request data from it, such as its member roster and present linkage.

[1] A list of data objects currently scheduled for transfer between this actor and one or more others.

[2] A list of all links to or from the actor, where to be "linked" effectively means to be "logged into," or "able to perform transfers with.

[3] Implemented using the Open Agent Architecture (Martin, David L. and Cheyer, Adam J. and Moran, Douglas B. 1999).

Client/Server Networks

If a group interoperates via a client/server network, the group manager acts as "server" for the group. Recall that, like all actors, there is a repository associated with the manager. This repository will serve as the shared "file space" for the group. Here, group members may post data objects that they wish others to download. Also, any data objects that are shared by the group will reside here.

Peer to Peer Networks

If the network topology is P2P (Peer to Peer), then logging in to the group manager should result in a link being created to each other member of the group. There is no "server" in this case. If a file is to be shared, a group member must host it on his or her own device. In fact, there is no single group manager in the case of P2P. A copy of the group manager will reside on every device. This distributed group manager must synchronize itself. For example, when an actor logs in to the group, the group manager on that actor's device must go out onto the P2P network and find the other managers, and set its state to their state.

A special case of a P2P network is a limited and/or directional P2P network, in which an actor links to some subset of the group (limited), and a given actor may only transfer in one direction with some other actor in the group (directional). This could be used to form a chain of actors in which data objects travel in one direction.

CML IN ACTION: BRINGING A LEARNING GROUP TO LIFE

Groups

Creating a group

As mentioned earlier, the teacher is the superuser of the ClassSync system, which gives the teacher the ability to create groups. The creation of groups has two stages—defining the group, and enabling the group. Once the group has been defined and enabled, students can participate in the group. To define a group, the teacher creates a group manager for the group. This act has two steps, assigning descriptors for the manager, and assigning it initial data.

There are four types of data associated with the group manager—data objects, a member roster, group affiliations, and a list of activities. The teacher creates a list of Universal Resource Names (URNs) of the data objects that the group should have at the start. Then the teacher creates a list of roles to be played by members of the group. Finally, if the group is to be a member of a larger group, the teacher identifies that group and assigns the subgroup's role in the supergroup.

Enabling a group

The teacher enables the group after it has been defined, and the system performs setup according to the group topology. For a Client/Server group, the system creates a group manager repository containing copies of the data objects assigned to the group, and schedules a bot to locate the students to add to the group. The division of students into groups can be done randomly, strategically (see Example), or according to a specific list. For a P2P group, there is no centralized repository, so the bot copies the group manager to each member and copies the data objects assigned to the group to one of the group member's repositories.

Participating in a Group

The system notifies students when they have been placed in a group. Students link to the manager to join the group and learn what their role is (this can require a login with a password). They can also find out who the other members are and whether they're logged in, what the group's data objects are, and what the group's goal or role is. Furthermore, they may also find themselves linked to the other members of the group if the group is a P2P group.

"Jigsaw" Groups

In the spirit of the "Jigsaw Classroom" approach (Aronson & Patnoe, 1997), a CML implementation could automatically create groups that join everyone whose roles in their existing groups are the same, with some default interaction topology. The teacher managing the system controls whether or not this function is turned on, and what the topology of an automatically generated jigsaw group ought to be.

Example

After using the IRE to demonstrate the work the students will be doing, our teacher begins the GLOBE activity by dividing the 30-person class into six groups and assigning two groups to each of the three measurement protocols. Each group of five has the following roles, filled by actors of type "Student": data collectors (3), data analyst (1), and a reporter (1) who compiles the group's write-up. The teacher specifies a group topology of P2P, though that may change when activities are assigned. Additionally, there is a group of groups called "Overall GLOBE Investigation" that includes all six groups. This group has six roles, two for each protocol, and each role must be filled by an actor of type "Group" with the appropriate description, e.g., "Humidity Investigators."

Next, the teacher must assign specific actors to roles. The teacher can do this by gestural input, or the system may offer some automated process operating under a teacher or author defined strategy. When assigning students to roles the teacher, or the automated process, might make use of actor descriptors. For example, it may create groups at random, but with the caveat that each group have gender balance. In the GLOBE activity example, the teacher may elect to assign the "natural leaders" in the class to the role of reporter. Also, in anticipation of the activity to come, the teacher in this activity elects to automatically generate a jigsaw group with P2P topology amongst all the data analysts.

Activities

Creating Activities

Activities are defined as having an input, an output, and some process by which the output should be generated from the input (e.g., using a tool controlled by CML or referred to by it, but outside the system). To create an activity with CML, input, output and process must be specified. Input and output are defined by specifying a semantic type of the data object. To specify process, the author must include a data object that provides instructions and, optionally, specifies the role of the actor who should do the activity. The process definition must also include sufficient information for the system to determine where to send the output data object when it is completed.

We differentiate between an activity definition, and an actual activity instance. Thus, a teacher can define an activity as having a certain type of input data object, a certain role of actor, and, a certain type of output data object. However, it isn't until assignment (or runtime, in programmer-speak) that specific values are filled in and the activity is instantiated.

Creating Linked Activities

A linked activity still has the same properties as a normal activity—input, process, and output. As mentioned earlier, the input is simply the input of the first subactivity, and the output is the output of the final subactivity. The actor associated with the process, however, must be a group if the subactivities are to be performed by multiple actors. (Otherwise, the actor is just the one actor that performs all of the activities.) Besides the group associated with the superactivity, there is the collection of activities itself and its link topology. The author must identify what these activities are and which links to which. Bear in mind, that we are still only defining the activity, not instantiating it, so this mapping of actors to activities is still in the abstract. That is, we are still only identifying *roles*, not specific actors.

Assigning Activities

ClassSync automates assigning activities to actors so that the process is the same regardless of the type or complexity of the activity. The teacher simply picks the activity, an input data object, and a group to which the activity is to be assigned. The assignment process then goes and finds each actor that is a member of the specified group that has the capability to do the activity. Having a "capability" simply means that the actor is of the appropriate role (or roles) within the group.

Example Activity Assignment

> In our GLOBE classroom, the investigation groups have been created, and now it is time to assign the investigation activities. The teacher has created data collection activities, an analysis activity, a write-up activity, and a discussion activity. The discussion activity is to be assigned to the "Overall GLOBE investigation" and its input is a data object that is composed of a union of all the collected data (which will be produced by the analysts). The data collection, analysis, and write-up activities compose a network activity called "X Investigation," where "X" is one of the three protocols (air temperature, pressure, humidity).

To assign the activities, the ClassSync system must, for each activity, identify every actor in the system that has the role associated with the activity. For instance, there is an activity for measuring temperature. The role associated with the activity would be "'data collector' who is a member of a group whose type is 'Temperature Investigators.'" (Note that we can define roles in ClassSync iteratively—"an X, which is a member of a Y, which is a member of a Z...") Altogether, the system should find six such actors, but it doesn't matter that we know this is the case ahead of time. Without changing anything about the activities, the teacher should be able to alter the number and type of actors in the class, and the system should still be able to handle it.

Once an actor is identified for assignment, the ClassSync system adds the activity to their activity list and, if appropriate, schedules a transfer with them to give them an input data object. When the assignment is made, the student or group should receive notification about the assignment. Once all the assignments have been made, the teacher indicates that the students may begin work using some start trigger associated with the overall activity. This trigger may be an initial input data object for the entire network of activities, or it may simply be a message to the top level group in the activity network telling it to "begin."

CLASSSYNC SUPPORTS COLLABORATIVE PROJECT BASED LEARNING

We have described in this paper how CML provides the infrastructure essential for collaborative project-based learning by coordinating the activity lifecycle, providing group administration services, and managing resources and communication processes. CML provides a language that specifies dynamic configurations of this infrastructure. Teachers interact with ClassSync at a high level by creating groups and assigning activities to them. ClassSync automates the details of creating a group by notifying students that they now belong to a group, by making resources available to the group, and enabling resource sharing and messaging. ClassSync automates the details of activity assignment, assigns roles to members, and transitions to the next activity when the activity completes.

CML is consistent with Activity Centered Design

Activity Centered Design (Gifford & Enyedy, 1999) represents a shift in the theoretical framework of CSCL from Learner Centered Design—which proves less suitable for collaborative models because of its focus on the individual—to a model in which learning happens within an activity system consisting of people, artifacts (tools and data objects, as per above), and tasks linked within a social context. The model is neither simply learner-centered nor teacher-centered; rather, learners draw upon resources such as the teacher, other students, or tools and data as they participate in an activity. We applaud this emphasis as a productive modeling framework for CSCL as well as the other forms of socially-situated and artifact-mediated instructional activity that take place in classroom workflows (e.g., Cole, 1996). Such an Activity Theoretic focus has its roots in work by Vygotsky (1978) and Leont'ev (1979), and has been used fruitfully in CSCW research (e.g., Bodker, 1997; Nardi, 1996).

CML fits neatly within this framework by providing a language for expressing the relations between the activity, actors, and tools/data, which operate as part of a dynamic system. The system is dynamic because the relations do not have to be fixed or tightly coupled, nor do the activities have to proceed on a fixed trajectory. Actors move from one activity to the next, have tools and data objects at their disposal, and create data objects/tools that they may share or exchange with other actors.

WHO BENEFITS FROM CML?

It is also worth highlighting what we consider to be the primary benefits from use of the ClassSync Modeling Language, for curriculum designers, students, teachers, publishers, and researchers in the learning sciences.

• Curriculum designers benefit from CML by having a means of expressing activities covering a wide range of interaction scenarios. CML provides a level of abstraction above the hardware and network, so a designer can specify activities that could run in a variety of settings.

• Students benefit because ClassSync gives them the ability to participate in a number of interaction topologies. ClassSync simplifies the technical hurdles of transitioning between these topologies through automatic configuration and resource management for easy access to information and people resources.

• Teachers benefit because ClassSync coordinates classroom workflow and simplifies the task of grouping students and managing the details of assigning work to groups. ClassSync enables real-time performance measurement and post-class playback of activity sequences for classroom reflection or teacher professional development purposes.

• Publishers can use CML tools to address the problem of scaling to cover entire curricula with authoring tools and reusable activity structures. CML, as a runnable formalism, also is testable, so that activities can be run in a simulated environment for quality assurance.

• Researchers in the learning sciences benefit from CML because activities may be instrumented to monitor and record the learning process; later, data mining techniques may be applied to the collected data, and results fed back to support the teacher's instructional decision-making.

CHALLENGES

We have outlined a specification for the ClassSync Modeling Language, but acknowledge that there are formidable challenges to implementing a working system and applying it to commonplace curriculum design and classroom use.

• Every modeling language faces a tradeoff between expressiveness and usability. As language complexity increases, authors may create richer activities, but the system may become unwieldy. We are seeking a workable balance in this tradeoff space that nonetheless will provide a powerful action augmentation framework for teachers.

• CML does not model everything of significance to learning interactions that occurs in a classroom (e.g., social exchanges, uses of tools that are not computer-controllable). There will always be a gap between system knowledge and tacit knowledge, between formal interactions with the devices and real-world interactions. Nonetheless, we expect CML can model centrally significant aspects of e-learning workflows.

• The ClassSync system may require a non-trivial amount of training for the teacher and students, who may not be familiar with handheld devices, much less information exchange over a wireless network. We expect a design research focus (e.g., Edelson, Gordin & Pea, 1999) can iteratively improve on such issues toward a readily learnable system.

• Any implementation of ClassSync is bound to face practical issues related to the particular hardware or network used. This may lead to significant differences in system capability or performance that impose constraints on the kinds of activities that are practical.

We anticipate that in our ongoing work to successfully develop CML, we will be applying iterative design techniques, involving authors and teachers in the design of the language and the authoring tool. We will need to conduct field tests of the resulting activities to verify that the language is sufficiently expressive, and develop a test framework for authors to use during development. We are employing a bootstrapping process (Engelbart, 1962) in which we use the products of our development and conduct synergistic activities that focus on specific interaction topologies and activities in specific domains as steps towards a complete system.

ACKNOWLEDGMENTS

Thanks to the many contributors from the WILD (Wireless Internet Learning Devices) project team at SRI International: Tristan de Frondeville, Chris DiGiano, Sarah Lewis, Judy Li, Charlie Patton, Jeremy Roschelle, Deborah Tatar, Phil

Vahey, and Wenming Ye. We gratefully acknowledge support from SRI International and the National Science Foundation.

REFERENCES

Aronson, E., & Patnoe, S. (1997). *The jigsaw classroom: Building cooperation in the classroom (2nd ed.).* New York: Addison Wesley Longman.

Barron, B. (2000). Achieving coordination in collaborative problem solving groups. *Journal of the Learning Sciences, 9*(4), 403-436.

Barron, B., Schwartz, D.L., Vye, N.J., Moore, A., Petrosino, T., Zech, L. & Bransford, J.D. (1998). Doing with understanding: Lessons from research on problem and project based-learning. *Journal of the Learning Sciences, 7*, 271-311.

Bodker, S. (1997). Computers in mediated human activity. *Mind, Culture and Activity, 4*(3), 149-158.

Borko, H., & Putnam, R. T. (1996). Learning to teach. In D. C. Berliner & R. C. Calfee (Eds.), *The handbook of educational psychology (pp. 673-708*). New York: Macmillan Publishing.

Cohen, D. K., McLaughlin, M. W. & Talbert, J. E. (1993). (Eds.), *Teaching for understanding: Challenges for policy and practice.* San Francisco, CA: Jossey-Bass.

Cole, M. (1996). *Cultural psychology.* Cambridge, MA: Harvard University Press.

Edelson, D. C., Gordin, D.N., & Pea, R. D. (1999). Addressing the challenges of inquiry-based learning through technology and curriculum design. *Journal of the Learning Sciences, 8*(3&4), 391-450.

Engelbart, D.C. (1962, October). *Augmenting human intellect: A conceptual framework* (Summary Report, AFOSR-3233). Menlo Park, CA: SRI International.

Finzer, W. & Gould, L. (1984). Programming by rehearsal, *Byte, 9*, 187-210.

Gifford, B.R. & Enyedy, N.D. (1999). Activity-centered design: Towards a theoretical framework for CSCL. In C.M. Hoadley & J. Roschelle (Eds.), *Proceedings of the Computer Support for Collaborative Learning (CSCL) 1999 Conference (pp. 189-196).* Palo Alto, CA: Stanford University [Available from Lawrence Erlbaum Associates, Mahwah, NJ]

GLOBE Program (2001, January). *The GLOBE Program.* Washington, D.C. (www.globe.gov)

Hammond, L. D. & Sykes, G. (2001). (Eds.), *Teaching as the learning profession: Handbook of policy and practice.* San Francisco: Jossey-Bass.

Leont'ev, A.N. (1979). The problem of activity in psychology. In J. Wertsch (Ed.), *The concept of activity in Soviet Psychology.* New York: M.E. Sharpe, Inc.

Little, J.W. & McLaughlin, M. (1993). (Eds.), *Teachers work.* New York: Teachers College Press.

Martin, David L. and Cheyer, Adam J. and Moran, Douglas B. (1999) The Open Agent Architecture: A Framework for Building Distributed Software Systems. *Applied Artificial Intelligence, vol. 13, no. 1-2, pp. 91-128, January-March 1999.*

Means, B., & Coleman, E. (2000). Technology supports for student participation in science investigations. In M.J. Jacobson & R.B. Kozma (Eds.), *Innovations in science and mathematics education (pp. 287-319).* Mahwah, NJ: Lawrence Erlbaum Associates.

Mehan, H. (1978). Structuring school structure. *Harvard Educational Review, 48*(1), 32-64.

Nardi, B. (1996). *Context and consciousness: AI and Human Computer Interaction.* Cambridge, MA: MIT Press.

Polman, J. L. (2000). *Designing project-based science: Connecting learners through guided inquiry.* New York: Teachers College Press.

Roschelle, J., Pea, R., Hoadley, C., Gordin, D., & Means, B. (2001). Changing how and what children learn in school with collaborative cognitive technologies. *The Future of Children, 10*(2), pp. 76-101. (Special issue on *Children and Computer Technology*, M. Shields (Ed.), published by the David and Lucille Packard Foundation, Los Altos, CA).

Salomon, G. & Globerson, T. (1989). When teams do not function the way they ought to. *International Journal of Educational Research, 13*, 89-99.

Schwartz, D. L., Lin, X., Brophy, S., & Bransford, J. D. (1999). Toward the development of flexibly adaptive instructional designs. In C. Reigeluth (Ed.), *Instructional Design Theories and Models, Volume II.* Hillsdale, NJ: Lawrence Erlbaum Associates.

Smith, D. C., & Cypher, A. (1998). Making programming easier for children. In A. Druin (Ed.), *The design of children's technology.* San Francisco: Morgan Kaufmann.

Vygotsky, L. S. (1978). *Mind in society: The development of higher order psychological processes.* M.Cole, V. John-Steiner, S. Scribner, & E. Souberman (Eds.). Cambridge, MA: Harvard University Press.

Zuboff, S. (1988). *In the age of the smart machine: The future of work and power.* New York: Basic Books.

F. (PEDAGOGY TRACK): COMPUTER SUPPORT FOR PROBLEM-BASED LEARNING

Collaborative Ways of Knowing: Issues in Facilitation

Cindy E. Hmelo-Silver

Rutgers, The State University of New Jersey

chmelo@rci.rutgers.edu

ABSTRACT

This paper describes a detailed analysis of a student-centered problem-based learning group. The focus of this analysis is to understand the goals and strategies of an expert facilitator. This was accomplished by examining the questions and statements that the students and facilitators generated and inferring the facilitator's goals and strategies. Studying facilitation in a face to face situation provides some guidance in designing support to use in an online problem-based learning environment; however, considerable adaptation is necessary as some facilitation can be built into the system but some facilitation may need to be done by a human tutor. Implications for CSCL system design for problem-based learning will be discussed.

Keywords

Problem-based learning, facilitation, student-centered learning

INTRODUCTION

One of the hallmarks of a constructivist classroom is its focus on student-centered discourse (Palincsar, 1998). In a typical teacher centered classroom, the teacher asks 95% of the questions; mostly requiring short answers (Graesser & Person, 1994). The typical mode of discourse is the IRE pattern in which the teacher initiates a question, generally aimed at getting a student to display their knowledge, the student responds, and the teacher evaluates that response. Thus the goal often focuses on having students learn facts. Teacher's strategies are influenced by their goals for teaching and beliefs about learning (Schoenfeld, 1998). In contrast, inquiry teachers have goals that include having students learn the facts but their goals go to higher levels as well. A study of inquiry teachers identified several different types of goals and strategies that are used (Collins & Stevens, 1982). They found that inquiry teachers' goals include having students learn theories and how the theories are derived. Inquiry teachers believe that it is important for students to be active agents in knowledge construction. This includes having students learn what questions to ask, how to make predictions from theories, and how theories and rules can be tested. Their analyses indicate that these teachers use different kinds of strategies to achieve these goals. For example, they may select appropriate cases and counterexamples to encourage the students to generate hypotheses, make predictions, reveal their misconceptions, and test their ideas. In inquiry teaching, the students are more active than in IRE discourse but the teacher still leads the discussion, working towards global learning goals but choosing strategies on the fly.

Social constructivist approaches to learning are said to be student-centered, with students driving the discussion and the teacher serving as the guide on the side (Palincsar, 1998). Determining exactly what that means and how student-centered learning can be facilitated are important in being able to implement constructivist approaches more broadly. One way to examine this is to analyze the goals, strategies, and tactics of a master facilitator. Understanding how an expert facilitates in terms of the goals, strategies, and tactics that he uses has important implications for training new facilitators and in designing CSCL systems. Examining group discourse in terms of who is asking questions, the nature of the questions asked, and the nature of the responses can provide some insight into characteristics of a student-centered classroom. This paper reports on a study of a specific student-centered learning environment, problem-based learning (PBL). PBL is widely used in medical schools (Barrows, 1988; Schmidt et al, 1996). PBL is an example of a cognitive apprenticeship (Collins, Brown, & Newman, 1989). In a cognitive apprenticeship, students learn in the context of solving complex, meaningful tasks. The role of the teacher is to make key aspects of expertise visible and making tacit thinking processes explicit. In PBL, students learn through solving problems and reflecting on their experience. They work in small groups guided by a facilitator. The role of the facilitator is guiding students on the learning process, pushing them to think deeply, and modeling the kinds of questions that students need to be asking themselves. The collaborative groups provide a forum for students to distribute the cognitive load and negotiate shared understanding as they solve the problem. This study analyzes the group discourse during two PBL sessions to better understand the learning process. It focuses on the interaction between a master PBL facilitator and an experienced group of PBL students.[1]

A PBL tutorial session begins by presenting a group, typically 5-7 students with a small amount of information about a complex problem (Barrows, 1988; Hmelo & Ferrari, 1997). From the outset, students question the facilitator to obtain additional information; they may also gather facts by doing experiments or other research. At several points, students pause to reflect on the data they have collected so far, generate questions about that data, and ideas about solutions. Students identify concepts they need to learn more about to solve the problem (i.e., learning issues). After considering the case with their existing knowledge, students divide up and independently research the learning issues they identified. They then regroup to share what they learned, and reconsider their ideas in light of what they have learned. When completing the task, they reflect on the problem to abstract the lessons learned, as well as how they performed in their self-directed learning and collaborative problem solving. This helps prepare the students for transfer (Salomon, Perkins, & Globerson, 1989).

While working, students use whiteboards to help scaffold their problem solving. The whiteboard is divided into four columns to help them record where they have been and where they are going. The columns help remind the learners of the problem-solving process. The whiteboard serve as a focus for group deliberations. The *Facts* column holds information that the students obtained from the problem statement. The *Ideas* column serves to keep track of their evolving hypotheses. The students place their questions for further study into the *Learning Issues* column. They use the *Action Plan* column to keep track of plans for resolving the problem.

METHODS

Data Sources

The participants in this study were five second-year medical students, who were experienced in PBL, and a master facilitator. Students worked on a problem for five hours over two sessions. The sessions were videotaped and transcribed. In addition, the researcher reviewed the audiotapes with the facilitator and interviewed him regarding his goals and strategies for particular discourse moves.

Coding and Analysis

The entire transcript was coded for the types of questions and statements in the discourse. All the questions asked were identified. They were coded using Graesser and Person's (1994) taxonomy of question types as well as several additional categories that were developed to capture monitoring, clarification, and group dynamics questioning (see Table 1). Three major categories of questions were coded. Short answer questions required simple answers of five types: verification, disjunction, concept completion, feature specification, and quantification. Long answer questions required more elaborated relational responses of nine types: definitions, examples, comparisons, interpretations, causal antecedent, causal consequences, expectational, judgmental, and enablement. The meta category referred to group dynamics, monitoring, self-directed learning, clarification-seeking questions, and requests for action. Any questions that did not fit into these categories were classified as uncodeable.

Statements were coded as to whether they were new ideas, modifications of ideas, agreements, disagreements, or metacognitive statements. Each of these statements was coded as to its depth. Statements were coded as simple if they were assertions without any justification or elaboration. These corresponded to responses to the short answer questions. These included verifications, concept completions, and quantities. Elaborated statements went beyond simple assertions by including definitions, examples, comparisons, judgments, and predictions. These would be responses to long answer question types 7-10, 14, and 15 in Table 1. Statements were coded as causal if they described the processes that lead to a particular state or resulted from a particular event (i.e., responses to question types 11-13). Statements were also coded as to whether they were read from the case information, repetitions of a previous statement, or uncodeable statements. An independent rater coded ten percent of the discourse; interrater agreement of greater than 90% was achieved.

RESULTS

Questions and Statements

Students were expected to ask a substantial number of questions. The meta questions were expected to be the major category for the facilitator. The distribution of questions is shown in Figure 1. Because these were experienced PBL students, they were also expected to generate a substantial number of this type of question. A total of 809 questions were asked, 466 by the students and 343 by the facilitator. The students asked 226 short answer questions, 51 long answer questions, and 189 meta questions. Of the short answer questions, the modal question type was to elicit the features of the patients' illness from the medical record, for example when Jim asked "Does it say anything about medications?"

[1] As in the PBL literature, the terms tutor and facilitator are used interchangeably in this paper.

Table 1. Categories of questions

Question Type	Description	Example
Short answer		
▪ Verification	Yes/no responses to factual questions.	Are headaches associated with high blood pressure?
▪ Disjunctive	Questions that require a simple decision between two alternatives	Is it all the toes? Or just the great toe?
▪ Concept completion	Filling in the blank or the details of a definition	What supplies the bottom of the feet? Where does that come from??
▪ Feature specification	Determines qualitative attributes of an object or situation	Could we get a general appearance and vital signs?
▪ Quantification	Determines quantitative attributes of an object or situation	How many lymphocytes does she have?
Long Answer		
▪ Definition.	Determine meaning of a concept	What do you guys know about pernicious anemia as a disease?
▪ Example:	Request for instance of a particular concept or event type	When have we seen this kind of patient before?
▪ Comparison	Identify similarities and differences between two or more objects	Are there any more proximal lesions that could cause this? I mean I know its bilateral.
▪ Interpretation	A description of what can be inferred from a pattern of data	You guys want to tell me what you saw in the peripheral smear?
▪ Causal antecedent	Asks for an explanation of what state or event causally led to the current state and why	What do you guys know about compression leading to numbness and tingling? How that happens?
▪ Causal consequence	Asks for an explanation of the consequences of an event of state	What happens when it's, when the, when the neuron's demyelinated?
▪ Enablement:	Asks for an explanation of the object, agent, or processes that allows some action to be performed.	How does uhm involvement of veins produce numbness in the foot?
▪ Expectational	Asks about expectations or predictions (including violation of expectations)	How much, how much better is her, are her neural signs expected to get?
▪ Judgmental:	Asks about value placed on an idea, advice, or plan	Should we put her to that trouble, do you feel, on the basis of what your thinking is?
Task oriented and meta		
▪ Group dynamics:	Lead to discussions of consensus or negotiation of how group should proceed	So Mary, do you know what they are talking about?
▪ Monitoring	Help check on progress, requests for planning	Um, so what did you want to do next?
▪ Self-directed learning	Relate to defining learning issues, who found what information;	So might that be a learning issue we can, we can take a look at?
▪ Need clarification	The speaker does not understand something and needs further explanation or confirmation of previous statement	Are you, are you, Jeff are you talking about micro vascular damage that then, which then causes the neuropathy?
▪ Request/ Directive	Request for action related to PBL process	Why don't you give, why don't you give Jeff a chance to get the board up.

The facilitator asked 39 short answer questions, 48 long answer questions and 256 meta questions. Short answer questions were often used to focus students' attention.

Long answer questions often asked the students to define what they had said or interpret information as for example when the facilitator asked a student "But I mean what produces the numbness at the bottom of the feet?" Meta questions were the dominant mode for the facilitator as he asked the students to evaluate one of their hypotheses "Well yeah, multiple sclerosis. How about that? How do you feel about that?..." These statements also included monitoring the group dynamics as he asked "So Mary, do you know what they are talking about?" The facilitator asked comparatively few content-focused questions. The distribution of question types differed for the facilitator and the students.

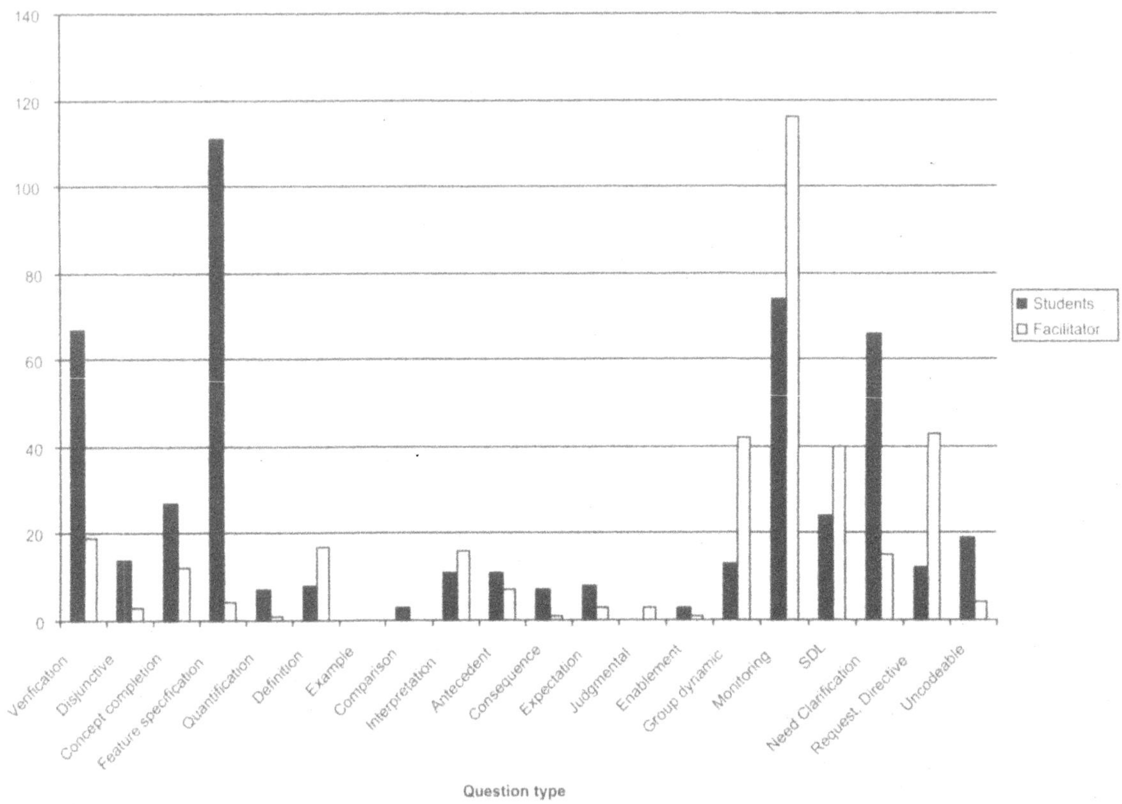

Figure 6. Distribution of question types

If the discussions were student-centered then it is reasonable to expect the students to do most of the talking. Moreover, if knowledge were being collaboratively constructed, the students' statements should be in response to previously introduced ideas. The facilitator should be offering few new ideas and making statements that are in the metacognitive category, centered around monitoring the groups progress in problem-solving and self-directed learning.

This was indeed the case. The facilitator made a total of 243 statements and the students made a total of 3763 statements. The distribution of statement types is shown in Figure 2. Clearly, the students are doing most of the talking. The distribution of statement types differed among the students and the facilitator. The facilitator made very few statements, rarely offering new ideas or modifying existing ideas. The facilitator was most likely to offer a comment monitoring the group's progress or encouraging students to consider that a poorly elaborated idea might become a learning issue. Both the metacognitive questioning and statements helped support the students collaborative knowledge construction as they build on the new ideas offered by others, expressing agreement, disagreement, and modifying the ideas being discussed. Of the first 4 categories of statements, the majority were simple statements (1641) but the students also made elaborated statements (464) and causal explanations (211).

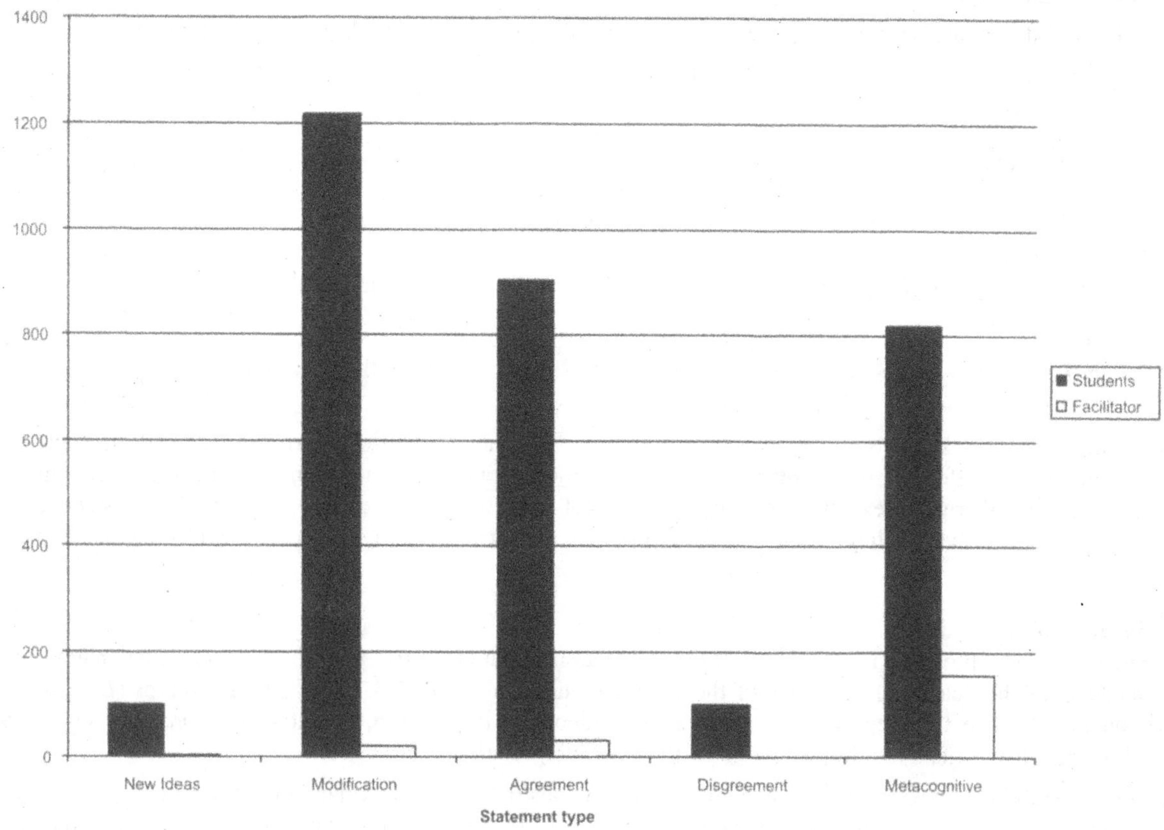

Figure 7. Distribution of statement types

While many of the statements taken individually were simple statements, taken as a collaborative explanation, they were elaborated, over several speakers and several conversational turns as occurred in this sequence after Barrows ask the students how the pernicious anemia hypothesis accounts for their concerns.

HB: Mary does that malnutrition vitamin B cover the, the things you were talking about just a minute ago? You were concerned about there's a number of different vitamins that may be involved.

MA: I hmmm.

HB: Can we just leave the, that hypothesis up?

MA: Oh yes. I think that's fine.

DE: Like pernicious anemia is a big one.

MA: Right. That must be the vitamin, the B.

HB: What, what's pernicious anemia?

DE: Uh, it's a deficient, deficiency of cobalamine.

MA: Vitamin B12, cobalamine or...

JM: Or folate.

MA: Or folate.

DE: Yeah, but it's not, that's not pernicious anemia. That's a, also another macrocytic anemia.

MA: Pernicious anemia is specifically.

JM: Oh. You're right. That's right.

DE: And um, you get anemia and you can also get eh, um, peripheral...

MA: Neuropathies.

DE: ... neuropathies.

HB: down there too?

CP: Technically pernicious, pernicious anemia is technically just the loss, the lack of intrinsic factor.

DE: The loss of intrinsic factor. So you don't absorb.

CP: And that's [unintelligible]

DE: You don't absorb.

CP: Right.

MA: Right. That's a good distinction. You see, we just...

CP: As opposed to like somebody who had part of their intestine removed and can't absorb.

MA: Right.

CP: But their ileum is gone and they can't absorb the B12. That's different than pernicious anemia.to vit, intrinsic factor.

This is collaborative because students all contributed different parts of the explanation. Barrows triggered the explanation but then different students offered different pieces of the explanation about pernicious anemia, what some signs might be (neuropathies) and what alternative explanations they can rule out (poor absorption of B12 in the gut). The students were themselves very metacognitive as they monitored their progress and understanding and considered their need for self-directed learning.

Goals and strategies

The fine-grained analysis provides useful descriptive information about the PBL tutorial. This is complemented by a qualitative analysis of the goals and strategies of the facilitator using a stimulated recall. The facilitator (Barrows) was interviewed on his goals and strategies while viewing the videotape. In addition, an interaction analysis session was conducted with a cognitive scientist to further elucidate the data interpretation.

The facilitator's overall goal emphasized that students needed to construct a causal explanation of how a disease leads to a particular pattern of signs and symptoms. He believed that students learned best through guided exploration of complex, ill-structured problem spaces. He focused on helping students become good reasoners as they looked for consistent mappings between different levels of explanations. Another important goal was helping the students become critical, self-directed learners who are cognizant of the limitations of their knowledge. His overall strategy was to use open-ended questioning and take advantage of the PBL routine.

One specific strategy that the facilitator frequently used was to push students for an explanation as he did in the example below when MA throws out the idea of multiple sclerosis as the cause of the patient's problem:

MA: Um, just given the idea that numbness in your feet, I had multiple sclerosis as a possibility. She is an older woman and multiple sclerosis, I believe, usually presents in the younger generation 30's and 40's, but it, it definitely can happen in an older person. So...

Facilitator: And tell us what multiple sclerosis is.

MA: Um, Multiple sclerosis is um, a progressive, it's a progressive and chronic debilitating disease um, where you get various points of sclerosis within the brain itself and it can affect different areas of um, of um, people's motor function. And it's called multiple sclerosis because there are multiple areas of these sclerotic plaques that occur in the brain.

Facilitator: What causes those plaques?

This serves the goal of placing the students' knowledge in public view and helping the students see the limitations of their understanding. Another strategy observed is that of revoicing (O'Connor & Micheals, 1993) in which the facilitator restates what a students has said.

MA: And another important um, hypothesis that's come is a vitamin B12 deficiency, which we've crossed out. Hah, because we didn't think she had any malnutrition. However, we found out that um, in the elderly there is a much, much higher prevalence of Vitamin B12 deficiency...

DE: And also I was just, happen to glance at it last night and um, 'cause I was just talking with my husband and, about the um, neurosyphilis and, and uh, the olivopontocereballer atrophy being pretty serious and progressive and, and I was thinking that vitamin B12 wasn't so much if you treated it. But it, I was reading that it's in a lot of the neur, uh, neural deficits are irreversible.

MA: Uh hmm.

DE: So it is, you know. It does put in my mind it's a more of a serious.

Facilitator: Now you people are saying B12 all the time and yet when you say we eliminated it, you're talking about pernicious anemia, right?

The facilitator has accomplished three goals here. First, he has taken the idea put forth by the students and clarified it for the group as he restated it. Second, he has legitimated DE's idea. She is a quiet but extremely thoughtful student and she is recognized in this move. Third, he made sure this very important idea did not get lost. Pernicious anemia is the cause of the patients' problem and was in danger of being lost from the discussion. Table 2 provides a sample of some of the additional strategies that served as useful facilitation tools.

This study demonstrates that, in PBL, the students do a substantial amount of question-asking and explanation construction indicating that the tutorials are clearly student-centered. Moreover, the teacher's role is that of metacognitive guidance and scaffolding the collaboration. Specific types of questions are strategically used in the service of learning goals. These questions serve as scaffolds that are faded as students internalize the questions (Hmelo & Guzdial, 1996). These results suggest that through this cognitive apprenticeship, students see the big picture and integrate large bodies of learning and are becoming socialized into their community of practice through their learning discourse.

Table 2. A sampler of additional strategies

Strategy	Goals
Summarizing	Ensure joint representation of problem
	Establish common ground
	Help students synthesize data
	Move group along in process
Map between symptoms and hypothesis	Elaborate causal mechanism
Generate/ evaluate hypotheses	Help students focus their inquiry
	Examine fit between hypotheses and accumulating evidence
Check that students agree that whiteboard reflects their discussion	Make sure all ideas get recorded and important ideas are not lost
Cleaning up the board	Evaluate idea
	Maintain focus
	Keep process moving
Creating learning issues	Knowledge gaps as opportunities to learn
Encourage construction of visual representation	Construct integrated knowledge that ties mechanisms to effects

APPLYING THE LESSONS LEARNED TO ONLINE FACILITATION

The analysis of an expert facilitator has important implications for providing tools for facilitating online collaboration as well as providing a basis for training novice facilitators in PBL. These results provide suggestions for conversational moves that facilitators might make and representations that could embody the learning goals and strategies that an expert facilitator uses. There are other issues that this analysis does not address as well—for example, how does facilitation need to differ between synchronous and asynchronous environments.

The role of the facilitator in a face-to-face discussion has several aspects. First, the facilitator needs to help maintain the agenda and manage time. Second, the facilitator needs to ensure that ideas are addressed at a deep, conceptual level. Third, the facilitator needs to keep the group moving and ensure that everyone participates. These roles are critical in an asynchronous facilitation but enacting them will have some qualitative differences. In face-to-face tutorials, it is critical to get to the learning issues before a session ends. Session boundaries are not always clear in online PBL. Online systems need to consider timeframes and embedded activity structures for accomplishing PBL activities to create these boundaries. It is more difficult to keep an online group moving without the visual cues available in face-to-face interaction. Finally, it is likely that the facilitator has an additional role in asynchronous PBL –helping the group to converge rather than continuing to diverge. Understanding how to address these differences is critical in developing systems to support both students and tutors in asynchronous discussion.

PBL provides a well-described approach to constructivist learning however it is labor intensive and requires one trained facilitator for each group of students, which is not always practical. Often novices are asked to facilitate with very limited training. Research by Derry, Seymour, Steinkuehler, and Lee (2000) suggests that facilitation is quite difficult for novices. Novice tutors may not always know how and when to intervene appropriately. In the novice tutors' struggle to facilitate, they may be overly directive as they try to guide the group's agenda and have difficulty dealing with the group dynamics. The questions that the expert asks can be incorporated as procedural facilitations for the novice tutor by providing hints that suggest different questions that might be useful to serve different goals in different stages of learning. The analysis of the questions asked has been incorporated into a set of procedural facilitations for student tutors in an Educational Psychology class for preservice teachers. Figure 3 shows an example of one of the four prompt cards that a novice facilitator might use during hypothesis generation. These types of hints might be incorporated into an online tutor tool kit. As well, annotated examples of discourse could be provided to model how and when expert facilitators intervene and when they stand back and allow the group to work issues out among themselves. Although this includes very basic information about PBL, it provides concrete examples of questions that the facilitator could ask.

2) GENERATING MULTIPLE HYPOTHESES

Students should brainstorm their first instincts about:

IDEAS: how to solve the problem

FACTS: information we know about the problem and from their own knowledge

LEARNING ISSUES: information we need to know

ACTIONS: what we can do to start solving the problem

The scribe will begin to write down what the group says on the white board/ big paper.

Ask for clarification of terms written down in the FACTS and IDEAS columns.

EXAMPLES:

- What does that term mean?
- What does "expert" mean in this case?

If students can't clarify or define their ideas, these become LEARNING ISSUES

Goal: To help students understand what they don't know.

Figure 3. Example prompt card for facilitators

If trained facilitators are a limited resource, then a distributed PBL system might offer an alternative way to deal with this limitation (Steinkuehler et al., in press). As noted in the previous section, the analysis of expert facilitation can be used to provide tools to support novices in tutoring. Asynchronous collaboration might offer opportunities for students to be more reflective than they might be in a face-to-face conversation, enabling deeper learning conversations. However, the slower pace of asynchronous PBL might make some of the strategies described above difficult to implement. The slower pace gives the facilitator more time to respond to issues going on in the group but there is a real danger that the flow of the dialogue might be lost. In the face-to-face tutorial, the students made 3763 statements and asked 454 questions. Online, students take many fewer turns and there are significant time lags in students' responses. This suggests that there needs to be some adaptation to accomplish PBL asynchronously. A pilot study was conducted in Spring 2001 with 2 groups experienced in face-to-face PBL using the STEP PBL system.[2] The STEP PBL system is an innovative web site designed to support facilitated problem-based discussions of video-cases (Derry et al., 2001). The site has a student module which helps structure the students collaborative PBL, a tutor toolkit to provide resources for facilitation, an asynchronous environment for online collaboration, video case materials, and hypermedia information resources that cover learning sciences content. The student module included a whiteboard, as in traditional PBL and the asynchronous environment was a threaded discussion, For the pilot study, an experienced tutor facilitated the groups. Students would log on at different times and at irregular intervals. This posed a major challenge when the facilitator would ask a student to explain what they meant and the student might not log on for several days by which time the conversation was on another topic. As in other CSCL systems, the responses to students' posts and whiteboard entries need to be flagged so students can respond. One possible solution to this problem would be to have the system email the participants (including the facilitator) whenever there is a new post to remind them to log in. Because of the nature of threaded discussions, there need to be mechanisms that make the flow of the online discussions more transparent to the participants.

[2] STEP website: http://www.wcer.edu/step

A CSCL system adapted for online PBL needs to have representations that support problem-based discourse. One way to accomplish this might be through anchored collaboration (Hmelo, Guzdial, & Turns, 1998) in which the whiteboard serves as an anchor for conversations. There needs to be a mechanism for the facilitator and other students to negotiate and discuss the contents of the whiteboards in an integrated fashion. Pilot work with the STEP PBL system suggests that integration of disparate workspaces is critical in distributing some of the facilitation onto the system and in maintaining the flow of the PBL tutorial session. A more integrated system might contain links and annotations that connect the discussion space to the whiteboard space.

Representations can also embody the goals of PBL. Consider the general goal of the facilitator to help students construct causal explanations that connect theories, data, and proposed solutions. Representational tools constrain student discourse to the extent that they support these goals—for example, a concept-mapping tool could support the construction of causal explanations to the extent that it is salient that students need to tie problems to solutions (Suthers, 2001). For example, the representation might emphasize what students need to observe in the problem (e.g., teachers goals, activity structures, assessments). Other visual representations might support other goals. It is critical that the various workspaces be integrated such that students map among the spaces, i.e., the whiteboard, asynchronous discussion, and other visual representations.

The sequence of activities is another way of offloading some of the facilitation task onto a system. Some of the expert facilitation strategies discussed above can be incorporated into the sequence of activities structured by the system. Students might be asked to generate summaries after some period of time and to compare their summaries and negotiate a joint summary of their problem representation and solution to date. The system might ask the students to update their hypothesis list whenever they log onto the system and ask them to explain why they are modifying their ideas as the expert facilitator does at regular intervals. As they are getting ready to log off, the system could have students compile a list of the learning issues they plan to research before the next time they log in. They might identify the resources that they used. This information could then be passed onto the facilitator as well as being posted to the group whiteboard as well as supporting the appropriate student activities.

CONCLUSIONS

Analysis of expert facilitation provides many valuable insights into what it means to do constructivist teaching. These insights fall into four categories. The first set of issues relate to how facilitators with varying levels of expertise can be trained and supported to be more like experts. The second is to provide guidance to offload facilitation functions onto an asynchronous PBL system. The third issue relates to embodying the goals and strategies of the expert facilitator into the visual representations that are available in the system. The fourth issue addresses how facilitating asynchronous and face-to-face discussions differ. These ideas for system design are hypotheses that need to be systematically tested to understand how PBL and other constructivist instructional models can be implemented to support productive discourse. Similar analyses need to be conducted of online facilitation to understand what it means to be an expert facilitator in an asynchronous environment.

ACKNOWLEDGMENTS

This research was funded by a National Academy of Education/ Spencer Postdoctoral Fellowship. I am especially appreciative of the assistance of Howard Barrows for being the subject of this data analysis and contributing to an ongoing discussion of these data and to Allan Collins for his assistance in data analysis. I also thank Sharon Derry, Constance Steinkuehler, and Matt DelMarcelle for the opportunity to apply the lessons learned in a preliminary attempt at online PBL. I think Uravi Trivedi for her tireless coding of the tutorial discourse.

REFERENCES

Barrows, H. (1988). *The tutorial process.* Springfield IL: Southern Illinois University Press.

Collins, A., Brown, J. S., & Newman, S. E. (1989). Cognitive apprenticeship: Teaching the crafts of reading, writing, and mathematics. In L. B. Resnick (Ed.), *Knowing, learning, and instruction: Essays in honor of Robert Glaser* (pp. 453-494). Hillsdale NJ: Lawrence Erlbaum Associates.

Collins, A. & Stevens, A. (1982). Goals and strategies of inquiry teachers. In R. Glaser (Ed.). *Advances in instructional psychology.* pp. 65-119. Hillsdale NJ: Lawrence Erlbaum Associates.

Derry, S. J., Seymour, J., Steinkuehler, C., & Lee, J. (2001, April). *From ambitious vision to partially satisfying reality: An evolving socio-technical design supporting community and collaborative learning in teacher education.* Paper presented at the Annual Meeting of the American Educational Research Association. Seattle, WA.

Graesser, A. C., & Person, N. (1994). Question asking during tutoring. *American Educational Research Journal, 31*, 104-137.

Hmelo, C. E., & Ferrari, M. (1997). The problem-based learning tutorial: Cultivating higher-order thinking skills. *Journal for the Education of the Gifted, 20*, 401-422.

Hmelo, C. E., & Guzdial, M. (1996). Of black and glass boxes: Scaffolding for learning and doing. In D. C. Edelson & E. A. Domeshek (Eds.), *Proceedings of ICLS 96* (pp. 128-134). Charlottesville VA: Association for the Advancement of Computing in Education.

Hmelo, C. E., Guzdial, M., & Turns, J. (1998). Computer support for collaborative learning: Learning to support student engagement. *Journal of Interactive Learning Research, 9*, 107-130.

O'Connor, M. C. Michaels, S.(1993). Aligning academic task and participation status through revoicing: Analysis of a classroom discourse strategy. *Anthropology & Education Quarterly*, *24*, 318-335.

Palincsar, A.(1998). Social constructivist perspectives on teaching and learning. *Annual Review of Psychology, 49,* 345-375.

Salomon, G., & Perkins, D. N. (1989). Rocky roads to transfer: Rethinking mechanisms of a neglected phenomenon. *Educational Psychologist*, 24, 113-142.

Schmidt, H. G., Machiels-Bongaerts, M., Hermans, H., ten Cate, T. J., Venekamp, R., & Boshuizen, H. P. A. (1996). The development of diagnostic competence: Comparison of a problem-based, an integrated, and a conventional medical curriculum. *Academic Medicine, 71*, 658-664.

Schoenfeld, A. (1998). Toward a theory of teaching-in-context. *Issues in Education*, *4*, 1-96.

Siegel, M., Derry, S.J., Kim, J., Steinkuehler, C., Street, J., Canty, N., Fassnacht, C., Hewson, K., Hmelo, C.E., & Spiro, R. (2000). Promoting Teachers' Flexible Use of the Learning Sciences through Case-Based Problem Solving on the WWW: A Theoretical Design Approach. In B. Fishman & S. O'Connor-Divelbiss (Eds.), *Proceedings of the Fourth International Conference of the Learning Sciences* (pp. 273-279). Mahwah, NJ: Lawrence Erlbaum Associates.

Steinkuehler, C.A., Derry, S.J., Hmelo-Silver, C.E. & DelMarcelle, M. (in press) Cracking the resource nut with distributed problem-based learning in secondary teacher education. *Journal of Distance Education.*

The STEP System for Collaborative Case-Based Teacher Education: Design, Evaluation & Future Directions

Sharon J. Derry, Marcelle Siegel*, John Stampen, and the STEP Team(1)

University of Wisconsin-Madison

Sharond@wcer.wisc.edu

ABSTRACT

We report research and development work with STEP (Secondary Teacher Education Project) Web, an innovative and complex web site designed to support learning through facilitated video case discussions in secondary teacher education programs. The goal of instruction with STEP is to help pre-service teachers acquire useful scientific knowledge about cognitive psychology and other learning sciences. STEP Web is currently being used and evaluated in connection with psychological foundations courses taught for teacher education majors at UW-Madison and Rutgers University. We report user preference data on web site design and related instructional formats, and provide evidence that the STEP approach can produce transfer and flexible use of course concepts.

Keywords

Instructional Web Sites, Video Cases, Case-Based Learning, Teacher Education, Problem-Based Learning

INTRODUCTION

Case-based instruction (CBI) refers to a class of pedagogical methods in which learners acquire subject knowledge through study and analysis of cases, often experts' solutions to real-world problems. For many years, CBI has been employed extensively in both preservice and inservice teacher education with the aim of helping teachers acquire pedagogical and theoretical knowledge that is grounded in situations like those they will encounter in professional practice (e.g., Shulman, 1992; Loucks-Horsley, Hewson, Love, & Stiles, 1998; Merseth, 1996). Typically, the instructional materials used with CBI in teacher education are written narrative cases of various types, such as authentic classroom dilemmas faced by practicing teachers (e.g., Harrington, 1995). Recently, however, there has been a strong, growing trend toward preference for video cases of classroom practice, a trend partly motivated by release of videotaped lessons from the Third International Mathematics and Science Study (TIMSS; e.g., Stigler & Hiebert, 1999). Case narratives are more convenient to develop and use than video cases, and they are easier for teachers to comprehend and study. However, researchers argue that such narrative cases oversimplify, and hence misrepresent, the "buzzing confusion" of true classroom life (e.g., Grossman, 1992, p. 228; Koehler & Lehrer, 1998), and that oversimplified problem representation during learning may contribute to later flawed reasoning in practice, such as "reductive bias" (e.g., Spiro et al., 1991). Video case-based methods may be an especially important form of professional development for preservice teachers, who may have little opportunity to experiment with instructional methods in classrooms (Putnam & Borko, 2000). Since classrooms in which education majors observe and practice teach often do not represent the ideals of school reform (Shulman, 1992), video cases can help provide better models for practice and visions of what is possible. Also, preliminary evidence indicates that video case methods in preservice programs may improve reasoning, produce more reflective practitioners, and produce lasting effects (e.g., Copeland & Decker, 1996; Tochon, 1999).

Motivated by such arguments, researchers are now designing and investigating various technologies and socio-technical infrastructures for making video cases more available and learning from video-case discussions more central to teacher professional development in the United States (e.g., Barab et al., 2000; Chaney-Cullen & Duffy, 1999; Derry & the STEP Research Group, 2000; Frederiksen et al., 1999; Lampert, & Ball, 1998; Marx, Blumenfeld, Krajcik, & Soloway, 1998). Some projects have produced stand-alone multimedia systems to support teacher learning by individuals or small groups. An example is CAPPS (Casebook of Project Practices), a multimedia system that scaffolds teachers as they study and learn from video cases of classroom practice (Marx et al., 1998). Other projects are attempting to promote online case-based teacher learning. For example, Barab et al. (2000) developed a video-based Internet technology that enables teachers to upload video of their classes and remain in their classrooms while they go online to observe and discuss how teachers in other sites are implementing state standards. Stigler (personal communication) and Goldman-Segall (2001) are also developing Internet technologies to support group discussions and learning from instructional video cases. A major online commercial initiative is Teachscape (http://www.teachscape.com), described by its web site as follows:

---

* Marcelle A. Siegel is now located at the University of California at Berkeley, SEPUP, Lawrence Hall of Science #5200, Berkeley, CA 94720-5200

(1) Other contributors included Constance Steinkuehler, Cindy Hmelo, Rand Spiro, David Woods, John Street, Youl-Kwan Sung, Julia Lee, Matt DelMarcelle, Jennifer Seymour, Paul Feltovich, Joan Feltovich, and Hakmo Koo

> Teachscape is building a national community of educators by sharing real-world examples of excellent teaching in practice, by creating opportunities for online and in-school dialogue on teaching and learning, and by integrating on-site professional development support.

Another example is STEP (http://www.wcer.wisc.edu/step; Derry & the STEP Group, 2000; The STEP Research Group, 2000), an innovative web site designed to support facilitated video case discussions in secondary teacher education programs. The site is currently being developed, used and evaluated in connection with psychological foundations courses taught for teacher education majors at UW-Madison and Rutgers University. This paper will overview the design and theoretical basis of the STEP site and related instructional procedures, report findings from evaluation studies involving its use, and briefly overview future directions, including deveopment of the STEP environment for online problem-based learning, described in another paper in this conference proceedings (Steinkuehler, Derry, Woods, & Hmelo, 2002).

THE STEP SITE

The goal of instruction with STEP is to help pre-service teachers acquire useful scientific knowledge about cognitive psychology and other learning sciences that can flexibly be applied to the design and analysis of instructional environments. Research has shown repeatedly that this type of transfer is a very difficult goal to achieve. Our premise is that high level transfer of professional teaching knowledge and skill can be attained with our approach, partly inspired by Cognitive Flexibility Theory (CFT) (e.g., Spiro, Feltovich, Jacobson & Coulson, 1991). A central argument of CFT is that many instructional approaches fail because they represent complex subject matter in an unrealistically simplified and well-structured manner. The most common kind of learning failure is reductive bias -- the tendency to over simplify approaches and solutions to complex problems encountered in the world outside of class. CFT holds that the goals of advanced knowledge acquisition in ill-structured domains must include flexible and adaptive knowledge transfer, a process whereby students spontaneously assemble an appropriate set of ideas as a basis for creating unique models of real-world problem situations. This goal requires instructional techniques that lead students to re-examine the same domain concepts on multiple occasions in the context of multiple real-world cases and problems.

Our instructional approach engages students in collaborative group problem solving supported by STEP Web, a complex network of interactive conceptual relationships among cases and ideas within the domain of learning science applied to teaching, and of tools for supporting navigation through and discussion of that domain. Thus, STEP Web represents a hypermedia network of instructional resources designed to support video CBI. These resources include:

- Cases—stories of lessons, and of student learning and development resulting from lessons, in actual classrooms—that include edited video of the classroom, expert commentary and case analyses, plus additional materials that supply information about context
- Instructional problems and projects that make use of cases and are designed to promote in-depth analysis and, through such analysis, development of knowledge about how to support student growth through instruction
- A network of case-related links to web pages and other resources discussing core concepts from cognitive psychology and other learning sciences
- An environment for supporting facilitated online asynchronous discussions of video cases (pbl online)
- Links to additional tools and resources that teachers can use to help them adapt and implement ideas acquired from study of cases

To convey knowledge complexity and promote transfer and cognitive flexibility, instructional strategies, which determine how students navigate and study the complex conceptual terrain, must encourage students to construct multiple understandings for cases and use concepts repeatedly in case analysis, in different combinations. The main strategy we are using to help meet these conditions is an adapted version of Problem Based Learning (PBL; (Barrows, 1988). PBL is a form of facilitated, small-group, student-centered instruction in which learners acquire subject matter by discussing, analyzing and reanalyzing case-based problems (e.g., redesign Mr. Smith's algebra lesson), and by conducting research to find material (e.g., psychological concepts and related instructional methods) as required for solving the problems. STEP Web is designed to be a resource for both online and face-to-face PBL in teacher education learning science courses.

Instruction with STEP Web ---An Example

In spring semester 2000, 55 students, enrolled in an educational psychology course that was the instructional centerpiece of their third semester in a four-semester secondary teacher education curriculum, were assigned to small groups of 5-7 students that studied together in a PBL format. During the semester, each student participated in two different PBL groups. Each group was assigned a case to study and a problem to solve using that case. For example, a case assigned to a group of science majors was "Students Get a Charge out of Static Electricity." This case, presented on STEP Web as readings, videos, and inquiry materials, tells the story of an actual science unit in a public school taught by a popular teacher and representing good traditional instruction. The problem was to advise Mr. Johnson (the teacher) on how to improve the unit and to justify the group's redesign in learning-sciences language. Our expectation was that students would redesign the lesson, developing a more authentic, inquiry-based approach for the unit.

After studying the case individually on STEP Web, students met with their groups to discuss the case. A teaching assistant trained to facilitate a specific group method known as Problem Based Learning (e.g., Barrows, 1988) guided each group. In accordance with this method, groups began by identifying learning issues—things they needed to learn more about in order to solve the redesign problem. Between classes, students researched assigned learning issues, bringing varied findings to their group discussions. STEP Web was made available as the primary research tool, which was used both during and outside of class. The links and navigational tools in STEP Web scaffolded students' research while allowing them to pursue interests in depth. Research beyond the materials in STEP Web was also promoted, since links led to other library and WWW resources.

Each problem required about four weeks to complete. The TA guided students through collaborative discussions of their research, during which time they identified positive and negative aspects of the instruction in the case and proposed new instructional solutions. In the third week they posted their redesign with explanations on a web conference for peer evaluation and consultation with experts, including scientists and educational experts. After revision, a group design report was submitted and evaluated as a course requirement.

USER EVALUATIONS OF STEP WEB

The STEP implementation at UW-Madison during spring semester, 2000, represented a process of continuous user-centered design in which students provided feedback that was used to upgrade and improve STEP Web throughout the semester. Early in the semester, intensive feedback was obtained from a small number of students who volunteered to be research subjects, but on March 7th and again on April 18th, all students were surveyed to obtain their feedback and satisfaction ratings regarding the web site.

Fifty-four students returned surveys on March 7; fifty returned surveys on April 18. On these dates, 48 and 46 students respectively reported using the web site as an instructional resource for their study and PBL research. Satisfaction with STEP Web as an instructional resource was 3.9 on March 7 and 4.1 on April 18, based on a rating scale of scale of 1 - 5 (not very satisfied to very satisfied). Students' comments initiated a number of improvements and changes throughout the semester. For example, the addition of a search engine was based on students' requests. Students' satisfaction with STEP Web [also referenced as the Knowledge Web, or the KW, in comments below] increased as the site was improved and students gained experience with it. For example, one student who participated in three surveys commented:

Feb 22: "KW - impressed me this week . . .I did not research outside of it. " (No rating requested)

Mar 7: "I am getting better at navigating the KW." (Rating = 4)

Apr 18: "I am starting to appreciate the knowledge web." (Rating = 5)

Other representative student comments:

"When I finally figured out how to use it, it was great." (Rating = 5)

"I like the newer KW." (Rating = 4)

"Much improved!" (Rating = 4)

"Some pages that could have helped weren't up." (Rating = 4)

"They [web pages] were quite useful but KW needs to be more easily navigated." (Rating = 3)

"I found the KW to be confusing in some of its explanations (Rating = 3)

In sum, most students in the UW-Madison course were pleased with the knowledge web by mid semester, but their comments indicated that further development and improvement is needed. Based on students' concerns, there is need to: 1. add to and improve resources on STEP Web; 2. improve navigation; and 3. provide instructional supports within the course to speed the process of learning how to use the site. We either have implemented or are currently working on these improvements.

STEP Web was also used at Rutgers University in a smaller course taught by an experienced PBL instructor. There it was positively rated despite being used at an early stage in its development. Based on fourteen students and a scale of 1 - 5 (not very satisfied to very satisfied), the web site was rated 4.6. The textbook used in the course, a best-selling educational psychology text, was rated 4.5.

EVIDENCE OF TRANSFER AND FLEXIBLE CONCEPT USE

The evaluation study at UW-Madison also produced evidence of growth in students' ability and propensity to activate and combine concepts from the learning sciences in the analysis of videotaped lessons. Also described in Siegel et al. (2001), our assessment approach was grounded in Hierarchical Schema Theory (HST; Derry, 1996), which claims that students should develop during a course in at least four different ways. One type of learning expected from a course is acquisition of new concepts, independent of how those concepts are activated and applied across contexts. Such acquisition is demonstrated if a student is able to define or use a concept correctly when expressly told to do. For example, consider the test item, "Define scaffolding and give an example." This question points directly to the concept that should be recalled and used to answer it. If a student develops only this level of performance, she has merely acquired unusable knowledge.

However, our goal was to help students acquire usable, flexible knowledge. Related to this goal, HST predicts three *additional* types of growth. Second, the course should increase students' general propensity to activate learning sciences ideas as frameworks for thinking about instructional situations. Third, not only should student teachers activate more learning science ideas in instructional situations, the activated ideas should be the most relevant and important ones for analyzing particular situations. Student teachers who activate more learning-sciences knowledge in thinking about instruction have grown to some degree, but students have developed further if they more frequently activate the ideas that more expert analyzers agree fit particular contexts. Fourth, student teachers should integrate ideas to construct coherent theoretical interpretations of situations. Concept activation supplies building blocks for this activity, but the construction of conceptual situation models requires the recalling, mapping and combining of concepts into coherent interpretations. Hence, although some growth is indicated when a course increases students' activation of appropriate concepts in instructional contexts for which those concepts are appropriate, there is greater growth if students discuss concepts within the framework of a coherent situational model. Here we report a preliminary analysis from a pretest-posttest assessment of these additional three types of course-related development predicted by HST.

Method

Of the 55 students who completed our spring 2000 course, 18 volunteers participated in this study. Two parallel versions of the test were developed, Test X and Test Y. Each version consisted of two video segments chosen from the Annenberg/CPB "Minds of Our Own" series (Schneps & Mintzes, 1997), each followed by an essay question. For example, video segment A from Test X depicted a good student completing an interview task both before and after a science lesson. The task showed that the lesson had not apparently improved the student's conceptual understanding of the flow of electricity in an electrical circuit. The student teachers in our study were asked to study the clip, reflect on it, and write a coherent statement about why the student's understanding did not improve as a result of seemingly good instruction.

A counterbalanced design was employed. That is, for the pretest (given in the beginning of the STEP course), half of the participants were assigned Test X and the other half were assigned Test Y. For the posttest (given during the last week of the course), participants were assigned the alternate test. The participants, who were paid for their time, were instructed to take home a compact disc containing the video segments, plan 45 minutes to devote to the task, and complete the entire test in one sitting. Neither test explicitly directed students to incorporate learning science concepts from the course into their answers; participants were notified that their responses would not be viewed or evaluated by their instructors.

After eliminating two subjects due to missing data, sixteen subjects remained, eight subjects in each of the two counterbalanced test conditions. Researchers who were "blind" to subjects' identities and time of testing coded and scored essays as described in the analyses below.

Activation of Course Concepts

Our first question was whether the course increased students' propensity to activate course concepts as interpretive frameworks for the videos. Researchers first identified key concepts from the course, and then determined the number of course concepts that each essay contained. Results, summarized in Table 1, indicated that students did spontaneously activate a greater number of course concepts for instructional situations presented in video cases, after the course.

Table 1. Descriptive statistics of the number of concepts included in pretest and posttest essays, by question.

	Question 1		Question 2	
	Pretest	Posttest	Pretest	Posttest
Mean	1.13	2.94	0.19	0.81
Standard Deviation	0.62	2.44	0.40	1.11
Range	0—2	0—9	0—1	0—3
N	16	16	16	16

Selective Activation of Most Relevant Concepts

Next we asked whether there was a trend toward increased activation of concepts determined, by more expert reasoners, to be particularly appropriate for the given video scenarios. Two doctoral students in Educational Psychology, who helped teach the course, took Test X and Test Y collaboratively. They identified a set of relevant concepts and selected from these the two or three most important "key concepts" for each video situation. For example, the key concepts for Text X, Segment A, were *misconceptions*, *prior knowledge*, and *tools*. Additional appropriate concepts were *hands-on learning*, *explanation-based learning*, *knowledge construction*, *zone of proximal development*, *assessment*, and *disequilibrium*. We then coded for and counted the number of appropriate and key concepts present in the student teachers' essays. We gave credit if students could either name a concept or correctly discuss it without using the exact term.

For both video segments, there was a marked pre- to posttest gain in number of situation-appropriate concepts activated. Examination of key concepts alone revealed the same trend. Gains for the most important key concepts averaged 1.38 for both questions combined; gains for the other appropriate concepts averaged 1.0. These results suggest that during the course, student teachers did develop in their tendency to selectively activate relevant learning-sciences concepts for different instructional situations.

Further examination determined that almost all key concepts identified by "experts" were also identified by student teachers following the course. Even for key concepts that were not explicitly mentioned, student teachers employed related theoretical ideas in their analyses.

Constructing Situation Models of Teaching

We also examined whether preservice teachers learned to adaptively integrate concepts into particular situational mental models of the instructional scenarios presented in the video segments. We developed a hierarchical taxonomy of plausible situational models. Each situation model was based on an underlying understanding of the interaction between teaching and learning, which can range from a simple transmission view (e.g., teaching is information transmission and learning is additive) to a more complex constructivist view (e.g., teaching is a form of assisted practice and learning is knowledge construction). We adapted our taxonomy from a heavily researched scheme developed by the Cognitively Guided Instruction project (e.g., Fennema, Carpenter, Franke, Jacobs, & Empson, 1996).

Table 2. Summary of Situation Models

Level	Situation Model in Brief
1	Teaching is showing and telling.
2	Students interpret instruction using prior knowledge.
3	Students' prior knowledge affects design of curriculum and classroom interaction.
4	Teaching is based on a developmental theory of disciplinary knowledge.

The hierarchical coding scheme included four levels of situation models of instructional contexts, briefly summarized in Table 2, as well as sublevels. At level 1, the respondent believes that for a student to learn science, a teacher has to show them or tell them (Fennema et al., 1996). A respondent at this level does not recognize the importance of students' prior conceptions. For example, a response might include a statement such as, "because the teacher never explained how to complete the task, the student never understood the concept." At level 2, the respondent begins to view disciplinary knowledge as important to learning (Fennema et al., 1996). We created several subcategories of this level, with higher subcategories being scored as 2.5. Respondents at lower levels recognized and minimally described the importance of prior knowledge. For example, one response began, "If the teacher was able to first find out what all his students knew...," but did not go on to connect this idea to an instructional approach. Students at higher levels expressed the idea that instruction must respond to students' prior knowledge. For example, one student blamed performance on misconceptions that "were not addressed during the lesson in a direct enough way." At level 3, teachers believe that student thinking should determine the evolution of curriculum and the ways a teacher interacts with individuals (Fennema et al., 1996). The teacher needs to interact with students to create challenging situations and conceptual conflict. For this stage, the teacher specifically assesses students' prior knowledge. Respondents at this level said the reason students in the video did not understand what was being taught was not only because the teacher did not assess prior knowledge, but also because the teacher needed to maintain an interaction with the students in order to teach more effectively and challenge students. For example, one student teacher stated, " It is the teacher's job to challenge those previously held views and to engage students in an authentic process leading toward that goal and assessed in a way that tests growth in knowledge/changes in knowledge against prior misconceptions." The most sophisticated situation model in our hierarchy was level 4. At this point, the teacher holds a developmental theory of disciplinary knowledge and, based on this viewpoint, has a sense of how to teach certain ways at certain times and why. (Fennema et al., 1996).

Our data indicated that before the course, student teachers often used level 1 models in which teaching is merely the one-way transmission of information. Level 2 models, in which prior knowledge of the student is recognized, were also used, and a few higher-level 2 models were utilized as well. On the posttest, only two people used level 1 models, a few used level 2 models, the majority used higher level 2 models, and four people constructed level 3 models. None of the participants, on either assessment, developed a level 4 situational model in which teaching is based on the trajectory of students' disciplinary knowledge. Table 3 summarizes these data.

Table 3. Situation Models Results

	Pretest	Posttest
N	16	16
Mean	1.84	2.31
SD	0.54	.68
Range	1-2.5	1-3

One important aspect to note about the quality of the essays is that the students, as well as the experts, did not employ single theoretical frameworks, such as information processing or Piagetian psychology, in video case analysis, but rather flexibly applied pieces from different theories. For example, a higher-level 2 discussion might incorporate concepts of transfer and working memory from information processing theory, but also mention cognitive apprenticeship, from sociocultural theory. Such observations provide additional evidence that the course and site design are promoting the goals of cognitive flexibility theory, as we intended.

Narrative Case Vignettes versus Video Cases Online

Data from the fall, 2000, implementation of the STEP course at UW-Madison were used to compare students' perceptions of lengthy PBL projects anchored to complex video cases embedded within STEP Web to brief PBL projects anchored to short case vignettes presented as written narratives. Figure 1 graphs students' ratings of PBL activities within three course sections representing different teaching certification areas. The rating scale asked students to judge the usefulness of the PBL exercise for helping them learn to teach. The data points labeled as cases 1, 3, and 4 show mean usefulness ratings for short PBL activities based on narrative case vignettes. Data points labeled Large PBL parts 1 and 2 show mean usefulness ratings at two points in time during a four-week activity based on a lengthy video case analysis. That the substantial upward shift in satisfaction at point 4 occurred for all sections at the time video cases were introduced and was maintained through the next testing period at point 5 strongly implies that students' perceptions of instructional usefulness was more favorable for the video-based PBL that is the standard instructional format for STEP courses. Thus, video case-based instruction may be preferred to the narrative case format typically used in teacher education.

CURRENT DIRECTIONS

STEP Web and its associated instructional model are complex, but results from several implementations show that the approach may be producing desired learning goals and that it is appreciated by students. Encouraged by the preliminary results reported above, we are now continuing three specific lines of work.

Expanding STEP resources, focusing specifically on the development of new and improved video-based instructional cases for five secondary teaching disciplines: mathematics, science, social studies, English and foreign language.

Figure 1
Mean Usefulness Rating
by Section/Case
[N= 68, n=59]

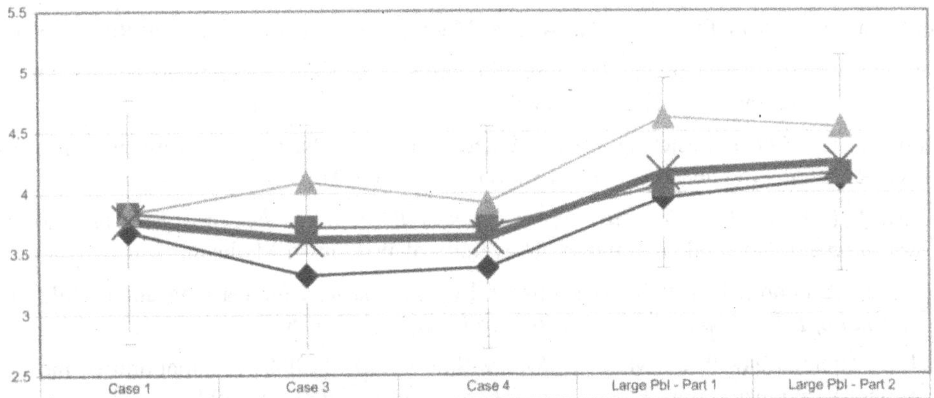

	Case 1	Case 3	Case 4	Large Pbl - Part 1	Large Pbl - Part 2
English/Social Studies	3.681818182	3.318181818	3.380952381	3.952380952	4.111111111
Math/Science	3.833333333	3.714285714	3.714285714	4.058823529	4.157894737
World Language	3.833333333	4.090909091	3.916666667	4.615384615	4.538461538
Class Mean	3.769230769	3.617021277	3.62962963	4.156862745	4.24

- Cognitive research that will guide design of better instructional cases and group procedures for case-based and PBL instruction in STEP Web. One interesting question in case design suggested by project collaborator Rand Spiro (personal communication; Spiro et al., 2001) is whether video instruction using computer-enhanced perceptual overlays that employ color, sound, and imagery to emphasize themes in video cases can accelerate teachers' acquisition of learning science concepts applied to classroom instruction. In collaboration with Spiro we are also planning to investigate whether such perceptual enhancements can highlight complex thematic interactions in video cases, helping learners acquire the ability to think flexibly and interpret classroom interactions from multiple perspectives.
- Research and development leading to more sophisticated conferencing tools within STEP. This line of work will enable us to offer a distributed (distance) form of problem-based learning instruction in STEP, which will permit improved course implementation on a large scale with fewer human resources. The STEP pbl environment, which has been beta tested at Rutgers, provides new users with early guidance in use of STEP Web, reducing the time required to become familiar with the complex site and its instructional procedures. The STEP pbl environment also supplies toolkits to support inexperienced facilitators and course managers. This work is described in more detail elsewhere in this proceedings (Steinkuehler et al., 2002).

ACKNOWLEDGMENTS

This work was supported by a grant from the Joyce Foundation, Grant #REC-0107032 from the National Science Foundation, and by the National Institute for Science Education, a cooperative agreement between the National Science Foundation and the University of Wisconsin-Madison. The ideas expressed may not be representative of positions endorsed by these agencies.

REFERENCES

Barab, S., Moore, J., Cunningham, D., & the ILF Design Team. (2000, April). *The Internet Learning Forum: A new model for online professional development.* Paper presented at the annual meeting of the American Educational Research Association, New Orleans LA.

Barrows, H. (1988). *The tutorial process.* Springfield IL: Southern Illinois University Press.

Chaney-Cullen, & Duffy, T. (1999). Strategic Teaching Framework: Multimedia to Support Teacher Change, *Journal of the Learning Sciences* 8(1), 1-40.

Copeland, W. D., & Decker, D. L. (1996). Video cases and the development of meaning making in preservice teachers. *Teaching and Teacher Education, 12*(5), 467-481.

Derry, S.J. (1996). Cognitive schema theory in the constructivist debate. *Educational Psychologist*, 31 (3/4), 163-174.

Derry, S. J. and the STEP Project Group (October, 2000). Taking STEPs toward infusing modeling and visualization technologies into teacher education. Paper prepared for NSF-sponsored workshop, Infusing Modeling and Visualization Technologies into Teacher Education, Washington, D.C.

Fennema, E., Carpenter, T.P., Franke, M.L., Levi, L., Jacobs, V., & Empson, S. (1996). Learning to use children's thinking in mathematics instruction: A longitudinal study. *Journal for Research in Mathematics Education 27* (4), 403-434.

Frederiksen, J. (1999). *Supporting professional development and improving practice using video case examples of classroom practices collected for that purpose.* Paper presented at the meeting of the Board on International Comparative Studies in Education, National Academy of Sciences Invitational Meeting, Washington, DC.

Goldman-Segall, R. (2001). Presentation at Annual Meeting, American Educational Research Association, Seattle, WA.

Grossman, P. L. (1992). Teaching and learning with cases: Unanswered questions. In J. H. Shulman (Ed.), *Case methods in teacher education* (pp. 227-239). New York: Teachers College Press.

Harrington, H. L. (1995). Fostering reasoned decisions: Case-based pedagogy and the professional development of teachers. *Teaching and Teacher Education, 11*(3), 203-214.

Koehler, M. J. (1999). *Designing case-based hypermedia tools to help teachers understand children's mathematical development.* Doctoral Dissertation, University of Wisconsin-Madison.

Koehler, M. J., & Lehrer, R. (1998). Designing a hypermedia tool for learning about children's mathematical cognition. *Journal of Educational Computing Research, 18*(2), 123-145.

Krajcik, J. S., Blumenfeld, P. C., Marx, R. W., & Soloway, E. (1994). A collaborative model for helping teachers learn project-based instruction. *Elementary School Journal, 94*(5), 483-497.

Lampert, M., & Ball, D. L. (1998). *Teaching multimedia and mathematics: Investigations of real practice.* New York: Teacher College Press.

Loucks-Horsley, S., Hewson, P. W., Love, N., & Stiles, K. E. (1998). *Designing professional development for teachers of science and mathematics.* Thousand Oaks, CA: Corwin.

Marx, R. W., Blumenfeld, P. C., Krajcik, J. S. & Soloway, E. (1998). New technologies for teacher professional development. *Teaching and Teacher Education, 14*(1), 33-52.

Merseth, K. K. (1996). Cases and case methods in teacher education. In J. Sikula (Ed.), *Handbook of research on teacher education* (pp. 722-744). New York: Macmillan.

Putnam, R. T. & Borko, H. (2000). What do new views of knowledge and thinking have to say about research on teacher learning. *Educational Researcher*, 29(1), pp. 4-15.

Schneps, M. H. (Executive Producer), & Mintzes, J. (Director of Research). (1997). Minds of our own [Videotape]. Washington, DC: Annenberg/CPB.

Shulman, L. (1992). Toward a pedagogy of cases. In J. H. Shulman (Ed.), *Using case methods in teacher education* (pp. 1-30). New York: Teachers College Press.

Siegel, M., Derry, S., Steinkuehler, C., Kim, J., & Seymour, J. (Apr, 2001). What and How Preservice Teachers Learn: Designing A Course that Fosters Development of Useful Theoretical Knowledge and the Assessment Methods to Capture It. Paper presented at AERA Annual Meeting, Seattle, WA.

Spiro, R. J., Feltovich, P. J., Jacobson, M. & Coulson, R. L. (1991a). Cognitive flexibility, constructivism and hypertext: Advanced knowledge acquisition in ill-structured domains. *Educational Technology, 31*(5), 24-33.

Spiro, R. J., Feltovich, P. J., & Coulson, R. L. (1992). Cognitive flexibility, constructivism, and hypertext: Random access instruction for advanced knowledge acquisition in ill-structured domains In T. M. Duffy & D. H. Jonassen (Eds.), *Constructivism and the technology of instruction: A conversation* (pp. 57-75). Hillsdale, NJ: Lawrence Erlbaum.

Spiro, R. J., Zaritsky, R., Feltovich, P. J., Coulson, R. L., Theta, J. (April, 2001). Teaching for transfer with digital video cases. Symposium paper presented at AERA Annual Meeting, Seattle, WA.

Steinkuehler, C. A., Derry, S. J., Woods, D. & Hmelo, C. (Jan 2002). The STEP environment for distributed problem-based learning on the WWW. Paper presented at CSCL 2002, Boulder, CO.

The STEP Research Group* (2000). Promoting teachers' flexible use of the learning sciences through case-based problem solving on the WWW: A theoretical design approach. In B. Fishman & S. O'Connor-Divelbiss (Eds.), *Proceedings of the Fourth International Conference of the Learning Sciences* (pp. 273-279). Mahwah, NJ: Erlbaum. (*M. Siegel, S. Derry, J. Kim, C. Steinkuehler, J. Street, N. Canty, C. Fassnacht, K. Hewson, C. Hmelo, & R. Spiro)

Stigler, J. W., & Hiebert, J. (1999). *The teaching gap.* New York: Free Press.

Tochon, F. V. (1999). Video study groups for education, professional development, and change. Madison: Atwood Publishing

The STEP Environment for Distributed Problem-Based Learning on the World Wide Web

Constance A. Steinkuehler, Sharon J. Derry, David K. Woods, Cindy E. Hmelo-Silver

steinkuehler@students.wisc.edu, University of Wisconsin–Madison

{SharonD; DWoods}@wcer.wisc.edu, University of Wisconsin–Madison

chmelo@rci.rutgers.edu, Rutgers University

ABSTRACT

Successful elementary and secondary educational reform requires analogous reform in teacher education; however, the standard undergraduate setting in schools of education poses considerable obstacles. In this paper, we describe the STEP environment for distributed problem-based learning (www.eSTEPweb.org), which represents one of many efforts to create a viable model for teacher education reform. Here, we describe our approach to creating a socio-technical infrastructure designed to help foster a knowledge-building community among preservice teachers, practicing teachers, and instructional staff. We highlight the online environment that supports student and staff coursework in the learning sciences component of a secondary teacher education curriculum.

Keywords

Problem-based learning, case-based learning, teacher education, conceptual change

INTRODUCTION

Successful elementary and secondary educational reform requires analogous reform in teacher education and professional development (Loucks-Horsley, Hewson, Love, & Stiles, 1998); if we want teachers to transform their classrooms from traditional "chalk and talk" environments into authentic "knowledge building communities" (Scardamalia & Bereiter, 1994), we must likewise transform ours. However, the standard undergraduate setting in schools of education at large universities poses considerable obstacles to such reform on both the concrete and conceptual level (Derry, Seymour, Steinkuehler, Lee, & Siegel, in press; Steinkuehler, Derry, Hmelo-Silver, DelMarcelle, in press): lack of space, scheduling constraints, insufficient and inconsistent staffing, training limitations, legal credentialing requirements, professional risks associated with instructional innovations, ideational fragmentation (Ball, in press) within teacher education programs that often engenders competing discourses or "voices" (Wertsch, 1991), and, in some courses, students' legitimate fear of theory (Simon, 1992). Together, such factors pose a considerable challenge to efforts to build sustainable knowledge building communities of teachers. The question is not *whether* to pursue such reform, however, but *how*.

No single technology or pedagogy can be a panacea for schools of education; however, well-designed *socio-technical infrastructures* (Barab, Kling, & Gray, in press) that are context- and community-sensitive might at least broaden our conception of what's possible in teacher educational reform. Online environments that are designed to be sensitive to the contexts in which they are embedded can make possible the accumulation of knowledge and practice of the communities they are to serve. Internet technologies hold great promise for teacher education programs by enabling teacher educators to avert many of the concrete barriers to reform efforts; for example, we can now provide students ample space (albeit virtual) for collaborative work and reduce the need to coordinate schedules by enabling "anytime/anywhere" interaction (Benbunan-Fich & Hiltz, 1999). In combination with pedagogies that provide a social structure for collaborative, student-centered activities, such technologies can be a viable solution for teacher educators searching for feasible ways to practice what they preach.

THE STEP SOCIO-TECHNICAL INFRASTRUCTURE

The Secondary Teacher Education Project (STEP) at the University of Wisconsin-Madison represents one of many efforts to create a viable model for preservice teacher education reform. STEP is an ongoing and continuously evolving research and development effort to design a socio-technical infrastructure — technical environment and related social structure and activities — that fosters and sustains knowledge-building communities among preservice and practicing teachers, instructional staff, and disciplinary mentors (subject-matter specialists). As discussed in Derry et al. (in press), our goal is to develop a technology-based distributed professional learning community in which instructional staff mentor teams of students who collaborate on instructional design projects which, when possible, are then implemented in the classrooms of local cooperating teachers. Through these instructional design projects, members of the community construct (and reconstruct) shared knowledge about teaching and learning on the basis of current research and theory and in the context of authentic practice, producing artifacts, such as model lessons, that would constitute an evolving communal knowledge base. This community is slowly evolving, with our current implementation representing an early intermediate stage of progress.

SOCIAL STRUCTURES & ACTIVITIES

This model is currently realized under the rubric of problem-based learning (PBL) and in the context of a foundations course in educational psychology. PBL is a collaborative learning method in which small groups of students, facilitated by an instructor or "tutor," learn content by solving problems (Barrows, 1985; Hmelo & Ferrari, 1997). We chose PBL as a framework for structuring students' collaborative design projects because we wanted to anchor students' design work in the context of real-world problem solving and replace passive acquisition of course content with authentic, student-driven inquiry. Previous experience with PBL in an undergraduate educational psychology course suggests that students engage with the course content and revisit educational psychology content across multiple cases (Hmelo-Silver, in press). Other research suggests that PBL leads to positive learning outcomes (Hmelo, 1998; Hmelo, Holton, & Kolodner, 2001). The design goal for our course is to develop students' propensity to *use* current theory and research in the learning sciences (fields of research on cognition and education such as educational psychology, cognitive psychology, and cognitive science) as tools for designing instruction — to foster *useful* knowledge, not inert information. Moreover, by situating instructional design in the context of collaboration rather than isolated independent practice, PBL activities should afford preservice teachers in our course the opportunity to engage in sustained collaborative work of the type we want practicing teachers to engage in.

Students in our course learn to apply the learning sciences to teaching through collaborative problem solving based on videocases of actual classroom instruction. The problem students are asked to solve is to develop an adaptation or redesign proposal for the instruction depicted in the videocase, based on learning sciences research. In order to solve each problem, students conduct an individual preliminary analysis of the videocase and then meet with their group online to share and negotiate their ideas, generate learning issues, conduct research, and then reason through their preliminary ideas in light of what they investigate. Once the group has completed their deliberations, each student composes his or her own final solution proposal, compares it to other solutions, and then reflects back on the products and processes so generated. This helps prepare the students to develop a flexible understanding of the concepts with the goal of having them transfer it to their professional practice. Students' instructional design projects, then, are the result of their individual and collaborative problem solving; later implementations of those projects in the classrooms of local cooperating teachers (where the students observe and teach) constitute a "test" of the feasibility of the design solutions generated.

In this way, pbl[1], as implemented in our course, serves as one enabling *social* infrastructure for supporting development of a knowledge building community by fostering the joint production and negotiation of community knowledge and skills in the form of shared practices and artifacts. Our modifications to the traditional PBL format were motivated by the work of Scardamalia and Bereiter's (1994) who state, "When we speak of schools as knowledge-building communities, we mean schools in which people are engaged in producing knowledge objects that...lend themselves to being discussed, tested, and so forth...and in which the students see their main job as producing and improving such objects. Restructuring schools as knowledge-building communities means...getting the community's efforts directed toward social processes aimed at improving these objects, with technology providing a particularly facilitative infrastructure" (p. 270).

TECHNICAL ENVIRONMENT

The *technical* infrastructure (www. eSTEPweb.org) we are now putting in place to facilitate both student and staff coursework consists of several overlapping modules designed to support the needs and functions of different categories of members within the community (see Figure 1). Using ZOPE, an open-source web application server, in combination with an extensive SQL database, we have now fully implemented a *Student Module* designed to structure and scaffold student work (discussed in detail below), a *Tutor Module* which provides a suite of tools and resources for instructional staff who tutor pbl groups, a *Course Manager Module*, which allows instructors to adapt elements of the students' environment to suit the local context and needs, and a *Research Module* which supports our own ongoing research and development work. We have yet to fully engage practicing teachers from local schools in our online community, although dialogues are beginning to take place.

Course Manager Module

The Course Manager Module will provide the basic functions necessary for establishing and tailoring our online pbl activities to a given context. Using this module, the "course manager" or instructor will be able to create the instructional unit or course by defining four things: (a) the *community members* and their roles (which students will be working together, which staff will be tutoring them, etc.); (b) *content materials* to be used (which problem and case will be used, whether all groups will work with the same problem or different problems, etc.); (c) which *tools and activities* are to be included; and

---

[1] We use "PBL" to refer to the Problem-Based Learning technique originally designed by Barrows (1985); we use "pbl" (all lowercase letters) to refer to the modified version of problem-based learning used by STEP. We maintain this distinction throughout our work in order to acknowledge the fact that we employ online *asynchronous* discussions while Cameron, Barrows & Crooks (2000) specify that such discussions should always occur synchronously. Our use of asynchronous rather than synchronous environments was a deliberate design decision; the rationale behind this decision is discussed later in the paper.

(d) the *time frames* in which the community members' activities are to take place. Based on these selections, the system assembles the appropriate tools and resources for both student and staff use.

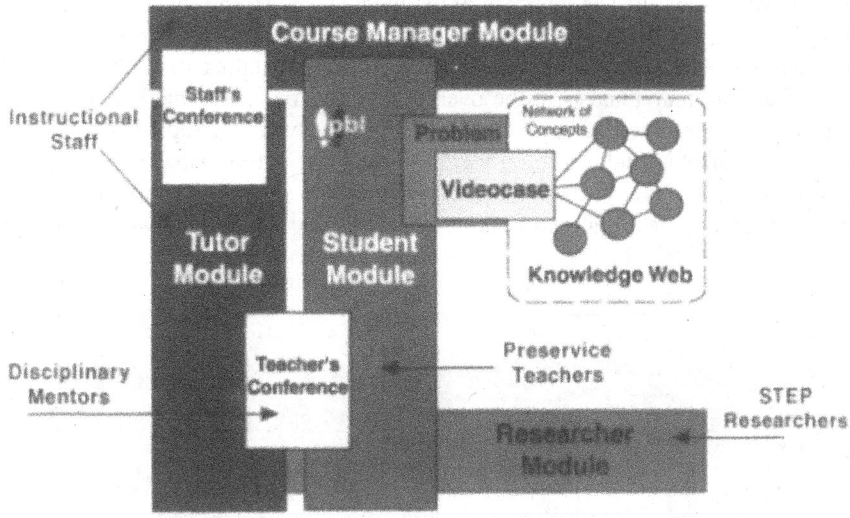

Figure 1. Diagram illustrating the interacting modules of the STEP online environment.

By providing course managers flexibility in selecting which content materials (b above) and tools and activities (c above) will be used, we hope to insure that our technical infrastructure is context- and community-sensitive by permitting adaptation of the system to local context. The resources, tools, and activities that comprise students' and staffs' pbl work help shape the community's accumulation of knowledge and practice; therefore, allowing flexible adaptation of the online environment to local needs and goals is critical. Toward this end, we provide a suite of options for each tool and activity wherever possible. For example, the instructor will be able to select the layout of the interactive tools that students and staff will use during their activities, from a set of pre-built options, and will be able to edit the headings of the tools in order to guide students' learning in different ways (cf. Suthers, 1999; 2000). He or she will also make certain resources available, such as previous successful solutions to the given problem, in order to tailor students' activities to the particulars of the local community goals and practical time constraints.

Tutor Module

In pbl, tutors play a critical role in determining what and how students learn throughout their activities; they monitor the flow of each student's activities, perform metacognitive functions for the group (e.g., probing students' reasoning, asking "why?"), and make educational diagnoses in terms of both product (knowledge) and process (critical thinking) (Hmelo-Silver, 2002). As argued in Steinkuehler et al. (in press), accomplishing these responsibilities is a challenge for the most seasoned tutors; for new staff members with little training who must facilitate several groups at once, it is a tall order indeed. The Tutor Module we are developing is designed to provide instructional staff the assistance, scaffolding and support necessary for successfully tutoring multiple online groups at once. Through this module, instructional staff working with groups can access an outline of suggested group activities, practical suggestions for guiding students' collaborative work "from the side" without being intrusive, and example "conversational moves" that can be used to probe students' knowledge and reasoning. In addition, we are developing online tools for diagnosing group interactions such as an "Interaction Matrix" that provides a snapshot of the level of engagement within each group and indicators of the equity of participation, a *Target Group Report* that summarizes solutions to the given problem that have proven successful in the past, and full access to each group member's products so that educational diagnoses can be made. Together, this bank of online tools and resources will scaffold *tutors* as they, in turn, scaffold *students* through the collaborative process.

Researcher Module

The technical environment of the STEP system not only will serve as the environment in which course activities and community collaboration occurs, it also will serve as our research instrumentation. The online system includes a system-wide monitoring and assessment component that will enable researchers and staff to diagnose and assess students' online products and processes. For example, it captures a "trace" of each user's activities (e.g., sequences of pages accessed) and data entries (e.g., students' responses to reflection questions, discussed below) for basic research, course management, and site/curriculum development purposes. Such data are stored in a protected database that can be "harvested" via the Research Module and easily exported to statistical software packages for subsequent analyses.

THE STUDENT MODULE

The Student Module, currently being tested, is at the heart of the STEP pbl system. It is here that preservice teachers engage in both individual and collaborative work. The interface of the module, shown in Figure 2, consists of three main elements: (1) a representational overview of the activities, (2) a suite of resources that remain accessible at all times, and (3) a center workspace. Together, these elements form a *digital dashboard*: work conducted in the center space is framed by a representation signaling where the individual is in the overall activity (top) and a bank of interactive tools and resources (left). Students navigate through the space using the "sidewalk" overview at the top of the browser or the *next* and *back* buttons; however, the system scaffolds students' progression through the activity space by dynamically tracing what each student has completed and then providing access to the next activity or session in the series based on this trace, thereby guiding students through the appropriate sequence of phases or *step*s and ensuring adequate attention to each.

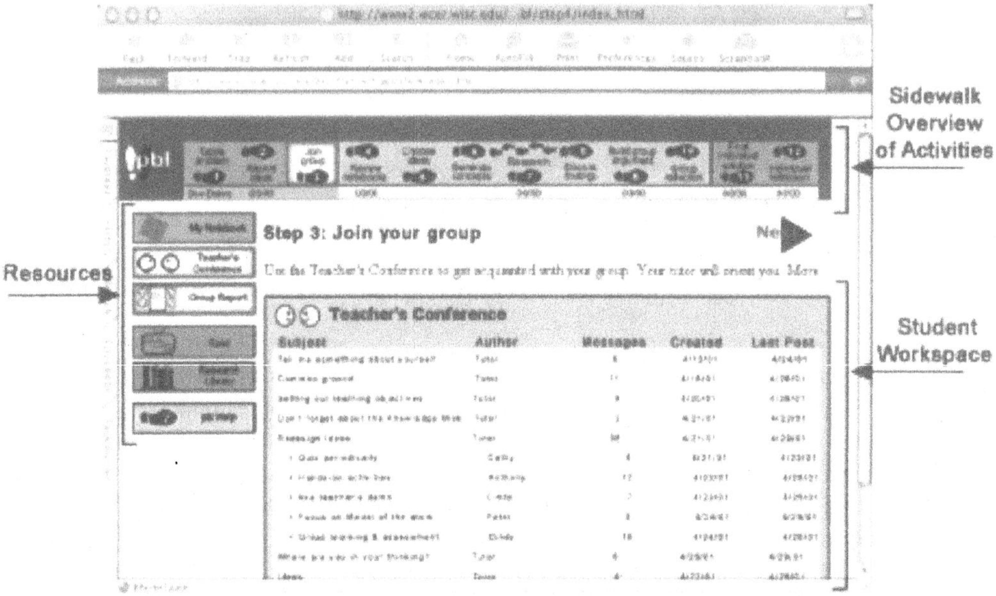

Figure 2. Interface of the STEP pbl Student Module Interface. The third step is active with the Teacher's Conference appearing in the workspace.

Overview of the Activities

Students' activities are represented as steps down a sidewalk and are organized into three main phases, distinguished in the interface by different shades of color. Figure 2 shows a series of 12 activity steps, however, the actual number and order is determined by the instructor, who can enable or disable particular ancillary activities as described above. Together, these three phases of activities are designed to prompt students to explicate the beliefs and assumptions about teaching and learning that they bring to the activity, to engage students in a collaborative activity and environment in which the import of learning science research to instruction can be negotiated and jointly reasoned through, and to facilitate individual belief revision and metacognitive awareness.

The first phase of activities (steps 1-2) is designed to help students mine the videocase in order to construct and make explicit their initial situation model (e.g., Derry, 1996) of the teaching and learning observed therein. During this session, students are scaffolded through a pre-analysis of the videocase designated by the assigned problem. After individuals complete the preliminary individual phase, having gained some initial experience with the purpose of the pbl activities and the opportunity to begin thinking deeply about the problem, they join their group (of five to six other preservice teachers enrolled in the course) and tutor online (step 3, shown in Figure 2 above) to develop a consensus solution to the problem that is justified in terms of the learning sciences. The goal of this central phase of activities (steps 3-10) is to help students *reconstruct* the situation model of teaching and learning they explicated during the first phase based on what they discover through investigation and online interaction with other peers.

Toward this end, members share and suggest solutions to the problem, synthesize a list of solution ideas they will commit to as a group, and then generate a list of related learning science concepts that need to be investigated. Students conduct research using the *Knowledge Web* (described below) and other online and offline resources and then return to the group discussion to reason through the import of their pooled research on the solution ideas they initially proposed, specifying not just *what* was discovered but also *how it bears on* the solution ideas discussed so far. In the third and final phase of activities (steps 10-12), each student writes an individual final solution proposal to the problem, compares and contrasts their solution with others, and then reflects back on both the products and processes resulting from their activities. This final phase allows individual assessment in addition to group assessment, which is necessary since teacher certification is based on individual performance. More importantly, however, these follow-up activities help students come to understand how their own understanding of the relationships among teaching, learning, and instructional redesign has been revised as a result of their group work.

Resources

A suite of tools and resources, located to the left of the workspace, is intended to scaffold and structure students' products and processes. Here, students can access online interactive tools for constructing their individual and group products (My Notebook, Teacher's Conference, Group Report) as well as general resources for the problem (the videocase, a Research Library, and pbl Help). Each resource, described separately below, appears as a second pop-up window that can be accessed at any time during the activities.

My Notebook

My Notebook contains all of the online tools students need to complete their individual work. Appearing as a tabbed sequence of four pages (Figure 3), My Notebook contains an *Initial Ideas* tool designed to structure each student's pre-analysis of the problem and videocase, a *Research Notes* page which provides online space for the student to take notes during their investigation into the research literature, a *Final Solution Proposal* page where each student enters a final individual product, and a *Reflection* page containing open-ended questions which prompt reflection on both product (e.g., "What limitations are there, if any, on implementing the solution you proposed?") and process (e.g., "What would you do differently next time?"). As discussed earlier, the course manager selects the layout and text prompts of each tool contained in My Notebook; which tool structure(s) are most effective for learning, however, is an empirical question we intend to pursue.

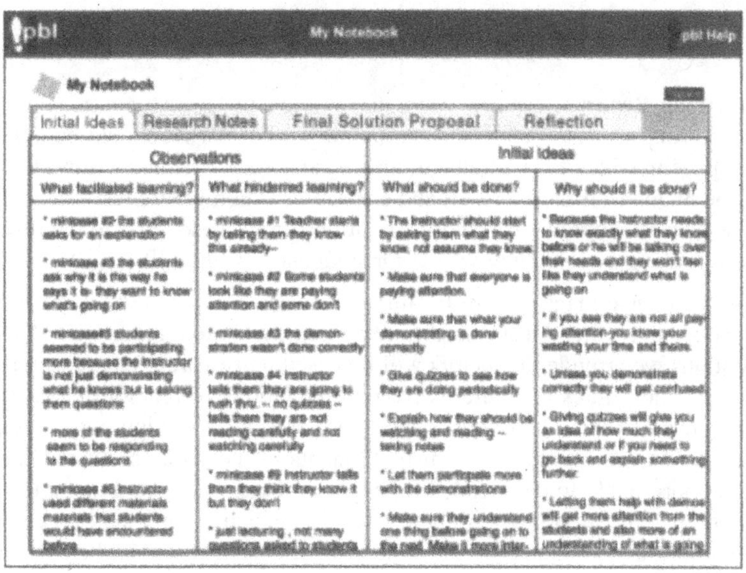

Figure 3. Interface of My Notebook. The first tab is active with the Initial Ideas tool appearing in the pop-up workspace.

Teacher's Conference & Group Report

During their collaborative work, students will make their knowledge and reasoning public through a combination of an asynchronous discussion *environment*, the *Teacher's Conference*, and strategically designed online group *product*, the *Group Report*. Our decision to use this combination of collaborative spaces was strategic (Steinkuehler et al., in press): Together, they translate student reasoning into public artifact.

Previously we conducted problem-based learning activities in the classroom using a face-to-face format. By moving collaboration to an online asynchronous environment, we are able to transform discussion from a temporal unfolding of talk to a cascade of inscriptions. Threaded discussions have been shown to have distinct advantages over synchronous discussions, fostering more serious and lengthy interactions (Bonk, Hansen, Grabner-Hagen, Lazar, & Mirabelli, 1998), more reflective responses (Davidson-Shivers, Tanner & Muilenburg, 2000), increased group interaction (Eastmond, 1992), more equitable communication patterns (Harasim, 1990), and enhancement of the quantity and quality of students' solutions to case-based problems (Benbunan-Fich & Hiltz, 1999). Used alone, however, the hierarchical organization of such tools can obscure rather than expose the group's line of reasoning (Hiltz, Johnson, & Turoff, 1986); because new posts are added chronologically, the content of each thread can become more and more diffuse, leading to "a sense of information overload and confusion about the intellectual focus of the community" (Hewitt, 1997). In order to prevent this outcome, we combine such discussion with a shared workspace for recording the group's consensus argument, the Group Report.

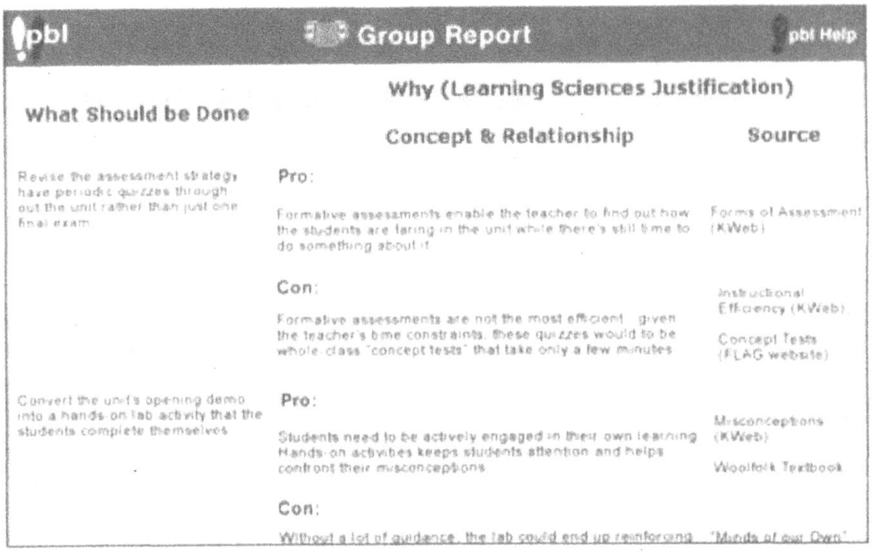

Figure 4. Interface of the Group Report, a collaborative pop-up workspace in which group members post their consensus ideas.

As depicted in Figure 4, the Group Report is a more elaborated version of the two columns of the Initial Ideas tool that individual students use prior to group work to record their initial ideas (i.e., "what should be done" and "why it should be done") with the addition of a space in which to cite both confirming and disconfirming evidence (for a classic discussion of "confirmation bias," see Wason & Johnson-Laird, 1972) and a space in which to cite the source of their claims. Using this tool, each group records its consensus solution ideas and the relationship of these ideas to the results of the group's pooled learning science research, making the group thinking visible for students and staff alike.

As with the Initial Ideas tool, the course manager will be able to select the layout and text prompts of the tool; although, again, we intend to empirically study the effects of different "representation guidance" (Suthers, 1999) on learning outcomes so that the set of options we provide instructors will be based on research. Our research on this issue follows the work of Suthers (2000), which demonstrates how alternative representations of relationships among claims and evidence shape the discussion of groups using them. The Group Report tool presented in Figure 4, for example, coordinates both individual and group activities by (1) making the constituent elements of the group argument (i.e., claims, pros and cons, evidence) salient and therefore more likely to be attended to, negotiated and elaborated upon, (2) making the relationships between these elements explicit, thereby providing a framework within which group members can negotiate how the results of their research bear on their solution ideas, and (3) makes the gaps or absences within the argument conspicuous, hence a topic for discussion. Different Group Report representations, then, should foster different forms of collaborative reasoning, making the design and systematic investigation of alternative tool formats a worthwhile avenue for future research.

Case & Research Library

The problems students solve in our environment will be structured around videocases of actual classroom instruction. We are beginning to develop a *Case Library* that eventually will incorporate a full spectrum of instruction — from innovative, research-based instruction to conventional pedagogical techniques — so that the preservice teachers taking our course are exposed to both *model instruction* (innovative pedagogies that are *not* always represented in the schools where they observe and teach) as well as *instructional problems* likely to be encountered out in the field. Using video rather than text exposes students to the complexities of in situ teaching practice, in all its "buzzing confusion"(Grossman, 1992), thereby deterring reductive bias (Spiro, Feltovich, Jacobson, & Coulson, 1991) and fostering high levels of transfer (Siegel, Derry, Steinkuehler, Kim, & Seymour, 2001; STEP, 2000). STEP research on the design and evaluation of collaborative case-based teacher education is extensive; for further discussion, see Derry & STEP (2002) in this volume.

Once the course manager selects the content materials students are to work with from the Case Library, the appropriate case and case-related materials (e.g., demographic information, the teacher's handouts and overheads, interviews with the teacher and/or students) are automatically made available to students from within the Student Module Interface. The Case Library is part of a larger section of our site called the *Knowledge Web* (Derry & STEP, 2000). The Knowledge Web is a densely interlinked network of learning science concepts connected to each videocase (see Figure 1). Each videocase, then, is linked to related learning science concepts that serve as a "jumping off" point for student research. Each page of this hypertextbook resource contains an overview of a given concept, examples of its application to instructional design, and a list of further resources for more in-depth research. In addition to the Knowledge Web, the Research Library also contains links and references to both online and offline research resources, including online journals, recommended websites, suggested textbooks, and relevant academic journal databases such as the Educational Resources Information Center (ERIC) and the American Psychological Association's Psychological Abstracts (InfoPsych).

pbl Help

Finally, students are also provided extensive online help resources that contain (a) elaborated explanations of each step in the activities, (b) a glossary of terms, (c) worked examples of each product, and (d) directions for how to use each resource and tool. The interface of this pop-up window is similar to the interface of My Notebook (Figure 3); each category of help resources appears as a tabbed page in a sequence of pages. This searchable resource is tightly integrated with the Student Module Interface: when opened, the materials related to the currently active activity or tool appear highlighted and in the main space of the pop-up window; disciplinary "jargon" appearing on activity pages is linked to definitions in a glossary; and each activity step prompting the creation of a product or artifact is indexed to related worked examples of that product.

ACCUMULATING KNOWLEDGE & PRACTICE

Our technology-based model for reform in teacher education has, to date, only been implemented in one course; however, the *socio-technical infrastructure* we are developing through a continual cyclical process of design, development, research, and redesign has tendrils out into the community (e.g., the cooperating teachers in the local schools where our students implement their instructional designs) and into other courses in teacher education both locally (University of Wisconsin-Madison) and nationally (Rutgers University), vertically (courses in different semesters) and horizontally (courses within the same semester) (Derry et al., in press). Our work has focused on the simultaneous development of a *social infrastructure* (pbl) for collaborative production and "worrying" of knowledge through the process of developing artifacts (instructional designs), and a *technical infrastructure* that can support this community in a context-sensitive way. Our current system is in its early intermediate stages and, given the bottom-up needs-based approach we take to its development, will surely evolve in ways we currently do not anticipate.

An intelligent "grounded" approach to development, however, would not be possible were it not for the fact that our socio-technical environment simultaneously serves as our research instrumentation. Behind the interfaces of our interlocking modules is an extensive database with the capacity to generate an ever-thickening history of use (Steinkuehler et al., in press). It is this thick history that guides our development in apt ways. Ongoing analyses of data from preliminary trials of our environment have helped us identify community members' needs, intersections between and within system components where we can increase the system's flexibility so that it remains community- and context-sensitive, and obstacles both students and staff encounter when working within the context of our course. With every such trial on our system, we gain one more layer of description: what the students and staff members did and the ways in which it was successful or unsuccessful, the challenges community members encountered and the ways they moved beyond them, and unanticipated issues that emerge. For better or worse, our monitoring and assessment systems traces and records nearly all user behavior, from minutiae such as which glossary terms Individual A accessed, in what order, and for how long, to more global information such as the percentage of students who successfully accessed the Knowledge Web. The trick is: *putting all these data in the service of current and future communities.*

Our site development strategy stems from our definition of "knowledge-building communities" as those focused on the joint production and negotiation of shared practices and artifacts: *accumulate wisdom and practical skill through repeated trials and then distribute it across resources, tools, and artifacts.* The online resources we are building "artifact" our community's accumulated wisdom; they provide newcomers (Lave 1991), whether they are researchers, students, or staff, access to the experiential knowledge members of our community have developed over time. Students' successful solutions are later archived as worked examples of each product that future students can access; productive research resources are later listed for student use; learning science concepts that previously proved useful for specific problems and videocases are compiled in a *Target Group Report* for tutors working with groups grappling with the same problem; frequent questions, misconceptions, and difficulties populate resources in the Tutor Module so that instructional staff can consider the ongoing deliberations of their current student groups in a broader historical context; and our own research on student and staff cognition within the environment is folded back not only into the course manager resources but also into very structure of the overall system design. In this way, we are able to provide an ever-thickening history for new members to access. Our hope is that, in so doing, we will help foster knowledge-building communities not only *horizontally* within each cohort of system users as they move through the system's activity space but also *vertically* among different cohorts over time.

CURRENT RESEARCH DIRECTIONS

We too are part of that secondary teacher education community though our participation not only as developers but also as *researchers*. We are embarking on three broad strands of research: (1) tutor cognition, (2) group interaction and individual cognitive change, and (3) longitudinal effects of our course on teacher practice. Our research on tutor cognition will include comparisons of expert versus novice tutor performance online, tests of the effectiveness of our Tutor Module system in scaffolding the performance of minimally trained and inexperienced staff, and development of a procedural model of what successful tutors do during group discussion, specifying the schematic conditions that elicit tutoring moves, what tutoring moves are made, and what results from those moves. Our plans for future research on the relationship between group interaction and individual cognitive change include comparisons of online versus face-to-face pbl group collaboration in order to characterize the impact of our system on group discourse, and investigation into the characteristics of the group argumentation our system fosters and the relationships between these characteristics and individual cognitive change (as evidenced by within-subject comparisons of pre-analysis and final solution proposals). Our most extensive research program, studies of the longitudinal effects of our course on teacher practice, entails several investigations and comparisons: assessment of the course's impact on students' concurrent practicum experiences and subsequent student teaching, multiple measures of students' perceptions of and attitudes toward the course, pretest/posttest comparisons and time-series assessments of student performance, attitude, and useful knowledge (i.e., ability to transfer), and examination of the relationship between these longitudinal data and performance on specific activities within the course.

Online technologies hold great promise for teacher education. When combined with the appropriate social structures, they enable us to imagine wholly new forms of community and collaborative work by widening the horizon of viable models for teacher education and professional development. In so doing, they broaden our understanding of what constitutes elusive entities such as "learning" and "community" in the first place. Online technologies make the concrete obstacles to reform in teacher education — limited physical space, uncoordinate-able schedules, physical distance, training and staffing constraints, etc. — more surmountable. Even the more subtle hurdles — professional risk, competing discourses, etc. — may eventually be overcome with the help of technology. Technologies "do not simply cross space and time; they also can cross hierarchical and departmental barriers" (Sproull & Kiesler, 1991, p. ix). Accomplishing this will require substantial time and sustained effort, yet it is our hope that the end, in this case, will be worth the effort. In the words of Michael Fullan (1993), "You cannot have students as continuous learners and effective collaborators, without teachers having the same characteristics" (p. 46).

ACKNOWLEDGMENTS

This work was supported by a grant from the Joyce Foundation, Sharon J. Derry, principal investigator, by the National Institute for Science Education, a cooperative agreement between the National Science Foundation and the University of Wisconsin-Madison, and by a grant (#REC-0107032) from the National Science Foundation's Research on Learning and Education (ROLE) Program, Sharon J. Derry and Cindy E. Hmelo-Silver, principal investigators. The ideas expressed herein are not endorsed by and may not be representative of positions endorsed by the sponsoring agencies. The authors are grateful to all members of the STEP community: Kate Hewson for humanizing the interface, Matt DelMarcelle for organizing the first out-of-house trial, Hakmo Koo for assuring usability for *all* individuals, Joan and Paul Feltovich for their ongoing intellectual counsel, John Stampen for his organizational resolve, Youl-Kwan Sung for his substantial work on the case interface, Julia Lee for her thoughtful critiques, Rand Spiro for his lively theoretical conversations, and Jenna Seymour for her contributions as both tutor and researcher in the course.

REFERENCES

Ball, D. (in press). Bridging practices: Intertwining content and pedagogy in teaching and learning to teach. *Journal of Teacher Education.*

Barab S., Kling, R., & Gray, J. (in press). Introduction: Coming to terms with community. In S. Barab, R. Kling, & J. Gray (Eds.), *Designing virtual communities in the service of learning.*

Barrows, H. S. (1985). *How to design a problem-based curriculum for the preclinical years.* New York: Springer.

Benbunan-Fich, R. & Hiltz, S. R. (1999). Impacts of asynchronous learning networks on individual and group problem solving: A field experiment. *Group Decision and Negotiation 8*(5), 409-426.

Bonk, C. J., Hansen, E. J., Grabner-Hagen, M. M., Lazar, S. A., & Mirabelli, C. (1998). Time to "connect": Synchronous and asynchronous dialogue among preservice teachers. In C. J. Bonk & K. S. King (Eds.), *Electronic collaborators: Learner-centered technologies for literacy, apprenticeship, and discourse*, (pp. 289-314). Mahwah, NJ: Erlbaum.

Cameron, T., Barrows, H. S., & Crooks, S. M. (2000). Distributed problem-based learning at Southern Illinois University School of Medicine. *Computer support for collaborative learning (CSCL '99): Designing new media for a new millennium*, (pp. 86-93). Mahwah, NJ: Erlbaum.

Davidson-Shivers, G., Tanner, E., & Muilenburg, L. (2000). *Online discussion: How do students participate?* Paper presented at the Annual Meeting of the American Educational Research Association, New Orleans, LA.

Derry, S. J. (1996). Cognitive schema theory in the constructivist debate. *Educational Psychologist, 31*(3/4), 164-174.

Derry, S. J., Seymour, J., Steinkuehler, C. A., Lee, J., & Siegel, M. A. (in press). From ambitious vision to partially satisfying reality: An evolving socio-technical design supporting community and collaborative learning in teacher education. In S. Barab, R. Kling, & J. Gray (Eds.), *Designing virtual communities in the service of learning.*

Derry, S. J. & STEP* (2000). *Reconceptualizing professional development: Collaborative video projects on the world-wide web.* Paper presented at the Annual Meeting of the American Educational Research Association, New Orleans, LA. (*Kim, J. B., Steinkuehler, C. A., Siegel, M., Street, J. P., Canty, N. G., Fassnacht, C., Hewson, K., Hmelo, C. E. & Spiro, R.)

Derry, S. J. & STEP* (2002). The STEP system for collaborative case-based teacher education: Design, evaluation, and future directions. *Computer Support for Collaborative Learning (CSCL '01).* Mahwah, NJ: Erlbaum. (*Siegel, M., Steinkuehler, C. A., Woods, D. K., Street, J., Sung, Y.-K., Lee, J., DelMarcelle, M., Hmelo-Silver, C. E., Spiro, R., Feltovich, P., Koo, H., & Seymour, J.)

Eastmond, D. V. (1992). Adult distance study through computer conferencing. *Distance Education, 15*(1), 128-152.

Fullan, M. G. (1993). *Change forces: Probing the depths of educational reform.* Bristol, PA: Falmer Press.

Grossman, P. L. (1992). Teaching and learning with cases: Unanswered questions. In J. H. Shulman (Ed.), *Case methods in teacher education*, (pp. 227-239). New York: Teachers College Press.

Harasim, L. (1990). Online education: An environment for collaboration and intellectual amplification, *Online education: perspectives on a new environment*, (pp. 39-64). New York: Praeger Publishers.

Hewitt, J. (1997). *Beyond threaded discourse.* Paper presented at the Annual WebNet Conference.

Hiltz, S. R. (1986). The 'virtual classroom.' Using computer-mediated communication for university teaching. *Journal of Communication, 36*(2), 96-104.

Hmelo, C. E. (1998). Problem-based learning: Effects on the early acquisition of cognitive skill in medicine. *Journal of the Learning Sciences, 7,* 173-208.

Hmelo, C. E. & Ferrari, M. (1997). The problem-based learning tutorial: Cultivating higher-order thinking skills. *Journal for the Education of the Gifted, 20*, 401-422.

Hmelo, C. E., Holton, D. L., & Kolodner, J.L. (2000). Designing to learn about complex systems. *Journal of the Learning Sciences, 9*, 247-298

Hmelo-Silver, C. E. (in press). Knowledge Recycling: Crisscrossing the landscape of educational psychology in a problem-based course for preservice teachers. *Journal of Excellence in College Teaching.*

Hmelo-Silver, C.E. (2002). Collaborative ways of knowing: Issues in facilitation. In G. Stahl (Ed.), *Computer Support for Collaborative Learning (CSCL '01).* Mahwah, NJ: Erlbaum.

Lave, J. (1991). Situating learning in communities of practice. *Perspectives on socially shared cognition*, (pp. 63-82). Washington DC: American Psychological Association.

Loucks-Horsley, S., Hewson, P. W., Love, N., & Stiles, K. E. (1998). *Designing professional development for teachers of science and mathematics.* Thousand Oaks, CA: Corwin Press.

Scardamalia, M. & Bereiter, C. (1994). Computer support for knowledge-building communities. *Journal of the Learning Sciences, 3*(3), 265-283.

Siegel, M. A., Derry, S. J., Steinkuehler, C. A., Kim, J.–B., & Seymour, J. (2001). *What and how preservice teachers learn: Designing a course that fosters development of useful theoretical knowledge and the assessment methods to capture it.* Paper presented at the Annual Meeting of the American Educational Research Association, Seattle, WA.

Simon, R. L. (1992). *Teaching against the grain: Texts for a pedagogy of possibility.* New York: Greenwood Publishing Group.

Spiro, R. J., Feltovich, P. J. Jacobson, M. J., & Coulson, R. L. (1991). Cognitive flexibility, constructivism, and hypertext: Random access instruction for advanced knowledge acquisition in ill-structured domains. *Educational Technology, 31*(5), 24-33.

Sproull, L. & Kiesler, S. (1991). *Connections: new ways of working in the networked organization.* Cambridge, MA: MIT Press.

Steinkuehler, C. A., Derry, S. J., Hmelo-Silver, C. E., & DelMarcelle, M. (in press). Cracking the resource nut with distributed problem-based learning in secondary teacher education. *Journal of Distance Education*.

STEP* (2000). Promoting teachers' flexible use of the learning sciences through case-based problem solving on the WWW: A theoretical design approach. In B. Fishman & S. O'Connor-Divelbiss (Eds.), *Proceedings of the Fourth International Conference of the Learning Sciences,* (pp. 273-279). Mahwah, NJ: Erlbaum. (*Siegel, M., Derry, S. J., Kim, J., Steinkuehler, C. A., Street, J., Canty, N., Fassnacht, C., Hewson, K., Hmelo, C. E., & Spiro, R.).

Suthers, D. (1999). Representational support for collaborative inquiry. *Proceedings of the 32nd Hawaii International Conference on the System Sciences (HICSS-32),* Maui, Hawaii: Institute of Electrical and Electronics Engineers, Inc. (IEEE).

Suthers, D. (2000). Effects of alternative representations of evidential relations on collaborative learning discourse. In C. Hoadley (Ed.), *Computer Support for Collaborative Learning (CSCL '99): Designing new media for a new millennium*, (pp. 611-616). Mahwah, NJ: Erlbaum.

Wason, P. C. & Johnson-Laird, P. N. (1972). *Psychology of reasoning: Structure and content.* Cambridge, MA: Harvard University Press.

Wertsch, J. V. (1991). *Voices of the mind: A sociocultural approach to mediated action.* Cambridge, MA: Harvard University Press.

Reflective Inquiry: Enabling Group Self-regulation in Inquiry-based Science Using the Progress Portfolio Tool

Eleni A. Kyza, Ravit Golan, Brian J. Reiser, Daniel C. Edelson

Northwestern University

{ekyza, rgolan, reiser, d-edelson}@northwestern.edu

ABSTRACT

This paper discusses how an inquiry-support software, the Progress Portfolio, can help students engage in reflective inquiry. We argue that self-regulation is one of the most critical components of reflective inquiry and present an empirical case of how the Progress Portfolio tool was designed to enable students to become self-regulated in their learning. Even though there is a rich literature on self-regulation, little has been written about group self-regulation in inquiry-based science. Preliminary results from a study with middle school students show that students do use the Progress Portfolio tool to engage in self-regulating cognitive activities, such as setting goals, planning, and monitoring their work.

Keywords

Reflective inquiry, self-regulation, middle school, inquiry-based science, computers, technology-supported learning.

INTRODUCTION

Inquiry-based science and current models of teaching & learning require that students become more active in their learning (AAAS, 1990). This is not an easy task, as students need to become accustomed to new modes of teaching, assume more responsibility over their learning than what has been traditionally expected from them, and learn to plan ahead, set, monitor, and evaluate their own goals and investigations. These changes create a need for students to become more independent learners.

Many factors interact with and contribute to learning in inquiry-based science. We argue that for inquiry-based science to be successful in overcoming the obstacles students face in inquiry-based science (such as organizing and managing complex data in ill-structured, open ended science investigations) while assuming the primary role in their own learning, students need to be engaged in *reflective inquiry* (Loh, Radinsky, Reiser, Gomez, Edelson, and Russell, 1997). According to Loh, Reiser, Radinsky, Edelson, Gomez and Marshall (2001), "*reflective inquiry* is a style of inquiry that encompasses both effective inquiry strategies (e.g. systematically collecting and interpreting data) and reflective activities (e.g., monitoring, periodically evaluating progress, and revising plans)". In order to support reflective inquiry, researchers at Northwestern University and elsewhere have designed tools like the Progress Portfolio, which will be described further down in this paper. The focus of this paper will be on how the Progress Portfolio tool can support reflective inquiry in collaborative learning environments in science, and in particular, how it can support one of its aspects, self-regulated learning in a collaborative learning situation.

REFLECTIVE INQUIRY AND SELF-REGULATED LEARNING

Figure 1 presents the factors that we define as belonging to the reflective inquiry framework and that we believe come into play in students' science learning. As Figure 1 shows, the following factors dynamically interact with and affect the learning process:

Students' self-regulation strategies

Prior (and evolving) understanding of the specific domain

Attitudes and beliefs

Interactions with peers and the teachers

Interactions with the instructional and learning materials

Since this paper will discuss one aspect of reflective inquiry, group self-regulated learning the latter will be the focus of the remaining discussion.

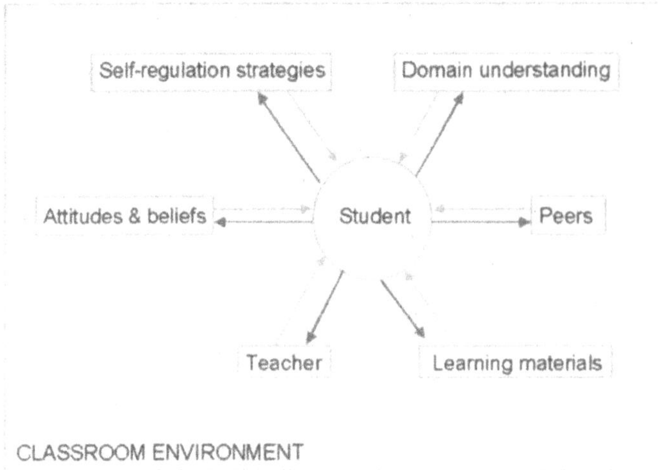

Figure 1: The Reflective Inquiry framework

The topic of self-regulation has a long history of research that emphasizes the fact that students with poor self-regulation skills achieve poorly in school (Zimmerman & Martinez-Pons, 1986, 1988). Even though not necessarily looking at learning solely from the self-regulation lens, many other researchers have pointed to problems with inquiry-based teaching that contribute to poor learning and are associated with self-regulation, as defined by the self-regulation literature. More specifically, in science, Carey (1989) has pointed out that students often do not understand inquiry while Shauble (1990) argues that reflection is difficult to achieve. Under such problematic situations, students' self-regulation and learning are reciprocally affected: if students do not understand how to do inquiry and if they do not take the time to be more reflective and think about what they are doing and why, then their self-regulation and learning will suffer.

According to Pintrich (1999), self-regulated learning is "an active, constructive process whereby learners set goals for their learning and then attempt to monitor, regulate, and control their cognition, motivation, and behavior, guided and constrained by their goals and the contextual features in the environment" (p. 453.) In inquiry based science, such self-regulation skills as setting and monitoring goals, planning, monitoring and evaluating one's performance, are critical for understanding and learning scientific content, in addition to developing general learning strategies. Even though students in inquiry-based science are expected to assume a great deal of responsibility in how to structure and conduct their investigations, when left alone to plan and conduct their investigation they often do not know neither where to begin nor how to proceed. In order to work on their own and also be able to communicate what they have been working on to their teacher, so that they can receive helpful guidance when they need it, students need supports to help them keep track of what they have been doing and help them plan ahead (Zimmerman & Martinez-Pons, 1988).

Most research on self-regulation has been conducted on individual students and, to our knowledge, very little has been written on how self-regulation functions within a group of students working together. In the study discussed in this paper we will be taking a new perspective on self-regulation, looking at how self-regulation evolves within a group using the Progress Portfolio tool. The Progress Portfolio described in the next section is a tool that was designed to scaffold students as they engage in inquiry-based investigations by providing scaffolds that can guide and support their investigation.

THE PROGRESS PORTFOLIO TOOL

The Progress Portfolio is an inquiry-support tool developed at Northwestern University (Loh, B., Radinsky, J., Reiser, B. J., Edelson, D. C., & Gomez, L. M., 1997) to help promote reflective inquiry. The Progress Portfolio is a general-purpose tool, flexible enough to be used to support both teachers and students in their roles and respective activities in a variety of inquiry-based investigations, by allowing users to create and customize templates that address their specific goals and needs. The scaffolds afforded by the tool were explicitly designed to help guide the learners to understand the goals of the task they are working with and find support in understanding both the content and acquiring general inquiry skills.

Progress Portfolio was designed to promote the following cognitive activities: 1) identifying important information, 2) planning, 3) process monitoring, 4) synthesizing, interpreting, and analyzing, and 5) communicating. We believe that all five of these cognitive activities contribute to self-regulated learning in inquiry-based, collaborative science learning. In trying to assess whether the Progress Portfolio tool achieves what it was designed to do, we looked at the scaffolds within the tool and studied whether they are contributing to any of these five cognitive activities. We will discuss the results of this study in the next section of this paper.

The scaffolds that comprise the tool can be broken down into four different categories. These structures can be described as follows:

1) *Scaffolds, like the data capture camera tool, that enable the user to move smoothly between the two environments* (the main investigation software and the reflective inquiry support tool), select and copy selected information from the one environment and paste it in the other (Figure 2, A).

2) *Scaffolds that enable the user to organize the selected information in meaningful to them ways:* To begin with, users can select to work with the templates their teacher has created or they can choose to create new page types to use for storing their data. Then, they can label, re-order and group the pages in any way that makes sense to them, they can create spaces for storing more data or for articulating what they see in the data, and they can link pages together. (Figure 2, B).

3) *Scaffolds that guide and facilitate articulation like the sticky notes and text boxes, accompanied by prompts.* Text boxes are usually structures that the designer of the template has put in place, along with a prompt to help guide the user to concentrate on the important points in the investigation -- these are usually areas or steps in solving a problem that would benefit from further reflection and articulation. Sticky notes are a more free form of expression and constitute a way for the users to specify with more accuracy the most important features of the data they have selected to store in their Progress Portfolio page. (Figure 2, C).

4) *Generic page layout and display scaffolds that allow easy management, searching and manipulation of all the information the user stores in the Progress Portfolio.* For example, all existing pages can be listed on the left-hand side of the window and clicking on any one of these displays the relevant information on the right hand side of the window. In addition, there is another display mode (not shown on Figure 2) that assists the users in preparing and giving presentations to communicate their findings to their peers and teacher. (Figure 2, D).

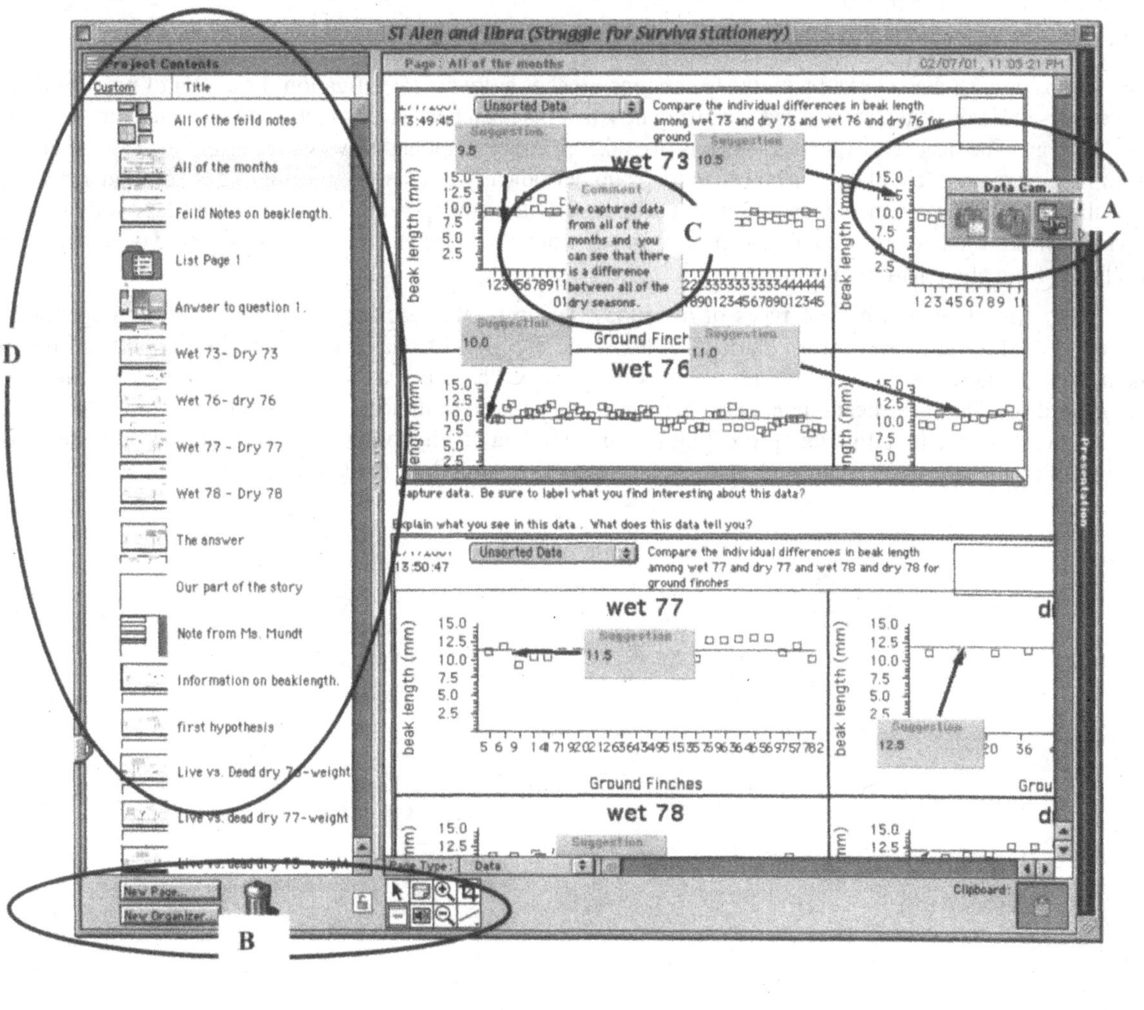

Figure 2: The Progress Portfolio scaffolds

HOW DOES THE PROGRESS PORTFOLIO TOOL HELP SUPPORT GROUP SELF-REGULATION?

Task and methodology

The discussion that follows is based on a study of an 8th grade science classroom, in an urban Chicago Public Schools setting. We collected data from three pairs of students, while they were enacting the *Struggle for Survival* curriculum (Reiser, B. J., Tabak, I., Sandoval, W. A., Smith, B. K., Steinmuller, F., & Leone, A. J., 2001). The *Struggle for Survival* is a LeTUS (Center for Learning Technologies in Urban Schools) evolutionary biology curriculum, designed for use in middle school, inquiry-based science classrooms. Through a variety of activities and the use of a software database, the *Galapagos Finches*, (Tabak, I., Smith, B. K., Sandoval, W. A., & Reiser, B. J., 1996), students investigate the reasons that led to the death of many finches on the Galapagos island of Daphne Major during the late 1970's. The unit is based on authentic scientific data gathered on Daphne Major. Through the use of the Galapagos Finches software students collect data to support their hypothesis on why many finches died and why some survived during the crisis years on Daphne Major. At the same time they were using the Galapagos Finches software, the students in this study were also using the Progress Portfolio software, to help them manage the information they thought would prove useful for supporting an evidence-based explanation. Figure 2 is also an example of how a pair of students created and labeled pages in their Progress Portfolio file to store important data (such as graphs) captured in the Galapagos Finches software.

Over a period of six weeks we videotaped the interactions between the members of the groups and between the groups and the teacher, the groups' presentations to their peers, and recorded all the actions that the groups took on the computer using the two software programs. Since one of the purposes of the study was to examine how the reflective inquiry system functions, we also conducted pre- and post- content assessments in order to understand how the students' domain understanding progressed, administered a student self-efficacy and attitudes survey (attitudes towards computers, group work and science), and interviewed the teacher and all members of the three groups case studied. This paper will present preliminary data on how group self-regulation strategies can be supported through the use of the Progress Portfolio.

How do groups work with the Progress Portfolio tool?

All three groups case studied worked with the Galapagos Finches software investigation for a total of nine sessions. For the majority of these sessions students worked independently from the teacher, having received some guidance from her during the first session. The teacher expected students to take primary responsibility for keeping track of their goals and monitoring their progress, circulating from group to group periodically to answer questions or probe students wherever she was expecting that they may encounter difficulties. Because of this and except for those major class-wide deadlines each group had to make their own decisions as to how much work they needed to complete every day. Each of the group sessions lasted from about half to one hour.

Students' work was structured by two types of deadlines, set up by the teacher as the investigation progressed: the first deadline concerned when to move from Phase A to Phase B. The goal of Phase A was for the students to investigate and document why so many finches were dying, whereas the goal of Phase B was to investigate why some finches survived whereas most died. The other deadline concerned two major peer presentations of the students' work: the first one took place in the middle of the investigation, presenting preliminary data and hypotheses, whereas the second one took place at the very end of the investigation when students were expected to present their final conclusions.

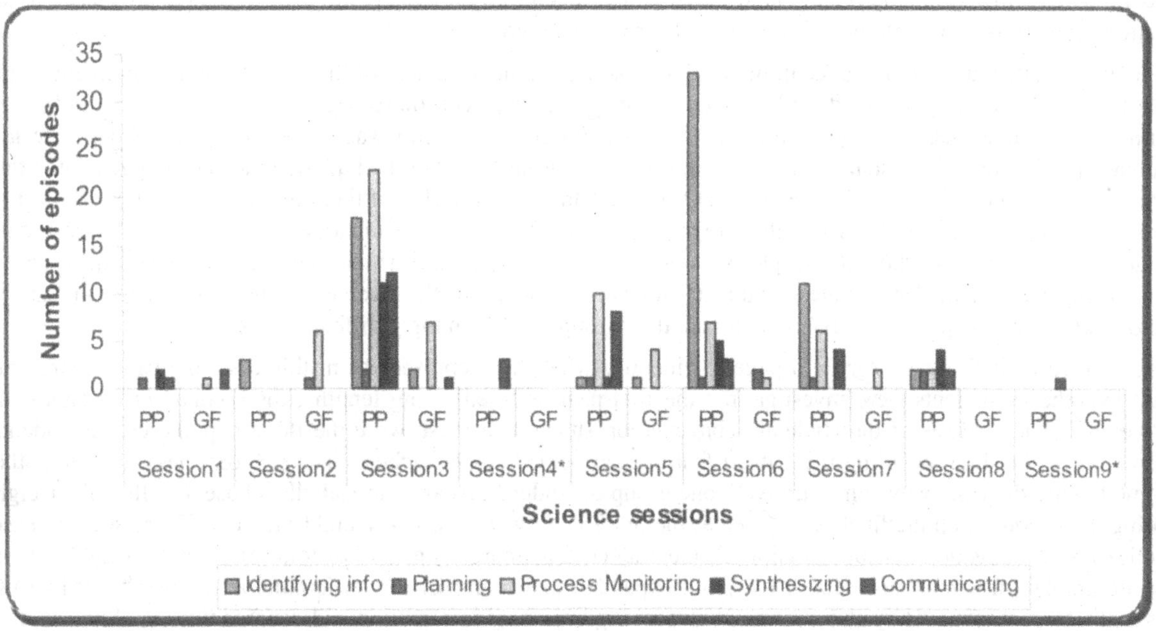

Figure 3: Cognitive activities, scaffolded by the Progress Portfolio tool, that promote the group's self-regulation.

Sessions with an * denote the days on which the students gave their peer presentations.

Figure 3 shows what the students were doing in each of the investigation sessions. The data graphed display all the instances when the students engaged with the five cognitive activities the Progress Portfolio tool was designed to foster. These five cognitive activities emerged after doing an analysis of the reasons behind the design of the Progress Portfolio. At the same time, an analysis of the classroom data collected also points to similar categories in what the students are doing while using the Progress Portfolio as a reflective inquiry tool. An explanation of how each of the episodes was categorized as belonging to one of the five cognitive activities follows. a) Identifying info: an episode was thought to belong to this category if students were selecting and storing data that they thought might be useful to support their proposed hypotheses. For example, observing an episode with a group capturing data graphs in the Galapagos Finches, selecting the ones they thought useful and pasting them in data boxes in their Progress Portfolio file would fall in this category. b) Planning, c) Process Monitoring: episodes belonging to these two categories were based on a combination of discourse analysis and an analysis of what the students were observed to be doing while working with the two software programs. "Planning" would require that students discuss with each other (or articulate in writing) what they should be doing next, as a result of their work with either environment, whereas a "process monitoring" activity would have the students discussions showing that they were monitoring and evaluating their progress. d) Synthesizing manifested itself in two forms: in the annotations that students wrote on sticky notes or on the text boxes and through their conversations with each other about the data they had in front of them. Finally, e) communicating, referred to all the episodes in which the students engaged in conversations that were not covered by the previous categories. A conversation that had students discuss different ideas about what their data meant, without resulting to "planning", "process monitoring" or "synthesizing" would fall under this category.

Even though the students could have been engaging in these activities outside of the Progress Portfolio, as is shown in Figure 3, students were engaging with these activities only either in the Progress Portfolio tool or in the Galapagos Finches in all episodes observed and coded. (In coding the data, episodes were also crosschecked to ensure that the students engaged in the above cognitive activities as they were using one of the four Progress Portfolio scaffold categories described earlier.) Another important point to notice is that as the investigation progresses, students spend more time working with their Progress Portfolio file. The data collected (videotaped interactions and records of groups' work on the computer) show that students' typical pattern of work was to identify the kinds of information they would need to gather in the Galapagos Finches software, generate the graphs and then capture the ones they thought useful and paste them in their Progress Portfolio file. From there on, students spent a considerable amount of time annotating their captured data (by either posting their own sticky notes, as Figure 2 shows, or by responding to the prompts accompanying the text boxes), and looking for patterns in the data that would help them understand which feature might have given the finches the advantage to survive. This pattern of work is representative of how all three groups worked.

Figure 3 shows that students did engage in the cognitive activities the designers of the Progress Portfolio intended them to, and that they were spending a considerable amount of time engaging with these cognitive activities while in the Progress Portfolio. At the same time, the information stored in the Progress Portfolio was purposefully selected by the group to support each pair's work. For instance, in Session 3, one of the groups case studied queried the data and generated thirty-six graphs in the Galapagos Finches software, and only selected and stored twelve of them in their Progress Portfolio file. This supports the argument that students use the Progress Portfolio to help them identify and organize important data. The Galapagos Finches data log, where the graphs are stored automatically each time the user generates a new query, are placed chronologically by default. Nevertheless, students did not simply paste the twelve graphs in one page in the Progress Portfolio or on a separate page each, but, in contrast, they grouped them in three different pages.

Students labeled their Progress Portfolio pages to identify what they represented: in this case, the pages represented the different hypotheses students were investigating: the first page is titled "wing length", the second "beak length" and the third "weight". The analysis of the students' conversation shows that these were the three hypotheses the students were contemplating at the time regarding the critical feature that helped some finches survive. From these three hypotheses of why some finches died and why some survived, one group of students, Adam and Isabelle, chose to follow the weight first, comparing the weight of all the finches between a) the dry 76 and wet 77 seasons, and b) the dry 77 and wet 78 seasons. In their following investigation session (Session 4), they added four more Progress Portfolio pages with weight data, adding eight more graphs (in comparison sets of two) and expanded their comparisons to looking at the weight of live vs. dead finches in different seasons. They also continued identifying important information and denoted this by adding sticky notes, which they annotated and connected to specific points on each graph, further explaining their points. They did the same with annotating the text boxes, responding to the prompts in place. These initial hypotheses were not all the hypotheses the students could have come up with, as more hypotheses could be derived from the available data. From this and from the next actions the students took, one may infer that students were careful to store information that would help them develop their working hypotheses –thus, the Progress Portfolio tool seems to be achieving its design purpose of helping the students manage and organize data, while at the same time contributing to students' cognitive engagement with the data, in regards to thinking about hypotheses, evidence, and planning the future steps in their investigation. Looking at the kind of comparisons students do as the nine investigation sessions unfold, one can see how through iterative discussions with one another and their teacher, and work in the Galapagos Finches and the Progress Portfolio software, students increasingly became more systematic in how they queried and thought about the data. For instance, at the beginning they were comparing data in almost a random manner (i.e. looking at dry 76 and wet 77 and dry 77 and wet 78 seasons); during one of their conversations with the teacher, she pointed to the group that it would be more useful for them if they looked at data more systematically. Over the subsequent sessions, one can see the group gradually doing a more careful query of the data, getting comparison graphs for both seasons in the years prior and during the drought on Daphne Major and looking for trends in the data over time.

An example from the data: how the Progress Portfolio scaffolds help the group's self-regulation

One of the most important supports in helping students become self-regulated learners has to do with guidance in deciding which investigation strategy they should use and where to go next. The question is how we can support students so that they can be self-regulating their learning in complex investigations, instead of getting lost in massive amounts of data or depending all the time on a more knowledgeable person for help. One way the Progress Portfolio tool deals with this issue is by allowing the creation of customized pages and prompts within these pages that can support learners with their investigation. Figures 4 and 5 show how two such pages, used in the study referred to in this paper, look like. Figure 4 is the "Planning your Investigation" page, whereas Figure 5 is the KWD page ("What do you know", "What do you want to know" and "What are you going to do"?). These pages were designed by the teacher and were given to the students as templates, which the groups filled with their own data. Overall, the students called upon four different page templates all created by the teacher, depending on the phase of the investigation they were at.

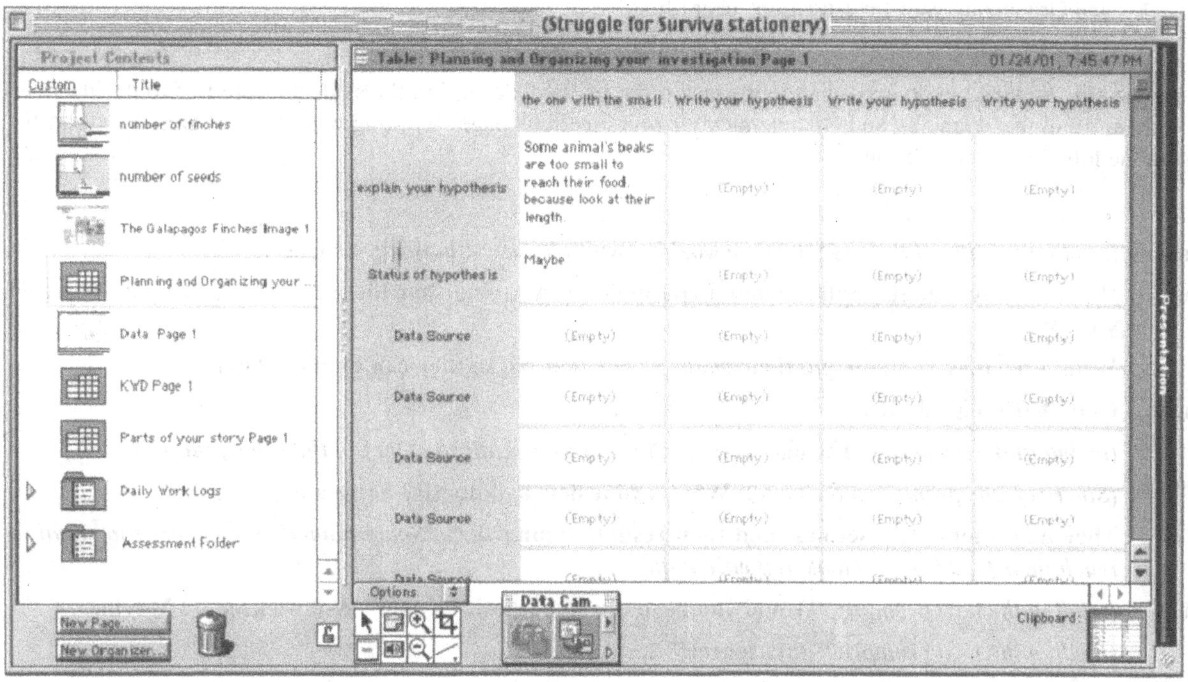

Figure 4: Planning and Organizing your Investigation Page

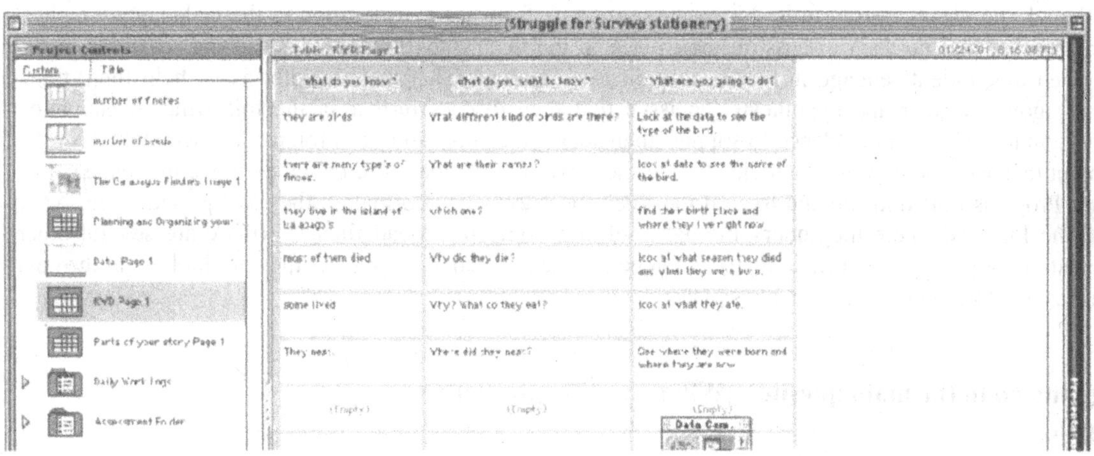

Figure 5: The KWD page

Another pair of students, Matthew and Jane, whose work is shown in Figures 4 & 5, was at the beginning of their first day of the investigative process when they decided to work with these two pages. They were just starting to think how they could go about making sense of all the data in the Galapagos Finches software in order to solve the problem of why so many finches were dying. Up to this point, the teacher had introduced them to the investigation and gave some brief details on how they could capture data from the Galapagos Finches and paste them in their Progress Portfolio file. When the teacher left, they continued working with their investigation alternating between the Progress Portfolio and the Galapagos Finches software. They captured some finch measurement data from the Galapagos Finches, which they then pasted in a new data page they created in the Progress Portfolio.

At the point of the following excerpt, the group has returned to the Galapagos Finches environment and has been exploring it for about ten minutes trying to come up with a plausible hypothesis on why the finches were dying. Matthew insists that they go back to the "Planning your Investigation" page in the Progress Portfolio and type in their hypothesis:

Matthew: I'm telling you, we had better go back and work in here [referring to the Progress Portfolio "Planning and Organizing your Investigation" page] first.

Jane: Yeah.

This is something they had to do according to the task setup by the teacher, but the students were free to decide when they were ready to fill in the "Planning and Organizing your Investigation" page. Working with their Progress Portfolio file they engage in the following conversation:

Matthew ***(reading the title of the page they are working with aloud)*: "Planning your investigation".**

Matthew: **Write our hypothesis...What is our hypothesis? I'm saying that there isn't enough food. What do you say?**

Jane: **Yeah. Like they're small and their beaks aren't that big so they can't get the food.**

Matthew: **Ooh, that's a good idea.**

Jane ***(typing in the template):* The one with... *(she continues until she types in the full hypothesis.)***

Jane ***(She reads the prompt on the page)*: What's your new hypothesis? Some animals eat...?**

They pause for a few seconds and then resume typing that "*Some animals' beaks are too small to reach their food because look at their length*".

Matthew ***(reading the next prompt)*: "Would you keep this hypothesis or not?" Will we keep it? Maybe...**

Jane ***(reading the next prompt)*: "Data source"...**

The above excerpt shows that the students are aware of the prompts in the Progress Portfolio (the page title "Planning and Organizing your investigation", and the cell prompts "Write your hypothesis", "Explain your hypothesis", "Status of hypothesis", and "Data source") and are actually guided by them to engage in a discussion about what their current hypothesis is. Even though the ideas referred to in this discussion come from their exploration in the Galapagos Finches, the session's transcript shows that no such discussion took place in the Galapagos Finches. Instead the scaffolds in the Progress Portfolio helped the students engage in a reflective discussion about what their hypothesis is, help them think about whether they are going to keep the hypothesis (an issue that they discuss further in the following investigation sessions) and prompt them to think about evidence to support their ideas (the "data source" prompt). Immediately after the students read the prompt that asks them to provide evidence for their hypothesis ("data source") they move to a page called "Data Page 1" in their Progress Portfolio file and look at the finch measurement information they had pasted there. After this, they go back to the Finches. There they query the data, selecting only the "dead finches" (there are several other subgroups in the population they could ask questions of) and generate the respective graphs. As they are looking at the data in the Galapagos Finches, the following exchange takes place:

Matthew: **I'm gonna go to the main question. What was the question again?**

Jane: **Am...why did so many finches die?**

Matthew: **Ok! Forget that.**

After this, the students complain about being confused by the program, go to the field notes section in the Galapagos Finches, click through the finch profiles very quickly and then return to the KWD page in their Progress Portfolio file. As Matthew and Jane later volunteered during the post-investigation interview, even though they started to look for evidence to back up their hypothesis, they ultimately became confused as to what they should do next. When they next returned to their Progress Portfolio file they found that articulating some of the things they already knew and reflecting on what they should do next using the KWD page helped them decide where to go next. In the post-investigation interview, they talk about their confusion:

Matthew: **We were thinking how we would find this and...we just did this once (*referring to the KWD page*).**

Jane: **Yeah, because when we first looked at the data we got confused.**

Matthew: **So we came back here. [*Pointing to their KWD page that is showing on the computer in front of them.*]**

Jane: **Like "what do you want to know" ? [*"What do you want to know" is the prompt on the KWD page.*] We wanted to know everything 'cause at that point the profiles, everything confused us.**

Now working with the KWD page, as Figure 5 shows, Matthew and Jane responded to the issues presented by the Progress Portfolio prompts ("What do you know", What do you want to know" and "What are you going to do"), spending the next 19 minutes on this. Figure 5 shows how their KWD page looks like when they finished entering the information they discovered using the Galapagos Finches software. They end their first investigation here –when they resume for the next investigation session, they remind themselves of what they had done and had not done, including the KWD page, and move on to look at data in the Galapagos Finches in order to compose an answer to what caused the death of so many finches. An analysis of their transcript shows that the data they looked at where consonant with their annotations in their KWD page (i.e. they followed up on what they wrote they wanted to find out when they typed the following answers in the "What are you going to do" column of the KWD page: "*look at what season they died and where they were born*", and "*locate what they ate*".)

CONCLUSION AND FUTURE WORK

As the preliminary analysis of the data points, the scaffolds within the Progress Portfolio tool are helping the students engage in the desired cognitive skills that the tool was designed for. Data from the three cases studied show that students were predominantly on task and conversed with each other and with their teacher about important investigation issues (identifying relevant information, forming hypotheses, seeking patterns and evidence) using the Progress Portfolio scaffolds (the pages, data boxes and annotation tools) as assistants in helping them manage their investigation (organize data and remind themselves of where they were in the investigation). As Matthew's and Jane's example shows, these scaffolds also provided the opportunity for students to engage in reflective inquiry, by affording meta-conversations concentrating on monitoring and evaluating the group's current progress and helping students self-regulate their learning, by gradually guiding their investigation.

Due to space limitations we cannot refer to all the examples of how the groups use the Progress Portfolio and how the Progress Portfolio scaffolds help the groups become self-regulated and reflective learners. In a nutshell, in the majority of the episodes coded thus far the groups spent a considerable amount of time, and in some occasions spent their whole investigation session for the day working with the Progress Portfolio scaffolds. During this time, they identified important data and stored them in their Progress Portfolio file, they responded to the text prompts designed by the teacher to elicit student conversation and explanation of what the data are saying, and added their own sticky notes to make their explanations more specific. In several occasions they engaged in discussions that brought each individual student's ideas to the foreground, helping the group move forward as a unit, while on other occasions, different opinions from the members of the group served as the initiator of discussions that, whenever possible, helped students create a shared understanding of what they were doing.

These are encouraging results about the role of the Progress Portfolio tool in promoting reflective inquiry. Our current analysis efforts focus on understanding in more detail the different kinds of reflective activities the groups engage with during their investigation in relation to the scaffolds in the Progress Portfolio and comparing across the three groups to find commonalities and differences. We will also be looking at each group to see how their self-regulation evolves over time and how the scaffolds help facilitate this process. In addition, our next round of data collection will try to examine and juxtapose reflective inquiry practices as students engage in similar inquiry-based investigations but without the use of the Progress Portfolio tool. We hope that this will enable us to better understand the true effect of such tools in collaborative inquiry-based science.

ACKNOWLEDGEMENTS

We would like to thank our teacher collaborator Jennifer Mundt-Leimberer for her important contribution to this work. This work was funded by the NSF KDI/ASSESS grant.

REFERENCES

AAAS (1990). *Science for all Americans: Project 2061.* New York: Oxford University Press.

Boekaerts, M., Pintrich, P. R. (Eds.) (1999). *Handbook Of Self-Regulation.* Academic Press Publishing.

Carey, S., R. Evans, M. Honda, E. Jay, and C. Unger. 1989. An experiment is when you try it and see if it works: A study of grade 7 students' understanding of the construction of scientific knowledge. *International Journal of Science Education,* 11(5): 514-529.

Loh, B., Radinsky, J., Reiser, B.J., Gomez, L., Edelson, D. C., and Russell, E. (1997). The Progress Portfolio: Promoting reflective inquiry in complex investigation environments. In R. Hall, N. Miyake, & N. Enyedy (Eds.), *Proceedings of Computer Supported Collaborative Learning '97*, 169-178. Toronto, Ontario, Canada.

Loh, B., Reiser, B. J., Radinsky, J., Edelson, D.C., Gomez, L.M., Marshall, S. (2001). Developing Reflective Inquiry Practices: A Case Study of Software, the Teacher, and Students. In K. Crowley, C. Schunn, & T. Okada, (Eds.), *Designing for Science: Implications from Everyday, Classroom, and Professional Settings.* Mahwah, NJ: Erlbaum.

Reiser, B. J., Tabak, I., Sandoval, W. A., Smith, B. K., Steinmuller, F., & Leone, A. J. (2001). BGuILE: Strategic and conceptual scaffolds for scientific inquiry in biology classrooms. In S. M. Carver & D. Klahr (Eds.), *Cognition and instruction: Twenty-five years of progress* (pp. 263-305). Mahwah, NJ: Erlbaum.

Shauble, L. (1990). Belief revision in children: The role of prior knowledge and strategies for generating evidence. *Journal of Experimental Child Psychology,* 49, 31-57.

Tabak, I., Smith, B. K., Sandoval, W. A., & Reiser, B. J. (1996). Combining general and domain-specific strategic support for biological inquiry. In C. Frasson & G. Gauthier & A. Lesgold (Eds.), *Intelligent Tutoring Systems: Third International Conference*, ITS '96, (pp. 288-296). Montreal, Canada: Springer-Verlag.

Zimmerman & Martinez-Pons (1988). Construct validation of a strategy model of student self-regulated learning. *Journal of Educational Psychology, 80*, 284-290.

Authors' addresses

Eleni A. Kyza, Ravit Golan, Brian J. Reiser, Daniel C. Edelson:

School of Education and Social Policy, Northwestern University, 2115 North Campus Drive, Evanston, IL 60208.

G. (PEDAGOGY TRACK): COMPUTER SUPPORT TO SCAFFOLD COLLABORATIVE LEARNING

Mapping Alternative Discourse Structures onto Computer Conferences

David Jonassen

University of Missouri-Columbia

Jonassen@missouri.edu

Herbert Remidez

University of Missouri-Columbia

Remidezh@missouri.edu

ABSTRACT

In this paper, we describe a constraint-based discussion board that we have developed. A number of discourse systems have sought to constrain the ways that learners converse by requiring them to classify the nature of the comments and replies to others' comments. Those systems imposed a single constraint system on learners. In our system, we enable users to adjust the structure and content of the system in order to support a variety of discourses, including argumentation, problem-solution, literary analysis, and any other kind of activity. We describe the rationale for the system and will demonstrate the results of two discussions during the conference.

Keywords

CSCA, Alternative Discourse Structures, asynchronous learning

INTRODUCTION

Computer support for collaborative learning (CSCL) is a rapidly emerging paradigm. An important focus of CSCL work is the development of discourse systems such as KIE (Bell and Linn, 1997), CaMILE (Guzdial, 1995), and the Collaboratory Notebook (O'Neill & Gomez, 1994), and CSILE (Scardamalia & Bereiter, 1994) that are intended to scaffold domain-specific conversations and problem solving. This paper describes the development and initial implementations of a web-based environment for constraining conversations depending on the nature of the discourse you wish to support. We describe an asynchronous conferencing environment for supporting shared meaning making among members of collaborative groups with different learning tasks. Groups engaged in an activity (laboratory, simulation) or groups who have been presented with an authentic problem by their instructor need to discuss the activities or problems in different ways. While most scaffolded conferencing systems support a single discourse structure, the scaffolded discourse system that we describe can be adapted to support alternative discourse structures.

WHY ARGUE? WARRANTS FOR ARGUMENTATION SCAFFOLDS

Effective collaborations require not only convergent activities but also shared meaning making. This shared knowledge occurs through conversations about the meaning of the activities and their outcomes experienced by the collaborative group. The goal of that conversation and the collaborative inquiry process that engages it is consensus building, which is socially mediated through discourse (Meyer & Woodruff, 1995). Knowledge results from the gradual convergence of informed opinion. As learners develop new ideas and contribute them to the discourse, agreement emerges in the development of shared knowledge. That shared knowledge is created through a process of convergent understanding and "gradual refinement" (Roschelle, 1992). Since the knowledge is shared and owned by the discourse community, it is not only apprehended better by the members but also more likely to be appropriated by the members. Such knowledge is more meaningful and lasting to the members of the community than that which is dispensed by the teacher or professor, because the members own the ideas. Dispensed knowledge is not shared and therefore not as likely to be appropriated by members of the community, especially new members. Shared understanding through consensus-building also supports the mutual interdependence of members of the discourse community, which is an essential characteristic of collaborative learning that is too often ignored.

When collaborations involve problem solving, especially ill-structured problem solving, argumentation is required. Argumentation is a fundamental process of social negotiation through informal reasoning. Most attempts at negotiation do not expose people's informal reasoning processes so that the group can reason collectively. In order to support social negotiation, it is essential to make this informal reasoning explicit (Senge, 1990).

How do we facilitate learners' development of argumentation skills? Cerbin (1988) proposed that direct instruction on reasoning skills based on an explicit model of argumentation. Leeman (1987) and Saunders (1994) advocated using Toulmin's (1958) model of argument in law education class to develop argumentation skills. Several researchers have also advocated direct instruction on the structure and notation of argumentation (Knudson, 1991; Sanders, Wiseman, & Gass, 1994; Yeh, 1998). However, research findings show inconsistent results: direct instruction does not always improve argumentation skills as expected. Some research indicates that direct instruction enhances argumentation skills (Sanders, Wiseman, & Gass, 1994), whereas other research demonstrates no positive effects for direct instruction on improving argumentation skills (Knudson, 1991).

Technology can support social negotiation and the explication of informal reasoning in the form of argumentation through computer-supported collaborative argumentation (CSCA). CSCA scaffolds negotiation of solutions in problem-based learning, the situation in which we have chosen to implement our web-based argument tool.

CSCA AS SCAFFOLDING

CSCA scaffolds may be of two types, threaded and constraint-based. The threaded discussion is a simple form of hierarchically structured, textual argumentation provided by discussion boards or bulletin board systems (BBS) (Zumbach & Reimann, 1999). The threaded discussion shows the list of all the messages with headings, so learners do not have to search through old messages unrelated to the discussion topic. In a typical use of the threaded discussion, an instructor specifies a topic heading in advance and has learners associate their input such as opinions, messages, or issues with the topic. Their inputs are organized around topics and subtopics (Klemm & Snell, 1998) that emerge in the discussion. That is, the discussion is not prestructured. Thus, the threaded discussion provides a medium for topically organizing a discussion (Scardamalia & Bereiter, 1994).

The second kind of conversation scaffold is constraint-based. The concept of constraints has been used in a variety of ways in the psychology literature. Reading researchers have explored syntactic and lexical constraints on meaning generation while parsing sentences. In problem-solving research, constraints are the set of possible combinations of values between variables in the problem to be progressively restricted (satisfied) during problem solving (Darses, 1991; Richard, Poitrenaud, & Tijus, 1993). Chi, Slotta, and de Leeuw (1994) describe constraint-based interaction in defined systems that behave according to principled interactions or two or more values in the systems. These interactions can be defined canonically. It is important to note that these constraints are implicit in the problem. Any conceptual system (from a simple sentence to a complex conceptual domain) consists of attributes with values that interact. Those interactions impose constraints on the psychological processes required to operate on that system. Those constraints must be satisfied or eliminated in order for the processes to be completed.

Constraint-based CSCA conversation scaffolds, on the other hand, are prestructured forms of conversation systems that impose different conversational ontologies onto the discussion. These ontologies make explicit the constraints involved in the conversation. They supply the explicit statements of the interactions among the attributes in the domain. Users supply the values for the attributes. Preclassifying conversational attributes to fit these sets of canonical relations constrains the nature of verbal interactions among conversants. The Belvedere environment, for example, provides four predefined argumentation constraints ("hypothesis," "data," "principles," and "unspecified") and three links ("for," "against," and "and") (Suthers, 1998). These constraints form the links or relations between the ideas that conversants produce.

Many of these constaint-based CSCA systems have graphical interfaces that utilize node-link graphs representing argumentation or evidential relationships between assertions (Suthers, 1998). Like semantic networking tools that provide visual and textual tools for developing concept maps, these graphical interfaces provide learners with a visualization of an argument, so they can view the entire argument and manipulate it with ease (Suthers, 1998). Visualizing argumentation enables students and faculty to see its structure, thus facilitating its more rigorous construction and subsequent communication (Buckingham Shum et al., 1997). It also helps learners visualize and identify "the important ideas in a debate as concrete objects that can be pointed to, linked to other objects, and discussed" (Suthers & Jones, 1997, p. 1). The primary purpose of most constraint-based conversation systems to date is to support the student's ability to seek warrants as supporting evidence for claims. Bell and Linn (1997) suggest that conjecturing (with warrants, as opposed to descriptions) to support arguments provides evidence that students are making scientific conjectures, which enables them to generate more cogent problem solutions.

CONTEXT: SUPPORTING THE CONSTRUCTION OF SHARED KNOWLEDGE IN UNIVERSITIES

While the construction of shared knowledge occurs naturally in authentic work groups (project teams, scientific communities, etc.), the structure and methods employed in most university courses do not support these processes. Most instructional activities, such as laboratories and writing assignments, are individualistic. However, trends toward to the integration of active and collaborative learning methods in large universities are changing the activity structures of many courses. Unfortunately, many of those efforts are only marginally effective because the students do not construct shared knowledge through discourse processes about the activities. They may learn how to cooperate adequately through division of labor, but socially constructing shared meaning about their activities requires that they know how to discuss their activities in meaningful ways. More often than not, students do not possess these skills, largely because they have seldom been encouraged or required to meaningfully discuss what they are doing. Student opinions are not sought or valued.

IMPLEMENTATION OF CSCA ENVIRONMENT

The scaffolded discourse environment that we are testing is derived from a generic asynchronous conferencing forum. When creating a new forum in our environment, instructors first much chose whether to create a scaffolded forum or a generic forum (see Figure 1).

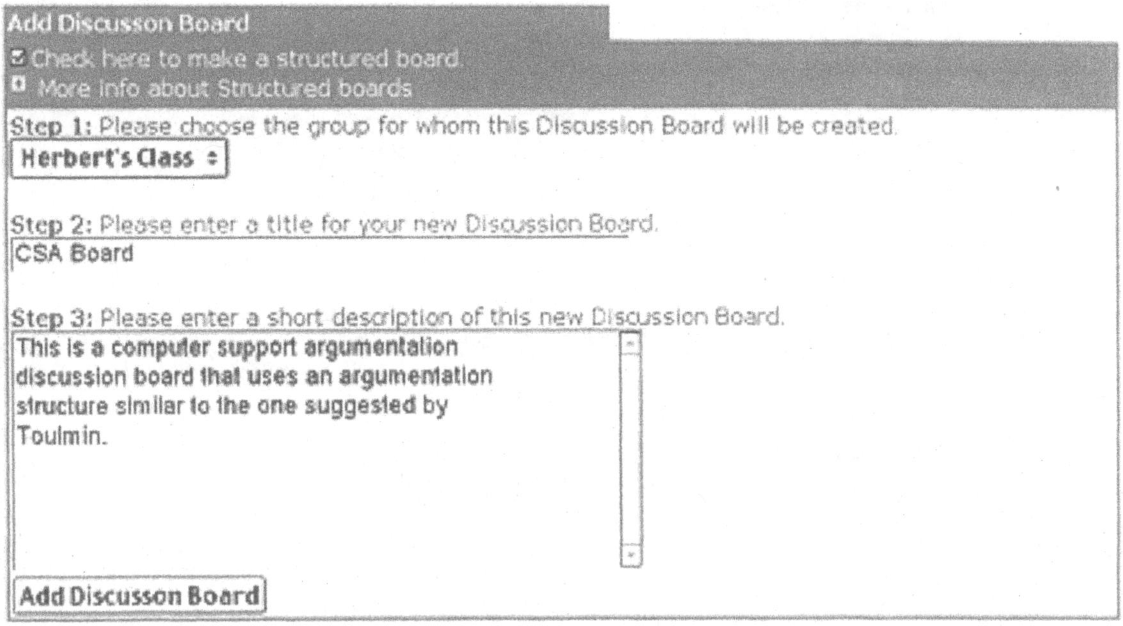

Figure 1. Creating a Discussion Board

If the instructor chooses to create a scaffolded forum, s/he must enter a title and description for the forum. Next, s/he defines the message types from which the student will be able to choose (ex: Problem, Solution Proposal, Support Proposal, etc.) and defines the name and the description for each message type (see Figure 2).

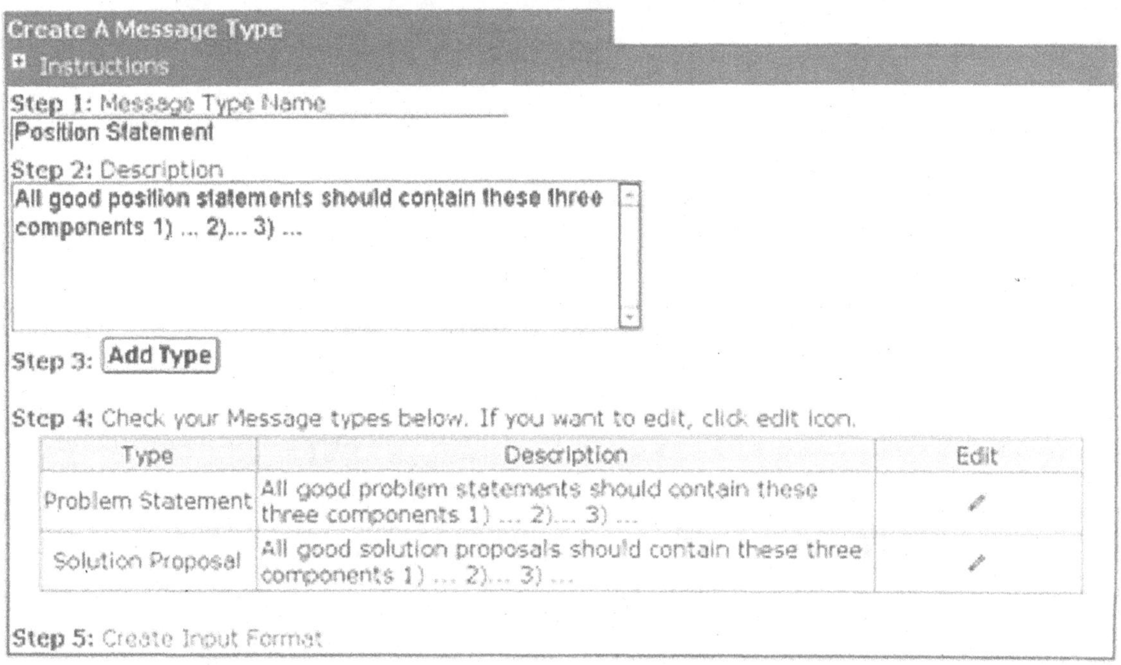

Figure 2. Creating Message Types

After specifying all the message types, the third step is to create the input format for each message type (see Figure 3). For example, an instructor can specify that all problem statements should be composed of a text block (a.k.a. text area in HTML) labeled "Problem Statement" and another text block labeled "People Affected by The Problem". Currently, the system only supports combining text blocks and text lines (a.k.a. text fields in HTML) to construct input types, but we anticipate enhancing the system to support other input types such as check boxes and pull-down menus. There is no limit to the number of text blocks or text lines that a message type can contain; however, all message types require a subject line.

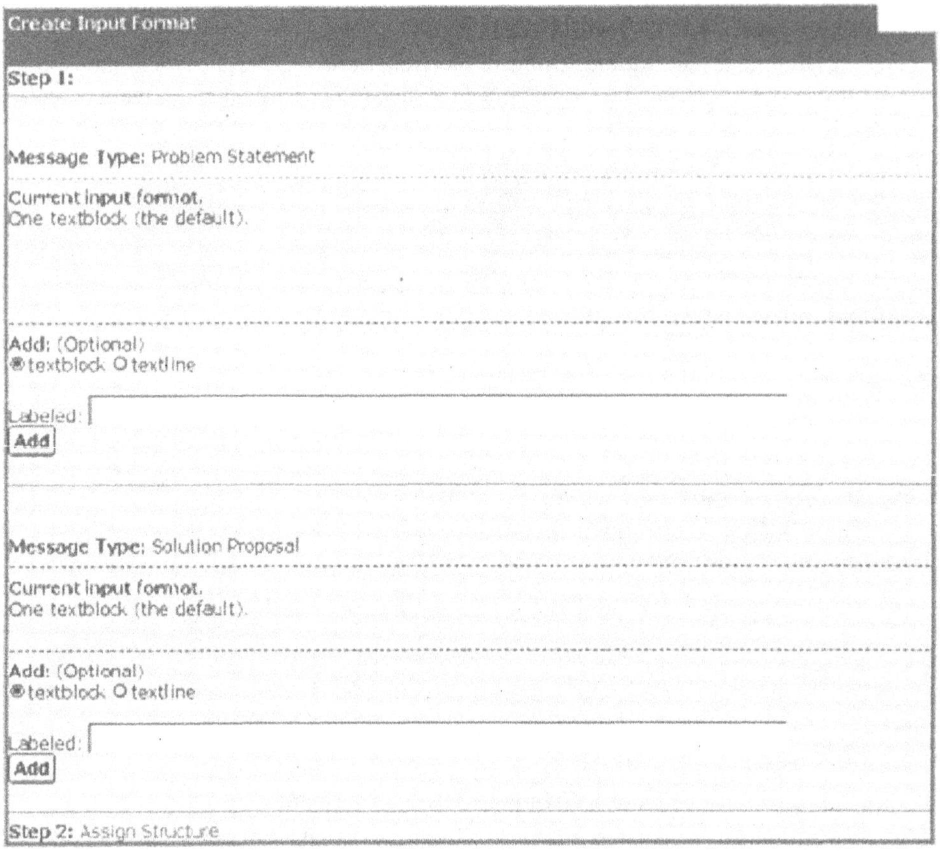

Figure 3. Creating the input format for message types.

The fourth step is to specify the relationships between the message types (see Figure 4). The instructor specifies the message type relationships by checking which message types are allowed to respond to other message types. For example, the discourse structure that we are testing defines 14 types of statements (see Table 1). Like Toulmin's argument structure, we have grouped the types of statements that make up an argument into four levels (problem, proposal, warrant, and evidence). The hierarchical structure that we have defined constrains users' comments and message response structures. At the problem level, the instructor posts a problem statement which student only can respond to using proposal-level statements. Proposal-level statements include solution proposals, position statements, and administration policy or law statements, and can be responded to with warrant-level statements. Warrant-level statements include support statements, clarify/re-interpret requests, rebut/reject statements, and problem redefinition statements. Warrant-level statements can only be responded to with evidence-level statements, which include facts/statistics/evidence, personal opinion/belief, personal experience/observation, theory/law, other's experience, and common knowledge. Although this defines the argumentation structure we have chosen to implement, the conferencing systems we are developing can be adapted to support multiple structures. After specifying the relationship the message types can take on, the fifth step is to create the board. In addition to supporting the creation of scaffolding structures, we anticipate the system supporting the ability to save, load, and share structures.

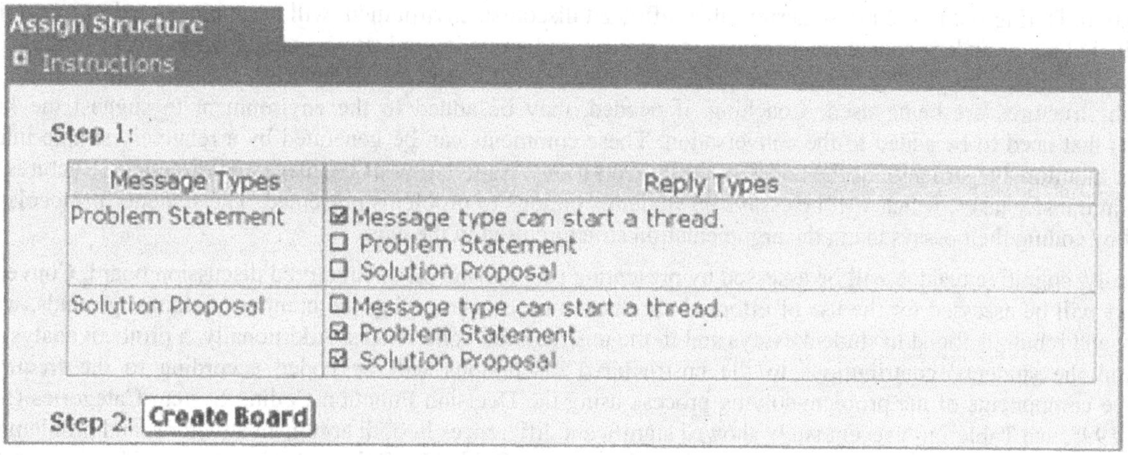

Figure 4. Defining relationships between message types.

The scaffolded discourse environment that we describe functions within the Shadow netWorkspace™ (SNS) (http://sns.internetschools.org). SNS is a Web-based work environment designed and developed to support schools and universities. Much like a personal computer's desktop SNS provides a personal workspace for organizing, storing and accessing files and an environment for running applications. SNS also provides the ability to create groups and for each group to have a "group desktop" for file sharing, communication, and collaboration. Because it is Web-based, teachers and students can access their workspaces from any computer that can access the World Wide Web, and partners (parents or mentors), who are unable to participate in schools because of time or distance, can participate in the netWorkspace. SNS is designed to be installed at individual school locations, has an Application Programming Interface (API) so others can develop applications for it, and is freely available under the open source (GNU Public License) so that anyone can participate in enhancing and supporting it. As with all SNS applications to date, the scaffolded discourse environment that we describe is available under the GNU Public License.

Problem Level

- Problem Statement

Proposal Level

- Solution Proposal
- Position Statement
- Administration Policy or Law

Warrant Level

- Support Proposal
- Clarify/Re-interpret Proposal
- Rebut/Reject Proposal
- Problem Redefinition Proposal

Evidence Level

Facts/Statistics/Evidence

Personal Opinion/Belief

Personal Experience/Observation

Theory/Law

Other's Experience

Common Knowledge

Table 1. Discourse structure being used in initial testing of scaffolded discourse environment.

ASSESSMENT OF LEARNING FROM SCAFFOLDED DISCOURSES

An important outcome of any professional education is the assimilation of the language and reasoning in the field. Students become scientists when they can use the language and discourse structures of the field to solve problems and engage in discourse communities about problems in the field. The scaffolding of that language acquisition and discourse structures is the purpose of the scaffolded discourse environment. Therefore, acquisition of those discourse structures will be the focus of evaluation. During the fall, 2001 semester, the scaffolded discourse environment will be implemented in two university classes, including an undergraduate teacher preparation class and an undergraduate course on comparative religions. Well-structured and ill-structured problems will be presented to students in each class. Their conversations will be monitored to see which structures are being used. Coaching, if needed, may be added to the environment to suggest the kinds of comments that need to be added to the conversation. These comments can be generated by a relatively simple intelligent agent that monitors the structure of the nodes in the conversation. Assimilation of language and discourse structures will be assessed in transfer tasks, which will be essays on student solutions to problems presented. The students' protocols will be analyzed by coding their essays using the argumentation structure used in the class.

Additionally, cognitive residue will be assessed by presenting problems in an unstructured discussion board. Conversations and essays will be assessed for the use of informal argumentation by classifying the number of claims, grounds, warrants, backings, and rebuttals found in student essays and in the unstructured conferences. Additionally, a protocol analysis of the essays and the students' contributions to the unstructured discussions will be coded according to the frequency of occurrence components of the problem-solving process using the Decision Function Coding System Categories (Poole & Holmes, 1995; see Table 2). A recent study showed significant differences in both argument structures and problem solving components between unstructured conferences and conferences scaffolded by Belvedere (Jonassen & Cho, in press). Their scores from the protocol analyses will be statistically compared to the number and proportions of statements from the unstructured computer conference. They will also be compared with essays from control groups who did not use the CSCA conferencing environment.

Results from these studies will be presented at the conference.

Problem Definition (PD)

Orientation (OT)

Criteria Development (CD)

Solution Development (SD)

Solution Approval (SA)

Solution Critique (SC)

Non-task Statements (NS)

Table 2. Poole & Holmes (1995) Decision Function Coding System

NEXT STEPS

Following the implementation and testing the scaffolded conferencing environment during the fall, 2001, we intend to develop alternative discourse structures and to implement those in other classes. Alternative discourse structures might include:

Argumentation:

Proposition, issues, positions, evidence, and arguments

Major premise, minor premise, conclusion, Cause/effect

Deductive: Rule-principle, premises, cases (instances)

Inductive: Cases (instances), generalization

Evidence: facts, opinions, stories

Illustration:	Example, similarity/dissimilarity
Problem/Solution:	Hypotheses, positions, arguments, evidence, conclusion, solutions, event conditions
Description:	Properties, characteristics, attributes, sequence, examples
Process:	System parameters, change, catalyst
Compare/Contrast:	Attributes, relationships, examples
Concept Elaboration:	Has analogy, has example, has attributes, has characteristics, has opposite
Decision Making:	Antecedent, condition/state, option, probable effect, weight
Case Analysis:	Problem, learning issues, rrgency, analysis, alternative, decision criteria, preferred alternative, implementation plan, missing information, assumption
Argument Analysis:	Questionable assumption, alternative explanation, counter example, evidence for, evidence against

ACKNOWLEDGMENTS
We would like to thank Abraham Ott for programming this discussion forum, Dr. Dale Musser, Dr. James Laffey, and the rest of the SNS development team for creating the environment in which this forum operates.

REFERENCES
Bell, M. C., & Linn, P. (1997, March 26). *Scientific Arguments as Learning Artifacts: Designing for Learning on the Web.* Paper presented at the AERA, Chicago, IL.

Buckingham Shum, S. J., MacLean, A., Bellotti, V. M. E., & Hammond, N. V. (1997). Graphical argumentation and design cognition. *Human-Computer Interaction, 12*, 267-300.

Cerbin, B. (1988, April 24-27). *The Nature and Development of Informal Reasoning Skills in College Students.* Paper presented at the National Institute on Issues in Teaching and Learning, Chicago, IL.

Chi, M.T.H., Slotta, J.D., & de Leeuw, N/A. (1994). From things to processes: A theory of conceptual change for learning science concepts. *Learning and Instruction, 4*, 27-43.

Darses, F. (1991). The constraint satisfaction approach to design: A psychological investigation. *Acta Psychologica, 78*, 307-325. Jonassen, D.H. & Cho, K.L. (in press). Effects ofd argumentation scaffolds on problem solving.

Klemm, W. R., & Snell, J. R. (1996). Enriching computer-mediated group learning by coupling constructivism with collaborative learning. *Journal of Instructional Science and Technology, 1*(2). (http://www.usq.edu.au/ electpub/e-jist/vol1no2/article1.htm).

Knudson, R. E. (1991). Effects of instructional strategies, grade and sex on students' persuasive writing. *Journal of Experimental Education, 59*(2), 141-152.

Leeman, R. W. (1987). *Taking Perspectives: Teaching Critical Thinking in the Argumentation Course.* Paper presented at the Speech Communication Association, Boston, MA.

Mauffette-Leenders, L.A., Erskine, J.A., & Leenders, M.R. (1997). Learning with cases. London, Ontario, Canada: Case and Publication Services, Richard Ivey School of Business, The University of Western Ontario.

O'Neill, D. K., & Gomez, L. M. (1994). The Collaboratory notebook: A distributed knowledge building environment for project learning. *Proceedings of ED MEDIA*, 94. Vancouver B. C., Canada.

Poole, M.S., & Holmes, M.E. (1995). Decision development in computer-assisted group decision making. *Human Communication Research, 22* (1), 1, 90-127.

Richard, J.F., Poitrenaud, S., & Tijus, C. (1993). Problem-solving restructuration: Elimination of implicit constraints. *Cognitive Science, 17*, 497-529.

Sanders, J. A., Wiseman, R. L, & Gass, R. H. (1994). Does teaching argumentation facilitate critical thinking? *Communication Reports, 7*(1), 27-35.

Scardamalia, M., & Bereiter, C. (1994). Computer support for knowledge-building communities. *The Journal of the Learning Sciences, 3*(3), 265-283.

Senge, Peter M. (1990). *The fifth discipline : the art and practice of the learning organization.* NY: Doubleday/Currency Press.

Suthers, D. (1998). *Representations for scaffolding coolaborative inquiry on ill-structured problems.* Paper presented at the 1998 AERA Annual Meeting, San Diego, California.

Suthers, D., & Jones, D. (1997, August). *An architecture for intelligent collaborative educational systems*. Paper presented at the 8th World Conference on Artificial Intelligence in Education (AI-Ed 97), Kobe, Japan.

Toulmin, S., Rieke, R., &Janik, A. (1984). *An introduction to reasoning*. NY: Macmillan Publishing Co.

Voss, J. F. (1991). Learning to Reason via Instruction in Argumentation. *Learning and Instruction, 1*(4), 337-50.

Yeh, S. S. (1998). Empowering education: Teaching argumentative writing to cultural minority middle-school students. *Research in the Teaching of English, 33*(1), 49-83.

Zumbach, J., & Reimann, P. (1999, December). Combining computer supported collaborative argumentation and problem-based learning: An approach for designing online learning environments. Paper presented at the Computer Supported Collaborative Argumentation Workshop at the CSCL 99 Conference, Stanford, California.

Scaffolding Group Learning in a Collaborative Networked Environment

Amy S. Wu, Rob Farrell, Mark K. Singley

University of Michigan
Ann Arbor, MI 48109
amyswu@umich.edu

IBM T.J. Watson Research Center
Yorktown Heights, NY 10598
{robfarr, ksingley}@us.ibm.com

ABSTRACT

Scaffolding students in a collaborative networked learning environment requires different instructional methods than in a traditional home or classroom setting. The goal of this research is to understand computer-mediated collaboration in an instructional setting in order to create an effective computer-mediated collaboration tool. We identify ways to support collaboration by examining the interaction and strategies employed by a peer tutor and teacher and between peers working in our collaborative learning environment. We found that supporting collaboration in an electronic setting requires diagnosing impasses, facilitating problem-solving interaction, and suggesting ways to divide the problem into sub-tasks.

Keywords

computer-mediated collaboration, tutoring, learning environments

INTRODUCTION

Proponents of collaborative learning claim that students in cooperative teams achieve higher levels of thought and retain information longer than students who work quietly as individuals (Webb, 1995). Students learning effectively in groups encourage each other to ask questions, articulate their thoughts, explain and justify their opinions, and elaborate and reflect upon their knowledge. Yet, the field of CSCL (Computer-Supported Collaborative Learning) continues to struggle to identify how best to support collaborative learning online as new communication technologies allow the learner to network with other learners (Berge, 1997) and as CSCL becomes an established research paradigm for electronic learning environments (Koschmann, 1996).

How does a collaborative networked learning environment impact the types of tutoring needed to effectively scaffold students? We report on a study that compares peer-mediated instruction and teacher-mediated instruction to inform scaffolding in a collaborative networked learning environment. The goal of this research is to investigate how peers and teachers support group learning in a networked environment so in the future, we can use this model to inform the design of electronic scaffolds for our learning environment.

THEORETICAL RATIONALE

The following sections provide a foundation and rationale for our work. A brief discussion of collaborative learning and technology-based learning environments will establish a framework for our study.

Collaborative Learning

Many educators and learning researchers have found promise in Vygotsky's (1978) social constructivist ideas about learning in a social setting. His notion of the zone of proximal development (ZPD) posits that children's mental development can be positively influenced by the assistance of an adult or more capable peer. The core concept of constructivism is that understanding and knowledge come from our interactions with the environment (Savery & Duffy, 1996). Studies suggest that communicating ideas in a group setting encourages self-explanation and justification, both of significant instructional value (Rogoff, 1990; Webb, 1991)

Different groupings of learners with or without tutors have been shown to be effective in improving student achievement. Bloom (1984) demonstrated that tutoring raises students' performance by .40 standard deviations with peer tutors and 2.0 standard deviations with experienced tutors. What strategies do experienced tutors use to facilitate learning? Graesser, Person and Magliano (1995) documented the techniques used by to facilitate problem-solving: *pumping* to expose student knowledge; *prompting* to supply the student with context to fill in missing information; and *splicing* to provide the student with correct information when they make a mistake. Other tutoring strategies found by Graesser et. al. include hinting, summarizing, elaborating, assessing, and providing feedback.

Research on peer interaction suggests that peers can mediate each other's learning. McCarthey and McMahon (1992) found that in a peer-tutoring situation, the discourse tends to be unidirectional, from the more knowledgeable student to the less knowledgeable student. Unfortunately, peers may not collaborate effectively. Nelson-LeGall (1992) suggests that with schooling, students perceive that competition and independent performance are increasingly normative, which may account for their failure to seek help from their peers and even from their teachers.

How does working with a peer compare to working with a teacher? In comparing the effectiveness of working with experts or peers, Salomon and Perkins (1998) note an interesting difference between expert tutoring and peer problem solving. Whereas tutors aim to facilitate the learning of the student(s), peers working together often aim just to accomplish the task. As a result, the individual learner often gets more of a chance to participate actively in the problem-solving effort when interacting with an expert tutor than with same-level peers. In fact, students working in groups appear to be more focused on finding the right answer than in mediating each other's learning (Vedder, 1985). Therefore, in many cases, an expert tutor may be needed to support peer problem-solving. Why scaffold collaborative learning? Despite studies (e.g. Webb, 1991) showing that social learning situations correlate with a wide range of positive outcomes – such as improved learning, increased productivity, and higher motivation – collaborative learning does not work for all learners. According to Brown and Palincsar (1989), "social interactions do not always create new learning; peer interactions vary enormously." (p. 397). Several researchers (King, 1994; Webb, 1995) have found that it is the nature of peer interaction that is perhaps the most critical factor mediating individual student achievement.

The human tutoring literature shows that expert tutors can effectively support students, and that peers can mediate each other's learning. However, these studies of tutoring are based on individual tutoring situations or face-to-face group instruction, which may not necessarily apply to networked learning. The next section explores technology-based learning environments that can support collaborative learning.

Computer Support for Collaborative Learning

Technology has taken on new roles in learning, providing students with the opportunity to interact with responsive, dynamic environments that support learning. These computer-based interactive learning environments have traditionally been designed to support a single student's needs. Interactive learning environments (ILEs) are commonly grounded in constructivist theories on learning, which emphasize that knowledge is something that a student constructs based on his or her prior knowledge and experience. ILEs are designed for a single student but may have a computer tutor to assist in learning. Computer tutors in interactive learning environments, also known as Intelligent Tutoring Systems (ITS), can diagnose the conceptual difficulties and misunderstandings of any student. Brown and VanLehn (1988) found that learning occurs when students encounter problems, at which point they need help to repair their incorrect procedures. The tutor, then, is able to intervene at those salient points.

CSCL environments, in addition to supporting learning of subject matter, also support students working together at a distance or at the same computer. These systems have the potential to enhance the effectiveness of peer interactions, by coaching peers as they work on problems and critique other students' solutions. A human or computer tutor can help structure the interaction, give advice when needed, and promote deepening of understanding. From studies of an ITS called Sherlock (Lajoie & Lesgold, 1989), Katz and Lesgold (1993) believe that the tutor has three main roles to play in collaborative learning situations: (1) provide advice on demand, (2) provide quality control over collaborative activities, and (3) manage peer collaboration. Our study also investigates the role of a tutor in a computer-support collaborative learning environment, but we conduct an empirical study with human tutors to answer this question.

Our study is designed to understand the effective strategies of human tutors in a CSCL environment, in which networked computers link the participants. What is the nature of peer and expert tutoring? How does such an environment impact the types of tutoring needed to effectively scaffold students? The goal of our research is to determine how best to support learning in a CSCL environment. Our long-term goal is to use the results of this study to inform our design of electronic scaffolds for a group of students working together on tasks requiring conceptual understanding.

METHOD

We conducted a small study that examined the role of a teacher or more experienced peer with one or two other students in a challenging problem-solving situation. We chose algebra as our subject domain because algebra provides concrete, well-defined problems on which students can collaborate. Our existing system, ALGEBRA JAM (Singley, Fairweather & Swerling, 1999), supported collaborative problem-solving and was an appropriate environment for exploring various collaborative arrangements.

Collaboration in ALGEBRA JAM

ALGEBRA JAM is a collaborative learning environment that supports teams of students as they collaborate synchronously and remotely to solve situated, multi-step problems involving algebraic modeling. Students are provided with resources containing information they need to solve an algebra word problem and given various tools to support collaboration.

The blackboard, shown in the top right of Figure 1, supports the participants as they share ideas about how to attack a problem, and monitor team progress. They can post the variables they need to compute as nodes in the goal tree. Any changes in the blackboard are reflected synchronously to other participants in the session; the students cannot make their work private. To aid in collaboration, a face of the user(s) with whom a student is collaborating is displayed in a panel to the right of the blackboard.

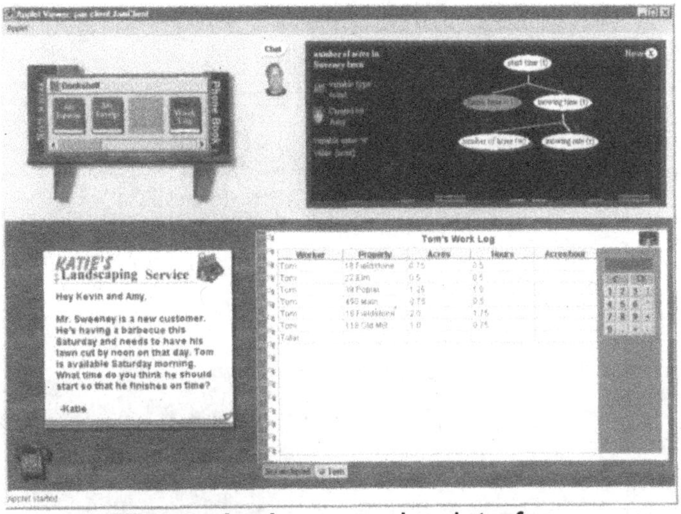

Figure 1 : ALGEBRA JAM interface

The tabbed workspace, shown in the lower right of Figure 1, is an area where students work with the various information resources required to solve the problem. The resources are dragged from the bookshelf in the upper left corner of Figure 1. Like the blackboard, when one participant performs an action in the tabbed workspace area, that action is reflected synchronously to all other participants. This is intended to encourage collaboration in that students can work together to write equations, perform calculations, model solutions, and evaluate each other's work.

Rather than provide a generic chat facility, ALGEBRA JAM allows learners to participate in threaded discussions tied spatially to the work products and interface objects with which they were working. Learners communicate with one another by typing a message while pointing to a particular object on the screen. Users can place a chat balloon anywhere on the screen to focus their conversation or chat about a particular action or object. To further support collaboration, users must identify the type of comment they are contributing. The goal is to encourage metacognition in students.

Participants

The participants were eighteen 8th-12th graders from summer school programs in the metropolitan New York area. The students who participated in the same groups knew each other. The teacher was a high-school math teacher with 22 years of teaching experience. The peer tutor was a student who also participated in our study as a (non-tutor) student and agreed to return in the role of a tutor in subsequent experiences.

Design of Study

We placed participants in one of four experimental groups as arranged in Figure 2. We observed three sets of participants in each condition.

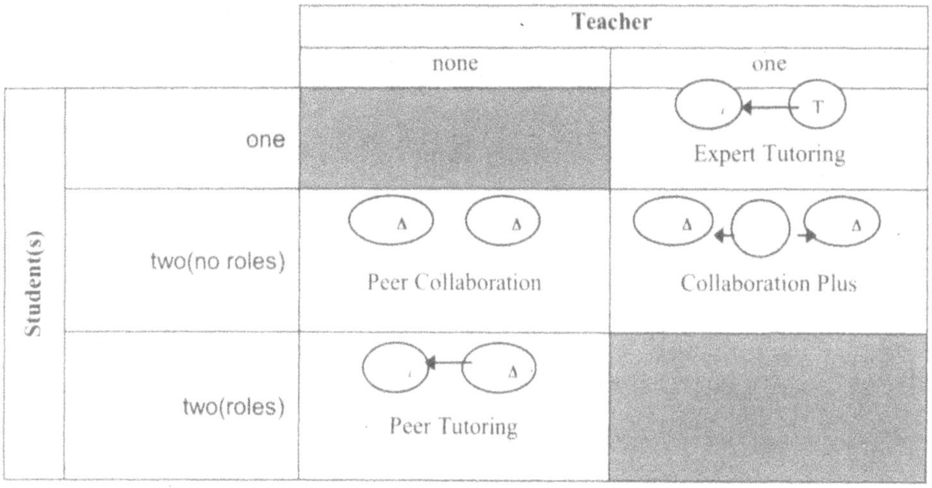

Figure 2: Experimental Groups

The "Expert Tutoring" condition involved one student working with one teacher. We expected that students in this condition would regularly consult the teacher for advice and suggestions. The "Peer Collaboration" condition involved two students working together without role assignment (i.e. neither student was told to tutor the other). We expected that when two students were present, they would work closely, collaborating on most decisions, since they were provided tools to support collaboration and a design that encouraged working together. "Collaboration Plus" involved two students working with a teacher. We hypothesized that students would approach the teacher more than they would consult one another for help. "Peer Tutoring" involved two students working together, in which one played the role of a tutor. The peer tutor had been given instruction on the problems before assuming the tutor role. We suspected that the peer tutor would be approached in a manner similar to how the teacher was approached.

Procedure

Prior to using the system, the participants were instructed on its features as we demonstrated a scenario between two users. The students working together were not directed on how or when to collaborate and were merely told that they would be working together using computers in different rooms. The students in the same groups knew each other previously. In the "Expert Tutoring" and "Collaboration Plus" conditions, the teacher was introduced as a resource if the student(s) encountered difficulties. The teacher was not provided direction on how frequently to provide assistance to the student(s). The teacher, placed in a separate room than each student, could see the events that each of the students saw on their computer. Each group of participants was given a set of three problems to solve in one hour using the system. Each problem involved a landscaping scenario in which students had to solve for variables such as mowing rate or the time to complete a job. The same resources were available on the bookshelf throughout the session.

Analysis

No measures were taken to assess learning because of the short timeframe in which the participants used the system and the design of the open-ended algebra problems. We focused on the nature of the collaboration and did not assess cognitive gains. From the transcripts of the chats, we analyzed the manner in which the human tutors offered assistance and responded to student successes and struggles. We also coded the participants' actions and decisions so we could identify general strategies and techniques employed by peer tutors and teachers when students encountered difficulties. We identified types of feedback offered by a tutor and calculated the number of times a tutor mediated the problem-solving effort.

FINDINGS

We present our findings at two levels. First, we examine the collaboration, or the flow of information, that occurred between participants in ALGEBRA JAM. We begin by looking at how often learning is mediated and by whom. Then, we discuss *how* the participants mediated each other's learning.

Modeling information flow

Information flow is defined as the sharing of meaningful, relevant information that assists in completing the task. We have modeled the information flow between participants in each condition to summarize our findings in Figure 3. The data to support these diagrams is discussed in the following sections. We had expected to see arrows between the two students in the collaboration conditions, but no useful information was exchanged between peers.

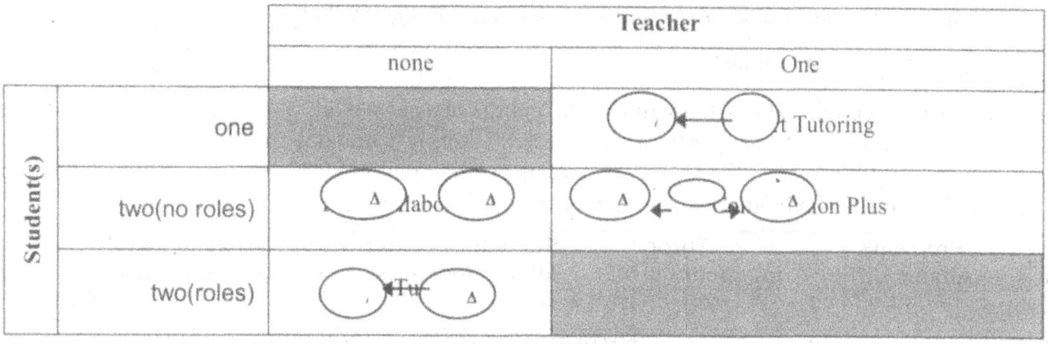

Figure 3: Observed information flow

In the "Tutor mediation" tables in this section (Tables 1, 2, and 3), we list the number of problems which the student(s) attempted, the total number of times the teacher intervened during the session, the percentage of interventions solicited by the student, and the percentage of interventions initiated by the teacher during that session. "Peer Collaboration" does not have a table since no tutor participated in that condition.

Expert Tutoring

In "Expert Tutoring", the students regularly consulted the teacher for advice and suggestions. Most of the information was flowing from the teacher to the student, as illustrated in Passage 1.

Tutor: Good, now how many more minutes is the first time besides 120?
Timmy: So is it 120.15?
Tutor: 120 minutes + 15 minutes =
Timmy: 135

Passage 1: Information directed from teacher to student

In the "Expert Tutoring" condition, most of the interaction involved the problem-solving process. On average, the student solicited approximately 45% of the teacher interventions in this condition; 55% were initiated by the teacher. Only one of the three students progressed past the first problem. Table 2 shows that his session was the only one in which the percentage of solicited interventions was greater than the percentage of tutor-initiated interventions.

Expert Tutoring	Problems Attempted	Tutor Interactions	Student-Solicited Interactions *n(%)*	Tutor-Initiated Interactions *n(%)*
Group 1	1	13	6(46.1)	7(53.8)
Group 2	2	9	5(55.5)	4(44.4)
Group 3	1	9	3(33.3)	6(66.7)
Average	1.3	10.3	4.7(45.0)	5.7(55.0)

Table 1: Tutor mediation for "Expert Tutoring"

Peer Collaboration

In "Peer Collaboration", where neither student was more knowledgeable than the other, the pair worked independently even when collaboration would have been more efficient. Students would do their own work, as evidenced by Passage 2 from our chat transcripts. We also saw in this condition the students were extremely off task.

Thomas: Did you do the problem?
Nick: I'll call you back in a minute
Thomas: Did you finish?
Nick: I'm going to try to finish the last problem...

Passage 2: Lack of peer mediation

Collaboration Plus

In "Collaboration Plus", where a teacher and a same-level peer are present for consultation, we found that neither the teacher nor the peer were asked directly for help. The teacher decides when to intervene to guide or redirect the students. The students did not share useful information, although they did interact more with a teacher present than they did in the "Peer Collaboration" condition without a teacher. They usually only interacted to encourage each other or put each other down, as in Passage 3.

Tutor: You have total acres and total hours. How do you get the rate?
Aaron: Ohhhhh my bad.
Brandon: Yes it is your bad.
Aaron: Shut up. I didn't hear you come up with some answer, Mr. I-know-it-all.

Passage 3: Peer interaction in "Collaboration Plus"

Sometimes, students would lead each other down the wrong path and the teacher would intervene. With multiple students, the teacher, instead of being solicited by the learner(s) as in "Expert Tutoring", initiates more of the mediation. Table 2 shows that a large percentage (90% average) of the tutor mediation in "Collaboration Plus" was tutor-initiated, compared to Table 2 in "Expert Tutoring" which showed tutor-initiated interactions averaging 55%.

Collaboration Plus	Problems Attempted	Tutor Interactions	Student-Solicited Interactions *n(%)*	Tutor-Initiated Interactions *n(%)*
Group 1	1	17	1(5.9)	16(94.1)
Group 2	3	10	1(10.0)	9(90.0)
Group 3	1	15	2(13.3)	13(86.7)
Average	1.3	14.0	1.3(9.7)	12.7(90.3)

Table 2: Tutor mediation for "Collaboration Plus"

Peer Tutoring

In "Peer Tutoring", the peer tutor was consulted in a similar fashion to the teacher in "Expert Tutoring". No fewer questions were asked than in the condition where a teacher was present. The peer tutor seemed to be an adequate substitute for the teacher in terms of answering questions and directing students. The following transcript passage, Passage 4, is an example of effective guidance by a peer-tutor.

Peer Tutor: No...what are u trying to find in the "Phillip" book?
Tremaine: The amount of acres that he mows per hour
Peer Tutor: Yes...his average rate of lawn mowing. How does one find an average?
Tremaine: Divide

Passage 4: Effective peer tutoring

Information was directed from the tutor to the student, just as we saw in the "Expert Tutoring" condition. As shown in Table 3, our data set demonstrates that a peer, with a lower average number of interactions, intervenes slightly less than a teacher. The average number of interactions between the teacher and the student was 10.3 in the Expert Tutoring condition (as shown in Table 2), as opposed to an average of 8.7 interactions in this condition.

Peer Tutoring	Problems Attempted	Tutor Interactions	Student-Solicited Interactions *n(%)*	Tutor-Initiated Interactions *n(%)*
Group 1	1	9	5(55.6)	4(44.4)
Group 2	2	7	2(28.6)	5(71.4)
Group 3	1	10	1(10.0)	9(90.0)
Average	1.7	8.7	2.7(31.4)	6.0(68.6)

Table 3: Tutor mediation for "Peer Tutoring"

Summary of Information Flow Findings

From studying the flow of information between participants, we found that when a teacher or peer tutor is present, information is directed from the tutor to the student. In contrast, in "Peer Collaboration" where another same-level peer was available for help, students did not exchange useful information with each other to mediate the learning process; the teacher initiated almost all the interaction in that condition. When two peers are working together with or without the presence of a tutor, the peers work independently and do not mediate each other's learning.

Instructional Strategies

We coded the types of strategies used by tutors, and we found five categories that are derived from Graesser and his colleagues' (1995) categories. We did not code the "Pure Collaboration" condition because we did not observe information flow between the students in those groups. The types of mediation we coded were *leading, prompting, hinting, probing*, and *diagnosing.* Figure 4 categorizes the percentage of interventions by both a teacher and a peer-tutor according to the instructional strategies they employed.

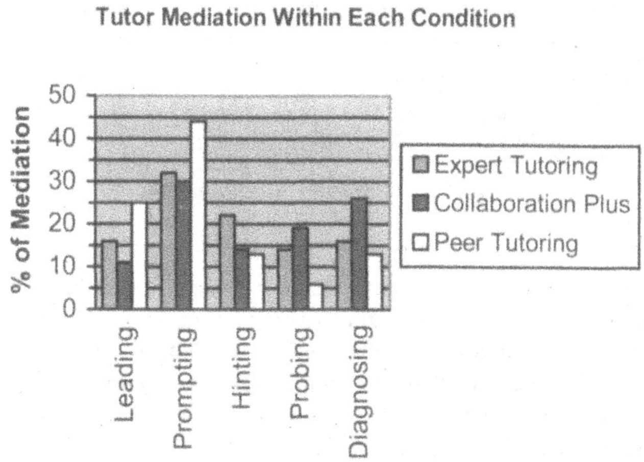

Figure 4: Instructional strategies graph

Leading

Leading differs from *prompting* in that in a leading strategy, the tutor is specifically directing a student to complete a task. Leading would mean answering a question such that it solves part of the problem, as illustrated in Passage 5. Peer tutors did almost twice as much leading as did teachers. A teacher used similar strategies whether working with one student or two simultaneously.

> **Timmy**: I don't know how to figure that out
> **Tutor**: The last column is acres divided by hour. That would be how much work Phillip did in 1 hour.

Passage 5: Example of *leading* by a teacher

Prompting

In *prompting*, tutors (either a peer or teacher) ask questions so that the student can arrive at the answer himself or herself. In Passage 6, the teacher is prompting the student to a particular answer. *Prompting* is the strategy that the teacher and peer tutor used most often when mediating learning.

> **Tutor:** Where would we find the information we need?
> **Timmy:** Phillip's timesheet
> **Tutor:** Good, now what does this tell us?
> **Timmy:** How many hours Phil worked
> **Tutor:** Ok, and what else?

Passage 6: Example of *prompting*

Hinting

Hinting differs from *prompting* in that hints usually take the form of analogies or reminders and may not relate specifically to the problem. Passage 7 illustrates hinting. The teacher employed the hinting strategy more often that did the peer tutor.

> **Tutor**: Remember what rate is?
> **Timmy**: Is it the consistency of something?
> **Tutor**: Heart rate we defined as the amount of work that your heart does in a given time.
> **Tutor**: So Phillip's rate would be ________?

Passage 7: Example of *hinting*

Probing

Probing involves the tutor asking questions to make sure a student understands the problem, as in Passage 8. A peer tutor seems to do less *probing* than a teacher to make sure an idea or concept is understood.

> **Tutor**: You already did his total acres so we just need the total time.
> **Timmy**: 19.669 acres in 19.669 total time
> **Tutor**: How did you get 19.669 for total time?

Passage 8: Example of *probing*

Diagnosing

Diagnosing is a strategy in which tutors provide feedback by evaluating the student's ideas and actions in the learning environment. As illustrated in Passage 9, *diagnosing* provides the student with immediate input about their progress. In our study, a teacher did more diagnosing than a peer tutor.

> **Tutor**: You are correct – John has mowed 15.75 acres before.
> **Tutor**: You are also right that there are 60 minutes in an hour.

Passage 9: Example of *diagnosing*

Summary

Primarily, human tutors in a learning environment take the learner through the problem by asking questions pertaining to the problem at hand. The teacher did less *probing* and *diagnosing* and more *leading* and *hinting* in the "Expert Tutoring" condition than in the "Collaboration Plus" condition. It also appears that a peer tutor prefers *prompting* followed by *leading* to mediate student learning. Overall, we found that the notion that a problem-solving partner is more knowledgeable, regardless of his or her status or teaching experience, seems to provide a student with more inclination to ask questions of the partner than in the case where the partner is a same-level student.

DISCUSSION

We had hypothesized that students in the "Expert Tutoring" condition would consult the teacher regularly for advice and suggestions. We saw in Table 2 that a student initiated more of the interaction in the case when he or she was able to solve a problem, whereas the teacher initiated more of the interaction when the student was struggling. This would be a logical result of students not knowing when to ask for assistance or what types of questions to ask. In responding to the student, we found that the teacher used *prompting* most frequently, followed by *hinting*. It seemed that the teacher expected the students to find the answers on their own with some direction.

We had hypothesized that students would work as equals in the "Peer Collaboration" condition, working together since they were information resources for each other in the environment. But the students had no prior training in how to collaborate and were not given explicit instructions on how to work together. Perhaps as a result, they proceeded as individual problem-solvers; there was no shared knowledge. Even though the participants in this condition were not complete strangers, they needed support in working together.

We had expected in the "Collaboration Plus" condition that we would see the teacher being consulted more often than the other student. However, in most cases, questions or remarks would not be addressed to either participant, and the teacher would be responsible for initiating the interaction. In "Collaboration Plus," the instructional strategies used by the teacher were primarily *prompting*, followed closely by *diagnosing*. We also noticed that the teacher aimed to facilitate the learning of the student, whereas the peer often aimed just to find the right answer. Furthermore, when students did interact, they often misdirected each other or moved off-task, requiring teacher intervention. This is more evidence that the collaboration process needs to be scaffolded in a networked environment.

Lastly, we believed that a peer tutor would be approached online by a student in a similar manner to a teacher. We found that the tutor initiated interaction more often than the student asked for assistance. Because of the nature of the task and the differences in expertise, the tutor assumes more of a traditional teacher role and thus dominates the dialogue. Unlike when the teacher was acting as the tutor, we found that the peer tutor almost half the time chose the more straightforward, simple instructional method of *prompting*, followed a quarter of the time by *leading*, another less sophisticated approach, to help a student.

IMPLICATIONS AND CONCLUSION

We conclude by returning to our research questions. How does a CSCL learning environment impact the types of support needed to effectively scaffold students? Which elements of peer interaction and teacher interaction are effective in supporting collaborative learning? We cannot make strong claims due to the size of our study, but our results suggest interesting areas for further exploration.

Design Implications

We noted general design implications from tutor-mediated instruction for designing support for groups of students working in electronic learning environments. In "Expert Tutoring," we saw that the teacher initiated more of the interaction when the student was struggling. Support for group learning should diagnose student progress and intervene at impasses. This is consistent with the findings of Brown and VanLehn (1988) described earlier. A human or computer tutor does not necessarily need to provide immediate feedback, but a model tracing student progress could ensure that students do not get too far off track.

Scaffolds in CSCL environments should also improve communication between students to accelerate their path along an acceptable solution trajectory. We saw in the "Peer Collaboration" condition that students proceeded as individual problem solvers with little useful information shared between them. As suggested earlier in this paper, discussing and explaining ideas to peers is a useful learning strategy. This suggests that supporting collaboration requires (1) diagnosing impasses to redirect incorrect solution paths, (2) facilitating problem-solving interaction to keep students engaged, and (3) suggesting ways to divide the problem into sub-tasks for which each participant can be responsible. These functions are somewhat similar to the findings by Katz and Lesgold (1993) of the role of the tutor in a collaborative situation, except that our results suggest that the tutor in a CSCL environment needs to be more pro-active in providing advice. Rather than leaving to students the responsibility for deciding when advice is needed, we believe the tutor needs to identify problems and provide redirection.

Finding the optimal balance of peer and expert tutoring strategies is an important research challenge. There are times when a knowledgeable expert is needed, and other times when a peer, to which ideas can be explained and justified, is appropriate. Our study suggests, however, that peers need to be instructed on how to collaborate before they can be effective at facilitating each other's learning. Experts also need to give students the chance to work together and correct each other before jumping in with the solution.

Conclusion

More research needs to be done to examine how traditional methods of tutoring differ when the participants are interacting over a computer. More studies should also explore how students learn differently with peers versus teachers in an electronic environment. This study demonstrated that the techniques used to scaffold learning in a CSCL environment are different from interactive learning environments. Not only does individual learning need to be supported, but the interaction between participants needs to be facilitated because outside of the social context of the classroom, it is easy for the students to become disengaged.

We have performed a small study that has looked more generally at the role of peers, a knowledgeable peer-tutor and a teacher put into an electronic tutoring situation. Our findings suggest that there are significant advantages for both knowledge-rich interactions and peer-to-peer collaboration. Designers of collaborative learning environments need to capture these advantages by developing scaffolds that can effectively lead, prompt, hint, probe, and diagnose in a way that supports team problem-solving without actively leading the team towards a predetermined outcome.

ACKNOWLEDGEMENTS

This work was supported by IBM T.J. Watson Research Center. We would like to thank Elizabeth Davis and Nichole Pinkard for their feedback and suggestions. We also thank the participants in this study.

REFERENCERS

Berge, Z. (1997). Computer conferencing and the on-line classroom. *International Journal of Educational Telecommunications*, 3(1): 3-21.

Brown, A., & Palincsar, A.S. (1989). Guided, cooperative learning and individual knowledge acquisition. In L. Resnick (Ed.) *Knowing, learning, and instruction: Essays in honor of Robert Glaser* (pp. 393-451). Hillsdale, NJ: Erlbaum.

Brown, J. and VanLehn, K. (1988). Repair theory: A generative theory of bugs in procedural skills. *Readings in cognitive science: A perspective from psychology and artificial intelligence.* San Mateo, CA: Morgan Kaufmann.

Cobb, P. (1994). Where is the mind? Constructivist and sociocultural perspectives on mathematical development. *Educational Researcher*, 23(7): 13-20.

Crook, C. (1994). *Computers and the Collaborative Experience of Learning*. London: Routledge.

Gall, S. (1992). Children's Instrumental Help-Seeking: Its Role in the Social Acquisition and Construction of Knowledge. In R. Hertz-Lazarowitz, V. Kirkus, & N. Miller (Eds.) *Interactions in Cooperative Groups.* New York: Cambridge University Press.

Graesser, A.C., Person, N.K., & Magliano, J.P. (1995). Collaborative dialog patterns in naturalistic one-on-one tutoring. *Applied Cognitive Psychology*, 9: 359-387.

King, A. (1994). Guiding knowledge construction in the classroom: Effects of teaching children how to question and how to explain. *American Educational Research Journal*, 30: 338-368.

Koschmann, T. (1996). *CSCL:Theory and practice of an emerging paradigm*. Mahwah, NJ: Lawrence Erlbaum Associates.

Lepper, M, Woolverton, M., Mumme, D., & Gurtner, J. (1993). Motivational Techniques of Expert Human Tutors. In S.P. Lajoie and S.J. Derry (Eds.), *Computers as Cognitive Tools*. Hillsdale, NJ: Lawrence Erlbaum Associates.

McCarthey, S. & McMahon, S. (1992). From Convention to Invention: Three Approaches to Peer Interactions During Writing. In R. Hertz-Lazarowitz, V. Kirkus, & N. Miller (Eds.) *Interactions in Cooperative Groups*. New York: Cambridge University Press.

Newman, R., & Goldin, L. (1990). Children's reluctance to seek help with schoolwork. *Journal of Educational Psychology*, 82, 71-80.

Rogoff, B. (1990). *Apprenticeship in thinking: Cognitive development in social context.* New York: Oxford University Press.

Salomon, G., & Perkins, D.N. (1998). Individual and Social Aspects of Learning. In P.D. Pearson & A. Iran-Nejad (Eds.), *Review of Research in Education.* 23.

Singley, M.K., Fairweather, P., & Swerling, S. (1999). Team Tutoring Systems: Reifying Roles in Problem Solving. In *Proceedings of Computer Support for Collaborative Learning*, Palo Alto, CA, 538-548.

Van der Miej, H. (1988). Constraints on question-asking in classrooms. *Journal of Educational Psychology*, 80, 401-405.

Vygotsky, L. (1978). *Mind in society: The development of higher psychological processes.* Cambridge, MA: Harvard University Press.

Webb, N.M. (1995). Constructive Activity and Learning in Collaborative Small Groups. *Journal of Educational Psychology*, 87(3): 406-423.

Webb, N.M. (1991). Task related verbal interaction and mathematics learning in small groups. *Journal forResearch in Mathematics Education*, 22 (5).

Wood, D., Bruner, J. & Ross, G. (1976). The role of tutoring in problem solving. *Journal of Child Psychology and Psychiatry*, 17(2), 89-100.

Why Scaffolding Should Sometimes Make Tasks More Difficult for Learners

Brian J. Reiser

Northwestern University

Reiser@northwestern.edu

ABSTRACT

There has been much interest in using software tools to scaffold learners in complex tasks, that is, to provide supports that enable students to deal with more complex content and skill demands than they could otherwise handle. Many different approaches to scaffolding techniques have been presented in a broad range of software tools. I discuss two mechanisms to explain how software tools can scaffold learners. Software tools can help structure the learning task, guiding learners through key components and supporting their planning and performance. In addition, tools can shape students' performance and understanding of the task in terms of key disciplinary content and strategies, thereby problematizing this important content. While making the task more difficult in the short term, by forcing learners to address these ideas, such scaffolded tools make this work more productive opportunities for learning.

Keywords

caffolding, interactive learning environments, science education

INTRODUCTION

There is much interest in education reform in using technology to support learners. One aspect of the argument for technology has been that software can be used to *scaffold* students, that is to provide enough support to enable learners to succeed in more complex tasks, and thereby to extend the range of experiences from which they can learn (Davis & Linn, 2000; Edelson, Gordin, & Pea, 1999; Guzdial, 1994; Quintana, Eng, Carra, Wu, & Soloway, 1999; Reiser et al., 2001). Scaffolding is a key element of the notion of cognitive apprenticeship, in which students can learn by taking increasing responsibility and ownership for their role in complex problem solving, with the structure and guidance of more knowledgeable mentors or teachers (Collins, Brown, & Newman, 1989).

There are many different approaches to scaffolding, and no common framework has yet emerged that can be used to provide design guidelines for scaffolded software. In this paper, I propose two general mechanisms by which software tools can shape tasks for learners in a way that makes their problem solving more productive, and thereby scaffolds their learning.

Traditional Approaches to Scaffolding

The term *scaffolding* has traditionally been used to refer to the process by which a teacher or more knowledgeable peer assists a learner, altering the learning task so the student can solve problems or perform tasks that would otherwise be out of reach. The conception is associated with Vygotsky's notion of the zone of proximal development, which characterizes the region of tasks between what the learner could accomplish alone and what he or she could accomplish (and master) with assistance (Rogoff, 1990; Vygotsky, 1978). It is important to stress the dual aspects of both (a) accomplishing the task and (b) learning from one's efforts, i.e., improving one's performance on the future tasks in the process. If learners are assisted in the task but are not able to understand or take advantage of the experience, the assistance will have been local to that instance of scaffolding, but will not have provided support for learning. Thus, scaffolding entails a delicate negotiation between providing support while continuing to engage the learner actively in the process (Merrill, Reiser, Merrill, & Landes, 1995).

In recent design research on interactive learning environments, this notion of scaffolding has been generalized to refer to aspects of software tools that assist the learners in making progress on what would otherwise be tasks out of their reach. Software scaffolding provides some sort of structure that helps make the learning more tractable for learners. For example, the software might provide prompts to encourage or remind students what steps to take (Davis & Linn, 2000), graphical organizers or other notations to help students plan and organize their problem solving (Quintana et al., 1999), automatic execution of lower level processes, or representations that help learners track the steps they have taken in the problem solving process (Collins & Brown, 1988; Koedinger & Anderson, 1993). In all these cases the software provides additional assistance beyond what a simpler, more basic tool would have provided, to allow learners to accomplish more ambitious tasks.

This work on scaffolded software tools has been very encouraging, and promises to be an important benefit in integrating technological tools into classrooms. However, there have been a wide range of approaches to designing software scaffolds, and almost as many design principles as there are working systems. Development of general guidelines for the design of software scaffolds first requires a general theoretical framework to characterize how tools can scaffold learners. How can we characterize the mechanisms by which software scaffolds assist learners?

There are a number of different ways one could carve up the space of software scaffolds. We could attempt to organize scaffolds according to the nature of the interface feature involved, such as text-based prompts, or hyperlinked representations. We could enumerate different functions scaffolds can serve, such as linking representations or helping learners break down complex processes into their subcomponents. Such analyses have clear utility. However, a principled articulation of scaffolding approaches must begin with a model of the task and the identification of the obstacles that learners face in performing the task (Quintana, 2001; Quintana et al., 1999; Reiser et al., 2001). A delineation of scaffolding strategies must be based on an analysis of what the target domain requires of learners, why the task is difficult, and finally how interacting with the tools can help learners overcome these difficulties, both to accomplish the task and to learn more effectively from the experience.

In this paper, I argue that there are two principal mechanisms by which software scaffolds can assist learners in mastering complex tasks. Following discussion of these two scaffolding mechanisms, I present some specific design principles consistent with this model, and describe their implementation in learning environments. To construct this argument, I will focus on scaffolding in the discipline of science. Much of the work on scaffolding tools has taken place in this domain, and there is a rich literature on the obstacles learners face. Furthermore, tools to access and interpret data are a central part of scientific investigations, so this domain is a productive context in which to explore the design of scaffolded tools.

THE NEEDS OF LEARNERS

Modern instructional approaches in science and mathematics emphasize learning by engaging in knowledge construction practices. In the case of science, this entails learning in the context of scientific investigation and argumentation (Edelson, 2001; Olson & Loucks-Horsley, 2000; Singer, Marx, Krajcik, & Chambers, 2000). These investigations often entail students learning general principles in the context of specific problem scenarios. Designers have developed approaches of problem-based learning (Cognition and Technology Group, 1990; Schank, Fano, Bell, & Jona, 1994; Williams, 1992) and project-based science (Blumenfeld et al., 1991) as a way of engaging learners in acquiring disciplinary knowledge in the context of solving particular problems, such as learning genetics by working through the tasks of being a genetic counselor (Bell, Bareiss, & Beckwith, 1994) or learning introductory physics by analyzing the quality of air in one's community (Singer et al., 2000). These approaches, while providing the potential to connect knowledge more effectively to real world contexts, also pose a particular type of challenge for learners. For this approach to be successful as a learning approach, students must not only construct solutions to the particular scenario, but must construct and analyze their solutions in terms of more general disciplinary content. In particular, students need to ground their reasoning in more general disciplinary strategies, and connect the explanations or arguments they construct to more general disciplinary frameworks. For example, if students are learning about mass and density by designing toy boats to carry loads, they need to analyze and synthesize their results and work toward physical explanations, rather than focusing only on the goal of the boat-building task (Schauble, Klopfer, & Raghavan, 1991).

Performing an investigation is a complex cognitive task that pushes the boundary of learners' content knowledge and processes. For example, the current education standards characterize the iterative processes of designing an investigation, collecting data, constructing and revising explanations based on data, evaluating explanations, and communicating arguments (Olson & Loucks-Horsley, 2000). This requires coordinating domain-specific processes and content knowledge, and metacognitive processes to plan, monitor, evaluate and revise these investigation plans. Thus, learners face challenges at several levels. The knowledge students are mastering includes conceptual knowledge, basic domain process skills, domain-specific strategies, and more general metacognitive processes.

Along with efforts to bring more ambitious science practices into classrooms, there has now been a rich set of empirical studies documenting the challenges that learners face. We briefly consider the main findings here in order to motivate the nature of the solutions that scaffolds can provide to these problems. Where does the complexity arise for learners in science?

Tacit expert knowledge: Sophisticated problem solvers relies on strategies for planning and guiding the reasoning. These heuristic strategies in science are needed to plan investigations, select data comparisons, and synthesize findings. These strategies are built upon on discipline-specific explanatory frameworks (Reiser et al., 2001; Tabak, Smith, Sandoval, & Reiser, 1996). A key challenge is that this knowledge is typically tacit for more experienced reasoners, and very much taken for granted. Instruction often fails to make these strategies explicit for learners.

Non-reflective work: Learners tend to focus on products rather than on explanatory and learning goals (Perkins, 1998; Schauble, Glaser, Duschl, Schulze, & John, 1995). The difficulty in managing investigations leads to little attention being given to reflection and reevaluation (Loh et al., 2001). Lack of content knowledge further complicates the process of evaluating the progress of an investigation.

Fragile and superficial understanding. Learners tend to focus on surface details, and have difficulty seeing the underlying structure (Chi, Feltovich, & Glaser, 1981). They may have difficulty mapping between related representations and instead become overly reliant on particular forms.

In summary, the task demands of engaging in scientific investigations reveal a system of challenges for learners. The ongoing cycle of planning and monitoring, sense making, and communication requires a number of processes that are likely contexts where assistance will be needed. Investigations require planning, in which students need to coordinate reasoning about hypotheses and reasoning about experiments or data comparisons that can be constructed to test hypotheses (Klahr & Dunbar, 1988). Constructing and pursuing that plan requires new disciplinary strategies, and poses metacognitive demands in continually monitoring, evaluating and revising that plan. In addition to help in managing this process, learners may need assistance in thinking through their own solutions in terms of the disciplinary content, so that they can learn about the discipline from the experience. Making sense of the data collected may require deep subject matter knowledge to interpret observations in light of disciplinary frameworks. Learners may need prompting to consider alternatives in light of initial support for a line of argument. They may need assistance in exploring the implications of the evidence they collect for the hypotheses they consider. They may not articulate their ongoing understanding, focusing instead on pragmatic goals of creating required products. They may need assistance in scientific discourse to move beyond description and communicate a scientific argument. In all these processes, the challenges of more superficial understanding, lack of access to tacit expert strategies, and a tendency toward non-reflective work create the need and opportunities for more supportive environments.

HOW CAN TOOLS HELP LEARNERS?

While traditional views of scaffolding have focused on social interactions as the source of assistance, the focus of the last two decades of research on the cognitive science issues in technology design has illuminated ways in which technological tools may provide some types of scaffolding functions. In considering how to help learners with these challenges, it is important to reconceptualize the learning problem from that of an individual working on tasks, perhaps with assistance of another more knowledgeable other, to focusing on the context in which the people are acting, the tools they use, and the knowledge embedded in this context. Rather than considering what the individual can accomplish, this view of distributed cognition focuses on what the system of person and tool can accomplish (Hollan, Hutchins, & Kirsh, 2000). The structure of a tool shapes how one interacts with the task and affects what can be accomplished.

One clear possibility for more supportive tools lies in automating aspects of tasks, and thereby restricting the part of the task for the learner needs to perform, potentially enabling them to focus on more productive parts of the tasks (Salomon, Perkins, & Globerson, 1991). This is the perhaps the most straightforward sense of scaffolding. For example, calculators can offload simple computations, allowing people to focus on other parts of the data manipulation tasks, such as considering what calculations to compose together to solve a problem. Word processors with spelling checkers can allow writers to focus more on the construction of their prose rather than devoting time to checking spelling in dictionaries. If offloading these aspects of the task enable learners to focus more effectively on the conceptually important aspects, and thereby learn from their experience, the tool has scaffolded that learning.

Tools can have even more dramatic effects on tasks in the way they shape the task itself. In fact, the nature of the tools we use can be a critical factor in how people think about the tasks they perform (Hutchins, 1995; Norman, 1987). This is particularly true when tasks involve accessing, manipulating, storing, or reasoning about information. Norman (1987) describes *cognitive artifacts*, or tools that are used to represent and manipulate information in a task. These tools can change the task in fundamental ways. The cognitive artifact becomes the vehicle through which the person interacts with the environment. It provides the representation of external states and the vehicle for manipulating the environment. Because of the central role of tools in effecting actions in information domains, the task cannot really be defined independent of the tools people use in the practice of that task (Bannon & Bødker, 1987). Thus, the nature of the task emerges from the interactions of people, subject matter, and tools, and the nature of the tool clearly affects how tractable the performance of a task is for learners.

Norman describes the problem of mapping between the external representation and what it represents. The goal of human-computer interaction design research is to make that mapping as transparent as possible. Cognitive artifacts can change the task for users in the way in which they represent and allow people to manipulate information. For example, direct-manipulation interfaces allow users to control a process by appearing to act upon it directly, through the visual metaphor (Hutchins, Hollan, & Norman, 1986). Visualization tools are designed to help users form deep models of an underlying system (Hollan, Bederson, & Helfman, 1997).

In the design of scaffolded tools, we can use this mapping to our advantage. Rather than striving only for transparency between the representation and the world it represents, we can bend that representation to instructional purposes. Cognitive artifacts provide a lever for designers to shape how learners think about tasks. In the next section, we consider how cognitive artifacts can be used to instructional advantage.

MECHANISMS OF SCAFFOLDING: STRUCTURE AND PROBLEMATIZE

How can tools provide scaffolding? First, let us revisit the definition of scaffolding as applied to science. There are two critical notions in scaffolding: (1) learners receive assistance to succeed in more complex tasks that would otherwise be too difficult; (2) learners draw from that experience and improve in process skills and/or content understanding. Focusing on the representational properties of tools puts us in a position now to consider how the specific design of the tool can support learning tasks.

I propose two complementary aspects of scaffolding in software tools — it can help structure problem solving, and it can provoke learners to devote resources to issues they might not otherwise address. We consider each of these in turn.

Structuring the Task

The first sense of scaffolding is the most straightforward — if reasoning is difficult due to complexity or the open-ended nature of the task, then one way to help learners is to make the task more structured. This may be done by providing structured workspaces, graphical organizers, decomposing functionality according to conceptual processes, or providing prompts. The structure of the tool may provide guidance as to what actions to take, their order, necessary aspects of work products, and so on. This type of structuring is a key characteristic of a number of different scaffolding approaches. For example, in KIE, structured prompts reminds students of aspects of the process they may otherwise neglect to perform (Davis & Linn, 2000). Model-It structures the task of modeling into plan, build, and test processes, and organizes relevant functions in each of those modes (Jackson, Krajcik, & Soloway, 1998). In the BGuILE ExplanationConstructor, structured workspaces can be used to remind students of the necessary components of their explanations, and can remind students about the criteria they should apply to evaluate their own work (Reiser et al., 2001; Sandoval, 1998). In these cases, the scaffolded tool addresses the obstacles of the investigation task by helping learners construct their plans, consider the possible actions relevant to each stage of the process, monitor the plan, and tie in relevant disciplinary ideas as they make sense and communicate about their data.

Problematizing Concepts

The second general approach is to make something in students' work more problematic (Hiebert et al., 1996). That is, the software tools help students see something as problematic that they might otherwise overlook. Rather than simplifying the task, the software forces students to encounter important ideas or processes. For example, if students are forced to use a menu to categorize the data they have collected, they need to consider the significance of the data. In the BGuILE ExplanationConstructor (Sandoval, 1998), students must make conceptual distinctions between the type of argument they wish to construct. In these cases, forcing students to apply these distinctions, which represent key conceptual ideas in the target discipline, can provoke debate, deliberations, and decisions that are all productive for students as they make sense of the findings of their investigation and manage its progress.

In this way, scaffolds can provoke students, "rocking the boat" when they are proceeding along without being mindful enough of the rich connections of their decisions to the domain content. This provocation may occur as the tools force them into decisions or commitments required to use the vocabulary and machinery of the interface. This type of scaffolded tool may create short-term costs, preventing students from rushing through their work in a problem without being mindful of the subject-matter issues that are the goal of the instruction. While this may be a short-term challenge rather than directly assisting with more expeditious solutions, such a tool may make the students' efforts in the problem a more productive learning opportunity.

The social context of collaborative problem solving is often integral to the problematizing nature of the tool. Students must make their understanding public when using tools that represent conceptual distinctions explicitly. Such tools require students to discuss disciplinary ideas decisions in order to effect actions in the tool. In this way, the artifact students use to examine data and record their interpretations becomes a vehicle for negotiation of understanding about the disciplinary ideas and their application to the task at hand (Roschelle, 1992).

These two mechanisms of structuring and problematizing are often complementary. The same characteristic of a tool designed to help structure students' engagement in a task, for example, by providing guiding prompts or making explicit a set of subtasks, may also problematize the disciplinary ideas, by requiring students to make sense of the options and connect their own work to these disciplinary ideas.

In summary, through these two mechanisms, scaffolds can help learners overcome some of the challenge of the complexity in the domain. Their work can be more productive and more effectively guided by expert strategies and understanding. In the next section we provide examples from our work on BGuILE learning environments that exemplify these complementary functions of guiding and problematizing in students' scientific investigations.

DESIGN PRINCIPLES: USING TOOLS TO MAKE THE TASK EXPLICIT

The design principles I present here address the learner obstacles of fragile understanding and accessing tacit expert knowledge. The key to the design approach is to help make the structure of the task more accessible to learners through the tools they use and the artifacts they create. Articulation plays a central role in the approach. We will help learners understand the tasks by requiring them to articulate their actions and encode their results in terms of disciplinary frameworks.

I will present two types of designs that attempt to help students understand and practice these investigation and argumentation strategies by making them explicit in both the tools students use and the work products or artifacts they create. We call these *strategic tools* and *strategic artifacts* (Reiser et al., 2001). I describe these two types of design features and then present examples of scaffolded tools that employ these strategies.

Strategic Tools: We structure the tools students use to access, analyze, and manipulate data so that the implicit strategies of the discipline are visible to students. When students interact with these tools they are led to articulate their interaction in terms of these strategies. For example, when students construct data queries they articulate their query in terms of the key distinctions in the types of comparisons used to build theory in the domain, rather than solely in terms of surface data parameters.

Strategic Artifacts: We design the work products that students create to represent the important conceptual properties of explanations and models in the discipline. For example, we have students construct hypermedia documents that make explicit the rhetorical structure of their arguments.

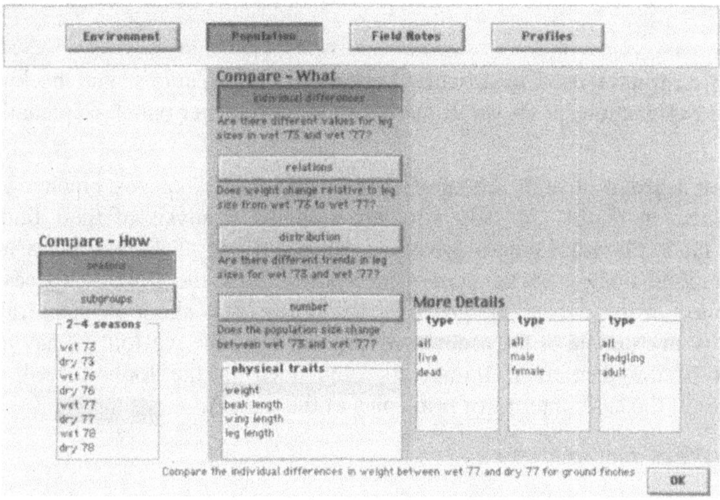

Figure 1. The query screen from The Galapagos Finches. The student has selected a comparison between seasons (first panel), and has selected "individual differences" as the comparison type (second panel). The particular constructed query is assembled at the bottom of the screen.

Strategic tools

Scaffolded tools can help represent more of the structure of the task for learners. We have designed the structure of *The Galapagos Finches* software as a strategic tool (Reiser et al., 2001; Tabak & Reiser, 1997; Tabak et al., 1996). The Galapagos Finches enables learners to investigate changes in populations of plants and animals in an ecosystem, and serves as a platform for learning principles of ecology and natural selection. The tool makes explicit the key strategies for examining ecosystem data — scientists can study a population through time (a longitudinal comparison) or split a population according to some dimension of interest, such as comparing male to female or young to adult (a cross-sectional comparison). These two families of comparisons are options students must select when constructing a query (shown as the choices "seasons" and "subgroups"). Similarly, students must articulate what type of comparison they wish to perform (looking at individual differences, relationship between two variables, and so on). In this way, students are led to articulate the strategic intent of a data comparison, rather than phrasing their action in terms of the surface details (see Figure 1). Similarly, in the ExplanationConstructor, disciplinary frameworks are represented in explanation guides that students use to ensure that their explanations address the key features of the framework (see Figure 2).

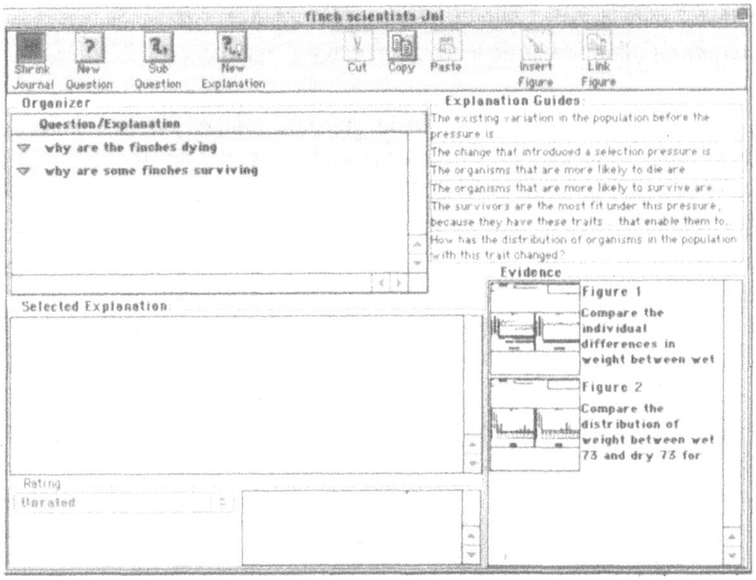

Figure 2. The ExplanationConstructor used to articulate questions, explanations, and backing support. The outline of questions, subquestions, and explanations is shown in the upper left Organizer panel. Explanation guides are shown in the upper right.

The following example from a group of high school students using the Galapagos Finches and ExplanationConstructor demonstrates how the explanation guides can help structure students' analysis of their findings. In this example, the students' attempt to satisfy the explanation guides provokes debate on one of the key ideas in the domain, the nature of traits. In considering whether their finding fits the goal of identifying traits, the group disagrees about whether food choice qualifies as a trait. In the course of this debate, the group brings in key ideas about physical traits and the relation between structure and function. This is an example of the problematizing nature of the scaffold — having to structure their analysis of their findings in terms of the theoretical framework embedded in the tools forced students to structure their understanding of the specifics of the case in terms of principles of the domain.

Evan: *(reading prompt)* "Environment causes…"

Janie: No!

Evan: Yeah, "to be selected for…"

Janie: Yeah, but that means like…

Evan: // what food they eat //

Janie: … organism with these trait

Evan: // the trait being the food

Franny: Yeah, that's right.

Janie: No, because like, if my trait is to eat steak, and there's no steak, I'm immediately gonna go to something else.

Evan: If you're only a vegetarian and you only eat… you don't eat meat, you're not gonna eat meat. Well, that depends…//

Janie: Are you insane!?

Franny: OK, OK. Don't think of people. Think of these guys (the finches). If they only eat one type of seed with their beaks and that seed is gone then they can't live anymore.

This example demonstrates the type of discourse we aim to create through the scaffolds. The structure they impose on students' work causes them to grapple with key disciplinary ideas such as the nature of a trait and the difference between a species' characteristic traits and learned behaviors. Decisions about the use of the artifact became the context for negotiation between the students of these important disciplinary ideas. Both sense making (interpreting the observed differences in individuals as candidates for traits supporting differential survival) and articulation were supported by the problematizing nature of the strategic tool.

Strategic artifacts

Just as the tools students use are structured to help them understand the task, we also structure the key work products students create to clearly represent important conceptual distinctions and task structure. Just as transparency in cognitive artifacts that people use can affect the ease with which they can achieve their desired ends in actions in the interface, here we aim for transparency in the artifacts people create. Our goal is for students to create artifacts that clearly represent the important strategic and disciplinary thinking they have performed in creating the artifact. Contrast this with more traditional artifacts such as verbal essays, in which the research behind the essay and the deeper argument structure embedded in the essay may be very difficult to discern.

In the Animal Landlord, students study examples of animal behavior to isolate and analyze the key components of complex animal behavior (Smith & Reiser, 1998). Students study examples of behavior sequences such as hunting or eating and deconstruct the complex sequence into what they see as the important causal events. For each event, students record their observation of the event and their inference of the importance of that event (see Figure 3).

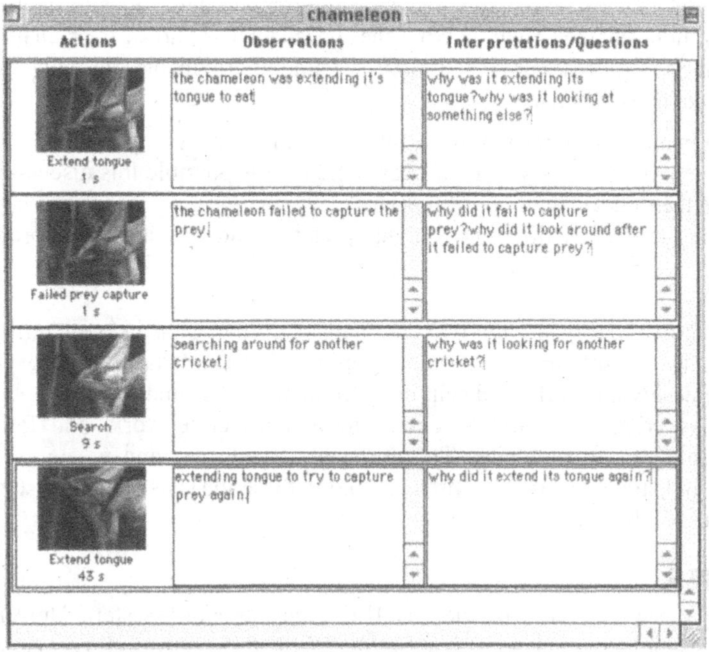

Figure 3. Strategic Artifacts from the Animal Landlord. Students decompose complex behavior into its constituents, categorize each constituent, and record their observations and interpretations.

The artifacts students create are structured to represent key aspects of the task. Students study complex behavior by decomposing a sequence into its constituents, represented by the rows of actions, and categorize each constituent, indicated in the label attached to the frame. Their analyses are structured into Observations (what we can see in the data) and Interpretations (what we infer from these observations) a key distinction in the scientific practice students are learning.

Again this provides both structure and problematizing. The structure prompts students to perform the subtasks of observation an interpretation. In addition, forcing them to categorize their observations pushes students to articulate their understanding and represent it in the artifact. The explicit distinction between observation and interpretation facilitates discussions geared at understanding the relationship between the two.

The following episode illustrates how the structure of the artifacts forces students to grapple with disciplinary content (Golan, Kyza, Reiser, & Edelson, 2001). This debate was recorded from a group of three 7th grade students who were watching a clip featuring two Golden Lion Tamarin monkeys eating a grape. One of the monkeys (the female) had the grape first and then the male took it away from her, jumped over her and moved to another branch. The students were arguing about the part in which the male Tamarin jumped over the female. Two of the students believed that was an instantiation of the "mount" behavior, while the third student did not agree. In essence this argument was about what "mount" means, is it merely contact between two animals or more than that?

S2: What did we observe as mount? (reading)

S1: No, that one is yours because I totally disagree with you guys!

S2: Good for you! Come on man, you see in the clip it just looks mounting, they got on top of each other.

S1: No, he jumped *over* her.

S3: She, she jumped over him…

S1: Whatever, she jumped over him.

S2: I know, but still, the contact…

S1: She jumped over him, doesn't matter, contact is not what you guys are talking about. Shoot, you are talking about like getting on top of each other and staying on top for a couple of minutes.

S3: No, no, no. We are not talking about that!

S2: No, no, not that, no, no, that's not. See, look, watch this contact. Boom! Look at that!

S1: Jumping *over*! *Over!*

This argument was finally settled by one of the researchers explaining to the students what the behavior "mount" means in the domain of animal behavior. This discussion surfaced students' implicit definitions of the behavior, an important step in learning to apply a categorization scheme. Again making these decisions as part of their analysis, and clearly representing these distinctions in the artifacts they create provoked these and similar arguments, surfacing disagreements and eventually refining students' definitions of these behaviors.

It is interesting that this disagreement had been brewing for some time in the group, but it had not been addressed. Had the group merely been asked to report a summary of their observations, it is possible this discussion would not have occurred. Forcing students to articulate their understanding and represent it explicitly using menu item labels and the Observation and Interpretation structure finally surfaced the differences in interpretation and provoked these productive discussions.

CONCLUSIONS

I have argued that scaffolding may occur through two complementary mechanisms, structuring and problematizing. Most accounts of scaffolding define support that helps students proceed through tasks. However, given the importance of connecting students' problem solving work to disciplinary content, skills, and strategies, it may also be important to provoke issues in students, veering them off the course of non-reflective work, and forcing them to confront key disciplinary ideas in their solutions to problems. The artifacts students use and create can be designed to map onto important disciplinary ideas and strategies, thereby problematizing these ideas as students use the tool to work through the task and represent the products of their work.

ACKNOWLEDGMENTS

This paper builds upon the design research of the BGuILE group at Northwestern University, and I am grateful to conversations with my colleagues Iris Tabak, Brian Smith, William Sandoval, Ravit Golan, and Elena Kyza about principles of scaffolding in learning environments. I am also grateful to my colleagues in the KDI/ASSESS group for discussion of these ideas, Joseph Krajcik, Danny Edelson, Elliot Soloway, Chris Quintana, and Betsy Davis, and to Bruce Sherin for many fruitful discussions. This research was funded by the James S. McDonnell Foundation, Cognitive Studies for Educational Practice, and by the National Science Foundation under grants #REC-9720383 to the Center for Learning Technologies in Urban Schools and #REC-9980055 to the KDI/ASSESS project. The opinions expressed herein are those of the author and not necessarily those of these foundations. For additional information about BGuILE software or curricula see: http://www.letus.org/bguile/

REFERENCES

Bannon, L. J., & Bødker, S. (1987). Beyond the interface: Encountering artifacts in use. In J. M. Carroll (Ed.), *Interfacing thought: Cognitive aspects of human-computer interaction* (pp. 227-253). Cambridge, MA: MIT Press.

Bell, B., Bareiss, R., & Beckwith, R. (1994). Sickle Cell Counselor: A prototype goal-based scenario for instruction in a museum. *The Journal of the Learning Sciences.*

Blumenfeld, P. C., Soloway, E., Marx, R. W., Krajcik, J. S., Guzdial, M., & Palincsar, A. (1991). Motivating project-based learning: Sustaining the doing, supporting the learning. *Educational Psychologist, 26*, 369-398.

Chi, M. T. H., Feltovich, P., & Glaser, R. (1981). Categorization and representation of physics problems by experts and novices. *Cognitive Science, 5*, 121-152.

Cognition and Technology Group. (1990). The Jasper series as an example of anchored instruction: Theory, program description, and assessment data. *Educational Psychologist, 27*, 291-315.

Collins, A., & Brown, J. S. (1988). The computer as a tool for learning through reflection. In H. Mandl & A. Lesgold (Eds.), *Learning issues for intelligent tutoring systems* (pp. 1-18). New York: Springer-Verlag.

Collins, A., Brown, J. S., & Newman, S. E. (1989). Cognitive apprenticeship: Teaching the crafts of reading, writing, and mathematics. In L. B. Resnick (Ed.), *Knowing, learning, and instruction: Essays in honor of Robert Glaser* (pp. 453-494). Hillsdale, NJ: Erlbaum.

Davis, E. A., & Linn, M. C. (2000). Scaffolding students' knowledge integration: prompts for reflection in KIE. *International Journal of Science Education, 22*, 819-837.

Edelson, D. C. (2001). Learning-for-use: A framework for integrating content and process learning in the design of inquiry activities. *Journal of Research in Science Teaching, 38*, 355-385.

Edelson, D. C., Gordin, D. N., & Pea, R. D. (1999). Addressing the challenges of inquiry-based learning through technology and curriculum design. *The Journal of the Learning Sciences, 8*, 391-450.

Golan, R., Kyza, E. A., Reiser, B. J., & Edelson, D. C. (2001). Structuring the task of behavioral analysis with software scaffolds, *Paper presented at the Annual Meeting of the National Association of Research in Science Teaching*. St. Louis, MO.

Guzdial, M. (1994). Software-realized scaffolding to facilitate programming for science learning. *Interactive Learning Environments, 4*, 1-44.

Hiebert, J., Carpenter, T. P., Fennema, E., Fuson, K., Human, P., Murray, H., Olivier, A., & Wearne, D. (1996). Problem solving as a basis for reform in curriculum and instruction: The case of mathematics. *Educational Researcher, 25*(4), 12-21.

Hollan, J., Hutchins, E., & Kirsh, D. (2000). Distributed cognition: Toward a new foundation for human-computer interaction research. *ACM Transactions on Computer-Human Interaction., 7*, 174–196.

Hollan, J. D., Bederson, B. B., & Helfman, J. (1997). Information visualization. In M. G. Helander & T. K. Landauer & V. Prabhu (Eds.), *Handbook of human-computer interaction* (pp. 33-48). Essex, UK: Elsevier Science Publishers Ltd.

Hutchins, E. (1995). *Cognition in the wild*. Cambridge, MA: MIT Press.

Hutchins, E., Hollan, J. D., & Norman, D. A. (1986). Direct manipulation interfaces. In D. A. Norman & S. Draper (Eds.), *User centered system design: New perspectives in human-computer interaction*. Hillsdale, NJ: Erlbaum.

Jackson, S. L., Krajcik, J., & Soloway, E. (1998). The design of guided learning-adaptable scaffolding in interactive learning environments. In C.-M. Karat & A. Lund & J. Coutaz & J. Karat (Eds.), *Proceedings of CHI 98: Human Factors in Computing Systems*, (pp. 187-194). Reading, MA: Addison-Wesley.

Klahr, D., & Dunbar, K. (1988). Dual space search during scientific reasoning. *Cognitive Science, 12*, 1-48.

Koedinger, K. R., & Anderson, J. R. (1993). Reifying implicit planning in geometry: Guidelines for model-based intelligent tutoring system design. In S. P. Lajoie & S. J. Derry (Eds.), *Computers as cognitive tools*. Hillsdale, NJ: Erlbaum.

Loh, B., Reiser, B. J., Radinsky, J., Edelson, D. C., Gomez, L. M., & Marshall, S. (2001). Developing reflective inquiry practices: A case study of software, the teacher, and students. In K. Crowley & C. D. Schunn & T. Okada (Eds.), *Designing for science: Implications from everyday, classroom, and professional settings* (pp. 279-323). Mahwah, NJ: Erlbaum.

Merrill, D. C., Reiser, B. J., Merrill, S. K., & Landes, S. (1995). Tutoring: Guided learning by doing. *Cognition and Instruction*, 315-372.

Norman, D. A. (1987). Cognitive artifacts. In J. M. Carroll (Ed.), *Interfacing thought: Cognitive aspects of human-computer interaction* (pp. 17-38). Cambridge, MA: MIT Press.

Olson, S., & Loucks-Horsley, S. (Eds.). (2000). *Inquiry and the national science education standards: A guide for teaching and learning*. Washington, DC: National Academy Press.

Perkins, D. (1998). What is understanding? In M. S. Wiske (Ed.), *Teaching for understanding: Linking research with practice*. San Francisco, CA: Jossey-Bass Publishers.

Quintana, C. (2001). *Symphony: A case study for exploring and describing methods and guidelines for learner-centered design*. Unpublished Ph.D. dissertation, University of Michigan.

Quintana, C., Eng, J., Carra, A., Wu, H.-K., & Soloway, E. (1999). Symphony: A case study in extending learner-centered design through process space analysis. In *Proceedings of CHI 99 Conference on Human Factors in Computing Systems*, (pp. 473-480).

Reiser, B. J., Tabak, I., Sandoval, W. A., Smith, B. K., Steinmuller, F., & Leone, A. J. (2001). BGuILE: Strategic and conceptual scaffolds for scientific inquiry in biology classrooms. In S. M. Carver & D. Klahr (Eds.), *Cognition and instruction: Twenty-five years of progress* (pp. 263-305). Mahwah, NJ: Erlbaum.

Rogoff, B. (1990). *Apprenticeship in thinking: Cognitive development in social context*. New York, NY: Oxford University Press.

Roschelle, J. (1992). Learning by collaboration: Convergent conceptual change. *The Journal of the Learning Sciences, 2*, 235-276.

Salomon, G., Perkins, D. N., & Globerson, T. (1991). Partners in cognition: Extending human intelligence with intelligent technologies. *Educational Researcher, 20*(3), 2-9.

Sandoval, W. A. (1998). *Inquire to explain: Structuring inquiry around explanation construction in a technology-supported biology curriculum.* Unpublished Ph.D. Dissertation, Northwestern University, Evanston, IL.

Schank, R. C., Fano, A., Bell, B., & Jona, M. (1994). The design of Goal-Based Scenarios. *The Journal of the Learning Sciences, 3*, 305-345.

Schauble, L., Glaser, R., Duschl, R. A., Schulze, S., & John, J. (1995). Students' understanding of the objectives and procedures of experimentation in the science classroom. *The Journal of the Learning Sciences, 4*, 131-166.

Schauble, L., Klopfer, L. E., & Raghavan, K. (1991). Students' transition from an engineering model to a science model of experimentation. *Journal of Research in Science Teaching, 28*, 859-882.

Singer, J., Marx, R. W., Krajcik, J., & Chambers, J. C. (2000). Constructing extended inquiry projects: Curriculum materials for science education reform. *Educational Psychologist, 35*, 165-178.

Smith, B. K., & Reiser, B. J. (1998). National Geographic unplugged: Designing interactive nature films for classrooms. In C.-M. Karat & A. Lund & J. Coutaz & J. Karat (Eds.), *Proceedings of CHI 98*, (pp. 424-431). New York: ACM Press.

Tabak, I., & Reiser, B. J. (1997). Complementary roles of software-based scaffolding and teacher-student interactions in inquiry learning. In R. Hall & N. Miyake & N. Enyedy (Eds.), *Proceedings of Computer Support for Collaborative Learning '97*, (pp. 289-298). Toronto, Canada.:

Tabak, I., Smith, B. K., Sandoval, W. A., & Reiser, B. J. (1996). Combining general and domain-specific strategic support for biological inquiry. In C. Frasson & G. Gauthier & A. Lesgold (Eds.), *Intelligent Tutoring Systems: Third International Conference, ITS '96*, (pp. 288-296). Montreal, Canada: Springer-Verlag.

Vygotsky, L. S. (1978). *Mind in society: The development of the higher psychological processes* (A. Kozulin, Trans.). Cambridge, MA: Harvard University Press.

Williams, S. M. (1992). Putting case-based instruction into context: examples from legal and medical education. *The Journal of the Learning Sciences, 2*, 367-427.

H. (PEDAGOGY TRACK): TEACHERS AND CSCL

Complexity, Harmony and Diversity of Learning in Collaborative E-learning Continuing Professional Development Groups

David McConnell

University of Sheffield

d.mcconnell@shef.ac.uk

ABSTRACT

In this paper I examine the learning dynamics of three collaborative, e-learning continuing professional development groups: specifically the degree of complexity, harmony and diversity in them. Two of the groups worked harmoniously, and successfully produced a collective end product. The other group exhibited extreme anxiety and division, and required extra resources from its members in order to sustain itself and produce its' collective end product. Anxiety became a major focus for this group, which had the effect of diverting it from effective collective production. I use these differences as a point of departure in order to consider the place of identity, control, ontological security and guilt in collaborative e-learning groups.

Keywords: e-learning, collaboration, groups, identity, control, ontological security, guilt, community.

INTRODUCTION

Collaborative e-learning in continuing professional development (CPD) higher education contexts is relatively un-common. Distance learning has long been a source of education provision in CPD contexts, but the shift to a new generation of distance learning involving course delivery entirely via the Web and Internet, and which involves collaborative group work as the main pedagogical method, is slow to emerge.

In this paper, I draw on research into a two year, part-time professional development e-learning Masters in Education course which is delivered entirely online and which has a pedagogic design focusing on collaborative and cooperative group work. The focus of the course is on e-learning itself. Further information on the background to the design of the course can be found in McConnell, 2001.

Participants are organised into small groups of between 7-10 members with a tutor. They work together for periods of between 16 and 32 weeks using Web-CT asynchronous forums and synchronous chat rooms for their communications and group work.

The collaborative issues and problems which the groups work on are characterised by the following:

- Complex: The problems and issues researched by these groups are defined by the groups themselves through processes of negotiation. They are usually complex, often ill-defined problems which are fertile ground for the production of mutual understandings and the construction of "shared resolutions" (Schon, 1983).
- Have a personal and professional focus: They are important to the members of the group, arising from concerns and interests they may have about their professional practice. The outcomes associated with the group work will be of benefit to the members in their professional practice.
- Require negotiation and communication to understand them: because the issues researched are invariably complex and ill-defined, the members of each group have to engage in considerable communication in order to understand them and in order to negotiate changes in their perception of the 'problem' and its resolution as their work progresses. Communication is both task oriented and socially centred. The groups function both as learning communities (Pedler, 1981; Snell, 1989) which have an interest in sharing, supporting and learning collaboratively in a social context, and communities of practice (Wenger, 1998) in which members are actively constructing understandings of what it means to be professional e-learning practitioners.
- Require an action research approach to progress them: The groups are encouraged to view their research and learning as "action research" (Carr & Kemmis, 1986; Elden & Chisholm, 1993; Whitehead, 1989; Winter, 1989), and they are introduced to the concept of action research in an earlier e-seminar. This provides them with a model of how to act together, which helps guide them in their work.

- Require a journey of learning: There are no specific pre-defined learning outcomes. Each group embarks on a learning journey which requires collaboration but which does not define in exact detail how they should work together or what the outcomes of their learning should be. In this respect, the groups are following a long tradition of adult-learning which supports openness and exploration (Boot & Hodgson, 1987; Cunningham, 1987; Harris, 1987), and which has a history in experiential learning groups (Reynolds, 1994; Davis & Denning, 2000).
- Involve a high degree of reflexivity: Learning in these groups is highly experiential, and the groups are therefore encouraged to be reflective and to use this as a source of learning (Boud and Walker, 1998; Moon, 1999).

There are usually significant differences in the learning dynamics of these groups, and in the way they negotiate and carry out their collaborative work, and in the way they produce their final product. It is some of these differences which I will examine here.

METHODOLOGY

I examined the activities of three e-groups which were working at the same time, but separately. In carrying out their work, members of each group produced approximately one thousand separate entries in their own asynchronous forums, which when printed amounts to at least 200 pages of text per group. Each group also used the Web-CT synchronous chat facility and as an example, members of one group participated in 15 synchronous chat sessions, each lasting at least one hour, which amount to over 100 pages of text.

I analysed the transcripts of the textual communications of the groups using a grounded theory approach (Glaser & Strauss, 1968; Strauss & Corbin, 1990). I started by reading the transcripts and making annotations in the margins indicating different features of the group's work such as shared ideas, disclosure, planning for chat sessions, summaries of chat sessions, the production of documents, discussions of the documents, joking, sharing professional practice, sharing resources, the production of timetables of planned work, reference to stakeholders and so on. As part of the procedure I also made analytical notes to myself highlighting possible interesting issues for investigation and analysis.

As the entries of each member of the group is numbered in the transcripts (along with dates and times and other contextual information), I was able to follow the various threads of the discussions with relative ease.

This first reading of the transcripts allowed me to 'get a feel' for the group's work and to immerse myself in the data. By a process of progressive focusing (Parlett, 1981) and constant comparison (Strauss & Corbin, 1990) issues of relevance and potential importance concerning the nature of the groups' work became apparent. I then looked in depth at these emerging issues, re-read the margin annotations and notes to myself, moving back and forward from the text of the transcripts to my notes. I then made a new set of notes on the particular issue and proceeded to engage in a new round of analysis in order to illuminate the issue in some detail (Parlett, 1981).

This qualitative research approach allows the emergence of sensitizing concepts, which are:

"...less specific suggestive ideas about what might be potentially fruitful to examine and consider, an emergent meaningful vocabulary that alerts the researcher to promising avenues of investigation" (Clarke, 1997).

rather than the generation of definitive concepts from data abstracted from their social milieus. The purpose is to remain close to the natural world being researched.

FINDINGS

In this section I present the findings relating to one group (group two), and in the following discussion section, I examine the degree of complexity, harmony and diversity in the three e-learning groups.

Two of the groups (groups one and three) worked harmoniously, and successfully produced a collective end product, which they were happy with. The other group (group two) exhibited extreme anxiety and division, and required extra resources from its members in order to sustain itself and produce it's collective end product. Anxiety became a major inward looking focus for this group, which had the effect of diverting it from effective collective production. It did produce a collaborative product, but one which the group was not entirely happy with. The patterns of work and communication of the three groups can be summarised as:

Group One: characterised by

Negotiation

Discussion

Agreement

Work and research

Collaboration

Production

Group Two: characterised by

Struggle –over leadership; over project focus and group processes

Argument

Changing minds and direction

Personality and identity

Anxiety

Learning conflict

Closed-ness: use faxes, chats, telephone, email as well as open forums. But this has not been agreed by members, but brought about by division and struggle to be productive

High introspection which "becomes" a major component of their project

Group Three: characterised by

Negotiation

Support for each other

Openness

Discussion

Agreement

Work and research

Collaboration

Production

Patterns of group two

In analysing the work of group two, several patterns of communication and group dynamics can be discerned which illustrate some of the problems they faced:

1.Members not replying to requests or questions from other members.

Throughout the life of the group it was evident that members often did not reply to requests and questions from other members. Analysis of the group's work shows that this involved:

Members posting summaries of decisions made by sub-groups in the asynchronous forums, and inviting (by name) those not present to comment on them, with not response from them.

A member taking time to reflect on the dynamics of the group and post her thoughts on why there were no replies, and receiving no response.

A member trying to get the group to discuss how they are working together, with no response.

Members posting sets of possible guidelines which had been devised by sub-groups for improving communications within the group as a whole – with no response from others

A member trying to summarise where they are in their group work, with no response (she was not asked to provide the summary, but in other groups when this happened members were always grateful and acknowledged the entry).

A member inviting others to brainstorm ideas about group effectiveness, with no-one participating

A member posting the final plan for the group's collaborative work after discussion in a group chat session: no one responds, and one person disagrees with its contents.

2. Anxiety

Members refer to themselves as being anxious, or to the group itself being in a state of anxiety over its work, including:

Perception that some members are deliberately contriving to produce division in order to examine its effects on the group.

Constant questioning and reflection about their own group processes

Their "struggle" (a term often used by some participants) to effectively collaborate.

Exclusion experienced by some – others making every effort to be inclusive

3. Strong personalities

Some individuals taking very strong views on issues and not being willing to negotiate around them.

Disagreement amongst individual members, sometimes extreme

Differences in perceived level of previous experience and expertise, leading to perceptions that some members were better equipped than others to fulfil certain tasks, or had greater experience and knowledge.

4. Decisions only being made by some members

In the early stages of the group's work, it proved impossible to find appropriate times when everyone could meet in the synchronous chat sessions to discuss their work and make decisions. Sub-groups met in the chat rooms and later posted in the asynchronous forum the outcomes of their discussions and any decisions made so that those not present could have their say. This proved unworkable as those not present began to question the focus and outcomes of the chat sessions, which often led to feelings of frustration by those who had attended. Decisions made had to be re-negotiated, which took time and also caused members to feel that little progress was being made.

5. Changing ground rules and focus of project

In addition, the interpretation of decisions made in chat sessions were often questioned afterwards in the asynchronous forums by some of those who had taken part in them. It seemed that the ground rules were being changed. This sometimes led to ill feeling and a degree of mistrust. Agreement on the focus of the group project was a major example of this. Considerable time and effort was put into negotiating the focus in several chat sessions, and on several occasions it seemed that the group had successfully negotiated what they should work on, only for the interpretation of that decision to be challenged afterwards in the asynchronous forum. The group never satisfactorily resolved this (and it emerged frequently throughout their period together as a point of argument and disagreement). They finally agreed that each member of the group should work on their own professional interests (according to how they individually interpreted that), and report back to the group on progress and findings in two/three weeks time. This is when the sub-groups were formed. At the end of this period the group opened a new thread to discuss their findings, and at this point they did begin to work collaboratively as a whole group.

6. The role of the Tutor

The tutor's role in the group was for some a source of anxiety. Reference was made to how tutors in other groups were participating by way of pointing out how their tutor "should" be working with them. However, there was division over the group's view of the role of the tutor. Some members were critical and looked for "stronger" tutor guidance. Others took the opportunity to publicly thank the tutor for his support, signalling that they thought he was doing a good job.

The lack of effective group functioning in the early stages of the group's work caused some members to seek "outside" (ie tutor) intervention to tell them what to do. This had the effect of forcing the tutor to make some important decisions on behalf of the group which were not therefore owned by the group. For example, at one point the tutor suggested that the group should have a manager, chosen from its members to help steer the group through its work. At another point he suggested that, because they had spent an inordinate amount of time negotiating their differences, they should "just get on with it" and work towards producing their product. Both these decisions were perhaps understandable given the circumstances, yet they had the effect of unwittingly dividing the group even further. Someone did take on the role of group manager, but was largely ignored by most members. The group members did "get on with it", but did so in their sub-groups, perhaps using the tutor's directive as a way of avoiding facing up to the divisions in the group.

7. The role of "closed" chat sessions

Compared to the other two groups, this group used the synchronous chat facility extensively. Chat sessions were very important in the life of this group, and a great deal of the work of the group was conducted in them compared with their use of the asynchronous forums. As we have already seen, not everyone could attend the chat sessions. So on some days one sub-group would meet in the morning and make certain decisions. Those who could not attend would often meet later in the day and try to 'catch up' on the work of the first group. This often had the effect of making those who attended the second chat session feel that they were working "at the tail end", having to address and essentially agree to an agenda devised by the other group. These sub-groups also used other "closed" forms of communication such as faxes, telephone calls and emails.

By contrast, the other two groups carried out the vast majority of their communications in the open forums where everyone could participate or follow what was happening.

COMPARISON OF THE GROUPS

In this section I draw-on the differences between what might be termed the traditionally "successful" groups and the "anxious" group as a point of departure in order to consider issues of identity, control, ontological security and guilt in collaborative e-learning groups.

Harmony, communication and conflict

Groups one and three have a high need to collaborate harmoniously. Their starting point is to make each group a really "good" collaborative group which works harmoniously, and they put considerable time and effort into ensuring this happens. They deliberately address the need to support differences and mutual recognition. They actively involve everyone in decision-making, group processes and production. They work in ways that are open and accessible to all members and make reference to this being an important requirement for success. They talk of "really wanting the collaborative project to work". They could perhaps be described as being "dutiful".

Group two supports difference but also uses it as a source of conflict. They bring "differences" to the forefront and use them constantly in negotiations and discussions. However, as a group they cannot seem to reconcile some important differences in a way that helps them work together and be productive. They therefore sub-divide to achieve their tasks. They also bring a high degree of closure to their group processes by the sub-groups using faxes, telephone, email and so on within the sub-group rather than conducting their work in the open forums, therefore making it impossible for others to participate and know what is going on. They never talk of "really wanting their collaborative project to work" as the other two groups do. They are perhaps less concerned with "duty" and less likely therefore to collaborate as a group and more likely to diverge, confront and question. Their high introspection causes them to constantly refer inwardly to themselves in a struggle to understand why they are working in the way they do. Therefore, experiential learning is high and the opportunity to investigate group dynamics is high. In a sense, this becomes the focus of this group's project. To some degree this group "contrives" (as some members put it) to produce its final product.

All three groups at some point divide their work so that sub-groups can focus on accomplishing particular parts of the overall product. Groups one and three formally and openly divide and come to an agreement about how the sub-tasks relate to the final product. They support each other in their sub-group work, which is open and accessible to all members of the group. Group two works in sub-groups by default – perhaps as a mechanism for avoiding conflict in the large group. They cannot easily find a way of working as a community. It seems people therefore form liaisons in order to deal with the lack of agreement over the focus of their project. Collaboration in the sub-groups is carried out in closed circles, with little communication between sub-groups or, at times, within the large group. There is some evidence of the sub-groups deliberately keeping their work closed from others.

However, group two does see itself *as a group* – there is evidence of them comparing themselves to the other two groups and using them and their work as a reference point for themselves.

Reflexivity within groups

Each group is highly reflective about its work and learning processes, but in group two reflection becomes something of an obsession, and actually becomes a major focus for the group without them collectively agreeing to it being so. It could be argued that in the absence of an agreed focus, this group "naturally" (because of its particular circumstances and dynamics) chooses its focus to be itself.

Considerable time, thought and energy is devoted to this by:

- the group struggling to understand itself. It has resource to communicating about its own dynamics as a way of explaining what is happening to itself, justifying its actions, controlling members actions, comparing itself to the other groups, accusing members about various aspects of their project work and generally ruminating on the sense of distrust within the group.
- Sub-groups devoting time in their chat sessions to trying to understand the group as a whole
- Individuals choosing to focus their research on finding out about group processes and dynamics

Contemporary psychological thinking about distrust in collaborative groups suggests that rumination and reflection is not always valuable in producing clarity regarding difficult situations or with producing insights into how to cope with them:

"..it seems reasonable to hypothesize that rumination about others' motives and intentions in situations where concerns about trust already loom large will increase individuals' distrust and suspicion of others' behavior. In particular, one might argue that the more individuals ruminate about the intentions and motives underlying the behavior of other actors with whom they are interdependent in a trust dilemma situation, the greater their tendency to make more sinister attributions regarding their behavior." (Kramer, 1999 p172).

The balance between taking time to ruminate and reflect, and that of leaving aside their differences and "moving on" cannot be an easy one to determine when a collaborative learning group is in the middle of a difficult dynamic. This group could have chosen not to spend time ruminating and reflecting. They could just have got on with the "task" of producing a final product. But by focusing on themselves and their struggle to collaborate I think they show a real and genuine concern for each other. To ignore the issues they are facing would be tantamount to saying that they did not care. But there is evidence throughout their discussions that, at the individual level, they do care. They are trying to look after themselves. This is evidenced in part by them continuing to communicate and not give up. They even remark on this themselves, showing that they have a high degree of self-awareness. They do share and discuss, they produce work, and they never talk of splitting up or giving up.

Group identity and self-identity

In his analysis of the self and society, Giddens (1991) suggests that:

"Self-identity (...) is not something that is just given, as a result of the continuities of the individual's action-system, but something that has to be routinely created and sustained in the reflexive activities of the individual" (Giddens, 1991, p52).

Drawing on the work of the psychoanalyst R.D.Laing, Giddens suggests that one way of analysing self-identity is to consider those whose identity is fractured or disabled. From such a viewpoint, the ontologically insecure individual may display one or more of the following characteristics. They

- lack a consistent feeling of biographical continuity; they cannot sustain a continuous narrative about themselves.
- are in a constant state of anxiety, which prevents them from carrying out practical actions
- fail to develop trust in themselves and their identity, and often subject themselves to constant self-scrutiny

Can the concept of self-identity and the analytical framework provided above be applied at the group level? For example, can a group be described as being "anxious"? The analysis of the work of the three groups shows that they are all highly reflexive: they are aware of themselves as groups and address their histories, development and their future. The anxiety amongst the members of group two may work towards producing a sense of the group that is fractured or disabled. Participants subject their behaviour and thoughts to constant scrutiny, which at times becomes obsessive. This group is obsessed about questioning itself in a way that none of the other groups are. The other groups do reflect on their processes and procedures and use this as a source of learning. But at times group two is very single-minded about this, and it pervades the life of the group. The group never seems to get over its anxiety about itself, and the members constantly discuss and scrutinise themselves and their actions.

What does group two feel in danger of? Not achieving its objectives? Not "working" as a group? Not "fitting" into the required model of an effective group (whatever that is)?

The group doesn't seem to know itself – a condition which Giddens (1991) suggests is necessary for ontological security. It seems to be struggling to find some kind of collective identity: some kind of ongoing narrative (Giddens p54) of itself. In a real sense it does not know who it is or where it is going. This seems to be a major source of anxiety. Members of the sub-groups try to work out how they came to be where they are, and how they can bring about change and development so that they can influence where the group collectively is going. But this is perhaps inevitably doomed to failure as long as it is the work of the sub-groups and not the work of the group as a whole. Factions, no matter how well intentioned and how insightful they are, cannot mend the fractured group. As long as some individual members are not involved in the project of making the group "better", it is probably the case that the group will not function well as a collective. If some members of the group are with-holding their engagement, then the other members of the group will either

- carry on the group's work without those people, or
- spend a lot of time and energy trying to understand why those people are engaging in the way they are, whilst at the same time not functioning as a group. They can function as sub-groups and get some of their work done, but the division will make it impossible for them to achieve a collective group product.

In the other groups there is a high sense of self-identity as a group. They seem to have a strong ongoing narrative, which they keep active throughout the collaborative project. These groups are inclusive and mainly work in harmony. Sub-groups evolve from collective work and discussion as a source of production which feeds into the main group task of producing the final product. Divisions, differences of opinion and so on exist, but the groups want to achieve and be successful, so they are handled with considerable understanding and willingness to be inclusive and supportive. The focus on the well being of the members of the groups seems to ensure this, as well as each group's need to succeed. These two groups work at establishing their identity, constantly creating and sustaining it through reflexive processes.

Control and ontological security

Implicit in the actions of groups one and three is a high degree of "routinised control" (Giddens, 1991 p56) which helps protect the members of these two groups against themselves. Their high need to collaborate and be productive within the agreed parameters of the course requirements may mean that each member monitors themself so as to prevent schism and division within the group. Competition and disagreement do exist, but are supported in subtle ways by processes of negotiation, give and take and reciprocity. Members are willing to "give" so long as that is taken as a criterion for existence in the group and for successful production.

Self-control can be a powerful mechanism in these two "successful" groups. The language used in these two groups is perhaps an indicator of this: it is always positive and the group members tell themselves that they are working well. They say they are collaborating and succeeding in their work. They sustain an ongoing narrative about collaboration and success, which is largely absent in group two. They believe what they say, and it has the effect of sustaining that belief. They trust each other in these circumstances. This helps produce a sense of ease within the group about who they are and how they are working. The effort needed to sustain the group is therefore greatly reduced, and with it any anxiety about the group is reduced. All of this helps the performance of the group.

On the other hand, the members of group two tell themselves they are not doing this and perhaps therefore reduce the chances of it happening? They come to believe that they cannot collaborate successfully. They cannot seem to begin to develop a positive ongoing narrative about themselves, let alone sustain it throughout their time together. This keeps the level of anxiety high within the group, which in turn has the effect of requiring extra resources from the members in their efforts to sustain the group. Their anxiety is a source of constant examination and questioning which diverts them from effective collective production.

There may be a need to control in order to produce harmony and effectiveness. The patterns of the work of the groups may indicate the ways in which control is established and maintained.

The conventionally "successful" groups discuss and support each other. Members do not go off and do their own thing. They do however work as sub-groups, but only after they have been given 'permission' to do so by the whole group. At other times the enthusiasm to achieve and be productive and the interest inherent in their collective work makes it possible for individuals to legitimately go off and work separately and not be punished or ignored for doing so. Group two does not easily perform and has not developed routines conducive to sustaining the group and its work. At the end of the collaborative work, this group is still trying to develop its routines. It is still negotiating with itself.

The way group two functions helps throw light on how the other two groups function, and vice versa. No one group is "typical", "correct" or "normal". Groups one and three may achieve collaborative and collective products which they are pleased with and which meet the requirements of the course. But group two learns in different ways: it learns about *itself*, and it learns about the dynamics of group-learning in difficult circumstances. Members may not choose to view this *as learning* or as being worthwhile, though several of them do in fact see the learning potential of this and say so. The members of this group may in fact experientially learn so much about collaborative group work that they are better equipped to participate and survive in future groups. Disharmony and division open up the group processes and make them available to the members for scrutiny in ways that do not occur in more harmonious and less divided groups. The experience may be difficult and challenging, but the potential to learn from it (if taken) can be high.

Outsiders

The MEd functions as a large learning community, with activities, structures and mechanisms which involve all participants outside of the particular groups. The concept of outsiders can function in at least two ways in this context:

1. when participants become members of a group, each group exists on its own, outside the community. Each group can "visit" the other groups and see how they are working, and compare their own group to the other groups. It is therefore possible for a group to feel like an outsider in this context.
2. individuals in each group can also feel like an outsider in their group, lacking the necessary personal and social relations to feel part of the group

We know that outsiders are able to "look- in" with insight through the experience of being at the edge (Goffman, 1971) They are part of something larger, yet set apart from it. They struggle to exist in the group and produce something worthwhile, but at the same time they are outside the group and view it as an outsider. This may also apply to groups, as well as to individuals. So in this virtual learning environment, group two can simultaneously carry on with its work towards producing a final product while also looking at itself in a search for some kind of identity. This e-learning medium allows this group to continue with their work whilst also continuing to try and understand themselves.

Defensivess is another trait of this group and another aspect of being an outsider. Some individuals are highly defensive, which is one way of protecting oneself against anxiety. Similarly, not contributing to the groups' work and not participating in discussions, and ignoring others' entries and questions directed at you are other ways of keeping one's identity. By these mechanisms, anxiety is kept to a minimum and to a level that can be dealt with. By choosing how often, and in what ways, one contributes to the group's work, you are staying in control (and to some extent, controlling the work of other members too) and therefore reducing the possibility of anxiety of one kind ie that which arises from confrontation and argument. This is, however, likely to produce other kinds of anxieties, such as feelings of guilt about not participating and about the effects of non-participation on others.

Guilt, trust and the community

Clearly the emotions of the members of these groups play an important part in shaping the work of the groups. Anxiety is present in all the groups to some extent, but is pervasive in group two. The members of this group talk of their "struggle" to collaborate, and at some time or other they all indicate a certain degree of guilt about the way they are interacting and behaving. Their identity does not match up to the implicit and explicit contract of collaborative learning ie to work together through processes of negotiation and participation. The existence of feelings of guilt pre-supposes people going against norms sanctioned by the group or community (Giddens, 1991). The very presence of guilt therefore suggests the existence of some kind of community.

At times trust is lost in group two between certain individuals. This has the effect of unsettling the group by raising questions about trust generally. Although it is never actually mentioned openly, a reading of the communication transcripts indicates an implicit lack of trust between one particularly strong-minded, and therefore significant, member and the others. Trust is present in the sub-groups, but not across all individuals. Their language and actions are indices of this. In the other two groups, trust does seem to exist across individuals. Members are loyal to each other. They do not abandon decisions made collectively after the event. We have seen that in group two there is a pattern of decisions being made only to be questioned afterwards, or abandoned altogether. To the members of this group, this feels like being betrayed. Groups one and three work hard at developing a sense of trust, and at individuals winning the trust of others in the groups. They are very open about themselves, their interests, worries and concerns. They actively support each other by making every effort to "listen" and respond quickly. They offer to share the workload. They show commitment to the members of the group and to ensuring that the group sustains itself and carries out its job of production. These are all characteristics of people with a well developed senses of identity (Giddens, 1991). These groups could be characterised as being highly sociable.

In group two, being sociable is openly questioned by the significant member. She says she is not interested in socialising or in getting to know the others. She is only concerned with getting on with the job of producing a collaborative product. This admission has profound effects on the other members of the group, and as we have seen, acts to stop them being productive. At the same time this person says she feels like an outsider, and talks of the group being made up of 'cliques' and being apart from her.

Although liking others, socialising and getting on with them is not always a necessary criterion for successful cooperation (Axelrod, 1990), it does seem that in the context of an adult learning environment such as this, there is a real need for a sense of trust and community. Trust is created by people taking time to listen to each other and to nurture an atmosphere of caring (Giddens, 1991). This helps produce feelings of security within the members of the groups. In trustful situations people are more likely to take risks with their learning, to push themselves and others beyond their present boundaries. This can be highly developmental, as well as more likely to produce useful insights into the groups' learning processes.

END PIECE

In this paper, I have attempted to examine issues of self-identity and group-identity in the context of e-learning groups, drawing-on concepts and frameworks derived from the examination of individuals in modern society. This has, I think, been a worthwhile exercise, which has offered interesting and potentially useful insights into the ways in which e-groups function.

Collaborative e-learning groups exhibit complex dynamics and diverse learning processes and outcomes. Pedagogical designers who ask learners to work in such groups need to be aware of this. It is all too easy to design-in group work in the assumption that the technology itself will "look after" the work of the group. This is unlikely to be the case (Mantovani, 1994).

One reviewer of a draft of this paper suggested I should conclude by suggesting ways in which to "better co-ordinate" the "problematic" group to bring it on the "right path". I am grateful for this reviewer's comments: they made me think hard about the issue. I am, however, reluctant to end the paper with a list of conclusions, or a set of procedures for the better co-ordination of the "problematic" group. To do so would be to suggest that as an observer I can easily translate my examination of the work of these groups into some general, pedagogical formula which will ensure that all such future groups work harmoniously and on the "right path". I am not entirely sure what the "right path" is, or should be, in such collaborative e-learning groups.

As I stated at the beginning of this paper, the collaborative issues and problems which these groups work-on are complex and are not defined in advance, but defined by the groups themselves as they proceed. It seems to me that the particular context of each group, the people involved, their different purposes and expectations and their personal and professional backgrounds and concerns are all likely to be influential in how the groups work. To suggest that we might be able to define in advance how each group should work, and provide a set of procedures that make that happen, is surely an impossible task? It is in the nature of experiential group-work that there will be diversity in the dynamics of learning. Each group exhibits a high degree of reflexivity and it is in these processes that perhaps their own individual understanding of what it means for them, in their particular context, to be on the "right path" might emerge? More research is needed in order to clarify if this is the case.

The role of the tutor in all of this is of course worthy of further examination too. As we have seen, tutor intervention has it's own consequences and the outcomes of any intervention cannot be fully anticipated. Once again, to suggest that tutor intervention will always put the group on the "right path" is to put too much hope in the skill, perception and facilitative ability of tutors. Certainly, tutors can learn from their experience of facilitating e-groups, and they can learn from reading about the ways in which such groups work. From this, the likelihood of them being more able to help groups in trouble will no doubt be greater. But they can never be sure of the outcome of any particular intervention. The outcome of each intervention is likely to depend on the context and circumstances in which the group is working at any one time. Once again, more research is needed to understand this.

The issues discussed in this paper – the "reflexive organisation of self" as Giddens puts it – are characteristic of the period we are living in. Reflexive self-control and moral imperatives appear to be guiding principles for the members of these collaborative e-learning groups. However, as we have seen, their application has different affects in each group. Seen from this viewpoint, this e-learning Masters course is highly moral in its explicit educational philosophy and in its learning processes. It perhaps can be seen in this light: as an example of the need to be self-referent in a post-modern society. Identity – of self and of groups – is something to be creatively worked-at in order to be sustained:

"The altered self has to be explored and constructed as part of a reflexive process of connecting personal and social change". (Giddens, 1991, p 33).

In the context of these e-groups, it would seem that this applies equally to individuals within the groups, as well as to the groups themselves.

ACKNOWLEDGEMENTS

I would like to thank the three anonymous referees for their helpful comments on this paper.

REFERENCES

Axelrod, R. (1990). *The evolution of cooperation*. London, Penguin Books.

Boot, R. and V. Hodgson (1987). Open Learning : Meaning and Experience. *Beyond Distance Teaching - Towards Open Learning*,. V. Hodgson, Mann, S and Snell, R. Milton Keynes, SRHE/OU Press.

Boud, D., Walker, D. (1998). "Promoting Reflection in Professional Courses: the Challenge of Context." Studies in Higher Education **23**(2): 191-206.

Carr and S. Kemmis (1986). *Becoming critical : education, knowledge and action research*. Brighton, Falmer Press.

Clarke, A. E. (1997). A social worlds research adventure: The case of the reproductive science. *Grounded theory in practice*. A. Strauss, Corbin, J. Thousand Oaks, Sage.

Cunningham, I. (1987). *Openness and learning to learn*. Beyond Distance Teaching, Towards Open Learning. V. Hodgson, S. Mann and R. Snell, SRHE/OU.

Davis, M. Denning., K. (2000). Online learning: frontiers in the creation of learning communities. In Proceedings of the Conference: *Networked Learning 2000 : Innovative Approaches to Lifelong Learning and Higher Education Through the Internet*, University of Sheffield.

Elden, M. and R. F. Chisholm (1993). "Emerging varieties of action research." *Human Relations* **46**(2): 121-142.

Giddens, A. (1991). *Modernity and self-identity: self and society in the late modern age*. Cambridge, Polity Press.

Glaser, B. and A. Strauss (1968). *The discovery of grounded theory*, Weidenfield & Nicholson.

Harris, D. (1987). *Openness and Closure in Distance Education*. Brighton, Falmer Press.

McConnell, D. (2000). Implementing Computer Supported Cooperative Learning. London, Kogan Page.

Mantovani, G. (1994). "Is computer-mediated communication intrinsically apt to enhance democracy in organisations ?" *Human Relations **47**(1): 45-62.*

Moon, J. A. (1999). *Reflection in Learning and Professional Development*. London, Kogan Page.

Parlett, M. R. (1981). Illuminative Evaluation. *Human Inquiry: A Sourcebook of New Paradigm Research*. P. Reason, Rowan, J. Chichester, J Wiley & Sons.

Pedler, M. (1981). Developing the learning community. *Management Self-development : Concepts and Practices*. T. Boydell and M. Pedler, Gower, UK.

Reynolds, M. (1994). *Groupwork in education and training: Ideas in practice*. London, Kogan Page.

Schon, D. A. (1983). *The Reflective Practitioner: how professionals think in action.* New York, Basic Books.

Snell, R. (1989). "Learning to work in a peer learning community." *Group Relations Training Association Bulletin.*

Strauss, A., Corbin, J (1998). *Basics of qualitative research: grounded theory procedures and techniques.* London, Sage.

Wenger, E. (1998). *Communities of practice: learning, meaning and identity.* Cambridge, Cambridge University Press.

Whitehead, J. (1989). "How do we improve research-based professionalism in education ? A question that includes action research, educational theory and the politics of educational knowledge." *British Educational Research Journal* **15**(1).

Winter, R. (1989). *Learning from experience: principles and practice in action-research.* London, The Falmer Press.

Reflective Communicator Roles in Preservice Teacher Team Email Discussions

Robert J. Beck, Richard S. Brown, Sue K. Marshall, Jennifer Schwarz
Department of Education, University of California, Irvine
rbeck@uci.edu

ABSTRACT
The objective was to model a type of effective team participant, reflective communicators, and their communications roles during four, eight-person preservice teacher team email discussions of their classroom observations. An aggregate statistical analysis revealed significant correlations between the quality of reflective observations provided, and the number and quality of responsive messages received from other team members. Conversely, high responsive message senders were associated with low quality messages. Reflective communicators were theorized to occupy a distinctive niche in the team, both as a source of high quality reflective observations and who engaged in high frequency, bi-directional responsive communications. Based on these criteria an individual analysis of the data revealed 13 reflective communicators among the 32 participants. Reflective communicators tended to communicate with other reflective communicators in groups containing multiple reflective communicators and increased these communications over time. Issues were raised concerning the rights of teams to assure them access to reflective communicator leaders.

Keywords
Reflective communications, team composition, message directions

INTRODUCTION
Recently, great importance has been placed on the value of teamwork skills in increasing learning and performance in education, military, and corporate settings (O'Neil, Chung & Brown, 1997). Morgan et al. (1986, p. 3) defined a team as "a distinguishable set of two or more individuals who interact interdependently and adaptively to achieve specified, shared, and valued objectives." Burke et al. (1993) concluded, however, that the demand for effective teams has outpaced the study of teamwork skills. They identified several overlapping conceptualizations of teamwork competencies that were relevant to the present study of preservice teacher teams, including: coordination (properly sequenced behavior and exchange of useful information); leadership (providing and accepting feedback, and help); and, communications (transmission and reception of support behavior). Several studies have reported that patterns of giving and receiving elaborated help are critical components of teamwork skills (Webb, 1993). Giving explanations helps senders of messages to reorganize and clarify material (Bargh & Schul, 1980); receiving explanations can benefit by filling in gaps of understanding or correcting misperceptions and strengthening connections between new information and previous learning (Mayer, 1984; Wittrock, 1990). However, both O'Neil, Chung and Brown (1997) and Brannick et al. (1993) have reported that the number of explanatory messages *sent* was negatively correlated with outcome measures, i.e., the more team members communicated the more their task performance suffered. Because of methodological choices, no study has yet been conducted on relations between the number and quality of messages *received* and outcome measures.

Researchers have found that group electronic communications promote the sharing of multiple perspectives that lead to the likelihood that one member will produce examples and interpretations hitherto unconsidered (Koschmann, et al., 1996; Feltovitch, et al., 1996). Reed and Bolstad (1991) found that in a word problem task involving mastery of an equation, students provided with both simple and complex examples outperformed all others, including those who had been presented with one example plus step by step procedures for solving word problems, in general. Exposure to multiple examples of concepts in particular performance tasks in collaborative learning may contribute to greater individual discrimination of the underlying concept.

This study was concerned with team communications that might be associated with individual preservice teachers' conceptual understanding of teaching standards as observed in field classroom activities through computer mediated teamwork. It was hypothesized that preservice teachers in computer mediated groups who exhibited particular teamwork skills, such as the frequency and quality of messages communicated, and who had access to multiple examples produced by the team, would also construct higher quality observations. Data concerning these communications skills associations would also contribute to the analysis of the characteristics and roles of a type of effective team member, *reflective communicators*, and lead to criteria for the equitable composition of teams.

METHOD

Task and Procedure

Using the California Teaching Standards for the Profession as a framework, teachers were set the task of observing and reporting on activities in their supervisors' classrooms that exemplified five different standards in weekly writing assignments. The five standards used were:

1.2 Uses a variety of strategies and resources to meet the needs of all students.

2.7 Create opportunities for students to become self-directed learners.

3.4 Develops and uses a repertoire of instructional strategies well suited to teaching to a particular subject matter.

4.5 Chooses and adapts instructional materials to make subject matter relevant to students' understanding of subject matter.

5.4 Uses a variety of assessments to determine what students know and are able to do.

Email listserv discussion groups were used to communicate observations of these standards. In addition, the teachers were asked to follow up by responding to particular participants for whatever reason they cared to. Whether in making observations or in responding to particular participants, all messages were addressed and copied to the whole group.

Sample

Thirty-two multiple subject teachers in a 5th year credential program were randomly assigned to four email groups of eight participants each. Of this group, 29 were female.

Data Analysis

Scoring Rubrics

Rubrics were developed for coding the email transcripts. One rubric was used to score the classroom *observations* about teaching standards. Three dimensions were scored (ascending scale): 1. Aptness, the extent to which students' observations were relevant to the standards (0, 1, 2 or cannot score); 2. Detail and context, the extent to which there was sufficient detail and context to explain what the teacher and/or students were doing in the classroom instruction (0, 1, 2 or cannot score); 3. Reflection, or the extent to which observations incorporated: (3.1) interpretations about teacher's strategy or student outcomes; (3.2) interpretations explaining why a strategy was beneficial; (3.3) questions; (3.4) connections to other observations; or, (3.5) alternatives considered (0-5 based on one point for each criterion, or cannot score).

A second rubric was applied to all *responses to observations*. These were scored for quality by two independent raters who achieved 90% agreement. This scale used the same criteria as the Reflection dimension above (0-5 based on one point for each of criteria, or cannot score).

Plan of Analysis

In Phase 1 of the study, the data were statistically analyzed by correlating measures of messages sent and received, reflective response quality and observation quality. Based on these findings, Phase 2 focused on an individual analysis that modeled the qualities and roles of effective communicators and their distribution in the four groups. In Phase 3, we examined communications among effective communicators in the four groups and over time.

RESULTS

Phase 1: A Correlational Model of Sending and Receiving Message Frequency and Quality Across Standards

A model was proposed concerning the interactions of sending and receiving messages, response quality and observation quality. Following previous findings, it was hypothesized that a negative correlation would obtain between the number of messages sent by individuals and their quality. In contrast, it was hypothesized that individuals who received a high number of messages would attract high quality responses, either because the latter would find their messages interesting and accessible, or because they perceived them as needing help. Therefore, a positive correlation was expected between the number of messages received and response quality received. If these high receivers did, in fact, construct interesting and accessible messages, then we would expect them to have relatively high observation scores, i.e., a positive correlation between number of messages received and observation scores. But, if high receivers had a negative correlation with observation scores, then this would give credence that they might need help and were perceived by others as needing help. Finally, it was speculated that a reciprocity principle might be operative concerning the number of messages sent and received and, therefore, that a positive correlation would be obtained between the two measures. We had no hypotheses concerning other iterations of these variables, i.e., between the number of messages respondents sent or received and, respectively, the quality they received or sent; or, between respondent quality sent and quality they received. The results are displayed in Figure 1. The results were significant for all predictions made concerning relations between number of messages sent and received and response quality. While significances at .05 are modest, given the small sample sizes of this study, and in most studies of teamwork, and the fact that all were in the expected direction, the findings were considered respectable. There was a negative correlation of -.366 ($p < .05$) between the number of messages respondents sent and the quality of those messages; and, a positive correlation of .484 ($p < .05$) between the number of messages respondents received and the mean response quality of the messages they received. Therefore, those who receive more messages tend to receive high quality messages and those who send many messages tend to be low quality message providers. Moreover, the number of messages sent was correlated significantly with the number of messages received (.413 $p < .05$) suggesting that some form of reciprocity principle was operative, but the direction of the effect is uncertain. It may have been the case that the number of messages received may have prompted respondents to send back a proportional number; and/or, the number of messages sent may have encouraged other participants to send back a proportional number. All other correlations were non-significant as expected. In addition, we investigated whether the relationships among variables between individual members within each group supported the hypotheses, or if there were non-hypothesized dependencies within any given group. The only significant correlations identified within each group supported the hypothesized model. No other relationships among the variables within a respondent group were significant.

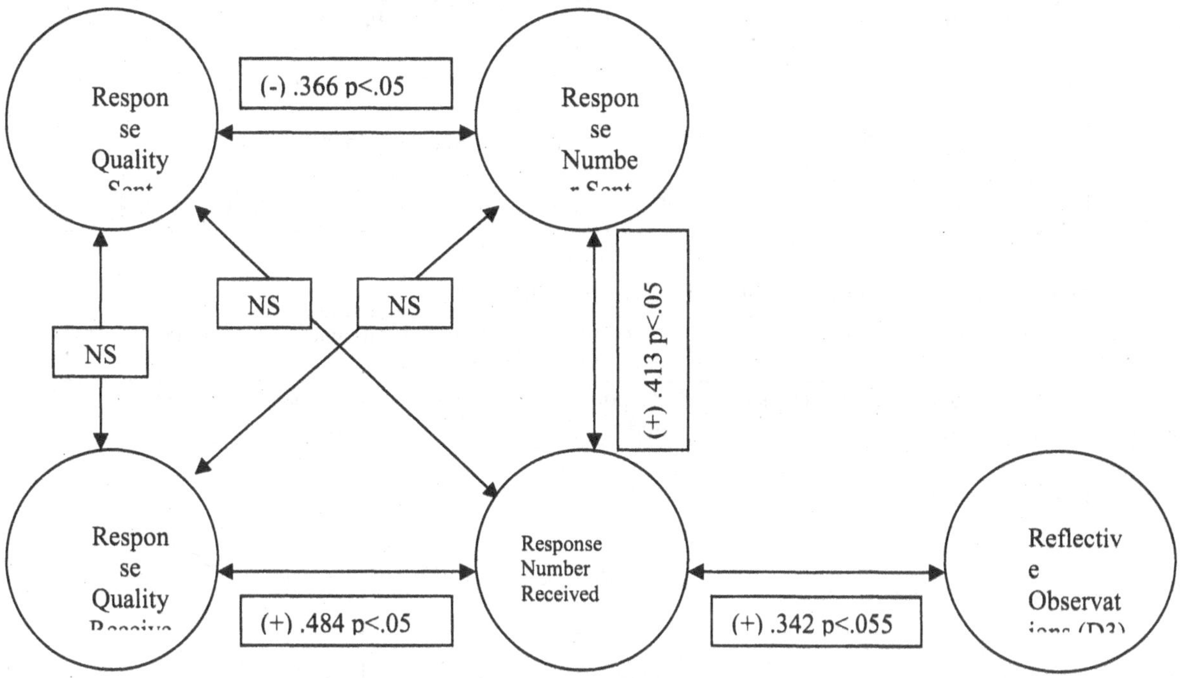

Figure 1. Correlational Model of Mean Number and Quality of Messages Sent and Received Across Standards. "NS" denotes that correlation is not significant.

The correlations for number of messages received and observation scores were less conclusive. Whereas, a modest significant positive correlation of .342 ($p < .055$) was obtained for the number of messages received and the observation reflections score (dimension 3), correlations with dimensions 1 and 2 were non-significant. This suggests that the number of messages received may be related to one's conceptual performance, but the effect is limited to teachers' competencies in elaborating their observations reflectively and not in making apt or detailed observations. However, this finding tends to support the conclusion that high messages receivers attract high quality messages because their observations are more reflective, not because they are perceived as needing help.

Phase 2: High Reflective Communicators and Distribution in Groups

In this phase of the analysis, we took a closer look at those individuals who received a high number of messages. Because of the significant correlation found between number of response messages received and reflective quality of observations (dimension 3 score), and also between number of response messages received and number of response messages sent, we characterized individuals who were high on all three of these variables as "high reflective communicators," and we looked at the way in which those individuals were distributed across the four email groups. This allowed us to explore the nature of their communication in a given group in our subsequent phase 3 analysis.

A quantitative score for "reflective communication" was computed for each participant. For each of three variables (dimension 3 score, number of responses received, and number of responses sent), participants received a sub-score of 3, 2, or 1, indicating their ranking in the top, middle, or bottom third respectively, among all participants. A sum of all three ranking sub-scores was computed to create a single reflective communication score, with a range from three to nine.

The next step was to identify the high reflective communicators and look at their group membership. Thirteen out of the thirty-two participants were identified as the "high" scorers; they received a reflective communication score between seven and nine, indicating a combination of threes, or threes and twos on the three sub-rankings. High reflective communicators were not evenly distributed among the four email groups, as illustrated in Table 1. While three of the groups had three or four out of eight members identified as high reflective communicators, Group 3 had only two such members, and their reflective communication scores were sevens. Thus even with random assignment to groups, the number of high reflective communicators was not equitably distributed.

Table 1. Distribution of high reflective communicators across email groups

Listserv Group	No. of High Scorers/ Their Reflective Communication Scores		No. of Lower Scorers/ Their Reflective Communication Scores	
Group 1	3	Scores: 9, 8, 7	5	Scores: 6, 5, 4, 4, 3
Group 2	4	Scores: 9, 8, 8, 8	4	Scores: 6, 6, 5, 4
Group 3	2	Scores: 7, 7	6	Scores: 6, 5, 5, 4, 4, 3
Group 4	4	Scores: 8, 8, 8, 8	4	Scores: 5, 4, 4, 3

Table 2. Summary of response messages among high reflective communicators

	Percentage of response messages sent by high reflective communicators that are received by other high reflective communicators		
Listserv Group	Responses messages up to the mid point	Responses messages from mid to final point	Reponses messages overall
Group 1 (3 "high" members)	42.85%	50.00%	46.88%
Group 2 (4 "high" members")	52.94%	71.42%	63.16%
Group 3 (2 "high" members)	25.00%	20.00%	22.22%
Group 4 (4 "high" members)	70.0%	82.61%	78.79%

Phase 3: Communications Among High Reflective Communicators

In this final phase, we investigated the nature of the communication within email groups, and any differences between groups, with a focus on the role of those identified as high reflective communicators. Within each group we looked at the number of response messages that high reflective communicators received from each other. We also looked at this data at two different points during the study to identify any patterns of change over time in the percentages of response messages sent and received among high reflective communicators: a) after the second round of observations and response messages had been sent (mid-time point); and b) after the fifth and final round of observations and response messages (final time point).

Table 2 summarizes findings about the response messages among high reflective communicators. There was a high level of responses sent and received among "high" members. Groups 2 and 4, each with four out of eight reflective communicator members, had 63.16% and 78.79% of their response messages sent and received among high reflective communicators. Group 3, which had only two reflective communicator members, had the lowest overall percentage (22.22%) of response messages sent and received among "high" members. A second finding from this analysis was the increase in percentage of response messages among high reflective communicators from the midpoint to the final round of responses, which was evidenced for groups 1, 2, and 4. We speculate that the reciprocity principle may be at work for "high" members. The more reflective communications high member send, the more they receive, and the effect may be compounded over time. Once again, Group 3, with only two reflective communicator members did not display the same compounding effect over time among its "high" members.

DISCUSSION

Identification of the reflective communicator type in teamwork communications has been supported by three kinds of evidence: (1) In an aggregate statistical analysis, significant correlations were found between those who received many messages, their observation reflection scores, and the quality of messages they received; (2) In an individual analysis, 13 reflective communicators were identified in the four groups. Those groups with the highest number of reflective communicators tended to communicate with each other more than they did with less reflective participants; (3) It was also found that reflective communicators in groups with three or four increasingly selected each other to communicate with over the course of the email discussions.

What possible roles might reflective communicators play in teamwork? While it is tempting to identify reflective communicators as leaders, or at least co-leaders, they were not so in the conventional sense, and this may be related to the nature of the task in this study. As the findings show, reflective communicators attract communications from other team members, including other reflective communicators. If reflective communicators lead then they do so by example. It is theorized that their initial high quality reflective observations were inviting and accessible to others, particularly those who were competent in reflective communications themselves. Reflective communicators speak in a relatively personal voice. By making interpretations, evaluative comments and speaking a language of wondering and questioning they reveal something of themselves, their points of view and opinions. By making connections to other experiences and offering alternatives to what was observed, they also reveal themselves as good analysts and comprehenders of the task. These are particularly valuable skills that might serve the needs of the group as a whole in this observational task: communicators who provide a strong flow of worked and reasoned examples of high quality observations and responses to others' observations. A follow-up qualitative study of the email transcripts would provide further evidence concerning these claims.

Even those who did not interact with reflective communicators were able to look on by reading the email texts created by them and so may have benefited by reading alone. But, perhaps, for this strategy to be effective in supporting low performers' reflective growth, it might require longer team projects than in the present case. While we can see how reflective communicators might serve the group, it is also apparent that a reflective communicator, by attracting many reflective communications, thereby receives more feedback on her own observations and reflections. She also receives a goodly flow of incoming high quality models of reflections, which could be subsequently adapted to personal use. And in recognizing and communicating with other reflective communicators concepts are exchanged in a uniformly high quality class. The richly competent, therefore, may benefit most, because their own communications have been multiply placed in context by other high quality communicators. And the rich communicators increasingly find and interact with other rich communicators. We are tempted to interpret this social grouping as adaptive for individual high reflective communicators, for they would obtain, potentially, a rich set of evaluative and contextual perspectives with which to view their own observations and could use these perspectives to create more interpretative, evaluative, responses themselves.

But, surely there is also a downside to these conclusions. We found that Group 3, which had only two marginally high reflective communicators, scored lowest in most of our performance indicators. It follows that it may be necessary to have a minimal critical mass of high reflective communicators in a group. From this perspective, once high reflective communicators are identified they could be equitably assigned to all groups. In the present context, three high reflective communicators might have been required in an eight-person group. One might also adopt rules or guidelines encouraging high reflective communicators to "communicate with those you might not ordinarily communicate with and provide support for such fellow team members." What is perplexing here is how to achieve such democratic ends, while at the same time exploiting the value of the interchange among high communicators and their high quality reflective text for all team members to read.

REFERENCES

Bargh, J. A., & Schul, Y. (1980). On the cognitive benefits of teaching. *Journal of Educational Psychology*, 72, 593-604.

Brannick, M. T., Roach, R. M., & Salas, E. (1993). Understanding team performance: A multimethod study. *Human Performance, 6,* 287-308.

Burke, C. S., Volpe, C., Cannon-Bowerts, J. A., & Salas, E. (1993). *So what is teamwork anyway?* Paper presented at the 39th annual meeting of the Southeastern Psychological Association, Atlanta, Ga.

Feltovitch, P. J., Spiro, R. J., Coulson, R. L., & Feltovich, J. (1996). Collaboration within and among minds: Mastering complexity, individually and in groups. In T. Koschmann's (Ed) *CSCL: Theory and practice of an emerging paradigm* (pp. 25-44). Mahwah, NJ: Erlbaum.

Koschmann, T., Kelson, A. C., Feltovich, P. J., & Barrows, H. S. (1996). In T. Koschmann's (Ed) *CSCL: Theory and practice of an emerging paradigm* (pp. 83-124). Mahwah, NJ: Erlbaum.

Mayer, R. E. (1984). Aids to prose comprehension. *Educational Psychologist,* 19, 30-42.

Morgan , B. B., Glickman, A. S., Woodward, E. A., Blaiwes, A.S. & Salas, E. (1986). *Measurement of team behaviors in a Navy environment* (Tech. Rep. No. 86-014), page 3. Orlando, FL.: Naval Training Systems Center.

O'Neil, Jr., H. F., Chung, G. WW. K., & Brown, R. S. (1997). Use of networked simulations as a context to measure team competencies. In H. F. O'Neil, Jr. (Ed.), *Workforce readiness: Competencies and assessment* (pp. 411-452). Mahwah, NJ: Erlbaum.

Reed, S. K. & and Bolstad, C. A. (1991). Use of examples and procedures in problem solving. *Journal of Experimental Psychology: Learning, Memory , and Cognition*, 17, 753-766.

Webb, N. (1993). *Collaborative group versus individual assessment in mathematics: Processes and outcomes* (CSE Tech. Rep. No. 352. Los Angeles: Center for Research on Evaluation, Standards and Student Testing (CRESST)).

Wittrock, M. C. (1990). Generative process of comprehension. *Educational Psychologist*, 24, 345-376.

Applying Technology to Restructuring and Learning

Mary Burns, Marylu Menchaca, Vicki Dimock

SEDL, University of Texas, SEDL

mburns@sedl.org, venus-v@mail.utexas.edu, vdimock@sedl.org

ABSTRACT

How can classroom teachers be assisted in developing constructivist learning environments supported by technology in schools with large populations of traditionally underserved students? What role does available technology and professional development and support play in allowing or promoting changes in teaching methods? Results of the Southwest Educational Development Lab project, *Applying Technology to Restructuring and Learning (ATRL),* indicate that teachers changed their classrooms practices and professional development coupled with access to technology was instrumental in that change. Teacher knowledge of how computer technology can be used to enhance learning and how to plan effective learning activities were shown to be more important than strong personal computer skills.

Keywords

Constructivist Learning Environments, Computer Supported Collaborative Learning, Professional Development.

INTRODUCTION

Classroom teachers are practitioners that need to be trained in developing constructivist learning environments supported by technology. Building bridges between research on learning and teaching and classroom teachers can provide the practitioner community and students with the benefits of the research efforts.

The *Applying Technology to Restructuring and Learning (ATRL)* project was aimed at developing an understanding of what is required to help and support classroom teachers in the process of learning to implement constructivist strategies and use new tools. The study examined school context issues, teacher qualities and the role of professional development. *Constructivism* was defined as a learning theory that "proposes that knowledge or meaning is not fixed. . . but rather is constructed by individuals through their experience. . . in a particular context" (Honebein, Duffy, & Fishman, 1991). *Constructivist learning environment* (CLE) was defined as a classroom in which "instruction is more a matter of nurturing the ongoing processes whereby learners ordinarily and naturally come to understand the world in which they live" (Knuth & Cunningham, 1991, p. 164). *Technology* was defined as computers, whether alone or in combination with other hardware, software, or networks.

The purpose of the intervention was to assist and support participating teachers in creating technology-assisted constructivist learning environments. ATRL project staff provided assistance in a variety of roles – technology consultant, researcher, designer, developer, and professional development facilitator. Project staff worked in three areas vital to the creation of these learning environments: planning, professional development, and follow-up assistance and support.

The research component of this project involved an *intervention study* with a two-tiered research design. *Tier One* was a collective case study of the approximately 150 classrooms, located across six school sites, whose teachers participated in 72 hours of ATRL professional development. *Tier Two* consisted of six detailed case studies of individual teachers whose experiences represented the process and the practices they employed in creating a constructivist learning environment within their classrooms. Both quantitative and qualitative data were collected and analyzed.

An analysis of several technology training curricula for classroom teachers revealed that technology skills training is frequently the primary focus with little or no emphasis on managing technology use (Sun, Heath, Byrom, Phlegar, & Dimock, 2000). However, ATRL teachers participated in professional development that modeled technology management in the classroom, as well as instructional strategies that teachers could immediately apply in their classrooms.

Establishing a theoretical framework

"Constructivism is not a theory about teaching, but is a theory about knowledge and learning," (Brooks and Brooks, 1993, p.vii) thus the ATRL project team developed a framework for understanding and exploring the implications of this theory for teaching. Through a review of the literature (e.g. Brown, Collins & Duguid, 1989; Duffy & Jonassen, 1992; Brooks & Brooks, 1993; Duffy & Cunningham, 1996; Jonassen, 1996; Maddux et al, 1997) the team arrived at a common understanding of constructivist learning theory which they distilled into the following six working principles of constructivism. These principles became the foundation for the ATRL project and were used for developing and carrying out each of the professional development sessions.

B. Learners bring unique prior knowledge, experience, and beliefs to a learning situation.

C. Knowledge is constructed uniquely and individually, in multiple ways, through a variety of authentic tools, resources, experiences, and contexts.

D. Learning is both an active and reflective process.

E. Learning is a developmental process of accommodation, assimilation, or rejection to construct new conceptual structures, meaningful representations, or new mental models.

F. Social interaction introduces multiple perspectives through reflection, collaboration, negotiation, and shared meaning.

G. Learning is internally controlled and mediated by the learner.

By developing and sharing these common ideas of how learning occurs, the ATRL team was able to create relevant and engaging learning experiences in professional development sessions that promoted collaboration and learner-centered activities.

Because the project team's goal was to effectively model authentic learning environments in its professional development sessions, they created activities that used limited numbers of computers rather than having a computer available for every participant, since teachers reported that comfort in managing limited resources was more important than expertise in any one application.

Models for managing technology in the classroom

Several models for managing technology in the classroom were also used throughout the professional development sessions. These models employed particular grouping strategies and were designed so that teachers could replicate them in their classrooms. These models are described below.

The Active Learning Environments learning stations model was designed with a thematic focus of "Your Community." The facilitator presented the activity and then functioned as a "consultant" for the remainder of the activity. With the goal of the project explained, teams of four to five rotated through three different "learning stations" to gather data and information about their community. One station used a digital camera to gather images, another station used a simple electronic spreadsheet to analyze data, and a third station used printed materials about the community. Each of the stations had roles for each of the team members as well as instructions for completing the tasks at that station.

The Navigator Model was another group approach designed by the ATRL team. This model was more technology intensive than the Active Learning Environments model, and it was designed so participants could learn to use a software application while learning about some content. In this model, several teams of four were given a different part of a concept to explore within their team. To do this, they were asked to create a "concept map" using concept-mapping software. While the team carried out its initial discussion, one person from each team attended "Navigator" training. Teachers selected for that role, spent approximately twenty minutes with the Navigators teaching them the basics of concept-mapping software. Once trained, the Navigators returned to their teams, and instructed the rest of the team the software. The Navigator could only give instruction and could not touch the keyboard. The rest of the team rotated using the keyboard so that everyone had a chance to use the software.

The Facilitator or Expert Model was designed to accommodate different skill levels of the participants. The facilitator/expert was a person who had some experience with the software and showed novice users ("students") how to use the software application. The facilitator/expert could not touch the mouse or keyboard. Each group had its own facilitator/expert and the role did not rotate within the group. This model was useful for carrying out more complex projects that required different skill sets and levels of expertise. When ATRL staff carried out this staff development session, it pre-assigned teams and distributed the technology skilled teachers across all of the teams with the designation that they would be the technology facilitator/expert for that team.

In *The Collaborative Grouping Model* all team members were responsible for creating a part of some final product. Other models included individual work, working in pairs, and working in groups of three or more.

In all cases, participants discussed the advantages and disadvantages of the different management models and also the appropriate uses of each model in their classrooms. Many opportunities were provided for teacher reflection about learning, classroom management of technology resources, and instructional strategies throughout the professional development sessions provided by the ATRL project.

Over the two years of the project, sixteen modules, seven videotapes, and multiple print resources for teachers were developed and incorporated into a professional development portfolio, *Active Learning with Technology*. Each of the sixteen staff development modules shared the following characteristics: They took into account teachers' understanding and beliefs about how students learn; They were supported by constructivist learning theory, both in terms of instructional approaches and the type of activity in which the learner engages; Utilized inquiry, problem-based teaching and learning; Used commonly available software found in classroom settings; Included two or more instructional strategies for managing a constructivist learning environment supported by limited amounts of technology; and they provided opportunities for teacher reflection on how different instructional strategies could be applied to their classrooms.

Follow-up assistance and support

Two major categories of follow-up assistance were also provided to participant teachers and school administrators. First, over the course of two years, project staff made regular follow-up visits to each participating site school in addition to the visits for professional development sessions. During these additional visits, staff observed participating teachers' classrooms, consulted with teachers individually and in small groups, and provided feedback, resources, technical support, and information based on teachers' concerns and needs. The ATRL staff also provided ongoing interactive assistance via the project's web site, a list server, e-mail interaction, and telephone conversations. Second, the ATRL staff developed a variety of materials designed to aid teachers in creating constructivist learning environments supported by technology.

Sites

Selected school sites included a school in Arkansas, Louisiana, Oklahoma, New Mexico and two Texas sites (SEDL's region) from each state in SEDL's region, with an additional site in Texas. The six site schools represented a variety of demographic and contextual characteristics in order to create a variable sample for the research study. Because of the selection criteria used for selecting the six site schools to participate in this research study, it is important to reiterate that this is a purposive sample, rather than a random sampling. This approach is consistent with the qualitative inquiry process (Borg & Gall, 1989).

DATA ANALYSIS AND RESULTS

Different data sources for analysis, both qualitative and quantitative, contributed to answering the research question. Quantitative data sources included: a project-developed observation protocol, and the *Teaching, Learning & Computing Teacher* survey (Becker & Anderson, 1998). Qualitative data sources included field notes, informal observations, unstructured interviews, case study interviews, lesson plans, staff development evaluations, and videotaped interviews and classroom episodes.

How can teachers be assisted in developing constructivist learning environments supported by technology? To inform answers to this research question, analyses of observation data included comparisons across the categories on the observation protocol to document which practices modeled during professional development were transferred into classroom practice. Comparisons of these categories, and of observation data, and of the computer skills self-assessment with field notes were also conducted.

The baseline computer skills checklist was compared with subsequent administrations of the checklist to look for relationships between teachers' technology skills and constructivist approaches. The computer skills checklist was also examined to gauge whether professional development session offerings to identify computer skills increase as a result of professional development sessions.

Analysis of videotaped teacher interviews and the in-depth case study interviews helped reveal the personal process of change that individual teachers must deal with when participating in an innovation. Interviews allowed teachers to discuss their fears and frustrations as well as successes and milestones in transforming their practice into constructivist classrooms supported by technology. Collaboration among teachers within instructional groups or among ATRL participants seemed to encourage teachers interested in creating CLEs. Simply talking about ideas with others helped teachers as one teacher explained, "I feel better now as I talk to other teachers, asking questions and sharing experiences. It makes me feel more open-minded, and willing to try new things."

The Teaching, Learning, and Computing Teacher survey asked teachers what they believed about teaching and learning and what support they needed to help them become the teachers they wanted to be. These data were compared to observation data to augment each teacher profile. As the participating teachers had received professional development designed to assist them in creating CLEs, it was hypothesized that rankings on constructivist practice and use of technology on the *Teaching, Learning, and Computing Teacher Survey* would be higher for participating teachers than in the national sample. The statistical method for this comparison was an Eta correlation ratio that measured the strength of relationships between the ATRL teachers and the national sample.

Part Two of the classroom observation protocol contained descriptors of observable characteristics of a constructivist learning environment supported by technology, regardless of content area or grade level. The descriptors in this protocol were formulated around the six principles of constructivism (mentioned previously). The descriptors for each of these six principles were coded on a scale from one to five by SEDL staff for each classroom observation. Each descriptor was then analyzed to determine the level of constructivist practice for each project teacher. Changes in mean scores from baseline to year one and year two were noted and regarded as an indication of change in practice. The five levels of constructivist practice observed for each descriptor were: (1) *Not evident*, (2) *Minimal*, (3) *Sometimes*, (4) *Frequent*, (5) *Regular practice*.

Results from the observation protocol were entered into an SPSS database and analyzed. Types of analyses included:

H. Cluster analysis, in order to sort cases by common characteristics into groups or clusters. This classification scheme allowed tracking of movement among teachers in terms of constructivist approaches.

I. Means tests, in order to determine teachers' "scores" in each of the descriptors in the observation protocol. These means were used to determine low, medium-low, medium-high, and high constructivist practices for each project teacher. Change in mean scores from baseline to the end of year one and year two were noted and regarded as an indication of change in practice if they achieved a significance level of .05 percent.

J. Cross tabulations of teachers' use of technology and level of use of constructivist approaches as recorded on the observation protocol during formal classroom observations.

Classroom Clusters

There was no one model or prototype of a constructivist learning environment. Rather, analysis of quantitative and qualitative data reveals that classrooms fell along various points on the continuum of constructivist practices. For the purposes of classification, classrooms were placed in clusters along a continuum of constructivist approaches: low, low-medium, high-medium and high. The classifications are comparative, not absolute, and indicate that these classrooms are low, medium, or high in relationship to one another. The purpose of placing classrooms in clusters was to categorize classrooms according to a set of common characteristics and to track the movement of these clusters over two years: Where did classrooms start out and where did they move? Did classrooms remain in their particular category over time and if so, why? Each category will be discussed below in greater detail.

As can be seen from Figure I those clusters that had the lowest baseline constructivist "scores" showed the greatest change in classroom practice; Those with the highest baseline constructivist "scores" showed the least change.

Figure 1: Changes in Cluster Mean Scores

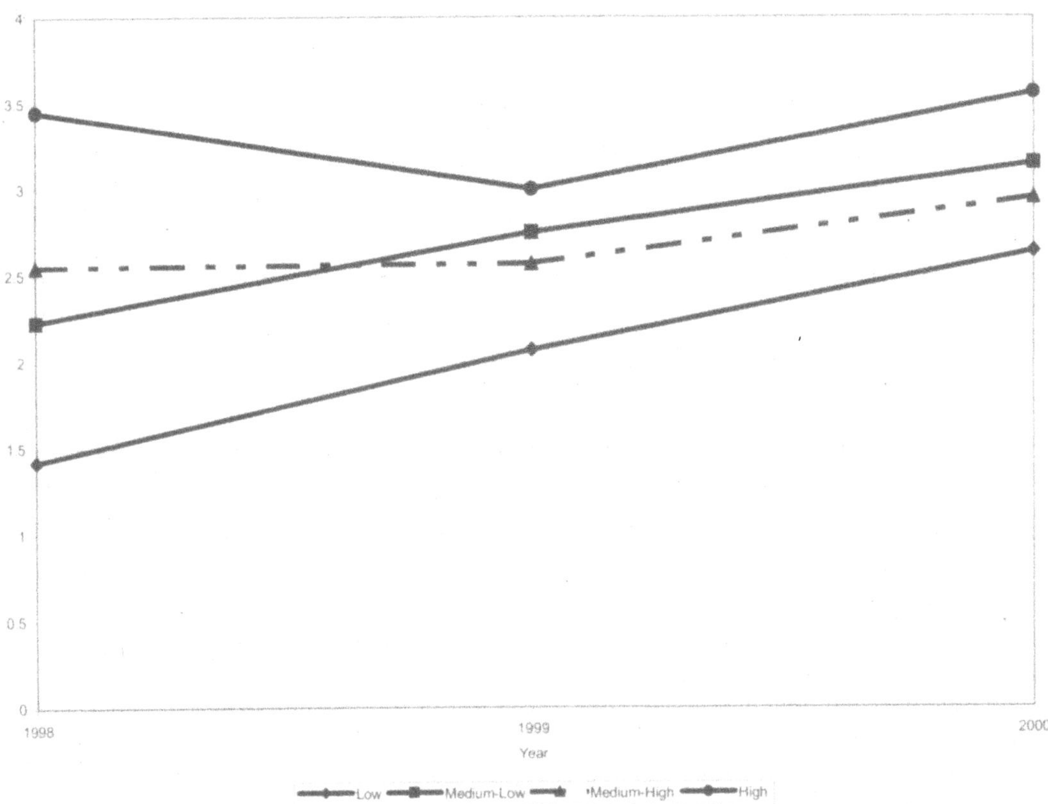

Low constructivism

Fifteen percent of classrooms observed at the end of year two of the ATRL project were identified as "low constructivism." This type of classroom fell on the lowest end of the constructivist spectrum with few or no constructivist practices. Low constructivist environments were teacher-centered: the teacher did most of the talking and the major class dynamic was whole group instruction. Typically, the teacher stood or sat in front of the class with students seated in rows. Such classrooms were characterized by a high degree of centralization and conformity. All students worked on the same activity at the same time. The teachers in this category worked with the whole class as a group, or rotated around the room to assist individual students.

Discourse was quite limited, consisting mainly of students responding to teacher-directed questions, usually providing short or rote answers. Student contributions or attempts to contribute were often not acknowledged and students were offered little opportunity to express their viewpoints or share their knowledge about a particular domain. There was usually little or no teacher-supported interaction between students. Though there may have been some use of small groups, there was often little student autonomy and students worked individually on teacher-assigned tasks.

Technology use: In terms of materials, traditional resources such as the overhead projector, textbooks, worksheets, paper and pencil, and the chalkboard were used. Though these classrooms may have had classroom computers, students infrequently or never used technology. When used, these classrooms tended to employ tools that mirrored traditional practices, such as students taking *Accelerated Reader* tests individually or the use of computers for teacher productivity.

Medium-low constructivism

By the end of year two, 24 percent of the formally observed classrooms were identified as medium-low constructivism. Medium-low constructivism classrooms differed from low constructivism classrooms primarily by the way they were organized for learning and by their use of technology—though the most obvious distinction between the two may be one of form as opposed to substance. Within these medium-low classrooms, students typically tended to sit together in groups working on a particular activity. Quite often these groupings were in the form of learning centers in which students were engaged in a number of discrete activities that were formerly conducted as a whole group activity. The worksheet was still prevalent in the low-medium constructivist classroom. Of the activities occurring at each station, approximately half may have been "open ended," that is requiring greater student creativity, problem solving, or greater student autonomy. Though students may have exchanged ideas on assignments, and were allowed to experiment and explore new ideas, students tended to be working together more individually than collaboratively.

The degree of collaboration varied across classrooms within this category. In some classrooms, students were arranged in loosely cohered groups, interacting with materials and to a much lesser extent, with one another, in solving problems. In others, the entire class was involved in the same activity at the same time. Though working in collaborative settings, students communicated very little or not at all, and the main communication pattern was still teacher to student(s).

Technology use: There was no pattern of technology use in a low-medium constructivist learning environment. For example, students in a low-medium constructivist classroom may have been engaged in an open-ended activity such as the creation of a product of their choosing, or in a more close-ended assignment, for example an *Accelerated Reader* test or word processing a report. Oftentimes, however, the computer activity was the most open ended, eliciting student creativity, problem solving or critical thinking skills.

While the teacher demonstrated activities, students engaged in some hands-on activities and more skilled students assisted less skilled students. The teacher solicited students' knowledge about a particular topic and generally offered more in-depth questioning of students' prior knowledge, understanding and opinion. However, patterns of communication were still predominantly teacher-student, versus student-student.

Medium-high constructivism

Approximately 32 percent of classrooms formally observed were identified as medium-high constructivism. Medium-high constructivist classrooms differed from medium-low classrooms in terms of substance rather than style. They were more learner-centered with the teacher in the role of facilitator or working with small groups of students. In such classrooms the teacher employed a variety of instructional methods, including class discussion, student writing, and responding to questions.

Students also worked in collaborative groups or pairs and typically interacted with a variety of materials: books, reports, worksheets, individualized instruction from the teacher, and the World Wide Web, to gain information. In some classrooms students were responsible for their own work, as opposed to a collaborative product. Some of the classrooms were characterized by teacher-led activities, but in such cases the teacher asked open-ended questions and solicited students' prior understanding. While the primary pattern of communication in medium-low constructivist classrooms was either teacher-student or a weak student-student pattern of communication, in medium-high constructivist learning environments the communication pattern was student-student and student-teacher.

While medium-high constructivist classrooms, like their medium-low counterparts, often employed learning stations, the activities in each tended to be more thematic and open-ended and the activities distributed. In other words, while students, at their various centers, may have been working on the same thematic unit, the activities at each station varied and students were not all doing the same thing at the same time. While students might not be organized into centers, they were in fact working either individually or collaboratively on multiple activities.

Technology use: A number of technology management models were evident in this medium-high constructivist environment. First, learning centers were employed in which students were provided with greater opportunity for communication, peer tutoring and collaboration, though the degree and kind of collaboration tended to vary across classrooms. None of the centers observed was thematically integrated, and some were based upon traditional content such as cursive handwriting and alphabetizing spelling words. In all of the centers the students interacted with each other by talking and discussing the task at hand, although in most of the centers students were responsible for their own written assignment or product for assessment.

A second model involved "concurrent groupings" where part of the class worked on a task at the computer while the rest of the class focused on another activity. Sometimes the activities were related to each other, for example in two classrooms, four pairs of students gathered information from the Internet to complete an assignment about a particular author. At the same time the remainder of the students who were not on the Internet wrote a personal response to the author about the story they listened to. In a third classroom, the majority of the class worked on a reading assignment for a class novel and a creative writing assignment, while two students worked with a student teacher on a *Hyper Studio* stack.

A third model involved all students having access to all computers. This model occurred in very specific settings—a library and computer lab—where access to multiple technologies was more prevalent than in the classroom. In the computer lab most students had their own computer, and in the library, groups of three to five students created a group presentation. Some of these students were practicing the oral part of their presentation, while other small groups worked at the computer. In all of the three models described above, as students were engaged in activities, the teacher either worked with another small group of students, or rotated among students, and offered assistance as needed. Though medium-high classrooms exhibited certain models of technology management there was no discernible pattern of technology use. Since activities in general tended to be more open ended, technology use also conformed to this pattern. Unlike the medium-low constructivist classroom, where the computer station activity may have been the most open ended and creative of the stations, there was no indication that this was so in a medium-high constructivist environment.

High constructivism

Twenty-nine percent of all classrooms formally observed were identified as high constructivism. The high constructivist learning environments differed from the medium-high constructivist learning environments in terms of the frequency and depth of student-centered approaches. These classrooms were characterized by students working together, autonomously, cooperatively and collaboratively, at their own pace and on a real world topic of their own choosing, with different groups conducting different activities simultaneously. Students appeared highly engaged and motivated by the curriculum and were allowed to come up with their own expressions of a problem they had solved or a product they had created.

In such high constructivist classrooms, the teacher was truly a facilitator or guide, typically circulating among students and observing student work. Most noticeable was that teacher talk, in relation to that of the students, was minimal. In most high constructivism classrooms, the teacher rarely talked to the class as a whole and answered questions or offered guidance only when it became obvious that students had exhausted all other forms of assistance. Further, within a high constructivist learning environment, the teacher appeared to be a co-learner with students, spending less time conveying information, and more time guiding students to sources of information. Field notes and formal observations noted that teachers in high constructivist classrooms often learned from and with students. Most often the learning took the form of some sort of new technology use but also included new concepts or facts within the subject area being studied. The research of Roehrig-Knapp & Glenn (1996) supports this "co-learning" role of the teacher in a constructivist learning environment.

Technology use: Students used several computer applications—on-line encyclopedias, the World Wide Web, presentation software, content-specific CDs, graphics software and word processing—for the purposes of research and expression. In all instances of high constructivist learning environments observed, students were independently using computers to solve problems, create intellectual products, produce written work, and other classroom activities. These classrooms had an atmosphere of inquiry and communication that encouraged student contribution and direction. Students in such a high CLE appeared to be highly engaged in the learning process and enjoyed a good relationship with their teachers. In such an environment the teacher was the model of a guide, facilitator, coach and mediator.

Typically, project teachers indicated that the constructivist approaches modeled in professional development sessions, were meaningful to their experiences. Teachers then seemed to utilize such approaches with or without technology with students. Further, as teachers became more comfortable with technology, they were more likely to let students use it. Once teachers allowed students to use technology and saw that many students had a certain amount of expertise, they were more likely to cede control of technology to students. Once this control was loosened and teachers saw that students worked well with technology and that their work improved as a result, they began to cede control in other areas, granting students' greater autonomy in their work.

Professional Development, Student Culture, and Constructivist Approaches

Findings indicate that many factors appeared to have influenced teachers as they changed their practice to accommodate constructivist practices supported by technology. Professional development opportunities appeared to have made a major impact on teachers' practice. Professional development that allowed teachers to construct professional knowledge about pedagogy, content, and technology, as well as strategies for managing the changing classroom environments seems to have brought about the creation of constructivist learning environments supported by technology. Peer support was instrumental for teachers as they changed their practice and also seemed to play an important part in the process of creating constructivist learning environments. This support came from colleagues or others such as an expert or leader.

As knowledge is a product of the activity, context, and culture in which it is situated, it is important for teachers to understand their community of practice. There was not much evidence that teachers drew upon students' diverse background in their classes. Further, teachers appeared not to harness the benefits of the culture, knowledge and language that minority families have to offer. According to Trueba (1999), teachers need to provide culturally different children with an environment that capitalizes on students' existing linguistic and cultural knowledge. If teachers acknowledge the richness of students' first language and the value of their life experiences and culture, the stage is set for student empowerment. It is crucial to create " ... a positive learning environment in which children become engineers of their own intellectual destiny and co-construct their future" (Trueba, 1999, pp 147).

The majority of the ATRL teachers seemed to know little about their students' background as reflected in their answers to a *Funds of Knowledge* (Moll, et al., 1992) questionnaire developed by the ATRL project. Ninety-one percent of the teachers who completed this questionnaire did not know if their students spoke languages other than English at home. In addition, 58% of the teachers did not share the ethnicity or the socioeconomic status of their students. In informal interviews, some teachers claimed that their students' background hampers their behavior and their willingness and ability to learn. It is possible that teachers did not ask students about their prior knowledge because they thought students knew little or nothing about the subject at hand.

For a student to open up and share what he/she knows, the student must trust the teacher and feel safe. It may be that this atmosphere was lacking in some classes and that when teachers did question students about cultural experiences, knowledge of a topic, etc., students were less inclined to respond. When students and teachers shared the same ethnicity/race more constructivist approaches, such as the use of prior knowledge were evident, even though such use appeared minimal and involved very visible or superficial aspects of culture, such as foods, celebrations, or heroes. Higher level approaches where students are permitted to view concepts and issues through the prism of their own culture were not reported. Although 54% of project teachers, had been exposed to diversity training, more research and training is needed in how to help teachers achieve classrooms where students feel safe and valued and where supportive relations with teachers and peers give children the opportunity to fully develop their talents and capacity.

RECOMMENDATIONS, CONCLUSIONS AND POINT OF VIEW

The study found four clusters of constructivist learning environments based upon variations in the intensity and frequency of constructivist approaches. The clusters were Low, Medium Low, Medium High and High. Within the clusters, classrooms shared many common characteristics. Teachers' change in practice was significant across the two years of the study.

We can assist teachers by providing them with collaborative groups where they can build peer support networks, and where they can share knowledge and gain assistance in the process of implementing new ways of teaching within their schools. Administrative support is critical to initiate and maintain change.

We need to know how to help teachers develop safe and empowering classroom environments for minority students and present models to them on how to use and be sensitive to students' funds of knowledge and cultural capital.

While the presence of technology may make teachers cognizant of the need to change instructional practice, it did not result in changing practice *per se*. Not only must we make technology available, we must increase teachers' understanding of how to employ technology in meaningful ways. For the teachers in this study, change appeared to occur with teachers' increased confidence/comfort using technology, supported by a collaborative group of other teachers in the school. As teachers participated in the ATRL professional development sessions, they learned to use technology, but, more importantly, became conscious of themselves as learners and more cognizant of best instructional practices. The teacher became less a repository of knowledge and more a general manager of learning in the classroom. The student role, in turn, was transformed from spectator to the protagonist in the learning process.

In the beginning stages of the adoption process of new constructivist teaching and learning strategies, it is important to count on close peer support and expert help in the development of lesson plans. In addition, the availability of opportunities for teachers to build confidence and comfort with the use of technology in a safe environment makes a difference in achieving the actual integration of technology tools in a constructivist learning environment in the classroom.

REFERENCES

Adams, S. & Burns, M. (1998). Connecting Student Learning and Technology. Austin: Southwest Educational Development Laboratory.

Banks, J. A. (1993). Multicultural Education: Historical Development, Dimensions, and Practice. In *Review of Research in Education* (19), 3-29. Washington DC: American Educational Research Association.

Becker, H. J. & Anderson, R. E. (1998). Teaching, Learning, and Computing: 1998. A national survey of schools and teachers describing their best practices, teaching philosophies, and uses of technology.

Becker, H. J., & Ravitz, J. (1999). The Influence of Computer and Internet Use on Teachers' Pedagogical Practices and Perceptions. In *Journal of Research on Computing in Education*, (31)4. Irvine: University of California.

Betsinger, A., Garcia, S. & Guerra, P. (2000). Research Report for the Organizing for Diversity Project, 2. Austin: Southwest Educational Development Laboratory.

Boethel, M. & Dimock, V. and Hatch, L. (1999). Putting Technology into the Classroom: A Guide for Rural Decision Makers. Austin: Southwest Educational Development Laboratory.

Boethel, M. & Dimock, V. (1999). Constructing Knowledge with Technology: A Review of the Literature. Austin: Southwest Educational Development Laboratory.

Borg, W. R., & Gall, M.D. (1989). *Educational research* (5th ed.). White Plains, NY: Longmans.

Brooks, J. G., & Brooks, M. G. (1993). *In search of understanding: The case for constructivist classrooms.* Washington, DC: Association of Supervision and Curriculum Development.

Brown, J. S., Collins, A., & DeGuid, P. (1989). Situated cognition and the culture of learning. Educational Researcher, 18.

Cognition and Technology Group (1992).

Dimock V. & Rood, M. (1996). The Emergence of an Online Community: The Use of Computer Mediated Communication to Support Implementation of Problem-Based Learning. Paper presented at the Annual Meeting of the American Educational Research Association, New York.

Duffy, T. M., & Cunningham, D. J. (1996). Constructivism: Implications for the design and delivery instruction. In D. H. Jonassen (Ed.), *Handbook for Research for Educational Communications and Technology* (pp.170-198). New York: Simon & Schuster Macmillan.

Duffy, T. M., & Jonassen, D. H. (1992). Constructivism: New implications for instructional technology. In T. M. Duffy & D. H. Jonassen (Eds.), *Constructivism and the technology of instruction: A conversation* (pp. 1–16). Hillsdale, NJ: Lawrence Erlbaum.

Greenfeld, P. M., Raeff, C., & Quiroz, B. (1995). Cultural values in learning and education. In B. Williams (ed.), *Closing the achievement gap: A vision for changing beliefs and practices.* Philadelphia: Research for Better Schools.

Honebein, P. C., Duffy, T. M., & Fishman, B. J. (1993). Constructivism and the design of learning environments: Context and authentic activities for learning. In T.M. Duffy, J. Lowyck, D.H. Jonassen, and T.M. Welsh (Eds.), Designing Environments for Constructivist Learning (pp. 87-108). New York: Springer-Verlag.

Glaser, B. G., & Strauss, A. L. (1967). *The Discovery of Grounded Theory: Strategies for Qualitative Research.* Aldine.

Honebein, P.C., Duffy, T. M., & Fishman, B.J. (1993). Constructivism and the design of learning environments: Context and authentic activities for learning. In T. M. Duffy, J. Lowyck, D. H. Jonassen, & T. M. Welsh (Eds.), *Designing environments for constructive learning* (pp. 87 – 108). New York: Springer-Verlag.

Jonassen, D. H. (1996). *Computers in the classroom: Mindtools for critical thinking.* Englewood Cliffs, New Jersey: Prentice-Hall.

Jonassen, D., Carr, C., & Hsui-Ping, Y. (1998). Computers as mindtools for engaging learners in critical thinking. *Tech Trends,*43(2) 24-32.

Knuth, R. A., & Cunningham, D. J. (1991). Tools for constructivism. In T. M. Duffy & D. H. Jonassen (Eds.), *Constructivism and the technology of instruction: A conversation* (pp.163-187). Hillsdale, New Jersey: Lawrence Erlbaum Associates.

Lincoln, Y. S., & Guba, E.G. (1985). *Naturalistic inquiry.* Beverly Hills, California: Sage.

Maddux, C. D., Johnson, D. L., & Willis, J. (1997). *Educational computing: Learning with tomorrow's technologies,* Second Edition. Boston: Allyn and Bacon.

Moll, L., Amanti, C., Neff, D., & Gonzalez, N. (Spring, 1992). Funds of Knowledge for Teaching: Using a Qualitative Approach to Connect Homes and Classrooms. In *Theory Into Practice*, XXXI.

Payne, K. J., & Biddle, B. J. (1999). Poor School Funding, Child Poverty, and Mathematics Achievement. In *Educational Researcher* (28) 6, 7.

Roehrig-Knapp, L., & Glenn, A. D. (1996). *Restructuring Schools with Technology,* 14. Boston: Allyn and Bacon.

Rogers, E. M. (1983). *Diffusions of Innovation* (3rd Ed.). New York: The Free Press.

Sandholtz, J. H., Ringstaff, C., Dwyer, D. C. (1997). *Teaching with Technology: Creating Student-Centered Classrooms.* New York: Teachers College, Columbia University.

Schifter, D. (1996, March). A constructivist perspective on teaching and learning mathematics. *Phi Delta Kappan,* 492-499.

Sun, J. Heath, M., Byrom, E., Phlegar, J., & Dimock, V. (2000). Planning into Practice. Durham, NC: Southeast and Islands Regional Technology in Education Consortium Partners.

Taylor, P. C., Fraser, B. J., & Fisher, D. L. (In press). Monitoring constructivist classroom learning environments. *International Journal of Educational Research,* pp. 1-11.

Trueba, E. T. (1999). Latinos Unidos: from cultural diversity to the politics of solidarity. Lanham, MD.

Constructing Collaborative Pedagogical Situations in Classrooms : A Scenario and Role Based Approach

Christine Ferraris, Philippe Brunier, Christian Martel.

"Systèmes communicants" team - Université de Savoie, campus scientifique,
73376 Le Bourget du lac cedex, France
christine.ferraris@univ-savoie.fr, christian.martel@univ-savoie.fr.

ABSTRACT
Most CSCL works put forward the fact that learners working together would only need a means of communication. We feel this is not always sufficient. We have focussed on the collaborative activity itself and the way of enhancing collaboration. We have proposed a general framework which gives the teacher the possibility of defining and constructing pedagogical collaborative situations. It is based on regulation functions allowing the teacher to manage groups, to define the roles played by the participants in a group and to describe the way actions can be performed (by means of scenarios). This framework has been implemented as an independent software that can be plugged into any collaborative application. It has already been tested with a collaborative drawing software for young children.

Keywords
Regulation, roles, scenarios, collaborative drawing application, constructing collaborative situations.

INTRODUCTION
Most CSCL works put forward the fact that learners working together would only need a means of communication. We feel this is not always sufficient. We think that the focus of attention would be the collaborative learning situations themselves and the way of enhancing the collaborative process. In what follows we present our approach, which consists in giving the teachers the means of defining, constructing and modifying these collaborative situations. We will first describe some applications designed in order to create situations in which learners had to collaborate or could discover the benefits of collaboration. We will then explain our approach and illustrate it on the collaborative drawing software intended for young children we have developed within the "cartable électronique"® project. We will first present the drawing software before showing how the teacher can construct collaborative pedagogical scenarios and presenting the underlying theoretical model. We will then present the very first results of the experiments which have been conducted in three schools.

COLLABORATIVE LEARNING SITUATIONS

A communication oriented approach
Cooperative learning has frequently been seen as a stimulus for individual cognitive development, through its capacity to stimulate collaboration and discussion between learners. Two major theoretical approaches explain the role of social interaction in the causation of cognitive development. In the Piagetian approach, cooperative learning is effective because it promotes the emergence of socio-cognitive conflicts due to different opinions and strategies employed by the partners (Doise, 1984; Perret-Clermont, 1991). In the Vygotskian perspective (Vygotsky, 1978; Wertsch, 1991), individual change is presented as the result of an internalisation of regulatory activities, such as co-constructive processes, through the mediation of language. In the situation of learner(s)-computer interaction, the computer is seen as a mechanism to support social interaction and to modify the nature and the efficacy of this interaction (Blaye, 1991; Mandl, 1992). Several experiments report highlighting positive effects of computer-based peer interaction.

So CSCL seems to be an interesting paradigm for learners to learn. That's probably why lots of CSCL environments are currently being developed. Most of the time, collaboration just relies on the fact that teachers can construct material about courses and make it accessible to learners, generally via a web-based interface. Teachers and learners also have the possibility of communicating by means of commonly-used media : chats, forum or videoconferencing. The focus is thus put on communication and document sharing : there is no real study of what could and would be a collaborative learning situation and how the computer could be used to support it.

Enhancing collaboration between learners
Some works have begun to focus on this particular aspect of CSCL, no longer concentrating on communication but rather on the collaborative activity to be set up. The first example we want to present here is the T3 collaborative writing tool (Tewissen, 2001) developed within the Nimis European project (Nimis; Hoppe, 2000). This tool allows young children to "write" words or small sentences phonetically, by assembling phonemes they can pick up from a phoneme table. It has been used to create a collaborative situation between two children. The phoneme table was split up : one of the children had to

work with the vowels while the other could only make use of the consonants. Therefore, to complete a word, both children had to work together.

Kidpad (Benford, 2000) is another example of software which was developed to enhance collaboration between children. It is a drawing tool with a shared drawing space. Children can draw together and they may not have at their disposal the same tools, for instance they may not have the same colored crayons. The originality of this software is that the colors of the crayons are mixed when the crayons are used on the same area. Children are thus invited to collaborate to create new colors and to enrich their drawings.

(George, 2001) and the European project NetPro (Markkanen, 2001) are also two other works in which a specific collaborative activity is considered and tools are developed to support it.

Constructing collaborative situations

The applications presented before have been designed in order to create situations in which learners had to collaborate or could discover the benefits of collaboration. They are based on predefined scenarios of collaboration that are encoded in software and that cannot be changed. Our approach is similar but goes one step forward : we want to give the teachers the means of defining, constructing and modifying these collaborative situations themselves by acting on the software. This will be done by means of what we call regulation functions. In what follows we will show how to construct these situations dynamically, through the example of a collaborative drawing application for young children we have developed.

THE EXAMPLE OF A COLLABORATIVE DRAWING APPLICATION FOR YOUNG CHILDREN

The collaborative drawing software

We have developed a collaborative drawing software within the "cartable électronique"® project (see below) in collaboration with teachers and pupils. It is intended to be used mostly in classroom settings, by children aged 5-6 years and by their teachers. It provides children with the means of working together to produce graphical realisations : drawings and graphics. Graphics has to be distinguished from drawings. It is also a drawing activity but a very constrained and directed one. It is used as a pre-writing activity, to develop fine psychomotivity. Children are told what to draw, where and how; they usually draw curves or "bridges" or "scales", because this is a way of preparing them to acquire the physical abilities for writing.

We have chosen to install the application not on classical hardware (like personal computers) but on pen tablets. These tablets have an interactive pressure-sensitive touchscreen. Children can draw on the tablet with a sensitive pen as if they were drawing with a real pen on a sheet of paper. Tablets are so much more usable by young pupils. Furthermore, they present the advantage of being easily carried, which is an important feature to consider, as we want children to be able to use the application in classroom settings but also at home.

The "cartable électronique"® project

In an attempt to address the issues of teaching and learning with technologies, Syscom has established the "cartable électronique"® project. It was inspired by the main object children carry every day when they go to school : the "cartable" (satchel or schoolbag), which contains books and pens, toys and drawing tools. Technology gives us the opportunity to reduce the weight of the "cartable" without losing its content. SysCom is working on this project in collaboration with educational organisations in France (the French Ministry of Education and local authorities representing the Ministry) and the Department of Savoie local government (Conseil Général).

The long-term goal of the project is to give each people in the education sphere (pupil, student, teacher, family,...) the possibility to access to several educational services anywhere anytime and to collaborate. The "cartable électronique" has three main axes of development. The first concerns hardware: people involved in the project participate in the design of computers adapted to children, mostly wireless ones, as mobility has to be taken into account. The second is the creation of a support on which services and applications can be put and proposed to teachers, children and their families. An educational web portal has already been developed to play this role. It has been designed as a CSCW environment based on the possibility given to its users to create and manage groups (Martel, 2001; Portail). The third is the services and applications one. The collaborative drawing application refers to the first and third dimensions.

Tools for drawing

The drawing application is designed around a series of graphical tools that children pick up and apply using the sensitive pen. The tools are:

- crayons of different thickness,
- a palette to choose the colour of the crayon,

- an eraser to do fine erasure,
- a rag to do rough erasure,
- stamps of various forms (letters, numbers, geometrical forms),
- an album to arrange the drawings done,
- scissors to cut out parts of the drawing (a part can then be put in the album or moved around the drawing in order to be pasted on it),
- an "undo" function which makes the drawing go back one step.

These tools can be accessed via the graphical interface shown in figure 1, on which Eloïse and Laetitia have collaboratively drawn a submarine.

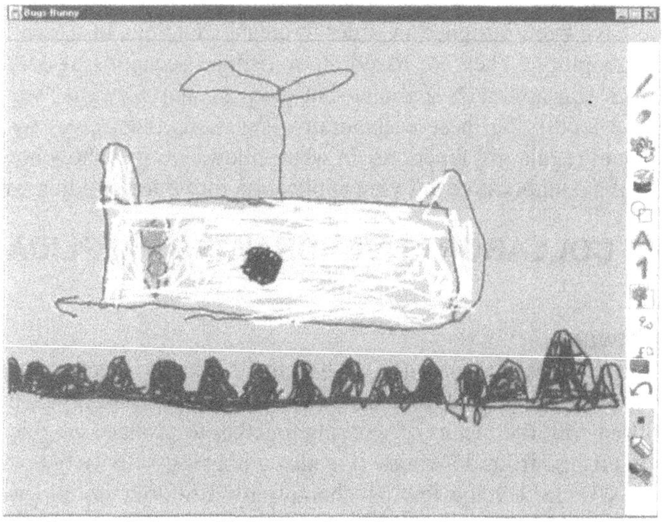

Figure 1: The interface of the collaborative drawing application

Drawing together

Children can choose to work together or on their own. When working together, each child belongs to one group. In a given group, each child has his/her own tablet and his/her tools. The children share the same drawing space but not the tools. When one child modifies something on the current drawing (by drawing, or erasing, or pasting, or cutting, …) on his/her pen tablet, the others immediately see what has been changed. It is a WYSIWIS approach, with strict synchronisation of the different children's views onto a shared workspace. Note that, as tools are not shared, the views onto the tools are not synchronised. Thus there is no problem of concurrent access to one tool. One child is either working alone, or as a member of a group. As soon as he/she becomes a member of a group, the drawing of the group appears on his/her tablet : he/she becomes immediately involved in the collaborative drawing process and can contribute to it. An individual drawing can thus be shared by the means of group definition.

Pedagogical challenges of the collaborative situation

When the teachers asked us to develop this software, they hoped that such a collaborative situation would be interesting for children to learn socialisation and develop oral expression, which are two important skills to acquire in primary education. The experiments we have conducted have actually shown that they were right. As was done in (Benford, 2000) or (Hoppe, 2000), the drawing software we have developed provides opportunities for children to discover the benefits of working together. They can choose with whom they want to draw and how to proceed: socialisation is thus encouraged by this means. Oral expression is encouraged by the fact that children, having to achieve a collective task, have the possibility of discussing and negotiating the way they are going to work (what are they going to draw ? on which part of the screen ? who does what ? etc.). They can also react to what is happening during the drawing process itself : for example one child can make suggestions about something new to draw; or they can discover together the need to define "rules" in their group ("hey ! you don't have the right to erase what I have drawn !"), which, once again, is a way of discovering life in a group.

Furthermore, they can be put in situations where one child can help and guide another. For example, in a situation where children have to make graphics (draw curves for example), one child having difficulties in drawing the curves and one who is quite a good "curves-drawer" can be members of the same group. So the second one will play the role of "assistant" for the first one : he will be able to help his friend, to show him how to make the right gesture, in the right direction, etc.

CONSTRUCTING VARIOUS PEDAGOGICAL SITUATIONS

The collaborative drawing software includes functions intended for the teachers allowing them to regulate the drawing activity. Regulation here resides in the possibility of defining pedagogical scenarios and submitting the collaborative activity to them. The teacher has the specific role of being in charge of the organisation and the management of the groups and, in a more general way, of all the mechanisms which regulate the group activity. He/she thus has at his/her disposal, through specific interfaces (see figures 2 and 3), functions allowing him/her:

1. to create groups,
2. to create roles and attributing roles to the participants,
3. to manage scenarios.

All these functions can be activated dynamically, even when children are involved in drawing. It is thus a good way of giving the teacher the means to influence the way the activity will proceed. It is a way of achieving flexibility in groupware and co-constructing the activity (Bourguin, 2001).

Creating groups

Creating groups consists in creating an empty group, naming it and putting children in it. For example, in figure 2, the teacher has created the "rabbits" and "classroom" groups. He/she is currently working on the "rabbits" one, which is represented physically by a square in figure 2. Defining who is a member of that group is just a matter of selecting the icon representing the pupil, dragging it onto the "rabbits" square and dropping it into the square. This has been done in figure 2 with "Bart" and "Duffy-Duck".

Dealing with roles

The management of roles entails two steps : creating them and attributing them to the children in one group. To create a role, the teacher has first to name it and to define a set of drawing tools (crayon, eraser, rag, ...) which will be attributed to the participant playing this role in the group. This may involve the children themselves : the teacher may ask a child the name of the role she/he wants to play, which tools she/he wants to have at her/his disposal, thus contributing to enhancing the imagination and creativity of the child. Associating tools to roles is done by means of "drag and drop" facilities. It is just a matter of picking up a tool and dragging it onto the role to whom the teacher wants to associate it. For example, in figure 2, the "big rabbit", "red rabbit" and "wizard" roles have been defined ; a "red rabbit" can only use the crayon and the scissors. The second step consists in attributing the roles thus defined to the children. This is done in the same way : just picking up a role and dragging it onto the pupil to whom the teacher wants to attribute it. In figure 2, Bart has the role of "big rabbit". So he will be able to use the tools associated with this role.

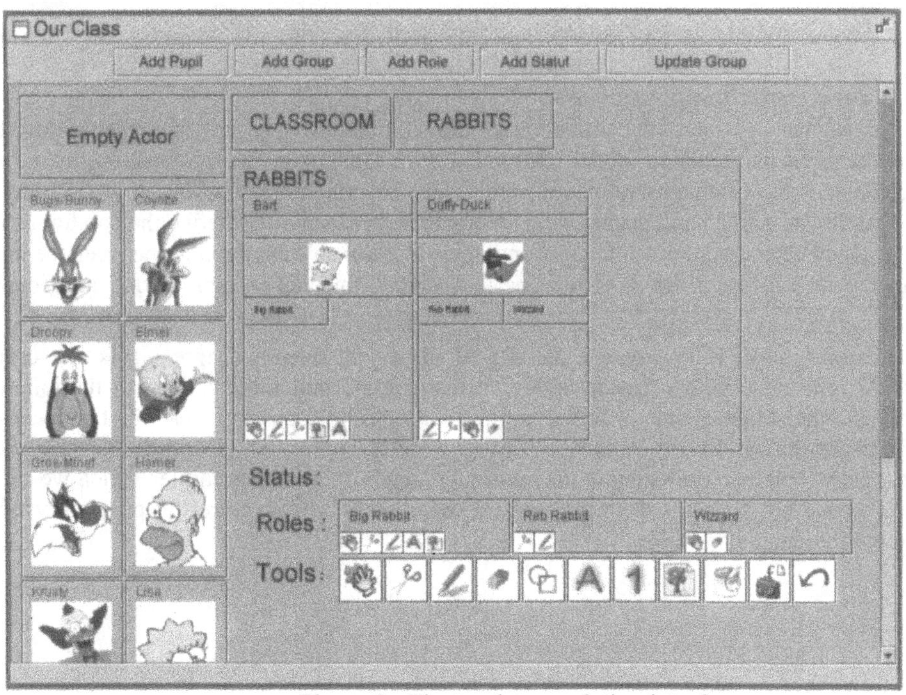

Figure 2 : The teacher regulation interface.

Dealing with scenarios

A *scenario* may be considered as a way of describing the laws, rules and effective uses of a group. It's a kind of story which describes how an interaction will be performed. It may be used to modify the way an action will occur in a group. It involves the members of one group through their roles. *"We can exchange tools"* is an example of a scenario. The teacher can "play" with scenarios in order to modify the collaborative situation. He/she can select the scenarios which will become active in a group from a set of predefined ones. This is also done by means of "drag and drop" interface facilities. For example, in figure 3, the scenario "before erasing, ask the big rabbit" has been chosen and put in the "rabbits" group. This will entail a change in the way the erasing tools can be used.

Note that defining scenarios (constructing them) is a particular function which, at the present time, cannot be handled by the teacher, as it supposes being finely aware of the theoretical model underlying the regulation process (see below). So it is handled by a person whose role is "administrator" (currently the designers of the software). We have developed a separate interface allowing the administrator to define scenarios and to link them to the methods invocation in the application code (Ferraris, 2000).

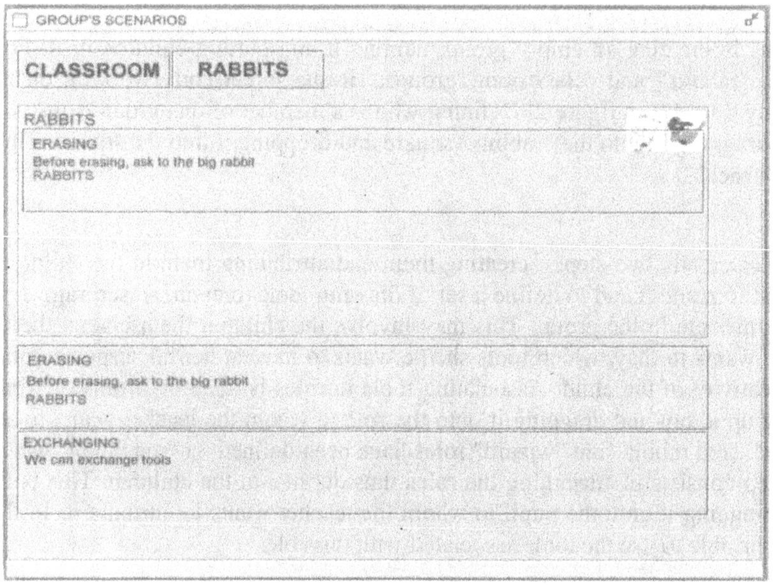

Figure 3: The interface for managing scenarios.

A more general model : the « participation model »

The interfaces offered to the teacher to regulate the collaborative drawing activity are just customized views of a general model of regulation that we call "the participation model" (Martel, 1998). This model is a proposition to take into account the social aspects of collaborative work, which most of the time are rarely supported in GroupWare. It proposes to consider the persons involved in a joint activity as active participants who can organise their activities, define the conditions under which they will be exercised and negotiate their commitment to these activities. It can enable compromise between the interests of the group and those of the individuals, between the dependencies that stem from relationships among individuals and their autonomy.

The objective of the participation model is to organise the shared space, the rules and agreements, the users and their actions or interactions. It is a conceptual model that describes, formalises and builds the context of the joint activity, the relationships of dependence and the structure of exchanges within the group. It proposes to describe the *arenas* (locations) where the activity will take place, the *interactive scenarios* guiding the interactions and the actions of the participants, and the participants themselves. They shall be represented in the arenas by means of computer entities which we call *actors* and are socially situated in the arenas by the *roles* they can play in them. They will acquire the possibility of acting and contributing to the joint activity through these roles.

The *interactive scenarios* describe the social protocols in effect in the group. They were inspired by the dialogue models of the University of Geneva (Roulet, 1985) that attempt to explain the succession and the interweaving of conversational exchanges. In the same manner, the scenarios will describe the possible exchanges between participants and define the possible sequence of these exchanges. This does not entail a rigid and deterministic description of the interactions between participants (which does not seem possible to us for most joint activities) but rather the furnishing of guides to help the participants govern their exchanges, such as is proposed by (Bider, 2000) for workflow. From a social point of view, the interactive scenario constitutes a means of subordinating the activity to the context (cultural, educational, commercial, technical, etc) in which it occurs and explains the typical sequences for each of these contexts.

Like many works in CSCW, we have been inspired by ethnomethodology and linguistics (Dourish, 1998; Goffman, 1981; Garfinkel, 1972; Rastier, 1989). We aim to give groupware users the means of co-constructing their environment. We share here the same approach as (Bardram, 1998; Bourguin, 2001; Fitzpatrick, 1995; Tolone, 1996).

Pedagogical challenges.

The regulation functions appear to be a good way of giving the teacher the means of creating various pedagogical situations. He/she can focus on the collaborative activity and imagine as many situations as possible to enhance collaboration. He/she can also involved the children in the definition of these situations and make them react to scenarios that were used or lead them to discover the need for rules.

Regulation is teacher-centered in this application. The teacher builds situations in which the children simultaneously play with tools and talk about them. The activity needs not only to be explained to the children but also to be negotiated with them, step by step. That's why we aim to move towards pupil-centered regulation, which will allow the children to take the activity in hand and to organize the framework of cooperation. This will take advantage of the reflexive feature of the regulation model.

TECHNICAL FEATURES

Concerning the drawing application

The application has been developed with the JAVA language and can thus be installed on various operating systems (we have already tried successfully to make it run on heterogeneous OS machines including Linux, windows NT and windows 95). We used the SWING package for the design of the interfaces and the RMI mechanism for communication between the tablets. In order to synchronize the updates on the shared drawing space, a server for each group has been implemented. It centralizes the events corresponding to the new pieces of drawing coming from the different tablets and redistributes them.

The Regulation level

The participation model has been implemented in JAVA as an independent software that can be plugged into any collaborative application, providing that the application has an API which allows the events generated by the users to be intercepted and to modify the methods invocation. The API must specify at least who is involved in the collaborative process and what actions can be performed (what tools are at the participants' disposal).

How the regulation level operates

In a non-regulated collaborative application, when a user activates a tool by acting upon the interface, the event generated by the interface modifies the application model directly. Our approach is to reroute the events and to send them to a specific regulation component called a *filter* that will be able to know if the actions corresponding to the events have to be regulated or not. If this is the case, the events will be transferred to the *decision center* which will treat them. This component is in charge of the management of the scenarios : it uses a *regulation motor* to select and activate them. The last regulation component is the *"execution mechanism"* which makes the connection between the actions in the scenarios and the method calls in the collaborative application.

ONGOING EXPERIMENTS

In order to validate our approach and the regulation functions, experiments were conducted in collaboration with a researcher from the department of psychology of the University of Savoie. They involved 43 children coming from three classes of three schools in the neighborhood of Chambéry (Savoie - France). The children were given in turn two collaborative tasks of drawing: a free one, which consisted in drawing what they wanted, and a constrained one, which consisted in reproducing a model of a drawing (a car, a house, ...) in which various colors and thickness of crayon were used. Groups of two or three children were constructed to manage these tasks. As one of the pedagogical challenges is to develop oral expression, the experiments were conducted in face to face settings. The children were thus able to see and speak with each other.

There were mainly two situations in the experiments : the first one during which traditional material was used (sheets of paper and real crayons), and the computer-mediated situation. For the latter, the drawing software was used with the interactive pen tablets in a regulated way and without regulation. The idea here was to compare a classical situation with the computer-mediated one, and a regulated situation with a non-regulated one.

The materials used to analyze the results of the experiments are the drawings done by the children and their verbalizations during the collaborative process. They are currently being analyzed, the drawings regarding their conformity to the given instruction, the verbalizations regarding the fact that they enhance collaboration or not. At the present time, we have only partial results, so we are not able to present full results in this paper (we will do it in a future publication). However, the initial results have already led us to establish the fact that regulation is useful in learning collaborative behavior. We expect the final results to confirm this conclusion. Meanwhile, we present in what follows the methodology defined to conduct the analyses. We are going to describe the way regulation can be analysed, the variables introduced to compare regulated situations and non-regulated ones, the outcome expected and the way collaboration can be measured.

How to analyze regulation: variables considered.

Two ideal models enabled us to explain the mechanism of regulation and to isolate relevant variables to experiment it with respect to the expected teaching considerations.

The instrumental theory, on the one hand (Rabardel, 1995), makes it possible to consider the tool not according to the uses prescribed or envisaged, but according to its capacity to be integrated by the subjects like a means to achieve their goals. This theory allowed us to isolate the conditions under which regulation should be effective before evaluating how it could support collaborative processes between two partners. The variation of the type of task (free task or constrained task) enabled us to show the importance of the specification of the conditions of learning. In the free situation of drawing, the children carry out the drawing of their choice. The only constraint is to manage prior agreement to the production of the drawing. In the situation of constrained drawing, the children must reproduce a model of drawing.

These two tasks do not refer to the same field of learning. The free situation of drawing refers to the field of creativity, whereas the situation of constrained drawing refers to the field of collaborative learning. The goal of regulation is mainly to support collaborative processes in the interaction between two partners, and not to support creative processes. It thus appears obvious that a facilitator effect of regulation will be expected in the situation of constrained drawing: regulation increasing the interdependence of the subjects in interaction and leading them to build a joint definition of the situation of training. In free situations of drawing, the model of learning implemented is creativity. However, constraining the activity of the subjects interacting does not appear relevant to support this type of creative learning. This variation of the conditions of learning thus enables us to expose the expected teaching considerations clearly, according to the adequacy of the characteristics of regulation with the characteristics of the task.

The goal of regulation is to support collaborative activity: the teaching situations will have to be defined according to this goal, and not in a general way, without consideration of the field of learning of reference. Eventually, this variation should make it possible for the teachers to use regulation in a relevant way, while enabling them to take into account the conditions necessary for the emergence of a collaborative process.

The theory of the activity, in addition, explains the effectiveness of the tool according to whether it is or not in the proximal zone of development of the subject, i.e. between what the subject is able to achieve alone and what it cannot do without external assistance (Kaptelinin, 1996). It will enable us to answer the question of the adequacy of the tool to the cognitive capacities of the children.

Practically, we thus chose to limit in this first phase of experiment the use of regulation to its simplest application, but also most fundamental: the fact of forcing the activity of the subjects or not, in allotting them turns at roles. When the activity is controlled, the tools are distributed between the two partners. Subject 1 does not have the same tools as subject 2. The idea is then to generate a complementarity between the two partners, a need for taking account of the actions of the other in the realisation of the task. When the activity is not controlled, the subjects have the same tools. They can thus carry out the task in an isolated way, without dialogue necessary with the partner before any action on the system.

The comparison of these two situations appeared necessary to us to validate the effectiveness of the mechanism of regulation on children of this age. Indeed, it is not so easy for children of that age to be decentred from their own point of view to take account of the point of view of their partner. We thus postulate a facilitator effect of regulation on the collaborative learning only if the situation of training generated is in the proximal zone of development of the child. The comparison of these two types of situations should enable us to account for the adequacy of the tool to the cognitive capacities of children of that age.

Expectations for the outcome of the investigations

The characteristics of the free task of drawing should promote processes of learning such as creativity, less compatible with the expected learning objective, which is collaboration. The characteristics of the task of constrained drawing should support processes of collaborative learning.

Regulation should increase the level of interaction of the subjects in the task of constrained drawing, by allowing the partners greater discussion and greater negotiation before any machine response. It should decrease their level of interaction in the free task of drawing, by supporting conflicts over resources and ideas.

Measures used

The measures used enabled us to analyze the two levels of interaction of a subject with his/her partner and the device. It relates to the cognitive aspects of the work of the subject in the course of action. The analysis of the course of action is carried out through the study of the interpersonal functioning communication. All the interactions were filmed and tape-recorded to allow this evaluation of the cognitive child work in the course of action. The method of analysis of the course of action consists of a synthetic-progressive method, which makes it possible to explain how the subject includes/understands new information on the basis of its knowledge. The chronicle of the course of action thus released makes it possible to account for the various stages of the inferential process of (1) proposition, (2) explanation, (3) execution and (4) control (Gilly, 1984; Saint-Pierre, 1998). This analysis of verbalizations also makes it possible to categorize the various cognitive acts according to whether they support the interaction or not. For example, the fact of proposing a joint action and of awaiting the answer of his/her partner is an action considered as supporting the interaction ("I draw the circle and you the square, ok?") whereas an isolated execution without preliminary dialogue with the partner is regarded as a negative cognitive act for the interaction.

A percentage of reduction in the initial actions of the subjects in particular units of language was also calculated, making it possible to account for the sequences of the actions, a long sequence being regarded as favourable to the interaction.

A percentage of stages in the correct sequence's inferential processes was also produced, making it possible to account for the respect of the actions and entries of language which respect the process of speech development. According to this process, a proposal must always be preliminary to an explanation or simultaneous with an execution, an explanation must be preliminary to an execution, an execution must follow a proposal or must be simultaneous with an explanation, a control must follow an execution.

A positive effect of regulation on the task of constrained drawing should be translated by a strong percentage of cognitive acts preliminary to the action (proposal, explanation) and a small percentage of concomitant or consecutive cognitive acts to the action (execution, control), a high percentage of cognitive acts supporting the interaction, an extreme percentage of reduction in the initial actions in particular units of language, a significant percentage of stages of the correct sequence's inferential processes. The effect of regulation on the free task of drawing should be translated by the effects opposite to those observed during the task of constrained drawing.

ASSESSMENT AND FUTURE WORK

The experiments are now finished and we are waiting for more detailed results. They have mainly focussed on the children at work and on the pertinence of regulation, as this have seemed to be the prerequisite of more complex ones. We think that we have now to pursue them by involving the teachers more. Actually, as one of the reviewers of this paper has noticed, it is probably a very new task for the teachers to design or to facilitate the designing of the scenarios and the cooperative situations. We thus particularly have to give them more time to think up pertinent and richer scenarios. We will work with them on the construction of those scenarios. Then we will have to enter the second and maybe most important phase of experimentation with the model: a learning situation intended no more for the children but for the teacher to manage scenarios.

We also have to work on a formalism that they would be able to manipulate via an appropriate interface in order to give them the possibility of constructing the scenarios themselves. We have actually noticed that this is done by the designers of the software as the formalism used to express the scenarios strongly relies on the participation model.

Finally, we will soon be focussing on the reflexive feature of the participation model. Actually, regulation can be considered as a collaborative activity which can itself be regulated. Within this activity, the teacher has the special role of "regulator". This role allows him/her to use the specific tools of regulation. It could be played by a pupil.

CONCLUSION

We have presented, through the example of a collaborative drawing application designed for young children, a generic framework of regulation intended for teachers to create original collaborative situations. Teachers can modify the way the drawing application operates by means of this framework. It is based on a theoretical model called "the participation model", which aims to take into account the social aspects of collaborative work.

ACKNOWLEDGMENTS

We want to thank very much Laurence FOUBERT-GAGNIERE who had led the experiments with the children in the schools, with the point of view of a psychologist. She is currently analyzing their results in a detailed way.

REFERENCES

Bardram J. (1998) Designing for the Dynamics of Cooperative Work Activities. *Proceedings of the ACM CSCW'98 conference*, ACM Press.

Benford S., and al. (2000) Designing Storytelling Technologies to Encourage Collaboration between Young Children. *Proceedings of the ACM DIS'2000 conference.*

Bider I., and Khomyakov M. (2000) Is it possible to Make Workflow Management Systems Flexible ? Dynamic Systems Approach to Business Processes. *Proceedings of CRIWG'2000, 6th international workshop on groupware* (Madeira, Portugal, October 2000), 138-141

Blaye A., Light P., Joiner R., and Sheldon S. (1991) Collaboration as a facilitator of planning and problem solving on a computer-based task. *British Journal of Developmental Psychology*, **9**, 471-483.

Bourguin G., and Derycke A. (2001) Integrating the CSCL Activities into Virtual Campuses : Foundations of a new Infrastructure for Distributed Collective Activities. *Proceedings of Euro-Cscl 2001*, (Maastricht, Netherlands, March 2001).

Doise W., and Mugny G. (1984) *The social development of the intellect.* Pergamon Press, Oxford.

Dourish P., and Button G. (1998) On "technomethodology": Foundational Relationship between Ethnomethodology and System Design. *Human Computer Interaction*, **13**, N°4, 1998.

Ferraris C., and Martel C. (2000) Regulation in groupware: the Example of a Collaborative Drawing Tool for Young Children. *Proceedings of CRIWG'2000, 6th international workshop on groupware* (Madeira, Portugal, October 2000), 119-127.

Fitzpatrick G., Tolone W. J., and Kaplan S. M. (1995) Work, Locales and Distributed Social Worlds. *Proceedings of the ECSCW'95*, (Stockholm, Sweden, September 1995), 1-16.

Garfinkel H., and Sacks H. (1972) *Contributions in Ethnomethodology*, Bloomington, Indiana University Press.

George S., and Leroux p; (2001) Project-based Learning as a Basis for a CSCL Environment : An Example in Educational Robotics. *Proceedings of Euro-Cscl 2001*, (Maastricht, Netherlands, March 2001).

Gilly M., and Roux J.P. (1984). Efficacité comparative du travail individual et du travail en interaction socio-cognitive dans l'appropriation et la mise en oeuvre d'une procédure de résolution chez les enfants de 11 à 12 ans. *Cahiers de Psychologie Cognitive*, **4**, 171-188.

Goffman E (1981) *Forms of Talk.* Philadelphia, Univ. of Pennsylvania Press.

Hoppe U., and al. (2000) Supporting collaborative activities in Computer integrated Classrooms - the NIMIS approach. *Proceedings of CRIWG'2000, 6th international workshop on groupware* (Madeira, Portugal, October 2000), 94-101.

Kaptelinin, V. (1996). Activity Theory : Implications for Human-Computer Interaction. In Nardi, B.A. (Eds), *Context and Consciousness: activity theory and Human-Computer Interaction*, Cambridge, Ma: MIT Press, 103-116.

Mandl H., and Renkl A. (1992) A plea for more local theories of cooperative learning. *Learning and Instruction*, **2**, 281-285.

Markkanen H. (2001) NetPro : methodologies and tools for Project Based Learning in Internet. *Proceedings of Ed-Media 2001, World Conference On Educational Multimedia, Hypermedia & Telecommunication,* (Tampere, Finland, June 2001).

Martel C. (1998) La modélisation des activités conjointes. Rôles, places et positions des participants. *Thesis of the University of Savoie*, September 1998.

Martel C., and Vignollet L. (2001) Educational Web Portal based on personalized and collaborative services. *Proceedings of ICALT (International Conference on Advanced Learning Technologies*), (Madison, USA, August 2001).

Nimis Project. http://collide.infomatik.uni-duisburg.de/Projects/nimis.

Perret-Clermont A-N., Perret J. F., and Bell N. (1991) The social construction of meaning and cognitive activity in elementary school children. L. B. Resnick, J. M. Levine, & S. D. Teasley (Eds.), *Perspectives on socially shared cognition,* Washington, D.C.: American Psychological Association.

Portail. http://portail.univ-savoie.fr:8080/cellule.

Rabardel, P. (1995). *Les Hommes et Les Technologies; approche cognitive des instruments contemporains.* Paris : A.Colin.

Rastier F (1989) *Sens et textualité.* Hachette, Paris.

Roulet E., Auchlin A., Moeschler J., Rubattel C. and Schelling M. (1985) *L'articulation du discours en français contemporain.* Peter Lang, Berne.

Saint-Pierre, M. (1998). Une approche pragmatique cognitive de l'interaction personne/système informatisé. *ALSIC*, **1**, 1, 27-36.

Tewissen F., Lingnau A., Hoppe U., Mannhaupt G., and Nischk D. (2001) Collaborative Writing in a Computer-integrated Classroom for Early Learning. *Proceedings of Euro-Cscl 2001*, (Maastricht, Netherlands, March 2001).

Tolone W. J. (1996*) Introspect: a Meta-level Specification Framework for Dynamic, Evolvable Collaboration Support.* Ph.D. Thesis. University of Illinois at Urbana-Champaign.

Vygotsky L. S. (1978) *Mind in society: The development of higher psychological processes.* Harvard University Press, Cambridge.

Wertsch J. V. (1991) A sociocultural approach to socially shared cognition. L. B. Resnick, J. M. Levine,, & S. D. Teasley (Eds.), *Perspectives on socially shared cognition,* Washington, D.C.: American Psychological Association.

I. (PEDAGOGY TRACK): CSCL IN THE BROADER SOCIAL CONTEXT

Web Resource Collaboration Center (WRCC): An Integrated Tool to Support Lifelong Learning

Joanna C. Dunlap

University of Colorado at Denver

Joni_Dunlap@ceo.cudenver.edu

ABSTRACT

Influenced by EPSS, generative learning, and intentional learning strategies, a Web-based tool – called the Web Resource Collaboration Center (WRCC) – was developed to support learning communities in building their own Web-based learning and performance support systems to support lifelong learning and professional development. Using various online communication and collaboration technologies, the WRCC is designed to not only enable learning communities to (1) build a learning and professional development resource that will provide them with immediate support and guidance and (2) help them develop structure, strategies, and skills for subsequent lifelong learning and professional development activities, but also (3) take responsibility for creating original resources that support lifelong learning and professional development.

Keywords

Lifelong learning, professional development, learning communities, EPSS, generative and intentional learning

INTRODUCTION

In the present climate of continual change and innovation, developing lifelong learning skills is a critical educational goal. To keep current in their fields, people have to be willing and able to continually update their knowledge and skills. The need for continuous learning is especially apparent in ill-structured domains—such as medicine, law, business, engineering, and information technology – because of the overwhelming explosion of information and technological advances. At the same time, employers want employees who can "retool" overnight; if organizational needs change at the speed of sound, then employees need to become lifelong learners and keep up with the pace. Many people look to the Web as an on-demand source to support lifelong learning and professional development activities. However, the Web itself is not necessarily designed to efficiently or effectively support these activities; Web resources are not organized by specific project, problem of practice, context, or domain, making it difficult to find what you need when you need it.

Although employees' ability to engage in lifelong learning and professional development has a direct impact on an organization's effectiveness in today's ever-changing marketplace, many employers have neglected the development of the skills needed to engage in perpetual learning activities. Organizations rely on short-term solutions, such as conventional training where trainers impart knowledge and procedures to employees using canned, inflexible instructional materials that often do not reflect the true complexity of an ever-changing work environment. (Unfortunately, this is the case whether we are describing instructor-led, computer-based, or Web-based training.) After the training activity is over, employees struggle with applying what they learned from their training experience to the demands of their jobs. Not only does the conventional training solution not accurately represent the on-the-job performance requirements, but also it does not prepare the employees to:

- Transfer the knowledge and skills to their specific job requirements,
- Extend the knowledge and skills presented during training to address increasingly complex job requirements, or
- Update the knowledge and skills presented during training when their job requirements change or the knowledge and skills change.

To address these shortcomings, some organizations have implemented electronic performance support systems (EPSS) to replace or augment conventional training. An EPSS is an integrated database of information, tools, learning experiences, resources, and guidance/advise designed to help people learn how to perform a task just-in-time and in context (e.g., on-the-job).

However, the problem with conventional training is also, in part, the problem with EPSS – as I discovered firsthand while working with the organization described below. Instructional designers working with content experts typically develop EPSS products. They create all of the tools, references, job aids, and tutorials to meet the generic needs of all the individuals who will access it. EPSS limits individualization because it assumes that everyone who needs to access the EPSS has the same performance issues, learning needs, and learning preferences. Issues of transfer, extension, and updating are not effectively addressed by EPSS. In addition, like with conventional training solutions, all of the higher-order thinking, problem-solving, and decision-making that goes into creating the "content" of an EPSS — all of the activity that helps people develop domain-specific lifelong learning skills — is done by the development team.

Facing the Challenge

A few years ago, I was hired by an information technology organization (let's call it *ITO*) to "get to the bottom" of why its elaborate EPSS which was available on the company's intranet was not being utilized by employees. The company had used its training and development resources to build this EPSS to help employees keep up with all of the new technologies they were expected to master for the various projects the organization was taking on. Since a front-end analysis was not actually conducted before the development of the EPSS (the decisions were made based on anecdotal information and a desire to use "cool" technology, which many of us are guilty of at some point in our development work), this is where I started. The employees liked that the EPSS provided a variety of resources (e.g., tutorials, white papers, job aids, business cases, etc.) to support their various learning needs and preferences. Instead of conventional training (which could not help them keep up with their changing needs), they wanted access to learning and professional development resources that would help them keep their knowledge and skills "cutting edge". So, although they were not against the idea of an EPSS, they did not believe that the developers of the EPSS understood what resources they needed, and certainly did not know how to present them in contextualized ways (e.g., resources that would help with one type of project vs. another type of project). They were also concerned that there was no way to capture the "here's how I did it" expertise of the people in the organization, and in the external community of practice. In addition, the EPSS was static – the information and tools related to the technologies these employees were using was constantly evolving and being upgraded. The most up-to-date information was being distributed on the Web. The EPSS was not dynamic enough to capture those changes, so the employees were using the Web to support their learning and professional development – albeit not very efficiently, which led to frustration. Bottom line, they had been cut out of the process, and believed that they were better judges of what was needed to support their learning and work.

This consultation led to my interest in developing a tool that would (1) take advantage of some of the structural qualities of EPSS, (2) harness the resources on the Web (since it was a distribution source for some of the most up-to-date information and tools), and (3) provide a structure for learning communities and communities of practice to build their own unique content to support both lifelong learning and professional development activities. To meet this challenge, we created a Web-based development tool called the Web Resource Collaboration Center (WRCC). This tool was designed to help learners take advantage of the wealth of resources available on the Web during on-the-job professional development as well as lifelong learning activities. Influenced structurally by EPSS and conceptually by generative and intentional learning strategies, the WRCC provides a structure for people in workplace and educational settings to generate their own, collaboratively built Web-based learning and performance support systems. After a number of redesign iterations based on continual needs assessments and formative evaluations with both organizational and higher education groups, the WRCC has been implemented in over ten settings. This paper describes the WRCC design decisions, and reports on the use of this tool with three specific learning communities.

STRUCTURAL AND CONCEPTIONAL FOUNDATIONS FOR THE WRCC

Based on my work with the ITO learning community, EPSS seemed to provide a good structural starting place as a way of organizing Web resources because it:

4. Provides an integrated database of learning and professional development resources;
5. Provides access to a variety of different resources to support people with different learning needs, preferences, maturity, style, and expertise; and
6. Is designed to help people learn in context, while they are on the job or working on a particular problem (although, because of the over-generalization of the content, EPSS does not do this well).

However, it still did not adequately address the need for knowledge building by the community itself to support their specific lifelong learning and professional development needs. Therefore, I turned to the literature for conceptual guidance. This led me to generative learning and intentional learning.

Generative Learning

Generative learning directs students to take responsibility for determining what it is about a particular domain they need to know, and then directs their activities accordingly to effectively research, synthesize, and present their findings (Cognition and Technology Group at Vanderbilt, 1992; Hannafin, 1992). Some generative learning activities provide students with a context or situation requiring them to take action (e.g., a problem that needs to be solved or a case that needs to be analyzed). Other types of generative learning activities require students to determine what it is about a particular content area they wish to know, and then take responsibility for answering their own questions through research and synthesis and representing the acquired knowledge in an organized and accessible way. This process of "generating" knowledge – instead of passively receiving information – helps learners develop structure, strategies, and habit for lifelong learning.

Schank and Jona (1991) describe generative learning in their discussion on the research method of teaching. Under the research method of teaching, students are asked to research a particular topic and then present their results to others (the class, a collaborative group, etc.). In this way, students are taking over the responsibility of information gathering, synthesis, and dissemination/presentation from the teacher. For this teaching method to lead to successful learning, students need to be allowed to select their own topics to research and report on, so that they have a real interest in proceeding with the assignment and have more control over their learning. Teachers often have to help students find something to research that is relevant and meaningful to them while still meeting learning objectives and outcomes – this requires strong teacher guidance, coaching, and scaffolding. Because students are responsible for selecting a topic, developing a question to research, making decisions about how to gather information, analyzing and synthesizing information, etc., they are engaging in activities that help to develop high-level thinking and problem solving abilities (Bruner, 1961).

Intentional Learning

Intentional learning requires learners to be actively in control of the learning process (Resnick, 1989). Palincsar and Klenk (1992) describe intentional learning as an achievement resulting from the learner's purposeful, effortful, self-regulated, and active engagement; it refers to the "cognitive processes that have learning as a goal rather than an incidental outcome" (Bereiter & Scardamalia, 1989, p. 363). Intentional learning's objective is to create a supportive structure in which students can engage in cooperative knowledge building as they move towards greater autonomy. Addressing students' need for higher-order thinking and learning skills, intentional learning helps students develop the general metacognitive and self-directed learning skills that facilitate autonomous lifelong learning (Palincsar, 1990; Scardamalia, Bereiter, McLean, Swallow, & Woodruff, 1989), specifically the abilities to:

- Monitor and assess how they learn, think, and solve problems, and make adjustments when necessary;
- Make maximum use of existing knowledge;
- Ask questions to identify knowledge deficits and set personal learning goals to address those deficits;
- Utilize learning strategies other than rehearsal to attain learning goals;
- Access, apply, and evaluate appropriate resources, including peers and teachers; and
- Manage the learning process (e.g., set goals, create action plans, identify appropriate learning strategies).

Students develop these skills by engaging in situations in which they need to build a body of knowledge based on their learning interests using a variety of information resources. Structure and teacher facilitation is provided throughout the knowledge building process to prompt, assess, and redirect – if necessary – students; again, like in generative learning settings, the teacher is very involved in guiding, coaching, and scaffolding students to ensure intentional learning outcomes. While building the knowledge base, students practice tactics for making claims, collecting evidence in support of their claims, and evaluating and responding to counterarguments from peers and teachers. Through this knowledge-building process, students reflect on specific aspects of their learning and thinking processes, and consider the effects of collaboration on each other's learning, such as the impact of opinion, bias, controversy, debate, and negotiation (Glaser, 1991).

Additionally, intentional learning prepares students for self-directed learning activities by helping them learn how to ask questions based on personal knowledge deficits and formulate learning goals to address those deficits. Research by Scardamalia and Bereiter (1991) indicates that students can learn to ask questions to guide their knowledge building, thus assuming more control and ownership over their learning activities. Because intentional learning emphasizes question generation to guide goal attainment, students acquire ownership over learning activities, find personal relevance during learning activities, and develop skills needed to be lifelong learners.

Common Instructional Strategies to Support WRCC Design Decisions

Generative and intentional learning approaches employ common instructional strategies to encourage lifelong learning and contextualized, relevant knowledge building. These strategies had a direct influence on the specific design components and use of the WRCC, specifically learner autonomy, collaboration, and reflection.

Learner Autonomy

To be autonomous learners, people have to know how to plan their learning: address learning needs, set learning objectives, employ learning strategies, utilize resources, and assess the overall process. They need to acquire more agency over their zones of proximal development by being self-directed learners. Barrows (1986) defines the process of self-directed learning as utilizing the following skills:

1. Identify and define a problem/learning need;
2. Identify, find, use, and critique resources for solving the problem or meeting the learning requirement;
3. Capture and apply information from resources to the problem or learning need; and

4. Critique information, skills, and processes used to solve the problem or meet the learning requirement (an especially important skill for using the Web).

Collaboration

Learning takes place in a social context; higher cognitive processes originate from social interactions (Vygotsky, 1978), with knowledge acquisition "firmly embedded in the social and emotional context in which learning takes place" (Lebow, 1993, p. 6). Conversation, communication, and establishing a community of learners are critical to the teaching and learning process (Pask, 1975). Collaboration:

1 Elevates thinking, learning, and problem solving to an observable status (Glaser, 1991), making students' metacognitive processes apparent. This provides students with opportunities for understanding and sharing these processes — refining, strengthening, and extending their metacognitive skills (Von Wright, 1992).

2 Gives rise synergistically to insights and solutions that would not come about individually; learners working together collaboratively can often successfully tackle complex problems that individuals working alone would not be able to handle.

3 Displays multiple viewpoints leading to the conceptual growth that comes from sharing perspectives and testing ideas with others (Bednar, Cunningham, Duffy, & Perry, 1991).

Reflection

The process of reflection is the ability to think about one's self as an intentional subject of personal actions and to consider the consequences and efficacy of those actions (Von Wright, 1992). This involves the ability to look at one's self in an objective way and to consider ways of changing to improve performance; in other words, it requires metacognitive skills. Von Wright (1992) defines metacognitive skills as "the steps that people take to regulate and modify the progress of their cognitive activity: to learn such skills is to acquire procedures which regulate cognitive processes" (p.64). Metacognitive skills include taking conscious control of learning, planning and selecting strategies, monitoring the progress of learning, correcting errors, analyzing the effectiveness of learning strategies, and changing learning behaviors and strategies when necessary (Ridley, Schultz, Glanz, & Weinstein, 1992).

THE WRCC COMPONENTS

After determining the structural and conceptual frameworks based on front-end analysis and a review of the literature, I started working with a computer programmer to develop a tool for learning communities to use to build their own lifelong learning and professional development systems. After a number of implementation and feedback iterations with organizational and higher education groups, we chose the best – at least for the moment – configuration of EPSS structure and generative and intentional learning strategies.

By creating a structure that supports collaborative knowledge building by the people who will actually be using the knowledge, the higher-order thinking, problem-solving, and decision-making involved in the selection and utilization of appropriate learning materials and performance support is done by those who can get the most out of the process. Additionally, because these activities happen within the framework of a learning community and are driven by the needs of the job, challenge, or interest at hand, the learning activities are contextualized, authentic, and meaningful. Therefore, the WRCC was designed to meet the following goals:

- Learning community members learn about the domain while they are locating, evaluating (which requires utilization of resources), organizing, and creating resources to support their learning and job performance activities – making the process relevant and productive;
- The content of the WRCC is information which has been applied/articulated from the perspective of reflective practice, making the WRCC a knowledge management forum;
- The WRCC is developed by and for the people involved in the project, challenge, context, or domain;
- Because the learning community controls the content, the WRCC can change and adapt based on the changing learning or professional development needs; and
- Once a WRCC is developed it can be used to support continued learning and professional development.

In this way, the WRCC was designed to not only enable a learning community to build a learning and professional development resource that will provide members with immediate support and guidance, but also help them develop structure, strategies, and skills for subsequent lifelong learning and professional development activities.

To provide a structure for these activities, the WRCC is broken into three EPSS-influenced functional areas that support the common instructional strategies – learner autonomy, collaboration, and reflection – prescribed by generative and intentional learning methodologies. The three functional areas are the Discussion Forum, the Link Manager, and the Resource

Construction System. [Note: These tools – written entirely in Perl – are not unique – there are similar tools available from a variety of sources. The impact is in the use and integration of the tools, and the fact that they are Open Source.]

The Discussion Forum

The Discussion Forum provides a structure for capturing the "here's how I did it" expertise that exists within the learning community itself, as well as information that is unique to the community (see Figure 1). Using the Discussion Forum, learners can post questions, issues, problems, etc., and receive feedback from other WRCC participants. It enables learning community members to work together to share ideas and work through challenges. It also provides a forum for coaching and mentoring activities.

Figure 1. Practitioner forum for JavaScript and PHP programmers

The Link Manager

The Link Manager helps learners collaboratively categorize, assess, and utilize Web-based resources. Learners use the Link Manager to categorize and critique resources found on the Web (see Figure 2). When a resource on the Web is added to the Link Manager, specific information (determined by the learning community based on their purpose) must be added, such as:

- The name and URL of the resource
- A description of the site
- Learning and/or professional development need/s addresses
- Type of learning supported and/or the complexity level of the site
- The site's strengths and weaknesses

Administrators who have different needs are able to customize the Link Manger to request different information from people submitting links. For example, the complexity level, strengths and weaknesses could easily be replaced with a single text area asking for a critique of the site and a popup menu with the options "thumbs up" and "thumbs down".

Figure 2. Example of the Link Manager completed entry

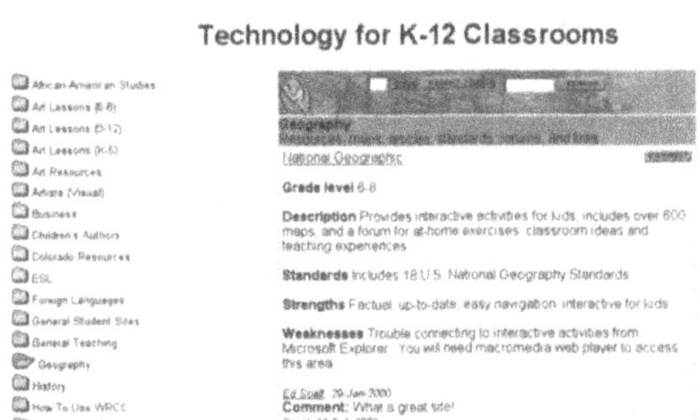

Resource Construction System

Sometimes there are learning and performance needs that cannot be effectively addressed using existing Web resources. This may be because the learning or performance need revolves around a new technology, or an organization-specific issue not well represented on the Web. Or, resources may be available on the Web, but not in a format that is effective for all learners. To address this issue, the WRCC provides a learner-centered tool for developing unique resources – the Resource Construction System (RCS).

The RCS combines the technologies of document sharing and asynchronous threaded communication to create an environment in which learners can collaboratively develop – from scratch – their own Web-based resources.

The document-sharing feature:

1. Enables learners to track and archive various versions of new resource documents,
2. Utilizes asynchronous threaded discussion technology to allow reflective discussion around the development of new Web-based resources, and
3. Provides easy uploading and downloading of resource documents for revision purposes.

The RCS allows the learning community to build their own Web resources online. To accomplish this a learner must first create a Project on the system. Once a project is added to the RCS, any number of documents may be added to the project (see Figure 3). Typically, documents added to projects are HTML documents.

Figure 3. Discussion Posting in Resource Construction System

Once a document is added to a project, learners may view the document through the System. Learners collaborate on changes, additions, and deletions that should be made to the document through a threaded discussion forum attached to the document. Once consensus is reached on discussed changes, one of the learners will make the actual changes to the document and then post a new revision to the RCS. The collaboration process then repeats for the new revision of the document if necessary. Each revision of a document has its own discussion forum. When browsing a project, learners are not only able to see any revision of a document, but they also see the historical discussion that took place over an older revision and may participate in the discussion of a current revision.

The RCS is very intelligent when handling HTML documents. When a new revision of an HTML document is added to the RCS, the RCS internally calculates the differences between the previous revision and the newly checked-in revision. As with any type of document, when a learner clicks on a revision's icon, they see the rendered document in a separate window. However, with HTML documents, if they click on the revision icon a second time, learners see the annotated version of new revision. Any text removed from the previous revision is shown in strikethrough text, and any text added to the previous revision is shown in a green font (see Figure 4).

Figure 4. Example of document under construction in the Resource Construction System

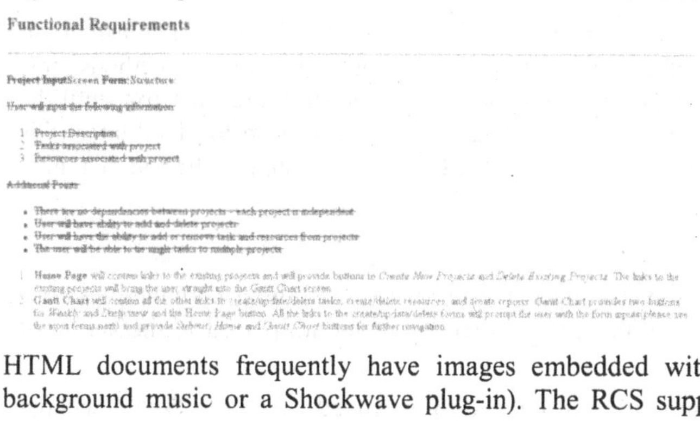

HTML documents frequently have images embedded within them and may have other media embedded (such as background music or a Shockwave plug-in). The RCS supports this by allowing learners to "attach" media to a given

document so that the document renders correctly when presented to learners. Although the RCS only annotates the differences between revisions of HTML documents, the RCS is capable of managing revisions of any type of document. Examples of different documents learners could collaborate on and revise include images, audio, video, PDF files, Microsoft Word documents, etc. Figure 3 shows the "Sam-I-Am" team working on HTML, text, and image documents to support their software design project.

Summary

The WRCC provides a structure for learning communities to engage in active knowledge building and collaborative construction of new resources based on specific lifelong learning and professional development goals and needs. It does this by employing the instructional strategies prescribed by generative and intentional learning – namely, learner autonomy, collaboration, and reflection – within an EPSS-like structure (see Table 1).

Table 1. Relationship of generative and intentional learning strategies to WRCC functional areas

	Discussion Forum	Link Manager	Resource Construction System
Learner Autonomy	Learners ask questions based on their own goals and needs.	Supports goal-driven activity: learners add to and access the Link Manager to locate resources to support learning goals. Learners decide what is included and excluded from the resource database. Provides access to variety of learning resources based on learning needs, goals, strategies, and preferences, and level of expertise/maturity.	Based on the needs and goals of the learners building the WRCC, learners determine what additional resources need to be built for inclusion in the Link Manager.
Collaboration	Learners are exposed to a variety of ideas, solutions, and perspectives because of the collaborative setting.	Guiding collaborative knowledge building: Because people are building the WRCC collaboratively, a variety of resources are collected and annotated based on different learning preference and stages. Building the content of the WRCC is a collaborative knowledge building process. The Link Manager is directly impacted by the extent to which the community actively contributes.	Learners work together to build new resources for inclusion in the Link Manager.
Reflection	Learners must reflect on what they know and don't know. To contribute to the community, learners must articulate and elaborate their understanding.	Learners annotate other's contributions, so the information about each Web resource continues to grow based on reflective use and practice.	Determining what new resources need to be created requires reflection (what new resource is required, who is the resource for, what is the best way to present the resource, etc.).

USE AND IMPACT OF WRCC

The WRCC has been implemented in both work-based learning communities – also referred to as communities of practice – as well as school-based learning communities (Gordin, Gomez, Pea, & Fishman, 1996). This means that the people who use the WRCC have a common purpose and share some background, language, or experience (Hildreth, Kimble, & Wright, 1998). For example, the WRCC has been used:

1. To support communities of practice in two information technology organizations and one training and development company (examples not provided due to proprietary content concerns);
2. To support school-based learning communities in both face-to-face and online programs at three different higher education institutions;
    (1) To support a hybrid learning community of K-12 teachers focused on technology integration issues in Colorado (http://carbon.cudenver.edu/public/wle/wrcc/techfork12/).

In all implementations of the WRCC so far, learning community involvement has been facilitated by me (as a consultant or faculty member) or by another faculty member. As prescribed by generative and intentional learning methods, this facilitation involves teaching people how to use the tool as well as guiding, coaching, and scaffolding their use until the community members are using and contributing to the WRCC without reminding or prompting from the facilitator (this period of facilitation also allows me to collect formative evaluation data to adjust the tool to better support lifelong learning and professional development needs in learning community settings).

Data Collection

Using pre and post questionnaires and WRCC log-in information, I collected data on three learning communities (one work-based, one school-based, and one hybrid) I facilitated to use the WRCC over a four month period in the spring of 2001 to answer the following questions:

- Can the facilitated use of the WRCC in a learning community setting lead to improved use of the Web – without the WRCC structure or facilitation – for learning and professional development activities?

- Can use of the WRCC for lifelong learning and professional development activities in a learning community setting lead to the development of some transferable lifelong learning skills: goal/need determination, action planning, learning strategy selection, and resource evaluation?
- Can facilitated use of the WRCC in a learning community setting lead to continued use – where *use* means continued utilization of the pre-existing resources and the addition of new resources – of the WRCC after the facilitation is removed?

Results

Work-based learning community: Information Technology Project Team

This community of practice had 11 participants who all actively participated in the WRCC during a software development project (although the project lasted much longer, my facilitation of their WRCC activities only lasted four months). Nine of the 11 original members continued to use and contribute to the Discussion Forum and Link Manager of the WRCC after my facilitation ended (the two members who discontinued had been transferred to a different project). The WRCC experience, as reported on a questionnaire, had a positive impact on how they used colleagues and technical texts as resources. Regarding use of colleagues, for example, the group reported being much more selective and specific about what questions they took to colleagues, as well as when they turned to colleagues for help; instead of going to a colleague down the hall immediately, the group was using each other and the WRCC for support first. In addition, when they did go to an external source for support, the members made an effort to capture the information for inclusion in the WRCC using the Resource Construction System.

School-based learning community: Web Developers

Fourteen graduate students preparing for careers as Web-based instructional designers participated in a semester-long, school-based learning community. During the semester, all members participated in building the content of the WRCC. After the semester was over – and my facilitation ended – only three members continued to contribute resources to the Link Manager, although all of them continued to access the WRCC and utilized the existing resources (from both Discussion Forum and Link Manager). In addition, over 300 peripheral participants (Lave & Wenger, 1991) have accessed the WRCC, with many people adding a link from their own Websites to it. Questionnaire results revealed very little impact on transferable lifelong learning skills; when using the Web outside of the WRCC structure, students reported more efficient searching skills based on higher order questions and more specific goal setting, but did not apply these strategies to library or colleague use.

Hybrid learning community: K-12 Teachers

This community of 19 participants was both a school-based and work-based learning community; although these teachers were involved in a graduate program at the time, they were actively participating in different communities of practice focused on technology integration in the classroom. During the four-month period, all members contributed and used all components of the WRCC. After my facilitation was removed, all but two members continued to access the WRCC, but only six of the original 19 continued to contribute to it. Additionally, over 200 peripheral participants have accessed the WRCC's Link Manager (although they did not add to the Link Manager). From the pre and post questions that asked the community members to describe their use of the Web to support learning and professional development activities, the WRCC experience did have an impact on their use of the Web, specifically how they searched for resources, how the evaluated resources, and how they used resources to support their needs. However, only three of the participants indicated a similar impact on their non-Web resource use; the majority of the group did not indicate making adjustments to how they used library or human resources.

Summary of Results

Consistently, the WRCC experience seemed to have a positive impact on continued, non-facilitated, non WRCC-structured use of the Web to support learning and professional development activities. Unfortunately, only the ITO group reported any improvement on their strategies when using non-Web resources (such as texts and colleagues). It is also discouraging to see that the school-based and hybrid learning communities no longer added to the Link Manager or Discussion Forum after facilitation faded. This may be due to discontinued facilitation, the end of the semester/grading period (although students did not receive a grade for participation), or diminished need to participate in the community. An interesting side effect seems to be the peripheral participation that happened once each of the two "open to the public" WRCCs were developed by the Web Developers and the K-12 Teachers, respectively.

DIRECTIONS FOR FUTURE RESEARCH

The development and implementation of the WRCC, and the initial examination of its impact on participants described above, leads to new directions for research. My immediate focus is on:

1. The impact of facilitation. Facilitation was included in the WRCC implementations because I followed the prescriptions of generative and intentional learning. However, would learning communities spontaneously use tools like the WRCC without initial facilitation? Can learning community members provide referents for contribution without someone initially acting as facilitator?
2. The difference between project-specific communities of practice (which may have more of an emphasis on workplace learning and on-the-job training as opposed to lifelong learning and professional development) and learning communities that form because of a common challenge (e.g., the K-12 teachers working together on technology integration issues) or interest (e.g., folks who participate in Slashdot.com).
3. Ways to improve the transfer of the lifelong learning skills being promoted through facilitated use of the WRCC to unfacilitated learning and professional development activities.
4. What would the results be if the participants had not been co-located? All three groups had face-to-face time with each other. Although the WRCC has been implemented in school-based distance learning communities, I have not explored my original research questions with these groups.

CONCLUSION

While creating their own WRCC to support their learning and professional development, learning community members practice and develop the very skills and strategies needed to engage in lifelong learning and professional development activities. The WRCC was designed to enable people to develop their own Web-based knowledge bases and learning and performance support systems. The activity of building a WRCC helps people learn about a domain, construct a knowledge base to support their future learning and professional development in that domain. Although further research is needed – leading to further improvements to the tool and facilitation of the tool's use – the WRCC shows promise as a tool to help learning community members develop the skills, strategies, and structure needed to engage in the type of lifelong learning and professional development activities that will help them stay current in their professions. [Note: To take a WRCC test drive or get your own copy, see http://carbon.cudenver.edu/~jdunlap/wrcc/]

REFERENCES

Barrows, H. (1986). A taxonomy of problem-based learning methods. *Medical Education,* **20**, 6, 481-486.

Bednar, A., Cunningham, D., Duffy, T., & Perry, J. (1991). Theory into practice: How do we link? In G. Anglin (Ed.), *Instructional technology: Past, present, and future* (88-101). Englewood, CO: Libraries Unlimited.

Bereiter, C., & Scardamalia, M. (1989). Intentional learning as a goal of instruction. In L. Resnick (Ed.), *Knowing, learning, and instruction: Essays in honor of Robert Glaser* (361-392). Hillsdale, NJ: Lawrence Erlbaum.

Bruner, J. (1961). The act of discovery. *Harvard Educational Review,* **31**, 1, 21-32.

Cognition and Technology Group at Vanderbilt (1992). The Jasper experiment: An exploration of issues in learning and instructional design. *Educational Technology Research and Development,* **40**, 1, 65-80.

Glaser, R. (1991). The maturing of the relationship between the science of learning and cognition and educational practice. *Learning and Instruction,* **1**, 129-144.

Gordin, D., Gomez, L., Pea, R., & Fishman, B. (1996). Using the World Wide Web to build learning communities in K-12. Journal of Computer-mediated Communication, **2**, 3. Retrieved May 5, 2001 from http://www.ascusc.org/jcmc/vol2/issue3/gordin.html

Hannafin, M. (1992). Emerging technologies, ISD, and learning environments: Critical perspectives. *Educational Technology Research and Development,* **40**, 1, 49-63.

Hildreth, P., Kimble, C., & Wright, P. (1998). Computer mediated communications and international communities of practice. Proceedings of Ethicomp '98, March 1998, Erasmus University, The Netherlands, 275-286.

Lave, J., & Wenger, E. (1991). Situated learning: Legitimate peripheral participation. Cambridge: Cambridge University Press.

Lebow, D. (1993). Constructivist values for instructional systems design: Five principles toward a new mindset. Educational Technology Research and Development, **41**, 3, 4-16.

Palincsar, A. (1990). Providing the context for intentional learning. *Remedial and Special Education,* **11**, 6, 36-39.

Palincsar, A. & Klenk, L. (1992). Fostering literacy learning in supportive contexts. *Journal of Learning Disabilities,* **25**, 4, 211-225.

Pask, G. (1975). *Conversation, cognition, and learning.* New York: Elsevier.

Resnick, L. (Ed.) (1989). *Knowing, learning, and instruction: Essays in honor of Robert Glaser.* Hillsdale, NJ: Lawrence Erlbaum.

Ridley, D., Schultz, P., Glanz, R., & Weinstein C. (1992). Self-regulated learning: The interactive influence of metacognitive awareness and goal-setting. *Journal of Experimental Education,* **60**, 4, 293-306.

Scardamalia, M., & Bereiter, C. (1991). Higher levels of agency for children in knowledge building: A challenge for the design of new knowledge media. *The Journal of the Learning Sciences,* **1**, 1, 37-68.

Scardamalia, M., Bereiter, C., McLean, R., Swallow, J., & Woodruff, E. (1989). Computer-supported intentional learning environments. *Journal of Educational Computing Research,* **5**, 1, 51-68.

Shank, R., & Jona, M. (1991). Empowering the student: New perspectives on the design of teaching systems. *The Journal of the Learning Sciences,* **1**, 1, 7-35.

Von Wright, J. (1992). Reflections on reflection. *Learning and Instruction,* **2**, 59-68.

The Motivation is the Message: Comparing CSCL in Different Settings

R. T. Jim Eales, Tony Hall, Liam J. Bannon

Interaction Design Centre,
University of Limerick, Limerick, Ireland.
jim.eales@ul.ie

ABSTRACT

In this paper, we attempt to draw comparisons between our research experiences of Computer Supported Collaborative Learning in the workplace, in schools and in universities. We present an outline description of our activities in each setting. As a possible contribution to foundational theory in CSCL, we focus on the crucial but complex issue of learner motivation. We argue that the dominant issues of motivation may vary from setting to setting but that CSCL can play an important role in engaging learner motivation in all settings. In particular, we consider the inauthenticity of most university education and consider how this might be addressed by CSCL.

Keywords

Learner motivation, workplace learning, school education, university education, situated learning, deschooling, authentic learning.

INTRODUCTION

This paper arose out of the realisation by the first author that he had been involved, in one way or another, with Computer Supported Collaborative Learning (CSCL) in a number of very different settings or domains. We reasoned that on the basis of our CSCL experiences in the workplace, K-12 schools and universities, it must surely be possible to draw some valuable general conclusions about the foundations of CSCL. Although we would confidently describe all our experiences as relating to CSCL, we also realise that because of variations in factors other than setting, it could be said that we are attempting to compare chalk with cheese (or as the Americans say, apples with oranges). The experiences occurred in three different countries: Australia, USA and England, (and we are now working on CSCL research in Ireland). All the countries are, however, predominantly English speaking, and national location seems to have been one of the least significant variables. The predominant technology also varied between the different research settings. In the K-12 schools, our main focus was on synchronous communication using videoconferencing, whereas in the university and workplace our focus was predominantly on asynchronous communication. Of perhaps most significance were variations in the "formality" of the learning perspective. In the workplace, we were exploring clearly informal learning strategies amongst workers, whereas at university level and in the K-12 schools, our perspective was more formal. The order or sequence of the experiences, it seems, has also had a marked influence on our overall conclusions about the value and priorities of CSCL. If the experiences had occurred in a different sequence our final impressions would perhaps have been very different.

This paper is not simply a series of personal CSCL recollections. We have attempted to find some common theme running through the paper connecting all the experiences. Collaboration, of course, was a common factor, but that is a defining characteristic of the field. The central theme that emerged from our reconsideration of CSCL in the different settings was the crucial issue of learner motivation. At first, it was not easy to recognise this common factor because the issues related to motivation where markedly different in the various environments. But slowly we began to realise that many of the principal conclusions we had previously drawn from our research, such as ownership, interest and authenticity, were all facets of learner motivation. We have long believed that motivation, while often overlooked, is perhaps the single most important factor in learning.

In this paper, although we make frequent reference to our practical experiences (including interview extracts from the participants), we focus primarily on the more theoretical issues relating to the value of CSCL in learning and education; and, of course, the crucial importance of motivation. We believe this reflects the foundational spirit of the conference. We do, however, apologise for not discussing in more depth the fine details of CSCL-based educational activities, but we can't help but feel this is like arranging deck chairs on the Titanic. Perhaps the ship of education is not about to sink but it does seem to be going around in circles. We argue for a radical agenda in the application of CSCL. We also apologise for concentrating on learning and educational practices (and particularly undergraduate education) rather than technological design issues. As pointed out by Bannon (1995), in CSCL there is a tendency to focus too much on the features of the technology, and not on the learning activities. In our practical CSCL experiments we have only very occasionally come up against obvious technical limitations.

We need to say something briefly about the language used in this paper. It does seem that educational terms exhibit a higher than average variation between the different versions of English. When we refer to K-12 schools (kindergarten to 12th

grade) we will use the term K-12 school. When we are referring to higher education we will generally use the term university. However, we use the terms students, teaching and schooling generically to refer to all formal education. A module is an individual class at university.

After a brief discussion of our most significant theoretical educational influences we describe our CSCL research experiences in the order in which they occurred. We begin by considering collaborative learning in the workplace; we follow with an outline of our K-12 school CSCL experiences and end the section with a description of our use of CSCL at university level. We attempt to draw some general conclusions from each of the experiences, in particular, relating to the theme of motivation. We then consider the issue of the inauthenticity of university education in more detail, and how CSCL can perhaps challenge this inauthenticity.

THEORETICAL INFLUENCES

Paul Goodman (1971) described schooling as a "mass superstition" which nobody opposes and for which nobody proposes alternatives. Our main theoretical influences are *situated learning* (Lave and Wenger, 1991, see also Brown et al, 1989, and Wenger, 1998) and *deschooling* (Illich, 1973, see also Reimer, 1971). Although at first these two theories may appear to have little in common, we believe, they both offer radical challenges to traditional ideas on learning and education. In addition, all theories based on social models of learning are influenced to some extent by the socio-cognitive theories of Vygotsky (1978).

Lave and Wenger (1991) explain situated learning as "...learners inevitably participate in communities of practitioners and that the mastery of knowledge and skill requires newcomers to move toward full participation in the sociocultural practices of a community" (p. 29). They describe the process by which newcomers become part of a community of practice as legitimate peripheral participation (LPP). They suggest that a "person's intentions to learn are engaged and the meaning of learning is configured through the process of becoming a full participant in a sociocultural practice. This social process includes, indeed it subsumes, the learning of knowledgeable skills" (p. 29). It should be noted that Lave and Wenger do not intend LPP to be an educational form or a pedagogical strategy – "it is an analytical viewpoint on learning, a way of understanding learning" (p. 40). They argue that learning through LPP takes place whatever the educational setting or even if there is no explicit educational setting at all. Consequently we cannot speak about situated learning and non-situated learning, all learning and all activity is situated. Interestingly, they note that in the examples they use to illustrate the concept of LPP there is very little observable teaching; the emphasis is on learning, not teaching, and often the most important and direct contributors to that learning are the peers of the participant.

In situated learning, and particularly in studies of communities of practice, motivation is rarely explicitly mentioned. Learner motivation is integral to the culture and expectations of the community and is expressed in terms of changes in social participation and cultural identity. However, it should be remembered that an important act of commitment takes place when the newcomer enters the community of practice and commits to eventually becoming a full participant.

From a situated learning perspective, we can see that in formal education the principal thing learned is schooling itself. It is the game itself that gets into the blood. Perhaps the most inauthentic aspect of formal education is the practice of grading. Illich (1973) suggests that "the institutionalized values school instils are quantified ones. School initiates young people into a world where everything can be measured, including their imaginations, and, indeed, man himself" (p. 45). Illich proposed *Learning Webs* as an alternative to schools. He outlined the kinds of resources required if one considered not what people ought to learn, but instead what kinds of things and people learners might need to be in contact with. He identified four kinds of learning resources: *Things* (educational objects), *Models* (skilled people), *Peers* (other learners), and *Elders* (educators-at-large). Illich also suggested that technology could be harnessed to provide a reference service for these resources.

Illich warned that education tends to become unworldly and the world becomes non-educational. For him, and for us, deschooling society means far more than just breaking out of schools; it means overcoming the schooling mentality throughout the whole of society. We cannot emphasize this point too much. Our experiences have shown that it is possible to escape the physical classroom only to find that you have taken the mentality of schooling with you.

CSCL EXPERIENCES

Workplace

We carried out "ethnographic" investigations into the *informal* learning strategies used by administrative workers to develop their computer-related skills (see Eales, 1994, 1995, in press). The setting was the administrative sector of the University of Queensland, Brisbane, Australia. The University, at the time, employed some 5,000 staff, had 25,000 students and an annual budget of over AUS$330 million. The administrative section of the university was divided into a number of departments using a wide range of software on several different hardware platforms. Our ultimate aim was to use our findings to inform the design of a computer-based collaborative support system. An important part of our research was to find an acceptable technical medium that allowed users to easily create or capture representations of their practice. To this end, we performed a number of experiments using recorded demonstrations as a means of sharing expertise between users.

Our investigations indicated that formal training played only a small part in workers' computer-related skill development but that informal collaborative learning was ubiquitous and important.

> Beverley: ... *there are people who have got more experience than others. But we all know each other and are helpful to each other. People will lend a hand. Well I don't know whether the boss would appreciate it going outside of the room but we do, you're not going to turn anybody down if they need any help. I don't anyway.*

Owned dilemmas related to computer-based skills were often referred to and appeared to represent important windows for learning, but although "communities of assistance" existed, expertise was often in short supply. Two of the departments had experimented with the appointment of semi-formal support persons in an attempt to supplement informal expertise. These support persons were expected to assist with the development of computer skills within a department. It was evident from our research, that any formalization of the support person role may well lead to a change in the fundamental relationship between the people with problems and the person providing support, often accompanied by a certain amount of tension. Narelle, a semi-formal support person, articulates the development of this dependency relationship.

> Narelle: *It's easier to run in and say "Narelle, is there a problem with this?" or "Narelle, do you know something about this?" than it is to try and do some trouble-shooting of your own.*

A sense of ownership of the problem or dilemma appears to be a vital motivating force in learning. When support is completely informal, the problem is owned by the learner and any assistance from other workers is based on mutual support. When the support role is formalized users may be encouraged to take a more passive attitude to their learning, becoming more dependent on the support person. Our research focused on how the levels of mastery or expertise in communities of assistance could be increased and how the problems could be resolved collectively without diminishing the all-important motivating sense of ownership?

In this particular workplace, there appeared to be a real need for some kind of technical augmentation to the existing collaborative support network. Ownership of the (learning) problems was manifest, collaborative relationships with other workers (learners) were strong, but learners appeared to be isolated from more expert practice. The expertise the workers had, they shared, but they needed ways to extend or develop their practice that did not violate the subtle rules of informal commitment and assistance. We believed that some kind of CSCL system, rather than individualised content delivery (e-learning), could make a positive contribution to the development of more expert practice amongst these workers. In summary, while commitment and motivation to learn were evident in this workplace, demonstrated by a clear collective ownership of skill-related problems, this motivation was nevertheless extremely fragile and could easily be lost.

K-12 Schools

The context for our investigation into K-12 school-based collaborative learning was a project group from Virginia Tech, Blacksburg, USA and the Montgomery County Public Schools (Virginia) supported by a major award from the U. S. National Science Foundation (see Eales & Byrd, 1997, Eales et al., 1999). The Learning in Networked Communities (LiNC) project sought to utilise the network infrastructure brought to the County by the Blacksburg Electronic Village (BEV) (Carroll & Rosson, 1996). Our particular interest was the support of web-based collaborative learning between the schools and between schools and the university. The project members included four science teachers from four different schools, two high schools and two middle schools. Two of the schools are in the Town of Blacksburg and are approximately 12 miles (19 km) away from the other two schools in a rural part of the county.

During our time on this project, the principal interest was experimenting with web-based desktop videoconferencing (DVC) between the schools and between the schools and mentors at the university. The videoconferencing provided a small window to the outside world that never failed to interest the students. Perhaps the most significant educational issue to emerge from our introduction of videoconferencing into the classroom was that many of the most active and competent system users were what might be termed "average" students. The particular demands of the videoconferencing medium appeared to empower and motivate a set of previously relatively disadvantaged students. The experienced teachers in the project first highlighted this characteristic of DVC. For example, one middle school student when asked which method of communication he preferred replied:

> Josh: *The video [DVC], because you actually get a chance to see and talk to the person rather than spending a lot of time typing.*

Videoconferencing introduces a new form of communication into the classroom that requires new skills. Many of those that demonstrated competency in this area were students who normally do not get the opportunity to excel in the classroom. Student motivation that developed during videoconferencing appeared to be transferred to areas where literacy skills are more central. For example, students coordinated videoconferencing sessions via e-mail messages and presented their final project reports in the form of web pages.

It seemed that students were motivated by the "reality" of videoconferencing with the outside world. Willis' (1980) classic ethnographic study of schooling in an English industrial town has some very interesting perspectives on the relationship between schooling and reality. Willis contrasts the motivations of the anti-school group, "the lads", with the more pro-school group, "the ear 'oles". One of the most interesting aspects of this study is that he follows the boys beyond the school into the workplace. Willis demonstrates that the counter-school culture of "the lads" has many similarities with the culture of the factory floor. If we take a perspective that equates the culture of the workplace with reality, it is possible to interpret the lads' rejection of school as a rejection of the inauthenticity of schooling. The "ear 'oles", on the other hand, are prepared to accept, at least partially, the alternative reality of the school. The lads left school as early as possible. The "ultra-realists" seem to be the first out the door of the school. CSCL, in its ability to afford sustained collaborative interaction with "real" people and situations outside the classroom, may be able to offer a valuable educational motivating force. This may have a specific positive influence on those students who typically perform badly within the current prevailing educational environment.

University

The context for our university-level CSCL "experiments" was a third year undergraduate module in Computer Supported Cooperative Work (CSCW) in the department of Computer Science and Information Systems at the University of Luton, England (see Eales, 2001). This module ran in 1999 and in 2000 and had 35 students on each occasion. The field of CSCW is concerned with the study of group activities and the design of computer-based technologies to support cooperative work (sometimes referred to as groupware). A particular problem (especially at undergraduate level) in CSCW education is that most students have only limited previous experience of computer-mediated group activities. An important part of understanding CSCW is appreciating the subtleties of group activities and group dynamics mediated by technology. Without this personal experience there is a danger that the learning will be overly theoretical and detached from the learner (Dewey, 1966). Our solution, which seemed appropriate, was to use a CSCW system to provide a hopefully authentic CSCW experience to underpin the teaching of CSCW theory. The software used was the Basic Support for Cooperative Work (BSCW) system (Bentley et al., 1997) developed at the German National IT Research Center (GMD) (**http://bscw.gmd.de/**). This system is essentially an asynchronous shared workspace system. Access to a group workspace requires only a standard web browser. The system supports a variety of information-sharing activities including structured discussions, uploading and downloading of documents and links to websites. The BSCW system was originally created as primarily a business tool but is being increasingly used for educational purposes (Appelt and Mambrey 1999). For us the system had a number of distinct advantages. It was easy to set up (we used the servers in Germany), it offered web-based access, was content-free, flexible and reasonably easy to use, in effect, an educational technology test bed.

The use and development of the shared workspace became an integral part of the learning experience for this module. Having taken the decision to use the system it then seemed appropriate to seek to use it to investigate novel ways of supporting learning. An important part of our investigation was the involvement of an authentic domain "expert". The expert was importantly not an academic but a practising researcher in CSCW, based at a major government research establishment in Australia.

The use of a shared workspace system as the basis for a learning environment obviously supports collaborative learning. Luton students typically represent an extreme range of abilities and this range was reflected in this particular module. Often, in instructor-led educational settings, students are unaware of the contributions from other students. The technology-facilitated group workspace made the contributions, views, and particularly the reflections, of all students more visible to the entire group, hopefully improving overall standards of scholarship and intellectual reasoning. Such a system can provide a level of participation and visibility that would be difficult to facilitate in a physical classroom.

In previous modules, where participation in a shared workspace had been voluntary, student use had been somewhat limited. We decided from the outset that the extrinsic motivation of 25% of the final grade for participation in the workspace was a necessary evil. Ideally we would hope that student reaction would be of this form:

> Enda: *Finally I think I would have contributed whether or not there was a grade involved, simply because it has been fun to use a new system like this!!*

However the more common student feedback was:

> Lisa: *There is no way I would have participated in BSCW if there was no grade attached to it. I find it takes too long wading through all the various folders and discussions that are going on, by the time I finish doing that I don't feel like replying to anything. The sole reason for my participation is the GRADE.*

We announced at the beginning of the course that there would be a grade for participation in the workspace and then rather naively hoped that the students would put the matter to the backs of their minds and just get on with participating. However, the issue of what constituted the right kind of participation was a recurring topic of discussion. Most students adopted the "sensible" strategy of mainly taking part in lecturer-initiated discussions or discussions that appeared to be important to the lecturer, (a kind of cyber-stalking). In this way, their contributions were sure to be noticed. These strategies clearly worked against many of the objectives of collaborative learning. For example, some students tried to initiate discussions of their own but other students did not respond. Student behaviour at times resembled pigeons pecking for seed in a Skinner box (a device for developing and measuring behaviouristic learning).

We consider access to the "authentic" to be a valuable resource. Our virtual expert had a significant influence on the activities and learning in the module. However, we would like to have magnified her influence. One of the main problems seemed to be that she had to come to terms with our university culture. In many ways the shared workspace became an extension of the module and of the university; a place where the standard "rules of schooling" applied. It seems we had tried to escape from schooling and to create a more authentic environment only to find that schooling had followed us. This student focus on getting a good grade is at the heart of what we term inauthentic learning. We intend to explore the issue of authenticity in more depth, and its relationship to CSCL, later in this paper.

MOTIVATION

What general conclusions, based on our experiences, can we make about motivation and CSCL? As we mentioned earlier, in trying to make generalisations across our experiences, to some extent, we are not comparing like with like. There were a number of significant variations other than the domain of interaction. However, rather than a disadvantage, these changes may have allowed us to experience a wider cross section of motivational factors.

We do not fully understand the complete geography of motivation, but we can make a number of tentative observations. We want to make a distinction between authentic and inauthentic motivation. Authenticity is a particularly complex philosophical concept, but in very simple terms, authentic motivation is related to a focus on the development of robust, long-term knowledge, whereas, inauthentic motivation is focused on assessment and the tactics of schooling, i.e., getting a good grade. Ownership of the learning problem appears to be a particularly powerful form of motivation. However, perhaps because it is so compelling, so demanding, this type of motivation is also very fragile. In the workplace, learners seemed only too ready to surrender their ownership in return for a reduction in the anxiety related to their skill development. Importantly, communities of practice appear to offer a model where commitment to the community retains ownership but spreads the burden of the learning problem across the whole community. Rather than surrendering ownership to a group of professional trainers, ownership of problems and the need to develop appropriate solutions is integrated into the collective objectives of the whole community. We feel that CSCL appears to offer opportunities to create technically augmented communities of practice that spread the burden of learning problems while retaining the all important ownership of those problems. For example, Scardamalia and Bereiter (1996) present the idea of knowledge building in communities as a way of facilitating superior education (or authentic learning) in schools.

Inauthentic motivation, on the other hand, often appears to represent a surrendering of ownership, of what is to be learned, in return for some extrinsic reward like a qualification. It also often allows the learner to adopt a more passive role. In its extreme form, "learners" have no interest in what they are learning, only in increasing their rewards and/or decreasing their efforts. We will argue later in the paper that this is inauthentic because the content and the rewards are misaligned. Knowledge within this kind of "learning" environment tends to only have short-term exchange value. In educational institutions, CSCL may offer opportunities to challenge deeply ingrained inauthentic motivation by bringing students into contact with authentic situations and problems from outside these environments. In particular, the ability of CSCL to introduce an element of "reality" into schools may engage those underachieving students who have previously largely rejected the inauthenticity of formal education.

AUTHENTIC LEARNING

From our current position in higher education, we find it hard to interpret our complete CSCL experience as anything other than "a journey away from reality and authenticity". In the workplace, at the informal level, workers had real problems that necessitated learning. In particular, they needed to connect with expertise and manage the time and effort associated with learning, but there was also a real sense of collective ownership of the problems. That is not to say, however, that inauthenticity does not exist in the workplace at other levels. In the classroom environment of the K-12 school, there was genuine interest in the glimpses of reality from beyond the classroom. In the university, although technology afforded many valuable "educational" experiences, undergraduates eschewed the authentic, remaining focused on the game of schooling or "getting a degree". In this section, we want to discuss in more detail the inauthenticity of most university learning and how this can perhaps be addressed by CSCL-based "virtual deschooling".

For many years, there has been debate about the fundamental basis of university education. One side has championed various professional or vocational skills specific to the age, whereas the other has advocated more theoretical general-purpose skills as being the best preparation for life after university. Accusations such as "dumbing-down" are levelled at one side and "living in ivory towers" levelled at the other. One thing, however, that unites both camps is their use of success in the real world as a yardstick to justify their theories and practices. This appeal to real world values or authenticity is an implicit aspect of all theories of education and has been a consistent ingredient in calls for educational reform. After all, who would propose a theory of education that prepared students only for a life in educational institutions?

Brown, Collins and Duguid (1989) offer the following definition of authenticity: "The activities of a domain are framed by its culture. Their meaning and purpose are socially constructed through negotiations among present and past members. Activities thus cohere in a way that is, in theory, if not always in practice, accessible to members who move within the social framework. These coherent, meaningful, and purposeful activities are authentic, according to the definition of the term we use here. Authentic activities then, are most simply defined as the ordinary practices of the culture" (p. 34). Koschmann et al. (1996) include the principle of authenticity as one of their six principles of effective learning and instruction. They summarise this principle as "Learning is sensitive to perspective, goals, and context, that is, the learner's orientation, goals and experiences in the learning process determine the nature and usability of what is learned; instruction, therefore, should provide for engagement in the types of activities that are required and valued in the real world" (p. 91). But just what are the types of activities that are required and valued in the real world? Resnick (1987) suggests that there are four broad characteristics of mental activity used outside of school that stand in marked contrast to mental activities developed in schools:

1. Individual cognition in school versus shared cognition outside school.
2. Pure mentation in school versus tool manipulation outside school.
3. Symbol manipulation in school versus contextualized reasoning outside school.
4. Generalized learning in school versus situation-specific competencies outside school.

Being aware of the value of authentic learning and facilitating authentic learning, are, of course, two different things. In particular, it seems difficult to understand what is currently going on in universities. University lecturers often seem to be motivated most by their own interests and what they believe is the inherent value of "their" subject. Nothing brings them back to "reality" quicker than a question from a student such as "will this be in the exam" or "are your lecture notes on your website?" There seems to be a paradox here. The education system constantly selects on the student's grades, and yet we are appalled by the "Frankenstein's monster" that our selection process creates. Of course, the more sophisticated students are adept at hiding their interest in the game of schooling.

A critical description of the education system by Jean Lave (1990) may help us to at least tease apart the most obvious competing versions of reality/authenticity. She argues "the problem is that any curriculum intended to be a specification *of* practice, rather than an arrangement of opportunities *for* practice (for fashioning and resolving ownable dilemmas) is bound to result in the teaching of a misanalysis of practice (...) and the learning of still another" (p. 324). From this we can identify three curricula:

- Curriculum 1 - The curriculum as an arrangement of opportunities *for* practice (for fashioning and resolving ownable dilemmas)
- Curriculum 2 - The curriculum as a taught specification *of* practice
- Curriculum 3 – The curriculum as a learned specification *of* practice.

To this list, we should add perhaps the most dominant curriculum (or possibly it is a meta curriculum). What Illich (1973) describes as the "hidden curriculum of schooling" – the curriculum as an arrangement of dilemmas related to performance. University students rightly understand that university is a community of practice where the "real" practice is getting a good grade and ultimately getting a degree, the rest is just window dressing. The owned dilemmas are dilemmas of performance not of learning or understanding. Ironically, the more inauthentic university education appears to be the more it supports the claims of situated learning. In that, in the university situation, most students quite successfully learn the tacit knowledge that will usually ensure their survival in that particular environment. What makes this practice inauthentic, however, is that it has little value outside of a university. We believe university education is particularly inauthentic because of the "front loading" of education. Most students go straight from K-12 school to university. By the time they reach university graduation they have been at school continuously for over fifteen years. No wonder then that in terms of intrinsic motivation most students are "running on empty", just trying to keep going long enough to finally get a degree.

SUPPORTING AUTHENTIC LEARNING

We agree with Fischer and Scarff (1998) that we need to go beyond the "gift-wrapping" approach, where new technology is merely wrapped around old frameworks for education. Authentic learning clearly needs to be collaborative, but CSCL also appears to offer the opportunity to *virtually deschool* education by bridging educational and outside worlds. Indeed, in the virtual, the issue of what is inside and what is outside becomes problematic. This means that CSCL systems, with their ability to support interaction with diverse remote communities are of value to all students and not just those involved in distance education.

In 1997 (Eales & Byrd, 1997), we outlined a preliminary three-level model of authentic learning. Our three levels were:

1. Engagement with information
2. Engagement with simulation
3. Engagement with authenticity

We still stand by our three-level model, however, we would define the levels a little differently (especially avoiding the self-referential third level description):

1. Engagement with authentic data and information
2. Engagement with authentic procedures and skills (usually involving simulation)
3. Engagement with authentic contexts

Our original aim in proposing this model was to distinguish the third level from the other areas claiming to be authentic learning. An important characteristic of the first two levels is that they imply a certain degree of pre-authentication (Petraglia, J., 1997, Barab et al., 2000). They depend to a large extent on an educator-derived definition of what is authentic, whereas third level authenticity is an emergent property of the interaction. In other words, attempts by educators to teach what is authentic rather than to facilitate student engagement with the authentic are unlikely to lead to authentic learning.

As outlined earlier, we have experimented with what we term Authentic Learning Environments (ALE's), networked technical systems allied to appropriate authentic learning activities. Our aim was to bring together university students and outside domain experts in a virtual environment, unfortunately the mentality of schooling is not that easily defeated. Although the environment provided a number of valuable educational experiences, the all-powerful collective motivation of getting a good grade ensured that the virtual space became an extension of the university, where university rules of reality held sway.

Currently, we are experimenting with connecting university students to well-established virtual communities with strong existing authentic motivations, what Brown and Duguid (2000) describe as networks of practice. Although we are generally pessimistic, we are interested in exploring whether virtual interaction can blur the distinction between inside and outside of the university and challenge the participant's identities as students (or degree-getters). There are obviously limits to the level of authentic engagement possible in undergraduate education. The inauthentic motivation of undergraduates is strong and we only have the opportunity to mount a small challenge (perhaps a single university module) to this prevailing perspective; what Carl Rogers (1969) termed "institutional press". Nevertheless, we believe CSCL at university level should be used to explore the limits of inauthenticity. An alternative role for CSCL systems as hi-tech skinner boxes will only serve to reinforce existing inauthentic practices.

CONCLUSIONS

We have suggested that motivation is an essential but often overlooked ingredient in successful learning. We have attempted to illustrate this with descriptions and discussion of our CSCL research experiences. CSCL by virtue of its defining characteristics of technically augmented collaborative learning appears to be uniquely suited to address both the issue of extending informal communities of practice and challenging inauthentic learning in educational institutions. To address these key issues, however, we need to continue to pursue a radical educational agenda in CSCL.

ACKNOWLEDGMENTS

We would like to thank Jim Welsh, Laura Byrd, Dennis Neale, Jack Carroll and Geraldine Fitzpatrick for their assistance in our CSCL research.

REFERENCES

Appelt, W. and Mambrey, P. (1999) Experiences with the BSCW shared workspace system as the backbone of a virtual learning environment for students. In *the proc. of ED-MEDIA '99,* Seattle, USA.

Bannon, L. J. (1995) Issues in computer supported collaborative learning. In O'Malley, C. (ed.) *Computer Supported Collaborative Learning*. Springer-Verlag, Berlin, Germany, 267-281.

Barab, S. A., Squire, K. D. and Dueber, W. (2000) A Co-Evolutionary Model for Supporting the Emergence of Authenticity. *Educational Technology Research & Development*, **48**,2,37-62.

Bentley, R., Appelt, W., Busbach, U., Hinrichs, E., Kerr, D., Sikkel, S., Trevor, J. and Woetzel, G. (1997). Basic support for cooperative work on the World Wide Web. *International Journal of Human-Computer Studies*, **46**,6,827-846.

Brown, J. S., Collins, A., and Duguid, P. (1989) Situated cognition and the culture of learning. *Educational Researcher*, **18**,1,32-42.

Brown, J. S. and Duguid, P. (2000) *The Social Life of Information*. Harvard Business School Press, Boston, MA.

Carroll, J. M., and Rosson, M. B. (1996) Developing the Blacksburg Electronic Village. *Communications of the ACM*, **39**,12,69-74.

Dewey, J. (1966) *Democracy and Education*. Free Press, New York, NY, (First published 1916).

Eales, R. T. J. and Welsh, J. (1994) Learnability through working together. In *the proceedings of OZCHI'94*, (Melbourne, Australia, 28th Nov - 2nd Dec 1994), pp. 27-32.

Eales, R. T. J. and Welsh, J. (1995) Design for Collaborative Learnability. In *the proceedings of CSCL '95*, (Indiana University, Bloomington, IN), pp. 99-106.

Eales, R. T. J. and Byrd, L. M. (1997) Virtually Deschooling Society: Authentic collaborative learning via the Internet. In *the proceedings of WebNet 97* (World conference of the WWW, Internet & Intranet), Toronto, Canada, November 1997.

Eales, R. T. J., Neale, D. C. and Carroll, J. M. (1999) Desktop Videoconferencing as a Basis for Computer Supported Collaborative Learning in K-12 Classrooms. In *the proceedings of ED-Media 1999* (World Conference on Educational Multimedia, Hypermedia & Telecommunications), Seattle, USA, June 1999.

Eales, R. T. J. (2001) Brewing ALE's: Creating Authentic Learning Environments. In *the proceedings of WebNet 2001* (World conference of the WWW and Internet), Orlando, USA, October 2001.

Eales, R. T. J. (In press) Supporting Informal Communities of Practice within Organizations. In Ackerman, M., Pipek, V. and Wulf , V. (eds). *Beyond Knowledge Management: Sharing Expertise*. MIT Press, Cambridge, MA.

Fischer, G. and Scharff, E. (1998) Learning Technologies in Support of Self-Directed Learning. *Journal of Interactive Media in Education*, **98**,4. [www-jime.open.ac.uk/98/4]

Goodman, P. (1971) *Compulsory Miseducation*. Penguin, Harmondsworth, UK.

Illich, I. (1973) *Deschooling Society*. Penguin, Harmondsworth, UK.

Koschmann, T., Kelson, A. C., Feltovich, P. J. and Barrows, H. S. (1996) Computer-Supported Problem-Based Learning: A principled approach to the use of computers in collaborative learning. In Koschmann, T. (ed.) *CSCL: Theory and practice of an emerging paradigm*. Erlbaum, Mahwah, NJ, 83-124.

Lave, J. (1990) The Culture of Acquisition and the Practice of Understanding. In Stigler, J. W., Shweder, R. A. and Herdt,G. (eds.) *Cultural Psychology*. Cambridge University Press, Cambridge, UK, 309-328.

Lave, J., and Wenger, E. (1991) *Situated Learning: Legitimate Peripheral Participation*. Cambridge, UK: Cambridge University Press.

Petraglia, J. (1997) *Reality by Design: The rhetoric and technology of authenticity in education*. Erlbaum, Mahwah, NJ.

Reimer, E. (1971) *School is Dead*, Penguin, Harmondsworth, UK.

Resnick, L. B. (1987) Learning in School and Out. *Educational Researcher*, **16**,9,13-20.

Rogers, C. R. (1969) *Freedom to Learn*. Merrill, Columbus, OH.

Scardamalia, M. and Bereiter, C. (1996) Computer Support for Knowledge-Building Communities. In Koschmann, T. (ed.) *CSCL: Theory and practice of an emerging paradigm*. Erlbaum, Mahwah, NJ, 249-268.

Vygotsky, L. S. (1978) *Mind in Society: The development of higher psychological processes*. Harvard University Press, Cambridge, MA.

Wenger, E. (1998) *Communities of Practice: Learning, meaning and identity*. Cambridge University Press, Cambridge, UK.

Willis, P. E. (1980) *Learning to Labour: How working class kids get working class jobs*. Gower, Farnborough, UK.

From Paralyzing Myths to Expansive Action: Building Computer-Supported Knowledge Work into the Curriculum from Below

Yrjö Engeström

University of California, San Diego and University of Helsinki, Finland

Yrjo.Engestrom@helsinki.fi

Ritva Engeström

University of Helsinki, Finland

Ritva.Engestrom@helsinki.fi

Arja Suntio

University of Helsinki, Finland

Arja.Suntio@helsinki.fi

ABSTRACT

Technology-driven CSCL solutions are often difficult to integrate into the instructional practices of a school community. We report on an intervention study in a middle school where the entire teaching staff engaged in a year-long effort to change their instructional practices by means of incorporating information and communication technologies in pilot curriculum units. The teachers set out to make pedagogical changes along two dimensions, from procedure-oriented drill to problem- and principle-oriented knowledge production, and from encapsulated classroom work to networked learning in partnerships between the school and organizations outside. They employed conceptual models to anchor their change efforts 'upward' in a long-term general vision. They also anchored their change efforts 'downward', in videotaped examples of classroom practice. Technical tools were subordinate to a pedagogical object. For the pedagogical object to gain momentum and become a true motive for the teachers, they needed to take expansive actions that moved them from myth-driven to object-driven discourse. These expansive actions were actions of redefining the students as capable, and consequently redefining a new model of teaching as possible.

Keywords

Computer-supported knowledge work, school change, expansive learning

INTRODUCTION

In the school year 2000/2001, we conducted a longitudinal intervention study at the Jakomäki middle school in Helsinki, Finland. The school is located in a socio-economically disadvantaged neighborhood of the city, with some 30% of the students coming from recent immigrant and refugee families. The school has 30 full-time teachers, all of whom participate in the intervention. The intervention, called Knowledge Work Laboratory, was a continuation and extension of a Change Laboratory intervention we conducted in the school in 1998/99 (Engeström, Engeström & Suntio, in press).

A central outcome of the intervention work in 1998/99 was a modeling of the inner contradictions of the teachers' activity system (Figure 1).

"...the inner contradictions of the work of Jakomäki teachers appeared only in latent forms, as dilemmas within components of the activity system, not yet as aggravated contradictions between components causing constant manifest troubles or 'double bind' situations in everyday practice. The two lightning-shaped arrows in Figure 1 represent the latent contradictions we found salient in the teachers' activity system. The first one (within the object) was manifested in the teachers' repeated talk about students as apathetic -- and in occasional utterances where they would contradict their very assessment. The second latent contradiction (within the instruments) was manifested in the teachers' repeated talk about the need to control the students' conduct -- and in occasional statements suggesting that the students should be trusted." (Engeström, Engeström & Suntio, in press)

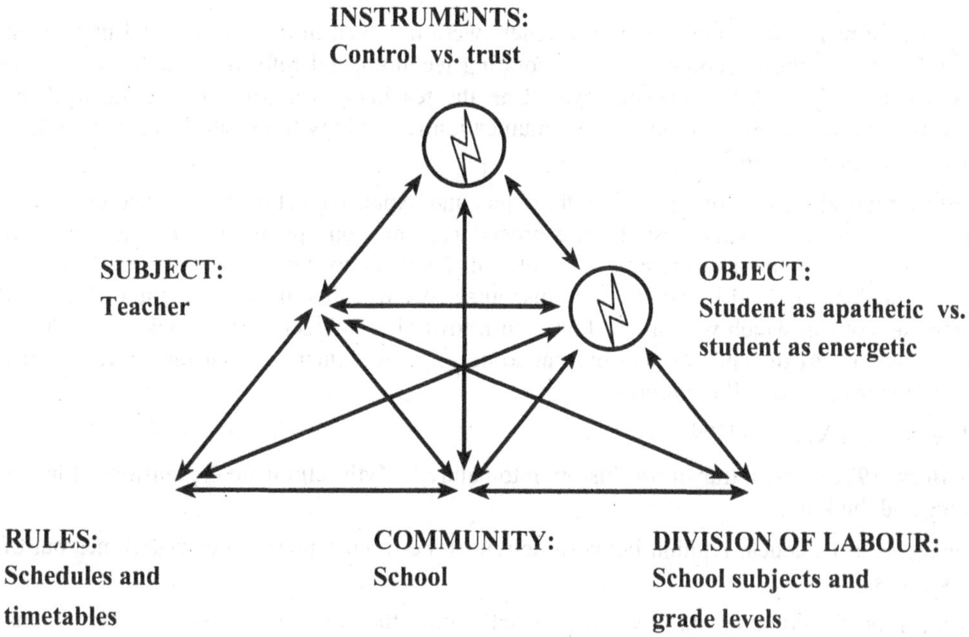

Figure 1. Inner contradictions of the teachers' activity system at Jakomäki middle school (Engeström, Engeström & Suntio, in press)

In the first intervention, we found that the teachers cherished a stubborn collective myth of their students as 'apathetic' beings who could not be trusted. What surprised us was that in spite of this paralyzing myth and the 'underdeveloped' state of the inner contradictions of their activity system, the teachers went on and created potentially expansive and quite durable changes in their work practices.

"In similar intervention studies we have conducted in other organizations (e.g., Engeström, 1999), the practitioners' involvement in serious and sustained change efforts has typically been explained by aggravated contradictions in the activity system. Such aggravated contradictions generate disturbances and double bind situations in everyday work, making it evident that something must be done.

In Jakomäki, this explanation works poorly. As we have already indicated, the teachers did not experience the kind of urgent pressure or pending crisis that would make expansive transformation a deeply felt necessity. Yet the teachers were very willing to design and try out new forms of practice. (…) Instead of dwelling on problems and their causes, they formulated calls for change. This is in stark contrast to our experiences in many similar projects, where the practitioners have interpreted the absence of crisis as a license to protect the status quo." (Engeström, Engeström & Suntio, in press)

Furthermore, we found that in Jakomäki the teachers had an unusually rich and strong relationship to their students' lives – that is, to the dynamics of their object. The 'staring back' of students' reality (Hargreaves, 1997, p. 6) is of course common to any school located in a tough neighborhood. In Jakomäki, the teachers seem unusually sensitive to and energized by this 'staring back' – paradoxically, in spite of their cherished myth of student apathy. As we concluded in an analysis of the first intervention (Engeström, Engeström & Suntio, in press): "Students may be talked about in negative, nostalgic and frustrated terms. But they are not deleted or covered up with the help of fashionable jargon."

Our hypothesis was that the teachers' ability to 'surpass themselves' (Bereiter & Scardamalia, 1993) demonstrated in 1998/98 was not an accidental phenomenon but an historically accumulated property of their activity system. Thus, in the intervention of 2000/01 we *first* of all expected to witness again such a movement from paralyzing myths to expansive action. We *secondly* assumed that this movement would be mediated by the teachers' turn to the students, that is, by anticipatory and actual involvement in students' expectations, reactions and lifeworlds.

In the intervention of 2000/01, the teachers specifically wanted to integrate tools of information and communication technology into their instruction. That is why the intervention was called Knowledge Work Laboratory. They wanted to do this as a step toward new pedagogical practices, not merely because it is fashionable to use computers in teaching. The teachers were very suspicious of technology-driven packages and models of instruction. We might add that our research group also has no particular interest to promote information and communication technologies, and certainly no preferred model or package that we would propagate. Thus, in groups of two to four members, the teachers selected pilot topics, curriculum units in which they applied information and communication technology to facilitate pedagogical change from below. Nine pilot units were formed, and 27 out of the 30 teachers were involved in their design and implementation. So the challenge here was to overcome the phenomenon of evaporating technological reforms brought in from the outside (Cuban, 1986, Tyack & Cuban, 1995). A key question was: Can the teachers as a collective create in their school a sustained movement that turns available information and communication technology tools into locally grounded means or infrastructures of serious pedagogical change?

In the following, we will first introduce the concepts of myth, object and expansive action as key theoretical constructs to be used in our analysis. We will also briefly describe the procedures and conceptual tools of the Knowledge Work Laboratory. After that, we will present and analyze data from the fall 2000 sessions of the Knowledge Work Laboratory, demonstrating the nature of myths expressed in the teachers' discourse. We will then move on to an analysis of data from the winter 2001 laboratory sessions in which we can see how a turn toward the object began to take shape and mediate a transition toward expansive action. At the end, we will present some very preliminary conclusions, aware of the fact that our analysis of the intervention process is still in progress.

MYTH, OBJECT AND EXPANSIVE ACTION

According to Roland Barthes (1972), "myth transforms history into nature." Myths eliminate the tensions of human activity from our ways of speaking and thinking.

"The world enters language as a dialectical relation between activities, between human actions; it comes out of myth as harmonious display of essences."

"Myth does not deny things, on the contrary, its function is to talk about them; simply, it purifies them, it makes them innocent, it gives them a natural and eternal justification, it gives them a clarity which is not that of an explanation but that of a statement of fact." (Barthes, 1972)

The language of myth " organizes a world which is without contradictions because it is without depth." In other words, myth hides away contradictions, it harmonizes and normalizes them.

Myth may be contrasted with the concept of object. According to Leont'ev (1978), the object is the true motive of activity. Object is the horizon of possible actions, a permanently unfinished project. As Jean Baudrillad puts it:

"In our philosophy of desire, the subject retains an absolute privilege, since it is the subject that desires. But everything is inverted if one passes on to the thought of seduction. There, it is no longer the subject which desires, it's the object which seduces. Everything comes from the object and everything returns to it, just as everything started with seduction, not with desire. The immemorial privilege of the subject is overthrown." (Baudrillard, 1990)

Karin Knorr-Cetina (2000) adds the important observation that today's expert activities are increasingly oriented at epistemic objects with extraordinary holding power, motivating force and developmental perspectives.

A move from myth-driven to object-driven talk and action requires expansive actions. By expansive action we mean actions which question the existing mythical definitions of the activity and redefine the object of activity in ways that radically broaden the scope of possibilities for the community (Engeström, 1987).

KNOWLEDGE WORK LABORATORY AND ITS CONCEPTUAL TOOLS

Before the actual intervention sessions, we fist videotaped lessons where teachers used information and communication technologies. After such a lesson, we asked the students and teachers (first separately, then jointly) to reflect and comment critically on the lesson – the commentaries were also videotaped.

In the first laboratory sessions in the fall of 2000, the teachers watched and discussed selected excerpts from the lessons and commentaries. On the basis of these discussions, the teachers selected nine topics and formed nine groups to design new curriculum units to serve as spearheads of change. Plans for the new curriculum units were presented and discussed in sessions in the winter of 2001. The new units were implemented in the spring of 2001, and implementation lessons were again videotaped. At the end of the school year, the new units and their implementation were assessed jointly.

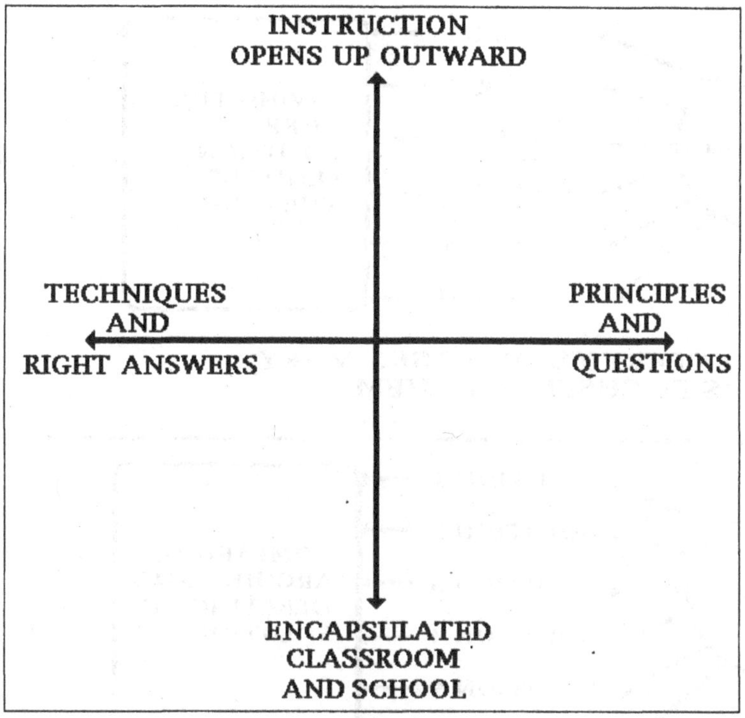

Figure 2. Two dimensions of change in instructional practice

Practices of school instruction and learning may be problematized along two dimensions: (1) the cognitive dimension, ranging from procedure-oriented drill to problem- and principle-oriented knowledge production, and (2) the socio-motivational dimension, ranging from encapsulated classroom work to networked learning in partnerships between school and organizations outside. We used this simple two-dimensional framework as a shared conceptual meta-tool in our intervention sessions at the school (Figure 2).

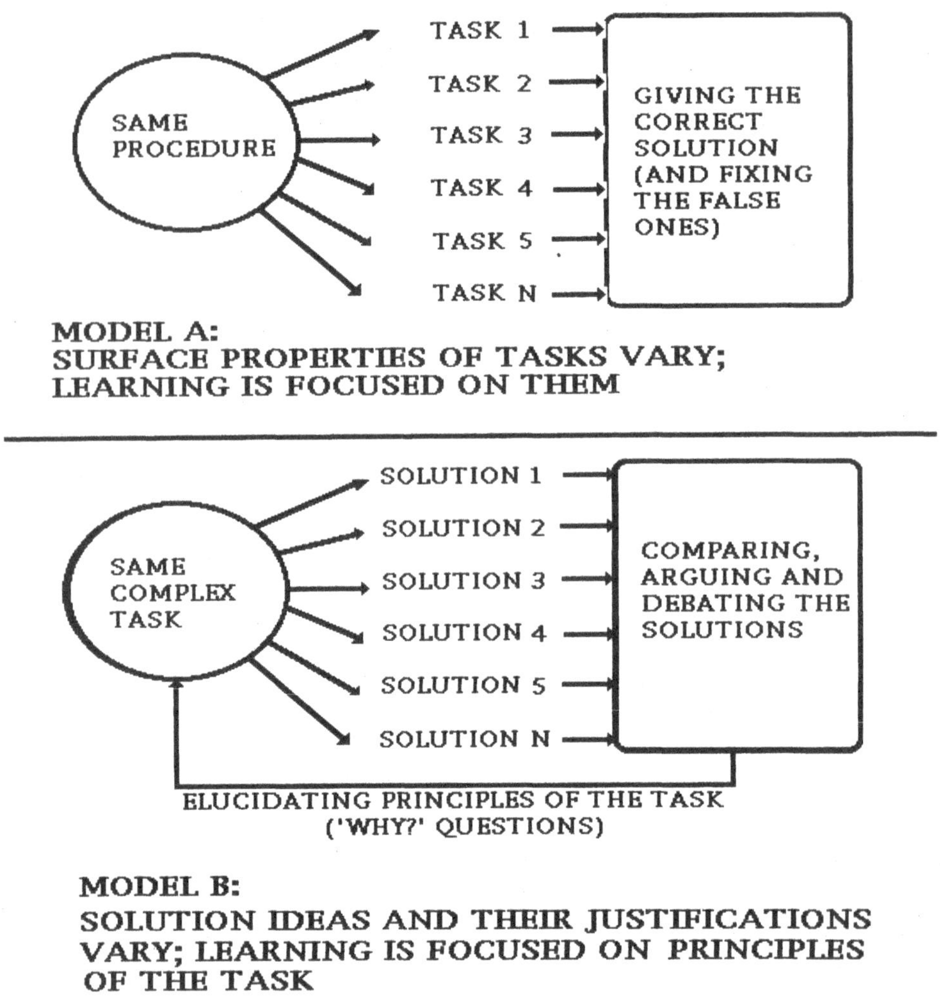

Figure 3. Two models of instruction: variation is the mother of learning

Another central conceptual tool we used in the laboratory sessions distinguishes between two basic models of instruction (Figure 3). This tool is based on Ference Marton's (personal communication) insight: variation is the mother of learning. In the traditional model A, variation is in the surface properties of basically similar tasks. In the challenging model B, variation is in the different solutions produced by students to a single complex problem or task.

FALL SESSIONS: PARALYZING MYTHS

In the first laboratory sessions in the fall of 2000, the teachers repeatedly explicated two myths that were used as warrants for rejecting the possibility of change in instructional practices. The first myth is crystallized in the statement "They just don't have the basic skills. And basic skills can only be learned by Model A." The second myth is condensed in the statement " Certain students only want to copy." Below is an example from the third laboratory session.

Excerpt 1: Laboratory session #3, November 1, 2000

DISCUSSION OF MODELS A and B

Teacher 13: As I see it, in order to be able to work according to model B, they must first learn the basics about the subject, they must have basic knowledge, and one almost has to do it according to the simple model A. Only when they have some knowledge about the subject, then one can go deeper.

The two myths seemed to be unshakable. The more we challenged and questioned them, the more solid they seemed to be. Against this background, we were quite relieved when the teachers actually did select topics and form groups for designing the pilot curriculum units.

WINTER SESSIONS: TURN TOWARD THE OBJECT

In late January, 2001, we started another set of three laboratory sessions, devoted to the presentation and discussion of the teachers' plans for the new units. We were struck by how different the tone of these discussions was compared to the ones held only some three months earlier. Pilot group 3 which designed a unit called 'Project work and ICT professions' is a case in point. During the planning process, the group took up and discussed their idea with the students who expressed enthusiasm for the idea of studying ITC professions by actually taking the roles of different professionals in a real production process. Such a discussion with students was *an expansive action*, quite atypical to the everyday instructional practice in the school. It meant that the teachers plan was not merely an ideal image; it was already grounded in *a turn toward the object,* the students and their concerns. Below is an example from the fourth session.

Excerpt 2: Laboratory session #4, January 31, 2001

PILOT GROUP 3: "PROJECT WORK AND ICT PROFESSIONS" (8th grade)

Teacher 3: Will all the students have sufficient skills? Such a question came up in our group.

Teacher 13: With us...

Teacher 4: They certainly will.

Teacher 13: Yes, they will. Our plan is that when the graphic artists, for example, are put into their own group, one of us, either me or Annie and possibly someone else will be there all the time available, helping them. And the content producers will get guidance from the Finnish language teacher, and so on.

Notice that Teacher 13 is the very same teacher who in Excerpt 1 insisted that complex tasks typical to model B cannot be used because the students do not have sufficient basic skills. Now she had been member of a pilot group which had designed a curriculum unit very much based on complex tasks of type B – and she insisted that the students will indeed have sufficient skills. This kind of change was pervasive throughout all the nine projects. There was practically no use of the two paralyzing myths in the three winter sessions. Excerpt 3 below sheds some light on the dynamics of this change.

Excerpt 3: Laboratory session #4, January 31, 2001

PILOT GROUP 3: "PROJECT WORK AND ICT PROFESSIONS" (8th grade)

Researcher:	Someone said that this is so fancy, did you mean too fancy? It is after all a fact that more and more young people go into those professions...
Teacher 6:	Well, and a certain part of the students... some small part of the students will be really into it.
Teacher 20:	And I think it is very good to try, it doesn't matter if you try to accomplish a bit too much. What have you got to lose, nothing!
Teacher 5:	Yes, and the outcome, it's not so clear what measures we use to assess it. I mean it's not the best outcome that you've got the fanciest CD-ROM and the timing and division into groups were the smoothest. It's an outcome and a result always when the process has worked...
Teacher 20:	...We will help the students as much as we can and that will lead to an outcome, whatever it'll be. If we do this in a traditional way, we won't learn from what we do now, and do it better next year, and so on. We can all only succeed in this.

Teacher 3: I guess many of us think that this pilot will waste, when you know those certain students, that it's a waste of time...

Teacher 5: Well, like Pat (Teacher 20) said, the idea was not to plan something traditional, where we pretty much write the students' correct answers ahead of time, that this is how they'll answer. Wasn't this supposed to be a <u>plan?</u>

In this excerpt, Teacher 6 and Teacher 3 questioned the plan of the pilot unit as being too fancyand unrealistically demanding – a waste of time for the majority of the students. Teacher 20 (Pat) defended the plan, pointing out that they had nothing to lose. Importantly, Teacher 20 was not a member of this particular pilot group. She was a teacher of immigrant students, used to having to find untraditional methods to reach students who do not know Finnish and have little idea of the workings of the traditional

Finnish classroom. Teacher 5 was a member of the pilot group. Challenged by the critics and supported by Pat, she nicely captured the pedagogical idea of model B, as an opposite to "something traditional, where we pretty much write the students' correct answers ahead of time."

PRELIMINARY CONCLUSIONS

In the case analyzed in this paper, the entire teaching staff of a middle school engaged in a year-long effort to change their instructional practices by means of incorporating in formation and communication technologies in pilot curriculum units. However, the means were not seen as the end – or to put in activity-theoretical terms, the tools were not confused the object. The teachers set out to make pedagogical changes along two dimensions, from procedure-oriented drill to problem- and principle-oriented knowledge production, and from encapsulated classroom work to networked learning in partnerships between the school and organizations outside. They employed conceptual models, in particular the models designated as A and B type of teaching (Figure 3), to anchor their change efforts 'upward' in a long-term general vision. They also anchored their change efforts 'downward', in videotaped examples of classroom practice. Technical tools were subordinate to a pedagogical object.

For the pedagogical object to gain momentum and become a true motive for the teachers, they needed to take expansive actions that moved them from myth-driven to object-driven discourse. These expansive actions were actions of *redefining the students as capable, and consequently model B as possible.* When pilot group 3 submitted its idea to discussion with students, it took such an expansive action which in itself redefined the students as capable of having meaningful points of view. On the other hand, the teachers' expansive actions of turning toward the object were in large part induced by and performed in debates in the laboratory sessions. In both Excerpt 2 and Excerpt 3, the optimistic articulation of students as capable and model B as possible happened through debate, in response to questioning, critique, and support. Of course these discursive expansive actions had to be accompanied by equally expansive practical actions in classrooms. The two require each other. The pulsating transitions between these different contexts of action are of crucial importance for the accomplishment of sustainable innovation from below in a school community.

REFERENCES

Barthes, R. (1972). *Mythologies.* New York: Hill and Wang.

Baudrillard, J. (1990). *Fatal strategies.* London: Pluto.

Bereiter, C. & Scardamalia, M. (1993). *Surpassing ourselves: An inquiry into the nature and implications of expertise.* Chicago: Open Court.

Cuban, L. (1986). *Teachers and machines: The classroom use of technology since 1920.* New York: Teachers College Press.

Engeström, Y. (1987). *Learning by expanding: An activity-theoretical approach to developmental research.* Helsinki: Orienta-Konsultit.

Engeström, Y. (1999). Expansive visibilization of work: An activity-theoretical perspective. *Computer Supported Cooperative Work,* 8, 63-93.

Engeström, Y., Engeström, R. & Suntio, A. (in press). Can a school community learn to master its own future? An activity-theoretical study of expansive learning among middle school teachers. In G. Wells & G. Claxton (Eds.) (in press), *Learning for Life in the 21st Century: Sociocultural Perspectives on the Future of Education.*

Hargreaves, A. (1997). Rethinking educational change. In M. Fullan (Ed.), *The challenge of school change: A collection of articles.* Arlington Heights: IRI/SkyLight.

Knorr-Cetina, K. (1999). *Epistemic cultures: How the sciences make knowledge.* Cambridge: Harvard University Press.

Leont'ev, A. N. (1978). *Activity, consciousness, and personality.* Englewood Cliffs: Prentice-Hall.

Tyack, D. B. & Cuban, L. (1995). *Tinkering toward utopia: A century of public school reform.* Cambridge: Harvard University Press.

Working and Learning Together: ICT Supported Learning in Small Businesses

Craig Thomson

Glenrothes College, Scotland

cthomson@glenrothes.ac.uk

ABSTRACT

Information and communications technologies (ICT) sit at the centre of lifelong learning policy in the UK. Considerable public expenditure is being applied to the creation of on-line learning and on-line learner information services. These are seen as having a major role in stimulating learning in small businesses. The small business sector has traditionally proved reluctant to engage in structured programmes of employee development. While policy is finding application through significant spending on new infrastructure, insufficient attention is being paid to the ways in which those in the workplace learn and learn about learning.

Drawing on research carried out in Scotland, this paper suggests that the development of ICT supported work-based learning will result in significant changes in learning relationships and in the sources from which learners seek support. The effective development of learning in small businesses is dependent on the radical changes in technology associated with ICT being matched by equally radical changes in the way that work-based learning is conceptualised and organised. In particular, the potential of new learning relationships must be recognised and taken fully into account in planning and implementing work-based learning programmes. While positive for learners and the businesses in which they work, the changes in roles and relationships which the adoption of this perspective will involve will challenge and are likely to marginalize traditional players in the learning market.

Key words

Work-based learning; small businesses; information and communications technologies; elearning

INTRODUCTION

This paper considers a range of points that are of particular relevance in gaining a clearer understanding of information and communications technology (ICT) supported work-based learning and elearning in small businesses. The context within which the paper has been prepared is provided by current developments in the UK generally and in Scotland specifically. Following the election of a Labour Government for the UK in 1997, learning rapidly became a central policy theme. This has been re-emphasised by the Scottish Parliament. Since its re-establishment in 1999 (after a gap stretching back to 1707), the Scottish Parliament has taken a vigorous approach to policy and, in line with wider policy objectives in the UK, has placed a high priority on education and training and the use of new technologies. It has described its objectives in these areas as the creation of a 'learning nation' (Scottish Executive, 2000) and ensuring that Scotland enjoys '... the fullest possible participation in the digital technologies in timescales that bring competitive advantage' (Scottish Executive, 2001).

As a consequence of these developments, the last two years of the 1990s and the first two of the new Millennium have seen the rapid development of the infrastructure required to enable learning and the provision of information for learners using Web-based systems. The Scottish University for Industry (http://www.scottishufi.co.uk) (SUfI), which operates as *'learndirect scotland'*, and the University for Industry initiative in England and Wales have made progress with the development of robust and effective managed learning environments (MLEs) and with organising and making available information on courses, learning materials and learning support. The SUfI / learndirect scotland offer is based around:

... the national network of learning centres which is currently being established (and) a database of some 60,000 learning opportunities, from basic skills such as numeracy and IT to masters degrees and continuing professional development (Scottish Executive 2001, p16)

SUfI's core objectives include stimulating the development and growth of learning in small businesses. A central theme of this paper is that for this to be achieved it has to be recognised that recent radical developments in learning technology must now be matched by equally radical changes in the ways in which work-based learning in small businesses is understood, organised and supported.

In the following section the term *small business* is briefly defined and explored. The paper moves on to describe and reflect on direct research with small businesses. Two specific sets of issues are identified and explored as being particularly relevant to understanding and developing work-based learning in small businesses. These relate, firstly, to potential *sources* of learner support in the workplace and, secondly, to the *forms* of support required by learners. As part of this central section of the paper, the meaning of the term 'work-based learning' is considered. A further section then reflects on how learners 'learn about learning' in the workplace. This is followed by a concluding section that reflects briefly on a number of the main points raised.

SMALL BUSINESSES

Businesses which are either small or are small/medium (SMEs) make up a very significant sector of the economy of the UK (Matlay 1997, p577). In all but one sector in 1996 (Hughes and Gray 1998, p7), over 99% of all businesses in the UK were SMEs (the exception was the electricity, gas and water supply sector). This translated into 42% of total national turnover and 46% of non-government employment. This is a pattern which repeats around the world. Internationally, "SMEs - defined broadly as fs with up to 500 employees - typically account for up to 99 per cent of all firms, 60 per cent of employment and 40 - 60 per cent of output in national economies" (UNCTAD 1998, p1). The broad definition of SMEs, that is, up to 500 employees, used within this quote is consistent with one of the definitions used by the EU (although EU definitions vary and can also be either 250 or 300). Other definitions of 'SME' include those based on criteria relating to growth rate, level of reserves and supply chain issues. (Hughes and Gray 1998, p10)

For the purpose of this paper, *small business* is used as a term to describe businesses towards the smaller end of the spectrum. Such businesses would typically not, for example, employ specialist human resource managers, operate a training department or enjoy other similar specialist staffing characteristics of larger businesses. Key characteristics are:

- the total number or employees is below 100
- the majority of the operation is in one locality (though not necessarily on one site)
- ownership and control remain within the business.

At the other end of the scale, small is not taken to include 'micro', a term that refers to businesses with five or less employees.

While these characteristics relating to size can be used to define small businesses in general terms, attempts to move the definition onto a more specific level tend to be unproductive. Small businesses vary widely in their area of activity and in the ways in which they are organised and operated. The sector includes everything from 'dot com' businesses working internationally to local trades (plumbers, electricians, joiners, etc), professions (lawyers, accountants, doctors, etc) and retail businesses. The small business 'sector' encompasses sole traders, partnerships, limited companies, charities and cooperatives.

The scale of the challenge faced by SUfI and by other initiatives that are aimed at stimulating learning in small businesses is underlined by the extent to which colleges, universities and other bodies supporting learning have failed to engage successfully with this broad and diverse sector in the past. Working with small businesses can prove difficult, costly and disappointing for organisations involved in education and training (Hughes and Gray 1998, p10). The smaller the business, the less likely they are to embrace or, more critically, to resource, formal programmes of education and training. As Gibb has pointed out in considering small firms' training and competitiveness, ".... training does not appeal to the small firms population for a variety of obvious reasons relating to time and resource" (Gibb 1995, p14). Furthermore, low levels of participation in learning in small businesses result only in part from demand-side problems. They can also be attributed to supply side failure in that many of the education and training opportunities that are made available to small businesses are inappropriate in terms of time, cost and location. Matlay draws attention to the point that many of the solutions offered to this sector were developed for other situations and with larger enterprises in mind:

> Expedient attempts to down-scale and forcibly fit large-scale training strategies to resource-starved small businesses have resulted in a relative paucity of materials focusing specifically upon the human resource needs of smaller firms. (Matlay 1997, p578)

The shift required to ensure that learning materials and methodologies are appropriate to small businesses is a significant one and the assumption that learning relationships (between learners and between learning providers and learners) that have failed in the past can be dusted off and used effectively in elearning has to be recognised as fundamentally flawed. Indeed, despite the fact that the strong proposition behind this paper is that ICT presents exciting and challenging new opportunities, its adoption in work-based situations may eventually prove to owe as much to the limitations of traditional learning as to the benefits that new technologies present (Helm 1997, p41).

LISTENING TO LEARNERS AND DEVELOPING MODELS

The paper now turns to focus on learners in these complex, diverse and challenging situations drawing on research with small businesses carried out in Fife, Scotland between 1997 and 1999 (Thomson, 1999). A central component of the methodology used in this research was the creation, use and review of a number of models that were established and developed by exploring theory and researching practice. Review of literature and exploration of development work being carried out in other parts of Scotland and in the UK more generally can be described as having provided the clay from which the models were initially formed. The more detailed shape that then emerged was based on direct research with a number of small businesses involved in a project in which they were connected by way of a managed extranet to a college of further and higher education. The models helped me to describe, to reflect and to theorise in these areas drawing mainly on a series of detailed, extended semi-structured interviews carried out in small businesses and with staff in the college. These were backed up by wider analysis of the businesses involved.

The models served two purposes. On the one hand, they were used as conceptual methodological devices to 'organise' and to reflect and, on the other, as practical 'tools' to describe, compare and consider the learning situations on which the research focussed. This was based on the position that models offer "... a form of explanation and are therefore closely related to understanding" (Lacey 1993, p127). The interviews with learners were divided into three stages. In the first stage, exploratory interviews were carried out with three learners in two separate businesses. The second stage involved interviews with twelve learners in four small businesses. One of the businesses visited in stage 2 had also been visited in stage 1. The third stage involved a return to this business and the development of a more detailed case study. Three interviews were carried out in stage 3 with learners who performed management roles and who, in addition to reflecting on their own learning, could provide an overview of the organisational context within which learning in the business took place.

In one session with small business employees, two learners were interviewed together. In all others the format was one-to-one and was largely unstructured. Analysis was carried out by marking up each interview and producing an individual summary. Second stage analysis was then carried out and an integrated summary was produced for each small business highlighting individual and common points and themes. The result was a set of source documents on three levels (backed up by audio tapes) - full transcript, individual summaries and SME summaries. The interviews with learners were part of a broader set of field research that included primary work with the 'learning provider', the college. One-to-one interviews were carried out with four college staff and focus group work with two cross-college groups of staff also contributed to the development of an understanding of the college's work with the businesses and with individual learners.

Two outline models were initially developed. The first of these was intended to illustrate *sources* of support for learners and the second the *forms* of support that appeared to be of most relevance to them. The initial understanding that had been developed and invested in these models was used as a basis on which to consider direct information provided by the interviews and other forms of investigation carried out. These highlighted the wide range of factors that shape the experience of individual learners in small businesses. Interviewees explored their social, learning and employment backgrounds; their roles as employees; their learning strategies and skills; and, the extent to which they found that ICT itself acted as a gateway or a barrier to learning. (Mainly a function of their familiarity with or fear of computers.) In addition to these individual characteristics, the research suggested that the experience of learners in small businesses is shaped by the forms of learning support available, by their ability to interact or engage with this support and, as part of this, by the social and organisational contexts within which learning takes place and support for learning is provided. The quality and coherence of learner opportunity can also be influenced by the lack of specialist human resource management and development skills and capacity in the business.

The developed versions of the two models initially produced are described briefly below. In addition to defining the shape of these models, the research provided an opportunity to identify and explore a wider range of factors relevant to successful ICT supported learning in small businesses. The importance of two further factors became increasingly apparent and resulted in the parallel production of two additional models (C and D) encompassing *learning skills* and the *learning context.*

It can be argued that the development of ICT supported learning in a small business has the potential to be a liberating experience. However, interviews with learners suggested that they require assistance if they are to acquire sophisticated learning skills and that interactions between the learner and the workplace and among learners are complex and, in some ways, contradictory. Learner comments suggested strongly that while they wish to have the freedom to develop as learners, they are likely to do this most effectively when the work-based context provides a structure, systems and other elements of control that are positive and supportive. If this is achieved, it can be argued that learners will benefit from an environment in which their learning is characterised by clarity and informed choice on their part as opposed to '...institutional control over the construction of the learner' (Gillard 1992, p182). Indeed, the paradox can be proposed that establishing broad, appropriate and collaborative structured contexts for work-based learners provides them with much more opportunity (and responsibility) to construct themselves as they learn and collaborate with other learners. Models C and D are described in a parallel paper which is currently in preparation.

LEARNING IN THE WORKPLACE

The points above relating to collaboration in learning and support for learners in the workplace focus attention on a specific question. What exactly is meant by work-based learning? In addressing this, it is important to bear in mind the primary function of the locations in which it takes place. Pillay, Brownlee et al. (1998, p240) point out that while workplaces can offer excellent learning opportunities, they are complex learning situations that have other priorities that, "...may hinder the learning process". Work-based learning takes place in locations that those involved recognise primarily as workplaces, not learning places. Problems resulting from lack of time, space or priority being applied to learning are common.

Within these complex contexts, the relationship between learning and work can take a number of forms as individuals observe, explore or self-instruct, receive on the job instruction, withdraw from the job to learn or are involved in various combinations of these and other options. In attempting to explore and understand this diverse set of potential forms of work-based learning, a useful distinction can be drawn between learning *at* work and learning *for* or *through* work (Reeve, Gallacher et al. 1998, p19).

The work of Jean Lave also presents terms and concepts that are helpful. Lave explores how people work and learn in dynamic, changing and developing contexts in which learning results from direct participation (Lave, 1993). In Lave's view the individual learner does not gain a discrete body of abstract knowledge to transport and reapply in later contexts. Instead, it is acquired by engaging in a range of processes under the attenuated conditions of *legitimate peripheral participation.* (Hanks 1991, p14) Lave emphasises the circularity of the relationship between learning and the workplace in a direct experiential sense: learning takes place in context, results from participation and develops through experience.

The direct research in small businesses described above provided an insight into situations in which a range of learning was taking place, some of which was contextualised and some, in an immediate, concrete or experiential sense, partly decontextualised. Learners were engaged in a range of activity including 'fully situated' learning (both supported by and not supported by ICT) in which they were learning through participation as part, for example, of their day-to-day work. It also included learning by way of transfer (or intentional instruction as Lave would have it) involving the computer as a medium of self-instruction or supported instruction. A further set of activity was also apparent (a point to which I return towards the end of this paper) that involved learning about learning. This was also fully situated as learners undertook a form of apprenticeship in learning and developed learning skills and strategies influenced by the culture and behaviour around them in the workplace.

SOURCES AND FORMS OF LEARNER SUPPORT

Review and reflection on the direct research carried out in small businesses combined with the interviews and focus group work with college staff provided an insight into how the development of ICT supported learning can be dominated by the technology and the materials involved. The specific needs of learners can be overshadowed by more abstract consideration of the availability and appropriateness of technology and materials. However, while it is important to see beyond the technology and to emphasise the centrality of learning and the learner, it is an oversimplification to suggest that technical issues should simply be set aside to allow pedagogy to be given its rightful place. The critical importance of the technology and, related to this, of the nature and format of materials in ICT supported learning has to be acknowledged and a balance achieved reflecting the fact that '... pedagogy and technology are ... fundamental and inseparable'. (Evans and Nation 1993, p197) The need to achieve this balance helped to define the shape of the first of the models, Model A, which highlights two broad sets of learner interfaces. The first of these, described as *transactional links*, relates to the range of potential supportive inter-personal transactions in which learners in small businesses might engage locally and at a distance. The second interface relates to the technology and the materials delivered or supported by this. These are described as *instrumental connections.*

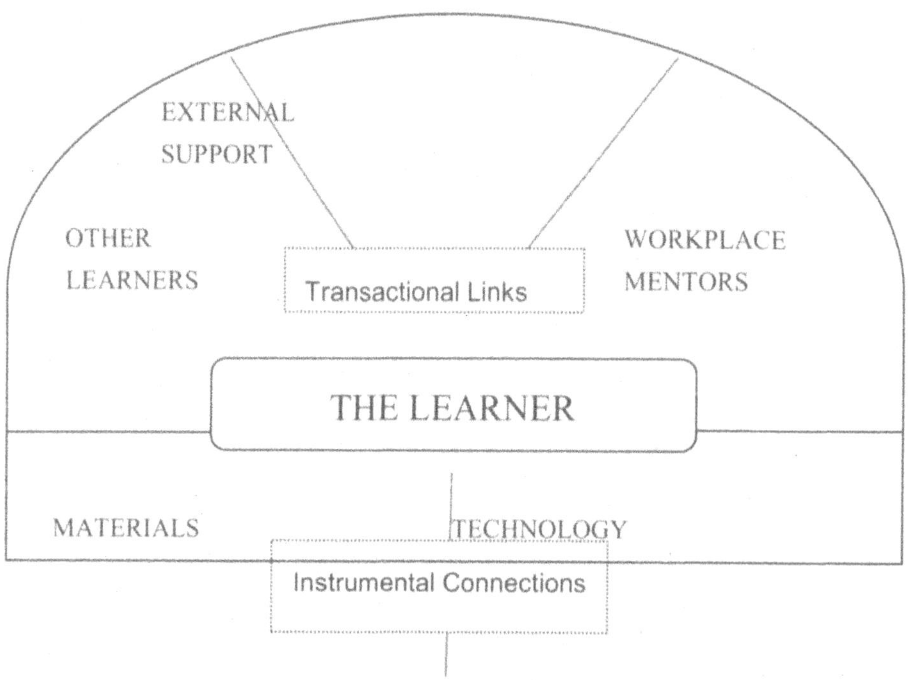

MODEL A: LEARNER INTERFACES

Model A is based on a third generation view of distance learning (Garrison, 1985; Nipper, 1989; Evans and Nation, 1993;Thorpe, 1998). The key elements of third generation distance learning are interactivity (Thorpe 1998, p270) and the integration of new technologies and materials with support for learning. As such, its development has been tied closely to the emergence of the information society. Garrison (1997, p3) describes a "... post-industrial model of teaching and learning at a distance" which "... incorporates highly interactive communications technology along with the ideal of both personalised and collaborative learning".

The framework within which learners in small businesses collaborate is reflected by the three principal transactional links identified in Model A. These are learners' potential points of contact with external support (such as college or university tutors), in-company support (workplace mentors) and other learners. The transactional links combine with the two principal instrumental connections or 'non-human' points of contact for learners (with learning materials and technology). These various components shaped Model A as illustrated.

In considering sources and forms of support together, two points drawn from the interviews with learners can be emphasised. Firstly, with only one exception, these in-depth discussions indicated a strong demand or desire for some form of supportive interaction. Secondly, the patterns and levels of support in place at the time of the interviews differed between learners and between businesses and tended largely to be unstructured and unplanned. In the small business that sat at the centre of the research, interviews carried out in three separate sets stretching over 15 months revealed that learner support tended to take place informally (albeit also on an ad hoc basis) through inter-colleague collaboration. Interviewees referred frequently to asking others in the workplace for help and to working with others in their learning. In part, this could be attributed to the lack of proactive support coming from the college providing their learning programmes. However, it also appeared to be defined by the internal dynamics of the business and, more specifically, by inter-employee relationships in the business.

Over the 15 months a learning community developed and within this, learners turned first to internal help from colleagues prior to considering external, expert support. Based on the accounts of the learners involved, it is possible to argue that the overall patterns of support that will prove most effective in small businesses using ICT in learning are likely to prove quite different from those in traditional work-based, and fundamentally different from traditional college or university-based settings.

This is not to suggest that one simple model (that is, that teachers support learners) can be replaced by another (learners support each other). The apparent position that emerged from the interviews suggested that the range of links used and the emphasis placed on them will vary from learner to learner with the permutations broadly defined by Model A. A factor relevant to the successful development of ICT supported work-based learning that can be drawn from this is that a range of potential forms of support should be available and learners should be clear about how to engage with each potential link in a pattern that meets their specific individual needs. Learning opportunities should be made available in a way that allows "... individualised and cooperative and collaborative kinds of learning to be combined" (Friedrich 1997, p34).

ICT opens the door to work-based learning in a small business moving on from the handing down or the handing on of information or skills from individual to individual. It has the potential to develop as a socially located exercise that rejects views of ICT supported learning as an individual exercise supported by a single umbilical link to a distant tutor. Much and potentially most of the social interaction can be local (that is, within the business) rather than distant. The lack of specialist or dedicated staff organising, delivering or supporting learning in small businesses makes the potential role of ICT doubly important in this respect.

While Model A identifies a set of points of interaction for learners, it does not include any indication of the forms of support required or provided at each interface. Rather than attempting to integrate these in (and complicating) the same model, these points were incorporated in a separate, linked model (Model B). The development of this followed a similar pattern to Model A. However, the initial outline drew significantly on a single source. In the mid-1980s during a period in which increasing priority was being placed in the UK on open learning as the way forward in further education, the Manpower Services Commission (MSC) funded the National Extension College to produce an 'Open Learning Toolkit'. Extracts from this in Lewis and Spencer (1986, p94). include the identification of the key roles of managers/teachers in open learning schemes when supporting learners. Their work has largely managed to stand the test of time in that it provided a basis on which to model the principal forms of learner support relevant to work-based learners in the 21st century.

As with Model A, the review of Model B drew on the interviews carried out with learners and took place in formal and informal discussions. This aspect of the research also benefited from work with staff in the college and drew significantly on the focus group sessions held there. Model B (along with Model A) was also critically reviewed in a workshop/focus group session made up of individuals from six separate colleges (one from each), one member of staff from an industry 'lead body' and one from an ICT content publishing company. The workshop had been organised as part of an ICT focused project and each of those present had an interest and involvement in the field.

A major distinction between Model B and Model A is that while ICT supported learning creates new sources of support, different points of contact and new collaborative relationships for learners in small businesses, the *scope* of support required by these learners does not appear to differ significantly from that required by them in traditional (same time/same place) settings.

SUPPORTING LEARNERS

Involves....

informing / advising / guiding / tutoring / counselling

any one of which may involve

communicating, facilitating, feeding back, reassuring, listening, inspiring, valuing, encouraging

MODEL B: LEARNER SUPPORT

Although the shape of Model B was influenced by the MSC Toolkit and its subsequent use by Lewis and Spencer, the assumptions behind it differ significantly. The assumption that the principal (or, indeed, the sole) relationship relevant to the learner is that with her tutor or teacher is rejected. Models A and B reflect the view that college, university or other tutors are simply one of a range of possible sources of help and support available to the learner. Internal support in the workplace is viewed as a central factor in this form of work-based learning.

The individual points relating to learner behaviour and expectations that shaped Models A and B were set within a complex context. Various internal priorities of the small businesses combined with systems, structure and other factors to complicate or simplify, reward or discourage and displace or accommodate learning. The picture that emerged was one in which small businesses each have their own cultures, relationships, rules and objectives. These shape how people work together and set the context within which they can learn together. Each of the small businesses in which research was carried out showed similarities to and also differed from each of the others. Similarly, the learners interviewed presented distinct pictures of themselves as learners, workers and individuals. They described learning contexts that combined individual variety resulting from the interdependence between and mutual influence of learning and context (Lave 1993, p5) and collective stability resulting from parameters specific to each business. The research highlighted the extent to which the organisational and cultural context of businesses are critical in shaping work-based learning and in setting internal limits to variation in the learning context. These limits are both implicit in terms of norms of behaviour (including learning behaviour and expectations) and explicit where tasks and standards of performance are specified in the form of job descriptions and learning plans (Scribner 1984, p15).

LEARNING ABOUT LEARNING

Interviews with learners provided an insight into the sources and forms of support that they require. The accounts of learners also indicated how they interact and collaborate as they learn about learning. While interviews with learners indicated their individuality as learners, there was also a strong indication that this aspect of their individuality was 'clustered' to a significant extent. Individuals interviewed in each small business revealed similar characteristics and expectation to learners in the same business. Similarities within single businesses did not always appear in the other businesses involved. Furthermore, clustered differences also appeared to exist between different locations in one of the small businesses involved (which operated from three separate sites with distinct groups of employees on each). Employees at one location revealed expectations and assumptions about learning which differed significantly from those which appeared to prevail at the other two sites.

These points make it possible to suggest that individuals develop assumptions about and commitment to learning and learning skills and strategies within a form of apprenticeship model. This is consistent with views of apprenticeship and communities of practice set out by Fuller and Unwin (1998, p158) who point out that such communities in the workplace are:

> … not only defined geographically, but also by the connections and relationships that are developed between its members and between them and the activity that brings them together.

New learners in such situations begin to learn and, closely influenced by their colleagues, to learn about learning. Their understanding and expectations about learning in the workplace (that is, in the specific workplace in which they are located) are critically influenced by the behaviour and expectations of their co-participants. Small businesses conform to the characteristics of communities of practice set out by Wenger (1998). Where behaviour is positive and expectations are high, this can be expected to influence new employees and new learners in the workplace positively as they work out the meaning of learning in that location. Within the workplace (as in other situations) "… people in activity are skilful at, and are more often than not engaged in, helping each other to participate in changing ways in a changing world" (Lave, 1993, p5).

CONCLUDING POINTS

ICT has the potential to stimulate the construction of new models and relationships in which access to and take up of learning in small businesses can be increased within structured programmes of relevant, appropriate education and training. Recent progress with the development of technology, environments and materials has been impressive. However, it cannot simply be assumed that better learning results from more technology, more challenging instructional media and more interactivity by way of communications media (Thorpe 1998, p271). Furthermore, little will be achieved if ICT is simply used as a medium to rework inflexible forms of interaction with small businesses and work-based learners that have failed in the past or to repackage learning solutions developed for larger work-based situations. New solutions are required. Experience to date, including the research described in part in this paper, suggests several points that are relevant to the form that these should take. Four sets of points are highlighted in this conclusion.

Firstly, work-based learning has to be recognised as multi-dimensional. It takes place in a variety of formal and informal situations, is based on a wide range of activities and encompasses a broad spectrum from hands-on activity to abstract learning. The format in which opportunities are presented and organised for learners has to be sufficiently flexible to reflect this diversity and to do so in a way that recognises that learning tends to be viewed as a secondary, optional activity in the workplace.

Secondly, and building on this point, learning environments and materials and the provision of support for learners have to be developed in a way that encourages and accommodates both the intricate patterns of collaboration and coparticipation that exist between learners and the complex interaction between learners and the workplace as a learning site. ICT creates the opportunity to develop new relationships based on new technologies, new materials and ever-faster telecommunications and should be harnessed to support the development of mutually supportive communities of learners composed of interdependent individuals. This will require the further development of learning support methodologies that recognise and foster both personalised and collaborative approaches to learning.

Thirdly, the lack of specialist human resource management capacity in small businesses has to be recognised as an important factor. Small businesses are most likely to engage with learning when its organisation and management are uncomplicated and when learning tasks and content can be related directly to business need and business development. It is important that technology, environments, materials and methodology all combine to support the management of learning and the development of explicit links between learning and the needs of the business.

Finally, the successful stimulation of learning in small businesses is critically dependent on the development of a new understanding of the sources of support that learners require and a clear appreciation of the forms of support most appropriate to them. As collaborative learning between and among learners develops, contact with colleagues and other learners and the availability of more comprehensive, self contained and inspiring learning materials are likely to mean that learners can increasingly be expected to view traditional forms of tutor support as optional, distant features. Changes associated with the information society, with the emergence of third generation distance learning and with the history and inherent characteristics of work-based learning in small businesses are fundamentally changing the 'geography' of learning. These changes are resulting in a move from distance *learning* to distance *tutoring*. ICT shifts the organisation, support and assessment of learning more firmly into a freestanding format in the workplace and, as a result, represents a challenge to the distance and traditional learning establishments to reconceptualise radically their relationships with the small business sector.

In the absence of an understanding of and a willingness to address points such as these, current broad policies in the UK aimed at the development of a learning society and specific lifelong learning initiatives such as SUfI will fail to attract and to benefit individual learners and workers and the small businesses in which they are employed.

REFERENCES

Evans, T. and Nation, D. (1993) *Reforming Open and Distance Education*, London: Kogan Page.

Friedrich, F. (1997) Transfer of Learning Technologies – the experience of the DELTA DEMO ESC Project, *Open Learning* **13(2):** 51 – 57.

Fuller, A and Unwin, L (1998) Reconceptualising Apprenticeship: exploring the relationships between work and learning, *Journal of Vocational Education and Training* **50(2):** 153-171.

Garrison, D. (1985) Three generations of technological innovation in distance education, *Distance Education* **6(2):** 235 – 241.

Garrison, D. (1997) Computer Conferencing: the post industrial age of distance education, *Journal of Open and Distance Education* **12(2):** 3 – 11.

Gibb, A. (1995) Small Firms' Training and Competitiveness: Building upon the small business as a learning organisation, *International Small Business Journal* **15:(3)** 13 – 29.

Gillard, G (1992) Deconstructing Contiguity, in Evans T and Nation, D. (eds) *Reforming Open and Distance Education,* London, Kogan Page.

Hanks, W (1991) Foreword, in Lave, J and Wenger, E. (eds) *Situated Learning: Legitimate peripheral participation*, Cambridge: Cambridge University Press.

Helm, P. (1997) Teaching and Learning with the New Technologies: for richer, for poorer, for better, for worse, in Field, J. (ed) *Electronic Pathways*, Leicester: NIACE.

Hughes, M. and Gray, S. (1998) *Promoting Learning in Small and Medium Sized Enterprises*, Coventry: The Further Education Funding Council.

Lacey, C. (1993) Problems of Sociological Fieldwork: a review of the methodology of Hightown Grammar in Hammersley, M. (ed) *Educational Research: Current Issues*, London: Open University Press.

Lave, J (1993) The practice of learning in Chaiklin, S. and Lave, J (eds) *Understanding practice: perspectives on activity and context,* Cambridge, Cambridge University Press.

Lewis, R. and Spencer, D. (1986) *What is Open Learning*? Cambridge: Cambridge University Press.

Matlay, H. (1997) The Paradox of Training in the Small Business Sector of the British Economy, *Journal of Vocational Education and Training* **49(4):** 573 – 589.

Nipper, S. (1989) Third generation distance learning and computer conferencing, in Mason, R. and Kaye, A. (eds) *Mindweave: communication, computers and distance education*, Oxford: Pergammon.

Pillay, H., et al. (1998) The Influence of Individual's Beliefs about Learning and Nature of Knowledge on Educating a Competent Workforce, *Journal of Education and Work*, **11(3):** 239 – 254

Reeve, F., et al. (1998) Can New Technology Remove Barriers to Learning? *Open Learning*, **13(3):** 18 – 26

Scottish Executive (2000) *Scotland: the learning nation.* Edinburgh, Scottish Executive Consultations.

Scottish Executive (2001) *Digital Inclusion: Connecting Scotland's People,* Edinburgh, Scottish Executive Publications.

Scribner, S. (1984) Studying Working Intelligence, in Rogoff, B. and Lave, J. (eds) *Everyday Cognition: its development in social context,* Cambridge: Harvard University Press.

Thomson, C (1999) *Developing information and communications technology supported work-based learning in small and medium sized enterprises: Thesis submitted for the degree of Doctor of Education.* Sheffield, University of Sheffield.

Thorpe, M. (1998) *Assessment and third generation distance education.* Distance Education, **19(2):** 265 – 286

UNCTAD (1998) *Note to Correspondents No 44*, http:/www.unctad.org/em/pub/pu98guen.htm

J. (TECHNOLOGY TRACK): SYNCHRONOUS COLLABORATION SUPPORT FOR CHILDREN

Understanding Children's Interactions in Synchronous Shared Environments

Stacey D. Scott, Regan L. Mandryk, Kori M. Inkpen

EDGE Lab
School of Computing Science
Simon Fraser University
Burnaby, BC V5A 1S6 Canada
+1 604 291 3610
{sdscott, rlmandry, inkpen}@cs.sfu.ca

ABSTRACT

Traditional computer technology offers limited support for face-to-face, synchronous collaboration. As a result, children who wish to collaborate using computers must adapt their interactions to the single-user paradigm most personal computers are based on. More recently, co-located groupware systems offering support for concurrent, multi-user interactions around a shared display have become technologically feasible. Unlike traditional groupware systems that provide multi-user interaction through the use of separate computers, these systems share the physical workspace, as well as the virtual workspace. These systems provide a unique mechanism through which children can interact with each other. However, ways to best utilize the technology in this manner has not been fully evaluated. This paper investigates how technological support for children's synchronous interactions facilitates their collaborative activities. In particular, we examined whether a shared workspace facilitates the development of a shared understanding during a computer-based collaborative activity. We present a field study that observed pairs of children playing an educational game in several display configurations. The findings from this research suggest strengths and weaknesses of various types of support for synchronous interactions and discusses issues related to the design and development of more effective computer systems to support children's face-to-face interactions.

KEYWORDS

Shared environments, co-located collaboration, Computer Supported Cooperative Work (CSCW), Computer Supported Collaborative Learning (CSCL), educational games, children, experimental evaluation, communication

INTRODUCTION

Despite the many technological advances to support distributed interactions, people still spend a great deal of time traveling to meet face-to-face with colleagues, family, and friends. Interacting in a face-to-face environment is very engaging. Numerous research and commercial endeavors have investigated technological advances in an attempt to capture the essence of face-to-face interactions when supporting people working at a distance (Fish et al., 1992; Gutwin et al., 1996; Inoue et al., 1997). Most groupware research assumes that face-to-face collaboration provides a richer experience and thus distributed groupware systems are often designed to recreate the feeling of "being there" (Gutwin et al.; 1996, Hollan & Stornetta, 1992; Inoue et al., 1997). However, an equally important endeavor is the exploration of how technology can enhance and improve users' co-located interactions. This is especially important when considering children's use of technology. Emergent environments such as home-use and portable computing are causing researchers to question the fundamental designs that society has adopted as representative of a computer. Traditional interaction paradigms, such as the one-keyboard one-mouse paradigm can be constraining to users and are slowly giving way to more flexible technologies, such as large screen displays (Pedersen et al., 1993; Streitz et al., 1994; Tani et al., 1994) and handheld computers (Myers at al., 1998). Still, these new technologies are not sufficiently addressing the needs of all users, specifically multiple children sharing machines in the classroom (Inkpen et al., 1999).

Distance learning is currently a major research and industrial focus worldwide while the re-design of hardware and software to support co-located learners in a classroom environment is explored less frequently. In most classrooms today, synchronous collaboration is supported in three different ways: 1) children working together at the same computer; 2) children working together on side-by-side computers; and 3) children working with others at a distance through networked computers. Understanding students' communication and interaction patterns in these three configurations can help us gain new insights into the strengths and weaknesses of each approach and discover issues related to the design of more effective interactive systems for face-to-face collaboration.

Our work investigates children's interactions while playing a puzzle-solving mathematics game in various collaborative configurations. We examine issues surrounding a shared understanding in a collaborative task. Much of the previous literature on cooperative learning suggests that shared goals, tasks, resources, and roles enhance shared understanding and allow for an effective cooperative learning experience (see Hymel et al., 1993 for an overview). This paper presents research related to co-located collaboration followed by a description of our field study, the methodology used, and the data collected. Empirical results are presented and analyzed. Finally, we discuss the impact of this work for supporting co-located collaboration, along with directions for future work.

BACKGROUND

The rich information available in co-located collaborative environments has spurred researchers to find novel ways of supporting multiple people working together around a shared display. Research in Single Display Groupware (SDG) (Stewart et al., 1999) has explored the development of co-located multi-user environments including connecting individual computers to one large, passive display (Tatar et al., 1991, Tani et al., 1994), creating large, shared interactive displays (Pedersen et al., 1993, Streitz et al., 1999), and providing multiple peripherals on a shared computer (Stewart et al., 1999, Myers et al., 1998).

These aforementioned studies have been primarily focused on supporting co-located collaboration in the workplace. While this is important groundwork, the domain of children working together in the classroom has unique issues and considerations. Children are smaller than adults, have no access to resources beyond what is provided at school or through their parents, and have different goals. While professionals and students both have the motivation of deadlines imposed by organizations or teachers, children need to experience enjoyment from their computer interactions in order to continue investigating the possibilities that technology has to offer (Inkpen et al., 1997). There are many exciting toys and leisure activities competing for children's time and interest. Children enjoy playing together and studies have shown that social interactions in a learning environment lead to significant learning benefits and that there are positive academic and social benefits to having children work together in groups (Hymel et al., 1993; Johnson et al., 1981).

In order to support children working together while maintaining the existing technological infrastructure available in most schools, current systems have been extended to accommodate multiple children using one computer. This has been accomplished using peripheral devices, such as styli (Bier & Freeman, 1991), joysticks (Bricker et al., 1999), and mice (Scott et al., 2000; Stewart et al., 1999), to provide multi-user interaction. However, most of these solutions still require specialized software development since most commercial software has been designed and implemented for use by a single user. Other research has investigated the use of smaller and less expensive handheld computers in the classroom to support collaborative educational activities (Mandryk et al., 2001), however, these devices are often not available in school environments.

Previous research suggests that shared displays provide certain advantages when computers are being used for collaboration (Inkpen et al., 1995). Sharing a display provides a shared artifact for collaborators to use in their conversation, which has been shown to increase attention and involvement during a collaborative task (Bly, 1988). Furthermore, research suggests that users subconsciously respond to computers as social actors, potentially complicating the task of discussing shared objects located on different screens (Reeves & Nass, 1996).

Although providing a shared display for co-located collaboration seems intuitive (i.e. it is a natural way to interact), research has not clearly demonstrated that a shared display system supports concurrent multi-user interaction as well as alternative display configurations such as side-by-side monitors, or distributed, networked computers. Children are very good at engaging in rich face-to-face social interactions. Research has shown that students can become more motivated and successful when these interactions are supported (Inkpen et al., 1999). Our study employed both quantitative and rich qualitative measures to elucidate why these designs are successful and to evaluate the effectiveness of several display configurations on a collaborative task.

FIELD STUDY

To better understand children's interactions in synchronous shared environments, we observed children playing a collaborative mathematical computer game. The children were given the opportunity to play the game in various configurations to support their collaborative interactions.

Students and Setting

Twenty-four grade seven students aged 11 to 13 (14 girls and 10 boys) from Lord Nelson Elementary School volunteered to participate in the study. Lord Nelson is located in a lower socioeconomic, culturally diverse area of Vancouver, British Columbia, Canada. Consent to participate was obtained from all children and their parents. The children played the game in the a small room off the school's library and the researchers remained in the room to monitor the equipment, address issues with the software, and take field notes of the children's interactions.

Children played the game using a personal computer with two universal serial bus mice. They used either one or two 19-inch monitors, depending on which collaborative setup they were playing in. When each student was given their own monitor, a VGA splitter was used to send the same output to the two monitors to simulate networked computers. This ensured that the hardware performance was consistent across all three playing conditions. Observations of the children's play were recorded by two video cameras, each with a lavaliere microphone. The children also wore audio headphones through which they could hear the output from their partner's microphone. While this was necessary in the distributed condition, it was also provided in the other configurations to minimize the novelty effect if the audio equipment. Although this decision was important for the quantitative analyses, it may have negatively impacted the qualitative data gathered from the non-distributed configurations.

Play Conditions

Children played the game in three different collaborative configurations: shared, side-by-side, and separated. In the shared configuration the subjects were seated beside each other, sharing a monitor (see Figure 1a). In the side-by-side configuration the subjects were seated beside each other, each having their own monitor (see Figure 1b). In the separated configuration, subjects were seated in the same room, each with their own monitor attached to the same computer, but visually separated by a divider (see Figure 1c). In each collaborative configuration, the children had their own mouse to control their own on-screen character.

Game Description

The game the children played was a mathematical game called Prime Climb (see Klawe, 1998), originally developed as a part of a distributed multi-player game, Avalanche. Prime Climb was modified to produce a stand-alone version that supported multi-user interactions on a single computer. The MID Java API (Hourcade & Bederson, 1999) was used to support concurrent, multi-user interactions within the game.

The goal of Prime Climb is to guide a pair of climbers to the top of a mountain, and to complete as many mountains (levels) as possible. To finish a level, players must work together to move on-screen characters to the top of a mountain consisting of stacked hexagon blocks. Players move to new positions by mouse-clicking on hexagons containing numbers. Two climbers are displayed on the screen (red and blue), each controlled by a cursor of the corresponding colour. The climbers are connected by a rope that can span at most three hexagons. Climbers can move only to a space adjacent to their current location and must avoid obstacles (goats, rocks, and trees).

The main rule of the game is that the two climbers can never be positioned on numbers that have a common factor other than one. If a player chooses an illegal number, their climber falls off of the mountain and begins swinging by the rope two levels below his/her partner. A swinging player must select a nearby number on the mountain to stop swinging. If a swinging player chooses an illegal number again, his/her partner falls and begins swinging. An additional feature of the game is an ice pick, located in the upper-left corner of the game window. Dragging the ice pick to the mountain and dropping it onto a hexagon decreases the value in the hexagon by one, to a minimum of one. When the players reach the top of a mountain, a new mountain appears for the next level of the game. Levels increase in difficulty by adding more obstacles, using larger numbers, and increasing the height of the mountains.

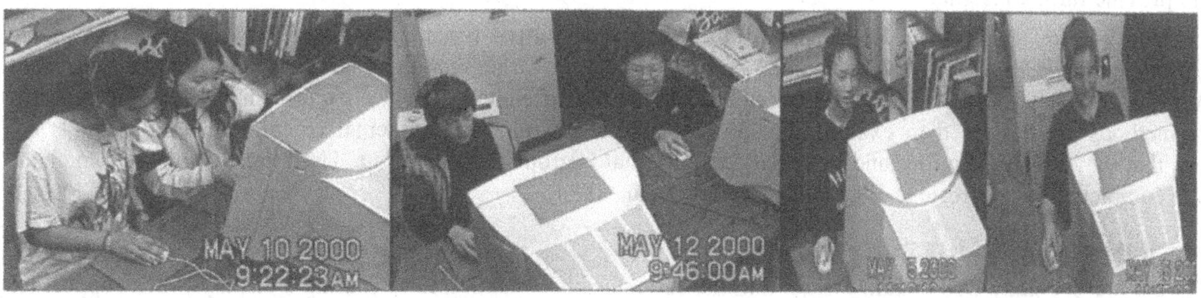

(a) (b) (c)

Figure 1: Kids played the game in three different display configurations. a) Shared display configuration, b) Side-by-side display configuration, c) separated display configuration.

Figure2 : Screen shot of the Prime Climb game.

Game Playing Sessions

Each pair of students was excused from class on three separate occasions and were given the opportunity to play the game in each of the collaborative configurations. During the first session, the students completed a background questionnaire to gather information on their exposure to computers and games. Following this, the rules of the game were explained and the children were given 15-minutes to play the game in one of the collaborative configurations. The children then returned for two additional 15-minute sessions to play in the remaining two collaborative configurations. After each session, the children filled out an interface evaluation questionnaire to elicit opinions on game difficulty, enjoyment level, and mutual understanding during their play. When a pair of students had completed all conditions, they filled out a post-experiment questionnaire to determine overall impressions of the game and feedback on the three collaborative configurations.

The study spanned two weeks, during which pairs did not play in more than one session on the same day. The order in which the children played the collaborative configurations was counterbalanced to avoid any order effects. Due to illness, two pairs were unable to complete the experiment and data for only 20 children were fully collected.

Data Analyses

Both quantitative and qualitative data were gathered from several sources during the study, including field notes, video, questionnaires, and computer logging. Computer log files tracked performance data including the number of mountains completed, the game events, and the number of errors. Verbal and non-verbal communications were analyzed from the video data using the MacShapa™ video analysis system. Inter-rater reliability was found to be high for both the verbal and non-verbal coding schemes. Video data for a subset of the participants were transcribed and annotated with corresponding field notes and computer log data. The conversation and gestures were coded and analyzed iteratively using the NVivo™ qualitative analysis software package (Richards, 1999). Three pairs, two female pairs and one male pair, were selected based on the order in which they performed the experimental conditions. Finally, questionnaire data from all pairs were analyzed to provide further insights.

The decision to employ qualitative techniques together with quantitative research methods is well supported in the literature. Both methods have their own strengths and are best used to address their corresponding research purposes (Maxwell, 1996). Quantitative methods are best used to examine the differences between experimental conditions whereas qualitative methods are best used to examine the process across or within experimental conditions. Both methods are empirical in that they involve rigorous and systematic inquiry that is grounded in the data. Used together, the two methods can be quite complementary (Firestone 1987; Miles & Huberman, 1994).

DISCUSSION OF RESULTS

The goal of the present study was to gain insight into the strengths and weaknesses of sharing a display, when support for concurrent activity is provided. Data were collected to promote understanding of students' interactions and communication patterns when collaborating in different display conditions. After a brief vignette, we present and discuss some of the insights gained during the study and subsequent analyses of the data. The vignette illustrates the type of interactions that occurred during the game play.

Betty and Sarah are trying to finish a difficult level as fast as they can and are finding it difficult to make it up the mountain without falling. Sarah is instructing Betty where she should go by calling out the numbers of where she wants Betty to move. Betty falls when she and Sarah move simultaneously without conferring on where to go. She suggests that they should use a strategy where she stays on odds and Sarah stays on evens. They take turns moving up the mountain and then begin to play in parallel when they are comfortable with their new strategy, sometimes calling out their intent by simply saying a number. Unfortunately, Sarah falls near the top and has nowhere to land without making Betty fall. Betty grabs the 'pick' and decrements a number above where Sarah is swinging so that Sarah could safety land there. Together they finish the level and Sarah does a 'chair dance' of excitement.

Multi-User Interaction Styles

When children work together, they often use a variety of collaboration styles, such as divide and conquer, or group consensus. The collaboration styles that are available to children working on a typical computer are restricted by the interaction technology (e.g., only one mouse and one keyboard). In this field study, the technology supported simultaneous multi-user interaction. Providing the children with this additional resource increased the potential flexibility of their collaboration process. However, the constraints of the game were determining factors as well. In particular, two rules of the game that affected the children's collaborative interactions were: 1) the players could move at most three positions away from each other; and 2) the validity of the number chosen by one player was related to the current position of the other player. These rules forced tightly coupled play and made it challenging to interact simultaneously. Nonetheless, informal observations during the children's sessions indicated that some pairs chose to interact concurrently. To help understand the type of interactions used by the children, including when they took advantage of the ability to interact simultaneously, we performed in-depth analyses of the experimental sessions for three of the ten student pairs. These analyses were based on the rough picture of the students' on-screen interactions that was provided by combining the computer logs with the session transcripts.

Given the rules of Prime Climb, the simplest interaction style is strict turn-taking. This allows the students to evaluate the partner's current number before choosing a new position. Interestingly, the pairs did not always use this interaction style. Although the players started the experiment using strict turn-taking, some players preferred to make multiple moves per turn, some pairs developed strategies that allowed players to select numbers independently of the partner's current position, and some pairs preferred to move up the mountain quickly, in parallel. The parallel interaction style required each player to anticipate the partner's next move and then to quickly choose a compatible number.

To mitigate the challenges of interacting concurrently within the game, some of the pairs negotiated play strategies. One pair developed a strategy based on the type of numbers each player should land on, creating an "odds or evens" strategy. This strategy worked well until the numbers became large. Others used short-term strategies that were sometimes unrelated to the numbers and therefore not particularly successful. For instance, players would climb along the edge of the mountain because they felt it would be easier. The players' goals also influenced their interaction styles. For example, the primary goal of two of the pairs who interacted concurrently seemed to be to finish as many mountains as possible during the session. Conversely, the players in a third pair had conflicting goals and rarely interacted simultaneously. One girl appeared intent on reaching the top of the mountains quickly, but her partner seemed more intent on having fun by antagonizing her.

Overall, the goals of the players affected their game strategy and the game strategy often affected the interaction style used by the players. Consequently, the children interacted in a variety of ways with the same hardware and software. Although the in-depth qualitative analyses were only performed on three pairs, the findings support informal observations made of the other 17 pairs during the experiment. This indicates that technology, especially multi-user technology, needs to be flexible to account for this variation in interaction styles.

Communication

Our presupposition with regard to display conditions was that a shared display would lead to a shared understanding of the workspace. When people view shared objects in the physical world, an individual has an understanding of both where the object is and where their partner is in relation to themselves. This helps provide an implicit understanding of how their partner views the object, potentially leading to a better shared understanding of the workspace. If artifacts in a virtual scene are analogous to objects in the physical world, this same result may hold for virtual objects on a shared display. However, it is unclear whether or not this phenomenon extends into shared virtual workspaces when users have separate visual displays or are in separate physical locations.

The results of this study suggest that reaching a shared understanding of the workspace was more difficult when the children were discussing on-screen objects in the conditions where they had separate visual displays. Consider Excerpt 1, which was taken from one pair of children playing in the side-by-side display condition. In this excerpt one player, Scott, has just tried to move to a number that shares a factor with his partner's current position. This action causes Scott's climber to fall off the mountain and start swinging below David's player. David suggests that Scott move to "the 7" and he points at that position on his own screen. Scott does not see where David is pointing though because Scott is still looking at his own display. While clarifying his suggestion, David looks at the mountain on Scott's screen, even though their two displays are showing the identical scene. This excerpt suggests that reaching a shared understanding regarding on-screen objects could be facilitated by sharing a physical display.

Excerpt 1. Two children playing the game in the side-by-side display condition.

[Scott's climber falls. David and Scott are both looking at their own displays.]

David: *Oh...come up!* [David points to his own display to show Scott where he should "come up". Scott is still looking at his own display]... *oh* [David seems to realize that Scott did not see where he was pointing]

[David leans back from his own monitor and turns to look at Scott's screen]

David: *Go to the 7...the bottom one.* [Scott continues to try to get his climber back on the mountain]

Scott: *This one?* [Scott is still looking at his own screen]

David: *Yeah.* [Scott's climber is back on the mountain. David turns back to his own screen and resumes playing]

Data gathered from the questionnaires also supports the notion that a shared display can facilitate collaboration. After completing each display condition, the students were asked to rate how well they understood their partner, on a five-point scale (one corresponded to 'always' while five corresponded to 'never'). A Friedman two-way analysis of variance revealed a marginally significant difference between the display conditions, $\chi^2(2,N=20)=5.5$, $p=0.063$. On average, students reported more strongly that they understood their partner in the shared condition (M=2.3, SD=1.3) than either in the side-by-side condition (M=2.7, SD=1.3) or in the separated condition (M=2.6, SD=1.4). A similar trend was also apparent in student's responses when asked, in each condition, how well they felt their partner understood them. These differences, although subtle, support the notion that a shared display can help foster a shared understanding. Students felt strongly that there was mutual comprehension in their communication when they viewed the virtual scene on the same physical display. However, in the side-by-side and separated condition, even though the virtual scene was identical when viewed on separate screens, these display configurations did not appear to evoke the same degree of response.

Effect of Display Condition on Student's Game Perception

If a shared display leads to a shared understanding of the workspace, it can be argued that it should be easier for students to work together and solve puzzles. After each experimental condition, the students were asked to rate how easy the game was to play on a five-point scale (one corresponded to 'easy' and five corresponded to 'hard'). A Friedman two-way analysis of variance revealed a significant difference for perceived ease of use between the display conditions, $\chi^2(2, N=20)=10.7$, $p<.01$. The students, on average, rated the shared condition as being easier to play (M=2.3, SD=0.9) than the side-by-side (M=2.8, SD=0.8) or the separate condition (M=2.9, SD=0.8). Since the students only played for a short amount of time (15 minutes), and because the software crashed during some of the sessions, it was not possible to compare the number of mountains (game levels) completed in each condition. As a result, the performance data could not be used to validate the students' perceptions of how easy it was to solve puzzles in each of the conditions.

Although these results are subjective, and may have been influenced by external factors unrelated to the display configuration (e.g. time of day, mood, partner's behaviour), they are also supported by the post-experiment questionnaire[1]. Fifteen of the twenty children stated that the shared condition was the easiest of the three display conditions to solve puzzles in ($\chi^2(2, N=20)=16.3$, $p<.001$). Thus, the children's perception that it was easier to play in the shared condition was consistent for both the evaluation of the interface after each condition, and the overall evaluation at the end of the study.

On the post-experimental questionnaire, the children reported why they found it easiest to solve puzzles in the shared condition. The majority of their comments related to the fact that they could communicate more effectively and could help each other when they were "right beside each other", in the shared display configuration. Table 2 groups the children's responses into several categories for each display configuration along with an example remark for each.

Table 2: Why children found the game easier to play in the different display configurations.

Why	# of Remarks	Example Remark
Shared display:		
Close to partner	7	"We were right beside each other so we knew what to do"
Ability to point and do things for partner	3	"If your partner didn't understand, you could do it for them"

[1] The post-experiment questionnaire was completed after all three display conditions were played. This allowed the children to express their preferences across display conditions. This questionnaire was in addition to the one the children completed after each condition to evaluate the specific display condition in which they had just played.

Better communication	2	"We could see each other and communicate better"
Same display	2	"Because we had the same screen"
No reason given	1	
Side-by-side display:		
Separate displays	2	"You get your own screen"
Ability to point	1	"They could point out what you're doing wrong"
Better understanding	1	"If you win you can see if she's happy or not, then you know what happened"
Separated Displays:		
Order related	1	"We did it last so we were getting used to the game"

Non-verbal Interactions Between Students

The impact of the display configurations on the children's non-verbal interactions with each other is important to understand. In the physical world, our non-verbal interpersonal interactions are very refined and play an important role in our activities. How a computer environment enhances or impedes these interactions will ultimately impact its effectiveness as a collaborative environment.

Pointing

The number of times children pointed in the various display conditions was gathered in the non-verbal coding of the video data. In general, the children rarely pointed in any of the display conditions. Overall, six occurrences of pointing were recorded in the shared condition, compared to two occurrences in the side-by-side condition, and one in the separated condition. In face-to-face activities, pointing while interacting with shared artifacts is common and often helps to augment the verbal communication. Our results, however, showed that this mode of communication was rarely utilized when children played in either of the two face-to-face conditions. This may be explained by the introduction of a virtual non-verbal communication channel, which becomes available when users are provided their own on-screen representation, e.g. their own cursor. It is possible that children chose to "point" using their cursor as opposed to their hand. Further investigation is required to understand how this extra communication channel augments or replaces physical gestures.

Looking at Their Partner

In both the shared display and side-by-side conditions, it was possible for the players to see their partner. However, video analyses revealed that players looked at their partner more often in the side-by-side display configuration (105 occurrences) than in the shared configuration (85 occurrences). Although this difference was not statistically significant, qualitative observations suggest that this trend is a result of students looking at their partner to increase awareness of their partner's actions in the side-by-side condition. Visual focus may also have played a role in the users' awareness of each other's actions. In the shared display configuration, the students' attention was focused on the same physical artifact (the computer screen); thus, their partner was relatively close to the player's center of visual focus. Conversely, in the side-by-side condition, both the separate displays and the increased distance between players caused partners to be further away from each other's center of visual focus when looking at their own displays. As a result, a player's awareness of their partner's actions may have decreased in the side-by-side condition causing them to actively look at their partner more often to see their partner's physical actions.

Enjoyment

After playing in each condition, students were asked to rate how much they enjoyed playing the game on a five-point scale (one corresponded to 'fun' while five corresponded to 'not much fun'). No significant differences between the conditions were found, $\chi^2(2, N=20)=4.1$, *ns*, and in general, the students rated all three conditions as being somewhat fun (shared: M=2.4, SD=1.4; side-by-side: M=2.75, SD=1.52; separated: M=2.6, SD=1.4). After playing in all conditions, students were asked to choose which condition was the most fun to play. Of the twenty students, nine chose the separated condition, six chose the shared condition, and five chose the side-by-side condition. This difference was not found to be significant, $\chi^2(2,N=20)=1.3$, *ns*. The children's explanations of their choices were grouped into several categories for each display configuration. These are shown in Table 3, along with an example remark for each category. The high variability of these results, compared with the results of which display condition was easiest to use, indicates that the children do not necessarily equate the easiest collaborative environment to the most fun environment. In fact, four students commented that they enjoyed the challenge of the separated display configuration.

Table 3: Why children found the game more fun to play in the different display configurations.

Why	# of Remarks	Example Remark
Shared display:		
Sharing a display made it easier	3	"It was easier with one monitor which made it more fun"
Can point at the display	1	"She can point out which ones for me to go to"
Miscellaneous	2	"It was the first time I played the game"
Side-by-side display:		
Beside each other, but had own display	2	"You have your own monitor but you can see your partner"
Can see partner	3	"You can see the expression on their face when you mess up"
Separated Displays:		
Needing the microphones	2	"You actually needed the mikes and it was cool"
Being separate was more challenging	4	"We couldn't see each other so it was more challenging"
Couldn't see partner's actions	2	"You couldn't see what the other was doing"
Miscellaneous	1	"It was similar to an Internet game and talking to a friend combined"

A second factor that contributed to children preferring the separate display configuration was the necessity of the audio equipment (headphones and microphones) for communication in that condition. The ability to use technology to communicate with a partner, when they were separated, was very engaging for the children. As a result, several children mentioned this novelty factor as their reason for preferring the separated condition. In contrast, the use of audio equipment in the other two configurations was not essential for communication given that they were face-to-face. Consequently, even though audio equipment was utilized in these two conditions, it appeared to be less of a contributing factor to children's engagement.

Playing with a partner also added to the children's enjoyment of the game. Analysis of the post-experimental questionnaires revealed that many of the students felt that having a partner made it easier to finish mountains (levels) in the game. This preference was expressed by fifteen students when they played the shared and the side-by-side conditions but only eleven students when they played the separated condition. This difference was found to be marginally significant, $\chi^2(2, N=20)=5.3$, $p=0.069$. Providing children with technology that supports multiple users allows children the option of playing or working on computers with friends.

CONCLUSIONS AND FUTURE WORK

The results of this work further our understanding of how children interact in synchronous shared environments. In particular, the physical proximity of participants, the ability to utilize gestures, and the use of a shared physical workspace, all positively influenced the students' collaborative experiences. In the physical world, these interactions are a natural part of our daily lives. Unfortunately, current technologies do not adequately support these interactions in a seamless manner. Continued work in this area is needed to fully understand its full potential for collaborative learning environments.

Although we observed many interesting trends, these results must be interpreted with caution. The small sample size, limited playtime, and high variability among the pairs limited these analyses. Although there were hints of behavioural change, fifteen minutes of play may not have been long enough for the children to develop an interaction style suited to a particular display configuration. Future longitudinal studies where subjects are given time to adapt to each display condition will help address such issues.

Other areas for future investigation include the type of collaborative task and the application domain. The present study required users to work together to reach the top of the mountain by solving mathematical problems. With such tightly coupled group work, partners may not have had the opportunity to explore alternative collaborative interaction styles afforded by each of the display configurations.

Most importantly, beyond all of the intricate analyses, we ultimately cannot forget the preferences of those who will inevitably interact with these systems. Some students vocalized that they preferred the shared display simply because they "had the same screen", but could not articulate why this configuration was important to them. Others were able to describe the essence of the shared display configuration. One student felt that the physical proximity and shared screen enhanced communication, while another commented that the shared display was easier to use because "cooperation [was] dynamically increased". Although this is a complex research endeavor, the children effectively captured the spirit and fundamental quality of the experience – having fun.

ACKNOWLEDGMENTS

This project was funded by NSERC and the TeleLearning NCE. We would like to thank the E-GEMS group at UBC for allowing us to use Prime Climb and for their assistance during our modifications. We would also like to thank Garth Shoemaker, Daryn Mitchell, Wai-ling Ho Ching, and Michelle Daly for their assistance with software development and video analysis. Thanks also to the other members of the EDGE lab for their assistance.

REFERENCES

Bier, E.A., & Freeman, S. (1991). MMM: A User Interface Architecture for Shared Editors on a Single Screen. In *Proc. of UIST '91*. 79-86.

Bly, S. (1988). A Use of Drawing Surfaces in Different Collaborative Settings. In *Proc. of CSCW '88*, 250-256.

Bricker, L.J., Bennett, M.J., Fujioke, E., & Tanimoto, S.L. (1999). Colt: A System for Developing Software that Supports Synchronous Collaborative Activities. In *Proc. of the Ed-Media Conference*, 587-592.

Firestone W. (1987). Meaning in method: The rhetoric of quantitative and qualitative research. *Educational Researcher*, (16), 16-21.

Fish, R.S., Kraut, R.E., & Root, R.W. (1992). Evaluation Video as a Technology for Informal Communication. In *Proc. of CHI '92*, 37-48.

Gutwin, C., Greenberg, S. & Roseman, M. (1996). Workspace Awareness in Real-Time Distributed Groupware: Framework, Widgets, and Evaluation. In *Proc. of HCI '96*, 281-298.

Hollan, J. & Stornetta, S. (1992). Beyond Being There. In *Proc. of CHI '92*, 119-125.

Hourcade, J. & Bederson, B. (1999). Architecture and Implementation of a Java Package for Multiple Input Devices (MID). Technical Report CS-TR-4018 University of Maryland.

Hymel S., Zinck B., & Ditner E. (1993). Cooperation versus competition in the classroom. *Exceptionality Education Canada*, 3:1-2, 103-128.

Inkpen, K., Booth, K.S., Klawe, M., & Upitis, R. (1995). Playing together beats playing apart, especially for girls. In *Proc. of CSCL '95*, 177-181.

Inkpen, K. (1997). Three Important Research Agendas for Educational Multimedia: Learning, Children and Gender. *Proc. of Educational Multimedia '07, Calgary AB, June 1997*, 521-526.

Inkpen, K.M., Ho-Ching, W., Kuederle, O., Scott, S.D., & Shoemaker, G.B.D. (1999). "This is fun! We're all best friends and we're all playing.": Supporting children's synchronous collaboration. In *Proc. of CSCL '99*, 252-259.

Inoue, T., Okada, K., & Matsushita, Y. (1997). Integration of Face-to-face and Video-mediated Meetings. In *Proc. of GROUP '97*, 405-414.

Johnson D.W., Maruyana G., Johnson R,T, (1981). Effects of cooperative, competitive, and individualistic goal structures on achievement: A meta-analysis. *Psychology Bulletin, 89(1)*, 47-62.

Klawe, M. (1998). When does the use of computer games and other interactive multimedia software help students learn mathematics? In *Proc. of the Technology and NCTM Standards 2000 Conference*.

Mandryk, R.L., Inkpen, K.M., Bilezikjian, M., Klemmer, S.R., & Landay, J.A. (2001). Supporting Children's Collaboration Across Handheld Computers. In *Extended Abstracts of the Proc. of CHI'01*, 255-256.

Maxwell J.A. (1996). *Qualitative Research Design: An interactive approach.* Thousand Oaks: Sage.

Miles M.B. & Huberman A.M. (1994). *Qualitative Data Analysis (2nd Ed.).* Thousand Oaks: Sage.

Myers, B.A., Stiel, H., & Gargiulo, R. (1998). Collaboration using multiple PDAs connected to a PC. In *Proc. of CSCW '98*. 285-294.

Pedersen, E. McCall, K., Moran, T., & Halasz, F. (1993). Tivoli: An Electronic Whiteboard for Informal Workgroup Meetings. In *Proc. of InterCHI '93*. 391-398.

Reeves, B., & Nass, C. (1996). *The Media Equation*, Cambridge University Press.

Richards, L. (1999). *Using NVivo in Qualitative Research*, SAGE Publications, London.

Scott, S.D., Shoemaker, G.B.D., & Inkpen, K.M. (2000). Towards Seamless Support of Natural Collaborative Interactions. In *Proc. of Graphics Interface 2000*, 103-110.

Stewart, J., Bederson, B.B, & Druin, A. (1999). Single Display Groupware: A Model for Co-present Collaboration. In *Proc. of CHI '99*, 286-293.

Streitz, N.A., Geibler, J., Haake, J.M., & Hol, J. (1994). DOLPHIN: Integrated Meeting Support across Local and Remote Desktop Environments and Liveboards. In *Proc. of CSCW '94*. 345-358.

Streitz, N.A., Geibler, J., Holmer, T., Konomi, S., Müller-Tomfelde, C., Reischl, W., Rexroth, P., Seitz, P., & Steinmetz, R. (1999). i-LAND: An Interactive Landscape for Creativity and Innovation. In *Proc. of CHI '99*, 120-127.

Tani, H., Horita, M., Yamaashi, K., Tanikoshi, K., & Futakawa, M. (1994). Courtyard: Integrating Shared Overview on a Large Screen and Per-user Detail on Individual Screens. In *Proc. of CHI '94*. 44-50.

Interfaces to Support Children's Co-present Collaboration: Multiple Mice and Tangible Technologies

Danaë Stanton,[1] Helen Neale[2], Victor Bayon[3]

[1]CREDIT, School of Psychology, [2]Virtual Reality Applications Research Team,
[3] Mixed Reality Lab
University of Nottingham
University Park
Nottingham
NG2 2RD
UK
[1]Danae.Stanton@nottingham.ac.uk [2]Helen.Neale@nottingham.ac.uk [3]Vxb@cs.nott.ac.uk

ABSTRACT

This paper summarises two different approaches using technology to support young children's collaborative interaction in a classroom setting. KidPad, a 2½D drawing package with zooming capabilities, was adapted for use with multiple mice and tangible interfaces. The first section of the paper focuses on a study carried out to evaluate the effect of multiple mice on children's collaborative behaviour at a desktop computer. Positive effects of the use of two mice included symmetry of mouse use amongst pairs and a greater degree of engagement in the task. However a number of usability issues were identified when children attempted to collaborate, particular problems were faced when the shared control was taken away, and one of the users took control, for example, when navigating. Different types of working styles were also evident between the one mouse and two mice conditions. The second section of the paper describes a move away from the desktop computer towards room-based technologies. Tangible interfaces to KidPad were developed in order to facilitate shared control over actions such as navigation where difficulties had been identified in a desktop situation. The visibility of action is highlighted as a fundamental element in the support of collaboration on a larger scale. Finally, future work and the potential of these technologies in encouraging shareable co-present interaction in a real school context are briefly discussed.

Keywords

Collaboration, children, evaluation, usability, tangible interfaces, single display groupware

INTRODUCTION

Group work with young children is well established in British schools (Galton and Williamson, 1992) and research in psychology and education has consistently demonstrated that working in pairs and small groups can have advantageous effects on learning and development, especially in young children (Rogoff, 1990; Topping, 1992; Wood & O'Malley, 1996).

The role of the computer in supporting collaborative learning has been examined (Barfurth, 1995; Crook, 1994, O'Malley, 1992). Littleton (1999) suggests that the computer is not just capable of supporting collaborative behaviour, but is unique in that it can transform the way in which collaborative activity is structured. A limited number of computers in schools and an emphasis on group work in the UK school curriculum means that it is important to examine "how new technology (can) serve effectively to resource collaborative arrangements for learning?" (p.122, Crook, 1994).

Traditional computer software and hardware has been designed with only one user in mind, two users must share a mouse and control over one cursor on the screen. This may result in an unequal balance between two children collaborating in this situation. For example, Light and Glachan's (1985) study found that boys are more likely to take control of the mouse when access was limited.

The aim of the KidStory project is to develop new technologies that support small group collaboration within the classroom. The main focus of this research is to support young children (aged 6 and 7) to collaborate in the creation and re-telling of stories, using technologies specifically design for this. Over the last 3 years researchers have built up a close working relationship with teachers and children in school. This has allowed children and teachers to influence technology design using a 'participatory' or 'co-operative' approach (for more information on the design process please see Neale, in preparation, Taxen, 2001). It has also meant that the authors have been able to assess the impact of technologies, designed to support collaboration, and modify, refine and improve them to take into account usability, functionality and issues regarding the school context.

The first part of this paper describes the development and use of multiple input devices. An evaluation study has been conducted to investigate the impact of 2 mice on pairs of children's story creation.

The second part of this paper focuses on tangible interfaces to KidPad to support group learning in the classroom.

MULTIPLE MICE TO ENCOURAGE CO-PRESENT COLLABORATION

Standard computer systems are designed to support single users working alone, however, within schools it is common for pairs or small groups to work together around a computer, and for them to collaborate on a shared task. Even though two or more children may collaborate verbally, only one child at a time has control of the computer. The recognition that group work around a single display is desirable for many groups of users has led to the development of software and hardware that is designed specifically to support this. There are a number of difficulties in developing computer systems that support multiple input devices, however recently technical advances have been made in Single Display Groupware (Stewart, Bederson and Druin, 1999).

Single Display Groupware (SDG) allows two or more co-located users to interact with a computer system simultaneously whilst feedback is provided via a single display screen. SDG therefore enables all participants to input to the same piece of computer-based work. This type of software could be used to support a number of different situations where two or more people are gathered around a computer, all commenting on, interacting with, or editing the same artefact.

Very few studies have been conducted to examine the effect of multiple input devices on collaborative interactions and so little is known about how they may influence behaviour. Reported here is a summary of the studies that have examined SDG use.

Inkpen, Booth, Gribble and Klawe (1995) examined children's use of commercial computer games, and found that they were more motivated when playing together on a single machine, as opposed to playing side by side on computers or by themselves. The effect of giving each user an input device, even if only one could be active at a time was then examined and significant learning improvements were found (Inkpen, Booth, Klawe and McGrenere, 1997). Preliminary results from a study of pairs of students working together using SDG to complete a problem solving task indicate that children using two mice demonstrate higher levels of activity and less time off task (Inkpen, Ho-Ching, Kuederle, Scott and Shoemaker, 1999).

Stewart, Raybourn, Bederson and Druin (1998) observed that children with access to multiple input devices seemed to enjoy an enhanced experience, with the researchers observing increased incidences of student-student interaction and student-teacher interaction as well as changing the character of the collaborative interaction. The children also seemed to enjoy their experience more, compared with earlier observations of them using similar software on standard systems. The availability of an input device for each child also suggests that no one child would be able to monopolise the task (Stewart et al, 1999). Stewart et al (1999) do however recognise that some negative effects on behaviour may occur with SDG use. For example, task completion may take longer, as no one user can direct the product, also the opportunity to work in parallel may mean that users in fact collaborate less than when they had to share one form of input.

Abnett, Stanton, Neale and O'Malley (2000) found some gender effects when using two mice with KidPad. Interaction with two input devices led to greater equity between gender pairings, while interaction when using one mouse led to poorer performance in mixed gender and male gender pairs.

Thus there is some evidence that the use of multiple input devices improves motivation, effectiveness of task completion (through parallel or co-operative work), equity of activity and time on task.

In some cases SDG applications have been specifically designed to *force* or *encourage* users to collaborate. In one study, multiple users were each given control of one aspect of an activity and therefore had to work together in order to reach their goal (Bricker, Baker and Tanimoto, 1997). Rather than forcing users to carry out actions, some SDG applications are designed to encourage people to actively take part in group activities (Sugimoto, Kunsunoki, and Hashizume, 2000) or to enhance the results of activities carried out when these are achieved by working collaboratively with others (Benford, Bederson, Akesson et al, 2000).

One of the major goals of the first year of the KidStory project was to develop technologies that supported collaboration around a desktop computer. As well as supporting multiple mice, software was developed to encourage children to work together. Two pieces of software 'KidPad' and the 'Klump' were developed with functionality's designed to encourage collaboration (Benford et al, 2000). Only KidPad is elaborated upon here as more extensive studies in schools have been undertaken with it.

KidPad is a collaborative authoring tool designed for children (Druin, Stewart, Proft, Bederson and Hollan, 1997). KidPad enables children to draw, edit and write stories using links to connect elements of their story. They can then use these links to 'zoom' to objects that may not appear within screen shot.

Figure 1. A typical KidPad story created by a class of 7-year-olds. Only one part of the story is visible. By zooming in/out or navigating left/right or up/down it is possible to view the other parts of the story or access blank space to create more content. In this case at that level of zooming it is only possible to view 1/9 of the graphical representation.

Collaboration with multiple input devices

An observation study was carried out where pairs of children were asked to complete a storytelling task in KidPad using either one or two mice. From the results of previous studies examining multiple mice use, as well as informal observations of KidPad use, it was hypothesised that the use of multiple mice would produce less off task behaviour and also greater synchrony of mouse use in line with Inkpen et al's (1999) findings. However, the study also aimed to explore, in detail, the effect of multiple mice on collaborative dialogue and computer-based interactions. Analysis was facilitated by mixing video capture of both the computer screen, and the children, enabling the development of a coding scheme (see figure 2). A detailed account of how the study was carried out and the outcomes in terms of collaborative behaviours can be found in Stanton and Neale (in preparation).

Method

Twelve pairs of children aged between 6 and 7 years used KidPad to carry out a creative task. Six of the pairs carried out the task using KidPad with only one mouse while the remaining six pairs used two mice. Children chose a classmate who they wanted to work with. The groups were balanced in terms of ability and gender. The children who took part in the study were familiar with the researchers who had been working in with the school for the previous eighteen months. They were also familiar with KidPad and its features.

Figure 2. Video capture of the children and on screen activity enabled analysis of talk and actions.

The study took place in the corner of the classroom during an academic lesson, usually English literacy. The children were introduced to the task and told that they were to use KidPad to recreate a poem. The poem used was 'Twinkle, Twinkle chocolate bar', a poem they had previously read in class. The children were encouraged to work together and were told that their KidPad story was to be presented to their teacher on completion.

Results

For the entire period of computer use, children's activities were recorded to identify whether they were active and on task; inactive but still on-task; or off task.

In the one mouse condition 42% of the time was spent actively drawing, writing or creating their story in comparison to 73.30% of the time with 2 mice. In the one mouse condition children were non-active (involved in the task, either watching what their partner was doing, instructing, or commenting, but not actually using an input device) 48.28% of the time while in the two mice condition the children were non-active 17% of the time.

Non attentive behaviour (such as looking away from the computer screen) was found to be low for both the one mouse and the two mice conditions 3.42% and 0.9% respectively. However in the one mouse condition there were cases where children were non-attentive for 9% and 16.22% of the time.

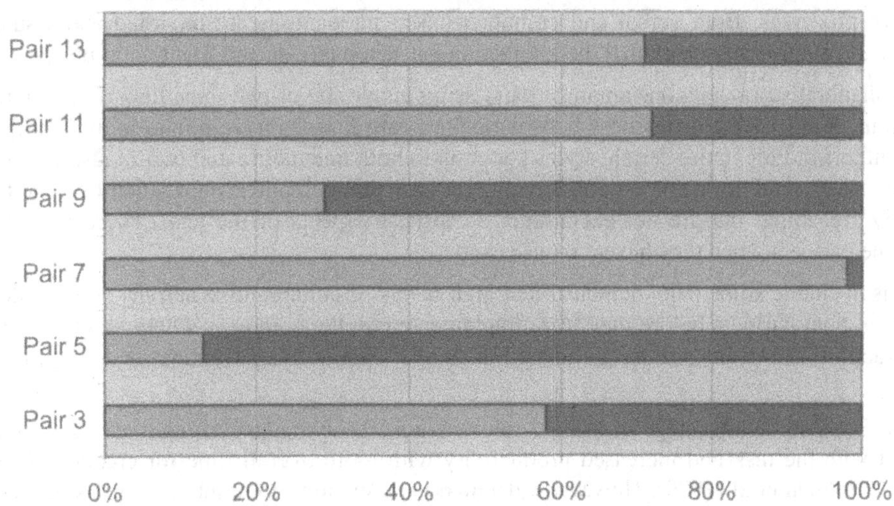

Figure 3. Distribution of mouse use between left-hand side and right-hand side (1 mouse)

Figure 3 and Figure 4 illustrate the distribution of active mouse use between the left-hand and right-hand partners. In the 2-mouse condition input was fairly symmetrically distributed. However in the one mouse condition the patterns are more asymmetric, with individuals dominating. For example, in pair 7 one of the pair has the mouse for 98% of the total task time.

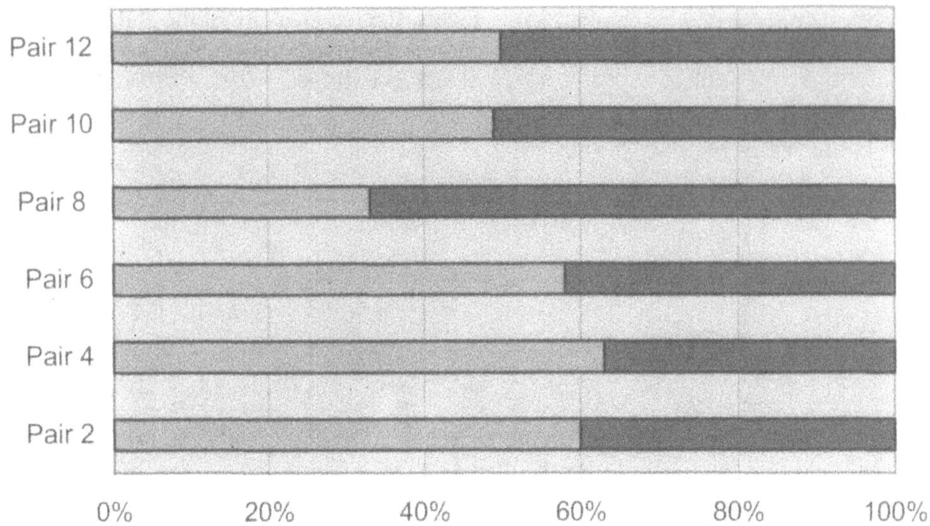

Figure 4. Distribution of mouse use between left-hand side and right-hand side (2 mice)

Access to the mouse does not necessarily portray the full picture of collaborative behaviour and it is important to look for indicators 'beneath the surface' to find out who is controlling the collaborative actions and contributing to the production of ideas (Cole, 1995). The person in control of the mouse may be physically active but not psychologically active. A more detailed analysis of the interactions between the pairs was carried out (for a more detailed account see Stanton and Neale, in prep). Previous work in this area has focused primarily on talk and less on actions, in the study presented here actions were analysed alongside talk as they often indicate important parts of the interaction such as acceptance of ideas or children may input ideas directly onto the computer without verbalising them.

Collaboration Networks have been used to code and represent collaborative interactions around the computer. This method was developed specifically to address some of the deficiencies in existing methods in the analysis and presentation of complex collaborative processes. Both verbal and computer-based interactions are recorded and visually represented in terms of the temporal and evolutionary path that the interaction has taken (Neale and Stanton, in press).

The exploration of collaborative interactions amongst pairs using either one or two mice identified a number of patterns of collaborative behaviour. Many of the differences between collaborative styles were due to individual differences between pairs; however, the authors did recognise certain styles common to both one mouse and two-mouse use. When two mice are available to the pair, they tend to work co-operatively, they create computer representations on their own, usually verbalising what they are doing, but are not encouraged to discuss aspects of the task. There is noticeably less verbal reciprocity between the partners when they have a mouse each.

When one mouse was available some pairs demonstrated high levels of collaborative activity, where ideas were discussed with contributions from both partners before they were implemented on the computer. Other pairs demonstrated low levels of collaborative interaction, where one partner dominated the work, leading to an asymmetric distribution of idea input and creation.

The evaluation study found some advantage of using 2 mice such as the symmetry of input afforded by 2 mice, the higher levels of engagement with the task and increased productivity with more overall time for creation. These results support work by others such as Inkpen et al (1999). However a detailed examination of the interaction taking place also uncovered different styles of behaviour attributed to the number of mice used and formally confirms some of the points raised by Stewart et al (1999). The use of 2 mice seems to encourage a co-operative and parallel style of working while we have found considerably more elaboration/extension of ideas taking place before these ideas are implemented on the computer when pairs share one mouse. On occasions when a pair has one mouse, low levels of collaborative behaviour have been observed, with one partner dominating and directing.

Multiple input devices at the desktop have been seen to facilitate pairs of children in actively working on a shared task at the same time. There are however a number of limitations to the ability of this type of technology to support small group work. Firstly the physical size of the output device means that it could never support more than a few users working simultaneously. At most 3 or 4 children could sit around and input to a single desktop computer. A number of usability problems related to multiple users have been identified from observing this technology in use. Most of the actions facilitated by the software enabled two or more users to work at the same time, a few of the actions only allowed one partner to carry them out, for example, navigation, often disabling or disrupted their partner from carrying on with their task. This often caused confusion and frustration.

TANGIBLE TECHNOLOGIES TO ENCOURAGE CO-PRESENT COLLABORATION

In this section tangible technologies are defined and reasons why they may be beneficial in terms of collaboration are outlined. One particular interface 'the magic carpet' is discussed, and some informal observations of use are detailed.

The approach taken within years 2 and 3 of the KidStory project to interface development has mostly focused on physical and tangible interfaces (see Stanton, Bayon, Neale et al, 2001). Physical in that the interaction is based on movement and tangible in that objects are to be touched and grasped.

In HCI research there has been a general move towards, and much support for, the development of tangible and mobile interfaces to facilitate computer use (e.g. Norman, 1999). Many of the types of interfaces that are being created support socially based activities. Research is being carried out using tangible and physical interfaces for children's play and learning (see Bobick, Intille, Davis et al, 2000; Ryokai and Cassel, 1999; Strommen, 1998). Other authors have developed devices to aid children's computational skills in a collaborative context, for example see 'curlybot' (Frei, Su, Mikhak and Ishii, 2000) and a study by, Kynigos and Giannoutsou (2001) which used GPS to examine spatial and orientation concepts when groups of 7 year olds carried out collaborative cartography. In spite of these recent developments, little is known about the influence of tangible technology on collaborative learning, particularly with children in a school environment.

In the KidStory project tangibles have been developed as interfaces that inherently support small group collaboration amongst young children. Much of this development was also based around the KidPad software, described in the above sections. When working in a school it became clear that if the teacher was to be involved in using the technology with a sub-set of her class, then the rest of the class needed to be able to participate in the experience in some way. Replacing a standard monitor with a large projected screen helped to accomplish this. A number of different input devices were used to allow multiple users to interact with KidPad carrying out different functions, for example, creating a scene, creating a sound, and navigating, were all carried out using different input devices. This section will focus on one particular input device 'the magic carpet'.

The Magic Carpet is a collaborative tangible interface based on 12 floor sensors, with 3 sensors arranged on each side to create a square. KidPad is usually projected onto a large screen in front of the carpet, providing a display that can be clearly seen by groups of users. Children interact with the Magic Carpet by standing on its pressure sensitive sides. This input device allows users to travel forwards into the KidPad scene, backwards to zoom out of the scene, and left and right (a separate input device was used to travel along a third axis, up and down). To travel forwards, users stand at the front of the carpet; to travel backwards they stand at the back, and so forth. The number of sensors activated at any time affects the viewpoint in KidPad. Multiple sensors may be activated at the same time altering the way in which the user navigates through KidPad. It is possible to, for instance, zoom in and move right by standing at the front and the right side of the carpet and activating the sensors on those sides of the magic carpet, or zoom in faster by standing and activating all 3 of the sensors at the back of the magic carpet.

The design of the magic carpet meant that interaction was scaled up, allowing larger groups of children to interact with the technology simultaneously. Sensors were widely distributed about the carpet, meaning that many children could use the carpet at the same time, in fact benefits were found by multiple users working together to navigate.

A key factor of moving technology into a larger space, providing room for objects to become organised spatially, is that the visibility of other people's actions is increased. Initially the magic carpet was used to re-tell stories created on a desktop version of KidPad. Informal observation of these sessions indicated that navigation using the magic carpet drew children's attention to the spatial features of KidPad and in contrast to the desktop a considerable amount of time was spent navigating. Navigation became a collaborative activity rather than a one-person process. The physical size of the carpet and the visibility of actions meant that group interaction was encouraged as well as navigation. The set-up enabled all of the group members to contribute and they worked as a team.

Figures 5, 6 and 7 illustrate a group of children using the magic carpet to retell a story to their peers. In the first image the children are all on the left hand side of the carpet moving the image on screen to the left. In the middle image one of the children is indicating that they are going in the wrong direction to get their pictures. The third image illustrates the move of all interactors to the right hand side of the carpet. By all working together to navigate they are moving faster than one child carrying out this action alone.

Figure 5 Children move the viewpoint by standing on the left-hand side of the

Figure 6 One child realises that they need to travel in the other direction and points in the direction she wants them

Figure 7 All of the children move over to the right hand side of the carpet to move the viewpoint in the other direction

These findings are only informal observations, however, an in depth evaluation of a spatially distributed tangible set-up has recently been carried out and is currently being analysed (see Stanton et al., in prep). Collaboration on a story creation task using tangible technologies is examined in terms of its ability to encourage and support collaborative behaviour. Four children used a variety of the tangible technologies, including the magic carpet over three sessions. The technology consisted of a large display in which they could input pictures (using PDA's, a webcam and a scanner) and sounds (using RFID tags) and navigation using an arrangement of sensors 'the magic carpet'. The children could then retell their story using bar-coded images and sounds. Pending results from this study will provide new information about how children collaborate when using tangible interfaces.

DISCUSSION

Until recently most of the technology developed to aid computer assisted learning was designed with one user in mind regardless as to the activities around the computer.

O'Malley (1992) presents three classifications of the role of the computer in collaborative settings. The third of her classifications is termed 'Learning mediated via the computer' where she describes the computer as a tool, which 'augments' collaborative learning with the technology designed for pair or group activities. With careful structuring of the activity, desktop KidPad with 2 mice fits neatly within this classification. However O'Malley suggests that there is probably a continuum of roles rather than a strict categorisation and we would suggest that tangible technology is further along that continuum. While asynchronous interaction is reported to allow reflection and reaction time, the visibility of actions when using tangible technologies allows multiple users to carry out synchronous interaction while maintaining awareness of the collective collaborative action.

Although there has been a rapid advance in the design and use of technologies, such as SDG and tangible interfaces, formal evaluation is still limited. Here we have outlined ways in which these two types of technology have been used to encourage collaboration in educational settings. A formal study evaluating the use of one or two mice indicates that two mice produce a more even symmetry of use and higher levels of task engagement. However mouse use reflects very different working styles with two mice favouring co-operative work and 1 mouse favouring more collaborative working styles. The potential of tangible interfaces for group activities in the classroom has been discussed; preliminary observations identify that the physicality of inputs, the spatial distribution of the set-up and the visibility of actions are important factors in aiding collaborative behaviour. Ongoing work aims to evaluate children's collaborative learning with tangible technologies.

The children using the technologies described in this paper have all been between 6-7 years old. Interaction with tangibles may be well suited to very young children because of their physicality, as mouse co-ordination skills or verbal ability would not limit children. One of the teachers involved in the project over the last 3 years stated that a major advantage of the tangible technologies was that the less able students (in terms of reading and writing ability) were able to express themselves.

Desktop KidPad and variations of KidStory tangible technologies continue to be used within classrooms, in pairs, small groups and for whole class sessions. The success of this integration is summed up in the Ofsted report (school inspection board in the UK) who state under "Good teaching, alongside a vibrant and rich curriculum, means that learning is effective: - Visitors to school add an extra dimension to the whole curriculum. An excellent example is the involvement of the Kidstory team from Nottingham University. The project aims to encourage the pupils to work collaboratively together, and it is very successful. It has been in place for three years, giving the pupils an opportunity to use a range of new technologies for communication. In the lesson seen pupils worked very effectively to create different parts of their story, using new technology."

ACKNOWLEDGEMENTS

This work has been conducted as part of the KidStory project funded by ESPRIT (#29310). The authors acknowledge support from project partners at CREDIT, VIRART and CRG University of Nottingham, SICS and KTH in Sweden and The University of Maryland, USA. We would particularly like to thank Ben Bederson for KidPad and his continuing enthusiasm in developing it (to download KidPad please see www.kidpad.org) and Camilla Abnett for her help with data collection. Thanks also to the teachers and children at Albany Infant School, Nottingham for their collaboration in this work.

REFERENCES

Abnett, C., Stanton, D., Neale, H and O'Malley (2001) The effect of multiple input devices on collaboration and gender issues. In the *Proceedings of European Perspectives on Computer-Supported Collaborative Learning (EuroCSCL)* 2001, March 22-24, Maastricht, the Netherlands. p.29-36.

Barfurth, M.A. (1995) Understanding the collaborative learning process in a technology rich environment: The case of children's disagreements. *In the proceedings of CSCL 1995.*

Benford, S., Bederson, B., Åkesson, K.-P., Bayon, V., Druin, A., Hansson, P., Hourcade, J., Ingram, R., Neale, H., O'Malley, C., Simsarian, K., Stanton, D., Sundblad, Y., & Taxén, G., Designing storytelling technologies to encourage collaboration between young children. *CHI 2000* pp. 556-563.

Bobick, A., Intille, S., Davis, J., Baird, F., Pinhanez, C., Campbell, L., Ivanov, Y., Schutte, A., & Wilson, A., The KidsRoom: A perceptually-based interactive and immersive story environment. *Presence: Teleoperators and Virtual Environments,* **8**(4), 367-391, 2000.

Bricker, L. J., Baker, M. J., & Tanimoto, S. L. (1997). Support for cooperatively controlled objects in multimedia applications. Paper presented at the *Proceedings of Human Factors in Computing Systems (CH'97)*, Atlanta, GA

Cole, K.A. (1995) Equity issues in computer based collaboration: Looking beyond surface indicators, *In Proceedings of CSCL 95*, http://www-cscl95.indiana.edu/cscl95/cole.html

Crook C. (1994) Learning within peer collaborations. In Charles Crook, *Computers and the Collaborative Experience of Learning*. Routledge, London.

Druin, A., Stewart, J., Proft, D., Bederson, B., & Hollan, J,. KidPad: A design collaboration between children, technologists and educators. *CHI97* pp. 463-470.

Frei, P, Su, V., Mikhak, B., and Ishii, H. (2000). Curlybot: Designing a New Class of Computational Toys. *In Proceedings of Human Factors in Computing Systems (CHI 2001)* ACM Press, pp.129-136.

Galton, M. and Williamson, J (1992) *Group work in the Primary classroom.* Routledge, London

Inkpen, K., Booth, K.S., Gribble, S.D. and Klawe, M. (1995). Playing together beats playing apart, especially for girls. *Proceedings of CSCL '95*

Inkpen, K. M., Booth, K. S., Klawe, M., & McGrenere, J. (1997). The Effect of Turn-Taking Protocols on Children's Learning in Mouse-Driven Collaborative Environments. *In Proceedings of Graphics Interface (GI 97)* Canadian Information Processing Society, pp. 138-145.

Inkpen, K.M., Ho-Ching, W., Kuederle, O., Scott, S.D. and Shoemaker, G.B.D. (1999). "This is fun! We're all best friends and we're all playing": Supporting children's synchronous collaboration. *Proceedings of CSCL 99*

Kynigos, C. and Giannoutsou, N. (2001). Seven year olds collaborating to construct a map using GPS and space representation software. In the Proceedings of *European Perspectives on Computer-Supported Collaborative Learning (EuroCSCL)* 2001, March 22-24, Maastricht, the Netherlands. p.364.

Littleton, K. (1999). Productivity through interaction: An overview. In K. Littleton and P. Light (Eds.) *Learning with Computers: Analysing productive interaction.* Routledge. Londonp.179-194.

Light, P. & Glachan, M. (1985) Facilitation of individual problem solving through peer interaction, *Educational Psychology,* **5**, 3-4, 217-225.

Neale, H.R. & Stanton, D. (In press) Evaluating verbal and computer-based interactions using collaboration networks. *Computer Support for Collaborative Learning. (CSCL) 2002.* Boulder, Colorado, USA. January 7th-11th.

Neale, H. Stanton, D. (in preparation) Supporting co-present creative tasks: design issues for Single Display Groupware

Neale, H., Stanton, D., Cobb, S. (in preparation) Development of children's collaborative storytelling technologies: Working with users in schools.

Norman, D. (1999) *Invisible Computer,* MIT Press.

O'Malley, C. (1992) Designing computer systems to support peer learning, European Journal of Psychology of Education, *7, 4, 339-352.*

Ofsted report (2001) www.ofsted.gov.uk/inspect/index.htm no. 194367

Rogoff, B., *Apprenticeship in Thinking: Cognitive Development in Social Context.* New York: Oxford University Press, 1990.

Roschelle, J and Teasley, S.D. (1991) The construction of shared knowledge in collaborative problem solving. In O'Malley (Ed) *Computer Supported Collaborative Learning*, Springer Verlag, Berlin. 67- 97.

Ryokai, K. & Cassel, J., Computer Support for Children's Collaborative Fantasy Play and Story Telling, *CSCL '99*, 1999.

Stanton, D., Bayon, V., Neale, H., Ghali, A., Benford, S., Cobb, S., Ingram, R., Wilson, J., Pridmore, T., & O'Malley, C. (2001). Classroom Collaboration in the Design of Tangible Interfaces for Storytelling. *In Proceedings of Human Factors in Computing Systems (CHI 2001)* ACM Press, pp. 482-489.

Stanton, D., Abnett, C., Bayon, V., Cobb, S. and O'Malley, C. (In prep). The use of Tangible Interfaces to encourage small group physical and social collaboration.

Stanton, D and Neale N. (in prep) Collaborative behaviour around the desktop: The effect of multiple mice on children's talk and interaction.

Stewart, J., Raybourn, E. M., Bederson, B., & Druin, A. (1998). When two hands are better than one: Enhancing collaboration using single display groupware. Paper presented at the *Proceedings of Extended Abstracts of Human Factors in Computing Systems (CHI'98).*

Stewart, J., Bederson, B., & Druin, A. (1999) Single display groupware: A model for co-present collaboration. *CHI99* pp. 287-288, 1999.

Strommen, E., When the interface is a talking dinosaur: Learning across media with Actimates Barney. *CHI98* pp. 288-295, 1998.

Sugimoto, M., Kunsunoki, F., & Hashizume, H. (2000, December 2-6, 2000). Supporting face-to-face group activities with a sensor-embedded board. Paper presented at the *Computer Supported Cooperative Work*, Philidelphia, Pennsylvania

Taxen, G., Druin, A., Fast, C., & Kjellin, M. (2001). KidStory: a technology design partnership with children. *Behaviour and Information Technology, 20*(2), 119-125

Topping, K., Cooperative learning and peer tutoring: An overview. *The Psychologist, **5***, 151-157, 1992.

Wood, D., & O'Malley, C., Collaborative learning between peers: An overview. *Educational Psychology in Practice, 11*(4), 4-9, 1996

Literacy Learning by Storytelling with a Virtual Peer

Kimiko Ryokai, Catherine Vaucelle, Justine Cassell
MIT Media Laboratory
[kimiko, cati, justine]@media.mit.edu

ABSTRACT

In this paper, we present Sam, an embodied conversational storyteller who tells stories interactively with children. Sam was designed to appear as a peer to preschool children, but to tell stories in a developmentally advanced way in order to model narrative skills important for literacy. Literacy learning - learning how to read and write, begins long before children enter school. One of the key skills to reading and writing is the ability to represent thoughts symbolically and share them in language with an audience who does not share the same background. Children learn and practice such important language skills in the informal setting of everyday storytelling with their peers and adults available around them. In particular, storytelling in a context of peer collaboration provides a perfect place where children not only learn language skills important for literacy, but also learn to be critical listeners of others' stories. Preliminary evaluation showed that by interacting with Sam, 5-year-old children's stories more closely resembled Sam's linguistically advanced stories with more quoted speech and temporal and spatial expressions. In addition, the children listened to Sam's stories carefully, assisting her and giving suggestions on how to improve them. With Sam, children not only learned new linguistic behaviors that are important for literacy, but also to become critical listeners of other's stories.

Keywords

Literacy learning, storytelling, peer collaboration, virtual peer

INTRODUCTION

While new technologies have been introduced into classrooms to prepare children for computer literacy, traditional literacy skills – the ability to read and write – remain critical for children's academic success and may also be aided by advances in technology and research. The acquisition and practice of skills leading to literacy begin in informal settings of everyday interactions with adults and peers, and are not isolated to formal, academic environments. In this paper, we address the specific discourse genre of *storytelling* as a bridge to literacy. Storytelling occurs in the context of peer play and while a fun activity for children, also involves emergent literacy activities that can bridge children's competence and knowledge of oral language with that of written language. We present and discuss a novel approach in supporting children's literacy learning, where technology is a listener of children's stories and can provide opportunities for children to practice and acquire linguistic expressions in oral mode that are useful for their later literacy skills. First, we provide background for the link between storytelling and literacy, and the importance of social interactions in literacy learning as children learn new linguistic skills in interaction with both adults and peers. We will then introduce Sam, an embodied conversational storyteller who can act as a peer to children in storytelling play, and discuss our preliminary findings with children.

Oral Storytelling and Literacy

Our research is based on the theory of emergent literacy. Emergent literacy theorists view children as "active hypothesis testers of their language who are in the process of becoming literate" (Teal & Sulzby, 1986). According to this view, literacy learning does not happen only in formal classroom settings, but also in informal settings, in both oral and written modes, and in collaboration and interaction with others.

Whitehurst and Lonigan (1998) distinguish between the "inside-out" and "outside-in" skills of literacy. Inside-out skills are concerned with children's phonological and syntactic awareness, and grapheme-phoneme correspondence, thus facilitating children's ability to decode information within a sentence. Outside-in skills are concerned with children's ability to take the meaning of a sentence from the context in which the sentence is placed. Therefore, children must bring in their knowledge about the world and apply that to the text. Children need both inside-out and outside-in skills for successful literacy learning. However, with development, the outside-in skills become increasingly important to children, as literacy learning is concerned more with comprehending text, and not just the decoding of letters in the text (Snow, 1983; Whitehurst & Lonigan, 1998).

Successful storytelling not only requires children to use decontextualized language, the language that is not bound to the concrete here and now (Snow, 1983), but it also requires them to "recontexualize" (Cameron & Wang, 1998). In Cameron and Wang's terms, children must be able to hold the audience's perspective in mind in order to reconstruct the context of a story in a way that is understandable for the audience. This ability to adopt an audience's perspective in recounting an event is crucial to literacy (Snow, 1983; Cameron & Wang, 1998). Storytelling, then offers a perfect place for children to practice such outside-in skills of literacy. Children learn these skills through interaction with both adults and peers.

Literacy Learning with Adults

Vygotsky defined the zone of proximal development as "the distance between the actual developmental level as determined by independent problem solving and the level of potential development as determined through problem solving under adult guidance or in collaboration with more capable peers" (Vygotsky, 1978, p.86). According to this theory, a child performs at a higher developmental level of abstraction and performance with a knowledgeable and skilled partner than he would achieve individually.

Adults act as the competent partner in emergent literacy activities to support children's literacy learning. With parents and teachers, children engage in many different kinds of conversations together: exchanging information, disciplining and socializing, and showing feelings. Within those various types of conversations, children are given opportunities for conversations that require syntactic planning, careful lexical selection, making explicit cross-utterance relationships, and integrating successive utterances into a particular structure (Nelson, 1996). For example, the use of rare words during parent-child book reading is correlated with children's vocabulary acquisition (Snow, 1993). Dickinson, Cote, and Smith (1993) found that preschool teachers' use of rare words during meal time and in free-play settings were positively correlated with story understanding and definitional quality (such as a cat is a kind of animal) in addition to vocabulary growth. Therefore, adults' conversations serve as a model for children in learning new ways of using language to express their thoughts and feelings.

Literacy Learning with Peers

While parents and teachers may not always be available to listen to children's everyday stories, peers are available and can also offer scaffolding to their co-equal status partners. Neuman and Roskos (1991) investigated how children provide the kind of expert-to-novice scaffolding adults may provide in literacy activities. Neuman and Roskos observed children engaged in instructional conversation with their peers – designating, negotiating, and coaching each others' literacy activities. Unlike in an adult-child relationship, children often took turns being the more capable peer according to the purpose of the play. Similarly, Stone and Christie (1996) found that children engaged in collaborative behaviors to help each other in literacy activities. In their mixed-age, K-2 classroom, they observed children collaboratively helping each other by modeling, inviting, assisting, directing, tutoring, negotiating, affirming, and contradicting to each other in literacy activities. Results from these studies suggest that the combination of literacy-enriched play environments and literacy-rich older primary-grade children in a mixed age play setting stimulates literacy behaviors. In addition, Christie and Stone (1999) with their studies of multi-age classrooms have shown that even younger children (supposedly less capable ones) could offer assistance to older and more capable ones. Therefore, peer interaction involves not just one-way transmission of knowledge from an expert to a novice, but more "multi-directional" interactions (Christie & Stone, 1999).

It is through dialogue with others in peer collaboration that children come to realize the unique functional potential of the various symbol systems in their society, including reading and writing (Vygotsky, 1978). In a comparison of collaborative teacher-child writing with collaborative child-child writing, Daiute et al. (1993) found that generally, teacher-child collaboration produced more elaborated classic narrative structure than peer collaboration. However, one pattern of teacher talk that was controlling was negatively correlated with more elaborative narrative. Peer collaboration did not produce a more classic narrative structure than teacher-child collaboration, but did produce elaborated narrative texts. Moreover, engaging in highly interactive peer conversation was positively correlated with the change toward writing in the third person. Daiute et al. concluded that the nature of social interaction around literacy may be more important than the absolute expertise of any partner.

RELATED SYSTEMS

Significant improvements in oral reading fluency and other literacy skills have been found with new developments in technology. Mostow et al. (1994) focused on inside-out skills of literacy and developed a reading tutor that gave appropriate feedback for children reading storybooks out loud. The reading tutor was found to increase oral reading fluency in children significantly. In contrast to Mostow's intelligent tutor approach, the Cognition and Technology Group at Vanderbilt used a situated learning approach in developing their Young Children's Literacy series (The Cognition and Technology Group at Vanderbilt, 1996). In it, anchored video stories challenged children to write a story to save the animals they saw in the video. Interaction with others was key to literacy learning as the teacher modeled the story writing activity for the children, and children worked together as a group. The series has produced significant improvements in children's word and sentence fluency and story complexity.

Our previous story listening system, StoryMat (Ryokai & Cassell, 1999) was a technologically enhanced play mat that recorded children's oral stories and movements of stuffed animals made on the mat, and played those stories as animations on the mat when the same or another child told a story at the same place. Through listening to peer stories on StoryMat, children told more imaginative and structurally advanced stories. Therefore, peer stories became models and through an opportunity to listen to peer stories, children told more sophisticated stories than they did alone. Our previous story listening system TellTale (Ananny & Cassell, 2001) recorded pieces of children's stories into the body parts of a plastic caterpillar. Through deciding how to arrange and segment story sequences, children's use of discourse connectives and story event language improved. These systems led us to questions about the potentially encouraging role of a partner's feedback on children's stories; for instance, could we foster children's storytelling skills in a way more specifically helpful for literacy by incorporating a kind of virtual companion who could be a listener of children's stories?

Chan and Baskin (1988) proposed "learning companion systems" which employed both an intelligent tutor and an artificial student that were both designed to be at about the same level as the student (both were non-embodied agents). The idea was that a student would learn from an intelligent tutor (in regards to programming LISP), but then was asked to teach the artificial student (learning companion) what he learned. By having the two tasks – learning by being tutored and tutoring, learning companion systems offer a learning protocol that is similar to "reciprocal teaching" (Palincsar & Brown, 1984) where children take both the teacher's and learner's role. While their preliminary results did not show significant improvements on problem solving tests, their interviews revealed that the students enjoyed teaching an agent over a real student because they felt it was like a game.

In the Teachable Agent project (Brophy et al., 1999) children learn ecology by teaching an agent about the subject. Brophy et al. found that children who studied in order to teach the agent did better on the post test than control children who studied just for the subject test, as the students who prepared to teach spent time trying to understand "the why" of the studies.

As evident from this literature review, there seems to be an advantage in making technology play a more social role in supporting children's learning. In literacy learning, such social interactions are important as they serve as opportunities for children to gain new knowledge about language and communication, and also to test their knowledge about language and how such knowledge becomes useful.

SAM

Sam is an attempt to have technology play a social role in supporting young children's literacy learning (Cassell, 2001). The Sam system has two components: Sam, an embodied conversational agent (who is designed to look like a child around age 6), and a toy castle with a figurine. Sam is projected on a screen behind the castle, and can both listen to a child's stories and tell her own. The figurine can exist in either the physical world or on the screen, so that Sam and the child can pass it back and forth between their worlds (Cassell et al., 2000). When a child arrives in front of the toy castle, Sam looks at the child and says, "Hi, I'm Sam!" After the child greets Sam, Sam tells a story as she moves the figurine around the castle, occasionally looking up to draw the child in to the story. When Sam finishes her story, she then says, "I'll put the toy in the magic tower so you can tell a story," and places the figurine inside the tower. When the child opens the door, she finds the figurine Sam had been playing with and tells her story. While the child does so, Sam watches the child (following where the child is moving the figurine with head and eye movements), nodding, smiling, and prompting, "What happens next?" When the child is done, the child gives the figurine back to Sam and the interaction continues.

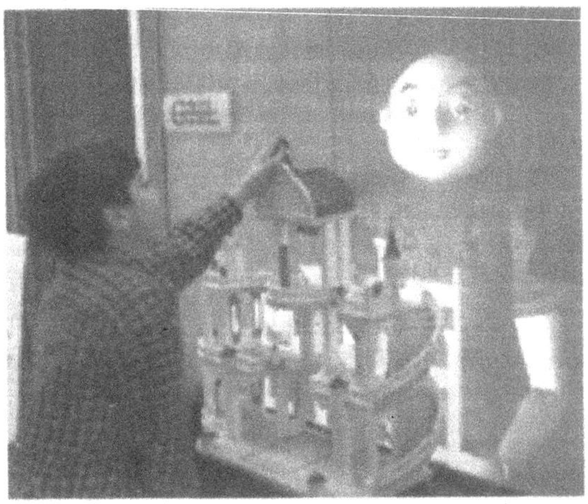

Figure 1. Sam with her toy castle

As discussed earlier, children model literacy skills from a competent partner. Sam acts as that partner as she tells stories using more advanced forms of linguistic expressions (quoted speech, and temporal and spatial information to give enough information for the audience to reconstruct the event). In interacting with precocious Sam who tells stories in developmentally more advanced forms than the child, the child may enter his/her "zone of proximal development" (Vygotsky, 1978). In Vygotsky's term, children develop through their participation in activities that are slightly beyond their competence, with the assistance of adults or more skilled children. In a way, Sam acts as that more skilled peer who can push the ability of the child a little further along. Our hypothesis is that by interacting with precocious Sam and listening to Sam's developmentally advanced stories, children model Sam's linguistic behavior and therefore, perform their storytelling task in a more developmentally advanced form themselves. Yet, because of Sam's peer-like appearance and the playful environment with the toy castle, Sam may offer both playful and collaborative activities, more than what an adult may offer. Our intention is for Sam to provide just the right amount of challenge. Sam's storytelling is more advanced than the child's, but not too advanced, as he is a partner who is just a head taller than the child.

Technical Implementation

Sam detects a child's presence through a microphone, and a motion detector sensor in front of the castle. When the child is playing with the toys and narrating, the system uses audio threshold detection to determine when to give feedback (backchannels such as "uh-huh" nods, and explicit prompts such as "and then what happened next?"). Swatch RFID tag readers are embedded inside of every room in the castle. The tag attached to the figurine tells the system which room in the castle the figurine is at. A switch in the door tells the system whether the figurine is inside of the magic tower and when the magic tower door is opened, so that the child will never see the physical and virtual instantiations of the toy simultaneously (when the door is opened and Sam has the figurine, it disappears instantly and Sam expresses surprise). In order to make Sam's character believable, Sam's stories and other utterances were recorded from a real child, as the quality of children's synthesized voices is still poor. The software is written in Java and C++ and can run on a single PC with a graphics acceleration card. The animation is displayed on a back-projection screen behind the castle.

SAM STUDY

To investigate Sam's role as a competent peer who tells stories using oral language important for literacy, we observed how children interacted with Sam and how her presence affected a child's use of decontextualized language, compared to children who played with a human peer partner.

The study was done in a "Wizard of Oz" setting where Sam's response was controlled by a researcher behind the screen. Thirty-one children volunteered for the study. All children were female and aged 5. Nine children played alone with a castle without Sam, 10 children played alone with a castle with Sam, 6 children played with a co-present playmate with a castle but without Sam, and 6 children played with co-present playmate with a castle and with Sam. All children played for approximately 15 minutes: 5 minutes introduction with an experimenter, and 10 minutes play session on their own. All the children's 10-minute play sessions were transcribed.

Sam as a Storytelling Partner

Sam's presence as a partner who told stories and invited children to tell their stories engaged both children who played alone and children who played with a co-present playmate. In taking turns with Sam and listening to Sam's stories, children seemed to use and explore linguistic expressions important for literacy learning. The following is an example of a child interacting with Sam:

Ann (age 5) is telling stories with Sam by herself

SAM: OK. Let me start. Today I'm going to ride horses in the meadow. My parents said I could ride the big horse named Star. Oh, no. Star has been stolen. I better go tell the sheriff. "Oh, sheriff, my favorite horse Star has been stolen and I don't know where she is." "Oh, no. No need to worry. A kind old lady from the other side of the forest has found her, and she is just coming back home." "Yippee! Thanks. Come on, Star."

SAM: I'll put the toy in the magic tower so you can tell a story.

ANN: Once upon a time there was a little girl and she went downstairs. She looked in the magic mirror. She went downstairs and looked in the mirror. And turned on the lights, and then went back up the stairs. And she looked at her magic, and she looked in the magic mirror, then went back downstairs, and there was her mom and dad. The end. Your turn to tell the story.

SAM: Cool! OK, let me start. I'm going to have a party and I'm going to invite whoever I want. My mom, the queen said I could. Oh look! Here Chris comes. I'm going downstairs to meet him. "Hi Chris, you're the first one here. What do you want to do?" "Well, we can go ask the mirror, who is going to come to your party?" "Oh yeah. Oh, mirror, who is going to come to my party?" "Oh, people from all the way over the land." "Oh yeah. Here, I see Cheryl, Brad, and Sean. Oh, this is going to be a great party." I'll put the toy in the magic tower so you can tell a story.

ANN: Once upon a time, there was a little girl who wanted her mommy and poppy, but she didn't have one so she could do anything she wanted. She hopped downstairs and then she saw the, she went upstairs and told the magic mirror that she wanted a mama and papa. The magic mirror told her that she couldn't get one. So she went back downstairs and she saw a monster. She went back upstairs to the magic mirror and said, "Magic mirror, why there's a monster?" and she went back downstairs and there wasn't a monster anymore. The end!

In the example above, Ann took turns with Sam, listened to Sam's stories, and in that process, her stories seemed to become more sophisticated. In her first turn, Ann's sentences involved very little complexity. Her speech was almost an eventcast (i.e. the form of "then she did this, and then she did that...") rather than a story with a causal connection between clauses (Labov, 1972).

Sam's stories were created to involve complicating actions (e.g. losing a horse) and resolution of stories (e.g. finding the horse). They also modeled advanced language, such as relative clauses (e.g. the big horse named Star), quoted speech (e.g. "Oh, sheriff..."), temporal expressions (e.g. *today* I'm going to...), and spatial expressions (e.g. a kind old lady from *the other side of the forest*). After hearing Sam's stories, Ann used more literate expressions,

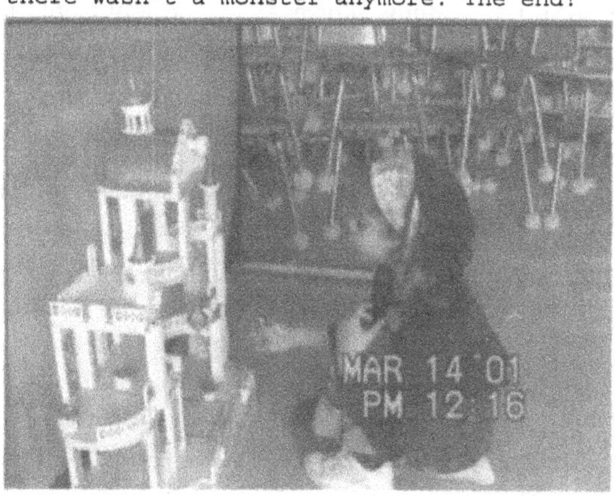

Figure 2. A child telling stories with Sam

such as relative clauses (e.g. "a little girl who wanted her mommy and poppy") and quoted speech (e.g. "she said, 'Magic mirror...'").

Two researchers coded together the occurrence of spatial expressions, temporal expressions, and quoted speech in the children's stories. Following Peterson, Jesso, and McCabe (1999), spatial expression was coded as definite information about *where* the event took place (e.g. "then the boy went to the *kitchen*") and temporal expression as explicit information about *when* the event took place (e.g. "he went downstairs *when he heard the noise*"). For the quoted speech, we coded for both direct speech with a framing clause (e.g. then she said, "Oh no!") and indirect speech such as "he said that he wasn't hungry" (Hickmann, 1993). The occurrences were tallied, and the numbers were then analyzed with respect to the time each child had to tell her story.

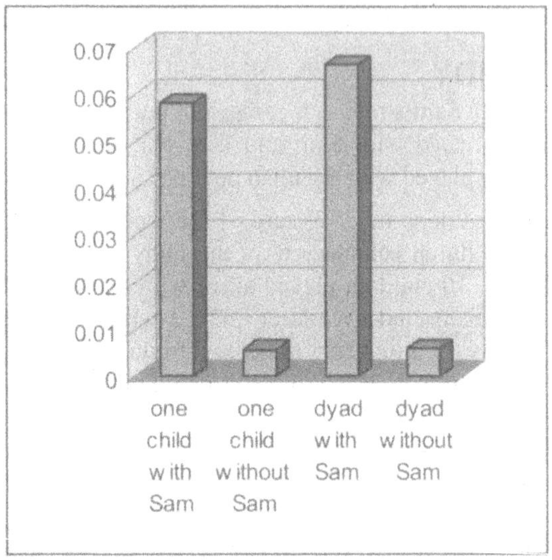

Figure 3. Mean frequency (tally of occurrences / total time) of spatial information

The presence of Sam dramatically increased the frequency with which children used quoted speech and temporal and spatial expressions. Figure 3 shows the mean frequency (tally of occurrences of expressions by each child / total time that child spent speaking) of spatial expression across the four conditions. Thus, for the dyads, the bar represents the mean frequency for each of the children in dyads. A full-factorial ANOVA revealed a main effect due to the presence or absence of Sam, $F(3, 24) = 68.04$, $p<.01$. There was no main effect for number of children (the one child vs. the dyad condition), nor were there any interactions. Children used significantly more spatial expressions when playing with Sam than they did alone, or with another child. Findings were equally significant for quoted speech ($F(3, 24)=10.58$, $p<.01$) and temporal expressions ($F(3, 24) = 30.52$, $p<.01$). The children in the "dyad with Sam" condition had equally high frequencies of quoted speech and temporal and spatial expressions as in the "one child with Sam" condition. This suggests that Sam succeeds in evoking literate behaviors even in the presence of a real flesh-and-blood playmate.

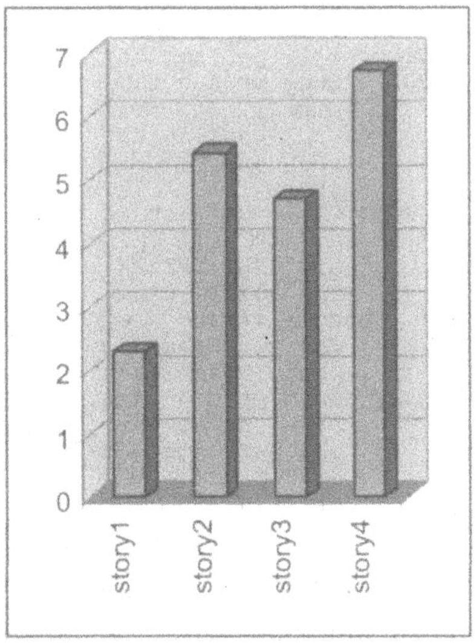

Figure 4. Mean number of spatial expressions per story

Was children's use of literate expressions attributable to the fact that Sam modeled these behaviors? In order to examine this question, we looked at whether the literate expressions increased over the course of the interaction with Sam. Remember that as the children took turns with Sam, every one of their stories was preceded and followed by a story by Sam. Figure 4 illustrates the mean number of spatial expressions per story produced by the children in the "one child with Sam" condition. The figure illustrates the increased amount of spatial expressions as the children tell their stories with Sam: the first story contained a relatively low number of spatial expressions, yet the number doubles and triples over the course of a child's interactions with Sam. The Pearson product-moment correlation test revealed a significant positive correlation between the chronology of stories and occurrence of spatial expression, $r=.35$, $p<.05$, and of quoted speech ($r=.27$, $p<.06$). No significant correlation was found for temporal expressions ($r=.065$). Interestingly, however, if one looks only at the first three stories, the use of temporal expressions does increase significantly over the stories. This suggests that children may have become tired after the third interaction, and no longer were able to push their linguistic behavior to its limits. Of course, a future study will investigate children's interaction with Sam over a longer term, as observation of stable linguistic improvements may require more than a few storytelling turns with Sam.

Unlike the children who played with Sam, children who played with another child without Sam treated each other as conversational partners rather than taking turns being the storyteller and the story listener. In the example below, the two children engage in fantasy/pretend play (i.e. the two children seem to be pretending to be at a house with a ghost) and talk to each other as a character in their play. As the two children are engaging in a conversation, rather than storytelling, their speech is more dependent upon contextual cues. For example, the child did not introduce or explain what "this" was in the utterance "You broke this..." because the referred item was immediately shared with her partner and in their conversation:

```
Wendy and Sarah (both age 5) are playing without Sam
Wendy:   You broke this after I had fixed it.
Sarah:   Not me.
Wendy:   It's probably the ghost.
Sarah:   There's no such thing as monsters. Did that door just open, or was it just my
         imagination?
Wendy:   It was just your imagination.
Sarah:   No. I think it was just the wind. I'm having nightmares.
Wendy:   Me, too.
Sarah:   I want to sleep. I want to sleep. I hope I am.
```

The children who played with Sam also shared the physical context with Sam (e.g. sharing the castle). However, Sam explicitly invited the children to tell stories and modeled decontextualized storytelling behavior. Further, because Sam's method of narration did not rely on contextual cues, the children's narration also became less context-dependent. In a way, the children and Sam shared the same invisible audience. Therefore, Sam's presence as a partner who took turns with children and told stories using diverse linguistic expressions appears to have been important in making the stories more sophisticated, fostering children's use of linguistic expressions in storytelling.

Sam as a Peer

Children seemed to perceive Sam as a co-storyteller and collaborator, as demonstrated below:

```
Ann (age 5) is playing alone with Sam. Sam finishes her story and gives the turn to Ann.
SAM:  I'll put the toy in the magic tower so you can tell a story.
ANN:  Once upon a time there was a little girl and she went downstairs. [eye gaze at the toy
      she is telling her story with] She looked in the magic mirror. She went downstairs and
      looked in the mirror. And turned on the lights, and then went back up the stairs. And she
      looked at her magic. And she looked in the magic mirror, then went back downstairs, and
      there was her mom and dad. The end. Your turn to tell the story. [gaze back at Sam]
```

Once Ann finished her story, she acknowledged Sam's turn by looking at Sam and saying, "Your turn to tell the story." Then Ann put the toy back to the magic tower for Sam to take it away. Many children acknowledged Sam's turn by giving similar "Your turn!" acknowledgement. When things were not clear, as in the following example, children seemed to "ask" Sam questions as if to check if Sam was OK:

```
Simone (age 5) is playing alone with Sam.
SAM:     Cool! OK, my turn. Today I'm going to ride horses in the meadow. [...] She is just
         coming back now. Whee! Thanks. Come on, Star. [pause]
SIMONE:  You done, Sam? OK.
SAM:     I'll put the toy in the magic tower so you can tell a story.
SIMONE:  What should I tell, Sam? Do you have an idea? [gaze Sam] Hmmmm.[gaze away]
SAM:     Tell me what happens next.
SIMONE:  Oh, the girl was happy.[...]
```

Simone seemed to regard Sam as a storytelling partner. So, when Sam finished her story, and did not immediately give up her turn, Simone asked Sam, "You done, Sam?" before she took her turn. Simone also seemed to consider Sam as a fellow collaborator. When Simone was thinking about what to tell, she looked at Sam and asked, "What should I tell, Sam? Do you have an idea?" Then, she gazed away while she thought about what to tell, a behavior one might observe from two real peers. Although we did not quantify eye gaze patterns used by children in the study, our observation leads us to believe that children looked back-and-forth from Sam to the castle in similar ways as they did when they were playing with another child. And, in fact, even with a co-present playmate, children seemed to take Sam into account. The following is an example from two children playing with Sam:

```
Amy and Beth (both age 5) are playing together with Sam. Beth has already told her story. Now
Amy is telling her story.

AMY:   And she ran upstairs. And she ran upstairs again. So, they didn't find her. And then
       they were surprised that it was all messed up. And they didn't even know who it was
       from. So, then, she came back down. And they said, Annabelle. Did you do this? And she
       said, no. And she was lying.
BETH:  So, her nose went big?
AMY:   So, then, the mother and father put her bed.
BETH:  Because she lied?
AMY:   Because she lied, and because she wasn't supposed to do that.
BETH:  OK. My turn.
AMY:   Sammy. I want Sammy to do it. I'll put it back. [Amy puts the toy in the magic tower for
       Sam to take her turn]
```

The two children seemed to collaboratively tell a story. While Amy is the main storyteller, Beth scaffolded Amy by giving some ideas (e.g. "What about Anna?" "Because she lied?"). When Amy finished, Beth tried to take the turn. However, Amy turned things over to Sam.. Thus, even with a co-present playmate, the children seemed to take Sam into account. In everyday storytelling, children become collaborators and facilitators of peer narrations (Preece, 1992). Thinking about Sam's turn and acknowledging Sam's role as a fellow collaborator is similar to what children go through with peers in everyday collaborative storytelling. Literacy learning is more profound in situations where children assist each other or collaboratively engage in activities than it is in parallel or solitary behaviors (Stone & Christie, 1996). In our experiments,

Sam seemed to play the role of an engaging peer, and was thus able to elicit linguistic behaviors predictive of future literacy.

Children Coaching Sam

Children not only seemed to regard Sam as a storytelling partner to model, but also as a peer to coach. We did not design Sam to be a character that explicitly elicited help from children. However, in interaction with Sam, children spontaneously helped Sam. The following is an example of a child "coaching" Sam:

```
Jane (age 5) is playing alone with Sam.
SAM:     Now what happens?
CHILD:   It's like this. Now it's a girl. Hi. [...] The End. Now it's your turn.
SAM:     Cool. OK, my turn. One day me and my friend[...] I'll put the toy in the magic tower so
         you can tell a story.
JANE:    [talking to Sam] Try to make a longer story next time. It's like this. The little boy
         was outside. He flipped all around and he went inside, he did a flip, [...] He went to
         sleep. That's the end!
```

Jane told a long story before Sam took her turn. After listening to Sam's story, Jane went on to model what she was looking for. "It's like this," she told Sam and then told her own, longer story, thereby coaching and modeling for Sam how to be a better storyteller.

The following is another example of a child correcting Sam:

```
Ann (age 5) is playing alone with Sam. Sam tells a story which Ann has heard before. Ann
interrupts Sam and comments that Sam has already told that story before.
SAM:    OK. My turn. I love dancing with the music. [...] They said that the lady from the other
        side of the forest was going to come, but she didn't show up.
ANN:    You already told that story!
SAM:    So, many people until my parents said I have to go to bed.
ANN:    Sam!
SAM:    I could have danced all night. When I grow up, I'm going
ANN:    Sam, you already told that story. You can still tell it though. Go ahead. [pause]
SAM:    I'll put the toy in the magic tower so you can tell a story.
ANN:    OK. Let's see. [pause]
SAM:    Why don't you tell me a story?
ANN:    Just a minute, Sam.
```

Ann listened carefully to Sam's story and commented that Sam had already told the story before. Ann was acting as a corrector of Sam's storytelling, but did so politely, allowing Sam to finish her story. In everyday storytelling, children become not only collaborators and facilitators, but also active critics and correctors of peer stories (Preece, 1992). Accordingly, Jane and Ann became critics and correctors of Sam's storytelling. Sam seemed to act as a co-storyteller, but also a peer the children felt responsible to critic and coach. By coaching, peers provide substantive input to one another's learning (Cazden, 1988; Rogoff, 1990; Neuman & Roskos, 1991). Therefore, children's interaction with Sam both as co-storyteller and as critic may contribute to them becoming critical thinkers who could evaluate and challenge others' linguistic behaviors.

Limitations

Sam's current response behavior is fairly limited. Sam was able to elicit collaborative behaviors from children, but could not follow up on the children's collaborative behaviors. For example, Sam did respond to a child's story by saying "Cool!" However, Sam was not able to give any specific feedback that related to the child's story. Somewhat surprisingly, given Sam's quite limited collaborative behavior, children still took Sam as a peer and continued to engage in collaborative behavior with Sam. We are currently investigating how Sam could relate to and incorporate children's story elements into her own stories through the use of keyword recognition techniques.

The scope of the study was limited in that it included only 5-year-old girls. Would interactions with Sam and her toy castle be engaging for both girls and boys? To children of what age range could this type of storytelling play be engaging and effective? We are designing Sam and her toys and stories to appeal to both girls and boys for our future study, as well as the age range appropriate for such an interface.

Finally, the children in the study played only once with Sam. However, in order to establish a longitudinal study, Sam's interaction with children needs to evolve over time. For example, Sam cannot simply greet "Hi, I'm Sam!" every time a child plays with her. How could Sam establish a long term relationship? Can Sam be a friend to a child? A study has shown that friends, compared to non-friends, resolved more conflicts and performed better at emergent literacy activities during pretend play (Pellegrini et al., 1998). We plan to investigate the kind of interactions and relationships Sam could have with children over a longer term.

FUTURE WORK

We are currently developing Sam in two directions: 1) designing Sam's stories with more precise features of outside-in literacy skills and 2) enhancing Sam's interactivity.

In order to more precisely model outside-in literacy skills, Sam's new stories will involve more decontextualized language (e.g. spatial and temporal information of stories), and perspective taking. A recent study has shown that children's ability to take multiple perspectives in storytelling is positively correlated with their mathematical skills (O'Neill & Pearce, 2001). We believe Sam could model such perspective taking by introducing and maintaining different characters in her stories. To encourage such perspective taking, we have also incorporated multiple figurines so that Sam and children can tell stories with multiple perspectives using the figurines.

In order to increase Sam's interactivity, we are investigating keyword spotting speech recognition technology. In addition to speech input, Sam's toy castle is being enhanced with more sensors to follow movements children make while they are narrating. For example, movement of furniture in the castle while children tell their story will be cues for Sam to give feedback to their actions. Finally, in order for Sam to produce the positive effect of multi-age collaboration where children learn by both modeling and coaching their peer (Christie & Stone, 1999), we need to have a more explicit model of a peer who could both teach and be criticized. Currently, we are investigating behavioral features of Sam that invite constructive criticism. With a more explicit model of Sam as a peer, we plan to further investigate children's literacy learning with Sam.

DISCUSSION

In summary, Sam became a partner for children to model their own stories after, as well as a peer in need of didactic coaching. The role of the "more capable partner" in the Vygotskian sense, changed fluidly between Sam and her human playmate, just like it does between real peers. This type of role change resembles a reciprocal model of peer assistance where children take both the teacher's and student's roles (Palincsar & Brown, 1984; Cazden, 1988), beneficial for collaborative learning in general.

Most importantly, Sam was able to model linguistic behaviors crucial for literacy. By taking turns with Sam and by listening to Sam's stories, the children's stories became more sophisticated and explicit through the use of quoted speech and spatial and temporal expressions. As such, children learned and practiced ways to gear their text more sensitively to an audience, which is one of keys to literacy learning.

By listening to Sam's stories and having Sam as their listener, children became both active learners and critics of others' stories. Unlike in traditional CSCL, where computers are enlisted to support learning between a teacher and pupils or to support collaborative learning between pupils, this work explored the role of computers as participants in collaborative learning. This work contributes to the field of CSCL as it illustrates how computers could play a more social role in supporting young children's literacy learning in familiar environments.

ACKNOWLEDGMENTS

We thank all the children who participated in the study, Thompson School, Vicky Rose, Linda Lin, Elisabeth Sylvan, Dona Tversky, Stefan Marti, Ian Gouldstone, Schuyler Horton, and the members of the Gesture and Narrative Language group at the MIT Media Lab.

REFERENCES

Ananny, M. and J. Cassell (2001). Telling Tales: A new toy for encouraging written literacy through oral storytelling. *Society for Research in Child Development biennial meeting*, Minneapolis, MN.

Brophy, S., Biswas, G., Katzlberger, T., Bransford, J. & Schwartz, D. (1999). Teachable Agents: Combining Insights from Learning Theory and Computer Science. In S. P. Lajoie and M. Vivet (Eds.), *Artificial Intelligence in Education.* vol. 50, pp. 21-28. Amsterdam: IOS Press.

Cameron, C. & Wang, M. (1999). Frog, Where Are You? Children's narrative expression over the telephone. *Discourse Processes*, 28, 217-236.

Cassell, J (2001). "Towards a Model of Technology and Literacy Development: Story Listening Systems." Tech Report ML-GNL-01-1.

Cassell, J., M. Ananny, Basu, A., Bickmore, T., Chong, P., Mellis, D., Ryokai, K., Smith, J., Vilhjálmsson, H., & Yan, H. (2000). Shared Reality: Physical Collaboration with a Virtual Peer. In *Proceedings of CHI 2000.*

Cazden, C. (1988). *Classroom discourse.* Portsmouth: Heinemann.

Chan, T-W & Baskin, A. (1988). Studying with the Prince: The Computer as a Learning Companion, *Int'l Conference on ITS.*

Christie, J. & Stone, S. (1999). Collaborative literacy activity in print-enriched play centers: Exploring the "zone" in same-age and multi-age groupings. *Journal of Literacy Research*, 31, 2, 109-131.

The Cognition and Technology Group at Vanderbilt. (1996). A multimedia literacy series that celebrates authorship and books. *Communications of the Association for Computing Machinery (ACM) on Learner-Centered Design,* 39 (8), 106-109.

Daiute, C., Campbell, C.H., Griffin, T.M., Reddy, M. & Tivnan, T. (1993). Young authors' interactions with peers and a teacher: Toward a developmentally sensitive sociaocultural literacy theory. In Daiute (Ed.) *The development of literacy through social interaction.* San Francisco: Jossey-Bass Publishers.

Dickinson, D.K., Cote, L.R. & Smith, M.W. (1993). Learning vocabulary in preschool: Social and discourse contexts affecting vocabulary growth. In W. Damon (Series Ed.) & C. Daiute (Vol. Ed.), *New directions in child development: Vol. 61. The development of literacy through social interaction* (pp. 67-78). San Francisco, CA: Jossey-Bass.

Hickmann, M. (1993). The boundaries of reported speech in narrative discourse: some developmental aspects. In John-Arthur, L. (Ed.) *Reflexive language: Reported speech and metapragmatics*, New York, NY: Cambridge University Press, pp.63-90.

Labov, W. (1972). The logic of non-standard English, *Language in the Inner City: Studies in the Black English Vernacular* (pp.201-240). Philadelphia, PA: University of Pennsylvania Press.

Mostow, J., Roth, S., Hauptmann, A.G. & Kane, M. (1994). A prototype reading coach that listens, *Proceeding of the Twelfth National Conference on Artificial Intelligence,* August 1994 (pp.785-792), Seattle, WA: American Association for Artificial Intelligence.

Nelson, K. (1996). *Language in Cognitive Development.* New York: Cambridge University Press.

Neuman & Roskos (1991). Peers as literacy informants: A description of young children's literacy conversations in play. *Early childhood research quarterly*, 6, 233-248.

O'Neill, D. & Pearce, M. (2001). A new perspective on the predictive relation between narrative perspective-taking ability in preschoolers and academic competence, (under review).

Palincsar, A.S. & Brown, A.L. (1984). Reciprocal teaching of comprehension-fostering and comprehension monitoring activities. *Cognition and Instruction*, 1, 117-175.

Pellegrini, A.D., Galda, L., Bartini, M. & Charak, D. (1998). Oral language and literacy learning in context: The role of social relationships. *Merrill-Palmer Quarterly*, 44, 1, 38-54.

Preece, A. (1992). Collaborators and Critics: The nature and effects of peer interaction on children's conversational narratives. *Journal of Narrative and Life History*, 2, 3, 277-292.

Ryokai, K. & Cassell, J. (1999). Computer support for children's collaborative fantasy play and storytelling. In *Proceedings of Computer Support for Collaborative Learning*, 1999, pp.510-517.

Rogoff, B. (1990). *Apprenticeship in Thinking: Cognitive development in social context.* New York: Oxford University Press.

Snow, C.E. (1983). Literacy and Language: Relationships during the Preschool Years, *Harvard Educational Review*, 53, 2, 165-189.

Snow, C.E. (1993). Families as social contexts for literacy development. In Daiute (Ed.) *The development of literacy through social interaction.* San Francisco: Jossey-Bass Publishers.

Snow, C.E., Tabors, P.O., Nicholson, P.A. & Kurland, B.F. (1995). SHELL: Oral language and early literacy skills in kindergarten and first-grade children. *Journal of Research in Childhood Education*, 10, 1, 37-48.

Stone, S.J. & Christie, J.F. (1996). Collaborative literacy learning during sociodramatic play in a multiage (K-2) primary classroom. *Journal of Research in Childhood Education*, 10, 2, 123-133.

Teale, W.H. & Sulzby, E. (1986). *Emergent Literacy: Writing and reading.* Norwood, NJ: Ablex.

Vygotsky, L.S. (1978). *Mind in society: The development of psychological processes.* Cambridge, MA: Harvard University Press.

Whitehurst, G.J. & Longian, C.J. (1998). Child development and emergent literacy. *Child Development*, 69, 848-872.

A Two-tiered Collaborative Design for Observational Science Activities in Simulated Environments

Tom Moher, Janet Kim, David Haas
Electronic Visualization Laboratory
University of Illinois at Chicago
moher@uic.edu

ABSTRACT
Elementary school science focuses on the early phases of science inquiry: observation, description, data collection, reflection, and reporting. Technologies afford opportunities to scaffold and extend the domains of inquiry, but successful adoption depends on their integration with classroom organization and practice. In elementary schools, small group and whole class activities dominate over solitary activity, and the effective use of traditional desktop computer systems has proven to be a difficult challenge for classroom teachers. Increasingly affordable large-format displays more naturally support small-group collaboration, but require careful activity design to maximize utility. We describe an activity design employing large displays that accommodates both the constraints of the classroom and the play experiences of children in support of observational science learning.

Keywords
Collaboration, science inquiry, large-format displays, elementary school

THE SNOOKERPUSS ADVENTURE
In Mr. Baez's fourth grade classroom, the talk was of the Snookerpuss, and whether there would be enough mushrooms—the Snookerpuss's favorite cuisine—to satisfy his ravenous appetite when he came out of hibernation*. In order to make their prediction, small groups of Mr. Baez's students had been conducting crop surveys in a large field and counting mushrooms during successive months of the growing season. Plotting their collective data on a graph and visually introducing a best-fit line, they developed a prediction of the number of mushrooms that would be available at the end of his hibernation. They confirmed their favorable prediction by sneaking into the field for a final count just before the hungry Snookerpuss awoke.

When they did their surveys, the children noticed that the field they were exploring contained different types of terrain (rock, sand, and grass). As they inventoried the mushrooms, the children took note of the underlying terrain, and later developed separate graph lines for each type. Concluding that the mushrooms grew most rapidly in the grass, they recommended that next year the mushroom spores be distributed in grassy areas to maximize yield.

In follow-up individual activities, the children described their surveying strategies, and developed new Snookerpuss predictions based on hypothetical data. Although the children had not previously been introduced to linear extrapolation, 75% of the students were able to construct a supported prediction. The next month, when the kids were formally introduced to the concepts of linear interpolation and extrapolation in their math textbooks, they repeatedly cited the Snookerpuss adventure.

The Snookerpuss Adventure took place over two rainy days in November 2000. The children were working in a simulated environment called "the Field," presented on a large-format multi-user display located in a resource room at their school. Kids "walked around" in small groups, navigating the simulated space and recording tallies, conditioned by terrain type. In a whole-class setting prior to the exploration, they had been introduced to the Snookerpuss's needs, and had discussed how they might be able to make predictions of future events based on historical data. The aggregation and plotting of the data, and the ensuing curve fitting and extrapolated prediction, was likewise a whole-class exercise. Overall, each child spent about 30 minutes using the display technology, and about two hours in small group and whole-class activities.

VIRTUAL AMBIENTS
The field used in the Snookerpuss Adventure is an example of a *virtual ambient* (Moher, et. al., 2000, 2001) —a configurable simulated environment used as the locus for children's scientific exploration. Virtual ambients are three-dimensional "first person" spaces within which users may navigate in space, scale, and time. Virtual ambients may be static or dynamic, but unlike traditional simulations, virtual ambients offer users no direct control over independent variables; they are designed to support observational, rather than experimental, sciences (AAAS, 1993; NCTM, 1998; NRC, 1996). Nothing that the user may do within a virtual ambient can affect the course of the underlying simulation. This constraint is

* The Snookerpuss's second favorite food is fourth graders

designed to reduce the cognitive burden of exploring complex input spaces (de Jong et. al, 1998; Friedler et. al, 1990; Jackson, et. al, 1994) by limiting young learners to familiar concepts and activities: moving around, seeing things at different scales, and imagining the past and future. It does not preclude the articulation and investigation of causal hypotheses; it simply shifts the burden from artificially *manipulating* preconditions to *finding* instances of varying preconditions in space or time.

Virtual ambients are intended as complements to, rather than substitutes for, accessible physical phenomena. Teachers often rely on accessible local environments to stimulate young learners' questions and to provide direct access to observable and measurable phenomena. Local environments have the advantages of convenience and salience, but they also have important limitations: they may emphasize activity over learning (Dewey, 1910), they may limit the domain of inquiry, and, at least in natural environments, they may constrain teachers' ability to scaffold learning by reducing complexity.

Activities employing virtual ambients typically address complementary learning goals. In the case of the Snookerpuss adventure, one goal was to help the children develop their understanding of transforming between numeric and graphical representations of data, linear best-fit, interpolation, and extrapolation. The other goal was to develop students' skills for conducting scientific inquiry, including planful investigation, navigational strategies within a survey space, observation of phenomena and recording of data, distribution of effort within an investigational team, reporting of their results, and the aggregation of data across teams in a large-scale project.

Virtual ambients share a motivational base with field- and video-based classroom investigation technologies in their focus on children's direct observations of phenomena (Smith & Reiser, 1998; Soloway et. al, 1999). Like video, virtual ambients benefit from their ability to focus attention to a manageable data domain; like field-based activities, they allow learners latitude in observational choices and practices.

In our work to date, we have deployed our virtual ambients on large-format displays (Figure 1). In the case of the Snookerpuss Adventure, students used an ImmersaDesk®, a 1.27m by 1.7m rear-projected video system with head- and hand-tracking employing lightweight shutter glasses to present a stereoscopic display, situated in a resource room at a local elementary school.

Figure 1. Children using virtual ambients deployed on an ImmersaDesk in school resource room

ACTIVITY DESIGN

The use of large format displays for presenting virtual ambients has facilitated activity designs involving groups of children engaged in collaborative investigations. Our motivation for these designs draws from several sources:

- The organization of activity—and even the physical layout of classrooms—in elementary schools is most frequently designed to support small group interaction. Moreover, from both logistic and economic perspectives, it is simply impractical to effectively schedule individual access to very scarce technological resources.
- Many children have substantial experience outside of school in collaborative virtual environments presented on large displays; the image of several children sitting cross-legged in front of a 32" television exploring complex video-game worlds for hours on end has become a cultural touch point for parents.

- Finally, we share the perspective that learning in a social context affords opportunities simply unavailable to the solitary learner.
- The large display enhances the children's sense of "immersion" in the virtual environment, and provides a closer approximation to the wide field-of-view available to learners in the natural world.
- Prior research supports the conjecture that peer collaboration plays a significant role with respect to the level of student engagement within virtual learning environments (Jackson, et. al., 1999).

A commitment to collaborative organization still leaves considerable latitude in the design of learning activities. Working with teachers at a local elementary school over the course of the past two academic years, we have developed a two-tiered approach that interleaves whole class and small group collaborative activities. A typical lesson trajectory, normally enacted over the course of a few days or weeks, includes the following components.

Reconnaissance. In order to enhance the students' ownership in the virtual environment, units typically begin with the selection of a small group "scouting party" whose responsibility is to make a brief visit to the environment, make initial observations and take some notes on what they saw, take some simulated "snapshots" of scenes in the environment, and then report what they found back to the whole class.

Establishing challenge/task/question. After the scouts describe what they saw, a research question is established in a whole class setting. The setting of the research question is a delicate balance between curricular goals and self-motivated children's inquiry. In some cases, features of the environment may lead children to raise questions consistent with the curricular goals; in other cases, the teacher may lead the children to a question by referencing environmental features that the scouts reported.

Operational planning. Once a research question is established, the teacher and students, again in a whole class setting, engage in an extended planning discussion in preparation for exploration in the virtual environment. Among the issued discussed are what data need to be collected in order to address the question (and the design of the data collection forms), how labor will be divided among the class to accomplish data collection, how accuracy in data collection can be enhanced, and the roles of individual team members during the exploration process. Data attributes in our studies have included such features as cardinality, shape, size, color, location (both coordinate data using a handheld device as a simulated GPS display, and categorically with respect to environmental attributes), and motion/gesture of animate characters in the environment.

Data collection. As the simulation environment is a single resource, data collection is accomplished serially, with individual exploration groups collecting the data assigned to them during operational planning. Depending on the technology, this may be achieved either through pull-outs (to access the ImmersaDesk in the resource room), or opportunistically planned by the teacher directly in the classroom (in the case of the plasma display).

Data investigation. Once all of the exploration groups have collected their data, the data are explored in small-group and whole class settings. Individual groups may initially work with their own data, but the data are compared among groups or aggregated across groups. In our studies, students have identified location- and time-based patterns, performed best-fit regression on time series data, developed conditional co-occurrence rules, and constructed and compared categorical distributions, among other activities.

Reporting. The unit is concluded by a reporting activity in which the students, either individually or in small groups, or as a whole class, develop an intellectual product that reflects both the process they undertook and the conclusions that they reached as a result of the investigation. This has taken the form of individual reports, group enactments, and whole class posters in our studies.

While the lesson trajectory is presented as linear, in practice it is often the case that activities undertaken at one phase may require backtracking to earlier phases of the investigation, in some cases to correct errors or resolve discrepancies, but also to undertake entirely new investigations based on accumulated experience.

COLLABORATION IN THE SNOOKERPUSS ADVENTURE

The Field

In the Field (Figure 2), students collaboratively explore a large (3000m x 3000m) "natural" terrain populated by up to eight different plant types. A standalone Java application allows the Field to be configured by selecting a plant type and clicking on the desired location. The Field itself has limited affordances: navigation, the ability to take "snapshots" automatically posted to a class web page, and the ability to plant an unlimited number of (biodegradable) "flags" in the ground. In the Field, the land mass is statically divided into regions in two independent ways: by the 3x3 orthogonal arrangement imposed by the picket fences ("sectors"), and by the differential texture maps (grass, gravel, sand) used on the ground ("terrain"). A standalone Java application allows the Field to be configured by selecting plant types and clicking on the desired locations, supporting learning objectives across a range of grade levels without requiring additional software development.

Figure 2. A mushroom in a rocky region of the Field.

In the Snookerpuss Adventure, we used only one of the nine regions, and created eight different configurations populated by varying numbers of mushrooms reflecting a time series over eight simulated months during the growing season. In the rocky portion of the field, the number of plants was held constant over the time series. In the sandy and grassy portions of the field, the number of plants grew as a linear function of time (Figure 3). The simulation for the month of June was intentionally excluded in order to create an opportunity to discuss linear interpolation.

Month	Rock	Sand	Grass	Total
March	5	5	5	15
April	5	6	7	18
May	5	7	9	21
July	5	9	13	27
August	5	10	15	30
September	5	11	17	33
October	5	12	19	36

Figure 3: Actual configuration of mushrooms by terrain type per month.

(The decision to use "perfect" data values in configuring the field drew from our experience with virtual ambient activities at other grade levels (Moher et. al, 2000). In prior activities, we had intentionally introduced noise into the data in an effort to move children away from the expectation that everything always comes out "right" in elementary school math and science. However, we found that the counting tasks in the virtual ambients were of sufficient difficulty that exploration groups almost never counted completely accurately; we also found that their errors included both undercounting and overcounting. Rather than introduce arbitrary "noise" into the data and risk further aggravating the children's own counting errors, we have settled on a strategy of using model values.)

Tier 1: Small-group collaboration

In the Snookerpuss Adventure, there were two types of small-group activities: scouting (open-ended reconnaissance enacted by a group of four students at the outset of the unit) and data collection (mushroom counting enacted by seven groups of two or three students during different simulated months).

The charge for the scouts was simply to explore the field and report back to their classmates; scouting was done prior to establishing the Snookerpuss scenario. The children took notes (Figure 4), and also took simulated photographs of scenes in the field that were assembled into a slide-show presentation that the children showed to the whole class using a video projector. Scouting took approximately 40 minutes.

The scouts collected information describing both the environment and the interface affordances (and limitations) of the system. They noted the different terrain types and the presence of the mushrooms and some ancillary plants. They also discovered that pushing one of the buttons on the controller caused a flag to be planted in the proximity of their position. They were intrigued by a software fault that caused them to get "stuck" in one portion of the field.

The students negotiated their own roles during the scouting activity. One student was the "driver," operating the controller that moved them around the field. A second student was the "photographer," deciding when to take snapshots and pushing the "shutter" button (actually, a key on a computer keyboard). The remaining two students were the note-takers.

Because the roles were viewed as differentially desirable, the children spontaneously (and quite smoothly) settled on a turn-taking regimen that allowed each student to serve in each role over the course of the activity. This worked well in terms of learner engagement, with the exception of the note-taking activity, where one student typically was temporarily resigned to watching another student write notes while offering suggestions (which were sometimes ignored by the scribe).

Figure 4. Notes taken by children during scouting activity.

Once the Snookerpuss research problem had been established in a whole-class session, six of the individual data collection groups took turns visiting the field. (The final data collection group served as "checkers" to test the predicted mushroom count developed from linear interpolation, but their activity was identical.) In class, the children had discussed the kind of data to be collected, and had developed a data table consisting of three labeled cells (one each for rocks, grass, and sand) within which they would make tally marks as they encountered mushrooms.

Drawing on the scouting experience, these groups were limited to two children apiece, as this would allow each child to have an active responsible role during data collection, with one child serving as driver and the other as data recorder. As with the scouts, turn-taking was unproblematic, with the children spontaneously sharing the two roles.

Accuracy of counting dominated discussion during the small group explorations. In the whole class setting, the children had discussed traversal algorithms for ensuring a complete count (see next section), and had decided to use the flags as a means of ensuring that individual mushrooms were not accidentally recorded more than once. Once they arrived in the virtual environment, however, they discovered that the traversal algorithms they had discussed were difficult to implement, and they began to explore alternatives.

It was interesting to note that five of the seven exploration groups settled on a similar traversal strategy that had not been raised during the whole-class discussion. Rather than treating the whole field as a homogeneous space to be covered, they used the "natural" terrain to break the region into smaller areas. While the field as a whole was too large to use "naked eye" observations to spot the mushrooms, this strategy was more effective in the smaller regions. Figure 5 shows one group's depiction of a "radial scan" strategy that they had used during their exploration.

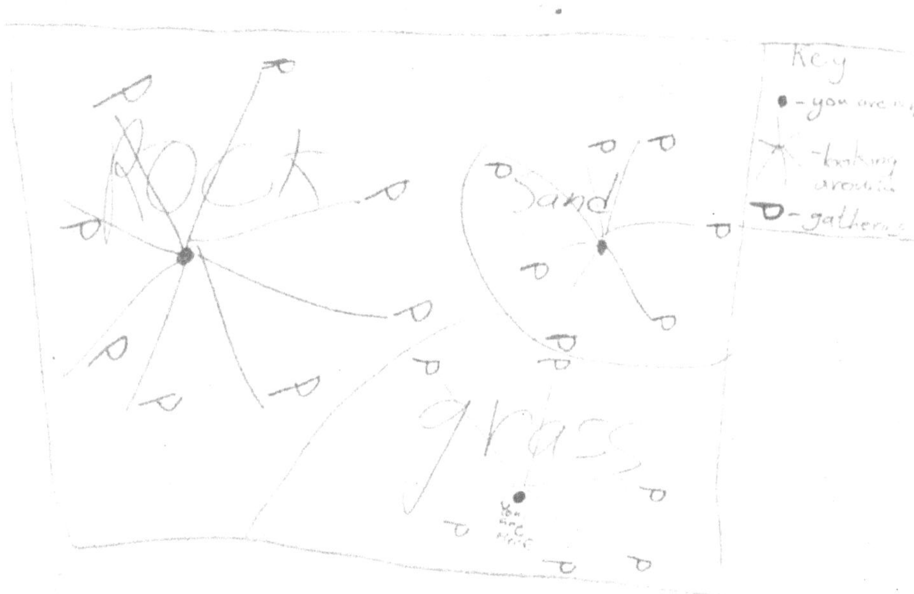

Figure 5. Terrain-based surveying developed by exploration group.

Tier 2: Whole-class collaboration

Whole-class collaboration was situated at two points during the unit, first in the setting the research question and planning of the exploration, and later in the aggregation and analysis of data leading to a prediction of mushroom count based on linear interpolation.

Following the scouts' report, the teacher built on their observations and told them about the Snookerpuss, a mythical creature who was *not* represented in the application. The absence of the Snookerpuss drew a mixed response; some were relieved at not having to face what was portrayed as a potentially dangerous creature, while others were interested in talking about his physical characteristics. (Later in the school year, when the children told a visiting member of the school board about the Snookerpuss, they imbued him with all sorts of interesting physical characteristics. "He's about 12 feet tall and brownish-green and he's really mean and he has really sharp teeth".)

The fourth graders enthusiastically accepted the story line, and understood that they would have access to a (simulated) time series of the field. Based on their prior knowledge, the children readily volunteered hypotheses about which growing medium they believed would be best for the mushrooms. While the students had been introduced to categorical bar graphs, they had not yet worked with quantitative line graphs, but the class did reach consensus that if they knew the history of the mushroom population, they might be in a position to make an estimate of future populations. ("If there was like 10 mushrooms the first month, and like 20 mushrooms the second month, there should be like 30 mushrooms the third month, and like that.")

Using an overhead projector, volunteers presented suggestions for the design of a data table that could be used for data collection. Some students suggested maintaining a list, with each item in the list being the type of terrain in which mushrooms were found, but that we later rejected in favor of the tally system with labeled cells.

A considerable amount of time was spent dealing with the accuracy of counting. The scouts had reported that the field was too large for them to simply look around and see all the mushrooms, and the children recognized they would need to develop a traversal strategy. The teacher prompted discussion by asking whether any of the kids mowed lawns, and if so, how did they make sure that they had cut all of the grass. The students responded by drawing a variety of traversal algorithms (back-and-forth with offset, diagonal, spiraling inward) that they thought might be effective. No consensus was reached on a single strategy; this was left to the individual exploration groups.

Following the exploration of the field by the data collection groups, the children returned to the whole class setting prepared to present their data. In what turned out to be one of the most engaging activities of the whole unit, the children came forward, group by group, to fill in their month's population counts on a transparency projected to the whole class (Figure 6). Initially, the teacher had asked that one representative from each group come forward; this was quickly rejected by the children, who insisted that the whole group come forward, and that each member of the group be allowed to enter some of the data on the form. (Note that the October data was not yet entered at this point in the unit; these data were added later *after* the children had developed predictions for the October mushroom population and the "checking group" had gone back to test those predictions.)

Figure 6. Aggregated data entered by children on overhead projector.

After the aggregate data had been entered, the each group proceeded to enter their point data onto a line graph, again at the overhead projector on a transparency sheet (Figure 7). For many of the students in the class, this was the first time that they had been asked to represent two-dimensional coordinate data, and the addition of a third variable (terrain type) depicted as multiple color-coded points on the same graph made the task even more complex. (As one child noted, "it looked like a bunch of stars".) Notwithstanding the lack of prior experience, the class collectively negotiated the process of representing the data on the graph. This period of the activity was characterized by a great deal of spontaneous interaction in the form of suggestions and constructive criticism. ("No, you're on the wrong line. Move it over to the right", "You've gotta use the red marker for that one", "You're reading your numbers wrong from the table.")

Once all of the groups had transcribed their tabular data onto the graph, the students were ready to draw in best-fit regression lines on which to base their predictions. Initially, the children suggested drawing line segments to connect the points. After some discussion, the students came to the realization that while this might be good for finding interpolated data (e.g., the missing June information), it would not provide them with a basis for extrapolation. With the teacher's guidance, they agreed that a single line which was "kind of in the middle of all the points" (in the words of one student) would let them predict mushroom populations into the future. With the help of many strongly vocalized suggestions, students drew best-fit lines on the graph.

Finally, the students discussed the meaning of the graph in relation to their research problem. They first concentrated on the critical question of whether the Snookerpuss's appetite would be satisfied. While there appeared to be universal consensus on the interpretation of the graph, there remained some debate on the Y-coordinate of the regression line. A tally of the student estimates is noted in the upper-right-hand corner of Figure 7. The Snookerpuss needed exactly 34 mushrooms to satisfy his appetite, so in spite of the individual differences, the class remained confident that there would be enough mushrooms when he awoke. The students also noted the differences in the growth rates by terrain; several of them talked about how some of the lines were "steeper" than the others ("like on a hill"), and there was strong agreement that the grass was the best place for mushrooms to grow ("and if you ran out of room on the grass, then you should plant them in the sand.") When the checking group returned with an actual count of 36 mushrooms in October (Figure 6), a cheer arose from the class.

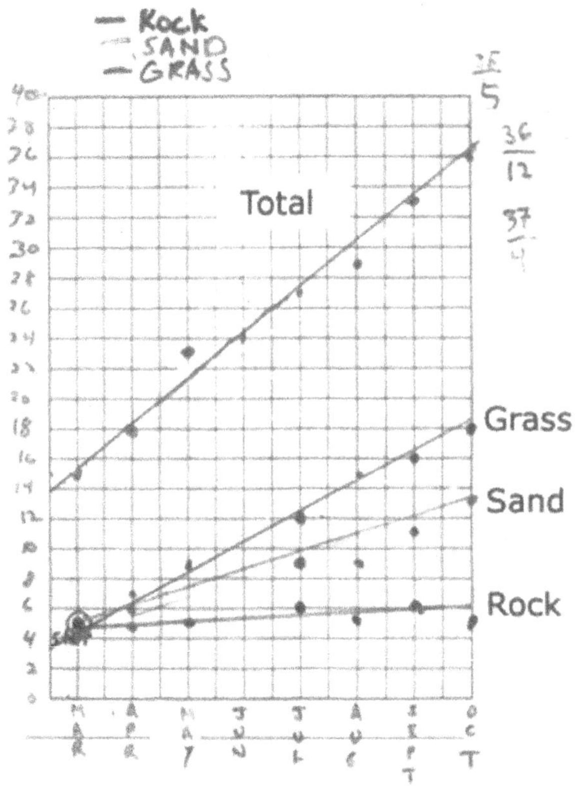

Figure 7. Student-drawn best-fit regression lines for mushroom populations

DISCUSSION

At both the whole-class and small-group tiers, the Snookerpuss adventure was designed to promote positive interdependence among learners. At the classroom tier, it was impossible for any individual group to predict the outcome (the October mushroom count) without the information provided by other groups. At the small-group exploration tier, the self-assignment of roles made it impossible for an individual student to gather the necessary data without the cooperation of their group mates.

In related research involving Shared Display Groupware (Stewart, et. al, 1999), Inkpen and her colleagues found that the presence of multiple input device had a significant impact on students' sense of engagement, as measured by off-task behavior and level of activity (Inkpen, et. al, 1999). Our qualitative experience mirrors the results in her study, with the difference that in the case of the Snookerpuss adventure, engagement increased as a function of children having a critical *role*, rather than necessarily having their hands on an input device. The responsibility for manual data recording appeared to compensate for the absence of a widget.

(Recently, we have begun to augment our virtual ambient systems with handheld devices directly supporting data collection; a test of manual vs. handheld data collection modalities might shed light on their relative merits. However, the availability of an electronic input device, even if more engaging, might not be warranted from a learning perspective; Holst (1996), for example, reported on a study in which the use of interactive computer graphics was associated with lowered mastery of content materials.)

How did children make sense of this activity: was it a game, or was it a math lesson, or was it a field? The fourth graders in this class were happy to suspend disbelief, and the language of both the small groups and the classrooms was of fields, mushrooms, and the Snookerpuss, and not of glasses, keyboards, or screens. In discussing the data in the whole class, the children never questioned whether their counts were "wrong," in spite of the fact that their data was not collinear. To the students, this was just a field, and this was just the way things were in this field.

What did the kids learn? As mentioned earlier, 75% of the children were able to use a data table to construct a graph, draw a best-fit line, and make extrapolated predictions in a post-test applied several days after the unit. On average, they were also able to articulate 3-4 distinct strategies for ensuring accurate counting. (In follow-up discussions with the children, they were very interested to know how accurately they had counted. The teacher related the importance of counting to recent events in the U.S. presidential election, which had taken place only a few weeks earlier.) More importantly, as reported by their teacher, the students continued to cite the Snookerpuss Adventure in subsequent lessons in mathematics and science through the remainder of the school year. While anecdotal, this evidence supports the conjecture that the activity was both memorable and meaningful to the students. Perhaps the most important outcome of the activity was the adoption among the students of an attitude of competence in the conduct of scientific investigations; in the words of one girl, "We're little scientists."

The activity structure exemplified in the Snookerpuss adventure has now been employed on a half-dozen units conducted at grades two, four, and six using different configurations of the Field to support different mathematics learning goals. It has proven to be a workable model for providing shared access to a scarce resource within a conventional school setting, and teachers have been able to easily integrate the small-group activities into their regular educational program. Innovative technologies embody potential that may only be realized by a deep sensitivity to the context of their deployment (Brown & Edelson, 1999), and the activity structure described here is intended as a small advance in that evolution.

We expect that technology advances will relatively render the marginal cost of using large displays—and even virtual reality systems—insignificant over the next decade. However, continuing personnel costs cannot be expected to decrease, so that a model based on adult-supervised pullouts is not sustainable in the long run. In our most recent projects, we have begun to explore the use of large-format displays (plasma panels) deployed directly in the classroom, under varying models of guided inquiry.

Figure 8. Children using virtual ambient deployed on a plasma panel in a sixth grade room

ACKNOWLEDGMENTS

The authors wish to express their gratitude to Victor Baez and his fourth grade students. We also wish to acknowledge the help of Andy Johnson, Yalu Lin, and Yongjoo Cho in the development of the Field application, the advice of Josh Radinsky and Marlynne Nishimura in the design of the unit, and the suggestions of the anonymous referees. This work was supported, in part, by the National Science Foundation's Graduate Students in K-12 Education (DUE-9979537) and Information Technology Research (EIA-0085946) programs.

REFERENCES

American Association for the Advancement of Science (1993) *Benchmarks for Science Literacy: Project 2061*. Oxford University Press, New York, NY.

Brown, M., and Edelson, D. (1999) A Lab by Any Other Name: Integrating Traditional Labs and Computer-Supported Collaborative Investigations in Science Classrooms. *Proceedings of CSCL '99* (Palo Alto, CA, Dec. 1999), 73-80.

de Jong, T., van Joolingen, W.R., Swaak, J., Veermans, K., Limbach, R., King, S., and Gureghian, D. (1998) Self-directed learning in simulation-based discovery environments. *Journal of Computer Assisted Learning*, **14**, 235-246.

Dewey, J. (1910) Science as subject-matter and as method. *Science*, **31**, 121-127.

Friedler, Y., Nachmia, R, and Linn, M. (1990) Learning scientific reasoning skills in microcomputer-based laboratories. *Journal of Research in Science Teaching*, **27**, 173-191.

Holst, S. (1996) Directing learner attention with manipulation styles. *CHI '96 Conference Companion* (Vancouver, Canada, April 1996), 43-44.

Inkpen, K., Ho-Ching, W., Kuederle, O., Scott, S. and Shoemaker, G. (1999) "This is Fun! We're All Best Friends and We're All Playing.": Supporting Children's Synchronous Collaboration. *Proceedings of CSCL '99* (Palo Alto, CA, Dec. 1999), 252-259.

Jackson, R., and Winn, W. (1999) Collaboration and Learning in Immersive Virtual Environments. *Proceedings of CSCL '99* (Palo Alto, CA, Dec. 1999), 260-264.

Jackson, S., Stratford, S., Krajcik, J., and Soloway, E. (1994) Making dynamic modeling accessible to pre-college science students. *Interactive Learning Environments*, **4**, 3, 233-257.

Moher, T., Johnson, A., Cho, Y., and Lin, Y. (2000) Observation-Based Inquiry in a Virtual Ambient Environment. In B. Fishman & S. O'Connor-Divelbiss (Eds.), *Fourth International Conference of the Learning Sciences* (Ann Arbor , MI, June 2000), Erlbaum, Mahwah NJ, 238-245.

Moher, T., Johnson, A., and Cho, Y. (2001) First-Person Science Inquiry in Virtual Ambient Environments. *CHI 2001 Extended Abstracts* (Seattle, WA, March/April 2001), 261-262.

National Council of Teachers of Mathematics (NCTM) (1998) *Principles and Standards for School Mathematics Electronic Version: Discussion Draft* (http://standards-e.nctm.org/1.0/normal/index.html).

National Research Council. (1996) *National science education standards*. National Research Council, Washington DC.

Smith, B. and Reiser, B. (1998) National Geographic unplugged: Classroom-centered design of interactive nature films. *Proceedings of CHI '98* (Los Angeles, CA, May 1998), 424-431.

Soloway, E., Grant, W., Tinker, R., Roschelle, J., Mills, M., Resnick, M., Berg, R., and Eisenberg, M. (1999) Science in the Palms of Their Hands. *Communications of the ACM*, **42**, 21-26.

Stewart, J., Bederson, B., and Druin, A. (1999) Single display groupware: A model for co-present collaboration. *Proceedings of CHI '99* (Pittsburg, PA, May 1999), 286-293.

K. (TECHNOLOGY TRACK): SYNCHRONOUS COLLABORATION SUPPORT FOR ADULTS

Evidence from a Series of Experiments on Video-mediated Collaboration: Does Eye Contact Matter?

Richard Joiner
Department of Psychology, University of Bath, UK.
r.joiner@bath.ac.uk
Eileen Scanlon
Institute of Educational Technology, Open University, UK.
e.scanlon@open.ac.uk
Tim O'Shea
Birkbeck College, University of London, UK.
Randall B. Smith
Sun Microsystems Laboratory, California, USA.
Canan Blake
Institute of Educational Technology, Open University, UK.

ABSTRACT
We report a series of studies on the role of eye contact in video-mediated communication. These are part of an ongoing research program, which is investigating the usefulness of the technological mediated collaborative problem solving for distance learning. Technological mediation consists of access to shared simulations and access to a variety of means of communication. The means of communication we have explored range from audio only contact to video mediated communication with or without eye contact. The motivating question behind this research program is 'what is different when members of a problem-solving group are physically separated but technologically connected?' The studies are set in the context of pairs of adults working with shared simulations of either physics or statistical experiments. The first set of studies investigated pairs working on a shared simulation of a physics experiment developed in SharedARK. The study compared remote technological mediated communication with communication that occurred during physical co-presence. There were no differences in performance, but the addition of computer mediated communication did influence the pattern of interaction. These experiments suggested that eye contact influenced problem solving. The second set of studies compared pairs and groups of threes and fours using a simulation of a statistic experiment developed in a system called Kansas. In these studies we compared learners with either video-mediated communication or audio only communication. The addition of the visual communication channel altered the pattern of interaction. The most recent study presents evidence that suggests eye contact facilitated conceptual understanding..

Keywords
Collaboration, Science, Simulation, and Evaluation

INTRODUCTION
In this paper, we discuss the role of eye contact in technologically mediated collaboration. This is discussed in the context of a ten-year series of experiments designed to explore the usefulness of the technological mediation of collaborative problem solving. The components of the technological mediation are access to shared simulations and access to a variety of means of communication with co-learners. These means of communication range from audio contact only to video conferencing with and without full eye contact. The purpose of this work is the desire to make the future use of such technologies by distance learners as effective as possible. Over the period in which these experiments have been run, there have been developments in the extent to which such technologies are available and affordable for schools and colleges.

This paper therefore reviews this work and as a consequence describes how the use of information communication technology alters the experience of learners in these settings. This programme builds on past work evaluating science based computer assisted learning software with both children in schools and adults in other settings (see e.g. Smith et al., 1991,

Scanlon et al., 1993, Taylor et al., 1993). The focus of the programme is to explore the potential of collaborating technologies for distance learning. The motivating question for the research programme is 'what is different when members of a problem solving group are physically separated then reconnected via this type of computer and communications technology?'

TASKS MEDIATED BY TECHNOLOGY

Introducing technology into a setting can have both predictable and unpredictable effects. It is our experience that using technologically mediated collaboration changes the nature of the activity in ways we had not predicted. We discuss these later in the case studies but first we review findings from other empirical studies of technologically mediated problem solving.

Early laboratory studies compared video-mediated communication with audio only communication on cognitive problem solving tasks and found no benefits of video mediated communication in terms of performance efficiency or quality (e.g. Chapanis 1975; Chapanis et al., 1972, Reid, 1977, Short et al, 1976, Williams, 1977). More recent studies have reported similar findings. Fish et al., (1992) compared the use of videophones with audio only telephones and found no difference in usage statistics. Kraut et al., (1996) compared participants working with an expert on a bicycle repair task, with video-mediated communication and with audio only and found no difference in the time taken or quality of the performance. In a follow up study Fussell et al., (2000) compared participants who were located side-by-side or connected via audio-video or audio-only links. They replicated their finding from the previous study and found no difference between audio-only and audio-video conditions in terms of the interaction or the performance of the participants in the audio Anderson et al., (1997) used a map task and found no differences in performance between those used video mediated communication and those using audio only communication.

Only in tasks involving conflict resolution and negotiation is there positive evidence for the benefits of video-mediated communication. Olson et al., (1995, 1997) reported that face to face or video-mediated communication produced higher quality designs than groups who used only audio only communication. Veinott et al, (1999) compared the performance of people explaining a map route to each other. Half were native speakers of English and half were non-native speakers of English. They found that non-native speakers benefited from video-mediated communication whereas there was no difference in performance of the native speakers who used video-mediated communication compared to those who used audio only communication. Thus research in this area seem to suggest that the benefits of video mediated communication are be dependent on the nature of the task.

Although commercial video conferencing systems are becoming more prevalent, there are a variety of parameters which require further examination to establish fitness for purpose. O'Malley et al., (2001) report on work in the Eye-2-Eye project which aims to provide comparative data in order to understand the different uses and cost benefits of different technologies. One of their interesting findings from this project is the decreased likelihood of lying when pairs were able to see each other using a videoconference compared to when they used an audio-only conference. Fulwood (2001) has investigated the problems in communication associated with the positioning of the camera in relation to the monitor. In this set-up direct eye contact is impossible and the lack of it was reported a problem by the users. His solution was to train them to gaze into the camera rather than the monitor.

CASE STUDIES OF SYNCHRONOUS COLLABORATION

We have been studying synchronous collaboration in the context of adults working on shared simulations. The main technological base has been provided by a number of systems designed by Randall Smith. The Alternate Reality Kit, ARK (Smith, 1992) was a system for creating interactive animated simulations implemented in the Smalltalk-80 programming environment. The Shared Alternate Reality Kit, SharedARK, (Smith *et al.,* 1991) and KANSAS, a network shared application space (Smith, in press) are prototype technologies for allowing students to work together at a distance from each other on a shared simulation while maintaining voice and eye contact. The following are two simulations used to explore the capabilities of the shared space for problem solving, the Running in the rain experiment and the Gameshow experiment.

The 'Running in the Rain' experiment

Our primary purpose in this experiment was to assess the usability of the SharedARK technology and to identify factors which were important in facilitating collaborative problem solving with this technology. We did this by comparing remote electronically mediated communication during collaborative problem solving, with that occurring during physical co-presence. These experiments involved eleven pairs of adults working at a simulation of an under-specified problem. Four of the pairs of participants used the video tunnel while working together on the simulation, three worked on the simulation as co-present participant pairs and two pairs worked remotely with only audio contact. We used the problem of whether to run or walk in the rain without an umbrella (De Angelis, 1987). Running means spending less time in the rain, but, on the other hand, since you are running into some rain, you might end up wetter than if you had walked.

In these experiments two users are in separate rooms with a workstation each, and communicate through a high fidelity, hands free audio link and with a camera /monitor device called a video-tunnel which enables both voice and eye contact through the use of a beam splitter and a mirror (see figure 1).

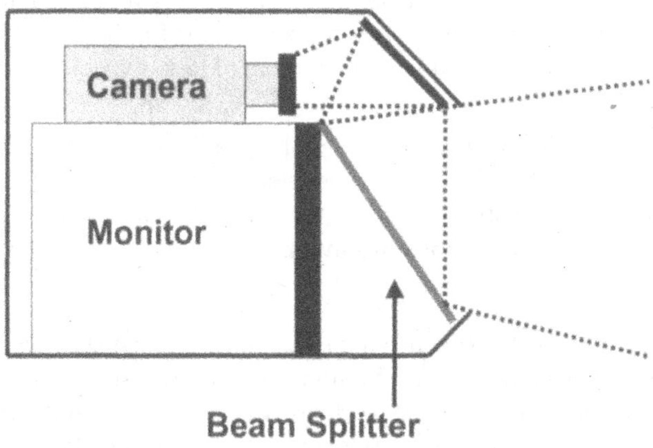

Figure 1: Video Tunnel

After an eight to ten minute introduction to the interface and the task, the participants were given a simulation containing a rain cloud, a rain runner and a device to control simulation parameters such as the speed and the direction of the rain and the wetness of the runner. During the introduction they are told that the object of the activity is for them to jointly agree when it is worth running in the rain. They are shown how to make the runner wider and narrower, how to make the runner move and how to switch the rain on and off. Participants were invited to use the simulation to test their ideas and after ninety minutes they were asked to report on their findings.

A data capture suite was used to capture video records of the interaction, which were then displayed in a four-way matrix. For pairs this meant capturing each user's screen and their video conferencing record. (For the larger groups a single shared screen was recorded with each individual user's video.) Video cameras were used to record task performance. One camera was used to record task performance. One camera captures the information displayed on screen. This data collection set-up was inspired by the development of the media space at Xerox PARC in the mid-eighties (see Bly et al., 1993), and then developed further in Rank Xerox research centre Cambridge where the running in the rain experiments were recorded. This facility was then developed in the Computers and Learning Research Group at the Open University where later experiments took place.

Four synchronous video signals made up of what was displayed on the two video-tunnel screens and the two simulation screens worked on by the participants. The video protocol was analysed by relating utterances made by participants to both events in working with the simulation and eye contact. Participants' activities and utterances from their verbal protocols were categorised according the type of activity in which participants were engaged, according to whether it involved the interface, (e.g. figuring out how to alter the rain runner's speed, or the rain runner thicker), the task (discussion about running in the rain or social interaction (e.g. laughing at jokes). These utterances were then further assigned to subcategories called meta-level activity, specific activity and recovery, which further describe the nature of the activity. For example, meta-level activity might be generating hypotheses, or discussing problem-solving strategies, specific activity might be talk generated in doing the task, and recovery from breakdown might be recovery from interface errors or misunderstandings during a conversation. Features of the dialogue are described in Taylor *et al.* (1993), and the type of augmented problem solving which was facilitated described in Scanlon *et al.* (1993), and the nature of the shared space and its role in establishing successful collaboration described in Smith *et al.* (1991).

This analysis revealed some interesting features. Use of the video channel was correlated with activity when participants were not directly manipulating the interface. We found several examples of jokes being cracked across the video channel. There are long periods where the video tunnel was not used at all, for example when objects are being manipulated or data points collected. However when the participants were talking about what they observe or suggesting hypotheses or planning experiments they look towards their partner through the tunnel. Another difference was that participants who could see each other were terser and less explicit. We hypothesised that a video channel might encourage non-interface specific activity and indeed meta-level discourse about the task was accompanied by much higher levels of eye contact than was specific talk about the interface. There was also considerable differences in the way that different pairs negotiated their problem solving

The unique shared space created by the participants using the technology is interesting. The use of overlapping (shared) and non-overlapping work areas seemed to have encouraged task division but also role division was fluid. Participants can both be face to face through the video tunnel and side by side looking at the SharedARK interface. This would suggest that pairs using the video tunnel might do better in solving the problem since being face to face facilitates patterns of mutual gaze. We thought that more productive problem solving might ensue. In considering the use that participants made of the video tunnel, which coincided with joint assent to particular decisions particularly at the planning phase. This side to side and face to face combination was not available to co-present pairs, and seemed to influence how role and task division takes place. In the audio-only condition there was more explicit negotiation of task division than in the video condition

In substance it appeared from this exploratory experiment that the addition of a video channel influenced the users activity by encouraging interaction about the problem Comparing the problem solutions produced by pairs on this task with written problem solutions (see Scanlon et al., 1993) the study demonstrated that the use of audio links and video tunnels does not attenuate the problem solving behaviour of pairs working on the task but in fact enhances it. In particular this experiment highlighted the importance of eye contact in joint problem solving.

The GAMESHOW experiment

This work informed the design of a second series of studies exploring a statistics-based simulation implemented in a distributed classroom environment designed by Randall Smith at Sun Microsystems called KANSAS. This allows several physically distributed users to move about in a 2D space (called "Kansas" because it is very extensive and flat not because it also stands for KANSAS: a networked shared application space.) Moving together and apart in Kansas will make and break audio connections. Users each have a window in which they can see their local portion of Kansas. Each user sees a small local rectangular portion of Kansas and can scroll their viewpoints across the vast surface, causing their rectangles to overlap in order to collaborate, or can move away from others to work alone. Our experiment here was conducted on a version of Kansas which supports up to 5 simultaneously active users (or, of course, up to 5 groups of users) and users can be given access to audio or both video and audio links between each of the 5 locations. Randall Smith has experimented with larger numbers of simultaneous users (see Sipusic et al., 1999 for another educational use of this technology).

We used a game show simulation of a well-known statistics problem- the Monty Hall dilemma to explore a number of related themes.

- The effect of working with a simulation on concept development in statistics.
- The influence of the bandwidth of the communication channels on the collaboration.
- The scalability of the collaborative experience.
- The usability of the interface design.

We have collected data on 6 pairs of participants, two groups of three and a group of four using the shared simulation augmented by audio communication. We also have collected data on five pairs who used a video tunnel to provide a video channel of communication, and a further four pairs working with altered video tunnels where there is no eye contact. In this paper, we are comparing data from pairs working with the video tunnels and pairs working with the altered video tunnels.

We are using a simulation of a well known statistics problem- the Monty Hall dilemma originating in an TV gameshow called 'Let's make a deal' where the gameshow host encouraged contestants to make a choice between three items, and then change their choice. This problem is non trivial and caused extensive correspondence between statisticians when discussed in a newspaper (see Hoffman 1999). The groups of participants were asked to explore the problem with the aid of a shared simulated game show setting, a shared note-taking tool and a remote human host. They communicate over an audio or video link. The game show host displays the consequences of their choices. We have recorded videos of adults at working together on the statistics simulation in different physical locations and observed their problem solving behaviours and the impact of the experience on their understanding of concepts in probability.

The participants were interviewed and given an individual pre-test questionnaires. The participants were told.

'You are a game show contestant. You have won through to the final round and your final challenge is to choose one of three doors. Behind one but only one of the doors is a Mercedes. You announce your selection but before you open the door the game show host 'helpfully' opens one of the doors which was not the one you have chosen. It doesn't have a car behind it. What should you do, stick to your original choice or change'

In the pre-test, they were asked individually to make a prediction and to give a reason for that prediction. Then they were introduced to their partners and given a shared simulation to conduct experiments. The time taken on the task ranged from 30 minutes to 90 minutes. After the simulated experiment, students still in their groups were asked to make a joint statement of their solution and to comment on whether it had changed from their individual statements. Then they completed an individual post test questionnaire to establish what their own opinion was. They were asked to state what they thought the best strategy for the game contestant to pursue. They also were asked to make a prediction about what the best strategy to pursue if the problem had four doors and the game show host opened two of them.

When groups devised simple highly focused ways of summarising the data that could be viewed in a single window they were much more likely to identify and resolve their mathematical misconceptions. The most elegant summary was a two by two matrix of success/fail versus stick/change where the appropriate cell was updated by one of the participants after each go at the game.

In this experimental situation we describe above, the learning experience was managed in part by the game show host and this raises another issue related to scalability- the issue of learner support. In this case the learning support demands appear to be much more acute than those found in the conventional classroom (see O'Shea, Smith, & Scanlon, 1997).

This system was designed to allow participants working collaboratively to solve particular problem. The particular focus here was on trying to understand how students could use a system which allowed them to conduct variable based practical experiments to help them develop their knowledge and understanding of a statistics topic. Simulations on computers can allow many experiments to be conducted quickly to develop an understanding of statistical topics. We found some success with this method (the majority of students made progress in their understanding of the problem in addition to the detection of many of the misconceptions about randomness cited above. Students however held widely differing views about how many trials of different strategies were necessary to build up a sensible picture of the outcomes of different strategies. A full account of their attempts is given in Scanlon et al. (1997).

As to the influence of the means of communication on collaborative problem solving, we were able to compare the behaviour of pairs communicating with an audio channel only or a video channel. The influence of the video channel was less marked than in the previous Shared Ark experiment in terms of pattern of discourse. Some pairs using audio were fairly terse, but some were quite discursive. The use of audio only however did require more interchanges clarifying task division. For example one pair communicating over audio only about their use of the shared note taking tool comment:

X	Sorry, D. am I blitzing you?
Y	Yeah I didn't realise that, so who is going to… what shall we do about... shall we have a procedure for making the notes so we both don't try and type at the same time?
X	**OK**
Y	**Shall I type in?**
X	You go ahead and type in yes

However, in some pairs, the access to and use of the video channel did lead to a better co-ordination of views between the two participants, what they thought the position was what they thought a good experiment to do was. One pair in particular used the video channel to explain their current view of the problem was even drawing diagrams to explain what they thought the explanation for the successful strategy was. In addition this pair's conversations over the video channel had a particular courteous quality

X	Do you want to do any more, or do you think we've..?
Y	*I'd quite like to try ten more with not changing*
X	**OK You're best at writing, do you think, it doesn't depend on who chooses does it?**
Y	I don't think so
X	It's the policies what count, so do you want to choose and I'll count this time?

We have also begun to analyse the effects of technological mediation on conceptual change. We compared the pairs using the video tunnel with the pairs using video-mediated communication without eye contact: in terms of the number of participants who changed from saying stick was the best strategy to saying that swap was the best strategy. Table 1 shows the results from this comparison.

	Change	No Change
Audio Only	2	4
VMC with Eye Contact	4	4
VMC without Eye Contact	1	9

Table 1: Number of participants who change their opinion.

Interestingly the pairs using the video tunnel were significantly more likely to change their opinion than participants using video mediated communication with no eye contact. The audio only and the VMC without conditions were collapsed together because in the table above more than 4 cells had an expected frequency less than 5 (Chi-squared = 5.5, df = 1, $p < 0.05$). This tendency to change made them more successful in there problem solving.

COMPARISON OF THE CASE STUDIES

The two systems described here differ in the extent to which the computer-based component and the audio-video component are distinct. In Shared Ark they are disjoint, as the audio /video is output to a device completely separated form the computer screen, while in KANSAS the audio/video is integrated with the interface. However more fundamentally for both systems the video and computational components are separate. For the use of the systems that we have explored this is not an issue, as we have used audio/video only for communication between learners but the possibilities of integration between video and simulation lead to possibilities for more extended experimentation.

Videoconferencing is an appealing possibility for distance education. Multiple video images can be displayed on a single monitor (for effects see Smith, in press). For pairs of students the augmented video contact of the video tunnel provided a sense of eye to eye contact . Multiple video sources can be displayed together but there is no way yet to simulate this improved eye contact for larger groups of users.

Comparing the two simulations they had some similar features but also some differences. For example, the Running in the rain simulation required more attention from participants, while the Game show simulation was more dependent on the successful use of the shared note-taking tool. In addition, in both experiments, as well as acting as an experimental resource, the shared notebook implemented on the screen became a shared focus for discussion (see e.g. Enyedy et al., 1997)

CONCLUSIONS AND FURTHER WORK

The motivating question for the research described here was to explore situations when members of a problem solving group are physically separated then reconnected via combinations of computer and communications technology. The provision of a simulation which members of the group could explore is a key feature of the systems we describe here. Our finding in general is that distributed problem solving can be supported by appropriate technologies without attenuation, but we have also noticed ways in which the interaction is altered by the technology. If we consider a pair of individuals working together in the same room, the way in which they interact will vary over time, their proximity will vary. When a technology is the medium of communication between two physically separated individuals the proximity relations will be altered. They will not be able to touch but equally they cannot remove themselves from the interaction without breaking it off altogether. They can work side by side while in the video condition be face to face with their partner. So although there may be a loss of quality in the communication via audio or video channels the proximity relations may be enhanced with an effect on talk about the problem. (See Smith et al, 1991 for further discussion of this.)

The key dimensions of variation which have been explored in these experiments are the number of learners working together, whether or not they are physically co-located, and the bandwidth of the communication channels available to them. The bulk of experience reported here is with pairs of participants communicating remotely over audio or video with physically co located pairs used to draw comparisons. Indeed the main result of this work is to develop a picture of the shared space created by shared simulations and video communication tools. In both cases, the participants quickly learn to use the simulations and come to terms with the shared audio-video-computer space in which they find themselves. The shared space created by this technology places participants into a kind of enhanced proximity in which it is possible to be simultaneously side-by-side and face-to-face. There is much still to be explored about how such workspaces can be designed to maximise the beneficial effects of collaborative problem solving. We can in these case studies demonstrate particular ways in which participants have used this rich shared resource to augment and facilitate their joint problem solving, which gives us considerable hope that such systems will be developed for distance learners. We find the role of eye contact in video-mediated communication is important in both our first and second set of studies.

Sometimes it has been claimed that the nature of the activity change caused by the use of technologically mediated collaboration alters the authenticity or reality of the learner's experience, either positively or negatively. However the change in the working practices of scientists over the last few years while we have been engaged in this research means that communication over networks as part of collaborative working is a now common part of the working practices of modern scientists. Therefore the context of this work which began as a laboratory investigation of an unfamiliar and futuristic setting for group working is one which today's students now accept as a reflection of the type of settings they may encounter in their future working lives. Students and teachers can confidently predict the continuing integration of information and communication technologies with other tools and educational researchers can expect to build and test virtual learning environments, focussing on identifying the different special properties of such new shared spaces.

ACKNOWLEDGEMENTS

The authors gratefully acknowledge the members of the Running in the Rain project team (Josie Taylor and Claire O'Malley) and Game show project team (Yibing Li, David Perry, Mark Treglown, Canan Tosunoglu).

REFERENCES

Bly, S., Harrison, S. and Irwin, S. (1993). Media Spaces: bringing people together in a video, audio and computing environnment. *Communications of the ACM*, **36**, 28-45.

Chapanis, A. (1975). Interactive Human Communication. *Scientific American*, **232**, 34-42.

Chapanis, A., Ochsman, R., Parish, R., & Weeks, G. (1972). Studies in interactive communication: the effects of four modes on the behaviour of teams during cooperative problem solving. *Human Factors*, **14**, 487-509.

De Angelis, D.(1987). Is it really worth running in the rain? *European Journal of Physics*, **8**, 201-202.

Enyedy, N., Vahey, P., and Gifford, B.(1997). Active and supportive computer-mediated reseources for student -to-student conversations. In Hall, R., Miyake, N. and Enyedy, N. (Eds.) *Proceedings of Computer Support for Collaborative Learning 97*, December 10-14 Toronto

Fish, R., Kraut, R., Root, R. and Rice, R. (1992). Evaluating video as a technology for information communication, *Communication of the ACM*, 36, 48-61.

Fullwood, C. (2001). Video-mediated gazing behaviour: training and advice for improvement of communication over video-mediated technologies. Paper presented at the *International Conference on Communication, Problem-Solving and Learning*. University of Strathclyde, June 25-29.

Fussell, S., Kraut, R. E., & Siegal, J., (2000). Coordination of communication: effects of shared visual context on collaborative work In the *Proceedings on the ACM 2000 Conference on Computer supported cooperative work* December 2 - 6, 2000, Philadelphia, PA USA.

Hoffman, P. (1999). *The man who loved only numbers*. London: Fourth Estate.

Kraut, R. E., Miller, M. D. & Siegel, J. (1996). Collaboration in Performance of Physical Tasks: Effects on Outcome and Communication. *Proceedings of the Computer Supported Cooperative Work Conference, CSCW'96*. (pp. 57-66). NY: ACM Press.

O'Malley, C.,Langton, S.,Anderson, A.,Doherty-Sneddon, G. & Bruce, V.(1996) Comparison of face-to face- and video mediated interaction. *Interacting with Computers*, **8**, 177-192.

O'Malley, C., Brundell, P., Lonsdale, P., Brooks, P., Asting, T., Heim, J., Schlieman, T., Skjetne, J. H., Hestness, B., Nilsen, S., Ulseth, T., Frowein, H. & Aaaby, C. (2001). Eye-2-Eye: Fitness for purpose of person-person communication technologies. Paper presented at the *International Conference on Communication, Problem-Solving and Learning*. University of Strathclyde, June 25-29.

O'Shea, T., Smith, R., Scanlon, E., Li, Y. (1997) Exploring the scalability of object-oriented environments that support synchronous distributed collaboration, *Proceedings of EDMEDIA-97*, Calgary.

Olson, J., Olson, G. & Meader, D. (1995). What mix of video and audio is useful for remote real time work. *Proceedings of CHI '95* (pp. 362-368). New York: ACM Press.

Olson, J., Olson, G. & Meader, D. (1997). Face to face group work compared to remote group work with and without video. In K. E. Finn, A. J. Sellen, S. B. Wilbur (Eds.) *Video-Mediated Communication* (pp. 157 – 173). Mahwah, NJ: Lawrence Erlbaum Associates.

Reid, A. (1977). Comparing the telephone with face to face interaction. In I. Pool (Ed.) *The social impact of the telephone*, (pp. 362-368). Cambridge, MA: MIT Press.

Scanlon, E., O'Shea, T., Driver, R., Draper, S., Hennessy, S., Hartley, J. R., O'Malley, C., Twigger, D.(1993). Twenty-nine children, five computers and a teacher, *Proceedings of the Fifteenth Annual Conference of the Cognitive Science Society,* Boulder, Colorado: Cognitive Science Society.

Scanlon, E., O'Shea, T. & Smith, R. (1997). Supporting the Distributed Synchronous Learning of Probability: learning from an experiment. In Hall, R., Miyake, N. and Enyedy, N. (eds.) *Proceedings of the Second International Conference on Computer Support for Collaborative Learning, CSCL '97* (pp. 224-230). New York: ACM Press.

Scanlon, E., O'Shea, T., Smith, R., O'Malley, C. and Taylor, J. (1993) Running in the rain-can a shared simulation help to decide? *Physics Education,* **28**,107-113.

Sipusic, M. J., Pannoni, R. L., Smith, R. B., Dutra, J., Gibbons, J. F. & Sutherland, W. R. (1999). Virtual Collaborative learning: A comparison between face-to-face tutored video instruction and distributed video instruction. Sun Microsystems laboratories Inc. TR-99-72. (Available at http://www.sun.com/research/techrep/1999/abtsract-72.html).

Short, J., Williams, E. & Christie, B. (1976). *The social psychology of telecommunications.* London: Wiley.

Smith, R.B. (1992) A prototype futuristic technology for distance education. In Scanlon, E. and O'Shea, T. (Eds) *New developments in Educational Technology.* Location: Springer-Verlag.

Smith, R. (in press) KANSAS: a dynamically programmable multi-user virtual reality. In O'Shea, T. and Scanlon, E. (Eds.) *Virtual learning environments and the role of the teacher.*

Smith, R., O'Shea, T., O'Malley, C., Scanlon, E., Taylor, J. (1991). Preliminary experiments with a distributed, multi-media problem-solving environment. In Bowers, J.M. and Benford, S.D. (Eds.)_*Studies in Computer Supported Cooperative Work: theory, practice and design.* (pp. 31-48). Amsterdam: North-Holland.

Taylor, J. A., O'Shea, T., Scanlon, E., O'Malley, C., & Smith, R., (1993) Discourse and Harmony: Preliminary findings in a case-study of multi-media collaborative problem solving. In R. Glanville & G. de Zeeuw (Eds.), *Interactive Interfaces and Human Networks.* Amsterdam: Thesis Publishers.

Veinott, E., Olson, J., Olson, G. M. & Fu, X. (1999). Video helps remote work: speakers who need to negotiate common ground benefits from seeing each other. *Proceedings of the CHI' 99,* (pp. 302-308). New York: ACM.

Fostering Collaborative Knowledge Construction in Desktop Video-conferencing. Effects of Content Schemes and Cooperation Scripts in Peer Teaching Settings

Markus Reiserer, Bernhard Ertl, Heinz Mandl

Ludwig-Maximilians-University Munich, Germany

reiserer@edupsy.uni-muenchen.de

ABSTRACT

Video-conferencing is expected to become increasingly important for tele-learning environments. In contrast to asynchronous, text-based computer-mediated communication, video-conferencing facilitates cooperation tasks that require highly frequent and continuous coordination. Typical kinds of such cooperation tasks are found in peer teaching settings. Despite the growing application of video-conferencing, only little is known about possibilities of enhancing collaboration in video-conferencing settings. This study investigates the effects of different types of support for cooperation on the learning outcomes of peer dyads in a video-conferencing scenario. The main research question is how cooperation scripts and content schemes enhance the students' cognitive activities and foster the outcomes of cooperative learning. Two factors were varied experimentally: The content scheme (with/without) and the cooperation script (with/without). 86 university students of educational psychology participated in the study. Each student of a dyad received a text dealing with a psychological theory in the field of the nature-nurture-debate. The students' tasks were (1) to teach their partners the relevant contents of their text and (2) to reflect ideas that went beyond the scope of the text. Results indicate that in particular the cooperation script enhances learning outcomes of collaborative knowledge construction.

Keywords

Collaborative knowledge construction, video-conferencing, content schemes, cooperation scripts

INTRODUCTION

Research on cooperative learning in video-conferencing has become increasingly interesting for educational psychology. The rapid developments in the field of information and communication technology suggest that video-conferencing will be intensively applied in educational institutions in the near future, since it enables synchronous forms of collaborative distance learning which allow very frequent and complex interactions. So far, research in this field has mainly aimed at investigating differences with respect to interaction and communication between video-conferencing and other modes of cooperation, in particular face-to-face and asynchronous text-based cooperation. Yet, only a few studies in the field of video-conferencing have focused on processes and outcomes in the context of learning. This study tries to bridge this gap by investigating effects of content schemes and cooperation scripts on processes and outcomes of collaborative learning in video-conference settings.

THEORETICAL FRAMEWORK

Contents, processes, and outcomes of collaborative knowledge construction in face-to-face and video-conference settings

Learning contents and learning processes

So far, only a few studies on video-conferencing have analyzed collaborative knowledge construction systematically. The analyses and descriptions of collaborative knowledge construction basically discriminate content-related and process-related aspects. Regarding the content level, a major question concerns the distinction between *on-task* and *off-task* contents. In particular, it has been analyzed to what extent, how frequently, or how adequately learners talk about relevant contents of the learning task (e.g. Cohen, 1994). Another aspect of content-related aspects that is especially relevant in the context of video-conferencing concerns the *coordination* of learning activities. When analyzing discourse processes in video-conference settings, Fischer, Bruhn, Gräsel, and Mandl (in press, b) distinguish between *task-related* and *technology-related* coordination. According to them, task-related coordination during collaboration is positively correlated with individual learning outcomes. Moreover, they conclude that there are no significant differences between collaboration in video-conferencing and in face-to-face settings, neither concerning task-related coordination nor concerning technology-related coordination.

In addition to discourse contents, other approaches include the analysis of process-related aspects of collaborative knowledge construction. Webb (1991), for example, analyzed explanations with different levels of elaboration, whereas Graesser and Person (1994) focused on questions in tutoring discourse. Fischer, Bruhn, Gräsel, and Mandl (1998) presented an approach that analyzed four processes of collaborative knowledge construction: (1) *Externalization* refers to the process of contributing prior individual knowledge. This exchange of different individual concepts is considered to be the starting point of negotiating common meaning. (2) *Elicitation* refers to the strategy of using the learning partner as a resource (Dillenbourg, Baker, Blaye, & O'Malley, 1996). Learners cause each other to externalize task-related knowledge: By asking questions, for example, they induce their partners to give explanations. Thereby, elicitation can be responsible for activating deeper comprehension processes (e.g. King, 1994). (3) *Conflict-oriented negotiation*, another aspect of collaborative knowledge construction, refers to the concept of socio-cognitive conflict (cf. Dillenbourg et al., 1996; Doise & Mugny, 1984). Socio-cognitive conflict occurs in situations in which learning partners externalize different or contrasting interpretations related to the learning task. This conflict often results in modifications of knowledge representations. (4) Apart from conflict-oriented negotiation, another way of reaching a consensus is the *integration* of different individual perspectives into a common interpretation or solution of the given task. However, although this form of consensus-building can be helpful under some conditions, it involves the risk of turning into a conflict-avoiding cooperation style. Considering current empirical findings, Fischer and Mandl (2000a) conclude that there are no substantial differences between video-conferencing and face-to-face settings concerning the processes of knowledge construction described above.

Learning outcomes

Research on cooperative learning focusses on different concepts of *learning outcomes*. Frequently, individual outcomes of cooperative learning are in the center of research interest. Therefore, cooperative learning efforts aim at the development of individual cognitive, socio-cognitive or affective abilities. In contrast to the focus on individual learning outcomes, other approaches emphasize the importance of collaborative outcomes, which are achieved by a joint solution of the given cooperation task (e.g. Scardamalia & Bereiter, 1993). In a recent study, Bruhn (2000) found that (1) dyads in the video-conferencing environment attained similar collaborative outcomes compared to dyads in a face-to-face setting, and that (2) learners in the two different settings did not differ with respect to individual outcomes. Similar to the findings concerning the learning processes, these results show that the different measures of learning outcomes do not differ substantially from each other in video-conferencing and face-to-face settings.

Another aspect concerning learning outcomes is the extent of *knowledge convergence* between the learning partners of a dyad or group. The concept of knowledge convergence refers to the degree to which individual learning outcomes of former learning partners are comparable in quality and quantity (Fischer & Mandl, 2000b). Aspects of knowledge convergence have rarely been considered up till now. Fischer, Bruhn, et al. (in press, b) presented empirical findings of a recent study that indicate that knowledge convergence is neither lower nor higher in video-conferencing than in face-to-face settings.

Fostering collaborative knowledge construction in face-to-face settings

The interactions described above, which are seen to be critical for effective cooperative learning, do not occur automatically. Typical barriers to effective cooperative learning are for example the diffusion of responsibility, social loafing, the dysfunctional division of labor, or a lack of learning skills on the part of the students (Johnson & Johnson, 1992). Renkl and Mandl (1995) specify important factors that are responsible for the success of cooperative learning: It depends on the nature of the given task, individual characteristics of the learners (which either support or interfere with cooperative learning activities) or the reward structure of the learning situation. Yet, the most critical kinds of interventions aim at fostering learning processes by guiding learners' interactions during collaboration.

One well-known and effective way to evoke learning activities in cooperative settings is to distribute different learning materials among the learners that should first be worked through individually. The subsequent cooperation task is to teach the learned material to each other. We label this kind of arrangement *peer teaching*, assuming that the learning partners possess similar learning skills but vary concerning the knowledge they acquired in the individual learning phase. Thus, peer teaching is distinguishable from peer-tutoring arrangements in which partners differ from each other in status and learning experiences with respect to the content (O'Donnell & Dansereau, 2000).

Peer teaching arrangements evoke learning activities by defining two different roles: the explainer and the learner. While the role of the explainer generally involves processes like providing information and responding to questions, the learner-role is defined by activities like asking questions. In this way, peer teaching settings trigger processes of collaborative knowledge construction in a 'natural' manner. Thereby, both the explainer and the learner may benefit from collaborating. For the explainer, learning by teaching is a significant mechanism that provides an opportunity to reformulate and extend knowledge structures. The learner, on the other hand, benefits from the one-to-one interactions in peer teaching settings: He or she not only gets the chance to immediately ask questions if necessary, but also to receive individual feedback by the explainer. Empirical findings (e.g. O'Donnell & Dansereau, 2000) indicate that peer teaching is an effective method of instruction. Yet, it has to be considered that peer teaching is a complex and complicated process of interaction which demands a great deal of the learners. Therefore, the question is how interaction and collaborative knowledge construction can be improved in peer teaching settings. At least two possibilities of fostering the interaction processes are conceivable: (1) supporting learners with content-specific structures which can facilitate the construction of new knowledge and (2) providing a cooperation script in order to evoke conducive processes of collaborative knowledge construction. Both treatments are considered to be helpful for cooperative learning in general. Therefore we will discuss both strategies in a broader context that goes beyond the scope of peer teaching settings below.

Pre-structuring task-specific contents. In order to improve collaboration by content-specific structuring methods, the learners receive some kind of visualization, such as a diagram or a table with central, yet abstract characteristics of the contents discussed during their collaboration. Fischer, Bruhn, Gräsel, and Mandl (in press, a) present empirical findings which indicate that content-specific structuring methods can foster processes and outcomes of collaborative knowledge construction. Dyads which worked with a pre-structured visualization tool not only externalized and elicited more task-related knowledge, but also benefited with respect to the quality of a collaborative problem solution when compared with dyads of a control group that received a non-structured visualization-tool. Suthers (in press) compares different kinds of representations (textual, graphical, and matrix) learners had to work on during collaboration in order to facilitate their learning processes and outcomes. According to him, the variation in the features of the representational tools can significantly affect the learners' knowledge building discourse. We assume that these kinds of content-specific structuring methods facilitate interaction processes in peer teaching by supporting both the peer in the explainer role and the peer who takes the role of the learner. They (1) can support the explainer in structuring the contents to be taught and (2) can provide 'anchors' for the learner to integrate the new knowledge.

Providing Cooperation Scripts. One of the most well known techniques which defines roles including specific cognitive activities is the *scripted cooperation* technique. It was developed for learning dyads and can be applied to a variety of tasks. A prototypical cooperation script used with a text comprehension task includes the following steps: (1) Both partners read the first section of a text, (2) partner A recalls the text information without using the text, (3) partner B provides feedback without looking at the text, (4) both partners elaborate on the text information, (5) both partners read the second section of the text, switch roles and continue with steps 1 to 4. Several studies have documented the effectiveness of this technique for cooperative learning (O'Donnell & Dansereau, 1992).

Another well-known instructional method for cooperative learning is *reciprocal teaching* (Palincsar & Brown, 1984). The reciprocal teaching technique designates roles that include the strategies questioning, summarizing, clarifying and predicting (Palincsar & Brown, 1984). Evidence for the effectiveness of these techniques results from numerous studies (Rosenshine & Meister, 1994). Studies about the effects of cooperation scripts usually compare groups who have been trained in applying the collaboration strategy with control groups which received no training. Thus, in contrast to methods merely using resource interdependence to evoke cooperation processes, techniques like scripted cooperation or reciprocal teaching generally include a prior training for the students working on a cooperation task.

A major advantage of techniques that explicitly aim at scripting cooperation – as described above – is that they support learners in effectively interacting with each other. So far, the effectiveness of these techniques has been documented mainly within face-to-face settings. Our approach is to apply these techniques within a video-conference setting.

Fostering collaborative learning in video-conference settings

Due to the rapid progress in the field of communication technology, video-conferencing is more and more becoming an application for everyday use and can also be expected to be a helpful extension concerning the design of new learning environments. Yet, up to now only a few studies on video-conferencing have raised the question of how to foster collaborative learning in video-conferencing. The question is, to what extent the approaches developed in face-to-face settings can also be applied to the context of video-conferencing. In general, we believe that interventions that have been shown to be effective in face-to-face settings as described above can also be helpful for fostering cooperative learning in video-conferencing. Yet, we also see some differences. Whereas techniques like peer teaching and the provision of content structures or cooperation scripts can be transferred to video-conference settings, the training of role skills in distance learning is an obstacle since the learners are located in different places. Yet, net-based learning environments provide the possibility to implement treatments not only by preliminary training but also by structured interfaces. This implementation strategy is well known in text-based computer-mediated learning environments. For example, Baker and Lund (1997) structured the text-based communication among learners working together on a problem-solving task by providing a structured communication interface which included so-called "communicative act buttons". These buttons aimed at facilitating the interaction between the learners and at encouraging the learners to engage in effective collaboration activities. Buttons labeled for instance with "Where do we start?" or "What should we do now?" tended to facilitate coordination and evoke meta-cognitive processes. Empirical findings indicate that the structured interface is able to promote interactions that enable learners to collaborate effectively on a problem-solving task.

AIMS OF THE STUDY

The aim of the presented study is to investigate two different possibilities to facilitate collaborative knowledge construction in video-conferencing. Therefore, we arranged a peer teaching setting in which two similarly experienced university students collaborated on a text comprehension task. Both learners were asked to teach each other the contents of a theoretical text they had read individually in a preceding text acquisition phase. The two variables varied in the experiment were (1) a text-based content scheme including guiding questions to facilitate collaborative text comprehension and (2) a cooperation script aiming at directing processes of collaborative knowledge construction. Both treatments were not implemented as a preliminary training of the participants. Instead we pre-structured the shared visual interface the learners worked on during collaboration. Our research questions are:

- How does the content scheme influence the learning outcomes in a video-conferencing peer teaching setting?
- How does the cooperation script influence the learning outcomes in a video-conferencing peer teaching setting?
- How does the interaction of the content scheme and the cooperation script influence the learning outcomes in a video-conferencing peer teaching setting?

METHOD

Setting

The scenario consisted of a desktop video-conferencing system including audio- and video-connection and a shared screen to support the dyads' knowledge construction. In this way, the setting allowed synchronous verbal communication and joint creation of text material. The shared application was realized with MS-Netmeeting 3.01. As text-editor we applied MS-Word 2000, an application that we expected to be well known among our participants and therefore easy to handle. This technical solution enabled the learners to alternately type or edit notes in the text-editor. Since we de-activated most of the Word-facilities, the participants were merely able to create text-material. The creation of tables or diagrams was not possible. The reason for this restriction was to focus the participants' activities on learning-relevant processes by reducing the amount of non-content talk.

Participants

96 students in their first semester who were enrolled in educational introductory courses at the Ludwig-Maximilians-University of Munich took part in this experiment. Participation was required for receiving a course credit at the end of the semester, even though learning outcomes of the experimental session were not accounted for the final students' performance appraisals. Dyads were set up and randomly assigned to one of four conditions (three experimental conditions and a control group). Learning partners in general did not know each other before the experimental session. The partners were seated in two different rooms where they stayed during the experiment. For data analysis we excluded 5 dyads, since in these groups at least one member had substantial problems with the German language.

Design

The design of the study is shown in Table 1. A 2x2 factorial design was formulated. The two factors were (1) content scheme and (2) cooperation script. Three experimental groups and a control group were formed. The experiment was conducted in one session that consisted of two main phases. During the individual text acquisition phase two different theory texts were distributed, one for each partner. In the following collaborative learning phase, the dyads were asked to work together using a desktop video-conferencing system to teach the contents of each text to the fellow learner. Thus, each learner took two roles: the *explainer-role* when explaining his or her theory to the fellow learner and the *learner-role* when receiving information from the partner. Two text documents (one per theory) were provided on the shared screen to allow the documentation of important discussion contents. In the *unscripted/scheme group,* the text documents were structured in such a way that they included several guiding questions stressing the content of that text which were supposed to direct the dyads' discussion throughout this phase. In the *scripted/non-scheme group*, the two text documents included instructions about the explainer- and learner-role in order to effectively direct the learners' interaction. Dyads in the *structured/scheme group* worked with text documents that included the guiding questions as well as the cooperation script. Participants in the *unscripted/non-scheme group*, which served as control group, worked with two text documents that only included the name of the particular theory as a headline without any further aids.

Table 1: Experimental design of the study.

		Cooperation script	
		Without	with
Content scheme	without	**unscripted/non-scheme group** (n = 12 dyads)	scripted/non-scheme group (n = 11 dyads)
	with	**unscripted/scheme group** (n = 10 dyads)	**scripted/scheme group** (n = 10 dyads)

Content scheme. The content scheme was implemented by a pre-structured shared text document that contained eight guiding questions. Table 2 shows the questions of the content scheme.

Table 2: Questions included in the content scheme.

Theory	Empirical Findings
• What are the most important concepts of the theory? • What are the main ideas of the theory?	• How was the theory examined? • What were the results of the empirical studies?
Consequences	**Individual Estimation**
• Which pedagogical interventions can be concluded from the theory? • Which limits of pedagogical interventions can be concluded from the theory?	• What do I like/dislike about the theory? • Which of my own experiences support/do not support the theory?

The structure of the scheme was adopted from Brooks and Dansereau (1983) and adapted in accordance with the purposes of our study. As can be seen in Table 2, the content scheme was divided into four sections comprising two questions each. The different sections stressed important aspects including concepts and main ideas of the theory, empirical findings, consequences and individual estimations regarding the theory. Participants were asked to generate answers to all questions and write them down in the text document. Both theory texts did not provide any information concerning the questions regarding the consequences and the individual estimation. By answering these questions, the participants were expected to draw conclusions that go beyond the scope of the texts.

Cooperation script. Learners in these conditions also received a pre-structured text document. This text document included a short description of the explainer- and learner-role and directed the learners' interactions during the collaborative learning phase by defining four steps of interaction: (1) explaining the text material (explainer) and asking comprehension questions (learner), (2) typing the information received (learner) and supporting the learner (explainer), (3) generating own ideas concerning the theory (explainer and learner individually), and (4) discussing (explainer and learner) and writing down the results of the discussion (learner only, see Table 3). An observer, who stayed in one of the two rooms, supervised the correct application of the specified roles and controlled the time in which the different tasks were to be completed. After the discussion of the first theory had finished, the partners changed roles and repeated the same procedure, now discussing the second theory. Time-on-task for each theory was 40 minutes.

Table 3: Steps and learning activities included in the cooperation script.

	Explainer	***Learner***
Step 1 (approx. 10 min.)	Explaining the text material	Asking comprehension questions
Step 2 (approx. 15 min.)	Supporting the learner's activities	Explaining and typing the information received in the shared text document
Step 3 (approx. 5 min.)	Elaborating on text information individually	
Step 4 (approx. 10 min.)	Discussing generated ideas with the partner	Discussing generated ideas with the partner and writing the results in the shared text document

Dyads in the unscripted groups received no instructions in structuring their interactions. According to the given time in the scripted groups, time-on-task for both theories was 80 minutes. The partners in the unscripted groups were able to decide how much time within this time period they wanted to spend discussing each theory. For example, if they decided to take 50 minutes discussing the first theory they only had 30 minutes left for the second theory.

Text materials

As mentioned above, two different theory texts were distributed between the two partners of each dyad. Both texts contained theories associated with the nature-nurture-debate. One partner read a text about "Attribution Theory" as developed by Bernhard Weiner, the other one about the "Theory of Genotype-Environment Effects" by Sandra Scarr. Both texts comprised approximately 1400 words each. The texts provided information on the foundations of the particular theory, its main concepts and on important empirical findings.

Procedure

Introduction and Pretests. At the beginning of the experiment, the dyad partners were seated in two different rooms and were informed about the aims of the session. They were told that at first they would learn about one theory with implications for the nature-nurture-debate individually, while their partner would learn a different theory, also concerning this topic. The task of the whole session would be to learn two important psychological-pedagogical theories. After that, the participants received the pretests as described below.

Individual text acquisition phase. In this phase, participants received a text either about the attribution theory or about the theory of genotype-environment effects. Each learner was informed about his/her task to explain the contents of the studied text to his/her partner after the individual acquisition phase. Both learners were given 25 minutes to read the text, underline important parts and take notes of the most important aspects if they wanted to. After that, the participants were given 10 minutes to think about how to explain the contents to their partners.

Collaborative learning phase. Prior to the actual learning interaction, participants were instructed on how to use both the video-conferencing system and the shared text documents. It was demonstrated how each partner could work on the same text document. Further, the participants were familiarized with the different tasks they had to accomplish according to the different conditions. The dyads were told that they should use the text documents as a worksheet providing a basis for discussion. The cooperation task required both participants to comprehend both theories as deeply as possible.

In all sessions, an observer stayed in one of the two rooms to supervise the correct performance of the particular tasks. In the scripted conditions, he/she also provided the participants with information about the time and switched from one phase to another. The collaborative learning phase took 80 minutes.

Posttests. After the collaborative learning phase, the participants were asked to complete three tests assessing their level of knowledge acquisition. The first test was a free recall-test for which participants were given 10 minutes to summarize both theories in approximately five sentences each. The second and third tests were the same as the tests conducted prior to the individual text acquisition phase (short answer- and multiple choice-test). For each test, the participants were given 5 minutes time for completion. At the end of the experiment, the participants were asked to complete a questionnaire concerning their motivation and the quality of their collaboration.

Data sources

Pretests. At the beginning of the experimental session, the participants were asked to fill out a questionnaire regarding biographical information and interest, social anxiety, uncertainty orientation, and text-processing strategies. Additionally, we conducted two knowledge pre-tests (one short answer- and one multiple choice-test) concerning concept-knowledge and deeper understanding of the theories to be learned. For analyzing the previous knowledge, we computed a combined cued recall measure consisting of the short answer and the multiple-choice test. In both cued recall tests the highest possible score was 12 points.

Posttests. The posttests included knowledge-tests regarding concept-knowledge and deeper understanding which were similar to the pretests described above. Both cued recall tests (short answer and multiple choice) are assumed to measure a deeper and more detailed understanding of the theoretical concepts and their relations. Again we computed a combined cued recall measure consisting of the short answer and the multiple-choice test. In both cued recall tests the highest possible score was 16 points. In addition, the students were asked to take a free recall-test concerning their recall of concepts of the theories learned during the experimental session. The maximum scores in the free recall tests were 22 points (Attribution Theory) and 27 points (Theory of Genotype-Environment Effects). Finally, we asked the participants to fill out a questionnaire regarding their motivation, and the quality of collaboration during the learning session.

Process data. All experimental sessions were recorded on videotapes. Additionally, we recorded processes (screen recording) and outcomes (Word-files) of activities concerning the collaborative representations. All process data serve as sources for discourse and other process analyses.

RESULTS

In order to control the effects of the pre-knowledge we computed a 2x2x2 Analysis of Variance (ANOVA) with the cued recall pretests as dependent measure. The between-groups factors were cooperation role (explainer or learner), content scheme (with or without) and cooperation script (with or without). Results showed no statistically significant differences between the groups neither regarding "Attribution Theory" nor "Theory of Genotype-Environment Effects".

In order to check if the two test types (free recall vs. cued recall) used in this study represent relatively independent knowledge measures, we computed correlations between the different outcomes. In fact, it turned out that the free recall and cued recall measures in both theories did not correlate significantly: The correlation between free recall and cued recall of "Attribution Theory" was $r = .06$ (*n. s.*), the correlation between free recall and cued recall of "Theory of Genotype-Environment Effects" was $r = .04$ (*n. s.*). Yet, we found that both free recall measures correlated significantly. The correlation between free recall of "Attribution Theory" and free recall of "Theory of Genotype-Environment Effects" was $r = .22$ ($p < .05$). There was no significant correlation between the two cued recall measures ($r = -.06$, *n. s.*). These results confirm our assumption that the free recall and cued recall measures represent two different types of knowledge. Therefore, we will treat each knowledge measure separately in our further analyses.

Below, results concerning learning outcomes in the different knowledge tests are presented. For a better illustration the results are described separately for each theory.

Attribution Theory

In order to analyze effects of the factors cooperation role, content scheme and cooperation script on learning outcomes we computed a 2x2x2 ANOVA with free and cued recall tests of "Attribution Theory" as dependent measure. Means and standard deviations of both measures are presented in Table 4. A significant effect of the cooperation role was found for the analysis of the cued recall score (F (1,78) = 19,78; $p < .01$). The participants who taught the Attribution Theory information significantly outperformed those who took the role of the learner (M = 11,03, SD = 1,91 and M = 8,92, SD = 2,37, respectively). Neither concerning the free recall nor the cued recall test no other effects reached statistical significance. That means that both treatments – content scheme and cooperation script – did not lead to significant effects on learning outcomes concerning "Attribution Theory".

Table 4: Results concerning free and cued recall of "Attribution Theory".

•		***Free recall*** of "Attribution Theory" M (SD)	**Cued recall** of "Attribution Theory" M (SD)
Explainer	unscripted/ non-scheme group	6,58 (5,16)	11,43 (1,56)
	unscripted/ scheme group	8,00 (4,16)	10,67 (2,65)
	scripted/ non-scheme group	7,36 (3,17)	10,78 (3,36)
	scripted/ scheme group	5,40 (4,67)	11,21 (3,94)
Learner	unscripted/ non-scheme group	7,55 (3,50)	9,28 (2,31)
	unscripted/ scheme group	7,90 (3,67)	8,14 (3,02)
	scripted/ non-scheme group	7,45 (4,95)	8,94 (1,71)
	scripted/ scheme group	6,00 (4,69)	9,26 (2,54)

Theory of Genotype-Environment Effects

With respect to the "Theory of Genotype-Environment Effects" we also computed an ANOVA with the factors the factors cooperation role, content scheme and cooperation script. Means and standard deviations of both measures are presented in Table 5. Again a significant effect of the cooperation role was found for the analysis of the cued recall score (F (1,78) = 8,15; $p < .01$). The peers who took the explainer role significantly outperformed those who took the learner role (M = 9,50, SD = 2,54 and M = 7,93, SD = 2,56, respectively). A slight effect of the cooperation role was also found in the free recall measure (F (1,78) = 2,83; $p < .1$). Again, the explainers outperformed their partners in the learner role (M = 10,90, SD = 3,81 and M = 9,35, SD = 4,29, respectively).

Table 5: Results concerning free and cued recall of "Theory of Genotype-Environment Effects".

•		***Free recall*** of "Theory of Genotype-Environment Effects" M (SD)	**Cued recall** of "Theory of Genotype-Environment Effects" M (SD)
Explainer	unscripted/ non-scheme group	11,25 (2,73)	9,19 (2,89)
	unscripted/ scheme group	10,20 (2,97)	9,31 (1,78)
	scripted/ non-scheme group	11,91 (4,16)	9,30 (2,91)
	scripted/ scheme group	10,10 (5,30)	10,29 (2,52)
Learner	unscripted/ non-scheme group	8,91 (4,78)	7,15 (3,50)
	unscripted/ scheme group	9,50 (4,03)	7,28 (1,79)
	scripted/ non-scheme group	10, 27 (3,50)	9,07 (5,98)
	scripted/ scheme group	8,70 (5,17)	8,27 (1,70)

Additionally a significant main effect was found concerning the free recall measure with respect to the factor cooperation script. This effect almost reached the .05 significance level (F (1,78) = 3,27; $p = .07$). Peers who cooperated in the scripted conditions outperformed the participants working without the cooperation script (M = 9,23; SD = 2,46 and M = 8,22; SD = 2,77, respectively). No other effects concerning the free and cued recall tests reached statistical significance. Hence, the content scheme did not show to have significant effects on learning outcomes concerning the "Theory of Genotype-Environment Effects".

DISCUSSION

Results show that peer teaching is an effective mean for structuring cooperation between two learners. Obviously, compared to traditional classroom instruction, peer teaching helps students to actively engage in beneficial learning processes (Graesser & Person, 1994). Yet, it must be considered that peer teaching supports particularly the learners who take the role of the teacher. The results presented above clearly indicate these advantages on the explainer's part: In both theories the peers in the teacher role outperformed their partners who were taught the learning material. These results correspond to findings of studies that also focussed on peer teaching (e.g. O'Donnell & Dansereau, 2000). At least two reasons can be assumed for explaining the teachers' advantages. First, the better outcome performance can be ascribed to the higher amount of time on task that the explainers received due to individual acquisition of the material to be taught. The second explanation refers to the relevance of the so called *generation effect*. Due to the generation effect overt verbal activity leads to better recall of information than listening to it (Slamecka & Graf, 1978). Therefore, learners who get the chance to explain knowledge to others in particular benefit from cooperative learning. The design of this study does not permit to decide which of both interpretations is more relevant. Yet, when findings of other studies are taken into account, both factors (more time-on-task and higher level of activation) should be responsible for the advantages on the teacher's part (cf. Lambiotte et al., 1988).

The results of this study showed no significant effects of the content scheme on learning outcomes. Therefore one might deny the relevance of this treatment. Yet, this conclusion is precipitate when considering (1) the learning activities evoked by the content scheme and (2) the knowledge tested in the outcome measures. The content scheme supported students particularly in elaborating on the learning material. Elaborations are assumed to mainly facilitate long term retention since they help connecting the learned material to the knowledge base. That means that the effects of the content scheme might have failed to appear because of testing the outcomes immediately after the learning session. Perhaps advantages of the content scheme would have appeared if learning outcomes had been tested again at a later time. Unfortunately, this was not possible for organizational reasons.

In contrast to the content scheme the cooperation script showed significant effects on learning outcomes. However, advantages of the scripted groups only occurred concerning the cued recall measure of the "Theory of Genotype-Environment Effects". One reason for the advantages of the cooperation script only in one theory might be that the effectiveness of the cooperation script is tied to the level of difficulty of the studied theory. A comparison of the outcomes of the two cued recall tests shows that the score of the "Theory of Genotype-Environment Effects" is lower than the score of the "Attribution Theory". This lower score indicates a higher degree of difficulty of the first theory. Therefore, the conclusion can be drawn that the cooperation script only shows effects with more complex learning material.

At present we can only present results concerning learning outcomes. In order to gain deeper insight in mechanisms of the varied treatments additional analyses of learning processes are needed. Therefore we are currently working on a category system for discourse analysis. According to the assumptions described in the theoretical framework, the categories include content-related and process-related aspects. The content-related aspects refer to activities concerning the coordination of the collaboration activities, the discussion of text material and the elaboration on information of the text. Process-related aspects comprise activities concerning elicitation, externalization, and conflict- or consensus-oriented negotiation of on-task contents as well as the distribution of task-related activities among learners (such as writing down information in the shared document). We assume that such a detailed analysis of discourse will enable us to reveal critical factors correlated with recall performance.

REFERENCES

Baker, M., & Lund, K. (1997). Promoting reflective interactions in a CSCL environment. *Journal of Computer Assisted Learning, 13*, 175-193.

Brooks, L. W. & Dansereau, D. F. (1983) Effects of structural schema training and text organization on expository prose processing. *Journal of Educational Psychology, 75*, 811-820.

Bruhn, J. (2000). *Förderung des kooperativen Lernens über Computernetze. Prozess und Lernerfolg beim dyadischen Lernen mit Desktop-Videokonferenzen* [Fostering cooperative learning in computer networks. Processes and outcomes of dyadic learning in video-conferencing]. Frankfurt am Main: Lang.

Cohen, E. G. (1994). Restructuring the classroom: Conditions for productive small groups. *Review of Educational Research, 64*, 1-35.

Dillenbourg, P., Baker, M., Blaye, A., & O'Malley, C. (1996). *The evolution of research on collaborative learning*. Oxford: Elsevier.

Doise, W., & Mugny, W. (1984). *The social development of intellect*. Oxford: Pergamon.

Fischer, F., Bruhn, J., Gräsel, C., & Mandl, H. (1998). *Collaborative knowledge construction with mapping tools* (Research Report No. 97). Munich: Ludwig-Maximilians-University, Institute of Educational Psychology.

Fischer, F., Bruhn, J., Gräsel, C., & Mandl, H. (in press, a). Fostering collaborative knowledge construction with visualisation tools. *Learning and Instruction.*

Fischer, F., Bruhn, J., Gräsel, C., & Mandl, H. (in press, b). Kooperatives Lernen mit Videokonferenzen: Gemeinsame Wissenskonstruktion und individueller Lernerfolg [Cooperative learning with video-conferencing systems: Collaborative knowledge construction and individual learning outcomes]. *Kognitionswissenschaft.*

Fischer, F., & Mandl, H. (2000a). *Being there or being where?* (Research Report No. 122). Munich: Ludwig-Maximilians-University, Institute of Educational Psychology.

Fischer, F., & Mandl, H. (2000b). *Knowledge convergence face-to-face and in an videoconferencing environment* (Research Report No. 123). Munich: Ludwig-Maximilians-University, Institute of Educational Psychology.

Graesser, A. C., & Person, N. K. (1994). Question asking during tutoring. *American Educational Research Journal, 31*, 104-137.

Johnson, D. W., & Johnson, R. T. (1992). Positive interdependence: Key to effective cooperation. In R. Hertz-Lazarowitz & N. Miller (Eds.), *Interaction in cooperative groups: The theoretical anatomy of group learning* (pp. 174-199). New York, NY: Cambridge University Press.

King, A. (1994). Guiding knowledge construction in the classroom: Effects of teaching children how to question and how to explain. *American Educational Research Journal, 31*, 338-368.

Lambiotte, J. G., Dansereau, D. F., O'Donnell, A. M., Young, M. D., Skaggs, L. P. & Hall, R. H. (1988). Effects of cooperative script manipulations on initial learning and transfer. *Cognition and Instruction, 5*, 103-121.

O'Donnell, A. M., & Dansereau, D. F. (1992). Scripted cooperation in student dyads: A method for analyzing and enhancing academic learning and performance. In R. Hertz-Lazarowitz & L. Miller (Eds.), *Interactions in cooperative groups. The theoretical anatomy of group learning* (pp. 120-141). New York, NY: Cambridge University Press.

O'Donnell, A. M., & Dansereau, D. F. (2000). Interactive effects of prior knowledge and material format on cooperative teaching. *The Journal of Experimental Education, 68*, 101-118.

Palincsar, A. S., & Brown, A. L. (1984). Reciprocal teaching of comprehension-fostering and comprehension-monitoring activities. *Cognition and Instruction, 1*, 117-175.

Renkl, A., & Mandl, H. (1995). Kooperatives Lernen: Die Frage nach dem Notwendigen und dem Ersetzbaren [Cooperative learning: The question concerning necessary and replacable conditions]. *Unterrichtswissenschaft, 23*, 292-300.

Rosenshine, B., & Meister, C. (1994). Reciprocal teaching: A review of the research. *Review of Educational Research, 64*, 479-530.

Scardamalia, M., & Bereiter, C. (1993). Computer support for knowledge-building communities. *Journal of the Learning Sciences, 3*, 265-283.

Slamecka, N.J. & Graf, P. (1978). The generation effect: Delineation of a phenomenon. *Journal of Experimental Psychology: Human Learning and Memory, 4*, 592-604.

Suthers, D. D. (in press). Towards a systematic study of representational guidance for collaborative learning discourse. *Journal of Universal Computer Sciences.*

Webb, N. M. (1991). Task-related verbal interaction and mathematics learning in small groups. *Journal for Research in Mathematics Education, 22*, 366-389.

Using Tools and Resources in Computer Supported Collaborative Writing

Gijsbert Erkens, Gellof Kanselaar, Maaike Prangsma, Jos Jaspers

Dept. of Educational Sciences
Utrecht University, The Netherlands
G.Erkens@fss.uu.nl

ABSTRACT

The relationship between collaboration processes, task strategies and the use of the tools and resources that the computer environment offers, may be crucial for the effects of computer supported collaborative learning. We are interested to find out how, within a computer environment, students collaborate, how they use the different tools we offer and how this influences the quality of the final product. A custom-made computer-supported environment (TC3) was implemented that enables pairs of high school students to collaborate in writing an argumentative essay. The essay had to be convincing and based on authentic information sources. TC3, a *groupware* program, offers the students as task related and communicative tools: a shared text editor, a chat facility, access to relevant sources of information and a private notepad. Furthermore, some facilities or tools were offered that might promote collaboration on the task: access to the chat history, adaptability of the display layout, marking and searching in information sources and counting the number of words in the shared text. From our analyses we may conclude that the tools and resources the students use during collaborative writing seem to reflect the writing strategies they adhere to and that the use of these tools and resources in the different phases of the collaborative writing process is related to the argumentative quality of the final product. Future research will focus on the effects of adding tools for text planning and linearization to the TC3 environment on the coordination processes of collaborative writing.

Keywords

Computer supported collaborative writing, tools, resources, argumentative writing

INTRODUCTION

A recent Dutch educational law has transformed the curriculum in the last three years of college preparatory high school. Among the changes, schools are required to provide support for students to do increasingly independent research, in order to prepare them better for college studies. Working and learning actively, constructively and collaboratively are seen as important parts of this program. The computer-supported, collaborative writing environment that we are developing is meant to fit within this new program. Through its active and interactive nature, the Information and Communication Technology (ICT) involved can emphasize both the constructivist and collaborative aspects of the curriculum.

Computer and telematics-based environments seem especially suited for collaborative learning by the variety of possibilities they possess: they integrate multimedia information sources, data processing tools and communication systems (time and place independent) in a single working environment (Bannon, 1995, Van der Linden, Erkens, Schmidt & Renshaw, 2000). Computer Supported Collaborative Learning systems (CSCL) are assumed to have the potential to enhance the effectiveness of peer learning interactions (Dillenbourg, 1999). As for the role of computers in education, the focus is on the construction of computer-based, multimedia environments: open learning environments that may give rise to multiple authentic learning experiences (Cognition and Technology Group at Vanderbilt, 1994). The cooperative aspect is mainly realized by offering computerized tools, that can be helpful for collaborating students in solving the task at hand (e.g., the CSILE-program of Scardamalia, Bereiter & Lamon, 1994; the Belvèdere program of Suthers, Weiner, Connelly & Paolucci, 1995). These tools are generally one of two kinds: task content related or communicative. Task related tools support the performance of the task and the problem solving process (Teasley & Rochelle, 1993). Communicative tools give access to collaborating partners, but also to other resources like external experts or information sources on the Internet. In this respect, the program functions as a communication medium (Henri, 1995). Programs that integrate both functions are generally known as *groupware:* they are meant to support collaborative work by sharing tools and resources between group members and by providing communication opportunities within the group and with the external world. In complex, open problem solving tasks students will have to decide when and where to use the task related and communicative tools and resources during the process of collaboration within the groupware environment. Furthermore, they will have to coordinate the use of shared tools and discuss their application.

COLLABORATIVE ARGUMENTATIVE WRITING

Writing clearly is an open task. Writing texts of any length has been shown to be a complex process in which several interrelated sub-processes can be distinguished, each with its own dynamics and constraints (Rijlaarsdam & Van den Bergh, 1996). We conceptualize writing argumentative texts mainly as a knowledge-construction (Galbraith, 1999) and problem-solving task. In this task, several informational units from internal or external sources must be generated, selected, collected, related to each other, and organized in a consistent knowledge structure. Furthermore the problem of convincing the reader by finding a persuasive ordering of arguments and contra arguments must be solved. This entails quite a few skills, among which social, cognitive, rhetorical, and cultural.

The main advantage of collaborative writing, compared to individual writing, is the presence of a workspace where the writers can receive immediate feedback. Argumentation by itself, according to Stein, Caliches & Bernas (1997), facilitated learning because it necessitates searching for relevant information and using each other as a source of knowledge. Furthermore, the discussions generated by the activity make the collaborators verbalize and negotiate many things: representations, purpose, plans, doubts, etc. Collaborating writers have to test their hypotheses, justify their propositions, and make their goals explicit. This may lead to progressively more conscious control and increased awareness of the processes (Giroud, 1999).

Planning argumentative texts

Theories of writing (Hayes & Nash, 1996) generally distinguish three types of activities in the writing process: planning (generating, organizing and linearizing content), formulating or translating (writing the text) and revising. Planning an argumentative text is a type of task whereby arguments need to be generated and ordered based on one's position and the audience's needs. Unlike in storytelling, the order of the content of an argumentative text does not inherently follow from the order in which events take place. During planning activities, ideas will probably be conceived and organized in a very different manner than in time – for instance, in argument clusters. Hence, linearization of the contents is needed before the ideas can be expanded into text, and again when a text is re-organized. Linearization, therefore, is an important part of argumentative writing (Levelt, 1989). Research at our department showed that an explicit parting of the idea organization and linearization phases during planning leads to an improvement of the quality of an argumentative text (Coirier, Andriessen & Chanquoy, 1999). It was apparent that converting the conceptual representation of ideas into linear text is a crucial problem for the writer who is producing argumentative texts. The proposed environment will endeavor to support students during these two phases with an ICT environment in which tools for conceptual organizing and linearization are integrated.

Much previous research has concerned itself with examining *preplanning*. Preplanning refers to planning activities that occur before the actual writing of the text. Such research has shown that preplanning can have a favorable effect on the quality of the text (Andriessen, Coirier, Roos, Passerault & Bert-Erboul, 1996). It is known that inexperienced writers seldom do preplanning (Alarmargot, 1997). Moreover, because of a lack of knowledge of the issues involved, when preplanning does occur in novices it is more likely to be a superficial sort of brainstorming, which is actually not much more than simple content-activation based on the terms used in the assignment. Bereiter & Scardamalia (1987) found this to be true for children. Torrance, Thomas, & Robinson (1996), likewise, found little idea generation based on rhetorical demands during preplanning for adult undergraduates (relative novices). Rather, their idea generation made a better match with a simple content-activation model. Also, the number and originality of ideas in the draft were not correlated with time spent preplanning. Preplanning for writing informational or argumentative texts, however, largely consists of searching, reading and annotating external information sources.

Lacking preplanning skills, supporting *online planning* becomes especially important for inexperienced writers. By online planning we mean the monitoring activities that occur during writing based on goals set, ideas, expectations and strategies (Van der Pool, 1995). These activities direct the process of knowledge construction during writing. Online planning activities, unlike preplanning, are generally linked more strongly to the local organization of the text. Preplanning, at least in experts, is more concerned with global issues like setting goals and determining overall organization and genre. In earlier research, the transition between preplanning processes and writing the actual text was found to be a stumbling block. Kozma (1991), Scardamalia & Bereiter (1985, 1987), and Schriver (1988) all found positive effects of teaching preplanning on the amount and/or the quality of preplanning, but not on the quality of the written text. The problem can lie in the linearization or the translation processes, both transitional processes.

In collaborative writing the partners will have to agree on both the content and the ordering of the text. Thus, reflecting on transitions becomes a natural process. Furthermore, the use of resources will have to be coordinated and discussed. In previous research, in which college undergraduates selected arguments and produced an argumentative text while collaborating in a groupware environment, differences in the argumentative discussion were found to correlate with the representation of the source material. It was found that in a task where the arguments appeared as pictures, more inferences were needed to deduce the usefulness of the information. The students discussed more new arguments in the chat discussion and more new arguments in their common argumentative text (Andriessen, Erkens, Overeem & Jaspers, 1996). Having to put the pictures into words must have helped. Thus, the constructive activities of organizing, linearizing as well as translating to the common text will have to take place in mutual deliberation, necessitating verbalization and reification of ideas. This negotiation, arriving at a shared knowledge construction and common task strategy, takes place in the collaboration dialogue between the partners (Erkens, Andriessen & Peters, submitted). The expectation is that more mutual coordinating activities in the dialogue result in a more consistent, shared knowledge structure and in a better mutual problem solution, that is a better argumentative text (also see Baker, 1999). Furthermore, computer support for content generation, organizing and linearization will help to make these planning activities explicit and negotiable. We are currently examining these two expectations in the COSAR project. This paper will focus on the question how students use and coordinate their use of tools and resources in the process of collaborative writing, and how the use of these tools and resources relates to the quality of the final written product.

COSAR PROJECT

In the COSAR project (COmputer Supported ARgumentative writing) we study electronic collaborative text production with respect to the relationship between characteristics of interaction on the one hand and learning and problem solving on the other (http://eduweb.fss.uu.nl/cosar). A groupware program (TC3: Text Composer, Computer Supported & Collaborative) was developed that combines a shared text editor, a chat facility and private access to internal and external information resources to foster the collaborative distance writing of texts. The project was meant for pairs of students (16-18 years old) working together in writing argumentative essays in the context of the Dutch language curriculum. The assignment was to choose a position pro or contra a current topic (cloning or organ donation) and to write a convincing argumentative text addressed to the Department of Public Health. The texts had to be based on recent articles from well-known newspapers published on the Internet. Each partner worked at his/her own computer.

The basic environment consists of four main windows (see Figure 1):

INFORMATION (upper right): This private window contains tabs for the task assignment and the information sources. Each student has different sources. Relevant parts of the sources can be highlighted, and the search button (bottom toolbar) allows students to cycle through the marked parts. On request of the teachers, copying and pasting from the information sources was disabled.

NOTES (upper left): A private notepad in which the student can make personal notes. Copying and pasting from the notes to the shared text is possible.

CHAT (lower left): The chat window is shared and *WYSIWIS* (‘*What you see is what I see*’). The lower chat box is for the student's current contribution; the other shows the incoming messages of his partner. The scrollable window holds their past dialogue: the chat history. Copying and pasting from the chat is disabled.

SHARED TEXT (lower right): A text editor (also *WYSIWIS*’) in which the shared text can be composed by taking turns with a turn-taking device. Turn taking is regulated by a traffic light (bottom toolbar). One student has the green sign and can write in the text, the other has a red sign. The student with the green sign can pass on his turn by clicking on the traffic light. The partner will get the green light and can then write in the text. A student with the red light who wants to write, can ask for the turn by clicking the traffic light. Both lights will turn to yellow and flash, signaling that the turn has been asked for. A word count button (bottom toolbar) can be used to count the number of words the text contains. It is possible to copy and paste from the shared text into the notes.

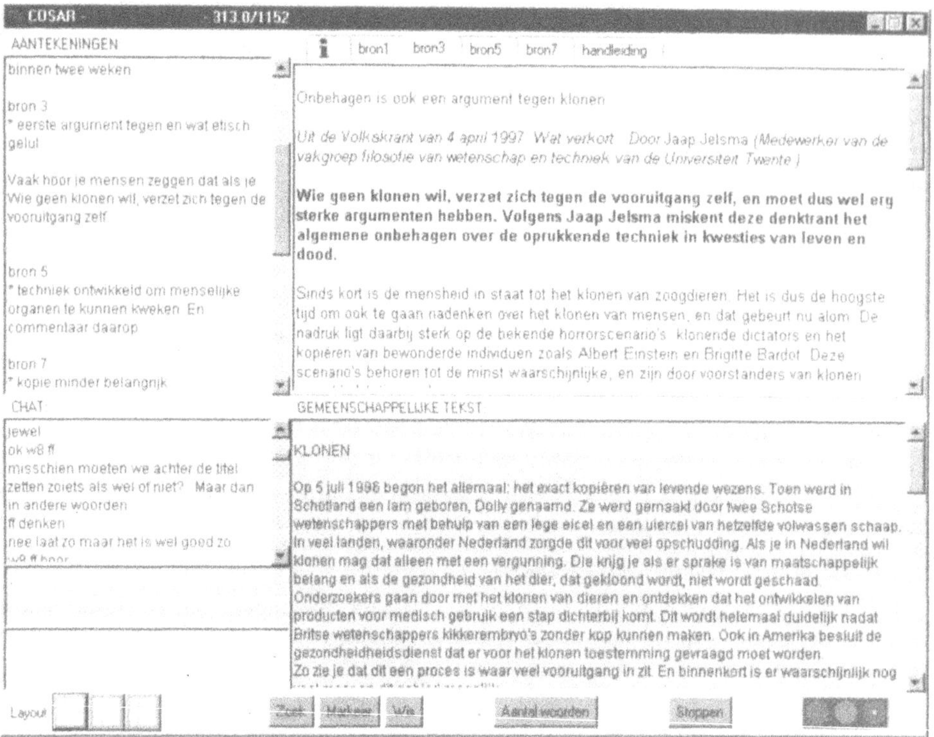

T

Furthermore, the students can change the layout, that is, resize the windows, of the basic TC3 environment by layout buttons (bottom toolbar). For reading information sources and making private notes the information window and the notes window can be enlarged. Another layout button will enlarge the lower windows (chat and shared text) for emphasis on the communicative and shared tools. The layout buttons change the layout of the TC3 environment individually. The last button in the bottom toolbar is the stop button. With the stop button the students can stop their collaborative work and continue at a later time. The students work on a text for about 6 hours, in most cases in 3-4 sessions on separate days. Clicking the stop button automatically saves all work in progress that is, all text, notes, highlights and chat history.

The program keeps a log file in which all actions in the separate windows and the chat discussion history are saved. This log file may be used to literally replay all keystrokes and thus the full collaboration between the students. The log file is also used to construct an activity and chat dialogue protocol for data analysis.

RESEARCH QUESTIONS

In a first study 40 pairs of students from two College Preparatory High schools (*VWO*) have written one or two argumentative texts on the topics cloning and organ donation in the basic TC3 environment. The evaluation of the students showed that, although criticizing technical flaws and drawbacks of the program (mainly in the first session), they were rather satisfied with this way of computer-supported collaborative learning.

In a second study, we have experimentally added two planning tools (a diagram visualizing the argumentative structure and an outliner function for the text) in order to determine the effect of sharing these tools on the argumentation in the discussion and on the resulting argumentative text. In this study 120 pairs of students from six schools participated. We are currently analyzing the results from the second study.

In this paper we will discuss results on three research questions in the context of the first study in the COSAR project:

- How do students use the tools and resources in order to coordinate their collaborative writing?
- How does the use of tools and resources relate to the argumentative quality and structure of the resulting text?
- Does the use of tools and resources differ in different phases of the writing processes, i.e. before and during the actual writing of the text?

In the next section we will discuss the method of analysis we are using to study the coordination of the collaborating students of the use of tools and resources during planning and writing the argumentative texts. In the following section we will present quantitative results on the three research questions. In the last section we will discuss some conclusions and further analyses we are planning to do.

METHOD OF ANALYSIS

Chat and activity protocol

Process oriented research in general is very laborious and consists of two consecutive analyses: a) single case analyses of protocols of the processes, and b) comparison of quantitative or qualitative characteristic features of the processes in the protocols that have been analyzed. If several protocols are to be compared, this can be an enormous task. We try to reduce the effort of protocol analysis by using the computer program MEPA (Multiple Episode Protocol Analysis), developed in our department at the University of Utrecht. The use of tools and resources is recorded by TC3 in a full action, keystroke based protocol. These protocols are automatically compressed into basic actions and converted into a MEPA data file. The actions with regard to tools and resources that are logged in the protocols are shown in Table 1.

Table 1. Actions categories for use of tools and resources

Actions	Description	Actions	Description
Chat	Chatting	To-manual	Opening the TC3 manual information
Layout	Using a layout button	To-notes	Activating the notes window
Mark-source	Marking in an information source	To-source	Opening a information source
Stop	Clicking on the stop button	To-text	Activating the shared text window
To-assignment	Opening the assignment information	Turn-ask	Asking for a turn shift by clicking the traffic light
To-chat	Activating the chat window	Turn-give	Giving the turn by clicking the traffic light
To-chat history	Activating the chat history window	Word count	Clicking on the shared text word count button

Argumentative quality and structure of the texts

We measured text quality with four measures and their mean score. Textual structure refers to the absence or presence of the formal units – introduction, body, and conclusion – and their composition. Segment score measures the quality of the argumentation at segment level – segments roughly coinciding with paragraphs. The argumentation score concerns the argumentative quality of the text as a whole, including introduction and conclusion. The audience score consists of three parts: presentation, level of formality, and empathy. Finally, the mean score of these four measures was computed for each text. Interrater agreement on five papers by two raters varied between 74-87% on these scores, resulting in satisfying Cohen's kappa's between .69 and .79. This grading of argumentative quality was accomplished separately and blind to the grades the teachers gave the papers following their own criteria.

Phases of collaborative writing

There are two points in the writing process that can be clearly distinguished: the first draft and the final draft. In between, one or more drafts are written. We have used these two drafts as anchors. The first phase refers to the period in the chat and activity protocol before writing the first draft, and so reflects the preplanning phase. The rest of the protocol is divided into two phases of equal duration. We expect the second phase to be characterized by more writing activities and the third phase by more revising activities. However, we view the three phases as units of time, not as specific activity periods.

RESULTS

Using tools and resources for coordinating collaborative argumentative writing

Our first question was: How do students use the tools and resources in order to coordinate their activities in writing an argumentative text? Table 2 shows the mean percentages and standard deviations for activation of the different tools and resources in the protocol. On average, the collaborative writing protocols contained 994 actions. Almost two thirds of these actions refer to the chat tool. It shows the crucial role that task oriented chat plays in coordinating the collaboration process. The next highest percentages are as we expected: using the shared text tool (11%) and reading the sources (6%). Counting the number of words in the shared text (5%), giving and asking for turns (4%) and marking in the information sources (2%) occur rather regularly if we take the total number of actions into account. The students seldom use the layout buttons, work in the notes or read the program manual.

Table 2. Total number of actions, mean percentages and standard deviations in the protocols

Actions	Mean	SD	Actions	Mean	SD
Chat	62.47%	9.70	To-manual	.25%	.31
Layout	.82%	.93	To-notes	.98%	1.12
Mark-source	2.30%	2.98	To-source	6.37%	2.98
Stop	.34%	.41	To-text	11.18%	2.59
To-assignment	1.18%	.69	Turn-ask	1.42%	.86
To-chat	3.46%	1.89	Turn-give	3.06%	1.58
To-chat history	1.32%	.84	Word count	4.85%	2.08
			Total number of actions	993.75	349.09

Is the use of tools and resources related to the quality of argumentative texts?

In this section we will describe the relations we found between tool and resource use frequencies and the scores for the argumentative quality of the texts. Table 3 shows the correlations between the action categories and each of the argumentative text scores.

We did not find significant correlations for textual structure, nor for overall argumentation. However, we found several significant correlations for each of the other text scores. The quality of the segments correlates negatively with the *total number of actions* (-.38). This seems to be an overall tendency, as this category also shows negative correlations for audience score (-.20) and the resulting mean score (-.24). This could mean that long chat and activity protocols result in lower quality texts. In other words, switching between tools and criss-crossing the computer environment might be detriment to the production of a high quality text, possibly because the students do not focus efficiently on the task at hand. In line with this possibility, we found that paragraph argumentation (segment score) correlates positively with *to-text* (.28). This strengthens the theory that paying closer attention to the text may lead to a better text, in this case at the segment level. However, we did not find correlations for *to-text* with any of the other text scores. Note that a high frequency of *to-text* does not imply that students also write in the shared text. It seems plausible that focusing on the shared text is an important influencing factor.

Table 3: Correlations between action percentages and text scores for all phases.

	Textual Structure	Segment score	Argumentation score	Audience score	Mean score
Chat	.01	-.07	.03	.17	.05
Layout	-.08	-.09	-.16	-.25*	-.19°
Mark-source	.01	-.01	-.05	.05	-.00
Stop	.16	-.01	.03	-.06	.02
To assignment	-.02	.06	.05	-.05	.03
To chat	-.01	.03	-.02	-.17	-.05
To chat history	.10	.05	.07	-.07	.04
To manual	-.02	.12	-.05	-.01	.00
To notes	.14	-.00	.09	.08	.09
To source	-.09	.07	-.09	-.19°	-.10
To text	.13	.28*	.03	.03	.12
Turn ask	.07	-.11	-.05	-.17	-.09
Turn give	-.07	-.06	-.02	-.26*	-.12
Word count	-.11	-.10	.05	-.09	-.05
Total no. of actions	-.08	-.38**	-.14	-.20°	-.24*

** Pearson correlation is significant at the 0.01 level (2-tailed); * significant at the 0.05 level (2-tailed);° significant at the 0.10 level (2-tailed).

The audience score correlates negatively with *layout* (-.25), *to-source* (-.19), *turn-give* (-.26), and *total number of actions* (-.20). Somehow, focusing on these activities seems to draw the students' attention away from their readers. Finally, the mean score – which is the mean of the other four scores – correlates negatively with *layout* (-.19) and the *total number of actions* (-.24). Again, text quality seems to be influenced by the length of the protocol and by focusing on the program rather than the writing task.

Differences in the use of tools and resources in different phases of the writing processes

The differences in use of tools and resources in the three phases of the collaborative writing process are visualized in two graphs in Figure 2 and Figure 3. Figure 2 shows the mean percentages of all actions in the three phases. The mean number of actions for each of the phases is 163.0 (sd.=103.1), 402.1 (sd.=206.8), and 428.6 (sd. =174.0), respectively.

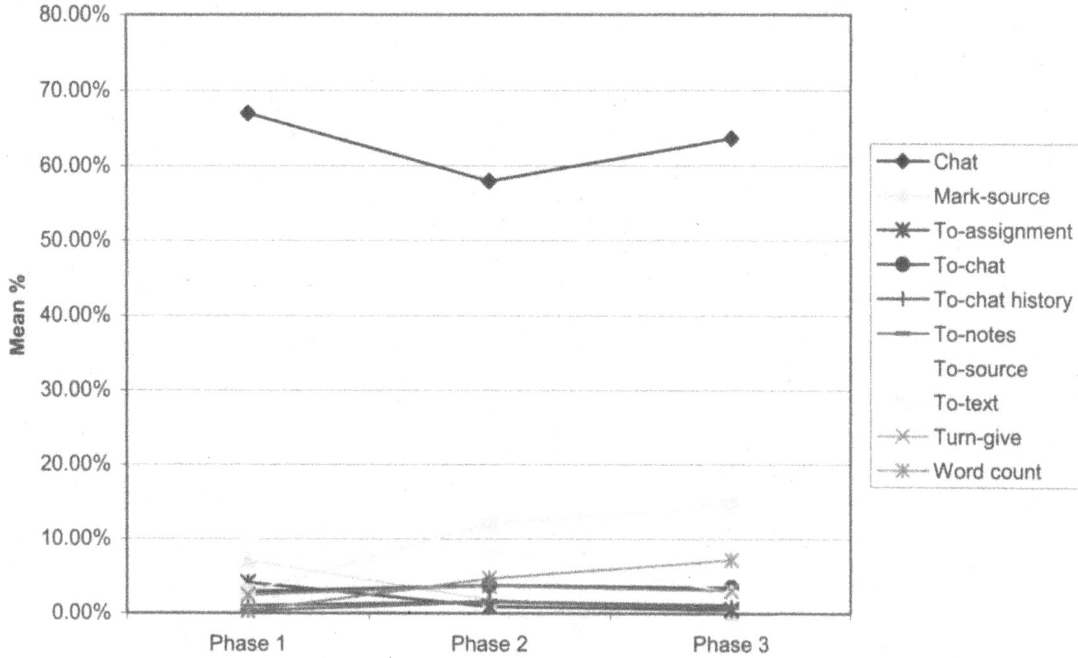

Figure 2. Trend graph including all action categories.

As can be seen in Figure 2, the *chat* activity relatively dominates in all three phases. The chat percentage clearly decreases (from 67% to 58%) and then increases again (from 58% to 64%): during preplanning and the final phase the students spend more time deliberating than during the highly productive middle phase. This is consistent with the findings by Kraut, Galegher, Fish and Chalfonte (1992), who found that subjects sought more frequent and richer communication during planning and revision phases than during the more solitary activity of drafting the text.

For better readability the chat action is excluded from the graph in Figure 3. As can be seen in this chart several action categories show a constant declining tendency, and often for obvious reasons. The categories *mark-source* and *to-assignment* are both activities naturally performed during the initial stages of the writing process. After all, when students leave marking sources and reading the assignment to the final phase, it will be too late to change the text. On the other hand, some categories show a rising tendency: *to-text*, and *word-count*. Again, this is hardly surprising, as these are activities naturally performed when the actual writing and revising are in full progress and the goal – that is, finishing the text – draws nearer. The mean differences for *total number of actions* show that the preplanning phase is a lot shorter than the other two phases that differ only slightly.

We found four categories showing a rising-then-falling tendency: *to-chat*, *to-chat-history*, *to-notes*, *turn-ask*, and *turn-give*. The latter might be explained by a change in co-operation between the students. At first, there is no reason to ask for turns, because there is nothing in the shared text yet. Later on, as they grow more familiar with the program and each other, the students start asking for turns in the chat window instead of using the *turn-ask* button for this purpose. From our observations we can confirm that most students seem to prefer this verbal communication to the flashing yellow screen caused by a *turn-ask*. However, the student evaluation showed that on average the students liked the turn taking system. For obvious reasons, virtually no *to-chat-history* is logged in the first phase. As the chat history grows, it can be used as a source: all arguments and viewpoints discussed earlier can be reviewed there. This explains the increased use of this window in the second phase. However, during the last phase there is less need for consulting the chat history, as the outline of the text has been clearly laid out by that time.

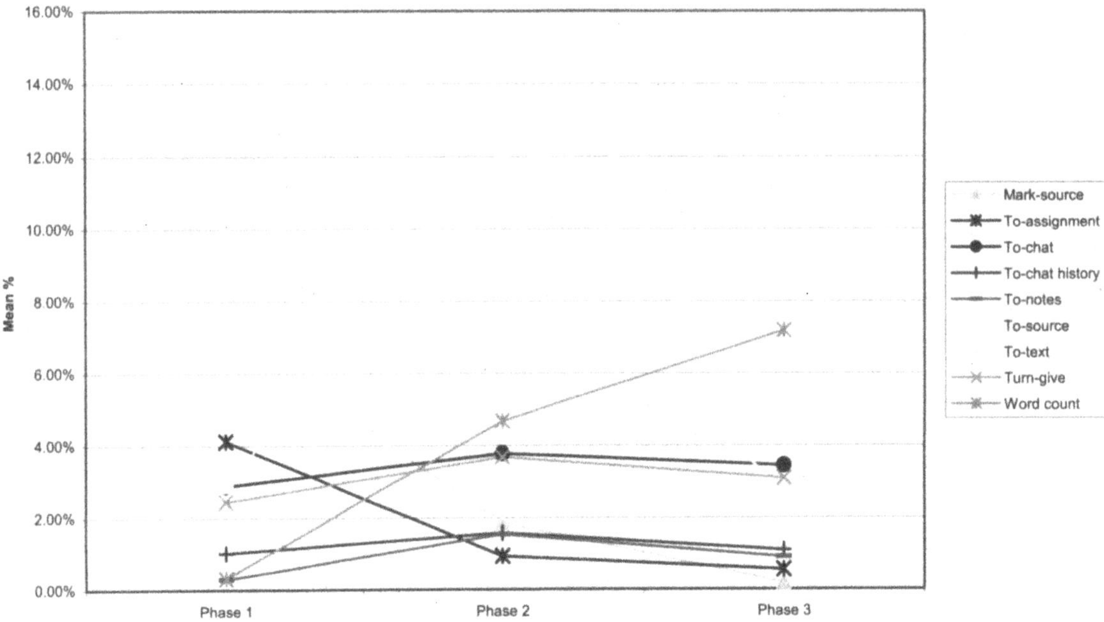

Figure 3. Trend graph excluding chat category

The tendency for *to-notes* can be explained with very similar reasons: the students read the sources first, before they start taking notes on them. The decrease between the second and third phases is caused by the fact that towards the end of the assignment all sources will have been read and annotated. The students know what is in their notes by then, and so they do not need to refer to them very often anymore during revision. However, reading – writing – taking notes – writing – revising does not seem to be the logical approach to planning and writing texts. It makes sense to take notes *before starting* to write the text, because you need to know about the content of the sources before you write about them. The students in this control group, however, only started to take notes extensively after they had already started writing the first draft.

Finally, *to-chat* was logged most frequently during the middle phase, and less frequently during the other two phases. This category was logged whenever a student clicked in the chat window without actually entering chat before moving on to a different window. The tendency for *to-chat* is in line with the tendency for *chat*: during the second phase, relatively fewer *to-chats* resulted in *chat*, thus resulting in a falling-then-rising tendency for *chat*.

DISCUSSION

This study posed research questions with regard to: a) the use of tools and resources by students in the TC3 groupware environment to coordinate their collaborative writing process, b) the relationship between the use of tools and resources and the quality of the written text, and c) the differences in the use of tools and resources during different phases (i.e. preplanning, writing and revising) of the writing process. So what is the relationship between the frequencies of tool use in the three phases of the writing process and the quality of the resulting text?

As we can see in the charts above, there are clear differences between the phases. However, the use of the chat facility is most frequent in all three phases. In a further analysis of the topics the students chat about, we found that 47% of the chat is about planning of the writing task on a meta-cognitive level, 36% of the topics are content related and 17% of the topics is not task related, social chat. Planning activities on a meta-level occur equally in all three phases of the collaborative writing process for low, medium and high quality texts. Discussion of specific content clearly occurs more often in the high quality text groups. Furthermore, we find that the higher the performance, the lower the occurrence of non-task, social chats.

In the pre-writing phase the students clearly make more use of the information sources, marking them and taking notes. Further analysis showed that *to-source* and *to-notes* frequencies in the first phase are, in fact, positively correlated to respectively the segment score ($r = .36$) and the textual structure ($r = .22$) scores. In the second phase of actual writing of the text the students show more activity in the shared text window and in the turn-giving device. Further correlation analysis showed a significant positive correlation between *to-text* frequency and the textual structure score ($r = .33$), the segment score ($r = .45$) and the argumentation score ($r = .21$). The third phase of writing shows an increase of chat activity, of text activity and of *word-count*. In the correlation analysis for the third phase only a small correlation is found between chat activity and the audience score (.19).

In our further analyses we will focus on the way the students explicitly discuss their use of tools and resources in the chat discussion. Furthermore, we will investigate the effects of adding tools for text planning and linearization to the TC3 environment on the coordination processes in collaborative writing.

ACKNOWLEDGMENTS

We would like to thank Marije van Amelsvoort for her help in these analyses.

REFERENCES

Alamargot, D. (1997). Processus de récuperation et d'organisation dans l'activité de redaction de texte. Effet de l'acquisition des connaissances réferentielles. These Doctorat de Psychologie. Université de Poitiers.

Andriessen, J.E.B., Coirier, P., Roos, L., Passerault, J.M., & Bert-Erboul (1996). Thematic and structural planning in constrained argumentative text production. In H. Van den Bergh, G. Rijlaarsdam & M. Couzijn (eds.) Theories, Models and Methodology in writing research (pp. 237-251). Amsterdam: University Press.

Andriessen, J.E.B., Erkens, G., Overeem, E., & Jaspers, J. (September, 1996). Using complex information in argumentation for collaborative text production. Paper presented on the First Conference on Using Complex Information Systems (UCIS'96), Poitiers, 3-6 Sept 1996.

Baker, M. (1999) Argumentation and constructive interaction. In J.E.B. Andriessen & P. Coirier (Eds.) Foundations of Argumentative Text Processing (pp. 179-203). Amsterdam: University Press.

Bannon, L.J. (1995). Issues in Computer Supported Collaborative Learning. In C. O'Malley (Ed.), Computer Supported Collaborative Learning (pp. 267-283). NATO ASI Series, Vol. 128, Berlin Heidelberg: Springer-Verlag.

Bereiter, C., & Scardamalia, M. (1987). The psychology of written composition. Hillsdale, NJ: Lawrence Erlbaum.

Cognition and Technology Group at Vanderbilt (1994). From Visual Word Problems to Learning Communities: Changing Conceptions of Cognitive Research. In K. McGilly (Ed.), Classroom Lessons: Integrating Cognitive Theory and Classroom Practice (pp. 157-201). Cambridge, Massachusetts: The MIT Press.

Coirier, P., Andriessen, J.E.B., & Chanquoy, L. (1999). From planning to translating: The specificity of argumentative writing. In J.E.B. Andriessen & P. Coirier (Eds.), Foundations of argumentative text processing (pp. 1-29). Amsterdam: Amsterdam University Press.

Dillenbourg, P. (1999). Introduction: what do you mean by "Collaborative Learning"? In: P. Dillenbourg (ed.), Collaborative Learning: Cognitive and computational aspects (pp. 1-19). New York: Pergamon.

Erkens, G., Andriessen, J.E.B., & Peters, N. (submitted) Interaction and performance in computer supported collaborative tasks. To appear in H. Oostendorp, Cognition in a Digital World. Hillsdale, NJ: Lawrence Erlbaum

Galbraith, D. (1999). Writing as a knowledge-constituting process. In: M. Torrance & D. Galbraith (eds.), Knowing what to write: conceptual processes in Text Production (pp.139-159). Amsterdam: Amsterdam University Press.

Giroud, A. (1999). Studying argumentative text processing through collaborative writing. In: J.E.B. Andriessen & P. Coirier (eds.), Foundations of argumentative text processing. Amsterdam: Amsterdam University Press.

Hayes, J.R., & Nash, J.G. (1996). On the nature of planning in writing. In C.M. Levy & S. Ransdell (Eds.), The Science of Writing (pp. 29-55). Mahwah, NJ : Lawrence Erlbaum Associates.

Henri, F. (1995). Distance learning and computer mediated communication: Interactive, quasi-interactive or monologue? In C. O'Malley (Ed.), Computer supported collaborative learning (pp. 145-165). NATO ASI Series, Vol. 128. Berlin: Springer.

Kozma, R.B. (1991). The impact of computer-based tools and embedded prompts on writing processes and products of novice and advanced college writers. Cognition and Instruction, 8, 1-27.

Kraut, R., Galegher, J., Fish, R., & Chalfonte, B. (1992). Task Requirements and Media Choice in Collaborative Writing. Human-Computer Interaction, 7, 375-407.

Levelt, W.J.M. (1988). Speaking: from intention to articulation. Bradford Books, MIT press, Boston MA, USA.

Rijlaarsdam, G., & van den Bergh, H. (1996). The dynamics of composing - An agenda for Research into an interactive compensatory model of writing : Many questions, some answers. In C.M. Levy & S. Ransdell (Eds.), The Science of Writing (pp.107-125). Mahwah, NJ: Lawrence Erlbaum Associates

Scardamalia, M., & Bereiter, C. (1985). The development of dialectical processes in composition. In D. Olson, N. Torrance, & A. Hildyard (Eds.). Literacy, language and learning: the nature and consequences of reading and writing (pp. 307-329). New York: Cambridge University Press .

Scardamalia, M., Bereiter, C., & Lamon, M (1994). The CSILE Project: Trying to Bring the Classroom into World 3. In K. McGilly (Ed.), Classroom Lessons: Integrating Cognitive Theory and Classroom Practice (pp. 201-229). Cambridge, Massachusetts: The MIT Press.

Schriver, K.A. (1988). Teaching writers how to plan: which planning heuristics work best? Paper presented at the meeting of the American Educational Research Association, St. Louis, MO, USA.

Stein, N.L., Bernas, R.S., & Calicchia, D. (1997). Conflict talk: understanding and resolving arguments. In : T.Giron (ed.) Conversation: cognitive, communicative and social perspectives. (Typological studies in language, volume 34). Amsterdam: John Benjamins.

Suthers, D., Weiner, A., Connelly, J., & Paolucci, M. (1995). Belvedere: Engaging students in critical discussion of science and public policy issues. In: Greer, J. (Ed.). Artificial Intelligence in Education (pp.266-273). Charlottesville, VA: AACE.

Teasley, S., & Rochelle, J. (1993). Constructing a joint problem space: The computer as tool for sharing knowledge. In S.P. Lajoie, & S.J. Derry (Eds,) Computers as Cognitive Tools (pp. 229-257). Hillsdale, NJ: Lawrence Erlbaum Associates.

Torrance, M., Thomas, G.V., & Robinson, E.J. (1996). Finding something to write about: strategic and automatic processes in idea generation. In C.M. Levy and S. Ransdell (Eds.): The Science of Writing (Pp 189-205). Mahwah, NJ: Lawrence Erlbaum Associates.

Getting in on the (Inter)Action: Exploring Affordances for Collaborative Learning in a Context of Informed Participation

Hal Eden

Center for LifeLong Learning & Design (L^3D)
University of Colorado at Boulder

ABSTRACT

Although considerable attention in the CSCL community has been on distributed-, Web-, or distance-learning applications, there is evidence suggesting that much of learning, particularly in open-ended problem-solving activities based on tacit information, does not occur in isolation but in face-to-face settings. This has led our research to explore ways to develop technologies and media that enhance participation, collaboration, and learning in face-to-face, copresent settings.

This paper explores the history of our research on developing such technologies in the context of our Envisionment and Discovery Collaboratory at the Center for LifeLong Learning & Design at the University of Colorado at Boulder, and discusses my research on interface design to support learning and participation in collaborative settings.

Keywords

Interface design, augmented reality, atoms and bits, participatory design, face-to-face interaction

INTRODUCTION

Considerable attention in the CSCL community has been on distributed-, Web-, or distance-learning applications. Certainly, it is appropriate to explore the new landscape that is opened by the removal of barriers of required copresence, and to understand the far-reaching implications of ready access to widely dispersed sources of information. However, there is evidence suggesting that much of learning, particularly in open-ended problem-solving activities [Arias, 1996] based on tacit information [Collins et al., 2000], does not occur in isolation but in face-to-face settings. Indeed cooperative learning advocates Johnson and Johnson include face-to-face interaction as one of the key features of their approach in which students discuss, teach, and explain to each other in promotive ways that "assist, encourage, and support each other's efforts to learn" [Johnson & Johnson, 1994]. Although it is may be possible to support such interaction at a distance, my research is exploring ways to develop technologies and media that enhance participation, collaboration, and learning in face-to-face, copresent settings.

Often the ability to access new, abundant stores of information is seen as a major breakthrough. However, for learning situations where the answer does not exist, access to all existing answers may be of little use. This is particularly true when the information needed to resolve a problem is tacit—part of the life experiences of multiple individuals who are impacted by the problem or may have crucial insights to bring to bear. Our work focuses on design problems that are typically "wicked" [Rittel & Webber, 1984]—ill-defined, ill-structured, unique, no completion criteria, no single "right" answer, large universe of solutions and potential steps, each problem may be a symptom of another problem, and whose solution path is strongly influenced by framing. Resolving such problems involves drawing on various viewpoints and perspectives and requires collaborative learning where participants learn from each other. In such situations, access to information alone is not sufficient [Arias et al., 1999].

It is also important to realize what the goals are for learning in a particular situation. Whereas much learning is focused on acquiring the skills and expertise necessary to operate within a domain in some competent, expert, or professional role, there are many situations where the goals for learning are quite different. Music appreciation does not necessarily have the goal of nurturing musicians, but of allowing people to enjoy the context, history, and to recognize various forms of music. Science and Technology Literacy has the goal of allowing a broader segment of the population to make these domains meaningful to their everyday lives—not necessarily to "do science." Our research has been exploring ways to support and encourage a similar form of learning in the area of citizen participation in decisions that affect their lives.

A CONTEXT FOR CITIZEN PARTICIPATION IN DESIGN

How can more than 261 million individual Americans define and reconcile their needs and aspirations with community values and the needs of the future? Our most important finding is the potential power of and growing desire for decision processes that promote direct and meaningful interaction involving people in decisions that affect them. Americans want to take control of their lives.[PCSD, 1996]

For citizens to have greater say within their community and for communities to benefit from the valuable insights that its citizens have to contribute, individuals need to become engaged in activities for which they have often had no training and in which they may have no desire to act in an expert or professional capacity.

Focus: Informed Participation

The key challenges for moving toward new forms of citizen participation include (a) addressing the paradox that citizens cannot really be informed unless they participate, yet they cannot really participate unless they are informed [Brown et al., 1994]; and (b) understanding that participation has limits that are contingent on the nature of each citizen's situation, the issues, the problems, and the institutional designs [Arias, 1989], as well as the available technology and media. However, a benefit of coming to grips with these challenges is that informed participation leads to ownership and a stronger sense of community.

Collaborative work vs. collaborative participation

Much of the focus on computer-supported collaborative work has been on using technology to support existing work cultures, i.e., communities of practice (CoPs) [Brown & Duguid, 1991; Wenger, 1998], which consist of practitioners who work as a community in a certain domain undertaking similar work. Some examples of CoPs are architects, urban planers, research groups, and software developers.

Even approaches aimed at interdisciplinary activities have tended to proceed from the assumption that those engaged in the activity are highly skilled in their respective field. However, the goal of collaborative participation is often different. Communities of interest (CoIs) [Fischer, 2001] bring together stakeholders from different CoPs, as well as those who may not be members of any established CoP to solve a particular (design) problem of common concern. Two examples of CoIs are (1) a team interested in software development that includes software designers, marketing specialists, psychologists, programmers, and users; and (2) a group of citizens and experts interested in urban planning who are concerned with implementing new transportation systems.

CoIs are characterized by their shared interest in the framing and resolution of a design problem. CoIs often are more temporary than CoPs: they come together in the context of a specific project and may dissolve after the project has ended. CoIs have great potential to be more innovative and more transforming than a single CoP if they are able to exploit the "symmetry of ignorance" [Rittel, 1984] as a source of collective creativity. Although there is a need to become informed about a domain in order to participate in design, decision-making, and input-giving processes, the goal is not generally to become more of an expert in the domain nor to become a member of the culture of the domain. The goal is to gain enough of an appreciation for the domain to be able to communicate with members of that culture while retaining the valuable views and perspectives from the participant's culture.

Fundamental challenges facing CoIs are found in building a shared understanding of the task at hand, which often does not exist at the beginning, but is evolved incrementally and collaboratively and emerges in people's minds and in external artifacts. Members of CoIs must communicate with and learn from others [Engeström, 2001] who have different perspectives and perhaps a different vocabulary for describing their ideas. Learning within CoIs is more complex and multi-faceted than *legitimate peripheral participation* [Lave & Wenger, 1991] in CoPs, which assumes that there is a single knowledge system towards whose center newcomers move over time.

Learning in CoIs requires *externalizations* [Bruner, 1996] in the form of *boundary objects* [Star, 1989] that have meaning across the boundaries of individual knowledge systems. Boundary objects allow different knowledge systems to interact by providing a shared reference that is meaningful within all systems. Computational support for CoIs must enable mutual learning through the creation, discussion, and refinement of boundary objects that allow the knowledge systems of different CoPs to interact. The interaction between multiple knowledge systems is a means to turn the symmetry of ignorance into a resource for learning and social creativity.

A BRIEF HISTORY: EXPLORING SUPPORT FOR INFORMED PARTICIPATION

We have found that an effective approach for understanding how to support participation is to look at other domains and how they have approached the problem. One of the foundations for our work on supporting collaborative participation is in the approaches pioneered by our urban planning colleague, Ernesto Arias, in the creation of physical simulations and games for use in fostering community participation and as learning tools for students in that domain [Arias, 1994].

Although our work focuses primarily on the processes our technologies must embody and interact with in order to support informed participation, it is impossible to create systems that operate solely at that abstract level. What we need is the context of a specific design domain to act as an "object to think with" and allow us to build a particular concrete instances to demonstrate the ideas and goals of our approaches. Urban design and planning is an ideal domain for this purpose as it gives rich domain content and environments as well as models of processes for design, problem solving, and interaction among people.

Physical Simulations & Games in Urban Planning

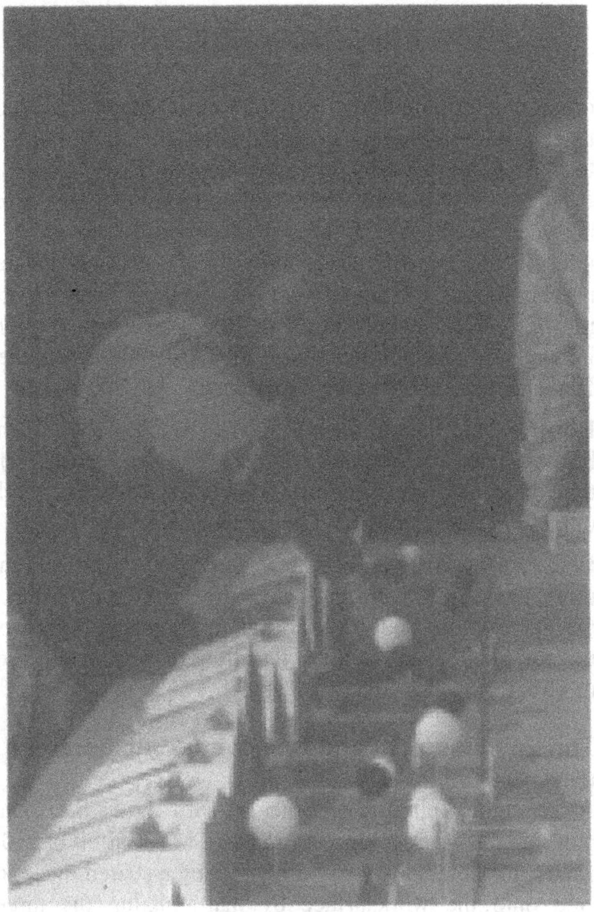

Figure 9: The Cole Neighborhood Redevelopment Project

As early as 1984 [Arias, 1984], this research recognized that early phases of design operate with what are known as *potential environments*—abstract representations of "the way things could be" such as plan drawings and maps that experienced designers manipulate with considerable ease. However, involving user communities in the design process requires communicating these potential environments to those communities who may not be as skilled at working with these abstract representations. This approach began to use *effective environments* to address this problem. (In the planing literature, the term "effective environments" connotes physical and social environments *as people experience and define them*. This is not a claim that these environments are effective for some specific goal.) Whereas physical models have been used extensively to display potential environments, they were not generally used as effective environments—to draw participants into interaction with the models and with each other and to support new forms of learning and creativity.

There are many examples of this approach—a notable example is the Cole Neighborhood Redevelopment Project [Arias, 1996]. In this project, models of the neighborhood were collaboratively constructed providing citizens a way of participating in the design process by interacting with problem through physical models (see Figure).

There were some limitations for this environment. It included computational support through a geographical information system (GIS) "on the side;" however, it was not integrated into the model. This caused a change in focus from the face-to-face interaction around the model to the GIS when issues appropriate to that system arose, resulting in a cognitive interruption. The system provided no means to model the dynamics of the neighborhood or the design process. Information generated in the process of the design sessions had to be manually gathered and recorded, which limited the ability to reuse and build on previous work.

The unique nature of each neighborhood required construction of a new model to match that particular situation. However, the creation of effective environment models can be viewed as developing languages of design that support human-to-human interaction, similar to Alexander's pattern language approach [Alexander et al., 1977]. From this perspective, many components and issues specific to these neighborhoods can be generalized and used to support learning in community, classroom, and design studio settings. This led to the creation of games that modeled the processes that took place (in the form of game rules) and reused the languages (the game pieces) that were developed in the neighborhood settings.

Figure 8: Mr Roger's Sustainable Neighborhood board game

The Mr. Roger's Sustainable Neighborhood board game [Spencer et al., 1997], developed by urban design students, is an instance of such a game (see Figure 8). By abstracting issues from real situations such as Cole neighborhood, the game confronted players with decisions on the social, economic, and environmental decisions that are faced in addressing issues of neighborhood development. In this game, participants take turns navigating through the neighborhood and are presented with various community design decisions (should a parking lot be added here, should a neighborhood focus be created there) that the players address as a neighborhood team.

The game supports learning in that it exposes students to issues of community development and to the challenges of achieving consensus in a community. However, the game situations are static and there is no support for extended exploration of the issues facing the players, which limits learning potential.

Computational simulations

As we began to explore how computational media might learn from and contribute to this work, an initial effort was made to explore how computational simulations could be used to enhance the board game approach. As a result, the Mr Roger's Sustainable Neighborhood simulation game [Perrone et al., 1997] was created (see Figure 9). The game board became a dynamic simulation that updates neighborhood situations based on decisions made by the players. Web support allowing the players to explore information and argumentation related to the issues they face enhances the learning experience.

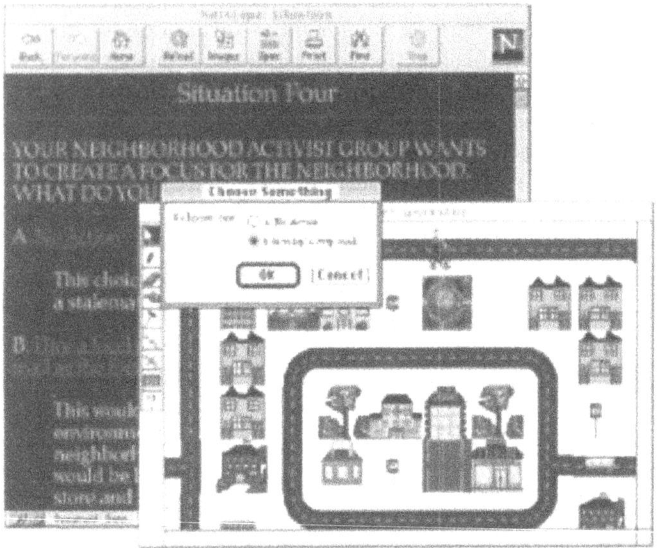

Figure 9: The Mr. Roger's Sustainable Neighborhood simulation game

However, the face-to-face, around-the-table nature of the board game was displaced by a computer environment that more naturally supports one person "driving" while others look over that individual's shoulders.

Based on the experiences and observations from creating these physical and virtual environments, we determined that it would be useful to develop an approach to draw on the complementary nature of the strengths and weaknesses of both forms of media (see Table 4).

The Envisionment and Discovery Collaboratory (EDC)

After some initial experiments with how horizontal worksurfaces and projection systems could be used to accomplish our goals, we developed the EDC (shown in Figure 10). By using a horizontal electronic whiteboard, participants work "around the table," incrementally creating a shared model of the problem. They interact with computer simulations projected onto the worksurface by manipulating the three-dimensional, physical objects that constitute a language for the domain [Arias, 1996; Ehn, 1988]. The position and movement of these physical objects are recognized by means of the touch-sensitive projection surface. In Figure 10, users construct a neighborhood through the use of a physical language appropriate for the problem by placing on the worksurface. This construction is a description of the setting of concern to the stakeholders and becomes the boundary object through which they can collaboratively evaluate and prescribe changes in their efforts to frame and resolve a problem. In the upper half of Figure 10, a second vertical electronic whiteboard presents information related to the problem-at-hand for exploration and extension. In the figure, a user is filling out a survey constructed from the model presented on the horizontal worksurface. The results of this survey are stored (for future exploration) and are also fed to the simulation, where the ramifications of the decisions specified in the survey can be explored. This work is described in more detail in [Arias et al., 2000] and more issues related to this paper are discussed in [Arias et al., 1999].

Figure 10: The Envisionment and Discovery Collaboratory

Table 4: Complementary strengths and weaknesses of physical and virtual environments and associated implications for learning (based on [Arias et al., 1997]).

Weaknesses of Computational Simulations	**Complementary Strengths of Physical Games & Simulations**	**Potential learning support through combination**
user must learn and work the interface	direct, naïve manipulability and intuitive understanding	from learning about the interface to learning about the domain and the problem
(sans haptics) little or no tactile feedback	tangible, tactile interaction	manipulative learning
individual interaction with computer the usual focus (either each with own computer or one person driving shared system)	mediation of communication and social interaction through 1. common focus 2. forms of "body language" in manipulation of physical	social interaction and collaborative learning
complex modeling needed to realize all constraints	natural constraints of physical objects (boundaries of the physical enforced)	constraints can provide structure to learning, can point out conflicts
Weaknesses of Physical Models	**Complementary Strengths of Computational Simulations**	
models passive, static representations, behavior not easy to visualize, all interpretation of meaning and dynamics by users	well-suited for dynamic models and visualization of behavior	learning aided by dynamic models and visualization
automatic feedback on consequences of decisions not provided	dynamic models can reflect the results of decisions	learning by understanding consequences of decision
fidelity to reality limited due to problems such as scaling. Alternate realities not easy to model	virtual models can span scales and constraint systems	learning effects of scale and interactions between levels of scales, learning in alternate realities, relaxed constraints
management and capture of information is difficult	can capture information and design results for analysis and future use	assessment tools, seeds for learning can be built upon, evolved, and reseeded

Informal assessment of the EDC.

We have used this system in numerous demonstrations of our work to transportation planners, urban designers, community members, researchers, and other visitors. The current state of development both at an overall system level and from the standpoint of low-level interaction has made it impractical to deploy in realistic settings as was our initial goal. However, in the context of our demonstrations, we have engaged the observers as pseudo-participants asking them to perform some basic design interactions and have observed several aspects of the interaction that pose limitations to the usability of the system. These observed limitations include

- The touch-screen technology of the SmartBoard was designed for single-user-at-a-time (single cursor) interaction. This required that users take turns (simultaneous actions created error situations, e.g., a row of houses between the two touches rather than just two single houses).
- The use of an interaction style characterized as "select-object/select-action/perform-action" causes the user to have to "work" the interface. This led to frequent "mode" errors [Lewis & Norman, 1986] (e.g., the user tried to delete an object when the "add" mode was active). Certainly, there are alternate interaction techniques that could lessen the overhead for the users, but the single-cursor limitation still requires that a linkage be made between the physical cursor and the current virtual object and allows only one object type to be active at a given moment.
- The user had to take explicit action to make the physical-virtual connection by pressing the object onto the touch screen rather than just placing it on top of it.
- Taken together these require the user to have a more abstract mental model of the interface to guide how they interact with the system. Often this model is separate from their model of how the domain object being manipulated should behave. Although individuals who are continuously engaged in these sorts of activities may be willing to learn this model as they work with the system, participants who have limited exposure to the system may not have the opportunity to form that model and may be left out of interaction. The challenge is to make it more accessible to them.

FOCUSING ON INTERACTION ISSUES TO PROVIDE ACCESS FOR LEARNING

As Table 4 describes, there are many ways that the blending of the physical and the virtual could create improved interaction for learning. Based on our assessment of the EDC, the most critical aspects necessary to make that environment available to users in realistic situations is to make the interface more accessible to participants. Specifically, the advantages of physical elements for naïve manipulability and mediation of communication will be the focus for the remainder of this paper. Others of the issues raised there are discussed elsewhere (e.g., [Scharff, 2002]) or will form the basis of future work.

Using a DGT Electronic Chessboard, we have created prototypes of the Participate-in-the-Action Board (PitA-Board, see Figure 11). The underlying technology consists of an 8-by-8 sensor grid that can determine the location and identity of 15 distinct transducers.

The new forms of interaction support that this technology provides include

- Multiple "points of control" rather than a single interaction cursor.
- Sensing pieces automatically when placed on board (rather than needing to explicitly press the piece onto the surface).
- Parallel interactions (rather than single-threads of interaction and errors when multiple simultaneous accesses are attempted)

Figure 11: The PitA-Board

These interaction capabilities form the basis for our initial investigation into direct and natural interaction techniques aimed at improving accessibility to our simulation environments.

Naïve manipulability

Utilizing the multiple "points of control" provided by the PitA-Board allows us to create a broader repertoire of direct interaction styles more closely tuned to the type of domain object being represented. For example some interactions that might be useful in the domain of transportation are

1. Tracking behavior: the virtual representation follows the physical piece (this could represent an individual moving through the space or an object whose location is subject to change)
2. Placing (Rubber stamp) behavior: placement of physical piece creates a virtual representation that remains when physical piece is removed (used to place items with known, fixed location—a house, store, or school)

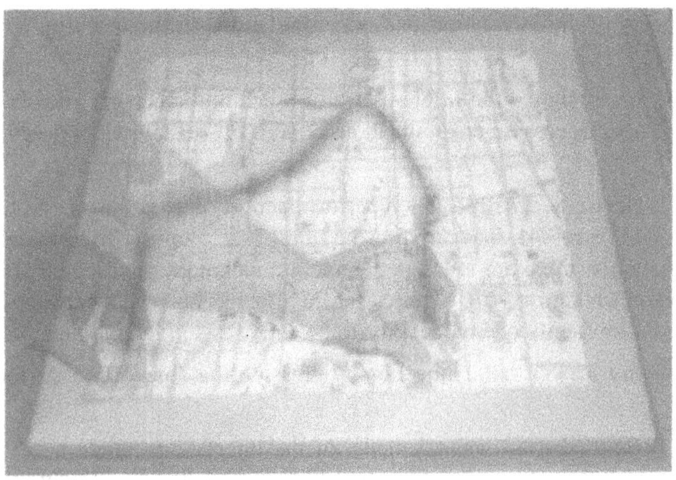

Figure 12: This multiple-exposure photo shows the user tracing out a bus route (enhanced for clarity) using a bus-route-drawing object.

1. Drawing behavior: piece is used to trace out a series of points that make up the object being created. (e.g., a road, a bus route—see Figure 12)
3. Launching behavior—placing a dynamic item: the physical piece indicates the initial location of an object that has dynamic behavior—if appropriate, the virtual object begins its dynamic behavior from that point. (e.g., bus, auto)

In addition to the interaction attached to domain-grounded objects, there will still be the need for interaction pieces that support control or inspection of the environment. For example, by having some virtual representations that no longer have corresponding physical pieces (such as a "placed" object) means that there needs to be some way to indicate that the virtual representation needs to be removed when it is no longer needed, which might require an "eraser" piece. A magnifying glass may be useful in some contexts to examine the attributes of an object.

The underlying idea is that the system allows the creation of affordances that are more natural to the situation being modeled and the design process being supported by the technology. The examples that are given here are only for purposes of illustration and were developed in an ad hoc manner (though based on observation of prior interactions) to demonstrate the concept. Future work will involve interaction with use communities to determine what affordances are best suited to the needs of users and to develop a repertoire of objects for a particular domain.

Mediation of Communication

In Arias' work with physical games and models it was observed that the physical pieces often become extensions of the speaker, allowing the speaker to provide emphasis or to extend her/his body language. In the hybrid environment, we envision that interaction using physical objects will allow the speaker to project that sense of extension into the virtual space.

By supporting a group interaction with the simulation, it is no longer just a user-computer interaction, but the environment becomes a form of media supporting conversations among participants (i.e., human-human communication mediated by the artifact) as well as collaborative "conversations with the material." [Schön, 1992] In this regard, the ability to interact in parallel becomes an issue. The question could be raised whether a conversational paradigm really requires parallelism and that problems with that aspect of the current interface might not be better mitigated by using concurrency control (e.g., locking or other turn-taking approaches).

Certainly, a top-level view of the conversational paradigm is one of turn taking based on a need (especially in larger groups) to avoid everyone talking at once so that participants can hear and be heard. However, a finer-grained inspection of conversations reveals that they are not strictly based on turn taking. Sometimes there are back-and-forth volleys as meaning and understanding are negotiated and grounding is achieved [Clark & Brennan, 1991]. Extra-verbal utterances (gestures, nods, shrugs, hyphenated glances) certainly happen without turn taking—and are also important parts of conversational grounding.

Furthermore, not all group interaction is conversational—there may be situations in which participant input could happen in tandem (e.g., a group leader asks everyone indicate where their house is in the neighborhood and each person places their house).

It seems that the goal for interaction with the computational environment is to match the characteristics of the interface/medium as closely as possible to the characteristics of the rest of the face-to-face environment. It is highly doubtful that anyone would bring a group of people into the same room and then ask them to use the telephone to talk to each other. The availability of parallelism provides a means to tune the interaction to the needs of the situation but does not imply that all interactions must occur in parallel.

Emerging opportunities for future evolution

The development of new ideas and approaches are generally accompanied by corresponding limitations that need to be acknowledged and understood. These limitations do not necessarily represent flaws or barriers to the use of this approach, but need to be understood as opportunities for further development and evolution.

By introducing multiple physical objects into the interface, they now have to be kept track of (where did that bus-drawing object go…?). In a completely virtual environment, the palettes organize tools and objects very neatly so that they, as well as the single physical object (the mouse), are generally easy to keep track of. A possible solution might be to create a "storage tray" to organize and keep track of the items.

This could also impact how many interaction objects one could manage. For example, in virtual palettes, there can be techniques, such as pop-ups or multiple palettes that provide access to a large number of tools/objects. Attempting to provide more and more features under this approach would create an unmanageable proliferation of physical cursor objects. On the other hand, the general goal of our approach is not upon an "experts" interface where every feature that anyone ever wanted is available—rather on a participant/learner interface, where the features important to the task at hand are there and directly accessible.

One could also argue that this approach violates some well-known principles of interface design, such as consistency of interaction: Why does this piece have one sort of behavior and another act differently? As I have discussed, I believe this is a desirable feature, but I would think that careful application of this feature—matching the behavior with the sort of object represented—is critical to its success.

There are also limitations based on the specifics of the "borrowed" technology. Since it was designed specifically as a chessboard, the granularity of resolution is coarse. Even so, the interface appears to be surprisingly effective. This may because the interactions of groups in design settings are usually not focused on fine-motor tasks. The grid technology also produces dead spots when the piece is at the edge of a square or placed between two squares, which is problematic in our system since the domain being modeled may not fit as neatly into a grid representation. The current system has a limited number of distinct sensors, which makes it difficult to have a large number of objects and track them reliably.

In our current system, we have tried to emphasize the grid outline to decrease the occurrence of problems, but it is not completely successful. These experiences with limitations will serve to guide future developments to better meet the goals that we have for participant interaction.

Related Work

Although the focus of this paper has been on the history and development of our current research and its implications for learning, it is important to acknowledge that it has been strongly influenced by a broad, rich research landscape. The perspective of ubiquitous computing movement [Abowd et al., 1998; Weiser, 1991] toward "breaking out of the desktop box" gave an initial, powerful impetus to think about how physical models could be enhanced by computation in varied ways. The importance of the tangible nature of physical interaction and its interaction with computations is underscored by the tangible media [Ishii & Ullmer, 1997] and graspable interfaces [Fitzmaurice et al., 1995] work. There are many efforts underway to address issues related to shared interfaces such as the Collaborage [Moran et al., 1999] and DiamondTouch [Dietz & Leigh, 2001] projects.

CONCLUSIONS:

This paper presents some promising approaches to interaction that focus on needs of face-to-face interaction among a group of users. Although it has been based on multiple prototyping cycles, there is still a need for closer evaluation and evolution with user communities. Limitations that we have encountered have resulted in tradeoff decisions, but strong initial indications that this may be well suited to face-to-face participant interaction.

Future work on this system includes assessment in more realistic settings using role-playing scenarios and application to actual community settings (e.g., the design of a new local bus route). Throughout these interaction with use communities there will be continued evolution of interaction techniques and studies of how the evolving systems supports participation and learning.

ACKNOWLEDGEMENTS

I would like to thank Gerhard Fischer, Ernesto Arias, Andy Gorman, Eric Scharffe, and Kyle Bygott for their collaboration in the development of the EDC concepts and prototypes and for feedback on drafts of this paper. Ben Bulsink of DGT Products, NL has been extremely helpful in providing us with materials to continue to develop the PitA-Board further. All of the members of L^{3}D have provided encouragement and feedback in the continued development of this work, which has been supported by NSF grants REC-9631396 and CDA-9529549 and the Coleman Family Initiative.

REFERENCES

Alexander, C., Ishikawa, S., Silverstein, M., Jacobson, M., Fiksdahl-King, I., & Angel, S. (1977) *A Pattern Language: Towns, Buildings, Construction*, Oxford University Press, New York.

Arias, E. G. (1984) "Resident Participation in Public Housing: A Conceptual Approach," In Vogt & Mickle (eds.), *Part 1: Geography-Regional Science*, ISA, Research Triangle Park, NC, pp. 131-138.

Arias, E. G. (1989) "The Contingent Nature of Participation and Housing Research.," *Guru Nanak Journal of Sociology—Special Housing Policy Issue*, 10(1-2), pp. 81-99.

Arias, E. G. (1994) "Decision Support in Locational Analysis: An Integrated Approach," *Proceedings of GIS '94*, pp. 129-143.

Arias, E. G. (1996) "Bottom-up Neighborhood Revitalization: Participatory Decision Support Approaches and Tools," *Urban Studies Journal—Special issue on Housing Markets, Neighborhood Dynamics and Societal Goals*, 33(10), pp. 1831-1848.

Arias, E. G. & Eden, H. (1997) "InterSim: Supporting Face-to-Face Collaborative Design," *Proceedings of CSCL '97.*

Arias, E. G., Eden, H., & Fischer, G. (1997) "Enhancing Communication, Facilitating Shared Understanding, and Creating Better Artifacts by Integrating Physical and Computational Media for Design," *Proceedings of Designing Interactive Systems (DIS '97)*, pp. 1-12.

Arias, E. G., Eden, H., Fischer, G., Gorman, A., & Scharff, E. (1999) "Beyond Access: Informed Participation and Empowerment," *Proceedings of the Computer Supported Collaborative Learning (CSCL '99) Conference*, pp. 20-32.

Arias, E. G., Eden, H., Fischer, G., Gorman, A., & Scharff, E. (2000) "Transcending the Individual Human Mind—Creating Shared Understanding through Collaborative Design," *ACM Transactions on Computer Human-Interaction*, 7(1), pp. 84-113.

Brown, J. S. & Duguid, P. (1991) "Organizational Learning and Communities-of-Practice: Toward a Unified View of Working, Learning, and Innovation," *Organization Science*, 2(1), pp. 40-57.

Brown, J. S., Duguid, P., & Haviland, S. (1994) "Toward Informed Participation: Six Scenarios in Search of Democracy in the Information Age," *The Aspen Institute Quarterly*, 6(4), pp. 49-73.

Bruner, J. (1996) *The Culture of Education*, Harvard University Press, Cambridge, MA.

Clark, H. H. & Brennan, S. E. (1991) "Grounding in communication," In L. B. Resnick, J. M. Levine, & S. D. Teasley (eds.), *Perspectives on Socially Shared Cognition*, APA Books, Washington, D.C., pp. 127-149.

Collins, A., Neville, P., & Bielaczyc, K. (2000) "Toward a Design Theory of Media for Education," *International Journal of Artificial Intelligence in Education*, 11, pp. 144-162.

Ehn, P. (1988) *Work-Oriented Design of Computer Artifacts*, Almquist & Wiksell International, Stockholm, Sweden.

Engeström, Y. (2001) "Expansive Learning at Work: toward an activity theoretical reconceptualization," *Journal of Education and Work*, 14(1), pp. 133-156.

Fischer, G. (2001) "Communities of Interest: Learning through the Interaction of Multiple Knowledge Systems," *24th Annual Information systems Research Seminar In Scandinavia (IRIS'24), Ulvik, Norway*, pp. (in press).

Johnson, D. W. & Johnson, R. J. (1994) "Cooperative learning in the culturally diverse classroom.," In R. A. DeVillar, C. J. Faltis, & J. P. Cummins (eds.), *Cultural Diversity in Schools: From Rhetoric to Practice*, State University of New York Press, Albany, pp. 57-73.

Lave, J. & Wenger, E. (1991) *Situated Learning: Legitimate Peripheral Participation*, Cambridge University Press, New York.

Lewis, C. H. & Norman, D. A. (1986) "Designing for Error," In D. A. Norman & S. W. Draper (eds.), *User Centered System Design, New Perspectives on Human-Computer Interaction*, Lawrence Erlbaum Associates, Hillsdale, NJ, pp. 411-432.

PCSD—President's Council on Sustainable Development (1996) *Sustainable America: A New Consensus for Prosperity, Opportunity, and a Healthy Environment for the Future*, President's Council on Sustainable Development, Washington, D.C.

Perrone, C., Spencer, S., & Arias, E. (1997) "Mr. Roger's Sustainable Neighborhood: A Visual Language Case Study for Community Education," In *Visual Languages '97 (Capri, Italy)*, pp. forthcoming.

Rittel, H. (1984) "Second-Generation Design Methods," In N. Cross (ed.), *Developments in Design Methodology*, John Wiley & Sons, New York, pp. 317-327.

Rittel, H. & Webber, M. M. (1984) "Planning Problems are Wicked Problems," In N. Cross (ed.), *Developments in Design Methodology*, John Wiley & Sons, New York, pp. 135-144.

Spencer, S., Perrone, C., & Goldstein, M. (1997) "Mr. Roger's Sustainable Neighborhood," In *Environmental Design Research Association Conference (EDRA) (Montreal, Canada)*, pp. 126-127.

Star, S. L. (1989) "The Structure of Ill-Structured Solutions: Boundary Objects and Heterogeneous Distributed Problem Solving," In L. Gasser & M. N. Huhns (eds.), *Distributed Artificial Intelligence*, Morgan Kaufmann Publishers Inc., San Mateo, CA, pp. 37-54.

Wenger, E. (1998) *Communities of Practice — Learning, Meaning, and Identity*, Cambridge University Press, Cambridge, England.

Learning Via Distributed Dialogue: Livenotes and Handheld Wireless Technology

Alastair Iles, Daniel Glaser, Matthew Kam, John Canny*

(iles@nature + dcg@cs + mattkam@cs + jfc@cs).berkeley.edu

University of California at Berkeley

ABSTRACT

This paper introduces a new learning technology for in-classroom and remote learning. The system and practice is called "Livenotes" and is motivated by the empirical success of peer learning methods, and by theoretical considerations of distributed dialogue among student peers as a facilitator of learning. The technical part of Livenotes is a collaborative whiteboard running on wireless handheld computers. We describe the system and the affordances we have developed for it to support the distributed dialogue model. We then examine the interactive dialogue that resulted from two classroom trials, using transcript captures, and analyze how users developed ways to navigate between pages, organize space on screens, determine whether the system was operational, and create social rapport. Finally, we suggest several issues that researchers can consider in designing collaborative software.

keywords

Livenotes, peer learning, distributed dialogue, shared whiteboard, collaborative note-taking, wireless handheld.

INTRODUCTION

Peer discussion is one of the most potent facilitators of classroom learning. Several previous studies of collaborative learning via computer support – such as the Distributed TVI experiments at Stanford (Dutra et. al. 1999) – suggest that fostering peer dialogue through technological aids can lead to better outcomes than traditional in-class instruction. They also show that – as in a synchronous newspaper editing system (Tanikawa et. al. 1999) – groups of students can work together to solve problems more effectively through peer dialogue with ample feedback and interactions than with a single central authority directing the process. They imply that seemingly non-sequitur conversation during less structured peer dialogue can actually lead to greater attention and thought by students. In addition, there is extensive evidence that learning is facilitated in small groups (e.g. Resnick et. al 1991; Slavin 1990).

These facts motivate further exploration of distributed dialogue during in-class learning. Livenotes is such an exploration. Developed by Matthew Kam at the Department of Computer Science at the University of California at Berkeley, Livenotes uses wireless communication and handwriting to allow a real-time conversation within a small group of students during a normal lecture, independent of the number of students in the physical classroom. We have tested this software in two graduate classes – one a lecture and the other a seminar – which we report on here. The program was originally designed for small groups of students to carry on a live discussion during the course of a lecture or presentation to supplement what they were learning directly from the instructor. Later, after user testing, we noticed that the technology would be appropriate for other kinds of discussion settings. Along with our pre-designed practice, we observed the emergence of a rich new practice among the users of Livenotes as they developed ways to communicate and coordinate their note-taking.

Following an introduction to Livenotes, this paper looks at how learning depends on the development of "rules" for communication in the Livenotes medium. It also investigates how groups of both designers and users chose to adapt and think about, dialogue-supporting technology in distributed ways. As such, we define distributed dialogue as a non-localized, yet collaborative activity. Such distributed dialogue may reveal unexpected, non-text-based patterns (e.g., highlighting points or deciding where to put input on a screen) in communication between people that verbal dialogue in the context of a classroom situation may obscure. Enabling these patterns to emerge in a classroom context can ease constructive dialogue in which students can engage in different threads of conversation and help teach each other through clarifying or adding to the teacher-led discussion. In this paper we reinforce the argument that: "Learning occurs as the co-construction (or reconstruction) of social meanings from within the parameters of emergent, socially negotiated, and discursive activity" (Hicks 1996, p. 136).

Our approach of writing on multiple graphic screens linked by wireless technology is similar to other approaches looking at distributed learning environments such as chat rooms or bulletin boards since it allows for free-from discussion. It extends longstanding educational arguments that students learn best by actively engaging each other in conversation, and recognizes

---

* Alastair Iles is a deaf postdoctoral fellow at the Energy and Resources Group. Daniel Glaser is an doctoral candidate in Information Design. Matthew Kam obtained his B.S and B.A. degrees from Berkeley in Spring 2001 and has enrolled in Berkeley's M.S. in Computer Science this Fall 2001. John Canny is Professor in the Department of Computer Science.

that each student has his or her own resources to contribute but may not have the opportunity to do so (e.g. as argued through Scardamaliea and Bereiter 1991). Wireless supported dialogue differs greatly from existing approaches because it not only involves people speaking by handwriting with each other in real time within a physical group situation, but also can support uncontrolled small group conversation in parallel with a broader level of controlled discussion (such as a lecture). Moreover, the wireless technology does not fully define what may be communicated and how, but allows users to develop potentially widely diverging styles of communication by themselves. In contrast, chat rooms and other similar media are heavily based on typed text, and operate via relatively centralized and fixed communication systems.

The initial results of testing Livenotes in the two graduate classes help illuminate some of its possibilities and problems in supporting distributed dialogue. We conclude that certain simple features are fundamental to creating an infrastructure where users can develop rules for negotiation and collaboration through free form, relatively unstructured dialogue. These features, however, are related to each particular context of use and may not be the same across different groups of users. We also analyze several key "socio-technical" features of the ways in which the technology was introduced and operated, with a view to assessing its benefits in small group collaboration and improving Livenotes later in 2001.

WHAT IS LIVENOTES?

Livenotes is a research software prototype and practice for collaborative note taking. It is a Java program that runs on Clio handheld tablets connected over a wireless TCP/IP network. The tablets and software are designed to be unconstraining and low-profile in their use. They can be used in many classroom settings without the necessity for direct access to computers (Figure 1a). Students can record handwritten notes on graphic screens that appear in real time on the Clios of their group members who are also running the software. Students, then, can exchange annotations and comments in the midst of the presentation. We chose Clio tablets because they were inexpensive, sufficiently small, light and portable to be used in a classroom setting, and their Windows CE 2.11 operating system could support a Java Virtual Machine. Livenotes was implemented in Java since it supported many Application Programming Interfaces (APIs) essential to the needs of this software such as multithreading, networking, and the Abstract Windowing Toolkit. In addition, Java programs, unlike their native code counterparts, are sufficiently hardware independent to run on most platforms. This is important for future flexibility in choice of hardware. Finally, the tablets that we currently chose can run on battery power for up to eight hours, thus facilitating prolonged note-taking.

Several important design choices were made to guide the anticipated collaborative learning. The program consists of a large shared whiteboard canvas, navigation bar, and a menu with a variety of options (Figure 1b). The canvas permits users to draw directly onto the canvas, using the stylus, with differently colored inkstrokes to identify each user. The inkstrokes are updated across all Clios belonging to the session via the wireless network connections. The navigation bar uses a "page" metaphor to signify that the main drawing area is only one of many numbered, sequential canvases. This navigation structure was chosen since we felt that users may get lost with a single scrollable page and it is a common strategy for electronic whiteboards. The menu bar is used to connect machines, save and load sessions, choose colors, and also to bring up a "presence indicator" window. This window helps users identify who else is online and what page they are currently looking at. A transcript of the note-taking can be saved for future reference, and can be exported to HTML. If desired, the transcript can be "played back" by being loaded onto the handhelds, though this is currently time consuming for client tablets due to network and hardware limitations of the Clio tablets. Various design options can be added to Livenotes as users desire: connection to a TV screen for broadcast to a room, private screens for separate conversation threads, and HTML export to websites or email for use by participants as notes. Further features may be added from time to time in response to user feedback.

A collaborative session is started by delegating a server role to a particular Clio or lap-top and connecting (multiple) clients to it, thus forming a star topological network. A computer can act both as a client and a server. Data compression has been an active area of research for allowing for responsive updating among the Clios on the wireless network. Tradeoffs between a highly reduced data format, low-cost compression schemes for the microprocessor, and data integrity of the inkstrokes has led us to a 50% savings in data format. In addition, thread timing and coordination is also being explored to find a more balanced updating scheme that will not overload individual machines and the network. For one user study, the wireless bridge between the Clio handhelds was already part of the computer science building while for another we brought in a small bridge for each session.

One precedent of a collaborative system using a shared graphical space is Belvedere (Suthers et. al 1997). Like Livenotes it allows for simultaneous access to a graphical space where users are able to create arguments. It differs from Livenotes though, since participants use a toolbar to create data, hypotheses, or unspecified textual input, which can be placed at a location on the whiteboard that they determine. Aside from keyboarding text, users can also create arrows between text boxes to agree, disagree, or join statements. There also is a window for bringing up hints—either through direct interaction with the instructor, or with an intelligent system.

Other precedents include the Distributed TVI (DTVI) experiments at Stanford University. These included probably the most comprehensive evaluations of a learning technology to date, but this is under the framework of students learning and being evaluated in a traditional lecture mode. DTVI allows small groups of students and a tutor to remotely collaborate through multiple video and audio channels to learn from a videotaped lecture (Dutra et. al. 1999). Although users are free to interact through audio and voice channels, there is no notion of collaborative drawing since the viewports are separated from each other. In DTVI, students regularly discuss the material, and half the students participate in roughly half of the discussions, so there is a high degree of participation. Outcomes correlate with the amount of interaction in the group. But surprisingly, there is no significant correlation with the relevance of the dialogue to the course material. Even apparently non-sequitur conversations among students enhance their learning. A second powerful peer learning technique is peer instruction (Mazur 1995). Peer instruction employs short episodes of dialogue in groups of students in a normal lecture classroom in response to questions from the instructor. Like DTVI, peer instruction has shown improvements in outcomes across many course topics.

DTVI and peer instruction have one feature in common: regular dialogue between a small group of students (less than seven) while the students are first encountering new material. In both cases, there is a practice to "steer" the dialogue toward the course material. In DTVI, a teaching assistant prompts students about the material, answers, and questions. In

Figure 1. a) (left) A Livenotes session—three users communicating as a small group. b) (right) What a screen capture of Livenotes looks like.

peer instruction, the instructor poses specific questions that the students must address during pauses in the lecture. Livenotes differs from these precedents because it is designed to run concurrently with a larger classroom conversation and tries to move the distributed dialogue to a number of tablets simultaneously without any central screen or authority (except a server to support the interplay). Consequently, differences in user personality and user familiarity with 'rules' of communication may affect how Livenotes is used in practice. Livenotes does not provide prefixed rules of communication so users are likely to make up these rules in the course of learning to use the technology.

USER ANALYSIS

BACKGROUND

Livenotes was first deployed in a graduate seminar in Human Centered Computing (HCC) in Berkeley's College of Engineering and then in an advanced seminar in Science and Technology Studies (STS) through the Energy and Resources Group. In both cases the technology was brought in after classes began (12th week in the HCC course, 5th week in the STS seminar) and hence played a supplementary role in structuring classroom activity. The analysis for the HCC course is based upon in-classroom observations of participant interactions by three of the paper's authors* and transcript analysis. The STS course analysis was also through observations of two of the paper's authors, in class discussion of the technology, unsolicited e-mail dialogue with classmates, transcript analyses, and questionnaires.

Starting in September 2000, the focus of the HCC course was to expand the theoretical foundations for research on computers and people through social systems that are broader than what is typically offered by a graduate computer science course on human-computer interaction. The HCC class was organized such that a student would first present and summarize the reading for that session, before the instructor further developed the topic and posed questions. Then small groups of about 4 students each would be formed to work out their responses and share them with the rest of the class. There were approximately 12 students in the class and most were affiliated with the College of Engineering.

* This is an acceptable data collection for educational researchers (e.g. Ball 1993)

During the 12th week of class, Livenotes was introduced into the class. The intention was to provide a parallel communication channel for students to concurrently discuss and clarify points during the student presentation and instructor lecture while it was happening. For that session 10 students were present and each of them was provided with a Clio tablet with the Livenotes software installed. The class separated into two user groups (and client-server networks), and used the Clio tablets extensively during both the student and professor's presentations. This was not surprising since all the participants were highly familiar with computer technology and there was an expectation that Livenotes would be used at some point. As the next section illustrates, even though the lecture was instructor-led, the students used the tablets selectively to discuss the material in a distributed fashion. During face-to-face group discussion, the Livenotes software lost the attention of students since they could not keep up with this fast paced environment. Livenotes lost the students' attention because they preferred to communicate verbally, and could not easily focus on the parallel distributed dialogue. During group summaries, one team leader used the tablet to read off his ideas to the instructor. The tablets were only used for one class, and a total of 13 pages were recorded for our analysis.

The STS seminar in Spring 2001 brought participants from a diverse set of disciplines together to discuss science as social and cultural practices. This was a high-level research seminar of 10-12 participants who engaged in extensive face-to-face interaction throughout. Participants came from a variety of disciplinary backgrounds (energy and environmental policy, medical sociology, political science, and education) and had different levels of familiarity with the subjects discussed. In each seminar session, participants took turns to present 3-4 readings each week, with another class member providing commentary, before opening the meeting up to discussion of several research questions posed by the leader. The aim was to generate input into each participant's dissertation or research project. One aspect of the seminar was taking notes for a deaf post-doctoral fellow who relied on peer note-taking to follow class discussion. Prior to the introduction of Livenotes, this note-taking took the form of recording by pen and paper, with the responsibility of being the scribe rotating between individual participants each week.

In the 5th week, Livenotes was introduced. The tablets were used for three classes, which generated 26, 34, and 28 pages of transcripts respectively that we could analyze. In contrast to the HCC class, many participants were unfamiliar with wireless computer technology. Additionally, not every seminar participant used Livenotes; some participants observed how their peers were using Livenotes but did not attempt to use Livenotes themselves. In the first class, three Clios were used, with two people taking notes for the deaf participant. In the second class, different people performed this note-taking role, but also engaged in distributed discussion. In the third class, the deaf participant was the session presenter and sought to make Livenotes a central part of the discussion. Five people participated actively, with four others observing passively for most of the time. We noticed that some people also joined the network by looking over a user's shoulder.

THE PROCESS OF INTRODUCING LIVENOTES

In both cases, the decision to introduce Livenotes into the class was top-down, made by the professor in cooperation with one or two students interested in the technology. There was little discussion of whether participants wished to try Livenotes out, or of what Livenotes might contribute to their classroom experiences. This may have affected the responses of the participants, in that some people—particularly in the STS seminar—expressed concern about the lack of discussion regarding the deployment of Livenotes. For them, the tablets simply appeared mysteriously in a meeting, without explanation as to why they were being used. In fact, one of the professors was worried that the way in which Livenotes was introduced may have influenced the seminar's social dynamics adversely.

KEY USAGE ISSUES

We observed many interesting phenomena during the trials, but choose to discuss three examples that bear particularly on future design considerations of Livenotes that may better support collaborative learning. We will refer to both trials because similar issues were raised by both seminar and lecture formats, and as such, may be relevant to any usage of Livenotes in general.

CONNECTING UP AND GETTING ON THE SAME PAGE

When starting Livenotes for the first time in a session, participants did not know whether Livenotes was operational. They did not know who were participating. The whiteboard canvas by itself could not indicate whether the network was working or if everyone was receiving and sending any handwritten messages. Additionally, throughout a session, people were repeatedly uncertain, on moving to a new page, whether others had also advanced to the page, or were still looking at earlier pages. It was possible for participants to open the "presence indicator" window to check if the individual Clio was connected to the server, who else were on-line, as well as the pages that these individuals were currently looking at. However, it was difficult for participants not already aware of this option to make use of this window.

Figure 2. Greetings dominated the first page of each session.

In both the lecture and seminar meetings, it was observed that many participants wrote brief messages to determine whether or not the wireless connection was transmitting these messages to the rest of the user group. Such opening messages included: "Can you receive?", "Hi", "Is this working?", or "Namaste". Sometimes, especially in the seminar, certain individuals would make little drawings to see if others could, or would, declare their presence by adding to the images. When moving between pages, individual users might write: "Is this page current?" or "Can anyone read this!?" The important observation is that users were able to create rules to decide whether or not the network was operational, based on their communication, rather than on the technology per se. Figure 2 illustrates the first page of one such session.

NAVIGATION AND SPACE MANAGEMENT

Two of the most pressing communication challenges that Livenotes poses are the distributed decision-making involved in navigating between and within pages, as well as in dividing up a page so that more than one user can participate. We found that although many different conversations and topics were jumbled together on the one page, users were nonetheless mostly able to coordinate how they would share their space and to work out ways to distinguish between the various conversation threads to a reasonable extent. Two observations were especially important.

First, people sitting far apart in the classroom often did not know whether or when they should move to a new page. However, they tested various symbols to either signal the need to change pages, or to ask if other people had changed pages. For example, in the 2nd seminar session, people used "Now we go to a new page", "page 4→", "p5?", "→", or "I got it!" in one corner of the page to communicate in this way. One user drew little arrows at the base of the page as if it was a continuous scrolling page.

Second, people did not always know whether or not others were paying attention to their input, or whether what they wrote was visible in the jumble of writing to the others. They could not rely on the kinds of cues that verbal, face-to-face communication can often provide. The conversation threads might not be easy to connect together. This differs from trying to find out if participants are all "on the same page", in that specific people may be concerned that their contribution is not being read or evaluated by the group. The social context matters greatly for how users resolve this issue.

We observed that a seminar session that was primarily note-taking by one or two people was fairly simple: the users would

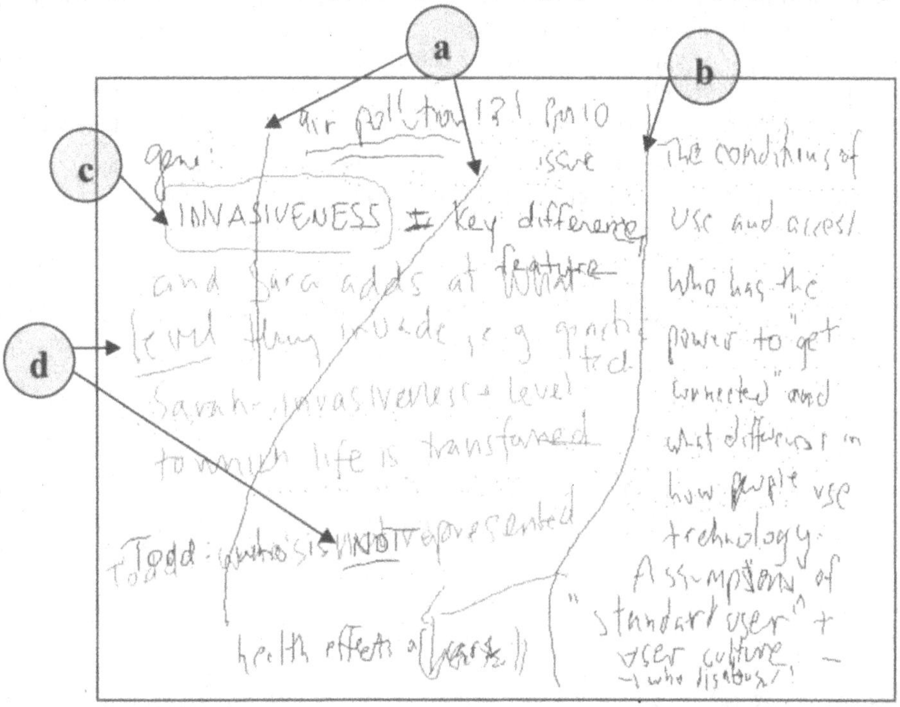

Figure 3. A screen capture showing a variety of elements including (a) linking together disjoint spaces of conversation (b) marking territory (c) highlighting someone else's points (d) highlighting one's own points for attention.

write in temporal sequence down the page in "sentences", with the inkstroke colors distinguishing between scribes. It was easy to follow the conversation thread, because there was just one, sometimes with little annotations by the deaf participant at the side. But when the sessions turned into a distributed discussion involving up to five people, space management changed markedly and new rules began to emerge. People would write phrases all over the page. They often highlighted specific parts of the page by drawing boxes or circles around their input (Figure 3a). In doing so, they tried to mark off territory for their input (Figure 3b). Quite commonly, participants underlined phrases to emphasize points (Figure 3c). Occasionally, a user would simply draw lines under two different contributions. Moreover, people often drew arrows or lines across the page to connect up widely scattered phrases to continue the thread and to pick up what they were saying because someone else was writing in the space (Figure 3d). Or they might put in a series of numbers next to phrases. These non-textual inputs help make Livenotes quite different from most other technologies for collaborative learning.

DISCUSSION, PLAY AND DRAWING

The kinds of communication that Livenotes enables can be multi-layered and reflect mutual teaching and clarification of points. We observed that users in the seminar would sometimes engage in overlapping dialogue: taking summary notes of the presentation (Figure 4a), commenting on issues raised by the presentation and perhaps "training" people less familiar with the topic (Figure 4b), engaging in "side" conversation unrelated to the topic (Figure 4c), or making humorous contributions (Figure 4d). However, it could be difficult for participants to determine whether or not a given input was related to the topic. Sometimes, users would identify a speaker by name to suggest that the reference was part of the group discussion. Nevertheless, even when a point followed the larger class discussion, there was a risk that it would not be resolved within the same time period and depth as the larger discussion. For example a user asked to clarify a small lecture point "can somebody give me an example of some 'organizational knowledge' that differs from individual knowledge?", while no less than seven responses over three full pages were provided. At the end of this heated exchange while turning back to the relatively laconic lecture a user unsurprisingly asked "so is anyone else having trouble listening & writing?".

Simultaneously, Livenotes can also provide a space for drawings and playfulness that do not necessarily follow the lecture or presentation, but that allow users to add a social dimension to their writing. People sometimes drew images on the page

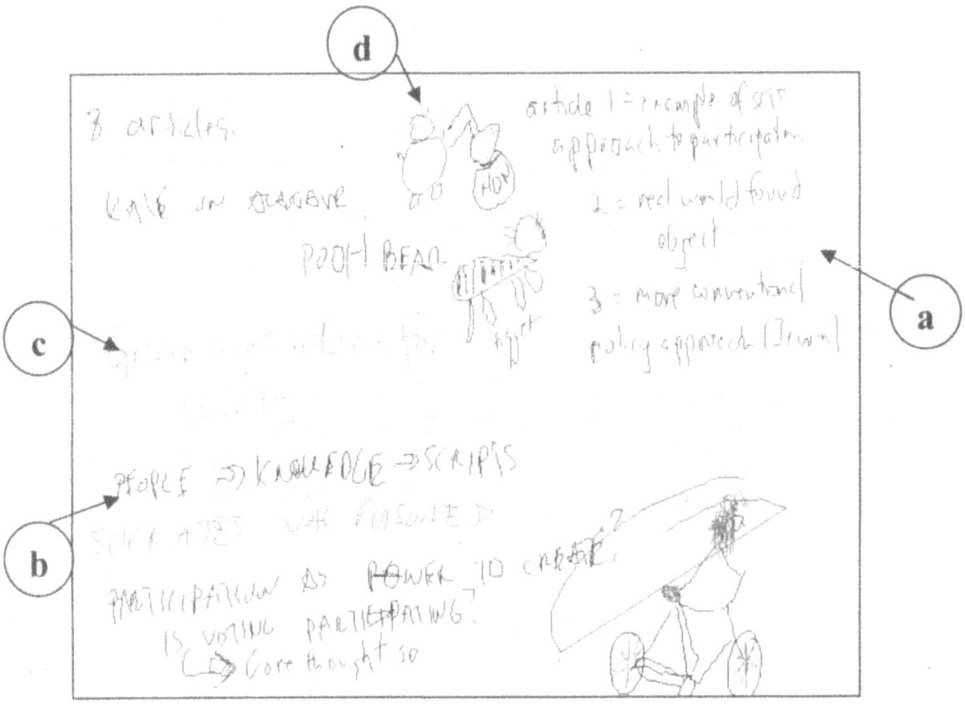

Figure 4. Transcript showing (a) summing up the lecture, (b) expanding on or developing lecture themes (c) an unrelated topic and (d) humorous interludes and drawings

alongside the textual discussion. These images could be humorous interludes or surprisingly novel attempts at clarification of discussion points. For example, an instructor in the STS seminar drew an egg representing a technical norm, while another less familiar with the literature in contempt of the idea drew Sigourney Weaver attacking the egg (as an alien), and the first participant responded, "the larva is in you" referring back to the topic of embodied knowledge. Similarly, Figure 4 shows drawings associated with Pooh the Bear (Figure 4d) while Figure 2 shows how participants in the HCC class drew ants creeping across the page and being devoured by a monster.

Strikingly, these drawings did not appear in the session where only one or two members were taking notes for the deaf participant. Usually, the humorous episodes were at the start or end of a session, so people may have been implicitly using these drawings as a means of getting accustomed to the wireless technology and to creating a rapport without necessarily talking verbally to each other. This illustrates how some participants may use drawings or play as a way to facilitate social interaction and to attract the attention of each other. Livenotes has the capacity to support this kind of activity because of its graphics-based interface, which permits free-form and informal expressions, whereas text-based interfaces are unlikely to permit it. However, we observed that some participants seemed to see such drawing and playfulness as detracting from the session's verbal dialogue, without considering how jokes may form part of this conversation.

In all these cases, participants actively created (or negotiated) solutions in the form of "rules", symbols, and governance of exchanges to be distributed across the participants. These solutions were based on communication and social norm-making that substituted for technical features not already built into Livenotes or the Clios. Interestingly, the behavior observed was often similar to the conventions generated by the deaf participant in his written conversations, in that he used arrows, underlining, circling, and other space management features.

QUANTITATIVE ANALYSIS

We performed an initial quantitative analysis of the third STS session transcript to start developing indicators of learning and user activity for our future research. First, we developed units of analysis based on our observations of user behavior, as described above. We counted the number of stylus marks that each user made on each canvas page, relying on pen colors. Next, we distributed these marks into two categories: management (how users control dialogue on the canvas) and content (what users say in relation to the classroom presentation). We then allocated the marks to the specific sub-categories that we created in analyzing the examples above, distinguishing between marks according to our judgment of how they fit into the overall dialogue. Our major conclusions were that:

- Management marks were almost as many as content marks (46.82% compared to 53.18%), suggesting that users not only discussed the lecture but also worked to manage their dialogue;
- The vast majority of content marks (83%) related directly to the lecture in some way, with only 12% of marks being on unrelated topics and humorous interludes, implying that Livenotes did facilitate in-group discussion, and that perceptions of Livenotes as dominated by play were ungrounded;
- One person (the presenter of the session: 45%) was expertly managing the dialogue – through linking points and marking territory – with the assistance of two other persons (who acted as notetakers for the presenters: 20% and 12% respectively), suggesting that Livenotes dialogue can be structured, and also that some users control whiteboard space more than others;
- In contrast, the same three users were more even in the number of their highlighting marks (31%, 28% and 28% respectively), yet produced far more such marks than other users, suggesting that highlighting is not only used more by some users but also differs from marking territory as a way to make dialogue clearer to other users;
- Two people out of six users produced almost all the drawing errors (74%), implying that they differed markedly in their ease with the technology from the others; and
- The vast majority of humorous interludes and drawings came in the first four pages of the transcript and one person accounted for 41%, suggesting that these not only are dependent on personality factors but also on the context (whether dialogue is starting, or is underway).

Breakdowns in use

We noticed several types of breakdowns in the usage of Livenotes — from the most basic technical failure of hardwire and wireless signals, to more socially contingent examples like users disengaging from the technology when they become overwhelmed in keeping up with the verbal and distributed whiteboard forms of discourse during classes. These breakdowns and, in some cases, recovery methods include:

- *Temporary technical disruptions:* Users experienced a number of interruptions including slow whiteboard responses to stylus inputs and server lag. Although it is often slower to write on the wireless tablets than with paper and pencil, some users took advantage of parallel note-taking—namely two or more people could write at once to track fast moving conversation. They could fill in information gaps side by side.
- *Multiple tasks and finite concentration:* People had various degrees of trouble following the discussion in the Livenotes user group Livenotes and the instructor-led discussion in the classroom. For some people, one means of coping with this was to abandon Livenotes altogether. Other users, however, appeared to be comfortable with switching between Livenotes and verbal conversations.
- *Frustration at the play witnessed:* Non-participants sometimes complained that the occasional smiles or laughter by the Livenotes users were at their expense. The sense of parallel conversations, which were often perceived as being unrelated to the session's topic, contributed to the tension between users and non-users of Livenotes. Non-users who had many users in their field of view but could not see the contents of the tablets were more critical than non-users who could share or look over a shoulder of a user to see the proceedings of the conversation within a Livenotes group.

These breakdowns further imply that the ability of the participants to engage in negotiations of the rules and symbols to facilitate the use of Livenotes is crucial in helping make the technology workable. This ability is affected by several variables that we plan to investigate in future trials and which we were not able to resolve through the few, yet varied, STS survey respondents. For example, one person described the stylus as being "completely too slow… uncomfortable" while another "liked it". A respondent wrote: "It was too hard to try to write coherently … I was always mentally very behind the discussion" while another "didn't think it was a problem [coordinating both conversations]". Nevertheless, there was some agreement where they did not like the idea of private notes since it would splinter the group even more.

DISCUSSION AND CONCLUSIONS

We conclude that, through Livenotes and handheld wireless screens, students can learn from each other during the course of a lecture or seminar in distributed and "horizontal" ways otherwise not possible. They can actively engage in discussion and commentary on lectures or presentations as these occur, thus enhancing their comprehension and ability to participate. Livenotes differs markedly from existing approaches to distributed learning that rely on typed text and relatively fixed technical and communication modalities. It is interactive dialogue that is distributed across a number of people, can take place in real time, can have many threads that can appear or vanish within a session, and can readily change in response to user participation. Wireless-supported dialogue allows much greater control over content and communication features to be given to users, instead of being imposed and moderated from the top-down.

This dialogue – as seen in Figure 4 for example – is often multi-layered, with people taking notes of the session, more experienced members explaining ideas to other, less knowledgeable people, and members engaging in what may seem to be peripheral conversation that nevertheless helps illuminate session topics. Even if students make erroneous statements of knowledge, they can be immediately corrected by other users or by teachers who may be involved, and their dialogue can be posted in various forms (email, web, or print) for further distributed comment and scrutiny. The inherent flexibility and whiteboard nature of Livenotes enables such free form, mutually correcting dialogue. In contrast, the enhanced, but text-based, DVTI system appears to be primarily based on lecture summaries instead of interactive dialogue (according to published transcripts available from www.sun.com/research.ics.notes.html). It is easier to maintain control over content through centralized and text-based systems, but this may inhibit the emergence of dialogue in small groups such as those that we observed.

In turn, we conclude that users can generate significant non-technical modifications to systems through engaging in the communication and social interaction enabled by Livenotes. We have found the effectiveness of the technology is highly contingent on the social context that it is being used in. In particular, users appear to generate social "rules", symbols, and conventions (often expressed in graphical or text-graphical forms) that fill in for missing or inaccessible technical features, and that enable communication to take place effectively. Livenotes allows this process of generation to occur because it is not "finished", depends on free form whiteboards, and has great flexibility built in. We have also realized that the ways in which deaf people engage in written conversations can provide valuable insight into how Livenotes might work in settings where hearing users write on handheld whiteboards and as a media for comparative purposes with the current development of Livenotes.

Designers of learning support systems, then, can gain much fruitful insight from studying how users work with technology. Drawing on the insights of the two trials to date, we recommend that, to make further advances in developing collaborative learning systems, designers consider the following:

- Systems need to be designed with flexibility and "unfinished" (comparatively unspecified) features to allow users to develop modifications through their communication activities. This facilitates negotiations between users in each particular context or use setting.
- Because some users became frustrated with the tablets since they demanded too much attention, different features should be added so that the user can participate at different levels of engagement. For example, their collaborative whiteboard could simply be tied to a group leader so that they do not need to worry about keeping up with navigation.
- Systems need to be designed to take account of how users may rely on communication and negotiation to deal with issues such as navigation between pages, space management on pages with multiple conversation threads and jumbled writing, and working out if users are "on the same page".

Finally, we are developing evaluation metrics for both adaptation and learning benefits of using Livenotes. This will include a typology of users, development of a protocol analysis to capture the multi-modal interactions with this media, and assessments on the utility of Livenotes in learning. Some of these indicators can be seen in our initial quantitative analysis. From our first trials, we identified familiarity with computer technology, preferences for typing versus handwriting, and the personality and multi-task capabilities as relevant user dimensions. Although we were able to make comparisons between the verbal and Livenotes conversations in section 3 of this paper, we are planning to set up video cameras to record classroom dialogue (with and without the use of Livenotes), to augment the data logs captured by Livenotes (e.g., to provide time logs of when users write on the canvas) with contextual information, and to interview participants before and after the introduction of Livenotes. We plan to cross-check these data sources against each other according to the timeline of the transcripts. We will also develop software tools to automate this analysis to some extent. These technical developments will play an important role in developing evaluation metrics with teachers on the effectiveness of Livenotes in the classroom.

REFERENCES:

Ball D. (1993) Halves, pieces, and twoths: Constructing and using representational contexts in teaching fractions. In T.P. Carpenter, E. Fennema and T. A. Romberg (Eds.), Rational numbers: An integration of research. Studies in mathematical thinking and learning (pp 157-195). Lawrence Erlbaum Associates, Inc, Hillsdale, NJ.

Dutra, J. Gibbons, J., Pannoni, R., Sipusic, M., Smith, R., Sutherland, W. (1999), "Virtual Collaborative Learning: A Comparison between Face-to-Face Tutored Video Instruction (TVI) and Distributed Tutored Video Instruction (DTVI)" Sun Microsystems Research Technical Report TR-99-72.

Hicks, D. (1996) Contextual inquiries: A discourse-oriented study of classroom learning. In D. Hicks (Ed.), Discourse, Learning, and Schooling (pp. 104-141). New York: Cambridge University Press.

Mazur, E., (1997) "Peer Instruction: A User's Manual", Prentice Hall, Upper Saddle River, NJ.

Resnick, L. B., Levine, J. M., Teasley, S. D. (Eds.) (1991), Perspectives on socially shared cognition. Washington, DC: American Psychological Association.

Scardamalia, M., Bereiter, C. (1991) "Higher levels of agency for children in knowledge building. A challenge for the design of new knowledge media". The Journal of the Learning Sciences, 1:37-68.

Slavin R.(1990) "Cooperative Learning: Theory, Research, and Practice", Prentice Hall, Englewood Cliffs, NJ.

Suthers, D., Toth, E., Weiner, A. (1997), "An Integrated Approach to Implementing Collaborative Inquiry in the Classroom", CSCL '97 Proceedings.

L. (TECHNOLOGY TRACK): ISSUES IN THE DESIGN OF ASYNCHRONOUS COLLABORATION SYSTEMS

Exploring the Lack of Dialogue in Computer-Supported Collaborative Learning

Mark Guzdial, Karen Carroll

College of Computing/GVU
Georgia Institute of Technology
guzdial@cc.gatech.edu
kcarroll@cc.gatech.edu

ABSTRACT

Research in collaborative learning has supported the hypothesis that dialogue between peers and between peers and teachers facilitates learning by the participants in the dialogue. Examples of these dialogues show dozens of turns (individual utterances by participants) in a single learning session. In contrast, measurements of interaction from computer-supported collaborative learning environments show that on-line dialogue looks much different, with an average of approximately one posting or less per student per week. Measurements of learning in these environments *do* suggest learning is occurring, but presumably, not based on the same kind of dialogue described in research on face-to-face collaboration. We explore explanations for how the learning is arising in CSCL environments based on the *Vicarious Learning* Project (Lee, Dineen, McKendree, & Mayes, 1999; McKendree, Stenning, Mayes, Lee, & Cox, 1998), but in the course of this explanation, two additional hypotheses emerge. We believe that some of the learning in CSCL environments occurs from the observation of the dialogue, the reflection induced by the *potential* of submitting, and in the interaction between the face-to-face and on-line environments.

Keywords

Measuring dialogue, measuring learning, empirical measurement of computer-supported collaborative learning

INTRODUCTION: IS THERE LEARNING IN COMPUTER-SUPPORTED COLLABORATION ENVIRONMENTS?

Dewey (Dewey, 1901) and Vygotsky (Vygotsky, 1978) both argued that all learning begins from a social context. Internal reflection and "monologue" are secondary effects that derive from previous social interactions. A peer discussion is a useful way of encouraging the kind of social interaction that leads to learning. Researchers on collaborative learning have found that collaborative discussions (competitive or cooperative) do facilitate learning (Cohen, 1994).

Learning scientists have described how dialogue leads to learning, especially, collaborative learning where a shared understanding is created through the dialogue (Jeong & Chi, 1997; Roschelle, 1992). Roschelle describes learning as arising from dialogue that follows a cycle of posing hypotheses, testing the hypotheses, and then discussing the results of the test and the formation of the next set of hypotheses. Jeong & Chi describes learning as resulting from a similar process of explaining to one another what each individual's understanding is, and then refining it based on what the individuals hear. A key characteristic in both the Roschelle and Jeong & Chi studies is that subjects are interacting with one another to a large extent. The posing of hypotheses, testing of hypotheses, and the generation of explanations described do not occur in a single utterance, but instead occur across dozens of utterances, including many non-verbal ones, in Roschelle's study. Roschelle's study identifies 49 turns between two students in less than one hour.

In the literature on computer-supported collaborative learning, we see nowhere near that level of interaction. Guzdial (Guzdial, 1997) showed that for a variety of asynchronous computer-supported collaborative learning environments (including CaMILE and newsgroups, Answer Garden (Ackerman, 1994), and CoNote (Davis & Huttenlocher, 1995)), students posted an average of less than one note (a contributed utterance in the shared, on-line space) per week. While we would expect more interaction in synchronous collaboration, asynchronous collaboration is the predominant mode in the research literature. Another way of looking at the interaction is in terms of the length of the discussion, which we can measure as the length of a *thread* (a series of notes posted in response to a single note). In newsgroups, one of the most popular environments for computer-supported collaborative learning (Terveen & Hill, 1998), the length of a thread in 18 classes was measured by Guzdial as averaging 2.2 notes. The implication is that the average discussion consisted of a note and a single note in response. Terveen & Hill found very similar results across hundreds of newsgroups on the Internet

(Terveen & Hill, 1998). A more recent study by Hewitt & Teplovs found that in seven graduate courses offered at a distance using the CSILE environment (Scardamalia, Bereiter, & Lamon, 1994) the average thread length was 2.69 (Hewitt & Teplovs, 1999).

All of these studies were measures of interaction only. There were little or no learning measures. One might presume that such little interaction implies that no learning is occurring. However, studies of CSCL use with similar interaction levels have demonstrated in the last couple of years.

- Miyake & Masukawa (Miyake & Masukawa, 2000) describe a system, ReCoNote, in which students explicitly create relations between notes, as well as post new notes. In their study, students in cognitive science did research and reported on their results in ReCoNote, and then later posted and discussed their research papers in ReCoNote. 57 students created 310 notes over a 15 week[1] period, for an average of 0.362 notes per student per week. If we consider a link between notes as another kind of utterance (referring to our definition of a note earlier), students posted an average of 0.58 notes per student per week. They mention that the number of logins by students was 749, which leads to 0.87 logins per student per week. Miyake & Masukawa report significant learning in cognitive science among the students, as measured by a qualitative analysis of their papers.
- A detailed study by Hoadley & Linn (Hoadley & Linn, 2000) focuses on a use of the SpeakEasy collaborative learning environment where eighth grade students debated the relationship between color and light over a four week period. Students participated in one of two conditions: An unmodified SpeakEasy discussion about the topic, and a SpeakEasy discussion structured around the perspectives of Kepler and Newton where the goal was to highlight the differences between Kepler's and Newton's views on color and light. In their studies, the average number of notes per student per week was 1.3[2]. The average number of logins per student per week was 0.825 (quite similar to the Miyake & Masukawa study). Hoadley & Linn found that all students learned significantly about color and light, but those using the historical forum learned more (in particular, they related the theories to the scientists). Surprisingly, the number of logins was the only measure that Hoadley & Linn found that correlated with post-test score.
- A new study by our research group at Georgia Tech has focused on a part of Freshman English Composition classes, comparing students using our CoWeb tool in a "close reading" activity with students not using technology for their "close reading" (Rick, Guzdial, Carroll, Holloway-Attaway, & Walker, 2002). Students in the CoWeb generated an average of 2.22 notes per student per week. Students were *required* to participate in the CoWeb, which leads to slightly higher averages, but 2.22 notes per student per week is still not anywhere near the rapid iteration of dozens of comments that we see in the work of Roschelle and Jeong & Chi. Students using the CoWeb did significantly better than the non-CoWeb-using class on class essays, especially in areas of vocabulary and organization of ideas, even though both classes scored about the same on the first assignments.

The finding that these results suggest is that learning is occurring in these computer-supported collaborative learning environments, despite the fairly low rates of discussion. But the interaction is not like what Roschelle and Jeong & Chi are describing, at least not in terms of the amount of discussion. What is the mechanism by which the learners are learning in these studies? Is it the shared understanding described by Roschelle and Jeong & Chi, or do the low rates of interaction suggest that something else is happening? In the rest of this paper, we describe a set of hypotheses for what the mechanism might be, and offer some interviews with students to support some of these hypotheses. Our opinion is that there is more than one kind of mechanism at work, just as there are several different learning mechanisms taking place in face-to-face learning.

HYPOTHESES ON LEARNING MECHANISMS

The first hypothesis to consider is that the shared understanding mechanism described by Roschelle and Jeong & Chi is also leading *in the same manner described* to learning in the computer-supported collaborative learning (CSCL) examples cited previously (Miyake & Masukawa, Hoadley & Linn, and Rick, et al.). We find little to support this hypothesis. The low rate of postings makes it unlikely that students are engaged in cycles of hypothesis formation, experimentation, and discussion (Roschelle) or in exchanged explanations (Jeong & Chi). One counter hypothesis might be that students are learning in the CSCL environments, but more slowly—that the entire term is a single learning session, and that the rate of discussion is appropriate when distributed across such a long time. We point out, however, that each of the studies is keeping pace with a face-to-face classroom. In the cases of Miyake & Masukawa and Rick, et al., the topics being discussed in the computer

---

[1] We are presuming here a 15 week semester study. Miyake & Masukawa describe their study as extending over a "half year" and describe their use as having four phases, the middle two of which were three weeks long each.

[2] Based on a reported average of 5.3 (SD=31) notes written per student over a four week period. Students were required to write at least three notes.

environment are appearing at the same time as the topics do in the traditional classroom—it isn't the case that all the observed discussion focused on a single topic so that shared understanding occurred.

We began this exploration with a hypothesis on where the learning was coming from:

- *Vicarious learning for shared understanding:* Students *are* engaged in the shared understanding mechanisms described by Roschelle and Jeong & Chi, but *vicariously*. That is, students sometimes do not post a note because someone else has already made the response or explanation they would make. Under this hypothesis, the mechanism for each individual's learning is the same as in the shared understanding model, but there are fewer utterances because students recognize their own understanding in others.

But in our search for evidence to support this hypothesis, two other possible explanations arose from the interviewing process:

- *Reflection stemming from the potential of posting*: Students encounter an idea in a forum, and reflect on it in order to create a posting, but in the end, they don't—perhaps because someone else posted the idea, or because they lose interest in the actual posting of a note. But in any case, the *possibility* of responding leads to an inquiry process that facilitates learning.
- *Relating on-line and in-class activities:* In the three CSCL studies cited, the on-line environment was an extension of an existing face-to-face class. Thus, studying the on-line space doesn't provide a complete picture of the learning. Students meet ideas in the on-line CSCL environment that they've heard in face-to-face class, or they take ideas from the CSCL environment into the face-to-face class for discussion or relate them to class assignments or topics.

All three of these hypotheses are consistent with Hoadley & Linn's observation that number of logins correlated well with learning outcomes. Students who log in more often are probably more likely to identify with other students and have vicarious learning opportunities. Students who log in more often may be more likely to be involved and reflective about the discussion. Students who log in more often are more likely to see connections between what's going on in class and in the CSCL environment.

EXPLORING THE HYPOTHESES

To explore why students were choosing *not* to post in a CSCL environment, we conducted a series of interviews in an English Composition class that was using the CoWeb (in a manner like that described in Rick, et al.) Through log files, we identified students who did post notes frequently into the CoWeb. We then identified a point when a frequently-posting student visited a discussion page and read it (or so we presume, based on length of time spent on the page) *but did not post a note to the discussion*. Because the CoWeb keeps every version of every page, we were able to reconstruct the page as it looked at the moment that the student read the page.

At the end of the same academic term, we were able to identify three students who matched these criteria. We asked them to explain why they chose not to post at that time, providing them with a printout of the page as it looked when they visited it. While the large time gap between the incident and the generation of an example is a problem if we were to consider these data as think-aloud protocols (Ericsson & Simon, 1980), we found that the example page served as a stimulus for a wider ranging discussion on why the students posted and when.

As mentioned our original hypothesis was that vicarious learning explained the learning-without-much-dialogue phenomenon. Our guide for the interview started from this hypothesis. We asked all three students the following questions, with questions added by the interviewer for elaboration or explanation of a confusing point:

- *It looks as if you read comments on this page, but didn't post. Can you remember why?*
- *Did you ever go with something to say and find someone else had already posted it? Did you ever come up with something to say, go away to think about it, and return to find someone else had said it?*
- *When you read comments which sparked something you wanted to say, did you generally post it right away or go away and think about it for a while first?*
- *Did you ever think of something to say and then bring it up later in class instead of posting?*
- *When you went to the CoWeb, did you usually go with something to say, or were you just browsing through other people's comments?*

Three students is admittedly a very small sample. We are not arguing that these students are representative of the whole class, nor that the mechanisms for potential learning that we identify are the only ones—they may not even be the most common ones. Rather, we see these interviews as *suggesting hypotheses* to explore further to explain the tension we point out in the literature between amount of discussion and evidence of learning. We conducted the interviews to develop some evidence for our first hypothesis. The fact that we found students offering stories of their experience that supported the first hypothesis and the two emergent hypotheses is significant in suggesting the *potential* of these hypotheses in explaining how learning can occur with little observable dialogue. In the sections below, we expand upon each of these hypotheses and offer students' comments in support of these hypotheses.

Vicarious learning for shared understanding

The *Vicarious Learning* Project (Lee et al., 1999; McKendree et al., 1998) studied how well students learned from experiencing the interaction between teachers and students as transcripts or video. The Vicarious Learning researchers recorded tutors working with students, or even students working together, then created transcripts and video segments from these recordings. New students would then study the transcripts and video segments. The result was that the new students learned as well as those recorded.

The goal of the Vicarious Learning Project was to show that transcripts of dialogues are an effective educational resource for future students. The mechanism of learning was that students would "identify" with the student in the dialogue and would benefit from the same explanations, and potentially have the same questions. They point out that "learning, particularly in higher education, requires learning about descriptions of the world, knowledge derived from someone else's experience, and from understanding someone else's arguments." Learning "vicariously" from recorded dialogues gives students the opportunity to practice learning from someone else's experiences.

What may be occurring in the three CSCL studies cited previously is a slight variation on the Vicarious Learning Project setting. Students in the same class are building the dialogue, but they are also observing others' dialogue. Students may not post if someone else has already made the posting that they were considering making. In this case, students recognize a shared understanding with others in the class, and they choose not to post because their contribution is already made. The end result is the kind of shared understanding that Roschelle and Jeong & Chi describe, but with fewer postings because of the identification with others' perspectives as described by the Vicarious Learning project.

Two of the students we interviewed described having this happen to them.

> K: Apparently, you looked at this page. My impression from looking at the CoWeb is that you posted pretty frequently. But this is one where you didn't post—where you looked at it and you didn't write anything. Do you remember this?
>
> Student P: Yeah, yeah, I remember this.
>
> K: Do you have any idea why?
>
> Student P: Oh, yeah, I saw this part, and I was going to answer it, but, I don't know, I,... before I could answer, somebody already came up with the answer, StudentC or StudentJ came up with the answer.
>
> K: Somebody said what you were going to say?
>
> Student P: Right
>
> K: So somebody already did it. Did that ever happen other times? Was that something that happened more than once for you, where people would answer what you were going to answer?
>
> Student P: It did actually, the open forum, it happened a couple of times, like I come there and I like look at people's questions, or something, and then go back, by the time I come back, like, ten more people have answered it.
>
> K: Did you ever find that you had a question you wanted to ask, and then somebody else had asked it already?
>
> Student P: A couple of times, yeah. Yeah. I guess, even if I did have a question, I mean, the questions were there, but it just didn't come out, somebody had already worded it, so I'm like oh yeah, I wanted to- I was wondering about this, too.

What's interesting in this exchange is that the student identifies that both generating an answer (like generating an explanation in Jeong & Chi's study) and questions (like generating hypotheses and questions in Roschelle's study) are happening vicariously for this student. Other students performed those answering and questioning roles that Student P would have posted, so the learning mechanism for each individual looks like the shared understanding model, but without the same level of interaction being evident in the on-line forum.

> K: Did you ever go with an idea of something you wanted to say and find that someone else had already posted it?
>
> Student Z: mm-hmmm. Several times. Yeah, like, with this, the whole Darwin related to creationism, there are some things that I probably could have added but I thought like, I don't know why I didn't, but like in retrospect I probably would have had some interesting discussions myself if I had, but like, I like when Student P, how he, I like reading what he writes, too, 'cause it's very interesting to me, 'cause he thinks sorta like I do; like he likes to have facts to base things up; I understand how he thinks, and like a lot of people in the class, a few of them have the same views and a few of them don't and I like, it just interests me, you know, kind of, I like how people think.

Student Z says that the event occurred several times that he was going to post, but found that his ideas were already posted. He also says that he noted a particular student who "thinks sorta like I do." Student Z also points out that he doesn't agree with all the views that he reads in the class forums, but it interests him to read them. That last point is echoed by Hoadley & Linn, "The most common benefit of SpeakEasy identified by interviewed students was that they could hear the opinions of others." The hearing of contrasting perspectives is an important part of the shared understanding mechanism described by Roschelle and Jeong & Chi.

Reflection from the potential of posting

All three of the students we interviewed talked about the role that *considering* whether to post and what to post had on their learning process. Students talked about doing research or going off to think about issues raised before making a posting—whether or not they actually did post. The role of the CSCL, then, is to start an inquiry process for the students, and that inquiry might not result in a posting into the CSCL environment. An asynchronous forum is particularly supportive of this mechanism because the delay in response during reflection doesn't impact the flow of the conversation.

> K: Somebody said what you were going to say?
>
> Student P: Right, like, I found stuff on this, I mean I came here, I saw this and I decided to do some research, so I went to some other web page and I looked it up and I found out stuff, I was actually ready to post, I come back, and somebody had already done it.
>
> K: Is that something that you would frequently do, to kind of look at what somebody else had said, and then go away to think about it yourself?

Student P: Um-hmm. That's probably what I did, yeah. Like I used this as kind of, you know, something that would help me think about a particular topic and a particular direction, like when you just read a book, it's really difficult to pick a subject and go in a particular direction, like if somebody thinks about something and gives a question, it's easier to channel your efforts towards a particular thing.

In this quote, student P describes going off to "do some research" in response to something that came up in the discussion. But someone else posted before he got back, so he didn't end up contributing to the discussion, but the learning benefit for him had already been gained.

> K: Suppose that you did have something to say, would you generally, say it right away or is it something you would go away and think about and come back to later, or?
>
> Student T: Generally I'll probably do it right away unless I'm just there browsing for whatever reason, if I don't really have that much time, I might go back and say later, and if I do that usually I'll also have thought about it some more and that may make me not want to write anything or it would give me more to write about.

Student T generally responds immediately, and doesn't go off to do "research" as did Student P. But sometimes Student T sometimes does carry the issues away to think about them further. In the end, there may be no posting at all, or the content of the posting may have improved due to the reflection.

> K: Sometimes people say that they would go and they'd have an idea of something they'd want to say but they'd want to go away and think about it a little bit before they'd come back and write it. But then maybe by the time they'd come back and write it, somebody else had written something to the same effect. Did you ever have that experience?
>
> Student Z: Maybe once or twice. Not too regularly. I usually try to like if I had something good , a good idea to post, I usually try to like, we were doing like group annotations or something I try to do it before the rest of my group so I could have what I already had, but like in the open forum it ended up a lot like that, kinda like I'd get there and I'm like, I see what it's been said and I try to think of something to add and I go and I come back and it's already been added.

Student Z sees a benefit in getting a posting in before the rest of "my group," but "maybe once or twice," Student Z did go off to think about the posting before making it.

Relating in-class and on-line activities

In all the CSCL studies cited, the CSCL environment is an extension of the class, an additional place to carry on discussion—or not. We found in our interviews a student who used the on-line space to gain additional perspectives on class discussion, and another student who said that he didn't post in the on-line space because all the issues were already discussed in-class.

> K: If you could just look at this and see if you can remember when you looked at it and why you didn't post anything.

> Student Z: Trying to remember…the majority of the time, when I looked at a page I was also trying to get other ideas from what the class was doing. See how the class was responding to things. 'cause usually from that, the class would pick up on attitudes of the teacher, and stuff like that; that way I can gear myself towards the teacher, 'cause every teacher you write to is different, had completely different writing style than I did in high school, and sometimes when I can go through, I can pick up other ideas and other views of things that are brought up in class, 'cause I think this was on like the open forum, and from that I can kinda understand what other people were thinking, and possibly get an idea of where the teacher wants us to go with things.
>
> K: Ok, so you're kind of using this as kind of an extension of class, in a way, and a way of getting information, more than as a forum for you to necessarily to put stuff out there.
>
> Student Z: Yeah, I probably looked over it and had an idea of something I could have posted but it just ended up that I looked over it and read it all and then kinda looked through it and tried to understand what everybody was thinking and then maybe I thought of something to post but I couldn't get it out or you know, different things happen at different times but I think with this one, I was just interested in what the class was saying, really.

Student Z is saying that he uses the on-line space to get a sense of the attitudes and ideas of the teacher (important for grading) and of the class overall, to better understand the class discussion. The role of the CSCL environment is not just a place to collaborate, but a place to gain perspective on other aspects of the class: Classroom discussion, and what the teacher is looking for on assignments. Benchmarking and understanding the unwritten assumptions are tasks that students struggle with in any class, and CSCL can help with these.

> K: Would there ever be a time when something would come up for you and maybe you wouldn't write it down but maybe it would be something you would think about and bring up in class, talk about in class later on?
>
> Student T: Not really, because generally we talk about it in class before we do the Open Forum thing, a lot of times. Except for a few subjects which, I think some of it was like the election and talking about monopolies and stuff, we generally talked about most of the stuff in class before, so most of the things I would have brought up in class I probably would have already said so instead of just waiting for the Open Forum. And so the Open Forum was just generally an afterthought type thing.

Student T is saying that one of the reasons why he doesn't post is because he feels that the discussion has already occurred in class.

The point of this hypothesis is that looking at the dialogue in the CSCL environment is only looking at part of a larger, multi-faceted story. A low rate of dialogue in the CSCL environment may imply that students are focusing at least some of their attention on classroom discussion, on completing assignments, or on some other learning activity in the class. The CSCL environment may serve as effective *support* for these other activities, thus explaining why learning may be occurring without a high rate of dialogue.

CONCLUSION: MULTIPLE PATHS TO LEARNING

We know from Roschelle and Jeong & Chi that learning can arise from collaboration. We know from Miyake & Masukawa, Hoadley & Linn, and Rick, et al that learning is occurring in computer-supported collaborative learning environments, even though the dialogue doesn't look much like what Roschelle and Jeong & Chi describe. In this paper, we have offered several explanations for where the learning may be coming from, despite the low rates of dialogue.

- Learning arises from the construction of a shared understanding, but students don't have to participate if others represent their questions and explanations.
- Learning arises from the inquiry and reflection triggered by ideas in the forum and the possibility of posting, even if no posting ever occurs.
- Learning arises from the set of activities in a classroom, and the CSCL environment is one support for those activities.

We see all three of these as likely, even among the same students in the same class, as seen in our interviews. In face-to-face classrooms, students learn from discussions, from hands-on activities, from reading, and even from listening to lectures. Learning in a CSCL environment is probably similar, with a variety of mechanisms leading to learning.

This paper is only presenting three possible hypotheses—there are probably others. The evidence for these hypotheses is weak—simply the comments of a small number of students in interviews. Identifying the hypotheses, however, is useful so that some may be further explored, developed into theory, and applied toward better design activities and environments that facilitate learning. Important next steps are to identify other hypotheses and to develop better evidence for explanations such as these for how learning is occurring in CSCL environments with low rates of dialogue.

ACKNOWLEDGMENTS

Funding for the CoWeb project is from the National Science Foundation Grant #REC-9814770 and the Mellon Foundation. Our thanks to our collaborators Barbara Ericson, Lissa Holloway-Attaway, Brandy Walker, Jim Greenlee, Joshua Gargus, Colleen Kehoe, Jochen Rick, Bolot Kerimbaev, and Kayt Sukel.

REFERENCES

Ackerman, M. S. (1994). Augmenting the organizational memory: A field study of Answer Garden. In R. Furuta & C. Neuwirth (Eds.), *Proceedings of CSCW'94* (pp. 243-252). Chapel Hill, NC: ACM.

Cohen, E. G. (1994). Restructing the classroom: Conditions for productive small groups. *Review of Educational Research, 64*(1), 3-35.

Davis, J. R., & Huttenlocher, D. P. (1995). Shared Annotation for Cooperative Learning. In J. L. Schnase & E. L. Cunnius (Eds.), *CSCL'95 Proceedings* (pp. 84-88). Bloomington, IN: Lawrence Erlbaum and Associates.

Dewey, J. (1901). *Psychology and Social Practice.* Chicago, IL: University of Chicago Press.

Ericsson, K. A., & Simon, H. (1980). Verbal reports as data. *Psychological Review, 87*, 215-251.

Guzdial, M. (1997). Information ecology of collaborations in educational settings: Influence of tool. In R. Hall, N. Miyake, & N. Enyedy (Eds.), *Proceedings of Computer-Supported Collaborative Learning'97* (pp. 83-90). Toronto, Ontario, Canada.

Hewitt, J., & Teplovs, C. (1999). An analysis of growth patterns in computer conferencing threads. In C. Hoadley & J. Roschelle (Eds.), *Proceedings of the Computer Support for Collaborative Learning (CSCL) 1999 Conference* (Vol. December 12-15, Stanford University, Palo Alto, CA,). Mahwah, NJ: Lawrence Erlbaum Associates.

Hoadley, C., & Linn, M. (2000). Teaching science through online, peer discussions: SpeakEasy in the Knowledge Integration Environment. *International Journal of Science Education, 22*(8), 839-857.

Jeong, H., & Chi, M. T. H. (1997). Construction of shared knowledge during collaborative learning. In R. Hall, N. Miyake, & N. Enyedy (Eds.), *Proceedings of Computer-Supported Collaborative Learning'97* (pp. 124-128). Toronto, Ontario, Canada.

Lee, J., Dineen, F., McKendree, J., & Mayes, T. (1999). Vicarious Learning: cognitive and linguistic effects of observing peer discussions : Presented at American Educational Research Association, AERA '99, Montreal, Quebec, Canada.

McKendree, J., Stenning, K., Mayes, T., Lee, J., & Cox, R. (1998). Why observing a dialogue may benefit learning. *Journal of Computer Assisted Learning, 14*(2), 110-119.

Miyake, N., & Masukawa, H. (2000). Relation-making to sense-making: Supporting college students' constructive understanding with an enriched collaborative note-sharing system. In B. Fishman & S. O'Connor-Divelbiss (Eds.), *Fourth International Conference of the Learning Sciences* (pp. 41-47). Mahwah, NJ: Lawrence Erlbaum Associates.

Rick, J., Guzdial, M., Carroll, K., Holloway-Attaway, L., & Walker, B. (2002). Collaborative learning at low cost: CoWeb use in English Composition, *Proceedings of the Computer Supported Collaborative Learning 2002* (pp. Submitted). Mahwah, NJ: Lawrence Erlbaum Associates.

Roschelle, J. (1992). Learning by Collaborating: Convergent Conceptual Change. *Journal of the Learning Sciences, 2*(3), 235-276.

Scardamalia, M., Bereiter, C., & Lamon, M. (1994). The CSILE Project: Trying to bring the classroom into World 3. In K. McGilly (Ed.), *Classroom Lessons: Integrating Cognitive Theory and Classroom Practice* (pp. 201-228). Cambridge, Mass.: MIT Press.

Terveen, L., & Hill, W. (1998). Evaluating emergent collaboration on the Web. In S. Poltrock & J. Grudin (Eds.), *Proceedings CSCW98* (pp. 355-362). Seattle, Washington, US: ACM.

Supporting Interaction Outside of Class: Anchored Discussions vs. Discussion Boards

A.J. Bernheim Brush[+]*, David Bargeron[+], Jonathan Grudin[+], Alan Borning*, Anoop Gupta[+]

Microsoft Research[+], {davemb, jgrudin, anoop}@microsoft.com

University of Washington* {ajb, borning}@cs.washington.edu

ABSTRACT

Newsgroups and online discussion boards have long been used to supplement class discussions. We describe a study comparing the use of two systems, WebAnn and EPost, to support class discussion of technical papers in a graduate course. WebAnn is a shared annotation system that supports anchored discussions on web pages, and allows users to easily associate comments with a particular paragraph, phrase, or word in the paper being discussed. EPost is a high-quality conventional discussion board system. In our study, students contributed almost twice as much to the online discussion using WebAnn. WebAnn also encouraged a different discussion style, focused on specific points in the paper. We expected WebAnn discussions to serve as a starting point for in-depth discussions in the classroom; but in fact, online discussions often competed with classroom discussions. We conclude with implications of the study for technology design and the process of its use.

Keywords

Annotations, online discussion forums, computer-mediated communication, educational technology

INTRODUCTION

Students and instructors are spending more time online. Many see this as a significant opportunity to encourage more educational interaction outside the classroom. Tools that support asynchronous collaboration hold potential as a convenient, flexible means of doing just that. Various systems, for instance online discussion boards, have long supplemented class discussions, but their use typically has been limited and optional, because not all students were assumed to have access to a system or the skills to use it. Today these restrictions are fading away, and we can harness the increasing ubiquity of online access and tools to promote educational discussion beyond the classroom door. But what is the best way to proceed?

Tools that support asynchronous collaboration allow discussion to happen when and where it is convenient, and help link what goes on outside of class while students do homework to what goes on in class. For instance, students can begin to discuss a reading assignment *while they are reading it,* instead of taking notes and waiting until they get to the classroom to express their reactions.

Online discussion boards have supported this in the past, but discussion board posts are divorced from the context of the assignment. To contribute a comment or question students must manually reconstruct the context of their remark before making it. That is, they must identify not only the paper or document being discussed, but perhaps also the section, paragraph, sentence, or word. Only after this is done can a discussion thread ensue. Further, the resulting discussion will not be readily available to other students as they read the paper.

Our shared annotation system, WebAnn, takes a different approach. It supports fine-grained annotation of web pages, so that students' remarks can be made and seen in the context that inspired them. Furthermore, annotations are shared, and can serve as anchors for threaded discussions. In this way, discussions around class material outside of class are captured for all to see, *and* they are directly linked to the materials—and the precise location within the materials—that they reference. This paper presents a study we conducted to evaluate the efficacy of WebAnn for supporting ongoing discussion outside of class.

The process of use that we envision for WebAnn is as follows. A student reads a paper on-line, and can at any point identify some text and type in a comment or question. This annotation then appears alongside in a separate frame with a visual indication of the associated text. It can either be a personal note or an entry in a public class discussion. The student will also see annotations left in the class discussion by previous readers, and can reply to those. With this facility questions can be asked or answered, opinions made known, issues identified, and discussions started. Using the WebAnn system, students can more easily participate in discussions of class materials, and discussion outside the classroom will flourish.

At least, that was the theory. To put our hypothesis to the test, we conducted a study in a graduate university course comparing WebAnn with EPost, a high quality discussion board system (EPost, 2001). The course focused on lectures and discussions of published research papers, and student assignments included making comments on the readings using the two systems. The study provided many insights into the value and appropriate uses of tools for support of discussion outside the classroom. For a variety of reasons, including access and the granularity of the discussion, student preference appears to slightly favor EPost. However, students contributed almost twice as much to the discussion using WebAnn. The nature of the class discussion was affected in ways not anticipated by the class or instructor. Based on our results we identified enhancements that will improve WebAnn, as well as important considerations for the process of using it.

The remainder of the paper is organized as follows. The next section briefly reviews related work. Then we describe the salient features of the WebAnn and EPost systems. We then outline the study we conducted to assess the efficacy of WebAnn in promoting discussion outside of class, and present the results. Finally, we discuss some of the implications of our findings, and provide some concluding remarks.

RELATED WORK

In this section we focus primarily on systems studied in an educational context. Word processors and co-authoring tools have gradually added commenting and revision features, although they are not yet as convenient as pen and paper. WebAnn incorporates some features of these systems. Like the commenting feature in Word, WebAnn allows comments to be attached to specific words or passages and it supports the viewing of the annotations and the original document in a single window. In contrast, CaMILE (Guzdial & Turns, 2000), Col•laboració (Col•laboració, 2001), and CoNote (Davis & Huttenlocher, 1995) support coarser granularities of context, with anchors to a threaded discussion of an entire web page or a section of a page or document. The first displays comments below the text, the second embeds a link to the discussion in the page, and the third is a discussion board in which a thread contains a link to the object being discussed. As our study indicates, tradeoffs affect design decisions regarding annotation granularity and presentation of source material. One solution may not be ideal for every setting. WebAnn allows us to explore the way people respond to the ability to identify precisely the context for a comment.

The intended user of annotation systems varies. Many systems that provide anchored comments or discussions, such as Quilt (Leland et. al, 1988), Prep (Neuwirth et. al, 1990) and Col•laboració, are intended to support co-authoring. The authoring and editing process is also a principal focus of commenting with Word (Cadiz et. al, 2000), which in its most recent versions supports anchored discussion threads. While WebAnn could be used for authoring and editing, in this paper we focus on its use for commenting.

In the educational context, bulletin boards and chats and other real-time communication systems have been used in distance education and to supplement face-to-face classes. In contrast to our study, studies of anchored online annotation systems have primarily focused on editing and commenting on student or instructor work. Hewitt and Teplovs (1999) is a nice study of the use of one such discussion board, CSILE, across many courses. In a study of CoNote (Davis & Huttenlocher, 1995), students were required to use the system to comment on project sites constructed by 3 others sets of students. CaMILE (Guzdial & Turns, 2000) was used to discuss short descriptions of assignments and review outlines for exams. The Collaboratory Notebook / CoVis system (O'Neill et. al, 1995) includes student-created notebooks on which instructors commented, as well as discussion boards.

One exception is CLARE (Wan & Johnson, 1994), in which a tool is used collaboratively to analyze scientific papers online through the creation of a highly structured hypertext of labeled annotations describing portions of the text as problems, claims, evidence, theory, concepts, and so forth. It also allows more general annotations categorized as critiques, suggestions, and questions. The interface and process of use of CLARE is very different from that of WebAnn: it is not first and foremost a discussion. Students first privately analyze the text, then view each other's analyses, at which point they can comment by creating new links. Threads are not presented visually. However, CLARE resembles WebAnn in the way that it anchors annotations on online representations of core course content.

Anchoring and context in education are used in a different sense in the anchored instruction paradigm developed by the CTGV group (CTGV, 1993). They discuss using materials such as videos to anchor assignments in the context of students' daily lives. We focus on anchoring discussions in the context of the text being discussed.

DISCUSSION SYSTEMS

In this section, we describe WebAnn, the online discussion system we implemented, and EPost, a discussion board that is part of the UW Catalyst toolkit.

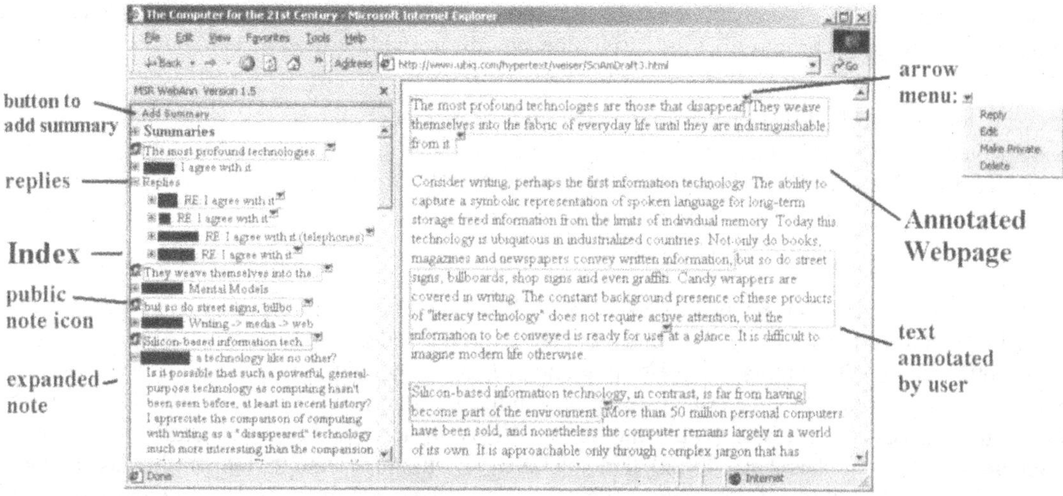

Figure 1: WebAnn interface embedded in Internet Explorer. On the right is the webpage being annotated, on the left is the index of notes and replies. Student names are blacked out to provide anonymity.

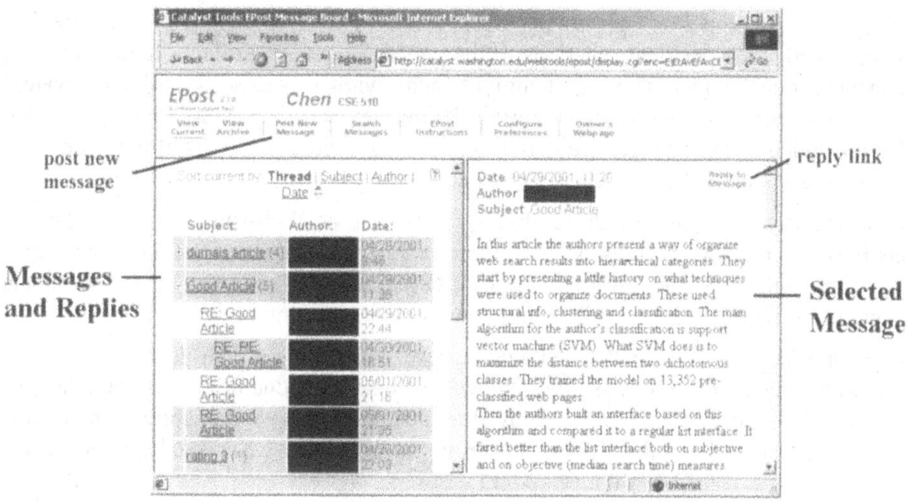

Figure 2: EPost, a threaded discussion board from the UW Catalyst toolkit. The left pane is the index of posts and replies. The right pane is the text of the selected message. Student names are again blacked out.

WebAnn

WebAnn allows text annotation on any web page. It is designed to support shared persistent threaded discussions that occur in a precise context. WebAnn is embedded in Microsoft Internet Explorer, and can be easily installed on any computer running Windows 2000. As shown in Figure 1, the web page being annotated is displayed on the right, and discussions on the page are shown in the index window on the left. WebAnn is adapted from an earlier system we built to experiment with robust annotations on web pages (Brush et. al, 2001).

To create a new note, a user selects the text to be annotated and chooses to "Add a Note" from a popup menu. A dialog box appears, into which the user types the note. The user can optionally make the note private. The new note is added to the index, and the text to which it corresponds in the page is outlined with a color unique to that user. Annotations are automatically made persistent in an internet-based annotation store.

Once an annotation has been created, it is available as a navigational aid in both the index and the page, so that clicking on it in the index, for instance, scrolls the web page until the outlined text is in view. Later on, the user can go back and edit or delete his or her notes (provided they do not have replies). To add a global note that applies to the entire web page, the user clicks the "Add Summary" button and follows the same procedure.

Threaded discussions grow when users reply to existing notes. To reply to a note, a user clicks the arrow menu next to the note (either in the index or the web page) and chooses "Reply." Replies are added to the index directly below the original note.

EPost

EPost, a University of Washington (UW) "Catalyst" tool (EPost, 2001), is a high-quality web-based threaded discussion board similar to a traditional newsgroup browser. EPost discussion boards are widely used at UW, and can be accessed using any HTML browser.

As shown in Figure 2, the left side of the EPost interface lists the original messages and replies, while the contents of the selected message is displayed on the right. To post a message, the user clicks on the "Post New Message" link at the top left, and to reply on the "Reply to Message" link. EPost supports several useful features, including filtering and notification options. For the class we studied, an EPost discussion board was created for each reviewed paper.

STUDY

To examine the tradeoffs between discussions anchored in-context and traditional discussion boards, we compared the use of WebAnn and EPost in a graduate-level Human-Computer Interaction (HCI) class taught at University of Washington during Spring Quarter, 2001. Two of the authors, Alan Borning and A.J. Brush, taught the course and served as teaching assistant (TA). In general, we wanted to assess the efficacy of WebAnn for promoting discussion outside of class and to see how this affected subsequent discussion in class. Would the use of WebAnn increase the overall amount and quality of discussion and participation? Other studies have found that anchored discussions lead to longer threads and greater participation (Guzdial & Turns, 2000). Beyond this, would WebAnn engage students more by encouraging more specific and pointed comments and stimulate more engaging discussion in class? We expected that the online and in-class discussions would be complementary, since the online discussion could be used to inform the in-class discussion.

Study Design

During the class students were assigned to read 2 or 3 papers per week as homework. For each paper, students wrote a brief review with two parts: a summary and some personal reactions to the paper. Students were also required to respond to at least one other student's comments for each paper. The total length of each review was expected to be equivalent to two or three paragraphs, and students could skip up to five reviews during the quarter. Reviews were 25% of a student's course grade, and it was expected that all students would receive full credit for them. Previous offerings of the course were similar, except for the requirement to post a reply to another student's comment.

This assignment format is a particularly good one for discussion systems such as WebAnn and EPost. To submit paper reviews using EPost, students posted a message containing both their summary and comments, and then replied to other students' posts. With WebAnn, students used the "Add Summary" button for the summary, and then anchored their comments and reactions throughout the paper by adding note annotations and at least one reply.

The class met Mondays and Wednesdays for 80 minutes. Student reviews were due on Tuesday at noon, and responses were due before class on Wednesday. We planned to make the reviews and responses due before the Monday class, but the inability of some students to access WebAnn from home forced the later due dates. Six women and five men enrolled in the class. Four students were from Computer Science; the others were from the Information School, Psychology, and Medical Informatics. One student was an employee of the UW library system.

The class alternated between using EPost and WebAnn in two-week blocks. During the 10 week quarter, students spent at least 4 weeks using each system, with an extra week on EPost at the beginning of the quarter and a final week of presentations when there were no paper reviews. On WebAnn weeks all papers were available in html to enable online annotation.

We fixed basic WebAnn problems and released two new versions during the first two weeks of its use, focused on improved annotation loading and rendering speed. For the final two weeks of WebAnn use, we introduced a version supporting direct editing of annotations (rather than having to manually delete and re-create a note to change it).

Data Collection

We archived the online discussion forums and surveyed students each week. An initial survey collected background information, and a final survey asked about their overall experience with in-class and online discussion. One author (not the instructor or TA) interviewed eight students at the end of the quarter.

Method	Number of Papers	Number of Messages	Messages Per Paper	Average Messages Per Author Per Paper	Average Replies Per Author Per Paper	Average Character Contribution Per Author Per Paper
EPost	13	299	23	2.23	1.15	2485
WebAnn	12	470	39.2	4.71	1.58	4401

Table 1: Student participation using EPost and WebAnn.

RESULTS

Online discussions easily exceeded the required participation level. WebAnn activity differed substantially from EPost discussion. One significant observation is that all students printed out and read paper versions of papers. This removes important potential advantages of WebAnn and affects its use and reception. Despite this, WebAnn was used more than EPost and the pattern of use provides guidance to the design and use of anchored annotation systems.

More participation using WebAnn

As we expected, the ability to anchor comments precisely led to more comments in WebAnn weeks, given that students would be likely to concatenate comments in EPost threads. Table 1 shows key per-author participation statistics using the systems. Using WebAnn, there was an average of 39 comments per paper, with EPost 23. Several students also remarked on the increase in survey responses. For example, "*I made more comments with WebAnn. With EPost I was disinclined to make minor or very contextual points—the kind it is easy to do with WebAnn. I also think I wrote more replies in WebAnn because it was easy to do so (and easy to see the context).*"

Students also replied more when using WebAnn. With EPost, the average number of reply messages per author in each discussion board was 1.15 (most students made only the one required response per discussion forum). Using WebAnn, authors averaged 1.58 replies per paper. A paired-samples t-test showed the averages were significantly different with $p < 0.03$. In fact, 8 out of the 11 students made more replies using WebAnn than using EPost. One student averaged a remarkable 3.33 replies per paper using WebAnn, and only 1.5 with EPost.

While we thought WebAnn annotations might be short, since students would not need to reconstruct the context for each comment, we were not sure how the total participation per student would vary since students would probably make more posts using WebAnn. We found that students wrote almost twice as much with WebAnn. Each student wrote an average of 4,401 characters per paper using WebAnn, compared to 2,485 characters per paper using EPost. These are significantly different based on a paired t-test ($p < 0.001$). Although increased participation in discussion does not necessarily imply enhanced learning, grades in this class included participation and there were no exams, so increased participation was considered a positive outcome.

General vs. Specific Discussion

The two systems support very different types of discussions. EPost discussion boards are completely separated from the paper being discussed, while WebAnn discussions are anchored directly to specific parts of the paper. As we expected, these differences affected the type of online discussion that occurred in the two systems, and this was reflected in student survey responses. For instance, one student observed that with WebAnn it was "*More difficult to make high level comments about [the] paper, [and] discussions usually focused on sentences or paragraphs ...*" and another noted that with EPost "*It's definitely harder to make pointed comments about these papers.*" In response to the final survey, one student said "*I think the comments were at a higher level in the E-Post system and more general opinions were presented*" and another said "*...the comments were more specific and numerous [with WebAnn]. I think this is because I could transfer notes I'd made on paper and section of text I'd highlighted directly to the annotation software.*"

Although the preference for more general or more specific discussions varied, many students observed that WebAnn led to more thoughtful, involved discussions. For instance, one student observed "*More scattered, but more insightful comments in WebAnn,*" while another saw "*More involved discussion—more back and forth,*" and a third said "*I think the quality of annotations and online discussion [with WebAnn] was better than with E-Post.*"

Week	1	2	3	4	5	6	7	8	9
System	EPost	EPost	EPost	WebAnn	WebAnn	EPost	EPost	WebAnn	WebAnn
1. Discussions in class were valuable	5 (11)	5 (11)	5 (11)	5 (10)	5 (10)	5 (10)	5 (11)	4 (9)	5 (6)
2. Online Discussions outside of class were valuable	4.5 (10)	5 (11)	4 (11)	4 (10)	5 (9)	4 (11)	4 (11)	4 (10)	3 (5)+
3. The review method [software] was beneficial to my learning	4 (9)	5 (11)	4 (11)	3 (10)	4 (9)	4 (11)	3 (11)	4 (10)	3 (5)+
4. I prefer this reading review method	*N/A**	*N/A**	*N/A**	2 (8)	3 (8)	4 (11)	4 (11)	3 (10)	5 (6)

Table 2: Median student ratings on a selection of questions from the weekly surveys. (1 is Strongly Disagree, 6 is Strongly Agree). Numbers of students who responded to a question are in (). *N/A**: There was not yet a basis for comparison. +Only 4 students participated in the online discussion this week, which may have impacted the ratings.

Student Preferences

Table 2 shows median student ratings on several key questions from the weekly survey. The ratings are on a 6 point Likert scale where 1 is "Strongly Disagree" and 6 is "Strongly Agree." Table 3 shows the median student ratings for key questions from the final survey, also on a 6 point scale where 1 is "Low" and 6 "High," except for question 6 where 1 is "Disagree" and 6 "Agree." Only the ratings for amount of time spent on software in Table 3 (concerning software trouble) were significantly different between the two systems based on paired sign test ($p < 0.02$).

Value of Discussion

In general, students gave high ratings to the value of discussions both in class and online throughout the course, and there is little quantitative distinction in the value of discussion supported by the two systems. In surveys and interviews students commented more specifically on the value of online discussion. Some examples: *"[online discussion] made the discussion [in class] a lot more interesting," "since they [online comments] are written, they are definitely more composed," "[through online discussion I] got to know people's opinions, the people who aren't as vocal in class,...having the online discussion encouraged everyone to participate in-class as well,"* and *"there were a couple of people who often dominated the class conversation, but they wouldn't dominate the online discussion because everyone got a change to talk."*

Finally, two interesting ratings from Table 2 are the 3's given to WebAnn in week 9 for questions 2 and 3. In this week, most students used their paper skips and only 4 students participated in the online discussion. This affected satisfaction with online discussion. One student commented: *"It's really boring when no one says anything."*

System Preference

Based on their subjective ratings, students preferred EPost slightly overall. However, with only 11 students the data are inconclusive, and individual student preferences varied. Table 2, question 4, illustrates that WebAnn preference ratings started low and rose over time. This may reflect the improved versions of WebAnn that were introduced. Table 3, question 6 shows that on the final survey both EPost and WebAnn received the same median rating, despite having encountered more technical and access problems with the WebAnn software. However, comparing a particular student's ratings of the two systems, for example, if they rated EPost a 4 and WebAnn a 3, we obtain more information: 5 students preferred EPost, 3 preferred WebAnn, and 3 had no preference. In this regard it is useful to keep in mind that by reading printed copies of papers, students lost the advantages of annotating and seeing comments of others as they first read a paper and were thus reacting primarily to the discussion features.

Comments on the final survey indicated that preferences for a particular method were based on a range of factors, including access and perceived quality and granularity of the discussions. Favoring the EPost system, one student said "*I didn't have [a]* preference. *[The] only issue was that I could use EPost at home.*" Another expressed a

System	1. "The quality of the online discussion was"	2. " My satisfaction with this method of online discussion"	3. "The quality of the in-class discussion was"	4. "My satisfaction with the in-class discussion"	5. "The amount of time I spent on problems with the software"*	6. "Overall I prefer this method"
EPost	4	5	4	4	1	4
WebAnn	4	4	5	4	4	4

Table 3: Median student ratings on questions from the final survey. For the first 5 questions 1 is Low, 6 is High. For question 6, 1 is Disagree, 6 is Agree. *The only significant difference is for question 5.

> "*slight preference for EPost because it allowed for more articulation of complete ideas/thoughts.*" A third observed that "*It was easier to understand other student's opinions by reading all their comments in a single message. Also, I think the comments were at a higher level in the EPost system and more general opinions were presented.*"

In favor of WebAnn, one student said "*I prefer WebAnn (later versions) over EPost. I think the quality of annotations and online discussion was better than with EPost. WebAnn allowed us to comment on specific portions of text, which was nice...*" and another observed that WebAnn was useful because students "*can comment on particular parts of the paper easily...*"

ISSUES AND OPTIONS

Based on the survey ratings and comments, most students felt that online discussion helped the live discussion start quickly and gave it focus. The online discussion space also provided an outlet for students who said less in class, and overall increased class participation. In addition to these successes, though, we learned a number of important lessons about incorporating online discussion into a class. We start by describing some of the major issues we encountered, then we discuss potential changes in technology and process that would help address them.

Student and Instructor Workload: In general, incorporating online discussion into the class created more work for the students and instructor by requiring everyone to keep track and participate in the online discussion at some level.

Although some students felt WebAnn led to more thoughtful online discussions, and clearly it resulted in more extensive online discussions, WebAnn required students to do more work to post their reviews. As noted above, although all papers for WebAnn discussion were made available in html format, all students printed them out to read. To enter WebAnn comments they had to go back and annotate the papers online. One student commented: "*I found WebAnn much more time-consuming to use, perhaps because I prefer to read on paper, and then had to go back through to do the annotations.*"

Should professors or teaching assistants participate online beyond reading or leave it as a space for students? We observed both, and each has advantages and disadvantages. In our study the instructor and TA generally participated very little (3 posts in EPost, 5 in WebAnn) beyond reading all messages. This was less work for the instructors and allowed students to take the lead, but meant questions could go unanswered or issues left undeveloped. One guest lecturer in a WebAnn week addressed most questions and issues students raised online, an approach used successfully for design reviews of student assignments using CoWeb (Guzdial et. al, 2000). Students seemed to appreciate the responses. One advantage of having the instructor, the TA, or even an expert in the field respond to students is that it may encourage students to go back and read through the comments. On the other hand, students may avoid controversial points if an author or known expert will reading them. In this case, one student deleted or edited one or more comments when he realized the paper author (the guest lecturer) might read them.

Online and in-class discussion: Before the study, we saw the online discussion as a complement to the in-class discussion, leading to a more engaging classroom discussion focused on issues raised online. Each week after student reviews and comments were due, the instructor and TA read all the comments and replies. The TA also created a list of interesting issues and comments to start in-class discussion if necessary. Some students found this helpful, but others commented: "*...[it would] be more effective if there were some way to better integrate online discussion with in-class discussion,*" and "*[class time] was redundant.*" Smoothly integrating the two was more challenging than we expected. In a sense, in-class and online discussion competed with one another.

Integrating online and in-class discussions was complicated by the timing of the online discussion and the differing amounts of participation in the online discussion (both posting and reading comments). Because weekly reviews were due Tuesday and replies were due Wednesday just prior to class, the time for students to read through responses was limited, a problem exacerbated by the fact that some could access the system only from home or from work. If a reply was added shortly before class it was unlikely that many students would read it. This negatively impacted the in-class discussion. A student who made a long or complicated reply on-line might not want to repeat it in class, even when asked to by the professor. As a result, interesting replies were not always picked up in class.

Differences in time commitments and interest levels led to varying student participation online, which could take a fair amount of time. Students who participated online often seemed uninterested in continuing that discussion for those who had not participated online. In one instance, following a spirited WebAnn discussion among six students, the professor tried to bring up the issue in class for further discussion. One student said there had already been a "*pretty good discussion on [the] board.*" This comment, along with others like it, ended the classroom discussion on the topic. The students who had participated online saw no need to discuss the topic further.

Global and specific comments: With WebAnn it was easy to make or understand focused comments but awkward to make general notes about large sections or even long paragraphs. Conversely, EPost required considerable context to comment on a particular point. Each tool readily supported one type of comment. The ideal tool would facilitate comments at multiple levels.

Focus of Attention: Online discussion systems face a tradeoff between focusing attention on threaded comments or on the document being discussed. CoNote (Davis & Huttenlocher, 1995) places links to content in threaded discussions; CaMILE (Guzdial & Turns, 2000) places links to discussion in content. WebAnn splits the focus between comments and document. (With EPost, only comments are viewed.) In the interviews, some students noted this tradeoff and suggested that more space be devoted to comment threads. When reading the document and making comments the document might be the focus, but these students did most reading on paper. When reviewing others' comments and replying, the comments might better be the focus. In fact students could adjust the size of the frames in WebAnn, but did not discover this.

Discussion overload: When examining student participation in the online discussion we found they contributed much more during the WebAnn weeks. While this suggests that anchored discussions in WebAnn encourage students to participate more, some students remarked that the number of comments and replies was overwhelming. Clearly, this could become an even larger problem with bigger classes. EPost discussions could also be problematic with large numbers of participants. This tradeoff between encouraging student participation in online discussions and keeping online discussions a "manageable size" has also been noted by Guzdial and Turns (2000).

Convenient universal access: As other studies have found, convenient access is critically important (Hmelo et. al, 1997). We were initially concerned with making sure all students had some access to WebAnn, which runs only on Windows 2000. However, it turned out that *where* students had access was also important. With EPost, 9 of the 11 students had access both at school and home. Using WebAnn, although all students had access either at home or school, only two students had access in both places. With access in only one location, students were limited in when and where they could do their reviews and participate in the online discussion.

Improvements to WebAnn

The subjective ratings and comments suggest the majority of students had a small preference for EPost, even though they contributed more using WebAnn. Factors including access, workload, software use, and different types of discussion seem to influence students. In this section we focus on technical improvements to WebAnn, or any other online discussion system, that might address issues raised by the field study.

Access: Making access as universal as possible by supporting more operating systems and browsers would enable students to review the discussion more often from more locations, and might improve participation in making and reading comments. Adding an offline mode would also help students with slower internet connections.

A more sophisticated solution might allow comments and replies to be sent through e-mail in addition to being added as web page annotations. When students did not have access to the annotation system, they would still receive annotations in e-mail. Replying to the e-mail would add their response to the online discussion. The MRAS video annotation system found this approach successful in a number of studies (Bargeron et al., 2001).

Filtering and Notification: Several students suggested adding filtering that exists in EPost to WebAnn: author-based filtering and identifying notes and replies that are new. Mechanisms that assist in quickly finding replies to a person's comments and highlight potentially interesting discussions based on collaborative filtering, perhaps by allowing students to rate each others' posts, could further reduce discussion overhead and student workload, making it easier to keep up with the online discussion.

Although EPost can notify students of the presence of new posts, only 3 students subscribed to this for one week of the study, suggesting a need for improvement. Notifications could summarize the comments made that day, rather than just alerting a student to the fact that comments were made. This could provide a sense of the ongoing discussion and encourage checking online for the full comments. Notification messages could include clickable links to take a student directly to the online discussion (Bargeron et al., 2001). Finally, an optional feature that notifies a note's author when someone replies could encourage more back and forth discussions.

Advanced notifications features have the potential to allow students to follow the online discussion more easily. This could support easier integration of online and in-class discussions, reduce student and instructor workload, and help students deal more effectively with discussions containing a large number of comments.

Supporting General Comments: Students wanted to add comments at many different levels, from general comments about an entire paper to specific comments on a particular issue. To better support online discussions, WebAnn needs a mechanism for easily commenting on larger document units, including paragraphs, sections, and the entire paper. Softening the display of anchors in the web page, perhaps with vertical lines in the margin instead of outlining the text, might make users more willing to overlap comments. More ambitiously, mechanisms for clearly supporting comments at every level of the document could be provided, perhaps through menu items that specify "comment on this document," "comment on this section," and so forth.

Allocating Screen Space: As noted above, the interface should clearly indicate that the annotation and document frames can be resized to accommodate a focus on threaded comments or a focus on the content.

Process Changes

Along with technological improvements, careful consideration of the process of use might smooth the experience of combining online and in-class discussions.

More time for reviews: It would have benefited students to have all online discussion before the first class of the week, and to have the review and replies due earlier to provide more time before class discussion for reading and responding. Scheduling class meetings for the end of the week could also address weekend access issues.

Summarize online discussion in-class: A short summary of the online discussion at the beginning of class might help cope with the different levels of on-line participation and frame an in-class discussion that builds on the online experience. Explicitly acknowledging students who took part in the online discussion could encourage other students to participate.

Consider instructor role: The pros and cons of active instructor participation online were noted above. On the whole, if instructors join the discussion late, it can provide an incentive for students to contribute to and review discussions. If online participation were not required—and some students felt mandatory replying to others' comments was artificial—this might be essential to motivate discussion.

Adjust the number of papers discussed online or in class: Using the online discussion for addressing fewer papers in more depth rather than for all the papers would reduce the amount of work. Dividing the papers into those that are discussed only on-line and those that are dealt with only in class would also reduce workload. Alternatively, classroom time could be focused more on other activities, such as demos and discussing student projects.

Reduce the number of students participating at any one time: To combat discussion overload, reduce workload, and help integrate online and in-class discussion, the number of messages students produce or read could be reduced. Students could be asked to comment on fewer papers, or participation could be made optional for large classes. Alternatively, students could be divided up into discussion groups, and each discussion group could briefly summarize in class what was discussed online, greatly reducing the number of messages a student must read.

Reduce assignments: Another approach for reducing student and instructor workload is to limit the number of assignments the students have, or to more dramatically reduce the time that is spent in-class. The broader issue is to consider what classes are best served by the technology. Possibly classes with less reading, (that students may be more likely to do online) would better exploit the value of anchored discussions. Or perhaps discussions could revolve around assignments and projects, which might have shorter blocks of text, as in Guzdial & Turns (2000).

CONCLUSION

Online anchored discussions hold great potential for extending in-class discussion beyond the classroom door. In our study, online discussions allowed the less vocal students to contribute equally and made in-class discussions more interesting, but integrating the online and in-class discussions was challenging. Rather than serving as a starting point for in-class discussions, the online discussions often competed with the classroom discussion. Students who participated frequently online seemed uninterested in addressing the same issues in-class with the rest of the students.

Because students in this class uniformly printed and read assignments on paper, many potential advantages in annotating in context were lost. Nevertheless, WebAnn led to more discussion, while requiring the greater effort of a second pass to add comments. With improvements in technology and appropriate process modifications, anchored discussions are an exciting avenue for distributed education and a viable tool to supplement classroom instruction.

ACKNOWLEDGMENTS

We are very grateful to the students in the class for participating in the study. We thank the UW Cataylst group, in particular Mark Alway, for their assistance. We also thank Cathy Marshall and Gina Venolia.

REFERENCES

Abowd, G., Pimetel, M., Kerimbaev, B., Ishiguro, Y., and Guzdial, M. (1999) Anchoring Discussions in Lecture: An Approach to Collaboratively Extending Classroom Digital Media. *Proc. CSCL 1999.*

Bargeron, D., Gupta, A., Grudin, J., Sanocki, E., and Li, F., (2001). Asynchronous collaboration around multimedia and its application to on-demand training. Proc. HICSS-34 Conference, CD-ROM.

Brush, A., Bargeron, D., Gupta, A., and Cadiz, J., (2001). Robust Annotation Positioning in Digital Documents. *Proc. CHI 2001*, 285-292.

Bullen, C.V., and Bennett, J.L. (1991) Groupware in Practice: An Interpretation of Work Experiences. Reprinted in Baecker, R.M. (Ed.) (1993) *Groupware and Computer-Supported Cooperative Work*, Morgan Kaufmann, 69-84.

Cadiz, J., Gupta, A., and Grudin, J., (2000) Using Web Annotations for Asynchronous Collaboration Around Documents. *Proc. CSCW 2000*, 309-318.

Collaboració, http://www.nada.kth.se/~henrry/Collaboracio.html

CTGV (1993) Anchored Instruction and situated cognition revisited. *Educational Technology*, 33 (3) 52-70.

Davis, J. and Huttenlocher, D. (1995) Shared Annotation for Cooperative Learning. *Proc. CSCL 1995*, 84-88.

EPost, UW Catalyst Toolkit, http://catalyst.washington.edu/tools/

Gay, G., Sturgill, A., Martin, W., and Huttenlocher, D. (1999) Document-centered Peer Collaborations: An Exploration of the Educational Uses of Networked Communication Technologies. *Journal of Computer-Mediated Communication,* **4**, 3, March 1999.

Guzdial, M. (1997) Information Ecology of Collaborations in Educational Setting: Influence of Tool. *Proc. CSCL 1997*, 83-90.

Guzdial, M. Rick, J., and Kerimbaaev, B. (2000) Recognizing and Supporting Roles in CSCW. *Proc. CSCW 2000*, 261-268.

Guzdial, M., & Turns, J. (2000) Effective discussion through a computer-mediated anchored forum. *Journal of the Learning Sciences*, **9**, 4, 437-470.

http://guzdial.cc.gatech.edu/papers/aera97/mbl.htmlHmelo, C. E., Guzdial, M., and Turns, J. (1997) Computer-support for collaborative learning: Learning to make it work. American Educational Research Association 1997 Annual Meeting, Chicago, Il. March 24-28. http://guzdial.cc.gatech.edu/papers/aera97/mbl.html

Hewitt, J. and Teplovs, C. (1999) An Analysis of Growth Patterns in Computer Conferencing Threads. *Proc. CSCL 1999,* 232-240.

Leland, M., Fish, R., and Kraut, R., (1988) Collaborative Document Production Using Quilt. *Proc. CSCW 1988,* 206-215.

Neuwirth, C., Kaufer, D., Chandhok, R., and Morris, J., (1990) Issues in the Design of Computer Support for Co-authoring and Commenting. *Proc. CSCW 1990*, 183-195.

O'Neill D.K., Edelson, D.C., Gomez, L.M., and D'Amico, L. (1995) Learning to Weave Collaborative Hypermedia into Classroom Practice. *Proc. CSCL 1996*, 255-258.

Wan, D., and Johnson, P. (1994) Computer Supported Collaborative Learning Using CLARE: The Approach and Experimental Findings. *Proc. CSCW 1994*, 187-198.

Collaborative Learning at Low Cost: CoWeb Use in English Composition

Jochen Rick, Mark Guzdial, Karen Carroll Lissa Holloway-Attaway, Brandy Walker

College of Computing / GVU Center School of Literature, Communication, and CultureGeorgia Institute of Technology Georgia Institute of Technology

{jochen.rick, guzdial, kcarroll}@cc.gatech.edu {lissa.holloway-attaway, brandy.walker}@lcc.gatech.edu

ABSTRACT

CoWeb is a collaborative learning environment used in many classes at Georgia Institute of Technology; it is an extremely simple domain-independent collaboration tool. Our aim is to show that such a simple system can sustain useful peer-to-peer and instructor-to-student interaction that fosters better performance and learning, without incurring a high cost. In this paper, we present evidence of the success of this tool in supporting learning at low cost in one environment—freshman-level English classes.

Keywords

CoWeb, low cost, close reading, English composition, collaborative learning

INTRODUCTION

In 1998, we introduced CoWeb (short for Collaborative Web-site) to Georgia Institute of Technology. Since then, we have been applying this simple collaboration technology to class contexts in different domains: architecture, computer science, mathematics, engineering, and English. Though we have developed a few specialized features, such as an equation editor to simplify sharing of mathematical equations, the CoWeb interface remains largely the same across these different domains.

This study examines the use of CoWeb in freshman-level English classes. In particular, we show both learning and cost effectiveness. By engaging students in collaboration, we can leverage the large numbers in classes to create greater opportunities for discussion, reflection, and (consequently) learning. Because the increased opportunity for learning is coming from the students themselves, the cost for the institution does not need to rise any further than simply providing oversight of the process. Thus, for relatively low costs (cost effectiveness), significant improvement can be made in class performance (learning effectiveness).

So, our use of CoWeb in English composition demonstrates that a simple and flexible collaboration tool can be effective for providing the benefit of collaborative learning while still being cost effective.

COWEB

CoWeb is conceptually based on the WikiWikiWeb* (or Wiki) by Ward Cunningham (Leuf & Cunningham, 2001). The Wiki is a web-site that invites all users to edit any page within the site and add new pages using only a common web browser; the text is edited in an HTML text area without special applets or plug-ins. The Wiki is an unusual collaboration space in its total freedom, ease of access and use, and lack of structure. The Wiki is inherently democratic—every user has exactly the same capabilities as any other user.

Like the Wiki, CoWeb looks like a fairly traditional web-site, except that every page has a set of buttons at the top that allow the user to do various things such as edit the page, (un)lock the page, or view the history of the page over time. Links between pages are easily created by referencing pages within the same site by name (e.g., *Page Name*). If a page with the given name doesn't already exist, a *create* link shows up next to the name upon save; clicking on this creates the new page (see Figure 1). CoWeb shares Wiki's democratic philosophy of equal power to all users. Though our usage is mostly set in classes, where there is someone in charge (the instructor), we find little reason to give more interface power to the instructor than to the students. The instructor naturally has social power that does not need to be reinforced by the interface. As one professor commented: "I just like the interaction that it enables. It's basically a whiteboard that everyone can write on. Protections are always kind of a pain."

* http://c2.com/cgi-bin/wiki

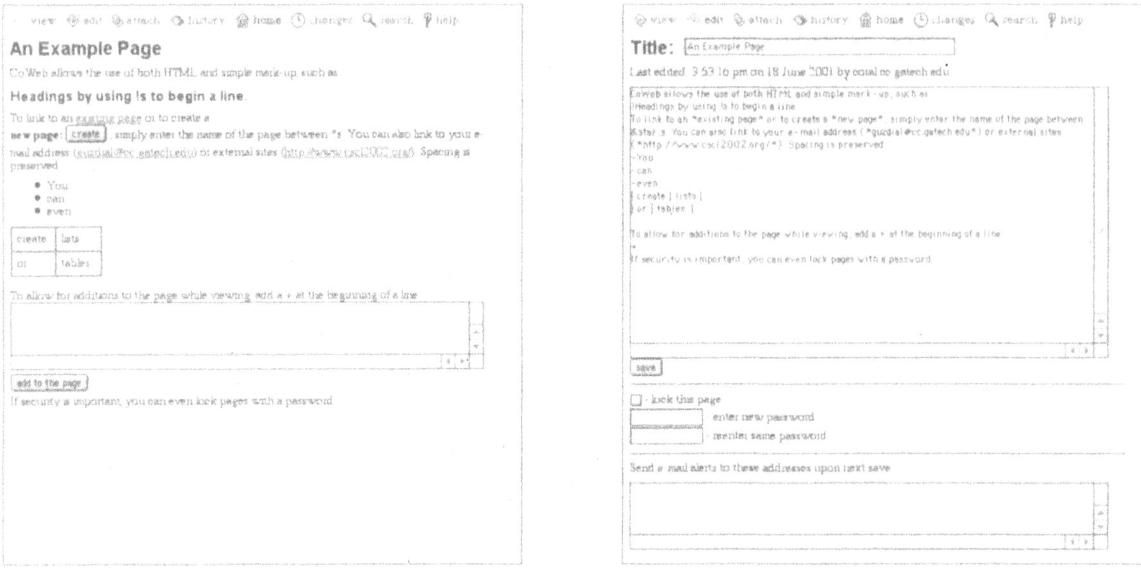

Figure 1: Viewing / Editing a CoWeb Page in a Web Browser

Through over a dozen iterations in the last three years, CoWeb has had features added and the interface streamlined to fit well into classroom use (Guzdial, Rick, & Kerimbaev, 2000). Over 100 class CoWebs are now in use at Georgia Tech. A wide variety of educational activities have been invented by instructors for their classes (Guzdial, Rick, & Kehoe, 2001), and we have catalogued some 25 common activities that we see tailored to meet specific class needs (Collaborative Software Laboratory, 2000).

COWEB USE IN ENGLISH COMPOSITION

In English composition, CoWeb is used for an activity called *close reading*, where prose or a poem for discussion is posted, and students comment upon it by inserting links directly into the prose or poem. Students then comment upon each other's comments and even use the same technique to comment upon each other's essays. Figure 2 illustrates two kinds of close reading activities. The left picture shows part of a CoWeb close reading assignment based on a chat session. Students completed a computer-based chat session based on classroom topics and assigned reading. The instructor then posted the contents of that chat session into the CoWeb. From there, students were instructed to find interesting parts of the discussion and create pages associated with the section. Basically, the students would find an interesting fragment and surround it with *s. When saving the page, they could create a new CoWeb page with that fragment as the title. So, the original chat session was preserved, but comments could be made on the most important sections of the chat session. The right picture of Figure 2 shows the same activity, except that the text to be annotated is a classroom reading, in this case from Karl Marx's "The German Ideology."

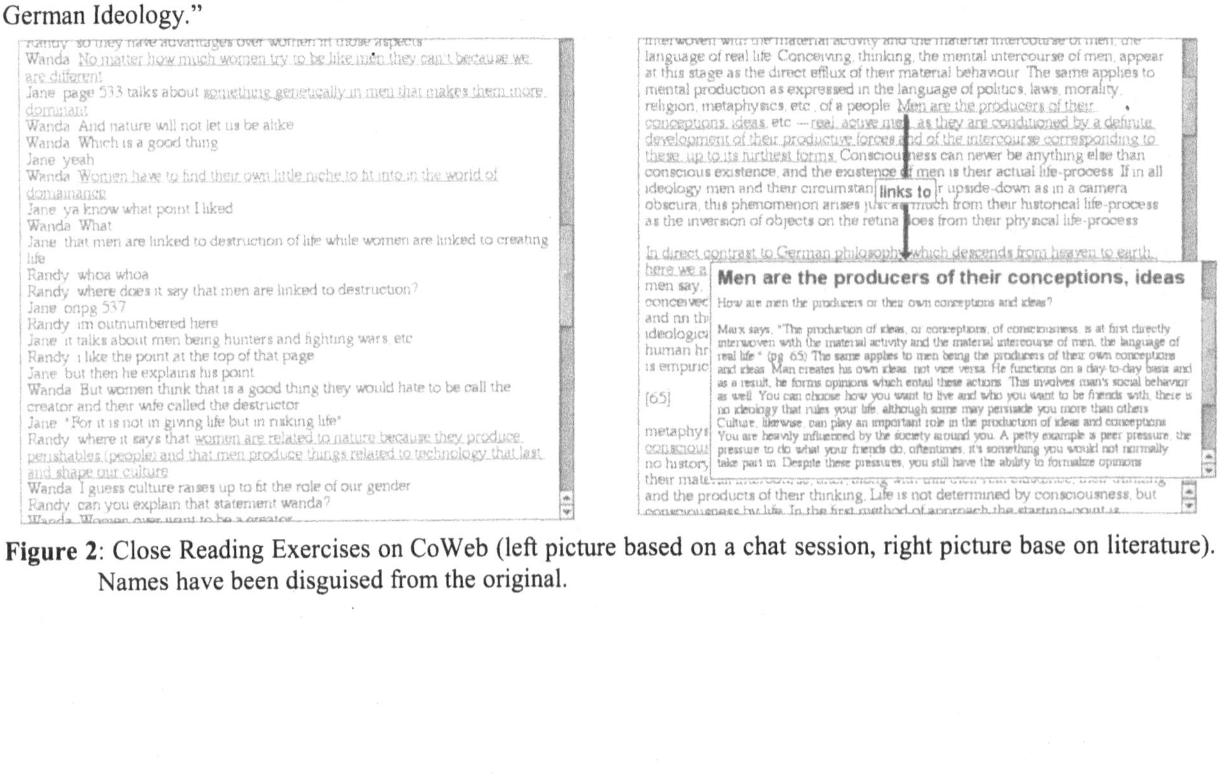

Figure 2: Close Reading Exercises on CoWeb (left picture based on a chat session, right picture base on literature). Names have been disguised from the original.

LEARNING EFFECTIVENESS

Learning effectiveness is the amount learned in relation to the cost for achieving that learning (i.e. time on task). In this section, we show our evidence for learning through use of CoWeb. Then, in the next section, we show that this learning benefit is achievable at a low cost.

We studied two sections of an English 101[(1)] class, taught by the same instructor. The first section (24 students) used CoWeb to complete various assignments[(2)]. The comparison section (25 students) did the same activities, but the students worked in a threaded-discussion on-line environment[(3)] on the close reading activities and individually on the essays. As each section did the same activities, student cost (effort) should be identical. To confirm this, we paid several students in both sections to track their time spent on the class; no notable differences between the groups were observed.

Through surveys, we find that the CoWeb section had significantly better attitudes toward collaboration than did students in the comparison section (Table 1). In addition, the CoWeb section received higher grades (grade breakdown: 7 A's, 10 B's, 3 C's, others F or W) than the comparison section (grade breakdown: 19 B's, 3 D's, others F or W), which indicates better performance and suggests better learning. In particular, the instructor noted that the CoWeb section showed more variance, thereby allowing A's to be assigned.

Statement	CoWeb Section	Comparison Section
I would rather work independently on assignments than in groups or teams.	3.83	2.81
I feel working with others on assignments is more helpful than working alone.	2.00	2.75
When working on team projects, I feel motivated by my sense of responsibility to the group.	1.78	2.69
I like doing teamwork.	1.89	2.75
I found it useful to relate my work to that of others.	1.56	2.50

Table 1: Attitudes toward Collaboration, where 1 is strongly agree and 5 is strongly disagree. $p < 0.05$ on a two-tailed t-test for all of these statements

We recognize that grades are not a precise measure of performance, and they are too large-grained to inform us about where any learning benefit may have come from. As such, twelve students were selected randomly from each section and their work rated by various criteria (Table 2). Five assignments were rated: two close reading assignments based on student-generated chat sessions (rated for the first 6 criteria, which we refer to as chat close readings), two close reading assignments based on literature (rated for the first 10 criteria, referred to as literature close readings), and one formal essay (rated for all 15 criteria). To keep individual bias to a minimum, two raters (one the course instructor, the other a colleague in the same department) rated each assignment on a scale of one to four (four being highest performance). No statistically significant differences were found in their ratings, and all criteria had better than 70% of the ratings identical. In each rating category, the CoWeb section outperformed the comparison section (in most, by a large statistically significant amount):

Category	CoWeb Section	Comparison Section	Difference
Engagement with Class Material	2.52	1.88	0.64
Foundation for Research	2.49	1.68	0.82
Reflective / Recursive Writing Practices: Authorial voice	2.30	1.58	0.73
Reflective / Recursive Writing Practices: Reflection and Exploration	2.24	1.49	0.75
Critical Vocabulary: Understanding	2.30	1.54	0.76
Critical Vocabulary: Application	2.28	1.33	0.95

---

(1) English 101 is a fictional course number, but the course is the Georgia Tech equivalent of English 101

(2) The CoWeb section was chosen at random and students did not know a priori which section would use CoWeb, so selection bias was minimized.

(3) The comparison class's on-line environment was similar to a Usenet newsgroup. The close reading text was the original posting and students replied to it with their annotations.

Formation of Critical Questions: Engagement with Topic	2.39	1.94	0.44
Formation of Critical Questions: Quality of Questions / Arguments	2.24	2.21	0.03*
Critical / Close Reading Skills: Analysis	2.29	1.97	0.32*
Critical / Close Reading Skills: Identification of Issues	2.36	2.06	0.31*
Research Skills: Locating Information	3.04	2.54	0.50
Research Skills: Using Information	2.75	2.00	0.75
Identification of Critical Sources	2.75	2.08	0.67
Engagement and Integration of Research Sources	2.71	1.75	0.96
Effective Use of Formal Essay Writing Conventions for Argumentation	2.79	2.21	0.58

Table 2: Writing Performance. $p < .05$ on a two-tailed t-test for all except *

On average, the students in the CoWeb section did significantly better on writing essays than the comparison section, particularly on issues of vocabulary and essay organization. Several categories show near 1.00 differences in performance; on a scale of one to four, one point of difference indicates a large difference in performance. For instance, on critical vocabulary application, the CoWeb section average is between 2 (chosen when "the student deploys these terms where appropriate in his/her writing, but most are misused") and 3 ("the student deploys most of these terms where appropriate in his/her writing, but occasionally misuses them"), while the comparison section average is between 1 ("the student never successfully deploys these terms where appropriate in his/her writing") and 2.

Clearly, CoWeb seems to engender better performance on these activities; however, we also wanted to get an idea as to whether there was a cumulative effect of CoWeb use over the term. As such, we looked at performance over the term on similar assignments. If CoWeb has a cumulative effect, the difference in ratings (i.e. performance-gap) should increase over time. Figure 3 shows that for each of the two assignment types noted earlier, the performance-gap increased over the term, though not by a large margin (.29 and .07 respectively).

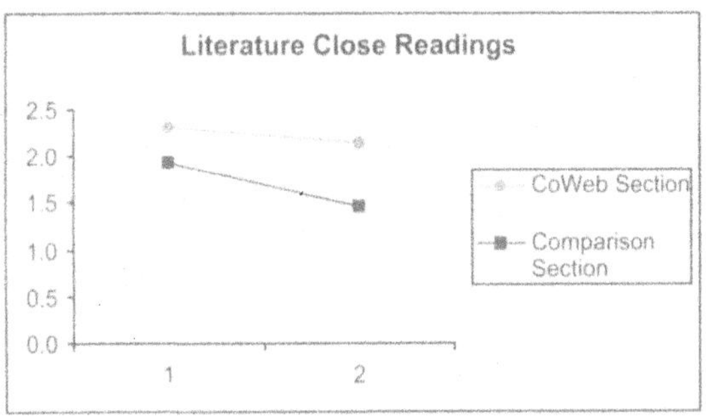

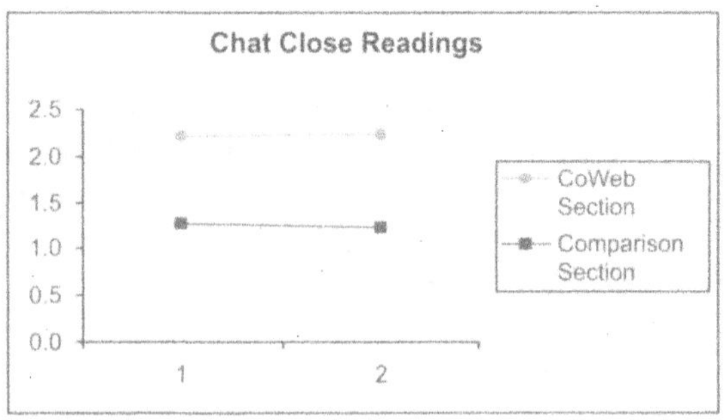

Figure 3: Graphs demonstrating that the performance-gap between CoWeb and comparison section increases over time on two different types of assignments

So overall, we conclude that CoWeb usage in close reading activities was effective for learning in this study. The performance of the students in the CoWeb section was significantly better by many key subject criteria over the comparison section. At the same time, attitudes towards collaborative learning improved. We speculate that these two factors are not independent; instead, as the use of collaborative learning proves beneficial, more learning will happen, which in turn improves the attitude towards collaboration. Furthermore, instead of just improving performance on the activity itself, CoWeb students show a cumulative learning effect.

COST EFFECTIVENESS

Now that we have shown learning effectiveness, it becomes important to look at costs. We aim to show that CoWeb use has both low infrastructure and human costs.

Infrastructure costs are negligible. Though a server was bought for this study, that server can support at least a dozen classes over many terms. CoWeb is a cross-platform and lightweight server application that can be run on virtually any hardware (in some cases, old 486's), so even a $1000 server can easily support many classes. Student access to internet-enabled computers is essential for CoWeb use; at Georgia Tech, there was no need to provide any infrastructure for this since it was already present. Nor is use of that infrastructure markedly increased, considering that students would need similar amounts of time for other applications for the same class (i.e. word processing). At other locations where the infrastructure is not in place, that cost may be prohibitive; however, this infrastructure is becoming very common. The CoWeb software is open-source freeware(4); thus, there are no software costs.

Administration costs too are negligible. Besides the tracking software (specifically used for gathering study data) and a couple of software upgrades (the CoWeb software is still actively being developed), an English professor (not a computer specialist) was able to administer the server without assistance. In total, the amount of administration time over the semester was less than an hour.

By far, the dominant cost factor in CoWeb use is instructor time. The instructor for the two sections, using self reporting, averaged about 2.5 hours per week devoted to CoWeb usage; this is quite reasonable as it is about the same amount of time as an office hours session. However, this does not give us a clear idea of how she spent that time or how student usage relates to instructor involvement.

In the term following our learning study, we set up CoWeb to log usage time. We did this for two instructors, teaching the same class (English 102(5)). The first (instructor 1) was the instructor for the original class, and here taught the follow-up course (class 1: 24 students, with 1 withdrawing). The second (instructor 2) was the second rater for the performance assessment. This was the first time this instructor used CoWeb, using one CoWeb for three sections of the same class (class 2: 64 students, with 5 withdrawing). As she was getting used to CoWeb, instructor 2 still relied on another web environment for the class; in contrast, all on-line activities for instructor 1 were done with CoWeb(6). The instructors did different activities with their class and have different styles of using the technology, so this data is a good cross-section of instructional uses. Table 3 summarizes instructor and student time on CoWeb.

	Class 1	**Class 2**
Average Not-Withdrawing Student Time	17.95 hours	8.13 hours
Total Student Time	412.84 hours	484.82 hours
Total Instructor Time	41.30 hours	57.35 hours
Total Student Time / Instructor Time	10.00	8.45

Table 3: Instructor and Student Time using CoWeb

What is most notable is that in both cases the ratio of total time spent by students to total time spent by the instructor is similar (10.00 and 8.45). One way to measure the cost effectiveness of an educational activity is to contrast the ratio of student to instructor time. By this criterion, lecture is cost effective. For each hour of instructor time input, there are *n* hours of total student time (24.00 and 21.33(7) respectively in our case) spent engaged in the learning activity. This number estimate is a bit high, considering it does not include preparation time for the instructor or absenteeism for the students. While lecture scores high marks on efficiency, it loses in learning effectiveness, as student involvement tends to be passive (particularly for large classes where cost efficiency would be high). In contrast, one-on-one tutoring, as may occur during office hours, can be quite active and engaging. Unfortunately, one-on-one tutoring is not economically feasible, with a ratio of 1.00 hour of instructor time to student time. The CoWeb ratios (around 9) on the other hand seem a reasonable compromise of the cost effectiveness of lower instructor time with the learning effectiveness of more active learning (as students construct artifacts).

Unlike lectures that have a high attendance level, time-spent using an educational technology can be highly varied. One scenario could have an exponential drop-off, with only a few students using the technology often. While the technology might have marked effects on these few students large enough to affect the class average, it probably wouldn't be considered a healthy situation in most schools. What we want to see is that the technology is reaching most if not all students.

---

(4) It can be downloaded from http://minnow.cc.gatech.edu/swiki

(5) Again, English 102 is a fictional course name.

(6) In the future, instructor 2 plans to only use CoWeb.

(7) 64 students / 3 sections = 21.33 student class hours per instructor hour

To look at the distribution of usage across students, Figure 4 plots student time on CoWeb from most usage to least usage. The vertical axis is the number of hours spent in CoWeb, and the horizontal axis represents different students, ordered in terms of the amount of time they spent in CoWeb.

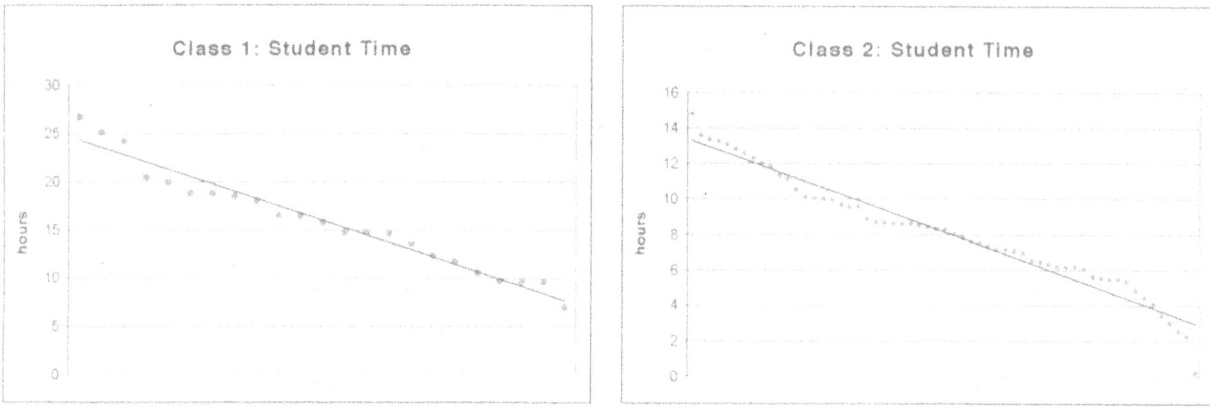

Figure 4: Distributions of Students' CoWeb Usage (from most use to least use)

What it shows is that while usage varies quite widely, it does so in a near linear way (for both classes). Also, in both cases, there seems to be a grouping around the class average with only a few doing significantly less or more. This grouping can be seen in the right graph where there is a dip below the line to the left of the center and a dip above the line to the right of the center. For an activity, like homework, a roughly linear distribution with a few doing significantly more or less than the average seems acceptable.

Are some activities more cost effective than others (i.e. requiring less instructor time for equal student effort)? If so, efficiency could then be improved by focusing on certain activities and dropping less efficient activities. To test this hypothesis, we recorded student and instructor time on CoWeb over the term (Figure 5—horizontal axis represents week intervals over the course of the term, and vertical axis represents time spent in the CoWeb during that interval). After looking at the data, interviews with the instructors were conducted to find out what activities occurred and how their time was spent.

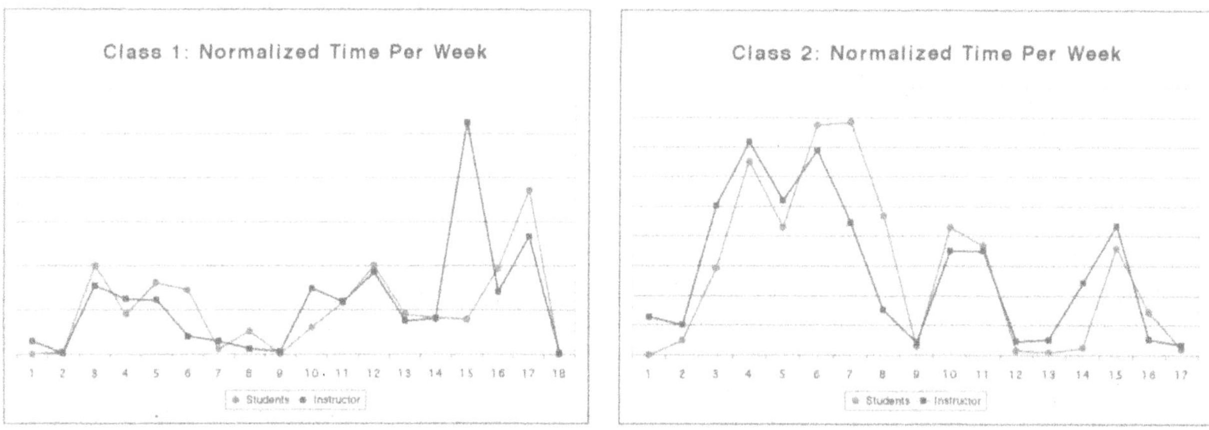

Figure 5: Distribution of Time per Week for Both Classes (Note: Week 9 is Spring Break)

A couple of conclusions can be drawn from this data. First, almost all of the time, the instructor put in some of the effort before the students; this can be seen particularly well for instructor 2, where instructor time seems almost shifted a week off the student time. So, a significant proportion of instructor time is spent on setting up the space; this observation was confirmed by both instructors during the interviews. Second, instructor time is closely linked to student time for each assignment. The only exception is week 15 for instructor 1, where she spent just over 10 hours on CoWeb; this time was mainly spent on grading. Instructor 2 did grading throughout the term. As such, there is no assignment for either instructor that is far more or less efficient. One way to explain this is that the amount of time that instructors and students spend on an assignment is closely related to the point value of the assignment; so, the original hypothesis about more efficient assignments is flawed.

Instructor 2 mainly used CoWeb for one large assignment worth 35 percent of their grade (weeks 2-12). Students worked in small groups (2-3 members) to investigate a decade from 1800-1912. Each group posted a timeline with a minimum of 10 significant science or technological innovations or discoveries identified in that decade; each member of the group researched one of these events in depth and wrote a five page paper on it. The purpose of this project was to provide a database of information about science and technology in the 19th century that students could use as background for their final project—to create a web-site to understand a 20th century phenomenon in terms of its origins or background in the 19th century. As such, CoWeb served as a research space where students could benefit from the work of their classmates. Although students had to link their final project to the class CoWeb for other students to see, the final projects were required to be traditional web-sites and could not be built in CoWeb. However, the instructor encouraged students to use CoWeb as a way to collaborate on their final project. Most of the use in weeks 13 through 16 is attributable to that voluntary collaboration.

Instructor 1 used CoWeb throughout the term for multiple smaller assignments. Students were required to complete three chat-based and one literature-based close reading assignments. Also, students posted summaries and discussion about the class reading. Instructor 1 also used the space as a way to distribute class readings and communicate deadlines and activities to the students. The largest chunk of student use came during weeks 15 through 17, when they worked on a final project. Like class 2, the final project for class 1 was for groups to build a web-site.

Unlike instructor 2, instructor 1 allowed students to do their web project entirely in CoWeb; four out of six groups decided to complete their projects entirely in CoWeb. So, students found interaction on CoWeb useful enough to use it instead of traditional web-site tools, such as Microsoft FrontPage™. As students tend to choose the most effective ways to accomplish their goals, this is further evidence of CoWeb's cost effectiveness (this time for students). Furthermore, Instructor 1 commented that the quality of the final projects was higher than previous classes as CoWeb-using students concentrated more on content than on looks. Although the instructor has always stressed content over looks, students creating web-sites tended to spend much of their time on looks. Since most web-page creation tools allow you to "mess around" easily with looks, it is only natural that students would find this aspect interesting. In contrast, it is almost painful to "mess around" with looks on CoWeb. Instead of being a detriment in this case, it was an advantage for learning effectiveness. If CoWeb usage were not seen as cost effective by the students, they would not have used it for their final projects, and the final assignment would not have been as effective for learning. So, it is important that instructor *and* students see a classroom technology as cost effective. In addition to CoWeb being a good environment for the final projects, instructor 1 observed a significant cumulative effect—the CoWeb class was already used to concentrating on content.

For instructor 1, all class activities, besides office hours and lecture, including grading, were conducted on CoWeb. Considering that lecture time was about 50 hours, roughly 40 hours spent on the class outside of lecture during a semester is quite efficient. The 41 hours observed through system logs also matches closely to instructor 1's self reported time of 2.5 average hours per week spent on CoWeb for the previous term, where the learning effectiveness was closely examined. While CoWeb's interface is easy to learn and we (the developers) have produced several guides on how to use it in the classroom, we expect a certain significant cost to be incurred from using a new technology for the first time. As instructor 1 already used CoWeb before and had taught this course before, her level of efficiency (10.00 total-student-time-to-instructor-time ratio) may have reached a stable efficiency saturation point. In contrast, this was the first time instructor 2 used CoWeb. As such, her total-student-time-to-instructor-time ratio would be expected to rise (slightly) over time, as she becomes more comfortable with the environment. Also, instructor involvement is highly dependent on teaching style. Instructor 1 views her CoWeb interaction as setting up the space for the students to work and then letting them "loose." In contrast, instructor 2's style is one of tighter control of what occurs in the space; she is actively involved in the running of the activities and likes participating along with the students. This difference in styles might cause instructor 2's saturation efficiency to be somewhat below instructor 1's. Even with different styles and uses, CoWeb usage remains cost effective for both instructor and student.

DISCUSSION

Use of CoWeb in the introductory English classes studied is a success, both from a learning perspective (the students were able to engage the curriculum actively) and a cost perspective (both fixed and variable costs were quite low). Collaborative learning activities are realizing their potential as a way of leveraging the numbers in the classroom to create a dramatically improved learning situation without a dramatic rise in costs.

The use of CoWeb in English composition has been remarkably independent of CoWeb development. Using CoWeb for close reading activities based on literature was invented by Greg VanHoosier-Carey, a fellow professor in the School of Literature, Communications, and Culture (Collaborative Software Laboratory, 2000). Close readings based on chat session were invented by the English 101 instructor. While we who developed CoWeb provided support such as answering questions and setting up monitoring programs, we did nothing to specify the usage of CoWeb in that domain. So, a simple collaboration tool (such as CoWeb or Wiki) can allow educators to take ownership of the technology and invent new uses that will be useful in their domain.

Though performance and learning improved in the collaborative learning case, student effort (time-on-task) remained the same. Guzdial and Carroll investigated this phenomenon; they found three possible causes for this effect (Guzdial, Carroll, 2002). First, vicarious learning can occur as students view each other's postings and try to understand the issues that their fellow classmates are engaging. Second, posting assignments to a real audience (i.e. fellow learners) provides an opportunity for reflection: students think deeply about the content before they post. Third, the on-line environment can provide support for and an extension of the in-class activities. By discussing the in-class activities in a forum where each student has a better chance of being heard, the average class performance is raised. The on-line environment gives students a clearer understanding of what is expected of them and how the lecture relates to the assignments.

ACKNOWLEDGMENTS

Funding for this project is from the National Science Foundation Grant REC-9814770 and the Mellon Foundation. Our thanks to our collaborators: Akbar Ladak, Joshua Gargus, Colleen Kehoe, Bolot Kerimbaev, and Kayt Sukel.

REFERENCES

Guzdial, M., Carroll, K. (2002) Explaining the lack of dialogue in computer-supported collaborative learning, *Proceedings of the Computer Supported Collaborative Learning 2002*. Mahwah, NJ: Lawrence Erlbaum Associates.

Guzdial, M., Rick, J., and Kerimbaev, B. (2000) Recognizing and supporting roles in CSCW. *Proceedings of CSCW'2000*, 261-268.

Guzdial, M., Rick, J., and Kehoe, C. (2001) Beyond adoption to invention: Teacher-created collaborative activities in higher education. *Journal of the Learning Sciences*, 10 (3), 265-279.

Collaborative Software Laboratory (2000) A catalog of CoWeb uses. Georgia Tech GVU Center Technical Report GIT-GVU-00-19, Georgia Tech GVU Center.

Virtual Communication in Middle School Students' and Teachers' Inquiry

Minna Lakkala, Liisa Ilomäki, Jiri Lallimo, Kai Hakkarainen

Department of Psychology, University of Helsinki
Minna.Lakkala@helsinki.fi

ABSTRACT

The aim of the study was to evaluate an innovative learning project in which middle school students and teachers completed chosen, group inquiries through virtual collaboration in a web-based learning environment. The students' task was to accomplish a cross disciplinary inquiry into cultural phenomena. Students worked mainly at home during the project and took much responsibility for their own work and course achievements. The investigators analyzed the content of the students' and teachers' communication in the web-based environment. The findings suggest that the virtual environment was used as a communication tool for organizing the collaborative work more than as a genuine knowledge-building tool. Also, the tension between the conventional school culture and the novel working practices apparently affected students' participation and patterns of activity in the course.

Keywords

Collaborative knowledge building, virtual learning, progressive inquiry, middle school

INTRODUCTION

This study concentrates on analyzing a virtual inquiry based learning project in middle school which differed from conventional school projects in many ways. Middle school students worked mainly off the school premises and communicated with each other and with teachers from home through a web-based learning environment. The project was organized under a very wide inter-disciplinary concept of culture, and it integrated students' work in several subject domains and school courses. The project was also untypical in that several teachers from different subject-domains took part in each group inquiry, jointly carrying out the pedagogical planning, and students' guidance and evaluation.

The teachers had an ambitious goal to introduce students to practices of *collaborative knowledge building*. Scardamalia and Bereiter (1994; 1999) have proposed that schools should be restructured towards knowledge-building organizations, in which students and teachers participate in the construction of collective knowledge as in professional research groups where the object of activity is solving knowledge-problems. The participating teachers were introduced by the researchers to the model of *progressive inquiry*, which has been developed by Hakkarainen and his colleagues (Hakkarainen & Sintonen, in press; Muukkonen, Hakkarainen & Lakkala, 1999) as a pedagogical model for promoting knowledge-building practices in schools with the support of collaborative technology. In progressive inquiry, students are guided to engage in a research-like process by defining problems and proposing working theories, using information sources and collaboratively formulating new higher-level problems and explanations. The methods were also new to the teachers, so they were genuinely in a novice's role themselves.

Another background goal for the evaluated project was to advance *virtual learning practices* on all levels in Finnish schools (Ministry of Education, 1999). There is a need to develop models for practical applications of technology-supported virtual learning in real school contexts. Most research and development that has been done on CSCL in lower school levels has been in face-to-face classroom situations (e.g., Salovaara & Järvelä, 2001). There are fewer studies of the challenges of collaborative knowledge building in distance learning situations. In this school project, one aim was to give the students an experience of technology-supported virtual working. The participating students did not belong to a traditional classroom community, but were gathered together especially for this course. Therefore, the challenges for organizing the learning community in the project can be compared to the challenges for building virtual communities in general. Elements that characterize successful virtual communities are e.g., shared goals and resources, active participation and reciprocal interaction, sense of belonging, trust in others, and shared context of social conventions (Schuler, 1996; Preece, 2000). According to Schuler (1996), development of a networked community requires organizing the mechanisms that "describe the general decision-making, responsibility allocating, and communication methods that will guide the group" (p. 338). In a study of university students' virtual learning process, Muukkonen et al. (1999) mentioned the issue of community building as one of the major challenges in using CSCL in education. They argued that to intensively participate in virtual learning environments, the students need strong community support to help induce them to participate.

The features of the virtual tool used for collaboration are of course important factors in facilitating the process. In this project the students and teachers used a web-based learning environment, in which the main collaborative tool was a quite typical threaded discussion forum. The same kinds of forums are widely employed as easy-to-use tools in learning situations. Guzdial and Turns (2000) have evaluated the effectiveness of the communication in selected virtual discussion forums for learning. They defined three necessary conditions for demonstrating whether the activity in the networked discussion supports learning: The discussion should be sustained (which they evaluated from the length of discussion threads), it should have broad participation and it should focus on class topics.

A third important dimension in studying innovations in schools is the effect of the whole *conventional school culture* on the new, collaborative process. As Engeström, Engeström and Suntio (in preparation) presented in their study of school change in the framework of cultural-historical activity theory, there are deep structural constraints in developing the school: Socio-spatial structure of the school work (separate classrooms, teachers working alone, isolation of the school from the environment), temporal structure (discrete and short lessons, test and grading phases etc.) and motivational and ethical structure (grading as a main motivational method). Bielaczyc (2001) has stated that the central challenge in implementing CSCL in schools lies in creating the appropriate social infrastructure for collaborative activity. She defines social infrastructure as having three levels: 1) A cultural level includes classroom culture and philosophy and norms established; 2) an activity level comprises the classroom practices and online activities in the process; 3) a tool level defines, how the participants structure the technological environment and use the possibilities of the CSCL tool. In the evaluated project the teachers' intention was deliberately to surpass the limits of the classroom and restrictions of separate subject domains, but they still acted in a conventional school context with no extra resources or changes in the official curriculum.

In summary, the framework for analyzing the challenges of the virtual school project was found in the interaction and contradictions of three elements, as Figure 1 describes.

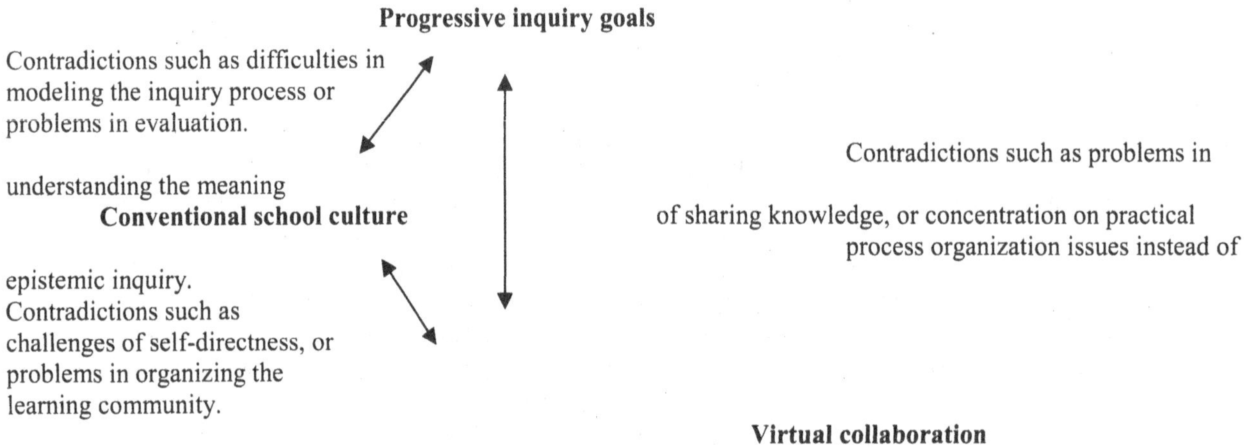

Figure 1. Dimensions for examining the virtual school project.

Research questions that are based upon the framework were as follows: 1) How was the socially shared character of inquiry realized in the participants' technology-supported communication? 2) What additional elements did the virtuality and distance work bring into the inquiry process? 3) How did the virtual inquiry practices fit with the demands of the conventional school culture?

METHODS

Setting and participants

The evaluated 'Culture course' was organized in Alppila School, which is a middle school in the city of Helsinki. The school is quite advanced and active in developing learning and teaching methods: The emphasis in all teaching is on cultural aspects of the phenomena under study; the studying is organized through courses that meet periodically, not fixed classes; the school has participated in various research and development projects for several years.

The investigated project had, at the end, 14 student participants (age 15-16) and 7 teachers (computer science, biology and geography, religion, history and philosophy, arts, music, Finnish language). The students volunteered to participate in the course. They were all quite high achieving and were meant to complete several regular school courses by participating in the Culture course. It was the students' last spring in the obligatory lower secondary school. The teachers did not participate full-time in the course, but were at the same time responsible for other school courses as usual. The computer teacher was a coordinator of the whole project; other teachers participated as experts and tutors of their own subject domain.

The goal of the Culture course was to deepen students' (and teachers') conception of culture, to give students an opportunity to get experience of distance learning and to introduce students to the progressive inquiry approach. Students were encouraged to produce an innovative cultural product as a final work of the course, not just a traditional project report. The students decided among themselves the actual topic of their inquiry. They worked mainly off the school premises during the course. There were seven common meetings at school, otherwise the students communicated through the web-based learning environment from home, or arranged face-to-face meetings with their small group members and the guiding teachers. The actual distance-working period lasted seven weeks from February to April, but the whole project started two months beforehand with some preliminary meetings.

The technology used in the course was a web-based collaborative software called Virtual Web School (VWS) designed by the Media Center of the Helsinki City Department of Education. A typical threaded discussion forum was the main tool for organizing the discourse. In addition, the learning environment included a chat tool and a text-based portfolio for students' private products, but they were not in active use in this course. It was not possible, for instance, to share documents through the VWS.

Data collection

The data that have been analyzed in this study included the database notes posted to the VWS environment during the course. Five (out of seven) joint meetings in school were observed and videotaped by the researchers. One researcher participated to two teacher meetings, where teachers planned the organization of the course. In addition we obtained various materials about course accomplishments, final works and written course evaluations.

Data analysis

Several quantitative measures of the features of the virtual discourse – such as number of the postings, distribution of postings in time, and length of the discussion threads – were counted from the discussion threads in the VWS.

The postings to the VWS database were also analyzed qualitatively using the methods of qualitative content analysis (see Chi, 1997) to evaluate the patterns of collaboration in the virtual learning community. The unit of analysis was one message or posting. Messages were categorized according to the main content of the message text: what appeared to be the main purpose or object of the posting in the discourse. The categories were derived from the several preliminary analyses of the data. The following five were used in the final classification:

1) `Content of the inquiry`: These messages represented students' problems, thoughts and explanations of the inquiry topics and subject domain concepts, descriptions of the content of their inquiry, and teachers' content-specific guidance.

2) `Community building`: Messages in this category represented general discussion relating to the common purpose of the learning community (progressive inquiry, collaborative work, accomplishing inquiry about culture), communication about the ways of using the virtual tools (organizing the forums, using sensible titles), and social aspects of the community (arranging a common meeting room, invitations to participate actively to virtual work).

3) `Process organization`: Messages in this category included communication that was needed for organizing the inquiry work of separate small groups (arranging meetings, asking help or comments, telling about information sources, making agreements of task completion).

4) `Course evaluation`: Messages in this category included questions, agreements and arguments about the rules for completing the project work, criteria for course grading and general timetables or deadlines.

5) `Other issues`: Messages put into this category included conversation about other topics or school activity unrelated to the project tasks, and nonsense test messages written by students in the practicing phase.

Each message was classified in only one of the content categories, according to its main content. Content analysis was performed using ATLAS/ti-program. To analyze the reliability of classification, an independent coder classified approximately 17% of all messages (randomly selected message threads from a general forum and all the messages from one group forum); the coefficient for rater agreement (Cohen's Kappa) was .85, which was considered satisfactory.

Other material and observational data from the course meetings and teacher meetings were used as complementary information to get an overview of the process, and to interpret the communication in the virtual environment in a larger context.

RESULTS

Structure and organization of the course

Below is a description of the structure and phases of the course.

Preliminary phase

The whole project started in the middle of December with a 1½-hour meeting in the school, when teachers introduced the course and its objectives to students. Students seemed to be insecure about the requirements and goals of the project. At least four high-achieving girl students who had originally reported to the project withdrew from it in the first meeting. They stated that it is 'safer' to work in traditional courses because they wanted to get the highest degrees to their final middle school report. In the middle of January, the computer teacher gave the participants a training session on the VWS-environment. Also the reasons for using the collaborative tool were discussed, and the general forum entitled 'Small talk' was founded for practicing. The teacher gave students a task to write their individual inquiry plans to the VWS forum entitled 'Working plans and starting theories' before the next meeting. In the beginning of February, the philosophy teacher arranged a brainstorming session in the school, meeting hall. Students planned the content of their inquiry work in the framework of various cultural dimensions (past-present-future, fact-fiction, etc.). Also discussed were decisions about the small groups, tutoring teachers and school courses that the students would complete. After the meeting the students continued the planning virtually in the VWS.

1st week

The fourth school period started in the middle of February when the students started their actual distance work. In the first week, the computer teacher gave a lecture about progressive inquiry at school; students formed small groups and decided the topics of their group's inquiry. The students formed 7 groups and formulated the following research topics: Biological effects of music (2 boys), Life in the Middle Ages (2 boys), Effects of genes and environment on a Finnish-Australian girls' life (2 girls), Japanese culture (1 girl alone), American Indian culture (2 boys), Comparison of Finnish and Canadian cultures (2 girls) and Aspects of religion and society (3 boys). Each group had a main, tutoring teacher, but all the teachers were meant to guide all students and give support especially to those students who were completing courses in their teaching subject. The students had chosen 2-6 school courses that they would complete by participating in the Culture course. At the end of the first week the students had another working session in the computer lab. Their task was to write to the VWS their group's research questions and starting theories, and comment on other groups' plans.

From 2nd to 6th week

During the next five weeks (from the end of February to the beginning of April) students did independent work and organized their group processes using the VWS. In the second week separate, specific discussion forums were founded for every group (everybody was allowed to participate freely in the group forums and the common forums). Students were guided to start the investigation of their research questions. During these weeks, students processed their work in their respective group forums but also discussed issues in joint forums. In addition they had face-to-face meetings with their own group and the tutoring teachers.

7th and 8th week

In the seventh week (in the beginning of April) there was a common face-to-face meeting, in which the groups commented on the state of each other's work. The teachers guided the students to think about high points and new interesting aspects in each group's inquiry work. After that day the small groups continued their process, mostly finishing their final work and making plans about how to present it in the closing event. In the last week (in the middle of April) there was a 4-hour closing event at the meeting hall. Each group presented its final work in a different way. The Middle Ages group had made a radio play; the Canada group had written an imaginary diary of a school girl who was visiting Canada as an exchange student. At the end of the week the students were called to school once more to write their evaluation of the course for the researchers. In the Culture course the students received credit for 61 courses in all, according to the agreements; 4.4 courses per student on average.

Amount of activity and threading of the virtual discourse

The participants posted 534 messages to the VWS database during the project (minimum was 3 messages of a boy student; maximum, 81 messages of a male teacher). Students (N = 14) posted 308 messages (Mean = 22.0, SD = 29.9) and teachers (N = 7) posted 226 messages (Mean = 32.3, SD = 26.0). Some of the messages were written by two or three students together. In the joint forum entitled 'Small talk' were 168 messages; in the 'Plans and theories' forum, 113 messages; and in seven, group forums there were 253 messages in all. In Figure 2 one can see how the volume of messaging varied in discussion forums during the course.

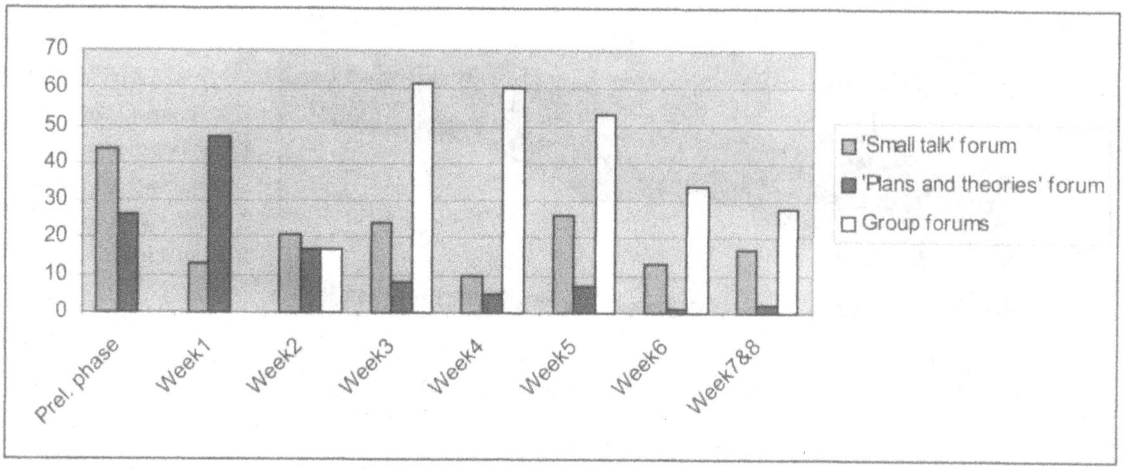

Figure 2. The number of messages in the discussion forums in course weeks.

In the beginning of the project, only the two general forums were in use. As Figure 2 shows, in the first, course week, the work was concentrated on the 'Plans and theories' forum according to the teachers' instructions. After the second week, the communication was transferred mainly to the group forums, and it was most active in the middle of the course.

In all the virtual forums together, there were 218 top-level messages (41% of all messages), which were considered as new initiations in the discourse. Of those messages, 97 (44%) were isolated messages that did not have any comments following, and 121 (56%) were messages that had at least one comment; e.g., they had started a new discussion thread. Mean number of messages in discussion threads (in the threads that included at least two messages) was 3.63 (SD = 2.15). The longest thread included 14 messages, and only three threads had more than ten messages. Studies from the elementary level (Lipponen et al., 2001) and university level (Guzdial & Turns, 2000) have given the same kind of results; that, in general, the discourse threads in virtual forums are quite short, which indicates that the inquiry, insofar as it is accurately reflected in the postings, is not very sustained or convergent.

There was a big difference in the use of each group's forum. Minimum number of postings in one forum was 13; maximum was 56. Mean number of postings in all group forums was 38.2 (SD = 14.9). We also counted the number of postings that the students sent to the forums of other groups. Only 8 (out of 253) messages in the group forums were written by students from the other groups; all other messages were written by the students of that group or by the teachers. After forming the small groups, the students obviously concentrated on their own work and did not contribute to other groups' work, although they where encouraged to do so.

Content of the virtual communication

Each posting to the VWS discussion forums was assigned to one of the content categories described earlier. The original goal of the project was to use the technology to support sharing and building of knowledge, which means sharing theories and explanations of cultural aspects in the students' inquiry. According to the content analysis, only 180 (34%) of the postings were about the Content of inquiry. The frequencies of other content categories were as follows: Process organization messages 129 (24%), Community building messages 105 (20%), messages about Course evaluation 67 (12%), and messages about Other issues 67 (10%).

The discussion forums obviously had different roles in the communication of the learning community. In the 'Small talk' forum half (50%) of the postings were community building messages, and about 25% were messages about issues unrelated to the common course goals. In the other joint discussion forum, the 'Plans and theories' forum, 64% of the postings were about the content of inquiry. In the seven group forums most of the communication was about the content of inquiry (42%) or process organization (42%).

The content of communication varied remarkably during the successive weeks of the course (Figure 3).

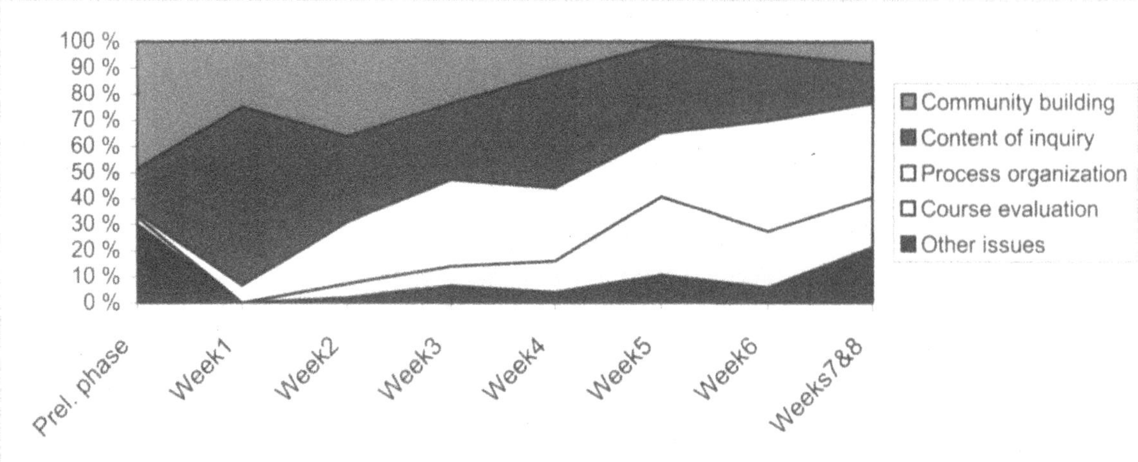

Figure 3. Change in the content of postings to the VWS discussion forums during the project.

As can be seen from Figure 3, in the beginning of the project, issues that were important for building up the learning community (common objectives and working methods) were dominant in the virtual communication. There were discussions about how to use the virtual tools, the importance of collaboration, and also plans to organize a joint working room for the course members in the school. Here is an example of messages assigned to the category of *community building*:

```
18.01.2000 14.45.04 About this Culture course (Thomas, boy student)
This is a fine system, but ... the possibility for real-time discussion is still
missing? Maybe an IRC-channel? For instance #alppila #culturecourse
#alppila_culturecourse ... And then we need of course a bot program to keep the
channel going, does anyone have a possibility to supply one?
Waiting for answers...

    18.01.2000 14.51.07 We need that later, we are not here [at school] all the time
    (Hannah, girl student)
    It is true that it would be useful because we need conversation, and it's not
    always sensible to use the telephone. This discussion forum is good, but it will
    probably be more differentiated; now this functions as a discussion medium. I
    support your idea!
```

The number of messages about other issues unrelated to the Culture course was large in the preliminary phase, probably because then the students and the teachers were practicing their use of the virtual environment. In the session in which the participants were trained to use the VWS environment, 42% (27) of the posted messages were classified as community building messages, and 32% (21) as messages about other issues. Teachers did not direct the first practices with the VWS to content-related inquiry work (a notice from a videotaped training session).

The number of messages in the *content of inquiry* category was largest in the first week of the course period, when there was also another hands-on session in the school. In that period students were guided explicitly to define their plans, questions and starting theories of their inquiry to the virtual forums. The following is an example of content-related discourse:

```
17.02.2000 19.37.53 Problems, group A (John, boy student)
1. How have the different cultures affected the development of humans?
2. How have the cultures spread out in the world and how have they affected each
other?
3. Collaboration with Thomas:
What were the basic differences between the culture of American Indians and the
western culture??
What affected the disappearance of Indians?
How did the Indians' nature-based culture work?
4. What is the Islamic culture like actually? Is it as bad as the media represent it?

    18.02.2000 13.46.40 A comment (Mathew, boy student)
    Good start, just continue!

    18.02.2000 13.43.31 Large topics... (Hannah, girl student)
    Large topics... good topics... the effects of cultures on human development, you
    should consider what things to examine... the appearance, ways of life, economic
    state, environment... it might be difficult to examine everything.
```

```
Effects on each other or the spreading... very good topic, but it is quite
difficult, at least those effects... should you examine some special culture?
Indians... on the other hand, if you have these large topics also, that topic is
quite restricted to a certain place and it is also a small one... but it is also
interesting.
About that Islamic religion I cannot say much.
```

Especially later in the course most of the content messages were about designing the content of the final work. Here is an example of the message from the Australian group:

```
23.03.2000 11.09.22 Answer Sorry, if...(Ann, girl student)
... sorry that we did not discuss with you before the course about including the
topics of religion into our work. But we have a lot of material about that topic.
First we are going to tell about the religion of aboriginals, totems and 'dreamtime'
and its myths. In addition we are going to compare their attitudes towards life to
ours, and to examine, how they experience our religion and our God. We thought also to
include something about Jesus...
```

Teachers' content-related postings were mostly guidance for the inquiry process. For example:

```
29.02.2000 08.39.28 I want information (Peter, philosophy teacher)
Do you remember, that I asked the other day for a list of your beliefs and conceptions
about the Middle Ages. I thought, that BEFORE you start to read Litzen's book etc.,
you should write your conceptions about what the Middle Ages are either as a mind map
or as an idea list. It can be a quite long list. Is Xena medieval? What about Conan?
You understand the usefulness of this, don't you? Don't be afraid of possible
"mistakes" - in this work you cannot make them.
```

According to the analysis, very little of the content-specific discussion was actual conceptual discourse or formulation of research questions and explanations. The students and the teachers did not actually use the virtual environment very much as a forum for collaborative knowledge building, or for sharing of knowledge productions. Most of the content-related knowledge construction probably happened in face-to-face meetings with the group members and the tutoring teachers, not through the VWS.

In the VWS the amount of *process organization* messages increased after the small groups were formed, and it continued to increase towards the end of the course. Many of the process organization messages handled daily, practical things such as arranging meetings or explaining activities to be done. The following is an example of process organization discourse in the Music group:

```
09.03.2000 17.09.11 How are you (Susan, music teacher)
What is the situation in the research about the biological effects of music, or are
you still planning it. Regards, Susan
    09.03.2000 22.48.04 Thanks, very well...(Jerry, boy student)
    we have started the research, but because the music made Mike sick, we have to
    "run" in the same place for a while.
        13.03.2000 10.32.44 Sharing the work (Rita, computer teacher)
        Would it be useful to share your work so that if the one is sick, the other
        can somehow continue the work before the time runs out.
```

During the course the students prepared a presentation of their course work and presented it in the closing event. Planning of the concrete presentation was also one dominant theme in the process organization messages. The discussions were more like those in traditional school projects where the form of the end product starts to dominate as the object of the work.

Toward the end of the course, questions about *course evaluation*, rules and study criteria started to interest the students more, and it seemed to have been a problem that the criteria were not clearly specified in the beginning. The original goals of the course had been quite advanced ideas about knowledge building and progressive inquiry, but towards the end the teachers and the students had to enter into agreement about course completion according to the curriculum. One of the longest and 'hottest' discussion threads (12 messages) in the virtual environment was about course evaluation and deadlines for the work. For example, one girl student had problems with understanding the idea of getting comments and revising the work:

```
30.03.2000 08.03.12 Returning the work (Peter, philosophy teacher)
Well, simply: you bring on the 5th the work you have. Some groups may be so ready, that
nothing can be added to the work. Most of the works consist of several parts. At least
some parts may possibly be improved? Maybe there is something to add, or to correct?
Why do you think that you cannot change the work that has been returned? This is not a
final exam.
Peter
```

```
01.04.2000 16.06.18 It cannot be changed, and that's it! (Ann, female student)
Our work is either ready, or then it is not. It is a sound whole, a story, and
there are two options: either we return it as a whole or we don't return it at
all.
```

Two female students even refused to come to the evaluation meeting after the course had ended because they had not yet come to an agreement with the teachers about their course grades. There was an obvious contradiction between the traditions and demands of the conventional school culture and the new goals of virtual, collaborative inquiry work.

Differences in the students' and the teachers' contribution to virtual communication

We wanted to examine whether there were differences in the students' and the teachers' activity in the virtual collaboration. The evaluated project was suitable for comparing students and teachers because there were so many teachers involved compared to the number of students, although most teachers' contribution to the project was rather small.

In Table 1 are presented the general frequencies and proportions of each message content category in the students' and the teachers' messages. The general content profiles did not differ much (correlation of the distribution was 0.71). According to $\chi 2$-test there was a significant difference between the groups ($\chi 2 = 26.8$, df = 4, p<.001). Cell-specific exact tests (Bergman & El-Khouri, 1987) were carried out in order to examine whether the observed frequencies in each cell deviated from what could be expected by chance alone.

Table 1. Contents of the students' and the teachers' messages in the VWS discourse forums.

	Students (N = 14)		**Teachers (N = 7)**	
Content category	f	%	f	%
Content of inquiry	104	34	76	34
Community building	65	21	40	18
Process organization	55*	18	74†	33
Course evaluation	40	13	27	12
Other issues	44	14	9*	4
Total	308	100	226	100

Note. Significance tests are based on binomial probability estimations (Bergman & El-Khouri, 1987);
* = Observed frequency smaller than expected by chance alone (p < .01);
† = Observed frequency larger than expected by chance alone (p < .01).

The results indicated that in the virtual communication, the teachers concentrated more than the students on organizing the group processes, although we expected that the teachers would take more responsibility for the advancement of epistemic and content-specific inquiry. Also intriguing is that both the teachers and the students took responsibility for organizing the work of the whole virtual community and keeping the virtual work active. A quite expected result is that the students had more postings than teachers, of other than project-related issues.

Another indication of the teachers' strong efforts to organize the group work through the virtual environment was the high proportion of the teachers' postings to the small groups' discussion forums. Teachers had written 57% (145) of the 253 messages in the group forums. Obviously, the students themselves did not use the virtual tool for their own collaboration, but did the actual work in face-to-face meetings. The virtual tool was used more as a communication channel between the students and the teachers.

DISCUSSION AND CONCLUSIONS

In this investigation we analyzed how middle school students and teachers succeeded in practicing virtual collaborative inquiry. We wanted to document the challenges encountered in applying new ways of working and to find indications of emerging innovative pedagogical practices. As Windschitl (1998) pointed out, qualitative research approaches are valuable in investigating phenomena in novel fields, such as technology-supported virtual learning applied in schools. The evaluated school project succeeded in surpassing many structural constraints in the school. Both the students and the teachers participated very enthusiastically and were motivated to experiment with progressive inquiry and virtual collaboration. The students took much responsibility for their distant work and completed many middle school courses from subject domains during the project. The final products of the small groups were large, multidisciplinary and unique cultural products.

First, we were interested in the realization of collaborative inquiry in the technology-supported communication. The features of progressive inquiry and joint knowledge construction were more obvious in the beginning of the course, when the teachers explicitly directed the virtual process towards formulation of research questions and theories about the cultural phenomena. Later in the course the web-based learning environment was not used for actual building of knowledge objects or for sharing expertise; the virtual communication (of both the students and the teachers) changed towards the organization of practical task-accomplishment issues. There are probably several reasons for this change. The organization of the course in sub-groups that had very divergent topics reduced the necessity for joint, knowledge sharing in the whole learning community. The web-based learning environment used did not have very sophisticated tools for higher-level knowledge building: the main collaborative tool was a threaded discussion forum, which did not allow sharing and modifying of joint digital artifacts, or did not include advanced built-in scaffolds for inquiry as CSILE (Scardamalia & Bereiter, 1994) or Future Learning Environment (Muukkonen et al., 1999). In addition, the students would obviously have needed more scaffolding in progressive inquiry, and more attention should have been given to the conceptual and theoretical goals of the course.

Second, we wanted to evaluate how the virtuality affected the inquiry process. Virtual work evidently needs a different kind of organization than CSCL practiced in face-to-face classroom situations. The great amount of communication concerning community-building issues in the beginning of the project indicates the necessity, mentioned by Schuler (1996), to make agreements of the collective work habits. Actually, in the virtual interaction, the students themselves quite skillfully took responsibility for issues of shared goals and social conventions. All the participants contributed to the virtual discourse, but the participation was quite unevenly distributed. The discourse was either not very sustained or not very topic-centered. The great number of process organization messages, especially in the small groups' forums showed that virtual collaborative inquiry needs a communication channel also for practical coordination of the work. More like epistemic inquiry, the communication resembled patterns of design process, as in a virtual project of textile students studied by Lahti, Seitamaa-Hakkarainen and Hakkarainen (2001), where over 20% of students' postings to a virtual learning environment were about process organization.

Third, we were interested in seeing how the virtual inquiry practices fit in the demands of the conventional school culture. The incompatibility of the new working methods and the school culture emerged as an important issue in the course. To begin with, some students withdrew from the whole course because they felt uncertain about getting the highest degrees in that way. Also, in spite of the high-level goals of the course for accomplishing collaborative multi-disciplinary inquiry, the teachers still had to grade students' work according to courses in the official curriculum. Based on the content analysis of the virtual discussions, we concluded that the lack of explicitly defined criteria in the beginning of the course caused problems to students both in planning the content of inquiry and in the timing of the work. In addition, the time of the course was not ideal for radical experimentation because the students were worried about their grades in the final, middle school report.

The participants had two demanding new challenges in the project at the same time: progressive inquiry and virtual work. A better structured process with commonly known and accepted goals, rules, and evaluation principles may have helped students to carry out a more profound inquiry process. If the participants had been more low-achieving students, they would have needed even more support and guidance. In general, children should have a possibility of practicing new working methods safely at school without the demands of grading; and growing up to a modern, knowledge building culture has to happen gradually throughout the whole school life.

ACKNOWLEDGMENTS

The first author was supported by grant from the Finnish Cultural Foundation.

REFERENCES

Bergman, L. & El-Khouri, B. (1987). Exacon: A Fortran 77 program for the exact analysis of single case cells in a contingency table. *Educational and Psychological measurement*, **47**, 155–161.

Bielaczyc, K. (2001) Designing Social Infrastructure: The Challenge of Building Computer-Supported Learning Communities. In Dillenbourg, P., Eurelings, A. & Hakkarainen, K. (Eds.) *European Perspectives on Computer-Supported Collaborative Learning.* Proceedings of the First European Conference on CSCL, March 22-24, 2001, University of Maastricht, the Netherlands.

Chi, M.T.H. (1997). Quantifying qualitative analyses of verbal data: A practical guide. *The Journal of the Learning Sciences*, **6**, 271–315.

Guzdial, M. & Turns, J. (2000). Effective Discussion Through a Computer-Mediated Anchored Forum. *The Journal of the Learning Sciences*, **9**(4), 437–469.

Engeström, Y., Engeström, R. & Suntio, A. (in preparation). Can a school community learn to master its own future? An activity-theoretical study for expansive learning among middle school teachers. Available: http://www2.ucsc.edu/people/gwells/CHATbook/Engetal.html.

Hakkarainen, K. & Sintonen, M. (in press) Interrogative approach on inquiry and computer-supported collaborative learning. *Science & Education.*

Lahti, H., Seitamaa-Hakkarainen, P., & Hakkarainen, K. (2001). The nature of collaboration in computer-supported designing. In Dillenbourg, P., Eurelings, A. & Hakkarainen, K. (Eds.) *European Perspectives on Computer-*

Supported Collaborative Learning. Proceedings of the First European Conference on CSCL, March 22-24, 2001, University of Maastricht, the Netherlands.

Lipponen, L., Rahikainen, M., Lallimo, J., & Hakkarainen, K. (2001). Analyzing patterns of participation and discourse in elementary students' online science discussion. In P. Dillenbourg, A. Eurelings, & K. Hakkarainen (Eds.), *European perspectives on computer-supported collaborative learning.* The proceedings of the First European Conference on Computer-Supported Collaborative Learning (pp. 421–428). University of Maastricht.

Ministry of Education (1991). Education, Training and Research in the Information Society. A National Strategy for 2000-2004. Available: http://www.minedu.fi

Muukkonen, H., Hakkarainen, K. & Lakkala, M. (1999). Collaborative Technology for Facilitating Progressive Inquiry: Future Learning Environment Tools. In C. Hoadley & J. Roschelle (Eds.) *The proceedings of the CSCL '99 conference*, December 12-15, 1999, Palo Alto (pp. 406–415). Mahwah, NJ: Lawrence Erlbaum and Associates.

Preece, J. (2000) *Online communities. Designing Usability, Supporting Sociability.* John Wiley & Sons, Ltd, West Sussex, England.

Salovaara, H. & Järvelä, S. (2001) CSCL in secondary school literature class - focus on students' strategic actions. In P. Dillenbourg, A. Eurelings, & K. Hakkarainen (Eds.), *European perspectives on computer-supported collaborative learning.* The proceedings of the First European Conference on Computer-Supported Collaborative Learning (pp. 537–544). University of Maastricht.

Scardamalia M. & Bereiter, C. (1994). Computer support for knowledge-building communities. *The Journal of the Learning Sciences*, **3**(3), 265–283.

Scardamalia, M. & Bereiter, C. (1999) Schools as knowledge-building organizations. In D. Keating & C. Hertzman (Eds.), *Today's children, tomorrow's society: The developmental health and wealth of nations* (pp. 274-289). New York: Guilford. Available: http://csile.oise.utoronto.ca/abstracts/ciar-understanding.html

Schuler, D. (1996). *New Community Networks. Wired for Change.* New York, NY: ACM Press & Addison-Wesley Publishing Company.

Windschitl, M. (1998). The WWW and Classroom Research: What Path Should We Take? *Educational Researcher*, **27**(1), 28–33.

Creating Context: Design-based Research in Creating and Understanding CSCL

Christopher Plekss Hoadley
SRI International and Stanford University
Christopher.Hoadley@sri.com

ABSTRACT
One of the biggest challenges in helping students learn via CSCL is embedding their work in appropriate social contexts and helping create a culture of inquiry and collaboration. This article describes how design-based research allowed the deliberate evolution of a set of tools and practices to help students collaborate effectively. The SpeakEasy, one of the earliest Web-based discussion boards, was evolved from prior discussion tools, adapted to an Internet-based science learning environment, and evolved to work with both online and offline classroom projects and practices. Research conducted as part of the evolution shows how social cues can be used to help students develop an integrated understanding of science. Implications for the design of socio-technical systems are discussed.

Keywords
Design, research methodologies, threaded discussion, science education

INTRODUCTION
This article describes a general approach to combining research and design in the creation of collaborative learning in an online tool. Rather than providing simple prescriptions on how to use the Internet for learning as determined by simple either/or comparisons, the "hard research" that is so lauded by the media, this article advocates a different approach to research and development in CSCL environments that is based on combining design and research. Research is important, and the defining characteristic of research is an empirical stance, a willingness to "listen to the data" and to look for patterns that hold true across time and space. However, as is true with most educational research, the simple studies and simple answers ("Which is best, A or B?") can be misleading. The tricky part of doing educational research on CSCL is in the details—interventions may take on widely varying forms depending on the teacher (if any), the learning context, and even the particular geographic location. In technology research in particular, many researchers ask questions that bely the role of context. "Is tool A better than tool B?" is a foolish question if one doesn't ever examine what is *done* with tools A and B. It's as if one tried to answer the question, "Are books better than pencil and paper in classrooms?" by running a carefully controlled study in which half the classrooms used each without regard to purpose. I advocate an alternative approach. In the past, work combining software design and research in education has been described as design studies, action research, or design experiments (Brown, 1992; Collins, 1992; diSessa, 1991), which I group under the label *design-based research methods*. In this article, I describe one program of research on a particular CSCL tool in which comparison studies were used to answer important questions, but every experiment was highly embedded in a web of efforts that blended creative technology and curriculum generation, proactive implementation, and iteration. This cycle of activities ensured that the comparisons examined by the research team made sense, and that the interventions we tested represent the best possible examples of their kind we could provide. By describing this example program of research, I hope to provide evidence that design-based research methods can and should play an important role in CSCL. In particular, intertwining design and research is especially important for establishing *collaborative contexts,* or activities and cultural structures that support collaboration leading to learning. Unfortunately, in much CSCL research essential components of collaborative contexts are implicitly codesigned by the developers of the technologies or the researchers, but they are not adequately recognized or reported in the research, reducing the applicability of the findings.

Design as a context of research
When we discuss *design*, we imply certain ideas about the character of the activities we engage in. First and foremost, design is purposeful and creative. In the story below, our purpose was fundamental to our approach: we were seeking ways to ensure that young students (in our case, 12- to 14-year-olds) were able to learn science, not only to develop theories about CSCL or learning in general. We were troubled by the deficits that seemed rampant, including disconnected knowledge that students might parrot but didn't understand and certainly couldn't apply to their own lives (diSessa, 1988; Linn, Songer, & Eylon, 1996). This actually set us apart from pure technologists in that our major goal was not to find application of technology, but to enhance learning.

A second defining feature of design is that design is open-ended. This is usually thought of as what makes design challenging (as compared to, for instance, "problem solving," Newell & Simon, 1972). However, open-endedness proves to be an advantage in educational technology research because it means our designs are well suited to the types of open-ended questions our research addresses, such as, "How can we best use technology to support reasoning in thermodynamics?" (as compared to, "Are computers better than filmstrips?").

Good design is iterative. The process of creating something to address a goal is repeated many times as the designed artifact or process is tested, observed, and refined. The iterative nature of design is often missing in research, but is vital in testing our interventions. By repeatedly creating, implementing, enacting, and improving our interventions, one begins to understand intuitively and empirically what works and what doesn't, and also which features of the design are essential and which are irrelevant to the goals. In typical design, especially typical software design, this type of refinement is an informal way of doing research—"user testing" can encompass experimentation that would pass muster with the most stringent research methodologists, but usually it is far more informal. The sage researcher uses mixed methodologies combining informal and formal methods according to costs and benefits (Neilsen, 1994). In the case of the research team I joined, we used this refinement cycle as an opportunity to listen to our data and to conduct studies that were robust because they were meaningful and were grounded in the extensive contextual knowledge that came from participating in the design process that created the intervention in the first place. As with scientific research in general, we used studies to test hypotheses and to ground us as we constructed falsifiable models and theories from our data.

Design narratives and their importance

One of the fundamental ideas in the scientific paradigm is replicability; a scientist's report of an experiment should include enough information to permit others to repeat the experiment. Unfortunately, this is often impossible in CSCL research, for two reasons: First, because our interventions are culturally embodied, the complexity of human nature may prevent us from adequately and completely describing our research context. This problem is well explored in the field of ethnography, and researchers turn to richer and richer descriptions (so-called "thick descriptions") of a research setting to communicate factors that may be relevant. A second, related idea is that educational research is often naturalistic and may be quasi-experimental, correlational, or descriptive. That is to say, often as researchers, we do not have the ability to control every variable, every iota of human experience in and around a classroom or learning environment, much less the out-of-school experiences students and teachers bring to their classroom lives. Because we cannot precisely engineer cultural context, we may not be able to exactly replicate an experiment. For these reasons, we may not be able to replicate others' findings since we may not be able to recreate exactly the conditions that they encountered. What this all means is not that empirical research in CSCL is hopeless, but rather that there is a high art to identifying which factors are most relevant to this particular situation and to communicating results in a manner that appropriately contextualizes them. While findings are not universal in the tradition of physical science research, they are often helpful to others in similar (but distinct) contexts. Rather than inscribing laws in some book of truth, the goal is to conduct research which leads to locally grounded theories and findings, and through application by experienced practitioners in other contexts, to uncover just how localized or generalizable research findings are.

In the context of design-based research, we must endeavor to meet the challenge of replicability by adequately describing our research. Not only is the researcher obligated to fully describe the tools he or she may have built, but also relate as fully as possible the context in which the tools are being studied, the activities and practices offered to the users, and, most importantly, the evolution of the context over time in response to the tools. Consider how infrequently educational technology research (even some CSCL research) carries this type of description; the usual study presents a technology fully formed as if it had risen from the oceans like Venus herself; describes, at best, little of how the technology was introduced into the research setting; and may not even describe how the technology was used before judging its "effectiveness" in learning by means of some (possibly unrelated) post-test.

Contrast the typical research paper with the notion of a design narrative. Narrative is a structure for conveying a series of related events, a plot. Narrative may omit details, but important agents, events, causes, and results are relayed. A design narrative describes the history and evolution of a design over time. It may not be as complete as, for instance, videotapes of the entire design process and all uses of the designed artifacts, but it does communicate compactly and effectively how a design came into being. By relating the design's changes over time, a design narrative can help make explicit some of the implicit knowledge the designer or designer-researcher used to understand and implement the intervention. Would that all interventional research included this kind of rich description of the "treatment" so that one might infer whether the results were applicable elsewhere.

Narrative is only one way of making sense of design-based research. In a number of cases, controlled studies helped inform the design decisions the research team and I made in implementing the interventions described here. Where appropriate, I allude to the experimentation or other data used to make our decisions. However, the goal of this article is not to provide a methodologically rigorous presentation of the myriad studies that informed our design, but rather to give the general shape of the design process and to describe what we learned in the large; by necessity, in covering more than eight years of work, I resort to a more sweeping and less detailed description.

Below, I make use of the design narrative form to describe the evolution of some of the collaborative technologies we researched and highlight the complementary roles of design and research. By reflecting on the evolution of the designs and research over time, one can see the strengths of this complementarity. The outcomes of our endeavors included locally applicable design principles (local sciences in diSessa's terminology) that help point the way to important overarching findings that isolate relevant factors in technologies' use (a more global science). We performed our methodological duty in trying to test some of our most important hypotheses with some of the strictest methodological techniques in place: controlled comparisons with random assignment, even double-blind coding of outcomes. For the details of these controlled comparisons, I refer readers to the cited papers. To really convey what happened, though, requires a story.

Designing for collaboration

This article is about some designs of technologies and activities that fostered collaborative aspects of learning, predominantly in the Knowledge Integration Environment (KIE) research project (Bell, Davis, & Linn, 1995; Hoadley & Bell, 1996) which developed software for Internet-based middle school science education. Collaboration research adds design complexity, is particularly sensitive to variations in context, and any intervention reverberates through the setting changing both the individuals and the social context. Time is required to see how the intervention settles into a more stable state as both individuals' practice and the group practices adapt to the new tools and possibly reach equilibrium. Here, I give a design narrative of work that provided rich contexts for studying how technology could scaffold student learning and knowledge integration in science. I will try to point out how technology, activity, and local culture interrelated in our studies and how our design stance helped our research, and vice versa. The central message is that by engaging in design on both a technical and a social level, one can arrive at valuable insights in how to foster computer-supported collaborative learning. This central point has been argued by others at a theoretical level (Koschmann, 1996); here, I argue it from the point of view of our research on Internet project-based learning tools.

THE SPEAKEASY DISCUSSION TOOL: A DESIGN NARRATIVE

The story of the SpeakEasy discussion tool takes place over a span of approximately eight years. SpeakEasy was one of the first two Web–based threaded discussion tools (along with HyperNews) that are so familiar to Internet users today, predating the introduction of the first Netscape browser. SpeakEasy has several unique features that have proven useful in fostering learning in science classes. In our last study, SpeakEasy discussion doubled the prevalence of correct conceptions in the student population and significantly improved partially correct conceptions. (Hoadley, 1999; Hoadley & Linn, 2000) To some extent, the point of this narrative is to describe how powerful technology can be in improving how students talk to and learn from each other. A second message is how beautifully subtle the relationships between tools and collaboration can be.

The story begins in 1992, before widespread adoption of the World Wide Web. Initially three people (Sherry Hsi, Christina Schwarz, and I) contemplated an interesting question: Could multimedia technology solve a problem educational researchers had; namely, that collaborative analysis of videotape was cumbersome and required same-time–same-place meeting in front of a videotape player? Hsi had recently seen some interesting uses of multimedia for messaging while interning at the Apple Multimedia Laboratory, and we each believed that we could help support asynchronous video analysis through similar technology.

Our design goal was straightforward: allow discussion of videotape among researchers who weren't in a single location at the same time. Like many design problems, this one capitalized on the potential of technology to make possible what had previously been impossible. We designed our initial prototype in HyperCard and dubbed it the Multimedia Forum Kiosk, or MFK. We examined prior interfaces such as Internet newsgroups (at that time, primarily an academic communication medium) and email mailing lists. We adopted an unofficial motto of "better than Net news" because we hoped to create a more reflective, less impulsive dialogue and, to the extent possible, avoid needless "flaming" (reactive, inflammatory comments that were more confrontational than the participant would contribute in a face-to-face discussion). Another important example we considered was Scardamalia and Bereiter's tool, CSILE (Scardamalia & Bereiter, 1992; Scardamalia & Bereiter, 1994; Scardamalia, Bereiter, McLean, Swallow, & Woodruff, 1989). We appreciated the ways in which CSILE encouraged reflective discourse, but we wanted to incorporate a more general discursive model than CSILE's (which was primarily science-focused), to foster a sense of community or awareness of others in the dialogue (CSILE didn't directly support social awareness), and to integrate video into discussions (Hoadley & Hsi, 1993).

Our tool had many common features (including a top-level organization by topic and threaded discussion) and several features which made it unique (Hoadley, Hsi, & Berman, 1995). First, it provided two collaboration spaces, one, the *opinion area*, allowed one comment per person on the topic which could be revised over time, while the second, the *discussion area*, allowed threaded discussion but did not allow revision of prior comments, only response. Secondly, the tool made use of *semantic labels*, or labels from a fixed set of choices (we borrowed this idea from Scardamalia and Bereiter, but while their categories were specific to scientific discourse, ours were aligned with a more general model of small group discussion: see Bales, 1969). Third, we made extensive use of social cues throughout the interface based on a theory of social representations. All comments were represented by face icons and all topics were introduced by a topic author. This tool underwent at least three major redesigns, with at least two incarnations as the Multimedia Forum Kiosk, and at least two incarnations as the Web-based tool, SpeakEasy. In this design narrative, I do not describe every design change (or even all of the major ones) but rather choose some to illustrate how our stance of design experimentation and design-based research led to new insights about generating collaboration for science learning.

Usability vs. conditions of use

Naively, we assumed that usability would be the primary indicator of success in our design. After creating the initial prototype, we tested the tool with subjects from an education research department using think-aloud analyses, time-usage analyses, and interviews. Our initial analysis did in fact demonstrate that the tool was usable—our test subjects were given no instruction and still managed to uncover and use every feature of the system, from reading and navigating comments to contributing their own comments in both the opinion area (nonthreaded) and discussion area (threaded). In one case, the think-aloud protocol provided direct evidence that our semantic types prompted reflective thinking and prevented a "flame." Interestingly, one of the first lessons we learned in this study (though we hardly noted it at the time) was the importance of seeding a discussion—adding not only a topic for discussion, but some sample viewpoints that would help initiate the discussion. By usability metrics, our system was a success already; people quickly figured out what it was for and how to use it, even people who hadn't used Internet newsgroups or, indeed, any online discussion tools other than email (Hsi, Hoadley, & Schwarz, 1992).

Our first field trial was less encouraging. The system was set up in a department lounge, and we undertook the time-consuming task of providing everyone in the department (around 30 to 50 people) with accounts, which involved laboriously taking and digitizing their photos. Since every member of the department had to pose for a photo, each person had at least some contact with the developers where we could explain to them the purpose of the system, more than we had done for our lab subjects. The topics we included were of general interest to members of the department (including both informal topics and comments on research data video segments). The accounts didn't even require learning a password, just choosing one's name from a pull-down menu. The location was frequented by most members of the department, as it contained mailboxes and was the location for well-attended, weekly community teas. We therefore hypothesized that people would participate in the online discussion, since the system addressed a known and professed need, and it didn't appear to provide any barriers to use.

Even so, the participation was underwhelming—each of four topics had approximately a dozen comments after an entire semester. We asked our friends and colleagues why they didn't participate, and heard answers like, "I don't have time," or, more tellingly, "I don't expect to do that sort of thing in the lounge." In fact, many people were discussing research in the lounge face-to-face, but the online system didn't really fit into the activity structure of the place. When people did use the system, they were often the only person in the lounge at the time (e.g., someone working late who had stopped in for a break or a cup of coffee). Once someone began using the tool, the arrival of additional people might spawn conversation over this artifact. This was an instructive first lesson on inserting our tool into existing settings and practices.

Designing functional activities and implementing conditions of use

Like many research and design projects, ours was subject to external constraints. What started as a small, unfunded project for researcher communication was repurposed. We received the first grant to study the system through a coalition of engineering schools, united in improving their undergraduate curricula through technology. This first grant was the result of what turned into an ongoing process of shopping our technology around, doing demos and presentations for anyone who would listen while trying to get expert design feedback from colleagues in HCI, education, and technology (Hoadley, Hsi, & Linn, 1993).

Initially, we took our tool into engineering classrooms on several college campuses, both graduate and undergraduate. At this time, we also started installing the tool elsewhere: a self-paced study center for undergraduates, a museum, the lobby of a college building. Partially through discussions with users, partially through comments students left in the system, and partially by comparing participation in the different settings, we realized that there were important preconditions for use (Hoadley, Hsi, & Linn, 1994; S. Hsi & C. M. Hoadley, 1994). The public installations turned out to be too idiosyncratic for us to understand what made some people use them and other people not, but the classroom experiences started giving us some consistent messages. First, we realized that students' use of the tool was directly related to their ability to access the kiosk running the software (remember, this was prior to widespread use of even the Mosaic browser), the degree to which the topics were perceived as relevant and interesting, and the degree to which the tool was integrated with their course. (Hoadley et al., 1994; S. Hsi & C. Hoadley, 1994) These findings seem obvious in hindsight, but addressing them is easier said than done, and involved significant exploration in our contexts. For instance, we thought of classrooms and public spaces as easy to access, but they were not because of the social discomfort caused by working on the kiosk in these spaces. Instead, laboratories provided a much more approachable venue, since students were used to being collocated with other students working on independent activities. Likewise, the perceived relevance and interest of the topics we posed came out differently than we expected. Topics that were highly controversial, or better yet, topics with diametrically opposed seed comments, were engaging. Generally, extreme viewpoints provoked reaction. Topics that we thought would be interesting to students (like discussing the strengths or weaknesses of the course) were too vague and provoked little interest.

Regarding integration with the course, we saw different instantiations of integration that supported the tool via the course and vice versa. In some cases, students felt they were better able to solve homework problems if they read and participated in the online discussion because the topics closely paralleled the technical content in class, and in other cases students participated because the instructor summarized comments in class and reacted to them, indicating a strong interest on the part of the professor. In many cases, anonymity played a big role in the participation, as students had few if any ways to communicate anonymously with their instructors besides our system. In some other cases, the asynchronous nature of the communication medium proved important; for instance, students with limited proficiency in English were able to participate in the discourse by taking extra time to read comments and prepare responses in English. The integration with the course also took some interesting twists. While some instructors actually provided participation grades for contributing comments to the system, we had nearly equivalent participation when an instructor read, summarized, and responded to student comments in class (this was a large course with nearly 100 students, and other opportunities to influence instruction were rare). The kiss of death, though, was superficial integration with the course—even if students were introduced to the system in class, if the instructor never mentioned the system again and didn't give grades on it, most students would opt not to participate. The few who did participate in these circumstances, interestingly, were often women or minorities. Without the in-class discussions and one-on-one interactions the kiosk provoked, the kiosk itself would have been a different intervention. Identifying the nature and scope of the intervention when the cultural changes provoked by our tools and activities were co-constructed simultaneously with use of the tools and activities made traditional before-and-after testing less meaningful. This coevolution of phenomena proved to pose a methodological challenge that would crop up repeatedly, one that is probably intrinsic to the problem of studying collaboration (Barab, Hay, & Yamagata-Lynch, 2001; Hoadley, 1999; Roth, 2001).

The overall lesson we learned, one which supports the strong design stance in our research, was that implementation and adoption required a lot of social design: designing activity structures that made sense in the local context, and implementing those designs either through our own participation in the community or (as was especially the case with sites we worked with at a distance) through communicating with leaders like faculty, teaching assistants, lab managers, and students about how to create their own successful activity structures in which the tool's use made sense. Had we simply scattered the tool to the four winds and tested outcomes, we might never have realized what conditions of use needed to be met, nor would we have been able to proliferate those conditions as a theme and variations in a wide variety of contexts. When testing new tools, as we were, any sort of research on effectiveness would have been meaningless without giving the tools a chance to succeed by helping establish best practices of use. This point bears repeating. Certainly, though one may study the outcomes of technologies in all the naturally occurring variations of use that might arise in the field, these studies may not answer the question we really want to know, which is: What will happen if the tool really takes root? Like the hypothetical study comparing blackboards to notebooks, we might get a lot of data but it doesn't address meaningful questions about how best to educate or support learning.

Evolving with the background (technology and culture)

Later in the development of the system, we began experimenting with our discussion tools in the Computer as Learning Partner middle-school science classroom (with 12- to 13-year-old students (Linn & Hsi, 2000). Initially, this experimentation began with the Multimedia Forum Kiosk technology and science-oriented topics (Hoadley, 1999; Hsi, 1997). There were important interactions between our tool and the culture of the classroom, interactions that evolved as tools influenced use and use influenced culture. Some elements of the local culture already supported use. For instance, students in this classroom (which had a 2:1 ratio of students to computers) were familiar with computers, and each student had some prior experience working on a computer. Likewise, the teacher had previously started a tradition of coming in to work on labs or computer work during lunch and immediately before and after school; the system benefited from these practices. Other aspects of the culture evolved in ways that we would not have predicted. For instance, the fact that the system was based on a sole kiosk (we actually had two computers in a single kiosk, but each student had an account on only one of the two machines) led to some interesting cultural outcomes. Initially, the single kiosk enhanced interest and face-to-face collaboration—students would gather around the kiosk and read over each others' shoulders as comments were made. The relative rarity of the kiosk machines made them more attractive, and soon "kiosk groupies" would frequently visit the machine as a social group outside of class time. Unfortunately, the emergence of these groupies began to erode access to the discussion for other students; the stronger the social bond between the groupies became, the harder it was for those not in the clique to access the machine. The teacher, who was aware of the problem, began to try different ways to ensure access, including a signup sheet for time on the kiosk and strategic shooing when clumps of people began to form around the machine. The teacher did not dissuade all groups from clustering around the machines, but rather based his actions on who else was in the room and whether they were likely to be encouraged or dissuaded by the current group near the kiosk (Hsi, 1997). This type of very nuanced design activity was only possible because the teacher was aware of activity around the machine (in part with the help of the researchers) and had a number of techniques to try to encourage equitable access. It is likely that in other circumstances different social issues would have arisen and required different interventions to allow all students to participate in the online discussion. Eventually, we moved to the Web-based SpeakEasy system which eliminated the problem of a single point of access, but raised other issues about which students had access to the Internet at home or other out-of-school locations.

Another aspect of our intervention coevolving with culture happened later, as the culture of technology changed outside the school. When we switched to the SpeakEasy tool from the MFK software (mid-semester), our students brought their prior practices easily to the networked version of the tool; and student participation rates escalated slightly but insignificantly. We found no differences in student comment length or quality. This switch occurred around the beginning of the KIE project, near the introduction of Netscape 2.0. At that time, we began to introduce Internet technology to the class by choosing a few students from each class period to be technology guides. At first, we saw an average of one or two students per class period (out of approximately 25 to 30 students in each class period) who had any experience with the Internet at all. Almost none of these students had experience with the World Wide Web. In an after-school session lasting about an hour, we gave the guides an introduction to the Web that included instruction on what hyperlinks looked like, how to click on them, and how to use the "Back" and "Forward" buttons to retrace their prior steps. The rest of the students got an abbreviated version of this tutorial and were encouraged to seek help from peer guides.

When students began to use the online discussion tool, they often perceived it to be a completely different social setting, with different expectations, than their familiar face-to-face counterparts such as in-class time or on the playground. Hsi documented how this worked to our advantage, as students expressed amazement not only that their peers could discuss science topics with them, but also that their peers had different ideas than they did about scientific phenomena. This eye-opening experience was described by many students in clinical interviews, and many students contrasted the rules of the new space with those in other social spaces, explicitly denying that they would ever have the same conversations with the same people (their peers at the school) face-to-face (in class or out). The ability of the teacher to "stake out" this new social territory as being for intellectual, student-centered, science-oriented discussion was a powerful point of leverage on the students' social interaction (Hoadley, 1999; Hsi, 1997).

Over time, this advantage dissipated due to changes in the cultural surround. Within three years of this initial run, the Internet went from being unknown to being ubiquitous. Not only did a majority of students come to class with knowledge of hyperlinks and browsers, they had favorite search engines, Web sites, and deeply held beliefs about what types of activity one would perform on the Internet. Our initial training needs decreased (no need to explain what blue, underlined text stood for) and student access from home and from the popular nearby library skyrocketed. However, students came to class with strong expectations about what online discussion was like. Increasingly, students would mention AOL chat rooms, email, and other online discussions in their interviews about the SpeakEasy, and it became more and more difficult to ensure that students held to the norms we tried to set in SpeakEasy. The teacher spontaneously began to differentiate the tool when introducing it to the class, by describing how special it was, how experimental, and so on, and by explicitly contrasting it with AOL chat. Maintaining the sense of our online discussions as new social territory required deliberate effort.

Likewise, we were aided by invoking cultural norms specific to the classroom environment. Students might not have had a good idea of what scientific explanation, argument, and questions looked like before coming to this course, but this was a genre the teacher could invoke as the students learned these concepts during the semester. This prospect in particular suggests how delicately intertwined the nature of the cultural practices and the nature of the tool itself are, and how locally (and temporally) specific they are. While one might think the 1990s are an exception to the rule due to the rapid growth of the Internet, in fact the technological and techno-cultural surround are always changing. Fads, new technology developments, and local culture will always mean our interventions are aimed at a moving target of existing culture.

Shaping collaboration through feature improvement

Given the plethora of external influences changing students' practices, do we as designers of technology have any leverage on the situation, any ways we can influence learning through the technologies? The answer is a qualified yes. In our work, we saw, again and again, how small changes in technology could have large and pervasive impact on behavior and practice. One of the most dramatic examples of this in our work occurred when the middle-school classroom got new computers; the classroom upgraded from Macintosh LC II computers to new, faster Power Macintosh clones. This change occurred mid-semester, so students had already begun working with our technology environment. Every detail of the user interface was the same, from the KIE software down to the operating system environment; only the speed of the computers differed. Overnight, student writing in their online assignments almost doubled, compared to their own work earlier in the semester and to prior semesters of student work. This experience serves as reinforcement of the idea that technology use *will* change over time, even if the tools we are studying don't themselves change. Likewise, it proves that the most powerful changes may come from the least expected places. Often, it is not what the computer makes possible, but what it makes easy, that proves to have the greatest impact. Because the rest of the research team and I had intimate contact with the environment under study, we could make mid-course corrections and help the students adapt to the technologies we provided and improve the affordances of our tools.

It is important to note that our design process was principled and relied on a specific, tentative model of how collaboration would foster learning. We recognized that poorly implemented collaboration could hinder learning as much as help (Linn & Burbules, 1993). Our model of productive discussion (after Hsi & Hoadley, 1997; Pea, 1992) dovetailed with the knowledge integration approach taken elsewhere in our research program. We faced two challenges: first, to ensure participation in discussion; second, to ensure the discussion was productive, meaning that it demonstrated the features hypothesized to be necessary (and possibly sufficient) for learning via discussion. Briefly, these features are: inclusiveness and participation (all members of the discussion are able to participate), the externalization of a repertoire of understandings or models of the domain (often different initial viewpoints), differentiation processes (where old models lead to new variants), linking (consideration of which models are coherent or incoherent), and selection (privileging or selecting the models that have the most explanatory power and coherence). In addition, as a component of a larger set of interventions (initially, the Computer as Learning Partner microcomputer-based laboratories (Linn & Hsi, 2000) and later the Knowledge Integration Environment suite of tools and activities) we had a responsibility to contribute to the overall goals of the project. We explicitly tried to help students develop their scientific epistemology through a coherent curriculum that included real-world experiences, laboratory experiences and inquiry, and critical examination of information resources from the Internet. Eventually, we succeeded in all these goals, although it took two dissertations to develop and implement a workable set of tools and activities, ensure that our tools were actually fostering productive discussion (Hsi, 1997), and demonstrate how this productive discussion leads to individual learning (Hoadley, 1999).

Anonymity: a highly context-dependent feature

Here, I describe the evolution of a set of technology features that helped support more equitable discussion practices among the students we worked with. Equity is an important issue, especially for middle-school science, where girls, who have higher achievement than boys in the primary grades, begin a downward trend compared to their male peers, presumably due to social factors. In particular, girls are often disadvantaged in classroom talk (AAUW Educational Foundation, 1992). Both because this is a recognized problem in participation, and because inclusiveness is an important component of our model of productive discussions, we had a deliberate goal of ensuring equitable participation by members of both genders. In our engineering work, we saw that the ability to communicate asynchronously, without needing to interrupt or take the floor to contribute, was an important force towards inclusiveness. (Asynchronous, text-based communication was also anecdotally related to the ability of non-native speakers of English to participate in the discussions in our engineering work.) We also saw that anonymity was important for participants who might not have social status but wished to express their views. This in particular conflicted with earlier theories that had driven our work: specifically, a theory that representations that included social context information and were socially engaging would promote ownership of ideas and motivate participation. It was for this reason that we had initially included face icons as part of the initial MFK system and had carried that feature through each iteration. However, we also heard that students were making use of anonymity in support of their participation, which would suggest that less social representations might be better. This became an important question for us as we investigated the role of identity in online participation and as we investigated how our system affected both genders.

The initial MFK system had a limited set of pseudonymous identities that people could use to contribute anonymously, such as Minnie Mouse. These icons were initially created to allow users to participate who had not been previously set up in the system. We also saw the possibility that they could be used to contribute anonymously and therefore made it possible to contribute using one of these pseudonymous identities even after logging in as oneself. Initially, we questioned whether consistent pseudonymity was important and several versions of the MFK were designed so that each person, when commenting anonymously, was given a separate anonymous identity, making it possible to identify which anonymous comments were made by the same or distinct individuals, even if the specific individual could not be identified. We did find in surveys that participants appreciated the ability to contribute anonymously. Some discussions were heavily anonymous (especially those discussing sensitive topics such as classroom atmosphere in the college engineering courses), while others had less anonymity. Interestingly, in one semester with the four engineering instructors, we noticed much less anonymity in the discussions of the two courses led by female professors than in the two courses led by male professors. Gender certainly seemed to be playing some role in the participation structures.

Hsi and I undertook a more careful comparison in the middle-school science classroom. Students were given free choice of anonymity, and girls contributed significantly more of the anonymous comments than boys (Hsi & Hoadley, 1997). Interviews with boys and girls revealed that the girls cited social safety (avoiding embarrassment) as the primary reason that online discussion was better than offline discussion. In what was expected to be a replication, we varied whether students were forced to attribute their comments to their real names and identities or were forced to attribute their comments. Surprisingly, we saw no significant differences between participation in the two groups, and no interactions between treatment group and gender (Hsi & Hoadley, 1997).

How could we explain these findings? In interviews with girls and boys in later semesters (with free choice of anonymity), girls often mentioned the option of anonymity as an important social feature that increased their comfort level in the discussion. Surprisingly, many of the girls who mentioned this *never made anonymous comments in any discussions.* As designers, we found this to be an exceptionally poignant example of a finding that would not have been uncovered without iterative design. We had created an interface feature that had important benefits for the collaboration without even being used! If use of the anonymity feature was independent of how the feature affected social comfort, how could we explain why some students used the anonymity feature while others did not?

It was around this time that we probed student beliefs about anonymity and attribution further. We surveyed, interviewed, and observed students to ascertain how they might view or use attribution in navigating or understanding student comments. Half of the students navigated the comments in the discussion (chose which ones to read or in which order to read them) on the basis of attribution, and students frequently stated that they liked being able to tell who had contributed a comment before and after reading the contribution. Many students explicitly said that they avoided reading anonymous comments. This contradicted the impression held by many girls that anonymity was an important safety valve to allow students to honestly and safely express ideas to their peers. It appeared that students were less likely to read anonymous comments, which defeated the inclusivity purpose of the anonymity feature, one of the central aspects of our theory of productive discussions. Students might feel empowered to contribute to the discussion if they could do so anonymously, but their ideas were not being heard by other students. Around this time, we switched from the stand-alone MFK system to the Web-based SpeakEasy.

We got our big break by examining who was making anonymous comments. We found that rates of anonymity were surprisingly consistent for any given individual over time. That is to say, the percentage of comments made anonymously by a person in one discussion correlated very highly with the percentage of comments made anonymously by the same person in a later discussion. Also, the percentage of comments made by a person in a discussion correlated with rates of anonymity for other students in the same discussion. Thus, some discussions had a large amount of anonymous participation by many individuals while others did not (Hoadley, 1999).

We finally uncovered a large part of the reason for anonymous contribution through informal observation and discussion with students in the classroom. Many students (not surprisingly) would skim the comments already in the discussion before contributing their initial opinion. If the students encountered mostly (or entirely) anonymous opinions, they themselves would contribute anonymously. This happened quite frequently since we had learned to seed discussions with comments to avoid an intimidating "blank slate" discussion. To avoid presenting these views as authoritative (coming from us as researchers), we added them anonymously. This anonymity would be perpetuated as increasing numbers of anonymous opinions accumulated, further discouraging students from contributing their views under their own name. The reason that some discussions had escaped this fate was that some students preferred to contribute before reading others' comments. These students were basing their decisions about comment attribution on their own sense of confidence rather than on the prior contributions.

Responding to this realization, we designed a simple intervention that would encourage students to participate with attribution. Resurrecting an interface design we had employed earlier, we changed the system to force students to contribute their opinion on the topic before browsing others' opinions. We had dropped this feature when we had introduced it previously because users were reluctant to state their views without exploring the topic (especially for science topics that were new to them), but we found this reluctance could be overcome. We also emphasized in our oral introduction to the system that students should revise their opinions as often as their views changed, even during their first login session, if change was warranted. The new feature and the new instructions had three benefits: students were less likely to comment anonymously (since they were basing their decisions on their own confidence rather than peer pressure exerted by the fictitious contributors of the seed comments), students were encouraged to develop a habit of revising their opinion area comments, and we as researchers got the beneficial side-effect of having a true student pretest for the topic (which was ultimately part of the data collection technique for our individual learning measures.) Overall, student participation—reading and writing comments—remained equally high as without the new feature (actually trending toward an increase), gender balance of contributions remained high (with trends favoring girls), and anonymity (which had inhibited other students from reading the comments) dropped significantly.

In this way, through a design stance and a close involvement with the classroom, we short-circuited what might have been a long series of expensive studies that would have misled us about how anonymity could benefit the discussion. Indeed, our view on anonymity in discussion changed from believing anonymous participation was evidence of inclusiveness to believing it was a threat to inclusiveness. By designing a new technology feature and some new activities around the feature, we were able to maintain the sense of safety in the discussion by allowing the option of anonymous participation, while greatly reducing the negative impact heavy use of that option previously implied.

Consider how differently this research might have unfolded if we had instead conducted laboratory studies. Certainly, since the discussions represented sustained effort on the part of the students, we would have had to make use of a demandingly long research protocol. The investment in subject hours required to run the experiment would have probably encouraged us to carefully pilot and then fix a particular set of instructions and a particular version of the interface. The iteration we conducted on a time scale of several years would have been far less likely. There is every likelihood we would have misinterpreted the role of gender and anonymity in the interface. Even if, by some miracle, we had uncovered the inconsistencies between girls attitudes as a result of the *presence* of the anonymity option versus the effects of *use* of the anonymity option, we wouldn't have had the informal observation that led us to not only a sensible explanation, but an easy remediation. This is the power of design-based research methodologies.

In this design narrative, I have described how a particular discussion tool coevolved with various activities in a context of learning science. The moral of this story is not about the particulars of the design of an online discussion system (this is another interesting story told elsewhere, as in Hoadley & Linn, 2000; Hsi & Hoadley, 1997). Rather, it serves as an example of the crucial interrelationship between the collaborative tool and the ways in which the tool is construed and embedded in local participants' activity structures. It also shows how a detective-like attentiveness to details and causes of social phenomena by participants (in this case, by the researchers and teacher) allows for a much greater degree of robustness, as idiosyncratic barriers to productive discussion can be sniffed out and addressed through (sometimes trivially easy) intervention.

CONCLUSIONS

Through this design narrative, I have described some of the advantages of a unified approach integrating design and research. First, as discussed in the section on conditions of use, not only usability but the development of conditions of use is a prerequisite to testing the tool in context; functional activities are part of the intervention along with the tool. Next, as demonstrated in numerous examples in the narrative, designed features do have powerful impact on collaboration and learning, but this impact is often hard to predict (such as the effective feature which is never used). Iterative design in context is an exceptionally good way to uncover these unanticipated consequences. Third, since local culture is a moving target, constant redesign and course-corrections are required throughout any interventional phase in research; by documenting change over time, the research is bolstered, not confounded. Lastly, the intimacy that comes with designing and refining tools and collaborative contexts during research can lead to important insights that can guide and support the research endeavor (as with the interpretation of anonymity findings). These anecdotes help illustrate why combining design and research can be not only a reasonable reaction to the complexity of tool use in cultural context, but also a beneficial one where design and research are each strengthened by the presence of the other.

ACKNOWLEDGMENTS

Many thanks to all my collaborators on the work in this paper, especially Sherry Hsi, the KIE Research Group, and the Learning and Design Underground. I thank the funders of our work including the National Science Foundation, the Spencer Foundation, and the Evelyn Lois Corey fellowhip. Special thanks to Ondine Hoadley Plekss for editing the manuscript.

REFERENCES

AAUW Educational Foundation. (1992). *How schools shortchange girls.* Washington DC: AAUW Educational Foundation.

Bales, R. F. (1969). *Personality and interpersonal behavior.* New York: Holt, Rinehart, and Winston.

Barab, S. A., Hay, K. E., & Yamagata-Lynch, L. C. (2001). Constructing networks of action-relevant episodes: An in situ research methodology. *Journal of the Learning Sciences, 10*(1), 63-112.

Bell, P., Davis, E. A., & Linn, M. C. (1995). *The Knowledge Integration Environment: Theory and design.* Paper presented at the Computer Supported Collaborative Learning '95, Bloomington, Indiana.

Brown, A. L. (1992). Design Experiments: Theoretical and Methodological Challenges in Creating Complex Interventions in Classroom Settings. *Journal of the Learning Sciences, 2*(2), 141-178.

Collins, A. (1992). Toward a design science of education. In E. Scanlon & T. O'Shea (Eds.), *New directions in educational technology.* New York: Springer-Verlag.

diSessa, A. (1991). Local sciences: viewing the design of human-computer systems as cognitive science. In J. M. Carroll (Ed.), *Designing interaction: Psychology at the human-computer interface* (pp. 162-202). Cambridge, England: Cambridge University Press.

diSessa, A. A. (1988). Knowledge in pieces. In G. Forman & P. B. Pufall (Eds.), *Constructivism in the computer age. The Jean Piaget symposium series.* (pp. 49-70): Lawrence Erlbaum Associates, Inc, Hillsdale, NJ, US.

Hoadley, C. M. (1999). *Scaffolding scientific discussion using socially relevant representations in networked multimedia.* Unpublished Ph.D. Dissertation, University of California, Berkeley, CA.

Hoadley, C. M., & Bell, P. (1996, Sept. 1996). Web for your head: the design of digital resources to enhance lifelong learning. *D-Lib Magazine.*

Hoadley, C. M., & Hsi, S. (1993). *A multimedia interface for knowledge building and collaborative learning.* Paper presented at the Adjunct proceedings of the International Computer Human Interaction Conference (InterCHI) '93, Amsterdam, The Netherlands.

Hoadley, C. M., Hsi, S., & Berman, B. P. (1995). *The Multimedia Forum Kiosk and SpeakEasy.* Paper presented at the ACM Multimedia '95, San Francisco, CA.

Hoadley, C. M., Hsi, S., & Linn, M. C. (1993). *Assessing curricular change with an electronic discourse tool.* Paper presented at the NSF Engineering Education Coalitions Evaluators Workshop, Baltimore, Maryland.

Hoadley, C. M., Hsi, S., & Linn, M. C. (1994). Innovative Assessment with the Multimedia Forum Kiosk: a Preliminary Report, *NSF Site Review, SYNTHESIS National Engineering Education Coalition.* Tuskegee AL: Tuskegee University.

Hoadley, C. M., & Linn, M. C. (2000). Teaching science through on-line, peer discussions: SpeakEasy in the Knowledge Integration Environment. *International Journal of Science Education, 22*(8), 839-858.

Hsi, S., & Hoadley, C. (1994). *The Multimedia Forum Kiosk Assessment Tool for Curricular Reform Evaluation* (Final project report): SYNTHESIS National Engineering Education Coalition.

Hsi, S., & Hoadley, C. M. (1994, April). *An interactive multimedia kiosk as a tool for collaborative discourse, reflection, and assessment.* Paper presented at the Annual Meeting of the American Educational Research Association, New Orleans, LA.

Hsi, S., & Hoadley, C. M. (1995). Assessing curricular innovation in engineering: using the Multimedia Forum Kiosk, *Annual Meeting of the American Educational Research Association.* San Francisco, CA: American Educational Research Association.

Hsi, S., & Hoadley, C. M. (1997). Productive discussion in science: gender equity through electronic discourse. *Journal of Science Education and Technology, 10*(1).

Hsi, S., Hoadley, C. M., & Schwarz, C. (1992). *Scaffolding Constructive Communication in the Multimedia Forum Kiosk* (Unpublished course report for EMST 291B): University of California at Berkeley: Education in Math, Science, and Technology.

Hsi, S. H. (1997). *Facilitating knowledge integration in science through electronic discussion: the Multimedia Forum Kiosk.* Unpublished Ph.D. dissertation, University of California, Berkeley, CA.

Koschmann, T. D. (1996). *CSCL, theory and practice of an emerging paradigm.* Mahwah, N.J.: L. Erlbaum Associates.

Linn, M. C., & Burbules, N. C. (1993). Construction of knowledge and group learning. In K. G. Tobin (Ed.), *The practice of constructivism in science education* (pp. 91-119). Washington, DC: American Association for the Advancement of Science (AAAS) Press.

Linn, M. C., & Hsi, S. (2000). *Computers, teachers, peers: Science learning partners.* Mahwah, NJ: Lawrence Erlbaum Associates.

Linn, M. C., Songer, N. B., & Eylon, B.-S. (1996). Shifts and convergences in science learning and instruction. In D. C. Berliner & R. C. Calfee (Eds.), *Handbook of educational psychology* (pp. 438-490). New York: Macmillan library reference.

Neilsen, J. (1994). Guerrilla HCI: Using discount usability engineering to penetrate the intimidation barrier. In R. G. Bias & D. J. Mayhew (Eds.), *Cost-justifying usability.* Boston: Academic Press.

Newell, A., & Simon, H. A. (1972). *Human problem solving.* Englewood Cliffs, N. J.,: Prentice-Hall.

Pea, R. (1992). Augmenting the discourse of learning with computer-based learning environments. In E. deCorte & M. Linn & L. Verschaffel (Eds.), *Computer-based learning environments and problem solving.* New York: Springer-Verlag.

Roth, W.-M. (2001). Situating cognition. *Journal of the Learning Sciences, 10*(1), 27-61.

Scardamalia, M., & Bereiter, C. (1992). An Architecture for Collaborative Knowledge Building. In E. De Corte & M. C. Linn & H. Mandl & L. Verschaffel (Eds.), *Computer-based learning environments and problem solving* (Vol. 84). Berlin: Springer-Verlag.

Scardamalia, M., & Bereiter, C. (1994). Computer support for knowledge-building communities. *Journal of the Learning Sciences, 3*(3), 265-283.

Scardamalia, M., Bereiter, C., McLean, R. S., Swallow, J., & Woodruff, E. (1989). Computer-supported intentional learning environments. *Journal of Educational Computing Research, 6*(1), 55-68.

M. (TECHNOLOGY TRACK): ISSUES OF REPRESENTATION IN CSCL

The Effect of Representations on Communication and Product during Collaborative Modeling

Simone Löhner, Wouter van Joolingen
Graduate School of Teaching and Learning
University of Amsterdam
simone@ilo.uva.nl, wouter@ilo.uva.nl

ABSTRACT
In this paper we investigate the effect of different external representations on the process and product of collaborative computer modeling tasks. Shared representations can significantly influence the processes of modeling and communication. In order to find the specific benefits of two different representations, we compare pairs working on a collaborative modeling task using a text based model representation with others using a graphical representation. The learners, secondary school students, used the modeling representation for two hours working on a task in the domain of physics. Results indicate that the two representations support different phases of the modeling process.

Keywords
Computer modeling, representations, simulation, collaboration

INTRODUCTION
Computer modeling and CSCL are two applications of information technology in education that have recently become more and more important. In the study presented in this paper we investigate the combination of working collaboratively (in this case in a face-to-face setting) and constructing runnable dynamic models.

The creation and manipulation of models by learners is increasingly recognized as a potentially powerful technique within constructive learning environments (Mandinach, 1988). In modeling environments, learners create executable models of phenomena in, for instance, physics or biology. This requires coordination and integration of facts with scientific theory rather than a mere passive collection of facts and formulas (Hestenes, 1987). Because a model is a conceptual representation of a real system that behaves in accordance with physical laws, creating models will help learners focus on conceptual reconstruction of reality and thus help constructing a unified and coherent view of science (Doerr, 1995; Hestenes, 1987).

Model building has been associated with constructing accurate and appropriate mental models. Through model building learners are able to 'run' their own mental model of a phenomenon (Jackson, Stratford, Krajcik, & Soloway, 1996) and it provides a way of asking whether they can understand their own way of thinking about a problem (Doerr, 1995).

When learners construct their models collaboratively, there is an extra benefit, because they also have to make their assumptions about the model relation they are working on explicit before adding it to the model. Modeling environments then serve as a shared artifact with which and about which discussion and co-construction of knowledge can be shaped. In this paper we focus on the role of a modeling environment as a collaborative workspace. One important property of such a workspace is the *shared representation* that is used to build the models. We discuss the properties of these representations and present an experimental study in which we compare two representations for models

Different ways of modeling
We distinguish two major categories of modeling in education, *expressive modeling* and *explorative modeling*. In *expressive modeling* learners try to externalize their thoughts about a domain by creating a model. Therefore expressive modeling makes ones mental models explicit, serving as a means for communication and negotiation of ideas. In expressive modeling there is no concept of a "correct" or "best" model. This can be the case where systems are considered for which no reference model is known or available or for which the model is too complicated to understand in detail, by the learners involved. Examples are models of populations, where the goal is to create and understand phenomena like the forming of clusters of population, with no claim that the model accurately describes the real world phenomena. The focus is on global understanding of phenomena and on the modeling process itself, and not so much on the rules of the domain.

In *explorative modeling* learners try to find a specific target model of a given domain. The target model is (more or less explicitly) present in the learning environment for example in the form of data or a simulation of the system to be modeled. The goal of explorative modeling is finding the rules governing the phenomenon under investigation using induction and thereby demonstrating an understanding of the domain that is being modeled. In our research we aim at explorative modeling. Learners collaboratively construct a model that explains given empirical data. Learners can retrieve the data that should be explained from a computer simulation that is also available in the environment. They can do experiments with a simulation and collect the data that can be compared with the output of the model they produce. Special to the situation is that in addition to the learner's model also the system model that can generate the data, is present in the environment, although it is not presented to the learner in an explicit way.

Representations and collaboration

Model representations are a means to construct models, but representations also serve as a vehicle for thought. External representations are not simply inputs and stimuli to the internal mind; rather they are so intrinsic to many cognitive tasks that they guide, constrain and even determine cognitive behavior and the way the mind functions (Zhang, 1997). Zhang calls this phenomenon 'representational determinism'. Zhang did his research on the influence of representation in problem solving activities, but we believe his conclusions will also hold for modeling tasks.

As representations play a role in supporting, guiding and constraining the cognitive processes in model building, we can also assume that they will have a strong influence on the way learners will communicate and collaborate when constructing models together. Suthers (1999) states: „...the mere presence of representations in a shared context with collaborating agents may change each individual's cognitive processes. One person can ignore discrepancies between thought and external representations, but an individual working in a group must constantly refer back to the shared external representation while coordinating activities with others..." (p.612). Tools in which learners can organize their knowledge, mediate collaborative learning discourse by providing the means to articulate emerging knowledge in a persistent medium, inspectable by all participants, where the knowledge then becomes part of the shared context.

As external representations can be tools for enabling and directing reasoning processes, the representation used for describing the model the learners are creating, is of paramount relevance to the way learners will engage in the modeling task. In (Löhner & Van Joolingen, 2001) a review is presented of several representations that are used in different modeling tools on the market, and an analysis is made of the different aspects of these representations. A distinction is made between the primary representation (text or graphics), qualitative or quantitative representations, primary model entities (variables or relations), the way complex relations are handled (by the modeler or by the system), the visibility of the simulation engine (need for programming by the learner), the amount of information that can be externalized and the amount of scaffolding a representation gives by preventing inconsistencies.

From the description of the characteristics it will be clear that representations can determine the modeling and collaboration processes to a rather large extent: representations determine the nature of the model that is constructed, e.g. qualitative or quantitative, and the process leading to it, e.g. by suggesting relations or offering sensible defaults.

Also it is clear that there is a trade-off between the various characteristics of the representations. For instance, it is impossible to let learners focus simultaneously on the structure of the model and the details of the relations constructed in a single representation. Choosing a graphical overview means emphasizing the qualitative model characteristics, choosing text implies a focus on the quantitative details of the relations. If the goal is to let the learner do both, the representation must offer different views of the model, like a zoom function on relations and/or variables. These are so called multiple external representations (MER's) (Ainsworth, 1999). Ainsworth shows that different representations used simultaneously can constrain each other's interpretation, construct deeper understanding or complement each other. In modeling for example the interpretation of a qualitative graphical model can be constrained by a quantitative textual model. The problem with MER's however is that, as Ainsworth shows, learners find it difficult to translate between the different representations.

There is also a trade-off between the ease of use of a representation and the expression power. An easy to use modeling representation may always yield a running model but the level of expression can probably not go deeper than semi-quantitative relations. A deeper specification could break down the internal simulation mechanism.

The two uses of modeling we identify, seem to put different requirements on the representations used for constructing the models. In the case of expressive modeling the optimal representation seems to emphasize qualitative views on the model and relations in the model also should be expressed qualitatively. Conversely, representations for explorative modeling should allow quantitative statements and should allow the system to generate quantitative data. However, the case is a bit more complicated. For some qualitative phenomena to occur in a model sometimes a more detailed specification of the model relation is necessary, for instance when phenomena depend on parameter values. In this case only qualitative input and output is not enough. On the other hand, qualitative representations used in models of a quantitative nature can help the learner in organizing the model and be an aid in finding the relations that should be specified.

THE MODELING ENVIRONMENT

In this paper we describe collaborative modeling by learners in a learning environment consisting of a simulation window and a modeling window (see Figure 13). The environment was built in SimQuest, an authoring system for discovery learning simulations (Van Joolingen & De Jong, in press; Van Joolingen, King, & De Jong, 1997). For the purpose of this study, SimQuest has been extended with a modeling tool. In the simulation window, the learners can conduct experiments on the system simulation by changing the values of the variables and starting the simulation. The simulation is dynamical, so variable-values can also be changed during the simulation. In the modeling window the learners can construct their own model. They can also run a simulation of their own model (a so called learner simulation) and thus compare the outcomes of the simulations of the two different models. The learners task is to construct build a model that gives the same results as the system model.

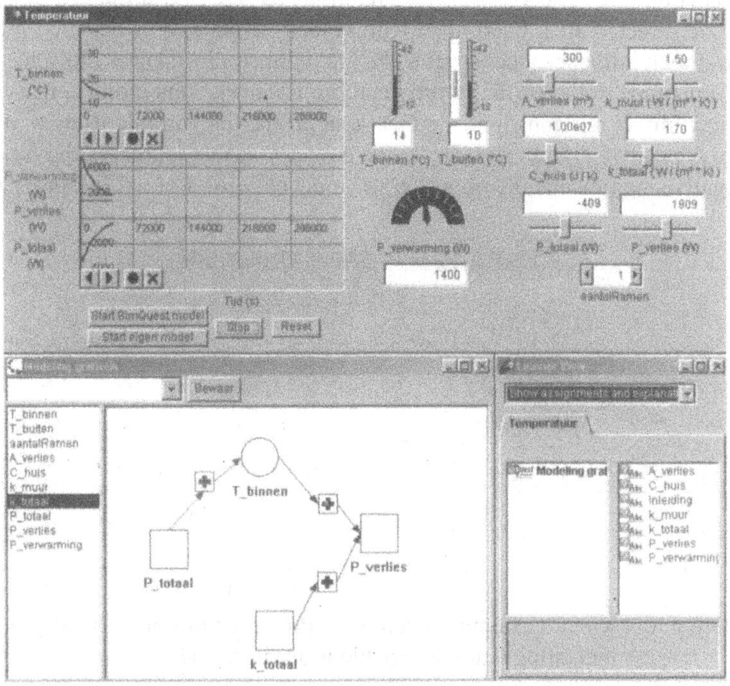

Figure 13 The collaborative learning environment with at the top the simulation window and at the bottom on the left side the modeling window and on the right side the explanations. The domain of the simulation in this case is heat and energy. The language of the environment is Dutch.

In the modeling environment there were two different possible representations. These were chosen to be as far apart as possible on the characteristics of (Löhner & Joolingen, 2001) in order to obtain a maximal contrast. In the following paragraphs the two representations will be explained in more detail

Textual representation

In the textual representation (see Figure 14), the learners type in the relations using algebraic equations. There are two types of equations, direct equations and rate equations. In a direct equation the learner specifies how a variable can be computed from others, for instance: "force = mass*acceleration". Rate equations take the form: "delta(velocity) = acceleration", where the delta indicates that the equation computes the change over time of the variable, not the variable itself. In essence, a rate relation is a first-order differential equation. The equations are not statements in a computer program, like DMS (Robson & Wong, 1985). Instead a simulation engine uses them to generate data and, for instance, takes care of the order in which they are executed.

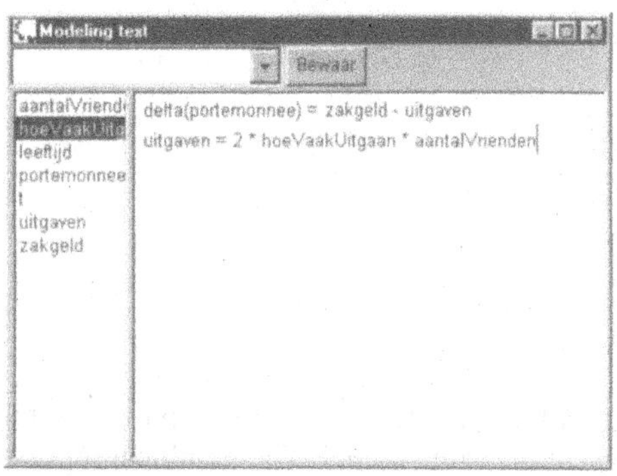

Figure 14 The textual modeling tool as present in the environment.

In the textual representation learners can, in principle, create variables by typing in their names. However only variables that are available in the underlying system simulation model in the learning environment can be made visible in the simulation interface. Here one of the consequences of the availability of a system simulation model becomes visible. The model defines a set of variables for modeling. This is different for modeling tools designed for expressive modeling, but inherent to the task at hand in which the model output needs to be compared with output from the simulation model.

Graphical representation

In the graphical representation (Figure 15), learners specify relations by drawing influence diagrams (inspired on Forbus (1984)), consisting of nodes and directed arcs. Each node represents a variable; arcs between two variables mean that the variable from which the arc is drawn influences the variable the arc points to. Influences are signed and exist in two flavors, similar to the rate and direct equations in the textual representation. Rate relations indicate that the influence specifies the change of the variable over time; direct relations indicate that value of the the variable itself is affected. The sign indicates the direction of the influence. A positive sign means that if the source variable increases the (rate of change of the) target variable also increases. A negative sign means the opposite, i.e. a decrease of a variable causes an increase of (the rate of change of) another.

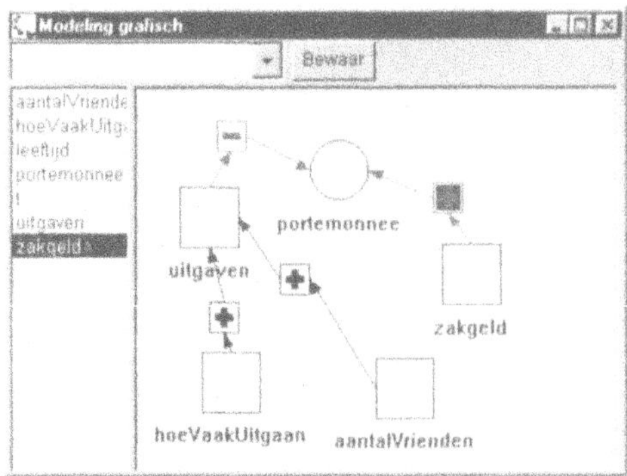

Figure 15 The graphical modeling tool with an example of a model. Rate relations are indicated in red, and point to a circle, indicating that the variable is a state variable.

To be able simulate the model in the graphical modeling tool and compare its output to the system simulation, the equations of the system simulation are used to determine the exact equations used for simulating the graphical model the learner creates.

As will be clear from the description, the graphical modeling language is qualitative. There is no precise specification of relations in the sense that the learner creates a single computational prescription that can compute the value of one variable from others. A feature of our graphical modeling tool, however, is that it can make non-local features of the model visible in the topology of the graph the learner is drawing. For instance, a feedback loop, an important modeling construct indicating that the change of a variable may be dependent on the size of the variable itself, is really visible as a loop in the graphical diagram as shown in Figure 16. The same model expressed as text does not emphasize the feedback loop character. Here the loop has to be constructed by substituting one relation in another.

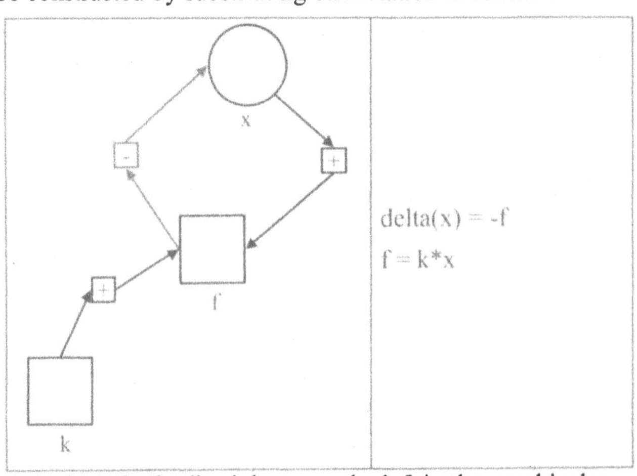

Figure 16 Difference in representation of a feedback loop, on the left in the graphical representation, on the right in the textual representation. Both models represent the same model. The graphical representation emphasizes the loop character of the model, the textual description focuses on the computational precision.

EMPIRICAL STUDY

The experiment was designed to explore differences in communication and modeling processes, as well as differences in the product of modeling, under influence of different modeling representations for explorative modeling. As the goal of the modeling task is explorative modeling, pairs of learners are asked to recreate the model present in the system (system model) by comparing it to a model they build themselves (learners model). Through building this model they are expected to gain a better understanding of the domain being modeled (temperature inside a house). The learning environment requires the students to induce rules about the domain being modeled from the data in the system model simulation (system simulation) and to come to an agreement about how to implement these rules in their learner model.

Method

41 secondary school students (grade 11) from three schools in the Amsterdam area participated in the experiment as part of their regular coursework. The students also received fl. 30,- (± 12 USD) for participating. The experiment took a total time of three hours.

First the students were tested for scientific reasoning skills with a test, adopted from the scientific reasoning part of the ACT (ACT, 2001). This took about 20 minutes. Then the students were tested for relevant domain knowledge on energy and heat (10 minutes). To get acquainted with the modeling environment each student individually worked through an instruction manual on an example model of personal finance, 'the contents of your wallet', for approximately 45 minutes. The students were randomly assigned to the two different modeling environments. After a short break the students were then divided randomly into pairs for the final modeling task. They spent about an hour working on a task on the temperature of a house. For this task they were given only a minimal instruction, to give them as much freedom as possible. During this task all actions in the learning environment were logged and also the students conversation was recorded. Finally the students were again given a domain knowledge test (10 minutes).

As the goal of this study also was to gain understanding of the modeling process, the students collaborated in a face-to-face setting. From a pilot study we learned that the communication between students was much more explicit when they worked face-to-face, than when they worked in a CMC setting.

The quality of the models the pairs constructed during the final modeling task was determined using a method similar to the one (Vollmeyer, Burns, & Holyoak, 1996) use (structure score). The score was obtained by adding the proportion of correct relationships and the proportion of correct signs of the relationships. (There were 23 possible correct relationships.) The score was then corrected by subtracting a penalty for redundant relationships. The score of the models could be in a range from 0 to 2. In the text representation it would be possible to break down the correct specification of the relationships even further (correct mathematical operation, correct weight), but to be able to compare the two representations we did not do that.

Expectations

We expect effects of the representation on the communication of the pairs during the modeling, on the modeling process and also on the product of the collaboration.

Because the graphical representation emphasizes the structure of the model, we expect students working with that representation to talk more about structural aspects of the model. For students working in the textual representation the emphasis will be much more on the precise form of the relation. We also expect that there will be more discussion and disagreement in the textual representation because it is less easy to just add a relation. In the text representation the students will be much more inclined to reach an agreement about the relation they are about to add, whereas in the graphical representation they can easily draw an arc and later delete it.

Therefore, one of our expectations about the collaborative modeling process is that there will be more experimenting with the model (changing, adding and deleting relations) in the graphical representation. For the textual representation we expect more experimenting with the simulations (learner as well as system) because the pairs need more data to reach the higher precision of the relations that is necessary. We also expect the pairs working in the textual representation to take longer before they actually start their first learner model simulation.

Finally for the product of the collaboration we expect better models in the graphical representation due to the better ability to experiment with the model, but on the other hand we expect the pairs working in the textual representation to have a better understanding of the found relationships.

RESULTS

Comparison of the two groups (graphical and textual) yielded no significant difference between the groups on the scientific skills pretest. Also there were no significant difference on grades in math and physics. Therefore we can assume equivalence of the two groups. The results of the domain test turned out to be unreliable. Also no differences were found between pre- and posttest on the domain for both groups, so the decision was made to discard the results of the domain tests.

Analysis of the data logged during the modeling session shows that the pairs working in the graphical representation run simulations of more different models (M=25.8, SD=11.1) than those working in the textual representation (M=16.4, SD=14.4). This difference is significant at an alpha level of 0.05.

The pairs working in the graphical representation also constructed more complex models. In their first models on average they used 6.1 (SD=3.7) relations, as compared to an average of 2.6 (SD=0.7) relations in the textual representation. The final models in the graphical representation also consisted of more relationships (M=10.7, SD=4 compared to M=7.5, SD=2.7 in the textual representation).

Not only were the models the pairs in the graphical representation constructed more complex, they also scored higher on our model structure score (score on the last model: graphical M=1.3, SD=0.6 and textual M=0.5, SD=0.4). All aforementioned differences between the representations are significant at an alpha level of 0.05. We found no correlation between the average score of the pairs on the scientific reasoning test and the model score of the last model.

	Number of different learner models	Number of relations in the first model	Number of relations in the last model	Model structure score of the last model
Textual	16.4 (14.4)	2.6 (0.7)	7.5 (2.7)	0.5 (0.4)
Graphical	25.8 (11.1)	6.1 (3.7)	10.7 (4)	1.3 (0.6)

Table 1 Overview of means and standard deviations (in parentheses) of some modeling process measures for the two representations (textual and graphical)

Although the number of simulations the pairs used was also higher in the graphical representation (see Table 2) the total time the pairs spent running both the system and the learner simulation did not significantly differ between the representations. Thus the pairs working in the graphical representation use more, but shorter simulations. The average number of simulations (both system and learner) per model was low (M=2.7, SD=0.6 graphical and M=3.2, SD=1.8 textual). This last difference is not significant. Also the time the pairs took before running their first self-made model was not significantly different (graphical M=6.7 min, SD=4.2, textual M=3.7 min, SD=2.1).

	Number of system simulations	Total time running system simulations	Number of learner simulations	Total time running learner simulations	Number of simulations (system and learner) per compiled model
Textual	17.9 (11.7)	10,8 min (8,0)	21.7 (14.7)	7,3 min (3.5)	3.2 (1.8)
Graphical	28.3 (12.6)	9.8 min (3.9)	39.0 (19.0)	10,8 min (4,1)	2.7 (0.6)

Table 2 Overview of means and standard deviations (in parentheses) of measures for the use of the simulation during the modeling process for the two representations (textual and graphical)

Influence of the representations on the communication

The two representations also give rise to different behavior of the collaborating pairs. In the graphical representations relationships can be drawn very easily, whereas in the textual representation the precise form had to be determined. Therefore in the graphical representation the focus of the conversation often jumps quickly from one relation to another.

A typical 'graphical' pair makes its relations on the basis of 'correlations' between the behaviors of variables. They look what happens when they change a variable, and then add those relation(s) to their model. In the textual representation often initially the same kind of reasoning is followed, but that is not enough for them to be able to add the relation to their model. They have to go deeper into specifying their relations. Sometimes the textual pairs express the need to just quickly sketch a relation. But also the graphical pairs are sometimes hindered by their representation, because it does not give them enough insight in what is actually happening in the model.

The following protocol fragment gives an example of the type of reasoning of a pair of learners working with a graphical modeling tool.

Students start a simulation of the system model (SimQuest model) and play around with the variables
A: OK, lets see. You see that P_total goes up, P_loss goes down.
B: Yes. P_total ... P_loss and T_inside.
A: Try what you can change here, in the SimQuest model. You can just ... with those sliders
A: No, not that one, not that one, not that ... That one. C_house. A_loss, A_loss?

B: Sure
A: K_wall? K_wall?
B: That too
A: K_wall has a relation to k_total. K_wall up, k_total up.
B: When k_total goes up, P_total goes... where? Up.
A: And temperature? I mean temperature outside? Temperature outside, OK, errr temperature outside that...
B: Number of windows
A: {writes} number of windows
B: That has an effect on k_total.
A: Wait a minute, what does it have?
B: It has an effect on k_total.
A: {writes} K_total, yes
B: K_total has an effect on P_total

In this protocol fragment, the students are playing with the simulation and are noting what happens when they change the value of an input variable on a purely phenomenological level. They do not actually think about the meaning of their findings, they just look for correlations in the behavior of variables. They also jump very quickly from one relation to the next. After this fragment, the students quickly add the relations they 'found' to their model. In the text representation this type of modeling is impossible. In the following fragment the learners would like to be able to sketch their model, but are hindered by their representation.

B: Let's start with P_heating, because … if that is higher then …
A: Huh? But that's not possible
B: {Asks researcher} So you write for instance … if the heating is turned up, the temperature inside increases … if it's low then the temperature decreases
R: Yes?
A: So how do I write that?
R: What exactly do you want to say? Because this is a textual modeling-tool. You have to be precise in what you want to say.
B: You can't say P_heating, the bigger …
R: No, you have to look at what exactly is happening

If they had been working in the graphical representation, this would not have been a problem. They could have just drawn the relation between the heating and the inside temperature, without having to think about an exact formulation. The student's working with the textual representation thus often have to spend a lot of time thinking about the mathematics behind the model, as can be seen in the following fragment.

A: So P_loss is…
B: Less
A: But what kind of relation is it? Isn't it a ehhh what's it called, exponential? Isn't it? That's this kind of formula, we have to make an exponential formula right?
B: Why don't we …
A: Well, that's why I said exponential thing. He but that is right, isn't it? That you're closer to a value, so the formula… No it isn't exponential it's zero.
B: Then it has to stay
A: No, because then it's a what's it called
B: Asymmetrical
A: Then it's a valley, valley yes then it's an asymmetrical. It's not x squared. Then you would get a downwards parabola right? That's not what it is.

But the graphical representation does present other problems. What the model is 'exactly' doing is not always obvious from the representation, as can be seen in the following fragment.

B: We probably should do more with the outside temperature. Cause look, if the temperature outside is higher, A_loss is also higher
A: Yes
B: Or errr lower. Should I put a minus?
A: Yes
Students add a relation between T_outside and A_loss to the model

…

A: A _loss is arealoss right? Squared meters
B: (unintelligible)
A: But what you're doing here, T_outside, that's in degrees Celsius, and you're subtracting it from squared meters.

What the students cannot see is that the negatively signed arrow they have drawn in their model does not represent a subtraction, but a division. Some students even express their dissatisfaction with the 'easy' graphical representation.

B: (Looking at another group) Oh, it looks difficult with the text tool
A: Is it difficult in text? I don't think so. Then you can at least see what you're doing!

CONCLUSION & DISCUSSION

The aim of this study was to explore the influences of different modeling representations on the communication process between collaborating learners, the explorative modeling process and on the results of the process. In a learning environment consisting of a simulation window and a modeling window, learners could experiment with a system simulation and try to build their own model of the domain (heat and energy). The two modeling representations used in the study were chosen to make the expected differences as large as possible.

The data indicates that the representation has a strong influence on both the modeling process and its results. This is apparent from the differences in activity and quality of the models. Activity is higher for the graphical group both for modeling and experimenting with the simulation, as well as the scores indicating the quality of the resulting models. From these results the graphical representation seems easier to use. The pairs made more complex models, which also scored higher on the quality measure we defined. But this representation also allows for a less deep specification of the relationships. Therefore the question is whether the graphical representation really leads to better understanding of the domain or if it just gives the students a better ability to try out possibly correct relations. The graphical representation seems to invite more experimenting with the model (more changes), probably because the commitment to a learner model relation is not as high as in the textual representation. In the textual representation the pairs have to spend so much time on formulating a relation they deem correct, that they are probably much more reluctant to delete it. Nevertheless the relations the pairs use in the graphical environment mostly seem very reasonable. They do not seem to be making their relations randomly, just to see what will happen, but seem to base their relations on 'common sense' reasoning.

The results on the use of the simulation in the two representations were not in line with our expectations. We expected the pairs working in the textual representation to use the simulation more than those in the graphical representation, and also we expected a higher overall use of the simulation. A reason for this minimal use of the simulation could be that the students are not used to using experimental data in such a way. Also the difficulty of the textual representation might have been a problem.

In the analysis of the communication of the pairs we have also seen the great influence the representations have on the communication. The different representations seem to support to different phases in the modeling process. The graphical representation leads the students too switching quickly from one relation to the next, and trying out every idea that seems to come up. This seems like a viable strategy for the beginning of a modeling process, when the learners do not yet have a clear idea about the model they are making. In the text representation this kind of modeling is virtually impossible. Learners have to actually think a relationship through before they can implement it. This seems like a preferable strategy for the latter part of the modeling process, when the model is brought into its definite form. Both forms of representation investigated in this study have their own particular role in the modeling process.

Therefore in realistic settings learners should use a mixed representation that providing the benefits of both the expression power of the textual representation and the easy experimenting of the graphical representation. But that alone is not enough. The modeling process has to be regulated by either the system or the learner, to make sure the representations are used for the right purposes and to help overcome problems that can be introduced by using MER's.

In our future research we plan on combining the representations, and manipulating the amount and form of the regulation of the modeling process.

ACKNOWLEDGMENTS

This research project is funded by the Dutch research organization NWO under grant number 411.21.115

REFERENCES

ACT, I. (2001). *ACT Assessment Homepage*. Available: http://www.act.org/aap/index.html.

Ainsworth, S. (1999). The functions of multiple representations. *Computers and Education, 33*, 131-152.

Doerr, H. M. (1995). *An Integrated Approach to Mathematical Modeling: A Classroom Study*. Paper presented at the Annual Meeting of the American Educational Research Association, San Francisco, CA, April 18-22.

Forbus, K. D. (1984). Qualitative process theory. *Artificial Intelligence*(24), 85-168.

Hestenes, D. (1987). Towards a modeling theory of physics instruction. *American Journal of Physics, 55*(5), 440-454.

Jackson, S. L., Stratford, S. J., Krajcik, J. S., & Soloway, E. (1996). Making Dynamic Modeling Accessible to Pre-College Science Students. *Interactive Learning Environments, 4*(3), 233-257.

Joolingen, W. R. van, & Jong, T. de (in press). SimQuest, authoring educational simulations. In T. Murray & S. Blessing & S. Ainsworth (Eds.), *Submitted to: Authoring Tools for Advanced Technology Learning Environments: Toward cost-effective adaptive, interactive, and intelligent educational software*. Dordrecht: Kluwer.

Joolingen, W. R. van, King, S., & Jong, T. de (1997). The SimQuest authoring system for simulation-based discovery environments. In B. d. Boulay & R. Mizoguchi (Eds.), *Knowledge and media in learning systems* (pp. 79-87). Amsterdam: IOS.

Löhner, S., & Joolingen, W. R. van (2001). *Representations for model construction in collaborative inquiry environments.* Paper presented at the First European Conference on Computer-Supported Collaborative Learning (Euro CSCL), Maastricht, The Netherlands, March 22-24.

Mandinach, E. B. (1988). *The Cognitive Effects of Simulation-Modeling Software and Systems Thinking on Learning and Achievement.* Paper presented at the Paper presented at the American Educational Research Association, New Orleans April 5-9.

Robson, K., & Wong, D. (1985). Teaching and Learning with the Dynamical Modelling System. *School Science Review, 66*(237), 682-695.

Suthers, D. D. (1999). *Effects of Alternate Representations of Evidential Relations on Collaborative Learning Discourse.* Paper presented at the Computer Support for Collaborative Learning (CSCL) conference, Stanford University, Palo Alto, CA, Dec. 12 - 15.

Vollmeyer, R., Burns, B. D., & Holyoak, K. J. (1996). The Impact of Goal Secificity on Strategy Use and the Acquisition of Problem Structure. *Cognitive Science, 20*, 75-100.

Zhang, J. (1997). The Nature of External Representations in Problem Solving. *Cognitive Science, 21*(2), 179-217.

The Effects of Representation on Students' Elaborations in Collaborative Inquiry

Daniel D. Suthers, Christopher D. Hundhausen

Laboratory for Interactive Learning Technologies
Department of Information and Computer Sciences
University of Hawaii at Manoa
{suthers,hundhaus}@hawaii.edu

ABSTRACT

In order to better understand how software design choices may influence students' collaborative learning, we conducted a study of the influence of tools for constructing representations of evidential models on collaborative learning processes and outcomes. Pairs of participants worked with one of three representations (matrix, graph, text) while investigating a complex public health problem. Focusing on students' collaborative investigative processes and post-hoc essays, we present several analyses that assess the impact of representation type on students' elaborations of their emerging knowledge. Our analyses indicate significant impacts on the extent to which students revisit knowledge and the likelihood that they will use that knowledge later.

Keywords

Collaborative representations, representational guidance

INTRODUCTION

External representations have long been a subject of study in the context of learning and problem solving tasks, with research showing that the choice of representation can influence an individual's conception of a problem and hence the ease of finding a solution (e.g., Koedinger, 1991; Kotovsky & Simon, 1990; Larkin & Simon, 1987; Novick & Hmelo, 1994; Zhang, 1997). This line of work has focused on individual problem solving. Little work has specifically compared the influence of alternate representations on collaborative learning processes (but see Baker & Lund, 1997; Guzdial, 1997). One might ask whether it is sufficient to extrapolate from individual to group problem solving: can we infer the effects of representations on groups by aggregating their effects on individuals? While we believe that much can be gained from such reasoning, we also believe that external representations play additional roles in group learning situations. Empirical research is not only necessary to validate extrapolations from individual studies to collaborative contexts, but also to examine new phenomena that emerge from the use of shared representations by distributed cognitions (Salomon, 1993).

External representations play at least three roles that are unique to situations in which a group is constructing and manipulating shared representations as part of a constructive activity. (1) *Initiating negotiations of meaning:* When an individual wishes to add to or modify a shared representation, there will be some level of obligation to obtain agreement or permission from one's group members. This obligation will lead to explication and negotiation of representational acts in advance of their commission. This discourse will include negotiations of meaning and shared belief that would not be necessary in the individual case, where one can simply change the representation as one wishes. Thus, the creative acts afforded by a given representational notation may affect which negotiations of meaning and belief take place. (2) *Serving as a representational proxy for deixis:* The components of a collaboratively constructed representation, having arisen from negotiations just discussed, evoke in the minds of the participants rich meanings beyond that which external observers might be able to discern by inspection of the representations alone. Residing in the shared context of subsequent interaction, these components can serve as an easy way to refer to ideas previously developed, this reference being accomplished by deixis rather than complex verbal descriptions (Clark & Brennan, 1991). In this manner, collaboratively constructed external representations facilitate subsequent negotiations, increasing the conceptual complexity that can be handled in group interactions and facilitating elaboration on previously represented information. (3) *Providing a foundation for implicitly shared awareness:* The shared representation also serves as a group memory, reminding the participants of previous ideas, encouraging elaboration on them and possibly serving as an agenda for further work. Individual work also benefits from an external memory, but in the group case there is an additional awareness that one's interlocutors may be reminded by the representation of prior ideas, prompting oneself to consider potential commentary that others will have on one's proposals. That is, it becomes harder to ignore implications of prior ideas if one is implicitly aware that one's interlocutors may also be reminded of them by the representations. In summary, there is good reason to believe that new representational effects worthy of study in their own right will be found in collaborative learning situations.

Further study is needed because these effects may differ between notational systems, and designers of representational tools for collaborative learning need to be informed of the implications of their notational design choices. Representational notations can differ on what information they are capable of expressing (Stenning & Oberlander, 1995), what information they make salient (Larkin & Simon, 1987), and what epistemic processes they suggest (Collins & Ferguson, 1993). We claim that the ways in which a collaboratively constructed representational artifact can play the three roles just discussed is sensitive to the notation's expressiveness and salience of information. Suthers (1999, 2001) calls this representation-specific influence *representational guidance*. See those publications for further discussion of the origins of representational guidance and a comparison of representations in CSCL systems. See also Toth et al. (in press) for a study of representational guidance in a classroom context.

To explore the ways in which representation impacts group learning, we have conducted an empirical study of the effects of representational tools on students' collaborative discourse and learning outcomes. In these studies, pairs of college science students investigated a problem in the area of public health. They used software based on one of three alternative representational notations (matrix, graph, or text) to compile data, hypotheses, and evidential relations, with the goal of coming to a conclusion about the cause of the problem. In our first analysis of the resulting data (Suthers & Hundhausen, 2001), we considered students' activity and talk surrounding evidential relations, as well as their learning outcomes as measured by a posttest and a post-hoc essay.

In this paper, we present new analyses that expand on our prior findings. These new analyses explore the influence of representational tool on participants' subsequent elaboration of the data items, hypotheses, and evidential relations that they represent. Elaboration may differ because the notations differ in salience of information (e.g., data and hypotheses are salient in graphs as visual shapes), and in whether they suggest consideration of relationships between new and previously represented information (e.g., the cells of a matrix prompt for consideration of *all* relationships between row and column items). From a pedagogical standpoint, representations that encourage elaboration of previously represented knowledge are beneficial in two important respects. First, they serve as *mediational resources* (Roschelle, 1994), facilitating collaborative interactions in which students elaborate on and refine the structure and content of their knowledge. Second, in encouraging elaboration of students' emerging domain knowledge, representations help students to integrate that knowledge with their existing knowledge, leading to better retention (Craik & Lockhart 1972; Stein & Bransford 1979; Chi *et al.* 1989).

The remainder of this paper is organized as follows. In Sections 2 and 3, we briefly review the design of the study, and our prior results. For a more comprehensive treatment, see Suthers & Hundhausen, (2001). Section 4 presents our new analyses. Section 5 discusses our general conclusions, and suggests avenues for future research.

STUDY DESIGN

Our study employed a single-factor, between-subjects design with three participant groups defined by the representational software they used: Matrix, Graph, and Text. All three groups were given the identical task of exploring an unsolved science challenge problem—presented as a series of textual web pages—by recording data, hypotheses, and evidential relations as they encountered them.

We recruited 60 students (32 women, 28 men) in self-selected, same-gender pairs, out of introductory biology, chemistry, physics, and computer science courses at the University of Hawai`i. Participants were all under 25 years of age, and had a mean grade point average of 2.99 (on a 4-point scale). All but three participants were native English speakers. (The three non-native speakers were fluent.) Participants were paid a $25 honorarium for their participation.

Pairs of participants used one of three different versions of software for representing data, hypotheses, and evidential relations. All three versions of the software had two distinct windows. Participants used the right hand window, identical in all three versions of the software, to move forwards, but not backwards, through a sequence of 15 pages that presented information relating to a science problem: the cause of a mysterious neurological disease on the island of Guam. The left-hand window contained a tool for constructing representations of the data, hypotheses, and evidential relations participants gleaned from the information pages on the right. This window varied by condition. The Matrix version contained a spreadsheet-like tool that enabled participants to type in data items along the left-hand column and hypotheses along the top row, and to select evidential relations denoted by "+," "-," or "?" in the corresponding cells. In the Graph version, the left window contained a tool based on Belvedere (Suthers et al, 1997) that enabled one to build a graph of nodes expressing data items and hypotheses, and links labeled "+," "-," or "?" representing evidential relations. The Text version contained a simple word processor into which participants could type data, hypotheses, and evidential relations in any way they wished.

At the beginning of the learning session, participants were given a brief (10-minute) introduction to the software they would be using. The experimenter read aloud and performed a demonstration while participants followed along. So that they could become acquainted with the software and the information-recording process, participants then worked on a warm-up science challenge problem (on mass extinctions), which was completely unrelated to the main problem. After 15 minutes, participants were instructed to stop work on the warm-up problem, and to move on to the main problem (on the neurological disease). Participants were given as much time as they needed to explore all 15 informational pages on the main problem. Following the learning session, participants were given 20 minutes to individually complete a multiple-choice post-test, and 30 minutes to collaboratively write an essay that discussed their hypotheses and the evidence for and against them.

PRIOR RESULTS

In previous analyses (Suthers & Hundhausen, 2001), we focused on participant talk and activities dedicated to evidential relations, as well as participants' learning outcomes. We predicted that participants who construct matrices would talk more about evidential relations than participants who construct graphs, and that both of these groups would talk more about evidential relations than participants who construct plain text documents. This prediction was made because the representation of evidential relations is no more salient than anything else in a textual representation; while graphs represent relations with an explicit object (a link) and carry with them the expectation that one construct such links; and matrices prompt for all possible relationships with empty fields. We also predicted that these process differences would lead to significant differences in learning outcomes. With respect to participant talk and activities, a content analysis revealed significant differences in the extent to which the three treatment groups tended to the topic of evidence. Specifically, our analysis found that, as compared to the Graph and Text groups, a significantly higher percentage of the Matrix groups' total on-task activity was dedicated to evidential relations. This result held for both their verbal talk and their representational acts with the software. Although Graph users had higher numerical counts of evidence-focused activity than Text users, there was no significant difference between these groups.

However, these process differences did not translate into learning outcome differences. We found no significant differences between the groups with respect to both post-test scores and the quality and quantity of information discussed in participant essays, although essay scores trended in the predicted direction. The lack of significance of learning outcomes was disappointing but not surprising. The total amount of time spent working with the tool was less than an hour. We speculate that this is not enough time for learning outcomes to develop fully.

ANALYSES OF ELABORATION

The results reviewed in the previous section furnish evidence for our general hypothesis that the type of representation students' use in collaborative scientific investigations will impact the focus of their discourse. We now turn our attention to an important related question: To what extent do the alternative representations encourage students to *elaborate on* previously represented items? This section presents several analyses that explore this question from different angles. Throughout these analyses, we use the term *elaboration* in the sense of *revisitation*, or subsequent consideration. Specifically, in our session transcripts, we classified as an elaboration any subsequent reference to an item, where a subsequent reference could take any of the following four forms:

- An explicit verbal reference to the item;
- An implicit verbal reference to the item through the item's representational proxy;
- A verbal or representational formulation of, or reference to, an evidential relation that includes the item (in the case of data items and hypotheses); or
- A representational change (e.g., changing an evidential relation from "supports" to "conflicts," or changing the particular wording of an item).

In addition, in order to increase the likelihood that participants' elaboration of an item was prompted by the representation, and not by participants' short term memory, we required that there be a reasonable delay between participants' initial representation of the item and their subsequent elaboration of the item. In particular, we counted only elaborations that took place while participants were viewing an information page that followed the page they were viewing when they initially represented the item.

Baseline: Representation of Items

To provide a baseline for our analyses of the impact of representation on elaboration, we begin this section by examining the extent to which participants represented information gleaned from the trail of web pages they encountered during the learning session. **Error! Reference source not found.** presents counts and percentages of data items, hypotheses, and evidential relations that students in each treatment group represented, both as mean counts, and as percentages of our *reference items*.

Table 5. Data items, hypotheses, and evidential relations each treatment group represented in learning sessions, both as mean counts and as mean percentages of the sets of reference items (standard deviations in parentheses).

	Graph		Matrix		Text	
	Count	%	Count	%	Count	%
Data	14.7 (0.5)	98.0 (3.2)	14.8 (0.6)	98.7 (4.2)	14.7 (0.7)	98.0 (4.5)
Hypothesis	3.8 (1.4)	57.5 (16.9)	5.3 (3.0)	72.5 (7.9)	7.2 (2.7)	80.0 (23.0)
Evidential Relations	9.2 (5.1)	25.0 (18.0)	47.5 (40.2)	63.2 (22.8)	15.0 (11.4)	30.9 (20.1)
Total	27.7 (5.6)	54.9 (11.3)	67.6 (41.8)	77.1 (12.4)	36.9 (13.3)	60.2 (12.0)

To interpret these data, we need to clarify two important questions: (1) what did we count as an "item?" and (2) what is a "reference item?" The answers to these questions are closely related. As one might have expected, participants chose to represent and relate information in different-sized semantic chunks. For example, upon reading the first information page, one pair created a single data item that read, "Northern Guam is a limestone plateau with high concentrations of calcium in the water." In contrast, another pair divided the same information into three separate data items: (a) "northern Guam," (b) "limestone plateau," (c) "high calcium in water." Clearly, both of these pairs represented the same information. In order to ensure that pairs who chose to divide information into smaller semantic chunks did not get credit for representing more items, we performed the same task as the participants in our study, creating in the process a set of 15 data items, four hypotheses, and 22 evidential relations that we believe a scientist exploring the materials would have created. These items, which we call *reference items*, served as normalized semantic units for our counts. Thus, in cases in which participants chose to represent smaller fragments of a given reference item, we collapsed all such fragments into a single item. Note that participants occasionally created items that were not in our set of reference items. (This happened most frequently in the case of evidential relations.) In these instances, we counted *each* such item, regardless of its chunk size.

Turning to the data themselves, we note several trends. While the three groups were identical in terms of number of represented data items, the Text group represented more hypotheses than the other two groups, as reflected by both the count and percentage of reference hypotheses represented. An analysis of variance (ANOVA) indicates that this difference is statistically significant (df = 2, F = 4.80, p = 0.0165); a post-hoc Tukey test reveals that the difference is between Text and Graph ($p < 0.05$). The Matrix group represented substantially more evidential relations than the other two groups, as reflected by both the count and percentage of reference evidential relations represented. This difference, according to an ANOVA, is statistically significant (df = 2, F = 7.21, p = 0031), with the differences lying between both Matrix and Graph (Tukey test, $p < 0.05$), and Matrix and Text (Tukey test, $p < 0.5$). This result echoes our prior results concerning discussion of evidence (Suthers & Hundhausen, 2001). Not surprisingly, the large difference in number of evidential relations represented translates into a statistically significant difference in overall number of items represented (df = 2, F = 6.68, p = 0.0044). Post-hoc Tukey tests show the difference, once again, to be between both Matrix and Graph ($p <0.05$), and Matrix and Text ($p < 0.05$). Finally, consider the mean counts in relation to our reference items. On average, participants represented 14.7 data items, 98% of our 15 reference items. This indicates that participants are in high agreement with us concerning the 15 data items to be gleaned from the materials. In contrast, Matrix and Text had on average more hypotheses than we did, and Matrix had far more evidential relations (47.5 compared to 22). Clearly, Matrix users were not as discriminating as we were in creating evidential relations.

Elaboration of Data and Hypotheses in Session

We now turn to our first analysis of elaboration, which considers the extent to which students revisited, within their learning sessions, the data and hypotheses that they initially represented. (Revisitation of non-represented items was negligible.) In accordance with our general hypothesis that representation type affects elaboration, we hypothesized that the Matrix group would revisit represented data and hypotheses more consistently than the Graph group, and that the Graph group would revisit represented data and hypotheses more consistently than the Text group. Our reasoning was that the Matrix representation encourages elaboration of data and hypotheses because it explicitly represents all possible evidential relations between the two (by cells to be filled in), and hence encourages students to reconsider represented data and hypotheses as they explore possible evidential relationships. In contrast, since the Text representation does not explicitly represent evidential relations, we reasoned that it would not prompt students to reconsider the data and hypotheses that they write down. We speculated that the Graph representation would lie somewhere in the middle of these two representations. Graph should encourage elaboration because data and hypothesis statements are reified as visual objects (shapes) arranged on the screen. The salience of these objects was expected to encourage subsequent discussion of the corresponding statements through reminding and ease of deixis. However, revisitations would be less frequent than in Matrix, because although Graph explicitly represents evidential relations by links it does not explicitly represent their absence, so it does not encourage exploration of all possible relationships.

Error! Reference source not found. presents the mean ratio and percentage of represented data and hypotheses that participants revisited in their learning sessions. (The denominators of the ratios are the sums of the counts of represented data and hypothesis items from Table 1.) As these numbers indicate, there exists a gap between both the Graph and Text groups, and the Matrix and Text groups. A non-parametric Kruskall-Wallis test of the mean percentages indicates that there does indeed exist a statistically significant difference (df = 2, H = 10.21, p = 0.0061), and post-hoc Fischer PLSD tests confirm that the difference lies between both Graph and Text ($p < 0.05$), and Matrix and Text ($p < 0.05$). These results confirm our hypothesis that Matrix and Graph are superior to Text for prompting elaboration on represented information.

Table 6. Mean percentages and ratios of represented data items and hypotheses that participants revisited within their learning sessions.

Graph		Matrix		Text	
Mean Ratio	Mean %	Mean Ratio	Mean %	Mean Ratio	Mean %
13.3 (3.7) / 18.5 (1.4)	71.9 (18.8)	12.2 (4.0) / 20.1 (3.2)	61.6 (21.5)	8.6 (4.3) / 21.9 (2.7)	39.3 (18.8)

Having detected general trends, we now turn to a more detailed analysis of actual reintroduction events. Specific questions to be addressed by this analysis include

- How often do participants actually get back to items that they revisit?
- Do they tend to get back to those items fairly recently after they represent them, or much later in the session, perhaps as their relevance becomes evident to a discussion?

We can answer these questions by examining logs of revisitation events indexed by (a) the number in sequence of the information page that was visible when the event occurred (there were 15 total information pages); and (b) the number of the segment in which the event occurred. A *segment* is a verbal utterance or a representational change that expresses a single thought or idea. (See Suthers & Hundhausen (2001) for details of coding.) Summary data from these logs are presented in **Error! Reference source not found.**.

Table 7. **Mean number of revisitations per data item/hypotheses, and the mean page and segment spans per revisitation**

	Graph	Matrix	Text
Mean # revisitations per item	1.7 (0.3)	4.7 (4.2)	2.7 (1.5)
Mean page span per revisitation	5.2 (1.7)	6.0 (1.3)	4.9 (0.6)
Mean segment span per revisitation	275.0 (203.7)	326.2 (114.2)	224.4 (83.8)

According to a nonparametric Kruskall-Wallis test, a marginally significant difference exists between the groups with respect to the mean number of revisitations per item (df = 2, H = 5.23, p = 0.0732). A post-hoc Fischer PLSD test indicates that the difference is between Matrix and Graph ($p < 0.05$). This analysis suggests that, while the Graph pairs revisited slightly more data and hypotheses than Matrix pairs, they did not revisit those items as often as did Matrix pairs.

With respect to the average page and segment span of each revisitation, a non-parametric Kruskall-Wallis test detects no significant differences (page span: df = 2, H = 4.51, p = 0.1047; segment span: df = 2, F = 3.42, p = 0.1805). We speculate that this lack of difference indicates that the sequencing of information in the pages, which dictates opportunities for elaboration, has more to do with when participants temporally revisit items than does representation type.

Elaboration of Evidential Relations in Session

We now consider the evidential relations that students represented and revisited in their learning sessions. Table 1 showed a significant difference in the percentage of reference relations represented, with Matrix representing more. However, the other groups may not have represented some of these reference relations because the data and hypotheses to be represented were not available. To rule out this explanation, we compare the extent to which participants actually represented relevant evidential relations upon representing the corresponding data item and hypothesis to be related. We focus on our set of 22 reference evidential relations because these are the only relations that we can reasonably expect participants to represent. **Error! Reference source not found.** lists the mean percentage of those reference evidential relations for which both relata were available that were filled in by participants across treatment groups.

Table 8. **Mean percentage of missing reference evidential relations that were represented. By *missing*, we mean evidential relations whose data and hypothesis components have already been represented.**

Graph	Matrix	Text
33.2 (21.8)	72.5 (25.8)	34.2 (23.6)

An ANOVA of these percentages (we can apply an ANOVA because the denominator is fixed) detects a statistically significant difference: (df = 2, F = 8.98, p = 0.0010) between groups. Post hoc Tukey tests show indicate the difference is between Matrix and Graph ($p < 0.05$), and Matrix and Text ($p < 0.05$). These results confirm our reasoning that Matrix users filled in significantly more evidential relations because of a property of the notation: the empty cells created when one represents a new data or hypothesis in the Matrix tool prompt users to fill in the "missing" evidential relations. In the other two representations, by contrast, "missing" evidential relations are not as obvious, so one is less likely to tend to them.

We now consider participants' revisitation of previously represented evidential relations. **Error! Reference source not found.** presents the mean ratio and percentage of revisited evidential relations. As these ratios indicate, subsequent elaboration of evidential relations was much more rare than elaboration of data and hypotheses, However, a non-parametric Kruskall-Wallis test of the groups' mean percentage of revisited evidential relations yields a significant difference between the groups (df = 2, F = 6.85, p = 0.0325). A post-hoc Fischer PLSD test shows the difference to be between Matrix and Graph ($p < 0.05$).

Table 9. **Mean ratio and percentage of represented evidential relations that participants revisited**

Graph		Matrix		Text	
Mean Ratio	Mean %	Mean Ratio	Mean %	Mean Ratio	Mean %
<u>0.2 (0.4)</u> 9.2 (5.1)	2.1 (4.4)	<u>7.3 (9.2)</u> 47.5 (40.2)	14.8 (20.4)	<u>0.8 (1.1)</u> 15.0 (11.4)	5.0 (7.3)

To explain the fact that participants revisited evidential relations less frequently than they revisited data and hypotheses results, we observe that evidential relations are already a syntheses of the domain information that participants encountered. Indeed, representing an evidential relation constitutes a more reflective activity than representing a data or hypothesis. We thus speculate that students tend not to see evidential relations as items that warrant further reflection. This is not to say that such reflection would not be valuable. For example, students might reflect on the warrants behind their inferences. However, getting students to reflect further on evidential relations appears to be a challenge for designers of collaborative representations.

We have two explanations for the difference in revisitations between Matrix and Graph. First, this difference may actually be symptomatic of a problem with the Matrix representation. While 46% of the revisitations of relations in Matrix were changes to the type of relation, there was only one change event in all of the Graph sessions and none in the Text sessions. We believe that Matrix users felt compelled to modify their relations much more often than other participants because they were prompted by the cells to invent relationships between items that were not particularly relevant to each other (as well as between items that were). The video data includes many examples of participants changing each relationship several times while they attempted to resolve the ambiguity.

A second explanation requires understanding relevant details of the software tools. In the Graph tool, one creates a new relation by selecting the appropriate relation's icon ("+", "-", or "?"), then selecting the statements that form the start point and endpoint of the link in turn. The method of changing the type of an existing link is entirely different: one must either right-click to obtain a link editor, or delete and then recreate the link. In contrast, the method of changing a relation in Matrix is identical to the method of creating it in the first place: one selects the cell of the matrix to obtain a menu of options. We speculate that there would be more revisitations in Graph if the method of modifying the relation became obvious while creating it. This observation illustrates the importance of considering one's instructional objectives even in the design of micro-level human-computer interactions.

Elaboration of Session Items in Essays

Our final analysis of elaboration considers the extent to which participants included represented items in their post hoc essays, which they wrote roughly 25 minutes after the learning session. In a sense, this is an analysis of *retention*: Do participants tend to remember and integrate into their own findings those items that they represented during the learning session? Consider this question with respect to two hypotheses. First, the null hypothesis is that there will be no relationship between representation and essay contents, and therefore no content differences between essays. Second, we might hypothesize that there is a relationship, but that it is independent of the particular representation being used: representing an item increases the likelihood that it will be remembered and included in the essay regardless of the representation. If this were indeed the case, then we would expect the Text group to include significantly more hypotheses in their essays than the Graph group, and the Matrix group to include significantly more evidential relations in their essays than the other two groups, because this is the pattern of representational counts found in Table 1. Departures from this pattern may indicate influences of the representations on retention for reasons other than the mere fact that the items were represented.

Error! Reference source not found. presents the mean number of data, hypotheses, and evidential relations participants included in their essays. ANOVAs suggest that half of our predication holds: The Text group included significantly more hypotheses than the Graph group (df = 2, F = 4.79, p = 0.0166; Tukey test: p < 0.5); however, there exist no differences between the groups with respect to number of evidential relations included in their essays (df = 2, F = 0.19, p = 0.8318).

Table 10. **Mean number of items included in essays**

	Graph	Matrix	Text
Data	9.8 (3.2)	10.6 (3.0)	10.5 (3.4)
Hypothesis	3.7 (1.3)	4.8 (1.1)	5.3 (1.1)
Evidential Relations	10.1 (5.9)	11.2 (4.1)	9.9 (5.3)
Total	23.6 (9.8)	26.6 (6.7)	25.7 (7.9)

Thus, more items represented in the session did not necessarily translate into more items discussed in the essay. This result admits the possibility that there may be group differences with respect to the percentage of "carryover" items: those data items, hypotheses, and evidential relations that were represented in the session and subsequently included in the essay. To test this possibility, we computed each group's percentage of represented-in-session items that were also included in the essay (see Table 7). Inspecting these percentages, we find that the Graph condition had a higher percentage of carryover items than both Matrix and Text. A non-parametric Kruskall-Wallis test indicates that this difference is statistically significant (df = 2, H = 6.48, p = 0.0391). A post-hoc Fischer PLSD test shows that the difference is between Graph and Matrix (p < 0.05).

Table 11. **Mean percentage of represented items included in essays**

	Graph	Matrix	Text
Data	63.1 (16.0)	66.2 (22.1)	64.3 (20.2)
Hypotheses	71.8 (25.1)	80.4 (28.5)	56.1 (14.7)
Evidential Relations	36.4 (33.1)	20.9 (23.0)	35.4 (29.9)
Total	55.4 (17.6)	36.2 (21.0)	48.9 (16.3)

In interpreting this result, note that Graph users were more focused with respect to what they represented in their learning sessions. Table 1 tells us that they were more selective than users of other representations in both the hypotheses and the evidential relations that they represented. Graphs prompt users to identify and represent *some* relationship involving each new item, but does not specify which relationship, and (unlike Matrix) does not encourage representation of all possible relationships. Thus pairs are faced with the need to discuss which relationship to represent, so they engage in a discussion of the possible relationships and their significance. We therefore speculate that Graph pairs are encouraged to engage in higher-order thinking when faced with the choice of how to connect a newly added item. In contrast, Text users (who had the most hypotheses in both the session representations and the essays, yet the least overlap between the two) were less discriminating in the hypotheses they represented, and were not prompted to evaluate these hypotheses in any particular way, so apparently reinvented hypotheses as they wrote their essays. (There is a marginally significant trend for hypotheses in Table 7 according to a Kruskall-Wallis test, df = 2, H = 5.27, p = 0.0716; 46% of the hypotheses in Text essays were new.) Matrix pairs may have filled in cells (47.5 cells on average) without being very discriminating of which relations are important, but were then forced by time constraints to select a smaller set of relations (11.2 on average) while writing their essays. This interpretation is corroborated by our coder's informal observation that some Matrix groups filled in the cells late in the session by systematically going down columns or across rows with minimal discussion, while Graph users usually linked items as they went, discussing each link.

DISCUSSION

Prior analysis of our data (Suthers & Hundhausen, 2001) showed that the exhaustive prompting of Matrix for consideration of all possible evidential relations leads participants to discuss issues of evidence more than users of other representations. The present analysis added the following results:

- Graph users represent the fewest items. Text and Matrix users represent more hypotheses than an expert might derive from the materials and Matrix users represent far more evidential relations than are relevant according to our analysis.
- Users of visually structured representations (Graph, Matrix) revisit previously discussed ideas more often than users of Text. Matrix users revisit prior data and hypotheses mainly to fill in the matrix cells that relate them.
- Revisitation of relations is rare except for Matrix users, who often modify their relations.
- The representational work done by Graph users has a greater impact on the content of their essays than the representational work done by users of Text or Matrix.

We draw several general conclusions from these results. The choice of representational notation for collaborative learning applications does matter. Representational notations can have significant effects on learner's interactions, and may differ in their influence on subsequent collaborative use of the knowledge being manipulated. Specifically, visually structured and constrained representations can provide guidance for collaborative learning that is not afforded by plain text. However, not all guidance is equal, and more is not necessarily better. For example, it is possible to over-prompt for consideration of irrelevant relationships. Whether the increased talk about evidence prompted by Matrix is valuable is a pedagogical decision that must be carefully considered in light of the possibility that many of the evidential relationships considered may be irrelevant. A representation such as Graph may guide students to consider evidence without making them unfocused.

We believe that each representation has its own strengths and weaknesses, and each may be the best choice for different cognitive tasks, learning objectives, and populations. In fact, our current version of Belvedere integrates three representational "views" (Graph, Matrix, and a Hierarchy representation not discussed here) of evidence models in one tool, providing an interesting platform for future studies. We speculate that Graph will be most useful for gathering and relating information by the relationships that motivated its inclusion; Matrix for subsequently checking that no important relationships have been missed and for scanning for patterns of evidence; and Hierarchy for performing selective queries on a complex evidential model.

There is of course a great deal of future work suggested by the studies reported here, ranging from further analysis of existing data to new studies. The analyses presented here only assess the extent to which students revisited represented items; they say nothing about the quality or depth of the exchanges in which items were revisited. What we really want to know is whether students are deeply reflecting on domain concepts and relationships. Ongoing work is analyzing the distribution of when relations were created and quality of the negotiations leading to each represented relation. An argumentation analysis of students' essays is also underway to determine whether there are any structural differences between the groups' essays. Subsequent analysis of our data will shift from comparison of group means to analysis of individual events, specifically to better understand how the different representations are appropriated as resources in support of collaborative discourse. Future studies currently being planned include attempts to replicate our results in distance learning contexts, with particular attention paid to the designed *integration* of discourse representations (chat and threaded discussion) with visual knowledge representations (Hoadley & Enyedy, 1999). We also plan to work with teachers in developing strategies for use of our multi-representational version of Belvedere.

ACKNOWLEDGMENTS

Laura Girardeau ran the study sessions, transcribed and coded the videotapes, and gathered much of the data analyzed in this paper. Michelene Chi provided valuable guidance and advice on the design and analysis of the experiment. This work was supported by the National Science Foundation under Grant No. 9873516. Any opinions, findings, and conclusions or recommendations expressed in this paper are those of the authors and do not necessarily reflect the views of the National Science Foundation.

REFERENCES

Baker, M. & Lund, K. (1997). Promoting reflective interactions in a CSCL environment. *Journal of Computer Assisted Learning, 13:* 175-193.

Chi, M. & Bassok, J. Lewis, M. Reimann, P. Glaser, R. (1989). Learning from examples via self-explanations. In *L. Resnick (Ed.) Knowing, learning and instruction: Essays in Honor of Robert Glaser,* pp. 251-282. Hillsdale, NJ: Lawrence Erlbaum Associates

Clark, H.H. & Brennan, S.E. (1991). Grounding in Communication. In L.B. Resnick, J.M. Levine and S.D. Teasley (eds.), *Perspectives on Socially Shared Cognition,* American Psychological Association, pp. 127-149.

Collins, A. & Ferguson, W. (1993). Epistemic forms and epistemic games: Structures and strategies to guide inquiry. *Educational Psychologist, 28*(1): 25-42.

Craik, F. I. M., & Lockhart, R. S. (1972). Levels of processing: A framework for memory research. *Journal of Verbal Learning and Verbal Behavior, 11*: 671-684.

Guzdial, M. (1997, December). Information ecology of collaborations in educational settings: Influence of tool. In *Proc. 2nd International Conference on Computer Supported Collaborative Learning (CSCL'97) (pp. 91-100).* Toronto.

Hoadley, C. & Enyedy, N. (1999). Between Information and Communication: Middle Spaces in Computer Media for Learning. In *Proceedings of the Computer Support for Collaborative Learning (CSCL) 1999 Conference,* C. Hoadley & J. Roschelle (Eds.) Dec. 12-15, Stanford University, Palo Alto, California. Mahwah, NJ: Lawrence Erlbaum Associates, pp. 242-251.

Koedinger, K. (1991). On the design of novel notations and actions to facilitate thinking and learning. *Proc. Int. Conference on the Learning Sciences,* pp. 266-273. Charlottesville, VA: Association for the Advancement of Computing in Education. Kotovsky, K. and H. A. Simon (1990). What makes some problems really hard: Explorations in the problem space of difficulty. *Cognitive Psychology, 22*: 143-183.

Larkin, J. H. & Simon, H. A. (1987). Why a diagram is (sometimes) worth ten thousand words. *Cognitive Science 11*(1): 65-99. 1987.

Novick, L. R. & Hmelo, C. E. (1994). Transferring symbolic representations across nonisomorphic problems. *Journal of Experimental Psychology: Learning, Memory, and Cognition, 20*(6): 1296-1321.

Roschelle, J. (1994, May). Designing for cognitive communication: Epistemic fidelity or mediating collaborative inquiry? *The Arachnet Electronic Journal of Virtual Culture.*

Salomon, G. (1993). Distributed cognitions: psychological and educational considerations. Edited by G. Salomon. Cambridge, England; New York, NY: Cambridge University Press, 1993.

Stein, B. S., & Bransford, J. D. (1979). Constraints on effective elaboration: Effects of precision and subject generation. *Journal of Verbal Learning and Verbal Behavior, 18*:769-777.

Stenning, K. & Oberlander, J. (1995). A cognitive theory of graphical and linguistic reasoning: Logic and implementation. *Cognitive Science, 19*(1): 97-140. 1995.

Suthers, D. D. (1999, January). Representational support for collaborative inquiry. In *Proceedings of the 32nd Hawai`i International Conference on the System Sciences (HICSS-32*). (CD-ROM). Maui, Hawai`i: Institute of Electrical and Electronics Engineers, Inc. (IEEE). Available: http://lilt.ics.hawaii.edu/lilt/papers/hicss99.pdf.

Suthers, D. D. (2001). Towards a Systematic Study of Representational Guidance for Collaborative Learning Discourse. *Journal of Universal Computer Science* 7(3), 2001. Electronic publication: http://www.jucs.org/jucs_7_3/towards_a_systematic_study

Suthers, D. & Hundhausen, C. (2001, March). Learning by Constructing Collaborative Representations: An Empirical Comparison of Three Alternatives. In P. Dillenbourg, A. Eurelings, K. Hakkarainen (Eds.) *European Perspectives on Computer-Supported Collaborative Learning, Proceedings of the First European Conference on Computer-Supported Collaborative Learning* (pp. 577-584). Universiteit Maastricht, Maastrict, the Netherlands.

Suthers, D., Toth, E., and Weiner, A. (1997, December). An integrated approach to implementing collaborative inquiry in the classroom. In *Proceedings of the 2nd International Conference on Computer Supported Collaborative Learning (CSCL'97)* (pp. 272-279). Toronto.

Toth, E., Suthers, D. & Lesgold, A. (in press). Mapping to know: The effects of representational guidance and reflective assessment on scientific inquiry skills. Accepted for publication in the journal *Science Education.*

Zhang, J. (1997). The nature of external representations in problem solving. *Cognitive Science, 21*(2): 179-217.

Influence of Authority on Convergence in Collaborative Learning

Teresa Hübscher-Younger, N. Hari Narayanan

Intelligent and Interactive Systems Laboratory
Department of Computer Science & Software Engineering
Auburn University, Auburn, AL 36849-5347
{teresa,narayan}@eng.auburn.edu

ABSTRACT

Teachers and students have established social roles, norms and conventions when they encounter Computer-Supported Collaborative Learning (CSCL) systems in the classroom. Authority, a major force in the classroom, gives certain people, objects, representations or ideas the power to affect thought and behavior and influences communication and interaction. Effective computer-supported collaborative learning requires students and teachers to change how they understand and assign authority. This paper describes two studies in which students' perceptions of authority led to learning difficulties while they were engaged in collaborative learning. Students converged on either a representation or representational style that they believed was authoritative instead of basing their choice on how well the available representations communicated a concept. Methods to help students avoid such premature convergence are suggested.

Keywords

Collaborative learning, authority, power, algorithm learning, computer-science students, college students, classroom

INTRODUCTION

It is often assumed in CSCL research that student ideas, understanding and communication styles are diverse, and that collaborative learning succeeds when the group can converge on a common understanding of a problem or concept. Students are assumed to be like scientists, looking at problems and concepts from different positions initially. Different understandings and knowledge are supposed to exist naturally in the student body.

On the other hand, often it is assumed that normal classroom practices are based on an information transmission model, where teachers present information to passive students. These two assumptions are mutually inconsistent. If all students obtain information primarily by absorbing it from one source, it is unlikely that they will have different knowledge and ideas.

The truth is found somewhere between these two positions. Students do differ and do not absorb information in the same way. However, they are often working with a similar set of assumptions, acquired from the same source. Students and teachers operate under a social system with methods for assigning, recognizing and understanding authority that makes it difficult for diversity to be recognized, acknowledged and effectively used by students.

A typical classroom is already a community of practice and learning. Teachers and students are not blank slates when they encounter Computer-Supported Collaborative Learning (CSCL) systems. College students, in particular, are not novices at assuming the role of student; they are skilled students with a lot of experience. They already have social roles, norms and conventions that effect social interaction and communication.

A major force affecting classroom communication and social interaction is authority, which gives certain people, objects, representations or ideas the power to affect thought and behavior. CSCL systems require students and teachers to change how they understand and assign authority. Students need to assume more authority, assign authority to their peers, and to value their own thoughts and ideas. However, this is not an easy transition to make.

Authority is often left out of the discourse of learning. Simon (1980) argues that authority has developed such a bad reputation that people avoid examining it: "A philosopher cannot discuss it without exposing himself to suspicion and malice. Yet authority is present in all phases of social life" (p. 13). Authority, he argues, is seen as unjust, unnatural, false and anti-democratic. But for a community to have common goals, communication and shared knowledge, authority is essential: A community needs "authority to unify its actions" (p. 50).

Authority is defined for this paper as the power to influence thought, opinion or behavior. People in authoritative positions, such as teachers in the classroom, can give students authority. Students can also gain some authority by citing authoritative sources, such as textbooks or lecture notes. Authority is what a person, idea or object needs to gain influence or power to change the thoughts of students.

The authority of participants in CSCL and of the representations they use for learning can have a negative effect on collaborative learning. A representation takes on the authority of its creator and the conventions they use. We found that for undergraduate students, whether or not a certain type of representation is used to build understanding has more to do with the authority of the representation, rather than its explanatory power.

In one study described in this paper, the students' perception of authoritative knowledge led them to difficulties when they engaged in collaborative learning. The students tried to use one representation presented by their instructor to answer all questions posed to them, regardless of whether or not it was an appropriate representation to use. They converged on a shared understanding based on one representation given by their instructor. Convergence early in the learning process is a hazard that is apparently difficult to avoid.

We also describe another study of students using the prototype of a system for supporting web-based collaboration called CAROUSEL (Collaborative Algorithm Representations Of Undergraduates for Self-Enhanced Learning). Students shared their own representations of algorithms anonymously, and viewed and evaluated each other's representations. In this study we found that the type and style of the representations converged over the course of five weeks. At the beginning of the study, many different types of representations were created, including ones with 3-D animation, sound and text stories. By the end of the study, though, most of the representations were explanatory graphics and text representations, without metaphors and analogy. These were similar to the representations one would find in the lectures students attended and in their textbook.

Feltovich and his colleagues argue that multiple representations will help students learn difficult concepts by making them view the concepts from different perspectives (Feltovich, Spiro, Coulson, & Feltovich, 1996). They argue that working in groups will necessarily bring multiple perspectives. However, our studies suggest instead that convergence is a likely occurrence, even when teachers or classroom conventions are not exerting authority during a learning activity. Students judged representations often on their ability to fit with cultural and classroom norms, rather than their ability to explain, communicate or enlighten.

This paper suggests methods to avoid early convergence and to encourage divergence with CSCL systems. Instead of ignoring the issue of authority, CSCL system developers are encouraged to acknowledge it and find productive ways to grant authority to students in learning contexts, taking into consideration their understanding and uses of classroom authority. Also, it is important to either adapt the system to the current social activities and arrangements in the classroom or to make it explicit how the social arrangement will change and have participants accept and take ownership of that change. The authority of a representation needs to be considered as a significant dimension in its power and in its ability to contribute to learning.

OBSERVING STUDENTS WHILE LEARNING ALGORITHMS

To discover what methods, representations, resources and strategies students use to learn about algorithms, a qualitative study was conducted with an introductory algorithm analysis class. Students were observed learning Quick Sort, a sophisticated sorting algorithm, and were then interviewed about the strategies they normally use to learn algorithms.

Quick Sort sorts a list of numbers as follows. If the list to be sorted contains zero or one number, the list is already sorted. Otherwise, the algorithm selects a number from the list; this number is called the pivot. Then, the list is partitioned into two lists such that one list contains all the numbers less than or equal to the pivot and the other list contains all the numbers greater than the pivot. Note that all the numbers in the former list are now smaller than the ones in the latter list. Then Quick Sort is recursively used to sort those two lists. Thus, the algorithm sorts a list of numbers by recursively partitioning it until lists of size one or zero are reached. Together with the previous observation, it follows that the whole list gets sorted.

Sixteen students enrolled in an introductory algorithm analysis class were observed and videotaped learning the Quick Sort algorithm and then answering a set of problem-solving questions, in six groups of two to three students each. Subsequently they were interviewed, either in groups or individually. The students in the study were told to bring their textbook and any other resources they generally use for leaning algorithms to the study. Once they arrived, they were shown a videotaped lecture on the topic. The videotaped lecture resembled the lectures they normally attended, i.e. it was presented by their instructor, who used only a white board and markers, his usual method of presenting the material. The students were given lecture notes, something that is normally given to them in their class, which summarized the material and presented the pseudocode of Quick Sort (i.e. a description of the algorithm that is not tied to a particular programming language). After viewing the videotape, the students discussed the lecture and worked together to answer questions given to them about the algorithm.

Studying student practices in this way has some ecological validity, since the students reported in the interviews that their most common method for studying was to study in groups and work on problems related to the topic. They regularly gathered together to study, complete homework problems and even program together. They reported that the way that they studied in groups for the study was similar to their normal practices, except in the study they were not familiar with all the members of their group. Students were grouped together randomly for the study, and the students in the study were quite different from each other. The students' sex, race, work experience, previous schooling, nationality and age varied considerably. Thus the study unintentionally grouped students together who had never met and did not normally study together. Despite this, and despite the fact that the students were not explicitly asked to collaborate with other members of their groups during the study, all students chose to work together and learn from each other, and all but one of the students reported enjoying working as a group in this experiment.

Problems with student learning of algorithms in this study could often be linked to the students' perception of classroom authority and what is considered authoritative knowledge. When the students were asked to answer questions that required using some other source than their lecture notes, they failed to answer the question correctly. They usually constructed an explanation based on their understanding of the lecture, rather than investigate the question using the textbook they had brought with them. The few students who did look at the textbook to answer these questions were not able to convince their peers to do the same or to consider their answers, even when their answers were correct. These other resources and the answers or understanding derived from them were not considered authoritative for most students in the groups.

The students in this study chose to consider a single representation presented by the instructor over all the other representations presented or available to them for understanding the algorithm. This graphical representation became central to their understanding of the algorithm, and they acted as if they would be able to understand everything about the algorithm by trying to reason using this one representation. The representation had acquired the authority of its presenter, their instructor, and the students believed by working out other examples using this single representation, they would be able to learn all they would need to know about this algorithm.

Classroom authority

CSCL researchers seem to give more authority to students in the classroom with their systems. They would have the instructor act more as a facilitator than an authority figure and give more agency and learning responsibility to the students (Koschmann, 1996). However, in many classrooms, the role of an instructor is to exert and control authority. Most instructors, including university instructors, are responsible for explaining new concepts and providing a learning environment, but as McCroskey and Richmond argue, exerting and using power effectively is also an important part of a teacher's job (1983). Instructors, though, usually do not acquire authority for its own sake, but instead they use power to gain authority to influence student-learning practices. Classroom management practices, such as giving assignments, motivating students to participate in learning activities, and helping students become better members of the class, rely on the teacher having authority (Richmond & Roach, 1992).

However, power and authority have to be granted, and in the classroom, the students hold the ability to grant authority. Although the institutional status of an instructor gives some initial authority, students must consent and comply with the teacher's plans for her to have authority. To say, as Jackson does (1976), that students have no agency or power in the classroom just because the students have to be there, ignores students' ability to resist. Richmond and Roach give the example of substitute teachers who are unable to gain authority and in extreme cases are driven crying from classrooms, to show how students can resist authority (1992).

College students primarily comply with authority, though, and the resistance that students create tends to be passive and partial, such as complying reluctantly, i.e. doing the minimum needed to pass the class, deceiving the instructor, and cheating. Student resistance can also be constructive, such as asking clarifying questions during class, assisting other students in learning the material, studying together, and providing constructive feedback. Constructive resistance to authority can help students become more active learners (Burroughs, Kearney, & Plax, 1989).

As noted earlier, most of the students in the study reported regularly participating in resisting authority, through collaborating on assignments, studying together and working together to understand the content. Constructive collaborative learning was already a natural, normal learning process for them.

Classroom contract

Students in the study appeared to believe in an implicit contract between the teacher and the class. This contract had been violated when in our study the students were asked questions that required them to do their own investigating rather than relying on the instructor's lecture. The students reported believing that what should and does happen in the classroom is that the teacher will tell them what to learn and how to learn it. They believed that if they were expected to know anything not explicitly said by the instructor, they should be able to be derive that knowledge by working out example problems given in class. In other words, if the student fails to learn something the teacher expects them to know, it's not that the teacher did not address the topic, only that they were not attentive enough to the details of what was said and what can be derived from what was given. Everything that needed to be learned should be in the lectures.

The students appeared to believe in a contract like the one described by Sizer in high schools. He describes students and teachers making a contract to reduce discomfort. The students are seen as trying to reduce stress and work, and teachers are seen as wanting to keep up an appearance of control. To come to an agreement, teachers don't demand much work and students behave (Sizer, 1984).

The attitude of the students in the study toward learning algorithms seemed to be that learning is something done in order to pass a test. They reported that they did not believe that the information learned in their classes would be applied outside of the classroom. They did not seem to engage in self-directed learning to learn about algorithms.

The students said during their interviews that they found the lecture notes provided by the teacher easier to understand and to use to study than their textbooks. They said generally they found the textbooks in computer science courses difficult to use. The lecture notes handed out by the instructor of this algorithms course gave more of an overview of the concepts covered in each lecture, provided less of the reasoning behind using a particular algorithm to solve a problem, used fewer mathematical symbols than the textbook, and gave less background information and comparisons with other algorithms. The lecture notes summarized the main concepts in the textbook, highlighting the key points from the lecture that the professor expected the students to know.

Most students reported not using the textbook until the night before an exam to reinforce the material in their lecture notes. The lecture notes were considered their most important learning resource, since the notes more honestly reflected the intentions of the instructor. The students did not believe they would need to use the textbook for learning. The implicit contract they believed they had with the teacher involved the teacher making it easier for them to learn the expected material and the students then would comply with that contract.

For similar reasons, students in the study relied on one graphical representation presented by the instructor in the videotaped lecture to answer all the questions about the Quick Sort algorithm. The students seemed to believe the contract would not be violated and that the representation could be used to answer all the questions posed to them. However, the questions posed to them could be correctly answered only by applying representations and concepts other than those explicitly covered in the videotaped lecture.

Learning problems arising from their adherence to the classroom contract

Most of the problems that students had in learning the Quick Sort algorithm in the study had to do with their reliance on an authoritative representation. They almost exclusively used and misinterpreted a single representation of the algorithm presented in the video (a recursion tree diagram, a type of diagram commonly used by experts to explain recursive algorithms). Groupthink (Janis, 1967) was a problem for all of the groups. Often the students would convince each other that explanations based on a faulty understanding of the algorithm were correct. They convinced each other that they did not need to use the textbook to answer the questions, and even decided not to accept correct answers that some group members derived from other sources such as the textbook.

The main learning strategy employed by students was to imitate an example presented to them by the professor on the videotape. The students seemed to believe that if they attacked problems in a way similar to how the instructor worked out the example in the lecture, drawing diagrams similar to the one they were given during the lecture, they would be able to correctly answer the questions. They did this, even though not all the information they needed to answer the questions was in that representation of the algorithm.

Although the recursion tree diagram is a representation often employed by experts, this diagram interfered with the students' understanding of the algorithm. The problem of incomplete understanding of the algorithm occurred because the students did not understand the *limitations* of this graphical representation. They believed it captured everything they needed to know about the algorithm, rather than just showing a partial and high-level view of the algorithm's execution. The instructor explicitly said while presenting this representation that all he was showing using this representation was a part of the algorithm, the recursive calls. Despite this, and despite the lecture and the pseudocode given to the students referring to other equally critical aspects of the algorithm (such as the partitioning step), students seemed to think that the recursion tree diagram was all they would need for learning and understanding the algorithm and answering the questions correctly.

All the students observed realized when they encountered questions about steps not explicit in the recursion tree diagram, such as the partitioning step or pointer manipulation, that their understanding of the algorithm was not complete. But instead of reaching out to other representations and explanations available to them, they struggled to invent answers to such questions. The information to answer these questions was available to them in their textbook. However, even when students were observed using the textbook, it was clear that they were frustrated and unable to integrate their knowledge from the lecture, their mental representation of the algorithm, and the description provided in the lecture with the descriptive material in the textbook.

All the students originally believed that if they worked out enough examples, drawing diagrams similar to the ones they were given during the lecture, and thought hard about the diagrams, they would be able to answer the questions. Instead of seeking the answers from other sources they tried to *derive plausible explanations* from one representation that did not contain any information that would be helpful with those questions.

Students converged on one representation and understanding of the algorithm. The instructor did use another representation during the lecture, the pseudocode. However, he spent more time explaining the algorithm using a recursion tree diagram, and thus, lent the graphic representation more authority. The selection of a representation to use to understand the algorithm had to do with the authority assigned to it, rather than its explanatory power. The learning problems found by this study are consistent with Milgram's studies on student obedience to authority (Milgram, 1963, 1965). Too much conformity can lead to Groupthink, during which a group converges on a poor decision or solution (Janis, 1967).

When Gifford and Enyedy studied how students used the Probability Inquiry Environment (PIE) (Vahey, Enyedy, & Gifford, 1999), they found that when students tried to reach a consensus on probability questions, they chose similar poor solutions (Gifford & Enyedy, 1999). The students, they say, often agreed on the first solution that they could agree on, rather than continue to consider and explore alternatives.

Students simplify things that are more complicated. They have a reductive bias, in which "only one of, or a small number of, the legitimate and useful ways a topic or phenomenon could be construed are recognized or considered, thus limiting understanding" (Feltovich et al., 1996). The students adopted a single representation and understanding and applied that representation, even when it was not appropriate to do so. "Students seem to prefer single models in learning and understanding. These restricted perspectives are then overextended in ways our research has shown to be detrimental to learning" (Feltovich et al., 1996).

CREATING, SHARING AND EVALUATING MULTIPLE REPRESENTATIONS

We propose that students should engage in an active process of representation *creation, sharing* and *collective evaluation* to combat this tendency of overextending authoritative representations. Students are more likely to accept representations as being incomplete and partial when created by their peers, rather than by an authority figure. Thus they may be better able to understand that different aspects of the algorithm need to be understood, and that different representations de-emphasize, as well as highlight, different aspects. By sharing their representations, they will be better able to compare their understanding with others.

We built a prototype system called CAROUSEL to help students create, share and evaluate their representations of algorithms. It was used in a pilot study with 12 students in a beginning data structures course. The system collected and displayed student-created representations and collected the ratings students gave to the other students' representations for certain characteristics of these representations, such as ratings for usefulness, understandability, familiarity, salience, contiguity, and pleasure.

The students created representations for three algorithms: the algorithm for generating Fibonacci numbers, the Selection Sort algorithm and the Merge Sort algorithm. After the students evaluated the representations, the average ratings on each characteristic for each representation were posted to the CAROUSEL web site along with the names of the authors of those representations.

At the beginning of the study, students chose to work with a wide variety of media, including text, graphics, sound and animation, based on their personal preferences. However, over the course of the study, the students converged on a simple style, one incorporating primarily simple graphics and text. For the first algorithm approximately 64% of the representations were text only, 9% were text and graphics, 9% included animation and sound, and 18% employed more complex media. For the second algorithm, the number of text-only representations decreased (37%), those with graphics increased (50%), and the use of animation and complex media decreased (18%). By the last algorithm, only text representations (57%) and representations with graphics (43%) were used.

Students were tested after they created representations to measure their knowledge of the algorithm. Initial results from the pilot study suggest that the constructive activities do help learning. For two of the three algorithms that were used in the pilot study, there was a significant positive correlation between creating and sharing a representation and test scores ($r=.635$, $p=.07$; $r=.663$, $p=.05$), compared to students who did not engage in these activities.

Missing contract/Missing authority

However, students find it difficult to communicate with each other when the authority of an instructor is missing. Stubbs (1983) studied how teachers control communication in the classroom. Teachers often control what is discussed, how much of it is discussed and how it is discussed. The teacher controls not only how much time they discuss something, but also how much time others have to respond. Also, for a student's solution to be considered correct, the student has to recognize an instructor's authority and has to adopt her methods of communication about the topic (Stubbs, 1983).

Similarly, students using Guzdial's CoWeb, a CSCL system that has students build knowledge collaboratively on the web, relies on the instructor's involvement and monitoring of student activity with the system. "The teacher's attitude and involvement is critical – since so many students were in the CoWeb mostly to hear from the teacher, a missing teacher might lead to less student involvement" (Guzdial et al., 1999). Even though students' attitude toward the classroom contract has changed with the use of CoWebs in the classroom and students no longer see the teacher as the main source of information, they are still placing authority in the teacher through valuing the teacher's opinions and teacher-approved discourse produced by students.

Even in classrooms where more progressive teaching methodologies are practiced, teachers often still maintain considerable control over what the students are doing. Edwards and Mercer studied classrooms where small-group learning was being used and found that although the students appeared to be working independently, the teacher was really controlling the discussion and actions of the group (Edwards & Mercer, 1992).

Studies of undergraduate students at Georgia Institute of Technology enrolled in classes where collaboration was part of classroom activities suggest that the students dislike and resist efforts to make them engage in collaborative learning (Hmelo, Guzdial, & Turns, 1998; Newstetter & Hmelo, 1996). One wonders whether these students were resisting the teacher's authority or the teacher's lack of adhering to their classroom contract. Jones' study of two New Zealand classrooms found that students exerted control over the teacher's curriculum and methods. The students in her study resisted when the teacher tried to have the students learn something other than facts, and did something other than lecture and testing on notes (Jones, 1989). Similarly, Oyler found that students shape teachers' actions in the classroom and can exert authority. The teacher in the study wanted the students to share some authority in the classroom, but she was not happy about how they exerted it (Oyler, 1996).

Students building authority based on convention

> *Our pilot study with CAROUSEL showed that when authority in terms of a person or instructor is missing, students build authority using other means. In the case of the pilot study, the students found authority in the representational styles used in the textbook and lectures. Over the course of the study, students moved from individualistic, metaphor and media-rich representations at the beginning of the study to an explanatory, example-based style with graphics and text. They converged on a style that mimicked what they saw in the textbook and lectures. At the beginning, one saw metaphoric stories and complex three-dimensional graphics, by the end of the study, one saw texts that primarily walked a student through an example and explained the steps of an algorithm clearly.*
>
> *One of the researchers rated all the representations in the study on a scale of 1 to 5 with 1 being a rating for representations that are least like a textbook or classroom explanation and 5 being a rating for representations that are most like a textbook or classroom explanation. These ratings increased over time with each new algorithm: the first algorithm had an average rating of 3.4; the second had 3.9; and the third had 4.7.*

Furthermore, the average of all the ratings the students gave each representation is significantly positively related to the rating of how similar that representation is to a textbook or classroom explanation ($F(1, 24)=3.9$, $p=.06$). Multiple linear regression analysis techniques were used to explore how the ratings of the representations' similarity to textbook or classroom explanations were related to the student ratings of different characteristics. The similarity rating's relations to students' ratings of usefulness, salience and contiguity are positive and significant ($F(1,24)=6.5$, 6.0, and 10.6 respectively, $p<.05$). In other words, how similar a representation was to a textbook or classroom explanation positively influenced student ratings for how useful that representation was for their understanding of the algorithm; how well that representation pointed out the salient features of the algorithm; and how well it was contiguous with (built upon) the other representations for that algorithm. For understandability and familiarity, the effect was also positive, but not significant. Interestingly, pleasure was the only student rating that was negatively affected by a representation's similarity to a textbook or classroom explanation, but the effect was not significant. Summarizing, how similar a representation was to a textbook or classroom explanation influenced what kind of rating a student gave to that representation, and usually, the more a representation was similar to what they saw in their textbook or classroom, the higher the rating was.

A follow-up interview with one of the participants in this study was consistent with this theory. During the interview, the student was asked to talk about each representation. He frequently talked about them in terms of doing things the "class way" or something being "teacher-like". He was then asked to rate the representations according to how "normal" they were. He responded, "By normal, do you mean most like what we see in class?" He was instructed to define it the way he thought was most appropriate, and he said that he thought "most class-like" was the most appropriate way to define normal. According to him, the best representations had the pseudocode, a picture or visualization of the algorithm and a plain-text explanation using an example. He explained, "It is really the best combo. Teachers do that."

However, at the beginning of the study, most students were turning in representations that did not look anything like the style he described. He was asked if he remembered what he thought when he was given the first assignment for the study. He replied, "Yeah. We were upset. You have to see when you're that young in college trying to do your best... When someone just tells you to get creative ... it is hard for me to get like that." The students felt a lot of anxiety about turning in the first set of representations, and they complained about not being given enough direction the day that they were due. The authority was missing, leaving them to create their own idea of what would be a "good" representation. They then seemed to be converging over time on the conventions and styles used in the classroom or found in the textbook.

When this particular student was asked about how he felt about the other students rating his work, he reported that he looked at them and competed with his classmates to get the highest rating. However, he was upset that the feedback he got was from his peers. "I don't trust my classmates as much as I trust professors," he said. The feedback did not carry enough authority for him. When asked how to improve the study, he thought the instructor rather than the other students in the class should do the rating.

RECOMMENDATIONS

In this section we present a set of recommendations for CSCL systems to effectively exploit the effects of authority. We have revised CAROUSEL in a manner consistent with these recommendations and are currently fielding and evaluating it with a similar, but larger scale study (60 participants, nine algorithms, and a duration of 12 weeks) in a junior level algorithms class during Fall 2001.

Allow students to both work alone and together

Having students participate in both dialog and monologue is critical for effective collaborative learning (Hoadley & Enyedy, 1999). Monologue does not depend on the context, social cue and interaction to communicate and interact with ideas, whereas dialogue has distributed control of the conversation among participants and involves interaction, common construction and sharing of ideas. Psychologists have argued that students should produce monologues of their own understanding (Chi, de Leeuw, Chiu, & LaVancher, 1994). However, making one's initial understanding available for further dialog is also critical for active learning.

Certain CSCL systems seek to balance student monologue and dialogue. The CoWeb system has students display individual work on web pages and then allows others to edit that work to create a dialogue about their understanding (Guzdial & Kehoe, 1998). CSILE (Computer-Supported Intentional Learning) supports students in collaborative knowledge building activities by creating a shared database that contains student representations of their knowledge. Students can author their own ideas and record them in the database, but their knowledge is linked to the knowledge already in the database, the social knowledge repository. The system promotes both individual reflection and group interaction with the knowledge base (Scardamalia & Bereiter, 1991). Hoadley and Enyedy (1999) used two different complimentary tools, SpeakEasy and SenseMaker, to support monologue and dialogue: SpeakEasy helps students have structured discussions, and SenseMaker helps students create an overview and integrate ideas.

Encourage divergence

Students need to be explicitly encouraged to diverge from cultural norms and disagree with each other, especially at the early learning stages. CSCL systems and teachers need to challenge students who believe that one representation can and does represent all aspects of a concept. Instead, students need to be encouraged to look for differences between representations and see the aspects that are obscured and hidden by any particular representation. Allowing students to work alone initially will likely encourage more divergence, but it alone will not prevent them from picking one representation among the many and using that one to the exclusion of others during collaborative learning. Integration and consideration of differences should therefore be explicitly encouraged.

Lessen effects of identity

Another important recommendation is to lessen the effects of identity within the system. Certain students in a class have more authority than others. As students reported in their interviews, students start college classes knowing which of their peers are more likely to receive good grades and understand the material. The representations or arguments of these students may carry more weight than those of others, encouraging convergence and the silencing of differences. So it is important in the early stages of a collaborative learning activity that student authors remain anonymous to lessen the effects of identity on convergence and engagement.

Rewrite the classroom contract

For collaborative learning to be successful in the classroom, the classroom contract has to be explicitly rewritten. Authority should be reassigned, based on input and agreement of both the teacher and students. Power and control are negotiated through interaction. Power does not reside in either the teacher or students, but instead is created between them. "A more dialectical and less functionalist perspective considers power and control as dynamic processes that are constructed and negotiated between teacher and students. ... It is through teacher-student communication that power is developed, attributed and maintained" (Staton, 1992, p. 173).

Authority cannot be successfully assigned by a computer system or even a social system such as the school system without the agreement of the participants as discussed earlier. For collaborative learning to be successful, the participants must make explicit the new terms and arrangement of authority.

For students and teachers to agree to a collaborative learning activity, it must be clear to both parties what the intended roles of the participants will be and what benefits one will receive from the additional responsibility and authority. One student who had used CAROUSEL in the pilot study said he felt that it needed to be clearer how the study was related to his class and how he was benefiting from it. "Tie the representation assignment with the class. ... It should have been more tied with our assignments every week," he suggested.

Gifford and Enyedy (1999) argue that CSCL environments should be designed by looking at the activities they are supposed to support. They argue that many CSCL systems do not fit with nor change the basic activities of the classroom, and therefore have little effect on the learning of students. They propose that CSCL systems should focus on supporting activities where learners and the teacher plan and participate in learning activities. CSCL systems have to be integrated into the social activities in the classroom. Successful classroom practices and authority are negotiated, rather than dictated by the teacher. Similarly, the authority given to a CSCL system has to be negotiated. The best learning environment is one that can flexibly adapt to the learning activities already negotiated in the classroom.

CONCLUSION

Authority was instrumental in how college students used, created or evaluated representations in the two studies described in this paper. Students converged on an authoritative representation or representational style and ignored the limitations of that representation or style and other available representations. The students' understanding of authority in the classroom discouraged the critical analysis and questioning of representations. Instead of evaluating a representation by looking at its content and how well that is expressed, judgments by students were based on how much time an instructor invested into a representation or how well a representation fit with the style normally used by textbooks and in lectures. This discouraged students expressing original viewpoints of the concept, and instead resulted in students looking at the same aspects of the concept in the same way.

Some argue that collaboration necessarily leads to a diversity of ideas. "It is more likely in a group that the limits of single interpretations or representations will be counteracted by alternative interpretations" (Feltovich et al., 1996, p. 36). However, how authority is assigned, recognized and resisted greatly affects whether this will happen. Instead of alternative interpretations arising in a collaborative learning setting, students may work to reinforce biases, to silence those with differing opinions and to reinforce a single view of looking at the concept. The students in our studies might have been better off if they were working alone rather than collaboratively.

Design of CSCL systems needs to consider how to manage and distribute authority. By changing the perception and assignment of authority, such systems must encourage students to diverge before converging, and facilitate critical analyses of different viewpoints and representations. This can be accomplished by explicitly changing the classroom contract, and having students do independent thinking as well as engaging in dialogic activities where anonymity of authorship is preserved at least initially.

ACKNOWLEDGMENTS

We thank Sadhana Puntambekar, Roland Hübscher and anonymous referees for their helpful comments and suggestions. This research is supported by the National Science Foundation under contract CDA-9616513.

REFERENCES

Burroughs, N. F., Kearney, P., & Plax, T. G. (1989). Compliance-resistance in the college classroom. *Communication Education,* **38**, 214-229.

Chi, M. T. H., de Leeuw, N., Chiu, M.-H., & LaVancher, C. (1994). Eliciting self-explanations improves understanding. *Cognitive Science,* **18**, 3, 439-477.

Edwards, D., & Mercer, N. (1992). *Common Knowledge: The Development of Understanding in the Classroom.* Routledge, New York, NY.

Feltovich, P. J., Spiro, R. J., Coulson, R. L., & Feltovich, J. (1996). Collaboration within and among minds: Mastering complexity, individually and in groups. In T. Koschmann (Ed.), *CSCL: Theory and Practice of an Emerging Paradigm* (pp. 25-44). Lawrence Erlbaum Associates, Mahwah, NJ.

Gifford, B. R., & Enyedy, N. D. (1999, Dec. 12-15). Activity centered design: Towards a theoretical framework for CSCL. Paper presented at the Computer Support for Collaborative Learning Conference, Stanford University, Palo Alto, CA.

Guzdial, M., & Kehoe, C. (1998). Apprenticeship-based learning environments: A principled approach to providing software-realized scaffolding through hypermedia. *Journal of Interactive Learning Research,* **9**, 3/4, 289-336.

Guzdial, M., Realff, M., Ludovice, P., Morley, T., Kerce, C., Lyons, E., & Sukel, K. (1999, Dec. 12-15). Using a CSCL-driven shift in agency to undertake educational reform. Paper presented at the Computer Support for Collaborative Learning Conference, Stanford University, Palo Alto, CA.

Hmelo, C. E., Guzdial, M., & Turns, J. (1998). Computer-support for collaborative learning: Learning to Support Student Engagement. *Journal of Interactive Learning Research,* **9**, 2, 107-130.

Hoadley, C. M., & Enyedy, N. (1999, Dec. 12-15). Between information and communication: middle spaces in computer media for learning. Paper presented at the Computer Support for Collaborative Learning Conference, Stanford University, Palo Alto, CA.

Jackson, P. (1976). *Life in Classrooms.* University of Chicago Press, Chicago, IL.

Janis, I. (1967). *Victims of Groupthink: A Psychological Study of Foreign Decisions and Fiascoes.* Houghton Mifflin, Boston, MA.

Jones, A. (1989). The culture production of classroom practice. *British Journal of Sociology,* **10**, 19-31.

Koschmann, T. (1996). Paradigm shifts and instructional technology: An introduction. In T. Koschmann (Ed.), *CSCL: Theory and Practice of an Emerging Paradigm* (pp. 1-24). Lawrence Erlbaum Associates, Mahwah, NJ.

McCroskey, J. C., & Richmond, V. P. (1983). Power in the classroom I: Teacher and student perceptions. *Communication Education,* **32**, 175-184.

Milgram, S. (1963). Behavioral study of obedience. *Journal of Abnormal and Social Psychology,* **67**, 371-378.

Milgram, S. (1965). Some conditions of obedience and disobedience to authority. *Human Relations,* **18**, 57-76.

Newstetter, W. C., & Hmelo, C. E. (1996). Distributing cognition or how they don't: An investigation of student collaborative learning. In *Proceedings of the International Conference of the Learning Sciences*, AACE, Charlottesville, VA, 462-467.

Oyler, C. (1996). *Making Room for Students: Sharing Teacher Authority in Room 106.* Teachers College Press, New York, NY.

Richmond, V. P., & Roach, K. D. (1992). Power in the classroom: Seminal studies. In V. P. Richmond & J. C. McCroskey (Eds.), *Power in the Classroom: Communication, Control and Concern* (pp. 47-66). Lawrence Erlbaum Associates, Hillsdale, NJ.

Scardamalia, M., & Bereiter, C. (1991). Higher levels of agency for children in knowledge building: A challenge for the design of new knowledge media. *Journal of the Learning Sciences,* **1**, 1, 37-68.

Simon, Y. R. (1980). *A General Theory of Authority.* University of Notre Dame Press, Notre Dame, IN.

Sizer, T. (1984). *Horace's compromise: The Dilemma of the American High School.* Houghton Mifflin, Boston, MA.

Staton, A. Q. (1992). Teacher and student concern and classroom power and control. In V. P. Richmond & J. C. McCroskey (Eds.), *Power in the Classroom: Communication, Control, and Concern* (pp. 159-176). Lawrence Erlbaum Associates, Hillsdale, NJ.

Stubbs, M. (1983). *Language, Schools and Classrooms* (2nd ed.). Methuen, London.

Vahey, P., Enyedy, N., & Gifford, B. R. (1999). The Probability Inquiry Environment: A collaborative, inquiry-based simulation environment. Paper presented at the Thirty Second Annual Hawaii International Conference on Systems Sciences.

SHORT PAPERS

These 100 papers were accepted in a highly competitive peer review process. They will be presented as interactive posters, where authors can discuss their work face-to-face with interested audience members. Due to space limitations, only two page summaries could be included in these Proceedings. Full papers will be available and searchable on a comprehensive CSCL 2002 DVD and on the CSCL website: http://cscl2002.org/ or http://cscl-home.org/.

A. ISSUES IN THE DESIGN OF CSCL SYSTEMS

Symphony-Q: A Support System for Learning Music through Collaboration

Fusako Kusunoki
Tama Art University
kusunoki@tamabi.ac.jp
Masanori Sugimoto
University of Tokyo
sugi@r.dl.itc.u-tokyo.ac.jp
Hiromichi Hashizume
National Institute of Informatics
has@nii.ac.jp

ABSTRACT
This paper describes the Symphony-Q support system for learning music. This system integrates a sensing board and a computer, and is used for collaborative learning in a face-to-face setting. One of the aims of Symphony-Q is to enhance music experiences: children who do not have music skills can easily participate in music learning, enjoy making sounds, and play rhythmically to music in collaboration with others. The paper discusses comments and feedback from school children and their teachers, which were collected during experiments with Symphony-Q carried out in a Japanese public elementary school.

Keywords
Music learning, music experience, collaborative learning, interaction, , sensing board, elementary school

INTRODUCTION
This paper describes a support system for learning music through collaboration. Several studies have indicated that it is very important for individuals to have rich music experiences, especially in their infancy, in order to fully develop their capability for music (Gordon, 1997).The system proposed in this paper, Symphony-Q, aims at enriching learners' musical experiences and developing their musical capabilities through the learning of tones, rhythms, and chords in an easy manner. Symphony-Q uses a sensing board that was developed by the authors. This board was applied to a support system for learning about environmental problems (Kusunoki, 1999), and electronically-enhanced board games. In Symphony-Q, a personal computer and the sensing board are linked together, and animations generated by the computer are projected onto the surface of the board through an LCD projector. When a learner places physical pieces on the board, the system makes different sounds based on their location, and changes the animations.

The features of Symphony-Q can be summarized as follows:

- CSCL for music: a group of learners sits around the sensing board of Symphony-Q, and uses it in a face-to-face situation. They can learn about tones, rhythms and chords through their interactions and communication, and enhance their own music experiences.
- Raising learners' motivations with games: learners with Symphony-Q can start learning music, as they would play a game, which is an effective way to motivate children to learn.
- Augmented reality: by integrating sounds, animations and a physical board, Symphony-Q creates an immersive learning environment. The system also supports learners who have difficulty using traditional input devices for computers (a mouse and a keyboard), or musical instruments. It enables learners to participate in music learning situations by directly and intuitively manipulating physical objects in the real world.

SYSTEM CONFIGURATION
Symphony-Q is composed of a sensing board, a personal computer, an LCD projector, a MIDI sound device, and audio speakers. The sensing board and the computer, and the computer and the MIDI sound device are connected through their serial interfaces. An animation of a musical instrument (for example, a piano keyboard) is projected onto the surface of the

board. When a physical piece is placed on a certain area of the instrument (for example, one of its keys), the corresponding sound is immediately emitted through the speakers.

One, two or three persons can use Symphony-Q. When it is used by a group of learners, Symphony-Q generates animations and sounds of multiple instruments at the same time. Each learner can select his or her favorite instrument and participate in an ensemble.

Figure 1. Example of using sensing board

The system changes animations based on learners' inputs. For example, if the pieces are placed correctly, a character on the board smiles and guides learners to the next question. If the pieces are not placed correctly, the character looks sad and prompts learners to try again. The background image of the animations also changes in relation to learners' scores from a pleasant atmosphere, for satisfactory performance, to a sad atmosphere for unsatisfactory performance, in order to raise learners' motivation and engagement.

CLASSROOM EXPERIMENTS

The experiments and evaluation of Symphony-Q were carried out in a Japanese public elementary school (in Yokohama, Kanagawa prefecture) from February to June 2001. The teacher in charge of the class and a music teacher were asked to use the system in their music lessons. Thirty school children (15 boys and 15 girls) in a fifth grade class participated in the experiments. The school children were randomly divided into 10 groups of three. After using the system, the children and their teachers freely discussed their experiences. All of the experiments and discussions were recorded by two video cameras. Post-experiment interviews were also carried out, and information by means of questionnaires was collected.

DISCUSSION

The system supported learners who were not skilled at manipulating conventional computers in school lessons. By supporting the intuitive manipulation of pieces and making the computer invisible, the system encouraged children to play and learn music. Many music learning support systems use traditional graphical user interfaces (GUIs) and input devices (Willams, 1998). Compared with these systems, Symphony-Q's learning environment has the potential to enhance learners' communication skills, interactions, and level of participation. Further experiments with Symphony-Q are required to address the finding that animations may disturb children's learning. In addition, it is not clear whether children can truly acquire musical knowledge and skills as a result of their interaction with the system. Another issue is related to the game feature of our system. Playing a game may direct learners to focus on the superficial aspects of the system, such as animations or characters, rather than on learning musical concepts, such as chords or rhythms. Achieving a balance between the game aspect and the learning of music are interesting and challenging problems that require investigation in the future.

REFERENCES

Gordon, E. (1997) A Music Learning Theory for Newborn and Young Children. GIA Publication Inc, Chicago, IL.

Kusunoki, F., Sugimoto, M., and Hashizume, H. (1999) A System for Supporting Group Learning that Enhances Interactions. Proceedings of CSCL'99 (Stanford, CA, December 1999) 323-327.

Williams, D. and Webster, P. (1999) Experiencing Music Technology (2nd Edition). Schirmer Books, New York, NY.

COALE: Collaborative and Adaptive Learning Environment

Nobuko Furugori [1], Hirotaka Sato [1], Hiroaki Ogata [2], Youji Ochi [2], Yoneo Yano [2]

[1] Systems Research Section, INES Corp.

[2] Department of Information Science and Intelligent Systems, Tokushima University

{furugori,sato_hiro}@ines.co.jp [1], {ogata,ochi,yano}@is.tokushima-u.ac.jp [2]

ABSTRACT

This paper proposes a new adaptive WBT (Web Based Training) environment for collaborative learning named COALE (Collaborative and Adaptive Learning Environment). COALE is an integrated environment of collaborative learning into individual learning based on WBT with active personalized awareness provider. We propose a personalized active recommendation system, which gives proper awareness at proper timing for each learner to support dynamic course organization aimed at effective and efficient learning.

Keywords

Collaborative learning, personalization, recommendation, awareness.

INTRODUCTION

This paper proposes a WBT (Web Based Training) system with active personalized awareness provider, named COALE (Collaborative Adaptive Learning Environment), to support dynamic course organization aimed at effective and efficient learning. COALE is based on the learner-centered concept. So the learners take the initiative of their own process of learning with proper supports from the environment, instead of given the next step from the system automatically through the intention of an author of the course. COALE has two keywords in its name: adaptive and collaborative. Adaptive features are realized by personalization. COALE supports learners' to select the next step learning material by personalized recommendation. The next step material selections settle the main road of the Course, step by step. COALE provides collaborative learning support to learners': to post shared knowledge and to discuss with co-learners. Note that we consider the posted shared knowledge as a part of the learning materials. Discussions and advices works to spread and deepen the learners' knowledge, therefore collaboration is considered to spread the width of the main road or to form branch roads of the Course.

COALE

Personalization is popular technique of web customization or e-commerce where user interface or contents recommendation is personalized according to the users' former activities (Hirsh, 2000). The major difference between such systems and COALE is the filtering criteria for the recommendation. The way of presentation of awareness information called the intervention type (Jermann, 2001) is "graphical visualization" and the level is monitoring among the three levels: mirroring, monitoring, and advising. This approach is similar to SharlokII (Ogata, 2000).

User Interface

Fig. 1 shows a display snapshot of the COALE prototype system.

Main Window (A): The right side window is the main place for individual learning action. A learner read and solves an exercise question, put an answer. The system checks the answer whether it is correct or not. By pushing the "explanation request" button, the system shows the explanation of the answer. Pushing the "show shared knowledge" button, the system presents a list of the shared knowledge for learners' selection. To put a shared knowledge, push the "knowledge input" button then an window for input will be opened. As for collaborative learning action, "request discussion" button works to open a chat request window for the first step of opening a discussion.

Contents Awareness Map (B): To select the next step exercise, learners select one of the recommended contents from the Contents Awareness Map. On the Map, a square mark represents a category, a circle represents an exercise question, which has not been correctly answered, and a diamond represents a question, which has not been learned. The level of difficulty of a question is reflected on their color. The orders of recommendation are displayed as a number at a side of the question title. The questions, which are graded as first and second, are presented in red text and given the order number. Learners can select a circle or a diamond to open the corresponding exercise question.

Learn*ing-mate Awareness Map(C):* To select a proper partner of discussion, learners can consult the Learning-mate Awareness Map. The nodes represent co-learners, exercise questions, and categories of questions. Corresponding marks are circle, diamond and square. Firstly and secondly recommended learners are in yellow color, presented with the order number. Moreover, up to two contents for these two recommended learners are displayed as their background knowledge. From third to seventh recommended learners are shown in gray circle.

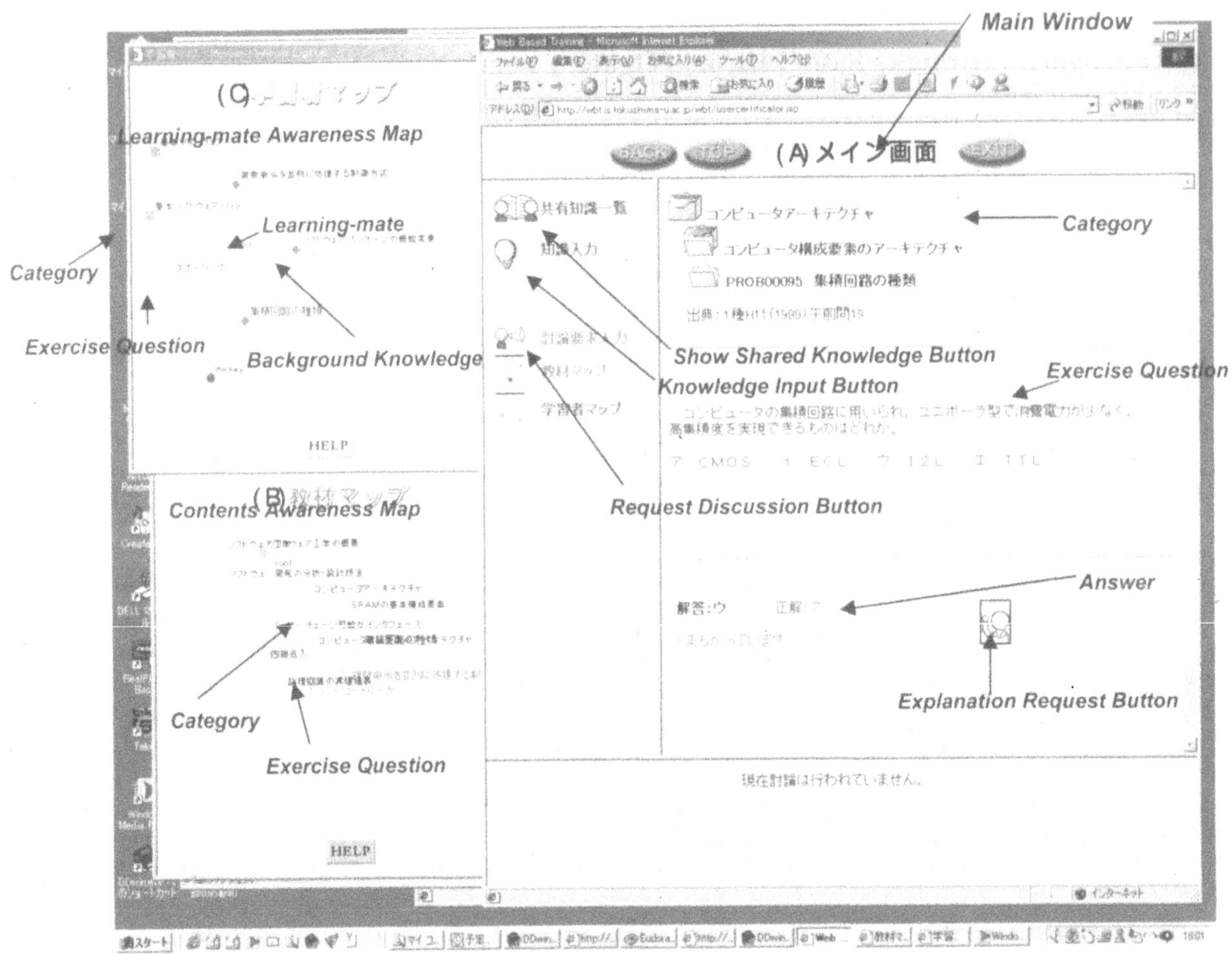

Fig. 1. Screen snapshot of COALE.

CONCLUDING REMARKS

This paper proposed two kinds of personalized active awareness provider. One recommends learning contents for the next step and the other recommends learning-mate for discussion. Both of them are presented as a visualized map using GUI, according to the history and the current state of learners' behavior. Because COALE follows the learner-centered concept, the final decision of selection is left to the learners. This work was supported in cooperation with the Information Technology Consortium, as a part of a project of the Information-technology Promotion Agency Japan.

REFERENCES

Hirsh, H., Basu, C., and Davison, B. D. (2000) Learning to Personalize. *CACM*, **43**, 8, 102-106.

Jermann, P., Soller, A., and Muehlenbrock, M. (2001) From Mirroring to Guiding: A Review of State of the Art Technology for Supporting Collaborative Learning. *Euro-CSCL 2001*, 324-331.

Ogata, H., Matsuura, K., and Yano, Y. (2000) Active Knowledge Awareness Map: Visualizing Learners Activities in a Web Based CSCL Environment. *Proceedings of The International Workshop on New Technologies for Collaborative Learning (NTCL) 2000*, 89-98.

Construction and Inspection of Learner Models

Juan-Diego Zapata-Rivera, Jim Greer

ARIES Laboratory. Department of Computer Science.University of Saskatchewan, Canada
{Diego.Zapata, Jim.Greer}@usask.ca

ABSTRACT

Learners working on the creation of conceptual maps become involved in a creative learning activity that involves "making sense" of new concepts and their relationships through modelling. These models can be seen as representations of the learners' understanding of a particular topic domain. During subsequent learning activities, students can reflect upon the models they have built. In addition to domain knowledge, models can contain information about learners' knowledge profiles and social aspects of learning. This paper explores different ways to interact with models in order to support reflection, negotiated assessment, and knowledge awareness. We have developed ConceptLab, a knowledge construction and navigation system that uses XML-based conceptual maps to represent the learner's view of the domain. ConceptLab has been used by students and teachers as part of an exploratory study carried out in a Colombian elementary school.

Keywords

Conceptual maps, Learner models, Collaborative and Negotiated Assessment.

INTRODUCTION

Constructivist environments promote reflection and meaningful learning. Computers should be used as cognitive tools helping learners to acquire responsibility for their planning, decision-making, and self-regulation (Lajoie, 1993). We claim that inspectable learner models can be constructed collaboratively or individually. Learners and teachers can inspect their models in order to support reflection and knowledge awareness. Learners can benefit by constructing models of the domain and later by looking inside these models and reflecting upon their content. Tools that make the learner model inspectable to learners and teachers promote reflection and interactive assessment. Teachers can use such tools to help students model their own understanding of the domain and also as assessment tools. One such tool, ConceptLab has been used by students and teachers as part of an exploratory study carried out in a Colombian elementary school. This paper presents ConceptLab as well as some preliminary results obtained from this study.

CONCEPTLAB

ConceptLab (Zapata-Rivera et al. 2000, Zapata-Rivera & Greer 2001), is a knowledge construction and navigation system that allows students to engage in collaborative construction of conceptual maps. These maps represent the learner's view about of the domain. ConceptLab considers the object resulting from the learner's work as his/her domain representation. Learner models in ConceptLab maintain basic learner information (i.e. preferences and personal information), the learner's current level of knowledge on every concept, social aspects of learning (i.e. helpfulness, eagerness, assertiveness, etc.), and the XML representation of the map (map structure, links, and presentation preferences).

Students and teachers can create their own maps collaboratively or individually. Students working in groups assume different collaborative roles (i.e. leader, speaker, resource manager, critic, and time vigilant) in order to co-ordinate their interaction. Students can use a predefined list of concepts (common vocabulary given by the teacher) or their own new concepts (in case they discover some original concept that is important and should be included in the system). We have experimented with students creating their models using paper, markers of different colours, and labels. A digital photograph of the paper model was used to integrate the model within ConceptLab as a conceptual "map".

Once the map is imported into ConceptLab, learning resources can be linked to the concepts in the map. Students can use their own map to access these resources. These resources can be suggested by the teacher (initial links) or by classmates. Students can use an existing map as a guide to study the content, or use ConceptLab as a learning tool to facilitate remembering, to create maps collaboratively, to share their maps, and to encourage discussions about a particular topic. Maps in ConceptLab can be overlaid with the knowledge profile of a particular student or group of students, integrating the system's or the teacher's view of the student's knowledge. In addition teachers can visualize how social aspects, such as: eagerness, helpfulness, assertiveness and self-confidence are taken into account in the overall assessment. Initial knowledge values are obtained from an initial pre-assessment quiz that feeds a Bayesian model that integrates information about the domain, self-assessment and social aspects of learning into a Bayesian network.

Through accumulation of evidence and Bayesian propagation, an estimate of the student's knowledge on every concept is available to be used within ConceptLab. Special interfaces have been designed to allow students and teachers to interact with the model. Students interacting with the model may realise what they really know or do not know and perhaps use this information to focus their learning activities. Learners and teachers use the model to engage in discussions that support knowledge reflection. We are interested in knowing how students and teachers will react to the model. What kind of support is needed in order to promote learners' reflection? What should be the teacher's role in this process? and how teacher and learners interact with the model during the creation, reflection, and negotiating based on the model.

EXPLORATORY STUDY

An exploratory study was conducted in May, 2001 in a classroom at the Joaquin Aristizabal, a Colombian public elementary school. Participants were eighty fifth grade students and six teachers. Students in a science class were introduced to the cell, were told about conceptual maps, ConceptLab, and learner models. Students were asked to create a map of a cell using paper, markers, and labels. They were prompted with some of the main concepts but were free to include some extra ones. Students worked in groups, dyads, or individually. The maps were fed into ConceptLab and students and teachers interacted with the graphical maps.

SOME PRELIMINARY RESULTS

Based on an initial analysis of the information gathered during the study, we report some general findings.

- *Students became engaged in learning while creating the map using these new and different kinds of media.*
- *Students understood their roles and were able to create group or individual representations of a cell.*
- *Students successfully explained their work as a group or individually.*
- *Student used books and asked questions more frequently than in traditional learning settings..*
- *Teachers were greatly surprised by students' participation during the whole experiment.*
- *Reflecting upon the model facilitates a new learning process.*
- *Explaining why (justifying learners' claims about their knowledge) facilitates learning.*
- *Dialogue between teacher and students was enhanced by ConceptLab.*
- *Evidence about students' social aspects of learning was useful to teachers.*
- *Teachers valued ConceptLab as a tool that supports negotiated assessment*

CONCLUSIONS

ConceptLab combines a knowledge construction tool and inspectable learners models. It has been interesting to begin to investigate the advantages of using these technologies to support learning and reflection. Different learning outcomes can be observed at different stages of the experiment. Support is needed to help groups to interact with a group knowledge profile. ConceptLab integrates constructivist and cognitive approaches by providing a set of tools that emphasises reflection and collaboration. More information about ConceptLab can be found on-line: www.cs.usask.ca/~rjz896

ACKNOWLEDGMENTS

We wish to recognise both the Natural Science and Engineering Research Council of Canada and COLCIENCIAS - Colombia for financial support of this research. We would like to thank teachers, observers and students at Joaquin Aristizabal Colombian elementary school especially Norelia Rivera for their participation in this exploratory study.

REFERENCES

Lajoie, S.P. & Derry, S.J. (Eds.). (1993) Computers as cognitive tools. Hillsdale, NJ: Lawrence Erlbaum Associates.

Zapata-Rivera, J.D., & Greer, J.E. (2001) Externalising Learner Modelling Representations. *Proceedings of the Workshop on External Representations of AIED: Multiple Forms and Multiple Roles. AIED2001*. 71-76.

Zapata-Rivera, J.D., Greer, J.E., & Cooke, J. (2000) An XML-Based Tool for Building and Using Conceptual Maps in Education and Training Environments. *ICCE 2000*. 755-762.

Using the Internet to Improve University Education: Problem-oriented Web-based Learning with MUNICS

Frank Fischer, Pamela Troendle, Heinz Mandl
University of Munich, Institute of Educational Psychology
Leopoldstr. 13, D - 80802 Munich
fischerf@edupsy.uni-muenchen.de

ABSTRACT
A principled approach to the design of problem-oriented, web-based learning at the university level is presented. The principles include providing authentic contexts with multimedia, supporting collaborative knowledge construction, making thinking visible with dynamic visualisation, quick access to content resources via ICT, and flexible support by tele-tutoring. These principles are used in the MUNICS learning environment, which is designed to help students of computer science to apply their conceptual knowledge from the lectures to complex real-world problems. For example, students may model the information flow in an educational organization with a dynamic visualisation tool. A main finding in the formative evaluation study with the prototype is the ignorance of the students concerning the additional content resources. This finding is discussed on the background of the well-known phenomenon of insufficient use of help systems in software applications.

Keywords
collaborative knowledge construction, dynamic visualization, problem-oriented learning, tele-tutoring, university education, web-based learning

PRINCIPLES FOR PROBLEM-ORIENTED, WEB-BASED LEARNING AND THEIR USE IN THE DESIGN OF MUNICS

In problem-oriented environments, (1) *authentic problem contexts* are seen as the starting points of learning processes. MUNICS(*)is based around an authentic multimedia case. As the content area is "distributed work groups", the case is about the inefficient distribution of information within an organisation. This case study represents a typical class of problems in computer science and a real-life scenario. The students are encouraged to actively request the information they need. Ideally, (2) *learners engage in collaborative knowledge construction* when dealing with these problems, discuss different perspectives and share their prior knowledge. In MUNICS, learners collaborate in small groups (three to five students). MUNICS offers multiple communication tools including a *chat tool* for synchronous communication and a *shared document repository* to facilitate co-operative document management. (3) *Making thinking visible with dynamic visualisation.* Especially when dealing with complex problems, visualization may enhance the construction of mental models of the topic and lead to deeper understanding. MUNICS includes the *Modeler Tool* (Koch et al., 2001) for collaborative dynamic visualization over the web. The tool enables modelling, analysis of static as well as dynamic aspects, and simulation of the flow of information. *(4) Quick access to content resources via ICT.* In problem-oriented learning, increasingly self-directed exploration of the problem and the task domain is emphasised (Gräsel, Fischer, & Mandl, 2001). MUNICS provides background knowledge like the hypermedia material of two lectures on the topic under consideration. For both lectures, *lecture notes* in HTML are available online. *(5) Providing flexible support by tele-tutoring.* Apart from content resources - a human tutor or an expert is available. Students can use the *chat tool* in the MUNICS environment to get in touch with the tutor.

Goals of the formative evaluation study

We implemented a prototype of MUNICS and conducted a formative evaluation study. The primary goal was to assess the extent to which the principles were realized in the prototype and what modification of MUNICS could improve objective and subjective learning processes and outcomes.

METHOD

(1) Sample. Eleven computer science students from the Technical University of Munich volunteered to test the learning environment. The participants were separated into learning groups of two or three students. (2) *Data sources, variables, and instruments*: As instruments to evaluate the realization of the principles we used (a) observation protocol, (b) a knowledge Test, (c) a personal data questionnaire; (d) a questionnaire concerning acceptance, (e) interaction protocols from the communication tools; (f) an individual work report and (g) a face-to-face group discussion at the end of each session. (3) *Procedure.* The session started with a short introduction about the purpose of the study and its course. Then students were asked to complete the questionnaire on personal data, followed by the prior knowledge test. After an introduction into the functionality of MUNICS, the students started to work on the problem. The learning group members were located in

different rooms, each equipped with a computer. After collaboration (approx. 2 hours), the learners were asked to complete the work report, the knowledge test, and the questionnaire on acceptance. Finally, members of the learning group discussed their experiences face-to-face.

RESULTS AND CONCLUSIONS

(1) Providing authentic contexts for learning. The observation protocols revealed that all participants used and explored the Interactive Problem Context intensely – this part of the work occupied about half of the overall working time. This observation is in line with the subjective evaluation of the learners. *(2) Supporting collaborative knowledge construction.* Questionnaire data indicated, that students accepted learning in small groups to a high degree. However, they rated the quality of collaboration for their own learning group as relatively low. The analysis of the interaction protocols revealed that the central focus of students' discourse was about coordination of. Conclusion: Scripted co-operation might structure learners' collaborative activities more appropriately. A main question is, how detailed such a script should guide the interaction. More controlled research on this issue is needed. *(3) Making thinking visible with dynamic visualisation.* Participants used the Modeler Tool collaboratively. Nevertheless, they evaluated the functionality and the usability of the tool to be still in need of improvement. The group discussion revealed that students felt restricted by the tool. On the other hand, the group discussions also showed that the dynamic representation was seen as very helpful for deeper understanding. Conclusions: This can be seen as the more general problem of finding the right specification level in designing representation tools. Domain-specific structures might facilitate collaboration by providing a kind of initial common ground (Fischer et al., in press). However, a highly specified structure might force more advanced students to change strategy. There is hardly any research on the interaction between the degrees of freedom of a representation tool and prior knowledge. *(4) Quick access to knowledge resources.* Most of the students hardly ever used the resources at all. Conclusions: At first glance, the phenomenon might be attributable to bad design of the online lecture notes. However, we argue that the problem points to a more general issue. Studies in different domains and with different tasks showed that students refrain from using background knowledge, glossary or help information, even when experiencing knowledge gaps (Gräsel et al., 2001). More basic research on this topic is needed which can shed light on psychological mechanisms responsible for this effect. (5) *Providing flexible support by tele-tutoring.* The facility of consulting the tutor was frequently used. Students emphasised the importance of the tutor. Moreover, they were satisfied with the support they received. Conclusions: The effect of an expert or tutor participating in peer collaboration is a neglected area of research. On the one hand, this might be detrimental to intensive and high-level negotiation processes, because there is someone who knows the right answer (so why have an argument?). On the other hand, a tutor can introduce the relevant topics, reducing the risk of collaborative construction of misconceptions and thematic vagabonding.

REFERENCES

Fischer, F., Bruhn, J., Gräsel, C., & Mandl, H. (in press). Fostering collaborative knowledge construction with visualization tools. *Learning and Instruction.*

Gräsel, C., Fischer, F., & Mandl, H. (2001). The use of additional information in problem-oriented learning environments. *Learning Environments Research, 3*, 287-305.

Koch, J. H., Schlichter, J., & Tröndle, P. (2001). Munics: Modeling the Flow of Information in Organizations. In P. Dillenbourg & A. Eurelings (Eds.), *euro CSCL 2001 European Perspectives on Computer-Supported Collaborative Learning* . Maastricht, NL: University Maastricht.

Applying Open Source Principles to Collaborative Learning Environments

Eric Scharff

University of Colorado, Center for LifeLong Learning and Design

scharffe@cs.colorado.edu

ABSTRACT

Open source software provides an example not only of a viable software development methodology, but also a model for collaborative construction of artifacts. Open source communities exemplify principles that are important in collaborative learning environments. This paper explores how open source efforts can be used as inspiration for the creation of collaborative learning experiences in a university course. Concrete public deliverables and use of collaborative technology help students explore ill-defined projects that are personally meaningful. This paper provides a description of open source principles, their role in designing collaborative learning experiences, the application of these principles in a university course, and the findings based on analysis of course projects and collaborative technology.

Keywords

Open Source, Swiki, CoWeb, undergraduate education

INTRODUCTION

One view of collaborative learning is as a compromise between two extremes of control. At one extreme, learning is a transmission of knowledge from instructors to learners. At the other extreme, learners choose the topics that are interesting to them and teachers serve as facilitators. In this dichotomy, collaborative learning is a compromise approach in which students and instructors both yield some control to create a more dynamic environment. Both extremes are similar, in that they imply a situation where one party is in control and the other acts in a more passive role. An alternative to this concept is to contrast "one-way" control models with a more community-oriented approach to learning settings (Rogoff, Matusov, & White, 1998). Participation in this manner transforms the roles and they become more shared and dynamic. This involves not a compromise between extremes but a departure from "one-sided" notions of control. Important to the community-oriented approach to learning is the notion of collaborative construction. Learners take an active role in constructing externalized artifacts in order to explore relevant concepts (Papert, 1980). Construction is a social activity involving both the artifacts created by the community and the relationships between community members (Shaw, 1996). This relation between learners and teachers may be asymmetric, and the roles may shift over time.

Open source software has been gaining attention recently as a viable software development methodology. In open source situations, diverse groups of individuals work together to create complex software systems. Much of this attention focuses on open source software as inexpensive alternatives to commercial software (Davis et al., 2000). One popular use of open source software is in teaching computer science principles such as operating systems and networking (Claypool, Finkel, & Wills, 2001; Nelson & Ng, 2000). Open source principles are also being used in MIT's "OpenCourseWare" project (Goldberg, 2001), in which all Web course materials will be free to the public. While this provides access to materials, it doesn't address the role the community will play in the evolution of academic resources or questions of intellectual property. An alternative perspective on open source involves the collaborative aspects of the open source communities themselves. Although open source communities may not be explicitly designed as collaborative learning communities, they exhibit many properties relevant to collaborative knowledge building activities. Open source communities provide a real-world example of how groups of individuals collaborate to create new software. Participants play an active role in the creation and refinement of software. The act of creating software is the vehicle through which the community learns about its own needs, explores solutions, and constructs something of benefit to the community.

In this paper, we will explore the relationship between collaborative knowledge construction and open source software. We will describe open source and how open source communities address problems in collaborative knowledge construction. We will then describe how open source principles were used in the design of a university course and some observations about that course. Finally, we will discuss the similarities and differences between open source and course situations as well as the challenges that face both types of collaborative learning situations.

ACKNOWLEDGEMENTS

The author would like to thank Gerhard Fischer for being receptive in transforming this course. The original course was developed by Ernesto Arias and Gerhard Fischer, without whom this research would not have been possible. The author would also like to thank Mark Guzdial and the rest of the Swiki team at Georgia Tech for providing an exciting environment that we could adopt and extend for this course. This research was supported by the National Science Foundation, grant ITR-0082915.

REFERENCES

Arias, E. G., Eden, H., Fischer, G., Gorman, A., & Scharff, E. D. (1999). *Beyond Access: Informed Participation and Empowerment.* Paper presented at the Conference on Computer Supported Collaborative Learning (CSCL '99), Palo Alto, CA, pp. 20-32.

Claypool, M., Finkel, D., & Wills, C. (2001). *An Open Source Laboratory for Operating Systems Projects.* Paper presented at the 6th Annual Conference on Innovation and Technology in Computer Science Education, Canterbury, United Kingdom, pp. 145-148.

Davis, M., O'Donovan, W., Fritz, J., & Childress, C. (2000). *Linux and Open Source in the Academic Enterprise.* Paper presented at the Conference on User Services: Building the Future, Richmond, VA, pp. 65-69.

dePaula, R., Fischer, G., & Ostwald, J. (2001). *Courses as Seeds: Expectations and Realities.* Paper presented at the European Conference on Computer-Supported Collaborative Learning 2001 (Euro-CSCL 2001), Maastricht, The Netherlands, pp. 494-501.

Goldberg, C. (2001, April 4). Auditing Classes at M.I.T., on the Web and Free. *New York Times,* http://www.nytimes.com/2001/04/04/technology/04MIT.html .

Guzdial, M., Realff, M., Ludovice, P., Morley, T., Kerce, C., Lyons, E., & Seukel, K. (1999). *Using a CSCL-Driven Shift in Agency to Undertake Educational Reform.* Paper presented at the Conference on Computer Supported Collaborative Learning (CSCL '99), Palo Alto, CA, pp. 590-599.

Papert, S. (1980). *Mindstorms: Children, Computers and Powerful Ideas.* New York: Basic Books.

Raymond, E. S. (1998). Homesteading the Noosphere. *FirstMonday,* *3*(10). http://www.firstmonday.dk/issues/issue3_10/raymond/index.html

Rogoff, B., Matusov, E., & White, C. (1998). Models of Teaching and Learning: Participation in a Community of Learners. In D. R. Olson & N. Torrance (Eds.), *The Handbook of Education and Human Development: New Models of Learning, Teaching, and Schooling* (pp. 388-414). Cambridge, MA: Blackwell.

Shaw, A. (1996). Social Constructionism and the Inner City. In Y. Kafai & M. Resnick (Eds.), *Constructionism in Practice* (pp. 175-206). Mahwah, NJ: Lawrence Erlbaum Associates.

Stallman, R. M. (1999). The GNU Operating System and the Free Software Movement. In T. O'Reilly (Ed.), *Open Sources: Voices from the Open Source Revolution* (pp. 53-70). Sebastopol, CA: O'Reilly & Associates.

Different Achievement in Online Oral History

Jason B. Ellis, Amy S. Bruckman

Georgia Institute of Technology
{jellis, asb}@cc.gatech.edu

ABSTRACT

The Internet has made it possible to incorporate adult mentors in the classroom in ways that it would have been difficult or impossible to do previously. As we move forward with such projects, it is important for us to consider what these adults contribute to the learning process. Palaver Tree Online is an online community that supports kids interviewing elders to build up a shared database of oral history. In this paper, we give a brief overview of two case studies of kids in Palaver Tree. In addition, we propose a new role for adults in aiding students having difficulty.

Keywords

Online community, oral history, children, adults, elders

INTRODUCTION

Projects like Foxfire (Wigginton 1985) have shown that oral history can provide opportunities for deep learning by connecting students with real people who have stories to tell. It is our hypothesis that students can gain a new perspective on history through these kinds of interviews with elders. Certainly, many elders have life stories to share. However what specifically students take away from such discussions with elders is unclear.

Palaver Tree Online is a constructionist (Papert 1991) online community aimed at exploring this issue. In Palaver Tree Online, kids interview elders and use what they learned to create online artifacts that share the stories with the world. Through two brief case studies, this paper contrasts the experiences of two groups of students in Palaver Tree Online during its use in a middle school classroom during the 2000-2001 school year. We give a brief overview of a more successful case followed by a less successful one and suggest a new role for elders in scaffolding the teacher in helping less productive students improve their work.

PALAVER TREE ONLINE

A Palaver tree is a West African tree that serves as the center of a village. It is a place where elders come to share their life stories and a place where the community comes to listen. Our aim is to create an online space that honors this tradition – a place where kids can hear history from primary sources.

The design of Palaver Tree Online (PTO) is based on three years of work in classrooms doing e-mail oral history (Ellis, Bruckman et al. 1999). One of the most important lessons we learned in this early work is that we are scaffolding a complex social process that involves students, teachers, and elders. Teachers need a way to recruit elders to work with their classes and manage their students online. We need to provide a comfortable place for elders to share their stories and other personal information online. Finally, we need to support kids taking the stories they hear from elders and creating online artifacts based on them. We call these artifacts PalaverStories.

We used the lessons learned from our e-mail studies to design PTO – a client interface and server infrastructure that aims to help the process of online oral history go more smoothly for all involved. The software helps carry through our interaction model and supports the roles of kids, teachers, and elders (Ellis and Bruckman 2001).

CASE STUDY OVERVIEW

We studied the use of Palaver Tree Online in one 8th grade Georgia History class over the course of six weeks. There were 21 students in the class and they worked in groups of two, with one group of one. Students visited the computer lab once or twice per week during the study. Each visit lasted one hour. We did extensive classroom observation, pre and post interviews with the kids and teacher, a student focus group, and student and elder surveys. We did post interviews with several elders as well.

Before getting started with PTO, students were assigned to read the Civil Rights chapter in their Georgia history textbook. They then spent a day in class brainstorming questions for elders. The first day in the lab, students reviewed discussions and PalaverStories from prior classes. The second day, each group of students was assigned an elder to interview, read the elder's profile, and posted initial questions for the elder.

Interviews consisted of a question and answer session between one elder and a group of kids over the course of two weeks (four sessions). After this, kids began work on their PalaverStories while many continued their discussions with elders for an additional two weeks (four sessions). Finally, each group made their projects available for feedback from elders and other kids. Feedback occurs in an anchored discussion (Guzdial 1997) that has the group's project as its focus. Kids spent the next two sessions giving each other feedback and reading the feedback they received from elders. A few groups made revisions to their PalaverStories based on elder feedback.

Our recent work has examined two groups of kids using PTO in detail: a more successful case and a less successful case. As there is not room here to give specifics on the cases, we will discuss them at a high level. In Case 1, students asked questions based on the elder's profile, heard stories about the elder's life, and created a PalaverStory that captured what they learned in a narrative that showed synthesis. In Case 2, students started in the same way but were never able to focus their interview questions to the same degree as the students in Case 1. The kids' follow-up questions showed little reflection on the elder's previous responses and the discussion got into little depth on Civil Rights. Just as they got further and further away from the subject matter at hand in their interview discussion, the PalaverStory created by these kids starts out well but gets confused and off-topic later.

Mid-way through project in Case 2, the teacher's intervention was needed. Due to the volume of messages, however, the teacher was unable to review the discussions at the level of detail required to detect these breakdowns on a regular basis. On the other hand, the elder simply tried to answer student questions to the best of his ability and may perhaps have felt that offering direction to the students would have been overstepping his bounds. How, then, do we aid teachers and elders in detecting and assisting students that are having difficulty?

Although there are numerous interviews going on, each of these is home to one elder. Perhaps, then, there is a role for the elder in identifying problematic discourses and alerting the teacher – a role similar to the One Sky, Many Voices staff members that monitor discussions (Lee and Songer 1999). Once an elder detects a problem, we could provide a mechanism for that elder to indicate the specific place in Palaver Tree that the teacher might want to pay special attention to. This would prompt the teacher to review the discussion and decide what (if any) intervention is necessary. Of course, for this scenario to work, elders must be keenly aware of what the students need to be doing in order to succeed, as O'Neill found in the CoVis Mentor Database (O'Neill, Abeygunawardena et al. 2000).

CONCLUSION

The Internet has made it possible to incorporate adults in the classroom in ways that it would have been difficult or impossible to do previously. As we move forward with such projects, it is important for us to consider what these adults contribute to the learning process and how we might scaffold this process. Here, we have briefly presented two case studies of students and adults working together online and described a new role for elders in the learning process. By connecting kids with adults eager to share their knowledge and encouraging students to explore interests in an appropriate framework, we believe educators can create important new learning experiences. For more detail on this work, see the project website at http://www.cc.gatech.edu/elc/palaver/

ACKNOWLEDGMENTS

We thank the teachers, kids and elders that have participated in this and previous studies of Palaver Tree Online. Generous financial support for this work is provided by Intel and IBM.

REFERENCES

Ellis, J. B. and A. S. Bruckman (2001). Designing Palaver Tree Online: Supporting Social Roles in a Community of Oral History. Proceedings of Computer-Human Interaction 2001. Seattle, WA: 474-481.

Ellis, J. B., A. S. Bruckman, et al. (1999). Children and Elders Sharing Stories: Lessons from Two Online Oral History Projects. Proceedings of Computer-Supported Collaborative Learning 1999. Stanford, CA: 151-158.

Guzdial, M. (1997). Information ecology of collaborations in educational settings: Influence of tool. Proceedings of CSCL 97. Toronto, Ontario, Canada: 83-90.

Lee, S.-Y. and N. B. Songer (1999). How Does Electronic Discourse Support Students' Scientific Inquiry In An Internet-Enhanced Collaborative Learning Environment? Annual Meeting of the AERA. Montreal, Canada.

O'Neill, D. K., H. Abeygunawardena, et al. (2000). The Telementor's Guidebook: A field manual for supporting inquire on-line, Ontario Institute for Studies in Education, University of Toronto: 61.

Papert, S. (1991). Situating Constructionism. Constructionism. I. Harel and S. Papert. Norwood, NJ, Ablex Publishing.

Wigginton, E. (1985). Sometimes a Shining Moment: The Foxfire Experience. Garden City, NY, Anchor Books.

Design of Augmented Creative Environments

Colin Beardon, Pelle Ehn, Lone Malmborg
Arts and Communication, Malmö University, Sweden
su1620@eclipse.co.uk pelle.ehn@k3.mah.se lone.malmborg@k3.mah.se

ABSTRACT

In this short paper we present the conceptual framework underlying research projects in a newly established research studio concerned with the design of technology-augmented creative environments. The studio investigates design-oriented collaborative environments for inspirational learning with demands on discovery and creative spaces. This is integrated with inquiries into artistic performance as creative practices. We have a collaborative learning research approach and emphasize the importance of place and body (synkinaesthetics) in collaborative learning. Important contexts are performing arts as creative practices and inspirational learning in design education.

Keywords
Creative practices, design education, inspirational learning, synkinaesthetics, performing arts

DESIGN OF LEARNING ENVIRONMENTS

Arts and Communication at Malmö University organizes research in cross-disciplinary design-oriented studios. A recently initiated research studio is concerned with the design of technology-augmented creative environments. We investigate the design of environments for learning, understood as places for collaborative creative activities, by addressing the fundamental intrinsic interplay between interactive media technologies, space (including architecture) and creative practices in design and the arts (especially, theatre and performance). The research work has a special focus on physical spaces and leading-edge technologies for rich multi-user multi-site interaction and ubiquitous computing, as opposed to the more traditional focus on individual personal-computer based learning.

Time, place and cooperation

New conceptions of learning can be summarized in three important concepts for future research which relate to the design of learning environments: *Time*: Learning takes place over a long period in life. It is a process of knowledge construction, which itself is knowledge-dependent; people use their existing knowledge to construct new knowledge. *Place*: Learning takes place in a variety of environments. Learning design has to take into account distributed cognition requiring knowledge in the head to be combined with knowledge in the world. *Cooperation*: Learning is part of collaborative processes in professional and educational settings. Education is incorporated as part of collaborative work activities fostering growth and exploration. These trends in learning research are supported by Resnick (1989), Norman (1993), and in learning theory by Lave and Wenger, (1991), Fischer (1996). A 'paradigm change' is on its way with learning environment, which will influence our whole everyday environment. Where the CSCW field mainly has been based on an integration of sociological and computer science perspectives, research on creative environments for learning should broaden the perspective to also encompass concepts, ideas and methods from design, architecture, cognitive science and the creative arts by strengthening the importance of space and of designing interactive systems which allow for the use of more senses. An important aspect of learning relates to the coupling of mind and body. Learning a process taking place in a community of practice; a creative activity supported by close interaction between senses and mind. We should design for synkinaesthetic interaction (Kirkeby and Malmborg 1995). Using a kinaesthetic approach to interaction design is also suggested by Svanæs (1997) as a way to design interaction with our physical environment. Svanæs uses the term 'kinaesthetic thinking' to signify direct cognitive operations on tactile-kinaesthetic sense experiences. Synkinesthetic interaction is to a large extent 'tacit' in the sense that it is not simply the manipulation of symbolic representations. Creation and expression of meaning is embedded in body movements.

Performing arts – the study of 'creative practices'

The study of how to design environments that support creativity benefits from the study of creative practices, or what people actually do when they behave in a manner that we generally agree is creative. Some of the clearest domains in which to study this are the creative arts, the crafts and theatre. This does not mean that we are only interested in developing environments to support this kind of creative work, but rather that we expect to find practices that have been devised in order to maximize creative potential. We hope to be able to learn from these practices, and to generalize from them in order to enhance creative practice in other human endeavours. We avoid the term 'creativity', concentrating instead upon specific practices: creative practice being seen as a mode of human interaction with the world. While technical practice adopts values such as formalism, information, logical reasoning, precision, detail, correctness and completeness, by contrast, creative practice tends towards communication, visual, spatial, textural and aural representations, ambiguity, abstraction, intuition and imagination. What is significant, is that the term 'creative' is here not simply applied to a particular individual, profession or occupation, but can be applied to any human endeavour. The co-existence of these two modes of interaction within the same project is problematic because of the different value systems they espouse. Our aim is to facilitate this co-existence in a constructive way. We aim to explore these issues of mediated communication through theatre performances that are both valid in their own creative terms, and explore key issues of representation and communication with respect to contemporary digital technologies. Through a series of performances we hope to produce interesting theatre that appeals to a theatre audience as well as raising and clarifying issues about communication within design. We think it may increase our understanding of technologically mediated communication and of spatial metaphors. But perhaps most significantly for this audience, it may lead to the idea of 'boundary practices' and their role in brokering design activities in communities where different stakeholders have not just different languages, but different value systems

Design education – the study of inspirational learning

We are interested in the design of technology-augmented environments for "inspirational learning" as it takes place in environments like the design studio or the master class in architecture, design and art. The inspirational learning environments that we envision are dedicated physical places where people in collaboration can establish and explore a particular thematic learning space by activating, manipulating, combining and assembling configurations of representational objects of mixed media origin. In such environments learning is stimulated by the presence of inspirational resources – images, music, film, samples of materials, everyday objects, which provide an element of surprise and discovery and help see things differently. An inspirational learning environment allows for novel forms of interactivity, such as: imprecise, fluid forms of categorizing inspirational material; digitally augmented physical 'things-to-think-with'; building one's own collection of material across digital media and physical objects; creating exhibitions of relevant materials within a project-specific environment, making one's learning experiences visible and sharing them with co-present and distant others. Especially we have found inspiration for this approach in the Wunderkammer concept (Büscher et al 1999), (Lainer and Wagner 2000). This is also the background for our ATELIER project (architecture and technology for inspirational learning environments). While many projects focus on distance learning, the ATELIER project starts out from face-to-face interactions with people and material artefacts in physical places and asks how we should enhance such environments to turn it into a resource for inspiration and creative learning. Inspirational learning and technologies will be explored at two sites: A "traditional" master-class in architecture, which is contrasted by the setting of an interaction design graduate program studio. While architects' work space is rich with multi-medial materials and artefacts, much of the interaction designers' work environment is concentrated in the screen, but at the same time more collaborative and open to exploring the possibilities of facilitating sharing and interactivity across temporal and spatial boundaries. The project will proceed through a combination of proactive ethnographic fieldwork and participatory design.

REFERENCES

Büscher, M, Kompast, M, Lainer, R, Wagner, I (1999). The Architect's Wunderkammer: Aesthetic Pleasure & Engagement in Electronic Spaces, Digital Creativity 10,1, 1-17.

Fischer, G. (1996) Learning & Intelligent Systems. NSF Symposium (June 26th 1996).

Kirkeby, O. F., and Malmborg, L. (1996) Imaginization as an approach to interactive multimedia. In: B. Gorayska (ed.) Cognitive Technology. North Holland/Elsevier.

Lainer, R, Wagner, I (2000) Silent Architecture - Narrative Technology. Digital Creativity 11,3, 144-155.

Lave, J., and Wenger, E. (1991) Situated Learning: Legitimate Peripheral Participation. Cambridge Univ. Press, NY.

Norman, D. (1993) Things that make us smart. Addison-Wesley, Reading, Ma.

Resnick, L.B. (ed) (1989) Knowing, Learning, and Instruction. Essays in Honor of Robert Glaser. Lawrence Erlbaum Ass, Hillsdale, NJ.

Svanæs, D. (1997) Kinaesthetic Thinking: The Tacit Dimension of Interaction Design. Computers in Human Behavior, 13, 4, 443-463.

Case Application Suite: Promoting Collaborative Case Application in Learning By Design Classrooms

JaKita N. Owensby, Janet L. Kolodner

Georgia Institute of Technology

(jowensby@cc.gatech.edu, jlk@cc.gatech.edu)

ABSTRACT

Transfer means extending what has been learned in one context to new contexts. This paper addresses the application part of transfer. For novice problem solvers, applying cases can be a difficult task. Case-based Reasoning (Kolodner, 1993; Schank, 1982) makes some suggestions for promoting good case application. Learning By Design™ (LBD) (Kolodner et al., 1998) builds on case-based reasoning and constructivist approaches to learning as well as classroom practices from problem based learning and communities of learners, to support both collaborative learning and learning from hands-on activities (Kolodner & Nagel, 1999). The software component to LBD, SMILE (Supportive Multi-User Interactive Learning Environment), was designed to promote the kinds of reflection that case-based reasoning suggests are needed to learn from experience. Among other tools, SMILE consisted of a Case Authoring Tool, whose role was to scaffold student's reading of an expert case such that they could write it up to present to the rest of the class. Although this tool did approach students' understanding of an expert case, it did not approach students' application of that case to their challenge. This paper reports on the Case Application Tool Suite (CATS), which supports four stages of case application – case interpretation, matching, solution application, and solution assessment. This tool suite builds on our experiences with scaffolding design discussions (with the Design Discussion Area (DDA)) and scaffolds both case application and collaborative learning in a project-based environment.

Keywords

Transfer, Case-based Reasoning, Learning By Design, SMILE, Reusing experience, Project-based Learning

CASE BASED REASONING INFORMING CASE APPLICATION and LBD

We all naturally engage in transfer from day to day, transferring our common sense across situations we encounter. But promoting transfer in classrooms seems to require a great deal of effort (Bransford, Brown & Cocking, 1999). Case-based reasoning, which focuses on learning from real-world experiences, provides a computational model of many of the processes involved in transfer (Kolodner, 1997), and also suggests how to promote transfer in the classroom (Kolodner, et al., 1996) and makes suggestions for promoting productive case application. Learning By Design™ (LBD™) was designed around the suggestions that the transfer literature and case-based reasoning make about how to promote transfer in the classroom (Kolodner et al., 1998; Hmelo et al., 2000). Students engage in activities where they use the science they are learning and try it out in the environment. Then they engage in reflective activities that help them make connections between goals, plans, and outcomes in their experiences, and they articulate their experiences to their peers, making explicit the science they've applied. This reflection and reporting are designed to help students turn their own and their peers' experiences into well-indexed well-articulated cases in their memories that they can use later as the need arises. Students also read expert cases and try to apply their lessons. Software that we've developed helps students interpret their own experiences and expert cases into memorable cases. SMILE's Design Discussion suite(Kolodner & Nagel, 1999) prompts students to articulate their design experiences in the context of presenting those experiences to the rest of the class. This analysis of their own experiences that they devise enhances the level of discussion among students in their small groups and as a class, informs their design decisions, and helps them justify those design decisions along the way. But up to now, we've had no software to help with applying those cases later.

We've been investigating the ins and outs of providing that help in the context of LBD's Erosion Challenge. A basketball court is going to be built at the bottom of a hill. The students are to make recommendations about how it can be built such that the hill does not erode onto the court. Two expert cases are presented: the Landslide Case and the Dust Bowl Case. The cases introduce students to agents that can aid in erosion and show students the types of decisions that must be made when planning to build. As they are addressing the challenge, the teacher helps the class reflect on what they can learn from the cases, reflect on what they've observed, reflect on what they've modeled in stream tables, and reflect on how to use that knowledge. Students use the cases to identify opportunities to make better design decisions based on the results of the experts and refer back to the expert cases to ensure that they have not overlooked important issues in their designs. Our software in support of case application is designed based on what the literature tells us is needed to promote analogical transfer, our experience with SMILE's DDA, and our observations of teachers helping their students successfully engage in the Erosion Challenge.

PROMOTING PRODUCTIVE CASE APPLICATION

Good case application\ requires several things. First, students need to understand the new situation well enough to recognize both the case they wish to apply and the task that they wish to apply the case to. Second, students need to be able to recognize what they know that might be applicable. Third, learners need a clear, diverse, easily retrievable library of cases to help them make connections, and they must have an environment that can prompt them to recognize when and which cases to apply.

Several of our teachers have done an exceptional job of scaffolding case application such that students become able to do it on their own. The most important thing we saw the teacher doing was helping students clarify their understanding of the source case and the challenge that they are currently working on. This was accomplished through helping students notice causality and sequencing, helping students identify the role that certain artifacts or items played in a case they were reading about, making sure that difficult vocabulary was identified and broken down. Teachers also expose students to a variety of cases, in addition to the ones provided by our unit, and helped students make connections between them and to the challenge they are trying to solve.

DESIGNING THE CASE APPLICATION SUITE

Watching our teachers, we've become aware that the software must scaffold two processes: understanding and application. Our experience with SMILE also provides suggestions about the design of software: (1) Each of the reasoning tasks students engage in during case understanding and application must be identified and each scaffolded specifically according to its needs. (2) Provide collaborative support for discussions within groups and across groups (Puntambekar, et. al, 1997). (3) Three kinds of scaffolding are useful in helping students articulate their ideas well: chunking, hints, and examples.

Keeping in mind both what we've learned from the Design Discussion Area and the difficulties of students in applying cases, we have created the tool suite to support four stages of case application—(1) gaining an initial understanding of the expert, peer case, or personal case (Case Interpretation); (2) thinking about how that understanding might apply in the new situation (Mapping); (3) guiding application (Solution Application); and (4) predicting the success of the new solution once the application has been made (Solution Assessment). For details, see http://www.cc.gatech.edu/projects/lbd/pub/index.html.

ACKNOWLEDGEMENTS

The McDonnell Foundation, NPSC, Georgia Tech, and NSF have supported this research.

REFERENCES

Bransford, John D. (Ed.), Brown, Ann L. (Ed.), Cocking, Rodney R. (Ed.). (1999). *How People Learn: Brain, Mind, Experience, and School.* Washington, D.C.: National Academic Press.

Hmelo, C.E., Holton, D.L. & Kolodner, J.L. (2000). Designing to Learn about Complex Systems. *Journal of the Learning Sciences.*

Kolodner, J. (1993). *Case-based Reasoning.* Morgan Kaufmann Publishers, Inc., San Mateo, CA.

Kolodner, J.L, Hmelo, C.E. & Narayanan, N. H (1996). Problem-based Learning Meets Case-based Reasoning. In D.C. Edelson & E.A. Domeshek (Eds.), *Proceedings of ICLS '96*, Charlottesville, VA.

Kolodner, J. & Nagel, K. (1999). *The Design Discussion Area: A Collaborative Learning Tool in Support of Learning from Problem-Solving and Design Activities.* Proceedings of CSCL '99. Palo Alto, CA, 300-307.

Sadhana Puntambekar, Kris Nagel, Roland H,bscher, Mark Guzdial, and Janet L.Kolodner(1997). Intra-group and intergroup: An exploration of learning with complementary collaboration tools. Proceedings of CSCL'97. Toronto, Ontario, Canada, 207-214.

Schank, R. (1982) *Dynamic memory.* Cambridge University Press, Cambridge, MA.

Compadres: Lightweight Support for Distributed Collaborators

Brian R. Johnson

Design Machine Group, University of Washington

brj@u.washington.edu

ABSTRACT

Design education has a strong reliance on passive presence awareness and unfocused interaction. This paper reports on Compadres, a system for support of distributed collaborators through creation of group presence awareness on the web. Compadres provides various configurable communications options, in both synchronous and asynchronous modes, including links for email, chat, and file transfer. It includes two levels of presence awareness: current status and an extended radar view providing "asynchronous presence." The system supports itinerant, or mobile, users (such as students) as well as situated users (such as faculty).

Our experiences with Compadres, which has been used by several classes and our research group, support those of others regarding the power of presence and messaging in supporting group cohesion, and indicate that it is possible to support infrequent or occasional collaboration as well as frequent interaction via the web.

Keywords

Web, collaboration, presence awareness, workgroup awareness, Compadres

INTRODUCTION

Design education, based on "studio" education and "project-based learning" has become something of a model for education. As pressures and opportunities increase to replace or supplement face-to-face educational models with computer-supported paradigms, it makes sense to look for insights within computer-supported design education. Donald Schön (1987) has written extensively about interactions within the studio and the role of what Goffman, (1963) calls "unfocused interaction" in the education of architects. The traditional design studio format is intended to create opportunities to overhear and observe interactions between others, including the studio mentor. Personal stereo systems and headphones are often banned during class hours as a consequence, even though students are working independently. Nonetheless, a number of experiments have been conducted using Internet and web-based collaboration tools to conduct "virtual design studios" involving design students collaborating on a project from different cities and time zones.

Research in Computer Supported Collaborative Work (CSCW) and Computer Mediated Communication (CMC) has often focused on support of distributed workers through digital replication of collocation communication options, particularly features of directed, or "focused" interaction (Dourish & Bly, 1992). Other research has found benefits from collocation of team members (Heath and Luff, 1996; Teasley, 2000), and some have found deleterious impacts of distributed work models in large corporations (Herbsleb, *et al.*, 2000).

Based on our own experience, we became interested in awareness and web-based workgroup presence. A survey of available tools supported the conclusion that a communications framework was needed, not a new communication tool. Task-oriented synchronous collaboration systems employing awareness have been shown to increase user satisfaction. Previous experience suggested that support for both asynchronous and synchronous communications was important. User Interface design guidelines suggested that simplification of the communication options would be good. The resulting system, by extending the communication functions of the user's computer environment, supports individual awareness of and participation in the group. It was first implemented in 1998 and has been undergoing informal evaluation and refinement since then.

THE COMPADRES FRAMEWORK

The Compadres system was developed to investigate unfocused interaction, through a web-based presence awareness and communication interface. Of particular interest is the support of loosely-coupled distributed groups. This encompasses not only full time workers, but also mutual support in seminar courses, on-line office hours for educators, distance education groups, and research groups.

Lightweight Client Interface

In Compadres we sought an extremely light-weight client with a focus on communication and a group presence monitor. No special hardware was to be required. A graphical web browser provides the client interface. The use of screen space was minimized. Data processing is handled by a web server application and "back-end" database. Users may use any networked workstation, including those in shared labs, and access Compadres by simply directing the browser to the correct URL.

The presence monitor (at the top of Figure 1) shows current group membership and individual connection status (through varied background colors–green for connected users, pink for absent ones). The display automatically refreshes several times a minute to reflect changing presence conditions within the group.

The Personal Data Page

Each user of Compadres has a personal data page (a portion of one is shown in the bottom area of Figure 1). This display provides the contact information that the individual wishes to share with other group members. The appropriate display is selected by clicking a name from the presence monitor at the top.

The "History" or "Extended Presence" Graphic

The personal data includes (center-right) a graphic showing presence over time. This gray-scale density map shows the pattern and relative amount of time this user was connected during the previous two weeks. It supports collaboration through "way-laying" behavior, and provides an "extended presence" indicator for asynchronous users.

Messaging & the "Door Sign"

When viewing the data page of a user, the one-line form may be used to write them a quick note. However, when viewing your own data page, this same input field may be used to quickly update the Door-sign activity status message (just below the photograph). Each individual's Door Sign is displayed as part of their data page.

CONCLUSIONS

Compadres has been made available experimentally as part of several courses (a total of around 40 people), and by members of our research group. After using the system for a period of time ranging from a few days to several months, they were asked to provide feedback. Responses indicate that the features mentioned above–presence monitor, personal contact data pages, and history graphic–were found valuable. These preliminary results suggest that Compadres does contribute to group identity and cohesion, and does present users with recognizable benefits.

Additional information available at http://www.caup.washington.edu/software/compadres/.

REFERENCES

Dourish, P. and S. Bly (1992) "Portholes: Supporting Awareness in a Distributed Work Group", in *Proceedings of SIG CHI '92*, pp 541-547.

Goffman, E. (1963) *Behavior in Public Places*, The Free Press of Glencoe.

Heath, C. and P. Luff (1996) "Convergent Activities: line control and passenger information on the London underground" in Y. Engestrom & D. Middleton (eds.) *Cognition and Communication at Work*, pp96-129, Cambridge: Cambridge University Press.

Herbsleb, J., A. Mockus, T. Finholt, R. Grinter (2000) "Distance, Dependencies, and Delay in Global Collaboration" in *Proceedings of CSCW 2000* (Philadelphia, December , 2000).

Schön, D. (1987) *Educating the Reflective Practitioner*, San Francisco: Jossey-Bass.

Teasley, S. et al., (2000) "How Does Radical Collocation Help a Team Succeed?" in *Proceedings of CSCW 2000* (Philadelphia, December , 2000)

Project-based Learning with CommSy

Michael Janneck, Wolf-Gideon Bleek

University of Hamburg, Department for Informatics

[janneck|bleek]@informatik.uni-hamburg.de

ABSTRACT

Project-based learning has long been an important element in teaching informatics topics, because it allows students to acquire important social and methodological competences in addition to professional competence. Groupware systems are increasingly used in such settings. In our paper, we present the didactic concept we have applied to more than ten cooperative educational projects over the last few years. We describe how electronic media have become an integral part of our concept and we introduce *CommSy* a web-based application, designed specifically to fit the needs of project-based learning.

Keywords

Project-based learning, learning communities, community system, CommSy

INTRODUCTION

Current work practice in the IT industry is characterized by cooperative work in small multidisciplinary teams. Therefore, social and methodological competences gain importance compared to professional competence, i.e. knowledge in a subject area. Obviously, those competences cannot be learned individually in lectures or traditional seminars, but require practice and being engaged in a real-world context. We address this problem by offering cooperative educational projects to our students with a didactic concept that focusses on authentic work practice. With the interdisciplinary mixture of students in our classes, the high number of "part-time students" (working a lot beside their studies) and the geographically dispersed campus of the University of Hamburg, our organizational setting suggests itself to the introduction of a groupware system into our didactic concept. Furthermore, by using electronic media in our educational projects, students can learn how to use computers to push their work and to communicate with their fellow project members.

PROJECT-BASED LEARNING

Our didactics for project-based learning is based on Dewey's (1966) educational philosophy. The following principles form the basis of our didactic concept:

- *Cooperative construction of a task:* Together with the students, we construct their task within a broad area given by the subject of the course. To be educationally valid, the task should be both, enjoyable and of practical relevance, and it must be demanding and provoke the desire for more information.
- *Teamwork:* The students work on the chosen task for the whole term. They organize their work processes themselves, and they have to thoroughly document their work process and their findings. Usually project teams are formed in groups of three to five students, to work on different aspects of the task.
- *Plenary sessions:* Weekly plenary sessions are used to handle organizational tasks and to reflect on the work process as well as for invited talks on relevant topics, for teaching basics, and for presenting preliminary findings. At the end of the term, the project group presents its results to a larger audience. Presenting results fosters a process of mutual teaching and learning among the students (Brown et al. 1993).
- *Coaching the learning process:* As teachers, we take on the roles of "coaches." Our job is to set the conditions and to give impulses to the project work.

According to Bastian and Gudjons, two activities are central to project-based learning:

- *Communication* plays a major role, because successful communication is the basis for all social interaction. That is coordinating team-work, negotiating positions and responsibilities within the team, sharing one's own perspectives on a given problem with other team members, and so on.
- The *handling of working material* is important, because a proper selection and rating of information sources is the basis for any informed decision made within the project. The presentation of work results in the form of new working material (e.g. reports) are the foundation for further project work.

SOFTWARE SUPPORT FOR PROJECT-BASED LEARNING

Software used in an educational project should support these central activities of project work. Therefore it should provide a means of computer-mediated communication, to allow students to discuss their topics without the plenary sessions. Information that should be shared by technical means are a list of the relevant literature, announcements, and other working material. Together with colleagues, we applied our didactic concept to more than ten projects over the last years. Computer support was first introduced in our projects by a mailing list as a tool for coordination and a shared directory to distribute documents. Later, we used Lotus Notes and Swiki in some projects and considered other tools as well. To better support our didactic concept with a software tool, we developed the web-based system *CommSy* as a suitable solution and found that it fits our needs more adequately.

*CommSy (*See http://www.commsy.org for more information on *CommSy* and our work) stands for *Comm*unity *Sy*stem and is a web-based system to support communication and coordination in project groups. *CommSy* supports communication in multiple ways: News and events can be announced, in a discussion forum, specific topics can be discussed, each member has a personal homepage to present him/herself to the group, and annotations can be made to every item in *CommSy*project room. Working material can be collected in a simple reference manager and put in context by attaching them to any other item (e.g. an announced event). A group-editor is available for cooperative writing of HTML documents. The following design principles distinguish *CommSy* from other software products:

- *Easy individual use:* Enabling individuals to easily use *CommSy* is a prerequisite for any project member to actively engage in the work without having to overcome technical barriers. We achieve this by implementing only required functionality and a simple structure across the whole system.
- *Transparency in cooperative usage: CommSy* gives special emphasis to user communities rather than individuals: *CommSy* is exclusively accessible to members of a certain group and each user's name is recorded with every item s/he creates. Every project room can be customized to help build a group identity.
- *No concept of roles:* "Ownership" is the sole access right in *CommSy*. Only the owner of an item may modify or delete it. Apart from this rule, every member of a *CommSy* is allowed to do everything and to see everything. There is no distinction between students and teachers. By that, *CommSy* reflects social manners we promote in day to day interaction with our students, like self-responsibility and commitment.

DISCUSSION

Introducing software to educational projects is a significant intervention in learning processes, it must therefore address the needs determined by the didactic concept. In the projects we offered to students during the last two years, we found that the use of *CommSy* is indeed a significant enhancement of our didactic concept. But the sole availability of a good software tool does neither automagically result in the sensible use of the software nor any use at all. It is important to negotiate conventions of software use early within a project. This is eased by the given structure of *CommSy*, but still one has to decide, for example, how often project members want to read new items or in which file format documents should be uploaded so that everyone can easily read and write them. In addition to those group-decisions, one has to individually judge the relevance of one's own items and how to present them to the group. We found that students reflected much more on their communication practice after the introduction of software, because it became an explicit topic. It was quite common, that new conventions and use practices were invented by them. Also, the project work was pushed ahead, because students had access to the working material of their team colleagues earlier, and access to the (preliminary) results of other project teams allowed for a broader insight into the subject area of a project. The work with literature received more attention, because all references were instantly available to all students without a big effort; it was thus attractive to add new references to the pool.

REFERENCES

Bastian, J., and Gudjons, H. (1994, 1998) *Das Projektbuch, Bd. 1 & Bd. 2.* Bergmann/Helbig, Hamburg, Germany.

Brown, A. L., Ash, D., Rutherford, M., Nakagawa, K., Gordon, A., Campione., J. C. (1993) Distributed Expertise in the Classroom. In Salomon, G. (publ.): *Distributed cognitions: psychological and educational considerations.* Cambridge University Press, UK, pp. 188–228.

Dewey, J. (1966) *Democracy and Education: An Introduction to the Philosophy of Education.* Free Press, New York, USA, first published 1916.

Mathematical Discussion System

Gabe Johnson
University of Colorado
johnsogg@cs.colorado.edu

ABSTRACT

The Mathematical Discussion System (MDS) enables students and instructors to hold embedded discourse in an online electronic text. These contextualized conversations are recorded and are able to improve the value of the text for students, instructors, authors, and publishers.

Keywords

embedded discourse, hypertext, SER, collaborative learning, discussion moderation

INTRODUCTION

While studying, students may encounter breakdowns in comprehension, and they may need to consult other resources before being able to move forward. In these cases, many people find a friend or a teacher that may be able to help. Another outlet for a struggling student can be the Internet. In both cases, the cause of the breakdown as well as the solution are rarely recorded. The MDS addresses this problem by reducing the distance between the source of the breakdown and a subsequent discussion. The discourse is recorded in the MDS for others so that if they need help on the same topic, there may be a discussion embedded in the relevant portion of the text. In a way, the text becomes a well-known place in which students and instructors can discuss course material without needing to be temporally or spatially collocated.

The MDS naturally supports the Seed-Evolve-Reseed [Fischer, et. al] process. Because the conversations are recorded within the original text, these discussions add value to the material. From the student point of view, using an online text that has conversations about the material may be much more useful than the same text without such embedded conversation. For instructors, the discussion forums can serve as an excellent way to understand what the students are struggling with, so that those topics can receive more attention in class. For book authors or publishers, embedded discourse can serve as embedded reader feedback, suitable for reference in future revisions. The original text serves as a seed; the discussions provide an evolution process for that seed; and the act of reflecting and changing teaching behavior, or the text itself, can be seen as reseeding.

PROTOTYPE DEVELOPMENT

During the summer of 2000, we built a prototype system to be used by an undergraduate differential equations course at the University of Colorado. We wanted to study how well such a prototype would facilitate learning and discussion between classmates and instructors.

In one manner of thinking, the electronic text provides a sort of "virtual place" for students and instructors to discuss course material within the context of course material. The electronic text becomes a location where readers can expect to find topical conversations. The discussion forums are very similar to today's Internet newsgroups, the MDS prototype provides a number of features (discussed below) to the discussion forums that extend the utility of standard newsgroups.

Due to the inherent attributes of an ASCII newsgroup, many students have found them to be inadequate modes of communication. For example, it is difficult to relate mathematical equations or other symbols not found on a QWERTY-keyboard. The MDS enables people to insert such symbols into their messages—addressing the limitation of ASCII-only newsgroups.

One major limitation of web-based discussion forums stems from the pull nature of web sites. In general, people happen upon discussions that interest them by browsing. It can be difficult to remain engaged in these forums because the user must actively look for new messages, rather than receiving them passively, as is the case with email [dePaula 2001].

People reading an MDS text are presented with colored squares next to each paragraph. These squares represent places where conversations take place regarding the surrounding paragraph. We call these squares hooks, because the conversations are thought to be hanging off the main text. These hooks are color coded to indicate activity. If there are new messages relating to the paragraph, the hook is red. Otherwise, the hook ranges from light blue (indicating a few messages) to dark blue (indicating many messages). When the reader clicks on a hook, a discussion forum interface is presented.

Users may not place their own hooks. In initial designs of the MDS, users were given the ability to create their own hooks based on arbitrary portions of text. Users could select a few words, sentences or even paragraphs, and comment on the selected text. This was problematic because after a number of people had created their own hooks, the page was visually cluttered. The hooks began to distract from the text of the page. We chose to give the page author the responsibility of marking up the page with hooks in order to avoid this problem.

Another problem inherent in online discussion forums is the presence of a large number of poorly thought out or erroneous postings. It is possible that a posting with incorrect content can lead students to believe things that are not true, but it is also possible that these 'bad' postings can be used to understand student's misconceptions and to use them as opportunities to set things straight. We have implemented a moderation system in the MDS which is very similar to the moderation system used by Slashdot [http://slashdot.org]. When a person reads a message and finds it to be particularly good or bad, he or she can give or take away a moderation point. After a number of people have read a message, it may achieve a good or bad moderation score. This score can be used to filter messages so that only messages above a certain threshold are displayed. Each user may set his own moderation threshold, so that all posts may be shown, or only the most highly rated posts are shown. This helps users sort out the potentially good messages from the large numbers of superfluous posts that are common within so many of today's newsgroups.

FUTURE WORK

The current MDS system remains a prototype. To better understand how the MDS can enhance learning, the prototype should be improved to a state that it can be used by a large number of students. Initially, we intended to use the MDS in a differential equations course at the University of Colorado, Boulder. Clearly, the MDS can be used outside of the domain of mathematics. We would like to study how the MDS is used by students in different fields such as engineering, the arts, and literature.

A clear design flaw in the current implementation of the prototype is that the seed text must be marked up by hand so that it can be used by the MDS. First, the text must be converted to HTML, then hooks must be inserted into that. This is a complicated process, and for our implementation to become more widely used, an easier method of marking up documents must be created. We would like to create a web page that serves as a proxy for marking up arbitrary HTML pages on the Internet so they can be used with the MDS. This way, authors can save their documents as HTML and put them on web pages, without having to convert their work for use with the MDS. In fact, authors may not even be aware of the MDS's existence—people could distribute a URL and ask other people to discuss that web page via the MDS proxy service.

The true test of the MDS prototype would be to conduct a full-scale study of the system within a real classroom environment. The primary aspect of the prototype we wish to study is the embedded discourse, but we would also like to study the usefulness of the features of the discussion forum enumerated above.

ACKNOWLEDGEMENTS

I would like to thank Dr. James Curry of the Applied Mathematics department for his support of this project. Thanks to Eric Wright and Rian Bogle for their role in building the MDS concept and prototype.

REFERENCES

Fischer, G. (1998) "Seeding, Evolutionary Growth and Reseeding: Constructing, Capturing and Evolving Knowledge in Domain Oriented Design Environments," Automated Software Engineering, 5(4), pp. 447-464

dePaula, R., Fischer, G., Ostwald., J. (2001) "Courses as Seeds: Expectations and Realities," Proceedings of the European Conference on Computer-Supported Collaborative Learning 2001 (Euro-CSCL 2001) pp. 494-501

Online Collaborative Learning as a Catalyst for Systemic Change in the Teaching-Learning Process Within a Multi-Campus Institution of Higher Education

Carlos Enrique Gonzalez, Paul Resta

Monterrey Institute of Technology and Higher Education-Mexico City
cegonzal@campus.ccm.itesm.mx

Learning Technology Center, College of Education, University of Texas at Austin
resta@mail.utexas.edu

ABSTRACT

This short paper describes an innovative and strategic cross-institutional collaborative project between Monterrey Institute of Technology and Higher Education (ITESM), Mexico, and the University of Texas at Austin (UT) to support systemic change in the teaching-learning process at ITESM. The purpose of the document is to share the scope, framework, content, and strategies for preparing faculty to serve as change agents, mentors and trainees of colleagues in the use of online and face-to-face collaborative learning strategies and tools. The UT-ITESM Summer Institute on Collaborative Learning and planned follow-on activities with 50 faculty is referred as one of the key components in such institutional effort.

INTRODUCTION

Higher Education has contributed to the development of societies throughout history. The Higher Education enterprise has shown its sustainability, adaptability and transformative capability during the last 800 years. But now it has "to develop the most radical transformation and renewal ever made" (UNESCO, 1998). Such transformation is often referred to as "The Learning Revolution" and will take place in a new era of global digital competition in higher education.

Consistent with this trend, ITESM is in the process of renewal and is changing the paradigm of the university. Monterrey Institute of Technology was founded in 1943 by a group of Mexican businessmen as a non-profit, private institution of higher education. Today, ITESM (http://www.sistema.itesm.mx) is a leading nationwide educational system of international scope with 31 branches in 27 cities throughout Mexico and subsidiary offices in North America, Latin America and Europe. SACS (Southern Association of Colleges and Schools) accredits all ITESM campuses that award bachelor's, master's and doctoral degrees. Currently, ITESM has a student enrollment of 93,000 and 7500 faculty members. ITESM offers high school, undergraduate and graduate programs in different fields such as Engineering, Computer Science, Architecture, Business, Social Sciences and Humanities.

According to ITESM mission statement (http://www.sistema.itesm/mision) a new educational approach is required. As business tries to keep pace with the changes brought about by globalization and technology, the need for skilled and flexible graduates has risen substantially. The desired educational philosophy of ITESM provides a focus on the students' development of knowledge, intellectual skills, and values and attitudes necessary to be effective and contributing members of Mexican society.

ITESM EDUCATIONAL PARADIGM

The redefinition and redesign of the ITESM teaching-learning process represents an institutional effort to develop individuals with deep knowledge in their academic field and with the desired attributes of honesty and integrity, the ability to be innovative and flexible, work collaboratively, think critically and solve problems, and start on the path as life-long learners. ITESM faculty is expected to transition from primary use of teacher-centered direct instruction and lecture-based teaching to the creation of more student-centered, interactive and collaborative learning environments. ITESM recognizes that the present teacher-centered focus on knowledge transfer and systematic instruction emphasizes individualized work, and uses few technological applications.

ITESM also recognizes that a plan must be developed to assist faculty members in migrating toward a new educational approach focused on knowledge construction and collaborative learning. This educational paradigm involves faculty integrating cognitive tools into their instructional practices and generating new learning environments in which students are more active and responsible for their own learning. To accomplish this goal it is essential to help the faculty transition from their present roles as information transmitters to facilitators of learning and for students to take greater responsibility for their own learning. ITESM's desired educational model emphasizes both knowledge and formative objectives; a set of predetermined values, attitudes and skills that must drive the teaching-learning process.

The ITESM Faculty Development Program (i.e. FDP) was designed to facilitate the transition to the new paradigm. It has a four-stage sequential framework lasting 350 hours for full time faculty members and 210 hours for part-time professors. In addition, ITESM required lap top computers of most students and provided lap tops to faculty and staff. A strong investment in Information Technology infrastructure for all ITESM campuses enabled high speed networks with huge capacity servers to host "redesigned courses" under *Learning Space* (a client/user-server application) within the Lotus Notes groupware environment.

UT-ITESM ONLINE COLLABORATIVE LEARNING PROJECT

With the technology infrastructure and learning resources in place, ITESM has focused its efforts on systemic change in the teaching-learning process by helping the faculty incorporate collaborative learning as an essential component of their teaching practices. To assist ITESM in accomplishing this goal, a cross-institutional collaborative project was designed to provide intensive faculty development and online support for a cadre of 50 faculty who will serve as change agents, trainers, and mentors to help other faculty in their home campuses understand the theories, strategies and technology tools of collaborative learning. The project involved close collaboration between ITESM, the University of Texas at Austin Learning Technology Center and the University of Minnesota Cooperative Learning Center in planning, conducting, and evaluating an intensive three week summer institute for an outstanding group of faculty members from ITESM branches.

The Summer Institute 2001 was held at the University of Texas at Austin and provided the participants with an opportunity to experience online and face-to-face collaborative learning as they themselves designed online collaborative learning components for their own courses. In doing so, ITESM faculty became part of a knowledge-building community in which they were able to share expertise and best practices, and assist each other in solving pedagogical problems of online learning.

The Institute provided participants with a specially designed Web-based course on Online Collaborative Learning (http://www.edb.utexas.edu/resta/itesm2001/) so that they would all experience the process of building virtual learning teams and participate in online collaborative learning projects and activities. An online collaborative learning environment was established to enable the participants to learn the tools and strategies for Computer Supported Collaborative Learning (CSCL). A virtual space using *First Class* groupware was created to enable the participants, who are distributed over the entire country, to continue to work together and support each other's efforts to change teaching-learning practices at their campuses. A metaphor of virtual ITESM Collaborative Technologies Center (CTC) was used in designing the virtual space and project activities. The participants were asked to be members of this new center that will serve as the catalyst for helping all ITESM faculty learn to use the new tools and strategies for collaborative learning.

During the three weeks, the participants also engaged in classroom learning activities focused on the theory and strategies of collaborative learning, face-to-face collaborative learning, the design of online collaborative learning projects, and the development of strategies and plans for the mentoring and training of faculty within their home campuses. Although the Institute was successful, the faculty members require continued and ongoing support as they plan and implement these strategies in their classes during the next academic year. Therefore, online support is provided and some follow-on activities are planned to support the individual, base group and regional group collaborative projects.

UT ITESM Summer Institute participants embody a critical mass that may influence the whole organization from a down-top perspective. It is recognized, however, that a parallel and intertwined top-down effort is also needed to support the ITESM faculty collaborative learning initiatives. Such an effort requires informing and engaging the institution's leaders in the effort and helping them in their role as transformational leaders if deep changes are to be made in the teaching-learning process.

In summary, ITESM has taken on an enormous challenge to transform the teaching-learning process across its 31 campuses. Such an effort is unprecedented and will involve change efforts on a massive scale. A key component of the change strategy is helping faculty integrate online and face-to-face collaborative learning into their instructional practices. It is recognized that this is not an easy effort and will be successful only with bottom-up and top-down leadership and support. This project will also provide a new environment and opportunity to explore new strategies for faculty development and support through the use of online learning communities and tools. The results of this effort will help inform other institutions of higher education facing similar challenges.

REFERENCES

UNESCO (1998) World's Declaration on Higher Education. World's Conference on Higher Education in the XXI Century. Paris.

Communityware Goes to School

Alessandra Agostini*, Monica Divitini**

*DISCO - University of Milano Bicocca, Milano, Italy

**IDI – Norwegian Univ. of Science & Technology, Trondheim, Norway

ABSTRACT

Schools are facing a new challenge. They must reverse the perishing of local communities, central to a democratic society, at the same time helping them to open to the world, also by teaching students the competencies needed to become citizens of the global village. In the paper we discuss how *communityware,* i.e. systems sustaining communities, can help educators in this challenge. The discussion is rooted in the experience of a school in Venice, Italy, with a communityware system, Campiello. The use of Campiello promoted the capabilities of students to manage knowledge, an active use of new technologies, and a learning process that involves the local community.

Keywords

Communityware, learning community, project-based learning, innovative interfaces.

1. INTRODUCTION

The Calvi School, for children aged 11-13, is located in Castello, a neighborhood of Venice that is still a lively and popular area, not only a tourist attraction. Its teachers all share the idea that the school must be an active subject in the neighborhood. To achieve this goal, they integrate traditional teaching with project-based activities designed for exploring historical, cultural and social features of the area. School projects are designed so to involve different disciplines, including in the effort external actors such as elderly and cultural associations. Most of the work is presented to the community during an annual feast. The effort of the teachers enlightens the school as a center for keeping alive community memory and building up community culture, activating a learning process that makes students more aware of their environment. It is however important to point out some difficulties experienced before the adoption of Campiello. First, it was problematic to motivate students and the projects often involved only a limited number of students. Second, the learning process failed to extend to the whole community. The results of the projects were in fact available only for a very limited period of time and in few places. After this they were archived, becoming very difficult to access. Even during this limited time, the reached population was limited, mainly students' relatives. Finally, the process had a limited continuity relying mostly on the continuity of the teaching staff. The representations of the outcomes of the projects (e.g., handwritten paperboards and video-recordings) made them difficult to update, integrate and access. To a certain extent each project was a world of its own. The possibility to activate a learning cycle where previous projects enrich the following ones and where the flow between the school and the community is continuous fully relied on the teachers. Aware of these limitations, the teachers agreed to collaborate to the design and experimental usage of Campiello (Campiello, 1997-2000; Agostini et al., 2000a).

Campiello aims at supporting the exchange of information among people living in and visiting art cities. Its goal is to turn local inhabitants and tourists into active participants in the creation of local knowledge, enhancing their chance to comment on, critique, and make use of it. Since a detailed description of the system is not possible, let us point out some of the main Campiello features. First of all, Campiello provides multiple user interfaces: large interactive screens, paper, and PC (Web). These interfaces have been selected for supporting ubiquitous access to knowledge and for assuring a high degree of accessibility and usability by the whole community (e.g., elderly). Second, Campiello stimulates an active usage of knowledge by providing different degrees of participation in the insertion, revision, and enhancement of knowledge. In particular, users can insert new items and topics; they can rate and comment existing items; they can answer to questions specified by the article's authors and point to additional materials. Finally, Campiello supports personalized interactions through recommendation of articles based on user preferences and past behaviors (Glance et al., 1998).

2. IMPACTS ON LEARNING

The involvement in Campiello had a strong impact on the Calvi School. First, we observed that Campiello played an important role in *reinforcing* the perception that students have of themselves as a learning community, assuring a greater continuity to the learning process. Gradually, teachers and students became aware of the possibility to take advantage of the "memory" built by previous students. Campiello fostered a trend that sees no longer isolated projects, but a learning cycle across years and classes, in a truly collaborative effort that involves students and teachers alike. Second, Campiello helped to *enlarge* the learning community by increasing the visibility of the produced material and assuring a wider audience. It proved to be a good way for connecting different generational communities, but also for connecting the school with other information providers. The support provided for this cross-fertilization is a relevant achievement of Campiello. In fact, often this would have not happened without Campiello, even when the material was already available through other communication media. What made the difference was the feeling that Campiello provided of a common ground. Campiello has also changed the capability of presenting the work of the school to "the world". Previously, projects were mainly designed to increase the awareness of students on their environment. Campiello involvement has allowed looking at a project as a communication media, acknowledging that as important as awareness are the exchanges with the external community that help to keep the environment alive. This leads us to the third point, the *improvement* of knowledge handling and exchange. Before the adoption of Campiello, the school projects were difficult to access, update, integrate, and reuse. The digital format of information and its management through a semi-structured knowledge base per se overcome these problems through various services (e.g., search, and easy modification). These possibilities reinforce the learning process making its outcomes more permanent. Moreover, in the previous years the teachers were forced, for practical reasons, to adopt a single format for each project. Thanks to Campiello, they have been able to integrate different media, e.g. combining text and pictures with audio and video. The richness of the media allows adopting the most suitable media, but it also allows teaching various techniques at the same time (e.g., writing, drawing, video-recording). The possibility to specify relations among different articles (possibly inserted by different authors) showed to enforce looking for correlation and learning by analogy. The awareness of the potential audience stimulated students to be concise and to adopt a writing style "attracting" readers. This lesson, according to teachers, is particularly relevant for students of this age, which often have difficulty in synthesizing concepts. Fourth, Campiello has fostered the appropriation of new technology. At the beginning of the collaboration, the school did not have any computer laboratory. However, at the end of the project the school was independent with respect to the design and production of electronic multimedia content, even if no formal training has taken place. From the educational point of view a strong impact of Campiello is the students' understanding of the Internet potentiality in term of being active providers of information instead of mere passive consumers. Students understood that Internet is different from a library where just expert people can add new books in the shelves. While at the beginning they knew just about the global accessibility nature of the media, at the end of the project they appreciated a broader range of characteristics such as the continuous and quick growth of the knowledge and, again, the possibility of being prime actors in this process.

Our experience shows that communityware can play an important role in making students feel as members of a community within a wider community. This feeling relies on the awareness of having a common *memory*, playing an active role in the construction of such a memory, and taking active part in the social practices for keeping it alive. As we have observed in Campiello, communityware can both facilitate the feeling of "belonging, having a common ground" and provide the technological substrate for keeping the community memory alive. For making this possible the system must support different participation forms, from simple fruition up to commenting and content production, in order to promote a smooth transition from peripheral participation to full membership in the learning community. In addition, based on our observations, we can claim that communityware can help students to grasp the basic competencies needed for becoming citizens of the "global village", both in terms of information management and active usage of new technologies. On the short term we think that schools can benefit from the involvement in existing communityware experiences. On the longer run, it is necessary to define a combined research agenda for educators and technologists to develop communityware that better meet the need of schools.

REFERENCES

Agostini A., Giannella V., Grasso A., Koch M., Snowdon D. (2000a): *Reinforcing and Opening Communities Through Innovative Technologies*. In M. Gurstein (Ed.), *Community Informatics: Enabling Communities with Information and Communications Technologies*, Idea Group Publishing, 2000, pp. 380-403.

Campiello (1997-2000): Esprit Long Term Research project #25572, PC interface available at: www.campiello.org

Glance, N., Arregui, D., Dardenne, M. (1998) Knowledge Pump: Supporting the flow and use of Knowledge in Networked Organizations. In U. Borghoff & R. Pareschi (Eds.), *Information Technology for Knowledge Management*, Springer Verlag, Berlin, 1998.

Using "Thinking Tags" to Improve Understanding in Science: A Genetics Simulation

Kimberley A. MacKinnon, Susan Yoon, Gail Andrews

Ontario Institute for Studies in Education of the University of Toronto (OISE/UT)
kmackinnon@oise.utoronto.ca, syoon@oise.utoronto.ca & gsandrews@oise.utoronto.ca

ABSTRACT

In this study, small wearable microprocessor-driven GroupWear tags (Thinking Tags) are pre-programmed to run a genetics simulation and used in a science classroom in order to investigate the effects on the nature and quality of discourse among students. Preliminary data suggest that Thinking Tags provide an effective method of instruction that can be used to address misconceptions in science that persist despite traditional pedagogical interventions.

Keywords

Science, technology, GroupWear, Thinking Tags, genetics, probability, participatory simulation, discourse

INTRODUCTION

Rosalind Driver, in her book titled *Children's Ideas in Science* (1985) discusses how children bring pre-conceived ideas about the world to science class, and that often these ideas have been reinforced from a very young age. Hence, science lessons may be perceived as counterintuitive when these ideas do not correspond to accepted theory. It is therefore important for students to be able to understand and evaluate a variety of conceptions. One means of accomplishing this goal may be via students' collaborative discourse since emergent ideas are brought out into the open and treated as artifacts that can be modified and improved (Bereiter, in press).

Heim (1991) states that, dominance and recessiveness of alleles is one of the most commonly misunderstood concepts in elementary genetics. Inheritance is an important and basic component in the study of genetics, yet it has been shown that students of all ages have much difficulty with its related concepts (Heim, 1991; Solomon, Johnson, Zaitchik & Carey, 1996; Banet & Ayuso, 1999; Weissman & Kalish, 1999; Lewis & Wood-Robinson, 2000). In a study by Lewis & Robinson (2000) students nearing the end of compulsory science education showed a marked level of misunderstanding, even of the most seemingly basic concepts of genetics. They explain that, "[a]lthough there was some recognition that sexual reproduction leads to an increase in genetic variation there was little awareness that this is the main purpose of sexual reproduction and is achieved through the process of fertilization – the fusion of genetic information from two different individuals" (p. 187).

THINKING TAGS IN SCIENCE

The MIT Media Laboratory has been at work developing small wearable microprocessors called *Thinking Tags* (Tags). These Tags are about the size of a small palm pilot and are equipped with infrared ports and sensors, lights and a small display panel however, they can also come with motors and various other sensory equipment.

A recent project at the MIT laboratory used these devices with children for the purpose of creating their own scientific instruments. Through a series of narratives they tell how the children, through working with the Tags, showed a marked level of motivation and critical capacity. They go on to say that, a constructionist "scientific instrument design has the potential for sparking interest in scientific issues among students who otherwise would avoid the subject altogether" (Resnick, Berg & Eisenberg, 2000).

One of the most salient features of the Tags is their ability to create a system of feedback, from which the students may gain increased understanding. Each Tag has the ability to send and receive information via an infrared signal, and can also display information, using lights, sounds and a mini digital display screen. Each of these features is then able to function in a constant loop of sending, receiving and displaying information, allowing students to obtain information from their Tag, almost instantaneously.

THE GENETICS SIMULATION

Using the programming language *Cricket Logo*, a simple genetics program was created to introduce students to some basic concepts related to inheritance. In the *Genetics Simulation*, each Tag is programmed with a specific genotype that is not initially known to the students. The only information given to the students is their eye colour (phenotype), which is either green (dominant) or red (recessive), and their task is to meet with other Tags and observe the total probability and random selection of eye colour of their "virtual offspring".

In the simulation, four lights, each lighting up as either green or red depending on the genotypes of both Tags that are meeting, denotes the total probability of eye colour (phenotypes) for the "virtual offspring". For instance, if a heterozygous green-eyed Tag met a homozygous red-eyed Tag, the total phenotypic probability would show as two green lights and two red lights. Then, to reveal the eye colour selection, students press a blue button on the Tag so that one of the lights is randomly selected to remain on, while the other three are shut off. Students then record this information following each meeting and discuss their ideas about the results.

DISCUSSION

Banet and Ayuso (1999) state that, "traditional teaching strategies have little effect on students' acquisition of meaningful understanding of inheritance, which suggests that significant changes should be made in both curriculum planning and the sequence of teaching" (p. 314). We believe that the *Genetics Simulation* provides a concrete experience with the underlying rules for the process of acquiring inherited characteristics, and we anticipate that the saliency of the experience will stimulate an interest and quality of critical discourse that would otherwise be missed using traditional pedagogical approaches.

Ongoing research using Thinking Tag technology has shown promising results for prompting student interest, critical discourse and conceptual understanding. A companion study that examines understanding the importance of dental hygiene among kindergarten students, has shown that participatory simulations can have a positive effect on conceptual development in very young children (Andrews, MacKinnon & Yoon, see this volume).

Preliminary pilot data from the *Genetics Simulation*, collected from two groups of graduate students, indicate that discussion during the activity appears to be mediated by content-based inquiries. Furthermore, students seem to become immersed in a "first-person experience" (Colella, n.d.), identifying with the characteristics of their Tag, and gathering information from their interactions within the group, suggesting that the technology has increased their effort at meaning-making. Current investigations will be examining the effects of the *Genetics Simulation* and the Thinking Tag technology with intermediate, secondary and graduate (non-science) students.

ACKNOWLEDGMENTS

Special thanks to Dr. Earl Woodruff and the Thinking Tag Committee at OISE/UT for their support.

REFERENCES

Andrews, G., MacKinnon, K. A. & Yoon, S. (2001). *Using "Thinking Tags" with Kindergarten Children: A Dental Health Simulation*. Poster session to be presented at the annual Computer Support for Collaborative Learning Conference, January 2002, Boulder, CO.

Banet, E. & Ayuso, E. (1999). Teaching Genetics at Secondary School: A Strategy for Teaching about the Location of Inheritance Information. *Science Education*, **84**(3), pp. 313 – 351.

Bereiter, C. (in press). *Education and Mind in the Knowledge Age*. Erlbaum, Toronto.

Colella, V. (n.d.). *Participatory Simulations: Exploring Dynamic Systems through Real World Interactions*. Retrieved from http://vanessa.www.media.mit.edu/people/vanessa/part-sims/index.html.

Driver, R., Guesne, E. & Tiberghien, A. (1985). *Children's Ideas in Science*. Open University Press, Philadelphia.

Heim, W. G. (1991). What Is a Recessive Allele? *The American Biology Teacher*, **53**(2), (February).

Lewis, J. & Wood-Robinson, C. (2000). Genes, chromosomes, cell division and inheritance – do students see any relationship? *International Journal of Science Education*, **22**(2), pp. 177 – 195.

Resnick, M., Berg, B & Eisenberg, M. (2000). Beyond Black Boxes: Bringing Transparency and Aesthetics Back to Scientific Investigation [Electronic version]. *Journal of the Learning Sciences*. Retrieved from http://el.www.media.mit.edu/groups/el/Papers/mres/bbb-jls/.

Solomon, G. E. A., Johnson, S. C., Zaitchik, D. & Carey, S. (1996). Like Father, Like Son: Young Children's Understanding of How and Why Offspring Resemble Their Parents. *Child Development*, **67**, pp. 151 – 171.

Weissman, M. D. & Kalish, C. W. (1999). The Inheritance of Desired Characteristics: Children's View of the Role of Intention in Parent-Offspring Resemblance. *Journal of Experimental Child Psychology*, **73**, pp. 245 – 265.

Collaborative Network-Based Virtual Reality: The Past, the Present, and the Future of the Virtual Solar System Project

Kenneth E. Hay, Dean M. Elliott, Beaumie Kim

University of Georgia

khay@coe.uga.edu delliott@coe.uga.edu bkim@coe.uga.edu

ABSTRACT

This paper and presentation describe an ongoing research and development effort to create a virtual reality environment in which students cohabitate, collaborate, and co-construct shared meanings of astronomical phenomena in an undergraduate introductory astronomy course. Initial versions of this environment addressed face-to-face and asynchronous methods of collaboration. The most recent iteration of our work incorporates the use of advanced networking technologies to enable synchronous collaboration between students in two primary collaborative learning activities: co-construction and co-habitation of virtual models of the solar system. Co-construction refers to multiple students working together to construct a common virtual model. Co-habitation refers to the ability to simultaneously experience the same virtual model from either common or multiple perspectives.

Keywords

Virtual reality, modeling-based inquiry, solar system

INTRODUCTION

Consider a scenario where groups of students studying solar eclipses collaboratively co-construct a shared world within a 3D Virtual Reality (VR) modeling environment. After creating the world, students position themselves to view the eclipse from different perspectives: one on the Sun, one on the near side of the Moon, one out in space, and four others at differing latitudes on the surface of the Earth. Visualization techniques they are using show the umbra and penumbra shadows of the moon as it approaches the earth. Similarly, they see the orbital paths of the moon and earth as well as the line of nodes. These students talk to each other on a networked party line where they describe their perspectives to each other in real time while watching the eclipse. They can tell each other what they see and when an eclipse is happening, and describe this to each other not simply in terms of the eclipse they see unfolding but in terms of their positions and the elements of their model that they have visualized. At critical times they stop the model and call everyone over to their perspectives, they lead each other from perspective to perspective exploring the interrelationships between the elements of their model. In the future they extend this collaborative exploration into collaborative prediction where they predict if an eclipse comes, and if it does, what kind it is, when it occurs, how fast it travels, and what kind of path it takes. The preceding scenario is our vision of what we are developing in the context of a collaborative, inquiry-based undergraduate astronomy course using non-immersive VR modeling and visualization software. This paper and presentation will begin by describing the theoretical and empirical foundations of an ongoing research and development effort to explore the educational potential of virtual reality in learning environments.

Virtual Solar System Project

The Virtual Solar System (VSS) project (Hay & Barab, 1998) is an education reform effort in undergraduate one-credit astronomy laboratory course. Students in the course create virtual 3D computational models of the solar system within a Modeling-based Inquiry pedagogical framework. Core inquiry activities currently include three themes: phases of the moon, eclipses, and seasons. Each activity begins with inquiry questions such as, "Can you create a model of a Sun-Earth-Moon system in which the Moon keeps the same face to the Sun throughout an entire Earth year?" It should be quite clear that students are unable to simply look up an answer to such a question in a textbook. Instead, they plan how they will build an appropriate model and determine what data they need. Next, students build their model, validate it, and revise it as necessary until the model works as planned. At this stage, the students' focus shifts to creating visualizations of the model that validate the model's suitability for answering the inquiry questions. Finally, they create a report containing their warranted conclusions, which must be supported with appropriate data and visualizations. Throughout the evolution of the VSS, we have used computer technologies to enable face-to-face, asynchronous, and synchronous collaborations among the students and the instructor.

RESEARCH: VSS + ASYNCHRONOUS COLLABORATION

Our investigation of whether asynchronous collaboration enhanced this learning environment began with a group of four learners in an exploratory study of asynchronous computer-supported collaboration. This group worked in a classroom setting for the first few weeks, then began working independently from home. In order to provide appropriate technology supports, we developed a course website that contained a range of course resources, grading utilities, assignments, asynchronous collaboration tools and communication facilities. The communications facilities included "ask the professor", a professor course messaging system, and a group threaded discussion area. This exploratory study indicated that students could effectively work independently in this environment and could effectively use the model building tools and access the informational resources. Much to our dismay, the students did not use the asynchronous collaboration tools at all. They reported that in order to use the VR software effectively they needed at least one hour of uninterrupted time, preferably two. They wanted help immediately when they encountered difficulties in order not to lose the flow they had established. The learners' solution to this collaboration problem was to use asynchronous communications to set a time for a phone call between classmates and to use that time to talk each other through problems while each was actively engaged with the software.

DEVELOPMENT: VSS + SYNCHRONOUS NETWORK-BASED COLLABORATION

We believe the immediacy of communication is related to the high level of learner engagement needed to work effectively in this complex cognitive environment. Once students were engaged they did not want to disrupt their flow. In order to resolve these issues, we are currently developing advanced network technologies that enable students to interact synchronously with their classmates and instructors. This model of computer-supported synchronous collaboration is designed to accommodate an anytime, anywhere learning model. Access to other students and the instructor will be possible in real-time, when their actual demands for collaboration arise. Using these synchronous technologies, students will also be able to co-habitate and co-construct within the same virtual world. Co-construction is similar to Resnick's (1996) third stage of distributed constructionism, collaborating on constructions. Co-habitation extends the learning experience by allowing students to gain multiple perspectives at the same time (re. earlier example). We have identified three primary types of network-based interactions: one to one interactions, small group interactions, and presentation interactions. One to one and small group interactions will be the primary interactions as students explore questions or as professors/teachers support students, and will be analogous to the current small group interactions that are found when students and teacher work together in our test bed at UGA. The presentation interaction will also be analogous to the current practices; nevertheless, they will require new networking strategies. In the presentation mode, students will present their findings to their entire class via the network. The size of the class could be anywhere from 20 to 300. The teacher would also be interactively engaged with the student, asking questions, probing ideas, and clarifying concepts.

CONCLUSIONS

We have made significant progress in the development of this technology. The initial stages were focused on developing the VR environment and curriculum to the point that students could efficiently and effectively construct their own models to answer inquiry-based questions. The focus of the past two years has been to examine the extent to which computer-supported collaboration allows learners to co-construct and co-habitate shared virtual worlds while investigating astronomical phenomena.

REFERENCES

Hay, K. E & Barab, S. A. (1998, April). *Building Worlds: Tools of Virtual Practice.* Paper presented at the annual meeting of the American Educational Research Association, San Diego, CA.

Resnick, M. (1996). Distributed Constructionism. In D.C. Edelson & E.A. Domeshek (Eds.), *Proceedings of the Second International Conference on the Learning Sciences*, Charlottesville, VA: AACE.

Moving Toward Knowledge-building Communities in Health Information Website Design

Jennifer Turns, Kristina Liu, Tracey Wagner
Program for Educational Transformation Through Technology
University of Washington
jturns@u.washington.edu, vrliu@u.washington.edu, tswagner@u.washington.edu

ABSTRACT

In this paper, we have described our work with the *Arthritis Source* website and our efforts to develop a community of learners in that context. We argue that given proper architectural support, efforts to listen to learners can effectively foster collaboration between the authors of an informational website and its visitors and help community building among its users through a dynamic knowledge base.

Keywords
Knowledge-building community, Community of inquiry, Informational website design, Content management system

INTRODUCTION

Informational web sites are not traditionally seen as collaborative technologies. In this paper, we wish to re-examine this common notion by describing the collaborative learning underpinnings of our current and future work on a medical information web site, the *Arthritis Source*. In this paper we discuss how the design of a medical information website has evolved to embody a knowledge-building community perspective (e.g., Brown and Campione, 1990; Scardamalia and Bereiter, 1994; Hewitt and Scardamalia, 1998) as the driving framework. This redesign transforms the *Arthritis Source* from its original state as a static, encyclopedic object into a community of inquiry and practice in which users learn from each other's questions and shape the growth of the knowledge base. In this effort, the designers, content authors, and users of the website each learn from the others.

Our redesign of the Arthritis Source has been guided by both the current research on medical information websites and by our own specific concerns. A variety of current studies on the roles and effectiveness of medical websites have discussed some common shortcomings and related design decisions (e.g., Berland et al., 2001). In our research, we have moved from describing the users and understanding the community of people we hoped to serve to focusing on the users' current knowledge and goals in visiting the site. In this project we have attempted to address some of these problems and also create a systematic solution to issues of content maintenance and site development that meet users' changing needs. Most importantly, we wanted to be able to help patients find answers to their questions concerning their conditions. We are working on a system of site architecture and content development that can be driven explicitly by both our understanding of site users' information needs and by site users' interactions with the site over time. As people use the site, they will collaborate with the content authors to create an information resource that serves users' purposes and will change with their needs. We are currently working toward a new vision for the Arthritis Source – a website that looks like an informational website, but is a community of inquiry.

DIVERSE LEARNERS, BUT SHARED NEEDS

Our earliest work with the Arthritis Source consisted of various efforts to "know thy learner" so that we could create a site that was more learner-centered (Turns and Wagner, submitted). We used a variety of methods to learn who was visiting the website and what they were doing during their visits. One of our most comprehensive activities has been our use of an online survey in which users of the site provide us with information about themselves and their visit (Turns and Liu, 2000). Based on survey results, personal interviews, and emailed comments, we know that while our user population is widely varied, there are some common needs and characteristics. The majority of the participants identified themselves as patients with arthritis (61%) or friends and relatives of an arthritis patient (8%). Patients have many different information needs and goals when they visit the site, but many patients share very similar needs. The complexity of some of these needs as well as the shared nature of the various goals suggests that a potential community of learners already exists. Patients also come to the site with existing knowledge, and sometimes with existing misconceptions. Many of these misconceptions are also shared (or originate from common sources), suggesting that patients may be positioned to benefit from previous visitors' learning—the essence of a knowledge-building community.

SUPPORTING A KNOWLEDGE-BUILDING COMMUNITY THROUGH DESIGN

The extent and complexity of the questions brought to the site by our learners convinced us quickly that no static system could effectively satisfy all the users. The knowledge-building community perspective suggested to us that instead we should design a system in which the learners influence the content, over time tuning the system to their needs.

At the center of our design is the site content, the result of a collaboration between arthritis patients and site designers in which the designers learned about the patients' information needs. The content of our site has changed dramatically as we have listened to the needs of the community.

This content, while accessible in the usual browsing mode, is also tailored via an open-source content management system to support a question-based navigation system. This system will allow learners to ask free text questions, and it will respond to them with authoritative, relevant text that has been developed to be learner-centered. The system will respond to such questions in two possible ways, each supporting a kind of community knowledge building. After a learner asks a question, the system returns several articles that may address the topic. If the learner cannot find any useful information by asking or rephrasing the question, he or she is invited to submit the question to the content developers. These developers will then be able to add appropriate content to answer the question or improve the search system.

Learners who receive useful answers from the system are benefiting from the knowledge-building efforts preceding their use. In the future, we hope to allow users to contribute to the knowledge embedded in the site by sharing with later users some of their constructions of the site. Learners who submit a question for the content developers contribute to the knowledge community both by driving content creation and by extending the designers' understanding of how to interpret questions.

This system only exists in partial form at the writing of this paper, so several challenges remain. One of the most important is assessing the individual and/or community learning that results from this enhanced architecture. As we move forward, we anticipate that we will also identify new opportunities to add learning features. Many additions are possible, and we need to think carefully about which will add to the knowledge-building community and which will merely distract.

Efforts to study web-based information systems in context of patient education and lifelong learning can shed light on issues broader than just health information websites. Issues such as learner-centered curriculum design, collaborative knowledge-building, and dynamic website content creation may be of interest to all information website designers.

ACKNOWLEDGEMENTS

This work has been supported by the Program for Educational Transformation Through Technology at the University of Washington. PETTT is a University Initiative Fund (UIF) program. We thank Dr. Frederick Matsen, Aaron Louie, Kristen Shuyler, Ralph Warren, and Scott Macklin for their dedication to this project. We also thank all of the users of the Arthritis Source who have participated in our studies.

BIBLIOGRAPHY

Brown, A. L. and Campione, J. C. (1990) Communities of learning and thinking: or a context by any other name, *Human Development,* **21**, 108-126.

Berland, G.K.; Elliott, M.N.; Morales, L.S.; Algazy, J.I.; Kravitz, R.L.; Broder, M.S.; Kanouse, D.E.; Munoz, J.A.; Puyol, J.A.; Lara, M.; Watkins, K.E.; Yang; and McGlynn, E.A. (2001) Health information on the internet: Accessibility, Quality, and Readability in Spanish and English, *Journal of the American Medical Association,* May 23/30: **285**, 20, 2612-2621.

Hewitt, J. and Scardamalia, M. (1998) Design principles for distributed knowledge-building processes, *Educational Psychology Review,* Mar, **10**, 1, 75-96.

Scardamalia, M. and Bereiter, C. (1994) Computer support for knowledge-building communities, *Journal of the Learning Sciences*, **3**, 3, 265-283.

Turns, J. and Liu, K. (2000) Online Survey Results. Technical Report.

Turns, J. and Wagner, T. (submitted) Listening to the learners: A case study in health information website design. *Society of Technical Communication's 49th Annual Conference* (Nashville, TN, May 2002).

Mediating Collective Discussions Using an Intelligent Argumentation-Based Framework

Marco A. Eleuterio (*)
PUC-PR/UTC
marcoa@hds.utc.fr

Jean-Paul Barthès
UTC, France
barthes@utc.fr

Flávio Bortolozzi
PUC-PR, Brazil
fborto@ppgia.pucpr.br

ABSTRACT

This paper briefly describes AMANDA(1), a framework for mediating collective discussions in distance learning environments. The objective of this framework is to help tutors achieve better results from group discussions and improve knowledge transfer among the participants. The overall idea is to organize the group discussion in an argumentation tree and involve the participants in successive discussion activities. The coordination of the discussion is made by a set of intelligent mechanisms which reason over the discussion and propose new interactions among the participants. AMANDA advances the discussion by generating progressive discussion cycles until a desired set of target conditions are observed. At each discussion cycle, the system redistributes discussion tasks among the participants to ensure a desired degree of agreement and participation among them. In this short paper we describe the underlying coordination principles and the use of knowledge models for producing natural language questions.

AN ARGUMENTATION-BASED STRUCTURE FOR THE DISCUSSION

The discussion is organized by an argumentation tree which links questions, answers and arguments. Each question proposed by the system (DE node) is linked to a set of answers (ALT nodes) given by the participants. Each answer has a corresponding sub-tree of arguments (ARG nodes). The ARG nodes express the intention to support or refute a given position presented by another participant. An ARG node is formed by its intention (full/partial support, full/partial refute) and by a free text expressing the proposition that holds the argument. The reasoning over the distribution and the nature of the ARG nodes is the basis for coordinating the discussion.

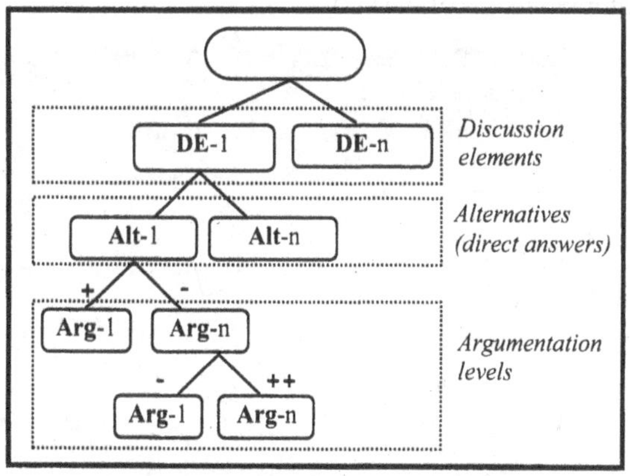

Figure 1: The discussion tree

THE TEMPORAL PROGRESS OF THE DISCUSSION

The discussion advances in periodic cycles, where the system distributes to each participant a specific discussion sheet (figure 3) containing either *questions* to be answered or *propositions* to be analyzed. At each cycle, the system receives the discussion sheets from all participants and builds the next discussion cycle by producing new discussion sheets (figure 4). The construction of a discussion sheet is intentionally made so as to promote the maximum degree of knowledge exchange among the participants. For this purpose, AMANDA uses a set of assignment mechanisms that reason over the discussion tree and propose new interactions among the participants. Some mechanisms attempt to detect potential discussion situations, such as participants that disagree over a certain answer, answers given by different participants to the same question and highly polemic positions. Other mechanisms attempt to assure that each participant takes part of all discussion elements with similar workloads. The discussion is advanced in cycles until a satisfactory set of conditions is achieved.

THE COORDINATION PRINCIPLE

The heart of the system is the way that AMANDA builds the discussion sheets at each discussion cycle. When opening a new discussion cycle, AMANDA analyses the current configuration of the discussion tree and decides to re-launch certain nodes, i.e. to create new nodes and strategically assign them to the participants. The choice among which nodes to re-launch is

---

* Sponsored by CNPq, Brazil

(1)AMANDA - Agent de Modélisation et ANalyse de Dialogues Argumentés - is a joint R&D effort between the Pontifical University of Paraná, Brazil (PUC-PR), the Technology University of Compiègne, France (UTC) and their respective partners Siemens Telecomunicações, Brazil and Cegos, France.

done by evaluating each node with respect to its sub-tree and assigning it a "re-launch priority value". The nodes chosen to be re-launched are then assigned to the corresponding participants as a result of the assignment mechanisms, as mentioned above. AMANDA is now ready to build the personal discussion sheets for the new discussion cycle. These discussion sheets are made available in HTML format to be fulfilled and sent back by the participants.

DOMAIN MODELING

The system uses a domain ontology and a task structure to represent the domain of discussion. They are used to produce natural language questions that can be turned into *discussion elements*, i.e. DE nodes for the discussion tree. The questions are produced based on the existing links among the concepts of the ontology, among the sub-tasks of the task structure and between the task structure and the ontology. This feature was proposed to help the tutors elaborate the questions to be launched for collective discussion. In practice, we were surprised how well the system can perform in producing well formulated questions provided that the models are well constructed. We also noticed that the *quality* of a question can also measure the quality of the domain modeling.

THE PROTOTYPE

AMANDA was developed in LISP and put into practice in four actual training situations. The results are promising and show that the system can efficiently coordinate a group discussion with very low effort from the tutor and a good degree of knowledge transfer among the participants. The prototype includes a tutor interface to view and edit the discussion tree (figure 2) as well as an editor for building the ontology and the task structure (figure 5). The system also features an HTML module (http server, PHP scripts and html files) which allows access to the system over the Internet. Below are some sample screens of the system.

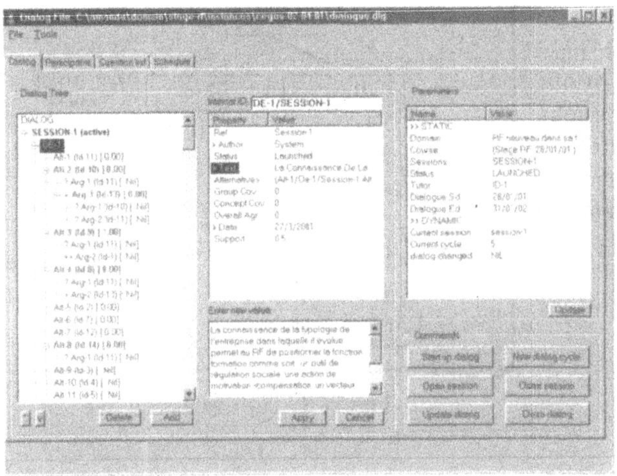

Figure 2: The tutor interface

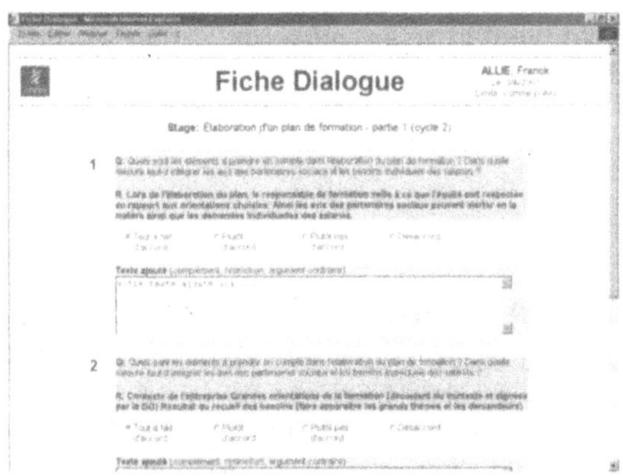

Figure 3: A discussion sheet

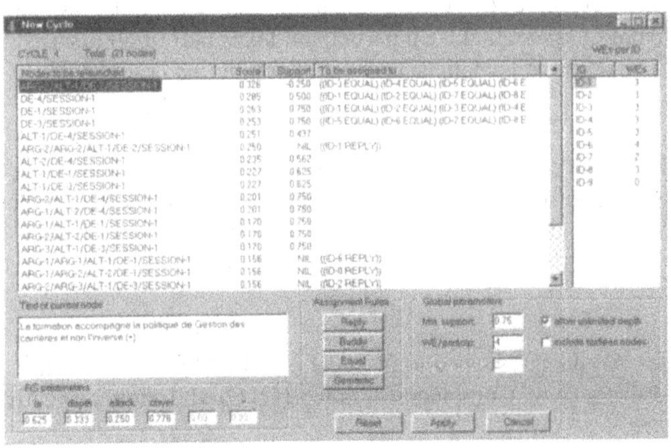

Figure 4: The interface for opening a new discussion cycle

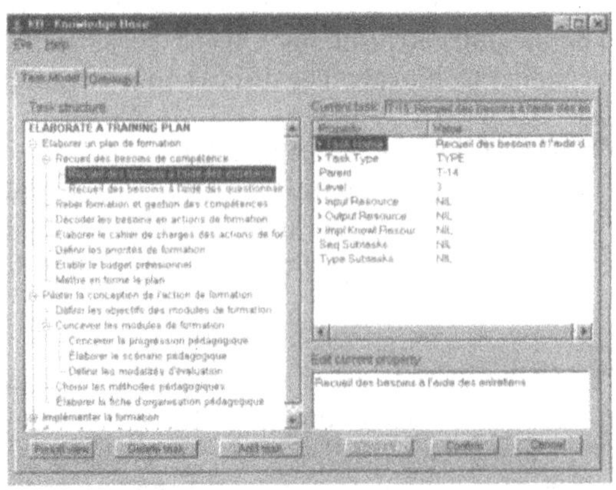

Figure 5: The domain model editor

VideoTraces: Rich Media Annotations for Learning and Teaching

Reed Stevens, Gina Cherry, Janice Fournier
University of Washington

ABSTRACT

This paper describes a computer-based video annotation environment with a variety of uses for learning and teaching. The *VideoTraces* system allows users to capture and annotate digital video, thus representing their ideas in a unique way. The system is based on research about the embodied nature of human knowledge and collaborative learning. In this paper, we report on two pilot uses of the system in very different settings (a science museum and a university dance course). We describe a range of ways in which people represent their ideas with *VideoTraces*, and argue that the system may be a general tool to support collaborative learning.

Keywords
Interaction, video, annotation, embodied knowledge

INTRODUCTION

Over the last two decades, ethnographically based field studies have described naturally occurring cognition and learning in a variety of settings. These studies argue against exclusively mentalistic conceptions of knowledge; knowledge needs also to be understood as *embodied.* Embodied knowledge is knowledge that is literally in the body—in the eyes and the hands of the knower (Stevens & Hall, 1998; Goodwin, 1994; Ochs et al., 1996; Suchman, 2000). Close analyses of interaction in which learning and teaching occur demonstrate a marvelous degree of coordination between participants, who used embodied representational resources of speaking, pointing, gesturing, and (sometimes) drawing. Joint attention, synchronous coordination of saying and showing,, and turn taking are primary resources that make these moments what they are as contexts for learning. Given that these sorts of teaching and learning situations can be hard to come by in many settings, are there ways to support expanded opportunities for these kinds of encounters between people through technology that build upon a principled understanding of human interaction and embodied knowledge?

THE VIDEOTRACES SYSTEM

This article offers a provisional and affirmative reply to this question by describing uses of a technology-based activity system called VideoTraces. The VideoTraces system was conceived of a number of years ago (Stevens & Hall, 1997), but became technically and economically feasible only with recent innovations in digital video technology. Through a simple computer interface, the system allows users to capture a piece of rich digital media (a video segment, an image, a piece of music), and to annotate it by talking and gesturing (using a pointer to record gestures), coupling descriptions of embodied experiences with the things they describe. The resulting "video traces" are then saved and can then be viewed, exchanged, and commented on by one's self and others.

VideoTraces is a system for people to *make* things with—in particular, to make representations of their experiences, embodied skills, understandings, and questions. It is also a system for people to learn with, both personally and collaboratively. Personally, people may learn by capturing, reflecting upon and re-presenting their own activities and ideas. Collaboratively, people may learn through conversation with the video traces produced by others.

This paper argues that this relatively simple system has a wide variety of possible uses for learning and teaching and in particular supports collaborative and distributed learning in new ways. Examples from two cases of pilot work, in which the rich media object that is annotated is a short segment of video, are presented here.

CASE 1: VIDEO TRACES AND INTERACTIVE LEARNING CENTERS

In Interactive Learning Centers like science museums, learning opportunities occur through interaction at exhibits and are often occasioned by observing the interactions of other visitors. These interactions are however ephemeral and usually too short for sustained inquiry to occur (See Stevens & Hall, 1997 for further details on these learning environments). VideoTraces provides an opportunity to encourage inquiry and support new interactions by allowing visitors to represent their own ideas and to leave a trace of these ideas with which other visitors can engage.

The VideoTraces system was tried at three science centers in United States. In these Interactive Learning Centers, visitors used the VideoTraces system to represent their ideas, explanations, questions, and perceptions about scientific phenomena modeled by exhibits. Our analyses suggest that visitors can use the system to make many types of traces that could be put to many different collaborative uses. The types of traces range from recognizable discourse genres such as well-formed questions and explanations to more informal conversational ones.

One way that VideoTraces provides for collaborative learning is in the joint production of the traces by multiple people. The other way it provides for collaborative learning is through distributed inquiry: visitors view, respond and link new traces to those made by other visitors. With this sort of viewing and linking capacity, visitors to science centers are able engage in inquiry with people they don't know and who could have visited a science center on a different day, month or even year. A third opportunity for collaboration addresses the "Field Trip Problem" - how to arrange experiences in the museum which connect with inquiry activities in classrooms. VideoTraces offers a way for students to make durable their ideas while in the museum that can then support further rich discussion and inquiry in the classroom (see Stevens & Hall, 1997 for elaboration of this possible use).

CASE 2: VIDEO TRACES AND DANCE COMPOSITION

Our second experiment with VideoTraces was with an undergraduate choreography class at the University of Washington. VideoTraces seemed like a natural fit with dance—a field in which people use their bodies to represent ideas and in which they make frequent use of videotape to document their work. VideoTraces provided learners with an opportunity to use video not simply as a medium for documentation, but as an interactive tool that supported reflection and the development of new ideas over time.

Students used VideoTraces in a number of ways to represent their ideas, including planning for rehearsals, documenting aesthetic intentions for the dance, and making connections between formal concepts and practice. Students used the pointer to indicate new potential pathways for movement or uses of the performance space.

There are a number of ways that VideoTraces can support collaborative learning in dance and other communities of practice. Choreographers could use VideoTraces to communicate with their dancers between rehearsals, allowing more effective use of rehearsal time. VideoTraces can also be used to comment on and critique the work of others. VideoTraces may also have a potential to significantly affect communication between students and instructors. Dance instructors rarely have a way to collect representations of students' *process* of creating a dance, and students' work is usually judged on the basis of what is successfully communicated in their final presentations. VideoTraces could be used by students to get feedback when they run into trouble while creating their dances and as a new form of assessment that encourages reflection and iterative refinement.

FUTURE DIRECTIONS

The significant differences in the two settings explored here suggest that VideoTraces may be a *generalizable* representational system that draws on peoples' everyday resources of watching, speaking, and pointing. Currently we also are experimenting with VideoTraces in a number of other learning environments where the embodied nature of knowing and learning are central. In addition to an expanding set of research settings, we will be pursuing the collaborative practices in the science centers and dance that we have described here.

CONCLUSIONS

Everyday interaction as a resource for learning and teaching needs neither repair nor augmentation. However, technologies such as the VideoTraces system that build upon a principled understanding of these resources can provide possibilities for intriguing new collaborations across time and space. Though we are still early in the life span of the project, we expect to count VideoTraces system as a successful tool if members of different communities continue to find in its generality and accessibility the capacity to represent the widest possible range of specific practices and ideas by which their communities are characterized and renewed.

REFERENCES

Goodwin, C. (1994). Professional Vision. *American Anthropologist* 96(3): 606-633.

Ochs, E., P. Gonzales, P. & Jacoby, S. (1996). "When I come down I'm in the domain state": Grammar and graphic representation in the interpretive activity of physicists. *Interaction and grammar*. E. Ochs, E. A. Schegloff and S. Thompson. New York, Cambridge University Press: 328-369.

Stevens, R. and R. Hall (1997). Seeing 'Tornado': How *VideoTraces* Mediate Visitor Understandings of (Natural?) Phenomena in a Science Museum. *Science Education* 81(6): 735-748.

Stevens, R. and R. Hall (1998). Disciplined perception: Learning to see in technoscience. *Talking mathematics in school: Studies of teaching and learning*. M. Lampert and M. L. Blunk. New York, Cambridge University Press: 107-149.

Suchman, L. (2000). Embodied Practices of Engineering Work. *Mind, Culture & Activity* 7(1 & 2): 4-18.

Introduction to the Shadow netWorkspace™

Joshua S. Gottdenker jsg0af@mizzou.edu
Herbert Remidez Jr. herbert@coe.missouri.edu
Ran-Young Hong rhe06@mizzou.edu
So-Yeon Yoon soyeony@yahoo.com
Chris Amelung AmelungC@mizzou.edu
Dale R. Musser MusserDa@missouri.edu
James M. Laffey laffeyj@missouri.edu
All from the Center for Technology Innovations in Education
111 London Hall, College of Education, Univ. of Missouri
Columbia, MO 65211
**(573) 882-8350 ** Fax (573) 884-5158
http://www.ctie.missouri.edu

ABSTRACT
Shadow netWorkspace™ (SNS) is a web-based CSCL environment designed and developed specifically to support schools and learning. SNS has been designed to facilitate the implementation of a learning community, wherein members (teachers, students, parents, etc.) have tools for representing, organizing, sharing and collaborating on their thoughts and efforts. The SNS environment may be installed locally for the learning community whether that is a school building, school district or consortium of teachers or schools collaborating on implementing a cross schools project. SNS is being provided for free, has an Application Programming Interface (API) so others can develop applications for it, and is open source so that everyone can participate in enhancing and supporting it. SNS includes tools such as secure login, well-defined user roles and group types, file system, calendar & task manager, chat & discussion boards, notes & document creator, and homework notification. The system's strength and potential for longevity lie in its Open Source (GNU Public License) development model, object and process oriented operating environment, and a robust application programming interface (API). Many schools (internationally) have downloaded SNS for trials and a number are currently engaged in pilot programs.

Keywords
Collaborative Network Learning, Open Source, Online Operating System, CSCL Infrastructure, netWorkspace

INTRODUCTION
Shadow is an Internet-based workspace designed to support the processes of learning and schooling. A quick and rough analogy is to imagine the desktop of your computer existing on the Internet. Using a browser, such as Internet Explorer or Netscape, you connect via a secure login to a SNS web-site and your personal netWorkspace. Here you find a desktop for accessing your files and applications. (Laffey et al. 2000)

There are many Network Learning Systems (NLS) both in existence and under development. Getting familiar with other systems can help you to understand SNS. Please refer to sns.internetschools.org in the publications section for a document entitled Systems Similar to Shadow netWorkspace for up to date NLS comparison information.

SNS is a server-side operating system, designed to be installed and operated within a local school to support an online learning community. In this way the school or community "owns" the Shadow implementation. They create the rules and policies, establish membership, add or remove software applications, and make it their own customized implementation. Ease of implementation and use is key to the success of SNS for school improvement. The hardware requirements for setting up and running this server will cost schools less than $1000 and most schools may simply designate an older Pentium-class computer to run the system.

The goal of the Shadow netWorkspace is to increase the capability of the students and teachers in a school/learning community to gain and process information and build and represent knowledge. A school-centered netWorkspace should facilitate the creation of artifacts representative of knowledge, and provide simple means to access, share and collaborate around those artifacts/representations.

EXTENSIBILITY & LONGEVITY
Shadow optimizes representation of learning and work in a networked environment, but is flexible enough to handle multiple methods of collaboration or learning. The learning/teaching method needs to be a local decision, allowing integration into other aspects of the local community. Computer support for methods of learning are expected to evolve as communities and developers experiment and refine new forms of learning and collaboration.

Therefore, we believe that it is important that a networked learning system evolve or be customized over time to be "useful" to the individual or community, rather than be simply a "usable" tool for some function that limits the flexibility for adaptation by the individual or community.

SNS is being developed as an Open Source project, which means that users will not have to pay to use the system. The Shadow networkspace operates on a Linux-based server and utilizes the Apache web server, MySQL, and Sendmail (All free software). The server-side operating system framework, application programming interfaces and core applications are written in Perl. As Open Source software, SNS is positioned to improve and evolve as more people implement and develop the system.

Developing sophisticated applications for the WWW is very challenging. There are many code snippets and technical how-to articles available, but web development is very different from traditional application development. The design of SNS as an operating system rather than a web-learning application provides a framework that simplifies the development and deployment of web applications. SNS also provides a secure consistent interface to these applications, with predefined individual roles and group structures with predefined rules. Thus bringing some of the favorable aspects of traditional application development to the fingertips of web-based application developers.

To illustrate how a web-based operating system designed to support learning would be useful to a school, consider this scenario. Lets say there are 10 schools that want to create new online communities and they each have small grants to hire a programmer to create their web-based environment. All 10 need to create a site where users need to login to the system and be treated appropriately based on their user type; 9 of the 10 want to have discussion boards; 8 of the 10 want to have chat rooms; and 7 of the 10 want some sort of file sharing. Each school has a different idea of how they would like to use these tools once their environment is built, but must wait for months of development before they can even begin to use their systems for implementing their online learning strategies. That's hundreds of hours of wastefully redundant effort. Wouldn't it be nice if there was a stable platform to start at? A platform that can provide all the base functionality schools are looking for and free-up their developers to begin working directly on applications that address pedagogical issues and learning strategies. Wouldn't it be nice if the platform simplified server-side programming so that developers had a robust library of system functions to rely on?

Programming a learning application within SNS involves utilizing preexisting system objects and defining new objects and processes to directly support a specific pedagogy. Discussion Boards and Chat Rooms can be associated with and accessed via groups. Programming for data input, display, and manipulation can be handled in an object-oriented manner with a rich set of system resources.

VISION

The vision for SNS includes the development and sharing of new pedagogical content, strategies and custom applications among the extended SNS community. Each local school or district owns their own community and they actively participate in the advancement of the global SNS community. As webquests are created in one locale, teachers elsewhere can share their strategies and applications to support group projects and learning. Currently, educators can share simple webquests via email, but SNS supports the sharing of full-fledged applications with secure roles and advanced file and data handling.

The idea is to employ two layers of Open-Source development: the first, the NLS, will function as a web-based operating system full of community support functionality, and the second, the core and custom applications and learning tools, will operate as processes and exist as content within the NLS to support specific learning and working strategies. The power is revealed when you consider an Open-Source NLS that supports the development of Open-Source applications that will operate within the freely and widely available web-browser platform.

REFERENCES

Laffey, J., Musser, D. & Espinosa, L. (2000) Shadow netWorkspace Learning Systems Project. *Proceedings of the International Workshop on Advanced Learning Technologies.* (Palmerstown North, New Zealand), IEEE Computer Society. pp. 188-189.

Collaborative Discovering of Key Ideas in Knowledge Building

Teemu Leinonen, Otso Virtanen, Kai Hakkarainen(1), Giedre Kligyte

University of Art and Design Helsinki, (1) University of Helsinki, Finland - teemu.leinonen@uiah.fi

ABSTRACT

In this paper, we describe our work-in-progress for developing Collaborative Discovering Tool (CoDi tool) that is meant for enhancing knowledge building discourse in the Future Learning Environment 2 (Fle2) system. Knowledge building discourse in the Fle2 type of systems usually leads to gradual accumulation of notes. We have found that users experience difficulties to get an overall picture of the knowledge produced and synthesize its advancement. By providing means for the participants to highlight key ideas, that they find particularly useful, the CoDi tool was designed to facilitate collective management of knowledge and inquiry and provide various visual representations of the database. We report results of a pilot experiment carried out with the CoDi prototype that appears to be a promising tool. However there are certain open questions concerning what are the social and pedagogical effects of highlighting ideas in different educational setting, how highlighting should be organized so that it would provide strongest support of knowledge advancement, and whether the results should always be shared not only by tutors but also by students. Regardless of the challenges, the development of the CoDi tool appears to open up an interesting line of inquiry that we would like to share with the CSCL community.

Keywords: Knowledge building environments, shared understanding, social awareness, design of CSCL systems, information design

KNOWLEDGE BUILDING WITH THE FLE2 SYSTEM

The main aim of computer supported collaborative learning (CSCL) environments is to provide students with advanced computer tools for knowledge production taking place in an interaction between the users (Scardamalia & Bereiter, 1993; 1994). In most of the CSCL applications (e.g. CSILE, CoNotes, Belvedere, Knowledge Forum) the knowledge production happens in a shared working space where students may carry out discussion by writing their notes. The Future Learning Environment 2 (Fle2), is a CSCL environment designed to support collaborative knowledge building and progressive inquiry (http://fle2.uiah.fi, see Leinonen, Raami, Mielonen, Hakkarainen, Muukkonen, 1999). The idea of progressive inquiry is to support a research-like study process, where the students themselves generate research problems, make hypothesis and search explanatory scientific information as a group (Hakkarainen, 1998; Hakkarainen & Sintonen, in press; Muukkonen, Hakkarainen, & Lakkala, 1999; Muukkonen, Lakkala, & Hakkarainen, 2001).

The current version of the Fle2's Knowledge Building (KB) module functions as a shared space for asynchronies dialogue and conferencing. The discussion is constructed around *Course Contexts* set by the tutor and all notes posted to the database are labeled with a *Category of Inquiry* (Problem, Working Theory, Deepening Knowledge, Comment, Meta-comment, Summary and Help) reflecting a step in process. Currently the knowledge building discussion of the group can be viewed as a thread or as a list of notes sorted by writer or by category of inquiry (Leinonen 2000). Testing of the Fle2 KB has shown the following pedagogical usability problems: (1) When the amount of the KB notes increases rapidly they are difficult to find and locate (knowledge-management challenge), (2) Other participants' activities are difficult to match (awareness challenge) and (3) the process of progressive inquiry appears for the students more as a linear process than a deepening circle (deepening-inquiry challenge).

An essential aspect of the Fle2's KB is that all knowledge artifacts (notes) are saved to the database. This way the Fle2 KB becomes an organizational memory of the group of learners. Effective organizational memory should be able to answer such questions as "Why did we do this?" and "How did such and such come to be the case?" (Conklin 1993). In the Fle2's KB a crucial problem is that when the amount of notes grows high investigating back to the history of the knowledge building process and making overall impression of the database becomes very difficult.

The study was focused on developing a new tool to solve the problems stated above related to the handling of information flows in a knowledge-building environment, making students more aware of the nature of the progressive inquiry process and aiming to increase participants awareness of their co-students thinking and the groups collective ideas.

CODI PROTOTYPE

The Collaborative Discovering of Ideas tool (CoDI tool) prototype was made for highlighting relevant material in the knowledge building notes. The students and tutor are able to review their individual highlights as well as group's highlights.

Figure 1 describes a user scenario of the CoDi tool. At first the students are working with the KB database according to the model of progressive inquiry by adding their own study problems, theories, and deepening knowledge in to the KB database. In some stage the tutor is introducing the CoDi tool for the students and asking them to highlight the most important ideas (paragraphs) from the notes in the KB database. After this the data related to the highlighting and the notes (writer, data, category of inquiry, link) are offered as alternative views of the content of the database. These visualizations can then be used as a starting point for further discourse.

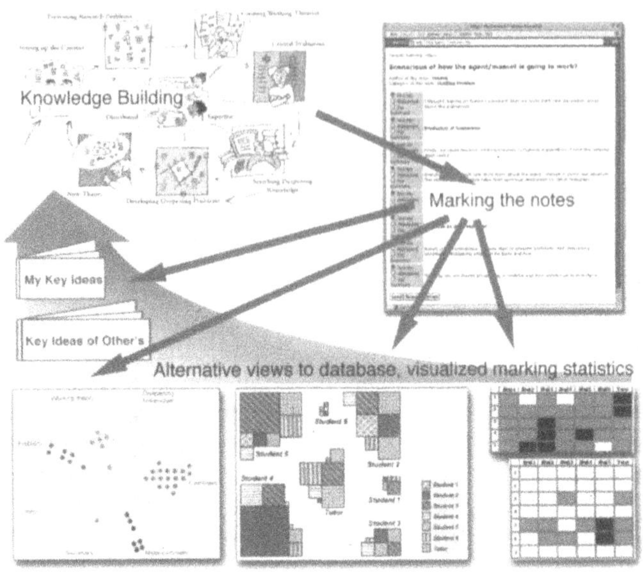

Figure 17: Knowledge Building, highlighting the notes and data provided for the users.

The experiment with the CoDI tool was carried out with students taking part in the study project on Design for CSCW/L carried out as part of the Future Learning Environment study project organized by the UIAH Media Lab at the University of Art and Design in autumn 2000. The study project lasted four months. More detailed description of the course and the class can be found from the http://www.euro-cscl.org database.

CONCLUSIONS

The main idea of the CoDi tool is that it offers the user the opportunity to select an interface that he or she is most comfortable (thread, list, map, etc. views). The CoDI tool gives an interesting possibility to combine and display many different levels of data at one glance. Users may take different views to the content of the KB database and use these views for browsing the database as well. The new views provided by the CoDi tool are: (1) *The KB Dartboard view* represents spatial relationships between notes values (calculated from the highlightings), (2) *The KB Social Blocks view* provides social network analyses of the groups activities, and (3) *The Key Idea Cluster views* of each note showing what paragraphs each participant has highlight (see Figure 1). The purpose of these views is to help participants to collectively assess progress of their knowledge building inquiry and navigate across the database with the help of the key ideas.

The prototype described in this paper offers interesting possibilities for students and teachers to define group's key questions and compare them with individual interests. It may also function as a learning process negotiation tool helping to orient and coordinate individual activity in the group context, raising discussions about other people's opinions, encouraging collaboration and possibly supporting reflection of learning and knowledge-building processes. The tool also helps to solve the problem concerning the representation of the KB-discussion, which should be more spiral in nature as indicated by the progressive inquiry model (see Hakkarainen, 1998; Muukkonen et. al., 1999). The solution proposed in this paper appears to be promising in terms of solving the problem of growing number of the knowledge-building notes.

There are still many open questions concerning pedagogical effects of the CoDi tool. We believe, however, that this kind of a tool or framework for tools would offer good possibilities to further developed Knowledge Building environments in other systems beside the Fle2 as well.

REFERENCES

Full paper with references is available in the following URL: http://www.uiah.fi/~tleinone/codi/

Simulating Pedagogical Agents in a Virtual Learning Environment

Silje Jondahl

Department of Information Science
University of Bergen
sjondahl@hotmail.com

Anders Mørch

InterMedia
University of Oslo
anders.morch@intermedia.uio.no

ABSTRACT

CoPAS (Collaboration Patterns Agent Simulation) is a simulation study carried out with the Wizard of Oz method. Students used a groupware system to solve a learning task in the domain of object-oriented analysis and design using UML (Unified Modelling Language) without meeting each other face-to-face. Simulated software agents (human experts) gave advice for various knowledge-intensive tasks, including tool use, domain (UML) understanding and peer-to-peer collaboration. Our findings indicate that agents can have an effect on collaboration by making users aware of collaboration patterns (division of labour, explicit roles, etc.) and by creating focus shifts in the users' interaction.

Keywords

Distributed collaborative learning, Wizard of Oz technique, software agent simulation, collaboration patterns

PEDAGOGICAL AGENTS

Pedagogical agents can interact with human learners in the context of their actions and activities in a virtual learning environment. It can sometimes even be difficult to distinguish an agent's actions from that of a user taking the role of an advising peer helping other users to solve a task in the environment (Johnson, Rickel & Lester, 2000).

We call our agents pedagogical interface agents, and our belief is that they should be developed on the basis of their perceived benefits for end users. Our interest is therefore not so much in development of algorithms or student models, but rather how the agents should intervene and behave in interaction with a group of collaborative peers.

There are different kinds of interface agents, including animated agents that simulate certain human behaviour, such as facial expression and body movement, and reactive agents that react to events in the environment and take action when they see an opportunity. The behaviour of reactive agents can be compared with a thermostat: when a certain temperature has been reached some action is taken (such as turning off the heat).

In CoPAS there are three types of reactive agents: 1) Tool agent, 2) Domain agent, and 3) Collaboration agent. The tool agent represents technical knowledge about how to use the groupware tools, and the domain agent gives advice about the concepts and relations in UML. The collaboration agent's knowledge base is built on theories of CSCL (Koshmann, 1996), principles of Genuine Interdependence (Salomon, 1992), and Collaboration Patterns (Wasson & Mørch, 2000).

SIMULATION STUDY

We used the Wizard of Oz technique to simulate the behaviour of pedagogical agents in a virtual learning environment (the TeamWave groupware). The participants were led to believe that they were using an implemented agent system, when in fact they were interacting with a simulation staged by human operators (Maulsby et al., 1993).

Three graduate students in our department acted as wizards. Each of them had a pre-assigned task to simulate one of the above agents. Their (perceived) participation in the learning environment were defined by a set of rules for when to act and what to say upon acting.

Six groups of students participated, and each group had three students. They were enrolled in the same undergraduate information systems class. The task for all groups was to create object-oriented analysis and design diagrams for an Internet banking system using UML (use case and class diagrams). Each group had 90 minutes at their disposal. The task constraints together with the constraints imposed by the Wizard of Oz technique were the main reasons for conducting a short duration experiment (i.e., the assignment was taken from a previous final exam, and the wizards may have revealed themselves if exposed for a longer period of time).

FINDINGS

The data was collected from notes, automatically recorded chat logs, and individual interviews conducted with the participants after the experiment.

Below is a chat log excerpt initiated by the wizard acting as collaboration agent (the wizard's messages was displayed in a pop-up window and not in the chat window). It was one of the most frequently issued messages:

Collaboration agent says: It can be useful to divide the work amongst yourself

B3.1 says: we should divide the tasks

B3.1 says: I can start with the class diagram...

B3.3 says: what about me, what should I do?

There were no obvious ways to divide the assignment equally among the group members (two tasks: use case diagram and class diagram; three members). The above comment by B3.3: *"what about me, what should I do?"* was discussed in the group interview. It turned out that two of the members knew each other well, whereas the third member did not know the others. She felt left out of much of the joint work. B3.2 gave the following comment when asked if knowing each other influenced division of work in their group. *"It certainly influenced our work, because one knows how to talk to a person you already know, and that can complicate collaboration with a third person who are supposed to be part in solving the same task"*

DISCUSSION AND IMPLICATIONS FOR DESIGN

Software agents are good at providing shared feedback when there are general principles that can be operationalized, but less useful for giving personalized assistance on the same principles. The feedback given to the students by the Collaboration agents was informed by such principles (e.g. Salomon, 1992, Koschmann, 1996, Wasson & Mørch, 2000), but it had sometimes unanticipated effects as illustrated in the above situation. One of the students felt excluded after a comment by the Collaboration agent. A human facilitator would have been able to resolve the situation more appropriately.

On the other hand, there were situations where the groups where happy to get feedback and to shift their focus of interaction. This can be explained by the term "breakdown". A breakdown makes room for learning and reflections about the joint work (e.g. Fischer 1994). Agents that create breakdowns may cause a shift in focus and indicate a new level of activity. We have found several indications of this, evidenced by a change in vocabulary after the intervention of an agent.

ACKNOWLEDGMENTS

We thank the three graduate students who acted as Wizards: Rune Baggetun, Karianne Omdahl and Trond Pedersen. This study is part of the DoCTA NSS project, and we are grateful for financial support from the ITU Program of the Norwegian Ministry of Church affairs, Education and Research.

REFERENCES

Fischer, G. (1994). Turning Breakdowns into Opportunities for Creativity, *Knowledge-Based Systems*, Special Issue on "Creativity and Cognition", Butterworth-Heinemann, Vol. 7, No. 4, 1994, 221-232.

Johnson, W.L., Rickel, J.W. and Lester, J.C (2000). Animated Pedagogical Agents: Face-to-Face Interaction in Interactive learning Environments, in *International Journal of AI in Education* (2000), 11.

Koschmann, T. (1996). Paradigm shifts and instructional technology: An introduction. In T. Koshmann (Ed.) *CSCL: Theory and practice of an emerging paradigm*, Mahwah, NJ: Laurence Erlbaum Associates, 1-23.

Maulsby, D., Greenberg, S. and Mander, R. (1993). Prototyping an intelligent agent through Wizard of Oz, *Proceedings of the Conference on Human Factors in Computing Systems(INTERCHI''93)*, Amsterdam, The Netherlands, ACM Press.

Salomon, G. (1992). What does the design of effective CSCL require and how do we study its effects? *SIGCUE Outlook Special Issue on CSCL*, 21(3), 62-68

Wasson, B. and Mørch, A. (2000), Identifying Collaboration Patterns in Collaborative Telelearning Scenarios. *Educational Technology & Society 3(3).*

Support for Object-Oriented Model Construction

Jakob Tholander, Klas Karlgren

Department of Computer and Systems Sciences
Stockholm University/Royal Institute of Technology
jakobth@dsv.su.se, klas@dsv.su.se

ABSTRACT

We discuss a design solution for a learning environment for students of object-oriented modeling. An overall goal in this work has been to ensure a design that is well grounded both theoretically and empirically. The design of the tools relate to central issues in cognitive apprenticeship and situated learning. Theoretical and practical design considerations are presented for each of the learning environment and results from empirical studies are discussed.

THEORY GROUNDED DESIGN

Theories of learning are important for the design of computer based learning environments but these cannot simply be applied and used in the process of design. (Jonassen & Land, 2000). We describe our design approach for incorporating cognitive apprenticeship and situated action in the design of a learning environment for computer science students of object oriented (OO) modeling. The purpose of object-oriented modeling is to create models of an enterprise that can be used for the subsequent design and construction of supporting communication and information systems. The learning environment consists of three tools aiming to support cognitive apprenticeship style learning for object oriented modeling (Collins, Brown, & Newman, 1989). Two of the tools (what we call expert problem solving tracks, and a library of modeling patterns) support aspects of authentic activity, i.e., an activity that help "students to foresee their participation in activities that matter beyond school" (Greeno, 1997, p.11). The third tool (a pedagogical assistant) support reflection and meta-cognition.

Theories that emphasize the situated properties of human action and learning (Lave & Wenger, 1991); (Collins et al., 1989) are very influential on current understandings of these phenomena and have been extensively used in analyses of learning (Jordan & Henderson, 1995). In our work we explore this new focus and the conditions it provides for designers of learning environments. An overall goal work has been to ensure a design that is well grounded both theoretically and empirically (Land & Hanaffin, 2000). This has led to two important design activities. The first was to explicitly state what aspects of the theoretical framework that we wanted to support in our design. The second activity came as a consequence of our theoretical framework which emphasizes learning in so-called authentic activities. This was to conduct studies on experienced conceptual modelers in order to get an understanding of how they acted when solving problems. The results of these studies were used to design particular aspects of the learning environment and in the evaluations of how learners interacted with the learning environment (Tholander, 2001).

Collins, Brown, & Newman provide a framework (cognitive apprenticeship) that designers of learning environments should consider (Collins et al., 1989). In our design we have identified the following aspects to be particularly important to consider in order to promote students to get engaged in the cognitive practices of conceptual modeling. First, learners should engage in *authentic problem solving* to develop skills that help them put knowledge into use. Knowledge of concepts and methods must not be learnt as abstract notions, but in a context where the practice of their use is uncovered. Second, *observation* of experienced practitioners' problem solving help student to develop their own problem solving strategies. Third, learners should practice to use experienced modelers' *language, concepts, and tools* in order to see the role of these concepts in practice. Fourth, learners should *reflect* on their own problem solving, and on their use of tools and concepts in relation to how experienced practitioners use these.

Learning and Doing Object Oriented Modeling

The first three aspects of our design focus above (authentic problem-solving, observing experienced practitioners, tool and language use) all include aspects of how experienced modelers go about in their problem solving. To be able to design tools for learners that support these aspects it is essential to ground the design in an understanding of how experienced modelers reason and carry out tasks. Therefore a think-aloud study with experienced modelers was conducted. The goal of the study was to find out characteristics about the different ways modelers solve problems in order to understand important elements of the cognitive practice they work in. The most important findings of the study were (see also (Karlgren, Tholander, Dahlqvist, & Ramberg, 1998)): First, in the problems experienced modelers face, they tend to identify familiarities with other problems which they have experienced and use these to solve the current problem, i.e,. they engage *in case based reasoning*. Second, they often go back and reflect on the overall nature and goal of the task, i.e., they show a high degree of *meta-cognitive thinking*. Third, they discuss with stakeholders how important concepts in the problem domain should be understood. They do not presuppose certain interpretations of the concepts based on their own ideas. Fourth, they refer to general problems and solutions that they often face in their everyday practice, i.e. they use *analysis patterns* (Fowler, 1997). Fifth, they proceed iteratively by solving sub-problems that they move back and forth between because they know that concepts are very dependent upon each other.

We have designed three tools to support students of object oriented modeling practice. *First*, expert problem solving tracks designed to support *authentic problem solving* (the first learning focus), *observation* (the second learning focus), and use of experienced practitioners *language, concepts, and tools* (the third learning focus). The purpose of this tool is to present modeling tasks that provide the same *kind of* problems and complexity which conceptual modelers face in the 'real world'. Through this tool we want the students to get exposed to scenarios that resemble authentic environments including how experienced modelers go about to solve complex problems and how they talk about them. Emphasis is on the authentic practices of experienced modelers and on the language they use.

Second, library of modeling patterns designed to *support authentic problem solving* and also use of experienced practitioners *language, concepts, and tools*. One of the goals of the project was that students should learn to create models at a level of abstraction that makes them reusable in future situations. Our way of supporting learners in this is through analysis patterns, which are abstractions of common knowledge in object oriented modeling. Our study on experienced modelers showed that these aspects are often referred to through analysis patterns. We view analysis patterns as representations of the *language, concepts and tools*, which the students should practice to use, not as special constructs that they should memorize.

Third, the pedagogical assistant provides comments with the purpose to encourage the students to reflect and think critically (the fourth learning focus). Students should not take their preconceptions about their solutions, their knowledge, and the problem domain they are modeling for granted. As the students construct their models, the assistant asks questions and gives critical remarks about why the students have created some particular objects or relations, comments about the way the student approaches the problem, or gives advice about good ways of approaching such a problem. We have created three types of comments, first, comments about some particular objects and relations in the model being constructed, second, about important issues in the enterprise that must be represented in the model, and third, about some general problematic modeling issues in the solution.

Two studies of students using the learning environment have been conducted. In the studies, students solved modeling problems with the learning environment for 60 minutes. An important finding was the collaboration that students engaged in. The tools became mediating artifacts between the students and something to use as support for discussion and to come up with new solutions from. The learning environment expanded the conceptual apparatus that the students could use to reason with and helped them to see their solutions from new perspectives.

Summary

In this work we have taken a well-defined theoretical position based on cognitive apprenticeship and situated learning. The point of this work has been to explicitly design solutions based on these models of learning in order to investigate how such models can and must be adapted to particular circumstances. The purpose has been to discuss how theoretical and practical issues have been taken under consideration in our design.

REFERENCES

Collins, A., Brown, J. S., & Newman, S. (Eds.). (1989). *Cognitive Apprenticeship: Teaching the Crafts of Reading, Writing, and Mathematics*. New Jersey: Lawrence Erlbaum Associates.

Fowler, M. (1997). *Analysis Patterns: Reusable Object Models*: Addison Wesley Publishing.

Greeno, J. (1997). On Claims That Answer the Wrong Questions. *Educational Researcher*, **26**(1), 5-17.

Jonassen, D., & Land, S. (2000). *Theoretical Foundations of Learning Environments*: Lawrence Erlbaum Ass.

Jordan, B., & Henderson, A. (1995). Interaction Analysis: Foundations and Practise. *The Journal of the Learning Science, 4*(1), 39-103.

Karlgren, K., Tholander, J., Dahlqvist, P., & Ramberg, R. (1998). *Authenticity in Training Systems for Conceptual Modelers.* Paper presented at the International Conference of the Learning Sciences, Atlanta, Georgia.

Lave, J., & Wenger, E. (1991). *Situated Learning: Legitimate Peripheral Participation*: Cambridge University Pr.

Tholander, J. (2001). *Students interacting through a Cognitive Apprenticeship Learning Environment.* Paper presented at the Euro CSCL, Mastricht, The Netherlands.

AudioExplorer: Multiple Linked Representations for Convergence

Jochen Rick
College of Computing / GVU Center
Georgia Institute of Technology
jochen.rick@cc.gatech.edu

ABSTRACT
The problem of convergence is an important one for designing collaborative-learning environments. Ideally, learning environments allow novices to work together to achieve convergence of correct understanding, without constant support from experts. In order to achieve this, software designers need to investigate properties of the environment that support convergence. One of these properties is multiple linked representations (MLRs). In this paper, I describe AudioExplorer, a learning environment where students, working in pairs, explore the physics of music. AudioExplorer is remarkable in its use of many linked representations; thus, it is a good environment to research the role of MLRs in the convergence process.

Keywords
Representation, software design, convergence, audio, inquiry-based learning

CONVERGENCE AND MULTIPLE LINKED REPRESENTATIONS
Jeremy Roschelle proposes that the "crux of collaboration is the problem of convergence (Roschelle, 1996)." Can two (or more) people working together reach convergence of understanding? Furthermore, is that convergent understanding closer to real understanding than the members of the group could have reached without collaborating? Roschelle shows that students (working in pairs) can achieve convergent conceptual change, using the Envisioning Machine (EM) software. EM is a direct-manipulation graphical simulation of particle dynamics (velocity and acceleration of a particle). Students are asked to manipulate position, velocity, and acceleration of a particle to match the motion of a simulated ball. Though students did not converge on everything that scientists know about velocity and acceleration, they did manage to work together to achieve better understanding. Since a typical classroom environment contains few experts (for the most part, one teacher) and many novices (students), creating learning environments where collaboration among novices is productive becomes necessary. So, what features of a learning environment support the convergence process?

MLRs can support the convergence process. In many scientific fields (such as mathematics and chemistry), phenomena can be looked at from different perspectives. For instance, in mathematics, a two variable relation can be looked at as an equation, graph, or table (Kaput, 1989). In chemistry, a chemical reaction can be looked at as the physical chemicals, the underlying reaction equations, the results of spectroscopy, etc. (Kozma et al., 2000). The power of multiple representations is that they emphasize different aspects of the same system. To understand each representation and how they are linked together is to understand the domain more completely than any one individual representation.

Both Kaput and Kozma assert that connecting multiple representations in a learning environment should be helpful for student understanding. This is based on the theory that students should be able to move between different representation and that each can inform the other. In chemistry, Kozma finds that experts move easily and often between different representations, while novices tend to get fixated on one representation (Kozma, 2001). Offering clear linkages between the representations should be a way to scaffold novices to go between them. As for convergence, MLRs offer the opportunity of different ways of exploring the same domain. Since the evidence displayed by the environment is multiple (more than a single representation), there is a greater chance that useful convergence dialogue will occur.

AUDIOEXPLORER
AudioExplorer is a computer environment to explore the physics of sound by examining the frequency domain. The frequency domain is a transformation of the sound signal into its frequency components. Since our ear perceives frequencies, examining the frequency domain is a useful way to understand the properties of music. The system consists of a music keyboard giving sound input into the computer (Figure 1); the AudioExplorer software displays the signal on the screen, which can then be analyzed by the students.

AudioExplorer is a tool for inquiry-based learning. The environment gives the users the opportunity to explore the subject (audio and music) and thereby discover the principles of the subject rather than passively learn about them. Thus, learning is active and students are encouraged to construct their own meaning.

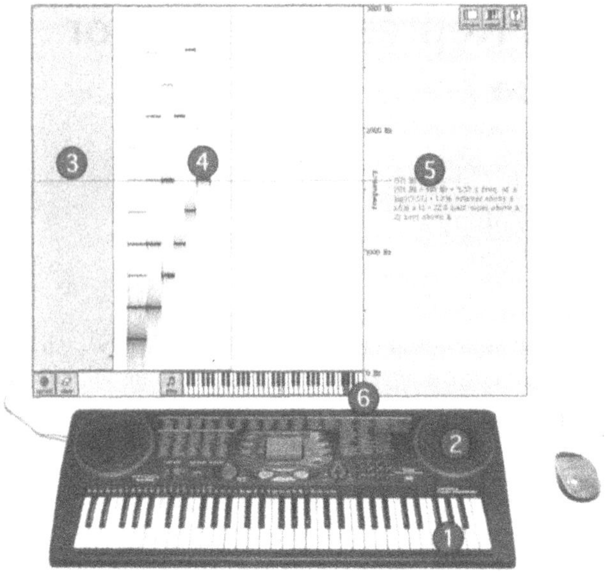

First, the student strikes a key on the music keyboard (point **1**). This produces a sound (point **2**). That sound is converted by FFT (Fast Fourier Transform algorithm) to an instantaneous frequency response notation (point **3**), where sonic energy is indicated by length of the line. The frequency response is recorded over time (point **4**), energy being indicated by darkness. Then, the student can use the analysis line to find out the frequency of the harmonics (point **5**); the students can drag the analysis line up and down by dragging on the spectrum graph to measure the exact frequencies. The calculations that the software shows (at point **5**) convert that frequency to the matching key and highlight it on the display's keyboard (point **6**). In the example in Figure 1, the fundamental harmonic is the key that was stuck originally by the student (point **1**). Thus, the multiple representations come full circle.

Figure 1: AudioExplorer usage set-up with numbers indicating representations

Each representation has different features that allow the users to look at the sound phenomena from different perspectives. So, each representation has different affordances that allow the user to better examine the domain. Each representation suppresses some aspects of the domain and emphasizes others, thereby supporting different forms of approaching the material. Perhaps most importantly, the linking of these representations creates "a whole that is more than the sum of its parts (Kaput, 1989)."

EVALUATION

In the extended on-line version of this paper, a formative evaluation of AudioExplorer is detailed. Students (working in pairs) were able to use AudioExplorer to engage the subject. They moved easily between the multiple representations and were able to understand the links between them. MLRs supported the convergence process. Significant learning was achieved with two learners and a supportive learning environment.

ACKNOWLEDGMENTS

My thanks go to the volunteers who used AudioExplorer, to Henry Valk who gave me guidance and an opportunity to test this software on a real audience, to Amy Bruckman's CS7465 class that gave me feedback on the design, to John Maloney and the Squeak community for their programming support, and to many who have given me insightful feedback on AudioExplorer.

REFERENCES

Kaput, J.J. (1989) Linking representations in the symbolic systems of algebra. *Research agenda for mathematics education: Research issues in the learning and teaching of algebra*, edited by S. Wagner & C. Kieran, pp. 167-194.

Kozma, R. (2001) Material and social affordances of multiple representations for science understanding. *AERA2001*.

Kozma, R., Chin, E., Russell, J., & Marx, N. (2000). The roles of representations and tools in the chemistry laboratory and their implications for chemistry learning. *Journal of the Learning Sciences*, 9(2), 105-143.

Roschelle, J. (1996) Learning by collaborating: Convergent conceptual change. *CSCL: Theory and practice of an emerging paradigm*, edited by T. Koschmann, Chapter 9, pp. 209-248.

A NetSeminar Design for Team-Based Learning in Professional Development Schools

Gary Obermeyer
Senior Associate
National Institute for Community Innovations
obee@nici-mc2.org

ABSTRACT

Professional Development School (PDS) partnerships offer a powerful leverage point for the improvement of student learning in the K-12 sector and a unique opportunity to experiment with new forms of online learning for the adults who work in and with schools. In this paper we present lessons learned in the design and delivery of online courses to teacher educators, classroom teachers, support personnel, and student teachers associated with the Virtual Professional Development School Consortium (VPDSC). This paper describes the NetSeminar model that is evolving through this work and considers implications for further development.

StoneSoup: A Contextualized Portfolio System

Jenny Robins

Graduate School of Library and Information Science University of Illinois Urbana Champaign

jrobins@uiuc.edu

ABSTRACT

Teaching and learning are social interactions that are impacted by contextual, situated factors within the learning environment. These factors include the past and present circumstances of the participants, their psychological and social characteristics, and the physical characteristics of the environment. Contextualized technological systems that take these factors into account. This paper contrasts contextualized and traditional computing. A description of the StoneSoup digital portfolio system is provided as an example of a contextualized CSCL application.

Keywords

CSCL, CMC, CSCW, context, situated, contextualize, portfolio, information structures, collaboratory

INTRODUCTION: THE IMPORTANCE OF CONTEXT

Teaching and learning are interpersonal activities that can be viewed as contextually situated. People draw on contextual understandings when making decisions about actions to take, and in interpreting the actions and responses of others (Dourish, 2001; Orlikowski, et al., 1995). Context refers to the environment in which interactions between people, or between people and things, emerge. It is understood in terms of both past and present circumstances. Context refers not only to physical characteristics, but also to psychological, historical, and social characteristics. It includes tasks to be accomplished, with their attendant goals, activities, and processes (Engeström, 1990; Nardi, 1996). Context is the stuff descriptions are made from, having to do with concrete circumstances, not abstractions. For example, from a physical perspective, K12 schools might seem contextually uniform. School buildings are easily recognized. But, when context is viewed holistically, schools and their classrooms vary widely and this impacts the type and extent of the adoption of computer supported collaborative learning (CSCL) technology. Improving the fit between technology and its application in the classroom means designing technologies that are more contextualized. This research addresses contextualized CSCL.

CONTEXTUALIZED SYSTEMS

In a traditional computer application, the system is designed with the view that goal states exist, and having been predetermined, procedures leading to these states can be coded into computer algorithms. This has resulted in work practices, organizational practices and physical environments that are designed around the functions of the computing system. In effect, computers order the environment, and humans obey the computers (Suchman, 1987). However, technology can be made to recede into the environmental background, while practices that draw on human skills, physical abilities and social practices can be fore-grounded. Computing systems can be made compatible with the social, organizational, cultural, physical and temporal activities of the people they serve, i.e. they can be designed to support contextual factors (Dourish, 2001).

Contextualized design takes advantage of the power of today's computers to create computing systems that emphasize flexibility over efficiency. Contextualized computing gives users the power to tamper with the system, execute it and circumvent it. It supports them in applying and adapting the system to the situation at hand (Schmidt & Bannon, 1992). One way to do this is to build computer systems as toolkits rather than monolithic applications. As opposed to one-size-fits-all packages, toolkits consist of small, stand-alone components that can be fitted together, as needed, by users through a bricolage process. Toolkits can also be made extensible, allowing users to add new components as they became available or remove components for use with other infrastructures. By configuring toolkits, users become co-designers of contextualized systems, adapting them to specific environments and needs (Dourish & Edwards, 2000). Rather than producing finished systems, this allows for the development of co-evolving social-technical environments. These bricolage systems enhance the role of users in computing systems and the role of computers in human systems. Computers can do the things that they do well, while humans do the things for which they are best suited.

While there is a need for increased flexibility in computing systems, there is a corresponding need for ways to represent that flexibility to users. One way to address the problem of representation in contextualized, bricolage systems is through the use of mediating information structures. These are structures that are meaningful to humans, but can also be interpreted by computers. Information structures organize and direct expectations regarding the presentation of information. Information structures impact human systems because of the way they are able to mediate between fixed objects, like documents and software, and flexible social practices (O'Day & Nardi, 2001). An information structure that can play multiple roles in a bricolage system is a common list. Creating lists is something humans are particularly good at. Processing lists is something computers are good at. Thus a list can function as a communication medium between humans and between humans and computers.

THE STONESOUP DIGITAL PORTFOLIO SYSTEM

StoneSoup portfolio units consist of student answers to a list of questions about their learning processes, activities and products. The StoneSoup digital portfolio system is a flexible, evolving tool that runs on a browser infrastructure. A digital portfolio system requires a critical mass of participating school districts in order for student information to be broadly available. However the learning objectives of school districts vary widely. Therefore, the system must simultaneously support the needs of numerous participating districts. At the same time, portfolios must be uniform enough to be processed across districts. Using StoneSoup, school administrators can adapt the question list so that it meets their learning objectives. Teachers have control over which questions are assigned to students and how long student answers need to be. However, the list remains consistent because, in all instances, StoneSoup uses a simple two-dimensional information structure. Portfolio questions can be answered using pencil and paper. But if the answers are input through an HTML form, they are stored as XML units on a school's local server. Answers can then be retrieved as HTML documents. These documents have a header that is customized for the school district, and answers are displayed using a standardized format. A centralized index to the XML units links student portfolios in all participating school districts, making them available when students transfer to new schools. Student units can be text-mined for resources and activities related to lessons units, giving StoneSoup a secondary role as an educational collaboratory. Visit StoneSoup at: http://www.stonesoop.org.

ACKNOWLEDGMENTS

The information structure used in this portfolio is derived from an information structure used by the Inquiry Page: http://inquiry.uiuc.edu, a project directed by Chip Bruce. This work was supported by the Graduate School of Library and Information Science at the University of Illinois, Urbana-Champaign.

REFERENCES

Dourish, Paul (2001). Seeking a Foundation for Context-Aware Computing. Human-Computer Interaction, 16,2-3.

Dourish, Paul & Edwards, Keith (2000). A tale of two toolkits: Relating infrastructure and use in flexible CSCW toolkits. Computer-Supported Cooperative Work, 9, 1, 33-51.

Engeström, Yrjö (1990). When is a tool? Multiple meanings of artifacts in human activity. In Y. Engeström, (Ed.) Learning, Working and Imagining, (pp.171-195). Orienta-Konsutit, Helsinki.

Nardi, Bonnie A. (1996). Chapter 4: Studying context: A comparison of activity theory, situated action models, and distributed cognition.. Context and Consciousness: Activity Theory and Human-Computer Interaction (pp. 7-15). MIT Press, Cambridge, MA.

O'Day, V. & Nardi, B.A. (2001). An ecological perspective on digital libraries. In A. Bishop, N. Van House, & B. Buttenfeld (Eds.).Digital Library Use: Social Practice in Design and Evaluation. Cambridge:MIT Press.

Orlikowski, W.J., Yates, JoAnn, Okamura, Kazuo & Fujimoto, Masayo (1995). Shaping electronic communication: The metastructuring of technology in the context of use. Organizaton Science, 6, 4, 423-444.

Schmidt, Kjeld & Bannon, Liam (1992). Taking CSCW seriously: Supporting articulation work. Computer Supported Cooperative Work, 1, 1-2, 7-40.

Suchman, Lucy (1987). Plans and Situated Actions: The problems of human-machine communication. Cambridge University Press, Cambridge.

Transparent Latecomer Support for Web-Based Collaborative Learning Environments

Torsten Illmann, Rene Thol, Michael Weber

Department of Multimedia Computing, University of Ulm, Germany

torsten.illmann@informatik.uni-ulm.de, rene.thol@gmx.de, weber@informatik.uni-ulm.de

ABSTRACT

In this paper we examine problems of synchronous collaboration of users in web-based learning environments. It is a strong challenge to develop efficient synchronous groupware systems which provide transparent collaboration of existing applications whereas participants may start at different points in time. Existing collaboration systems either provide transparency or the accommodation of latecomers. We developed a transparent support for accommodating latecomers which may be integrated in any Java-based groupware system on the web.

Keywords

CSCW, CSCL, Synchronous Groupware, Latecomer Support, State Migration, Serializable Java User Interfaces

INTRODUCTION

Virtual and especially web-based learning is popular. Within the project "Docs 'n Drugs - The Virtual Policlinic" (Illmann, et al., 2000) we are developing a web-based and case-oriented training systems for medical students. Students learn to come to case-based decisions by answering questions or interpreting/examining findings displayed as multimedia elements. Since the system is already embedded in the curriculum of medical students at the University of Ulm, it is often used and many cases are currently in development. Web-based applications realized as Java applets enable to process and create cases.

A big challenge of such systems is to support shared learning and authoring in location-independent groups. One distinguishes between synchronous and asynchronous collaborative learning.

When evaluating existent synchronous collaboration frameworks for our system, we noticed a system called JASMINE (Saddik, et al., 2000) which provides transparent synchronous collaboration of Java applets and applications. Unfortunately it does not support latecomers. That means that all participants of a collaborative session must start the program at exactly the same time.

In this paper we present a transparent support for latecomers of UI-based applications in Java. We outline how synchronous collaboration in Java can be achieved and describe how transparent latecoming can be supported. We integrated our implementation in the JASMINE system.

JAVA AND COLLABORATION

To realize synchronous collaboration in Java, applications or applets may be used. Since applets are special-designed Java applications for the WWW, they are a good choice for implementing collaborative applications in Java. Applets reside on a web server. On request, they are transferred to and executed on the client computer with the permission to communicate with the web server host. These are ideal conditions for implementing a collaboration framework in Java with applets.

A sophisticated collaboration framework should be able to support collaboration for any existing applet. If there are fix interfaces to meet, applet programmers have to know the interfaces and the applets do not run without the collaboration framework any more. To achieve this goal of transparency, the framework must integrate collaboration in the applet without the applet's knowledge. Its main task is to transparently forward UI events to all other participants within the current session. Forwarding events happens in three steps: Catching events, distributing them and triggering them to the user interface on the other location(s).

1. To catch all UI events, one may traverse the total UI component tree (starting from the root pane) and subscribe to each component for all possible events. This mechanism is quite time and data expensive. Another possibility is the registration of a general callback at the default UI toolkit of Java for all events using the method `Toolkit.getDefaultToolkit().addAWTEventListener`.
2. Events which have been caught have to be distributed to all other participants. This includes the transformation of them into a serializable structure which contains an index of the component they have been released on. The distribution may be performed by a central dispatch server where participants of this session are registered or by using a multicast-capable publish/subscribe communication infrastructure.

3. When a remote event is received, it has to be triggered to the corresponding component on which it originally has been released. The index identifies the component and the event is triggered by the `dispatchEvent` method of the component.

LATECOMING

Based on the ideas described above, a transparent support for latecomers has been developed. All applications that are commonly used by several users must be grouped to a collaborative session. If a latecomer is willing to accommodate collaborative applications that are already running at one or several other locations, two tasks have to be ensured by the collaboration framework:

- The state of the collaborative applications has to be transferred to the latecomer.
- During the transmission of the state (which lasts some time) none of the collaborative applications may change their state .

In order to transfer the application's state, one has to choose one collaborative applications that overtakes this task. To avoid problems to capture the program counter and local stack frames (Truyen, 2000), we must ensure that the control flow of the chosen application resides in the main event loop. Furthermore, we suppose that the application consists of only one running thread and has no open connections to resources such as files or databases. Taking these requirements into account, we may serialize the whole applications with starting from the root pane using the Java serialization mechanism (Sun, 2001). This mechanism requires all objects to be serializable. Fortunately, standard Java classes (except above mentioned exclusions) and elements of the Java UI framework (Swing and AWT) are already serializable. Unfortunately, event listeners which are subscribed to UI components are not serializable and therefore get lost or produce undesired exceptions during transmission. The only way to fix that problem transparently is to patch the base interface of all event listeners, the `java.util.EventListener` by extending the `java.io.Serializable` interface. Hence, all other event listeners (standard and custom ones) automatically get serializable by inheritance. Using that small patch , the serialized application can be transmitted to the latecomer's location. There, the application is deserialized, prepared for collaborative use and shown to the latecoming user.

The second task for latecomer support is to lock all collaborative applications simultaneously in order to avoid state-changing events during transmission. Since a simultaneous invocation of these operations without a synchronized common physical time among all participants is not possible, all applications are requested to disable asynchronously. User events that occur before all applications have acknowledged to be blocked are buffered in a message queue and have to be sent to all applications (except the initiating one) after the latecoming process.

FURTHER INFORMATION

To get more detailed information of this work a longer version of this paper may be accessed at http://www.docs-n-drugs.de. This version includes a detailed introduction, a quantitative analysis, related work and a discussion of problems and limitations of this approach.

REFERENCES

Truyen, E., et al. (2000) Portable Support for Transparent Thread Migration in Java, *Proceedings of ASAMA'2000*, (Zuerich, Germany, 2000), Springer, 29-43.

El Saddik, A., Shirmohammadi, S., Georganas, N., Steinmetz, R. (2000) JASMINE: Java Application Sharing in Multiuser INteractive Environments. *Proceedings of IDMS '2000* (Enschede, Netherlands, 2000), Springer, 214-226.

Illmann, T., Weber, M., Martens, A., Seitz, A. (2000) A Pattern-Oriented Design of a Web-Based and Case-Oriented Multimedia Training System in Medicine. *Proceedings of IDPT '2000* (Dallas, USA, June 2000), Social Science Computing Review.

Sun Microsystems Inc. (2001) Java Object Serialization Specification, ftp://ftp.java.sun.com/docs/j2se1.3/serial-spec.pdf, visited 10.10.01

Integrating Palm Hand-held Technology into the Web-based Inquiry Science Environment (WISE)

James D. Slotta, Douglas B. Clark, Britte Cheng

Graduate School of Education, The University of California, Berkeley

slotta@socrates.berkeley.edu

ABSTRACT

We describe a program of research to explore how Palm Pilot technology can facilitate inquiry activities in K-12 science and mathematics curriculum. This research was conducted within the context of the Web-based Inquiry Science Environment (WISE) project, which addresses fundamental questions concerning the role of inquiry and technology in science education. Working in close collaboration with two large school districts, we developed new approaches for integrating Palm applications into existing WISE curriculum. We developed a sophisticated and generalized solution to enable hand held survey and observation forms that can be uploaded into a class data set.

Keywords

Inquiry, Palm Pilots, Learning Environment, Handheld, Curriculum, Science Education, Internet, Web

WISE: THE WEB-BASED INQUIRY SCIENCE ENVIRONMENT

This paper will present an innovative application of hand held technology for science education. For the past seven years, the Web-based Inquiry Science Environment (WISE) project, funded by the National Science Foundation, has explored the most effective designs for inquiry activities that draw upon the wealth of available Web resources. The designs of the WISE learning environment, inquiry curriculum and assessments are based on a pedagogical framework called Scaffolded Knowledge Integration. This framework, developed by Dr. Marcia Linn and her colleagues (Linn and Hsi, 2000), has been developed through twenty years of classroom research with technology and inquiry (Linn and Songer, 1982, Bell, Davis and Linn, 1995; Slotta and Linn, 2000).

WISE offers a powerful browser-based learning environment for middle and high school inquiry science projects. Students work collaboratively in these projects, actively using materials and software from the World Wide Web. In one project, students evaluate the health of a local creek, modeling the factors that contribute to pollution. In another, they compare two competing theories about why deformed frogs are appearing in American waterways. On the left-hand side of the student's Web browser window, WISE provides an "inquiry map" that coordinates all project activities. Students click on steps within this map, resulting in Web materials, pop-up notes or hints, or any of a variety of other tools and features, such as online discussions, journals , causal maps, data visualizations, and an argument editor. Throughout the WISE project, students are scaffolded by the Inquiry Map as they work collaboratively to perform carefully designed inquiry projects

This learning environment technology is accompanied by teacher support tools that enable classroom management, student assessment, monitoring of student work and formative feedback during a project run. Teachers choose from a library of projects, each accompanied by a lesson plan, assessments, scoring rubrics, connections to standards, and opportunities to customize the project to local issues and curriculum topics. The reader is invited to go to our project Web site (*http://wise.berkeley.edu*) where s/he will find rich descriptions of the WISE learning environment, the project library, teacher supports, and an html slide show. Many projects are available, in all science topics for students in grades 4-12. More than 2000 teachers have run WISE projects in their classrooms.

We have researched the effectiveness of WISE activities for student understanding in a wide range of classroom studies. All WISE activities are assessed by pre-post and embedded assessments of students' understanding of the science content. WISE fosters lifelong science learning skills related to critique of evidence, debate of arguments, and design of personally relevant solutions (Linn and Slotta, 2000). We have also begun to research the challenges faced by science teachers as they adopt our innovative technology and inquiry methods. Working in close partnership with two large school districts -- Denver Public Schools (Colorado), and Desert Sands Unified School District (California), we have helped science teachers integrate WISE activities with their courses, and developed networks of WISE mentors within the districts to help offer support

In conjunction with these school district partnerships, we were recently awarded a grant of 500 Palm IIIc devices from *The SRI Palm Education Partnership*. In researching effective uses for hand held technology in education. we proposed to develop Palm activities that would benefit from the scaffolding of the WISE technology and inquiry curriculum. We sought to enable new kinds of activities like data collection, surveys and field observations. The resulting student-collected data could then be uploaded for subsequent use within the WISE activities.

WISE USE OF HAND HELD TECHNOLOGIES

We seek to leverage the strength of the WISE technology and curriculum to provide powerful new applications for hand held technologies. The scaffolding of the learning environment, and the instructional context of WISE inquiry projects will allow meaningful new possibilities for the use of these hand held computers in meaningful ways. For example, working in the *WISE Genetically Modified Foods* project, students download a carefully designed survey into their Palm Pilots, then interview their friends and family between classes or after school (e.g., collecting age, gender, dietary habits, and beliefs about GM Foods). The survey data from all students is then be uploaded into WISE, providing a collaborative data set for the students to use as they debate whether GM foods are dangerous. Alternatively, Palm Pilots could be used for field survey and data collection in the *WISE Healthy Creeks* project, or to help guide students as they visit the aquarium in conjunction with the WISE *Aquarium Conspiracy* project. Such activities put the hand held computer to good use in service to a broader curriculum context.

We identified four "distinctive features" of Palm Pilot computers that expand the functionality of WISE: (a) *portability* for remote functions like surveys and data collection; (b)*beaming* to enable students to share information or receive supplemental information while performing observations, (c) *touch screen functionality*, to enable ease of data input, and (d) *synching capability* to allow data upload and download from a PC and even from the Web. We sought to develop a system that would enable diverse educational applications, capitalizing on these four distinctive features. We therefore sought a general solution that would support diverse form data input into Palms for subsequent use within a WISE project . We were challenged to develop a solution for downloading information from our Web server to the student's Palm Pilot cradle, and a corresponding upload process where students "hot synch" their Palm Pilots, to transfer data from the Palm to their PC, and then on to our Web server.

WISE-PALM INTEGRATION: HOW WE SOLVED THESE PROBLEMS

We began our design process by articulating detailed user scenarios and system requirements. Based on these functional specifications, we articulated four main technology functions that would be required. (1) Palm data entry: some means of enabling students to input form data into a hand held computer was necessary. (2) Authoring of data entry forms: some generalized means of form authoring, to enable a wide range of Palm activities. (3) Interfacing Palm and WISE platforms: some means of downloading the blank input forms from the WISE project to the Palm application, and then returning the data back to WISE. (4) Data display and manipulation: some way of assembling and presenting the data into a meaningful format for students to use within their WISE browser window.

The result of our efforts is the WISE-Palm *Survey Your Surroundings* application. For any WISE project, a survey or set of observation forms are defined, each accommodating one Palm screen with a set of controls (e.g., check boxes, radio buttons, text entry fields) that are generally configurable. One item at a time is displayed, enabling the student to progress step-wise through the interview or observations. The software saves all of the form entries until the student "submits" his or her observations through the AvantGo custom Hotsync and ultimately into the collaborative database. Once loaded into WISE, the data can be viewed by students in aggregate form. Using data visualizing tools developed at Berkeley and elsewhere, students look at graphs, and plots of different categories of their data in an accompanying WISE project, scaffolded by hints and reflection notes.

This hand-held survey tool provides a perfect application for Palms within the broader context of a WISE inquiry project. Students are able to ask questions of their personal environments, then upload the data to be observed in aggregated form--providing a powerful source of inquiry content. In the process, students learn to evaluate information sources, to develop syntheses and clarity on issues that are confounding to others, to use data for knowledge development, interviewing skills, assessment practices, and self-monitoring opportunities.

REFERENCES

Bell, P., Davis, E. A., & Linn, M. C. (1995). The Knowledge Integration Environment: Theory and design. In J. L. Schnase & E. L. Cunnius (Eds.), Proceedings of CSCL '95, Bloomington, IN (pp. 14–21). Mahwah: Erlbaum.

Linn, M. C., & Hsi, S. (2000). Computers, Teachers, Peers: Science Learning Partners. Mahwah: Erlbaum.

Linn, M.C. & Slotta, J.D. (2000). WISE Science. Educational Leadership. Alexandria: Association for Supervision and Curriculum Development

Slotta, J., & Linn, M. C. (2000). How do students make sense of Internet resources in the science classroom? In M. In Jacobson, M. J. & Kozma, R. (Ed.), Learning the Sciences of the 21st Century. Hilldale, NJ:LEA

Use of the CANTOR System for Collaborative Learning in Medical Visual Object Recognition

Hans H. K. Andersen[a], Verner Andersen[b], Birgit G. Skov[c]

[a,b] Risø National Laboratory, System Analysis Department, Roskilde Denmark

[c] Gentofte University Hospital, Department of Pathology, Gentofte, Denmark

ABSTRACT

This paper reports from a user requirement, design and evaluation study on supporting collaborative learning by visual perception in the medical education domain. The CANTOR (Converging Agreement by Networking Telematics for Object Recognition) system can briefly be described as a tool that support collaborative consensus making when classifying sets of medical images or objects in medical images An evaluation experiment showed that using CANTOR seems to give a better learning effect than by using traditional methods.

Keywords

Visual Learning, Collaborative Medical Classification, Consensus Making

INTRODUCTION

As in many other domains learning in medicine is a life-long process. To specialize in pathology, for example, can last for up to ten years. Standardization of the learning processes is also needed to ensure a standardized high quality output of the medical work. In this paper we focus on the collaborative processes involved in learning to recognize, and to create consensus with respect to classifying, visual objects in medical images. Traditionally many of these processes have been of the master / student type. That is, the student learn how to classify under close supervision of an expert. This is a rather learning effective but costly educational activity and the level of expertise available may vary from place to place. The question is how better to support the collaborative learning processes and standardize the level of expertise within a group of students through training using the same system.

The CANTOR system support collaborative consensus making by letting a group of students view, share, compare, rank, and finally join individual and / or mutual classification results. In this way the system that stimulate learners to make maximum use of their cognitive potential (Scardamalia et al., 1989). CANTOR is based on the idea of self-regulated learning Schunk, 1989; Zimmermann, 1986) and it supports asynchronous distributed collaborative learning (Johansen, 1988).

EVALUATION EXPERIMENT

The objective of this experiment is to get a qualitative assessment of the usability of CANTOR for learning of 'students' within the domain of lung cancer histo-pathology. Six 'introductory doctors' from Denmark participated in the experiment. It is current practice to use a WHO booklet to learn how the different morphological features look like. The student can inspect sections of the book and compare the pictures with the microscopic image of the tissue to be classified.

The introductory doctors diagnosed individually 30 cases of lung cancer presented by slides as a base line test of their initial skill. After this introduction they were split into two groups, and they were allowed about two hours for training, one group using the CANTOR system and the other group using the standard WHO text book. Following this session they were all diagnosing 31 lung cancer cases. The improvement or deterioration for each participant was tested comparing the new success rate with the base line results. Since the two groups were small and the number of images shown limited, only qualitative results were obtained.

RESULTS

Figure 1 shows the average number and variation of correct pre-training and post-training diagnoses on person level approximated with normal distributions based on 30 and 31 classifications, respectively. If the increase in the mean value of correct diagnoses relative to the average of the variations before and after the training is taken as a measure of improvement, this value is about three times larger for the CANTOR training than for the textbook training. However, this is strongly influenced by the spreading of performance of the trainees, and this spreading is for the textbook trainees by chance nearly twice the magnitude of the CANTOR trainees. Furthermore, as indicated before, the two groups are too small to make any real quantitative significant conclusions from the results.

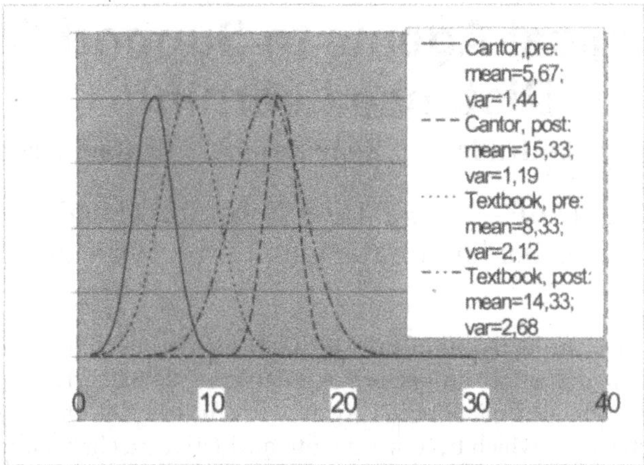

Figure 1 The correct diagnoses on person level approximated with a normal distribution regarding average and deviation. The scaling of the curves is arbitrary.

Following the session the group of physicians not using the CANTOR system were introduced to the system by their colleagues having used the system for a couple of hours. This introduction and the fact that all six physicians hereafter were able to benefit from the system by making diagnoses and making self control of these - by using the CANTOR tools - indicated the user friendliness of the system.

The session was concluded by a discussion concerning the usability and user friendliness of the CANTOR system for education and training of cancer diagnosis. Except for minor suggestions related to the user interface, the general opinion of the participating physicians was very positive. They found the system not only valuable, but also inspiring due to the tools allowing direct feedback of their performance as compared to the expert opinion, and allowing objective indication of personal improvement by the Kappa value.

In general the experiment indicates that CANTOR (still just seen as a qualitative indication) is just as good and may be even better than the textbook as an education tool, i.e., is has at least the same educational and training effect as textbooks. The scores provided by the students on a usability questionnaire indicated that the components of the CANTOR software that allow the classification of (objects in) images and for the comparison of classifications and the inspection of differences were well appreciated.

CONCLUSION

The experiment have shown that CANTOR is a valuable tool for learning and training. Using CANTOR seems to give a better learning effect than by using textbooks. The study are, however, limited since only six test persons were available. Using the CANTOR system in learning and training of medical persons could be more cost effective due to the increased computer supported collaborative learning effect replacing to a high degree the need for presence of real experts. Indeed, in front of a difficult diagnosis, a young isolated pathologist may greatly benefit from the CANTOR expert databases as well as the consolidation of the standards for disease classification.

ACKNOWLEDGMENTS

This work has in part been funded by the European Commission project CANTOR, Telematics Healthcare, HC4003

REFERENCES

[1] Johansen, Robert: (1988). *Groupware. Computer Support for Business Teams*, The Free Press, New York & London

[2] Scardamalia, M., Bereiter, R.S., Swallow, M.J., and Woodruff (1989). Computer-supported intentional learning environment. *Journal of Educational Computing Research*, 5, 51-68.

[3] Zimmerman, B. J. (1986). Becoming a self-regulated learner: Which are the key sub-processes. *Contemporary Educational Psychology*, 11, 306-313.

[4] Schunk, D. H., (1989). Social-Cognitive Theory and Self-Regulated Learning. In B. J. Zimmerman and D. H. Schunk (eds.), *Self-Regulated Learning and Academic Achievement: Theory, Research, and Practice*. New York: Springer-Verlag

Using Pedagogical Agents to Support Collaborative Distance Learning

Patrícia Jaques* **Adja Andrade**** **João Jung*** **Rafael Bordini*** **Rosa Vicari***

* PPGC, ** PGIE – Federal Uiversity of Rio Grande do Sul
{pjaques, jjung, bordini, rosa}@inf.ufrgs.br, adja@inf.pucrs.br

ABSTRACT

In this paper, we describe an animated pedagogical agent which assists the interaction among students in a virtual class within a collaborative communication tool, either on-line or not, motivating them, correcting wrong concepts and providing new knowledge. This guiding agent we call Collaboration Agent will consider not only cognitive capabilities of students, but also social and affective characteristics, which becomes a more qualitative mechanism for collaboration among students and learning. The considered agent is being modelled as part of the multi-agent architecture of the project "A Computational Model of Distance Learning Based on Socio-Cultural Pedagogical Approaches".

Keywords

Pedagogical Agents, Dialogue Analysis, Communication Tools

INTRODUCTION

To support the interaction among students, collaborative systems provide tools that facilitate online interaction, such as chat, bulletin board and discussion lists. These software are good mechanisms for conversation among students, but they do not provide any guidance or direction for the student during or after the dialogue sessions (Soller, 2001).

The agent considered in this work, called Collaboration Agent, is being modelled as part of the multi-agent architecture of the project "A Computational Model of Distance Learning Based on Socio-Cultural Pedagogical Approaches" (Andrade et al., 2001).

DESCRIPTION OF THE ENVIRONMENT

The architecture of the system consists of four types of artificial agents – Diagnostic Agent, Mediating Agent, Collaboration Agent and Semiotic Agent – and human agents (students and tutors). Further details about the system can be found in (Andrade et al., 2001). The tutoring system may function as an individual tutor, where the Mediating Agent presents pedagogical contents to the student in accordance to his/her profile and cognitive style, or as a facilitating system of collaboration, where the Collaboration Agent monitor and mediate the interaction among the students with collaborative tools.

In this article, we will focus on the system as a collaborative tool. In this case, the Collaboration Agent has an important role. Its function is to promote and to mediate the interaction between groups of students using collaborative tools (e.g., chat, discussion list, and bulletin board). In that way, it supports the students during the interactions, stimulating them when they appear unmotivated, presenting new concepts and correcting wrong conceptions. In the next section, we describe the functionalities of the system as a collaborative tool.

We can better understand the implementation of this environment through a scenario. Let us imagine a student, using his/her computer (at home or at work), connected to this system through the Internet. A Mediating Agent will be sent to the user's machine and it will monitor his/her activities. The Diagnostic Agent will suggest to the Mediating Agent a pedagogical tactic and the contents to be presented based on the inferences on the student model. The Mediating Agent will request the contents to the Semiotic Agent, which will show it to the student.

When a Diagnostic Agent verify that there is a gap between a student's actual and potential learning, so that it is necessary the intervention of some facilitators (i.e., other more capable colleagues and/or tutors), it will make a request to the Social Agent. Then, the Social Agent creates a Collaboration Agent that will invite the students to participate on an interactive session through a collaborative tool. The Collaboration Agent will monitor the discussions among the students intervening, when necessary, as mentioned above. It will connect itself to the chosen collaborative tool, as if it were a normal user of the tool, which gives the Collaboration Agent greater realism.

COLLABORATION AGENT IMPLEMENTATION

Due to its social function – to communicate with students, to promote and monitor the interaction among students – it would be interesting for the Collaboration Agent to have an interface that would allow it to exploit students' social nature. In fact, one of our main concerns is to better exploit the social potential of the students to improve their learning, and studies demonstrate that people interacting with animated characters learn to interact with other humans (Huard, 1998).

Therefore, we chose to represent it as an animated character who has a personality and which interacts with the student through messages in natural language.

Thus, as in human social interactions, the Collaboration Agent must be able to and show and perceive emotional responses. Learning is a comprehensive process which does not simply consists of the transmission and learning of contents. A tutor (in this case, the Collaboration Agent) must promote the student's emotional and affective development, enhancing his/her self-confidence and a positive mood, ideal to learning. The way in which emotional disturbances affect mental life has been discussed in the literature (Goleman, 1995). He recalls the well-known idea that depressed, bad-humoured and anxious students find greater difficulty in learning.

In order to interact with the student in an adequate way, the agent has to correctly interpret his/her emotions. Therefore, it is necessary for Collaboration Agent to have not only a student cognitive model, but also an affective one. We are going to use the student model proposed by (Bercht et al., 1999), which considers the affective states such as effort, self-confidence and independence.

In collaborative learning, the group is an active entity; therefore, the system must contain information that refers to the group as a whole. This information generates a group model, which is built and maintained by the Collaboration Agent. The Collaboration Agent can build the group model from the individual student models, which are obtained from the interactions between the students and their Mediating Agents, and updated by the Diagnostic Agents. The group model can also be obtained from the observation of the group as a whole.

Still, it is necessary to have in mind the responsibility about the use of affective agent architecture for interaction with the user, especially in the education. Often we observe that agents have attitudes that are not suitable to students' mood (e.g., if an agent gets sad when the student could not carry out an exercise). This kind of attitude may generate a disturbed reaction in the student, making him/her more anxious and less self-confident. It is necessary to identify which behaviours are appropriate to promote a mood in the student that provides better learning conditions.

The Collaboration Agent will carry out the analysis of the student's dialogue based on statistical methods, such as pattern matching, message categorisation and information retrieval (Soller, 2001). The messages will be generated in natural language, using dialogue models and frames. We intend to base this analysis on the work in (Jaques & Oliveira, 1999) (Jaques et al., 2000).

CONCLUSIONS AND FUTURE WORK

This research is currently in the phase of implementation design and specification. The phase of study of the pedagogical architecture and computational modelling is concluded. This work is the result of a research project in the area of Artificial Intelligence applied to Education that intends to create a computational framework (in which the pedagogical agents are part of it) to support collaborative learning.

REFERENCES

Andrade, A. F.; Jaques, P. A.; Vicari, R. M.; Bordini, R.; Jung, J. (2001) A Computational Model of Distance Learning Based on Vygotsky's Socio-Cultural Approach. *Proceedings of the MABLE Workshop,* AI-ED.

Bercht, M.; Moissa, H.; Viccari, R.M. (1999) Identificação de fatores motivacionais e afetivos em um ambiente de ensino e aprendizagem. Proceddings of SBIE'99 (Curitiba, November 23-25) (Poster).

Goleman, D. (1995). *Emotional Intelligence.* Objetiva, 19995.

Huard, R (1998). *Character Mastery with the Improvisational Puppets Program.* Technical Report (KSL-98-11) – Stanford University.

Jaques, P.; Andrade, A.; Moraes, M.; Móra, M. C (2000). Uma Arquitetura de Agente para a Análise Qualitativa da Interação em Ambientes de Educação a Distância. Proceedings of SBIA (Maceió, November).

Jaques, P.; Oliveira, F. M. (1999) Software Agents for Analysis of Collaboration in a Virtual Classroom. Proceedings of AI-ED99 (Le mans).

Soller, A. (2001) Supporting Social Interaction in an Intelligent Collaborative Learning System. *IJAIE*, 11.

Networked PDAs in a Community of Learners

Knut Lundby, Ole Smørdal, Anniken Larsen, Annita Fjuk
InterMedia, University of Oslo, Telenor R&D
knut.lundby@intermedia.uio.no

ABSTRACT
'Knowledge access in distributed training. Mobile opportunities for medical students' ('KNOWMOBILE') is exploring just-in-time functionality with Internet based educational resources on personal digital assistants (PDAs). Intended for life long learning in a variety of health professions, this specific project concentrates on medical students during their assignment to the primary health care sector. The project is conducting experiments in the fall 2001 focusing how students in face-to-face as well as in distributed communities of learners, use the net to access and apply relevant knowledge sources and build collaborative support structures for their training practice. The project is reported on http://www.intermedia.uio.no/prosjekter/knowmobile

KEYWORDS
Net-based learning, Communities of practice, Mobile terminals, Collaborative portal, Medical students

INTRODUCTION
KNOWMOBILE is an exploratory research and development project. The case is the tenth semester of the new curriculum in the medical school at the University of Oslo, when the students are on assignment at local hospitals and general practitioners offices in Southern Norway. The project focuses on how the dispersed learners, in a variety of local contexts, use mobile handheld equipment to access the net for relevant medical knowledge and information. The use of networked PDAs is understood and researched in relation to and as part of collaborative learning activities. The learning communities are emphasized, with a focus on how PDAs could offer access.

MIX MODE COMPUTER SUPPORT FOR COLLABORATIVE LEARNING
Networked computers facilitate *distributed learning*, which includes the *mediation* of learning activities by a constellation of various tools and signs with appropriate pedagogical approaches to collaboration and social interactions. These tools and signs include Internet services, Web-based groupware, multimedia shared spaces, videoconferencing technology, interactive 3D applications on the one hand, and text processing programs, drawing and painting programs, spreadsheet applications on the other. They shape and mediate the goals and courses of actions, increasingly taken place in collaboratively based learning environments. Thus it is important to derive a framework for design from a rich theoretical basis, in order to address various issues and aspects that are important for designing tools and signs that will be useful when introduced in collaborative learning (Fjuk & Smørdal, 2001).

Understanding interaction and collaboration patterns for various net-based learning environments is important in order to use these patterns explicitly in the pedagogical and technical design (Krange et. al., forthcoming). We regard it particularly interesting to combine the use of web and mobile terminals. Development, introduction and engagement in net-based learning activities implies that pedagogical, technological and organizational aspects must be considered a systemic whole. We regard it a goal to contribute to design and implementation of a net-based community of practice, where the students may critically reflect and discuss experiences from their practice.

NET-BASED COMMUNITIES OF PRACTICE
The medical students in this case study are subjected to a work-oriented assignment to the primary health care sector. This implies that students' own experience and problems in their practice should be the main motivation for participation and engagement in the net-based community of practice they relate to. When students and their tutors in cooperation establish a social and net-based community of practice, tutor supported reflections and discussions are possible. According to the literature (Salomon, 1993; Dirckinck-Holmfeld, 1995), successful learning processes in net-based environments are both contributed to and dependent on a series of elements:

- The actors are genuinely interdependent in order to reach their goals.
- They have an individual responsibility for a collective product, the collective process and their own learning.
- The actors must develop a collective product by means of argumentation and negotiation.

However, these elements are not trivial to support by means of text-based and asynchronous communication facilities (such as email and web-based groupware).

EXPERIMENTS IN LOCAL CONTEXTS

The medical students have their assignments in a local hospital for six weeks, then at a general practitioners office for an additional six weeks. All students are part of a distributed group solving two problem-based projects together, using a web-based learning environment. In addition, students are co-located with respect to their hospital, and some share apartment during their assignment. The medical students are offered PDAs (HP Jornadas) with standard software, such as a note-taker, an audio-recorder, email client, and online and offline browsers. We have selected three local contexts for introducing the mobile PDAs. This is for comparing and contrasting user experiences in various communities of practice:

Co-located Community of Learners

Five students co-located to a hospital and sharing an apartment are functioning as a learning community, e.g. discussing their day-to-day experiences over breakfast and dinner. We have introduced networked mobile terminals and IP-zones (wireless access to Internet plus a collective medical portal) where they work and live. This is to facilitate communication within the community of learners, using a high-speed network and always-connected mobile terminals.

Partially Co-located Community of Learners

Five students partly co-located during their assignments, but travelling back to their usual homes. We have introduced mobile terminals for them with GPRS access to the Internet. This is to facilitate communication within a community of learners regardless of location, e.g. from their homes.

Distributed Community of Learners

Eight distributed students, participating in a project group. The group is put together in order to solve two problem-based tasks requiring discussions, hypothesis generation and assessing net-based learning resources. We have introduced mobile terminals that must be synchronized with a desktop computer. This is to investigate their combined support for communication in a distributed learning community.

PROJECT PARTNERS

KNOWMOBILE is a project under Nordunet 2, an Internet research program financed by the Nordic Council of Ministers and by the Nordic Governments. Project partners are the Faculty of Medicine, Department of Informatics and InterMedia, University of Oslo, Telenor R&D, Ericsson, Hewlett-Packard and Umeå University. A reference process with medical schools in other Nordic countries is part of the project.

REFERENCES

[1] Fjuk, A and Smørdal, O (2001) Networked Computers' Incorporated Role in Collaborative Learning. In Euro CSCL 2001, Maastricht, The Netherlands.

[2] Krange, I., Larsen, A., Ludvigsen, S. and Fjuk, A. (forthcoming) Describing construction of knowledge through identification of collaboration patterns in 3D learning environments. Accepted to CSCL 2002.

[3] Dirckinck-Holmfeld, L. (1995) Project Pedagogy as the Foundation for Computer Supported Collaborative Learning. In: Collis, B & G. Davies. (Eds), (1995) Innovative adult learning with innovative technologies. IFIP Trancelations A-61, North-Holland.

[4] Salomon, G. (1993) No distribution without individuals' cognition: a dynamic interactional view. In: Salomon, G. (Ed.). Distributed cognitions: Psychological and educational considerations. Cambridge University Press, New York.

NetWorked Learning Systems

Herbert Remidez, Joshua S. Gottdenker, James M. Laffey, Dale R. Musser, Ran-Young Hong, Linda Espinosa, Christopher J. Amelung

herbert@coe.missouri.edu, jsg0af@mizzou.edu, laffeyj@missouri.edu, musserda@missouri.edu, rhe06@mizzou.edu, espinosal@missouri.edu, chrisa@coe.missouri.edu

Center for Technology Innovations in Education, University of Missouri-Columbia

ABSTRACT

New network-based learning systems are coming into use that offer the possibility of integrating curriculum support systems with student information systems as well as changing the metaphor of the Internet from library to workspace. We call these integrated and process-oriented systems Networked Learning Systems (NLS). An NLS is tentatively defined as a program or set of programs designed to operate over a network and support users as they undertake tasks or participate in processes related to learning. Computer Supported Collaborated Learning (CSCL) is one important type of process that can be enabled by NLS. Schools already have begun to adopt NLS. To adequately support CSCL in schools, it is necessary to understand the types and dimensions of networked learning systems currently available. This poster describes in detail one networked learning system, Shadow netWorkspace™ (SNS) (http://sns.internetschools.org), and highlights several other available networked learning systems.

Keywords

Networked Learning Systems, Shadow netWorkspace

INTRODUCTION

New network-based learning systems (NLS) offer the possibility of integrating curriculum experiences and student information systems as well as changing the metaphor of the Internet from library to workspace. Shadow netWorkspace™ (SNS) (http://sns.internetschools.org) is an NLS being developed by the Center for Technology Innovations in Education at the University of Missouri-Columbia (http://www.ctie.missouri.edu). SNS was designed to facilitate the implementation of a learning community, wherein members (teachers, students, parents, etc.) have tools for representing, organizing, sharing, and collaborating on their thoughts and efforts. Much like a personal computer's desktop, SNS provides a personal workspace for organizing, storing, and accessing files and an environment for running applications. SNS also provides the ability to create groups, and for each group to have a "group desktop" for file sharing, communication, and collaboration. These features help SNS become both an information space for organizing, storing, and accessing files and a social space in that SNS users have roles (e.g., teachers, students, parents, etc.) that structure the system interaction and are part of groups that share, communicate, and collaborate. Because SNS is web-based, teachers and students can access their workspaces from any computer that can access the World Wide Web, and partners (parents or mentors) who are unable to participate in schools because of time or distance can participate in the Internet-based workspace.

SNS is freely available to all users. It can be installed locally for a learning community, in a school building, school district, or consortium of teachers or schools collaborating to implement cross-school projects. It comes with an Open Source License (GNU Public License) and an Application Programming Interface (API) so others can develop applications for it and participate in enhancing and supporting it. Systems like SNS are somewhat primitive instances of the environments we envision for schools as learning organizations. These systems must advance through evolutionary and learning processes of their own.

RELATED NETWORKED LEARNING SYSTEMS

- Blackboard (www.blackboard.com) offers several proprietary software packages to support course delivery, portal services, and transaction processing. Blackboard, WebCT (www.webct.com), and eCollege (www.ecollege.com) are the three most popular networked learning systems currently in use by schools.
- Mimer Desk (www.mimerdesk.org) is an Open-Source groupware environment designed for a wide variety of uses such as web-based learning, project collaboration, and community support.
- SchoolMation (www.schoolmation.com) is a web-based school management system that is very management-oriented. It contains a nice grade book and course/assignment organization functions, and is freely available under an Open Source license.
- Authenticated User Community (AUC) (http://auc.sourceforge.net/) is an intranet system designed for use in a K-12 setting. AUC offers file transfer, email, class calendars, discussion boards, and much more. It is also freely available under an Open Source license.

- ILIAS (http://www.ilias.uni-koeln.de/ios/index-e.html) is a web-based training platform jointly developed by the University of Cologne, the Faculty of Economics, Business Administration and Social Sciences at the University of Cologne, the Sal. Oppenheim Foundation, and the Department of Education Science and Research of the State of Northrhine-Westphalia.

SUMMARY

New network-based learning systems are coming into use that offer the possibility of integrating curriculum support systems with student information systems as well as changing the metaphor of the Internet from library to workspace. We call these integrated and process oriented systems Networked Learning Systems. CSCL is one important type of process that can be enabled by NLS. Schools already have begun to adopt NLS. To adequately support CSCL in schools, it is necessary to understand the types and dimensions of networked learning systems currently available. This poster describes one networked learning system, Shadow netWorkspace™ (SNS) (http://sns.internetschools.org), and highlights several other available networked learning systems.

REFERENCES

Laffey, J., Musser, D. & Espinosa, L. (2000) Shadow netWorkspace Learning Systems Project. *Proceedings of the International Workshop on Advanced Learning Technologies*. (Palmerstown North, New Zealand), IEEE Computer Society. pp. 188-189.

B. QUANTITATIVE ANALYSES OF CASE STUDIES AND THEIR IMPLICATIONS FOR CSCL

Solo, Together, Apart: Evaluating Modes of CSCL for Learning a Problem Solving Task

Tim Wright, Andy Cockburn

University of Canterbury, New Zealand

{tnw13,andy}@cosc.canterbury.ac.nz

ABSTRACT

This paper describes an experiment that examines how computer supported collaboration influences how children learn to solve a simple puzzle. We found that collaboration resulted in relatively poor performance during a 'training' period, but that it appeared to aid puzzle comprehension during a later 'testing' period. Results also showed that girls found it harder than boys to solve the puzzle when collaborating.

Keywords: Learning, educational technology, groupware, empirical studies.

INTRODUCTION

Computers in schools remain, at present, a relatively scarce resource. Although primarily designed for single-user use (one keyboard, one mouse, and one screen), computers in schools are often used as collaborative devices with several simultaneous users. In this style of use, there is contention for input devices. To overcome the apparent limitations of contention for input devices, synchronous groupware technology can allow multiple users, each with their own computer, to simultaneously work with a shared computer-supported artifact such as a puzzle, virtual world, or interactive story. As computers in the classroom become more commonly available, it is feasible that synchronous groupware applications could be used to allow new styles of collaboration with local and remote students. Although feasible, will groupware be beneficial?

The precise questions addressed in this paper are as follows. First, do children learn problem-solving tasks better when working alone or when collaborating? Second, which hardware and software configurations for synchronous collaboration best support learning? Third, are there differences in the ways that boys and girls interact with, and collaborate around, computer systems? Our goal is to further the concrete empirical foundations of research in Computer Supported Collaborative Learning (CSCL).

EXPERIMENTAL DESIGN

The experiment investigates the effectiveness of three different modes of computer supported collaborative learning in supporting children learning how to solve a particular puzzle*. The puzzle used is the 'eight-puzzle'which consists of a three by three grid with eight numbered pieces and one empty slot. Users work towards a particular target configuration (such as the one shown in the figure) by sliding pieces into the empty slot. In our user interface, mouse clicking any tile that is adjacent to the empty slot causes the tile to slide into the vacant position. The tile's movement is rapidly and fluidly animated, providing a clear indication of the direction of motion.

Each of the fifty participants, aged ten and eleven, was asked to solve the eight-puzzle a total of ten times, with five trials in a 'training' phase, and five trials in a 'testing' phase. Each participant was assigned to one of three collaboration conditions for the training phase, and in the testing phase all participants solved the puzzle alone using the single user version of the system. The first 'solo' training condition acts as a control, and involves using a single-user version of the puzzle. In the second 'contention' training condition, two participants shared access to the interface used in the 'solo' condition. In the third 'groupware' training condition, two participants, each with their own computer, screen and mouse, shared access to a strict-WYSIWIS (What You See Is What I See) implementation of the puzzle. The only visual difference between the groupware interface and the solo one was the addition of telepointers, which reveal the location of the other user's cursor in

* The experimental design is similar to that described by O'Hara and Payne (1998).

the display.

After solving the puzzle five times in the training condition, all of the subjects, regardless of their training condition, moved to the testing phase in which they solved the puzzle a further five times on their own. The interface used in the testing phase was identical to that used in the solo condition. Figure 1 summarises the difference between the three conditions used during the training phase and the one condition used during the testing phase.

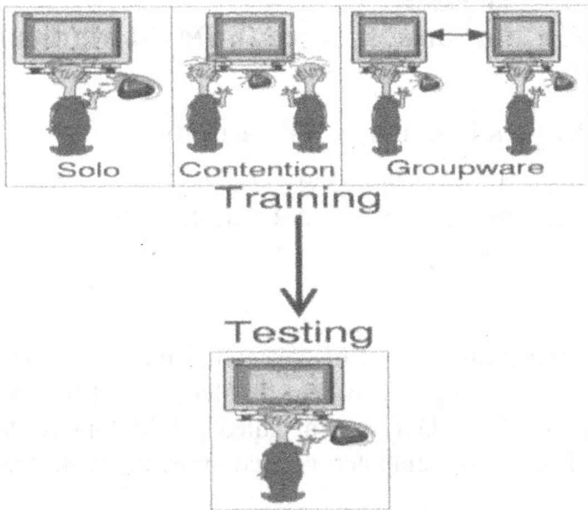

Figure 18: The participants were split into three groups for the training phase, but they all performed the testing phase individually.

RESULTS

Evidence of learning

Through the five trials in the training phase, the mean time to solve the puzzle was 235 seconds (σ 118), with a mean move count of 203 (σ 84), and an inter-move latency of 1.55 seconds (σ 0.22). During testing, these values all decreased, with means for solution time, move counts and inter-move latency of 167 (σ 78) seconds, 169 (σ 74) moves and 0.99 (σ 0.22) seconds. These are all reliable differences: $F(1,42)=16.23$, $p<.01$, $F(1, 42)=6.2$, $p<.05$, $F(1,42)=37.36$, $p<.01$. This reveals that the subjects successfully learned the puzzle.

Learning as a factor of training condition

The main effects for the training condition were not significant for any of the three measures. The mean solution time for the solo, contention and groupware conditions were 194 (σ 95), 200 (σ 82), and 207 (σ 134) seconds ($F(2,42)=0.114$, $p=.89$). This is unsurprising given that the sampled data includes the highly variable performance of the subjects during their initial learning trials.

There is a marginally significant interaction between training configuration and phase (training or testing) for the move-count dependent variable: $F(2,42)=2.89$, $p=.067$. The solo subjects took slightly more moves to complete the puzzle in the testing phase than the training phase (increasing from 180 to 185). The subjects in the two collaborative training conditions (contention and groupware), however, showed a relatively dramatic improvement from training to testing.

To summarise the impact of the three different training conditions on learning, when tested the subjects trained in the collaboration conditions took fewer moves and solved the problems more quickly (on average), but this is not a reliable observation. However, during training, the collaboration subjects took more time and more moves to solve the puzzle (on average) than the solo subjects did, but again this is not a reliable observation.

An analysis of gender showed that girls took slightly longer than boys to complete the puzzle (on average, but not significant), but roughly the same number of moves. However, girls seemed to perform particularly poorly when being trained using a collaborative system. The girls' poor performance during training did not appear to influence their learning the puzzle.

CONCLUSION

Results show that the children successfully learnt the puzzle. The three training configurations did not yield significant differences in the children's performance during testing, although the mean task completion times were lower for those that trained collaboratively. Girls in the collaborative training conditions took longer and more moves to solve the puzzle during training than those in the solo condition, but this had no obvious impact on their ability to solve the problem during testing. In essence, our results lend further support to prior studies indicating that collaboration neither hinders nor helps learning.

ACKNOWLEDGMENTS

This research was supported by a New Zealand Royal Society Marsden grant. We are in the debt of Ilam, Merrin and Westburn primary schools for allowing us access to their students. This work benefited from collaboration with Jane McKenzie, Bruce McKenzie, Michael JasonSmith, Geoffrey Xu and Ben Schmidt.

REFERENCES

O'Hara, KP. and Payne, SJ. (1998) The Effects of Operator Implementation Cost on Planfulness of Problem Solving and Learning. *Cognitive Psychology*, **35**, 34–70.

Text Forum Features for Small Group Discussions with Facet-Based Pedagogy

Steven Tanimoto[1], Adam Carlson[1], Justin Husted[2], Earl Hunt[1],Josef Larsson[1], David Madigan[3], Jim Minstrell[4]

[1]University of Washington, [2]Amazon.com, [3]Rutgers University, [4]Talaria Inc.
tanimoto@u.washington.edu, carlson@cs.washington.edu, elladan@eskimo.com, ehunt@u.washington.edu, jlarsson@cs.washington.edu, madigan@stat.rutgers.edu, jimminstrell@talariainc.com

ABSTRACT
We describe an approach to teaching that engages students in small-group discussions of conceptual material. Then we describe software that mediates the discussions with an online textual newsgroup-like system that has special features to support a pedagogical approach that deals explicitly with student preconceptions. Our system, called INFACT-FORUM, is part of a larger CSCL system called INFACT that supports student discussion, computer-assisted assessment, display of student progress data, and support for pedagogical intervention.

Keywords
facet, misconception, learning, collaborative, software, CSCL, assessment, text, conferencing, group discussion, mark-up, annotation, visibility, hide, concept, newsgroup, writing, pedagogy.

INTRODUCTION
In a recent report recommending methods for improving student learning (NRC 1999), recognizing student preconceptions and using them to engage the students is given a high priority. A particular methodology for discovering and working from students' preconceptions is sometimes called "facets" of understanding. A facet is a particular conception, often naïve or limited in its consideration of the relevant factors or phenomena, and it can be considered as an approximate understanding of some concept (Minstrell, 1992). The question arises as to how best to diagnose student facets. One method is to use a series of questions with multiple-choice answers. The DIAGNOSER project takes this approach (Hunt and Minstrell, 1994). It has the advantage that questions can be designed to get directly at student facets within a relatively short time. Furthermore, the reliability of the diagnoses can be high. One drawback of the multiple-choice approach, however, is that some students do not like the traditional, test-like format. Furthermore, students are not involved in collaborative learning (see, e.g., Scardamalia and Bereiter, 1996) while they are responding to the questions. An alternative approach to eliciting and diagnosing facets involves the students in focused, small-group discussions, and uses their expressions in that context as the basis for diagnosis.

THE INFACT TEACHING CYCLE
In Figure 1 is shown a process diagram of the teaching cycle when using the INFACT approach. The first event in the cycle is the posting, by the instructor, of a challenge question for consideration by the students. Students are given approximately 24 hours to make individual responses to the question. These responses are only visible to the instructor(s) and their authors until the "curtain" is raised to make them visible within their particular groups. Group discussion proceeds until day 5, when each group is required to post a consensus answer to the original challenge with either an agreed upon single answer or a synthesis of remaining differences. Diagnosis by the instructor(s) can begin as soon as individual posts are available, and continues until enough assessment data is available upon which to safely base interventions appropriate to each student. The diagnosis process itself may be interactive, if the teacher chooses, so that the teacher may request clarification from a student before entering a facet diagnosis in the database. The teacher may also wish to email each student as a method of acknowledgement of the student's efforts in the discussion. The email message itself could contain suggestions for the individual student. The next step in the general process is for the teacher to identify general trends in the groups or class as a whole by requesting visualizations of the facet assessment data just collected. These trends would typically suggest particular teaching interventions to an experienced instructor. The instructor then implements the interventions, which might consist of any of the following: joining in on group discussions and posting suggestions or leading questions; offering a link to some web-based resource; or making adjustments to the memberships of the groups.

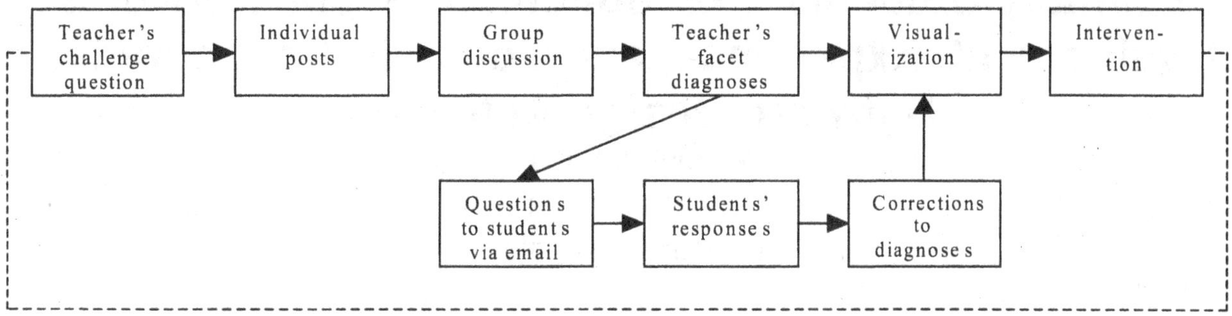

Figure 1. The INFACT pedagogical cycle. The period of the cycle is normally 1 week.

If additional time is available, there could be additional subcycles of group discussion, diagnosis, and intervention. However, in practice, there is seldom time for much iteration on that level.

The INFACT approach to assessment poses several challenges not faced by the multiple-choice questionnaire method of DIAGNOSER. The first of these is the necessity of structuring the small-group discussions so that there is a high probability that students will reveal their facets as they participate. The second of these is the challenge of making accurate diagnoses efficiently from the students' writing. This short paper is concerned primarily with the former and how the software itself can help structure the discussions.

INFACT-FORUM

In order to best support our teaching process, we decided to implement a custom textual conferencing facility. As a part of the INFACT suite of tools (Tanimoto et al, 2000), we call this INFACT-FORUM. Its features can be grouped as follows: (a) user account administration, (b) messaging, (c) visibility control, (d) support for annotation and assessment. Perhaps the most unique features of INFACT-FORUM are its controls, available to administrators, for the visibility of student messages. While it is common in text-conferencing systems to provide moderators with ways to delete or hide offensive or off-topic messages, INFACT-FORUM, as a system to support diagnosis of individual student preconceptions, allows an administrator to make student responses to the teacher's questions hidden from other students, either indefinitely or until a particular time. We refer to this feature as "the curtain," because unhiding a student's message is like raising the curtain on a stage to reveal something anticipated. The teacher raises the curtain to begin the group discussion phase of the cycle. For simply censoring, there is a facility for an administrator to hide a message from all users, without upsetting the thread structure in any way. Keeping the curtain lowered for the first phase of a discussion helps to keep each student's initial response to the challenge question an individual response rather than a response informed by peers. This provides a mechanism by which to engage every student in the discussion by forcing them to commit to an interpretation or possible solution before benefit of group ideas. The possibility of later raising the curtain permits all students to then share their personal views of the challenge without having to retype it or re-express it.

ACKNOWLEDGMENTS

Thanks to the National Science Foundation for partial support of this project under Grant CDA-9616532. Thanks also to other INFACT project contributors, including David Akers, Johann Ammerlahn, Nick Benson, Jeremy Baer, Jeff Phillips, Shirley Gaw, Jennifer Wright, Virginia Stimpson, and Andrew Schafner.

REFERENCES

For a more detailed description of INFACT-FORUM and more references, see the web-based version of this paper.

Hunt, E., and Minstrell, J. (1994). A cognitive approach to the teaching of physics. In McGilly, K. (ed.), *Classroom Lessons*. Cambridge, MA: MIT Press, pp.51-74.

NRC (1999). *How People Learn: Bridging Research and Practice*. Nat. Res. Council. Wash., DC: Nat. Acad. Press.

Scardamalia, M., and Bereiter, C. (1996). Computer support for knowledge-building communities. In T. Koschmann (ed.), *CSCL: Theory and practice of an emerging paradigm*. Mahwah, NJ: Lawrence Erlbaum Associates.

Tanimoto, S., Carlson, A., Hunt, E., Madigan, D., and Minstrell, J. (2000). Computer support for unobtrusive assessment of conceptual knowledge as evidenced by newsgroup postings. *ED-MEDIA 2000*, Montreal.

Elementary Students' Perceptions of Social Networks: Development, Experience, and Equity in Collaborative Software Design Activities

Yasmin B. Kafai

Graduate School of Education & Information Studies, University of California, Los Angeles

kafai@gseis.ucla.edu

ABSTRACT

More recently, the analysis of social networks in computer-supported collaborative learning environments has received more attention. Less attention has been given to how the participants themselves see collaborative patterns and trends. Towards that end, we interviewed 131 fourth and fifth-grade elementary students at the end of four different ten week-long collaborative software design projects and asked them to describe the type of help they had either given to or received from team members and other students in their class. Technical help with programming problems was by far the most prominent type of help given or received. The frequency of helping interactions not only increased over the course of two design projects but also became more varied. Distribution of helping interactions became only more equitable in a second design project. The discussion addresses methodological issues in using students' perceptions of helping interactions in social network analysis, the nature of students' social resources, the impact of experience, and issues of gender equity in computer-supported collaborative learning.

Keywords

Social network, learning through design, interview analysis, helping interactions, gender differences

INTRODUCTION

Researchers such as Lave and Wenger (1991) see collaborations in apprenticeships as a form of legitimate peripheral participation that allow participants' enculturation into the social practices of a community. Others, such as Moll and Greenberg (1990), focus on social resources within the larger community and talk about the importance of mobilizing 'funds of knowledge' within a classroom for learning. Helping interactions between members have been seen as an instrumental aspects of a community of learners (e.g., Webb & Palincsar, 1996). Many project-based learning environments have made helping interactions an integral feature of their design in the form of getting students to explain and share their understanding (e.g., Blumenfeld, Marx, Soloway, Krajcik, Guzdial, & Palincsar, 1991). The present study builds on research that analyzed helping interaction patterns in students' apprenticeships (Ching 2000) and complements it by focusing on students' perceptions of these helping interactions in their teams and class during a collaborative software design project (Kafai, 1996). It contributes to research on social networks found in computer-supported collaborative learning environments with the goal to examine not only individual contributions but also relationships among peers (Nurmela, Lehtinen, & Palonen, 1999; Palonen & Hakkarainen, 2000).

For that purpose, we asked elementary students in interviews conducted at the end of ten weeklong collaborative software design projects to describe the type of help they had either given to or received from project team members and other students in their class. Students, working in mixed-gender teams, developed their own research questions and implementing instructional software designs as answers. To facilitate helping interactions, student teams were comprised of more or less experienced students. For that purpose we distinguish in accordance with Lave and Wenger (1991) between students as old-timers, i.e., having participated in a previous software design project, and newcomers, i.e., being new to instructional software design activities. This approach resembles models of cognitive apprenticeship (Collins, Brown & Newman, 1989) with the important distinction that not adults but students with previous experience are configured as the more able participants. We used the interviews to develop social network diagrams (Frank, 1998; Wordham, 1999) to visualize participation patterns and relationships between class members. Our analyses included four classes: two parallel classes in the first year (one class had teams with old-timers and newcomers; the other class only newcomers), and two consecutive classes in the second year with teams of old-timers and newcomers—all taught by the same science teacher. In this context, we followed fifteen students from being newcomers in the first year to becoming old-timers in the second year. We examined several aspects: (1) in which ways students described the social resources available in form of other class members, newcomers and old-timers alike, (2) how such social networks develop over time within a classroom community over the course of two consecutive projects, (3) the perspective of students who transitioned from newcomers to old-timers within the project, and (4) the distribution of helping interactions within classes.

Our results indicate that help with programming problems was by far the most prominent type of help given or received. According to students' reports, the frequency of helping interactions not only increased over the course of two design projects but also became more varied including technical, science and design help. Distribution of helping interactions became only more equitable in the second design project.

In contrast to previous studies, this research was based on spontaneously generated reports of helping interactions by participants rather than observational data or logfile analysis. A comparative observational analysis conducted by Ching (2000) identified different forms of helping interactions around programming issues and confirms that students' perception of helping interactions seem to carry reasonable validity. The positive aspect of the old-timers' presence in teams came in form of help with programming problems. Old-timers also modeled helping interactions for newcomers who are prospective old-timers. The most promising finding appears in the second design project in the same academic year, when not only old-timers but also newcomers were more experienced in project work. Our findings also indicated gender differences in receiving and requesting help. Even in the longitudinal study of old-timer boys and girls we found these gender differences. However, our analysis of programming tests revealed no significant gender differences: old-timer girls are as proficient as old-timer boys in programming are. When we examined the outside helping reports, we found that boys and girls were equally frequent in the position of 'class experts'. It is possible that larger social forces are at play here. For example, it is known that boys tend to play in larger groups than girls do. One could speculate that boys tended to view other boys within their teams and outside of their teams as part of their expanded social network whereas girls tended to limit themselves to within team helping. It is also possible that girls see helping interactions more as 'common practice' and consequently tend to underreport them. Whatever the explanation, it is perplexing to find that gender differences are eradicated in programming proficiency but still replicated in helping structures. While this points to success on some levels, it also indicates that creating equitable learning environments is not just a matter of skill equality.

ACKNOWLEDGMENTS

This research was supported by an Early Career Award from the National Science Foundation. I would like to thank the teacher, Cathleen Galas, and her elementary students at the UCLA Corinne Seeds Elementary School for their participation in the Learning Science by Design research project over the past five years. Cynthia Ching and Kate Muir participated in conducting the interviews; Kate Muir, Meredith Roberts, Van Phan and Melissa Cantu assisted in transcribing and coding the interviews.

REFERENCES

Ching, C. C. (2000). *Apprenticeship, learning, and technology: Children as oldtimers and newcomers in the culture of learning through design.* Unpublished doctoral dissertation, University of California, Los Angeles.

Collins, A., Brown, J. S. , & Newman, D. (1989). Cognitive apprenticeship: Teaching the crafts of reading, writing and mathematics. In L. Resnick (Ed.), *Knowing, learning, and instruction: Essays in honor of Robert Glaser* (pp. 453-494). Hillsdale, NJ: Lawrence Erlbaum Associates, Inc.

Frank, K. A. (1998). Quantitative methods for studying social context in multilevels and through interpersonal relations. *Review of Research in Education*, **23**, 170-216.

Kafai, Y. B. (1996). *Learning science by design.* Proposal to the National Science Foundation, Washington, DC.

Lave, J. & Wenger, E. (1991). *Situated learning: Legitimate peripheral participation.* Cambridge: Cambridge University Press.

Moll, L.C., & Greenberg, J. B. (1990). Creating zones of possibilities: Combining social contexts for instruction. In L. C. Moll (Ed.) *Vygotzky and education* (pp. 319-348). New York: Cambridge University Press.

Nurmela, K., Lehtinen, E., & Palonen, T. (1999). Evaluating CSCL log files by social network analysis. *Proceedings of CSCL'99* (Palo Alto, CA, December 1999). Lawrence Erlbaum Associates, 434-444.

Palonen, T. & Hakkarainen, K. (2000). Patterns of interaction in computer-supported learning: A social network analysis. *Proceedings of ICLS'2000* (Ann Arbor, MI, June 2000), Lawrence Erlbaum Associates, 334-339.

Webb, N. & Palincsar, A. (1996). Collaborative learning. In D. Berliner (Ed.), *Handbook of Educational Psychology* (pp. 345-413), New York: Macmillan.

Wortham, D. W. (1999). Nodal and matrix analyses of communication patterns in small groups. *Proceedings of CSCL'99* (Palo Alto, CA, December 1999). Lawrence Erlbaum Associates, 681-683.

Promoting the Coordination of Computer-mediated Interdisciplinary Collaboration

Nikol Rummel, Hans Spada, Fabian Hermann, Franz Caspar, Katrin Schornstein

Psychologisches Institut, Albert-Ludwigs-Universität Freiburg, Germany
e-mail: <last name>@psychologie.uni-freiburg.de

ABSTRACT

The goal of this research is to promote the coordination of computer-mediated interdisciplinary collaboration of partners with complementary expertise. Efficient collaboration is shown to depend strongly on the quality of the coordination activities. A first experiment investigated the effects of different technical realizations of computer-mediated collaboration on the coordination of activities. It revealed that especially a well-balanced sequence of phases of joint work and individual working phases was central for the quality of the problem-solving process. The goal of a second experiment was to test the effectiveness of promoting this coordination by vicarious learning from an exemplary computer-mediated collaboration. By combining two strands of research – studies on worked-out examples and work on vicarious learning from dialogue and discourse – we show a new and theoretically well-founded way to strengthen collaborative competence.

EXPERIMENT 1: EFFECTS OF DIFFERENT TECHNICAL SETTINGS ON THE COORDINATION OF ACTIVITIES

The goal of the first study (see also Hermann, Rummel & Spada, 2001) was to investigate the effects of different technical realizations of a collaborative setting on the collaborative process and its efficiency. The collaborative task (in both experiments), was the solution of psychiatric case studies. Dyads of advanced medical and psychology students were asked to jointly formulate a diagnosis and a therapy plan making use of their complementary expertise. The main coordination demands (cf. Malone and Crowston, 1990) of the task were to identify and sequentiate different types of activities (i.e. content-related discussion and decisions, writing text) and to identify which parts of the task had to be solved together and which could be dealt with individually. A 2 x 2 design with eight dyads of participants in each cell was implemented varying the following factors: (1) A high-end videoconferencing system with shared text-editor was compared with a more "conservative" system, including e-mail and an audio connection (via telephone). (2) A condition with prescribed collaboration phases was compared with an unscripted condition. In the scripted condition, the goal was to foster an optimal coordination of the collaborative work.

With regard to the *quality of the final solution* the telephone and e-mail conditions turned out to be significantly better than the videoconferencing conditions. The differences in the unscripted conditions can be illuminated by looking at the *collaborative process* itself. In the unscripted condition with telephone and e-mail all work patterns showed collaborative <u>and</u> individual work phases, whereas some dyads in the condition with videoconference and shared text-editor tended to work <u>only</u> collaboratively (4 of 8 dyads). The difference between the two conditions was significant (Chi=5.33, F=1, p=.02). The best explanation of this finding might be that in the videoconference condition the strong support of joint activities kept some dyads from task division and working individually. The result is corroborated by a lower quality of final solutions for those dyads that did not work individually at any time: They produced poorer solutions (AM=.31 percent of met criteria) than dyads working both, jointly and individually (AM=.39). This result is statistically significant (t=1.89, F=1, p=.04, onesided). It is in line with the result, that the scripted collaboration with phases of individual and joint work yielded better solutions.

These results indicate, that the coordination of individual working phases with phases of joint work is of central importance for the quality of the problem solving process and its outcome. However, while a prescription of coordination might work in the initial phase of a collaboration it seems not to be a very promising strategy for longer periods of collaborative work. Therefore, in a second experiment we pursued the goal to have dyads of participants with complementary domain knowledge acquire collaborative competence.

EXPERIMENT 2: VICARIOUS LEARNING FROM WORKED-OUT EXAMPLES OF COMPUTER-MEDIATED COLLABORATION

In the second study, a new instructional measure for promoting the coordination of computer-mediated synchronous collaboration was introduced, which integrates (1) the concept of worked-out examples (e.g. Renkl, 1997), and (2) that of vicarious learning from dialogue and discourse (Stenning, McKendree, Cox, Dineen & Mayes, 1999). The learning effect of a worked-out case study – presented as a model of an ideal collaboration – on process and outcome of a subsequent computer-mediated collaboration (application phase) was to be analyzed and compared to the <u>learning effect</u> of scripted collaborative problem-solving and the performance of a control group. Vicarious learning from the modeled collaboration was expected to promote students competence to collaborate during the application phase. In comparison, scripted collaboration is known to be an efficient method to support collaboration online. However, the question was whether it had the potential to trigger learning and promote the competence for collaborative work and its coordination. The design of the study is shown in the table below. Two experimental groups and one control group were formed consisting of nine dyads each.

		Vicarious learning from an exemplary worked-out collaboration	**Learning from scripted collaborative problem-solving**	**Control group**
30 min.	**Technical instruction**	✔	✔	✔
15 min.	**Material (case study 1)**	✔	✔	–
120 min.	**Experimental learning phase (case study 1)**	observing a worked-out modeled collaboration	scripted collaboration	–
15 min.	**Material (case study 2)**	✔	✔	✔
120 min.	**Application phase (case study 2)**	free collaboration	free collaboration	Free collaboration
30 min.	**Posttest**	✔	✔	✔

Process and outcome of the dyads' collaboration during the application phase of the experiment were analyzed to investigate the learning effects of the two experimental variations on the promotion of the competence for the coordination of computer-mediated collaborative work and its outcome. To gain information about the *collaborative process*, log-files taken during the application phase were analyzed to identify patterns of individual and joint phases of work. The amount of individual work (in minutes) has been found to decrease from the vicarious learning condition (M = 52,8) to scripted collaboration condition (M = 44,6) and the control condition (M = 40,7). Moreover, the control group showed strongly diverging patterns ($SD_{control} = 28.64$; $SD_{scripted\ collaboration\ learning} = 12.43$; $SD_{vicarious\ learning} = 11.86$) . To corroborate this finding, the difference between model pattern and empirical patterns was analyzed statistically. The exemplary (optimal) length of individual work phases was compared with the empirical data by computing the absolute differences ($M_{vicarious\ learning} = 9.33$; SD = 7.92; $M_{scripted\ collaboration\ learning} = 13.33$; SD = 11.35; $M_{control} = 26.56$; SD = 18.08). The result shows a significantly higher deviation for the control condition and the scripted collaboration learning condition compared to the vicarious learning condition ($F (2,40) = 4.23$; $p < .05$).

Obviously, dyads in the vicarious learning condition learned from the modeled collaboration and therefore showed a coordination pattern similar to the one presented to them in the worked-out example. In comparison, dyads in the scripted collaboration group transferred less from the first (scripted) to the second (unscripted) collaboration. In the control group a considerable amount of collaboration patterns showed much joint activity and not enough parallel individual work, but also a great deal of variance with regard to these variables. It has yet to be proven whether these firsts results can be confirmed by the results for the *quality of the joint solution* as well as the performance on the *posttest*. Further results on those dependent variables will be presented at the conference.

REFERENCES

Hermann, F., Rummel, N., & Spada, H. (2001). Solving the Case Together: the Challenge of Net- based Interdisciplinary Collaboration. In P. Dillenbourg, A. Eurelings, & K. Hakkarainen (Eds.), *Proceedings of the First European Conference on Computer-Supported Collaborative Learning*. Maastricht, NL.

Malone, T.W. & Crowston, K. (1990). What is coordination theory and how can it help design cooperative work systems? In F. Halasz (Ed.) *Proceedings of the Conference on Computer- Supported Cooperative Work* (pp. 357-370). Los Angeles, CA: Association for Computing Machinery.

Renkl, A. (1997). Learning from worked-out examples: A study on individual differences. *Cognitive Science*, 21, 1-29.

Stenning, K., McKendree, J., Cox, R., Dineen, F. & Mayes, T. (1999). Vicarious learning from educational dialogue. In C. Hoadley & J. Roschelle (Eds.), *Proceedings of the Computer Support for Collaborative Learning (CSCL) 1999 Conference*. Mahwah, NJ: Lawrence Erlbaum Associates.

An Experiment using Software Agents for Dialogue Analysis in Collaborative Distance Learning

Patricia Augustin Jaques pjaques@inf.ufrgs.br PPGC-UFRGS – Brazil

Flavio Moreira de Oliveira flavio@inf.pucrs.br PPGCC – PUCRS - Brazil

Rosa Maria Vicari rosa@inf.ufrgs.br PPGC-UFRGS - Brazil

ABSTRACT

Trends in distance education show a growing emphasis in collaborative learning, stimulating students to exchange ideas and information. A collaborative environment, however, will demand a higher effort from the teacher, who will supervise all discussions among learners, so that they do not deviate from the intended topic for a lesson. Moreover, the information proceeding from interactions among students will provide to the teacher features that allow an individual evaluation of each student and his course. In this way, this paper describes a first experience using a multi-agent architecture that is able to monitor communication tools in a distance-learning group.

KEYWORDS: CSCL, Educational Dialogue Interaction Analysis, Software Agents.

MOTIVATION

The motivation for the development of the system that we propose here resulted from some interactions with distance learning educators (we had the assistance of some distance learning teachers of Pontifical Catholic University of Rio Grande do Sul - PUCRS). It was observed that there were not tools to aid a teacher to monitor the interactions among students. According to the educators, collaborative classes generate a great number of interactions, which is difficult for the teacher to monitor, and it results in little time to accomplish other important tasks in the class. Therefore, we decided to implement a multi-agent system to monitor and analyze collaboration that provides to the teacher information that will help him/her in the evaluation of the students and of his/her course.

SYSTEM SPECIFICATION

The multi-agent system proposed is composed of four agents. Three of them, witch we call collecting agents, are responsible for gatheringdata on the messages generated by the collaboration tools: discussion list, newsgroup and chat. There is an agent responsible for each tool. The fourth agent, the teacher's agent, when asked by the teacher, requests analysis made by other agents and shows them to the teacher.

Each agent has its own local database, which stores the collecting data. After this process of data collecting, that is periodic, the agent does the analysis. When the teacher decides to see the analysis, he will ask to the teacher's agent. That agent will request to the others agents that will send the name and the address of the file containing the analysis. The teacher's agent will do a local copy of the file and will show the analysis to the teacher. The collecting agents are located in the teacher's local folder, where the e-mail and the newsgroup's messages are stored, and can be installed in any machine chosen by the teacher.

INFORMATION COLLECTING

While reading new messages, the collecting agents look for data that will be used for posterior analysis. This information is stored in a database that has the following fields: ID (message identifier), Sender, Reply (it identifies a news thread), Subjects, Sub-subjects, Date, Time and Tool (chat, news or discussions list).

The subjects and sub-subjects are identified in the messages subject (just in e-mails or news) or by keywords in the message content. The agents consider as keywords all the nouns found in the text. In order to check the syntactic and morphological meaning of these words we are using a lexical-morphological (Lexicon) dictionary of the Lexis project (Lima, 1997) and a thesaurus that is supplied by the system.

DATA ANALYSIS

In the next step, the collecting agents do the analysis, based on data stored in their databases. The period of the analysis can be **default** (which analyzes all messages sent after the last analysis), or teacher can ask interaction analysis that happened in a certain **period** of time. There are three kinds of associations that can be identified by the agent in the analysis:

<u>Student-student</u>: It identifies which students interact more with each other.

<u>Student-subject</u>: The agent gets information about which subjects each student discusses more.

<u>Student-student-subject</u>: The agent identifies which subjects are of greater interest for a specific group of students.

Besides all associations mentioned above, it is possible to have access to some statistical analysis based on data gathered in on the messages. At a first moment, the information originated from the analysis is exhibited as table charts.

More details about the specification of the system can be obtained in (Jaques & Oliveira , 1999).

VALIDATION AND CONCLUSION

For the implementation of the system proposed, we used the Java Agent Template framework (JAT) version 0.3 (http://java.stanford.edu). All functionalities of the agents were implemented using the Java language (http://java.sun.com).

The proposed system was used for the analysis of chat interactions in the virtual discipline of Introduction to Computer Science of the PUCRS (http://www.pucrs.br). For the prototype's validation, the system was used to analyze chat meetings' logs of a virtual group. Messages were in Portuguese.

The analysis of the interactions of the virtual group allowed us to observe that the architecture and the types of analysis showed are appropriate for the desired objective of supplying information to the teacher that is able to aid him/her to monitor its student's interaction. It does not fit to the system to be the only evaluation mechanism of collaboration among students. The teacher's final evaluation and accompaniment are indispensable. The tool, however, can be used as an aid resource to the teacher.

We observed, also, that the analysis would be more precise to the related subjects if some deeper method of semantic analysis, i.e. discourse analysis (Grosz and Sidner, 1986), were used instead of keyword search.

The validation allowed us to observe that new aspects should be considered for larger efficiency of the system:

Expressions: Some subjects are formed for more than one word and they lose the meaning when it is just considered one of the words. For example: programming language.

Orthographic Mistakes: The language used by the students in the interaction tools is quite informal and has many orthographic mistakes and abbreviations that are not considerate by the agents. A possible solution is to create an agent that performs orthographic correction of the messages before they be analyzed.

Improvement of the interface of the Teacher's Agent: The teacher's agent shows the results of the analysis in text, in a simple way. To provide better visualization of the results for the teacher, the interface can be improved inserting hypertext mechanisms that would allow to the teacher to link among the available information.

On-line Prototype: Currently, the agent accomplishes the analysis of the log files of chat meeting. Another way would be the agent to work on-line, where he/she is connected to a virtual conference (chat meeting) and, during the section, it does the analysis and it show the results in the moment in that the conference is happening.

The limitations observed in this work, help us to model a new online system that will analyze the student's messages; and assist and guide the students in communication collaborative tools. This system is modeled as an animated pedagogical agent and it is part of the multi-agent architecture of the project "A Computational Model of Distance Learning Based in the Socio-Cultural Approaches" (Jaques et al., 2002).

REFERENCES

Andrade, A. F.; Jaques, P. A.; Vicari, R. M.; Bordini, R.; Jung, J. (2001) A Computational Model of Distance Learning Based on Vygotsky's Socio-Cultural Approach. *Proceedings of the MABLE Workshop* (San Antonio, Texas, May 19-23). X International Conference on Artificial Intelligence on Education.

Grosz, B.; Sidner, C. (1986) Attention, Intentions, and the Structure of Discourse. *Computational Linguistics,* Cambridge, v.12, n.3, p.175-204.

Jaques, P. A.; Andrade, A. F.; Vicari, R. M.; Bordini, R.; Jung, J. (2001) Pedagogical Agents to Support Collaborative Distance Learning. Proceedings of CSCL 2002. Colorado, EUA.

Jaques, P.; Oliveira, F. (1999) Software Agents for Analysis of Collaboration in a Virtual Classroom. Proceedings of AI-ED99. Le mans: L'Université du Maine.

Lima, V. L. S. de; Abrahão, P. R.; Paraboni, I. (1997) Approaching the dictionary in the implementation of a natural language processing system: toward a distributed structure. In: Workshop on String Processing. Valparaiso.

Using EPO to Stimulate Learning in the Health Sciences

Leo Plugge*, Paul Kirschner, Gaby Lutgens, Jan Vermunt

Stichting SURF / Maastricht University

plugge@surf.nl / *paul.kirschner@facburfdaw.unimaas.nl* / *g.lutgens@mmi.unimaas.nl* / *j.vermunt@educ.unimaas.nl*

ABSTRACT

Maastricht University is renowned for its use of Problem Based Learning (PBL) as the primary educational form since 1976. Although PBL has been immensely successful (Schmidt, 2001) it also has its drawbacks, such as the paucity of 'real' collaboration. This article describes an educational experiment aimed at implementing Project Centered Learning (PCL) for part-time students at the Health Sciences faculty supported by an Electronic Project Environment (EPO in Dutch). The results show that PCL is a good educational method for third year students in the Health Sciences and that the EPO offers a valuable support to the group work of these students who live all over the country. The study also reveals some aspects of PCL and EPO that need rethinking and possibly revision in further experiments.

Keywords

Collaborative learning, Project-centered learning, Computer Supported Collaborative Learning, Distributed learning groups, Part-time students, Health Sciences

INTRODUCTION

Problem Based Education (Barrows & Tamblyn, 1980) has been the central tenet of education at Maastricht University (MU) since its inception. While still successful, educational designers are beginning to question whether this educational method is suitable in teaching students to rely more on each other to find relevant information for solving new problems. To make thing even more complicated, these new problems are usually ill defined requiring excellent group decision-making skills.

One alternative to PBL is Project Centered Learning (PCL). PCL activates students to learn both the content and the processes of their chosen field by having them work collaboratively in teams on a project to deliver a product within a well-defined time span. Not only are the projects authentic, but also the work situation is authentic. Students work in teams performing the roles that they would perform if they were actually in a working environment.

This contribution describes an experiment in which a commercially available electronic project environment (EPO) was used to facilitate PCL with two groups of third year part-time students at the Health Sciences faculty at MU. The environment is based on the Basic Support for Cooperative Work project of the German National Research Center for Information technology. (Appelt, 1999; Bentley et. al, 1997) The primary goals of the experiment were to increase collaboration and active studying behavior. The students in this study are geographically dispersed, work differing shifts, meet only once a week, and have hardly any contact with each other between the meetings.

METHODS

Twelve third year part-time students from the Health Sciences faculty (3 males, 9 females) took the course *Making decisions about healthcare*. The students were randomly divided into two groups of six persons. Additionally, a tutor and a technical assistant were assigned to each group.

The project environment consisted of a private and a group space. The group space contained a document archive, discussion forum, project calendar, task and Gantt planning facility, contacts, participant's directory, wastebasket, group announcements, and web based help system. The environment is accessible through a web browser.

The course was consisted of three subprojects. The final task required an integration of the previous two subprojects. Each subproject ended with a joint report and an oral presentation by the members of the group. The course lasted for 64 days; each subproject approximately 3 weeks. Meetings took place on a Friday every fortnight.

To evaluate the experiment, three measurements took place: pre-experimental, intermediate, and post-experimental (all questionnaires). The first questionnaire contained items from the Computer Attitude Scale (CAS) (Nickel & Pinto, 1987), and from the Computer Understanding and Experience Scale (CUE) (Potosky & Bobko, 1998). Additionally, data was gathered from the daily activity logs produced by the electronic project environment.

---

* Requests for reprints should be addressed to Dr. L.A. Plugge, Stichting SURF, P.O.Box 2290, 3500 GG Utrecht, The Netherlands

RESULTS

The results show that the experiment was successful in many ways, while at the same time providing insight into the problems of PCL that need to be resolved.

First, there is the pleasure the students reported about working in teams on a project. They enjoyed working together on an end product, and it stimulated them to combine theory and praxis. The students also reported that the study time was higher than in PBL, that it stimulated discussion more, and appealed more to relevant professional skills than PBL. However, the students also reported that the theoretical knowledge acquired was fragmented. The cause behind this feeling of fragmentation is the division of labor during the project. Each student studied a different part of the subject and had to rely on reports from others.

The EPO proved to be a very good means of supporting asynchronous collaboration. The results clearly show that the students appreciated the EPO capabilities to exchange documents, discuss problems and plan their activities. It is interesting to note, that the students' mediocre computer skills did not affect their achievements in a negative way. They experienced EPO as a useful tool and fun to work with. In other words, contrary to what is often reported, computer skills are not a dominant factor of success in using an electronic environment.

Finally, the results showed that the students clearly had to get used to this open-ended type of education. They had to learn how to plan their study, they had to spend more time studying, and that it broke up their normal studying routine. This was, however, exactly one of the objectives of the experiment.

CONCLUSIONS

Overall, the educational model, the project work and the collaboration all appreciated highly by the students, as well as the EPO. The experiment succeeded in increasing time spent on studying and in spreading study activities across the whole week. In general then, it can be concluded that this experiment met its objectives. PCL turned out to be a good educational method for third year students in the Health Sciences and the EPO offered a valuable support to the group work of these part time students who lived all over the country. However, there is room for improvement concerning the fragmentation of the acquired knowledge, the clarity of the learning objectives, and the size of the projects. Some questions remain. This study was done with part time students who lived far apart from each other. This does not mean that the EPO works in the same way for full time students who meet each other frequently in the faculty buildings. A next experiment will address this issue.

REFERENCES

Schmidt, H. (2001). 3900 Alumni geven hun mening: Effecten van probleemgestuurd onderwijs na het afstuderen [3900 alumni give their opinion: Effects of problem based education after graduation]. *MCMLXXVI-MMI*. Jubileum book on the 25th anniversary of the university. Maastricht: Universiteit Maastricht.

Barrows, H. S., & Tamblyn, R. M. (1980). *Problem-based learning: An approach to medical education*. New York, NY: Springer Verlag.

Appelt, W. (1999) WWW Based Collaboration with the BSCW System. *Proceedings of SOFSEM'99*, Springer Lecture Notes in Computer Science 1725, p.66-78.

Nickel, G.S., and Pinto, J.N. (1986) The Computer Attitude Scale. *Computers in Human Behavior,* 2: 301-306.

Potosky, D. & Bobko, P. (1998). The Computer Understanding and Experience Scale: A self-report measure of computer experience. *Computers in Human Behavior,* **14**, 2: 337-348.

Synchronizing Group Interactions with Lecturing Video in Agent-based Asynchronous Virtual Classroom

Hiroaki Ogata, Kenji Matsuura, Yoneo Yano
Faculty of Engineering, Tokushima University
2-1, Minamijosanjima, Tokushima, 770-8506, Japan
Email: ogata@is.tokushima-u.ac.jp
URL: http://cscl.is.tokushima-u.ac.jp/ogata

ABSTRACT

This paper tackles to develop and evaluate the asynchronous virtual classroom, called AVC, which enables learners to participate in at anytime and from anywhere. Its environment provides on-demand multimedia learning-materials, e.g. videos of the lecture, slides and web pages. To utilize the two types of learning resources, on-demand materials and asynchronous interactions, the system synchronizes links and reproduces them toward efficient learning. To realize that, a software agent participates to the classroom behalf of a real learner and replays the past interactions along with the video. Besides this, we propose the model that a software agent recommends the suitable interactions for the current learner according to his/her interest.

Keywords
Asynchronous virtual classroom, Video on demand, Collaborative annotation, and Software agent.

INTRODUCTION

We have proposed the system, called AVC (Asynchronous Virtual Classroom), which allows learners to use at anytime and anywhere (Matsuura et al., 1999; 2000). The system provides multimedia learning materials, e.g., video of the lecture, slides, and text-based communication tools such as a bulletin board system. The basic idea is that the AVC system enables learners to share the past interactions about the leaning material, and reuses them appropriately for the later participants. To utilize the past action logs (question, answer, and annotation) that were stored in the same classroom, the system employs a software agent, which simulates the past interactions as an animation. In the reproduction, each statement appears on a series of relative time in the virtual classroom. The past activities have to be synchronized with the learning material. As is often case with an asynchronous system, it is easily figured out that the difficult situation to communicate with others (e.g., unless anyone asks another person, none exists at the same time) will occur among asynchronous participants (Ogata et al, 1996; 2000). Therefore, the system bridges asynchronous participants by notifying others' activities in her/his absence at the same classroom and by reproducing their activities in order of the relative timestamp when s/he joins the same classroom again.

Through the past experimental use, we found a critical problem to be solved that the subsequent learners often felt stress to read past discussions with a video. This problem was caused in a case that many topics were included in one discussion room and some contexts appeared at random based on absolute timestamp. However, this was originated from the framework itself essentially. The most characteristic point of the AVC system is to synchronize the past interactions with on-demand learning materials. In other words, the system must update the contents of the past interactions on the video's time-line. Nevertheless, both of them have their own time span. Hence, this paper proposes the new idea to solve this problem, which is the adaptive support for synchronizing interactions with on-demand video-based learning materials in an asynchronous virtual classroom.

Figure 1 shows an example of AVC interface. A learner can watch on the video in frame (A), where the learner can control the video, e.g., jumping to a video section. Frame (B) shows slides or web pages of the lecture with the video synchronized. The learner can annotate on them. Frame (C) and frame (D) shows a 3D virtual classroom. The learner can walk around in the virtual space. Frame (E) shows the animated reproduction of the asynchronous dialogues among learners along with the video time line. The system sorts out the discussions based on her/his curiosity. In this frame, the picture of each user is shown in the left side and his/her statement is shown in the left side. A learner can add the statement by clicking one of the statements in (E). Moreover, the leaner can enter the statement in frame (F) after stopping the video and selecting the type of his/her agent's face and its behavior and the type of statements. In this way, the asynchronous dialogues can augment.

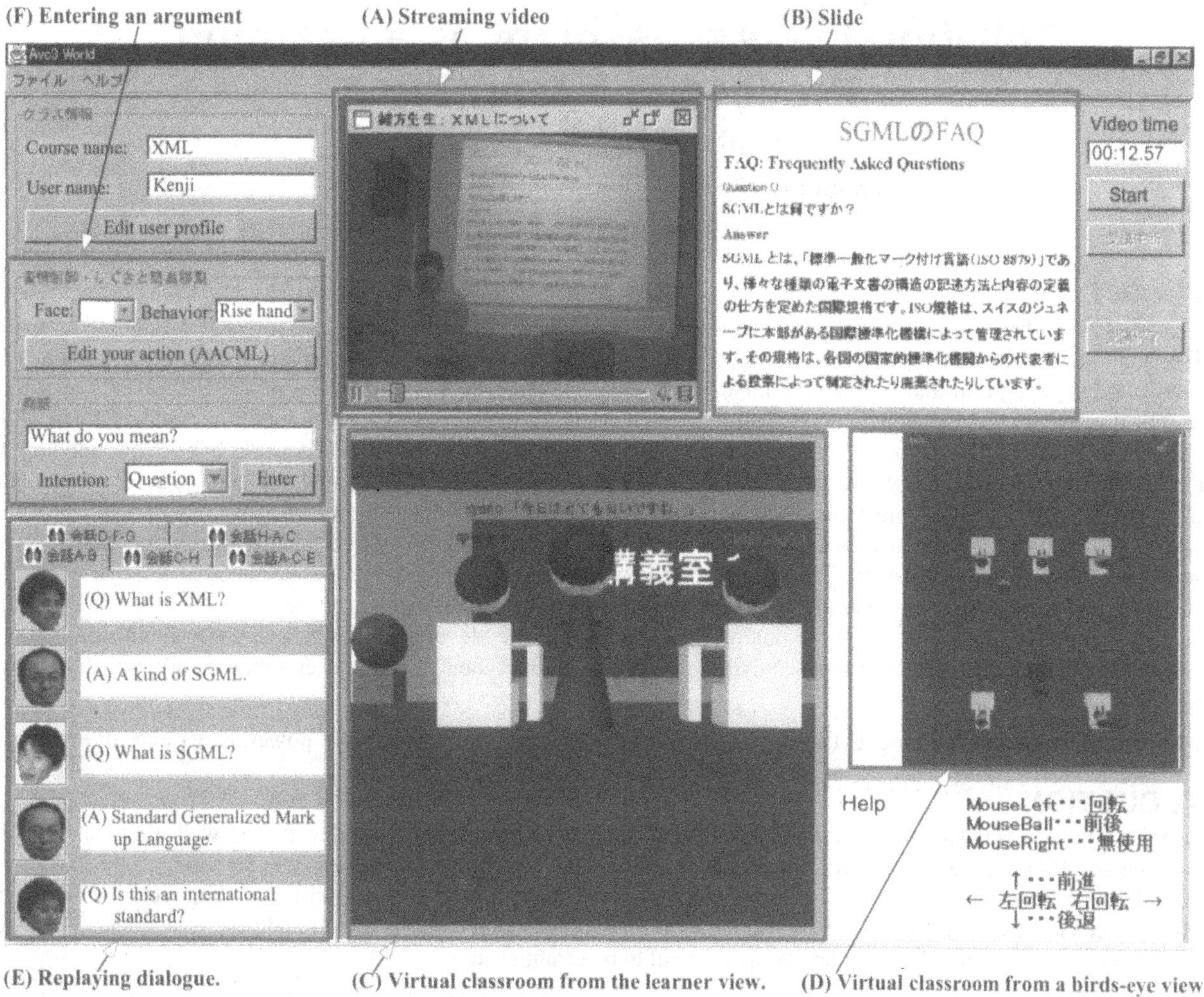

Figure 1: A screen snapshot of AVC.

CONCLUDING REMARKS

This paper introduces the interface agent to act for real learners in a same classroom. This agent reproduces the past interactions to the current learner on behalf of the absentees. These reproduced dialogues are sorted based on the priority of each learner's curiosity and filtered by the time span of section of the video. This work was partly supported by the grant to the research project at Doshisha University named "Intelligent Information Science and It's Applications to Problem Solving in Engineering Fields", and the Grant-in-Aid for Scientific Research No.13780121, No.12558011, and No.11878032 from the Ministry of Education, Science, Sports and Culture, Japan, from the Ministry of Education.

REFERENCES

Matsuura, K., Ogata, H., & Yano, Y. (1999). Agent-based Asynchronous Virtual Classroom, Proceedings of International Conference on Computers in Education 1999, in Cumming, G., Okamoto, T., Gomez, L., (Eds.), Advanced research in computers and communications in education, Vol.1, pp.133-140.

Matsuura, K., Ogata, H., & Yano, Y. (2000). Agent's contribution for an Asynchronous Virtual Classroom, Proceedings of ITS 2000, in Gauthier, G., Frasson, C., VanLehn, K. (Eds.), LNCS1839, Intelligent Tutoring Systems, pp.344-353.

Ogata, H., Matsuura, K., & Yano, Y. (1996). Knowledge Awareness: Bridging between Shared Knowledge and Collaboration in Sharlok, Proceedings of Educational Telecommunications 1996, pp.232-237.

Ogata, H. & Yano, Y. (2000) Combining Knowledge Awareness and Information Filtering in an Open-ended Collaborative Learning Environment, International Journal of Artificial Intelligence in Education, Vol.11, pp.33-46.

Collaborative Assessment as a Learning Process in E-learning

David McConnell

School of Education, University of Sheffield

d.mcconnell@sheffield.ac.uk

ABSTRACT

This paper examines the various ways in which students talk about their experience and perceptions of collaborative review and assessment as it occurs in e- learning environments. Collaborative review and assessment involves the student, their peers and tutor in thoughtful and critical examination of each student's course work. The process involves two stages: review and discussion of the student's work with a view to bringing different critical yet supportive perspectives to the work. This is followed by the use of two sets of criteria to make judgements on the student's work: one set provided by the student, the other by the tutor. The purpose of collaborative assessment is to foster a learning approach to assessment and to develop a shared power relationship with students. From analysis of face to face interviews, examination of e-learning discussions and student completed questionnaires, a set of analytic categories was developed describing the learners' experiences of collaborative assessment. The paper focuses on analysing and discussing these categories of experience. The research shows that collaborative e-learning assessment helps students move away from dependence on lecturers as the only or major source of judgement about the quality of learning. Students develop skill and know how about self and peer assessment and see themselves as competent in making judgements about their own and each other's work, which are good lifelong learning skills.

Keywords: collaborative e-learning; collaborative assessment; assessment criteria; shared power; experience of learning.

INTRODUCTION

The case for involving students in some form of self and peer assessment in higher education is well established in the literature (eg see Boud, 1995, 2000; McConnell, 1999, 2000; McDowell and Sambell, 1999; Somerville, 1993; Stefani, 1998). Student involvement in their own assessment is an important part of the preparation for life and work. Although by no means universal, there is now a wider belief in the educational and social benefits of self and peer assessment. The place of self and peer assessment in e-learning has, however, still to be established.

What effects, if any, does self and peer assessment have on students approaches to learning? If students are actively involved in decisions about how to learn and what to learn and why they are learning. And if they are actively involved in decisions about criteria for assessment and the process of judging their own and others work, then their relationship to their studies will probably be qualitatively different to those students who are treated as recipients of teaching and who are the object of others' unilateral, assessment. Because students in cooperative and collaborative learning situations make important decisions about their learning and assessment, there will be no need for them to seek cues from staff about assessment or seek to find ways of "playing" the system. They determine the system themselves, in negotiation with other students and staff.

How does this work in practice, and what do students think about this form of assessment? The categories under which students' experiences are analysed and discussed include:

- From unilateral to collaborative assessment
- Enjoyment, frankness, anxiety and tension
- Responsibility to others and submission of assignments
- The development of collaborative assessment skills
- Insights into assessment
- Access to others' learning
- Motivation to learn
- Intrinsic versus extrinsic validation of learning

CONCLUSIONS

Collaborative assessment in e-learning communities is not only possible it is desirable. It supports the collaborative work of the community. It is not merely a technique to be applied to students, but a value-laden approach to learning and teaching which seeks to involve students in decision making about the assessment process and how to make judgements on their own and each others learning. It is an integral part of a whole with many benefits for those participating in it. Above all else, it seeks to foster a learning approach to assessment.

This research indicates that students involved in collaborative e-assessment actively and critically reflect on their learning and on the benefits of collaborative assessment. It also shows that these new Web-based electronic learning environments are well placed to support the complexity of this form of assessment. The architecture of e-learning systems such as Web-CT supports students in the reflective learning and assessment process.

The outcomes of this research indicate that collaborative review and assessment helps students move-away from dependence on lecturers as the only or major source of judgement about the quality of their learning. They move to a more autonomous and independent situation where each individual develops the experience, know-how and skill to assess their own learning. It is likely that this skill can be transferred to other lifelong learning situations and contexts. Equipping learners with such skills should be a key aspect of the so-called "learning society" (Boud, 2000).

The openness of the collaborative assessment process is crucial to its success. Whereas most assessment techniques are closed, involving only the student and their teacher, collaborative assessment has to take place in an open environment. (cf Ames, 1992 (as quoted in Boud, 2000) who thinks all feedback should be private). As we have seen, learning relationships have to be fostered, and trust developed and maintained in order for collaborative assessment to succeed. The balance between critique and support is very important, yet at times very fragile. Peers and tutors are involved in collaborative learning and support throughout this course. But they are also called on to review and assess each others work. In a learning community or community of practice this is not only possible but it is desirable. We cannot bring in strangers to this community to assess learning. That would endanger the sense of community and undermine the learning relationships that each learning set has developed. The community' knows' itself and has developed a very strong sense of identity. But it also has to be able to reflect on its work, and be critical of each member's learning. This I think is achieved with some success in this particular context.

Overall this research shows the importance students attach to learning and assessment processes which take place in a social environment. This is a major theme, which is constantly referred to throughout the interviews and in the online discussions. Its importance cannot be over-stated. It is not only a major factor in supporting and motivating distant learners and in helping them overcome feelings of isolation. It also points to the benefits of social constructivism and social co-participation in learning, especially in continuing professional development contexts. Not only do adult learners enjoy learning in social settings, they are quick to appreciate the potential benefits afforded by collaboration in the learning and assessment process. It is no less so in collaborative e-learning environments.

SELECTED REFERENCES

Boud, D. (1995). Enhancing Learning through Self Assessment. London, Kogan Page.

Boud, D. (2000). "Sustainable assessment: Rethinking assessment for a learning society." Studies in Continuing Education **22**(2): 151-167.

McConnell, D. (1999). " Examining a collaborative assessment process in networked lifelong learning." Journal of Computer Assisted Learning, **15**(September).

McConnell, D. (2000). Implementing Computer Supported Cooperative Learning. (2nd edition) London, Kogan Page.

McDowell, L., Sambell, K. (1999). Students Experience of Self Evaluation in Higher Education: Preparation for Lifelong Learning?, Paper presented at the Bi-annual conference of the European Association for Research on Learning and Instruction (EARLI), Gothenburg, August 24-28 1999

Somerville, H. (1993). "Issues in assessment, enterprise and Higher Education: the case for self-, peer and collaborative assessment." Assessment and Evaluation in Higher Education **18**(3): 221-233.

Stefani, L. (1998). " Assessment in Partnership with Learners." Assessment and Evaluation in Higher Education **23**(339-350).

Developing Cognitive Prerequisites to Support Inquiry Learning in a Computer Environment

Alla Keselman, Deanna Kuhn

Post-Doctoral Fellow
Department of Medical Informatics
Columbia University
ak454@columbia.edu

Professor
Teachers College
Columbia University
dk100@columbia.edu

ABSTRACT

Present work describes an intervention, which improves students' inquiry learning skills by facilitating their understanding of multivaraible causality.

Keywords

Inquiry learning, knowledge acquisition, scientific reasoning, metacognition, mental models, goal-based scenarios

INTRODUCTION

Inquiry learning is an educational method, in which students engage in authentic scientific investigation activities. Typically, such activities involve exploring multivariable causal systems, with the goal of inferring causal relationships among the variables. The popularity of the method is reinforced by the advent of technology in schools. Through computer simulations, students can access complex biological, environmental and social systems, previously inaccessible to school labs. Yet, psychological research on scientific thinking warns educators that children and adolescents often experience difficulties with various stages of experimentation. They generate imprecise hypotheses, design inconclusive experiments, and tend to reject or misinterpret data that does not fit into their pre-existing theories (Kuhn, Zohar, Andersen & Garcia-Mila, 1995). Attempts to provide direct instruction in experimental strategies typically result in a very limited transfer of skills. Kuhn (in press) suggests that students' difficulties with scientific investigations extend beyond the level of performance, reaching into the meta-level. What is lacking is a clear understanding of task objectives, and metastrategic competence in selecting and monitoring performance-level strategies. Recent work, conducted by Kuhn and colleagues (Kuhn, Black, Keselman & Kaplan, 2001) suggests that many adolescents may also have deficient models of multivariable causality, in which the effects of individual variables are neither additive nor consistent. The present study is an attempt to strengthen students' scientific reasoning skills by improving their meta-level understanding of experimentation and refining their models of multivariable causality. Over the period of seven weeks, three groups of students engaged in a computer exercise, with the objective of identifying environmental features associated with earthquake risk. All students worked in rotating dyads, thus strengthening their mastery of strategies through externalized cognition. For the students in the control condition, their work was limited to engaging in the performance level exercise. Students in the practice condition received some support, aimed at improving their understanding of causality. Finally, students in the instructional condition received the most support. We hypothesized that by the end of the study, students from the instructional condition will show the greatest improvement in their scientific thinking skills, followed by the practice group students.

METHOD

The study followed pretest-intervention-posttest design. Participants in the study were seventy-four students from three six-grade science classes of a New York City public middle school. One class was assigned to each of the three study conditions. The main task in which students engaged repeatedly in the course of 5-7 sessions was a Macromedia Director computer program called Earthquake Forecaster. The task presented a multivariable environment characterized by 5 features (type of bedrock, snake activity, radon gas levels, water quality and s-wave rates) potentially instrumental in affecting the outcome – the risk of an earthquake. Each feature could assume one of the two possible levels (e.g., low or high), while the outcome assumed 4 levels (low, medium-low, medium-high and high). In a goal-based scenario, students were placed in the position of junior earthquake forecasters. They had to find out which of the five features played a role in causing earthquakes and learn to predict earthquake risk. Students investigated the environment by varying levels of the 5 features and observing resulting outcomes. In addition to participating in the main task exercise, students from the practice and instructional conditions also engaged in weekly paper-and-pencil prediction practice exercises. The exercises involved making and justifying risk predictions for Earthquake Forecaster instances presented by the researchers. The aim of the prediction exercise was to reinforce the understanding of the additive nature of multivariable causality. In addition to the main task and the prediction practice, students from the instructional condition also received weekly instruction in making predictions of flood risk, aimed at advancing their models of multivariable causality. In these sessions, the primary investigator modeled combining the effects of all causal features in order to derive the outcome. To equate time on task, students from the control and practice groups engaged in weekly discussions of scientific studies, relevant to middle school curriculum.

RESULTS AND DISCUSSION

After viewing each instance of the program, students had an opportunity to draw inferences about the features of the system. In analyzing the results, we relied on Kuhn's theory of knowledge acquisition (Kuhn et al., 1995). This theory suggests that students whose knowledge acquisition skills are weak have difficulty distinguishing between theory and evidence as the sources of knowledge, and using evidence to modify their theories. At this early point of the continuum, students are likely to state that something is true, because they "just know it." The experimental evidence is not implicated. At a somewhat more sophisticated level, students begin to appreciate the role of the evidence in the process of knowledge acquisition. Yet, they view a single experimental instance as providing sufficient information to draw conclusions about all the features of the system. The next step in knowledge acquisition skills involves making inferences based on comparisons (albeit uncontrolled) of instances. Finally, the most sophisticated level requires designing a controlled comparison between two instances, and subsequently drawing a correct inference about the feature under investigation.

As hypothesized for the present study, the gain in scientific reasoning skills was greatest in the instructional condition, followed by the practice condition. Yet, results of the study suggest that students from all three conditions derived benefit from participation. Repeated measures ANOVA yielded overall significant time effect for the number of unique instances students viewed within a program run, the proportion of evidence-based responses and the number of valid inferences about the causal status of the program features. This suggests that repeated engagement in self-directed investigations alone may lead to some improvement in students' scientific skills. This finding is consistent with previous research on scientific thinking (Kuhn, Zohar, Andersen & Garcia-Mila, 1995). Use of the evidence, however, was greater in the practice and instructional than in the control condition. For example, although students from all conditions showed pre- to posttest increase in the proportion of evidence-based responses, the improvement was greater in the practice and instructional conditions. Moreover, students from the instructional, but not from the practice and control conditions, demonstrated an improvement in the number of inferences, drawn on the basis of multiple records. This suggests that an intervention that drew the students' attention to the additive and consistent nature of individual effects in multivariable systems improved their understanding of the role of comparisons in experimentation. This improvement was maintained in a transfer task. Finally, as a result of their superior investigation strategies, students from the instructional group also showed a pre- to posttest improvement in their knowledge about the causal status of the features of the program.

Overall, this work supports the notion that both metacognitive understanding of task objectives and strategies as well as normative models of multivariable causality serve as prerequisites for developing scientific reasoning skills. Consequently, both need to be present in an effective intervention that aims to support students' inquiry learning. Future studies may focus on the interaction between metacognition and the understanding of causality, and on the process of development of normative causality models.

REFERENCES

Kuhn, D. (in press). Why development does (and doesn't) occur: Evidence from the domain of inductive reasoning. In R. Siegler & J. McClelland, eds., *Mechanisms of cognitive development: Neural and behavioral perspectives.* Mahwah NJ: Erlbaum.

Kuhn, D., Black, J., Keselman A., & Kaplan, D. (2000). The development of cognitive skills to support inquiry learning. *Cognition and Instruction, 18*, 495-523.

Kuhn, D., Garcia-Mila, M., Zohar, A., & Andersen, C. (1995). Strategies of knowledge acquisition. *Monographs of the Society for Research in Child Development*, 60(4, Serial No. 245).

Interactive Representations for Reflection in Group Simulations

Mike Dobson , Julie-Ann Sime, Michael Pengelly

Lancaster University

m.dobson@lancaster.ac.uk

ABSTRACT

A set of tools is presented within the theoretical framework of activity systems that is designed and developed to reify the communication acts of team members to support reflective learning. An evaluation tests the acceptability of the tools used within two multi-agent virtual reality simulations. We explore the affordance of the tools and issues around their acceptability in two experimental user populations.

Building and Maintaining the Common Ground in Web-Based Interaction

Kati Mäkitalo, Päivi Häkkinen
University of Jyväskylä, Finland
kati.makitalo@ktl.jyu.fi
Piritta Salo, Sanna Järvelä
University of Oulu, Finland

ABSTRACT
In this paper, the main purpose is to explore how participants establish and maintain the common ground in the computer-based conferences. Previous studies assume that before the participants can reach the deeper level interaction and learning, they have to gain an adequate level of common ground (Dillenbourg, 1999; Baker et al., 1999; Veerman, 2000). Subjects were 68 pre-service teachers and 7 mentors from three universities who participated in the web-based conferencing course for eight weeks. The results assume that in deeper level discussions it is essential that participants, especially fellow students did give not only the evidence about their own understanding by using written feedback, but also give the support to their co-students and show their attitudinal reaction in their replies.

Keywords
Common ground, feedback, electronic discussion, grounding, web-based interaction

INTRODUCTION
An adequate level of mutual understanding is a prerequisite in collaborative learning activities. In order to construct the common ground, individuals share mutual understanding, knowledge, beliefs, assumptions and pre-suppositions. The common ground can be constructed and maintained during the interactive process called grounding, which requires a joint effort by participants who meet each other at the first time in computer-mediated communication environment. (Baker et al., 1999) At the beginning of interaction, mentioning of facts and proposals in the presence of another, processes of diagnosis and feedback are essential for building the common ground (Baker et al., 1999; Brennan, 1998). There are four communicative factors, which may arise problems in maintaining common ground: contact, perception, understanding and attitudinal reaction (Allwood et al., 1991). The purpose of this study is to increase knowledge about web-based interaction and learning by exploring the mechanisms of augmenting and maintaining the common ground.

METHODS
This study is a part of the Finnish research project SHAPE (Sharing and Making Perspectives in Virtual Interaction: Järvelä & Häkkinen, 2001; Saarenkunnas et al., 2000). The subjects of the study were pre-service teachers in the USA, University of Indiana (N=35), and Finland, Universities of Jyväskylä (N=12) and Oulu (N=21). The students' learning task was to construct and maintain their case discussion and to summarise the discussion in the middle of the computer-supported learning course period and also at the end of it by using an asynchronous web-based learning environment called ProTo.

DATA COLLECTION AND ANALYSIS
The data of this study contained 36 written case discussions. In each discussion there were from 4 to 26 messages, in total 449 messages. Multi-phase analysis procedure was used in the following way:

A level of discussions (Progressive and Deeper level discussions; Järvelä & Häkkinen, 2001)

Types of postings (Comment, Suggestion, Experience, New Point/Question, Theory)

Cross-references to the other postings

A type of feedback

RESULTS
Results show that 18 case discussions out of 36 were categorized to the progressive level and the other half to the deeper level discussions. The progressive level discussions involved plenty of comments, experience-based postings and postings with new points or questions and some cross-references. Deeper level discussions involved a lot of theory-based postings as well as new points or questions and plenty of cross-references. Results show that 49% of the total amount of postings included the written feedback of some kind. The number and type of students' feedback are reported in Table 1. The difference of the feedback used by students in different levels of discussions is statistically significant

(p=0.094). Especially, standardized residuals are statistically significant in the use of supporting feedback by students. There were no differences found in the feedback use of mentors in different levels of discussions or between students and mentors.

Table 1. The feedback use of students in progressive and deeper level discussions

Types of Feedback	**Progressive Level Discussions**	**Deeper Level Discussions**	**Total**
1. Agree/disagree feedback	39	29	68
	45,9%	30,9%	38,0%
2. Personal feedback	17	16	33
	20,0%	17,0%	18,4%
3. Notifying feedback	13	21	34
	15,3%	22,3%	19,0%
4. Supporting feedback*)	4	15	19
	4,7%	16,0%	10,6%
5. Comparative feedback	7	7	14
	8,2%	7,4%	7,8%
6. Explaining feedback	5	6	11
	5,9%	6,4%	6,1%
Total	85	94	179
	100,0%	100,0%	100,0%

Person Chi-Square Value=9.414, df=5, p=0.094<0.1 *)Standardized residuals are statistically significant

CONCLUSION

These results imply that students provided valuable peer feedback, particularly task- and social oriented supporting feedback, which might lead into the constructive discussion (See also; Hara et al., 2000). Further analysis of maintaining mechanisms of web-based discussion will be demonstrated in the presentation.

REFERENCES

Allwood, J., Nivre, J. & Ahlsén, E. 1991. On the Semantics and Pragmatics of Linguistic Feedback (Gothenburg Papers in Theoretical Linguistics No. 64). Sweden: University of Gothenburg, Department of Linguistics.

Baker, M., Hansen, T., Joiner, R. & Traum, D. (1999) The role of grounding in collaborative learning tasks. In P. Dillenbourg (Ed.) Collaborative learning. Cognitive and computational approaches. Advances in Learning and Instruction Series. Amsterdam: Pergamon, 31-63.

Brennan, S. E. (1998) The grounding problem in conversations with and through computers. In S. R. Fussell & R. J. Kreuz (Eds.) Social and cognitive approaches to interpersonal communication. Mahwal, NJ: Erlbaum, 201-225.

Dillenbourg, P. (1999) Introduction: What do you mean by "collaborative learning"? In P. Dillenbourg (Ed.) Collaborative learning. Cognitive and computational approaches. Advances in Learning and Instruction Series. Amsterdam: Pergamon, 1-19.

Hara, N., Bonk, C. J. & Angeli, C. 2000. Content analysis of online discussion in an applied educational psychology course. Instructional Science 28, 115-152.

Järvelä, S. & Häkkinen, P. (2001, in press) The levels of web-based discussions – using perspective-taking theory as an analysis tool. In H. Van Oostendorp (Ed.) Cognition in a digital world. Lawrence Erlbaum.

Saarenkunnas, M., Järvelä, S., Häkkinen, P., Kuure, L., Taalas, P. & Kunelius, E. (2000) NINTER – Networked Interaction: Theory-based cases in teaching and learning. Learning Environments Research 3, 35-50.

Fostering Computer Supported Collaborative Learning with Cooperation Scripts and Scaffolds

Armin Weinberger, Frank Fischer, Heinz Mandl

Institute of Educational Psychology, Ludwig-Maximilians-University of Munich, Leopoldstr. 13, 80802 Munich

weinberg@edupsy.uni-muenchen.de, fischerf@edupsy.uni-muenchen.de, mandl@edupsy.uni-muenchen.de

ABSTRACT

The study investigates collaborative learning of small groups via text-based computer-mediated communication. We analyzed how two approaches to pre-structure communication influence participation, individual knowledge transfer, the convergence of participation and the convergence of knowledge among peers. We varied the factor scripted cooperation and the factor scaffolding in a 2x2-design. 105 university students of Educational Psychology participated. Results show that scripted cooperation was most and scaffolding least beneficial to individual transfer, knowledge convergence and participation in comparison to open discourse.

Keywords

CSCL, knowledge convergence, shared knowledge, participation, scripted cooperation, scaffolding, cues, cued interaction, computer-mediated communication, text-based communication, case-based learning environments

BACKGROUND AND GOALS OF THE STUDY

In collaborative, problem-oriented learning environments groups of learners are supposed to discuss and solve cases in an active and reflective way. However, learning in open discussion rarely seems to result in equal and high participation and equally distributed high individual transfer. Studies on CSCL show that these negative effects are usually replicated or even increased in new, technology-rich learning environments (e.g. Fischer & Mandl, 2001). This study investigates instructional means (*scripted cooperation* and *scaffolding*) to support participation and individual transfer of knowledge in case-based CSCL environments. Moreover, we analyze to what extent convergence of participation and convergence of knowledge of the learning partners can be fostered in CSCL.

Text-based, computer-mediated communication offers the possibility to structure the learners' discourse and can be designed to guide users through certain successive activities (Scardamalia & Bereiter, 1996). Scaffolding and scripted cooperation can be implemented with cues that have been previously inserted into messages of learners in order to pre-structure communication and possibly influence reflection and thereby also learning outcomes. These methods may substitute extensive training and adaptive feedback by co-present experts. On this background, the study investigates the effects of cued scaffolding and scripted cooperation and their combination with regard to (1) participation and the convergence of participation within a learning group and (2) the individual knowledge transfer and knowledge convergence.

METHOD

After a pre-test including a problem case participants of all conditions of the 2x2-design were asked to individually study a three page description of attribution theory, which is standard curriculum content. After this individual phase, the learners worked together on three cases communicating via a web-based discussion board in which the cued scaffolding and the cued cooperation script were implemented (see *figure 1*). The collaboration was followed by an individual post-test that included another case. Time-on-task was 3 hours in all four conditions.

Cues of scaffolding and of cooperation script were automatically inserted into the messages of the learners. The cues of scaffolding were questions about the case. Thus, the students' task was basically to respond and jointly elaborate on the given cues. The cues of the scripted cooperation was supposed to support students to take over the role of an analyzer for one of the three cases and the role of a critic for the remaining two cases.

Collected data include learning prerequisites (motivation, interest, anxiety, etc.), participation (e.g. words produced), participation convergence (similarity of participation inside one group), individual knowledge transfer (inferences of theoretical concepts on case information) and knowledge convergence (sum of shared inferences, i.e. inferences which two or three participants of one group had in common in the individual transfer case).

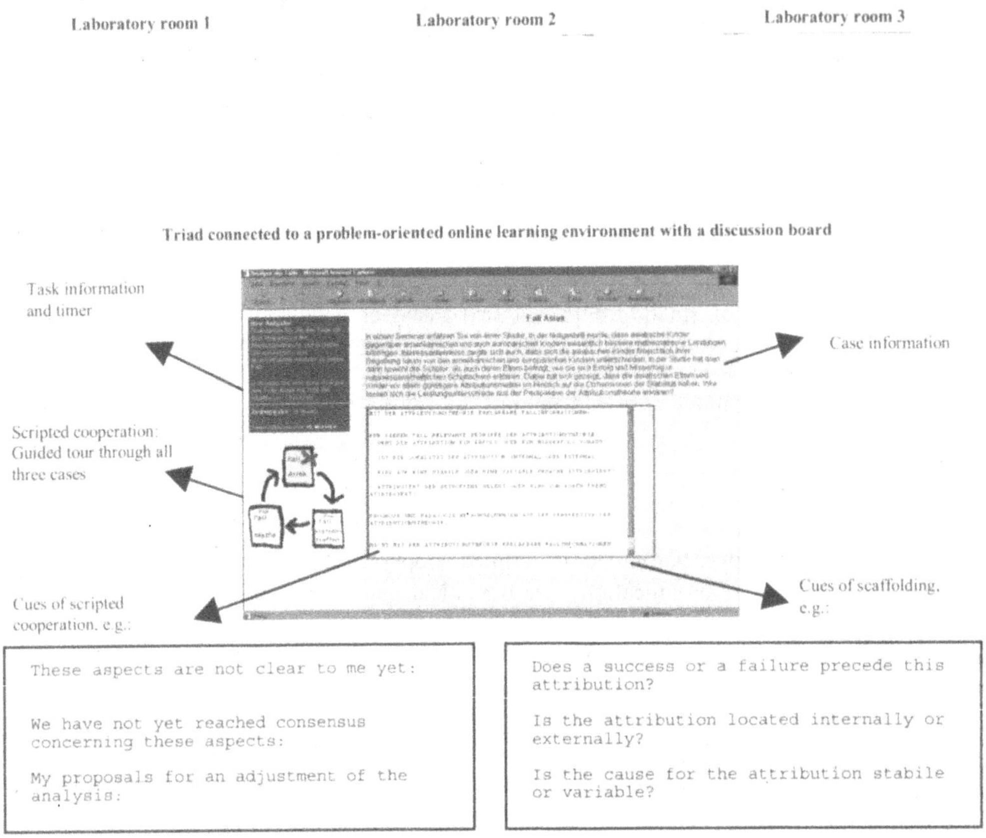

Figure 1: The experimental setup and the online learning environment. In the upper part you can see three participants in separate rooms communicating via a discussion board that is illustrated in the lower part.

RESULTS AND CONCLUSIONS

The findings show that participation, participation convergence, individual knowledge transfer and convergence of knowledge can be influenced not only by the preliminary training and moderation of collaborative learning, as studies have shown before, but also by the cue-based implementation of scripted cooperation and scaffolding into an online learning environment that structures the learning discourse itself.

The *cued cooperation script* proved to support learners substantially in comparison to open discourse regarding participation, convergence of participation, individual knowledge transfer and knowledge convergence. It was possible to replicate the positive effects of former research on scripted cooperation with scripted cooperation implemented with cues. Learners appeared to be encouraged to confront their ideas with those of their partners, reflect on the differences of perspectives, and sometimes modify their initial point of view.

A *cued scaffolding* of problem-oriented collaborative learning did not show substantial effects on participation or participation convergence, but was significantly least beneficial to the individual knowledge transfer and knowledge convergence in comparison to the other treatments. Maybe, the scaffolding did not foster the transfer as effectively as the other treatments, since important processes of learning failed to take place. Like a checklist, it may have facilitated the identification of relevant problems and their solution during the collaborative phase, but did not support the participants in developing a conceptual understanding of their own. Consequently, an integral part of scaffolding should be the fading of this kind of support. Maybe the scaffolding rather fostered individual than collaborative approaches to solve the cases. A joint effort to reflect on the application of theoretical concepts to case information may not have appeared relevant to the learners, as the scaffolding suggested an individual approach to solve the cases. We are currently investigating the discourse regarding collaborative knowledge construction in order to confirm or reject these hypotheses.

REFERENCES

Fischer, F., & Mandl, H. (2001). Facilitating the construction of shared knowledge with graphical representation tools in face-to-face and computer-mediated scenarios. In P. Dillenbourg, A. Eurelings, & K. Hakkarainen (Eds.), *Proceedings of euro-CSCL 2001* (Maastricht, NL, March 2001), 230-236.

Scardamalia, M., & Bereiter, C. (1996). Computer support for knowledge-building communities. In T. Koschmann (Ed.), *CSCL: Theory and practice of an emerging paradigm* (pp. 249-268). Erlbaum, Mahwah, NJ.

Multiplicity & Flexibility as Design and Implementation Features – A Case Study of a Web-Based CL Community for Diverse Learners

C. Y. Janey Wang
University of Texas at Austin
janeywon@mail.utexas.edu

Paul E. Resta
University of Texas at Austin
resta@mail.utexas.edu

ABSTRACT

This presentation describes multiplicity and flexibility as important factors in designing online collaborative learning environments. The presentation: (1) describes the design features of an award-winning Web-based course using extensive online collaborative learning; (2) examines and discusses four aspects and specific features of the course that supported multiplicity in design, development, implementation, and assessment; (3) discusses implications for future course design and research of online collaborative learning environments.

Keywords

Multiplicity, flexibility, Web-based learning, collaborative-learning, design, community, diversity

INTRODUCTION

John Dewey said, "The main purpose of instruction is to prepare the young for future responsibilities and for success in life." (Dewey, 1938, p. 17) In Asia, Confucius said, "Education should be provided indiscriminately. Teaching should be tailored discriminately."

The Internet provides unique opportunities to prepare learners for "future responsibilities" and "success in life," as well as tailoring instruction to meet individual learner's needs, interests, and strengths from diverse backgrounds.

The presentation describes the context, assumptions, objectives, and structure of an award-winning Web-based collaborative-learning course, *Instructional Technology Management and Planning (ITPM),* offered in the spring of 2001. This course received the "National Distance Learning Course Award" from the University Continuing Education Association and the instructor received the "2001 Excellence in Distance Learning Teaching Award for Higher Education" from the U.S. Distance Learning Association.

This presentation describes how and why multiplicity and flexibility were incorporated in the design, development, and implementation of an online course that emphasized collaborative learning. Essential features addressing multiplicity and flexibility will be discussed including: multiple course representations, tools, communication types and channels, support, interactions, flexible course structure, personalized communication and feedback system, and cultural-sensitivity to better meet the needs of learners from diverse backgrounds.

ONLINE COLLABORATIVE LEARNING

Collaborative learning strategies and online learning communities are increasingly incorporated within Web-based courses. Within these communities learning is derived from the negotiation and construction of knowledge among members. Based on emergent instructional needs, this curriculum is not static, but evolves throughout the design, development, implementation, and course revision process. One of the challenges in creating cooperative and collaborative learning communities is how to engage students' participation and interaction. To engage learners, the tasks should satisfy individual and group goals. The presentation describes the ways multiplicity and flexibility can help facilitate learner engagement and participation in the collaborative learning process.

SUMMARY

THE COURSE CONTEXT

The ITPM course was situated in a virtual environment where students met through online interactions. An authentic virtual environment with authentic tasks was created based on the metaphor of a hypothetical school district, Mustang Independent School District (MISD), composed of five schools. Data were derived from actual U.S. school districts, while problem- and project-based approaches to learning were employed. The major product was the "technology plan" that students produced collaboratively. In order to learn how to obtain funding support, each group also wrote a grant proposal based on their technology plan.

To accomplish course requirements, online socialization and communication were essential, as were extensive cooperation and collaboration among learners of diverse backgrounds. Authentic tools were employed to support the development of the strategic technology plan including the TechBuilder suite of tools and survey forms. In addition special spreadsheet forms were used for budget development, hardware and software inventories, as well as other tools such as GANNT charts for project scheduling. WebCT and Vcampus courseware were employed to provide access to course content and virtual environment. FirstClass groupware was also used to support the collaborative activites of the virtual planning teams. For synchronous interaction, the online chat function was used. Learners participated in monthly videoconferences on campus (face-to-face) or by way of network Webcasts, which served as a monthly forum for guest experts' discussion of relevant topics, teams to share their work, and instructor to answer student questions or give advice. The course contained eight modules; module tasks progressed from simple to complex.

Learners were either on-campus students at University of Texas, Austin or distance-learning students employing "TeleCampus" from across Texas, Georgia, and New York. On-campus students had the option of meeting the instructor, staff, and peers face-to-face or through the Internet while off-campus students could only connect via the network and phone communication.

MULTIPLICITY AND FLEXIBILITY: DESIGN FEATURES FOR DIVERSE LEARNERS

Multiplicity refers to the multiple ways of presenting and delivering course material, channels of communication, activity offerings, and learning strategies. Flexibility refers to the welcoming of and openness to questions and suggestions, timely support, options for learning tasks, and provision of individualized feedback throughout the course. Four major course aspects were observed to address multiplicity and flexibility including: course content and structure; communication tools, channels, and types; support, accessibility, and feedback; and performance assessment.

Multiple learning contexts and activities were provided in the ITPM course, such as self-learning, small group, cross-group learning, and whole class forums and interactions. Multimedia (text, audio, video, simulation) and multiple tools (TechBuilder, StaR Chart, Technology Profile Tool, and Milken Professional Competency Assessment) were structured for aesthetic representations and cognitive task engagement. Multiple course activity options were provided in consideration of divergent interests, values, and backgrounds of students. Multiple sources and kinds of support and feedback – as well as multiple channels of communication – were made available, including the instructor, a teaching assistant, administrative and technical staff, outsourcing consultants, area experts, and community members. Multiple assessment methods used to maintain student accountability included evaluations by the instructor, by self-evaluation, and by peers. Multiple instruction approaches were employed to motivate students of various cultures, intellectual levels, motivation, and interest.

Flexibility in design involves knowledge of and sensitivity to cultural diversity. It also requires enhanced understanding, communication, and instructional content and options tailored to the needs of the individual learner. In the ITPM course, students were encouraged to think "outside of the box" in looking beyond the obvious, and to value multiple perspectives. This entailed students seeking out relevant resources and utilizing their knowledge and creativity rather than confining themselves to traditional ways of thinking and learning. Because no plan is perfect, course content and schedule adjustments were made as necessary throughout the implementation process. Flexibility in meeting emergent needs of diverse learners required careful monitoring of the learning processes and individual student progress in order to make appropriate adjustments and modifications in schedule, approaches, and methods employed. For example, when technological failures or technical setbacks occurred, individual support and scaffolding was provided to accommodate learners' unforeseen personal problems and difficulties. A weekly newsletter provided announcements, clarifications, information updates, and reminders.

Students' end-of-course evaluations revealed positive results and feedback, as did students' peer and product evaluations. ITPM students' end-of-module reflections expressed enthusiasm about their learning throughout the semester. Students expressed their satisfaction with the tools they were exposed to, tasks they had accomplished, and the online social and collaborative skills acquired through group interactions. Based on our experience with the course, we have found that considerations of multiplicity and flexibility on various aspects of design, development, and implementation phases are important elements in the success in online collaborative learning environments.

REFERENCES

Dewey, J. (1938). Experience and education. New Jersey: Collier Book.

Structuring Group Learning within a Web-based Science Inquiry Program

Louise Yarnall, William R. Penuel

Center for Technology in Learning, SRI International

louise.yarnall@sri.com and william.penuel@sri.com

ABSTRACT

With an increased emphasis on inquiry in science education nationwide, we examined trends in the ways science teachers organized students into groups to implement one prominent one Web-based science inquiry program, Global Learning and Observations to Benefit the Environment (GLOBE). Our study focused on survey and case study data that SRI International collected as part of its ongoing evaluation of GLOBE (Means et al., 2001). We hypothesized: (1) teachers who are active in implementing an inquiry-based science program more frequently employ collaboration for cognitively complex activities than teachers who are less active implementers; (2) active teachers use collaboration more over time; and, (3) active GLOBE teachers who organize learning by collaborative groups perceive greater learning benefits than active teachers who rarely used collaboration. Our study confirmed that active teachers of an inquiry-based science program use collaboration more over time, but they are no more likely than less active teachers to see collaboration as beneficial to student learning. We also found that active teachers were likely to use collaborative small groups primarily to support data collection and reporting tasks to make them fit better into the classroom schedule than for data analysis and interpretation.

Keywords

collaboration, science inquiry, classroom culture

INTRODUCTION

The emphasis on scientific inquiry standards (AAAS, 1993; NRC, 1996, 2000) has led more teachers to incorporate collaborative projects and investigations into classroom practice. . Two decades of cognitive research cite many benefits of collaboration on student learning, especially in science (Dansereau, 1988; Forman & Larreamendy-Joerns, 1995; Jeong & Chi, 1997; NRC, 1999). In this study, we wanted to examine teachers' reasons and actual practices for using student collaboration to teach one prominent inquiry science program, Global Learning and Observations to Benefit the Environment (GLOBE). GLOBE is a seven-year-old international science and education program that involves elementary and secondary students in 9,658 schools in 95 countries. Backed by NOAA, NASA, NSF, the Environmental Protection Agency and the Departments of Education and State, GLOBE attempts to improve science achievement and environmental awareness by having K-12 students collect data about atmosphere, water, soil, and land cover, report those data regularly to a central Web site, and analyze those data via Web-based visualization tools. More than 10,000 teachers have been trained in GLOBE since its beginning, and there are 5.7 million pieces of student data reported. We hypothesized active U.S. GLOBE teachers probably used collaboration more often for more cognitively complex types of GLOBE activities than less active teachers -- a random sample of U.S. teachers who had been trained in GLOBE but who were reporting less data to the GLOBE Web site. We also hypothesized that active GLOBE teachers would use collaboration more over time, and that they held more positive perceptions of the pedagogical benefits of group work than less active GLOBE teachers.

METHODOLOGY

We analyzed data collected from 390 active U.S. teachers and 131 active international teachers who were selected because their classes regularly submitted data to the GLOBE Web site from December 1999-February 2000. We also analyzed data from a random sample of 512 teachers trained in the United States between June 1998 and August 1999, and who generally chose not to implement GLOBE or who reported less data. We also used case study data featuring interviews and observations collected during site visits to five GLOBE sites across the United States. To test our hypotheses, we aggregated data from our GLOBE Year 5 evaluation (Means et al., 2000) that compared how frequently active teachers and less active teachers organized students into six possible social configurations (single student, small group, multiple small groups, whole class, adult, no one) to engage in five different categories of GLOBE activity (data collection, data entry, data exploration on Web, data analysis, learning activities). To check for changes in use of collaboration over time, we compared two years' of teacher surveys. To compare perceptions of learning benefits, we divided perception data into two groups at active GLOBE teachers: frequent and infrequent group users.

RESULTS

The results showed that active GLOBE teachers used collaboration more than less active teachers for the procedural tasks of data collection, data entry, and exploring data on the Web site. Active GLOBE teachers did not differ from less-active GLOBE teachers in their use of small groups to support more cognitively complex tasks such as student-led discussions of

GLOBE data, preferring to a whole class, teacher-led discussion. In our case studies of active GLOBE schools, we did observe teachers engaging students in collaborative inquiry into data discussion, but we also observed group work being used as a way to manage data collection activities. At the same time, active GLOBE teachers organized students into groups more in 1999-2000 than they did in 1997-98. Active GLOBE teachers' use of small groups for data entry increased 12 percent. More than 90 percent of active GLOBE teachers and 82 percent of less active GLOBE teachers perceived similar benefits to collaboration, both for improving group skills and data understanding.

CONCLUSION

Our findings raise questions about why collaboration is used primarily for aspects of science inquiry related to data collection and reporting rather than data analysis and interpretation in active GLOBE classrooms. The study shows that teachers believe students can effectively learn about data collection while working in groups, yet they have not used student groups more for the tasks of discussing, analyzing, and interpreting data. It may be this finding is partly a result of our selection procedure, which focused on teachers' frequency of data reporting. It may be that a high proportion of teachers who report the most GLOBE data may be more focused on classroom management than engaging students in group inquiry. It may be that most teachers are overwhelmed by the complexity of GLOBE's collection procedures or lack materials to scaffold other phases of student-led inquiry. GLOBE has addressed this problem by adding an inquiry element to its professional development programs. An alternate explanation is that teachers and students may perceive that data collection is a cognitively complex task, and one that is critical to helping students understand scientific practice. For example, group-using active teachers had more confidence in students' data collection abilities than non-group using teachers. Finally, it may also be that in the GLOBE program, the small collaborative group is becoming what Saxe (1991) would call a hybrid form, one that merges the practices and goals of science culture into the classroom culture. The study suggests that teachers need special support to engage student groups in more complex tasks of data analysis and interpretation.

REFERENCES

Doise, W., Mugny, G., & Perret-Clermont, A. (1975). Social interaction and the development of cognitive operations. *European Journal of Social Psychology,* **5**, 3, 367-383.

Forman, E.A. & Larreamendy-Joerns, J. (1995). Learning in the context of peer collaboration: A pluralistic perspective on goals and expertise. *Cognition and Instruction,* **13**, 4, 549-564.

Dansereau, D.F. (1988). Cooperative learning strategies. In C.E. Weinstetin, E.T. Goetz, & P.A. Alexander (Eds.), *Learning and study strategies: Issues in assessment, instruction, and evaluation* (pp. 103-120). Orlando, FL: Academic Press.

Jeong, H. & Chi, M.T.H. (December 1997). Construction of shared knowledge during collaborative learning. *Computer Support for Collaborative Learning '97 Proceedings*, 124-128.

Means, B., Korbak, C., Lewis, A., Michalchik, V., Penuel, W. R., Rollin, J., & Yarnall, L. (2001). *GLOBE Year 5 evaluation.* Menlo Park, CA: SRI International. (soon to appear: http://archive.globe.gov/sda-bin/wt/gh/GRR+L(en)+Dg(gmx/el)Gn(GLOBE~20Program~20Evaluations)

National Research Council. (1999). *How people learn: Brain, experience and school.* Washington, DC: National Academy Press.

Saxe, G.B. (1991). Culture and cognitive development: Studies in mathematical understanding. Hillsdale, N.J.: L. Erlbaum Associates.

Developing Online Communities of Practice in Preservice Teacher Education

Melissa J. Poole

University of Missouri-Columbia

poolem@missouri.edu

ABSTRACT

Despite attempts to encourage greater teacher collegiality, the privacy of the classroom persists. Online communication tools offer opportunities for teachers to overcome these boundaries in professional communities of practice. This study of two cohorts of preservice teachers sought to determine if they were successful in building community in class and online and to examine factors that may have enhanced or impeded their ability to create community. Findings suggest that the physical and pedagogical contexts of the classroom and the way the communication tools are implemented are important factors in their use.

KEYWORDS

Preservice teacher development, collaborative learning online, communities of practice, community tools

INTRODUCTION

Despite a variety of strategies for encouraging greater collegiality in teaching, teaching remains, for many, a private endeavor. Yet, studies of co-present and emerging online teacher communities (Calderwood, 2000; Grossman, Wineburg, & Woolworth, 2000; Schlager, Fusco, & Schank, 1998; Westheimer, 1998) demonstrate the potential for teachers to develop effective communities of practice. Preservice teacher development is an ideal time to introduce teachers to the tools that can provide them opportunities for continued learning within a community of practice online. What follows is a report of a study of two cohorts of preservice teachers – secondary science and secondary English education majors – who began to build communities of practice both in class and online.

CONTEXT OF THE STUDY

In the 1990s, the College of Education at the University of Missouri revised both its curriculum and its technology infrastructure, building a new computer lab and providing laptop computers to everyone in the program. The Center for Technology Innovations in Education developed new software to facilitate preservice teachers' reflection, communication, and collaboration—the Interactive Shared Journaling System. Increasing interest in and demand for tools that provided course information online provided incentive for the College to license Blackboard's CourseInfo.

METHODS

Sample

This study is part of an NSF-funded study of the class of 2001 throughout their time in the teacher development program. It focuses on two cohorts of preservice teachers (PSTs) in secondary science education and secondary English education, over the course of their last two years in the program. Six PSTs in each cohort were selected for the case study.

Data Collection and Analysis

The researcher observed the PSTs' education courses in science and English, observed their interactions online, and interviewed six PSTs in each of these two cohorts each semester. Data analysis for this study included analysis of interview transcripts, archived communications online, and observation field notes.

RESULTS

Secondary Science Education

The first semester, the class met in a traditional classroom with student chairs in rows facing a teacher's desk at the front. The second semester was in a science lab where students sat in rows facing the instructor. Neither arrangement facilitated communication and collaboration among the PSTs. The Journal tool allowed users to post reflections and share them with others in the Journal community. The science education professor who led the course in the first two semesters assigned a series of Journal entry topics and teams with whom PSTs were to share their entries. Journaling counted only 5% of the total grade. In the third semester, PSTs were able to return to the renovated education buildng. Smaller tables in the room were rearranged for multiple groupings, providing more opportunity for communication. Much of the structure of the course was relaxed but use of the Journal was dropped. Over time, the face-to-face interactions of this group evidenced several markers of community—shared experiences, shared responsibililties within class, and a shared identity as science education majors. While there was a noticeable absence of an entrance ritual for the group, the PSTs created an exit ritual in the form of a carry-in dinner hosted by one of the PSTs. Several developed long-term meaningful relationships. Yet online participation via the Journal was limited to the assigned tasks. Most appeared to be relieved when the Journal assignments were dropped.

Secondary English Education

From the first, this syllabus of this sequence of classes espoused a model of learning through practice and from one another. In the first semester, the class met in a traditional classroom where chairs were most often arranged in rows facing the front. Occasionally students met in smaller "reader-response" groups, but there was generally little time for student-student interaction. In the second semester, the instructor asked the students to arrange the chairs in one large circle for each class meeting. CourseInfo was adopted and the discussion board became a regular means of communication among students. PSTs posted over 500 messages, discussing the books they were reading, giving feedback on theeir peers' microteaching lessons in class, and discussing other topics that emerged in class and in their field experiences. In the third semester, the class moved back to a more teacher-centric physical layout in the renovated education building, with desks facing the front, to take advantage of the new presentation technologies. Use of the discussion forum was limited to PSTs reporying on their field experiences. Through their face-to-face interactions, members of this cohort showed signs of developing community through shared experiences in this class and other English classes they had in common. They developed a shared identity as English education majors and reorganized a local chapter of NCTE (MUCTE). There was a noticeable absence of any entrance ritual in the first semester, but the instructor in the second semester created both an entrance ritual—through in class and online introductions—and an exit ritual in the form of a social gathering at the end of the semester. Connections made then carried into the third semester, but there was no exit ritual at the end of their three semesters together. Overall, participation online waxed and waned over the three semesters as greater or lesser importance was given to the online dialogue as integral to class communication.

DISCUSSION

Both groups evidenced the formation of a community of practice through their co-present interactions. Signs of community in the science education cohort did not emerge until the third semester, when the classroom and pedagogical structure were more relaxed and the use of the Journal tool was abandoned. The Journal tool did not serve them well as a community tool. Signs of community in the English education cohort emerged and peaked in the second semester. Changes physical and pedagogical structure and the addition of the CourseInfo discussion board helped to build stronger community ties. Participation in class and online increased dramatically. Despite the move to a modern, spacious, and technologically-enhanced classroom in the third semester, online participation appeared to diminish, ending in silence rather than a flurry of good-byes and a closing celebration. Clearly, the physical and pedagogical contexts of the classes mattered as much as the tools. At the same time, the way the tools were used—the importance they were given in the curriculum and the structure of the expected communications — had an effect on how PSTs used them to develop online communities of practice.

ACKNOWLEDGEMENTS

The author would like to acknowledge the assistance of the other members of this research team and the contribution of the preservice teachers in this study. This study was funded by NSF REC 9725214.

REFERENCES

Calderwood, P. E. (2000). *Learning community: Finding common ground in difference*. New York: Teachers College Press.

Grossman, P., Wineburg, S, and Woolworth, S. (2000). *In pursuit of teacher community*. Paper delivered at the Annual Meeting of the American Educational Research Association, New Orleans, April.

Schlager, M., Fusco, J., and Schank, P. (1998). Cornerstones for an on-line community of education professionals. *IEEE Technology and Society*, 17 (4), 15-21, 40.

Westheimer, J. (1998). Among school teachers: Community, autonomy, and ideology in teachers' work. New York: Teachers College Press.

Supporting Discourse in a Synchronous Learning Environment: The Learning Protocol Approach

Hans-Rüdiger Pfister
Knowledge Media Research Center (KMRC), Tübingen, Germany
r.pfister@iwm-kmrc.de

Martin Mühlpfordt
Fraunhofer IPSI, Darmstadt, Germany
mamue@ipsi.fhg.de

ABSTRACT
Lack of coordination and coherence among contributions is a typical problem with the use of chat for netbased learning. We propose so-called learning protocols to increase coordination, coherence, and, hence, the efficiency of learning via chat. Learning protocols are system controlled cooperation scripts: Participants explicitely identify the reference and the type of their contributions, and the order of contributions is predetermined. As an example, the explanation protocol is described and empirical results confirming that structured discourse leads to superior learning are presented.

Keywords
Cooperative learning, learning protocols, cooperation scripts, netbased learning

INTRODUCTION
We focus on the usefulness of synchronous text-based chat for cooperative learning discourses. In traditional face-to-face settings, the effectiveness of cooperative learning is well established (Slavin, 1995). Cooperation can be further improved using so-called *scripted cooperation*. Scripted cooperation implies the application of a more or less rigid schema, i.e., a set of rules and stages according to which the cooperation proceeds (O'Donnell & Dansereau, 1992). Empirical evidence with respect to positive effects on knowledge acquisition is mixed, though generally supportive (Huber, 1999; Slavin, 1995). However, according to Hesse, Garsoffky and Hron (1997), there are special problems with discourse in virtual environments: (i) lack of *social awareness*, (ii) insufficient *group coordination*, (iii) deficient *coherence* of contributions. What we call *learning protocols* are types of scripted cooperation, which are completely controlled by the system (Pfister et al., 1998), and intended to overcome the deficiencies of virtual discourses in cooperative learning environments.

LEARNING PROTOCOLS
A learning protocol requires that learners make explicit what is usually implicit in face-to-face discourse. We define learning protocols by four features: (1) *Explicit reference*: For each new contribution, the referred to concept (word, sentence) is explicitly specified. The reference is represented by an arrow visible for all learners. (2) *Typed contributions*: For each contribution, its type is explicitely specified, such as a question, an explanation, etc. (3) *Role assignment*: Each participant is assigned a definite role such as learner, tutor, explainer, or commenter, depending on discourse type. (4) *Message sequencing*: The succession of contributions is controlled according to a pre-determined pattern.

The Explanation Protocol: An Experimental Test
The explanation learning protocol instantiates a discourse of type "mutual explanation" (Hron et al., 1997), in which a complicated concept is explained. A tutor serves as the main source of knowledge. The explanation protocol works like this: (i) The topic is introduced by a short initial text; (ii) each learner has to contribute in turn; (iii) a contribution is made by first indicating the reference, second, the type of message is selected (Question, Explanation, or Comment), then the message is send to the public chat pane; (iv) depending on the message type, the next contributor is determined: if a question has been asked, the tutor is required to give an explanation; otherwise, the next learner is required to submit his contribution.

We compared a net-based discourse using the learning protocol with an equivalent discourse using conventional free-text chat as a control condition. Additionally, the type of knowledge was varied: one domain was "earthquakes", and the second domain was a philosophical topic on "knowing and believing". A total of 24 subjects participated in the study, put together in groups of three, in a distributed setting. Participants worked through both knowledge domains successively (max. 25 min.). The learning goal for the earthquake domain was "to understand the causes and consequences of earthquakes", for the philosophy domain "to understand the meaning of the concepts knowing and believing". Directly following each session, a knowledge test was applied.

The effect of the learning protocol was tested with the test score of the knowledge tests as the dependent variable (range 0 to 17). The mean scores in the earthquake domain were 12.08 ($SD = 2.65$) for the experimental condition, and 8.67 ($SD = 1.93$) for the control condition. As expected, participants in the experimental condition learned significantly more than participants in the control condition, $t(22) = 3.61$, $p < .01$. The mean test scores for the philosophy domain were 9.04 ($SD = 1.59$) for the experimental condition, and 8.21 ($SD = 1.54$) for the control condition; the difference turned out to be not significant.

DISCUSSION

Note that the results are preliminary based on a small sample (N = 24), and only a post-test was applied. We are currently running experiments using a larger sample and a pre-post-test design. However, the positive effect of the learning protocol in the earthquake domain is quite strong, and in the philosophy domain the difference is in the expected direction. This confirms the potential of learning protocols to enhance immediate knowledge gains from net-based discussions. It also shows that the efficiency might depend on the type of knowledge domain.

Several questions remain and need to be studied further. Which features of the learning protocol are essential for knowledge acquisition? The need to indicate the referent of each contribution is assumed to lead to a more coherent cognitive representation; if a coherent representation in fact mediates learning gains is an open question. The role of message typing is also far from clear. Not entirely unexpected is the finding that learning protocols work better in some knowledge domains than in others. One might assume that the explanation protocol is better suited for declarative knowledge acquisition in science or technology oriented domains, whereas other learning protocols might be better suited for philosophical or ethical domains.

ACKNOWLEDGMENTS

This research is funded by the German Research Council (DFG) as part of the priority program "Net-based knowledge communication in groups". Many thanks go to Martin Wessner, Mareike Hennings, Werner Müller, Mareike Geisen and Annette Conzelmann for valuable comments and for conducting the experiments.

REFERENCES

Hesse, F. W., Garsoffky, B., & Hron, A. (1997). Interface-Design für computerunterstütztes kooperatives Lernen. In L. J. Issing & P. Klimsa (Eds.), *Information und Lernen mit Multimedia* (pp. 252-267). Weinheim: Psychologie Verlags Union.

Hron, A., Hesse, F. W., Reinhard, P., & Picard, E. (1997). Strukturierte Kooperation beim computerunterstützten kollaborativen Lernen. *Unterrichtswissenschaft, 25*, 56-69.

Huber, A. A. (1999). *Bedingungen effektiven Lernens in Kleingruppen unter besonderer Berücksichtigung der Rolle von Lernskripten.* Schwangau: Huber.

O'Donnell, A. M., & Dansereau, D. F. (1992). Scripted cooperation in student dyads: A method for analyzing and enhancing academic learning and performance. In R. Hertz-Lazarowitz & N. Miller (Eds.), *Interaction in cooperative groups. The theoretical anatomy of group learning* (pp. 120-141). New York: Cambridge University Press.

Pfister, H.-R., Wessner, M., Beck-Wilson, J., Miao, Y., & Steinmetz, R. (1998). Rooms, protocols, and nets: Metaphors for computer-supported cooperative learning of distributed groups. In A. Bruckman, M. Guzdial, J. L. Kolodner & A. Ram (Eds.), *Proceedings of ICSL 98* (pp. 242-248). Charlottesville, VA: Association for the Advancement of Computing in Education (AACE).

Slavin, R. E. (1995). *Cooperative learning: Theory, research, and practice* (2nd ed.). Needham Heights, MA: Allyn and Bacon.

Coaching Collaboration in a Computer-Mediated Learning Environment

María de los Angeles Constantino-González
Dept. of Computer Sciences
ITESM Campus Laguna
aconstan@campus.lag.itesm.mx

Daniel D. Suthers
Dept. of Information and Computer Sciences
University of Hawai`i at Manoa
suthers@hawaii.edu

ABSTRACT
We evaluated a pedagogical agent that coaches collaborative problem solving by tracking student participation and comparing students' individual and group solutions. The software coach encourages negotiation when differences are detected between solutions, and encourages participation in other ways. Evaluations based on expert judgment and on students' behavior shows that the quality of the advice was good and that the coach helped guide the collaborative session, although specific areas for improvement were identified.

Keywords
collaborative distance learning, intelligent agents, entity-relationship modeling, socio-cognitive conflict

INTRODUCTION
A communication channel by itself does not guarantee effective collaboration between distance learners. Participants should be guided to help students leverage the advantages of learning with others. Yet it is difficult for human facilitators to guide many teams working synchronously. Several systems have been designed to guide online synchronous collaboration (Jermann, Soller & Muehlenbrock, 2001). Most of these systems use restricted menu-driven or sentence-opener interfaces to track students' dialogue and give guidance based on dialogue models. Wanting an approach that would not excessively restrict natural language interaction and would not require extensive knowledge engineering for each domain, we investigated the potential of a basic ability to detect semantically interesting differences between two representations of problem solutions, coupled with simple tracking of individual's quantity of participation, feedback given, and discussion. A software coach was designed based on the Socio-Cognitive Conflict and Cognitive Dissonance theories, and implemented as part of a computer-mediated environment in which students construct Entity-Relationship (ER) diagrams as solutions to database modeling problems. ER modeling was selected due to its collaborative nature and its use of easily compared representations. This paper reports on how students used and evaluated the coach's advice.

COLER
COLER (COllaborative Learning environment for Entity-Relationship modeling) is a web-based collaborative learning environment in which students can solve database-modeling problems. COLER is designed for sessions in which students first solve problems individually, and then work synchronously in small groups to develop group solutions. A personal coach gives advice based on conflicts between the contents of individual and group diagrams and on imbalances in students' participation. Several heuristic control strategies were specified to recognize relevant learning opportunities and to provide for the selection of appropriate advice. Details are provided in Constantino-González & Suthers (2001) or Constantino-González et al. (2001).

EVALUATION
COLER's performance was judged by comparison to expert judgment, student impressions, and how students responded to the advice. Five sessions were conducted, each with a different team of three students who were taking or had taken a database course. A domain expert also participated. Participants were located in different rooms, each containing a computer with COLER installed and Internet access. Students worked on an ER modeling problem individually for about 30 minutes. Then they initiated the collaborative session. At the end of the two-hour session, students answered a questionnaire regarding COLER's performance. The papers cited above reported on evaluations of the quality and coverage of advice and of the role of various knowledge-sources in generating this advice. This paper focuses on how students used and evaluated the coach's advice.

COLER's advice was codified according to videotapes and chat transcripts. Advice was codified as Taken if the coached student performed the action suggested by COLER; Ignored if the coached student didn't follow the advice; Not Longer Needed when the situation changed just after the advice was given; and Not Evaluated when there was not enough information to empirically determine the advice status or when system failures occurred. The students took 40% of the total advice instances while 28% was ignored. Not Longer Needed advice represented 21% of the total advices, and 11% could not be evaluated. Overall, students took 59% of the evaluated advice that was still needed at the time it was given. The

Expert categorized most of the advice taken by the students as "reasonable." Some ignored advice was evaluated as reasonable while others as "so-so." Most of the ignored reasonable advice suggested discussion of a difference without mentioning its specific type. So-so ignored advice was computed because of misspellings in names. Several Feedback and Continue Task advices, which are based on timeouts, were not longer needed since they were given just when conditions in the environment changed. This problem can be eliminated by re-checking conditions before giving the selected advice.

Advice rated by students as "useful" included pointing out differences between their solutions, encouraging them to share and discuss their ideas, to explain their reasoning, and to contribute to the group diagram, and suggesting that they verify their work when their contribution to the group was different from their own individual work. Advice was generally rated as useful only when students could do something in response. Almost all of the advice was given at appropriate times; however, some advice was given just after the action suggested was performed. Most of the students thought that the presence of a coach during the session helped guide and coordinate the collaborative session and establish the group dynamics required in collaborative learning. Most students said they reaffirmed their ER knowledge and learned about collaboration during the session. Some students suggested that more specific advice be given, and that additional types of messages be included, for example helping to solve the problem, indicating common mistakes in the diagram and giving feedback on how they are doing. Other students suggested that the coach compare individual solutions and then give suggestions related to what it finds different. Students also indicated that sometimes advice should be given to the whole group instead of just to individuals.

CONCLUSIONS

We found that reasonable advice could be generated based primarily on comparing students' individual and group solutions and on tracking student participation, although some refinements are needed to eliminate sensitivity to spelling errors and ensure that the advice is still applicable before it is given, and other knowledge sources will help increase the range of advice given. The approach should generalize to all domains in which students construct formal representations of problem solutions that can be compared for significant differences.

ACKNOWLEDGMENTS

Constantino-González was funded by ITESM Campus Laguna and by CONACYT, and Suthers was funded by the Presidential Technology Initiative and NSF's Learning and Intelligent Systems. We thank our many colleagues at ITESM and the University of Pittsburgh for their collaboration and support.

REFERENCES

Constantino-González, M. A., Suthers, D. D. & Icaza, J. (2001). Designing and Evaluating a Collaboration Coach: Knowledge and Reasoning. In J. D. Moore, C. L. Redfield, W. L. Johnson (Eds.) *Artificial Intelligence in Education, Proc. 10th Conference on AI-ED,* San Antonio Texas, May 19-23 2001, Amsterdam: IOS Press, pp. 176-187.

Constantino-González, M. A., & Suthers, D. D. (2001). Coaching Collaboration by Comparing Solutions and Tracking Participation. In P. Dillenbourg, A. Eurelings, K. Hakkarainen (Eds.) *European Perspectives on Computer-Supported Collaborative Learning, Proc. First European Conference on CSCL,* Universiteit Maastricht, Maastrict, the Netherlands, March 22-24 2001, pp. 173-180.

Jermann, P., Soller, A., & Muehlenbrock, M. (2001). From Mirroring to Guiding: A Review of State of the Art Technology for Supporting Collaborative Learning. In P. Dillenbourg, A. Eurelings, K. Hakkarainen (Eds.) *European Perspectives on Computer-Supported Collaborative Learning, Proc. First European Conference on CSCL,* Universiteit Maastricht, Maastrict, the Netherlands, March 22-24 2001, pp. 324-331.

Analyzing Sequential Data in Computer-Supported Collaborative Learning

Dietmar Janetzko[1], Frank Fischer[2]

[1]Institute of Computer Science and Social Research, University of Freiburg, Germany
dietmar@cognition.iig.uni-freiburg.de
[2]Institute of Psychology, University of Tübingen, Germany
frank.fischer@iwm-kmrc.de

ABSTRACT

Representations and changes between them play a major role in cognitive development (e.g., Vosniadou, & Brewer, 1992) and education (e.g., Hewson, Beeth, & Thorley, 1998). By definition, change of representations is also indispensable for collaborative work since a common understanding or shared knowledge can only be achieved by a partial convergence of the knowledge structures of the collaborating subjects. This articles presents and discusses knowledge tracking (KT), viz., an approach to analyze cognition on the basis of symbolic sequential data. We present and discuss the methodological aspects of KT and delineate the Web-based computer program (knowledge tracking engine, KTE) set up to run KT-analyses (http://www.knowledge-tracking.com). An empirical study in collaborative learning is taken to exemplify the usage of KT in analysis of computer supported collaboration.

Keywords

Shared knowledge, network representation of cognition, probabilistic model, change of representation, sequential data

KNOWLEDGE TRACKING

Knowledge tracking (KT) is a psychometric method that carries out a diagnosis of cognitive representations. Knowledge tracking can be used in a *confirmative* or in a *generative* mode. The former provides a rationale to decide which of some candidate theories (relational structures) explains a sequence of data best.[(1)] The latter may be pursued to generate a relational structure on the basis of some start-up structures such that the newly generated structure fits to the data best (Janetzko, 2000).

The Data: Sequence of Concepts. The input of data required by knowledge tracking is a sequence of symbols or concepts (e.g., the sequence of the concepts CAT, DOG, FISH, MOUSE etc.) that refer to the sequence of states in a Markov process. This kind of data may be easily obtained in studies of computer supported collaboration or think aloud studies.

The Theory: Relations and Structures. Knowledge tracking needs a theory to analyze sequences of symbolic data. To specify a theory we have to select one or many simple semantic relations (e.g., `x is-a y` or `x communicates to y`). On the basis of a relation we may then add a set of concepts that are taken to instantiate the relations. We end up with relational structures. A very simple relational structure can be described in a Lisp-like notation as (is-a (MOUSE MAMMAL) (HORSE MAMMAL) (SHARK FISH) (HERRING FISH) (FISH VERTEBRATE) (MAMMAL VERTEBRATE)).

Calculating Goodness of Fit Scores. In KT, the theory, viz., one or many relational structures, is taken to calculate goodness of fit scores on the basis of sequences of symbolic data. A goodness of fit score describes how well a sequence of symbolic data can be explained by a relational structure.

The Knowledge Tracking Engine: Using Knowledge Tracking via the WWW

The web-site `http://www.knowledge-tracking.com` allows visitors to carry out remote analyses of data on the basis of the knowledge tracking engine (KTE). Users may upload data and theories and use KT either in the confirmative or in the generative mode.

USAGE OF KNOWLEDGE TRACKING TO ANALYSE SHARED KNOWLEDGE

Recent work in CSCL indicates that *knowledge convergence* in collaborative learning might be an important factor for conceptual change (Roschelle, 1995). Knowledge convergence could be defined as the increasing similarity of subjects with regard to process and outcome of knowledge construction (Fischer & Mandl, 2001). We investigated, to what extent collaborators converge with respect to process and outcomes of problem-oriented collaborative learning in text-based computer-mediated communication. Moreover, we compared two different instructional conditions with regard to their effects on knowledge convergence. Both conditions were structured by a specific type of collaboration script (e.g.,

---

(1) By *explanation* we refer to the theory-based prediction of data.

O'Donnell, 1996): A *macroscript* mainly sets a common goal and prescribes major steps. In contrast, a *microscript* is more fine-grained in regulating the learners interaction.

Participants and design. We re-analyzed data of 18 subjects from a recent study (Reiserer, Ertl, Weinberger, Fischer, Mandl, & Jahn, in press). Subjects worked together in distributed groups of three learners (triads) in one of the two different script conditions of a one-factorial design.

Procedure. Learners worked on standard personal computers with 400Mhz and 128 MB RAM located in separated places. They communicated via text-based CMC facilities. The main components of the learning environment were a text-based computer conferencing system and a video lecture.

Results. As data sources we used transcripts of the discourse of the learner as well as learners` text production in the pre-test and in the post-test. In so doing, we identified all scientific concepts explicitly stated or paraphrased in the students' essays in the sequence of their occurrence. Thus, data were simply sequences of concepts, which is a format easily to be analyzed via knowledge tracking. First, we conducted a comparison between results from the pre-test and post-test (analyzed via the expert structure) and the random structure. There was a significant difference between the pre-test and random structure (z-= - 1,67; $p< .05$) as well as the post-test and the random structure (z =-2,54, $p< 0.005$) of both groups and the random structure, showing that subjects had prior knowledge that clearly increased during the collaboration. Second, we assessed the degree of convergence that was initiated by either the microscript or the macroscript condition. To assess convergence of knowledge we used the structures derived from traces (generative mode of KT) of subjects of each triad to analyze the traces of subjects of each triad (confirmative mode of KT) avoiding of course circular assessments. In this way, scores for the convergence of knowledge in the microscript and the macroscript condition were determined. A comparison of both script conditions revealed a marginally significant difference in favour of the macroscript condition (z = - 1,47 $p< .07$).

REFERENCES

Fischer, F. & Mandl, H. (2001). Facilitating the construction of shared knowledge with graphical representation tools in face-to-face and computer-mediated scenarios. In P. Dillenbourg, A. Eurelings & K. Hakkarainen (Eds.), *European Perspectives on Computer-Supported Collaborative Learning* (pp.230-236). Maastricht: McLuhan Institute.

Hewson, P. W., Beeth, M. E., & Thorley, N. R. (1998). Teaching for conceptual change. In . G. Tobin & B. J. Fraser (Eds.), *International handbook of science education* (pp. 99-218). Dordrecht, Netherlands: Kluwer.

Janetzko, D. (2000). Selecting and generating concept structures. In R. Roy (Ed.), *Knowledge management - A micro-level approach.* London: Springer.

O'Donnell, A. (1996). Effects of explicit incentives on scripted and unscripted cooperation. *Journal of Educational Psychology, 88 (1),* 74-86.

Reiserer, M., Weinberger, A., Ertl, B., Fischer, F., Mandl, H., & Jahn, K. (in press). *Scripted collaborative learning in text-based computer-mediated communication - A pilot study* (Research report 140). Munich: University of Munich.

Roschelle, J. (1996). Learning by Collaborating: Convergent Conceptual Change. In T. Koschmann (Ed.), *CSCL: Theory and Practice of an Emerging Paradigm* (pp. 209-248). Mahwah, NJ: Erlbaum.

Vosniadou, S., & Brewer, W. F. (1992). Mental models of the earth: A study of conceptual change in childhood. *Cognitive Psychology, 24(4)*, 535-585.

Evolving Shared Experience in Distributed Learning Environments

Grégory Bourguin
CUEEP/Laboratoire TRIGONE
Lille University of Science and Technology
gregory.bourguin@univ-lille1.fr
Anders Mørch
InterMedia
University of Oslo
anders.morch@intermedia.uio.no

ABSTRACT

Distributed learning environments such as groupware give two or more users the means for working together remotely on a shared task. This activity is more than the sum of single users working on their own to solve the same task. Although most people will agree about this, there is neither agreement nor much discussion in the literature on how coordination and collaboration skill should be distributed between users and computer tools. We present a new approach that uses a process model adapted from Activity theory to guide our efforts. The model outlines steps towards capturing *crystallised experience.*

Keywords
Distributed learning environments, shared experience, crystallized experience, Activity theory, end-user tailorability

INTRODUCTION

Certain actions like negotiating how to work and coordinating disjoint contributions distinguish group work from the work of single users. User experience is an important asset in individual work. In this article we address user experience in distributed settings and we ask the following questions: What is shared experience and how can it be useful when collaborating in remote settings? Our working hypothesis is that shared experience will be useful for supporting collaboration and coordination in distributed environments. Our experience is based on previous studies in building (Bourguin and Derycke, 2001) and testing (Wasson and Mørch, 2000) single-user and multi-user systems in different settings. The convergence of our ideas, which has evolved independently in two different laboratories, suggests that our approach may apply to other settings as well.

BASIC CONCEPTS AND PROCESS MODEL

We have adapted a set of concepts from Activity Theory (AT) and Computer Supported Collaborative Learning (CSCL). The rationale for this is to help us understand and explain the processes leading to crystallization (as a collaborative activity) and crystallized experience (a system property). Crystallized experience is externalized user (mental) experience materialized in physical artifacts. This is a result of a crystallization process, which in its final stage entails end-user tailoring of a computer system.

The concepts we adopt are the following: breakdown, reflection, knowledge building, and crystallisation. A breakdown according to AT is an inability to reach the object of the activity. After a breakdown the participants may have to switch to another level of participation in order to continue, which we call reflection. Reflection is an activity on a different level of abstraction than the activity that triggered the reflection. We call the former meta-level activity and the latter base activity. At the meta-level, reflection on the base activity is possible.

A person uses his internal (mental) experience for understanding the breakdown and its cause, and (if successful) is able to determine an approach for resolving it. In a cooperative work setting, the meta-activity may itself become the topic of a cooperative activity. When internal experience (reflection) is accompanied or replaced by public talk (debate), group discussion, or other means to externalizing the breakdown situation we refer to this as belonging to the realm of knowledge building, a concept and process introduced by Scardemalia and Bereiter (1996). The meta-activity may lead to a transformation of the activity's context. This may result in a reformulation of the task and its elements (object, tools, rules, division of labor, etc.).

In this paper we are primarily concerned with the transformation of tools. However, a tool will often (implicitly) contain a built-in representation of the rules and the division of labor of the activity in which the tool is used. Resolving a breakdown by implementing a work-around inside the tool that caused the breakdown is at the hart of the approach to shared user experience we pursue in this paper. When users are able to modify a tool, this is to a large extent a result of their past experiences (in designing and using similar tools). Modifications will thus reflect its users' experience. Crystallised experience is shared experience materialised inside a transformed tool. A second goal is to be able to reuse and disseminate crystallised experience in new user activities. As new users reuse a (modified) tool the experience crystallised inside it is also reused. New users may encounter breakdowns and this may require further adaptation of the tool, which again will bring new experiences to the fore. Only to the extent that these experiences are identified, externalised, crystallised and made available as (materialized) parts inside tools can they have a lasting value.

DESIGN ISSUES

A computer system is an artefact supporting some users' activities. We want to create systems that will allow other users to adapt it to their needs by building on the previous users' crystallized experience. From our point of view, each system adaptation contains some amount of experience from its users. We want to develop CSCL environments that can capture user experience useful for collaboration and coordination in groups in the context of distributed collaborative learning. For end users to be able to participate in the crystallization process computer tools have to be adaptable during use, i.e. supporting end-user tailorability (Mørch, 1997). However, the creation of a tailorable system is not a simple problem. We believe that a balance have to be found between users' motivation for realising a modification task and the computational effort to be expended by them for understanding the problem and solving it. First, we need to create a system with an understandable foundation as seen from the users point of view. Second, we want to realise this with existing technology. We have therefore embarked on a component software approach (Szyperski, 1997) for building end-user tailorable systems because one of the biggest obstacles to understanding computer systems is a lack of building blocks that match the users' cognitive thought processes. A framework for this is called DARE (Distributed Activities in a Reflective Environment) (Bourguin G., Derycke A., 2001). DARE proposes a global platform for CSCW allowing users to adapt their working environment at runtime. Users' adaptations are made on task, tool, and role components. According to the processes and concepts described above, we believe that DARE users' experience is crystallised inside the components they adapt while using it.

DISCUSSION

We have embarked on a cumbersome journey from two different starting points. One the one end, we have identified the importance of user experience for understanding the design and use of tools and shared (crystallized) experience for communication and collaboration in distributed settings. One the other end, we have developed a solution framework (DARE) for building computational support for crystallized experience. We have not yet completed our journey and the two paths do not join. However, we have adopted and further developed a set of concepts and distinctions we hope can be useful for other researchers in CSCL and CSCW. We strongly believe that for shared experience to have a lasting value it must be tightly integrated with the artifacts that mediate collaboration. A long-term goal of our work is to record experience that captures domain-oriented base activity and not only the experience for building and tailoring the systems.

ACKNOWLEDGMENTS

The first author would like to thank the members of the DARE project at the TRIGONE lab at USTL. The second author would like to thank the members of the DoCTA NSS project at the Universities in Bergen and Oslo.

REFERENCES

Bourguin G., Derycke A. (2001), Integrating the CSCL Activities into Virtual Campuses: Foundations of a new Infrastructure for Distributed Collective Activities. *Proceedings of First European Conference on Computer-Supported Collaborative Learning* (*Euro-CSCL 2001*), Maastricht, the Netherlands, March 22-24, Pierre Dillenbourg et al. eds., pp. 123-130.

Mørch, A. (1997), Three Levels of End-User Tailoring: Customization, Integration, and Extension. In *Computers and Design in Context*. M. Kyng & L. Mathiassen (eds.). The MIT Press, Cambridge, MA, pp. 51-76.

Scardamalia, M. & C. Bereiter (1996), Computer support for knowledge-building communities in T. Koschmann, ed., In *CSCL: Theory and practice of an emerging paradigm*. Lawrence Erlbaum, Mahwah NJ, USA, pp. 249-268.

Szyperski, C. (1997), *Component Software: Beyond Object-Oriented Programming*. Addison-Wesley.

Wasson, B. and Mørch, A. (2000), Identifying Collaboration Patterns in Collaborative Telelearning Scenarios. *Educational Technology & Society 3(3).*

Modelling and Supporting Learning Activities in a Computer-integrated Classroom

Andreas Lingnau, Ulrich Hoppe
University of Duisburg, Germany
{lingnau,hoppe}@informatik.uni-duisburg.de

ABSTRACT
We have implemented ubiquitous computing technology in a primary school setting to support rich classroom activities particularly in the field of early literacy. After initial tests have corroborated the benefit of this technology with respect to attaining curricular goals and to better supporting learner-centred classroom methodologies, we are now exploring specific intelligent support mechanisms, e.g., to inform participants - both teachers and pupils - about automatically assessed learning opportunities.

Keywords
Early learning, literacy, intelligent support, collaborative learning analysis, ubiquitous computing

INTRODUCTION
Computer supported collaborative learning is often identified with "virtual learning" in distance scenarios. In contrast to this, we have pursued the idea of enriching face-to-face classroom situations with embedded computing technologies. The technological approach was deliberately subordinated to grown curricular goals and pedagogical traditions. Recently, we have been able to demonstrate the benefits of such "computer integrated classrooms" in a specific learning domain (Tewissen et al., 2001). In this paper, we elaborate how specific forms of online support can be generated in computerised classroom environments. The classroom as such is a collaborative scenario with different roles (e.g., teachers, learners, peer helpers) and resources (network, archives, software tools, physical devices). In our view, automatic support functions are not meant to guide and control classroom learning processes globally but to locally enrich the situation, e.g., by informing participants about learning opportunities and affordances.

Within the European NIMIS project ("Networked Interactive Media in Schools", cf. NIMIS, 1998), computer integrated classrooms have been set up in associated primary schools. Both hardware selection and software design have been orientated towards the special needs of early learners. The classroom design was based on principles of "ubiquitous computing" (Weiser, 1991) (Fig. 1). To give the pupils easy access to our computing facilities a special JAVA based software has been developed which replaces the Windows desktop. As a standard mode the desktop supports partner work by allowing two children to be logged in at a time at one workplace.

Fig. 1 The NIMIS classroom in Duisburg

The concept of a "computer integrated classroom" (CiC) is essentially targeted at fostering collaboration between pupils. In Duisburg, the focus was set on the process of learning how to read and write. Adapting a new method called "Lesen durch Schreiben" (Engl.: Reading Through Writing, RTW) which was originally introduced in Switzerland (Reichen, 1991) the application T³ ("Today's Talking Typewriter") has been developed. It is a phonetics based approach for teaching reading and writing. Pupils get access to the complete range of phonemes in the form of a palette with letters from the very beginning. Thus children are able to write words by combining letters from a "phoneme table", even though they are not yet able to read. In abstract terms RTW inverts the usual sequencing of the analytic task of de-coding (reading) and synthetic task of encoding (writing). T³ is designed for usage with pen based interactive screens and behaves similar to the known procedure with pencil and paper in the normal classroom. (Fig. 2, cf. Tewissen et al., 2000).

INTELLIGENT SUPPORT

T^3 is enhanced to provide two different kinds of intelligent support, using the *Support Agent Architecture* developed by Prada et al. (2000). It facilitates intelligent agents which are not explicitly visualised but functionally embedded in the T^3 workspace.

Phonetic diagnosis

To provide automatic support for the children's' phonetic writing it is important that target words are known by the system. (In phonetic writing, it is practically impossible to infer a target word from only two or three starting letters.) If a target word is known, a phonetic diagnosis can be performed by comparison which allows for sophisticated forms of intelligent feedback. T^3 provides a pre-selection of target words on so called "theme pages". The phonetic comparison between the target word and the writing product of the child is done by an algorithm that is based on a phonetic classification. It detects incorrect substitutions, missing and "wrong" phonemes.

Fig. 2 Phonetic writing with T^3

Writing Support

There are two different intelligent agents in T^3. Both use the phonetic diagnostic algorithm. The first agent provides an embedded, "implicit" feedback during the writing process. Depending on the learning phase, the writing agent will first only analyse phonemes which are clearly pronounced and later also those which are not emphasised. The agent gives hints by "moving" the letters in the workspace to form a gap at the position where a phoneme is missing.

The second kind of support offers a selection of "peer experts" to those children who have problems detecting correct phonemes in a target word. The phonetic diagnosis determines the correctness values from the content of the workspace. If the score of the writing result exceeds a predefined limit the information is stored in a database. From this database, peer helpers will be selected according to their specific strengths. The mediation of peer helper is based on the methodology of "multiple student modelling" (Hoppe, 1995). The offer of peer helpers stimulates collaboration, which can take place outside the system in the classroom (by natural face-to-face communication) as well as inside the system in a special collaborative mode of T^3.

PERSPECTIVES

The intelligent support will be evaluated and improved in close cooperation with teachers. The indicators for the different stages of writing skills will be tested and checked against the teachers' expectations and observations in the classroom. A specific challenge lies in determining the point in time when learners start to read. This is particularly difficult since the overt actions in the system are only writing actions.

ACKNOWLEDGMENTS

Parts of this work has been funded by the European Esprit project No. 29301, "NIMIS". We thank our NIMIS partners and especially the teachers and pupils of the associated schools for their participation and creative input.

REFERENCES

Hoppe, H.U. (1995). Using multiple student modeling to parameterize group learning. In *Proc. of AI-ED '95*, 234-241, Washington D.C., August 1995: AACE.

Prada, R., Machado, I. & Paiva, A. (2000) TEATRIX: Virtual Environment for Story Creation. In *Proc. of ITS 2000*, 464-473, Montreal, June 2000: Springer.

Reichen, J. (1991). *Lesen durch Schreiben.* ("Reading through Writing"). Zürich, Switzerland: Sabe

Tewissen, F., Lingnau, A. & Hoppe, H.U. (2000). "Today's Talking Typewriter" Supporting Early Literacy in a Classroom Environment. In *Proc. of ITS 2000*, 252-261, Montreal, June 2000: Springer.

Tewissen, F., Hoppe, H.U., Lingnau, A., Mannhaupt, G., Nischk, D. (2001). Collaborative Writing in a Computer-integrated Classroom for Early Learning. In *Proc. of E-CSCL 2001*, Maastricht, Netherlands, March 2001.

Weiser, M. (1991). The computer for the 21st century. *Scientific American* 9/91, 66-75.

The Digital Workbook Students Constructing their Curriculum

Håkon Tolsby
(hakont@hum.auc.dk)
Dept. of Communication; Aalborg University; Kroghstræde 3;
DK-9220 Aalborg Oest; Denmark. Tel: +45 9635 9086. Fax: +45 9815 9434

INTRODUCTION

The purpose of this paper is to demonstrate a constructivist strategy of organizing Internet-based learning. The goal has been to design a learning environment that is open, student centred and problem based, in which the student is given control of the situation instead of being controlled, and which provides the student with sufficient structure and support to solve the problems and to reflect on the experiences (Dewey 1915).

The pedagogical tool discussed in this paper is called the digital workbook. It is not an advanced piece of technology. It is more a strategy for organizing and structuring Internet-based learning, where one takes advantage of the Internet as a constructivist and democratic tool.

The experiences of using the digital workbook come from a course in computer science given at Ostfold University College in Norway. The subject matter was "local area network and intranet", and there were 115 students attending the course, among them 17 distant students. Further there was only one teacher assigned to the course, sitting off-campus in Denmark, and two student assistants on campus. Consequently there were several challenges to overcome when designing a problem based learning environment for this course. The advantage was that the students were skilled in using computers.

THE DIGITAL WORKBOOK

The digital workbook is inspired by the portfolio pedagogy. It is a framework for structuring and collecting the work of the student. The aims of the workbook are: to effectuate knowledge building, to support communication and the sharing of experiences, and to provide assessment based on samples demonstrating authentic student work and focusing on the student as a problem solver. The course was carried out without ordinary lectures. It was organized around the framework provided by the workbook. Each student was supposed to construct his/her own workbook and publish it on the WWW.

In order to give direction in the learning process (Dewey 1915), the workbook was divided into four chapters, covering different aspects of the subject matter. In the first chapter the student was asked to describe his/her learning goals and motives for attending the course. The learning goals were expected to be reflected in the workbook. The next three chapters covered different main aspects or disciplines of the subject matter. Further there were organized several activities to each chapter. The main activities were related to producing content for the chapter. These activities raised different problems spanning from the concrete and general to the experimental, and they were meant to cover the different stages of an experiential learning cycle (Kolb 1983).

The problems the students were expected to work on were the following: giving an overview of the current technology; describing a "real" case to which they should prescribe solutions; choosing a technological problem to discuss and elaborate; carrying out a practical implementation and reflecting upon the experiences. The structure of these activities was deliberately kept relatively open. The learner was allowed to shape the problem according to his/her own experiences and interests. The student was expected to make the problem his/her own and identify with it (Dewey 1915).

Other activities had supporting functions. They were means to aid the student in elaborating on the problems and writing the chapters. Extensive study resources had been prepared for each problem to support the students in constructing their workbook, such as well-structured Web pages covering the basics of the subject matter. The students were also encouraged to look up external sources on the Internet and in the library. Additionally they received individual tutoring as well as written feedback to each chapter, and there were online discussion facilities (web-conferences) where they could raise and discuss problems and solutions.

The students were free to work on the activities whenever they preferred to. This meant that there were a variety of ways of traversing the terrain in order to meet the problem-solving approach and to answer the learner's enquiry. Learning is a dynamic process and the student could return to the different problems and elaborate further on them after obtaining more insight and knowledge. They were allowed to work with the problems of the workbook during the whole semester, which meant they had the possibility to engage in a process of learning at their own convenience. Additionally, the students were encouraged to visit each other's workbooks, discuss them and exchange experiences.

THE INQUIRY

The students' experiences of the digital workbook were researched using different methodologies: observation, questionnaires and interviews. The analysis of this empirical material indicates that different learning patterns were developing as a consequence of using the digital workbook, and it raises some interesting questions that will be briefly discussed below.

EXPERIENCES

An experiential learning style. The learning stories told by the students indicated that the students were indeed working in an experiential manner. They returned to the problem repeatedly after reflecting on it and doing more research, and after gaining more insight and practical experience. They emphasized that it was the problem-oriented tasks in the workbook that they really felt they learned from, when they were required to describe their own case for implementing a network and when they had to research a self-defined problem within the subject. These were the tasks they claimed that they returned to repeatedly. They also acknowledged the digital workbook as a learning tool. They characterized the workbook as being the motivating factor, and emphasized that they could form the workbook after their own interests and experiences.

- "The workbook makes you remember more of the theory. Students who attended this course last year without the workbook, don't remember anything at all" (male student).

Copying, or constructing knowledge? Copying was observed in the workbooks, but not as a general phenomenon. The students only copied when they solved general and shallower problems. For example when they were asked to give an overview of the technology, they copied from each other and from the study resources on the Web. These parts of the workbook are therefore remarkably similar for all of the students.

However, in the problem-oriented activities where the students were asked to define problems themselves and where they could present their own experiences, there is no noticeable copying. As one student remarked in an interview, "It is not possible to copy when you work with these topics". As a result all workbooks are different and with an individual profile.

- **Loneliness and distress at the price of flexibility.** The digital workbook provides a very flexible working style, and many students appreciated that (30% in the questionnaire). The problem is that just as many found the workbook overwhelming. A typical comment is that the workbook requires considerable discipline and that there is little pace provided by the design. The students also found it difficult to know where to begin and what was expected of them. They also complained that they got little feedback from the teacher.

As an observable consequence about half of the students postponed the work with the workbook until the last weeks before assessment. Some did this deliberately because it suited their work and life situation, but many did it because they were not motivated to start earlier.

Collaboration or comparison? We had expected that the students would collaborate. What we found was that the students were showing their workbooks to each other (except three students), and they explained that they were using the workbooks as a ground for discussions and for getting feedback. Additionally, the students were browsing each other's workbooks regularly and were interested in comparing their own work with that of their peers to get inspiration. Still there was no genuine collaboration (Salomon 1995). The workbook is an individual project and publishing on the WWW alone is not sufficient to stimulate collaboration.

CONCLUSION

The digital workbook appears to function as a design concept for a constructivist-learning environment. The workbook creates an environment where knowledge is constructed and where learning is experienced through activity and reflection, and most students adapted to the new learning model.

The negative result is that some 30% of the students felt lonely and distressed and were not motivated to work with the workbook. This can be expressed as the dilemma between designing for maximum flexibility and putting more effort in controlling the learner, and between designing for individual contra social learning.

One solution to the problem could be to allow the students to work in project groups and to make the digital workbook a shared resource of the group, visualizing shared experiences.

The experiences with the digital workbook and the results from the research are not conclusive. There is thus a need for more research on these types of arrangements in order to develop a coherent and stimulating digital learning environment that will benefit both students and teachers.

REFERENCES

Dewey John (1915). Democracy and Education. An introduction to the Philosophy of Education. The Free Press. ISBN 0-684-83631-9.

Kolb, David A (1983). Experiential Learning: Experience as the Source of Learning and Development. Prentice Hall. ISBN: 0-132-952-610.

Salomon, G (1995). What Does the Design of Effective CSCL Require and How Do We Study Its Effects? CSCL 95.

Advancing Understanding of Learning in Interaction: How Ways of Participating Can Influence Joint Performance and Learning

Brigid Barron, David Sears

Stanford University

barronbj@stanford.edu

ABSTRACT

An enduring issue for CSCL researchers involves developing methods of assessing collaborative interaction and tracing the quality of collaboration to learning outcomes. One critical question for research is whether we can identify relational and/or interactional resources that are important for generative collaboration. In this presentation, we will share research that examined the relationship between student interactions, group success, and subsequent individual performance on the same and a related problem solving measure.

Keywords

Alignment of goals, mutuality in interaction, joint attention, transfer of learning, quality of collaboration.

INTRODUCTION

Success in joint endeavors is often attributed to the knowledge-base resources that individuals uniquely bring to a collaborative situation. While individual resources are essential, recent research suggests that attention must also be paid to the ecology of relations that develops within interactions that make it possible (or not) for knowledge and other cognitive resources to be accessed, functionally expressed, and shared among group members. A number of accounts suggest that the quality and nature of collaboration within groups can differ even given objectively similar situations, and that while interactions emerge over time, and fluctuate on a moment-by moment basis, they can also be characterized broadly as falling on a continuum of productive interdependence. For example, Forman & Cazden (1985) found that different patterns of interaction emerged even given the same problem to solve. They described three styles of working together, "Parallel," "Associative," and "Cooperative," that evolved in the context of Piagetian isolation-of-variables problems and were characterized by increasing degrees of coordination. These findings point to a need to articulate further the dimensions of interaction and their potential consequences. The current research focuses on the relationship between the quality of interaction (as indicated by responses to solution proposals), group performance, and learning outcomes in the context of a mathematical problem solving activity.

METHODS

Participants

The data set includes twelve groups of high-achieving sixth grade students whose scores on the problem formed a bi-modal distribution. Triads were composed of same gender participants.

Materials and Procedures

The first episode in a series called *The Adventures of Jasper Woodbury* (Cognition and Technology Group at Vanderbilt, 1997) provided the mathematical problem-solving task used in this study. In order to solve the problem, students had to collect data embedded in the video presentation. Students solved the problem in same-gender groups of three. (see Barron, 2000a,b; Sears, Barron, & Strobel, 2001 for more detail).

RESULTS

Analysis of Response Patterns

The results from our coding of group interactions address two main questions: 1) Do the pattern of responses to correct proposals of students in successful and unsuccessful groups differ significantly; and 2) Do the pattern of response pairs differ significantly according to group success? All responses to correct proposals were categorized as engaged responses or non-engaged. Engaged responses took up the proposal in conversation and accepted or discussed it. Non-engaged responses included no verbal response or rejection of the proposal without rationale. As shown in Table 1, Chi square analyses indicated that successful groups made significantly more Engaged responses and significantly less Non-Engaged responses than unsuccessful groups, (*Chi sq.* (1) = 22.2, p = .000). Independent t-tests revealed that the proportion of Engaged responses produced by successful groups ($M(7)$ = 66.46% (±7.47%)) was significantly higher than that of unsuccessful groups ($M(4)$ = 41.75% (±26.04%), t = 5.904, $p < .05$). Thus, our analyses suggest that the groups did differ significantly, and in the direction that one would expect. It is interesting to note that the proportions are nearly inverted, with successful groups producing a fairly high rate of Engaged responses (66.46%) while unsuccessful groups produce a fairly high rate of Non-Engaged responses (58.75%).

In addition to looking at individual responses to correct proposals, we examined response pairs. It is important to realize that when people work in groups, often one person's response is taken to be the group's response, especially if the other group members remain silent. Thus, to determine whether responses to correct proposals were different at the group level (e.g. both partners) and not just at the individual level between successful and unsuccessful groups, we examined response pairs. Chi square analysis indicated that successful groups and unsuccessful groups differed in their production of pair types (Engage & Engage, Engage & Non-Engage, or Non-Engage & Non-Engage), (*Chi sq.* (2) = 24.9, $p = .000$). An independent t-test indicated that the successful groups (M (7) = 3.47% (±6.05%)) produced a trend toward a significantly lower proportion of Non-Engage & Non-Engage response pairs than unsuccessful groups (M (4) = 30.46% (±35.31%)), ($t(1) = 4.215$, $p = .07$). The differences between the two other possible response pairs were not significant. Thus, these results suggest that one characteristic of the interactions of unsuccessful groups includes a lack of responsiveness or reciprocity. Again, it is worth noting the magnitude of the difference in this lack of give and take between unsuccessful and successful groups. As shown by the percentages above, the proportion of Non-Engage response pairs produced by unsuccessful groups was nearly 10 times greater than the proportion produced by successful groups.

Mastery and Transfer Performance

Independent t-tests revealed that students in successful groups performed significantly better than their peers in unsuccessful groups on both the mastery test ($M_{successful}$ (7) = 96.8% (±14.6%), $M_{unsuccessful}$ (4) = 68.1% (±32.2%), $t = -3.53$, $p = 0.0013$, $df = 31$) and the transfer test ($M_{successful}$ (7) = 93.6% (±16.3%), $M_{unsuccessful}$ (4) = 73.7% (±32.9%), $t = -2.34$, $p = 0.026$, $df = 31$). Thus, we can see that students in successful groups showed more Engaged responses as well as greater performance.

CONCLUSION

These results suggest that better collaboration, as measured by the production and acceptance of correct proposals, is associated with group performance and greater individual learning. To advance research on CSCL issues we need to continue to define features of interaction that are linked to qualities of mutual engagement, quality of joint work, and individual learning. This work is a step in that direction.

REFERENCES

Barron, B.J. (2000a). Problem solving in video-based microworlds: Collaborative and individual outcomes of high-achieving sixth-grade students. *Journal of Educational Psychology, 92*, 391-398.

Barron, B. (2000b). Achieving coordination in collaborative problem solving groups. *The Journal of the Learning Sciences*, 9(4), 403-436.

Cognition and Technology Group at Vanderbilt (1997). *The Jasper Project. Lessons in curriculum, instruction, assessment, and professional development.* Mahwah, NJ: Erlbaum.

Forman & Cazden (1985). Exploring Vygotskian perspectives in education: The cognitive value of peer interaction. In J.V. Wertsch (Ed.), Culture, communication, and cognition: Vygotskian perspectives (pp. 323-347). New York: Cambridge University Press.

Sears, D.A., Barron, B., & Strobel, K.R.(2000). Coding collaborative interactions in a math setting: Attempting to identify discourse patterns that lead to group acceptance of correct proposals. Paper presented at the American Educational Research Association (AERA) Conference, Seattle, WA, April 2001.

Supporting Children's Collaborative Authoring: Practicing Written Literacy While Composing Oral Texts

Mike Ananny

Media Laboratory,
Massachusetts Institute of Technology
ananny@media.mit.edu

ABSTRACT

This paper presents the theory, design and evaluation of a new type of computer-supported collaborative interface intended to help young children practice certain oral language skills critical for later written literacy acquisition. Based on a theory of "emergent literacy", this paper describes a toy – TellTale – designed to let young children create, share and edit oral language in a way similar to how they will eventually create written language. Two user studies were conducted. The first suggests that paired children of different SES use different social and linguistic strategies to establish cohesion and that purely syntactic measures of narrative coherence are not sensitive enough to describe children's collaborative language play. A second pilot study investigated how groups of children used TellTale. Although results are not conclusive, TellTale also seems to be an engaging interface for group authorship.

Keywords

Emergent literacy, collaboration, authoring, language, play, toys, socio-economic strata.

INTRODUCTION

Old distinctions between collaborative learning, group play and language instruction are changing as both digital media and our relationship with technology evolve. By carefully designing technology-enhanced language toys that give children control over both the structure and content of their language, young children may be able to engage in literacy activities previously thought to be too advanced for their age. This research addresses a particular aspect of this new opportunity.

Specifically, it claims that a tangible technology-enhanced toy – TellTale – that supports collaborative construction of oral language can help children practice certain skills crucial for later written literacy. TellTale's interface is designed to support "externalized meaning-making" (Wells, 1981) and "emergent literacy" (Whitehurst and Lonigan, 1998) through collaborative oral story construction.

TELLTALE: A TOY TO SUPPORT COLLABORATIVE LANGUAGE PLAY

TellTale (shown at left) is a caterpillar-like toy with five modular, colored body pieces and a head. Children can press a button on each of the five body pieces to record 20 seconds of audio into that body piece. The child can then play back that audio by pressing the body piece's record button. The body pieces detach from each other and can be arranged and rearranged in any order. At any point the child can attach the toy's head to the body in order to hear the entire story (*i.e.* the audio recorded into each of the five pieces) played in sequence. The child can also record over the audio in any body piece at any time. All body pieces are identical in functionality and are designed to help children reflect upon the structure and content of their stories.

EVALUATING TELLTALE: TWO STUDIES

While an earlier study (Ananny & Cassell, 2001) found that TellTale's segmented interface successfully encourages individual children to create cohesive narratives, the two studies described here were designed to investigate how children use TellTale during collaborative language play. Due to space restrictions, only very brief descriptions of both studies are given here. For a complete presentation of both studies, please see the on-line version of this paper.

User study #1: TellTale and Paired Authorship

The goal of this study was to investigate the specific kinds of collaborative techniques paired children use to establish coherence within a jointly-authored TellTale story and, secondarily, how children of different socio-economic strata (SES) may use different strategies to establish narrative cohesion. A total of 22 native-English speaking children (5 low-SES dyads, 6 high-SES dyads) ranging in age from 6,1 to 7,6 participated in the study.

Overall, children from different socio-economic strata tended to engage in different behaviors during collaborative storytelling. An initial analysis of only the quantitative data may interpret low-SES children's high percentage of co-occurring utterances and low percentage of syntactic connectives as an indication that they are less able to engage in good turn-taking behavior and that they are less aware of their co-participant. But the qualitative data suggest that this may not be the case for two reasons: low-SES children appear to be using more subtle (*e.g.* non-syntactic, paralinguistic and non-verbal) strategies to indicate turn-taking during story construction. Also, despite the high percentage of co-occurring utterances in low-SES children's recordings, these children consistently incorporated elements of their partner's utterances concurrently. In contrast, children from high-SES tended to establish coherence using syntactic connectives between consecutive recordings.

The location of conjunctive phrases also suggests an interesting new finding. In both high- and low-SES conditions, children were more likely to use connectives to link the beginning of their recordings to the previous recording and less likely to use connectives to link the end of the recording to the subsequent recording. This reliable pattern suggests that, when children are establishing narrative coherence, they may be more focused on linking with previous content than planning for coherence with future content.

User Study #2: TellTale and Group Authorship (A Pilot)

Although this study was only a pilot investigation, several interesting observations were made about children's collaborative language play with TellTale. A total of 7 children in two groups participated in this study: four 7-year old girls in one group; three brothers aged 3, 5 and 7 in the second group.

In both groups, children worked together to build stories. Children frequently debated exactly what should be recorded in each body piece. At one point in the 7-year old girls' group, the story became complex and there was much debate over exactly what should be said in the fourth body piece. One child wrote with a crayon on a piece of paper exactly what she thought should be said – "so we'll know for sure" – indicating that these children were comfortable mixing written authorship with oral storytelling during the play session. In the other session, a 7-year old creatively used TellTale to solve his brothers' problem. After the 5-year old and the 3-year old had recorded into four of the five body pieces, they expressed concern that there was only one body piece left. The 7-year old brother then held down the record button on the fifth body piece while playing back the first four. In effect, he "copied" the first four body pieces into the fifth, freeing four body pieces for new audio.

CONCLUSION

While TellTale supports only certain kinds of language play, its design and evaluation suggest that there is a new opportunity to use media technology to support children's emergent literacy development and collaborative play. One user study found that children of different socio-economic strata use different strategies to establish cohesion during joint construction of oral stories; and that children's use of conjunctive phrases may indicate a preference to link with previous content over planning for future content. A second pilot study suggests that TellTale may also support authorship among more than two children.

ACKNOWLEDGMENTS

Special thanks to Professor Hiroshi Ishii and Professor Justine Cassell for their collaborative guidance. Thanks also to Dr. Bakhtiar Mikhak and Jean Barnwell for help thinking through and building this project. This work was generously supported by LEGO and the MIT Media Laboratory's Things That Think and Digital Life consortia.

REFERENCES

Ananny, M. & J. Cassell (2001). "TellTale: A toy to encourage written literacy skills through oral storytelling." Presentation at Winter Conference on Text, Discourse & Cognition, Jackson, USA. January 28-30, 2001.

Wells, G. (1981). "Language, literacy and education." In Wells, G. (Ed.), *Language Through Interaction*. Cambridge: Cambridge University Press.

Whitehurst,G.&C.Lonigan(1998)."Child development and emergent literacy."*Child Development* 69(3),pp.848-872.

Using "Thinking Tags" with Kindergarten Children: A Dental Health Simulation

Gail Andrews, Kimberley A. MacKinnon, Susan Yoon

Ontario Institute for Studies in Education at the University of Toronto (OISE/UT)
gsandrews@oise.utoronto.ca, kmackinnon@oise.utoronto.ca & syoon@oise.utoronto.ca

ABSTRACT

According to many dental professionals, the decay effects from the accumulation of sugar on teeth are a very difficult concept for young children to learn. Playing the dental hygiene game with Thinking Tags not only brings context into the classroom, but allows children to work with digital maipulatives that provide instant feedback. Instead of watching a demonstration of the accumulation of sugars on a screen or being told about dental health, this simulation allows 5-year old children to experience improving or decaying dental health without any real adverse effects. Small, wearable, microprocessor-driven tags were brought into the kindergarten classroom to simulate the decay process, providing information and creating a discussion about teeth. This program was effective and enthusiastically received by this age group.

Keywords

Science, technology, thinking tags, dental health, participatory simulation, discourse

INTRODUCTION

The principles of situated learning are that a) knowledge needs to be presented in an authentic context, and that b) learning entails social interaction and collaboration (Lave, 1999). An example of applied situated learning psychology is a Thinking Tags game designed to show children the concept of accumulation. Building on this basic concept, children are able to learn that sugar on the teeth can accumulate and over time cause tooth decay. Many dental professionals believe that this concept is thought to be too difficult for children to comprehend. In fact, the Canadian Dental Association recommends that children at this age should not be responsible for their own dental care (CDHA, 2000). Although the values of brushing are taught at this age, basic science concepts, which lie behind dental health, are not readily taught to this age group. Apart from an underdeveloped level of responsibility, it may be presumed that children are not able to grasp the complex concept of interactions of sugar on the teeth over time, which can cause cavities.

Resnick, Berg & Eisenberg, (2000) show that a constructionist "scientific instrument design has the potential to spark interest in scientific issues among students who otherwise avoid the subject altogether". We aim to show that by concentrating on the most basic ideas relating to accumulation and applying the pedagogy of situated learning, we can successfully teach this difficult concept to children as young as five.

THINKING TAGS AND DENTAL HEALTH

The MIT Media Laboratory has been at work developing small wearable microcomputers called *Thinking Tags* (Tags). These Tags are about the size of a name badge and are equipped with infrared ports and sensors, lights and a small display panel. With these tags, children are given the opportunity to concretely explore abstract scientific ideas. Furthermore, studies with digital robotic bricks show students using the bricks were required to examine classic feedback strategies, which they might not otherwise formally investigate until university (Resnick, 1998). This exploration of feedback and emergence allows insight into scientific thinking, the basic building blocks for activities such as data collection and control.

Digital manipulative objects can be also be programmed to demonstrate interactive behaviours. When programmed in this way, digital tools, like children's mechanical structures and toy model sets before them, provide insight into the type of interactive behaviour from which more complex systems arise (Resnick, Martin, Berg, Borovoy, Colella, Kramer, and Silverman, 1998). Due to its ability to allow students to explore feedback, emergence and control, this area of research may have many potential educational benefits. Digital tools can help students learn complex concepts by breaking those concepts down into basic levels and observing the behaviours that arise from these simple interactions. Students have the ability to tackle these concepts well before they are ready to learn them in an abstract, formalized educational setting. It is necessary then, to provide them with the tools to grasp them.

THE DENTAL HEALTH SIMULATION

Kindergarten aged children wear computerized Thinking Tags, that, through kinetic make-believe, show them the health status of their "teeth". In the Dental Health Simulation, children are asked to wear the Tags for a short period of time while they pretend to "feed" on various food items placed around the room. The food items have other Tags buried inside them, which emit information via infrared signals as to the amount of sugar contained in a serving of that specific product. Sugar amounts vary from food to food, with sugared cereal being the highest and water having no sugar value at all. Furthermore, a time-delay feature was added to simulate the temporal relationship between accumulation and decay. After a specific time, calculated according to the amount of sugar accumulated (more sugar means less time), healthy teeth (indicated by five green lights on the Tag turn red, indicating a state of dental decay. Children then have thirty seconds to get to the brushing station before one of their teeth, or LED lights, turns red permanently, indicating the presence of a cavity.

RESULTS & DISCUSSION

Our Thinking Tag game has been designed to introduce children to the concept of accumulation. Students made comments such as, "I'm eating the crackers" and "I have a cavity!", suggesting that they were able to personally identify with the characteristics of their Tag. The first-person experiences demonstrated in the study shows the extent to which children are drawn into the game, therefore enhancing the context for learning. Once the props were removed, children again referred to the Tag as "it".

The children were also observed collaborating with one another, urging their peers to brush their teeth when the lights on their Tag had turned red, suggesting that meaningful interaction is not impeded by the technology. It seems to be the case that the nature and quality of student discourse is in fact enhanced through the use of the Thinking Tags. Some of the children commented that "You brush before they go red!", indicating that they were able to identify proactive measures, before any observable evidence of decay had taken place.

Early work with this simulation suggests that 5-year olds are able to grasp the concept of accumulation of sugar. When the children were asked if they learned anything while they were doing this activity, they commented that they learned "not to eat too much" of the sugary foods. However, several questions still need to be addressed, including: Are children building on one concept after the other? What effect do the presence of classmates and the discourse have on learning? Furthermore, the temporal element in the simulation seems to indicate an important learning advance in children this age and future research may continue to explore the relationship between game time elapsed and amount of sugar.

ACKNOWLEDGMENTS

Special thanks to the Thinking Tag Committee at OISE/UT for their support.

REFERENCES

Canadian Dental Association Health Advisory (2000). *Your Dental Health, Children's Teeth.* Ottawa, Ontario. Courtesy CRHA (Calgary Regional Health Authority). [Web Resource] Available: http://www.cda-adc.ca/public/your_dental_health/childrens/cleaningenglish.html

Lave, J. (2000) *The Principles of Situated Learning.* http://tip.psychology.org/lave.html

Resnick, M., Berg, B & Eisenberg, M. (2000). Beyond Black Boxes: Bringing Transparency and Aesthetics Back to Scientific Investigation. *Published in Journal of the Learning Sciences.* [Web Resource] Available: http://el.www.media.mit.edu/groups/el/Papers/mres/bbb-jls/

Resnick, M. (1998). Technologies for Lifelong Kindergarten. *Educational Technology Research and Development*, vol. 46, no. 4.

Resnick, M., Martin, F., Berg, R., Borovoy, R., Colella, V., Kramer, K., and Silverman, B. (1998). Digital Manipulatives. *Proceedings of the CHI '98 conference*, Los Angeles, April 1998.

Presumptive Literacies in Technology-Integrated Science Curriculum

Kimberley P. Williams, Louis M. Gomez

Center for Learning Technologies in Urban Schools, Northwestern University
(k-williams1@northwestern.edu), (l-gomez@northwestern.edu)

ABSTRACT

In this paper we explore the multiple literacies presumed in the design of inquiry curriculum created at the Center for Learning Technologies in Urban Schools (LeTUS). The current design of LeTUS inquiry-based, technology embedded science curriculum presumes a facility with, and strategic use of literacies on the part of students who enact the curriculum. Here literacy means two things: deriving meaning from patterns in knowledge domains like science and facility with different information forms. We use teacher interviews and on-line discussions to expose presumptive literacies in design and learners' literacy challenges and offer suggestions that teacher modifications to these units can inform future design to support literacy in science.

Keywords: technology supported science curriculum, literacy, universal design

INTRODUCTION

Advanced learning technologies coupled with inquiry-based curricula can offer students access to powerful ideas in science as never before. For example, tools like Geodyamic data base and World Watcher makes visualizations of Earth's structures and data about its processes available to students and teachers in ways that fit into classroom activity. These tools, in theory, will allow all students to engage in more authentic analysis of current problems like the impact of global warming on the average temperature changes in our hemisphere or how to find earth's plate boundaries from earthquake and volcanic activity data. Curriculum projects like those at the Center for Learning Technologies in Urban Schools (LeTUS) (Gomez & Marx 1999; Krajick et. al. , 1998) and inquiry-focused projects(e.g. WISE) aim to create learning environments that make this sort of ambitious science a regular part of children's science learning. This is a challenging endeavor with many roadblocks. Nevertheless LeTUS and others are creating a substantial collection of technology-infused science units that are finding growing utility in urban classrooms. Heretofore our efforts at achieving utility have centered on matters like technology access, scaffolds to learners' prior knowledge, and technology usability. These are, and will for some time, remain important issues. We have devoted relatively less attention to the simple notion that learners must be literate to use these units. In this paper we focus on the literacy demands for urban children embedded in modern inquiry-based curricula. We now conjecture, and will later demonstrate, that, with respect to literacy, urban and second language learners lack the necessary literacy skills to use many of the curricular materials and tools of current inquiry based, technology integrated science curriculum.

To date a great deal of research has addressed how to create tools and materials to provide scaffolds (Edelson et. al., 1999; Loh et.al., 1998 that provide access and support for connecting students' prior knowledge to the opportunities to learning in curriculum, and deepen conceptual understandings in science domains. A central characteristic of these materials, whether graphics, text, or media-based, is that they heavily engage students' literacy skills. We conjecture that the very scaffolds that are designed to help students learn science may be inaccessible because they presume skills that students do not possess.

The Presumptive Literacies Study

The Presumptive Literacies Study was created to understand how to foreground the literacy demands of LeTUS curriculum and how to design literacy supports within the curricula units. The project has three phases: (1) document the literacy demands of the curricula; (2) engage in university researcher-teacher researcher collaborative design teams to design literacy-based modifications to the units, (3) beta test the modifications in LeTUS classrooms, and develop a set of principles to support literacy and linguistic needs in LeTUS science curriculum.

Method

We engaged in a multi-methodological (interviews, on-line reports, classroom observation not reported here) approach to data collection. For the purposes of organizing and analyzing the resultant data, we used a constant comparative research approach. When we were satisfied that the final categories represented the literacy demands and teacher strategies themes we began to conduct micro level analyses of each theme. The goal of the micro level analyses was to more fully describe the themes and to develop a set of principles for supporting the literacy that is engaged in LeTUS science curriculum.

FINDINGS

Results suggest that the LeTUS curriculum assumes that students require minimum support for, or have an adequate skill set to draw from, to do at least the following seven literacy-based activities: (1) conduct internet research; (2) identify research-relevant information; (3) recognize, record, and organize necessary information from science-related and documentary video; (4) interpret dynamic databases, scientific visualization graphs and systems modeling tools; (5) add research data to and organize information within advanced learning technology software; (6) access relevant background knowledge (often text-based) and make connections to current content and process requirements of activities; (7) organize and communicate research findings, especially utilizing multi-media tools. If curricular use requires these, and other, literacy skills and students do not even recognize these as genres with specific structure, students' access to the powerful ideas and tools of science made possible by inquiry-based techniques will be blocked. The data suggest that the literacy-centered curriculum modifications reported here fall into 10 topical areas; 1) accessing and building on prior knowledge; 2) vocabulary development, 3) deepening concepts; 4) providing students with tools to organize their learning and "hang their knowledge on, 5) building an awareness of patterns in information genres; 6) increasing reading comprehension; 7) focusing inquiry 8) data interpretation using multiple sources; 9) communicating complex ideas using multiple genres; 10) ongoing individual and collaborative assessment.

CONCLUSIONS

At the beginning of this report we claimed that little attention has been paid to the notion that learners must be literate to use inquiry-based, technology embedded curricula. We have attempted here to call attention to the literacy demands for urban and second language learners in these curricula and have used teacher modifications of these curricula as a lens into understanding how to deepen content and process understanding while supporting literacy skills. In sum, we believe designers of inquiry curricular and supporting materials need to embark on two courses of action. First, designers need to engage in reflective critique of materials themselves to make the literacy demands visible. Second, designers need to pioneer a new set of techniques that will help in using science (and other curriculum as well) as sites to directly support secondary literacy skills. We believe that teacher adaptation is one important lens to help us see literacy demands and to see how to better support children in using literacy to learn.

ACKNOWLEDGMENTS

This research was supported through a grant from the Joyce Foundation for the study of Literacy Design Challenges in Progressive Curriculum and National Science Foundation support to the Center for Learning Technologies in Urban Schools (LeTUS). Last but certainly not least, we thank the teachers for allowing us to gain insights into their practice and theories about how to improve student learning in inquiry curriculum.

REFERENCES

Edelson, D. C., Brown, M., Gordin, D. N., & Griffin, D. A. (1999, February). Making visualization accessible to students. *GSA Today*, 9(2), 8-10.

Gomez, L., & Marx, R.W. (1999). At the nexus of challenging curriculum design, learning technologies, and school transformation: The first year of the Center for Learning Technologies in Urban Schools. Symposium presented at the annual meetings of the American Educational Research Association, Montreal, Canada.

Krajcik, J., Blumenfeld, P. C., Marx, R. W., Bass, K. M., & Fredricks, J. (1998). Inquiry in project-based science classrooms: Initial attempts by middle school students. The Journal of the Learning Sciences, 7, 313-350.

Loh, B., Reiser, B.J., Radinsky J., Edelson, D.C., Gomez, L.M. and Marshall, S. (1998). Developing reflective inquiry practices: A case study of software, the teacher, and students. Published in Designing for Science: Implications from Everyday, Classroom, and Professional Settings.

Moje, E.B., Collazo, T. and Carrillo, R. (2000, April). Maestro, What is Quality?: A Study of Scientific Literacy and Reading Achievement Beyond the Primary Grades."Paper presented at National Association for Research in Science Teaching. Orlando, FL.

Task and Interaction Regulation in Controlling a Traffic Simulation

Patrick Jermann
TECFA – University of Geneva, Switzerland
Patrick.Jermann@tecfa.unige.ch

ABSTRACT

In collaborative problem solving, metacognition not only covers strategic reasoning related to the task but also reasoning related to the interaction itself. The hypothesis underlying this work states that regulation of the interaction and regulation of the task are closely related mechanisms and that their co-occurrence facilitates coordination. These assumptions are tested experimentally with a traffic simulator. The results show that co-occurrence of task and interaction regulation allows quicker solving of the problem, thus better performance. The experimental treatment aims at observing the effects of interaction meters on the accuracy of subjects' estimation of their participation. Interaction meters are visualization tools that represent the number of contributions related to the discussion and to the implementation of the solution.

Keywords

Metacognition, task regulation, interaction regulation, reflective tools, interaction meters

INTRODUCTION

In this paper, we present results from an experimental study investigating two aspects of metacognition at work in collaborative problem solving, namely, task and interaction regulation. The task we used consists of controlling a traffic simulation by tuning the green-red periods of traffic lights in order to reduce waiting time at intersections.

Task regulation is one aspect of metacognition as defined by Schoenfeld (1987) and Brown (1987). It includes knowledge about one's own cognitive processes, action regulation and control, as well as intuitions and conceptions about the context the activity takes place in. We focus here on the second aspect, which includes planning forthcoming actions, supervising current activities and evaluating past actions. In its initial formulation, metacognition is described as a mechanism in individual problem solving. Does the concept of metacognition scale up to a group of individuals who solve a problem? Nickerson (1993) asks this question in the context of the distributed cognition approach (Salomon, 1993). This approach considers a group of persons and the tools they use as a single cognitive system and the question is if such a system also has metacognitive skills.

Interaction regulation consists of organizing work inside a group by defining roles or defining and assigning sub-tasks to participants. We make the general hypothesis that simultaneous regulation of task and interaction is more efficient than regulation of the task alone because it leads to a better coordination of actions.

In order to address the question of the conditions that foster integration of task and interaction regulation we designed a tool that functions like a mirror for the pair's activity. This approach consists in coaching and regulating the interaction as it unfolds (Jermann, Soller & Muelhenbrock, 2001). Subjects are presented a constantly updated visualization of their participation while they solve the task. We refer to these dynamic visualizations as interaction meters. They represent participation in talk and task related actions through bar charts that show the number of messages and the number of problem solving actions. The design rationale of interaction meters is that they might give subjects a better representation of their participation as well as of the role they play in the problem solving process. Interaction meters reify participation and work organization. Our hypothesis is that interaction meters help subjects build and maintain a more accurate model of interaction.

METHOD

In order to test our assumptions, we designed two types of interactions meters. The first compares subjects by representing their participation side by side as two bars ('comparative' condition). The second represents participation cumulated across subjects, i.e. one bar chart represents the sum of the subjects' contribution to discussion and another bar chart represents the sum of the subjects' problem solving actions ('cumulated' condition).

Subjects were recruited through the subject pool associated with introductory psychology classes offered by the University of Pittsburgh. 98 undergraduate students participated in the experiment that was held at the Learning Research and Development Center (LRDC). The pairs were assigned randomly to either the control condition (without interaction meter) or one of the two experimental conditions. The complete duration of an experimental session was about two hours including a 40 minutes long tutorial and a 60 minutes long collaborative problem solving phase.

A snapshot of the simulation tool can be found online at http://tecfa.unige.ch/~jermann/sputnik/snapshots.html

RESULTS

The goal of the subjects was to bring the average waiting time of cars below 20 seconds and maintain it below this limit for 2 minutes. After examining dialogues produced by the 49 pairs, we decided to drop 6 pairs from the analyses. Out of 43 pairs, 39.5% (N=17, referred to as 'failed') failed and 60.5% succeeded (N=26). Due to the high percentage of successful pairs, we further distinguished between the pairs that reached the objective in less than half an hour (N=10, 23.3%, referred to as 'super') from those who succeeded in more than half an hour (N=16, 37.2%, referred to as 'normal').

Pairs that solved the problem in less than half the time allocated are differing from others by several simple traits: they talked relatively more than they executed problem solving actions (F=6.137, p=0.05 with LSD post hoc test; 'super' > 'normal', p=.020 and 'super'> 'failed', p=.001); they produced elaborated plans more frequently (F=2.915, p=.066 with LSD post hoc test; 'super' > 'failed', p=.021). But most important, and supporting our hypothesis that the co-occurrence of task regulation and interaction regulation would lead to a better performance, 'super' successful pairs more frequently produced planning sequences containing explicit references to one member of the group (F=4.233 p=.022 with LSD post hoc test; 'super'>'failed' p=.01 'super'>'normal' p=.015). In other terms, when deciding "what to do", these pairs also tend to decide "who does what".

The results concerning estimation of participation in problem solving actions were compatible with our hypothesis, suggesting that the 'comparative' version of the interaction meters is more helpful than the 'cumulated' version and than the absence of interaction meter. The correlations between the estimation of participation in tuning and the effective participation are r=.744 (p=.000, N=26) for the 'comparative' interaction meter, r= .404 (p=0.41, N=26) for the 'cumulated' interaction meter and r=.403 (p=.018, N=34) for the condition without interaction meter. There is no difference between the comparative and cumulated conditions when comparing the number of times subjects visited the interaction meters. However, on a 7 point lickert scale from very often to very rarely, subjects in the comparative condition stated that they looked up the interaction meter more often (m=3.1, sd=1.4704) than the subjects in the cumulated condition (m=4.23, sd=1.3309) (F=9.797 p=.003). Results for the estimation of participation in discussion were less clear maybe due to the fact that discussion, by essence, requires both individuals to participate, and estimating a difference in participation for such a collaborative activity might sound misleading.

So far, we focused the analysis of results on subject's estimation of participation in the interaction, but other components of a psychological model of interaction would be interesting to investigate. For instance, we might investigate whether subjects are able to perceive roles and what kind of tool would be useful to raise their awareness about their function in the group.

REFERENCES

Brown, A. (1987). Metacognition, Executive Control, Self-Regulation, and Other More Mysterious Mechanisms. In F.E. Weinert & R.H. Kluwe. Metacognition, motivation and understanding. Hillsdale, New Jersey: Lawrence Erlbaum Publisher.

Jermann, P., Soller, A., & Muehlenbrock, M. (2001). From mirroring to guiding: A review of state of the art technology for supporting collaborative learning. Proceedings of the First European Conference on Computer-Supported Collaborative Learning, Maastricht, The Netherlands, 324-331.

Nickerson, R.S. (1993). On the distribution of cognition: some reflections. In G.Salomon (Ed) Distributed Cognition (pp. 229-261). Cambridge University Press, New York.

Salomon, G. (Ed)(1993). Distributed Cognition. Cambridge University Press, New York.

Schoenfeld, A. H. (1987). What's All the Fuss About Metacognition ? In Cognitive Science and Mathematics Education. Ed: Alan H. Schoenfeld. London: Lawrence Erlbaum Associates.

Proximity and View Awareness to Reduce Referential Ambiguity in a shared 3D Virtual Environment

David Ott, Pierre Dillenbourg

Geneva Interaction Lab - TECFA
University of Geneva (Switzerland)
David.Ott@tecfa.unige.ch , Pierre.Dillenbourg@tecfa.unige.ch

ABSTRACT

This contribution investigates the role of virtual space on social interactions during collaborative tasks. We previously observed that MUD users rely on spatial positions to refine the conversational context and thereby facilitate mutual understanding. Supporting mutual understanding is a main challenge of CSCL research. We explore how this may happen in a continuous 3D space (VRML). Our first hypothesis was that the proximity of the emitter to the referred object clarifies the referential context. Our second hypothesis stated that the receiver uses gaze awareness in order to guess which object the emitter refers to. The experiment results confirmed the first hypothesis, surprisingly rejected the second hypothesis and reveal complex interactions between the two.

Keywords

Virtual space, virtual reality, collaboration, proxemics, view awareness

INTRODUCTION

Many CSCL environments are based on a spatial metaphor: a virtual campus includes rooms, buildings, etc. Why ? Besides the motivational role and the navigational role of the spatial metaphore we think that virtual space would play a functional role in collaboration among peers. This hypothesis arose from findings of a series of studies using a text-based virtual reality (a MOO environment) to create the task that subjects had to perform (Dillenbourg & Traum, 1999). We observed that the rate of acknowledgment was significantly higher when two subjects were located in the same virtual room (Dillenbourg, Mendelsohn & Jermann, 1999). Moreover, the delay of acknowledgment was significantly shorter in virtual co-presence. The implicit assumption behind these observations is that subjects pay attention to spatial awareness information. In another experiment (Montandon, 1996) using a task that requires spatial coordination, we suppressed the spatial awareness messages that are automatically generated by a MOO environment. The subjects compensate this information loss by performing specific user locating commands. These results reveal a mechanism that goes beyond co-presence effects: if there is a clear structural mapping between the problem space and the virtual space, reasoning on mutual positions is reasoning on collaboration strategies, or, in other words, *spatial awareness supports coordination at the task level.* We observed another functional role of space. The room that also includes one agent or key object seemed to be used by subjects as the by-default context to disambiguate utterances. This observation may develop our functional understanding of virtual space: we hypothesize that *spatial awareness supports grounding by providing subjects with the contextual cues necessary to refer to objects*. Understanding how a virtual environment may facilitate the construction of a shared understanding is a key challenge of CSCL research and the main goal of the experiments reported here. These preliminary observations were bound to the room paradigm of MUD environments. Would our preliminary observations be confirmed in a more systematic experiment using a continuous space, i.e. in space where rooms do not simply define in/out relations, but where distance matters?

METHODOLOGY

We constructed an experimental 3D VRML Virutal Environment (VE) where two subjects (N=20 pairs) are required to collaborate to solve a simple object-matching task. The subjects are seated in different computer rooms and can only interact with their partner through the VE. The multi-user 3D VE constructed for use in the experiment is figurative, and poor in details. The task (10 randomized rounds) is for both subjects to locate a target object from amongst nine objects located in the VE, to communicate their (the emitter's) finding to the partner using a structured communication interface and then for the partner (the receiver) to confirm or reject the proposition. During the task the target object is always shown in the upper portion of the viewpoint. All of the nine objects are cuboids, and are highly similar to each other; therefore the object-target matching task is far from straightforward. A quick glance at objects in the VE is insufficient to ascertain a match with the target object, subjects must, rather, take time to explore the objects in detail. The representations of the subjects in the virtual space, i.e. their avatar, are simple red cones. While a user explores the VE his avatar moves accordingly in the VE. Each user sees the avatar of his/her partner (or can decide to look at it), but being inside their own avatars the subjects cannot see themselves. The use of simple upright cones, as avatars, was a crucial experimental choice, as this representation carries no information on the orientation of the avatar. Therefore, there is no way for a user to tell the field of view of the partner on the VE. We provided the users with a view awareness tool: every object in the field of view of the partner's avatar is highlighted using a different color to those objects out of their field of view. The presence or absence of this awareness tool constitutes the experimental condition of the study. Position and orientation of the avatars in the VE are logged every second. Avatar actions, such as the manipulation of objects, or communication using the structured interface, are also logged. From this raw data we computed several measurements (dependent variables) like various distance measures of the emitter to the reference object and an ambiguity measure consisting of the sum of examined objects by the receiver prior to his answer, i.e. the greater the number of manipulated objects the greater the ambiguity of the situation. We postulate the following hypotheses:

- *Hypothesis 1: The proximity of the emitter to the referred object clarifies the referential context.* We think that although there is no explicit way for the emitter to reference the target object, the emitter still can use a collaborative feature of space, i.e. proximity, to identify the reference object. The nearer the emitter to the referenced object the less ambiguous is the referential context for the receiver.
- *Hypothesis 2: The 'view awareness' clarifies the referential context.* By providing the view awareness tool we think to facilitate the receiver's task. Sequences with view awareness should be less ambiguous and therefore have a clearer referential context.
- *Hypothesis 3: The distance from the emitter to the referred object should increase with the 'view awareness'.* According to (Clark and Wilkes-Gibbs, 1986, cit.in Clark & Brennan, 1991) 'least collaborative effort' principle, conversing partners tend to minimize their collaborative effort. The redundancy of context disambiguating clues, i.e. proximity and view awarenss, should lead to a slackening of the collaborative effort when possible, that is, the proximity to the object. In conditions with view awareness the emitter will tend to be more distant from the referenced object.

RESULTS & CONCLUSION

Results show that distance is positively correlated to the number of examined objects. Though the correlations are relatively small, three out of the four distance measures are highly significant. Thus, we consider hypothesis 1 to be confirmed. We didn't observe any difference between sequences with or without view awareness ($p=.983$). Hence, the second hypothesis is invalidated. Finally, although, distance measures to the referred object tend to be greater in the condition with the awareness tool, an ANOVA revealed no significant interaction between view awareness and proximity.

In conclusion, we say that users may use some features of virtual space, namely distance, to support a core mechanism in collaboration, defining the referential context. It still remains an open issue for us to dissociate to which extend the emitter's move to the object was due to the task constraints or reflect a deliberate deictic move. It only indicates that, when the emitter *has to* perform this move for task-specific constraints, then the receiver is able to use this information to disambiguate references. This information may however be used by CSCL designers for instance to decide how they position objects in virtual space.

BIBLIOGRAPHY

Dillenbourg, P., Mendelsohn, P. and Jermann, P. (1999). Why spatial metaphors are relevant to virtual campuses? In J. Levonen & J. Enkenberg (Eds.) Learning and instruction in multiple contexts and settings. Bulletin of the Faculty of Education, 73. University of Joensuu, Finland, Faculty of Education.

Dillenbourg, P. and Traum, D. (1999). Does a shared screen make a shared solution ? International Conference on Computer Supported Collaborative Learning, Stanford, décembre 1999.

Montandon, L. (1996) Etude des mécanismes de coordination spatiale dans un environnement virtuel de collaboration. Mémoire de Diplôme d'Etudes Supérieures en Sciences et Technologies de l'Apprentissage. Non publié. TECFA, Faculté de Psychologie et des Sciences de l'Education, Université de Genève.

Clark, H. H. & Brennan, S. E. (1991). Grounding in communication. In L. B. Resnick, J. Levine & S. D. Teasley (Eds), Perspectives on Socially Shared Cognition. APA, 1991.

Intentional Integration Supported by Collaborative Reflection

Miyake, N., Masukawa, H., Yuasa, K., Shirouzu, H.

School of Computer and Cognitive Sciences, Chukyo Univerisy

nmiyake@sccs. masukawa@grad.sccs. yuasa@grad.sccs. shirouzu@sccs. {chukyo-u.ac.jp}

ABSTRACT

The skills for thematic, or intentional, integration of independent pieces of research, a highly difficult but important task in academic training, is analyzed (Study 1) and supported by collaborative reflection (Studies 2 and 3). The results indicate that simple scaffolds combined and embedded in a collaboratively reflective curriculum can support this highly complex task.

KEYWORDS: Intentional integration, thematic integration, collaborative reflection

INTRODUCTION

In advanced collaborative classrooms, learners must not only study selected topics in groups but must also integrate such contributed pieces of work to understand the overall theme. In study 1, we found advanced students actively decompose each work into structural pieces and recompose them to form an entirely new structure. Study 2 tries to support such steps with simple scaffolds like card arrangement, embedded in thematically well-formed classroom activities. In Study 3, repetitive collaborative reflection was enforced on summary presentations of several independent research pieces, which resulted in the juniors understanding the topic better. The overall results indicate that simple scaffolds combined and embedded in a collaboratively reflective curriculum can support the highly complex task of intentional integration.

STUDY 1

PROCEDURE

Groups of cognitive science major students, ranging from sophomores and graduate students to a professional researcher, were asked to integrate five independent introductory articles on human intelligence ("Exploring intelligence," Scientific American Present 1998, Japanese edition). Fifteen cards were prepared to represent three structural elements of a research paper, "research background," "main findings," and "implications." The 15 cards were used for integration in this study. The sophomores read the articles in a jigsaw-puzzle fashion. The cards were expected to serve as scaffolds. Sophomore groups and five other mixed groups of juniors, seniors, graduate students and a professional researcher arranged these cards onto an A3-size sheet of paper, to support writing the summary by collaboratively reflecting upon them.

RESULTS

The task took 30 to 60 minutes depending on the experience of the subjects. Three typical layouts from the three group categories are shown in Fig. 1. Card number 1 means that the card is taken from article No. 1 and so on. Figure 1 a) was prepared by sophomores, who mostly preserve the independence of each article. Figure 1. b) was prepared by juniors to seniors lead by an advanced doctoral student, with a chunk consisting of three "research background" cards from three different articles. Figure 1 c) is a product of a professional researcher, which shows a complete reconstruction of the structural elements of the original articles, in clear contrast to a) and b). The professional researcher actively decomposed the pieces so that she could entirely reconstruct a new integrated view of them.

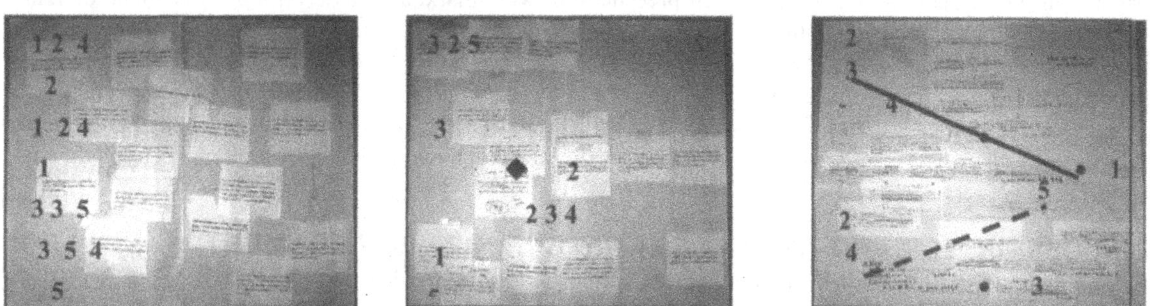

a) b) c)

Figure 1: Card arrangements of integrating independent articles.

This card arrangement environment is now computer implemented and usable for further explorations.

STUDY 2: PROCEDURAL SUPPORT FOR INTENTIONAL INTEGRATION

PROCEDURES

In order to see whether specific scaffolds are possible for professional-like integration, sophomores in cognitive science classes were asked to extract important pieces from original articles and record them onto small cards, and then to thematically integrate them by arranging the cards two-dimensionally. The visibility and the tangibility of the cards and their arrangement are expected to raise the chances of collaborative reflection, which then would raise the quality of the summaries. The task was to integrate three independent pieces of work, "sensory deprivation," "intrinsic motivation and spontaneous learning," and "the negative effect of rewards on intrinsically motivated behavior." The extraction of the cards was further guided by the same set of questions focused on structural elements used for all the articles. For the experimental group, the cards were colored differently according to the questions, so that the same color would guide the gathering and comparison of the answers to the same questions to facilitate the reconstruction. Seventy-six sophomores participated in this study. Forty formed 12 groups, to whom colored cards were given. The other 36 students were divided into 12 groups to whom only white cards were given. At the end of the task, they summarized their integrations individually. The entire process was technologically supported with note-sharing and presentation systems.

RESULTS AND IMPLICATIONS

More than half the subjects who used the colored cards could give detailed summaries, while less than 10% in the control group (white cards) did the same. At the end of the individual reading session, the ratio of the sophomores who extracted the main points with sufficient detail was found to be 54% in the experimental group compared to 21% in the control group. This conspicuous difference between the conditions suggests that the color-coded cards helped the experimental group students to yield richer resources for later collaborative reflection.

STUDY 3: REPETITIVE COLLABORATIVE REFLECTION FOR THEMATIC INTEGRATION

Study 1 clearly showed that intentional integration skill was acquired through long-term experience, for which classrooms rarely provide enough chances. Study 3 investigated the effects of repetitive exposure of integration in collaborative reflection in an attempt to supplement such professional experience. Twenty-eight junior students in our cognitive science course were required to create repetitive presentations to the class on seven studies of Wason's selection task: the original Wason experiment, the thematic bias studies, the pragmatic reasoning schema studies of Cheng and Holyoak, and Cosmides' social contract theory. They worked in seven groups.

A typical thematic integration would include explanations of the classic, laboratory-based human reasoning skills research, and more situated, or everyday cognition studies. It would also include how Cheng and Holyoak reconsolidated them from a cognitive psychological stand point with their new construct of "pragmatic schemas." A typical "lecture" on this topic would run in this fashion but is not easily absorbed by the students. In one of the first author's surveys, at the end of the semester course, only two out of 86 students could explain how the pragmatic scheme worked, the core construct of the Cheng and Holyoak paper.

PROCEDURE

The task given to these 28 students in this class was to construct a 15-minute talk to sophomores on this topic. During the six-week course with two 90-minute classes per week, the students were asked to give three short, preparatory talks and one final, full-scale talk to the class, with ample time for class discussion as a chance for collaborative reflection.

RESULTS AND IMPLICATIONS

At Week 4, only one out of seven groups could start structural integration of the pieces. At the time of their presentation in the fifth week, five groups gave highly structured presentations, integrated in the sense that they decomposed parts of each research to restructure the entire set of seven studies. Their presentations were marked with descriptions like dichotomizing experimental approaches of logical reasoning studies against more situated views. This indicates that the students in their junior years have the basic capability to integrate research pieces by decomposing, identifying and restructuring the constructs of the research. However, careful analyses of the content reveal that the presentation quality is distinctively different from that which a normal professional researcher would produce (in particular, they tended to lack precise descriptions of pragmatic schemas, how it works and/or its development), showing that they can make use of better supports, if available.

GENERAL DISCUSSION: TOWARD THE INTEGRATED SUPPORT ENVIRONMENT

The acquisition of appropriate skills for proper intentional integration requires more than a single technological support in one course College courses, particularly the ones in an interdisciplinary field like cognitive science, should be more integrated with each other, and should be conducted in a technologically rich environment. In such a learning environment, students from their first year to graduation can gradually participate in and take advantage of the collaborative reflection so that they can incorporate it into their meta-cognitive repertoire.

Components of an Optimal Online Environment

Christine Alexander

United States International University

calexan3@san.rr.com

ABSTRACT

Experts were polled in the area of Computer Supported Collaborative Learning (CSCL) research to determine components of an optimal constructivist/collaborative online learning environment. One hundred seventy-seven panelists were asked to participate. Eighteen panelists responded contributing 93 components. They were then asked to rate these components on a scale of 0-7. Thirteen panelists responded. The components were then ranked according to average score. The top ten ranking components were calculated. The "Most Popular" components rated "5" or better, were determined by majority. A third round seeking a consensus was attempted.

Keywords

Constructivist, collaborative, online, Delphi Poll, top-ten components, "most popular" components

PURPOSE

The purpose of this study was to determine components of an optimal constructivist/collaborative online learning environment.

RESEARCH DESIGN

In this study, a Delphi Poll was utilized. Expert opinion is used to determine components of optimal constructivist/collaborative learning environment since a thoroughly explored model has yet to appear in the literature. The individual responses remained anonymous; however, a list of the panelists' names and their institutions appeared on the questionnaires.

PANELIST DETERMINATION

The panel members are experts in the field of CSCL research. All of the panel members have been conference presenters at the CSCL Conference held at Stanford University in December of 1999. The range of expertise includes international researchers in the fields of computer science, instructional design, organizational systems design, communications, and educational technology. The researchers hailed from universities, government research laboratories, and private industry.

PROCEDURE

The procedures used in this study were successive rounds of a questionnaire. The first round asked participants to provide their own five components of an optimal constructivist/collaborative online learning environment. Round two asked the panelists to rate all of the 93 components resulting from round one on a scale of 0-7. Round three attempted a consensus of the "most Popular" components. The rounds were sent and received via e-mail.

FINDINGS

Two types of results were generated from the data. First, each statement rating was averaged. These ratings were then ranked in order from highest to lowest. The highest average rating received a score of 6. Second, "Most Popular" components rated "5" or better, were determined by majority.

The top ten ranking components were:

- #1: Peer interaction.
- #2: Sharing the results of your efforts with others.
- #3: Collaborative knowledge construction.
- #4: A way of negotiating group consensus or conclusions.
- Equally ranked #5: A means of motivating, focusing and scaffolding the discussion; a shared workspace.
- Equally ranked #6: robust technology (easy access, ease of use, etc.); and continuity over time and space, such as provided by threaded discussions.
- Equally ranked #7: Somebody facilitates interaction, this requires the possibility to monitor what is going on during interaction; and some facility for students to communicate (synchronously or asynchronously).

- #8: Associated curriculum framework. The accompanying curriculum should provide a framework that promotes collaboration, construction, reflection, peer review, etc.
- Equally ranked #9: Presence of the collaborators, either through digital/electronic means or colocation; accountability for one's collaborative actions, that is others are aware of authorship, without explicit signing required; an active role of mentor; support, encouragement, and challenge from the other people (co-learners & mentors) involved, being taken seriously by others, and being given room to play; construction: students are given tools that let them fairly easily generate their own representations (drawing, animations, text, etc); clear temporal organization: synchronous and asynchronous participation can both be supported.
- Equally ranked #10: Scaffolding to help students with the tasks they are involved in as well as with the collaboration itself; collaborative technology that helps participants communicate as well as share intermediate technical results; sharing: student can view other students (public) work; persistence of the discussion to support group and individual reflection over time.

"Most Popular " Components rated "5" or better by a majority of the panelists were:

- Presence of the collaborators, either through digital/electronic means or colocation.
- An active role of mentor.
- Associated curriculum framework.
- Peer interaction.
- Clarity of how to participate.
- Sharing the results of your efforts with others.
- Careful representation of users to each other.
- Optimal awareness functionality.
- Communication and peer review.
- People engaged in personally meaningful projects.
- Somebody facilitates interaction.
- Patterns or templates for knowledge representation or structuring, based on didactical valid principles, that can be used as a staring point for constructive activities and critical reflection.
- Teacher designers.
- Face to face sessions included in overall scheme.

The "most popular" list is more significant than the "top ten" list. The "most popular" list was determined by a consistency of high scores rather than averaged high scores. The consistent high score is more significant in a poll with a small number of respondents. The consistent high scores removes some skewing of results that takes place due to the extreme scoring of a few respondents. The "most popular" list should be used as the essential components in future models of an optimal constructivist/collaborative online learning environment.

SIGNIFICANCE

A working model of an optimal constructivist/collaborative online learning environment is needed in the field distance education. The results of this study provide needed guidelines for designing optimal collaborative learning environments. These findings generated a definitive list of essential components for constructivist/collaborative online environments as determined by a majority consensus of experts in computer supported collaborative learning research.

ACKNOWLEDGMENTS

I thank all of the panelists participating is this study. I also thank my dissertation committee members, Maria Fernandez, Holly Wilson, and George Stamos, at United States International University.

Webtanks for Knowledge Management: Web-based Collaborative Learning Environment

Zann Gill
Director of Program Development
BEACON (Bio-Evolutionary Advanced Concepts for NASA), a think tank
RIACS, NASA Ames Research Center
650-604-4370 sgill@mail.arc.nasa.gov

ABSTRACT
My assignment at NASA Ames Research Center is to develop a program plan for a think tank, BEACON (Bio-Evolutionary Advanced Concepts for NASA), that brings together cross-disciplinary teams to conceive the next generation of NASA technology and scientific research across IT and Fundamental Biology. A "webtank" (think tank on the web) is being developed to support think tank activities. Prior to implementing a webtank for BEACON, I initiated collaboration with the SETI Institute on their development of a high school integrated science curriculum (astronomy, geology, biology, and the evolution of technology) where students explore how the concept of evolution underpins and integrates these disciplines. Curriculum requirements for the final *Evolution of Technology* module provided an opportunity to develop, pilot, and test a self-organizing collaborative web environment, or webtank, to be later adapted, augmented, and extended to support BEACON. SETI established a systematic method for pilot testing and field testing all elements of the curriculum, and so offered a useful webtank testbed.

KEYWORDS
Computer-supported, web-enabled, intranet, collaborative learning

INTRODUCTION
Webtanks (think tanks on the web) can be designed to serve as guides, frameworks to facilitate collaboration, and knowledge management repositories, supporting students, designers, and inventors in team innovation. High school students in *Voyages Through Time*, SETI's new, integrated science and technology curriculum will form teams and collaborate to conceive new inventions. The webtank supports their invention process as a

- **series of prompts** to help student designer/ inventor teams generate innovative, integrated design concepts for their new inventions;
- **way to facilitate collaboration,** enabling students to interact with other students around issues that arise as they design and integrate those projects into a larger, collaborative plan;
- **framework to structure archives and resources** in order to reTRACE creative processes that have occurred in this environment.

COLLABORATIVE KNOWLEDGE-MAKING AND MANAGEMENT
I define *information* as "interpreted data," while *knowledge* is "information in action." Knowledge management is often equated with databases and information storage. If instead, knowledge management is integrated into a collaborative knowledge-making process, users post their knowledge resources to share. Critical to successful knowledge management is having a framework that facilitates and supports collaborative knowledge-making, so the webtank is designed to serve two complementary functions:

- A repository, offering a knowledge management framework for information resources and project archives (passive mode), and
- A think tank "prompt", providing process support for invention and collaborative problem-solving and capability to record sessions (active mode).

Users click back and forth between passive and active modes. Collaborators use document libraries (passive mode) to prepare for collaborative problem-solving sessions (active mode). The meetings themselves, and the ways the meetings use these resources, can be captured (active mode), permitting later analysis of what worked and what didn't, as well as refinement of the knowledge management system based on its continual assessment in use. So a Continual Survey Questionnaire capability supports ongoing development. It can gather qualitative metrics from the perspectives of learners, team leaders or teachers, and website developers (concerned with knowledge management, scalability, and maintenance).

Yale University Professor Irving Janis studied why committees fail by analyzing a number of case studies from public policy. If Janis was correct in stressing the importance of each individual's perspective for group process, then a webtank to support self-directed learning and innovation will require mechanisms to retain individual identity within the larger group process. Drawing an analogy between collaborative problem-solving and evolution supports this position; having a lot of cells doesn't make an organism complex; it's still just a lot of cells. Differentiation is a prerequisite for complexity in cells as in collaborative group learning.

In the active mode a Webtank Integration Broker supports collaborative transactions, so potential collaborators can bring their project ideas and find others with whom they can collaborate on a "bigger picture" that combines multiple projects. Complementing the active mode, at the end of a problem-solving session the webtank, again in passive mode, evaluates individual web entries and archives process records with multiple mechanisms for search and matching, requiring metadata and search capabilities. Some of the process record-keeping and archiving can be automated and could benefit by adapting AI tools for knowledge acquisition, indexing and retrieval. Additional technical challenges include design of a scalable environment that will self-organize as it scales up, establishing centralized human manual control and coordination that can gradually be replaced by decentralized autonomous agent control.

Conclusion

Webtanks can serve as petri dishes to culture the creative process, so that "invisible observers" can study how performance in this environment. Though any theory about the creative process is hard to prove, my premise is that a partial correlation can be drawn between individual creative process (unobservable) and group design and concept formation, where the invention process is open to view. NASA, with its vast network of collaborating universities, has need for better knowledge management systems so that a range of institutions working on aspects of the same problem from different disciplinary perspectives can more effectively collaborate. A problem-focused webtank necessarily crosses institutional boundaries, starting small to develop to test knowledge management strategies in its own document collection, data and project archives and to develop a system that can later be extended. Webtanks can pioneer a new type of intranet, one that is project or program-based, rather than institution-based, providing a foundation for emergent intelligence in distributed smart systems of the future.

ACKNOWLEDGMENTS

I would like to acknowledge the collaboration with The SETI Institute, in particular Jane Fisher, Project Director Curriculum Development for *Voyages Through Time.*

REFERENCES

Gill, Zann. Webtank Assessment: Performance in Web-based Collaborative Learning Environments. Human Systems 2001: Exploring the Human Frontier. Houston, Texas, June 20-22, 2001.

Gill, Zann. Webtank Design: intranet support for collaborative problem-solving. HCI International 2001. New Orleans, 5-10 August, 2001 also published in Systems, Social, and Internationalization: Design Aspects of Human Computer Interaction vol 2. edited by Michael Smith and Gavriel Salvendy. N.J.: Lawrence Earlbaum Assoc. 2001. P. 292-6.

Gill, Zann. Webtanks: Tools for Learning by Design. Siggraph 2001. Los Angeles, 12-17 August 2001.

http://www.arl.org/newsltr/213/assess.html and http://www.wcer.wisc.edu/nise/cl1/flag/goals/goals.htm

Janis, Irving. Groupthink: A Psychological Study of Policy Decisions and Fiascoes. Boston: Houghton Mifflin, 1984.

Smith, Reid and Farquhar, Adam. "The Road Ahead for Knowledge Management" in *AI Magazine*, *American Association for Artificial Intelligence,* 2000.

C. QUALITATIVE ANALYSES OF CASE STUDIES AND THEIR IMPLICATIONS FOR CSCL

Supporting Chinese Distance Learners through Computer-Mediated Communication – Revisiting Salmon's Model

Peter J Smith, Swee Noi Smith

Deakin University

pjbs@deakin.edu.au, ssmith@deakin.edu.au

ABSTRACT

Salmon's (2000) proposed model for the effective development of on-line communication and collaboration between student suggests that on-line socialisation forms an early and important component of establishing required levels of comfort and skill. In this paper we review research with Chinese learners that suggests that some adjustments to Salmon's model may be advisable for these students. Specifically, the model is redeveloped to provide a more structured experience, and to use that structure to develop on-line skills, such that the development of comfortable socialisation is seen as an on-going process rather than only an early enabler.

Keywords

Computer-mediated communication, Chinese learners, on-line socialisation, on-line structure

PREVIOUS RESEARCH FINDINGS

Over the last few years interest has increased in research focussing on the provision of distance education programs to identifiable clienteles. Jegede (1999) observed that knowledge of clientele is becoming a major issue facing distance education, while Calder (2000) has echoed this view and pointed to its importance in terms of service to students.

Apart from the issues of course design and content sensitivity towards different cultural groups, there is evidence of different forms of learning approaches, and learning strategies. Smith, Miller and Crassini (1998) showed, in their study of the approaches to learning by Chinese university students, as measured by Entwistle and Ramsden's (1983) *Approaches to Studying,* that Chinese students are not surface/rote learners, and that anxiousness over a fear of failure among Chinese students is associated with surface learning behaviours. An Efficiency Orientation identified in their research indicates that Chinese students are strategic in their selection of what to study, motivated by success in academic results. Later work with Chinese students by Smith and Smith (1999) noted a need for support in the effective organisation of study, and the development of conceptual frameworks.

Baron (1998) described the provision for CMC study group formation to reflect the collaborative learning behaviour that may be expected in a collectivist Confucian Heritage culture. Findings were that these study groups were not widely used, with the students preferring the lecture format provided through the on-line subjects. While the announcements area was well used, along with the on-line subjects and the resources, the chat facilities were not frequently visited, although Baron detected a growing usage. There is a clear connection here between Baron's findings and those of Smith, Miller and Crassini (1998) and Smith and Smith (1999). Chat rooms by their nature are largely unstructured, and do not clearly lead to enhanced assessment outcomes. Accordingly, they are probably not seen as other than fairly superfluous activity to Chinese learners.

REDEVELOPING SALMON'S MODEL FOR CHINESE LEARNERS

Salmon (2000) has proposed a five-stage model whereby participants gradually increase their involvement in, and commitment to, CMC as they become more comfortable and proficient with the environment. As the stages progress, so does the sophistication of the interaction and the learning outcomes. These five stages are:

- *Access and motivation*
- *On-line socialisation*
- *Information exchange*
- *Knowledge construction*

- *Development towards more self--direction in the CMC environment*

The difficulty with the model as it stands, for Chinese learners at least, is the positioning of on-line socialisation as an early stage of the process, and the leveraging off that socialisation for development into the later stages of the model. It is proposed here that on-line socialisation cannot be relied upon with Chinese learners to provide the platform of comfortable communication and that, rather than being established as an early stage in the process, this form of socialisation needs to be developed as an ongoing process within a structure and a purpose that is connected to the program of study. On-line socialisation, it is argued, needs to be developed through other parts of the process, and comfort with that form of communication viewed as an on-going development throughout the process, rather than just an early and enabling stage.

Our suggested modification to the Salmon model is shown in Figure 1 below, with more detailed explanation provided in the longer CSCL2002 paper.

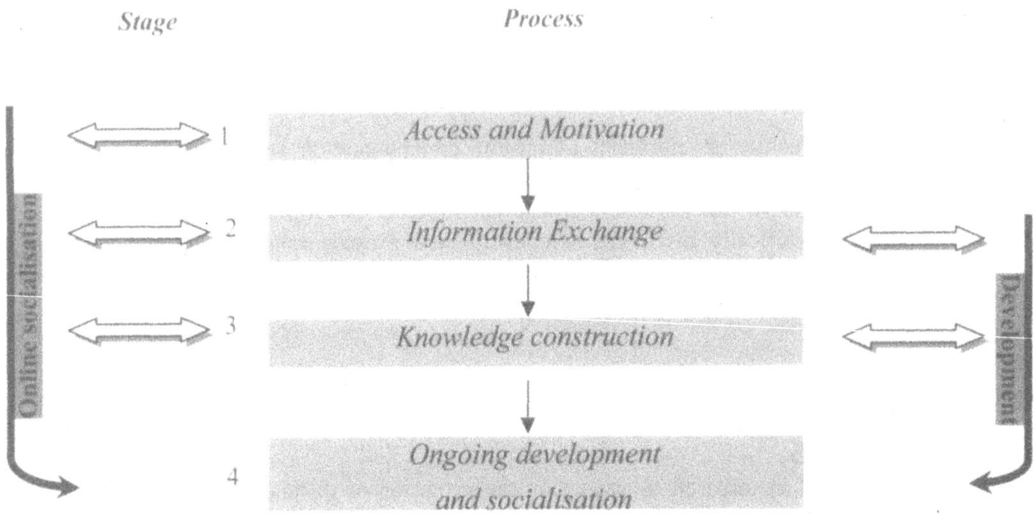

Figure 1: Representation of proposed on-line activity sequence for Chinese students (adapted from Salmon, 2000).

CONCLUSION

Our redevelopment of Salmon's (2000) model, it has been argued, provides for a set of on-line learning development strategies that are better suited to the characteristics of Chinese learners identified through the literature. Additionally, we would argue that there is evidence for the applicability of our revision of Salmon's model to much broader groups of distance learners than only Chinese, but we have further work to undertake before being confident of this wider application.

REFERENCES

Calder, J. (2000) Beauty lies in the eye of the beholder. *International Review of Research in Open and Distance Learning,* **1**, 1, www.icaap.org/iuicode?149.1.1.10.

Entwistle, N. & Ramsden, P. (1983) *Understanding Student Learning.* Nichols Publishing Company, New York.

Jegede, O. (1999) 'Priorities in open and distance education research; opinions of experts and practitioners within the Commonwealth', paper presented to the Pan-Commonwealth Forum on Open Learning, Brunei, March.

Salmon, G. (2000) *E-moderating: The Key to Teaching and Learning On-line*, London, Kogan Page.

Smith, P.J. & Smith, S.N. (1999) Differences between Chinese and Australian students: some implications for distance educators. *Distance Education,* **20**, 64-80.

Smith, S.N., Miller, R.J. & Crassini, B. (1998) Approaches to studying of Australian and Overseas Chinese students. *Higher Education Research and Development*, **17**, 261-275.

Design Experiments for Integrating a CSCL Technology into Japanese Elementary Science Education

Jun Oshima#, Ritsuko Oshima#, Isao Murayama#, Shigenori Inagaki*, Hayashi Nakayama+, Etsuji Yamaguchi+, Makiko Takenaka*

#Shizuoka Univ., Japan, *Kobe Univ., Japan, +Miyazaki Univ., Japan
joshima@oshima-7.ed.shizuoka.ac.jp

ABSTRACT

We designed CSCL-based science lessons for 4th and 6th grade. The CSCL technology we used was Knowledge Forum (KF), the second generation of CSILE software. In the first year, we designed the lesson in which KF was used as an extra communication tool. Goal-sensitive assessments for the lesson showed that students did not frequently discuss on the lesson concepts in a cognitive manner. The lesson design in the second year was revised by providing students with cognitive scaffolds so that they could more articulately discuss their thoughts as objects. Comparative analyses manifested that students in the second year were more engaged in science activities through social construction of their knowledge on KF. Design principles we found to be effective are discussed.

Keywords

CSILE, Knowledge Forum, design experiments, Japanese elementary science education

INTRODUCTION

"Computer-Supported Intentional Learning Environments (CSILE)" proposed by Scardamalia, Bereiter and their colleagues is an educational philosophy for the design of computer-supported learning environments (Scardamalia, & Bereiter, 1996). CSILE software is a communal database system in which learners are allowed to externalize their thoughts mainly in the form of texts or/and graphics called "notes," then engage in collaboratively organizing their knowledge as objects to advance their communal understanding as a whole. This communal database structure has been found to provide learners with opportunities to be involved in knowledge advancement through distribution of their expertise, and to eventually facilitate learners' conceptual understanding of complex scientific phenomena in comparison with traditional instructions. (Oshima, Scardamalia, & Bereiter, 1995).

DESIGN EXPERIMENTS AS EDUCATIONAL RESEARCH

The design experiments is not just compiling all we have known on learning, but an attempt to blend expertise from different areas. In our design experiments, we referred to the basic system of the community of learners by Brown and Campione (1996). In the community of learners, the basic components are research (student-directed learning), information sharing, consequential task (i.e., students' recognition of their knowledge as applied to problem solving in the future), deep disciplinary content (beyond textbook levels), and students' reflection on their own activities (i.e., metacognition). In the framework, our challenge for the curriculum design was to effectively use KF to facilitate students' sharing information and reflection.

ACTIVITY STRUCTURE IN JAPANESE ELEMENTARY SCIENCE EDUCATION

In Japanese elementary schools, teachers have a widely shared framework of science activities for students to do in the classroom which we think is similar to the community of learners. The activities are supported by Japanese school cultures (Linn, Lewis, Tsuchida, & Songer, 2000). Students are regularly educated to listen to others and collaborate with one another in small groups. They are also required of reflecting on their own activities in the classroom with their classroom goals determined by themselves at the beginning of the year. Thus, students' dispositions to learning help them to engage in the organized science activity. Science activity at Japanese elementary schools is well-structured based on instructional goals to make students think of science through their investigations as involvement in authentic science activities.

DESIGN EXPERIMENTS ACROSS TWO YEARS

LESSON PLAN 1: "NATURE AROUND US" FOR GRADE 4

We planned the lesson for sixteen periods (a period was 45 minute long). The lesson started with the teacher's attempt to connect his students' interests to learning goals in the lesson. After the training session for KF, students in small groups conducted their investigations on how plants and insects changed in the winter out of the regular schedule. The lesson was proceeded with several cross talks in the classroom. Students were encouraged to report what they found in their investigations on KF and then comment on one another. Further, in the final stage of the lesson, students were asked by the teacher to discuss "how plants and insects look like in the winter."

LESSON PLAN 2: "AIR AND HOW THINGS BURN" FOR GRADE 6

Students were expected to understand that oxygen is needed for things to burn in the air, then why and how things stop burning in relation to the existence of oxygen in the air. Based on our lessons from the first year, we invented the followings as scaffolds: (1) The lesson plan was designed so that students were more concerned with conceptual understandings by structuring students' activities as theory building through construction of their explanatory models. (2) Students were instructed to report, on Knowledge Forum, their thoughts in a specific form of scientific thinking such as hypotheses, experimental designs, predictions, results, and their discussion. (3) The participatory structure of students' science activities was more articulately designed. (4) Researchers and graduate students regularly discussed with students on their modeling, hypotheses, experimental designs, or their interpretations on results. (5) We changed the interface so that students could more easily recognize and use the database as a tool for their reflection. One feature was a graphical view to show them their understanding in progress. Secondary, we created a new sub-window called "diary."

RESULTS AND DISCUSSION

One of remarkable differences between the two years was that the second year students reported their thoughts in more cognitive or socially cognitive manner. The teacher did not consider that the difference was from the difference in ages. Rather, he thought that it was more difficult to have students at the older age engage in social knowledge construction. In Japanese schools, we usually see older students (particularly, at junior high schools) not report any ideas in the classroom or be afraid of expressing themselves. In the second year, we designed students' activities at individual, small group, and whole class level. KF was used mainly for reflecting on their and others' work at the small group level. The teacher and students also used notes in KF for presenting their thoughts in front of the class. Thus, they had articulate objects to talk about for improving their understanding in the collaborative manner. Our video research in progress has manifested that teacher and students talked in more cognitive or socially cognitive manner in face-to-face discussion as well as on KF.

ACKNOWLEDGEMENT

This study was financially supported by the research grant of the Ministry of Education and Science, Japan (Grant #: 11480030). We would like to thank students and teachers who welcomed us as action researchers and collaborators for their curriculum design. We also thank Hiromi Nagai, Hidefumi Nomura and Yoshihito Endo for their help in coding data.

REFERENCES

Brown, A. L., & Campione, J. C. (1996). Psychological theory and the design of innovative learning environments: On procedures, principles, and systems. In L. Shauble & R. Glaser (Eds.), *Innovations in Learning: New Environments for Education* (pp. 289-325). Mahwah, NJ: Lawrence Erlbaum.

Linn, M. C., Lewis, C., Tsuchida, I., & Songer, N. B. (2000). Beyond fourth-grade science: Why do US and Japanese students diverge? *Educational Researcher, 29*(3), 4-14.

Oshima, J., C. Bereiter, & Scardamalia, M. (1995). Information-access characteristics for high conceptual progress in a computer-networked learning environment. *Computer Support for Collaborative Learning '95*, Bloomington, IN, USA. Mahwah, NJ: Lawrence Erlbaum.

Scardamalia, M. and C. Bereiter (1996). "Student communities for the advancement of knowledge." *Communications of the ACM* **39**(4): 36-37.

Examining Synchronous Tutoring in a Virtual World

Maria Beatrice Ligorio

University of Salerno (IT) – Visiting Scholar University of Nijmegen (NL)

bealigorio@hotmail.com

Alessandra Talamo

University of Rome (IT)

Alessandra.talamo@uniroma1.it

Robert-Jan Simons

Utrecht University (NL)

r.simons@ivlos.uu.nl

Keywords: Virtual community, on-line tutorship, new learning, constructivism, discourse analysis

TEORETHICAL FRAMEWORK

The role of the tutor within a virtual community assumes specific features. First of all, because the concept of community fosters certain processes, and second of all technical features of the virtual environments in which the community lives are taken in account. The community assumes as its central focus group organization and sharing common goals (Brown and Campione, 1990; Lave and Wenger, 1991). The context-situated learning is relevant and connected to the idea of "distributed" knowledge (Salomon, 1993). According to this perspective, the tutor should push participants towards a more central participation, should fosters the social interaction, and should support the "emigration" of the knowledge from one source and its "appropriation" by the others. This paper explores the tutors' on-line role in a learning environment called Euroland.

THE EUROLAND PROJECT

Euroland is a virtual community composed by students, teachers and researchers from the two countries (Italy and The Netherlands). The community designed, built and populated a three-dimensional (3D) world. The content of the world included several "cultural" Houses, such as Houses of Food, Music, Art, and Travel.

The virtual world was constructed using the Active Worlds (AW) software (http://www.activeworlds.com) and through an action-research methodology (Ligorio, 2001). The software used differs from a Multi-user Objects Oriented environment (MOO) because virtual objects can contain other virtual objects and they can be visualized from the inside.

The community of Euroland was composed of seven groups of students (4 Italian and 3 Dutch), their teachers, some occasional visitors, a cross-national research group and three on-line tutors with different competencies. The students ranged in age from 9 to 14 years. The community connected to Euroland during the 1999-2000 school year. The interdependence principle (Salomon, 1993) was applied by asking the students from one country to build the cultural Houses for the other country.

DATA ANALYSIS AND RESULTS

The on-line chats are the main source of data. The three tutors participated with the 57% of the total utterances in chat. Two different analysis systems are combined and qualitative analysis is provided.

The first analysis is carried out with a category system dedicated to the analysis of tutor interventions' (utterances) and describes how the Euroland on-line tutors exploit their actions within the virtual community. Three independent researchers checked the interventions' categorization. The uncertain cases were discussed until an agreement had been reached.

The category system of tutorship comprises the following four different functions (Ashton, Roberts and Teles, 1999; Talamo, Zucchermaglio & Ligorio, 2001): Managerial, Social, Technical, and Pedagogical.

Results show that the most relevant function is the managerial (20% of the total tutors' interventions). This function seems to match with the potentialities of the chats (Talamo & Ligorio, 2002). The other functions are carried out through the other communication tools embedded in the virtual environment (a mailing list available for the project, a discussion forum), in certain cases off-line and often face-to-face, within the classrooms.

The second type of analysis is done through the discourse analysis and it is aimed at showing the interactive dimension of tutoring a chat-based community. Discourse analysis provides significant data on the social construction of shared meanings in the community. Talk is considered as social action (Antaki, 1994) and contributes to identifying the functions put into action through talk by the community members. The development of tutorship is, in the case of Euroland, mostly negotiated in "talk in interaction" (Schegloff, 1992).

The chats were selected on the basis of relevant events in which the tutorship functions are more evident: a) Newcomers' arrival; b) Members talking explicitly about tutors' actions; c) Other members acting as tutors.

The chat analysis showed that tutorship is also the result of a negotiation process between tutors and students. During the presentation, chats' excerpts will be presented proving that: a) tutorship is a fluid, situated and dynamic process; b) tutors share their functions with the other members of the community.

CONCLUSIONS

In this project, the tutorship on-line was aimed at establishing a virtual community of learners. Tutoring on-line is a complex action, performed through four different functions: managerial, social, pedagogical and technical. The function performed most on-line is the managerial.

The discourse analysis shows that, in specific situations, the other members of the community cover some aspects of the tutorship. This result shows that a virtual community of learners has been established and, at the same time, new features of on-line tutorship are highlighted.

REFERENCES

André, E., Rist, T., & Müller, J. (1997). WebPersona: A Life-Like Presentation Agent for Educational Applications on the World-Wide Web. *Proceedings of the workshop Intelligent Educational Systems on the World Wide Web, 8th World Conference of the AIED Society*, Kobe, Japan, August 18-22.

Antaki,C. (1994). Explaining and Arguing. *The social organization of accounts*. London: Sage.

Ashton, S, Roberts, T., & Teles, L. (1999). Investigating the Role of the Instructor in Collaborative On-line Environments. *Poster presented at the Conference Computer Supported Collaborative Learning '99*, Stanford, December 12-15.

Brown, A.L. & Campione, J.C. (1990). Communities of learning or a context by any other name. In D. Kuhn (Ed.) *Contributions to human development*, 21, 108-126.

Lave, J., & Wenger, E. (1991). *Situated learning: Legitimate Peripheral Participation*. Cambridge: Cambridge University Press.

Ligorio, M.B. (2001). Integrating communication formats: synchronous versus asynchronous and text-based versus visual. *Computers and Education*. Vol. **37**, 103-125.

Salomon, G. (1993). No distribution without individual's cognition: a dynamic interaction view. In G. Salomon (Ed.) *Distributed cognitions. Psychological and educational consideration*. Cambridge, Cambridge University Press, 111-138.

Talamo, A., & Ligorio, M.B. (2001). Strategic identity in the cyberspace. In G. Riva & C. Galimberti (Eds), special issue of *Journal of CyberPsychology and Behavior, The mind and the Web: Psychology in the Internet age*, **4**, 109-122.

Talamo, A. Zucchermaglio, C., & Ligorio, M.B. (2001). Communities' Development in CVEs and sustaining functions of on-line tutorship. In G. Riva & C. Galimberti (Eds), *CYBERPSYCHOLOGY: Mind, cognition and society in the Internet Age*. IOS Amsterdam. 186-208 http://www.emergingcommunication.com/

Minority Students' Participation in a Knowledge Building Community: A Sociocultural Perspective

Anita Slater, Jan van Aalst
Faculty of Education, Simon Fraser University
Burnaby, B.C., V5A 1S6
slater@sfu.ca

ABSTRACT

Minority students' participation in on-line discourse is discussed with reference to sociocultural perspectives on discourse and learning, which suggest that cultural and linguistic minority students' opportunities for full participation may be diminished, negatively impacting their learning.

Keywords: Discourse, appropriation, community of practice

INTRODUCTION

Part of an ongoing study aimed at facilitating and examining the use of Knowledge Forum (a online database program which allows students to engage in communal knowledge building), the present study was conducted in an 11th grade class in a suburban British Columbia high school, where Knowledge Forum was used for a six week period during a unit on nuclear physics. Scardamalia, Bereiter and Lamon (1994) suggested that the differences in the participation levels of different types of students (e.g. high and low achievers, males and females) were all but eliminated when an earlier version of Knowledge Forum (Computer-Supported Intentional Learning Environments, or CSILE) was used. We wanted to find out if the participation levels and learning of the minority students in this class was enhanced by the use of Knowledge Forum. At the conclusion of the unit, we conducted semistructured interviews (in addition to other means of data collection such as classroom observation and analysis of the online discourse) with three minority students during which we asked them to discuss their experiences in their physics class.

SOCIOCULTURAL PERSPECTIVES ON LANGUAGE AND LEARNING

This project was informed by sociocultural perspectives on language and learning according to which language (or discourse) is not a neutral code but rather a set of symbolic resources which are appropriated by differently positioned people to accomplish particular purposes, and which dialogically creates and renews our social world(s). In this view, the acquisition or appropriation of language is not unproblematic. Bakhtin (cited in Gee, 1996) wrote: "The word in language is half someone else's. It becomes "one's own" only when the speaker populates it with his own intention, his own accent, when he appropriates the word....Prior to this moment of appropriation...(the word) exists in other people's mouths, in other people's concrete contexts, serving other people's intentions." This view of the necessity of actively appropriating "the word" which exists in the mouths of others fits well with Lave and Wenger's (1991) notion of learning as participation in a community of practice. In order to learn, newcomers must be afforded opportunities for meaningful participation; however, this may not be easy when there are oldtimers who are already experts at the community's discourse, and one must appropriate their words. Some newcomers may be afforded more opportunities for participation than others. Communities have unspoken but generally accepted power relations which powerfully impact perceptions of who is entitled to participate in given situations. Toohey (2000) found that minority students' opportunities for participation were negatively affected by ongoing subordination efforts of some mainsteam students.

MINORITY STUDENTS IN A CLASS USING KNOWLEDGE FORUM

This initial research provided only slight support for suggestions that minority students' participation levels increase when on-line as opposed to face-to-face discourse is used. There was some indication that the slower pace of discourse was an advantage, however, two of the three students never contributed notes to the database which were written in their own words. As one student commented: "Um, the writing remained a long time, so I was just afraid to make any mistakes or errors in the, in my notes so I just find the information on (the internet) and I just copy it and paste it in Knowledge Forum." The reluctance to engage in the type of risk-taking that would have been required to make her error-prone English public may be linked to sentiments expressed by all three students about how they believe they are perceived and treated by many mainstream students. As one student bluntly stated: "There's racism, of course". When asked how that would affect his participation in physics class he said he would "Maybe just, say nothing."

The experiences which the students we spoke with reported suggest that their learning was negatively affected by their status as minority students in at least two ways. First, they must learn complex subject matter in what is for them a relatively unfamiliar language. Second, they are subject to subordination efforts such as racist remarks and exclusionary behaviour leading them to limit their participation, whether in face to face interaction or in on-line discourse. It is also possible that minority students' contributions may elicit fewer responses in the online discourse than those of other students. Further research is required to investigate this possibility.

APPROPRIATING THE WORD

This preliminary investigation of a beginning knowledge-building community has led us to renew our commitment to investigate ways that students are differentially able to appropriate classroom discourse and participate in classroom activities. Research efforts are needed to find ways to empower minority students to enhance their participation, and to take the risks which are crucial to successful learning. A shift in the way minority students are thought of has been suggested by Ross MacDonald (1999), who called for a paradigm shift from a conception of minority students as deficient (e.g. in language and cultural capital) to one of minority students as ambassadors to multiple ways of thinking and knowing. Such a perspective on diverse ways of knowing fits well with notions of collaborative learning, and with the goal of enabling a great diversity of students to come together in productive and respectful communities of practice.

ACKNOWLEDGEMENTS

We would like to thank the students we spoke with and their teacher for their participation in this work. This work was supported by a Standard Research Grant to the second author and Marlene Scardamalia from the Social Sciences and Humanities Research Council of Canada.

REFERENCES

Gee, J.P. (1996). Social linguistics and literacies. Bristol, PA: Taylor & Francis.

Toohey, K. (2000). *Learning English at school: Identity, social relations and classroom practice.* Clevedon, UK: Multilingual Matters.

Lave, J. & Wenger, E. (1991). *Situated learning: Legitimate peripheral participation.* Cambridge UK: Cambridge University Press.

MacDonald, R. B. (1999). Fueling up at the disciplinary crossroads: Advantaging nontraditional and minority students in interdisciplinary programs. *Bulletin of Science, Technology and Society*, **19**, 2, 144-146.

Scardamalia, M., Bereiter, C. & Lamon M. (1994). The CSILE project: Trying to bring the classroom into world 3. In Kate McGilly (Ed.) *Classroom lessons: Integrating cognitive theory and classroom practice.* (pp. 201-228). Cambridge, MA: Bradford Books/MIT Press.

Working Hard in the 'Office': An Ethnomethodological Study of On-line Workshops

Jacki O'Neill — Salford University — jackioneill@hotmail.com

David Martin — Lancaster University — d.b.martin@lancaster.ac.uk

Hasan Al-Matrouk — Manchester University — hasan@cs.man.ac.uk

David Wastell — Salford University — d.wastell@salford.ac.uk

ABSTRACT

This paper demonstrates the usefulness of ethnomethodology as a perspective for studying CSCL, with excerpts and findings from a case study of on-line workshops conducted using Office Hours Live. Ethnomethodology, with its focus on the detail of practical action and interaction, provides a particularly useful way of understanding whether and how CSCL technologies can support such interaction. The paper highlights important issues for the design of technology and the organisation of on-line.

Keywords

CSCL, Office Hours Live, ethnomethodology, synchronous learning, distributed learning

CSCL AND ETHNOMETHODOLOGY

One way in which ethnomethodology can bring fresh insights to CSCL is through the evaluation of operational systems to generate issues and requirements for redesign. In this short paper we will elucidate this approach through brief examples of problematic phenomena that arose in workshops on e-learning conducted using a new CSCL technology[1] (Office Hours Live), a multi-media, synchronous, distributed, web-based communication technology. It is purported to enable the type of real-time interaction on-line between educators and students hitherto only possible in *"physical academic venues"*.

Ethnomethodology, which can be usefully employed alongside other methods of systems design, has a very particular focus, which is on witnessing and honestly reporting social action and interaction. It is important not to confuse ethnomethodology with the more familiar term *ethnography*, which simply denotes the material (or data) that constitutes a literal record of the social activity as it actually occurred. Such ethnographic materials include: detailed field notes from participant-observation, pictures and copies of artefacts (particularly, in this case, technology in use) and recordings; visual, audio and text chat. What is distinctive about ethnomethodology is its orientation to this material. Instead of imposing a theoretical structure or attempting to create a grounded theory from the material (Glaser and Strauss), ethnomethodology looks for the achieved social structure and orderliness manifest in the ethnographic record. It highlights how this is created and oriented to by the participants themselves, *in-and-through* their actions and interaction (Garfinkel, 1967; Sharrock & Anderson, 1986).

TECHNOLOGY AND ANALYSIS

Office Hours Live consists of two 'rooms', the 'lecture hall' and the 'office'. Both support the presentation of slides, web pages and applications, text chat, participants list, live audio and a feedback tool. In the lecture hall only the presenter can talk to the participants (one-to-many audio), in the office multi-way audio is available. The examples demonstrate the usefulness of this approach in highlighting design issues. In the first example below, the participants have changed rooms from the lecture hall to the office and a problem arose with Dave Watson's audio. This illustrates the ***increased workload*** that arises from detecting and repairing problems using these technologies particularly the ***mixed media confusion*** resulting from multi channel communication. Text (gray) and audio (italics) are interspersed in the transcript:

Hanif: *"hello, hello, hello. Can you hear me now? (Long pause...) I think you can hear me now. Can you speak please? Push on and hold on the CTRL key then speak. I hear you well Nadia, Ian, Dave? Mustafa I hear you very well. Hello Janet, I hear you well. You know better than me Janet right? Is everybody there now?"*

Janet: *"Dave."*

Hanif: *"Are you there, can we hear your voice."*

Hanif: *"You can speak by holding down the CTRL key and start speaking. We can go on with the rest of the session now."*

Janet says: "he's not on the audio list"

Janet: *"Dave is not on the audio console any more, I am not quite sure what has happened to him?"*

watson says: "I get a message from Hear me saying…"Cannot open Wave out device...close any applications using play back device"

Hanif: *"Okay, so I think. Dave, Do you have problems with Audio?"*

Janet: *"He cannot hear you, use text Hanif."*

watson says: "I am going to log out and log in again…bye for now!!!"

---

[1] For further examples and greater depth of analysis we refer the reader to the full paper which can be obtained from d.b.martin@lancaster.ac.uk

Hanif (reading Dave's message in chart area) *"I get a message from Hear me audio error, close other tools using audio... I will log off and come back again. Okay Dave see you in a while."*
Janet: *"Hanif he could not hear what you are saying."*

Hanif begins making an audio check. Janet seems to note that Dave has not spoken, uttering "*Dave*", then typing *"he's not on the audio list"* before re-iterating this vocally. Dave types in his error message. Hanif asks whether Dave has problems before Janet's message directs him to the text chat. Hanif finally reads out Dave's message, and Janet repeats that Dave could not hear Hanif. Here we see the type of difficulty that can arise using mixed communication media, particularly in cases ***where technical difficulties arise***. These archetypal difficulties of the technology would not arise in face-to-face communication. The technology requires monitoring *two* channels (audio and text) to pick up and understand. Being ***both presenter and facilitator (P-F)*** makes this task more difficult for Hanif. One solution would be providing a **status monitor** showing current access to communication channels.

In another example illustrating the strength of this form of detailed analysis, we show how despite the shared interface, problems of interpretation can occur between participants and the P-F. For example, participants took unexpected time to complete certain tasks and were engaged in conversational ***pre-work*** around the problems of completing them. This led to problems for the P-F who ***could not locate the source of the trouble***, that is whether the tasks were being undertaken, since the system gave him *little indication of the activities of the participants*. The system only showed the conversation, not that the tasks were being undertaken. The actions that the P-F then took compounded the problems of the participants in undertaking the tasks. This suggests the need for a **presenter's indicator** showing the activities of the participants. One simple resolution could be to indicate to the presenter when participants are interacting with the slides, either entering text, scrolling, or other indicators of interaction.

In the full paper we discuss a number of further organisational and technical issues arising from these studies. These include: *noting the time spent* ***performing systems checks and setting up; the disruption to event flow*** *caused by changing rooms during workshop; the effects of participants* ***multi-tasking*** *in their own locales; and the potential usefulness of* ***fully integrated interfaces*** *for such applications.*

CONCLUSIONS

Our ethnomethodological studies have shown clearly how the medium of presentation (the technology)interacts with the material presented and its manner of presentation to create multiple problems. Despite the best efforts of the participants and the presenter to address these problems the workshop was severely disrupted, leading to frustration on all parts. Real-time, distributed CSCL is increasingly possible with the development of technologies like Office Hours. This paper reveals that such technologies provoke extra, on-going work for participants to establish the grounds for learning to take place. This raises issues concerning the quality of the educational experience currently possible. The sort of reflective evaluation facilitated by ethnomethodological study enables such design issues to be highlighted and new requirements generated, for example adding feedback features like the presenter's indicator and status monitor.

REFERENCES

Garfinkel, H. (1967) *Studies in ethnomethodology*. Prentice Hall: Englewood Cliffs.

Glaser, B. & Strauss, A. (1967). *The discovery of grounded theory*. Prentice Hall: Englewood Cliffs.

Sharrock, W.W., and Anderson, R.J. (1986). *The ethnomethodologists.* London, UK: Tavistock.

Considering Technical, Social & Organizational Contexts in Systems to Support Teacher Learning

Greg Shrader, Robb Lindgren, Neera Waingankar, Ryan Daily, Louis Gomez

Northwestern University – Center for Learning Technologies in Urban Schools, Evanston, IL

gshrader@northwestern.edu

ABSTRACT

This paper presents the results of a field trial of the Living Curriculum (an on-line professional development resource for teachers) examining use, utility and usability. Results show limited use of the system, but high utility for the teachers that did use it. Usability results suggest some design improvements but by and large show that teachers were readily able to use the system. Limited use is attributed to a failure to account for the context of use. Future research in this area should attend realistically to the technical and social constraints of schools.

Keywords

social context, performance support, teacher learning, on-line learning, design research

INTRODUCTION

This paper presents the results of a field trial of the Living Curriculum (LC); a case-based performance support system designed to help teachers learn to teach project-based science (Krajcik, Blumenfeld, Fredricks & Soloway, 1998) curricula by coupling video cases to curriculum over the Internet. The goal is for teachers to learn from those video cases as they teach the projects. This study examines the *use*, *utility* and *usability* of the LC. Do teachers use the system? Do they find it useful when they do? Finally, from an HCI perspective, is the system usable? In the interest of space we refer you to our CSCL '99 paper (Shrader & Gomez, 1999) for a description of the system.

METHODS & RESULTS

The participants in our study were all Chicago Public School teachers with at least 10 years experience who were planning to teach a project-based science unit called ReNUE between January and April of 2000. Participants were assigned to 2 groups (4 teachers per group). The "Scheduled User Group" committed to use the LC on two week intervals with an interviewer present. The "Independent User Group" had access to the LC but made no commitment to a schedule of use. We conducted pre and post-interviews with all participants. We also observed and videotaped the Scheduled User sessions and maintained a server log of all LC interactions. Results of the study are reported in the two categories: Quantitative analysis of use patterns and qualitative analysis of the scheduled user sessions.

Use Patterns: A total of 6 sessions were logged by the *Independent Users*; 4 by User 1 and 2 by User 2. Most of that use was motivated by the interaction with a professional development facilitator (not associated with this study) who recommended specific LC content to help a teacher experiencing difficulty teaching part of the project. All of the *Scheduled Users* logged sessions as planned but only User 4 logged independent sessions. It is interesting to note that our data are confounded by the fact that all of the participants were also registered in a graduate course supporting their implementation of ReNUE. All 4 of User 4's independent sessions occurred after the class ended. We also know that at least 2 teachers outside of our study used the LC; for one the LC was her sole PD resource.

Analysis of Scheduled User Sessions: To explore the utility and usability of the LC we now examine the video and interview data from the scheduled user sessions. All the videos from the scheduled user sessions were reviewed and coded by the interviewers. Those coded videotapes were then subjected to interaction analysis at team research meetings (Jordan & Henderson, 1995). The main results are outlined below.

- Teachers' time and computing skills: Our scheduled user data suggest that *teachers' time* was a significant barriers to use. Users frequently expressed an intent to use the LC independently between sessions, but rarely did. All of the teachers sampled had adequate basic *computing skills* and could locate and navigate the LC. However they needed help configuring their browsers by installing the Quicktime plug-in.
- Design and Usability: All scheduled users consistently complained about the *size and the quality* of LC videos. In some cases the video was streaming too slowly. In other cases the 160x120 pixel video was too small. The LC *organizes video cases* by indexing several videos to each project lesson plan and uses a schematic diagram of titles to point users to the individual videos. Users did not understand that organization.

- Utility of the LC: Our scheduled users all used the system to browse the curriculum pages until they found an activity of interest and then linked to the video for that activity. In both the scheduled user sessions and the post interviews teachers reported that the LC was useful in three ways: to plan their lessons, to review lessons that they had already taught, and to get help with difficult lessons (e.g., modeling).

DISCUSSION & CONCLUSION

We undertook this study to examine the use, utility and usability of the LC. Our *use* results were disappointing. Data suggest that use is constrained by teachers' access to connected computers, time, and technology skills. Despite these limitations we found that the teachers who did use the LC found *utility* in that use. They used it to plan their teaching, to build confidence in their teaching, and to address instructional problems in their classrooms. Finally with respect to *usability* we found room for design improvements but in general found that teachers easily learned to navigate the LC. We are encouraged by our utility and usability results. Of course those results only matter if we can address the barriers to use. For that reason we focus the remainder of our discussion on the question of use. We begin our discussion by addressing access and technical support from a social context perspective and then consider the larger context of use.

Access to computers and the Internet as well as limited technical proficiency are not surprising findings. Both are knowable conditions of the user population. The distribution of computing skill among the teaching population roughly mirrors that of the working population at large. The teachers in our study could use a computer to read mail, browse the web or produce documents. Difficulties arose when they were asked to install plug-ins. Access has two dimensions. In simple terms teachers do not have access to enough Internet connected computers. More importantly, they do not have access to adequate technical support. With adequate support the browser software would have been updated and the plug-in problem would not have arisen. But understanding the problem does not let us off the hook. Our job is to design for our clients' environment. Use of the LC suffers because we depend on an idealized computing infrastructure that does not exist. Our future success will depend upon our ability to execute a design that will be usable in school environments.

While the volume of use during this study was clearly disappointing we take encouragement from two results. First, when teachers did use the LC they found it useful. More importantly there were two contexts that fostered use. Teachers used the LC during scheduled use sessions with an interviewer. They also used it at the recommendation of PD facilitators to address specific problems. These two uses have one thing in common: social context. We are reminded of Vermeer's (in process) work on the social/organizational environment in which knowledge management systems are used. Vermeer argues that use of knowledge management systems depends on careful consideration to the design of use contexts. The goal cannot simply be to design systems that identify, represent and share practice but to design explicit organizational contexts within which the resulting system will be used. Through the design of our study we happened upon two social contexts that promote use (interviews and PD interactions). Future research in this area must take the social and organizational context of use seriously both as it relates to the design of the tools themselves (e.g., making them usable within the infrastructure of schools) and as it relates to the way the tool fits into the school context. A longer version of this paper with a more detailed analysis appears in the electronic version of these conference proceedings.

REFERENCES

Jordan, B., & Henderson. (1995). Interaction Analysis - Foundations and Practice. *Journal of the Learning Sciences, 4*(1), 39-103.

Krajcik, J., Blumenfeld, P. C., Marx, R. W., Fredricks, J., & Soloway, E. (1998). Inquiry in Project-Based Science classrooms: Initial attempts by middle school students. *The Journal of the Learning Sciences, 7*(3 & 4).

Shrader, G. W., & Gomez, L. M. (1999). *Design Research for the Living Curriculum.* Paper presented at the Computer Supported Collaborative Learning, Palo Alto, CA.

Vemeer. (In Process). *Untitled.* Unpublished Dissertation, Northwestern University, Evanston, IL.

Facilitating Knowledge Convergence in Videoconferencing Environments: The Role of External Representation Tools

Frank Fischer, Heinz Mandl
University of Munich, Germany
fischerf@edupsy.uni-muenchen.de

ABSTRACT

The study analyzed how two types of graphical representation tools influence the way in which dyads use shared and unshared knowledge resources in different collaboration scenarios, and how learners represent and transfer shared knowledge under these different conditions. We varied the type of graphical representation (content-specific vs. content-unspecific) and the collaboration scenario (videoconferencing vs. face-to-face). 64 university students participated. Results show that learning partners converged in their profiles of resource use. With the content-specific external representation, learners used more appropriate knowledge resources. However, learners in the videoconferencing scenarios differed from learners in direct collaboration in how they use the representation tools.

Keywords

Collaborative knowledge construction, knowledge convergence, external representation, shared knowledge, videoconferencing

BACKGROUND OF THE STUDY

Knowledge convergence. A question central to research and practice of computer-supported collaborative learning is, how locally distributed learners manage to converge with respect to their knowledge. In this paper we therefore focus on a theoretical aspect which seems both, highly relevant for the field and so far neglected by empirical research: The aspect of knowledge *convergence* (Roschelle, 1996). In our analysis we consider two main aspects of knowledge convergence: (1) *Process convergence.* We investigate how group members use the knowledge available to collaboratively construct new knowledge in discourse. Moreover, we analyze how learning partners converge with respect to their discourse focus. It is plausible that cooperation partners develop a kind of collaborative style - even in short-term problem solving activities. (2) *Outcome convergence.* If group members learn together they can construct *shared cognitive representations.* The study of Jeong and Chi (1999) showed that only a relatively small portion of the knowledge, which a dyad constructed in collaboration, is actually represented by both of the learners. A further question is to what extent learning partners are similarly able to *apply* the knowledge in new contexts.

Facilitating knowledge convergence with shared external representations. Shared external representation tools might help to improve discourse in computer-supported collaborative learning scenarios (e. g. Fischer, Bruhn, Gräsel, & Mandl, in press). We distinguish between two types of external graphical representation: (a) *Content-unspecific representation*: Tools like shared whiteboards should support interaction between collaborators by providing them with the possibility to visualize graphical elements and written notes. The subject area as well as the task type does not play a role in the design of these tools. In (b) *content-specific representation*, the degrees of freedom of the external representation are constrained by task-related structures. We expected that the provision of this task-related structure in content-specific representation tools would promote the construction of shared knowledge because of a representational bias (Suthers, 2000).

Videoconferencing. It is unclear to what extent the conditions of videoconferencing have an impact on process and outcome convergence. Up to this point, no systematic studies on this topic have been conducted. A smaller amount of convergence is possible, for the development of similar positions might be mediated through nonverbal and para-verbal aspects. For example, the lack of eye contact, differences in the visual fields of the partners, as well as the reduced possibility to make deictic gestures in a video conference could serve as hindering factors. However, empirical studies rarely show any differences between videoconferencing and face-to-face conditions concerning the outcome (O'Malley et al., 1996).

RESEARCH QUESTIONS

(1) Do learning partners converge with respect to discourse focus, knowledge representation, and knowledge transfer? (2) Which effects do the kind of external representation, the collaboration scenario, and their combination have on process and outcome convergence?

METHOD

(1) Sample and design: Sixty-four students of educational psychology volunteered in this study. The participants were separated into dyads and each dyad was randomly assigned to one of the four experimental conditions in a 2x2 factorial

design. We varied (a) the cooperation scenario (face-to-face vs. computer-mediated) and (b) the type of external representation tool (content-unspecific vs. content-specific). Time-on-task was held constant in all four conditions. (2) *Task and learning environment*: Students in both conditions had to work on complex cases in the domain of education. The students' task was to prepare a common analysis of the case. While working on a case, students were provided with a representation tool to visualize their developing solution. Dyads in the *content-specific representation tool* condition worked with a computer-based mapping tool, which provides cards for case information as well as cards for theoretical concepts. Positive and negative relations can be used to connect cards. Learners in the *content-unspecific representation* condition worked on a computer tool with the functionality of a simple graphic editor. (3) *Variables and data sources*: Learning discourse and individual oral evaluation of cases were transcribed and analyzed with respect to the following categories: (a) Discourse focus. Here we distinguish situational, conceptual, application-oriented (the relation of a concept to a case information), and strategic foci. (b) To determine process convergence we computed a similarity index on the basis of the discourse focus categories..(c) As an indicator of outcome convergence we took the quantitative as well as the qualitative differences between the knowledge test results of the learning partners. (4) *Procedure*: After a prior knowledge test, students were made familiar with the learning environment. Next, learners worked together on three cases. The collaboration was followed by an individual post-test.

RESULTS AND CONCLUSIONS

Results. (1) First, we compared real dyads to nominal dyads (i.e., two learners out of the same experimental condition, who have not learned together). We found higher convergence in real dyads at nearly every discourse focus category as well as for the global similarity measure based on these categories. Second, results concerning outcome convergence showed that real dyads do not differ from nominal dyads with respect to the representation of shared and unshared knowledge. However, more shared knowledge is transferred in real dyads as compared to nominal ones. (2) Compared to the content-unspecific representation, the content-specific representation fosters the use of conceptual and application-oriented focus. This indicates a representational bias effect of the content-specific structure given with the representation tool. (b) We analyzed the quantitative convergence of the learning partners concerning knowledge application in the individual transfer case. Interestingly, for content-specific representation, the convergence is similarly high in both collaboration scenarios. However, for the content-unspecific representation, convergence is low in physical co-presence and high in videoconferencing.

Conclusions. (1) We found evidence for process convergence: Learning partners strongly converge to a common profile of resource use. (2) Our findings concerning the shared representation tools could be seen as support for Suthers (2000) representational bias assumption: Learning partners talk much more about specific conceptual aspects, if the external representation provide a task-specific structure. (3) Content-specific representation tools might provide an initial coordination for learners in that they have some task-relevant categories already in their joint problem space as a preliminary common ground. (4) Collaborative knowledge construction and knowledge convergence is neither hampered nor facilitated by the characteristics of our videoconference. (5) The same external representation tool might fulfill quite different functions for the process of knowledge convergence in different collaboration scenarios.

REFERENCES

Fischer, F., Bruhn, J., Gräsel, C., & Mandl, H. (in press). Fostering collaborative knowledge construction with visualization tools. *Learning and Instruction.*

Jeong, H., & Chi, M. T. H. (1999). *Constructing Shared Knowledge During Collaboration and Learning.* Paper presented at the AERA Annual Meeting, Montreal, Canada.

O'Malley, C., Langton, S., Anderson, A., Doherty-Sneddon, G., & Bruce, V. (1996). Comparison of face-to-face and video-mediated interaction. *Interacting with Computers, 8*(2), 177-192.

Roschelle, J. (1996). Learning by collaborating: Convergent conceptual change. In T. Koschmann (Ed.), *CSCL: Theory and practice of an emerging paradigm* (pp. 209-248). Mahwah, New Jersey: Lawrence Erlbaum Associates.

Suthers, D. (2000). *Initial Evidence for Representational Guidance of Learning Discourse.* Paper presented at the Proceedings of International Conference on Computers in Education, Taipei, Taiwan.

Network and Content Analysis in an Online Community Discourse

Maarten de Laat
University of Nijmegen
m.delaat@ped.kun.nl

ABSTRACT
The aim of this paper is to study interaction patterns among the members of a community of practice within the Dutch police organization and the way they share and construct knowledge together. The online discourse between 46 members, using First Class, formed the basis for this study. Social Network Analysis and content analysis were used to analyze the data. The results show that the interaction patterns between the members are rather centralized and that the network is relatively dense. Most of the members are involved within the discourse but person to person communication is still rather high. Content analysis revealed that discourse is focused on sharing and comparing information.

Keywords
Social Network Analysis, content analysis, networked expertise, community of practice, organizational learning

INTRODUCTION
The aim of this paper is to study the nature of networked expertise within an organization, and the way its members share and construct knowledge together. In a learning organization, workers are stimulated to share and develop knowledge together. Workers tend to form networks of expertise to facilitate individual learning, collaboration and to discuss work related problems together. Sometimes these networks transform into communities of practice. In a community of practice (COP), participants, who share a common interest for the field they work in, come together to help out each other, solve problems, and share and create knowledge collaboratively. Over time these mutual interactions and relationships build up a shared body of knowledge and a sense of identity. They constitute an informal, social structure initiated by members and reflecting on their collective learning (Wenger, 1998).

This study focuses on the exchange of information through a CSCL-environment (First Class) within the Dutch police organization. The members of this network frequently exchange information and discuss work related problems together. Their shared interest for drugs issues in criminal investigation resulted in the establishment of a shared practice. This network can be characterized as a community of practice because of voluntary engagement, existence of this network over time (two years), and realization of a shared practice (Wenger, 1998).

The way people participate in expertise networks provides insight in the process of learning. A CSCL environment provides ideal possibilities to study interaction patterns between the members of a network. Social network techniques can be used to describe patterns of relationships between individuals. Insight in communication patterns within a certain network alone is not enough. Also the content of the discourse must be taken into account (Henri, 1992; Gunawardena, Lowe, & Anderson, 1997). This way information can be gathered about the quality of the learning and the social construction of knowledge.

METHOD
An existing community of practice within the Dutch police organization was studied to analyze the interaction patterns and quality of the discourse. They used the program First Class as a communication tool in which the discourse took place. In this study we focus on the following questions:

1. *How active are the members in the discourse?*
2. *Who are central participants in the discourse?*
3. *How dense is the participation within the network?*
4. *What is the quality of the discourse?*

Subjects and procedure
Communities of practice can't be built they emerge. Therefore we followed an existing community of practice within the Dutch police to analyze their activities. This COP consists of 46 members who are affiliated with or conducting drugs related investigations. They use First Class as an electronic environment to discuss work related problems, exchange information and to maintain their expertise. First Class is a communication forum that facilitates an asynchronous discourse. The members operate in a shared workspace in which they can read and write messages. The data that was analyzed during this study is from the period of January till June 2001.

Instruments

To answer the research questions we successively used the following instruments. First Class generates log-files about the activity of the members. Social network analysis (SNA) is used to analyze the social structure of the COP. First we conducted centrality measures to find the central participants within the network, than we conducted a density analysis to describe the overall linkage between the participants, and finally we visualized their interaction pattern using multi dimensional scaling. To assess the quality of the discourse the coding scheme from Gunawardena et al. (1997) was applied. This coding scheme examines the negotiation of meaning and social construction of knowledge in CSCL-environments.

RESULTS AND DISCUSSION

The results indicate that the members are relatively well engaged in this COP. They wrote 233 messages to the entire network, with an average of 5,07 (SD 6,72; min 0, max 32) messages per person. 14 members of the community did not write any message to the whole group. In total the written messages were read 7486 times with an average of 162,74 (SD 83,15; min 1, max 249) per person. Centrality measures indicate that the interaction patterns between the members of this network are rather centralized. All the members sort of gel around the more active members of this COP. There are no subgroups within this COP, and most of the members are somehow involved within the discourse. Some members are more passively engaged in this COP, and that the person to person communication is still rather high. This might be attributed to the culture of the police organization, where there traditionally is a lot of face to face communication. People tend to share information and solve problems through their personalized networks. Density calculations indicate how active the members are involved in the discourse. In the case of sending and reading the messages that were exchanged through First Class the COP had a density of 57%. The quality of the discourse in terms of social knowledge construction remains mainly in the phase of sharing information (72% of the messages). However the members of this COP want to use First Class not just as a tool for sharing information. Their intention is to recognize drugs related trends throughout the whole country and to develop collaboratively an approach to meet those new developments. This involves not just processes of sharing information, also discussion and negotiation resulting in construction of knowledge are necessary to maintain and develop their expertise. A suggestion to stimulate this process of knowledge construction is to form small subgroups around central discussion themes to develop deep understanding, and use all the members of the COP for feedback on their results and input of new trends and information.

REFERENCES

Gunawardena, C. N., Lowe, C. A., & Anderson, T. (1997). Analysis of global online debate and the development of an interaction analysis model for examining social construction of knowledge in computer conferencing. *Journal of Educational Computing Research, 17*(4), 397-431.

Henri, F. (1992). Computer conferencing and content analysis. In A. R. Kaye (Ed.), *Collaborative learning through computer conferencing*. London: Springer-Verlag.

Scott, J. (1991). *Social network analysis: A handbook*. London: Sage.

Wasserman, S., & Faust, K. (1997). *Social network analysis: Methods and applications*. Cambridge: Cambridge university press.

Wenger, E. (1998). *Communities of practice: Learning, meaning, and identity*. Cambridge: University Press.

Connecting Formal and Informal Discourses to Create Yet Another Zone of Learning

Hideyuki Suzuki
Ibaraki University
hideyuki@suzuki.or.jp

Hideo Funaoi
National Institute of Multimedia Education
funaoi@nime.ac.jp

ABSTRACT

In this paper, we focus on the "Question-Answer" function of the SOUTO system; the hypermedia authoring system, and classroom activities where learners make hypermedia compositions with SOUTO and discuss their compositions with the function mentioned above. Field tests of the system reveal that; 1. The Question-Answer function reconfigures social relationships in the classroom and thus creates a foundation for collaborative learning, 2. The Question-Answer function creates a field of informal talk, 3. The SOUTO system provides a foundation on which both formal and informal talks are constituted and woven together, and thus, transition between them is enabled. Based on these findings, we suggest that educational systems should be designed as mediators that hybridize school-like activities and non-school-like activities.

Keywords

supporting discussion, reconfiguring classroom activities, informal conversation

INTRODUCTION: CONSERVATIVE CSCL VS. RADICAL CSCL

CSCL researches can be roughly divided into two types. One is the conservative CSCL research that is based on existing concepts of what 'learning' and 'school' are, and contributes, as a result, to maintaining the present form of school and classroom activities. The other is the radical CSCL research that endeavors reformation of conventional school activities and culture. This paper focuses on our project that exemplifies the radical CSCL research. In the project we are endeavoring to reconfigure the existing relationship between learners and teachers, learners and learners as well as learners/teachers through CSCL systems design and thus to establish yet another zone of learning in school. In the following sections, we show (1) SOUTO system, the hypermedia authoring system, (2) how the system contributes to reconfigure conventional social relationships in classroom, and then discuss (a) significance of less formal personal exchanges in collaborative learning, (b) hybridization strategy for the radical CSCL research.

DESIGNING SOUTO SYSTEM AS A TOOL FOR RECONFIGURATION

SOUTO (creator/thinker) is a hypermedia authoring system that boasts skeleton set of functions to treat multimedia materials and simple GUI that allows learners to access the functions without difficulties. The Question-Answer function of SOUTO is designed to facilitate learners' conversation on their compositions. This function enables learners to create question or answer cards and put them onto the questioned/answered cards in a composition (fig. 1). The authors consider that the Question-Answer function contributes to reposition the interwoven agents, i. e., learners, teachers, compositions, and so on, that constitute the classroom.

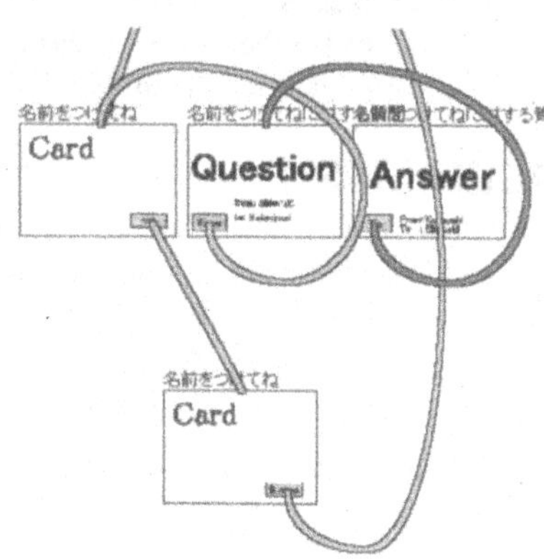

Fig.1: Juxtapositional view of question/answer cards and the composition

OBSERVATION IN SOUTO CLASSROOM

Commitment to peer learners: During question-answer activities in SOUTO classroom, it was observed that learners were encouraged to see their peer learners as audience of their compositions. The authors presume that the Question-Answer function, which establishes learner-learner information pathway, contributes to the emergence of this learner-learner relation.

- **Compositions as multivoiced products:** In many cases information exchanged through question-answer was imported into their compositions when they were revised and thus the compositions were imbued with the others' voices. This process turned the compositions from individual facilities into collective artifacts.

Emergent region of personal talk: While formal and public language was used in compositions, vivid colloquialism filled with personal talk, joking, capering, decrying, and irresponsibility, appeared in question and answer cards.

- **Hybrid language and hybrid identity:** SOUTO system juxtaposed formal school language (compositions) with personal language (question-answer). On this mingled region of public and personal, learners lived two different "I"s simultaneously. One is the public "I" who engaged in school-like activities, the other is the personal "I" who engaged in emotional and private reciprocation of words with their peers.

DISCUSSION

The region of personal talk was full of the carnivalistic characteristics (Bakhtin 1968) such as abusive language, anger, parody, mutual mockery, and degradation of authorities. In addition, it was observed that the region was ruled by laws incommensurable with that of school-like activities. It is fair to consider that the region of personal talk appeared as the carnivalistic world in relation to the school-like activities.

SOUTO appeared as a boundary object upon which different languages, i. e., personal language and school language were constituted and woven together, and thus, transitions among them were enabled. SOUTO was a tool for making hypermedia compositions into a product for classroom activity, it was also a tool for person-to-person small talk about the composition. This hybridism allowed the students to construct their learning based on both of the regions. Hybrid tool ensures hybrid learning.

What is the significance of this hybridism? From the viewpoint of learning through conversation, this hybridism assures creative nature of conversation. Bakhtin (1984) discusses that carnivalistic nature is essential to creative conversation where knowledge is constituted through the interaction/negotiation among interlocutors. From the viewpoint of school reform, this hybridism is expected to constitute yet another zone of learning. The region of carnival is an integral part of students' lives and their reality as students. However, it has been excluded when student activities are organized as formal learning activities. Making learners stand between a school-like world and the carnival world provides the possibility to realize an unprecedented learning activity with the missing part, or the region of carnival, as one of the constituents. The newly formed zone of learning is a field where school-like activities are questioned and relativized. It is also a field where learning is anchored to both sides of school life, i. e., classroom activities and small talk, and where the students appear as hybrid agents.

CONCLUSION

Observation in the SOUTO classroom showed the Question-Answer function reconfigured the existing social relation in the classroom. However, what we saw in the classroom was not a monolithic "alternative activity" brought about by the function, but rather a continuous constitution of different regions where students stand on the intersection of these regions.

This study suggests that systems for radical CSCL should be designed as boundary objects that constructively produce conflict between existing school activities and carnivalistic activities, and establish traffic between them. The point of this design strategy is not to replace school-like activities with "non-school-like activities", but to make these activities encounter and hybridize into yet another zone of learning. It is important that, in this work, the school-like activities are not concealed from the students, but are visualized for them and thus repositioned by the juxtaposition with the other activities.

ACKNOWLEDGEMENTS

This study is supported in part by the Grant-in-Aid for Scientific Research (B-11558013, 1999-2001) & (B-13558023, 2001) from the Japanese Ministry of Education, Culture, Sports, Science and Technology.

REFERENCES

Bakhtin, M. (1968). Rabelais and his world. Iswolsky, H. (Trans.) MIT Press

Bakhtin, M (1984). Problems of Dostoevsky's poetics. Emerson, C. (Trans.) Manchester University Press

Disinhibition in a CSCL Environment

James M. Hudson, Amy Bruckman
Georgia Institute of Technology
{jhudson, asb}@cc.gatech.edu

ABSTRACT
In this paper, we explore the IRC Français foreign language learning environment. This environment offers little more than a text-based chat system with a few features to make writing in a foreign language easier. Despite the limited structure, conversations online exhibit strong differences from conversations in the classroom, even when the teachers and students remain constant. We offer some explanations for these findings based on interviews conducted with a number of the teachers and students.

Keywords
Computer-Mediated Communication (CMC), Inhibition, Foreign Language Learning, Text, Equality, Chat

IRC FRANÇAIS
Over the past two years, we have involved students in online language learning conversations using text-based chat in a number of ways. Typically, seven to ten students participate in a conversation hosted by a teacher or a native speaker. This host, who is not necessarily the teacher of the students participating, acts as a party host would: s/he provides the seed to start the conversation and then participates like any other conversant. The host periodically takes more control of the conversation if the discussion seems to be waning. These conversations take place using IRC Français(1), a real-time, text-based chat client that allows students to converse over the Internet. The design of this system is described in (Hudson & Bruckman, In Press). The ehtory of this project can be found in the electronic version of this paper. Below, we briefly describe a study using two language classes over the course of a semester. These studies involved observing conversations in the classroom and online. Interviews were also conducted with a subset of the students participating. These teachers – Marie(2) and Philippe – illustrate the changes that occur in the discourse patterns of students using this type of online environment.

CONVERSATION IN THE TRADITIONAL CLASSROOM
In talking about her French class, one student succinctly summarized the trend seen in a number of classrooms:

> [The teacher] talks most of the time, actually. Literally, I maybe get in two to three sentences in class of me actually speaking. [...] It's a bit awkward sometimes because she'll pose these questions. It's supposed to be a free forum for anyone to answer and try to get a discussion started. Maybe we're just not comfortable enough with each other yet to actually do that. So, everyone just kind of sits there and she'll go around the circle prompting you to respond to the question. Everyone takes their seven seconds in the limelight and says something. And that's it.

This pattern of interaction occurs in conversations in many foreign language classrooms. Typically, a foreign-language instructor plans to have a classroom conversation on a given topic. Therefore, the conversation begins with the instructor asking a general question to the class in order to start discussion on that chosen topic. The instructor, then, waits while the students quietly struggle to avoid eye contact. Eventually, the teacher calls on a specific student; the general question is repeated and aimed at the chosen student. The student gives the professor an answer and then breathes a sigh of relief as another "victim" is chosen. This pattern continues with the instructor varying aspects of the general question while calling on specific individuals. As such, the instructor usually comments between each student comment, initiating a question and frequently reiterating the student answer. This is not unlike the traditional initiate-respond-evaluate (IRE) cycle seen in many classrooms in all academic disciplines (Newman, Griffin, & Cole, 1989). Not only does this lead to instructors saying significantly more in classroom discussions than the students, it leads to instructors acting as the gatekeeper to conversations. All comments must pass through the teacher. Also, student inhibition naturally leads to instructor dominance even with the best of instructors. The teachers we observed were both excellent instructors, but were unable to avoid being the dominant voice in the classroom.

CONVERSATIONS USING IRC FRANÇAIS
IRC Français-based conversations, however, seem to have little in common with classroom discussions. The same group of instructors and students (though in different combinations) approach conversations differently depending on whether they

---

(1) http://www.cc.gatech.edu/elc/irc-francais/

(2) All teacher names have been changed.

are held online or in the classroom. Students tend to talk more; instructors, less. More complex conversations arise. Marie,

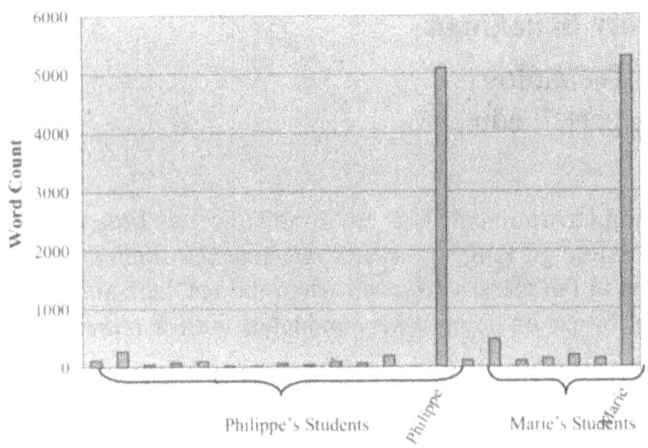

Figure 1: In the traditional classroom, teachers (Marie and Philippe) speak significantly more than any student.

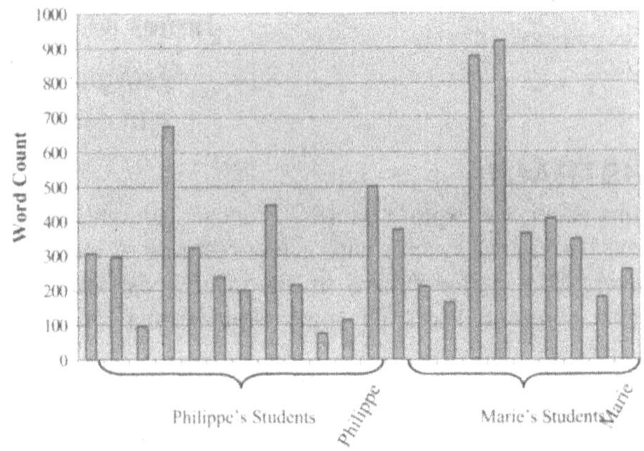

Figure 2: In the online environment, participation is much more egalitarian.

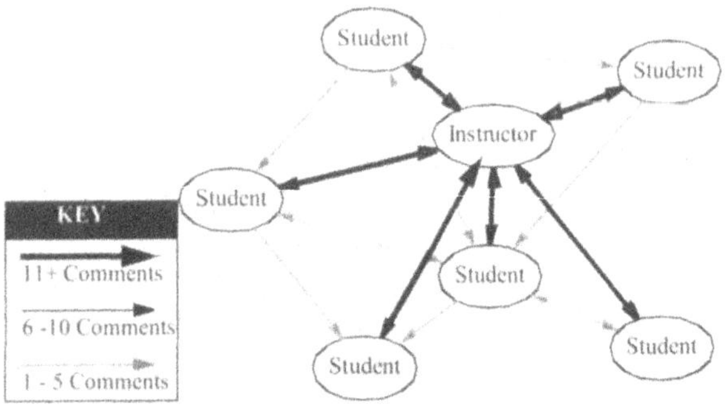

Figure 3: In Marie's traditional classroom, a social network analysis illustrates that she is the pivotal figure.

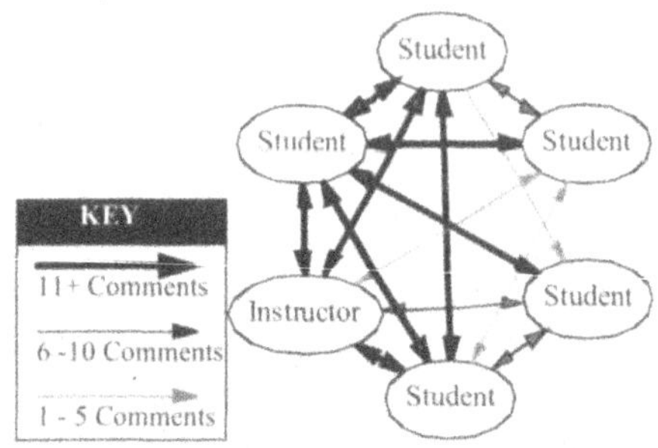

Figure 5: In Marie's online discussion, a much more democratic relationship between all participants emerges.

for example, became the pivotal figure in the *classroom* largely because no one answered her attempts to begin discussions. When she asks a general question *online*, however, she frequently receives a flood of responses. Almost all students seem to participate in the conversations with no provocation. As a result, she could relax control and let the conversations develop among the students.

DISCUSSION

These studies lead us to suggest that inhibition is reduced online in a number of ways. Particularly salient is the fact that discussions occur in almost real-time. Comments are not shown until the student decides to submit them. Struggling to formulate a grammatically correct comment does not hold up other in the class. As one student said, "People are not staring at you when you're talking. You're not put on the spot, basically. If you want to respond to something someone says, you can. And if you don't, you don't." The lowered inhibitions, subsequently allowed to the students to feel more comfortable sharing information with one another. As a result, a better, more supportive community of learners developed. Another student felt, "It's ok that I was going to make mistakes speaking French [online]. I'm not a native speaker and even if I were, I would make mistakes. That helped me realize that I could speak and that I wasn't going to be ridiculed for anything I said. … I'm not scared to speak French now." Further research is necessary to analyze why these changes occur in the online environment.

REFERENCES

Hudson, J. M., & Bruckman, A. (In Press). IRC Français: The Creation of an Internet-based SLA Community. *Computer Assisted Language Learning*.

Newman, D., Griffin, P., & Cole, M. (1989). *The Construction Zone: Working for Cognitive Change in School*. New York: Cambridge University Press.

Studying Social Aspects of Computer-Supported Collaboration with a Mixed Evaluation Approach

A. Martínez[1], Y. Dimitriadis[2], B. Rubia[3], E. Gómez[2], I. Garrachón[1], J. A. Marcos[1]

[1]School of Computer Science Eng.
University of Valladolid
amartine@infor.uva.es

[2]School of Telecommunication Eng.
University of Valladolid
{yannis, edugom}@tel.uva.es

[3] Faculty of Education
University of Valladolid
rubia@doe.uva.es

ABSTRACT

Studying and evaluating real experiences that promote active and collaborative learning is a crucial field in CSCL. Major issues that remain unsolved deal with the merging of qualitative and quantitative methods and data, especially in educational settings that involve direct as well as computer-supported collaboration. In this paper we present an evaluation methodology and its application to a university course that took place during the last two academic years. We have developed EL2AM, a tool that allows an automatic processing of computer logs using social network analysis. It has been used jointly with a commercial qualitative research tool in order to support the evaluation process. Experimental results allow us to reflect and draw conclusions on the changes of attitudes towards collaboration experimented by the students along the course.

Keywords

Qualitative and quantitative evaluation, social network analysis, project-based learning, ethnographic methodology.

INTRODUCTION

Evaluation of innovative curriculum experiences is a complex task that needs several perspectives in order to be fully understood. The application of computer networks to real classrooms provides a wide range of possibilities for interaction (Crook 1994), which demand a variety of evaluation methods. Computers can also generate automatic data logs, which offer new opportunities for evaluation, but at the same time present problems of data management and interpretation. We have applied social network analysis (Scott, 2000) to the automatic evaluation of *participatory* aspects of learning (Sfard, 98). Social network analysis is an approach that focuses on the study of patterns of *relationships* between *actors* in communities and therefore it is suitable for the study of social aspects of interactions in learning communities.

Our research goal was the study of the evolution of attitudes towards collaboration of the students in a real case that used BSCW (http://www.gmd.de) and other telematic tools as a means of collaboration. Automatic analysis of the data logs was complemented with traditional fieldwork data in order to study how the actual use of the software tools (measured with the social network analysis techniques) reflected the evolution of the ideas about collaboration in the classroom.

In the rest of the paper we briefly outline the evaluation techniques and tools we have used, as well as the results of their application to a real case.

QUANTITATIVE AND QUALITATIVE EVALUATION METHODOLOGY

As mentioned beforehand, our approach to evaluation combines qualitative and social network analysis in order to assess how the educational design and the tools used for its support favour collaboration among students of individualistic tradition. Qualitative analysis was based on students' questionnaires and formal observations performed along the semester. The social network analysis techniques were applied to the event logs generated by BSCW and to a special set of questionnaires. From all the possible social network measurements, we were interested in those giving information on structural properties of the network, such as *cohesion*. We used *density* and *degree centralisation,* as they measure the extent to which all members of a population interact with all other members (Scott, 2000). Graphical representations of the networks called *sociograms* were also used in our study.

We have developed a tool called EL2AM (Event Logs to Adjacency Matrices) that performs several on the event logs provided by BSCW. First, a *parser* translates the non-standard format of the original files to XML, providing a more intuitive view and avoiding several redundancies detected in the BSCW logs. Then, a *configuration module* allows the researcher to select and configure the network she wants to analyse, selecting the type of network, the period of time, and the set of nodes to be included in the study. The above mentioned measurements are then calculated and presented to the researcher in tables. As an additional output, EL2AM provides files in a format accepted by commercial packages such as UCINET or Krackplot. A particular contribution of EL2AM is that it calculates measurements on two-mode networks that other commercial tools do not provide. The results obtained with EL2AM and social network analysis have been integrated in the qualitative evaluation using NUDIST Vivo, a well known qualitative analysis tool.

This evaluation method has been applied to an educational project in which we have been involved for the last two academic years. It consists in the introduction of project-based learning with case-studies in a course on Computer Architecture in studies of Telecommunications Engineering of our university (Dimitriadis, Martínez, Rubia, and Gallego, 2001). In order to face the problems posed by the individualistic and passive culture in Spanish university, the project promoted collaboration by different means. Students were organized in pairs that had to deliver three reports along the course. A final report was written in bigger groups of up to four pairs that shared the same case study. The students were encouraged to use BSCW to maintain asynchronous discussions and to share information. For the study, we considered collaboration at three levels: intra-group, inter-group and at a classroom level.

With the automatic measurements we perceived a lack of use of some of the computer–mediated communication means, which was confirmed by the overall analysis that showed that the students preferred to interact directly with their mates in the classroom. The social network measurements obtained with EL2AM allowed us to observe how the interactions mediated by BSCW increased during the period in which the groups were writing the final report. The fact that they had a common goal promoted collaboration, and this was reflected in the use of the system. The analysis also showed how BSCW helped to mediate interactions in which students *indirectly* shared their information and ideas with the rest of the classroom. We finally observed how the educational project and the tasks the students had to perform helped them to develop new collaborative attitudes beyond the ones they reflected in the initial questionnaire.

CONCLUSIONS AND FUTURE WORK

We have presented an evaluation methodology in which different views complement each other in order to gain a better understanding of the processes under study. Log files give information about the actual use of the computational environment, difficult to grasp by other means; social network analysis applied to these data provides a new insight in the social interactions that are established through the use of the tools; finally, qualitative analysis provides information that is needed to increase the validity of the study.

The design of EL2AM, that relies on a XML intermediate file as the source of data, makes it possible to apply it to the study of other systems, as long as they provide enough information so as to represent the interactions in the format that has been defined. The application of EL2AM to the analysis of new systems will also help to improve the definition of the interactions represented in the XML file.

Here we have outlined part of the results of the evaluation that was actually performed. These results have been considered to inform the design of the new semester and the refinement of the evaluation process, which is currently taking place. Additional information on this project can be found at http://www.infor.uva.es/~amartine/LAO.

ACKNOWLEDGMENTS

The authors want to thank to Raquel Díaz, Mª José Gallego, César Osuna and to the rest of the EMIC group. Special thanks to all the students that eagerly participated in this academic program. Partial financial support for this research project was given by the JCYL, Spain (VA18/99, VA117/01), the Ministry of Science and Technology in Spain and the European Funds for Regional Development (TIC2000-1054) and the EU Leonardo Programme.

REFERENCES

Crook, C. (1994) *Computers and the collaborative experience of learning.* London, U.K: Routeledge.

Dimitriadis, Y., Martínez, A., Rubia, B., and Gallego, M. (2001) Cooperative Learning in Computer Architecture: An educational project and its telematic support. In *Proceedings of the Conference of Frontiers in Education, FIE 2001*, to appear.

Nurmela, K., Lehtinen, E., and Palonen, T. (1999). Evaluating CSCL log files by Social Network Analysis. In *Proceedings of Computer Supported Collaborative Learning, CSCL'99*, pp. 434-442.

Sfard, A. (1998) On two metaphors for learning and the dangers of choosing just one. *Educational Researcher*, **27**, 2, 4-13.

Scott, J. (2000) *Social Network Analysis. A handbook.* 2nd ed. London, U.K: Sage.

Rich Social Interaction in a Synchronous Online Community for Learning

Deborah Tatar, James Gray, Judith Fusco

SRI International CILT and SRI International SRI International

deborah.tatar@sri.com, jim.gray@sri.com, judi.fusco@sri.com

ABSTRACT

Synchronous online communities for learning have been criticized because participant contributions do not seem to build on each other. But overt measures of building do not adequately characterize the nature of communication in successful real-time interaction. Other factors, such as whether the participants understand the meaning of remarks, the light in which they are presented, and the *joint project* the group is engaged in may ultimately prove to be more directly related to learning prospects. This paper starts the process of thinking about these more subtle measures in the context of one example from one session in TAPPED IN.

Keywords

Online communities for learning, teacher professional development, joint projects, discourse

BACKGROUND

TAPPED IN is a technology available to teachers that purports to address the need for continuing professional development by providing an open, engaging and partially self-organizing real-time online community. TAPPED IN (www.tappedin.org) is conceived of as a virtual place similar to a college campus. Participants can conduct real-time online chats in the various rooms and buildings on the campus. TAPPED IN has met with remarkable success at a face level: an average of 700 members and 1600 guests log hours every month. Over a recent 8-month period of time, those members who logged in participated on an average of 11 occasions and had an average session length of 51 minutes. The time spent was particularly significant because it was volunteered by a group of people (teachers) who by definition already lead busy lives and because there was no direct, material incentive for participation.

This pattern of use suggests that the participants are receiving something of value. Yet, evaluating whether this is something of significance to learning poses a dilemma. Online communities have been criticized because participants appear to build on or elaborate each other's ideas rarely (Herring, 1999). But building may be only a rough measure of the conversational coherence that collaborative learning requires. Psycholinguistics, conversation analysis, and sociolinguistics point to the importance of factors such as understanding the meaning of remarks, the light in which they are presented, and the ability of the group to form satisfactory *joint projects* (Clark, 1996; Goodwin & Heritage, 1990). These more subtle indicators of responsiveness probably provide a better characterization of whether the communicative needs of participants are being met.

This paper presents evidence that participants are able to move from the joint project or activity of criticizing badly designed Websites, to the more complex activity of responding to a Website designed by someone who is at once present and a stranger---a sophisticated socio-cognitive accomplishment. Single cases such as this are important when a proof of concept is at stake or to make arguments about possibilities, as we do here.

SHIFTING JOINT PROJECTS

The structure of the seminar involved presenting different "Internet Inquiry" websites for critique. During the discussion of the first web site, a novice participant, Helen, mentions to the leader, Marty, that she has created an InternetInquiry about the Titanic (see Transcript 1). Helen is able to use the sophisticated technique of making an indirect offer---a statement with the potential to be treated at face value as a comment about the previous web site or taken up as an offer by Marty (Brown & Levinson, 1987; Clark, 1996). Helen also positions her offer through minimization: "It needs some updating" and "I've learned a lot since then." These minimizations probably have several functions: they act as an implicit request for reassurance, they lessen the imposition of her request and they show that the site has some emotional significance for her. Showing something of one's own in a public forum can be a significant personal and social risk, and teachers are often overly critical (Grossman, Wineburg, & Woolworth, 2000).

Marty chooses to interpret her remark as an offer. He encourages her to show her work by: 1) direct invitation to do so; 2) making her site the very next order of business; and 3), when she demurs, giving the further encouragement of "Awww... you're among friends here."

Transcript 1: The Offer to Show the Titanic Site (other remarks edited out)

16:58:14 Helen Marty, I did an internetinquiry on the Titanic which needs some updating now; however, I have learned more since then. It was my first internetinquiry. I don't know how much experience the last person had had.

16:58:36 Marty Shall we look at yours next Helen?

16:59:05 Helen It may be that disaster site.

16:59:29 Marty Awww... you're among friends here. Type /project and the URL. Close doesn't count.

16:59:48 Helen It is <TitanicURL>.

16:59:49 Marty Wait til we're done with this one, though.

One result of this exchange is that Marty and Helen have developed a project to show her site: she has mentioned, he has proposed and she has agreed. Another result is that Marty and Helen have set up a social situation in which she is going to take the risk of showing her site and he has indicated that a certain climate of response will prevail.

In part, their public discussion of the plan is a cue to the rest of the group that they will have to change their project from one of pure criticism to something else---if the rest of the group is paying attention and understands the force of the discussion. Difficulty maintaining topical discussions, such as that reported in other online forums, may be related to lack of focused attention. In TAPPED IN, people are also presumably multi-tasking, looking at the previous web sites, and pursuing different lines of thought and conversation. Marty reinforces the need by saying "OK... let's shift gears a bit and look at a person-made disaster. It's by Helen, who's right here, so be gentle."

The group appears successfully to have made a change in their joint project. People appear to pay Helen not only the compliment of their particular remarks, but also the compliment of their relatively sustained attention. 76 seconds pass between the projection of the site and the first comment. Other sites projected during the session elicited first relevant comments at 28, 31, 61 and 68 seconds. Additionally, most unusually, there are no public side conversations during the time when people are looking Helen's site or during the discussion, and indeed only one whisper during the discussion. There is some direct praise. People address her directly. Criticism, still a major purpose of the gathering, is mostly softened by praise.

By contextualizing our analysis in the on-going discourse, we are able to illuminate how Helen and her colleagues were able to engage in focused real-time behavior in an online setting, thus successfully redirecting their joint project. Through the investigation of relatively subtle patterns of online discourse in tandem with more overt ones, the field can continue to reveal the kinds of social processes that lead to learning and development online.

ACKNOWLEDGMENTS

This research was supported by the National Science Foundation, through their Center for Innovative Learning Technologies (CILT) (grant # 9720384), and a grant to SRI International to develop methods for the study of online teacher professional development (REC-9725528).

REFERENCES

Brown, P. E., & Levinson, S. C. (1987). *Politeness: Some universals in language use.* Cambridge: Cambridge University Press.

Clark, H. H. (1996). *Using Language.* Cambridge: Cambridge University Press.

Goodwin, C., & Heritage, J. (1990). Conversation Analysis. *Annual Review of Anthropology.*

Grossman, P., Wineburg, S., & Woolworth, S. (2000, April, 2000). *In Pursuit of Teacher Community.* Paper presented at the AERA, New Orleans.

Herring, S. (1999). Interactional Coherence in CMC. *Program in Linguistics*, 25.

Pianos, not Orchestras

Jochen Rick
College of Computing / GVU Center
Georgia Institute of Technology
Jochen.Rick@cc.gatech.edu

ABSTRACT

Would you rather that your children learn to play the piano, or learn to direct an orchestra? In this paper, I apply the poor learning environments perspective to this question. I conclude that learning environments should be like pianos, not orchestras.

Keywords

education theory, theatre theory, software design, poor learning environments

INTRODUCTION

Resnick, Bruckman, and Martin begin their paper, "Pianos Not Stereos: Creating Computational Construction Kits," with a simple question:

Would you rather that your children learn to play the piano, or learn to play the stereo?

The stereo has many attractions: it is easier to play and it provides immediate access to a wide range of music. But "ease of use" should not be the only criterion. Playing the piano can be a much richer experience. By learning to play the piano, you can become a creator (not just a consumer) of music, expressing yourself musically in ever-more complex ways. As a result, you can develop a much deeper relationship with (and deeper understanding of) music (Resnick, Bruckman, & Martin, 1996).

They go on to show how computational construction kits can enable a new class of piano-like environments to be produced. While I wholeheartedly agree with their position that educational software designers should try to produce pianos and not stereos, I feel the more dangerously seductive rival for the piano is the orchestra, not the stereo.

Would you rather that your children learn to play the piano, or learn to direct an orchestra?

This is a much tougher choice; the orchestra is more tempting than the stereo. Like playing the piano, directing an orchestra can be a rich experience. By directing an orchestra, you also become a creator (not just a consumer) of music. As with the piano, you might even develop a deeper relationship with music. Additionally, directing an orchestra has a seductive novelty, because only a limited few have the means to do it.

Creating rich and complex orchestra-like environments follows the current trend of software systems. However, despite the numerous interesting technical issues that would arise evolving such systems, it is not a fruitful design strategy if what we (educational software designers) want is personal commitment and deep understanding.

POOR LEARNING ENVIRONMENTS

There exists a deep analogy between theatre and education. With this analogy, theories in either domain can be translated into corresponding theories and inform the practices of that other domain. Because theatre has several advantages over education, mapping theatre theories into the education domain is particularly informative.

Here, I focus on the theatre theory of Jerzy Grotowski, whose work revolutionized the way many thought about theatre (Grotowski, 1968). I translate his theory of a poor[(1)] theatre to arrive at a design theory for educational technology called poor learning environments (PLEs); in particular, I find that Grotowski's poor design aesthetic is useful for designing learning environments that encourage *personal commitment* and *deep understanding*.

In many modern theatres (both community and professional stages), the performance of a play has been trimmed to its surface elements. With around four weeks of rehearsal, the actors barely have time to memorize their dialogue and the scenic action. Almost all of the deep work on character, plot, and theme has been ignored in favor of the surface-level elements that are the least common denominator for a performance to take place. Grotowski posits that this alarming trend is due to the modern stage trying to compete with its successful spin-off, the screen of the cinema and television. He finds that the stage has been trying to compete with the screen on exactly the qualities that the screen will always beat the stage—in richness.

---

(1) In Grotowski's sense and the one used in this paper, "poor" does not mean "bad." Instead, it simply means "a lack of wealth."

Grotowski's remedy is simple: "If it [the theatre] cannot be richer than the cinema, then let it be poor." Instead of trying to compete on surface elements, Grotowski shifts the focus of the stage theatre back to the actor and the essential power of the actor to convey emotions, feelings, and ideas. As such, he asserts that the stage does have a place without having to compete with the screen on its terms.

Just as Grotowski finds that the modern stage has deteriorated because of its focus on superficial elements, I find the modern education system to be lacking. Because of the screen, the stage has tried to satisfy viewers with ever decreasing attention spans that demand action and immediate gratification. Similarly, as the amount of knowledge in the world has increased (in some fields dramatically), more and more is seen as common knowledge for every student to have a glimpse of. Instead of deeply understanding domains, today's students are being exposed to so many fields that no field can be covered thoroughly enough to be deeply understood. Instead of really understanding systems and how separate elements work together, students are bombarded with surface-level knowledge that is easy to test. In theatre, the emphasis of the screen on surface qualities, such as looks and special effects, has encouraged stage performances to try to match those qualities. In education, quiz shows, like Jeopardy™, encourage the notion that what makes a person "smart" is being able to answer many questions across numerous fields. This enforcement of surface-level traits causes society to forget what is really important—communication of ideas and deep understanding.

My remedy for education is the same as Grotowski's remedy for theatre: let it be poor. I claim that Grotowski's sentiment should be applied to computing environments too; we should create poor computing environments.

PIANO AS POOR LEARNING ENVIRONMENT

What makes the piano a better learning environment than the orchestra for learning music? The PLEs perspective allows us to answer this question: it is poorer.

The piano is the poorer instrument, because it simplifies much of the essence of music. You can only play notes on the scale. The pattern of octaves is easily evident from the layout of the keys—12 keys up equals an octave up. It is fairly easy to strike a key and have the note sound pleasing. Even the tuning is simplified; pianos are usually tuned to sound equally pleasing in any key, while other instruments would sound unpleasant if tuned that way. The piano's sound is not changeable and notes will only sound slightly different depending on how they are struck. In contrast, orchestras contain many instruments that are better suited for producing certain sounds. An orchestra can produce a richer fuller sound than a piano.

Even if it was possible for a novice to control an entire orchestra, playing the piano is the better choice for deep understanding of music. Although instrumentation might be better explored by directing an orchestra, it is a relatively surface-level feature of music. Understanding how notes relate to one another in a systematic manner is more important for understanding how music works and what it takes to really create (compose) music. For this, the poor piano is better than the rich orchestra. Furthermore, the orchestra would not match the deep personal commitment that some novices develop for the piano, because deep personal commitment requires more than mastery of surface-level features.

Computing environments can offer rich learning environments that are impossible without computers. Computers could be used to create an environment where a novice can direct an orchestra (if only virtually). The PLE perspective informs us that, though this is a possible direction for software development, it is not the most fruitful direction if what you want is deep understanding and personal commitment. Instead, computers should enable new kinds of pianos—poor learning environments where the learner can directly engage the domain to achieve deep understanding.

ACKNOWLEDGEMENTS

My thanks go to the people who through dialogue, discussion, and critique have helped me to refine these ideas into their current form.

REFERENCES

Grotowski, J. (1968) *Towards a Poor Theatre*. London, England: Methuen & Co Ltd.

Resnick, M., Bruckman, A., Martin, F. (1996) Pianos Not Stereos: Creating Computational Construction Kits, *Interactions*, vol. 3, no. 6 (September/October 1996).

The Ethnography of Distributed Collaborative Learning

Frode Guribye, Barbara Wasson
InterMedia - Department of Information Science
University of Bergen
P.O. Box 7800, N-5020 Bergen, Norway
Frode.Guribye@ifi.uib.no; Barbara.Wasson@ifi.uib.no

Keywords
Ethnography, distributed collaborative learning, infrastructure, computer-mediated communication

SUMMARY

A major challenge for today's researchers studying 'online' learning is how to design their studies. The ostensibly simple question of *what and how* to collect and analyse data becomes a major obstacle. Recent theoretical developments emphasise that learning, communication and knowledge construction are embedded and distributed in the social and cultural context where they 'naturally' occur, and inseparable from these contexts as an object of research (see e.g. Suchman, 1987; Latour, 1987; Cole & Engeström, 1993; Hutchins, 1995). Some 'ground-breaking' studies that have expanded and, to a certain extent, had an impact on the understanding of learning and knowledge construction have been based on detailed ethnographic research (e.g., Lave, 1988; Lave & Wenger, 1991).

Ethnographic research represents a long tradition for studying various forms of social processes in everyday life situations. Ethnography or, more generally, qualitative methods have been used extensively in educational research, for example when studying classroom culture and interaction, but also when dealing more explicitly with technology. However, 'traditional' ethnographic approaches do not readily suit distributed ICT environments, and there are some inherent methodological issues with which ethnographers have to deal when entering a setting in order to study distributed collaborative learning. In this paper we argue that, by taking these issues into consideration, ethnography becomes an adequate and fruitful approach for studying learning as process, interaction, and practice also in distributed settings.

There is a growing body of literature about ethnographic studies conducted in the fields computer-mediated communication (see e.g. Hine, 2000) and computer supported co-operative work (see e.g. Harper, 2000). These are fields of research closely related to CSCL and the results, findings, and experiences made in these fields are relevant for the discussion of ethnography of distributed collaborative learning.

We focus on studying distributed collaborative learning with the techniques, methods, and analytical perspective of ethnography. Distributed collaborative learning is commonly placed in hybrid settings, where the participants engage in computer-mediated communication as part of some sort of institutionalised education. There are thus some inherent issues, both new and old, that need to be taken into consideration when doing ethnography in distributed learning environments. Addressing these issues, we emphasise the role of technology and information infrastructure and how this might impact the learning situation, but also how it can be used as a resource in ethnographic research. In addition, we discuss how to observe, participate and immerse oneself in these technologically dense environments. This includes presenting and exploring concepts such as *virtual observations* and *technological immersion*, but also discussing more common topics like *access* and *the role of the researcher*. Another important aspect of ethnographic studies is the devotion to an empirical grounding of the research, which again presents methodological challenges when studying students working online and in distributed settings.

In particular, we emphasise the specific circumstances for studying distributed learning environments as hybrid settings, and pay special attention to the role of the mediating artefacts and how to approach these analytically. In the full paper the ideas and methodological issues are illustrated by presenting empirical examples from and experiences made in one of our research projects – DoCTA (Wasson, Guribye & Mørch, 2000). In this way we forefront ethnography as a fruitful approach for studying and describing the complexity and contingencies of distributed learning in an informed and structured way.

ACKNOWLEDGMENTS

This research (as part of the DoCTA project, http://www.ifi.uib.no/docta) was funded by The Norwegian Ministry of Education, Research and Church Affairs (KUF) under their Information Technology in Education (ITU) program. Thanks to Liam Bannon, Berner Lindström, Hans Christain Arnseth, Eugene Guribye, and Eskil F. Andreassen for valuable comments on earlier versions of this paper. An earlier version of this paper was also presented at the Nordic Interactive Research School - Discourse and Interaction in CSCL, InterMedia, Oslo, May 2001. We also want to thank the anonymous reviewers for giving helpful feedback on this paper.

SELECTED REFERENCES

Arnseth, H. C., S. Ludviksen, B. Wasson & A. Mørch (2001) Collaboration and Problem Solving in Distributed Collaborative Learning. In P. Dillenbourg, A. Eurelings & K. Hakkarainen (Eds.), *European Perspectives on Computer-Supported Collaborative Learning: Proceedings of Euro-CSCL 2001*. Pp. 75-82.

Bannon, L. (1989) Issues in Computer-Supported Collaborative Learning. In C. O'Malley (Ed.) *Proceedings of NATO Advanced Workshop on Computer-Supported Collaborative Learning.*

Bowker, G.C & Star, S. L., (1999) *Sorting Things Out: Classification and its Consequences*. Cambridge: MIT Press.

Burgess, R. G. (Ed.) (1982) *Field Research: A Sourcebook and Field Manual*. London: George Allen & Unwin Ltd.

Clifford J. & G.E. Marcus (Eds.) (1986) *Writing Culture: The Poetics and Politics of Ethnography*. Berkeley, CA: University of California.

Cole, M. & Y. Engeström (1993) A Cultural-Historical Approach to Distributed Cognition. In Salomon, G. (Ed.) *Distributed Cognitions, Psychological and Educational Considerations*. Cambridge: Cambridge University Press.

Dillenbourg, P., Baker, M., Blaye, A. & O'Malley, C. (1996). The Evolution of Research on Collaborative Learning. In P. Reimann & H. Spada (Eds.). *Learning in humans and machines. Towards an interdisciplinary learning science*, 189- 211. London: Pergamon.

Fjuk, A. & S. Ludviksen (2001) The Complexity of Distributed Collaborative Learning: Unit of Analysis. In P. Dillenbourg, A. Eurelings & K. Hakkarainen (Eds.), *European Perspectives on Computer-Supported Collaborative Learning: Proceedings of Euro-CSCL 2001*. Pp. 237-244.

Hakken, D. (1999*) Cyborgs@Cyberspace: An Ethnographer Looks to the Future*, NY: Routledge

Hammersley, M. & P. Atkinson (1995) *Ethnography. Principles in Practice*. London: Tavistock. 2nd Ed.

Harper, R. H. R. (2000) The Organisation in Ethnography : A Discussion of Ethnographic Fieldwork Programs in CSCW. *Computer Supported Cooperative Work: The Journal of Collaborative Computing*. Vol. 9, No. 2, pp. 239-264.

Hine, C (2000) *Virtual Ethnography*. London: SAGE

Hutchins, E. (1995) *Cognition in the Wild*. Cambridge, MA: MIT Press

Jones, S. G. (Ed.) (1999) *Doing Internet Research: Critical Issues and Methods for Examining the Net*. London: SAGE Publications Ltd.

Koschmann, T. (1996) Paradigm shifts and instructional technology: An introduction. In T. Koschmann (Ed.) *CSCL: Theory and Practice of an Emerging Paradigm*, 1-23. Mahwah, NJ: Lawrence Erlbaum Associates.

Latour, B. (1987) *Science in Action: How to Follow Scientists and Engineers through Society*. Milton Keynes, England: Open University Press.

Lave, J. (1988) *Cognition in Practice: Mind, Mathematics and Culture in Everyday life*. NY: Cambridge University Press.

Lave, J. & E. Wenger (1991) *Situated Learning: Legitimate Peripheral Participation*. NY: Cambridge University Press.

Marcus, G. E. (1995) Ethnography in/of the World System: The Emergence of Multi-Sited Ethnography. *Annual Review of Anthropology*, Vol. 24, pp. 95-117.

Star, S. L. and K. Ruhleder (1996) "Steps toward an Ecology of Infrastructure: Design and Access for Large Information Spaces," *Information Systems Research*, Volume 7:111-134.

Star, S. Leigh, (1999) The Ethnography of Infrastructure. *American Behavioral Scientist*, Vol. 43 No.3, pp 377-391. New York: Sage Publications, Inc.

Strauss, A (1993) *Continual Permutations of Action*. New York: Aldine de Gruyter, Inc.

Suchman, L. (1987) Plans and situated actions. Cambridge University Press.

Wasson, B., F. Guribye & A. Mørch (2000). *Project DoCTA: Design and use of Collaborative Telelearning Artefacts*. Oslo: Unipub.

Walk a Mile in Students' Shoes – An Approach to Faculty Development on Integrating Web-Based Collaborative Learning into Instruction

C. Y. Janey Wang

University of Texas at Austin

JANEYWON@MAIL.UTEXAS.EDU

ABSTRACT

This presentation focuses on teachers' experiences and perceptions of their assuming the student role during an intensive faculty development workshop. The workshop, ITESM Summer Institute, hosted at the University of Texas in Austin in June 2001, was a three-week cross-institutional and cross-discipline professional faculty development workshop on cooperative and collaborative learning attended by faculty members of ITESM (Monterrey Institute of Technology and Higher Education System) from throughout Mexico. This presentation: (1) provides information about the workshop program, activities, and participants; (2) examines and discusses workshop participants' feedback about their learning; (3) discusses implications for future faculty development studies.

Keywords

Web-based learning, collaborative learning, faculty development, technology integration, students' perspectives

INTRODUCTION

Integrating technology into curriculum has received increased attention over the past decade (National Science Board, 1992), as have faculty development and the integration of technology into teaching and learning. (Shapiro, 1999; Frayer, 1999) Nancy Shapiro discussed how learning communities could be extended "beyond classroom walls" while "challenging the separateness of the curricular and cocurricular." She said, "This integration requires collaboration among administrators, faculty, and staff responsible for the academic and social dimensions of the undergraduate experience" (Shapiro, 1999, p. 110) .

Resistance to change is common in faculty development and is especially acute when technology integration is at stake. In their discussion of resistance to faculty development, Turner & Boice (1986) suggested viewing resistance "constructively," distinguishing active from passive resistance, and utilizing "objective analysis" rather than "emotional reaction."

This ITESM Summer Institute was a cross-institutional collaborative effort between ITESM in Mexico, the University of Texas at Austin, and the University of Minnesota. Hosted by U.T. Austin, the intensive three-week professional faculty development workshop, which emphasized the integration of technology into teaching, was attended by 48 ITESM faculty members from throughout Mexico.

FACULTY DEVELOPMENT

To enhance student learning, Frayer (1999) suggested encouraging faculty to network and learn good practices from colleagues; stimulating faculty to refine their learning goals in relation to technology; providing faculty resources and "technology-enhanced pedagogical strategies"; and rewarding successful practices as key strategies for creating a campus culture conducive to assisting faculty integration of technology into instruction. As a faculty developer, Frayer (1999) said that she found that faculty were rethinking their teaching and learning process through the implementation of technology integration. A few approaches mentioned as catalysts to spur goal reevaluation includes school-wide integration, online courses offerings, summer institutes for faculty, and roundtable discussions.

The ITESM Summer Institute sought to engage teachers in intensive learning and hands-on processes, to encourage teachers to examine the relationship between knowledge and the social-emotional aspects of learning, and to recognize and experience the role of technology in learning. ITESM, Mexico expected its faculty members to demonstrate progress in their instructional design utilizing strategies learned, resources explored, and realization of the changing roles of teacher. As the catalyst for changing teacher practice, the workshop provided participants – who were from across Mexico – the opportunity to network with and learn from colleagues, to redefine their instruction and learning goals, and to integrate technology into their curriculum. These workshop goals mirrored Frayer's (1999) strategies for spurring goal reevaluation.

SUMMARY

This presentation, based on a preliminary study, explores the perceptions of ITESM (Mexico) faculty members' experiences in assuming the role of student in an online collaborative environment where cooperative and collaborative teaching and learning strategies and technology were emphasized. Through hands-on activities and collaborative learning experiences, participants explored three major aspects in the workshop – cooperative learning, collaborative learning, and faculty development – while assuming the role of student in the online learning environment.

Participants' daily workshop reflections, two end-of-workshop surveys, and the researcher's observation journal were used as data sources to illuminate participants' experiences of and insights into "walking a mile in their students' shoes," as well as their perceptions of the effectiveness of the workshop.

The workshop was geared specifically to assist participants in learning strategies in the development of Web-based collaborative learning courses and institutional action plans. Various hands-on activities – both face-to-face and online – were employed to engage participating teachers. These activities included cooperative-learning, collaborative-writing, WebQuest, rubrics design, collaborative learning project design, and institutional action plan design. Social learning, group dynamics, and the interplay that occurred among different cultures and minds were reported as highlights of their learning experience as students in this collaborative learning.

Among 48 participants, 15 respondents reported that prior to the workshop they were not familiar with the rubrics design, but that after the workshop, participants reported that they will use the rubrics they designed at the workshop as an alternative assessment tool for peer and product evaluation in their future courses. Another 25 respondents reported coming to the realization that course design strongly influences students' learning experiences. While a well-planned curriculum is essential, flexibility and on-going student support and feedback throughout the process are equally crucial. Superficial interactions--rather than meaningful and constructive learning--may easily occur in the online learning environment, some participants concluded. They indicated that instructor and facilitator feedback is even more important in the online learning environment than in face-to-face settings.

As administrators and instructors, respondents thought that students' needs are sometimes easily forgotten and that instructors sometimes lose perspective and fail to take into account students' needs when setting course requirements and goals. By assuming the student role, participants experienced first-hand what online learning entails, how to effectively collaborate with others, and what they should be aware of when designing a course utilizing online learning or collaborative learning strategies. They reported that many teachers tend to focus on cognitive and task aspects of learning rather than socio-emotional learning aspects. After this workshop, respondents reported gaining a better understanding of time constraints and other personal aspects of the student learning experience.

Future studies may focus on how these faculty members change their teaching practices, implement various strategies learned directly and indirectly from this experience, and how realizations gained in this workshop impacted their post-workshop course designs.

ACKNOWLEDGEMENT

The ITESM Summer Institute was conducted by the Learning Technology Center director (U.T. Austin), Dr. Paul E. Resta, Dr. Edythe Johnson Holubec of the Cooperative Learning Center at the University of Minnesota, and Dr. Marilla Svinicki (U. T. Austin), in collaboration with Carlos Enrique, Patricia Diaz, Cecilia Valdez, and Francisco Ayala from ITESM, Mexico. Special thanks to Rafael Cota for providing the workshop snapshots and rubric survey, and to Guillermo Espinosa for providing information of ITESM (Mexico) expectations for participants.

REFERENCE

Frayer, D. A. (1999). Creating a campus culture to support a teaching and learning revolution. *Cause/Effect*, **22**, 2, 10-17 & 50

National Science Board (1992). *Science and technology integration in Europe and influences on U.S.-European cooperation : a report of the National Science Board* Committee on Europe in 1992. Washington, D.C.: National Science Foundation

Shapiro, N. S. & Levine, J. H. (1999). *Creating Learning Communities - A Practical Guide to Winning Support, Organizing for Change, and Implementing Programs*. Jossey-Bass Publishers, San Francisco, California.

Turner, Jim L. & Boice, Robert (1986). Coping with resistance to faculty development. In *"To Improve the Academy – Resource for student, faculty, & institutional development."* A Joint_Publications of "The Professional & Organizational Development Network in Higher Education" and "The National Council for Staff, Program and Organizational Development."

Presuppositions about "Good Communication": An Assessment of Online Discourse

Susan Bagley Koyle, Mark Aakhus

Department of Communication
Rutgers, The State University of New Jersey
4 Huntington St., New Brunswick, NJ 08901-1071
bagley@scils.rutgers.edu aakhus@scils.rutgers.edu

ABSTRACT

This study investigates the online discourse generated by a class of student interns regarding dilemmas they experienced in their work life. The interns use an application designed to foster a dialectical record of their experiences and differences of opinion about how to understand those experiences. We use discourse analysis to explore the students' presuppositions about good communication in the online text. We describe how students' presuppositions that good communication is "open and honest" often conflicts with their experience of superior-subordinate relationships. We suggest that conflicts with presuppositions can be used to facilitate further reflective learning and to shape the online dialogue.

Keywords: Collaborative Learning, Reflective Learning, Internships, Professional Development, Discourse Analysis

A central part of reflective learning (Schön, 1983) is the uncovering and questioning of assumptions. Reflective learning depends on learners surfacing their assumptions about the world that are represented in the actions they take to handle everyday dilemmas. Thus, in order to learn from experience, it is necessary for learners to reflect on how they make decisions and the assumptions that those decisions are based on. This study explores how an online communication forum of student interns was designed and implemented to foster students' ability to reflect on everyday choices in a manner that helps them develop more sophisticated ways of framing problems and taking action. The data for this study is drawn from an online archive of dilemmas ("updates") that students experienced and wrote about as well as responses to those dilemmas made by classmates.

When an initial update is responded to in an oppositional way, the interaction becomes an argument (Hutchby, 1996). This perspective allows an examination of what respondents treats as arguable and what normative codes participants use to identify what is arguable. This dialectical exchange helps make visible normative and factual presuppositions about communication at work and in professional life. Thus, a key focus of this study includes an examination of what respondents call out and presuppose about the accounts they are responding to. While the topics of the updates varied, most of the dilemmas ultimately dealt with how the student could best resolve or handle a dilemma in terms of communicating with a superior or co-worker. Whether it was how to articulate a grievance about lack or recognition to a boss or how to tactfully turn down a request for a date from a co-worker, students were primarily concerned with achieving what they perceived to be good communication in a professional environment. One of the major findings of the analysis of updates was that despite frequent reasoning based on the presupposition that "open, honest communication" would resolve conflict and prevent misunderstandings, many of the dilemmas that were presented in the online forum did not actually reflect this assumption.

We have also found enormous practical value, and we suspect learning value, in developing and teaching the student participants search strategies to help them make sense of the large database of messages produced in the online venue. For example, students were given the assignment to analyze their online work during the semester and compare the advice they gave in responses and their own actions. They were to consider whether there was a difference between the advice they gave to others and what they actually did and why this might be the case. The application allows participants to uncover and question their own assumptions, with the goal of developing reflective learning. It also allows an analysis of the online discourse to understand the students' presuppositions about communication in a professional setting

SELECTED REFERENCES

Aakhus, M. (November, 2000). Virtual dialectics: Support for critical reflection in on-line, experience-based learning communities. Paper presented at the National Communication Association Convention, Seattle, WA.

Craig, R. and Tracy, K. (1995) Grounded practical theory: The case of intellectual discussion. Communication Theory, 5, 258-272.

Hutchby, I. (1996). Confrontation talk: Arguments, asymmetries , and power on talk radio. Mahwah, NJ: Lawrence, Erlbaum Associates, Publishers.

Morrill, C. (1995). The Executive Way. Chicago: The University of Chicago Press.

Schön, D. (1983). The reflective practitioner: How professionals think in action. New York: Basic Books, Inc.

Distributed CSCL/T in a Groupware Environment

Simon B. Heilesen, Mia Cudrio Thomsen **Robin Cheesman**

Roskilde University Copenhagen Business School Roskilde University

simonhei@ruc.dk mt.dps@cbs.dk robin@ruc.dk

ABSTRACT

Using FLE2 groupware (Future Learning Environment 2, http://fle2.uiah.fi) we have tried to integrate a distance education course into the regular academic programme at Roskilde University, Denmark. The course was offered jointly by two universities, attracting students and involving teachers from both institutions. The practical and pedagogical problems encountered are discussed, and it is suggested that while net-based teaching may be suitable only under certain circumstances in a normal academic programme, skills of communicating and working in an online environment are important qualifications that should be introduced broadly into academic life.

Keywords

Future Learning Environment 2, net-based collaboration, net-based learning, online courses, resource sharing.

SHARING A COURSE USING FLE2 (FUTURE LEARNING ENVIRONMENT 2)

Roskilde University accepts quite a few foreign students, and there is a need for many courses in English. A way of broadening the scope of our programmes may be to share teachers and students with other universities. In Spring 2001 the Communication, Journalism and Computer Science Dept. at Roskilde offered a course in *Methods in Internet Research* in collaboration with the Media Studies Dept. at Aarhus University, Denmark.[1)] The 3 ECTS points course (European Credit Transfer System) included two face-to-face classes: An initial introduction to FLE2 and a summing up at the end of the course. All other activities were net-based. 38 Danish and international students participated actively. The course was divided into four "net seminars", each one lasting a week and introducing a selected theme from the vast field of inquiry. Each seminar was run by a different instructor (located in Aarhus, Lyngby, Roenne, Denmark, or Gothenburg, Sweden) who assigned tasks to be performed and topics to be discussed by the students who were divided into four groups. A final week was reserved for the students to write an essay.

FLE 2 is designed to support a pedagogy consisting of problem based learning (PBL) and inquiry learning (see: http://fle2.uiah.fi/pedagogy.html). In the course in question we have not adhered strictly to the progressive inquiry pedagogy, nor have we used the system as intended by its creators. FLE2 is a groupware system meant to supplement face-to-face classroom work. We have used it as a conferencing and collaborative work tool in what has been primarily a distance education course. For this kind of use FLE2 is not optimal.

LESSONS LEARNED

Net-based education is demanding for instructors as well as students

In terms of drawing upon distributed competences the course was quite successful. In terms of efficiency, however, it was not. The course was extraordinarily time consuming for all involved, and we experienced both practical and pedagogical problems. Coordinating two programmes at different universities proved complicated, curricula not yet being geared for that eventuality. Getting the students up and running in the system was unexpectedly time consuming. Achieving an acceptable level of proficiency in using FLE2 involved a fair amount of extra work, and it had a negative impact on the pace of the course. Instructing in the use of an online system is a one-off investment, but in terms of time spent on technical matters it is a heavy one for the first online course that the students attend.

All instructors were familiar with the techniques of online teaching. We had of course coordinated the syllabus in advance and had outlined roles and responsibilities. But in our conventional shyness of encroaching upon the practices of a colleague we failed to agree in detail upon pedagogical methods. Thus the students experienced four rather different personalities and approaches to online tutoring ranging from laissez faire to zealous participation in even the smallest event. The free choice of teaching methods has no future in this kind of online teaching.

Only a few of the students had prior experience with online courses. Most of our students expected a smaller workload than in a traditional course, and the amount of work involved in getting acquainted with FLE2 and participating in discussions took them by surprise. Adapting to the new way of working in an online environment was indeed a real obstacle. In the beginning most of them felt uncomfortable and exposed having to write notes in the threaded discussions. We had a few lurkers. But those students who did overcome the initial shyness grew increasingly bold in contributing to the discussions, and some ended up being quite keen on the net-based way of working. Students interviewed by the evaluator indicated that the course had been a rich learning experience as well as a frustrating one. Most students spent too much time on tasks that normally take only a few minutes in an ordinary conversation. Also the interface did not appear all that intuitive, and navigation seemed slow and complicated. Part of the blame should be placed on the course designers and not on the software, as we will discuss below.

Making decisions

Making decisions is difficult in net-based collaboration and learning. Some decisions are of course unavoidable. But in general, students should not be given even simple choices that seem so natural in the classroom. Let a group of students choose between working on problem A or problem B, and the result will be a meta-discussion going on for days. As a tool for making decisions, the chat included in FLE2 is far more efficient than threaded discussion. But chat is only manageable with a small number of participants working in synchronous mode. We also noticed that some students were reluctant to make chat decisions involving the entire group.

Allowing things to take time

The course had a tight schedule rather like lectures in a classroom. This proved to be a mistake as most discussions took some time to get going. We observed a proportional relation between duration and intensity of the discussions. One should consider carefully whether or not a subject is suitable for a net-based course. In-depth analysis of a relatively narrow theme would probably be more suitable than the broad introduction that we have attempted. But all in all you should expect to cover less ground in an online course than in a conventional classroom course.

Group composition and size

Since most of the assignments involved discussion rather than project work we assumed that large groups would be appropriate. Assigning students from two institutions and from many countries to work together in four large groups, however, provided for a heterogeneity that made it difficult to establish a sense of community and obligation to contribute for the common good. Also being so many in each group may have encouraged lurking.

Avoiding clutter

The course was presented in FLE2 as an online syllabus, listing all four seminars in chronological order. Initially this provided a good overview of the course. But as the number of contributions grew, so did complexity, and working with the system became a protracted affair. The print media logic of the course presentation turned out to be counterproductive in the online environment where speed and accessibility are all-important. It would be better to break up the course into a series of shorter courses, one for each net seminar. However, presenting just one fragment of the course at a time may result in a kind of tunnel vision, robbing the student of an understanding of the course as a whole. Probably a better solution is to introduce a kind of "fish eye perspective".

Looking ahead

In 21st century society it will become an important qualification to be able to communicate and work collaboratively in net-based environments. It certainly should be taught at the university level, but getting started is hard. The course in Internet Research Methods has demonstrated some of the difficulties involved in integrating net-based teaching into a conventional academic programme. Many new skills are to be mastered – both for students and for faculty, and in early courses the problems of adapting to the new setting tend to dominate.

NOTES

1 Faculty for the course was Joergen Bang, Aarhus University, Robin Cheesman, Simon Heilesen and Eva Ekeblad, Roskilde University. Teemu Leinonen, Medialab, Helsinki, participated in technical discussions, and Mia Cudrio Thomsen, Copenhagen Business School, evaluated the course. This paper is *not* part of the FLE2 software evaluation project and does *not* deal with the functionality and pedagogical qualities of the system. It is a report on a teaching experiment that could have been performed in several other conferencing systems.

Ethnomethods as Resources for Developing CVEs in the ITCOLE Project

Alessandra Talamo
University of Rome – University of Salerno
Alessandra.talamo@uniroma1.it
Maria Beatrice Ligorio
University of Salerno
bligorio@unisa.it

Keywords: Ethnotechnology, synchronous communication, Collaborative Virtual Environments (CVEs), Conversation Analysis

INTRODUCTION

ITCOLE is a project funded by the European community aimed at designing software for collaborative knowledge building supporting a virtual learning community. The software is designed so to represent metaphorically the model of Learning by Inquiry. In this paper we propose a methodology to assess the contextual uses of the software, as to further develop synchronous communication tools.

ETHNOTECHNOLOGY AS A RESOURCE FOR TOOLS DEVELOPMENT

Synchronous communication fits the requirements of recent advances in educational research. Studying learning processes, even more when they occur in collaborative contexts, can benefit from the study of "emic" descriptions (Duranti, 1997) of the context itself. An emic description is the reconstruction of the meanings valuable within a community in the way that is explicitly expressed by the members during the interaction. Thus, studying synchronous communication allows the recording of the mediated forms of talk during the interactions. Furthermore researchers are allowed to describe, in an ecologic way, how the learning process proceeds during the collaborative work at a distance.

Ethnomethodology and discourse analysis (in that it allows emic descriptions of interactive contexts), integrated by the recent methodological research about on-line interactions, are now considered as the appropriate methods to analyse data from synchronous communication. From a methodological point of view, this implies the analysis of the negotiation of shared meaning in the discursive interaction within members, while they occur. This can also allow the study of interactions in mediated talk within not-experimental settings, like in spontaneous educational communities. Conversation and discourse analysis look for order and regularity in human actions, in the place of they observable intersection, that is in the ways in which persons organize their encounters with others, in the ways they regulate the shared activity and with which attribute meaning to artefacts, even technological, with which they interact (Schegloff, 1989). The discursive perspective (Duranti, 1997) is able to grasp the social complexity of the negotiation practices, considering as the unit of analysis the activity system of the community (instead of single individuals). Communities use technology in their social and material context, attributing to them shared meanings that are developed and defined through the continuous negotiation of their possible uses (and not-uses), benefits, disadvantages and peculiarities. This negotiation process explains how the use of each technology is shaped and developed by different communities of practice. Pre-existing shared practices act as essential mediators among the intended (by technical developers) meanings of technology and their actual use in the daily practice of each specific community. In this perspective, virtual environments are not a substitute of the real experience. In virtual environments the interaction is closely related to life out of the screen. Virtual environments are not something different from real life, but rather, a follow up of the reality based on the additional resources coming from the interaction at a distance (Carlini, 1998). The use of "community" as central unit of analysis of cultural ergonomics research leads to consider human action as always built by answering to other persons, in social contexts of inter-subjectivity (see: http://www.vepsy.com/communication/book1/cap11.pdf)

As Grossen and Pochon (1997) propose, there is actually a need for the development of an *ethnotechnology*, a specific field for studying the impact of technology raised from the observation of a mismatch among the users' way of tools' implementation and the functions for which the developers had planned them (Gaudin, 1988). Ethnotechnology is so conceived as the ethnographic study of the concrete usage of technological solutions. Perriault (1989) developed the concept of logic of usage ("logique de l'usage") in order to define the function that users assign to the technology. The logic of usage can differ significantly from the one that the developers followed while developing the tool itself.

Grossen and Pochon (1997) highlight the following issues: (a) human-computer interaction consists "of an indirect dialogue between users and designers"; (b) This sort of "indirect dialogue" is the result of an interpretative activity based on reciprocal assumptions on each others representation of the tool's functions; (c) The "indirect dialogue" is developed in a specific context (p. 283). The ethnotechnology, allows the re-construction of an "emic" description of the meanings that users ascribe to the logic of usage of proposed tools. From this point of view, ethno methods are certainly useful to describe in an ecologic way the context (even in its technological feaures) as the participants perceive and define it. Moreover, an innovative use of the ethnotechnology can be foreseen by implementing the Conversation and Discourse analysis as tools for checking and improving the usability of technological devices in a situated way. Ethnomethods highlight also the role played by the additional resources in the interaction within the CVEs. Through conversationa and discourse analysis, it can be observed how those additional resources (for instance the graphical dimension or the chat on-line) can be used in a strategic way during the interaction at a distance. Recent studies (Talamo and Ligorio, 2001; see also Talamo and Ligorio, 2001 available in:

http://susanna.catchword.com/vl=7522993/cl=38/nw=1/rpsv/catchword/mal/10949313/v4n1/contp1-1.htm), show how specific aspects of visual interaction, such as the visualization of the virtual objects or the embodiment of the users in the *avatar*, are rhetorically made salient during the interactive discourse, depending on the content discussed or on the goals participants have in mind.

TESTING MEMBERS' USAGE

We plan to use Conversation analysis for testing some functionalities of the ITCOLE environment. Conversation analysis allows to investigate some basics aspects of interaction in technological environments, such as: (a) the interactive functionality among users; (b) the interactive functionality between users and the technological solutions developed, (c) the users' interaction with virtual objects; (d) the tutoring functions of teachers and project managers, (e) how the leading learning theory (learning by inquiry) is perceived by users.

The qualitative data are then actively included in planning strategies as resources for connecting developers' representation of users' need and expectations, and to make the tools more effective. Some examples will be provided during the presentation.

Based on these assumptions, the methodology chosen in designing the ITCOLE software takes in account contributions from the users' experience of the synchronous environment. Usually, the external representation of objects included into the interface is completely in charge of the software designers. In the ITCOLE project the way in which users implement the software is intended as their "voice" in designing the technological environment.

REFERENCES

Carlini, F. (1998) Un plus di realtà [More than real], in: Jacobelli, J. (ed.) *La realtà del virtuale [The real of virtual]*, Bari, Laterza.

Duranti, A. (1997) *Linguistic Anthropology*, Cambridge Mass, Cambridge University Press.

Gaudin, T. (1988) *Les Métamorphoses du future*, Paris, Editions Economica.

Grossen, M., and Pochon, L.O. (1997) Interactional Perspectives on the Use of Computer and on the Technological Development of a New Tool: The case of Word Processing, in: Resnick, L.B., Salijo, R., Pontecorvo, C. and Burge, B. (Eds.) *Discourse, Tools and Reasoning. Essays on Situated Cognition*, NATO ASI Series, Berlin, Springer, 265-287.

Perriault, J. (1989) *La logique de l'usage, Essay sur les machines a communiquer*, Paris, Flammarion.

Schegloff, J.(1989) Harvey Sacks' lectures on conversation: an Introduction/memoir, *Human Studies*, 12, 185-209.

Continuous Evaluation of Web-based Cooperative Learning: The Conception and Development of an Evaluation Toolkit

Shirley Holst, Torsten Holmer

Fraunhofer Institut integrierte Publikations- und Informationssysteme, Germany
{holst, holmer}@ipsi.fhg.de

ABSTRACT

In this paper we propose the concept of continuous evaluation, which combines existing evaluation approaches in the construction of an evaluation toolkit consisting of guidelines, methods and software tools for the monitoring, analysis and optimization of cooperative learning. The concept of continuous evaluation is interesting to those who wish to make systematic evaluations of CSCL systems. It describes those evaluation activities, which are appropriate when planning and designing CSCL, during early field studies, and throughout the ongoing maintenance of established courses. The aim of continuous evaluation is to build up a suite of evaluation methods and tools to be used by course organizers, authors, tutors and learners, which are tailored to a specific e-learning setting and are iteratively improved over time.

Keywords

Evaluation, quality assurance, cooperative learning, web-based learning, formative evaluation, data logging, participatory evaluation

THE CONTINUOUS EVALUATION APPROACH

The current explosion in the use of new web-based technologies to support cooperative learning brings many new challenges for those evaluating the effects of these new tools and methods on the learning process. Existing methods for the evaluation and quality assurance of CSCL systems, in particular criterion catalogues, have been heavily criticized for their lack of theoretical and empirical foundations (Fricke, 2000). Traditional evaluation approaches are not sufficient to tackle the evaluation of web-based cooperative learning. Evaluation in this area is difficult because many factors influence the cooperative learning process, which are always changing. This makes it necessary to make adjustments to the cooperative tools and learning methods to fit particular settings and emerging requirements. Therefore, there is a need to develop methods and tools for the formative evaluation of cooperative e-learning, which support course organizers, authors, tutors, learners (we call these the course 'stakeholders') to monitor and optimize their learning process at runtime. We should aim to provide sufficient information, so that they can reflect on their own activities and take effective action to improve their learning activities themselves.

We introduce our *continuous evaluation* approach to evaluating web-based cooperative learning in order to address the above needs and criticisms. This approach culminates in the construction of an evaluation toolkit (which we call the Quality Suite) consisting of guidelines, methods and software tools for the monitoring, analysis and optimization of cooperative learning. Drawing on established theories of cooperative learning we are creating models of learning that explain and predict the behavior of learners, tutors and learning groups with a particular technology in particular e-learning settings. Based on these models, we operationalize our evaluation measures in terms of specific behaviors, that are observable during the completion of a specific cooperative task. Via a series of laboratory and field evaluation activities, within representative e-learning settings, these models are being explored and tested. Thereby, the factors which contribute to effective learning are identified. The resulting Quality Suite provides methods and tools to support course stakeholders in their respective roles within these learning settings.

THE EVALUATION TOOLKIT

The evaluation toolkit (the Quality Suite) will consist of the following tightly interwoven three elements: Guidelines, Monitoring Tools and the Questionnaire Generator.

Guidelines for how to arrange effective cooperative learning will be used by the various stakeholders of the learning process in order to plan or improve their learning activities, to give new ideas for ways in which the tools can be used, to illustrate best practice examples and to support troubleshooting.

Secondly, we extend data logging methods, which have effectively been used to analyze online behavior in groups (Holmer and Streitz, 1999, in order to support the ongoing monitoring and optimization of learning at runtime. The *monitoring tools* will gather information about the learning process via both unobtrusive data logging and via brief online questionnaires that learners and tutors fill out at particular stages of the learning process. The questionnaires can be made to appear automatically after certain events (e.g. immediately after performing a cooperative activity). The data is then automatically analyzed and made available in summarized form to course tutors, giving them a useful overview of how cooperative learning is taking place in individual cooperative exercises as well as across the whole course.

Thirdly, the *questionnaire generator* will help those evaluating a course to apply known quality criteria in order to generate questions about the learning process, which can be answered by the learners, giving feedback to the tutor about the course. The evaluator selects those quality criteria that are particularly relevant at the time, and the software selects appropriate, pre-defined questions from a database of quality criteria and an associated pool of questions. The questionnaires can also be used to enquire about critical incidents, which may have occurred.

EMPIRICAL FOUNDATIONS

The following three evaluation types are contributing to the empirical foundations of the quality suite:

The *Internal Evaluation of Cooperative Episodes* assesses the usability of tools and the utility of the cooperative activities independently of any specific course setting. Laboratory studies are used to predict the effects of particular features and cooperative learning methods on the learning process;

The *Evaluation of Course Effects* assesses the effect that cooperative episodes have on the ongoing learning process. In particular, we want to establish what effects the cooperative learning activities have on individual learning activities. We monitor changes in learner behavior immediately before cooperation (e.g. preparations that are made before taking part in a cooperative episode) and also afterwards (e.g. the reviewing activities of the learners after the cooperation is completed);

The *Investigation of Moderating Variables* investigates how other factors, such as learning style or type of content, interacts with the acceptance, appropriateness and effectiveness of particular types of cooperative learning activity.

STATUS

We are developing the Quality Suite in the ALBA project, which is almost one year underway at the time of publishing. We are cooperating closely with our partners (the German software company, SAP AG; and the vocational training institution, CJD Maximiliansau) in both corporate and public education settings to gather requirements for the Quality Suite. In a series of field studies, the toolkit will be developed, used, and iteratively improved. The L^3 learning platform, is the test bed for many of our studies. The L^3 project (Life Long Learning as a basic need) is a predecessor to ALBA, in which cooperative services for the L^3 learning platform were conceptualized, developed, and evaluated (Wessner and Pfister, 2000).

ACKNOWLEDGEMENTS

We thank our colleagues for their contributions to both the L^3 and ALBA projects and for discussion of this paper.

REFERENCES

Fricke, R. (2000) Qualitätsbeurteilung durch Kriterienkatalogue. Auf der Suche nach validen Vorhersagemodellen. In Schenkel et a. (2000). pp.75-88.

Holmer, T., and Streitz, N.A. (1999) Neue Möglichkeiten der Analyse der Mensch-Computer-Interaktion zur Evaluation von computerunterstützten Gruppensitzungen. In: U. Arend, E. Eberleh, K. Pitschke (Ed.): *Software-Ergonomie '99. Design von Informationswelten*, pp. 137-148, Stuttgart, Teubner, 1999.

Wessner, M., and Pfister, H.R. (2000) Points of Cooperation: Integrating Cooperative Learning into web-based courses. In Proceedings of the International Workshop on New Technologies for Collaborative Learning. NTCL 2000, Awaji-Yumebutai, Hyogo, Japan, Nov. 27-29, 2000, pp. 33-41.

Interaction Repertoire in a Distance Education Community

Lars Svensson

Laboratorium for Interaction Technology
University of Trollhättan Uddevalla
lars.svensson@htu.se

ABSTRACT

This paper presents results from a study focusing on text-based electronic interaction in a distance educational setting. The analysis of the interaction identifies three typified genres, labeled *Query, Feedback and Smalltalk*. Together they constitute a shared interaction repertoire with marks of a new social landscape for education with changes in roles and behaviours that are important to grasp for designers as well as teachers.

Keywords

Interaction, Community, Distance Education, Genre, Social Situation

INTRODUCTION

Over the last years, the Internet has become a melting pot where traditional media has merged and collided, resulting in fruitful combinations and new functionality (Braa et al. 2000). From the perspective of Distance Education this means a technological platform with support for dynamic distribution and organisation of hypermedia course material, but also support for more flexible interaction, e.g. chat-rooms, computer conferences and news groups. The use of ICT should not be understood merely as neutral improvements in educational efficiency, but also in terms of changes to the social systems. When communicative patterns change, social and cultural change follows (Sproull and Kiesler 1991). A similar point is made by Meyrowitz (1985) who claims that the use of an electronic media changes and restructures the social situation with respect to the available social information, the audience and the different roles that defines the situation. And indeed, the perhaps most important outcome from using the Internet in Distance Education, is the social dimension it has introduced. The ease, at which informal contact can be initiated amongst students and teachers, is in strong contrast to the demand of structure and planning, necessary in distance education based on correspondence or teleconferencing. Subsequently, the web has become a media where *learning communities* can form and evolve.

In previous research on interaction within an educational setting, the focus is often set on interaction processes directly relating to the technology-mediated collaborative learning activities themselves. For instance, Baker et al. (1999) explores how students need to engage in processes of grounding, i.e. the interaction necessary to establish sufficient common ground to complete a collaborative task and Wasson and Mørch (2000) presents collaborative patterns expressed by small groups of students using various types of groupware. Furthermore the research has been dominated by an emphasis on control and rigour, using voluntary subjects and constructed tasks for experiments with short duration. There is a need to complement this research with studies that expands beyond such narrow foci to encompass longitudinal studies of all processes within the practise of education, and to study how groups of "real" students in real situations choose to use and make sense of ICT. Such a holistic perspective is argued to be vital in order to understand today's distance education as a social practice (Wenger, 1998) where motivation, engagement (Nuldén, 1999) and relations play a central part in a distributed learning community.

THE CASE

The object of the study presented in this paper is a distance course in Mathematics and Statistics. It is the first course in a three-year program for 52 students located in six communities in the vicinity of a Swedish University college. The primary technologies used in the course were videoconferencing and a system for web based education, called DisCo. The system provides a web site with course material and support for communication, primarily through email and a threaded discussion forum. Drawing on the concepts of genre repertoire proposed by Yates and Orlikowski (1994) the text-based interaction between students and teachers were analysed in order to identify typified patterns that could be said to constitute genres of communication.

The email interaction and the entries on the discussion board showed three fairly distinct genres of communication (Query, Feedback and Smalltalk). Together these genres constitute a repertoire for electronic interaction within the course community. The elements and characteristics of this repertoire paints a picture of how community members (students and teachers) accomplish their work, and in what ways the use of electronic media associates to changes in work practice and interaction norms (Orlikowski & Yates 1994, Meyrowitz 1985).

DISCUSSION

The Query genre is at the core of the collective goal of meeting the objectives of the course curriculum. In doing so students use their community of peers and teachers as collaborative resources, (Fjuk, 1998). In addition, the rich occurrence of Smalltalk and Feedback that were found shows how students are motivated to engage in the creation and maintenance of a mutual community. This community building involves several mechanisms of establishing a "we-notion", thereby creating boundaries and identity for the community, (Wenger, 1998). It also involves the development of a shared vocabulary and indexicality (Star, 1999). Smalltalk is argued to relate to the processes of creating identity and interpersonal relations. Feedback, is about the ability to influence and shape the community culture, where discussions could be seen as negotiations of what constitutes the norms of the community, (Wenger, 1998, Orlikowski & Yates, 1994). The discussion forum provided a shared arena where the community history could be exposed, and an interaction repertoire that made common sense to the community could be negotiated.

The data is not the result of a well-designed and controlled experiment, but rather an emergent and non-moderated expression of student-initiated interaction, which is argued to add substantial validity to the interaction repertoire as being rooted in realistic conditions. This does not imply that the genres are generic and exhaustive, and the most interesting aspect is not the composition of genres, but rather the actual use (Orlikowski & Yates 1994). The novelty of the social situation (Meyrowitz 1985) is partly relating to the way the genres coexist, thereby mixing activities traditionally typical for a classroom, an evaluation questionnaire and a student café. It also relates to the public nature of a shared discussion forum where the entire community is the audience of activities that are traditionally more private.

This could imply that design of software and course concepts should appreciate the potential of moving beyond the roles and behaviours of traditional schools and classrooms. Embracing and inviting socialising behaviour such as the Smalltalk and Feedback genres found in this study, rather than isolating it to separate digital cafés not only helps in attracting students to common discussions but also aids in the negotiation of a common ground that is essential for collaborate learning.

REFERENCES

Baker, M.& Hansen, T. & Joiner, r. & Traum, D. (1999) The role of Grounding in Collaborative Learning Tasks. In *Collaborative Learning: Cognitive and Computational Approaches*, pp 31-63, Amsterdam, Pergamon

Braa, K & Sørensen, C & Dahlbom, B (2000) *The Planet Internet, Challanges Facing Informatics*, Studentlitteratur, Lund Sweden

Nuldén, Urban (1999) *e-ducation, Gothenburg Studies in Informatics*, Report 15, Gothenburg University, Sweden

Orlikowski, W & Yates J. (1994). "Genre Repertoire: The Structuring of Communicative Practices in Organizations," *Administrative Science Quarterly* 39: 541-574.

Sproull, L & Kiesler, S (1992) *Connections: New ways of working in the networked organization.* The MIT press, Cambridge, Massachusetts,

Star, S. L. (1999) It's Infrastructure all the way down, *American Behavioural Scientist*, 43: 377-391.

Wasson, B. & Mørch, A. (2000) Identifying collaborative telelearning scenarios. *Journal of Educational Technology & Society,* 3 (3) IEEE, USA

Wenger, E. (1998) *Communities of Practice: Learning, Meaning and Identity*, Cambridge U P, NY, USA

Fjuk, A. (1998) *Computer Support for Distributed Collaborative Learning: Exploring a Complex Problem Area*, Dr. Scient. Thesis 5, University of Oslo, Dept. Of Informatics, Norway

Meyrowitz, J (1985) *No Sense of Place: The Impact of Electronic Media on Social Behaviour*, Oxford UP, NY, USA

Multi-Dimensional Tracking in Virtual Learning Teams An Exploratory Study

J. Zumbach[1], M. Mühlenbrock[2], M. Jansen[2], P. Reimann[1], H.U. Hoppe[2]

[1]University of Heidelberg, [2]University of Duisburg, Germany

zumbach@uni-hd.de

ABSTRACT

We present a shared workspace application for co-constructive tasks with functions for tracking, analyzing and feeding back parameters of collaboration to group members. The interdisciplinary approach is based on an integrative methodology for analyzing collaboration behavior and explicit surveyed data of group members' attitudes. In an exploratory study, we examined the influence of the feedback function, with the long term perspective of enriching collaboration processes in real communities of learners.

Keywords

Co-Construction, Motivation, Learning Communities, Shared Workspaces, Action Analysis

MULTI-DIMENSIONAL TRACKING IN VIRTUAL LEARNING TEAMS

Collaborative learning can be organized and orchestrated in a number of ways. For instance, Learning Communities (LCs) are groups that focus on building shared knowledge and, in doing so, also gain individual knowledge. Learning communities that work together for weeks and months must maintain a certain level of coherence and stability. This means that, in addition to task completion, psychological factors concerning the well-being of the group as a whole and the well-being of their individual members have to be considered. From a social psychology perspective, McGrath (1991) suggested in his TIP theory three success factors for learning communities, i.e. *production function*, *group well-being*, and *member support*. These factors are even more important in virtual groups that communicate via low-bandwidth channels e.g. discussion boards. In particular, social cues are lost when communication is limited to media that do not convey non-verbal information about other users' behavior and appearance. In our approach, we experiment with techniques to (a) dynamically *elicit* emotional and motivational state of the group members and (b) to *feed* this information *back* to the group by making use of *visualization* techniques for highlighting trends over time and for pointing out individual deviations from the group average. Although our long-term goal is the support of learning communities, we based our first exploratory study on ad-hoc groups that worked together for only a number of hours. In this study we were mainly concerned with methodological considerations: How can implicit and explicit collaboration parameters be tracked, used in order to analyze interaction and, by means of feedback, be used to support collaborative learning?

Supporting and analyzing co-construction in replicated shared workspace environments

We seek to advance the state of art of computer science methodologies with respect to computer-based analysis of cooperative activities in the context of CSCL and knowledge communication (Dillenbourg, Baker, Blaye & O'Malley, 1995). The focus is on the analysis of *directly observable* operations on visual objects in shared workspace environments, which support both spatial metaphors and direct manipulation. The analysis of activities is making use of the logic of the problem space, thus leading to principles of "operational semantics" for the analysis and support of collaboration. For our study, the application EasyDiscussing provides a shared workspace with a set of typed cards that can be dragged from a palette and dropped at an arbitrary position within the workspace. In addition, there is an overview panel, a chat interface with typed contributions, and a feedback component to visualize quantitative measures such as the number of each user's contributions in the chat and the shared workspace. All user actions in every component of this application are logged to an XML-based protocol that represents the type of action such as adding, deleting or changing nodes or edges together with further parameter that represent the objects involved, the user, and the time and date among others. The analysis of the user activities is based on performance oriented recognition of activity and interaction (Muehlenbrock, 2001). In a user interface with mainly free text input, an activity is analyzed concerning the *sequence* of actions involved, the *context* of their application (i.e. same object, connected objects, etc.), the *users* involved (same user, different users, etc.), and the contribution's *type* (e.g. question and answer). Patterns of activities have been defined formally for an automatic analysis. For instance, the activity "node_reference" is performed by a group of users if one user adds a node to the shared workspace and another user subsequently adds an edge that is partially based on this node (and could not have

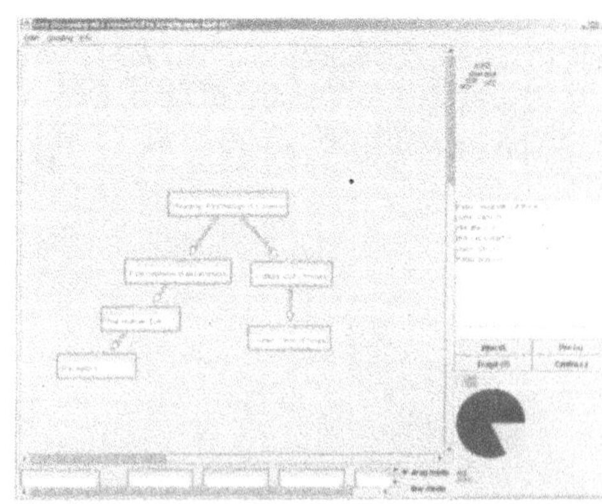

been created without that node). Another type of interaction ("node labeling") is signaled when some user adds a node and a different user puts in some text. For our study, 18 activities including variants have been defined. A sample analysis of a multi user session shows that 88 sequences can be recognized, and seven sequences involved more than one user and hence are interpreted as some interaction. In addition, the analysis indicates that one of the three users is a frequent initiator of activities, whereas another user tends to complete the interaction.

A first analysis of socio-emotional and task-analytic parameter feedback

In an explorative study we examined parameters influencing group processes during a co-constructive learning task using the shared workspace EasyDiscussing. The main idea of the study is the investigation of how groups can be affected by feedback of their own socio-emotional parameters and what kind of interaction patterns take place during a co-constructive design task. We use a combined top-down/bottom up analysis: On the one hand, we collect data by using traditional psychometric methods. On the other hand, the collaboration platform itself allows a detailed tracking of user behavior and a semantic analysis of interaction patterns during collaboration. Nine subjects (= three groups) participated in an experimental condition with the tracking of interaction as well as motivational and emotional parameters directly displayed as graphical feedback to each group. Three other groups in a control condition did not get any automatic feedback about interaction, motivational and emotional parameters. The task for all groups was the same: To collaboratively re-design a linear text into a didactically structured online-text. This design task had to be fulfilled by using EasyDiscussing tool and online learning resources. All subjects had to perform a multiple-choice pre- and a post-test regarding knowledge about didactical screen design. The results of subjects' performance in pre- and post-test concerning domain knowledge revealed no significant differences but both groups mastered the post-test significantly better than the pre-test. There were also no significant differences between both groups regarding the emotional state and motivational parameters, but interaction of repeated measurement and motivation became significant. A more detailed view on subjects' discussion structures showed a more frequent use of *pro* and *contra* postings in the experimental group. The automatic detection of interaction patterns in subjects' discussion yielded a significant difference in the number of dyadic interactions. A view on correlations between participation in dyadic interaction revealed significant correlations between use of the pre-structured argumentative icons of "pro" (0.82, $p<.05$) and "contra" (0.71, $p<.05$). In addition, we found a significant correlation between initiating a dyadic interaction and the use of questions (0.74, $p<.05$).

Summary and further work

In this paper we stressed the role of external representations as a result of a group's natural interaction. Overall we could show some effects of tracking parameters of group interaction and feeding them back to the group members. Further experiments and analyses are needed to investigate the role of this kind of protocols in detail and improve the quality the feedback. From a methodological perspective, our experiment is an example of what can be achieved by combining different analytic measures to gain more insight into group processes. The technical prerequisites are flexibly definable shared workspace environments, mechanisms for logging and analysis, and appropriate feedback techniques including visualization.

Acknowledgements: This research has been supported by grants of the German Science Foundation (DFG) to Ulrich Hoppe (HO 2312/1-1) and Peter Reimann (RE 814/11-1). We thank Johann Pixner for helpful contributions.

REFERENCES

Dillenbourg, P., Baker, M., Blaye, A. & O'Malley, C. (1995). The evolution of research on collaborative learning. In P. Reimann & H. Spada (Eds.), *Learning in humans and machines: towards an interdisciplinary learning science* (pp. 189-211). Amsterdam: Elsevier.

McGrath, J. E. (1991). Time, Interaction, and Performance (TIP). A Theory of Groups. *Small Group Research, 22*, 147-174.

Muehlenbrock, M. (2001). *Action-based Collaboration Analysis for Group Learning*. Amsterdam, The Netherlands: IOS Press.

Computer Support for Participatory Designing – A Pilot Study

Pirita Seitamaa-Hakkarainen [1], Henna Lahti [2], Marjut Iivonen[2], Kai Hakkarainen[3]

[1] Savonlinna Department of Teacher Education, University of Joensuu

[2] Department of Home Economics and Craft Science, University of Helsinki

[3] Department of Psychology, University of Helsinki, Finland

Henna.Lahti@Helsinki.fi

ABSTRACT

The present study analyzed whether and how students working in the collaborative learning environment (Future Learning Environment, FLE2) were able to share their design process with the intended user of the product. Six teams of first-year university-level textile students (N=24) participated in design course, in which they solved an authentic design task -- designing bags of EuroCSCL conference. The methods of social network analysis were applied to study interaction between all participants. A qualitative content analysis was carried out by analyzing the interaction between statements posted to the FLE2 database by two of the design teams. The results indicated that in the case of more successful group, the expert user took a role of co-designer by participating in the design process through evaluating ideas produced by students.

Keywords

Collaborative designing, knowledge-building environments, participatory design

INTRODUCTION

Collaboration is essential aspect of professionals' practical activity in the field of modern design. The idea of giving an "expert user" an important role in designing relies on the notion of participatory designing. Participatory design emphasizes the importance of acquiring relevant information from the end user of the product and ensuring that the product manifest the end user's viewpoint. The present study aimed to investigate aspects of teacher and expert users role in a participatory design process, specifically: 1) to explore how teacher and expert users worked in the virtual design environment to jointly advance students' design process; 2) to investigate the participatory design and the expert users' contribution to the design teams' collaborative design process.

The present study relies on the Future Learning Environment FLE2 (Leinonen, Mielonen, Seitamaa-Hakkarainen, Muukkonen, & Hakkarainen, 1999; http://FLE2.uiah.fi). The data were collected from a 13-week collaborative design course, and students were using FLE2 -environment during design process. In the study the participants were 24 first-year – university students and the students worked in six design teams. The design task was a very authentic and complex -- design task: the students were asked to design and produce functionally and aesthetically delightful conference bags to the EuroCSCL conference. Each of the teams had its' own "expert user" (i.e., an avid conference goer), and they participated in the design process by providing information about conference bags and conferences in general in the FLE2- environment. In order to analyze the participants' role in the social interaction of networked designing the social network analysis (Scott, 1991) was used to study participants' social position in the collaborative design process. The participants' positions in the networked discussions were analyzed using Freeman's degree as a centrality measure. The second level of analysis i.e., qualitative content analysis was conducted to teacher's and expert users' participation in design process. This detailed analysis was, limited to the database produced by two of the design teams, teacher and expert users. We selected team 1 and 2 because expert users appeared to participate rather actively in these teams. The knowledge-building messages posted to the database were segmented into propositions representing one main idea (Chi 1997). The classification schema consists of several categories but we are limiting our results analysis only one category. The reliability of classification; the coefficient for rater agreement was .88, which was considered satisfactory.

RESULTS

The entire database consisted of 211 Knowledge Building messages. The students posted 149 messages, on average 6.2 messages per student (minimum was 0, maximum 26 messages) to FLE2's database during the course. The teacher posted 35 messages, and the expert users posted 27 messages. Team members' activities and expert users' participation varied considerably from one team to another. The analysis indicated that the participants' social network had a relatively centralized structure (92% in the case of sent, and 82% in the case of received messages). The teacher's extremely high betweenness value indicates that she was mediating information between the teams and expert users. The students did not actively comment on design process across the teams. Team 4 appeared to be the most productive in posting KB messages, and the number of their sent and received messages was higher than those of other teams. Team 3 did not participate in virtual designing as actively as the other teams. Teams 1 and 2 appeared to have most active expert users, whereas in Team

6's expert user did not participate (for technical reasons) in the ongoing discussion. The analysis indicated that the students' network of interaction was not very dense; specifically, 0.22 (SD =0.86) for symmetrized data (direction of commenting ignored). Detailed analyses indicated that the teacher distributed her coaching efforts equally across design teams.

We analyzed more closely two design teams, with respect to interaction between the teacher and the users. Teams 1 and 2 posted 72 knowledge-building messages, consisting 293 design statements. There appeared to be significant differences between the teams' designing concerning how student used information and acquired knowledge as well as feedback from the expert users (df=7; χ^2= 46.3; p< .001). While all teams were provided information of expert users' conference experience, only Team 2 explicitly requested experts to comment on their design. The teacher's and expert user's contribution to Team 2's design process appeared to focus on helping to evaluate students' ideas. Moreover, Team 2 students also asked for more feedback (f=14; 8%) from their fellow members than did Team 1 (f=4; 3%). Both teams received an approximately equal amount of statements representing expert users' experience during their designing and both expert users were active and supported students' designing by providing their own experiences with conference bags. Team 1 acquired, however, much more information from the users outside the present network environment by interviewing some other conference goers (f=24; 20%). In the case of Team 2, the expert users gave feedback about the students' ideas twice as often (f=31; 18%) as in the case of Team 1 (f=9; 8%). Team 1 produced design ideas, but they did not ask for any direct feedback for their ideas, from the teacher or the users.

DISCUSSION

In general, it appears to us that participatory designing (i.e., including the expert user as a designer's partner) is indeed possible to arrange in the FLE-environment. Our previous studies have indicated that there are two important aspects of designing that virtual design environments may scaffold: defining the design context and acquiring new information. In the case of Team 2's design process, the expert user directly provided his or her own experiences and feedback for the participants about their solutions. Students of Team 1 also acquired outsider users' experiences but did not rely on interaction with the expert user while testing their design ideas. In Team 2's design process, the teacher and user became more involved in the students' designing since they were actively invited to the discussion of the relative merits of solutions. The user and teacher became more co-designers with the students even if they did not directly provide new solutions or sketches. An essential aim of the present study was to facilitate direct student-expert partnership, i.e., provide the students with access to authentic expert users' knowledge so that the student designers might apply it. In the present case, however, the activity of the user also varied: Either the student did not ask the active user's contribution, or the volunteer expert user did not have enough time to participate in the virtual design process. It might be important to improve the participants' awareness of what is going on within a networked learning environment (e.g., setting up a notification system that transmits information about students' activities to the expert users), so that very busy experts could follow what students are doing and provide timely feedback for students.

REFERENCES

Chi, M. T. H. (1997) Quantifying Qualitative Analyses of Verbal Data: A Practical Guide. *Journal of the Learning Sciences* **6,** 271-315.

Leinonen, T., Mielonen, S., Seitamaa-Hakkarainen, P., Muukkonen, H., & Hakkarainen, K. (1999) FLE – Tools Prototype: A WWW-Based Learning Environment for Collaborative Knowledge Building, *Proceedings of ENABLE99* (Enabling Network-based Learning), June 2-5, 1999 Espoo, Finland.

Scott, J. (1991). *Social network analysis.* A Handbook. London: Sage Publications.

Collaborative Problem Solving using an Open Modeling Environment

C. Fidas[1], V. Komis[1], N.M. Avouris[1], A. Dimitracopoulou[2]

[1]University of Patras, Patras, Greece

[2] University of the Aegean, Rhodes, Greece

fidas@clab.ee.upatras.gr, komis@upatras.gr, N.Avouris@ee.upatras.gr, adimitr@Rhodes.Aegean.gr

ABSTRACT

An innovative learning environment, enabling collaborative modeling activities, is introduced in this paper. ModelsCreator 3.0 (MC3) supports semi-quantitative, quantitative and qualitative reasoning during modeling activities of collaborating young children. MC3 is also an open environment in terms of primitive modeling entities, models and collaborating partners. Synchronous modeling activity can be performed at a distance using MC3, based on a mechanism of light multiple processes (reactive agents) residing in collaborating hosts.

Keywords: Computer supported collaborative learning, open learning environments, computer supported collaboration, semi-quantitative modeling

INTRODUCTION

A number of software tools have been developed during the last years that support learning through modeling (e.g. Teodoro, 1997). ModelsCreator (MC) is a learning environment that supports expression of different kinds of models, mostly for students 11-16 years old. It integrates dynamic models: semi-quantitative, quantitative, and executable decision making models as well as static qualitative models (concept maps), with special emphasis on semi-quantitative modeling (Komis et al, 2001, Dimitracopoulou et al, 1999). The most recent developments of ModelsCreator (MC version 3.0, MC3), reported here, have been in two directions: (i) Transformation of MC in an *open modeling system* and (ii) support for synchronous and asynchronous *collaborative development of models* by distant groups of young students.

OVERVIEW OF THE MC3 ARCHITECTURE

MC3 permits the collaborative building, testing and validation of models. The main functionality of the environment relates to the **Activity Space** where the models can be built, shown in figure 1. This space contains tools necessary to construct models, tools to represent models in alternative ways and tools that can run the models. In order to design a model, students have to insert primitive entities, set their properties and create relations between them. A part of the library of available **primitive entities** is shown on the left of the Activity Space, in figure 1, while on the right there is the list of available (semi-quantitative) **relations**. The relations are represented through symbols. For instance, the relations of analogy or inverse analogy are represented by the symbols:↑↑, ↑↓, (see figure 1) expressing reasoning such as: "If one entity increases, the other one might increase, or decrease". The students can use a variety of simple relations that correspond to hidden algebraic formulas.

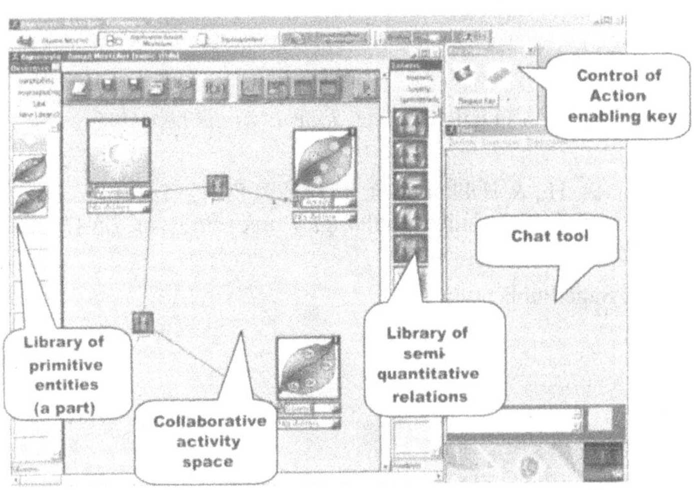

Figure 1. The ModelsCreator v3. User Interface during model building

MC3 is an open modeling system since it provides the possibility through an **entity editor** and open libraries to create new entities with various properties and behavior as well as new compound entities, models and problems. The MC3 system architecture and functionalities that enable this open character are: (i) A *repository* of publicly available modeling entities that has been created and made available to the learners community in a common Server, (ii) *Search mechanisms* and web-based interface to this repository, (iii) provision has been made to support unique identities (GUID) of any developed object (entities, models, problems) at the local host level, and entities-exchange mechanisms have been established (iv) user protocols of collaboration for synchronization of shared activity space and online update of users' heterogeneous libraries have also been defined.

Collaboration in MC3 is enabled both through asynchronous and synchronous interaction of distance partners. The integrated **chat facility**, shown on the right of figure 1, permits exchange of free-text messages between collaborating partners. Also a synchronous and asynchronous **object exchange tool** has been implemented. The Activity Space in this case becomes a drawing space of synchronous collaboration, in which one of the two collaborating partners can insert primary objects (concepts and relations), through direct manipulation. The supported protocol of interaction permits to the two partners to exchange roles, playing either the passive or the active role. The active partner is the one who can manipulate objects in the activity space. Variations and enhancements of the standard protocol involve a mechanism for interleaving text messages and action in the form of *sticky notes* (see Fidas et al. 2001). Additionally alternative protocols for controlling *ownership of parts of the model* have been devised, so that collaborating partner cannot modify parts of the solution that have been built by another partner. These also support the collaboration analysis framework OCAF, discussed in Avouris et al. (2002).

CONCLUSIONS- EVALUATION STUDIES

The MC3 environment presents many interesting new features that need to be extensively evaluated. The first phase of this evaluation, involved experimentation with specific functionalities. One experiment studied the effect of heterogeneous or missing primitive object libraries in problem solving. The result of this experiment was that the available functionality and tools allowed students to proceed with building models by collaboratively searching for missing primitive objects or develop new ones at run time, when required. One remark relating to this experiment concerns the extensive use of text-based messaging tools in this cognitively demanding activity. A second experiment involved variations on the *solution ownership protocols*. It was proven that even slight variations of the developed interaction protocols affect the use of the tools and pose new demands in terms of cognitive tasks requested by the users. More experiments and investigations are currently planned, exploring grounding mechanisms during individual and collaborative construction of new primitives (entities and sub-models) for problem solving and modeling in sciences. The creation and use of these constructed primitives during various collaborative modes constitutes also a research direction for our team. Additionally an extended large scale use by learners communities of five European countries is planned in the frame of a new European project.

ACKNOWLEDGMENTS

Financial support has been provided by the IST2000-25385/ModelingSpace Project of the European Union and the ModelsCreator/Pinelopi Program of the Greek Ministry of Education.

REFERENCES

Avouris N.M., Dimitracopoulou A., Komis V., Fidas C. (2002), OCAF: An object-oriented model of analysis of collaborative problem solving, Proceedings CSCL 2002, Colorado, January 2002

Dimitracopoulou A., Komis V. Apostolopoulos P. & Politis P. (1999). Design Principles of a New Modelling Environment Supporting Various Types of Reasoning and Interdisciplinary Approaches, in *Proc. of 9th Int. Conférence of Artificial Intelligence in Education,* IOS Press, Ohmsha, pp. 109-120.

Fidas C., Komis V., Avouris N.M. (2001). Design of collaboration-support tools for group problem solving, *Proceedings PC HCI 2001*, December 2001, Patras, Greece.

Komis V., Dimitracopoulou A., Politis P., Avouris N. (2001). Expérimentations exploratoires sur l'utilisation d'un environnement informatique de modélisation par petits groupes d'élèves, *Sciences et Techniques Educatives*, Vol. 8, no 1-2, pp.75-86.

Teodoro V.D. (1997). Modellus: Using a Computational Tool to Change the Teaching and Learning of Mathematics and Science, in "*New Technologies and the Role of the Teacher*" Open University, Milton Keynes, UK.

Full paper at: http://www.ee.upatras.gr/hci/Publications.htm

Talk, Silence and the Study of Situated Action

Ivar Solheim

Department of Educational Research, University of Oslo and Norwegian Computing Center[1] solheim@nr.no

ABSTRACT

This theoretical paper discusses some conceptual and epistemological issues in the study of situated action in CSCL environments, especially focusing on ethnomethodology (EM) and conversation analysis (CA). It is argued that EM and CA approaches provide relevant and fruitful research strategies and methodologies. Some theoretical and epistemological peculiarities, weaknesses and biases of the approaches are identified and discussed. Finally, activity theory is briefly discussed as a potential alternative methodological and theoretical approach.

Keywords

Situated action, discourse analysis, ethnomethodology, conversation analysis, computer supported group work.

INTRODUCTION AND MOTIVATION

The ideas discussed in this paper have partly been inspired by some concrete methodological challenges that I have met in my study of the interaction between computers and students in classrooms. A basic challenge for my methodological framework rooted in analysis of talk-in-interaction, was the fact that the students I observed only talked occasionally to each other during their work. This raises of course some specific methodical issues concerning application of the appropriate devices for mapping the interaction. Obviously, a mere recording of the talk is in this case not sufficient as a tool to map the actual interaction going on in this group. I chose, probably appropriate, to use video camera to tape the interaction between the students and the computers in order to map not only the interaction with the computers, but also non-vocal communication, gestures, gaze, the character and function of hesitations and absences etc.

However, these more methodically and technically oriented issues are not my main concern in this paper. It seems to me obvious that it would be wrong to reduce my problem to merely a question of finding the appropriate methods and techniques for mapping the interaction. Several broader methodological, epistemological and philosophical issues must be addressed. For example: Are the conceptual tools of CA appropriate for analysing silence and unspoken utterances? To what extent can pupil's learning processes be accounted for within this framework? What is the epistemological status of spoken utterances compared to the unspoken within the framework of CA? Is the methodical strategy of CA focusing on moment-to-moment turn-taking in talk neglecting the importance of other significant, but less observable structures? Most fundamentally, to what extent can the possible constraints of CA as an empirical strategy reflect more fundamental challenges or problems in the philosophical and epistemological foundations of EM/CA?

A DISCURSIVE ANALYTIC PERSPECTIVE ON SOCIAL ACTION AND LEARNING

Inspired by Wittgenstein's later writings, Harold Garfinkel's ideas of ethnomethodology, and especially the ideas for discursive psychology (Edwards, 1996, Potter and Edwards, 1992), my work has been based on an understanding of *language as action* and *talk as accountable action* reflecting the participants' own concerns, orientations and intentions. According to this view, the researcher should not look for "hidden" representations and motivations or unobservable social structures, but concentrate on the accountable, observable, and detailed talk-in-interaction of people, in my case interaction between students doing computer assisted project work. I have been particularly attracted to CA, which has been presented "as a solution to EM's problem of the 'invisibility' of common sense" (ten Have, 1990). This approach directs the focus on the detailed interaction and construction of meaning through talk. For example, if one wishes to study how or to what extent students "learn" in the interaction with computers, the researcher should be paying attention to what students are actually doing and saying when they use computers in their daily work.

DISCUSSION

In a critical discussion of EM and CA, I relate my arguments loosely to my initial methodological problem of applying EM/CA in a context where the participants evidently do communicate in their cooperative work, but where this only to a very limited extent is reflected in "ordinary" conversation between the members of the group.

I appreciate CA as a part of the methodical fundament of discourse analysis. But as I read the works of many conversation analysts and ponder the character of the research program, I am increasingly struck by a peculiar narrowness and disembodied, and to some extent empiricist, character of many CA studies. In my view this is due to certain theoretical

[1] In the academic year 2001 and 2002 I am a visiting researcher at the Center for Lifelong Learning and Design, Department of Computer Science, University of Colorado et Boulder. Email: ivar@cs.colorado.edu

peculiarities and biases, more specifically the idea of rationality as accountability, the premise of the knowledgeable actor and the exaggerated epistemological and methodological status of speaking turns and sequential organisation of utterances. In particular, and here I follow Michael Billig's (1997) critique, the study of central issues as repression of knowledgeability and absences and silence in dialogues, seem to require additional or alternative theoretical and methodological frameworks.

Activity theory has been presented as an alternative to CA and discourse analysis (Engeström, 1999), but in my view activity theoy does not offer significant insights in the study of the finegrained aspects of sociality and human interaction, especially human-computer interaction, which is the focus of the present paper.

By way of conclusion, I consider EM and CA to be highly relevant and valuable research strategies and methodologies in the study of situated interaction, and especially in CSCL environments. The major strength of CA lies in the idea that conversational meaning is to be situated in the sequence. Its most powerful idea is undoubtedly that human interactants continually display to each other, in the course of interaction, their own understanding of what they are doing. This, among other things, creates room for a dynamic, interactional view on human-computer interaction. EM and CA seem particularly relevant to the study of human-computer interaction since these processes are often complex to analyse because also the computer is involved as an interactant in its own right, albeit not human.

For the further development of CA within a discursive analytic framework it seems important to also include analysis and interpretation of "unspoken utterances" which are not directly observable, but which leaves traces. Theoretical concepts from e.g psychoanalysis and rhetorics, may seem relevant in addressing the challenges presented in the beginning of this paper (for other phenomena, other theories may seem interesting). But a prerequisite for such application of theory should be that the inferences and theorizing are derived and traced from actual interaction in its situated context, non-vocal or vocal.

ACKNOWLEDGMENTS

I thank Hans Christian Arnseth, Vibeke Grøver Aukrust, Sten Ludvigsen, Roger Säljö and Svein Østerud, for helpful suggestions and comments on a previous version of the paper.

REFERENCES

Billig, M. (1997) The dialogic unconscious: psychoanalysis, discursive psychology and the nature of repression, *British Journal of Social Psychology*, **36**, 139-159.

Billig, M. (1996) *Arguing and Thinking*, 2nd Edition. Cambridge: Cambridge University Press.

Edwards, D. and Potter, J. (1992) *Discursive Psychology*. London: Sage.

Edwards, D. (1996) *Discourse and Cognition*. London. Sage

Engeström, Y. (1999) "Communication, Discourse and Activity" (manuscript)

Have, P. ten (1990) 'Methodological issues in conversation analysis', *Bulletin de Méthod.Socio.*, Nr. **27** (June): 23-51

Garfinkel, H. (1967) *Studies in Ethnomethodology*. Englewood Cliffs: Prentice Hall.

Schegloff, E. 'Whose text? Whose context?', *Discourse & Society* (1997) **8**: 165-87,

Suchman, L. (2000) Embodied Parctices of Engineering Work. In *Mind, Culture and Activity*, **7**(1&2)

Wittgenstein, L. (1953) *Philosophical Investigations*. Oxford: Blackwell.

Resources for Coordination in Collaborative Telelearning

Rune Baggetun
InterMedia
University of Bergen
runeb@ifi.uib.no
Anders Mørch
InterMedia
University of Oslo
anders.morch@intermedia.uio.no

ABSTRACT

We have analyzed data from a field study in collaborative telelearning (Wasson, 1999). The goal of the study was to investigate how the students used a set of groupware tools to coordinate learning activities. We have used concepts from collaborative telelearning and coordination mechanisms (Schmidt & Simone, 1996) as analytic framework. Our findings indicate that students coordinate many activities by implicit, locally adopted resources instead of fully developed mechanisms. Three implicit resources were identified and named (no initial discussion, asymmetry of knowledge, and different expectations). These resources were not associated with any specific groupware features, but referred to the students' background knowledge and subjective interpretation. We end the paper by suggesting how implicit resources in distributed learning environments can play a role similar to how non-verbal cues – such as gesture and facial expression – play a role in face-to-face interaction, but without imitating human body language.

Keywords

Collaborative telelearning, distributed collaboration, coordination, explicit resources, implicit resources

DISTRIBUTED LEARNING AND COORDINATION

We have studied a distributed collaborative scenario over a period of four weeks. The participants were students enrolled at three educational institutions in Norway. They were assigned three activities requiring collaboration. A groupware system was used to mediate the interaction. The central research question we have asked is how the students coordinated their activities with the groupware facilities they had available.

Coordination can broadly be defined as how to support, manage, and justify collaborative interaction. Coordination has also been defined as "articulation work" (Strauss, 1985): the organization of work that accompanies work (contacting people, scheduling meetings, division of labor, etc.) to ensure the latter's successful completion. We have identified three main strands of research of relevance to collaboration systems: 1) Executable coordination mechanisms (e.g. Dourish & Bellotti, 1992), 2) Articulated coordination mechanism (e.g. Schmidt & Simone, 1996), 3) Coordination theories (e.g. Malone & Crowston, 1992, Wasson, 1999). The notion of coordination mechanism we use in this paper is adapted from articulated coordination mechanism (Schmidt & Simone, 1996), with some added modifications. Our focus has been to identify the shared artifacts and articulation work the students have used to coordinate their activities. We take a socio-cultural perspective in our analysis and have studied the scenario from different views (Wertsch, del Río & Alvarez, 1995). The most important technique was observation of the students as they worked. This was augmented with more traditional HCI-oriented usability studies, such as data logging and user satisfaction questionnaires.

FINDINGS

Our findings pertain to coordination at the tool use level and are summarized as follows. There were no prior agreement or discussion among the students for how to use the different tools before they started on the assignment. This would often lead to unanticipated situations. Most notably the students would use different tools to accomplish the same task. When there were no procedures for how to use the tools and none had been developed by the students nor suggested by us, the use of tools depended upon students' prior skills and new ideas for how the tools could be used. When interaction between students required several rounds of turn taking the expectation for what constituted a complete action sequence would often be interpreted differently.

Our findings are different from past work on coordination mechanisms by revealing personal choice and style as key factor in coordination rather than procedures and mechanisms. The styles were easily amenable to local interpretation and mutual adaptation. They were not built into the groupware, but dynamically "built" by the students during interaction with each other. That is why we call them *implicit resources* to stress their informal and subjective characteristic.

DISCUSSION

We argue in the full paper that implicit resources should be seen as the "virtual equivalent" of body language since body language (facial expression, body position, gesturing, etc.) and our implicit resources are associated with informal, situation-specific cues people indirectly use and take for granted in collaborative interaction (i.e., a kind of tacit knowing). These resources provide an important awareness of other people's activities and their level of participation.

IMPLICATIONS FOR DESIGN

We propose an approach to system design - inspired by Polanyi (1958) and his concept of *peripheral awareness*, which is different from past work on coordination and awareness (e.g. Dourish & Bellotti, 1992). Instead of imitating body language in support of computational awareness (e.g. multiple cursors, different views, interaction histories, etc.), we use it through analogy. Our findings indicate that collaborative telelearning can be more efficient if more attention is paid to informing the participants about affordances and constraints of coordination and collaboration. This can be achieved by a technique we have dubbed "conceptual awareness on demand". A conceptual level adds a new dimension to collaborative telelearning and exploits the distributed nature of this form of interaction. By bringing generally useful information about coordination and collaboration to the users' attention in ways that are different from face-to-face situations we go "beyond being there" (Hollan & Stornetta, 1992).

The current activity in the DoCTA project (DoCTA NSS) includes designing, developing, and field-testing a "pedagogical agent" system that will instantiate these principles and provide for this kind of peripheral awareness. In this phase we reuse ideas developed by others in the areas of software agents for collaborative applications, including the work on knowledge-based critics (Fischer et al. 1991) and coaches (Suthers & Weiner, 1995).

ACKNOWLEDGMENTS

The authors would like to thank the other member of the DoCTA project at the University of Bergen (Barbara Wasson, Eskil Andreassen, Frode Guribye, Hege Higraff, Øyvind Meistad, Trond Pedersen, Kurt Rysjedal, Helge Underhaug, and Jo Wake). We thank Weiqin Chen and Sten Ludvigsen for comments on an earlier draft. We are grateful for funding from the ITU (IT in Education) program of KUF (the Norwegian Ministry of Church affairs, Education, and Research).

REFERENCES

Dourish, P. and Bellotti, V. (1992). Awareness and Coordination in Shared Workspaces. *Proceedings of CSCW'92*. ACM Press, pp. 107-114.

Fischer, G., Lemke, A.C., Mastaglio, T. and Mørch, A.I. (1991). The Role of Critiquing in Cooperative Problem Solving. *ACM Transactions on Information Systems*, Vol. 9, No. 3, pp. 123-151.

Hollan, J. and Stornetta, S. (1992). Beyond Being There, in R.M. Baecker (ed.), *Readings in Groupware and Computer-Supported Cooperative Work*, Morgan Kaufman, 842-848.

Malone, T.W. and Crowston, K. What is Coordination Theory and How Can It Help Design Cooperative Work Systems? *Proceedings of CSCW'90*. ACM Press, pp. 357-370.

Polanyi, M. (1958). *Personal Knowledge: Towards a Post-Critical Philosophy*. The University of Chicago Press.

Schmidt, K. and Simone, C. (1996). Coordination Mechanisms: Towards a Conceptual Foundation of CSCW Systems Design. *Computer Supported Cooperative Work*, 5(2-3), pp. 155-200.

Strauss, A. (1985). Work and the Division of Labor. *The Sociological Quarterly*, Vol. 26, No. 1, pp. 1-19.

Suthers. D. and Weiner, A. (1995). Groupware for Developing Critical Discussion Skills. *Proceedings of the ACM Conference on Computer Supported Collaborative Learning*, Hillsdale NJ: Lawrence Erlbaum Associates.

Wasson, B. (1999). Design and Evaluation of a Collaborative Telelearning Activity Aimed at Teacher Training. *Proceedings of CSCL'99*. ACM Press, pp. 659-666.

Wertsch, J. V., del Río, P. & Alvarez, A. (1995). Sociocultural studies: history, action and mediation,. In J. V. Wertsch, P. del Río & A. Alvarez. (Eds.) *Sociocultural Studies of Mind*, Cambridge: Cambridge University Press, pp.1-34.

Design Reviews with Remote Critics in an Asynchronous Environment

Colleen M. Kehoe
GVU Center/Georgia Institute of Technology
colleen@cc.gatech.edu

Keywords
Design, jury review, critics, collaborative website, asynchronous

INTRODUCTION

A familiar activity to students of design is the design review – where students present their work-to-date to receive feedback and guidance from others. They take place throughout the term, providing students with multiple opportunities to present and develop their ideas (Schön, 1987). At Georgia Tech, we have been exploring how simple technologies can be used to increase opportunities for dialog in the design studio by expanding the range of topics, ways of participating, and set of participants in that dialog. One thread of this research deals with using remote critics in design reviews. Using technology, remote critics are able to view students' work and comment on it without traveling to the studio. In addition to solving some logistical problems of bringing visitors to the studio (e.g. scheduling, expense), we speculated that allowing remote critics to participate in design reviews had the potential to not only expand the set of participants in the dialog, but to change it in fundamental ways.

This paper documents the design and development of one activity called Student-Curated Galleries. In this activity, groups of students in a freshman studio in the College of Architecture used the web to present their work to remote critics who left comments for each of them. It was implemented using a technology called a Collaborative Website or CoWeb. A CoWeb looks and acts like any other website with one important exception: anyone can add new pages to the site or edit the pages which are already there using a standard web browser. (For details of the CoWeb and its uses, see (Collaborative Software Lab, 2000)).

DESIGN AND DEVELOPMENT

The Student-Curated Galleries activity was strongly influenced by our previous experience using remote critics in the original CoOL Studio project, which took place the previous year (Zimring et al., in press). CoOL Studio demonstrated that students and remote critics could interact successfully using the CoWeb. Students were able to represent their projects sufficiently so that they could be understood and commented on by the critics. Equally important, critics were able to participate with virtually no instruction and using only standard browser software. Even with these successes, CoOL Studio provided many lessons for future reviews with remote critics (for specifics, see (Zimring, et al., in press)).

One of the ideas inspired by CoOL Studio was that rather than showing each student's work individually, as is usually the case in design reviews, students would group their work into thematic galleries. In these galleries students would be responsible for "curating" them – for deciding on a theme, selecting images that explore that theme and writing about them. The pedagogical goal was for students to reconceive their designs in terms of the themes and how they related to the other projects in the gallery. Simultaneously, they would have to take into account the strengths and limitations of an online presentation and decide how to convey their ideas clearly to the critics. One instructor agreed to try the activity in her studio and so the research team worked with her over several months to develop the details. The final design for the galleries is shown in Figure 1.

Major design decisions about the online environment and the review activity included:

- The galleries would have a uniform format, designed by the research team and instructor, which students would have to work within. This decision was made to make the activity more manageable for students, and at the same time allow us to create a fairly sophisticated presentation for the galleries.
- The gallery format was designed to strictly limit the number and sizes of the images to keep download times reasonable for critics. Students were also instructed on how to change the compression and resolution of their images to make the file sizes smaller.

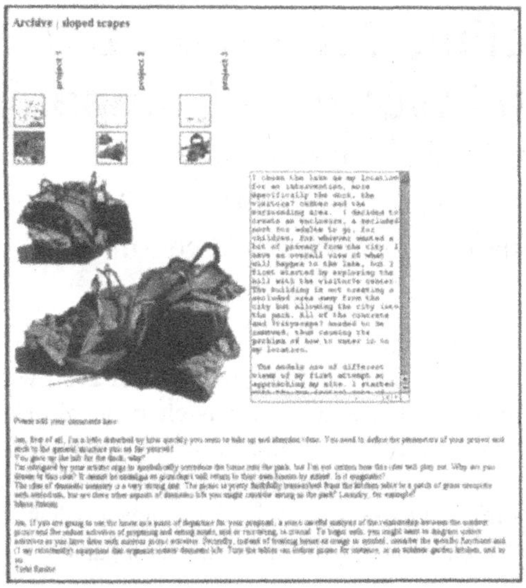

Figure 1. Detail of one gallery with an image from Project 2 in focus (right). Text to the right of the image is from the student; text below is from the critics.

- Several projects, related by a common theme, were displayed simultaneously on a single page. The goal was to allow critics to compare projects side-by-side, so instead of using a long, scrolling page, we used a "fish-eye" (Furnas, 1986) scheme for laying out each gallery. Students' images are shown in thumbnail and the critic can click on one of the thumbnails to bring it into focus. When an image is in focus, a larger version of it is displayed along with accompanying text that the student has written.
- There was a single comment space for each gallery. Within it, critics could comment on a specific project, compare projects, or comment on the gallery and theme as a whole. Using a single comment space meant that critics could easily read what other critics had written. We also hoped that it would encourage students to read the comments for the whole gallery, not just those related to their project.
- To make the creation of images more manageable, students worked on small format paper that could be scanned in a single pass. Arrangements were also made to use a digital camera to photograph their three-dimensional models, eliminating the intermediate steps of developing and scanning regular photos.
- Because the project was only six weeks long, on-line reviews were scheduled to replace, rather than duplicate or supplement in-person reviews. Two on-line reviews were scheduled, alternating weeks with in-person reviews.
- Students would spend about three days preparing their on-line presentations from the drawings and models they had previously created. Critics were given a five-day window in which to visit the galleries and leave their comments. The aim was to allow critics a reasonable amount of time to participate, but to make the window small enough that the comments would still be relevant to the students' projects.
- Critics were provided with background information and an explanation of the exercises the class had done via email before the review. This information was also included in the gallery along with an explanation of the 2CoOL project, brief instructions for using the CoWeb, and a "Sign-in" page for each critic where he or she could introduce themselves and practice using the CoWeb.

CONCLUSION

The design of the Student-Curated Galleries activity addressed many of the problems discovered in our previous use of remote critics, but it was not without its own set of difficulties. Many of these related not to the specific technology but how the activity changed by going from a familiar, face-to-face activity to a novel, asynchronous, computer-mediated one. A discussion of how this activity was different from a typical design review for the participants and how this impacted the outcome of the activity is available in the online version of this paper.

REFERENCES

Collaborative Software Lab (2000) *A Catalog of CoWeb Uses*. GVU Tech Report 00-19. Georgia Institute of Technology, Atlanta, GA. (ftp://ftp.cc.gatech.edu/pub/gvu/tr/2000/00-19.pdf)

Furnas, G.W. (1986) Generalized fisheye views. *Proceedings of ACM CHI'86* (Boston, MA, April 1986), 16-23.

Schön, D. A. (1987) *Educating the Reflective Practitioner*. Jossey-Bass Publishers, San Francisco, CA.

Zimring, C., Khan, S., Craig, D., ul-Haq, S., Guzdial, M. (in press) CoOL Studio: Using Simple Tools to Expand the Discursive Space of the Design Studio, Automation in Construction.

Organizational Learning - Enabling Self-organized Knowledge Logistics for a Health Insurance Company

Peter Mambrey[1], Volkmar Pipek[3], Markus Rohde[2], Markus Won[3]

[1]Fraunhofer FIT.CSCW, [2]Agenda Consult, St. Augustin; [3]ProSEC, Univ. of Bonn; (Germany)
mambrey@gmd.de,{pipek, won}@cs.uni-bonn.de, markus.rohde@agenda-consult.de

ABSTRACT

CSCL at the workplace is subject to the special characteristics of a situation where learning is not the primary task of the learners. The gap between the goal to work efficiently and the need to increase qualification and skills is even wider in organizations which operate in knowledge-intensive markets and where responsibility and autonomy characterize the work style of geographically distributed workers ("Virtual Organizations"). Classical learning methods have to be complemented by a lightweight knowledge-sharing infrastructure ("knowledge logistics"). In this contribution we describe a method of introduction of knowledge logistics which reflects that gap and offers support for self-organized settings for learning at work. We present our approach by describing the case of the field service of a German health insurance company.

Keywords

CSCL, knowledge management, organizational learning, virtual organizations, self-organization

INTRODUCTION

Virtual Organizations (Mowshowitz 1997) have three characteristics which complicate its capability to change: Its actors are usually geographically distributed (less social interaction), have a higher degree of autonomy (diversity of cultures and ideas) and collaborate usually via an IT-Infrastructure. Here, learning at work always competes with other, more "productive" work tasks, and the higher degree of autonomy of the actors can disturb learning cooperation. By describing the case of a German health insurance company (GEHICO) we show our way to introduce what we call self-organized "knowledge logistics" into a virtual organization.

In our methods, we feel inspired by research from the fields of CSCW (esp. groupware introduction), organizational learning, and collaborative and self-organized learning. We tried to combine all that to answer our key question: How to introduce and maintain self-organized knowledge logistics in a virtual organization.

Organizational Learning Challenges for a Health Insurance Company

The German Health Insurance Company (GEHICO) is one of the top ten health insurance companies in Germany with a turnover of more than 800 million dollars. Within its field service, a group of around 100 persons, covering all regions of Germany, is specialized on the contact management with free health insurance agencies (agency field service - AFS). Most of them are experienced insurance agents and work with GEHICO as freelancers. Each AFS agent is responsible for one German region (in very populated areas several agents work in one region), which is why AFS agents rarely meet each other. The usual way for becoming an AFS agent is the participation in the corresponding training program after working several years as an "ordinary" insurance agent in the field service. The training is organized as a series of workshops with around five to eight participants. GEHICO has about 15 trainers responsible for the qualification of the field service. Besides training services for becoming an insurance agent or an AFS agent, they also offer free skill trainings like negotiation, rethorics, etc. Some of the trainers are employees, some are freelancers.

The described setting given, our measures to improve organizational learning (continuous, faster learning cycles) in the field service of GEHICO mainly aim at: First, complementing the classical learning measures and the associated communication patterns with decentralized, computer-based measures and communication. A shift away from workshop-focused concepts towards computer-based collaborative learning concepts is also intended. Second. shifting the learning practice from a "managed", prescriptive learning organization to a more self-organized, demand-oriented practice. Therefore, it is necessary to introduce tools and establish practices of continuous expertise sharing related to the trainings attended and the daily work practice, to reorganize roles with regard to a more continuous, practice-related qualification concept ("Teachers" become "Qualification Consultants"), and to collect experiences with collaboration via internet-based media. We developed a concept for the introduction of such self-organized knowledge logistics which we believe can also be applied to other introduction processes of CSCL concepts.

A CONCEPT TO INTRODUCE SELF-ORGANIZED KNOWLEDGE LOGISTICS

What we call self-organized knowledge logistics is a conglomerate of technical systems and organizational practices and conventions which allow for of a high degree of flexibility and easy ways of re-negotiating and reorganizing collaborative structures. For the technical system for *self-organized* knowledge logistics two points are of importance: it should be easy to connect to the system wherever the user is, and the content should be easily restructurable by users (including setting appropriate access rights easily to build restricted or private areas). The technical system of our knowledge logistics was programmed on the basis of the web-based groupware BSCW.

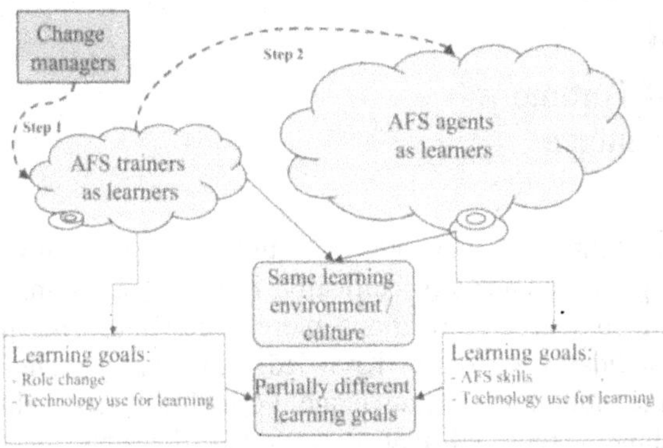

Figure 1: Introducing a knowledge logistics system

Our concept is also inspired by the work of Kafai (1991) and Pedersen (1930), who developed methods where higher-grade kids taught lower-grade kids. The interesting aspect for our context is that all "teachers" were "students" *in exactly the same learning setting* before. They do not only have the necessary knowledge with regard to the learning goal, but they also have experience in *how to learn in the setting given.* Therefore, they are also able to transmit a culture of learning. We adopted this idea by working first with a multiplier group, and then with our "real" target group.

Our approach can be best described by a process and an inner loop which is realized in steps 2 and 3 of the process. The process has the steps: Gathering the needs of the target group (here: AFS members), introducing "self-organized knowledge logistics" (system and practice) to a multiplier group (Choosing an appropriate multiplier group involves assessing them as sufficiently similar to the target group; we believe the trainers fulfill that requirement), and finally introducing the "self-organized knowledge logistics" to the target group. Figure 1 shows how this process works in the case of GEHICO. The learning goal of "technology use" is inherent to the method and dominates the other learning goals in the beginning. Learning goals are only weakly described, they mainly influence the material which is being put into the technical system. The inner procedure is the introduction itself which works according to the following pattern: Designing an initial system and presenting it within daily work scenarios, supporting users in system exploration, agreeing on learning goals with and for the users (including support for appropriate training; technology use is most likely always one of the first issues there), continuous evaluation and redesign (together with the users, shifting attention away from technology use to the core learning requirements of the user group).

We should stress that the existing training concept (mainly workshops) will be integrated in this method. We expect that it is necessary that there are opportunities to meet for a learning group which uses the knowledge logistics. The existing trainings will initiate as well as complement the online learning groups.

The most important question in this context is whether our concept works and if we can manage to change the learning in the way described above. It is also interesting for us to see how the role concept of the "classical" trainers will change during the process of becoming moderators of a new style of learning. At last we have to observe the use of our BSCW-based knowledge logistics system. Here the main question is how systems generally have to be designed to support self-organized continuing training processes. Due to this question we will conduct feedback workshops regularly which can be used to identify change requirements.

We believe that our method can at least serve as a first step to systematically deal with the introduction of CSCL systems into organizations and work setting.

REFERENCES

Kafai, Y.B. and Harel, I. (1991), *Children's learning through consulting: When mathematical ideas, programming knowledge, instructional design, and playful discourse are intertwined.* In: Harel, I. and Papert, S. (eds.) Constructionism, Ablex, Norwood, NJ, pp. 85-110.

Mowshowitz, A. (1997) *Virtual Organization.* Communications of the ACM, 40 (9). 30-37

Petersen, P. (1930), *Schulleben und Unterricht einer freien allgemeinen Volksschule nach den Grundsätzen Neuer Erziehung. (Großer Jena-Plan Bd. 1)*, Weimar, Germany.

Teacher Candidate Perceptions of Telementoring in Knowledge Forum

Jim Hewitt

OISE / University of Toronto

jhewitt@oise.utoronto.ca

ABSTRACT

The success of traditional email-based telementoring rests on the ability and inclination of students to maintain open channels of communication with mentors. Telementoring in learning environments (specifically, Knowledge Forum) may offer strategic advantages by making the day-to-day evolution of student investigations more accessible. This paper describes an experiment in which University of Toronto teacher candidates worked as Knowledge Forum telementors in four elementary school classrooms. Research findings support the notion that Knowledge Forum provides valuable contextual information for mentors. Additionally, teacher candidates reported that they found the experience of electronically mentoring a Knowledge Forum class to be professionally valuable.

Keywords

Telementoring, pre-service education, computer-mediated communication, learning environments

INTRODUCTION

The rapid growth of the Internet offers exciting new possibilities for classroom learning. In recent years, it has become increasingly feasible to use email to forge electronic mentoring, or *telementoring* relationships between students and subject-matter experts outside the schools. To date, telementoring experiments have focused almost exclusively on the use of email as a communications medium (e.g., Harris & Jones, 1999; O'Neill & Gomez, 1998). The current research breaks with this tradition and investigates the possibility of situating telementoring discourse within the context of a computer-based learning environment.

The full potential of telementoring has yet to be realized. Research suggests that traditional mentor-mentee models require careful preparation and ongoing monitoring to prevent failure. For example, in a study by Harris and Jones (1999), over one-third of the telementoring relationships were abandoned prematurely. Breakdowns such as these are commonplace, and perhaps understandable. The success of telementoring rests heavily on the ability and inclination of students to keep mentors informed about their goals, their discoveries, and the challenges they are facing. Some students have difficulties in this regard. It is an unfortunate reality that those learners who could most deeply benefit from a mentoring relationship are often the ones that have the most trouble carrying out and sustaining a productive series of email exchanges.

In conventional telementoring arrangements, students spend part of their time investigating a particular problem, and part of their time exchanging email with mentors. This system is inherently inefficient because it divides the students' attention. One way to bring these two worlds together is through the use of collaborative learning environments. Tools like Covis (Edelson, Pea, & Gomez, 1996), Virtual University (Harasim, 1993) and Knowledge Forum (Bereiter, in press) allow students to work together in an electronic learning community. Within Knowledge Forum, for example, learners define research problems and then assist each other by contributing theories, discoveries, questions, and information to the on-line database. Providing telementors with electronic access to a Knowledge Forum database would enable them to follow, in detail, the evolution of student investigations. This would provide mentors with a deeper sense of the students' work than they would likely acquire through email exchanges alone. At the same time, it would reduce the need for students to keep mentors constantly apprised of developments. Students would instead conduct their investigations in their on-line learning environment, while mentors observe remotely and offer assistance as necessary.

METHOD

This study explores the advantages and limitations of mentoring through Knowledge Forum. Seven teacher candidates from the one-year University of Toronto teacher education program served as mentors. After a brief telementoring preparation program, these individuals worked over the Internet in the Knowledge Forum databases of a nearby elementary school. The teacher candidates were divided among four classrooms: grade 1, grade 3, grade 4 and grade 5-6. The goals of the research were to: a) determine the degree to which teacher candidates could glean, through their virtual visitations, an understanding of student-led Knowledge Forum investigations; b) identify difficulties experienced by the teacher candidates during their online interactions; and c) explore teacher candidates' perceptions regarding the educational efficacy of telementoring as a professional development activity.

The data consist of teacher candidate interviews, written teacher candidate reports, two videotaped conversations between teachers and teacher candidates (lasting approximately an hour each), researcher field notes, and records of online mentor-mentee exchanges. Two parties identified reoccurring themes in the transcripts: the author of this paper and by a researcher who was not previously part of the telementoring experiment.

FINDINGS AND CONCLUSIONS

The interview data and written reports indicate that telementors had few difficulties following Knowledge Forum discourse and analyzing the progress that students were making in their investigations. The Knowledge Forum databases provided mentors with an extensive corpus of student work. In fact, mentors reported that there was sometimes too much information. Since the teacher candidates began mentoring in the middle of a unit, they were initially faced with a significant number of notes to read. As one mentor remarked, "I must admit that I was overwhelmed by the vast 'web of knowledge' that the students had created online."

The telementoring experience appeared to benefit the mentors as much, and possibly even more, than the mentees. All teacher candidates were impressed by the degree of agency that students were afforded in their investigations. They felt that their Knowledge Forum activities were much more student-centered than anything they had witnessed during their practice teaching sessions. One remarked:

"I am starting to understand that… the acquisition of rote knowledge is secondary to the development of theories and the ability to test theories and ask the right questions of other people's theories…. I must <as a teacher> create an atmosphere that allows students to take risks and not be afraid of making mistakes"

Some of the responses from teacher candidates suggest that the telementoring experience may have affected their pedagogical beliefs. One teacher candidate claimed that the experience changed the way that she interacts with her own children.

"<My> dialogue with my own two daughters <aged 8 and 9> changed as a result of this exposure…. We have adopted an open-forum type of attitude at home where questions, theories, ideas, opinion whether right or wrong are welcome in discussions…"

The research also uncovered two problems. First, the teacher candidates were accustomed to structured, teacher-centered pedagogies, and were unsure how to best support students in Knowledge Forum. This points to a need for effective telementoring models and more extensive mentor training. Second, teacher candidate messages sometimes closed down student discourse. The reason for this is unclear. Further research is required to determine why mentor contributions sometimes cause threads to end abruptly, and to explore possible ways of rectifying the problem.

If the approaches employed by this research can indeed transform teacher candidate beliefs about thinking and learning, then there may be potential for making telementoring a more central part of a teacher education program. Since Knowledge Forum preserves a record of interaction, mentor-mentee discourse could theoretically be extracted and made a subject of analysis in pre-service classes. This would provide pre-service programs with tremendous opportunities to link educational practice to educational theory.

REFERENCES

Bereiter, C. (in press). Education and Mind in the Knowledge Age.

Edelson, D., Pea, R., & Gomez, L. (1996). Constructivism in the collaboratory. In B. G. Wilson (Ed.), Constructivist learning environments: Case studies in instructional design, (pp. 151-164). Englewood Cliffs, NJ: Educational Technology Publications.

Harasim, L. (1993). Collaborative in cyberspace: Using computer conferences as a group learning environment. Interactive Learning Environments, **3**(2), 119-130.

Harris, J. B., & Jones, G. (1999). A descriptive study of telementoring among students, subject-matter experts, and teachers: Message flow and function patterns. Journal of Research on Computing in Education, **32**, 36-53.

O'Neill, D. K., & Gomez, L. M. (1998). Sustaining mentoring relationships on-line. Paper presented at the ACM Conference on Computer-Supported Cooperative Work, Seattle, WA.

"Letting go of the reins:" The Evolution of Pedagogy in an Online Graduate Program

Karen Sheingold

Princeton, NJ; ksheingold@mindspring.com

Linda Polin

Pepperdine University; 400 Corporate Pointe; Culver City, CA 90230; lpolin@pepperdine.edu

While many online graduate level courses mirror traditional face-to-face didactic teaching (Institute for Higher Education Policy, 2000), some programs are taking advantage of the rich opportunities for interaction online to create courses that embody social constructivist approaches. These emphasize the importance of communities of practice (Lave & Wenger,1991; Rogoff, 1994) and of students' engaging actively with each other, with experts, and with the material to construct their own understanding (Gergen, 1995; Wilson, 1993). This paper explores the evolution of one professor's pedagogy over the course of a year's teaching in an online master's program grounded in these approaches. The study uses two different methods—interview and analysis of newsgroup threads.

The professor we studied, 'Pat', is an experienced teacher who has taught in higher education for a decade, as well as in both middle and high schools. Having taught online at another university, she had joined this program because of her interest in pursuing online teaching in more depth in an institution with impressive leadership that 'wanted to grow.' The 13- month program in which Pat teaches includes three face-to-face meetings of students and professors. The remainder of the program is online, and includes synchronous class meetings as well as other online tools-- newsgroups, web pages, groupware, chat shells, email.

METHODS

We interviewed Pat after she completed her first year in the online program.The 40-minute unstructured phone interview was analyzed for consistent themes that emerged with respect to Pat's experience. In addition, we analyzed newsgroup threads from two of Pat's classes (three sections in all), one in the fall and one in the spring.

THE TEACHER'S REPORT: WHAT THE INTERVIEW TELLS US

Four themes emerged as central—being herself, responding to the group:letting go of the reins, valuing community, and getting support.. The first theme emphasized the challenges for Pat of figuring out how to 'be herself' online and get 'some of the things that work for me face-to-face to work in that synchronous environment.' She uses several strategies to bring her own culture and personality to the online environment, but still sees this as a challenge.

Regarding the second theme, Pat is very clear about having made a significant change in her teaching—giving more control to the group. "..I had to learn to be more responsive to the group and their questions, not just posting question after question, but allowing some of the discussion to arise from their interest with it. So really letting go of the reins more."

The third theme focuses on the community that this program helps students develop, in part because each cohort of 20 goes through the program together. She emphasizes the close bonds the students develop, because they communicate about and help each other with many different things. " So …what they get is a …network even beyond what a lot of faculty have in that they have a group of peers that they can contact in lots of different scenarios again and again..."

Finally, Pat talks about how important the program leaders have been in enabling her to develop as a teacher. For example, the program director "doesn't get in your way on anything. She's sort of waiting to see what you want to do, but she's also there to support you…"

CHANGES OVER TIME: WHAT THE NEWSGROUPS TELL US

The messages in each newsgroup were coded by who initiated them (teacher or student) and by content categories (e.g., Logistics, Assignment). In the fall, the course newsgroup contained 537 postings covering 85 subject headings, with slightly more than half of the topics put into play by the teacher. Logistics is the most frequent category, with postings that explain the syllabus, the schedule of online chat sessions, and the assignments, as well as the use of small groups and pairs to do course work. The balance of the initiated discussion is focused on Assignments and Resources, not on Discussion, to which only 7 of the 85 threads are devoted. Apparently, students are busy completing and turning in assignments, without much opportunity for construction of knowledge through dialogue in threaded newsgroups. This function must take place in the synchronous 'chat' sessions, which occur less than once a week. Although few threads are coded as Reading Question, this category reflects a traditional college course approach, which begins with the professor asking a question about the readings.

In the second semester, Pat relinquishes dominance of the topics in the threaded discussion. Down from 51.8%, the percent of topics initiated by the teacher is 37.3% and 38.5% in each section, respectively. Similarly, she ceases to ask Reading Questions.Furthermore, there is a general shift away from Logistics onto Discussion Topics. This reflects a shift in how students participate. Instead of formal assignments and reading questions, Pat now asks students to lead fellow students, to formulate an initial prompt for discussion in newsgroup and /or online. This request fulfills the same function as previous formal questions and reading assignments—getting students to think about the material. Now, however, the postings are largely student initiated (71% and 58.1%) extensions of course topics.

DISCUSSION OF FINDINGS

In becoming an online teacher in this master's program, the professor learned a great deal and changed her pedagogy. 'Letting go of the reins' required that she give up some old strategies—e.g., posting questions to structure the online discussion—as well as adopt some new ones—e.g., giving students the responsibility for structuring a reading discussion. Her comments suggest that she saw this change as being responsive to students and as creating more meaningful learning opportunities for them..

While it is remarkable that such a visible shift took place in less than one year, many factors were supportive of this change. First, Pat herself wanted to learn how to continue to teach well in this new environment. Moreover, she came to the program with considerable experience in teaching and comfort with technology. Second, the structure and philosophy of the program, as well as its leadership, was supportive of her taking risks and developing. And, finally, the technology made a significant contribution. It provided feedback about the effectiveness of her teaching and about the engagement of her students. She 'listened' to what the students were saying to her online.

This case suggests how we might investigate teachers' development on line more broadly. It underscores the value of using more than one method. Using both, the results indicated clearly that Pat had indeed given over more control to the students. The newsgroup analyses showed explicitly the changes that occurred in who initiated conversations and in what they were about. The interview indicated that this was a change that Pat herself was aware of and considered important.

Learning to teach in an online environment is complex and challenging. It offers possibilities that face-to-face teaching does not, while removing the visual and auditory immediacy of the face-to-face classroom. Making or constructing one's way as a teacher in this new space is likely to be a developmental process that takes place over many years. As teachers gain confidence, take risks, experiment with the technology and the pedagogy, and see themselves as part of a community in which practice itself is evolving, we will observe developments that we may not now be able to predict, let alone imagine.

REFERENCES

Gergen, K. J. (1995). Social construction and the educational process. Chapter 2 in Steffe & Gale (eds.) Constructionism in education. Hillsdale, NJ: LEA.

Institute for Higher Education Policy (2000). Quality on the line: Benchmarks for success in Internet-based distance education. Washington DC: Institute for Higher Education Policy. Also available at: http://www.ihep.com/quality.pdf

Lave, J. & Wenger, E. (1991). Situated learning: Legitimate peripheral participation. Cambridge: Cambridge University Press.

Rogoff, B. (1994). Developing understanding of the idea of community of learners. Mind, Culture, and Activity, 1. 209-229.

Wilson, A. L. (1993). The promise of situated cognition. Chapter 7 in Merriam (ed.) An update on adult learning theory. San Francisco: Jossey-Bass.

Assisting and Assessing the Development of Technological Fluencies: Insights from a Project-based Approach to Teaching Computer Science

Brigid Barron, Caitlin Martin, Eric Roberts, Alex Osipovich, Michael Ross

Stanford University
Barronbj@stanford.edu

ABSTRACT

University-school partnerships hold great promise for establishing innovative computer-science curricula and investigating how students learn and appropriate technologies for their own use. Here we highlight an interdisciplinary design work and describe a novel approach to the assessment of student growth.

Keywords

Design experiments, alternative assessment, teacher professional development, project-based pedagogy

INTRODUCTION

In 1997 the National Science Foundation asked the Computer Science and Telecommunications Board (CSTB) of the National Research Council to initiate a study that addressed the subject of *information technology literacy*. The study's rational was the increasing ubiquity of information technology in daily life and the importance of beginning to define what everyone should know in order to empower all citizens to participate in this new era. Increasingly, information technology is not only an efficiency tool but is fundamentally changing academic disciplines ranging from the biological sciences to the study of history. The results of the committees' work was a report entitled *Being Fluent with Information Technology*. Rather than use the term 'literacy' the authors of the report opted for the label 'fluency' and defined it as the capacity to reformulate knowledge, express oneself creatively, adapt to change and to continually learn in order to apply technology to work and personal lives. The committee defined a tripartite approach to fluency (or "FITness") with equal attention to intellectual capabilities, domain-general information technology concepts, and contemporary information technology skills. Schools potentially play an important role in developing youths' technological fluency and in bridging gaps between youth with more or less home access to computing opportunities. However, research on the use of computing in schools shows that only a small proportion of teachers use computers in ways that might enhance various aspects of technological fluency (Becker & Riel, 2001). Long-term, university-school partnerships in which new practices, curriculum, and assessment strategies are treated as on-going design problems and approached jointly by researchers and teachers hold major promise for bridging theory-practice gaps. The design experiment we report here is based on the assumption that new teaching practices can be scaffolded in a learning-by-doing framework for integrating multiple kinds of resources for professional development and learning. This assumption is supported by research in other domains (e.g. see Barron et. al., 1998) and emphasized in new perspectives that highlight the need for teaching to be viewed as a learning profession (Hawley & Valli, 1999) and supported by participation in "communities of practice".

Interdisciplinary Design Work

Since the fall of 1998, a group of faculty and students at Stanford University has been engaged in this multi-year design experiment to create, implement, and assess a new computing curriculum for the public secondary schools in Bermuda. The project is a collaborative effort of the Computer Science Department and the School of Education and draws heavily on both knowledge domains. The computer science team provides the technical knowledge necessary to develop the curriculum content, the implementation skills needed to develop interactive computer-based teaching tools, and extensive experience in teaching computing concepts to college students with widely varying interests. The School of Education team provides expertise in the design and study of the learning environment – a process that involves learning theory, curriculum development, professional development, and assessment strategies. By working together, the two groups create a synergistic environment that has proven enormously valuable. In our work we organize our curriculum around project-based learning opportunities that allow students to learn content in the context of creating meaningful artifacts. The design was guided by earlier work on project-based instruction and follows the design principles articulated by Barron, et al. (1998).

Assessment Strategy for Making Complex Learning Outcomes Visible

A challenge for researchers attempting to investigate the effects of innovative curriculum on student learning is to develop assessments that are sensitive to the multiplicity of outcomes that are theoretically predicted. This is particularly true for innovations that include new technologies that frequently transform the nature of tasks and what it means to know. Our systems for measuring change in knowledge and even processes such as problem solving are fairly well developed. We are less able to measure more complex yet highly valued outcomes such as changes in the ability to collaborate, manage projects, carry out research, persist in the face of difficulty, learn from social and material resources, and use tools to meet novel ends. These are the kinds of learning processes that are not only knowledge-based but involve social competence and emotional resilience.

To capture the development of these fluency-related processes we have created an approach to assessment called artifact-based interviewing. This novel method centers on eliciting learning narratives by cueing student memory and perspectives using students' project-based work. An interview protocol was developed that begins by asking students to lead the interviewer through their completed design work. The interviewer follows with a series of 45 questions in six areas. These include 1) learning of technological skills; 2) knowledge and use of design processes; 3) research skills; 4) collaborative work processes; 5) motivation and engagement; and 6) project sharing with peers, parents, teachers and other community members. These interviews yield student talk that allows us to characterize their level of fluency on multiple dimensions. We have found evidence of student growth in conceptualizations of collaboration, understanding of design and coding processes, knowledge sharing beyond the immediate community, and self-directed learning using networked resources. In addition to these interviews we measure pre to post-test change on paper and pencil measures of knowledge, motivation, perception of learning sources, breadth of technological experience, and knowledge sharing. We are also carrying out longitudinal case studies with a small number of students in order to capture their experiences, decision making and technological fluency development across the first three years of high school.

SUMMARY AND CONCLUSIONS

Our design-experiment work demonstrates the significant broadening of the content and pedagogy of traditional computing courses that can be obtained by working closely with teachers using research supported design principles. Our work has established new approaches to assessment. Traditional assessment tools are not well-designed for detecting the development of technological fluencies. They are even less suited to identifying what we might call far-transfer outcomes that are linked to school-based learning experiences but that have distal yet powerful self-perpetuating learning consequences for the student. These include self-initiated arrangements for further learning or learning that travels between the student and those in the community that the student lives within. Our findings thus far suggest that these kinds of outcomes do occur and that it is worth our while to reflect on how we might best document them in the service of creating more and better opportunities for generative learning.

REFERENCES

Barron, B., Schwartz, D.L., Vye, N.J., Moore, A., Petrosino, T., Zech, L. & Bransford, J.D. (1998) Doing with understanding: Lessons from research on problem and project-based-learning. *Journal of Learning Sciences*, 7(3&4), 271-311.

Becker, H. & Riel, M. (2000) Teacher professional engagement and constructivist-compatible computer use. Report from the Center for Research on Information Technology and Organizations, University of California, Irvine and University of Minnesota.

Hawley, B. & Valli, X. (1999) The essentials of effective professional development: A new consensus. In Linda Darling Hammond and Gary Sykes (Eds.), *Teaching as the Learning Profession: Handbook of Policy and Practice*. SanFransisco, CA: Jossey-Bass.

National Research Council. (1999). *Being fluent with information technology*. Washington, DC: National Academy Press.

INTERACTIVE EVENTS

An extensive program of interactive events parallels the paper sessions. These include demos and hands-on demonstrations. The events are organized into the following categories:

- Collaborative Workspaces
- Community and Culture
- New Media
- Online Communities
- PDAs and Ubiquitous Computing
- Professional Development
- Representational Scaffolding

A. COLLABORATIVE WORKSPACES

Virtual CSCL 2002: Making the Most of CSCL 2002 by Extending it Virtually

Elke Hinrichs, Marcus Specht

Fraunhofer Institute for Applied Information Technology FIT

{elke.hinrichs, marcus.specht}@fit.fraunhofer.de

"Virtual CSCL 2002" is aimed at extending the process of knowledge sharing and creation by conference participants, organizers, tutors and authors before, during and after the conference. We will provide a collaborative learning support server, ALE-BSCW. ALE-BSCW consists of a course authoring and learning environment (ALE) and a Shared Workspace System (BSCW). Conference participants may register with the ALE-BSCW server and may view the uploaded material, comment on it, add their own documents, engage in discussion forums and much more; any Web browser will suffice to access ALE-BSCW. The server will remain available after the conference for participants to stay in contact and cooperate. In the following, we will very briefly describe the two components of the "Virtual CSCL 2002" server: ALE and BSCW.

ALE – *A*DAPTIVE *L*EARNING *E*NVIRONMENT

The ALE framework utilizes hypermedia technology and AI (Artificial Intelligence) methods to deliver individualized hypermedia instruction. The framework is comparable to our previous ACE framework described in (Specht, Oppermann, 1998). Two different learning strategies are supported by ALE: expository learning, where students follow predefined paths through learning material, and exploratory learning, where students explore learning material on their own. Furthermore, awareness information integrated into the ALE learner portal and course interface support synchronous and asynchronous learning in learner groups.

Besides the adaptation of a goal oriented instructional process, the integration of cooperative learning components into ALE enables the support of a wider range of learning activities and the support of individual styles of learning. Students can learn in ALE not only by discussing with other students but also by following the individualized guidance of a pedagogical agent through all available learning material. The only criteria for a successful learning path are the test results of a student at the end of a learning unit or even a curriculum.

The ALE architecture consists of four main models: the *structural model* describes the learning units of the domain and their interrelations and dependencies, the *content model* comprises the concepts to be learned, the *pedagogical model* contains pedagogical strategies and diagnostic knowledge and the *learner model* stores the preferred settings of a learner, the domain concepts and learning units a learner worked on, and the interface components used by the learner.

When students log into ALE they enter an individualized learner portal, where they may book courses, contact courseware authors and other learners, maintain and update their profile, and access a collection of resources linked to that page. Additionally, students get awareness information about current online discussions, teachers' online lessons in their courses booked, and co-learners that are present on the ALE server. From their personal ALE portal they start working on their courses booked.

Based on the learner model, the content model, the structural model, and the pedagogical model, the presentation component of ALE selects appropriate learning units and generates individual hypermedia documents. When a learner requests information about a learning unit, the ALE system checks if the learner has already mastered the requested unit or has seen some material about this unit. In a second step the system looks up relations and available material for the requested unit. In a third step the presentation component retrieves a plan for presenting the unit depending on the available learning material for this unit, the knowledge of the learner, and the teaching rules and pedagogical specifications of the course author. The retrieved plan describes the presentation of the requested unit, which is translated into HTML by the presentation component. Throughout the whole course the learner's knowledge is tested so that the system can adapt to the dynamically changing knowledge, interests, and preferences of the learner.

BSCW – *B*ASIC *S*UPPORT FOR *C*OOPERATIVE *W*ORK

The BSCW system is a Web-based groupware system around the *shared workspace* metaphor. A BSCW server (a standard Web server extended by the BSCW functionality through the Common Gateway Interface) manages a number of shared workspaces – repositories for shared information, accessible to the members of a group via any normal Web browser. Registration with a BSCW server and administration of a workspace user group is performed in a self-organized manner:

by default no system administrator's action is required for user administration and workspace set-up. The only pre-requisites to become a BSCW user are an email address and a Web browser.

A workspace may contain different kinds of information, represented as information objects arranged in a hierarchical order. A shared workspace can contain different kinds of information such as documents, graphics, audio/video, URL links to other Web pages, threaded discussions, member contact information and more. The contents of each workspace are represented as information objects arranged in a folder hierarchy.

The main features of the system are (for details see (Appelt, 1999), (Bentley, 1997) and http://bscw.gmd.de/):

- *Authentication and security*: Identification of clients by basic name/password scheme or X.509 Client Certificates. BSCW runs well with SSL (Secure Socket Layer) compatible Web servers and thus supports encrypted data transfer.
- *Version management*: For joint document production, documents may be put under version control. Additionally, documents may be locked to prevent document replacement or upload of new versions by other users.
- *Discussion forums*: Threaded discussion forums may be set up in any shared workspace for closed group discussions in context. Discussion forums may additionally be attached to documents like "post-its".
- *Group awareness*: The *event service* of the BSCW system provides users with information on the activities of other users. Events are triggered whenever a user performs an action in a workspace, such as uploading a new document, reading an existing document, editing a document etc. The system records the events and presents the recent events to each user. Event notification may be individually configured to be rendered in-system by event icons or via email, both direct or in aggregated daily activity reports.
- *Access rights management*: The system contains a role concept which allows for flexible and fine-grained access rights settings. While some roles are system-defined (manager, administrator, member, anonymous user), others may be defined by the users themselves: for instance the roles of *teacher* and *student*.
- *Interface to synchronous communication*: Through this interface users can specify synchronous sessions and launch respective tools, e.g., audio/video conferencing software or shared whiteboard applications.
- *Customization*: Through user preferences the users can modify the system interface to some extent, e.g. to what detail information on the server should be displayed. Additionally, system administrators may almost entirely replace the user interface by providing their own XHTML and CSS user interface templates.
- *Multi-language support*: The interface of the system can be tailored to a particular language by straight-forward extensions. Various language versions have been created and published by users of the system.

The Fraunhofer FIT institute is operating a public BSCW server since October 1995 where everybody is invited to register and create workspaces free of charge. As of October 2001, more than 70,000 users have registered on FIT's public BSCW server and the server software for local installation has been downloaded several thousand times.

REFERENCES

Appelt, W. (1999) WWW based collaboration with the BSCW System in: J. Pavelka, G. Tel, M. Bartosek (Eds.), *SOFSEM'99: Theory and Practice in Informatics*, Springer Lecture Notes in Computer Science 1725, Berlin.

Bentley, R., Appelt, W., Busbach. U., Hinrichs, E., Kerr, D., Sikkel, S., Trevor, J., Woetzel, G. (1997) Basic Support for Cooperative Work on the World Wide Web. *International Journal of Human-Computer Studies,* **46**, Special issue on Innovative Applications of the World Wide Web, 827-846.

Specht, M., and Oppermann, R. (1998) ACE, Adaptive courseware environment. *New Review of Hypermedia and Multimedia*, **4**, 141-161.

Specht, M. (1998) Adaptive Methoden in computerbasierten Lehr/Lernsystemen. *Psychology*, G.R. Series, **1**, University of Trier, Trier.

Think.com

Sheila Hunter

Oracle Corporation, Redwood Shores, California, United States
Sheila.Hunter@Oracle.com

ABSTRACT

Think.com is a free, web-based environment for primary through secondary students and educators. Think.com supports online learning communities with the tools and space to create and share their work online. Both students and teachers have the ability to easily *create*, *communicate* and *collaborate* with their peers in an online environment. Integration of Think.com into the curriculum provides students an exciting new venue for learning, and facilitates global communication and collaboration within a learning community.

Keywords

Create, Communicate, Collaborate, K12, Online Learning Community

INTRODUCTION

Think.com is a unique tool that allows educators to participate in a collaborative learning community for primary and secondary education. It is currently available in the United States and the United Kingdom, with pilots in New Zealand and Chile. Learn more about Think.com during our two CSCL sessions and in the Collaboratorium.

CLASSROOM USAGE

The following two examples show two ways that educators may use Think.com to increase the learning opportunities offered to their pupils. Both examples are from the United Kingdom because Think.com was initially piloted there and hence has the longest observed usage in Britain.

Think.com Facilitates International Collaboration

The WebPlay project gives children the chance to interact with peers across the world, broadening their standard classroom learning. Think.com gives the children simple Internet tools to create their plays in a safe environment over the web. Through this collaborative project, schools write and produce a play across the Internet. The project brings primary school children from the UK and the USA together. Five schools in South London and 110 pupils from Los Angeles are writing and producing plays that will be shown over the Internet. The tools within Think.com allow children to effectively collaborate on the project. With its brainstorms, debating and email facilities, Think.com provides a unique platform for the WebPlay project. When the plays are finished they will be shown using the Internet so the children can see the results of the project.

The Merton Education Business Partnership and Southwark Education Business Alliance in the UK, along with the Los Angeles Unified School District in United States, developed WebPlay. Actors and staff from *Polka Theatre for Children* also joined the project, and will assist with script writing and provide workshops to the pupils and teachers taking part. *Polka* will also perform a play specially written for WebPlay entitled "Moon Shadow", to UK children involved in the project, then travel to the USA on 16th March to perform and coach the children in America. Using the Internet the children are able to exchange notes, review the play and also exchange ideas for their own productions.

Think.com Motivates Disaffected Students

Fiona Garrett of Boston Spa School was awarded a DfEE (Department for Education and Employment) Best Practice Research Scholarship this year. Below, she shares her research of the use of Think.com with disaffected children.

"My research project focuses on a group of students who are categorized in school as 'disaffected' and part of my role is to teach English to these students who are following a year eleven 'alternative curriculum'. My research project combines Think.com and this particular group of students. The question I chose to examine was: "Can the use of Think.com and consequently membership of an online community alter/improve the learning outcomes of a group of 'disaffected' students?"

A profile of the students is integral to this project. All students were in year 11 and had been classified as 'disaffected'. They had been identified towards the end of year 10 as either very disruptive, poor attendees, or consistently failing in most areas of the curriculum and consequently 'switched off'. This group of students was enrolled in an alternative year 11 course with the following objectives: to withdraw students from main stream; provide them with the opportunity to do a combination of work experience, college courses and continue studying core subjects but in small groups with work differentiated to meet their specific needs.

My hypothesis was that the students in this group were poorly motivated towards work. They had displayed this lack of motivation by rejecting their entitlement to the national curriculum in one way or another and consequently earning a place in the group. Thus in order to improve motivation and encourage the students to use a variety of skills, they had to be exposed to something that would provide a catalyst to motivation. I considered Think.com to be a system designed to offer something suitably new and interesting resulting in a positive change in motivation and work ethic.

The research is primarily ethnographic supported by in-depth qualitative interviews and some analysis of written work completed before and after exposure to Think.com. I have come to a range of conclusions:

- The ability to interact freely with other members of the community offers important learning gains.
- The natural differentiation that the technology allows is ideal for a group of this kind.
- The girls seemed more interested initially in the idea of a 'global' audience for their ideas.
- Think.com gives the students the ability to construct an identity through word. This is interesting for a student who has avoided using words for many years.
- Feedback from the virtual audience has a very important impact on the students' view of their own page and motivation towards the project.
- The lack of pressure on the students to produce an assessed piece of work gave them the freedom to control the content rather than have it dictated to them.
- Most students need to see the potential of the site the first time they look at it in order to feel inspired.
- Students need to recognize that they control the content, and there are consequences for inclusion of inappropriate content.
- With a group of 'disaffected' students, relationship with the teacher is of critical importance.

Essentially the impact of Think.com has been a change in motivation. Learning how to use the system and taking ownership of their own pages meant students who would normally have to be forced to work in class or who refuse to do anything perceived as work became independent learners. They accessed their sites in their own time and made use of the system without me prompting them to log on. Both confidence and motivation have massive educational benefits. Students who engaged with Think.com learnt a variety of new skills, not least how to set up their own page, but also communication skills, writing skills, layout and organizational skills. Think.com provides a new audience for students who don't trust the audience in school. They are able to construct a new identity and receive genuine feedback from people who don't know their reputation or usual behavior. There are no expectations.

Think.com offers a working space that instantly 'looks good'. Many of these students are used to very poor work in terms of style and quality and don't want to produce output as they know their work will be difficult to read, messy and embarrassing. Think.com offers a very coherent, well-organized space that they can be instantly proud of. Think.com gives them 'space'. Think.com offers a certain level of instant outcomes for the student. It doesn't take long to have something tangible on your page. This speed is important to students who give up very quickly if they can't see an outcome. They are not restricted to constructing 'teacher friendly' work. They can use their space to show something about themselves. It allows them to work independently and not have the teacher breathing down their neck. A lot of these students have not worked in school for many years. It puts a lot of pressure on them when they do have to work and they react badly to being watched.

It has been an interesting project with a wide range of conclusions and applications for future work with similar disaffected students."

ACKNOWLEDGMENTS

The Think.com team thanks WebPlay and Fiona Garrett of Boston Spa School in England.

B. COMMUNITY AND CULTURE

Technology and Collaboration in Informal Learning Environments: A Comparison of Community Technology Initiatives

Robbin Chapman, Leo Burd
MIT Media Laboratory
rnc@media.mit.edu, leob@media.mit.edu

ABSTRACT
In response to increasing concerns about the "digital divide" – the gap between those who benefit from digital technologies and those who don't – a growing number of community technology initiatives (CTIs) have emerged to realize the potential of digital technologies to underserved community members. Although CTIs share many common goals and procedures, there are also important differences. In this paper, we examine the role of collaborative learning and technology in two CTIs, the Computer Clubhouse (http://www.computerclubhouse.org/) and Committee for Democratization of Information Technologies Sao Paulo (http://www.cdisp.org.br/), and raise issues to be considered in the construction or improvement of effective community technology initiatives.

Keywords
Collaborative learning, community technology center, community technology initiative, constructionism, digital divide, telecenter.

INTRODUCTION
In this paper, we examine the role of collaborative learning and technology in the Computer Clubhouse (CC) and the Committee for Democratization of Information Technologies Sao Paulo (CDISP). At the end, we raise issues to be considered in the construction or improvement of effective community technology initiatives. CC is a network of after-school CTIs for underserved youth, ages 10-18 years old. Modeled on the constructionist theory of learning (Papert, 1980), members learn by working on projects of their own interests in an environment that fosters exploration, creativity and interaction. Projects range from Web site authoring to filmmaking, music recording, graphic design, and crafts and robotics. CDISP is a Brazilian organization that partners with community centers in the construction of "Schools of Information Technology and Citizenship" (EICs). At these centers, members from underserved communities, mostly teenagers, attend computer classes and use technology for their personal and community development.

COLLABORATIVE LEARNING AND TECHNOLOGY IN CC AND CDISP
Both CC and CDISP see learning, technology, and collaboration as empowering tools for underserved communities. These organizations create environments where people not only have access to technology, but also learn and practice a variety of attitudes and skills that are important to their personal and social life. For instance, a common Clubhouse artifact is a large, oval table around which community members gather to work on projects, share ideas, learn from each other, and forge relationships. Clubhouse walls provide a venue for showcasing member projects and inspiring new projects and collaborations. CDISP schools offer courses in which people learn basic computer skills by developing community-related projects -- such as newsletters, homepages and price comparisons -- addressing locally relevant issues that range from violence to teen pregnancy, drug abuse, and professional skills development.

The direct exchange of experiences among people from different ages, backgrounds, and social levels is of central importance to the two CTIs. For example, CC adult mentors expose members to innovative ways of engaging technology and serve as role models for identity development (Resnick, 1998). Mentors provide members the opportunity to see adults learning and developing projects. In the CDISP model, members develop a sense of citizenship by engaging in the Committee campaigns and decision-making process. Once a month CDISP hosts a "barn-raising" party in which expert technicians and novices from all social levels get together to fix the machines to be used in new EICs.

CC provides members with professional-grade graphic and multimedia design tools, a recording studio, movie and digital image capturing tools, robotics and other computational construction tools. There are typically eighteen high-end computer workstations and several dedicated computers for music and movie constructions. In contrast, CDISP schools have five to ten mid-range computers with mainly utility tools such as text processors, Web browsers and email programs, and no printers. CDISP schools have this configuration because they rely heavily on local used-equipment donations.

ISSUES TO BE CONSIDERED

CC and CDISP each address the digital divide issue but with different emphasis. Their individual perspectives reflect how they deal with collaborative learning and technology. For CC, they are used for creativity and identity development. For CDISP, they are used to promote citizenship development. The two CTIs aren't mutually exclusive in their approaches, though. One could envision an organization that combines the project-based learning and mentoring of the CC model with the community participation and governance of the CDISP approach.

It is interesting to note that, in most cases, neither organization applies technology directly to support collaborative learning. Technology is used as a medium of personal expression. Collaboration happens locally, without digital mediation. However, in order to expand and enhance their respective models, the two CTIs are widening their focus from local to inter-community collaborations. Without technology, these long-distance interactions cannot happen. This is where the tools they are using fall short. For instance, Clubhouse tools don't support collaborative project development or sharing of ideas across CC sites. Likewise, CDISP's technologies don't help communities exchange experiences or participate in the governance and strategic-planning process. Moreover, face-to-face interactions and member sense-of-connectedness to their community is still a critical element of the studied CTI's perceived effectiveness. Neither organization wants to lose this at the expense of expansion.

Our study about the relationship between technology and collaborative learning within CC and CDISP has raised important issues regarding construction or improvement of effective community technology initiatives. We believe that similar studies of other initiatives would contribute to enhancement of the CTI model, as a whole.

ACKNOWLEDGMENTS

Many thanks to Professor Mitchel Resnick, Head of the Lifelong Kindergarten group at the MIT Media Laboratory for his advice and support.

REFERENCES

Kobashi, R. Y. (2001). Information technology 'for and by' low-income communities in Sao Paulo. *Proceedings of Development by Design, 2001* (Cambridge, MA, June 2001). To be published.

Lave, J. & Wenger, E. (1991). *Situated Learning: Legitimate peripheral participation*. Cambridge, UK: Cambridge University Press.

Papert, S. (1980). *Mindstorms*. Basic Books. New York.

Resnick, M., Rusk, N., and Cooke, S. (1998) The Computer Clubhouse: Technological Fluency in the Inner City. In *High Technology and Low-Income Communities*, edited by D. Schon, B. Sanyal, and W. Mitchell. MIT Press.

Multicultural Issues in the Design, Evaluation and Dissemination of CSCL Systems

Masanori Sugimoto
University of Tokyo, Japan
sugi@r.dl.itc.u-tokyo.ac.jp
Daniel D. Suthers
University of Hawai'i at Manoa, USA
suthers@hawaii.edu

ABSTRACT

This paper describes an overview of a panel that will be held as an interactive event in CSCL2002. Multicultural issues in design, evaluations and dissemination of CSCL systems are discussed. Four outstanding panelists will share their rich experiences, and propose how multicultural issues should be considered and examined in the context of system design and development and practice in school education, what problems should be dealt with, and how information technologies can contribute to promoting multicultural learning. Discussions are not limited to the panelists: active participation from the audience will be welcomed.

Keywords

Learning in multicultural situations, collaborative learning, information technologies

INTRODUCTION

This paper describes an overview of an interactive penal to be held at CSCL2002. Multicultural issues are critical in today's internationalized and networked society, and should be deeply considered in CSCL research since one of the theoretical backgrounds of CSCL is mutual learning among people of different knowledge and backgrounds. Heterogeneity can be an opportunity for promoting collaborative learning, and CSCL systems should support people in overcoming their cultural differences and establishing mutual understanding.

Recent development of information technologies (Internet, WWW etc.) seems to give us ideal opportunities for applying CSCL in multicultural situations. However, it is not easy in practice. We face some serious problems, such as the "digital divide" comprised of disparities in access not only to computers, but also to well-trained teachers and useful digital resources. Another problem is how to construct mutual respect among people of different cultures and communities. For successful mutual learning, a critical precondition is to recognize differences among individuals, allow them to equally participate in a learning situation, and construct mutual understanding through interacting with each other.

We believe that emerging technologies should be useful tools for dealing with multicultural issues in CSCL. Therefore, we need to investigate (1) how we should use technologies to enhance mutual learning in multicultural situations, (2) what kinds of learning resources are necessary for establishing mutual respect, (3) whether we can create models of collaborative processes among different communities/cultures, and (4) how computational systems can play a role in supporting these processes.

ORGANIZATION OF THE PANEL

In this panel, four panelists who have been actively working in their own fields will discuss multicultural issues for design, evaluations and dissemination of CSCL systems through their rich experiences and perspectives. The panelists will show several interesting findings. One example is that cultural identities of individuals make them aware of their own uniqueness and differences, and this enhances mutual respect of different cultures. This example gives us a hint for content design of multicultural CSCL systems. Another example is that different communities and generations should not have excessive expectations of each other at the beginning of collaboration processes, but should work to establish expectations. The panelists have so far put their ideas into practice in various situations such as primary schools, local communities, and office environments. Based on these realistic and well-grounded experiences as well as those of audience members who have engaged in CSCL/multicultural activities, we will share lessons learned, and explore new possibilities and approaches for design, evaluation and dissemination of multicultural CSCL systems.

Each panelist will talk about their activities and demonstrate their own system in an interactive manner. Each presentation will be followed by a discussion period. As this panel is one of the interactive events, active participation from the audience will be welcomed.

The panelists have different backgrounds, cultures and knowledge. Their approaches and objectives are not the same. Therefore, multicultural issues will be investigated from different perspectives in this panel. Experiences shown by the panelists will make discussions realistic and well grounded. Through interactive demos and audience participation, active discussions and mutual understanding not only among panelists but also the audience will be pursued.

The panel will be beneficial for people who are interested in human-computer interaction, computer supported collaborative learning, computer supported cooperative work, and multicultural education. Topics discussed will range from system design and evaluations to practice in real settings, so researchers, system developers, business persons, and school teachers will be able to participate from their own standpoints.

BIOGRAPHIES OF THE PANELISTS (ALPHABETICAL ORDER)

Ms. Bonnie Bracey is a Lucas Fellow, and was a member of the National Information Infrastructure Advisory Council appointed by President Clinton working with Vice President Gore and the Department of Commerce in helping to frame the documents that provided the national visions for the use of technology. She is an outspoken advocate for teacher involvement in the exploration and visioning of the use of technology as a tool. She has been helping teachers all over the world in national and global outreach on special initiatives. She has been working on issues of digital equity, digital divide, and digital bridges that are inclusive of multicultural issues. She won the *Top25 Women on the Net 2001*.

Dr. Amy S. Bruckman is an assistant professor at college of computing, Georgia Institute of Technology. Her work is generally on constructionist learning online. In one of her projects "Palaver Tree Online", kids interview elders to learn about history from people who have lived it (for example, learning about civil rights from older African-Americans). Through several pilot studies, she found some interesting themes: how to find ethnic diversity online, differences between elders' perspectives and teachers' expectations, and so forth. They are key themes for designing and evaluating multicultural CSCL systems.

Dr. Shigeru Miyagawa is a professor in the Department of Linguistics and Philosophy and also in the Department of Foreign Languages and Literatures, both at the Massachusetts Institute of Technology. He has been working for "Star Festival", a learning support system about the quest for one's identity in a multi-ethnic and multi-cultural society. This system is now used in elementary schools in Boston and Hawai`i, and other school districts are considering adoption, in order to encourage young people to explore their own cultural identity while learning about Japanese culture and history. His works are not only related to design and evaluation issues of multicultural learning support systems, but also strategies for their dissemination.

Dr. Kumiyo Nakakoji is an associate professor at Graduate School of Information Science, Nara Institute of Science and Technology, Japan, and a senior researcher at a Japanese software industry. One of the key ideas of her work is "Three C's (Culture, Communication and Creativity)", as applied to software development, multimedia authoring, and design. She has especially been interested in open source software development processes and collective creativity: how computational systems support interaction with people of different backgrounds, bridging between communities of different cultures and promoting mutual understanding.

Design Principles for Educational Software

Yael Kali, Nathan Bos, Marcia Linn
Center for Innovative Learning Technologies
Jody Underwood
Educational Testing Service
Jim Hewitt
University of Toronto

ABSTRACT
This interactive session at CSCL 2002 will present, and add to our ongoing study of design principles for educational technology. We are seeking to capture key findings of the field using a three-level framework, including these interlinked components: educational goals, design principles, and software features.

Keywords: design, design principles, educational technology, representation, visualization

Education takes place in a complex system and needs methods matched to the challenges. We view education as a design science like architecture (Alexander, 1977) computer science (Simon, 1985; Moran and Carroll, 1996), manufacturing (Wright, 2001) and medicine. All these fields evidence creative innovations that succeed in complex settings.

This interactive session represents our attempts to capture the collective breakthroughs in our field and to enable researchers to benefit from the successes and failures of others. The initial impetus for this project came from a workshop on visualization and modeling at the CILT conference in the fall of 2000, where it was acknowledged that methods for communicating design knowledge between projects were inadequate. To progress as a design science, educational researchers need new ways to communicate and build on each others' work.

To pursue these goals we have formed a group including researchers from eight University projects and three commercial design companies. This group has since collaborated both online via email, and offline at CILT-sponsored workshops.

Project Methods

The first step in our process was to develop a rubric for identifying and presenting design principles. We quickly found that identifying 'principles' are not enough, because this information is usually too decontextualized to be useful. The current rubric calls for principles to be connected to one or more higher-level educational goals that they address, illustrated with one or more proven examples, and accompanied by designer's observations about tradeoffs, pitfalls, appropriate contexts of use, and evidence of effectiveness. We considered many variations on this structure, and refined the rubric with an iterative process of team discussion, obtaining feedback from colleagues, and attempting to analyze existing projects with draft versions of the principles. The goal was to have a rubric that 'felt right' for designers trying to articulate their principles, but was also useful to outsiders in understanding and applying principles to new projects. The current rubric is instantiated in an online database,.

With a fairly stable framework in place, we developed an online database, designated for the use of computer-based curricula designers. Since then, the task has been to aggregate and synthesize design principles from many different projects, and to feed them into this mutual design-principles online database. (**http://cilt.berkeley.edu:8080/design**

Framework for describing design principles

The database is built on a three level hierarchical framework with these three components:

Educational goals-- addressing a specific prl of the field. Each goal is related to one or more design principles.

Design principles-- the rational behind features in software. Each principle addresses one or more educational goals, and is illustrated by one or more features.

Software/curriculum features -- This includes attributes of features needed in order to make them communicative such as: Background and rationale, Illustration of the feature, Recommendations of how to use the feature, Use case scenarios, References & web links. A feature can exemplify one or more design principle.

This framework is illustrated in figure 1. One strength of the database lies in the "many-to-many" type of connections between the three hierarchical levels of the framework. These connections make it possible to search or browse the database from one of several starting points. For example, one could browse the database with a particular educational goal in mind, and find multiple related principles that other designers believe help address this goal, as well as tradeoffs and possible pitfalls of this design principle, and example software features where this design principle is implemented. Alternately, one could start the browsing with the database's principles, or the software features. Providing multiple access points will, we hope, accommodate different audiences (designers, researchers, educators) who will come to the database with different purposes (creating new designs, evaluation, customization etc.).

At CSCL 2002 we will present the framework and example principles, and then participants will join facilitated small groups to discuss the project. Small groups will feedback on the rubric or suggest new principles. The workshop will finish with presentation and discussion of small group work.

ACKNOWLEDGMENTS

We would like to thank the members of CILT, who provided frequent feedback at all stages of this project, and participants in previous design principles workshop, who contributed their ideas and experience to this effort.

REFERENCES

Alexander, C., Ishikawa, S., & Silverstein, M. (1977). A pattern language : towns, buildings, construction. New York: Oxford University Press.

Moran, T.P. and Carroll, J.M. (eds.) (1996) Design Rationale: Concepts, Techniques, and Use, Lawrence Erlbaum Associates, Mahwah, New Jersey.

Simon, H. A. (1985) The Sciences of the Artificial. MIT Press, 2nd edition.

Wright, P. (2001). 21st Century Manufcturing, Prentice Hall.

Figure 1: The structure of the database

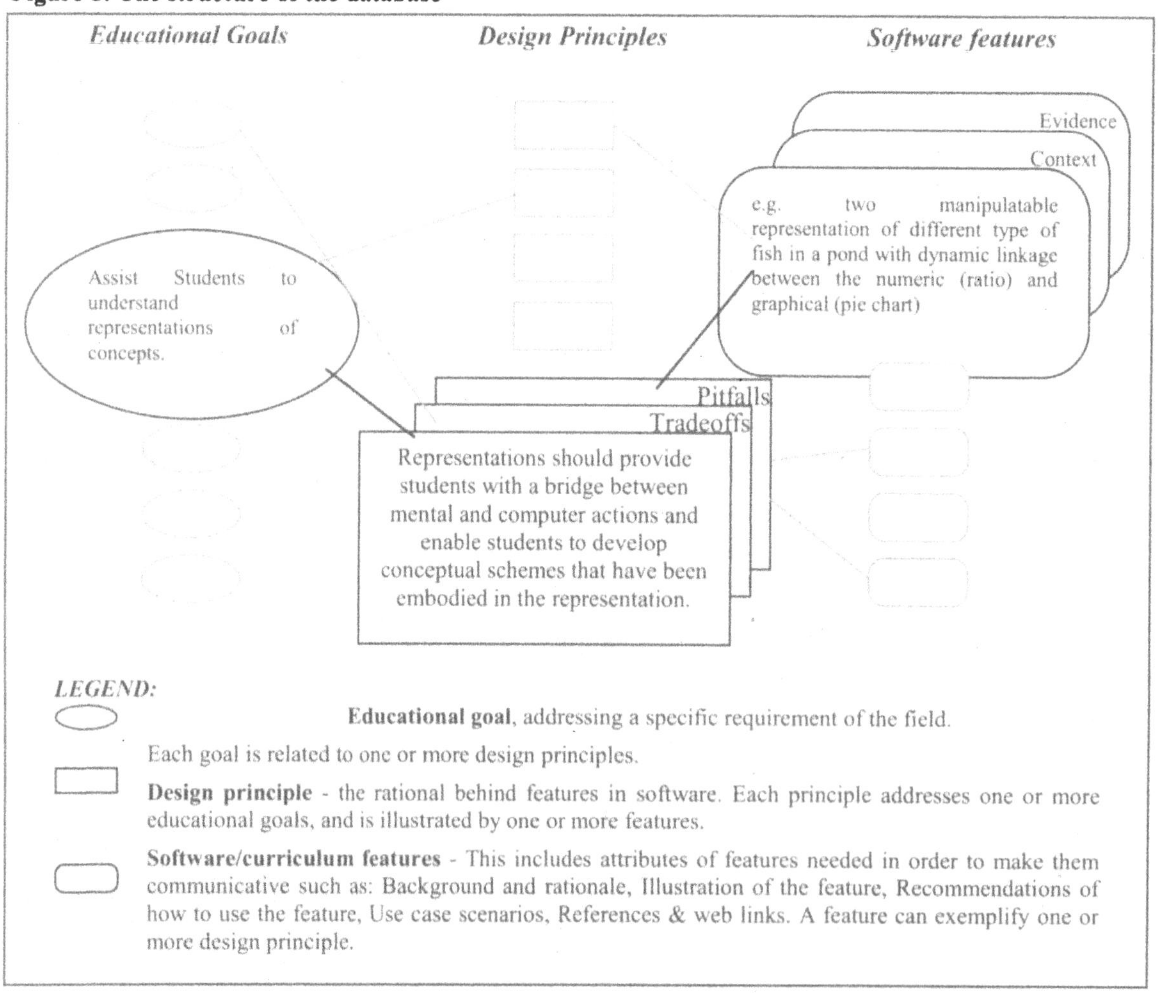

C. NEW MEDIA

Supporting Collaborative Design by Communities of Interest with the Envisionment and Discovery Collaboratory (EDC)

Ernesto Arias, Hal Eden, Vanessa Empinotti, Gerhard Fischer, Andrew Gorman, Shin'ichi Konomi, Eric Scharff

Center for LifeLong Learning & Design
College of Architecture and Planning (Arias, Empinotti)
University of Colorado

ABSTRACT

A major role of new media is not to deliver predigested information to individuals, but to provide the opportunity and resources for social debate, discussion, and the creation of new knowledge. In *collaborative design*, the knowledge to understand, frame, and resolve problems does not exist, but is constructed and evolved during the process, exploiting the power of "symmetry of ignorance" and "breakdowns." From this perspective, access to existing information and knowledge (often seen as the major advance of new media) is a very limiting concept.

To illustrate this theoretical approach towards collaborative learning, the participants in this interactive event will engage in collaborative design activities supported by the *Envisionment and Discovery Collaboratory (EDC)*. The EDC merges physical interaction, handheld devices, simulations, end-user modifiability, and evolving web spaces to support a) the integration of problem framing and problem solving, b) the creation of shared understanding articulated as externalizations, and c) computer-supported learning among stakeholders.

We will design the interactive event such that the participants will form a *community of interest* (defined by their collective concern with the resolution of a design problem) as they take on the roles of stakeholders from various communities of practice (such as city planners, transportation designers, and citizens). The event will illustrate the possibilities and limitations of the EDC for providing unique and innovative computer support for collaborative learning.

OBJECTIVE

Participants in this interactive experience will

- Learn about the challenges and opportunities faced by participants in collaborative design settings;
- Develop a deeper understanding of the nature of wicked design problems;
- Work with some of the technologies being developed to support collaboration and participation at L^3D;
- Experience the strengths and weaknesses of our approaches;
- Bring back insights from their participation to the overall conference discourse; and
- Have an opportunity to participate in our research by providing us with feedback.

DESCRIPTION

The EDC [Arias et al., 1999; Arias et al., 2000] is a unique, immersive environment that provides stakeholders new opportunities to engage in active knowledge construction supported by new techniques in human-computer interaction.. The EDC uses:

- physical interaction (using SmartBoard touch screens and PitA-Board [Eden, 2002] interfaces)
- handheld wireless devices (PDAs, QueryLens(1)),

(1) http://www.cs.colorado.edu/~L³D/clever/projects/querylens.html

simulations providing for end-user modifiability (built in substrates such as AgentSheets and Squeak), and

evolving web spaces (using DynaSites, LivingBook, and SPIDER) utilizing open source principles [Scharff, 2002].

This proposed interactive experience will engage all participants in playing the roles of various stakeholders (representing members of different communities who come together in a community of interest), using the EDC to explore, frame, and attempt to reach a resolution in the context of the following problem scenario.

> Colorado's rich history of mining has provided a colorful flavor to the development of the state, along with a legacy of environmental problems. The EPA has targeted mine sites near the towns of Vanessaville, Sharffeton, and Edensburg for cleanup. In working with residents to develop a viable approach to the environmental reclamation that is needed. However, they must address resident fears of increased tax burdens, the stigma that can accompany "Superfund" designation, potential depression of property values, and skepticism regarding the severity of the problems and their impacts. The perceptions of residents vary greatly depending upon their location (upstream, downstream, distance from watershed features)
>
> The planners face a difficult challenge in bringing together members of the community in a way that promotes civic discourse leading to a resolution of the challenges that are faced.

The participants will work together to resolve this community problem by constructing and modifying neighborhood model—placing and moving physical objects that represent objects such as houses, parks, schools, and bus stops. In doing so, they will engage in collaborative knowledge construction, creation of boundary objects for shared understanding, end-user modifiability of computational environments, and engage in innovative processes to construct new content.

We will conclude this interactive event with session at the conference site on Friday, in which the participants' experience with our interactive event can be brought back into the overall conference discourse. We will show videotape portions of the EDC interactive event to playback for the session attendees who did participate in the experience to ground the discussion, and will ask those who did participate to form an informal discussion panel on the challenges for learning and participation that the EDC is working to address.

REFERENCES

Arias, E. G., Eden, H., Fischer, G., Gorman, A., & Scharff, E. (1999) "Beyond Access: Informed Participation and Empowerment," Proceedings of the Computer Supported Collaborative Learning (CSCL '99) Conference, pp. 20-32.

Arias, E. G., Eden, H., Fischer, G., Gorman, A., & Scharff, E. (2000) "Transcending the Individual Human Mind—Creating Shared Understanding through Collaborative Design," ACM Transactions on Computer Human-Interaction, 7(1), pp. 84-113.

Eden, H. (2002) "Getting in on the (Inter)Action: Exploring Affordances for Collaborative Learning in a Context of Informed Participation," In Proceedings of CSCL '02 Conference on Computer Supported Collaborative Work.

Scharff, E. D. (2002) "Applying Open Source Principles to Collaborative Learning Environments," In Proceedings of CSCL '01 Conference on Computer Supported Collaborative Learning, pp. (elsewhere in this publication).

Modelling and Supporting Learning Activities in a Computer-integrated Classroom

Andreas Lingnau, Ulrich Hoppe

University of Duisburg, Germany

{lingnau,hoppe}@informatik.uni-duisburg.de

ABSTRACT

We have implemented ubiquitous computing technology in a primary school setting to support rich classroom activities particularly in the field of early literacy. After initial tests have corroborated the benefit of this technology with respect to attaining curricular goals and to better supporting learner-centred classroom methodologies, we are now exploring specific intelligent support mechanisms, e.g., to inform participants - both teachers and pupils - about automatically assessed learning opportunities.

Keywords

Early learning, literacy, intelligent support, collaborative learning analysis, ubiquitous computing

INTRODUCTION

Computer supported collaborative learning is often identified with "virtual learning" in distance scenarios. In contrast to this, we have pursued the idea of enriching face-to-face classroom situations with embedded computing technologies. The technological approach was deliberately subordinated to grown curricular goals and pedagogical traditions. Recently, we have been able to demonstrate the benefits of such "computer integrated classrooms" in a specific learning domain (Tewissen et al., 2001). In this paper, we elaborate how specific forms of online support can be generated in computerised classroom environments. The classroom as such is a collaborative scenario with different roles (e.g., teachers, learners, peer helpers) and resources (network, archives, software tools, physical devices). In our view, automatic support functions are not meant to guide and control classroom learning processes globally but to locally enrich the situation, e.g., by informing participants about learning opportunities and affordances.

Within the European NIMIS project ("Networked Interactive Media in Schools", cf. NIMIS, 1998), computer integrated classrooms have been set up in associated primary schools. Both hardware selection and software design have been orientated towards the special needs of early learners. The classroom design was based on principles of "ubiquitous computing" (Weiser, 1991) (Fig. 1). To give the pupils easy access to our computing facilities a special JAVA based software has been developed which replaces the Windows desktop. As a standard mode the desktop supports partner work by allowing two children to be logged in at a time at one workplace.

Fig. 1 The NIMIS classroom in Duisburg

The concept of a "computer integrated classroom" (CiC) is essentially targeted at fostering collaboration between pupils. In Duisburg, the focus was set on the process of learning how to read and write. Adapting a new method called "Lesen durch Schreiben" (Engl.: Reading Through Writing, RTW) which was originally introduced in Switzerland (Reichen, 1991) the application T^3 ("Today's Talking Typewriter") has been developed. It is a phonetics based approach for teaching reading and writing. Pupils get access to the complete range of phonemes in the form of a palette with letters from the very beginning. Thus children are able to write words by combining letters from a "phoneme table", even though they are not yet able to read. In abstract terms RTW inverts the usual sequencing of the analytic task of de-coding (reading) and synthetic task of encoding (writing). T^3 is designed for usage with pen based interactive screens and behaves similar to the known procedure with pencil and paper in the normal classroom. (Fig. 2, cf. Tewissen et al., 2000).

INTELLIGENT SUPPORT

T^3 is enhanced to provide two different kinds of intelligent support, using the *Support Agent Architecture* developed by Prada et al. (2000). It facilitates intelligent agents which are not explicitly visualised but functionally embedded in the T^3 workspace.

Fig. 2 Phonetic writing with T^3

Phonetic diagnosis

To provide automatic support for the children's' phonetic writing it is important that target words are known by the system. (In phonetic writing, it is practically impossible to infer a target word from only two or three starting letters.) If a target word is known, a phonetic diagnosis can be performed by comparison which allows for sophisticated forms of intelligent feedback. T^3 provides a pre-selection of target words on so called "theme pages". The phonetic comparison between the target word and the writing product of the child is done by an algorithm that is based on a phonetic classification. It detects incorrect substitutions, missing and "wrong" phonemes.

Writing Support

There are two different intelligent agents in T^3. Both use the phonetic diagnostic algorithm. The first agent provides an embedded, "implicit" feedback during the writing process. Depending on the learning phase, the writing agent will first only analyse phonemes which are clearly pronounced and later also those which are not emphasised. The agent gives hints by "moving" the letters in the workspace to form a gap at the position where a phoneme is missing.

The second kind of support offers a selection of "peer experts" to those children who have problems detecting correct phonemes in a target word. The phonetic diagnosis determines the correctness values from the content of the workspace. If the score of the writing result exceeds a predefined limit the information is stored in a database. From this database, peer helpers will be selected according to their specific strengths. The mediation of peer helper is based on the methodology of "multiple student modelling" (Hoppe, 1995). The offer of peer helpers stimulates collaboration, which can take place outside the system in the classroom (by natural face-to-face communication) as well as inside the system in a special collaborative mode of T^3.

PERSPECTIVES

The intelligent support will be evaluated and improved in close cooperation with teachers. The indicators for the different stages of writing skills will be tested and checked against the teachers' expectations and observations in the classroom. A specific challenge lies in determining the point in time when learners start to read. This is particularly difficult since the overt actions in the system are only writing actions.

ACKNOWLEDGMENTS

Parts of this work has been funded by the European Esprit project No. 29301, "NIMIS". We thank our NIMIS partners and especially the teachers and pupils of the associated schools for their participation and creative input.

REFERENCES

Hoppe, H.U. (1995). Using multiple student modeling to parameterize group learning. In *Proc. of AI-ED '95*, 234-241, Washington D.C., August 1995: AACE.

Prada, R., Machado, I. & Paiva, A. (2000) TEATRIX: Virtual Environment for Story Creation. In *Proc. of ITS 2000*, 464-473, Montreal, June 2000: Springer.

Reichen, J. (1991). *Lesen durch Schreiben.* ("Reading through Writing"). Zürich, Switzerland: Sabe

Tewissen, F., Lingnau, A. & Hoppe, H.U. (2000). "Today's Talking Typewriter" Supporting Early Literacy in a Classroom Environment. In *Proc. of ITS 2000*, 252-261, Montreal, June 2000: Springer.

Tewissen, F., Hoppe, H.U., Lingnau, A., Mannhaupt, G., Nischk, D. (2001). Collaborative Writing in a Computer-integrated Classroom for Early Learning. In *Proc. of E-CSCL 2001*, Maastricht, Netherlands, March 2001.

Weiser, M. (1991). The computer for the 21st century. *Scientific American* 9/91, 66-75.

3D Multi-user Virtual Worlds for Education: Knowledge Building in the Vlearn3D.org Community

Margaret Corbit

Cornell Theory Center
corbitm@tc.cornell.edu *contact

Bonnie DeVarco

MEDIA TERTIA
devarco@cruzio.com

ABSTRACT

This Interactive Event features a selection of projects of members of the Vlearn3D Community, a group that is focused on early development and research surrounding the use of multi-user virtual worlds for education. Participants will meet developers and users of the wide variety of worlds in the Activeworlds Educational Universe (AWEDU) and will become acquainted with projects under development in such environments as Adobe Atmosphere. The Activeworlds platform is a modular 3D environment in which all content is developed online in realtime. This facilitates distributed group collaboration across geographical distances. Projects will demonstrate various ways that bridges are being built between age groups, languages and cultures in educational virtual worlds. All projects will show how the collaborative construction of social artifacts, peer-to-peer activities and knowledge building define the learning experience. We will tour art, science, language learning, and information science worlds and meet some of their inhabitants (embodied and visible to each other as "avatars"). The program will combine a projected presentation, an overview of the technology and introduction to the projects, with the opportunity to interact with the worlds and their developers on their own through a bank of desktops.

Keywords

Constructivism, desktop 3D, avatars, Virtual worlds, collaborative virtual environments, knowledge building, knowledge networks, knowledge space

EVENT DESCRIPTION

This event will begin with an introduction to the people and projects that will be featured through a series of web pages with screenshots and photographs of distributed participants. A short hands-on tour through the navigation interface of 3D virtual worlds will follow. Tours and demonstrations will include an interactive science fair exhibit created by teens with support from online mentors, an immersive 3D interactive painting, a garden that grows in response to use of a digital library, and a visit with a group of college bound high school students in their mentoring/counseling worlds.

The defining feature of a modular 3D environment is its combination of social space scaled to the user, geospatial referents for navigation and multiple media that can create and foster a social setting that has both permanence and flexibility. All objects can be linked to web pages or media or have a sequence of actions or interactivity added to them through automated scripts. When a world is constructed, it can continually grow through a large base of users/builders. Since it is built in realtime, building activities are, by nature, collaborative.

Specific CSCL theories are being implemented and explored in a variety of ways using the synchronous collaboration and visualization tools available in virtual worlds or in conjunction with asynchronous communication tools such as the Web Knowledge Forum [Bereiter]. A virtual world provides a social environment in cyberspace where groups can grow together for a common purpose in an educational setting. Some worlds such as the *Virtual High School* look like realistic classrooms displaying examples of peer-to-peer, constructivist exercises such as a student-built chemistry "webquest" or a theme-based gallery. [VHS Scenarios] The *City Theme* project [Svensson] supports language learning by allowing students to represent linguistic concepts through the collaborative building of "cultural artifacts" in 3D. These student-built "cities" interrelate to and embody the conceptual frameworks presented in their 2D web pages and are excellent examples of collaborative knowledge building. [Stahl] Likewise, the *Tomato Islands* in Cornell Theory Center's SciFair world represent the collaborative learning experience of building teams.

Other projects such as *Euroland* demonstrate how the shared building of an environment can provide opportunities for "active knowledge building" and visualization by allowing students to design, implement, perform and evaluate their environment collaboratively [Ligorio]. Informal science learning worlds such as Cornell Theory Center's *SciCenter* demonstrate how the scale and interactivity of 3D objects used to teach basic concepts in genetics can increase students' understanding of abstract concepts and offer opportunities for group problem-solving [Corbit, M., DeVarco, B; Maher,

Corbit]. Other worlds such as Borderlink's *LinkWorld* and UC Santa Cruz's *EcollegE* provide opportunities for peer to peer support that allows college bound students to receive tutoring, counseling and orientation activities with each other and with university students in virtual high school and university settings. With geographic, architectural and cultural verisimilitude, these orientation worlds become social environments that support the zone of proximal development where collaborations with participants who are more skilled are needed and make opportunities for this mentoring available beyond geographic boundaries. [Cole, M., Wertsch J.]

Finally, because a cluster of virtual worlds can reside in an interconnected educational "universe," information sharing and knowledge networking [Dede] can occur through a growing global "community of practice." [Schlager, et.al.] This network participates in regular roundtables and events as well as an annual online conference in cyberspace [DeVarco, Corbit]. These activities take place in the same medium as the projects themselves. Through this workshop we hope to provide CSCL participants with a wide-ranging introduction to virtual 3D environments and the varied ways in which they are currently being used for distributed collaborative learning.

REFERENCES

Bareiter, C. 2001. "Knowledge Forum, a Second Generation CSILE Product – Testing and Research Results" http://www.learn.motion.com/Research.html

Cole, Michael, Wertsch, James. "Beyond the Individual-Social Antimony in Discussions of Piaget and Vygotsky" http://www.massey.ac.nz/~ALock/virtual/colevyg.htm

Corbit, M. & B. DeVarco. 2000 "SciCentr and BioLearn: Two 3D Implementations of CVE Science Museums." *Proceedings of the Third International Conference on Collaborative Virtual Environments, CVE 2000.* http://www.acm.org/pubs/citations/proceedings/chi/351006/p65-corbit/

Dede, Chris. 1999. "The Role of Emerging Technologies for Knowledge Mobilization, Dissemination, and Use in Education." Commissioned by the Office of Educational Research and Improvement, U.S. Dept. of Education. http://www.virtual.gmu.edu/SS_research/cdpapers/mobilpdf.htm

DeVarco, B., Corbit, M. 2001. M. *Vlearn3D 2000 - Live3D, Learn3D Conference Transcripts and Screenshots.* http://www.vlearn3d.org/conference/proceedings.html

Maher, Christopher, Corbit, Margaret. 2001. "Creating Genetic Applications for Informal Science Learning in Multi-User Virtual Environments or Virtual Worlds." http://www.people.cornell.edu/pages/cam46/weticedraft5.htm

Ligorio M.B., Trimpe J.D 2000. "Euroland: Active Knowledge Building Through Different Formats of Mediated Communication" Dept. Of Educational Psychology Katholieke University of Nijmegen (NL) http://pluk.wau.nl/Euroland/SharedFolder/Communication_Formats.doc

Schlager, M., Fusco, J., Schank, P. 1998. "Cornerstones for an On-line Community of Education." Stanford Research Institute. http://www.tappedin.org/info/papers/ieee.html

Stahl, Gerry. 1999. "Perspectives on Collaborative Knowledge-building Environments: Toward a Cognitive Theory of Computer Support for Learning" Position Paper, *Computer-Supported Collaborative Argumentation for Learning Communities*, CSCL'99 Workshop, 11th-12th Dec., 1999, Stanford University. http://d3e.open.ac.uk/cscl99/Stahl/Stahl-01.html

Svennson, Patrik. 2001. *The City Theme – Virtual Weddings Project 2001.* http://www.eng.umu.se/city/

VHS: Learning Scenarios in the Virtual High School. University of California, Santa Cruz. http://www.vhs.ucsc.edu/vhs/storyboard.htm

C-VISions: Socialized Learning through Collaborative, Virtual, Interactive Simulations

Yam San Chee, Chit Meng Hooi

School of Computing, National University of Singapore

cheeys@comp.nus.edu.sg

ABSTRACT

Today's cheaper personal computers with improved computational power have made the technology of networked desktop virtual reality environments accessible to typical end users, including students. This paper describes C–VISions, a collaborative virtual environment developed to support interactive and collaborative learning using virtual simulations. The research effort is grounded on the principles of active, experiential learning and constructivist/social constructivist ideas, with their attendant commitment to group sense making, discourse-based learning, and community building processes. The paper also provides an overview of the system's design and implementation. Finally, we explain the current status of the research effort and articulate plans for future work.

Keywords

Networked virtual environments, desktop virtual reality, collaborative learning, interactive simulations, experiential learning, constructivism

INTRODUCTION AND MOTIVATION

Educators and educational technologists often harbor visions of how computing technology might be leveraged upon to powerfully engage student learning. In practice, these visions are usually tempered by constraints related to the computational power of the hardware required and the cost of technology. Fortunately, rapidly increasing levels of hardware performance accompanied by falling costs has meant that students today have ready access to much more powerful personal computers than in the recent past. This development provides an opportunity for educators to push the technology envelope in pursuit of their vision.

One particular technology that is receiving greater attention in education is that of networked virtual environments (Singhal & Zyda, 1999). Such environments make prominent use of two system technologies: virtual reality and networking. While virtual reality (VR) technology has been available for many years, its application to the domain of education has been a specialist field limited to researchers with the resources to develop fully immersive VR applications. The rise of the Internet, however, has given rise to a new genre of distributed environments for chatting and socialization that include a desktop VR component, allowing users to share a three-dimensional (3D) virtual space. In this space, users are represented as avatars. They can navigate within the 3D worlds and interact with other users as well as virtual objects in the worlds albeit in fairly limited ways. Some of the most well-known systems of this type include *Active Worlds*, *blaxxun*, and *Community Place*. Damer (1998) provides a comprehensive, albeit somewhat dated, review of such virtual environments.

The goal of the C–VISions project is to harness networked desktop virtual reality technology to create a powerful and engaging collaborative environment for student learning. This technology was chosen because it is capable of supporting several important learning objectives. These objectives include experiential learning, simulation-based learning, inquiry-based learning, guided exploratory learning, collaborative learning, and socialized, community-based learning. The C–VISions environment seeks to foster these kinds of learning in the domain of science education, including physics, chemistry, and biology. We have chosen to focus on the desktop variant of virtual reality because it is readily accessible today. At the same time, it avoids the potential difficulty of motion sickness induced by the fully immersive virtual reality variant.

RESEARCH BACKGROUND

As stated by Normand (1999), "the essence of collaborative virtual environments (CVEs) is the use of natural spatial metaphors, together with the integration of participants and data within the same and common spatial frame of reference" (p. 218). The most established, well-known, and successful research work involving VR for general education (as opposed to medical education) can be traced to the Human Interface Technology (HIT) Lab at the University of Washington, Seattle, and to *Project ScienceSpace* at George Mason University. Both these research efforts, however, are based on fully immersive VR that makes use of head-mounted displays and data gloves. At both locations, the technology has been deployed mostly in a stand-alone, non-collaborative learning mode. A less well-known example of the use of educational VR is Virtual Explorer from the University of California, San Diego, where the researchers have created an immersive, highly interactive environment for learning human immunology (Dean et al., 2000).

Findings from the HIT Lab suggest that students engaged in a virtual world learning environment found it fascinating and enjoyable. They were highly motivated to learn the concepts and skills necessary to design and model objects, with their associated behaviors, so that they could build their own virtual environments (Bricken & Byrne, 1993). A study by Winn et al (1999) also suggests that building a virtual environment improved low-ability students' understanding of the virtual environment content; however, it had no effect on high-ability students. Unlike the focus of allowing students to build their own virtual environments adopted at the HIT Lab, much of the effort at *Project ScienceSpace* focuses on using immersive VR to convey abstract scientific concepts and to aid complex conceptual learning (Salzman, Dede, Loftin, & Chen, 1999). *ScienceSpace* represents a systematic program of research that deals with physics. Three multisensory learning environments have been created: *NewtonWorld*, dealing with Newton's laws and the laws of conservation, *MaxwellWorld*, dealing with electrostatics, and *PaulingWorld*, dealing with molecular representations and quantum-molecular bonding. These science learning environments are unique in that they were designed explicitly to allow students to "enter into" the world of the phenomenon being studied, namely, the conservation of momentum, electric fields and potentials, and ionic versus covalent bonding. In this regard, the researchers have employed the technology in a sophisticated manner to allow students to experience phenomena that cannot otherwise be experienced in the real world.

Research that employs desktop VR for education and learning is more scattered and less established. One example is DEVRL, Distributed Extensible Virtual Reality Laboratory, a joint research project between Lancaster University, Nottingham University, and University College London. The objective of this project, which has probably ended, was to build a shared virtual physics laboratory. This work is not well reported. In contrast, a better publicized related research effort that also involves the three mentioned British universities is the COVEN (COllaborative Virtual ENvironments) project (Frécon, Smith, Steed, Stenius, & Ståhl, 2001; Normand, 1999). Unlike DEVRL, however, the COVEN research effort has a technology focus and is not oriented to applications for learning. Like DEVRL, it makes use of the DIVE toolkit as its development base.

Empirical evaluation of learning using desktop VR is still in its infancy. A weak example can be found in Mills & de Araújo (1999). In this example, the researchers sought to compare a desktop VR group and a non-VR group on the effectiveness of learning a management technique. They employed desktop VR in a stand-alone mode and hoped to exploit visualization capabilities afforded by the technology. Their study found no statistically significant difference between the two groups. Viewed critically, however, the researchers made poor use of the technology, and the study was poorly conceived and operationalized. It should be evident, therefore, that the field of desktop VR in education and learning remains open and requires focused and systematic research.

TECHNOLOGY ASPECTS

When using desktop VR, the most prominent aspects of technology experienced are the 3D virtual world browser and the interaction style for interacting with the system. While 3D representation techniques and difficulties are fairly well understood from a computer science viewpoint, the design of an interaction style for 3D worlds still requires considerable research. In general, there are three types of interaction task that need to be supported: navigation, selection/manipulation, and system control (Bowman, Kruijff, LaViola, & Poupyrev, 2001). The design of an effective 3D interaction style will depend greatly on the domain in which the technology is applied and on the kinds of task that must be supported.

The introduction of networking technology to desktop VR allows the virtual worlds to be shared. Many technical hurdles must be overcome to implement a networked virtual environment successfully. Achievement of this goal, however, creates an environment where users can experience a shared sense of space, a shared sense of presence, a shared sense of time, a way to communicate, and a way to share objects and experiences (Singhal & Zyda, 1999).

There are other critical, but less apparent technology components at work in a networked virtual environment. A database is needed to support the persistence of object states in virtual worlds. Implementation of the technology also raises difficult issues relating to realtime, multi-user processing, the maintenance of world consistency across multiple client computers, the handling of concurrent events, and the design of a system architecture that will readily support scaling to a large number of concurrent users. In addition, the incorporation of audio communication and video streaming provide desirable, more advanced features that require implementation of realtime media streaming.

PEDAGOGICAL BASIS

The design of C–VISions is rooted firmly on active, experiential learning (see, for example, Dewey, 1916/1980) and constructivist/social constructivist principles (see, for example, Fosnot, 1996). Boethel and Dimock (1999) provide an excellent critical review of how technology can be used to support knowledge construction. According to Doolittle (1999), the basic epistemological tenets of constructivism are:

- Knowledge is not passively accumulated; rather it is the result of active cognizing by the individual.
- Cognition is an adaptive process that functions to make an individual's behavior more viable given a particular environment.

- Cognition organizes and makes sense of one's experience; it is not a process to render an accurate representation of reality.
- Knowing has roots in both biological/neurological construction and social, cultural, and language based interactions.

In light of the above, the technology of VR is leveraged upon to instantiate active, experiential learning. We provide an environment where students can engage in focused science inquiry by running simulations, asking "what if?" questions, changing simulation parameters, and observing simulation outcomes. As Winn (1993) persuasively argues, immersive VR technology is especially empowering for learning because it supports a direct, first-person experience of learning. This argument holds true also for desktop VR environments despite a weakening of the multisensory dimension of experience.

Shared experiences that revolve around shared objects in a virtual world (for example, a rolling billiard ball or a streamed video clip) create a natural and authentic context for a discourse-based learning community. The context motivates students to articulate their ideas and understandings to one another, thus fostering an environment for peer-assisted learning and reciprocal tutoring. In C–VISions, both text-based chat and audio-based chat are supported to support discourse-based learning.

As researchers, we recognize the importance of helping students to make the transition from first-person, experiential learning to third-person, symbolic learning. To this end, C–VISions includes a set of collaboration tools comprising a shared electronic whiteboard and a shared mind-map editor. The shared whiteboard allows students to express and represent their ideas in symbolic as well as graphical terms. We also recognize the need to support abstraction and critical reflection. The shared mind-map editor serves this purpose. In addition, the C–VISions virtual world browser includes a visualization tool that allows students to call up graph plots of interesting phenomena on demand. Our intention and hope is that the supporting tool set will facilitate the needed transition from experience to mentation.

The Experiential Learning Cycle proposed by Kolb (1984) summarizes what we hope to achieve fairly well (see Figure 1). Active experimentation yields concrete experience that provides the basis for reflective observation which eventually leads to abstract conceptualization, and the cycle iterates. In the process, students' understandings are transformed both extensionally and intensionally while comprehension is grounded in apprehension.

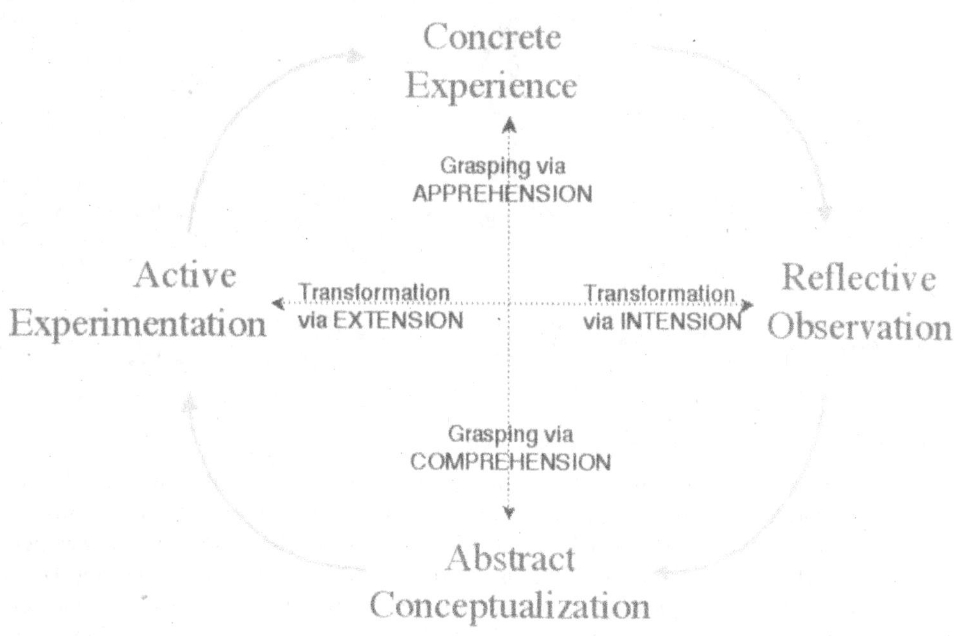

Figure 1. Kolb's Experiential Learning Cycle

Other authors have also highlighted the special advantages that can accrue from using VR for learning. Foreman (1999) values the sophisticated programmability of simulated objects and the simultaneous telepresence and collaboration of geo-distributed learners. He draws attention to three important features. First, avatar worlds are suited to developing actionable knowledge as opposed to knowledge for knowledge's sake. Second, avatar environments are leveraged effectively when they support learner-centered team work. Third, avatar worlds endowed with diverse learning resources support a discovery approach to education. The learning resources may include audio and video on demand, archives of images and schematics, conventional texts, search tools, objects that can be manipulated and queried, and programmed bots. Bricken (1990) extols the use of the computer as a reality generator, allowing the user to become a participant in the computational space where students are involved in activities that require explanation and extrapolation. Constant virtual world feedback provides a continual validation of understanding in a very personalized form of learning. The technology is able to create a superset of reality and to allow students to learn through what-if scenarios. It provides a natural interface semantics, allowing students to act out their ideas rather than saying them. Students can also be empowered to participate in virtual world construction.

THE C-VISIONS ENVIRONMENT

In this section, we provide a description of the C–VISions system in its current state of development. We use the description of one particular simulation world to highlight key features of the environment. We also explain the basic system design and implementation.

System Description

The C–VISions learning environment is modeled as an interconnected virtual environment consisting of four levels. Level 3 is designated the Social World (see Figure 2). The Social World is a general community location for users to mingle and chat. Users are placed in this world when they first log in to the system.

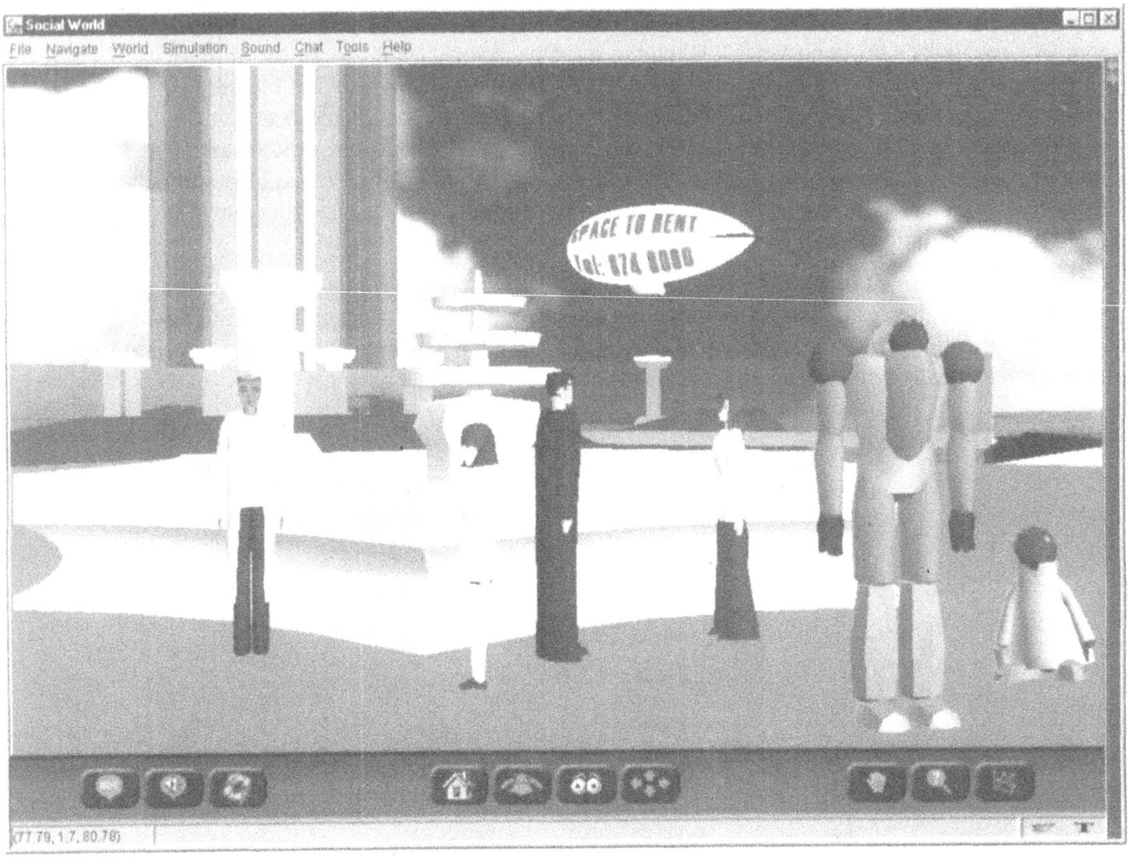

Figure 2. C–VISions Social World

C–VISions focuses on supporting science learning. Level 1 of the environment, located below (virtual) ground level is the Chemistry World; level 2, ground level, is the Biology World. Level 4 houses the Physics World. At present, the chemistry and biology worlds are virtual worlds that contain no learning simulations. We have, however, developed three learning simulations in the Physics World. These are the Battleships World, the Vacuum Chamber, and the Billiard World. We chose to focus initially on the domain of physics because it is well known that students' understandings of physics phenomena are replete with misconceptions derived from real-world experience and intuition (see, for example, McCloskey, 1983).

The top-right corner of the virtual world browser shows two arrows pointing in opposite directions. These arrows are used to call up and to put away a separate display pane that contains information related to the world the user is currently in. This information is particularly useful for orienting students to the context and purpose of the learning simulation objects that they are interacting with. It also provides them with useful tips for interacting with the simulation and some science concepts for exploratory learning. Figure 3 illustrates the extended information pane of the Vacuum Chamber. The lips icon and the "T" (for Text) icon below the tool bar allow users to turn on/off system messages in (synthetic) voice mode and in text mode. Text mode messages are displayed in the horizontal strip to the immediate left of these icons.

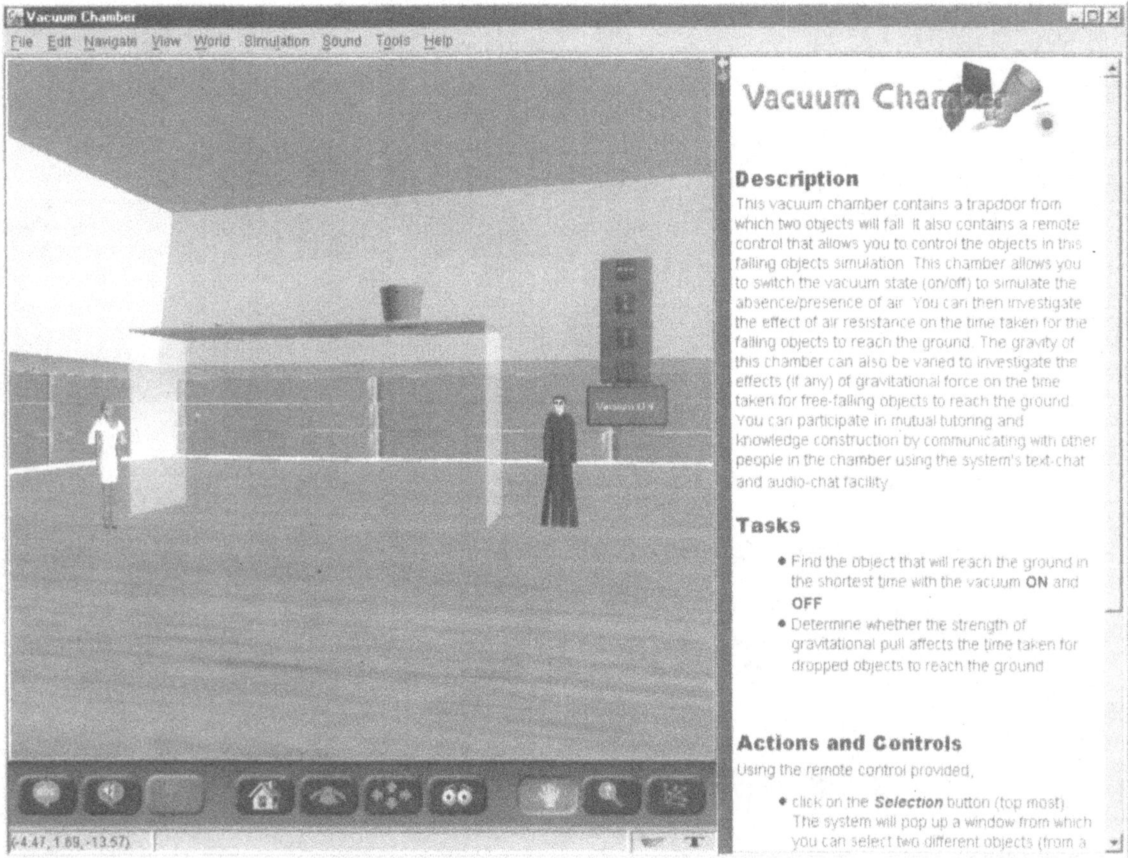

Figure 3. Vacuum Chamber information pane

Example World: Billiard World

The Billiard World is shown in Figure 4. It contains a billiard table with two balls and a cue stick for striking the balls. In the Billiard World simulation, students can learn about mass, velocity, acceleration, conservation of momentum, friction, and the coefficient of restitution.

Navigation and change of viewpoint

The four buttons in the middle section of the tool bar at the bottom of the virtual world browser denote *Home*, *Navigate*, *Strafe*, and *Look* respectively. The *Home* button allows users to reset the view to a default viewpoint. The *Navigate* button allows users to move forward and backward and to turn left and right. The *Strafe* button allows users to move left, right, up, and down in a vertical plane. The *Look* button allows users to change their viewpoint—left, right, up, and down. The interaction style we have defined for the use of these buttons is click-and-drag. Several alternative interaction styles are possible. We plan to investigate the alternatives systematically at a later date, to identify which style is easiest to learn and which style is most efficient to use. Together, these four buttons allow users to alter their viewpoint and to navigate within the virtual environment. Collision detection has been implemented. Users can deactivate this feature, if they wish, from the Edit menu. To teleport from one environment to another, users can either navigate to the lifts located in the central lift shaft that connects the four levels of the virtual environment, or they can teleport via the *Navigate* menu in the system's menu bar.

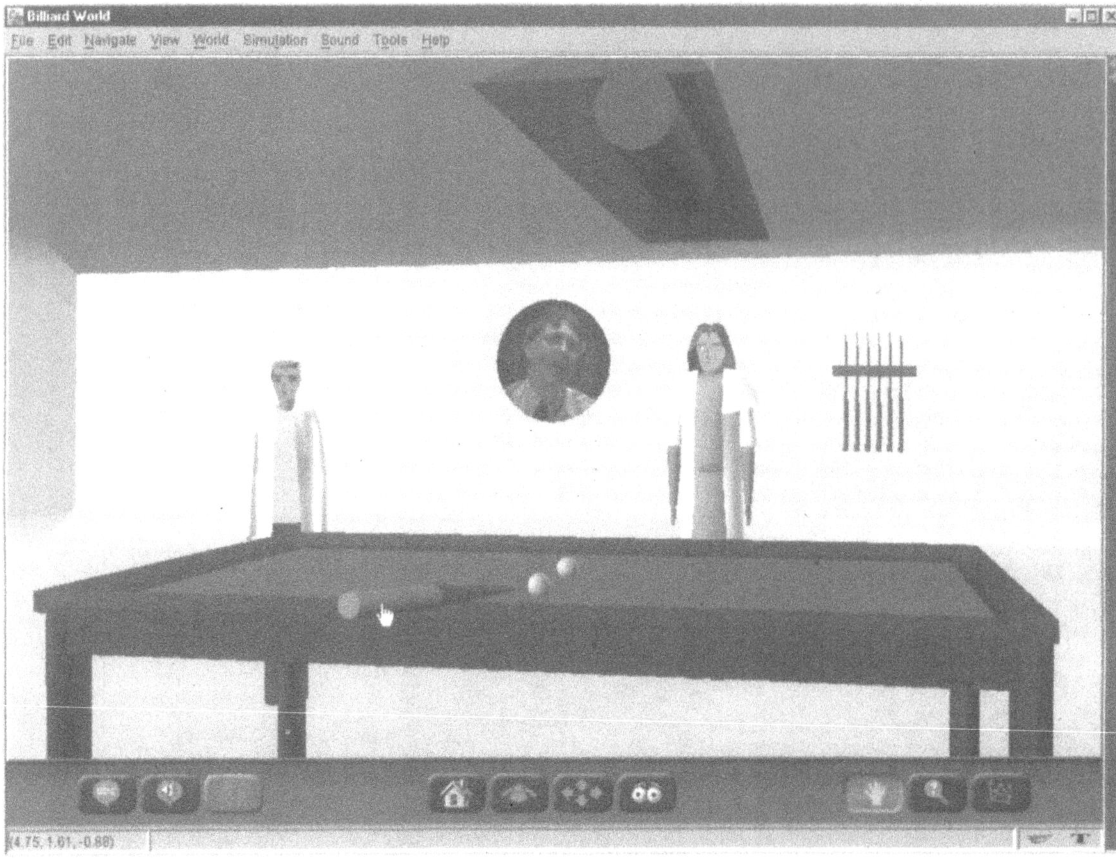

Figure 4. C–VISions Billiard World

Object manipulation and interaction

Objects that can be manipulated in the virtual world are known as "live" objects. To enter object manipulation mode, users select the *Hand* icon (the highlighted icon in Figure 4). As users move the mouse cursor over the virtual world browser in this mode, the cursor icon changes to something semantically meaningful when the cursor is positioned over a "live" object. We refer to these cursor icons as "hot" icons because they provide feedback to users that some action can be immediately executed on the object over which the cursor is positioned. In Figure 4, for example, the cursor icon showing the hand with the pointing finger indicates that the cue stick can be used to strike the billiard ball at which the cue stick has been aimed. The highlighted rear half of the cue stick serves as a reinforcement of feedback that the stick can be thrust forward to hit the billiard ball at which it is aimed. Certain interactions with objects are more difficult to design than others because they require a set of sequential, discreet steps. Using the cue stick to strike the billiard ball is such an example. Users must first select the cue stick to indicate that it is the object that they wish to interact with (initially). The cue stick must then be aimed at the billiard ball the user intends to strike so that a coupling between the cue stick and the target billiard ball can be established. Finally, (the system state shown in Figure 4), the user must select the rear end of the cue stick and thrust it forward to strike the target billiard ball. Research on the design of 3D user interaction styles in desktop virtual worlds is in its infancy as suggested by Bowman et al (2001). This is an avenue of research that we intend to pursue.

Object inspection and editing

C–VISions has been designed and implemented to allow users to inspect the properties of critical simulation objects in realtime and to modify the property values on the fly. This functionality is activated by selecting the *Inspect* button, denoted by the magnifying glass icon. (This feature is not illustrated due to lack of space.) Selection of the Editor tab foregrounds the pane that allows editable values to be changed. This functionality allows users to modify the value(s) of critical object properties, re-run the simulation, and observe the changes.

Event visualization

C–VISions provides an event visualization function that allows students to replay the most recent simulation event and to view the plotting of graphs of that event in a synchronized fashion. This function is evoked by clicking on the *Visualization* button on the bottom right of the task bar. Figure 5 illustrates how the most recent event can be reenacted in the mini world browser on the left. As the billiard balls move as a result of one ball being initially struck by the cue stick, the graphs on the right hand side unfold. The figure shows a plot of distance traversed relative to time. Other graphs showing plots of horizontal and vertical speed and acceleration can be selected from the pull-down menu shown. The design intention is to allow students to inter-relate and make sense of the different graph plots. It creates the context for inquiry and discourse-based learning about the phenomena of mass, velocity, acceleration, friction, and the conservation of momentum and helps to reify these abstract concepts. The provision of this tool is consistent with Bowman et al's (1999) advocacy of an "information-rich" virtual environment.

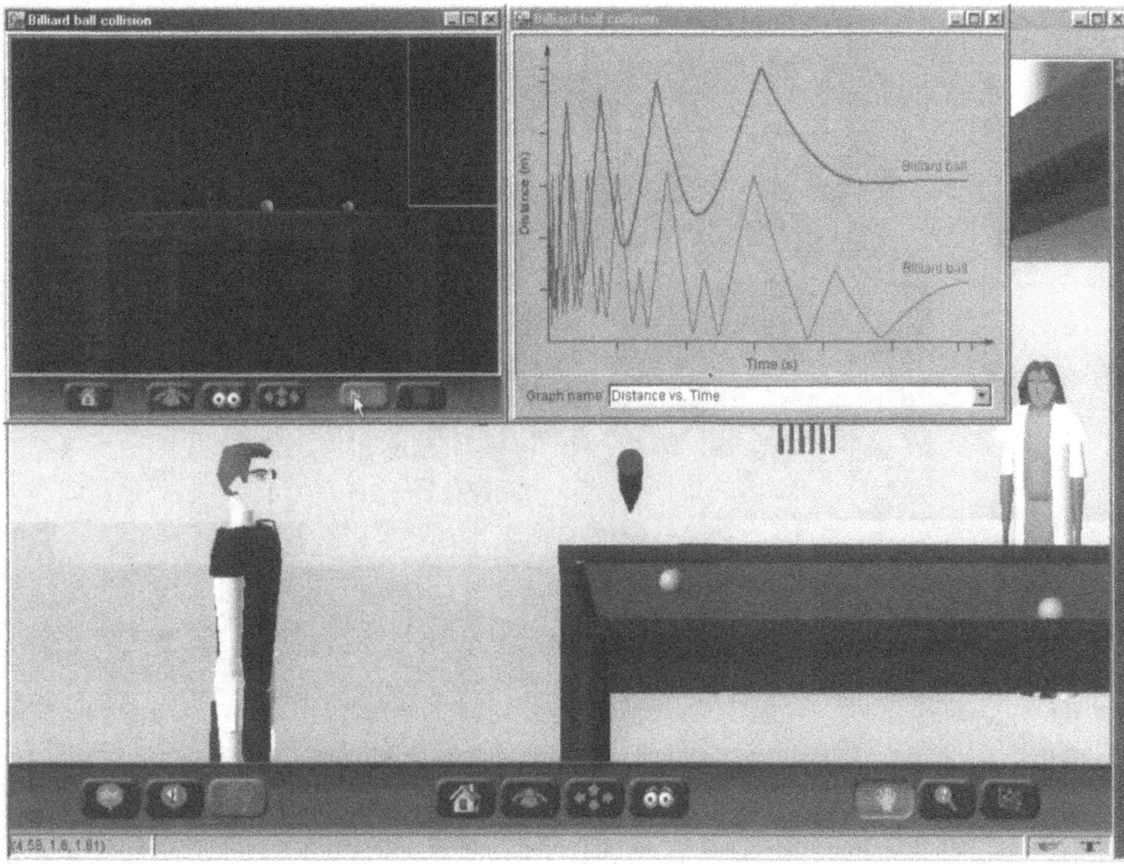

Figure 5. Event visualization in C–VISions

Realtime video streaming

C–VISions allows students to share video resources with other students located in the same virtual world. To do so, students simply drag the movie file from the computer desktop onto a virtual screen in the virtual world. The video is then streamed to all computers and played concurrently in the browser of all students in the same world. This functionality allows video material to be used as a shared referent for sense making dialog. Of course, it can also be used for the purpose of entertainment in the Social World. Figure 6 illustrates the operation of realtime video streaming. Control buttons on the posts of the virtual screen allow the initiator of the streamed video to terminate and to replay the video.

Communication

C–VISions supports student-to-student communication via text chat as well as audio chat. These functions are activated by the two buttons on the extreme left of the tool bar (see Figure 6). As suggested by Riva (1999), virtual reality is not only an environment for first-person experience, it is also a communication environment. The communication tools provided here are vital for discourse-based collaborative learning.

Collaboration tools

Finally, C–VISions also incorporates collaboration tools to support higher level representation and organization of ideas. This function is activated by the third button, from the left, in the tool bar. The collaboration tools provided are a shared electronic whiteboard and a shared mind map editor.

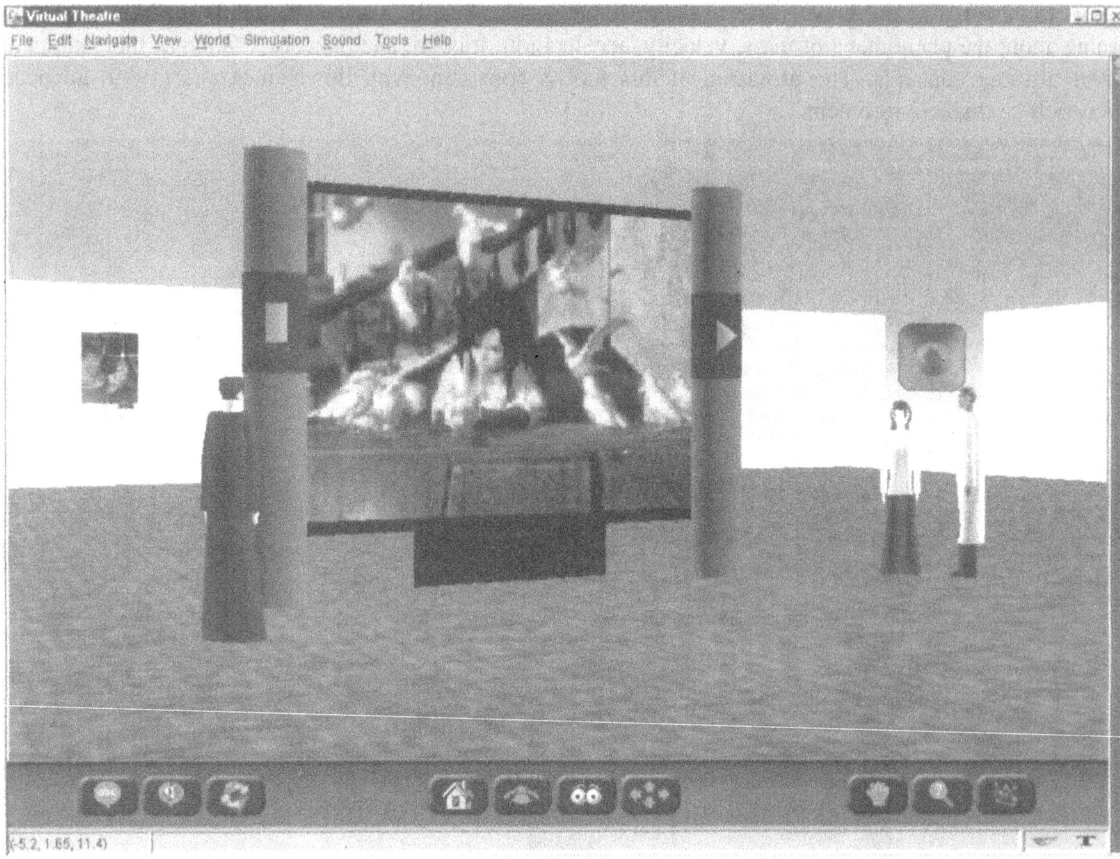

Figure 6. Realtime video streaming in C–VISions

System Design and Implementation

C–VISions has been designed from the outset to be a generic, object oriented software framework—the VISions© framework—that can be customized to different applications of the same genre. For example, it can be used to create military simulations or e-commerce applications. C–VISions is implemented entirely in Java and Java3D. Its design is based on the Model–View–Controller (MVC) architecture derived from the Smalltalk programming language. The Model component implements the virtual world, virtual objects, and the underlying laws that govern the behavior of the virtual objects. The View component implements the virtual world browser. It listens for events and renders them in the 3D browser. It also implements collision detection. The Controller component implements support for actions taken by the user in the virtual world browser.

The network component of C–VISions propagates virtual world events from every user to all other users in the same virtual world. There are two types of events. Semantic events are handled by TCIP/IP. User location change events are handled by UDP. To support object persistence, the state of all objects in the virtual world is constantly recorded onto a database. Conflict resolution for concurrent events has also been implemented.

The system-level flow of control and event propagation is depicted in Figure 7. When users interact with objects, the virtual world is informed of property changes made to the object. The virtual world updates the associated view and propagates these events to other client computers via the network to achieve synchronization of world state on all clients. Every event is tagged with the time of occurrence so that the order of events can be preserved and kept consistent across all clients at all times.

The virtual world (Model) on every client computer propagates events encapsulating changes to virtual objects. Upon receiving such events, the virtual objects update themselves and route the event to event listeners. The virtual browser (View) then interprets the events received from the virtual world and renders the updated geometric representations of all affected virtual objects. A more detailed explanation can be found in Chee and Khoo (2000).

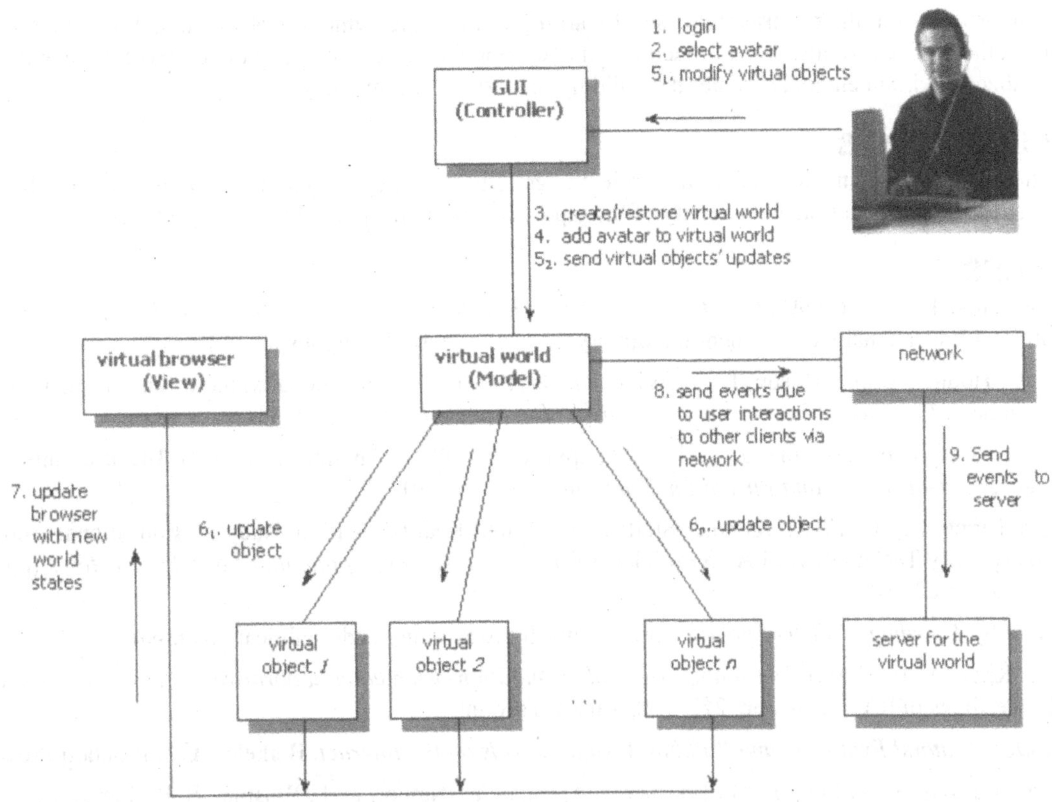

Figure 7. Schematic of control flow in C–VISions

CURRENT STATUS AND FUTURE WORK

The C–VISions system has been in development for close to two years. This time frame gives a sense of the design and development effort involved. A beta Version 4 of the system was released in late June 2001, and a full release Version 1 was launched on 31 August 2001. The C–VISions client can be freely downloaded via the Internet. As the system was built to be accessible via the Internet and to be used by schoolchildren, both from home as well as from school, we have had to address many practical networking issues (eg. bandwidth and fast vs. slow connections, firewall and security restrictions). As it is not possible to instantiate the heterogenous Internet environment within a University network for testing purposes, we have been forced, of necessity, to rely upon incremental, public releases to test our system, and this is what we have done.

C–VISions needs several improvements. For example, the audio chat system needs to be enhanced to be on par with the text chat system in supporting virtual world localization; it is currently a global audio chat system. Our collaboration tools also need to be improved to better support participant co-awareness in coordinated learning activities. Active work is in progress on both these fronts. We also plan to support avatar animation and gestures in the near term.

For the future, we plan to continue populating the virtual environment with more simulation worlds. Upon system deployment, we plan to commence empirical research of how students learn with our system and to begin exploring relationships between the design of the system with the types of concepts or skills to be learned and with individual learner characteristics. On the user interface front, we plan to study desktop 3D user interaction styles. We also hope to create a modified version of the system that supports immersive VR. On the technology front, there are many challenging issues still to be tackled. Chief among these are the issues of scalability, distributed interaction support, failure management, and high-level semantic modeling for application of the system core to other domains. At the broader social and human-computer interaction level, we also wish to research issues related to the genesis and maintenance of virtual communities and to temporal and spatial dimensions of operating in 3D virtual environments.

CONCLUSION

In this paper, we have set out our research work and vision for collaborative, simulation-based learning in desktop VR environments. Our focus on the desktop variant of VR has the benefit of making the technology widely accessible. From the perspective of pedagogy, our efforts are rooted firmly in active, experiential learning and the ideas of constructivism/social constructivism. We have explained the potential power of VR-based learning, especially in respect of shifting the learner's experience of education from a third person, disembodied perspective of knowledge to a first person, embodied perspective, using the technology to reify concepts to be learned, and providing the technology scaffolding to help students transition from the experiential base of learning to the more symbolic, abstract, and reflective modes of the learned mind. In the process, we also hope to facilitate the development of communication, collaboration, and coordination skills in a socialized environment and to foster the building of learning communities.

ACKNOWLEDGMENTS

The contribution of the following students to the project is gratefully acknowledged: Yong Bing Khoo and Siew Mun Ng. The project is supported by a National University of Singapore research grant, R–252–000–033–112.

REFERENCES

Boethel, M., & Dimock, K. V. (1999). *Constructing Knowledge with Technology: A Review of the Literature.* Austin, TX: Southwest Educational Development Laboratory. (http://www.sedl.org/pubs/tec27/)

Bowman, D. A., Hodges, L. F., Allison, D., & Wineman, J. (1999). The educational value of an information-rich virtual environment. *Presence: Teleoperators and Virtual Environments, 8*(3), 317–331.

Bowman, D. A., Kruijff, E., LaViola, J. L. J., & Poupyrev, I. (2001). An introduction to 3-D user interface design. *Presence: Teleoperators and Virtual Environments, 10*(1), 96–108.

Bricken, M., & Byrne, C. M. (1993). Summer Students in Virtual Reality: A Pilot Study on Educational Applications of Virtual Reality Technology. In A. Wexelblat (Ed.), *Virtual Reality: Applications and Explorations* (pp. 199–217). NY: Academic Press.

Bricken, W. (1990). *Learning in Virtual Reality.* (http://www.hitl.washington.edu/publications/m-90-5/)

Chee, Y. S., & Khoo, Y. B. (2000). *Designing extensible simulation-oriented collaborative learning virtual environments.* In Proceedings of ICCE 2000, pp. 222–230, Taipei, Taiwan.

Damer, B. (1998). *Avatars! Exploring and Building Virtual Worlds on the Internet.* Berkeley, CA: Peachpit Press.

Dean, K. L., Asay-Davis, X. S., Finn, E. M., Friesner, J. A., Imai, Y., Naylor, B. J., Wustner, S. R., Fisher, S. S., & Wilson, K. R. (2000). Virtual Explorer: Interactive virtual environment for education. *Presence: Teleoperators and Virtual Environments, 9*(6), 505–523.

Dewey, J. (1916/1980). *Democracy and Education.* Carbondale: Southern Illinois University Press.

Doolittle, P. E. (1999). *Constructivism and Online Education.* (http://www.tandl.vt.edu/doolittle/tohe/tohe2.html/)

Foreman, J. (1999). *Avatar Pedagogy.* (http://horizon.unc.edu/TS/vu/1999-11.asp/)

Fosnot, C. T. (Ed.). (1996). *Constructivism: Theory, Perspectives, and Practice.* NY: Teachers College Press.

Frécon, E., Smith, G., Steed, A., Stenius, M., & Ståhl, O. (2001). An overview of the COVEN platform. *Presence: Teleoperators and Virtual Environments, 10*(1), 109–127.

Kolb, D. A. (1984). *Experiential Learning: Experience as the Source of Learning and Development.* Englewood Cliffs, NJ: Prentice-Hall.

McCloskey, M. (1983). Intuitive physics. *Scientific American, 248*(4), 114–122.

Mills, S., & de Araújo, M. M. T. (1999). Learning through virtual reality: a preliminary investigation. *Interacting with Computers, 11*, 453–462.

Normand, V. (1999). The COVEN project: Exploring applicative, technical, and usage dimensions of collaborative virtual environments. *Presence: Teleoperators and Virtual Environments, 8*(2), 218–236.

Riva, G. (1999). Virtual reality as a communication tool: A sociocognitive analysis. *Presence: Teleoperators and Virtual Environments, 8*(4), 462–468.

Salzman, M. C., Dede, C., Loftin, R. B., & Chen, J. (1999). A model for understanding how virtual reality aids complex conceptual learning. *Presence: Teleoperators and Virtual Environments, 8*(3), 293–316.

Singhal, S., & Zyda, M. (1999). *Networked Virtual Environments: Design and Implementation.* NY: ACM Press.

Winn, W. (1993). *A Conceptual Basis for Educational Applications of Virtual Reality.* (http://www.hitl.washington.edu/publications/r-93-9/)

Winn, W., Hoffman, H., Hollander, A., Osberg, K., Rose, H., & Char, P. (1999). Student-built virtual environments. *Presence: Teleoperators and Virtual Environments, 8*(3), 283–292.

D. ONLINE COMMUNITIES

Developing a Shared Language for Discussing Networked Learning Systems

Herbert Remidez, Joshua S. Gottdenker, James M. Laffey, Dale R. Musser, Ran-Young Hong, Linda Espinosa, Christopher J. Amelung

herbert@coe.missouri.edu, jsg0af@mizzou.edu, laffeyj@missouri.edu, musserda@missouri.edu, rhe06@mizzou.edu, espinosal@missouri.edu, chrisa@coe.missouri.edu,

Center for Technology Innovations in Education, University of Missouri-Columbia

ABSTRACT

New network-based learning systems are coming into use that offer the possibility of integrating curriculum experiences and student information systems as well as changing the metaphor of the Internet from library to workspace. We will call these integrated and process oriented systems Networked Learning Systems (NLS). A NLS is tentatively defined as a program or set of programs designed to operate over a network and support users as they undertake tasks or participate in processes related to learning. CSCL is one type, albeit an important one, of process that can be enabled by NLS. This interactive event is intended to help participants build a shared language to facilitate discussions related to NLS. Through participation in a series of online and face-to-face activities, participants will build knowledge of many networked learning systems currently available, identify important dimensions of these systems, understand what aspects of those dimensions are important and why, and develop an understanding of how the work they are doing relates to the field of NLS. Participants in this session will undertake the online activities within the Shadow netWorkspace™ (SNS) (http://sns.internetschools.org), a NLS being developed by the Center for Technology Innovation in Education at the University of Missouri-Columbia.

Keywords

Networked Learning Systems, Shadow netWorkspace

EVENT DESCRIPTION

One week prior to the conference, those wishing to participate should email Herbert Remidez at herbert@coe.missouri.edu and notify him that they would like to sign up for the CSCL interactive session titled "Developing a Shared Language for Discussing Networked Learning Systems." Interested parties will receive directions on how to access a set of activities that guide them through reviewing a collection of similar systems, related white papers, and research publications. While undertaking these activities, participants will use the Shadow netWorkspace's communication support tools to collaboratively identify important characteristics and dimensions of networked learning systems. Participants will then come together for a face-to-face at the CSCL conference to discuss their findings, continue building a shared vocabulary for discussing NLS, and discussing how their work relates to the field of networked learning systems. To enhance participants' learning, the co-presenters will interact with participants throughout the online and face-to-face activities.

EXAMPLES

Participants will employ SNS to complete a series of online activities designed to help them build their knowledge of networked learning systems. These activities will guide participants through the exploration and identification of important dimensions of networked learning systems. As part of these activities, participants will employ functions of SNS such as asynchronous and synchronous communication tools, workgroups, and the file management system. A face-to-face session will then follow where participants will undertake activities designed to help them share their new knowledge and continue building a shared vocabulary for discussing NLS.

L^3 - An Infrastructure for Collaborative Learnflow

Martin Wessner, Peter Dawabi, Jörg M. Haake

GMD – German National Research Center for Information Technology
Integrated Publication and Information Systems Institute (IPSI)
Dolivostr. 15, D-64293 Darmstadt, Germany
{wessner, dawabi, haake}@darmstadt.gmd.de

ABSTRACT

In this paper we sketch an approach to integrate courses for individual learning into a powerful CSCL environment by using the Point of Cooperation (PoC) approach. We show how PoCs can be set up to create a collaborative learnflow, which exploits individual learning phases as well as different phases of asynchronous and synchronous collaboration. The implementation of the PoC approach in the L^3 project is presented.

Keywords

CSCL, collaborative learnflow, Point of Cooperation (PoC), L3.

MOVING FROM INDIVIDUAL TO COLLABORATIVE LEARNFLOW

How can new learning technologies support cooperative learning? In general, three basic types of learning processes can be differentiated in computer supported learning: Individual learning, synchronous and asynchronous collaborative learning:

Individual learning describes a scenario with a single learner performing a learning activity without others (such as peer learners or tutors). This includes activities such as reading a text, watching a video, reflecting on a picture or writing a summary. The learner can control the learning process, e.g., the speed and the number of iterations.

Synchronous collaborative learning is based on immediate learning together with peer learners or tutors. Here, the learner has less control over the learning process. Activities must be coordinated with the other group members.

Asynchronous collaborative learning happens when a learner manipulates an artifact (such as a document or a message), which has been or will be handled by one or more peers or tutors at a different point in time. Here, the learner has more control over the learning process opposed to synchronous collaboration, e.g. w.r.t. time and place.

Usually, a learner is confronted with different kinds of problems while working on a course. In order to deal with these problems without switching between different learning environments, an ideal learning environment should support flexible coupling and combination of the mentioned learning scenarios during a learning process. Concretely, the learner should be able to switch between synchronous and asynchronous communication in an intuitive way: If the learner needs immediate connection, the required tools should provide the demanded communication channels instantly. Alternatively the learner should have immediate access to asynchronous communication channels if there is no need or opportunity for real-time communication with a peer learner or a tutor.

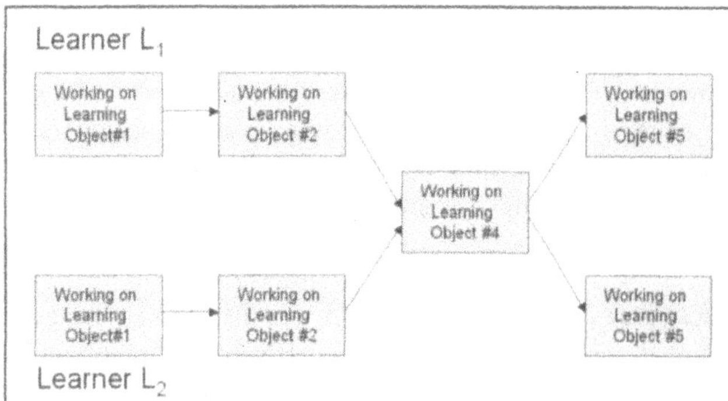

Figure 1: Collaborative learnflow of the learners L_1 and L_2

We consider a course as a set of learning objects interlinked by relations. Each learning object describes a learning activity to be performed (such as reading material, performing an exercise). The course resembles a schema definition of potential learner behaviour, i.e. in each phase of the learning process the learner can proceed to another learning object to extend her knowledge. The learnflow describes a concrete sequence of activities in that schema. During individual learning in a course, the learner initiates his learnflow by performing the start activity, e.g. reading the title page of the course. He extends his *individual learnflow* stepwise with each new learning activity he performs in the course; the learnflow consists of a sequence of activities.

If a course can be used by a learning group in the way that learners perform (some of the) course's activities together then we define the collaborative learnflow as the graph consisting of the individual learnflows where activities, which are performed collaboratively, are merged. Figure 1 shows the collaborative learnflow of two learners, which collaborated on Learning Object #4. During cooperative learning, the *collaborative learnflow* defines the joint behaviour of the learning group and the interactions between the learning partners.

We call an oportunitiy to cooperate given a specific learning context a *Point of Cooperation (PoC)* (see Wessner & Pfister, 2000 for more details). We call a cooperative activity an *intended cooperation* if it is logically and didactically incorporated into a course at a specific position in the course. The corresponding component in the learning environment is called an *Intended Point of Cooperation (IPoC)*. From a structural point of view IPoCs are treated in the same way as non-collaborative learning objects: IPoCs are related to other learning objects of the course. With IPoCs the course author can define "when", i.e. at which position in the locigal course structure, "what" cooperative activity should be performed. The cooperative activity is defined by a set of parameters, such as group size, duration, instructions, learning material, tools, and structure (a system-controlled cooperative learning method). Depending on the nature of the cooperative activity the group has to perform, we distinguish a number of IPoC types., e.g. group discussion, collaborative brainstorming, pro/con-dispute, cooperative text processing. An IPoC is integrated into a course as a learning object. Thus, an IPoC can use the knowledge about the author's intentions to support the user in his collaboration. Using PoCs smooth transitions between the individual and collaborative learning scenarios can be achieved: A user starts in individual learning. If the user encounters an IPoC in the course, the user can initiate an intended collaborative learning activity. Because the actual performing of the collaborative activity depends on runtime requirements, especially the availability of peer learners, encountering an IPoC and activating it are two separate steps. Otherwise the non-availability of peers would block the learner. Upon ending the IPoC tool the learner is back to individual learning.

IMPLEMENTATION: THE L^3 PROJECT

In the L^3 project, which stands for 'lifelong learning', twenty organizations cooperate to develop an integrated Internet-based learning infrastructure for life-long learning and continued training. The partners include infrastructure and technology providers, content providers, training organisations, and research institutions with a didactical or technical focus. In L^3, web-based courses consists of a number of learning objects. Especially, a learning object can be an IPoC, as explained previously. IPoCs are defined as learning objects by the author during the course design using an IPoC editor. E.g. for a brainstorming activity definition, the author defines group size, duration, topic, seed words and instructions for the intended brainstorming activity. The course material is presented in a web browser to the learner. An additional tool, the L^3 Communicator provides the means to start IPoCs after they have been reached in the course material by the learner. The so-called PoC-Pool, a view of the L^3 Communicator, is used to manage all IPoCs of a learner. The actual instantiation of an IPoC is a non-trivial task, e.g. participants need to be selected according to appropriate criteria, matching communication tools have to be activated, and the results of the cooperation processes need to be handled. Learning groups are formed manually by a tutor or automatically by the system. A number of tools supporting specific cooperative learning methods, i.e. the IPoC types mentioned above, have been developed. Currently, version 2 of the platform has been deployed to ten learning centers throughout Germany in 2001. Authors were trained in special workshops to integrate collaborative learning into their courses. We are preparing a large-scale evaluation of the L^3 environment to learn about the usability and the acceptance of the PoC approach.

Compared to existing CSCL environments an environment based on the PoC approach supports individual and collaborative learnflows. With PoCs, course authors can flexibly define collaborative activities integrated with the course w.r.t. to group size, learning method, duration etc. Thus, in the environment presented here, learnflows cover individual and collaborative learning scenarios and feature a variety of collaborative learning methods. In general, this approach allows new ways to represent and analyse group learning behaviour.

ACKNOWLEDGEMENTS

Thanks go to Daniel Tietze, Badie Garzaldeen, Martin Mühlpfordt, and Jessica Rubart for help with implementing the L^3 software. The L^3 project is funded by the German Ministry of Education and Research (grant 21B8196B).

REFERENCES

Wessner, M., Pfister, H.-R. (2000). Points of cooperation: Integrating cooperative learning into web-based courses. Proc. of the Workshop "New Technologies for collaborative learning" NTCL 2000, Japan, November 2000.

Dialogue – A Web Based Communication Tool Supporting Learning Communities

Barbara Shelly

Project Director, The Living SchoolBook, Syracuse University
030 Huntington Hall, Syracuse, NY 13244
bashelly@sy.edu http://lsb.syr.edu

Patricia Tinto

Teaching and Leadership, Syracuse University
School of Education, 152 Huntington Hall, Syracuse, NY 13244.
pptinto@syr.edu http://lsb.syr.edu

ABSTRACT

The Dialogue application is an innovative web-based communication tool that extends classroom boundaries and supports collaborative instructional goals. A key feature is the workspace environment in which professional dialogue is modeled and nurtured. For example, students in teacher preparation programs initiate dialogue that link the preservice teachers' university-based learning with field related experience in public schools. Another aspect is the shared dialogue across K-12 schools around student centered research projects. The Dialogue applications enables equal partnerships with community agencies, university students, and families. It supports networking and timely feedback to resolve issues. Additional features sustain communication and educational requirements of a learning community within a school and across semesters.

DESCRIPTION

The Dialogue Project has several facets. In its narrowest interpretation it is a web based application which provides the features needed by an instructor to create an online community (Conrad, 2001). However, this definition does not distinguish the Dialogue application from commercial software promoting online work. It is in the type of features that Dialogue becomes unique. These features center around the construction of conversations and resources and the sharing of information to promote understanding among all members of a community.

Dialogue's design and its features are envisioned by a team seeking to create a tool to meet the pedagogical needs of specific courses within the Syracuse University School of Education and K-12 classrooms. The instructors for these courses teach from a constructivist perspective, value the creation of conversation as an essential element in their courses, and look to the students to generate ideas and materials that will become resources for other class members both within the specific course and for students to follow in later semesters. In addition, the certification programs within the School of Education have their students in cohorts that move through specific sequences of field-related work. In several cases, the cohorts have moved from a group of students simply being in the same program to an active learning community. Creating a hierarchy that allows for communication among related courses is also part of Dialogue. At present, the hierarchy connections are realized through the ability to make announcements that are sent to all related communities via their "parent" community.

The Dialogue project has three discussion forums, called conversations. All conversations my be classified and titled allowing the members and the administrator to organize and sort postings for research, archiving, and portfolio building.

There are community-wide conversations that are shared with all members of the community. These community-wide conversations give each class member the opportunity to share products such as a lesson concept map, a photograph or an original historic document. A member may initiate or reply to a posting.

One-to-one conversations are for those events that are to be shared between a community member and the administrator, or between student and instructor. Multiple instructors are possible. One-to-one conversations may by replied to or commented on by the instructor. Comments appear attached to the posting. All comments are accumulated in a student's file across the life of the community and for the membership life of the student.

Small group conversations are among community members but private to the members of the small group community. The community administrator or instructor sets up the membership of each small group and selects the conversation format. Members may belong to more than one group within the larger community and with varying life-spans within the life-span of the whole community. Small groups may vary in the number of members. Conversation topics may be pre-determined by the instructor or initiated by group members.

Resources for each class such as a syllabus, videos, original documents, and other informative pieces are open to the entire community through the resource feature. Links to other web sites as well as video, audio or images may also be in the resource area. A community directory holds each member's profile of information to be shared with other members.

Through use of the Dialogue some of the lessons learned are in the area of interface design. These include the need for consistent display of images such as login, d-mail, and help across the multiple pages; the need for submission areas to be self-contained; the need for navigation to be non-linear and based on the use of a breadcrumb trail; and the need for consistent and specific vocabulary facilitating the multiple workspaces.

Other lessons include those that link pedagogy and design. These include that the display format of conversations makes a difference in the level of engagement in the conversation; that the management of small group conversations must be flexible and provide for a wide variety of types of groups; that the teacher's philosophy of instruction makes a difference in how Dialogue is seen as an instructional tool and determines the amount and level of use; and that student use and satisfaction with the tool increases with the percentage of communities to which they belong using the tool.

Dialogue has thus far been most useful to those communities based on the belief that students have a right and a responsibility to interact with different students and that they become resources for each other (Wexler & Tinto, in press). Questions that arise when infusing technology into such a course are: What kinds of conversation do you, as instructor, want to support? What kinds of conversations and use of resources will help students view an event through more than one perspective or lens? What kinds of conversations and resources will form a basis for students to construct their understanding of the content of the course? and What are the most appropriate technological tools to achieve these goals?

REFERENCES

Conrad, C. (2001). The dialogue project. Syracuse University School of Engineering Senior Thesis, Syracuse, NY.

Wexler, D. & Tinto. P. (in press). Active learning in the classroom: creating multiple learning spaces with technology. In S. Tice & P. Englot (Eds.) Handbook on University Teaching. Syracuse University Press, Syracuse, NY.

E. PDAS AND UBIQUITOUS COMPUTING

The Impact of Distributed and Ubiquitous Computational Devices on the Collaborative Learning Environment

Eric Klopfer
Massachusetts Institute of Technology
klopfer@mit.edu
Earl Woodruff
OISE/UT
ewoodruff@oise.utoronto.ca

ABSTRACT
Recent advances in small, personalized computing devices have made possible distributed and ubiquitous computing within the classroom. This creates a fundamentally different environment from one that has 4 or 5 desktop machines per classroom (Soloway et al., 2001). In this paper we sketch out the impact that Thinking Tags can have on the teaching and learning environment.

Keywords
Participatory Simulations, Wearables, Decentralized Systems, Distributed Computing, Collaborative Discourse

INTRODUCTION
Participatory Simulations use small, wearable computers to involve people in simulations that are mediated, in part, by technology (Colella, 2000). Each participant wears a small computer, called a Thinking Tag (Borovoy et al., 1996), that executes rules and keeps track of important information during the simulation. The computers themselves are brightly decorated with legos and are adorned with two displays – a two-digit LED and a series of 5 colored LEDs. The devices communicate through infrared, and are extremely simple, making them almost transparent to the participants during the simulation. The simulation results from the interactions between the rules that are programmed into the computers and adopted behavior. For instance, in the first activity developed for this platform, participants met each other and information was passed that may have infected an individual's tag. Working collaboratively, students determined the rules by which the virus starts and gets passed around.

Colella's research has shown that this technology can simultaneously engage a wide range of students in scientific investigation and discovery. To capitalize on the potential of these tools and further the research we have developed new simulations for this platform. These include:

- *Big Fish Little Fish* immerses participants in the fight for survival, as little fish scavenge for food and big fish attack little fish, and provokes an examination of the roles of collaboration and competition in systems.
- *Tit for Tat* allows participants to investigate how cooperation can evolve in communities over time as they play the classic Prisoner's Dilemma with each other to try to gain the most points.
- *Dental Health* encourages children, through kinetic make-believe, to mingle about the room and "snack" on foods or "brush" to get their teeth clean. Lights on a thinking tag display healthy and diseased imaginary teeth. The goal is to maintain healthy teeth throughout the game
- *Genetics* engages students in a simulated inheritance situation. Each Tag is pre-programmed with a genotype that is to be discerned by students as they meet with other Tags and observe the total probability and random selection of eye colour resulting from each encounter.
- *Issues Based Science* uses the Tags to publicly display the stance and values students hold on the issue of genetically modified foods. Students use this public information to decide whom they wish to try and convert to their position.

CLASSROOM IMPLEMENTATION
Currently, the goals for the Thinking Tag technology are two fold: (1) to investigate how teachers can use the Tags to improve science teaching, and (2) to explore how the Tags can help us understand the collaborative learning process.

Addressing the first goal, we have developed strategies to help teachers create more powerful learning experiences for their students. Our experience with the StarLogo Community of Learners workshops (Colella, et al., 1999) in which we teach teachers to develop their own models of complex, dynamic systems using StarLogo suggests that this is an effective professional development strategy. Clearly, for one teacher, the workshop pinpointed the beginning of his involvement with integrating technology into his classroom, "...When we both saw the kind of scientific thinking and redesigning and re-experimenting and re-editing which we don't have time to do—or don't take time to do—in our labs. We could, but we don't. [With the tags] the kids could change their variables in any way they wanted to, and that was an incredibly powerful experience for them." Another teacher combined the Tit for Tat game with computer simulations and a game in which the students had to develop cooperative strategies in order to consume the most M&Ms using four-foot long spoons. This combination created collaborative discourse unlike any that the teacher had seen before. Students brought in references from history, social science and even the popular show "Survivor" in which they described the first season's winner as a "defector" and the second season's winner as a "cooperator." Yet another teacher ran the disease simulation in his seventh and eighth grade science classes over three days. However, unlike in our workshop where the primary goal of the activity is to gain a deeper understanding of systems, this teacher adapted the activity to fit into a unit on epidemiology and combined the tag activity with related written assignments on specific diseases. This activity generated interest on the part of both the teacher and the students to create a modified version of the disease game to reflect characteristics of other viruses.

Our second goal of using the Tags to explore collaborative learning processes points to three emerging themes. The first is that the Tags make some of the covert collaborative process in social constructed knowledge overt. When 4 and 5-year old children were involved in the dental health activity it became apparent that they were watching what happened to each other's tags. On the surface their behavior appeared very individualistic and non-collaborative. Closer examination indicated, however, they were using the collective data to form their ideas about when to brush and the consequences certain foods had on one's teeth. The second theme is that the public display of first-person information on the tags highlights interactions between the affective and cognitive domains. Students in the issues based science activity, for example, became visibly nervous when another student approached them displaying a tag that indicated no one had managed to change her mind. "She's scary!" one of the group noted as they tried to avoid talking to her. The third theme features the role of evidence in what Scardamalia has called epistemic agency. Epistemic agency involves assumption of control over one's knowledge-building processes. Participants in the genetics simulation activity give us some insight into this process when they overtly formulate critical hypotheses and then seek individuals with tags that will give them the data they need.

NEXT STEPS

As distributed and ubiquitous computing devices become more common place, other researchers (Soloway et al., 2001; Wilensky & Stroup, 1999) are porting similar activities to more common devices such as Palm OS devices and programmable calculators. Therefore, one of our next steps is to systematically analyze how the Tag specific affordances impacts collaboration. At this point we conjecture that the unobtrusive, fun, simple and non-technical nature of the tags can provide a qualitatively different experience for the participants.

ACKNOWLEDGMENTS

Support for this research is provided, in part, by the the Imperial Oil Center for Science Math and Technology at OISE/UT as well as the MIT Media Laboratory and MIT Teacher Education Program.

REFERENCES

Borovoy, R., McDonald, M., Martin, F., & Resnick, M. (1996). Things that blink: Computationally augmented name tags. *IBM Systems Journal,* **35**, 3, 488-495.

Colella, V. (2000). Participatory Simulations: Building collaborative understanding through immersive dynamic modeling. *Journal of the Learning Sciences,* **9**, 4, 471-500.

Colella, V., Klopfer, E., & Resnick, M. (1999). StarLogo Community of Learners Workshop. *Logo Exchange, Journal of the ISTE Special Interest Group for Logo-Using Educators,* **17**, 2.

Soloway, E., Norris, C., Blumenfeld, P., Fishman, B., Krajcik, J., & Marx R. (2001) *Log on Education Handheld Devices are Ready-at-Hand. Communications of the ACM,* **44**, 6.

Wilensky, U. & Stroup, W. (1999). *Learning through Participatory Simulations: Network-Based Design for Systems Learning in Classrooms.* Paper presented at CSCL '99. Stanford University, CA.

Using Handhelds to Support Collaborative Learning

Kathleen Luchini, Chris Quintana, Michael Curtis, Richard Murphy, Joseph Krajcik, Elliot Soloway, Daniel Suthers*

University of Michigan, *University of Hawai`i at Manoa

{kluchini, quintana, micurtis, murphyr, krajcik, soloway}@umich.edu; suthers@hawaii.edu

ABSTRACT

Research suggests that collaborative classroom activities offer many benefits for learning. To collaborate successfully, students need adequate tools to share ideas and resources, develop and support arguments, and cooperate to solve problems. Handheld computers are emerging as a flexible and portable solution that provides students with "ready to hand" support to engage in collaborative activities anytime, anywhere. Handhelds can also be coordinated with desktops to support small group collaboration when larger workspaces are needed.

Keywords

Handheld computers, collaborative learning, wireless Internet, concept maps.

INTRODUCTION

While traditional K-12 education models focus on individual learning, abundant research has led to an emerging understanding of the benefits of collaborative learning. By cooperatively completing shared tasks, students can generate ideas, explore concepts, share resources, and construct arguments to build deeper understanding. In order to participate fully in collaborative activities, students must have access to a wide variety of information, understand the processes and skills required by the task, and become proficient in new terminology and content materials. One way to address these needs is to use a Scaffolded Work Environment, or SWEts (Luchini, Oehler, Quintana, & Soloway, 2001). While desktop SWEts like Symphony (Quintana, Eng, Carra, Wu, & Soloway, 1999) and Belvedere (Suthers, Toth, & Weiner, 1997) are powerful tools for learners, too often desktops in schools are confined to labs and libraries and the student-to-computer ratio is too high to allows students regular access to the machines. Handheld devices (such as Palms and PocketPCs) offer the opportunity to provide each student with their own computer. The mobility, flexibility and instant access of handheld devices means that they are "ready to hand," allowing students to engage in highly collaborative activities anywhere, anytime (Soloway et al., 2001). To help students use handheld devices as learning tools, the Center for Highly Interactive Computing in Education (hi-ce) at the University of Michigan has developed several educational applications designed specifically to take advantage of the mobility, flexibility, and easy collaboration engendered by handheld computers. Yet, desktop and projected workspaces will still play an important role in group activities, providing additional workspace that enables students to compare their work while also benefiting from the scaffolding of SWEts. In this paper we introduce some of of our handheld applications and describe an activity scenario for coordinated use of handheld and desktop educational applications. This scenario will be simulated in the conference interactive session.

EDUCATIONAL APPLICATIONS FOR PALM DEVICES

Hi-ce has developed a number of educational applications for use on Palm devices (Table 1). These programs have been used successfully in a number of classrooms in Michigan, and hundreds of copies have been distributed to educators across the country. The applications provide a wide range of features, and are designed to be both educational and academically flexible. These programs are available free of charge at http://www.hi-ce.org/palms.

Table 1: Educational Applications for Palm Devices

Application	Description
PiCoMap	Allows students to create, share, and explore concept maps consisting of nodes connected by directed arcs.
Fling-It	Allows students to instantaneously "fling" websites from a desktop computer to their handheld devices for off-line reading to build a personal library of websites with reference materials, news, reading materials, etc.
Go 'n Tell	Combines the Kodak PalmPix camera and a Palm computer to allow students to take pictures, annotate them, share the resulting "scrapbook pages" with each other, and instantly create a website displaying their work.
Cooties	A virus-transfer simulation. Teachers determine parameters for "coodles"—Cooties characters that "live" on students' Palm devices. Coodles meet each other via beaming, and some coodles will become "sick". Students then collaborate to determine which coodles were initial carriers and trace the virus transmission path.

CLASSROOM EXPERIENCES

During the 2001-2002 school year, hi-ce is working with two eighth grade science classes at Greenhills School in Ann Arbor, Michigan, to study how students can use handheld devices to collaborate. We provided each student with a Compaq iPAQ running Windows CE. The handhelds have a wireless network card for Internet access, and can "beam" data using infrared technology. We wrote a concept mapping tool for the iPAQs called Pocket PiCoMap, which allows students to build collections of nodes indicating main ideas and directed arcs connecting them (Figure 1). The teacher asked the class to make individual concept maps, exchange maps with a partner (by beaming), and then write comments about their partner's map using the "Map Notes" feature and beam the annotated map back to its owner. The collaborative activity of exchanging and critiquing each others' work led many students to discuss various ideas and revise their own maps to include additional information or different perspectives.

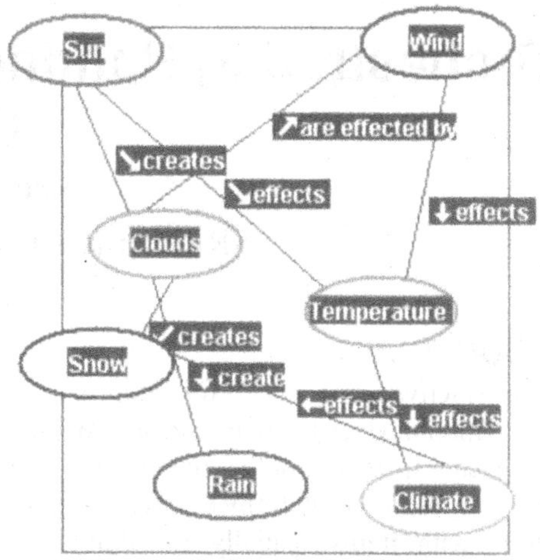

Figure 19: Student's Weather Concept Map

COORDINATING DESKTOP AND HANDHELD APPLICATIONS

Hi-ce and the Laboratory for Interactive Learning Technologies of the University Hawai`i at Manoa are working together to explore the synergy between handheld and desktop tools for helping students collaborate. While handheld computers can offer each student access to personal computing, the limited screen space of handheld devices suggests a remaining role for desktop systems to support group work, where the higher student-to-computer ratio is not an issue. In our CSCL 2002 interactive session we will explore an activity scenario in which individual work done on handhelds is transferred to the desktop for small group and full group manipulation and discussion of the knowledge artifacts. Individual concept maps are first constructed on handhelds and refined by pairwise collaborations using infrared networking as described above. Then these maps are uploaded to a PC into a version of Belvedere (Suthers, Toth & Weiner, 1997) designed to support comparative concept mapping. Small groups of learners display their concept maps side by side and merge them into a consensual knowledge artifact. The juxtaposition of individual work confronts students with alternate conceptions and prompts the justification of their own choices (activities known to improve learning), while the visual representations also help coordinate and ground their conversations. In classrooms with projection devices the resulting group maps might then be merged into a class-wide concept map. Grounded in this hands-on experience, interactive session participants will discuss strategies for maximizing the potential of both handheld and desktop devices for education.

ACKNOWLEDGMENTS

Microsoft, Intel, Palm Inc., National Science Foundation Grant Number NSF ITR 0085946 and a Graduate Research Fellowship supported the hi-ce efforts. National Science Foundation Grant No. 9873516 supported the Belvedere efforts. Any opinions, findings and conclusions or recommendations expressed in this material are those of the authors and do not necessarily reflect those of the National Science Foundation. We would also like to acknowledge Andrew Carra, the original PiCoMap developer; Chris Farah, Nayan Nandihalli, Kyle Reese and Adam Wieczorek for their work with the PocketPC project; and David Burger, Bruce Harris and Nick Ni for bringing Belvedere and PiCoMap together.

REFERENCES

Luchini, K., Oehler, P., Quintana, C., & Soloway, E. (2001, 2001). An Engineering Process for Constructing Scaffolded Work Environments to Support Student Inquiry: A Case Study in History. Paper presented at the ICALT 2001, Madison, WI.

Metcalf, S. J., Krajcik, J., & Soloway, E. (2000). Model-It: A Design Retrospective. In M. J. Jacobson & R. B. Kozma (Eds.), Innovations in Science and Mathematics Education: Advanced Design for Technologies of Learning (pp. 77-115). Mahwah, NJ: Erlbaum Assoc.

Quintana, C., Eng, J., Carra, A., Wu, H. K., & Soloway, E. (1999). Symphony: A Case Study in Extending Learner-Centered Design Through Process Space Analysis, Human Factors in Computing Systems: CHI '99 Proceedings (pp. 473-480). Pittsburgh, PA: ACM.

Soloway, E., Norris, C., Blumenfeld, P., Fishman, B., Krajcik, J., & Marx, R. (2001). Handheld Devices are Ready-at-Hand. Communications of the ACM, 44(6), 15-20.

Suthers, D., Toth, E., and Weiner, A. (1997, December). An integrated approach to implementing collaborative inquiry in the classroom. In *Proc. 2nd International Conference on Computer Supported Collaborative Learning (CSCL'97)* (pp. 272-279). Toronto.

Orchestrating Handhelds in the Classroom with SRI's ClassSync™

Chris DiGiano, Charles Patton

SRI International, Center for Technology in Learning

chris.digiano@sri.com

ABSTRACT

In our interactive experience, we address the problem of a teacher or other leader managing the use of electronic communication devices by their students. We have embedded the control elements into the physical class structure itself so that the teacher may control the interactive system by moving about the classroom and interacting with the devices therein. We have shifted control from a teacher-controlled display in a static location to a teacher's dynamic control that is interactive with items spatially distributed in the room. Our demonstration shows how this orchestration can be accomplished with low-cost infrared communications as opposed to more expensive radio-based solutions.

Keywords

Handhelds, design, wireless networking, classroom workflow

INTRODUCTION

In the next few years, advances in handheld computing, and wireless networks will enable portable 1:1 classroom computing with ubiquitous networking. Even more so than with desktop computers, technology employing Wireless Internet Learning Devices (WILD) enable individual learners to participate in synchronous collaborative learning experiences. However, this technology will undoubtedly shift the role of the classroom teacher. Whereas in traditional lecture classes the teacher is often characterized as the "sage-on-the-stage" and in modern CSCL contexts as the "guide-by-the-side," a new metaphor is needed to capture the role of the teacher in a WILD classroom.

WILD classrooms will demand that teachers manage real-time performance of classroom activities. Management tasks include (a) distributing and collecting work, (b) enabling students to collaborate in groups, (c) monitoring real-time progress with respect to learning objectives, and (d) controlling cheating, note-passing, and other disruptive communications. All of this must be accomplished without overburdening the teacher, compromising the already limited handheld battery life, or pushing the cost out of the reach of the educational market.

In our demonstration, we explore a new metaphor where the teacher is a "conductor" or "orchestrator" of classroom performances involving their students. The teacher attends primarily to group performance, not to each individual student. Moreover, the teacher, like the conductor, has responsibility for choosing and sequencing the material to be performed (the curricular activities), interpreting the performance, and guiding it toward its desired end. As in rehearsal, the conductor might direct groups of students to practice something alone, or in small groups. During performance, the teacher will work to ensure that all parts are "heard," that everyone gives their best performance—directing attention towards the students who need the most encouragement while keeping the overall performance moving forward. Moreover, like a conductor, the teacher will want to monitor individual participation to ensure that all the students are productively contributing to the classroom performance.

CLASSSYNC

We have drawn on SRI's expertise in mobile ad hoc networks, handheld devices, security, learning sciences, and educational technology research and development to assemble a suite of technologies collectively known as ClassSync™. ClassSync makes it possible, for the first time, for teachers to orchestrate the flows of work and conversation among wireless classroom participants in a manner that transparently maps onto how teachers routinely manage classroom work and conversation flow.

Teachers interact with ClassSync at a high level by creating groups and assigning activities to them. ClassSync automates the details of creating a group by notifying students that they now belong to a group, by making resources available to the group, and enabling resource sharing and messaging. ClassSync automates the details of activity assignment, assigns roles to members, and transitions to the next activity when the activity completes.

As a sample ClassSync-enabled application, we have created, for the Palm PDA, a version of the classic Gopher client and enhanced it with text and image editing as well as revising the protocol for infrared beaming. We use this sample application to illustrate the key ideas of our system. The Palm-based ClassSync also demonstrates how orchestration can be accomplished with low-cost infrared communications as opposed to more expensive radio-based solutions (e.g. Airport or IEEE 802.11b.)

ABOUT THE INTERACTIVE EXPERIENCE

The objective of the interactive experience is to give participants a hands-on sense of what it would be like to be a teacher or student in a WILD classroom. Participants will each be given a Palm device and asked to take part in a role playing activity. One will be selected as the teacher and the rest will assume the role of students. The activity will involve the following 5 phases:

1. Introduction Phase

The goal is to introduce basics of Palm operation including turning on and off, choosing menus and applications, and using the pop-up keyboard, and introduce the beaming concept by creating a business card and beaming it to a neighbor.

2. Take Attendance Phase

The goal is to introduce the notion of beaming points, illustrate switching beaming point configurations on the fly, illustrate a take-attendance capability, insure all participants have Gopher installed with appropriate contract, familiarize the participants with Gopher basics, and illustrate the concept of contracts

3. Preparing Teams Phase

The goal is to introduce the process of posting documents with the Gopher application, introduce the notion of share pair contracts, show basic typical operations involved for a teacher to form a new group, and introduce differentiated beaming points and how their configuration can be switched on the fly.

4. Collaboration Phase

The goal is to illustrate the use of beaming in a collaborative activity, and demonstrate the fun side collaboration and illustrate how it can be controlled.

5. Quiz Phase

The goal is to illustrate the mass distribution of contracts, illustrate the element of 'consideration', and show how the system can dynamically limit access.

ACKNOWLEDGMENTS

Thanks to the many contributors from the WILD and SimCalc teams: John Brecht, Mark Chung, Tristan de Frondeville, Jim Kaput, Sarah Lewis, Judy Li, Roy Pea, Jeremy Roschelle, Deborah Tatar, Phil Vahey, and Wenming Ye. We gratefully acknowledge support from the National Science Foundation, SRI International, Palm Inc., and Texas Instruments.

F. PROFESSIONAL DEVELOPMENT

Video Cases for Teacher Learning: Issues of Social and Organizational Design for Use

Greg Shrader, Barry Fishman, Sasha Barab, Kevin O'Neill, Gary Oden, Dan Suthers

Northwestern University, University of Michigan, Indiana University, Simon Fraser University, the University of Pittsburgh, and the University of Hawai'i

gshrader@northwestern.edu

ABSTRACT

This paper provides the foundation for an interactive symposium on the design of web-based systems to support teachers' professional development with videos of exemplary teaching practice. Five existing systems are examined against a common framework examining their design in terms of the models of use that they support.

Keywords

case-based learning, teacher learning, use models, design research

INTRODUCTION

Over the past several years, researchers in the Learning Sciences have undertaken a variety of efforts to use interactive media to design systems that ground teacher learning in reflective examinations of practice. This paper considers five such projects that each provide teachers with access to videos of exemplary teaching practice delivered over the web. While all of the projects integrate video, they do so in varied contexts and employ very different use models for the role of video in supporting professional development. It is the understanding the strengths and challenges of these diverse activity frameworks that is of central importance to the CSCL community. The goal of the paper is to set the stage for a critical examination of the use models as well as the task and activity structures underlying each project. We begin with a brief description and comparison of the systems.

THE SYSTEMS

The Living Curriculum (Shrader, 2000; Shrader & Gomez, 1999) and Knowledge Networks on the Web (KNOW) each couple video of exemplary teaching practice to project-based science curricula as a way of supporting the in-situ use of those specific materials. NetLearn also features videos of exemplary practice, but as the focal point for site-based communities of teachers and instructional leaders seeking to implement standards-based reform. NetLearn video clips are part of a suite of tools designed to help teachers and administrators develop an "eye" for teaching that enacts the "Principles of Learning" (Resnick & Hall, 1998), and assist them in understanding their interdependencies. In a related way, The Inquiry Learning Forum (Barab, MaKinster, Moore, & Cunningham, in press) uses teaching video as the focal point for a distributed community of educators interested in building their capacity to employ inquiry-based instructional strategies in their classrooms. These videos and their accompanying reflective case studies serve as anchor points for online discussions and community building. Finally, the IPLP Video Case project makes use of the Teachscape professional development system in a pre-service context. In the tradition of Lampert & Loewenberg-Ball (1998), faculty are working to integrate the use of video cases focusing students on exemplars of theory in action into their courses.

THE FRAMEWORK

Like any technological innovation, online professional development must be responsive both to the needs of learners and of the social and organizational contexts in which they work. Each project makes different assumptions about the kinds of activity structures through which teachers will interact with video cases of teaching, and how these can be integrated into the organizational settings of schools and districts. Our goal is to initiate a discussion that unpacks and analyzes those assumptions. In preparation, we describe each of the projects against the following framework.

How are teachers intended to use the video cases? Both the Living Curriculum and KNOW are designed as performance support systems providing opportunities for teachers to learn as they plan and teach the underlying project-based science units. Teachers browse the lesson plans online where they can view the associated video and examples of student work. KNOW adds a community discussion tool for teachers, which serves as a source of community-generated knowledge. In NetLearn, teacher leaders and administrators examine video examples of teaching practice in relation to the Principles of Learning, annotating and discussing these videos with online tools. In the IPLP project teachers in university based teacher preparation courses use Teachscape video cases as part of their course work. In the ILF, inservice teachers use the videos as part of workshops and professional development opportunities, while pre-service teachers use it as part of their course work.

What are teachers expected to learn through interaction with the video? Living Curriculum and KNOW users are expected to learn how to employ project-based science methods, including the integrated use of educational technology, in their classrooms. NetLearn users are expected to learn to recognize the Principles in action and how to assist their own teachers in implementing these principles. The goal of the IPLP project is to improve teachers' ability to reflect on teaching practice as well as their mastery of content, pedagogical and pedagogical content knowledge relevant to the teaching methods courses in which they are enrolled. Teachers in the ILF project are expected to gain a richer perspective on the contextualized practices of their colleagues, with the video serving as a jumping off point to rich discussion.

How is the use of cases motivated by CSCL-relevant theory and research? The Living Curriculum was conceived as a case-based performance support system designed to provide teachers with a just-in-time learning resource to support their transition to project-based pedagogy. KNOW uses individual teaching sessions as the unit of analysis for teachers. The use of video cases in NetLearn is itself motivated by the Principles being studied, including Accountable Talk and Learning as Apprenticeship. The use of cases in the IPLP project is intended to connect the theoretical propositions taught in teacher preparation courses to concrete exemplars in practice. The use of the videos in the ILF project is as starting points towards building a community of practice.

How is the activity around the cases supported? By linking video directly to lesson plans the Living Curriculum affords teachers an opportunity to learn from cases as part of their planning process. In addition, designers assumed that teachers would find the system useful as a resource to find solutions to instructional challenges that arise when they teach the projects. KNOW is used as one component of a broad professional development effort. NetLearn is unique in providing technology to support the activities of an existing national community of educators. It is intended to extend the work of this community beyond limitations imposed by face to face meetings. IPLP faculty integrated the use of video cases into courses by developing a series of assignments. In one assignment students utilize video cases as a resource to design instruction to meet specified learning goals. In the ILF, in addition to having information about the videos (class context, lesson plans, examples of student work, connections to standards, and other relevant resources) the videos themselves are situated in a larger framework of multiple types of participant structures (asynchronous discussions, library of resources, bounded groups of teachers with similar content interests, professional development modules) with the goal of connecting teachers to teachers.

CONCLUSION

An examination of these questions is essential at this time because their answers define models of use through which teachers may or may not interact with the learning environments. Like any technological innovation the critical limiting factor for these systems is not the technology design (though that is a precondition for use) but the social and organizational design through which technology systems are integrated into work practices. The "bets" placed on use models and activity structures are critically important to the eventual success or failure of these efforts. Moreover, as systems like these enter the commercial marketplace the questions driving future research are not how to build and scale the underlying technologies, but how and under what circumstances such systems can effectively be woven into the organizational lives of teachers and schools. We offer this session as a benchmark of current progress and as an opportunity to refocus our research enterprise on questions of use.

REFERENCES

Barab, S. A., MaKinster, J., Moore, J., & Cunningham, D. (in press). The Inquiry Learning Forum: A new model for online professional development. *Educational Technology Research and Development*

Lampert, M., & Loewenberg-Ball, D. (1998). *Teaching, Multimedia and Mathematics: Investigations of Real Practice.* New York: Teachers' College Press.

Resnick, L. B., & Hall, M. W. (1998). Learning organizations for sustainable education reform. *Daedalus*, 127, 89-118.

Shrader, G. W., & Gomez, L. M. (1999). *Design Research for the Living Curriculum.* Paper presented at the Computer Supported Collaborative Learning, Palo Alto, CA.

The Knowledge Loom: Supporting School Improvement Through Online Dissemination of Best Practices and Collaborative Inquiry to Put Them into Action

Martin Huntley, Mary Anne Mather, Stephanie Feger

Northeast & Islands Regional Educational Laboratory, The Education Alliance, Brown University
(Martin_Huntley@brown.edu, Mary_Anne_Mather@brown.edu, Stephanie_Feger@brown.edu)

ABSTRACT

The Knowledge Loom (http://knowledgeloom.org) web site, its companion Professional Development Workbook, and content partner data-input interface are examples of technology-supported tools intended to build learning communities that develop teaching expertise. The goal is to collect distributed teaching and learning knowledge and begin the process of weaving it into a rich tapestry of understanding of teaching and learning. The Knowledge Loom is a place where the work of educational researchers and practitioners comes together to put what works in teaching and learning into practice.

KEYWORDS

professional development, community building, technology, collaborative inquiry, interactive tools, K-12, best practices, proven practices, research-based, research to practice, collegial sharing, knowledge building

INTRODUCTION

Margaret Riel, Associate Director at the Center for Collaborative Research in Education, notes that "Expert teacher knowledge is not routinely recorded, negotiated, and stored in community spaces for use by new members of the community." Riel cites *The Knowledge Loom: What Works in Teaching & Learning* (http://knowledgeloom.org) as an example of a Web-based resource that exemplifies a new way of thinking about teacher expertise. The Knowledge Loom supports community-oriented models of professional development in four ways: (1) free, easy-to-use, online access to rich content about exemplary practices in K-12 education; (2) a suite of interactive tools that encourage broad sharing of educational practice/experience; (3) a Workbook that outlines a series of collaborative inquiry activities focused around Knowledge Loom content; (4) a Web-based administrative interface that allows selected content partners to regularly add content to the best-practices database. The Knowledge Loom is the 2001 recipient of the Distinguished Achievement Award in the category of technology-supported professional development from the Educational Publishers Association.

WHAT IS THE KNOWLEDGE LOOM?

The Knowledge Loom is a rich database of proven educational practices structured around theme-based collections called "spotlights." Spotlights contain lists and explanations of best practices, supporting success stories from schools and teachers, pointers to research, links to related resources that can be found on other Web sites, and a set of interactive tools that prompt users to input knowledge of their own. In some cases, these interactive tools include a threaded panel discussion with experts in the field. The goal is, through a series of both on site and online opportunities, to collect fragments of teaching and learning knowledge and experience from participants and begin the process of weaving them into a rich tapestry of understanding of teaching and learning.

HOW DOES THE KNOWLEDGE LOOM SUPPORT PROFESSIONAL DEVELOPMENT?

Teachers sometimes say that the best kind of professional development comes from talking with other teachers—they can get advice that feels practical and relevant. The Knowledge Loom and its companion Professional Development Workbook are predicated on the value of educators talking together, sharing their insights, and asking questions together. But in order for this exchange to be meaningful and effective, the discussion must be focused around educationally sound content, like the content provided on The Knowledge Loom. Educators access The Knowledge Loom collections to locate selected information, as needed, for school improvement planning and inspiration, pose important questions for answers from both local colleagues and others knowledgeable in the field, and contribute expertise via the various interactive components. Sometimes growing professionally simply means finding colleagues with whom to bounce ideas around. The Knowledge Loom and companion Workbook present many opportunities to exchange ideas and broaden understanding about effective education practice, whether the colleagues are in the same school/district or across the country.

HOW IS CONTENT PROVIDED?

The database content presented online comes from many places, including professional and technical assistance partner organizations (some funded by the U.S. Department of Education), private developers/providers of educational products and services, and individual teachers and administrators in schools and districts. The Knowledge Loom regularly develops and spotlights best practice information about topics that concern K-12 educators today. These currently include literacy, equity, technology, math, school organization, community involvement, and professional development. An Web-based administrative interface is provided for content provider organizations to input their information and findings, and link these to appropriate best practices, stories, and resources for appropriate search results. In addition, interactive tools located throughout the web site are available for all users to add their own threads of wisdom and experience to the content.

WHY A KNOWLEDGE LOOM?

The loom as a metaphor suggests a work in progress, a workspace where selected and varied threads are drawn together to craft a cohesive, unique, and useful fabric. The Knowledge Loom web site offers an online workspace where education-minded users can weave distributed threads of information and experience together in such a way as to create a fabric that wears well on their own conditions, needs, and visions for excellence in teaching and learning. The Knowledge Loom provides the content that supports collaborative professional development initiatives.

OUTLINE OF PRESENTATION/DEMO

Online tour of The Knowledge Loom to learn how to access theme-based best practices, success stories, supporting research, and resource links for ongoing professional development and action planning.

Demonstration of the asynchronous panel discussions and other online tools that are part of the suggested professional development activities.

Presentation of The Knowledge Loom Professional Development Workbook and Facilitator Guide as a companion resource that leads participants through a series of online and face-to-face collaborative inquiry activities using Knowledge Loom content.

Unveiling of the new content-partner administrative interface that allows expert content providers (professional and technical assistance organizations, government agencies, and individual schools and districts) to make direct submissions of their content to the Knowledge Loom database.

Audience discussion about the implications of a tool like The Knowledge Loom for effective school change. Sharing ideas about the expansion of the Workbook into an interactive workspace for both small-group and broadcast knowledge sharing and decision-making for effective teaching and learning, and discussion about developing an online course focused on the Workbook activities.

ACKNOWLEDGEMENTS

From October 1998 through December 2000, the United States Department of Education assigned resources to the Northeast and Islands Regional Educational Laboratory (LAB), a program of The Education Alliance at Brown University, to develop a "...sustainable, customer-driven, distributed repository/database of information on best practices in teaching and learning." After talking to many educators, the LAB realized that a "repository" was not enough. Our vision was The Knowledge Loom—a comprehensive electronic environment that moves from information delivery to information creation, from data to people, from a learning library to a learning community. The Knowledge Loom Professional Development Workbook and Facilitator Guide is a continuation of that work—to bring the best-practice content presented on The Knowledge Loom in a practical way to districts, schools, and classrooms through collaborative professional development activities.

REFERENCES

Riel, M. (2000) New designs for connected teaching and learning. *White paper for the U.S. Department of Education: Secretary's Conference on Educational Technology* (http://www.gse.uci.edu/mriel/whitepaper/learn4.html).

Investigating Physics: An Intimate Look at an Online Inquiry-based Graduate Science Course

Andee Rubin, Sue Doubler

TERC

Cambridge, MA

Andee_Rubin@TERC.edu

ABSTRACT

In this paper, we describe a new online course, Investigating Physics, which is part of an online master's degree in science education. The course is firmly rooted in the pursuit of scientific inquiry as a pedagogical model and we discuss here what design issues and solutions arise from this commitment to inquiry and in what ways the course supports the creation of a learning community that supports and extends students' growth in scientific thinking.

Keywords

Online master's degree, scientific inquiry, investigating physics, learning community

Introduction

Everywhere where we look, there are new online courses, from high school through graduate school. Serious conversation about important design aspects has proliferated more slowly, however, and the definition of a set of perspectives from which to analyze online courses has barely begun. This is a difficult task, since educators rarely agree on ways to analyze face-to-face learning interactions either.

Therefore, it is important that the conversations we have about online courses include pedagogical decisions as well as decisions about the online structure of the course. We describe here a course whose designers constantly returned to the pursuit of inquiry as a pedagogical model and, we believe, arrived at some interesting and new ways to think about the issues that arise when inquiry is the guiding principle of course construction.

Investigating Physics

Investigating Physics is the third in a series of six online courses that make up a fully online master's program for elementary and middle school teachers in Science Education , developed collaboratively by TERC and Lesley University. The program seeks to "re-open the door to science" by providing teachers with a safe environment where they can think hard, work collaboratively, and extend their science understandings. Totaling 33 credit hours, the program helps teachers increase their knowledge of physics, biology, earth science, engineering and ecology, while exploring new ways to support their students' science learning. As they develop their own expertise with computer-based technologies, they learn ways to enhance their students' learning with technology as well.

Creating a course that takes serious a commitment to learning science through inquiry presents many design challenges. In the Investigating Physics course, as well as the other courses in the program, we have successfully used the following design features.

The courses are designed to be solid science courses, but written for an audience that has often had negative school experiences with science. In the case of physics, people's memories were especially painful and some began the courses quite tentatively. The Investigating Physics course is on forces and motion—especially Newton's Laws. The aim of the course is for participants to see Newton's Laws in their own everyday actions by taking the perspective of a physicist. To guide the students' in their scientific thinking, one of the two instructors for the class is a scientist.

Each course is designed with an explicit focus on inquiry as a tool for learning – and teaching. This is not a simple task; it is easy to give lip service to inquiry, but more difficult to ensure that understanding develops through inqury - especially online. This is where the learning community fostered by the course is most important. As explained in more detail below, participants' interactions with one another, which are carefully supported by the course structure, are the major place that understanding unfolds from the investigations carried out by each course participant.

A key aspect of inquiry fostered by the course is first-hand experimentation carried out in course participants' homes. In Investigating Physics, a kit of materials is mailed to participants before the course begins - it contains a low-friction cart, several balls, some spring scales - simple materials that cost little and could be used in a classroom as well. Each course session begins with, first-hand experimenation that demands close observation; participants record their results in their journals, which then form the basis for their online conversation during the week.

In each course in the program, there is a dual emphasis: on science and on pedagogy. In the Investigating Physics course, the pedagogical emphasis is learning how to conduct interviews with children to understand their scientific ideas.
During the course, each student conducts interviews with several children on the same topics they are studying themselves, and transcribes and analyzes portions of each interview to share with other participants. In order to support this aspect of the course, there is a second instructor, who is a science educator. Both instructors interact with the students in the various forums described below.

Video is used in two different and, we have found, highly effective ways. In a more common use, there are video segments of interviews of the kind they are learning to conduct. These were designed and produced especially for the course. The other use of video is more unusual. We include short t video clips of motions that take place over too short a time to be analyzable in normal time. Participants can view these videos in slow motion and can analyze them frame by frame. Most of the videos in the course are less than one second long. Participants follow the path of objects they are studying by putting an overhead transparency over the screen and marking the series of positions the object is in as the frames advance. This creates a trace of the motion of the object and is the basis for many of the participants' discussions

An important part of students' learning is the study of different mathematical representations for motion, some conventional, others tailor-made for the medium in which they are working. In many online courses, the only thing participants can share is text. We explicitly gave students the ability to share graphs and other sketches with one another, using Powerpoint. This turned out to be an important part of the course, as sometimes the only way students could communicate their analysis of a motion scenario was through a diagram

Of course, all this takes place in a learning community which is the result of several features of the course. Early in the course, students are divided into several teams of five or six people. This is their "study group," the students with whom they will explore the science, share their interviews and offer personal support. Students communicate with one another in three separate forums. In the Physics Forum, students discuss the data they have collected, their analysis of it and further questions it evokes. This is where students also share graphs and sketches to illustrate their analysis. In the Learning Forum, the conversations center on interviews with children, including bits of transcript and analysis. Because all participants ask similar questions in their interviews, they are able to compare both their interviewing techniques and what they discovered about the child they interviewed. We added a third forum after the course began: the Motions in your Life Forum, in which participants describe places in their lives where they find the kind of motions and forces they are studying. There is also a place to share more personal trials and tribulations and to ask for support: Charlie's Café, named after a "real" café at Lesley.

We've learned a great deal about designing such a course, and in the process we have generated enough data (i.e. the online conversations) to keep many Ph.D. Candidates busy for years. We hope this is indeed what happens, since the analysis of these data can reveal much more about how online courses work.

G. REPRESENTATIONAL SCAFFOLDING

External Representations for Collaborative Learning and Assessment

Sadhana Puntambekar[1], Agnes Stylianou[1], Dan Suthers[2], Chris Hundhausen[2], Teresa Hübscher-Younger[3]

[1]Neag School of Education, University of Connecticut, [2] Laboratory for Interactive Learning Technologies, Department of Information and Computer Sciences, University of Hawai`i at Manoa, [3]Computer Science and Software Engineering, Auburn University

{sadhana, agnes.stylianou}@uconn.edu, {suthers, hundhaus}@hawaii.edu, teresa@Eng.Auburn.EDU

ABSTRACT

This interactive session brings together researchers and educators interested in using external representations to facilitate and assess learning. The session will juxtapose four systems, each of which takes a different design approach. The representations include concept maps, metaphorical textual descriptions or visualizations for helping students learn in complex domains such as science or programming.

Keywords

External representations, concept maps, algorithm visualizations

INTRODUCTION

External representations in many forms (e.g. concept maps, animations, visualizations, etc.) are now increasingly being used in interactive learning environments under the assumption that they provide affordances that are significantly different from expository environments (Jacobson & Archodidou, 2000; Suthers, 2001). External epresentations are believed to be especially helpful in helping students learn in complex domains such as science (e.g. White & Fredrickson, 1998) or programming (Hansen Schrimpsher & Narayanan, 1998). External epresentations can accentuate relevant characteristics of a concept and make higher-order relations more accessible. Collaborative learning can be enhanced through the negotiations that arise when co-constructing representations and through the subsequent role that collaborative representations play in coordinating discussion. Four systems, using external representations in different forms will be presented in this interactive session. Of the four, ALVIS (Hundhausen) and CAROUSEL (Hübscher-Younger) use algorithm visualizations and CoMPASS (Puntambekar) and Belvedere (Suthers) use concept maps as external representations.

ALVIS

ALVIS (ALgorithm VIsualization Storyboarder) is an interactive algorithm visualization system designed to make constructing a visualization as easy as constructing a "storyboard" out of simple art supplies such as construction paper, scissors, glue, and pens. We will demonstrate the ease with which one can create "cutouts"—virtual scraps of construction paper—and lay them directly out on the ALVIS animation surface. Underlying ALVIS is SALSA (Spatial ALgorithmic Language for StoryboArding) a high-level, interpreted language for programming animations based on spatial relations. We will demonstrate how one programs an algorithm visualization in SALSA by creating a *spatial analogy* of the algorithm to be visualized. Finally, we will describe three key features of ALVIS specifically designed to support conversations about algorithms: (1) fine-grained execution control; (2) dynamic mark-up; and (3) dynamic modification. Drawing on ethnographic studies of algorithm visualization construction and presentation exercises in an actual undergraduate classroom, we will illustrate the ways in which these features, along with specific features of "low fidelity" (sketched) visualizations, mediate and facilitate meaningful conversations about algorithms. We also consider ways in which algorithm visualization construction and presentation exercises can form the foundation for assessing students in an undergraduate algorithms course.

CAROUSEL

CAROUSEL (Collaborative Algorithm Representations Of Undergraduates for Self-Enhanced Learning) helps students engage in an active process of algorithm representation *creation, sharing and collective evaluation.* Learners relying on a single representation of an algorithm often misinterpret the limitations and specifics of that representation. A representation highlights or emphasizes different aspects of a concept and places less emphasis on or even ignores other aspects. A complete understanding is more likely to emerge from multiple different representations of a single concept. Students do not consider all representations equally, however. Representations similar to those presented by their instructor are often invested with more authority. Students are more likely to accept representations as being incomplete and partial when created by their peers. Thus they may be better able to understand that different aspects of the algorithm need to be understood, and that different representations de-emphasize, as well as highlight, different aspects, when creating, sharing and evaluating their peers' representations. We plan to demonstrate how the software supports the sharing of representations and the collective evaluations and discussion of representations. We will illustrate how student representations changed over time and show the variety of the style of representation as well as the variety of content.

CoMPASS

CoMPASS uses situational, dynamic concept maps to aid navigation and to scaffold students in their understanding of Physics. The system has two tightly integrated parts - a textual representation of the content units and a visual representation in the form of concept maps. Both views change dynamically as students choose the concepts. The maps are constructed and displayed with a fisheye based on the strength of relationships between the concepts. There are two main components of CoMPASS. First the software uses conceptual representations for navigation. Students' navigational paths are used to create representations of student learning. The 'pathfinder' graph theoretic technique creates a graphic representation of students' navigational patterns. Students' collaborative representations can be used (a) for assessment of student learning and (b) to assist teachers in getting insights into common misconceptions of a group of learners. Second, CoMPASS allows students to create their own maps. These can be created by a 'drag and drop' mechanism from the system map. Preliminary studies using CoMPASS have shown that students have a richer understanding of the domain and of the interconnectedness of the concept when they used concept maps for navigation. We are studying how student representations can be used to assess student learning, and the roles of student and system representations to scaffold learning.

BELVEDERE

The Belvedere project explores the use of visual knowledge representations to help make scientific reasoning and argumentation more accessible to students. Belvedere 3.x enables students to construct evidence models under any of three representational views: graph, matrix, and hierarchy, and to move freely between these views. External representations constitute an important resource for collaborative learning, particularly when they are constructed and manipulated by the learners. When learners are constructing a shared representation, the necessity of making a joint decision concerning the representational components to be created can lead to negotiations of meaning. Once created, these representations can facilitate subsequent reference to complex ideas through deixis, and can remind participants of these ideas, leading to further elaboration. Recent empirical work with Belvedere has focused on the "representational guidance" hypothesis, which states that the ways in which a given representation plays these roles will depend in part on the characteristics of the representational toolkit itself: what it prompts for, what aspects of represented information are made salient, and what cannot be represented at all. Results from a study testing his hypothesis will be summarized. The next step is to understand how to move between representations in order to most effectively support different subtasks of an inquiry process.

REFERENCES

Hansen, S., Schrimpsher, D., & Narayanan, N. H. (1998). Learning algorithms by visualization: A novel approach using animation-embedded hypermedia. *Proc. Third International Conference on the Learning Sciences.*

Jacobson, M. J. & Archodidou, A. (2000). The knowledge mediator framework: Toward a design of hypermedia tools for learning. In M. J. Jacobson & R. Kozma (Eds.), *Innovations in Science and Math Education*, 117-162.

Suthers, D. D. (2001). Towards a Systematic Study of Representational Guidance for Collaborative Learning Discourse. *Journal of Universal Computer Science* 7(3), 2001. Electronic publication: http://www.jucs.org/jucs_7_3/towards_a_systematic_study

White, B. & Fredrickson, J. (1998). Inquiry, Modeling, and Metacognition: Making science accessible to all students, *Cognition and Instruction.* 6(1), 3-117.

Integrating Collaborative Concept Mapping Tools with Group Memory and Retrieval Functions

H. Ulrich Hoppe, Katrin Gaßner

University of Duisburg, Germany

{hoppe,gassner}@informatik.uni-duisburg.de

ABSTRACT

The provision of shared visual representations is considered to be an important facilitator for creative processes in group working and learning scenarios. Although reusability is an inherent feature of computerised representations in general, a comparative analysis of existing tools shows clear deficits in this respect. We are convinced that reusability and thus sustainability of the results of co-constructive group work can be much enhanced by integrating visual environments with functions for indexing, archiving and retrieval to support the construction of group memories. This is exemplified with a new tool which supports creative working groups in the area of "trend monitoring" and technology transfer. This is an example of organisational learning, but also more standard learning scenarios may benefit from this technology.

Keywords

collaborative visual languages, co-construction, group memory, life-long learning

INTRODUCTION

The co-constructive use of shared visual representations is considered to be an important facilitator for creative processes in group working and learning scenarios. The perspectives range from small learning groups in educational scenarios to learning organisations. The basic function supported by shared visual representations is *externalisation*. According to Nonaka (1994), externalisation plays an important role in "organisational knowledge creation", namely in that it supports the transition from tacit, individual to explicit knowledge.

In computer-supported collaborative learning scenarios, shared workspaces with more or less specific visual representations are used to facilitate and to enrich synchronous communication and collaboration. Typical applications are group discussions (Conklin & Begeman, 1987; Streitz et al., 1998; Hoppe et al., 2000; Gaßner, 2001), scientific argumentation (Suthers et al., 1997), scientific modelling (v. Joolingen, 2000; Pinkwart et al., 2001), group design (Stahl, 2000). According to Hoppe & Plötzner (1999) shared workspace environments support the following types of cognitive processes within the learning group:

- *coordination* of individual contributions or action through external constraints of the shared workspace,
- *reification* of contributions as manipulable objects,
- *"mise en relation"* (in a Piagetian sense) by visually relating individual contributions to each other using a spatial metaphor,
- *reuse* of group results (e.g., for reflection, comparison, further elaboration).

Reusability is, of course, an inherent feature of computerised representations in general. Yet, a critical analysis of existing tools shows that it is usually not very explicitly supported (see below). The main concern appears to be the provision of a rich, flexible and expressive environment for the collaborative sessions, i.e., the collaborative session is essentially conceived as a closed event. We are convinced that reusability and thus sustainability of the results of co-constructive group work can be much enhanced by integrating visual environments with functions for indexing, archiving and retrieval to support the construction of group memories.

Similar orientations have been developed from a knowledge management perspective (e.g., Borghoff & Pareschi, 1998) or from the needs of supporting collaborative design activities (Stahl, 2000). A combination of concept mapping techniques and discussion support in the IBIS tradition with group memory functions has also been pursued in the Compendium approach (Selvin et al., 2001). Although we share the basic orientations, our approach is different in so far as it evolved as a smaller bottom-up activity, driven by the practical need of adapting an existing collaborative visual language framework to the needs of certain creative group processes.

ANALYSIS OF EXISTING SYSTEMS AND TOOLS

The following synopsis and comparison is targeted at *collaborative visual language environments*. In general, we see these as characterised by these features:

- provision of shareable representations in visual, graph-structured format
- co-constructive editing facilities

- support of certain methodologies for brainstorming, knowledge management, learning, etc.

An early account of the notion of "visual languages for co-operation" which is very much congruent with our understanding has been given by Lakin (1990).

Examples

The *gIBIS* system (Conklin & Begemann, 1987) is an early example of using visual languages to represent and elaborate arguments during a design process. It is used cooperatively yet asynchronously. It is based on a conceptual representation but does not provide operational semantics in the sense of automatic processing. The visualisation of the arguments and ideas is expected to make the design process more rational. As a spin-off, a documentation is obtained and important concepts may be explicitly recognised.

Another example that stresses more the aspect of workflow semantics is the *SEPIA* system (Streitz et al., 1992). SEPIA, developed for the cooperative design of hypermedia documents, offers four types of visual languages: planning, argumentation, content and a rhetorical space. Particularly the argumentation space uses a graph representation derived from S. Toulmin's argument patterns. The generation of some types of contributions in one workspace causes the automatic generation of an adequate object in another, which is an invitation for further exploration. The SEPIA system has later been modified to support face-to-face meetings and discussions. This system called *Dolphin* supports also free-hand-drawing and handwriting (Streitz et al., 1998). Since Dolphin is based on SEPIA, though not every SEPIA feature is offered, we will treat the "union" of the two systems as one.

In the *CSILE* environment (Scardamalia et al., 1992) learners construct knowledge cooperatively by creating a base of learning material which integrates graphics and text. This "community database" is extended through critical annotations of documents which capture a flow of a discussion and knowledge refinement. The working procedure is distributed and asynchronous. Documents in the database are not linked but can be searched which allows using existing material in several contexts. Although CSILE is not primarily based on a structured visual representation, we have considered it since it is a collaborative learning environment with interesting group memory features.

The *Belvedere* system (Suthers et al., 1995) was designed to teach students scientific argumentation. It uses a graph notation similar to SEPIA's rhetorical space. It offers two types of content objects, data and hypotheses. By using the system, argumentation rules such as "hypotheses not supported by data are not accepted" should be understood. Via an agent, the system analyses the developed structure and points out missing relations. In recent versions, co-operation is supported by the means of a shared workspace environment (Suthers et al., 1997).

The *CardBoard* environment (Gaßner et al., 1998) allows for creating multiple visual languages by parameterising a general shared workspace environment. A particular language profile specifies the syntax of the respective visual language in terms of a set of relations ("connector cards"), their argument slots, and the basic object types ("content cards"). To add semantics in terms of domain models or knowledge bases, an interface is provided that transfers actions from the visual language environment to the semantic plug-in component (Mühlenbrock, Tewissen & Hoppe, 1997). This architecture allows for flexibly defining semantically enriched tools, such as, e.g., a cooperative editor and simulator for Petri Nets (Wagler, 1998) or a discussion environment (Gaßner, 2001). The same plug-in architecture has also been used for analysing action patterns in collaborative learning and problem solving scenarios (Mühlenbrock & Hoppe, 1999).

Comparison

We will use the following *criteria* to classify collaboration support systems under the perspective of supporting knowledge management and a knowledge flow, e.g. for organisational learning (criteria are not meant to be descriptive not to judge the systems as better or worse):

- *Domain independence*: Specific methods such as cooperative text planning or brainstorming need specialised tools. The question is how flexibly the system can be adapted to different representations and forms of usage.
- *Shared workspaces* (and shared objects) are essential for cooperative work in distributed, both distance and face-to-face, scenarios. The reification feature depends on shared objects.
- Applicability in *synchronous mode*.
- Applicability in *asynchronous mode* (e.g., discussion threads or group archives).
- Flexible *definition of language syntax*: It should be easy to define different visual representations on a syntactic level without having to reprogram the system.
- *Externally definable semantics*: The provision of mechanisms to plug-in components defining object semantics or operational semantics (e.g. in modelling applications). Enables intelligent background processes to support the workflow as well constraint-checking of solutions.

- System driven *interpretations of states or processes* can support special perspectives on the visual maps. This can increase the awareness for the users.
- *Repositories* can be provided not only for storing and accessing intermediate or final products, but also to store processes or action histories. Can be combined with annotation facilities.
- *Replicated architectures* in which application data are synchronised but maintained autonomously in several places of the distributed environment allow for flexible sharing models (co-existence of private and public workspaces) and robustness (recovery).
- *Integration of common media formats* (text, graphics, sound, animations) is important for a unified knowledge management across different representations and tools.
- *Free-hand input*: In our experience, free-hand input facilities (hand writing, sketching) are particularly well-suited to support informal, creative processes, as e.g. in brainstorming sessions where typing is disruptive.
- Explicit *support of process models* means that the system supports different working phases or working goals, usually in accordance with certain discussion styles or learning methods.
- *Media repositories*: Independent of the products developed with the specific tool, repositories of foreign material in common formats can be provided. Here, good retrieval functions are of particular interest.

	Belvedere	***CardBoard***	**CSILE**	**SEPIA/ Dolphin**	**GIBIS**
Domain independence	o	+	+	+	+
Shared workspaces	+	+	-	+	-
Asynchronous work	?	-	+	+	+
Synchronous communication	+	+	-	+	-
Flexible definition of language syntax	-	+	-	-	-
Externally definable semantics	-	+	-	-	-
System driven interpretation of states or processes (filters)	through agents	through plug-in	-	-	-
Repositories	product repository	action protocol, no product DB	+	product repository	+
Replicated data maintenance	-	+	-	-	-
Process models (workflow support)	argumentation patterns	- (Gaßner et al.,1998) + (Gaßner, 2001)	(implicit)	different visual languages for diff. phases	+
Integration of common media formats	-	+	+	+	-
Free hand input	-	+	-	+	+
Media repositories	(in learning material)	-	+	-	-

Table 1: **Comparison of collaborative environments**

The distribution of positive marks indicates that the design of these systems was very much targeted at the first group of features. The second group of criteria is inspired by the engineering of standardising and "factoring out" certain generic functions that has guided an essential portion of our work on CardBoard. Replication (criterion 9) is of more general interest since it allows for very flexible forms of interaction in synchronous mode.

Generally, the last two groups of criteria reflect in some way or other system features which are desirable to support the sustainability and reusability of the work done in a collaborative environment. Yet looking at the distribution of marks, here, gives a too positive picture. Even if specific support is provided, there is one restriction: information access functions and "indexed archives" are usually confined to the products of the system itself, i.e., there is no real interoperability to share knowledge elements with external sources (e.g., by importing resources from the web or by exchanging elements with a general corporate memory). So, the main problem is that current systems are not *open*! We will particularly address this challenge in the case study reported below.

Extensions of collaborative visual language environments

In most cases, the development of more or less generic visual language environments aims at obtaining easy-to-communicate visualisations rather than at providing (seem-)formal machine-interpretable representations. The focus is on interactive tools and interfaces to represent a domain or support a certain task, not on system-internal structure and semantics. In contrast to the generic cooperative environments mentioned, specific tools like STELLA (http://www.hps-inc.com) or Rational Rose (http://www.rational.com) provide visual interfaces for existing model semantics, as e.g. "system dynamics" in the case of STELLA or UML in the case of Rational Rose. They (implicitly) use visual languages and provide a complete semantic interpretation to augment relations between nodes by operations.

A recent example of a collaborative learning environment based on a domain-specific visual language is the COLER system (Constantine-Gonzalez & Suthers, 2000). COLER supports the co-construction of entity-relationship (ER) models for database modelling. A current redesign and reimplementation of the CardBoard environment (JavaCardBoard) is focussed at supporting different kinds of more or less formalised visual languages, including Petri nets and system dynamics models, which can be mixed and combined with free-hand annotations (Pinkwart et al., 2001).

It was also Suthers (1999) who studied and reflected the impact of different visual tools and representations on collaborative learning discourse ("representational bias"). Typically, concrete representation systems come with inherent characteristics which favour or inhibit certain aspects and thus influence learning and working styles.

CASE STUDY: SUPPORTING TREND MONITORING IN SMALL TEAMS

In the following we will describe a modification of the CardBoard environment which has been developed to support small working groups monitoring new trends in science and technology. As a result, a new system, called *FreeStyler* has been developed based on the requirements defined and assessed with two application sites: the technology transfer department (TTD) of our university and a "pilot development group" in a large European company. Although the scenario is not primarily a learning scenario, it involves aspects of organisational learning and the incremental building of a group memory.

Since the role of TTD is to act as a transmission interface between university and industry, a "trend" cannot be determined by a retrospective of cases but rather as a combination of existing information and new requests the TTD receives. Information connections result in a structure that is the TTD-perspective on a trend and its information context. The daily work of TTD consists largely of personal consulting through which individual solutions for co-operation opportunities have to be found (Figure 20). More or less static information prepared for the web turned out to be not adequate for such a dynamic process and was also not well-suited to support internal information exchange. The consulting process includes phases in which only hand-written notes are useful, phases where information is exchanged and phases in which multiple media have to be put into a common context.

From a representational and media point of view, the system supports free-hand input to be able to smoothly support informal creative processes, structured representations (discussion graphs, models) as well as certain visual representations of data collections. All these features are equally interesting for many learning scenarios such as scientific argumentation and modelling.

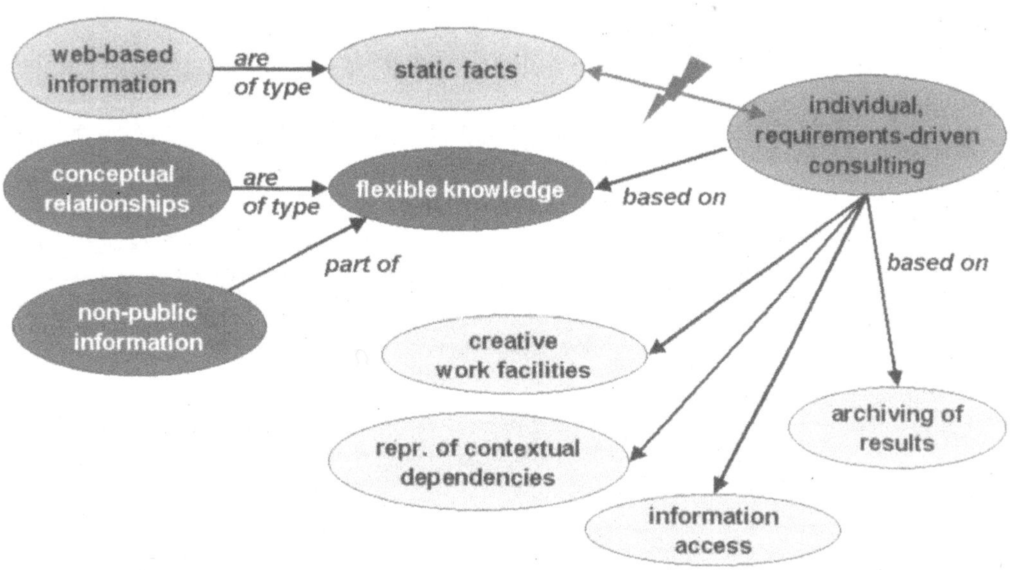

Figure 20: **Basic dependencies and requirements**

For the TTD, trend monitoring and consulting is a continuous, long term process as shown in Figure 21. In most cases, hand-written notes are taken during a first telephone contact and are a basis for further meetings. Open questions are fixed to be further annotated and elaborated on, new documents are added or old documents are linked. Such a preparation of materials represents the input for a later meeting that might lead to another accumulation of media and materials.

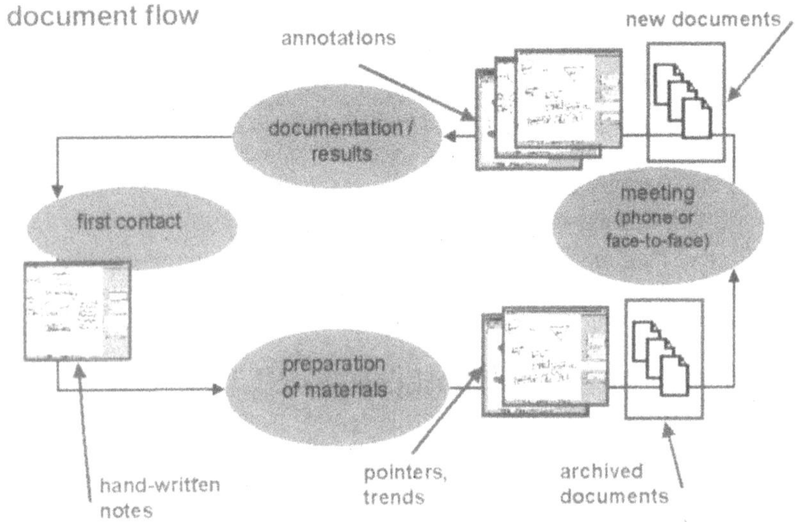

Figure 21: **Document flow related to trend monitoring**

It is a general observation, that externalisation forms the bottleneck of knowledge management projects which try to integrate dynamic process information. In our approach, we provide semi-structured, heterogeneous representations which can be refined and grow. The document flow does not introduce new procedures or formalities as compared to the original process which was only partially computerised. The benefit that we expect to gain by providing integrated support for this process lies in the avoidance of representational discontinuities and of interoperability deficits.

Technical features

In the following, the main features of the TTD knowledge management system are introduced. Figure 22 shows the overall system architecture and main interactions. The user interface is introduced in the next subsection which also includes an example of the evolution of a document.

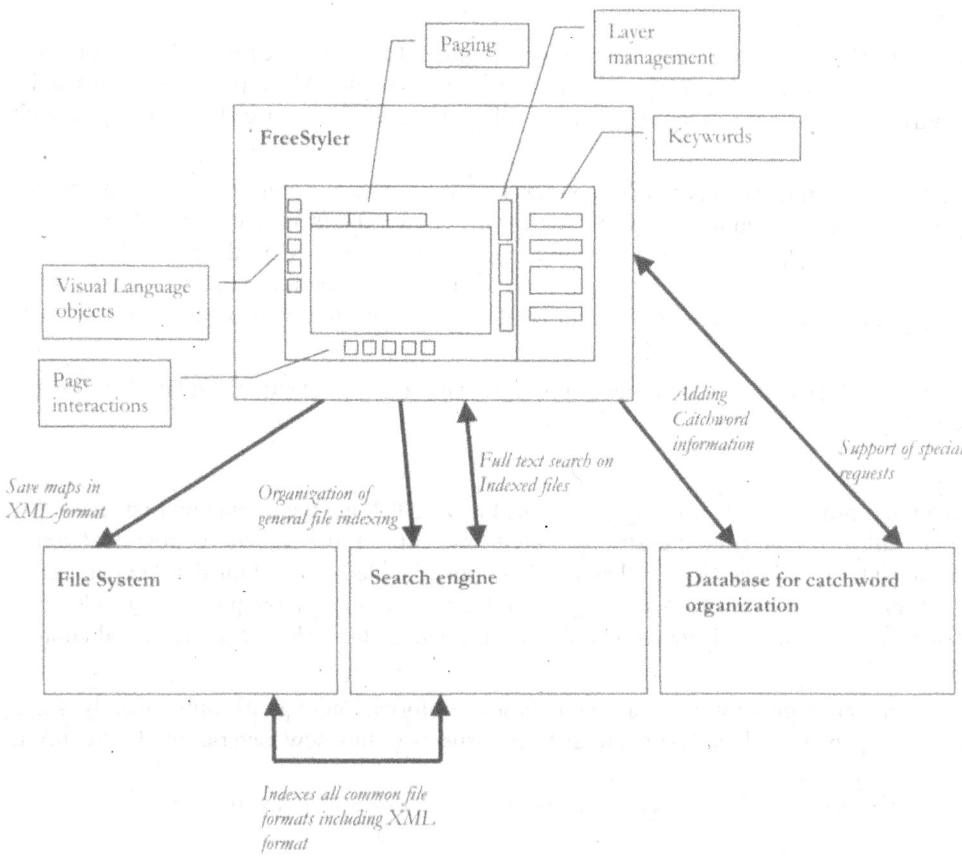

Figure 22: **System overview**

Visual language

FreeStyler is a Java application that interacts with a powerful search engine (*Verity*, cf. www.verity.com) and a database system. A visual language is used to structure the content. Predefined shapes provided on a palette represent different input types to distinguish different elements in the elaboration and analysis of an issue. A clear distinction of contribution types using shapes and colours supports the interpretation of material by other users. Hand-written annotations can be added flexibly.

Easy paging through workspace elements

The application offers pages to structure a document. By the use of "page tabs" (on top of the workspace) it is easy to go directly to a page without scrolling. Pages can be named by the user. Each page offers, in turn, a couple of layers in order to stratify different levels of input. There are layers for hand-written input and for the entries. The layer sequence can be changed and can be switched off. This allows for representing different levels of detail and different perspectives.

User-definable hyperlinks

User-definable internal links can be added as specific elements to the workspace. Their content is the link address which points to another page represented by its marker. It is possible to add multiple markers to pages which are shown as headers on the page tabs. Another entry type can also be used for external links to URLs and files. According to the file type, an appropriate viewer is selected and invoked when the node is activated.

Embedding of objects representing data collections or documents

The same type of entries that are used for external links are also used to represent document collections.

Embedding query objects

List entries also contain query results of the search engine which realises a full text search on the common file formats e.g. .doc, .pdf, .xml, .txt, etc. Using the Java Native Interface the query is handled by a Dynamic Link Library which uses the API of the search engine. The result is given back to the application and the retrieved documents are listed in the list entry. There they can be accessed interactively. The associated database offers other query possibilities: It allows for associating keywords with files and to ask for newest keywords and e.g. connections among keywords. To express these queries, the Java-SQL interface is used.

XML format

The developed materials are called "maps", following the idea of concept mapping. They are saved in XML format using the Java DOM interface. In connection with the search engine which is also able to search XML format, the maps can be searched as well. Using the keywords, which are also saved to the XML files, maps can be interrelated using the search engine.

The TTD working process includes both synchronous and asynchronous co-operation. The search mechanisms support also the asynchronous access to documents. The development of materials by different authors is intended and supported. Integrated mail facilities allow for notifying group members about new occurrences. To reach more flexibility, documents can either be referred inside the mail or the whole document can be sent. For the latter, it is possible either to send the XML file or a version transformed to a graphics format. Mailing lists can be defined during the work with a document for automatic notification.

Currently, FreeStyler is either used individually or in face-to-face meetings with a big interactive display. Mostly, co-operation occurs in asynchronous mode.

Example

The following group of figures show the process of developing a map. In Figure 23, FreeStyler contains first notes that have been entered during a telephone call. A person from industry has asked for a contact to a university group that works on the topic of fuel cells. The notes include typical questions at that stage for more detailed elaboration. The "client" asked for references to former projects and for information on the topic in general. He is also interested in published results. The right hand side of the application window contains the keyword entry section (for indexing). Here, also name and address of the contact person are noted.

Figure 24 shows the result of a first preparation phase wherein a user adds some information requests. Subsequently, some pages have been added. The links on the page (small circles) relate different aspects to this new material put to the linked pages.

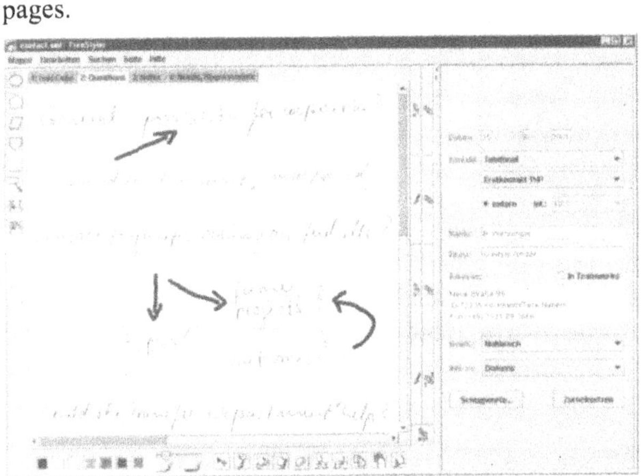

Figure 23

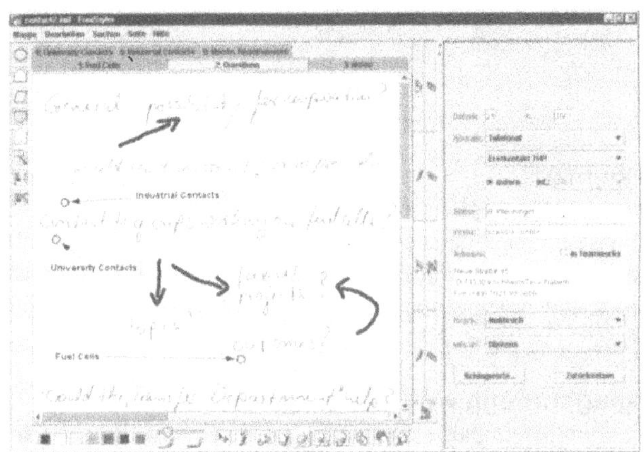

Figure 24

Figure 25 represents a page with institutional contacts. The institutions are listed in entries that are again related to corresponding URLs. Later, during a meeting, it is a very easy to follow that link for more information and, e.g., to discuss the relevance of such a contact. This is a typical activity during a meeting with experts because the TTD itself does not have detailed content expertise for each scientific field or topic and cannot decide on beforehand which contact might be interesting for an industry partner. On the right hand side of the screen, a web browser has been invoked with a requested URL. If the content of the list node had been a file path, the appropriate viewer would have been called to show the file by double clicking on the node.

Figure 26 shows a more content oriented page that might be a central part of a trend documentation. The map represents information on "fuel cells". Therefore, general concepts and background information are combined in a structured way. In this figure, multiple entries are integrated: Some entries represent information associated with the trend. Another is a graphical entry. The opened dialogue allows for searching the indexed documents of the file system concerning the requested concept. This dialogue window covers a list node with results from a previous request.

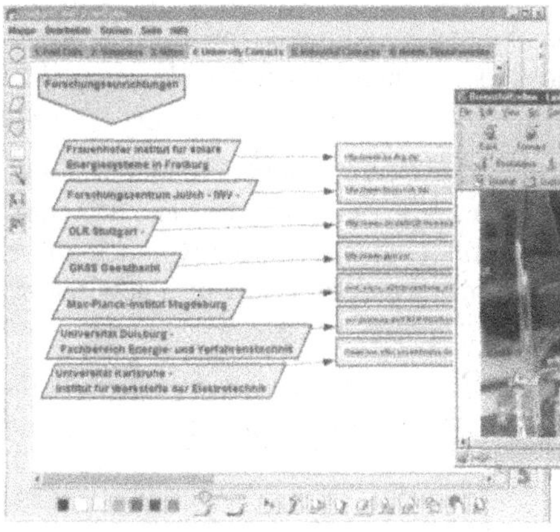

Figure 25

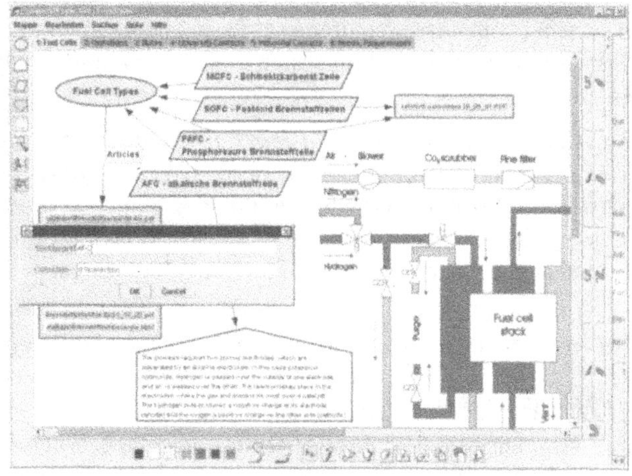

Figure 26

Figure 27 shows the possible use of FreeStyler for concept mapping enhanced with free hand annotations. The dialogue supports the request for files that are associated with special keywords. Based on the result, the concepts in this map can be related to available other material.

Figure 28 is an example of a comprehensive representation that is easily re-usable. Based on a geographical map, internal links are added which show where contacts to fuel cell producers are available. The links point to other FreeStyler pages that give more information about this concrete company.

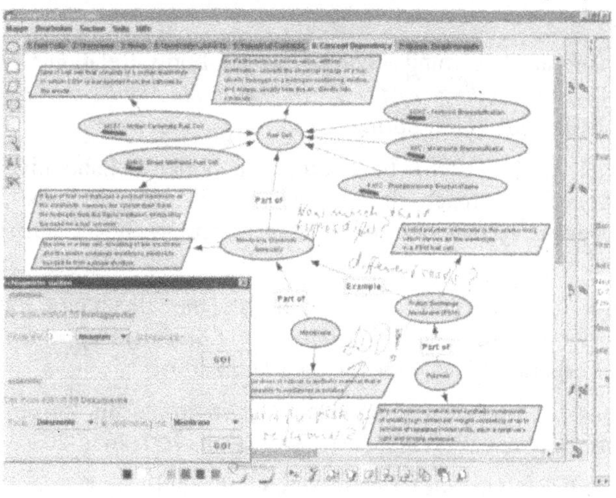

Figure 27

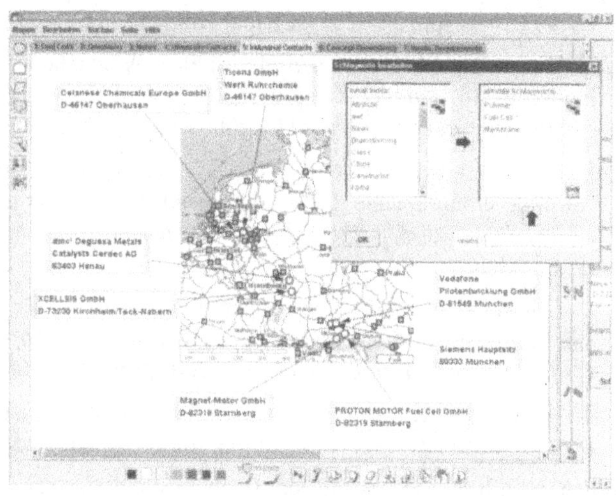

Figure 28

Through a dialogue, a FreeStyler map can be indexed with keywords. Already existing keywords are shown on the left. Putting a new keyword, the list on the left goes to the alphabetically closest existing word to avoid the entry of similar and potentially redundant keywords (synonyms – homonyms).

DISCUSSION

FreeStyler is currently being evaluated in everyday use in our TTD. At a first glance, organising technology transfer is still a tough problem, in contrast to which the use of FreeStyler is smooth and straightforward. Detailed evaluation results will be available soon.

We see the following analogies between our case study in trend monitoring and general functions for collaborative learning environments:

- The "trend monitoring" activity corresponds to learning activities in which students themselves explore a given theme or problem by searching relevant information, associating and elaborating this information and by documenting the results. This is typical for problem-based learning (Koschmann et al., 1996), but also for other types of open learning situations.
- "Trends" in our scenario correspond to "themes" in learning situations. FreeStyler allows for treating themes as moving targets, i.e., for moving from one are of interest to others, while maintaining a structured record of what has been done.

- The system is *open* (see requirements formulated above) in that it can search and integrate external sources in arbitrary format as long as the standard search engine is able to handle these. References to external sources are objects within the system.
- The system maintains a *base of index terms* in the form of a rudimentary thesaurus. We would implement a full thesaurus support only if practically needed. Yet, we have already identified one very interesting feature: The detection of new terms in our TTD application may indicate a new trend (an "innovation") which is usually much more interesting than the assignment of an already existing term. Accordingly, in learning, the appearance of a new theme may indicate new learning opportunities and may trigger certain types of "innovative" group processes.

Technically, the FreeStyler system is currently unified with the new version of the CardBoard environment which supports various palettes of languages at a time (e.g. to facilitate modelling). Also this opens new application perspectives.

ACKNOWLEDGMENTS

We thank Jörg Dixkens and his colleagues from the TTD for his valuable input and insightful suggestions. In the implementation work we were strongly supported by our student collaborators Martin Fendrich and Stefan Buschmann. This work was partially supported by grants from the Ministry of Science and Technology of the Federal State of Nordrhein-Westfalen and Mannesmann Pilotentwicklung (now Vodafone).

REFERENCES

Borghoff, U. M. & Pareschi, R. (1998). *Information technology for knowledge management.* Berlin, Heidelberg, New York: Springer.

Conklin, J. & Begemann, M. L. (1987). gIBIS: A hypertext tool for team design deliberation. In *Proceedings of Hypertext'87* (pp. 247-251). Chapel Hill (North Carolina).

Constantino-Gonzalez, M. A., Suthers, D. (2000). A coached collaborative learning environment for Entity-Relationship modeling. In Gauthier, G., Frasson, C., VanLehn, K. (eds.), *Proceedings of the 5th International Conference on Intelligent Tutoring Systems* ITS 2000 (pp. 252-261), Montreal, June 2000: Springer.

Gaßner, K., Tewissen, F., Mühlenbrock, M., Loesch, A. & Hoppe, H. U. (1998). Intelligently supported collaborative learning environments based on visual languages: a generic approach. In Darses, F. & Zaraté, P. (eds.), *Proceedings of 3rd International Conference on the Design of Cooperative Systems* (pp. 47-55). Cannes (Frankreich).

Gaßner, K. (2001). Architecture of a Cooperative Discussion Environment based on Visual Languages. In. Dillenbourg, P., Eurelings, A. & Hakkarainen, K. (eds.). *Proceedings of the European Conference on Computer-Supported Collaborative Learning* (EuroCSCL-2001) (pp. 261-268). Maastricht, The Netherlands, March 2001.

Hoppe, H. U., Gaßner, K., Mühlenbrock, M. & Tewissen, F. (2000). Distributed visual language environments for co-operation and learning: Applications and intelligent support. In *Group Decision and Negotiation, 9(3)*, 205-220.

v. Joolingen, W. (2000). Designing for collaborative discovery learning. In Gauthier, G. Frasson, C. & VanLehn, K.(eds.), *Proceedings of the 5th International Conference on Intelligent Tutoring Systems* ITS 2000 (pp. 202-211). Berlin et al.: Springer.

Koschmann, T., Kelson, A.C., Feltovich, P.J. & Barrows, H.S. (1996). Computer-supported problem-based learning: a principled approach to the use of computers in collaborative learning. In Koschmann, T.D. (ed.). *CSCL: Theory and Practice of an Emerging Paradigm* (pp. 83-124). Hillsdale, NJ: Lawrence Erlbaum.

Lakin, F. (1990). Visual languages for co-operation: a performing medium approach to systems for cooperative work. In Galegher, J., Kraut, R. & Egido, C. (eds.). *Intellectual Teamwork* (pp. 453-488). Hillsdale, NJ: Lawrence Erlbaum.

Nonaka, I. (1994). A Dynamic Theory of Organisational Knowledge Creation. *Organization Science* **5** (1), 14-37.

Pinkwart, N., Hoppe, H.U., & Gaßner, K. (2001). Integration of domain-specific elements into visual language based collaborative environments. Accepted for *Proceedings of CRIWG 2001* (Int.'l Workshop on Groupware, Darmstadt, Germany, September 2001).

Scardamalia, M. & Bereiter, C. (1992). An Architecture for Collaborative Knowledge Building. In De Corte, E., Linn, M.C., Mandl, H. & Verschaffel, L. (eds.), *Computer-Based learning environments and problem solving (NATO ASI Series, Vol. 84)* (S. 41-66). Berlin Heidelberg: Springer-Verlag.

Scardamalia, M., Bereiter, C., Brett, C., Burtis, P. J., Calhoun, C. & Smith Lea, N. (1992). Educational applications of a networked communal database. *Interactive Learning Environments, 2(1)*, 45-71.

Selvin, A., Buckingham Shum, S., Sierhuis, M., Conklin, J., Zimmermann, B., Palus, C., Drath, W., Horth, D., Domingue, J., Motta, E., Li, G. (2001). *Compendium: Making Meetings into Knowledge Events*. The Open University, Milton Keynes (UK), KMI-TR-103 (www.kmi.open.ac.uk/tr/papers/kmi-tr-103.pdf).

Stahl, G. (2000). Collaborative information environments to support knowledge construction by communites. *AI & Society* 14, 1-27.

Streitz, N., Geißler, J., Haake, J. & Hol, J. (1998). DOLPHIN: Integrated meeting support across Liveboards, local and remote desktop environments. In Fankhauser, P. & Ockenfeld, M. (eds.), *Integrated publication and information systems*. (S. 57-74). Darmstadt: GMD IPSI.

Streitz, N., Haake, J., Hannemann, J., Lemke, A., Schuler, W., Schütt, H. & Thüring, M. (1992). SEPIA: A cooperative hypermedia authoring environment. In *Proceedings of the 4th ACM Conference on Hypertext(ECHT'92)* (pp. 11-22). Milano (Italy).

Suthers, D. D. (1999). Representational bias as guidance for learning interactions: A research agenda. In Lajoie, S. P. & Vivet, M. (eds.), *Artificial intelligence in education* (pp. 121-128). Amsterdam: IOS Press.

Suthers, D., Toth, E. E., and Weiner, A. (1997). An integrated approach to implementing collaborative inquiry in the classroom. In *Proceedings of CSCL '97* (Int.'l Conf. on Computer Supported Collaborative Learning, Toronto, Canada, December 1997), 272-279.

Suthers, D., Weiner, A., Connelly, J. & Paolucci, M. (1995). Belvedere: Engaging students in critical discussion of science and public policy issues. In Greer, J. (ed.), *Proceedings of the 7th World Conference on Artificial Intelligence in Education* (pp. 266-273). Whashington DC (USA).

TrendMonitoring (1999). Funded by the Ministry for Schools, Science, Economy and Research of the State Nordrhein-Westphalen (Gemany). *http://www.uni-duisburg.de/THP/trendmonitoring/*

Wagler, F. (1998). Erstellung eines Petrinetz-basierten Steuerungsmechanismus zur Behandlung von Turn-Taking-Regeln in Gruppen-interaktiven Spielen (Development of a petri net based controlling mechanism for the handling of turn-taking rules in interactive group games). Unpublished masters thesis. University of Duisburg, Department of Mathematics and Computer Science.

WORKSHOP PROGRAM

Qualitative Methods and the Use of Videotaped Data: A "Data Session"

Curtis LeBaron, Rogers Hall, Timothy Koschmann, Yrjö Engström

Videotape is an increasingly popular tool for researchers within CSCL and allied fields. Participants in this workshop will consider questions and issues related to the use of videotaped data. How are videotaped data successfully collected? How might videotaped data best be analyzed? How might analysis of videotaped data be coordinated with other sorts of data collection and analysis? What are the advantages and disadvantages of videotaped data? After the panel organizers make introductory remarks participants will conduct a "data session" around videotaped data of "real" interaction within a PBL (Problem-Based Learning) classroom.

PURPOSE

The CSCL community of researchers seems to be in the process of finding (and negotiating) its methodological footings. On one hand, CSCL scholars have inherited the methodological debates of more established disciplines (e.g., the extent to which phenomena can and should be studied "in the moment" through first-hand observation). On the other hand, CSCL researchers face new methodological problems and issues as they grapple with new computer technologies and their pedagogical potentials (e.g., trying to observe and document learning among students who are geographically distributed and asynchronous users of technology). One research tool that is currently being considered and debated within CSCL and allied fields is the collection and analysis of videotaped data. For instance, at the most recent AERA conference (2001), dozens of panels related to the use of videotaped data in research projects. The following questions are especially timely and relevant to the CSCL community:

- How are videotaped data successfully collected?
- How might videotaped data best be analyzed?
- How might analysis of videotaped data be coordinated with other sorts of data collection and analysis?
- What are the advantages and disadvantages of videotaped data?

In the proposed workshop, we will address these questions and related issues. After the panel organizers make introductory remarks (i.e., explain their own uses of videotaped data in research approaches that are somewhat contrasting), workshop participants will conduct a "data session" around videotaped data of "real" interaction within a PBL (Problem-Based Learning) classroom. Data sessions are a routine practice of some qualitative researchers, who meet informally to examine data together (viewing it repeatedly and carefully) such that observations and findings inductively emerge. In addition to analyzing the videotaped data together, workshop participants will have opportunities to discuss the questions listed above, and other relevant topics.

INTENDED PARTICIPANTS

We solicit the participation of qualitative researchers who have experience working with videotaped data and are actively engaged in video analysis. Researchers that have not used videotaped data, or who are only beginning to collect and analyze videotape, or who are not currently conducting video analysis would probably not benefit from this workshop and are therefore discouraged from applying. The focus of the workshop will be on qualitative methods, so quantitative researchers are discouraged from applying. Because data sessions work best with a relatively small group of researchers, participation within this workshop will be limited to 24 people (including the 4 organizers).

ORGANIZATION

This half-day workshop will be organized as follows:

1. Welcome, introduction to topic (Koschmann, 5-10 minutes)
2. Methods presentation #1 (LeBaron, 15 minutes)
3. Methods presentation #2 (Hall, 15 minutes)
4. Methods presentation #3 (Engeström, 15 minutes)

5. Introduction to videotaped data (Koschmann, 5-10 minutes)
6. Data session (group analysis and discussion, 2 hours)

All necessary materials for this workshop will be provided on site. No preparation is needed prior to the workshop.

CHAIR

Timothy Koschmann
Department of Medical Education
Southern Illinois University
School of Medicine
P.O. Box 19230
Springfield, IL 62704-9230
(e-mail: tkoschmann@siumed.edu)

ORGANIZERS

(1) Yrjö Engeström
Center for Activity Theory and Developmental Work Research
P.O.Box 47
00014 UNIVERSITY OF HELSINKI
Finland
&
Laboratory of Comparative Human Cognition
University of California, San Diego
9500 Gilman Drive
La Jolla
CA 92093
USA
(email: yrjo.engestrom@helsinki.fi)

(2) Rogers Hall
School of Education
University of California, Berkeley
Berkeley, CA
(email: rhall@socrates.Berkeley.edu)

(3) Curtis D. LeBaron
Department of Organizational Leadership & Strategy
Marriott School of Management
TNRB 590
Brigham Young University
Provo, UT 84602
(email: lebaron@byu.edu)

Integrating CSCL Environments and Digital Libraries

Mary Marlino, Tammy Sumner, Mimi Recker

The purpose of this workshop is to promote discussion and collaboration between developers of CSCL environments, digital library developers and user communities. This topic is an important and complex one, and is comprised of both technical and social challenges. With a few notable exceptions, these research strands have not integrated their efforts in any meaningful or scalable manner. Towards this end, we are looking for a group of researchers and practitioners who are willing to work together in a workshop to identify challenges and opportunities for the integration of a variety of CSCL environments and digital library applications.

CONTACTS:

Mary Marlino (marlino@ucar.edu)

Tammy Sumner (sumner@colorado.edu)

Mimi Recker (mimi.recker@usu.edu)

PURPOSE:

The purpose of this workshop is to promote discussion and collaboration between developers of CSCL environments, digital library developers and user communities. This topic is an important and complex one, and is comprised of both technical and social challenges. With a few notable exceptions, these two research strands have not integrated their efforts in any meaningful or scalable manner. Both sets of technologies are now at the "post-infancy" stage; CSCL environments have been shown to be powerful and effective for a variety of purposes in many applications, including scientific visualization, general and discipline-specific problem solving, and content mastery. Digital libraries typically offer access to a managed collection of electronic information, with associated services, and are now rapidly emerging as promising teaching and learning tools in a variety of disciplines. This emergence has been supported by almost a decade of research on basic digital library technologies, and by a substantial interest among several funding agencies, notably the National Science Foundation. The full agenda for digital libraries is an ambitious one; in addition to providing access to quality resources, they are in many cases also promising to serve as the "intellectual commons" or "community center" for a particular discipline. As such, they attempt to address a full range of issues in the teaching and learning endeavor. Many CSCL environments pull together a variety of digital library-like content, in effect, creating purpose-built digital libraries. Clearly, the opportunities for important synergies between these two groups are timely and urgent.

INTENDED AUDIENCE:

We solicit the participation of researchers, educators, practitioners, and industry representatives who are actively engaged in the development, design, software implementation or classroom implementation of collaborative learning communities, tools for teachers and students, and interactive feedback and assessment. We also solicit input from developers of digital libraries, researchers who investigate basic digital libraries technologies, and consumers of digital library services. The workshop is designed primarily for people involved in such ongoing research and practice but is open to the general CSCL audience. We are looking for a group of researchers and practitioners who are willing to work together in a workshop to identify challenges and opportunities for the integration of a variety of CSCL environments and digital library applications.

ORGANIZATION:

This full day workshop will take place on Monday, January 7 and will be organized into two parts. The morning session will be devoted to demonstrations of CSCL environments and digital library projects. The afternoon session will provide an opportunity for a discussion of possible integration scenarios and outline issues that may result from the discussion. Participants should be prepared to demonstrate a particular CSCL environment or digital library.

BACKGROUND:

All workshop organizers have extensive experience with digital libraries. Marlino is the PI of the Digital Library for Earth System Education, a community-owned facility dedicated to offering high-quality resources that foster learning about the

Earth at all educational levels. DLESE users include learners and instructors in all venues, many of whom are also contributors and developers of educational resources and tools, providers of scientific knowledge, and evaluators of DLESE materials. Prior to this, she was Director of Educational Technology at the United States Air Force Academy in Colorado Springs.

Sumner is the co-PI of DLESE, and is responsible for the technical leadership of the project. In addition, she has research interests and experience in the development of on-line communities, collaborative learning tools, and usability issues. She is an Assistant Professor of Computer Science at the University of Colorado and is affiliated with the University's Center for LifeLong Learning and Design.

Recker is the PI of the Instructional Architect project, a curriculum creation and integration service for the National SMET Digital Library. Her research interests include digital libraries, using the Internet in education, and artificial intelligence and cognitive science in education. She is an Associate Professor in the Department of Instructional Technology at Utah State University.

Designing Computational Models of Collaborative Learning Interaction

Patrick Jermann, Martin Mühlenbrock, Amy Soller

Computational models are computer-based representations that help to describe, explain, and analyze patterns of human behavior. Recently, we have seen a considerable amount of interest in using computational models to both represent the interaction, and better understand the process of collaborative learning. Because these processes are complex, and include coordination of both cognitive and social aspects of learning, understanding and supporting group interaction is particularly difficult. Modeling the processes involved in collaborative learning may help us to better analyze and dynamically support collaborative learning activities on-line.

Many different types of computational models exist. Some help to identify group members' roles, others help scientists understand specific aspects of collaborative learning, such as knowledge sharing or cognitive conflict. Computational models that focus specifically on social factors may be applied to many different domains, while those designed to facilitate task oriented interaction may be bound to a particular domain. In this workshop, we will discuss the requirements for modeling different aspects of interaction. For example, what data are needed (e.g. participation statistics, coded dialog, task-based actions) to construct and maintain different types of models, and how should this data should be represented? This workshop will aim to address these questions, and others along these lines. A complete list of issues for discussion is available at the workshop homepage.

PURPOSE

Computational models are computer-based representations that help to describe, explain, and analyze patterns of human behavior, and predict future behavior. Recently, we have seen a considerable amount of interest in using computational models to understand the processes of collaborative learning. Because these processes are complex, and include coordination of both task and social learning activities, understanding and supporting group interaction is particularly difficult. Modeling the processes involved in collaborative learning may help us to better analyze and dynamically support collaborative learning activities on-line.

Many different types of computational models exist. Some help to identify group members' roles, others help scientists understand specific aspects of collaborative learning, such as knowledge sharing or cognitive conflict. Computational models that focus specifically on social factors may be applied to many different domains, while those designed to facilitate task oriented interaction may be bound to a particular domain. In this workshop, we will discuss the requirements for modeling different aspects of interaction. For example, what data are needed (e.g. participation statistics, coded dialog, task-based actions) to construct and maintain different types of models, and how should this data should be represented? This workshop will aim to address these questions, and others along these lines that are listed below.

Issue 1: Components of computational models

What types of models exist, and how do they differ?

There are many variables that may help to characterize collaborative interaction. Are there key indicators (e.g. participation) that allow us to characterize interaction in any case?

What information, and what components are needed to develop models suited to analyze various aspects of collaborative learning interaction?

How much and what kind of contextual, domain specific information is needed? What are the benefits gained, and perhaps the generality lost by including contextual information in a computational model? Can we reuse AI's work and lessons learned?

Issue 2: Moving from the conceptual level to implementation.

What sort of information should be coded and logged, and at what granularity? What compilation or abstraction methods are needed to construct a computational model from a logfile describing the group interaction?

How do conceptual models (in terms of, for example, roles, conflict, constructive argumentation) translate into computational models that can be represented and manipulated by a computer?

What is the technical cost (existing techniques, intensive computation) of making the theoretical indicators we deal with operational?

Issue 3: Towards a generic description of interaction

Is a unified representation of interaction possible/desirable ? For example, would it be useful to have a "Standard Collaborative Interaction Description Language" (SCIDL)? What about a Standard Collaborative Interaction Log Format (SCILF) ?

How can we compare and evaluate different models of collaboration across research disciplines? Will a unified scheme help? Would visualization tools based on a unified scheme help shape pedagogic interventions?

INTENDED AUDIENCE

The design of computational interaction models requires all the parties involved in CSCL to work together. We therefore encourage researchers, developers and practitioners in the CSCL field to participate to the workshop. As the workshop relies on discussion amongst participants we would like to limit the size of the audience to 40 people.

ORGANIZATION

The workshop will be organized for a full-day, and will consist of three or four sessions depending on the number of position papers received. Each session will address a particular issue and start with a group of three short presentations (20 minutes + 5 minutes for questions). The presentations will be followed by group discussion focused around the questions addressed by the presentations.

RELATED INFORMATION

This workshop is being organized, in part, because of the interest raised at Euro-CSCL 2001 from the chairs' review paper and as a follow-up to ECAI-2000's related workshop:

Jermann, P., Soller, A., & Muehlenbrock, M. (2001). From mirroring to guiding: A review of state of the art technology for supporting collaborative learning. Proceedings of the First European Conference on Computer-Supported Collaborative Learning, Maastricht, The Netherlands, 324-331.

ORGANIZERS

Patrick Jermann

Learning Research and Development Center

University of Pittsburgh

pjermann@pitt.edu

Martin Muehlenbrock

Xerox Research Center Europe

Martin.Muehlenbrock@xrce.xerox.com

Amy Soller

Learning Research and Development Center and

Intelligent Systems Program

University of Pittsburgh

soller@pitt.edu

ORGANIZING COMMITTEE

Pierre Dillenbourg
TECFA - University of Geneva

H. Ulrich Hoppe
University of Duisburg
Dept. of Mathematics/
Computer Science

Alan Lesgold
School of Education
University of Pittsburgh

The Learning Grid

John Cherniavsky, Eric Hamilton

SHORT DESCRIPTION

The notion of Grid computing has arisen with the desire to use computational, communication, and content resources on the internet efficiently and effectively in solving scientific problems. The origin of the term as now used is from the Supercomputing 97 Conference in which a demonstration, involving using 3600 processors from 15 sites in U.S., Germany, and Sweden to solve scientific computing problems in 10 application areas, was given using software from the GLOBUS project that made the coordination of these computations possible. In this workshop we would like to explore the use of the GRID for learning - thus the term Learning GRID. The workshop goal is to formulate a plan for using Grid technologies in the establishment of a Learning Grid. In particular, a desired outcome will be a determination of priorities for Grid development and areas of research requiring support in order to make the Grid an effective learning tool.

PURPOSE

The notion of Grid computing has arisen with the desire to use computational, communication, and content resources on the internet efficiently and effectively in solving scientific problems. The origin of the term as now used is from the Supercomputing 97 Conference in which a demonstration, involving using 3600 processors from 15 sites in U.S., Germany, and Sweden to solve scientific computing problems in 10 application areas, was given using software from the GLOBUS project that made the coordination of these computations possible.

The PACI centers and the Terascale computational resource centers are building a nationwide Computational Grid - called the GRID. The project involves the software integration of computational, communication, and data resources in a wide area network similar to the tasks that operating systems perform with single processor systems. It is envisioned that the GRID would be similar to the nationwide phone system in that anyone, anywhere with internet access could get a computational dial tone that would allow them the use of the GRID to accomplish the tasks they wish using the full resources of the computers, data, and communications available on the internet. Since 1997, the GRID notion has become international with individual countries developing their own GRIDs and the European Union proposing the development of a European-wide GRID.

The GRID has been primarily thought of as a resource for computational scientists. In this workshop we would like to explore the use of the GRID for learning - thus the term Learning GRID.

The Learning GRID, inheriting capabilities from the GRID, will support seamless, universal access to information, seamless access to computation, and seamless access to collaborative communication technologies such as wireless, collaborative virtual environments (CAVES for example), virtual net communities, and collaboration applications that require broadband communications.

The topic of this workshop is the formulation of a plan for using the GRID technologies in the establishment of a Learning GRID. In particular, a desired outcome of this workshop will be a determination of priorities for GRID development and areas of research requiring support in order to make the GRID an effective learning tool

Since this workshop is being held in conjunction with the CSCL meeting, this workshop will have an emphasis on the use of the GRID for collaborative learning . This will be accomplished through:

- ·brief presentations of the existing GRID architecture from GRID architects
- summary of virtual meeting/presence research and requirements for its use
- summary of virtual collaborative experiments and virtual collaborative scientific instrument control
- development of examples of effective collaboration scenarios
- identification of a research and development roadmap to a Learning GRID over the next ten years
- the use of a Learning GRID in K-12, university, vocational, training, and learning for life applications

The presentations will be short and the majority of this workshop's work will be done through participant discussions. A workshop report will be generated.

INTENDED AUDIENCE

We solicit the participation of practitioners and researchers who are engaged in distributed learning activities.

ORGANIZATION

This 1/2 day workshop will consist of an initial session of short invited and submitted presentations on GRID Technologies and applications of GRID affordances to distributed learning. This will be followed by small group brain storming and a whole group discussion. A workshop report on the recommendations of the group will be written.

ORGANIZERS

John Cherniavsky
Education and Human Resources Directorate
National Science Foundation, Room 855
Arlington, VA 22230
email: jchernia@nsf.gov

Eric Hamilton
Division of Research, Evaluation, and Communication
National Science Foundation, Room 855
Arlington, VA 22230
email: ehamilto@nsf.gov

Evaluating Current Capabilities and Future Research Issues in the Use of Online Course Portfolios

Eugene S. Takle, Elsebeth K. Sorensen, Daryl Herzman

SHORT DESCRIPTION

The purposes of the workshop are to (1) examine the theoretical basis for use of online portfolios to enhance individual and collaborative learning, (2) explore current uses, with focus on strengths and weaknesses, and (3) formulate a research agenda that will enable the educational community to accelerate deployment of effectively designed online portfolios in support of individual and collaborative learning. We will use online portfolios as a means of experiencing and sharing ideas about the use of this technology for enhancing the individual and collaborative learning environment through structured dialog, collaborative work, and peer evaluation. The intended outcome is to create a special issue of a relevant journal on portfolios that will serve as a status report on use of portfolios and a launch point for future research and deployment of student online portfolios.

PURPOSE

Online portfolios are viewed as tools in the computer-supported collaborative learning environment that can enhance use of higher-level thinking skills in the learning process. However, the foundation for such tools in learning theory and experience in deploying such tools in either on-campus or distributed learning environments are limited. The purposes of the workshop are (1) to examine the theoretical basis for use of portfolios to enhance individual and collaborative learning, (2) to explore current uses, with focus on strengths and weaknesses, and (3) to formulate a research agenda that will enable the educational community to accelerate deployment of effectively designed online portfolios in support of individual and collaborative learning. We will use online portfolios as a means of experiencing and sharing ideas about the use of this technology for enhancing the individual and collaborative learning environment through structured dialog, collaborative work, and peer evaluation. The intended outcome is to create a special issue of a relevant journal on portfolios that will serve as a status report on use of portfolios and a launch point for future research and deployment of student portfolios.

INTENDED AUDIENCE

Faculty members from colleges and universities who have used, seek to use, or conduct research on use of electronic portfolios in the learning environment. Ideal workshop size is 30 participants representing a spectrum of teachers and researchers. Faculty members designing and delivering distance education courses are encouraged to participate.

ORGANIZATION

Online portfolios will be issued to each participant, and each participant will be assigned to an online small group for conducting collaborative work (using personal portfolios with features for supporting collaboration and group work). A calendar of activities will be provided that requires each participant to enter biographical information, to add to the knowledge base on online virtual portfolio (research on online virtual portfolios, outline of needs and opportunities, literature search on online portfolios, etc.), to participate in online threaded discussion on portfolio topics, and to participate in a group peer review of online submitted materials (submitted to workshop organizers). The face-to-face workshop at CSCL2002 will consist of a series of papers selected (with assistance of collaborative online peer review) from those submitted online and a panel discussion (panelists selected with assistance of collaborative online peer review) on use of electronic portfolios. Open discussion will also be scheduled.

REVIEW

Registered participants will be divided into small groups, each group being assigned a private group portfolio. Each group will be asked to review one or more papers submitted for possible presentation at the conference in January and for inclusion in the set of papers to be submitted for a special issue of a journal.

ORGANIZERS

Eugene S. Takle
gstakle@iastate.edu

Department of Geological and Atmospheric Sciences
Department of Agronomy
3010 Agronomy Hall
Iowa State University
Ames, IA 50011 USA
Voice: 1-515-294-9871
Fax: 1-515-294-2619

WORKSHOP CO-ORGANIZERS

Elsebeth K. Sorensen
eks@hum.auc.dk
Department of Communication
Aalborg University
Kroghstraede 3
DK-9220 Aalborg Oest, DENMARK
Voice: +45 9635 9077
Fax: +45 9815 9434

Daryl Herzmann
akrherz@iastate.edu
Department of Agronomy
3010 Agronomy Hall
Iowa State University
Ames, IA 50011 USA
voice: 1-515-294-2551
fax: 1-515-294-2619

Documenting Collaborative Interactions: Issues and Approaches

Sadhana Puntambekar, Rosemary Luckin

The aim of the workshop is to look at the different approaches used to document collaborative learning and inform the design of the next generation of CSCL tools. We will be looking into different ways to document collaborative interactions, factors that affect collaboration as well as their effect on learning outcomes, and the development of a community of learners.

PURPOSE

In recent years several approaches have been put forth to document interactions in collaborative environments. Methods of analysis have spanned across the quality, quantity and social as well as affective aspects of collaborative interactions. Approaches to document collaborative interactions have included analyses of thread lengths, interaction patterns, and time-based interactions as well as analyses of notes written and read over several collaborative sessions. Further, researchers have also studied collaborative dialogue and used videos to coordinate screen activity with dialogue.

Although these approaches have been extremely valuable, we are yet to understand many issues related to the nature of successful collaborative interactions and their effect on learning outcomes. Research has shown that collaborative interactions are influenced by several factors such as the composition of the pairs or groups, the nature of the task, the nature of the tool, and the culture of the classroom or environment in which CSCL tools have been used. In addition, the development of a community of learners has also been recognized as an outcome of successful collaborative interactions. If learning in a collaborative environment can indeed foster the development of a community of learners, we need to identify ways to document the emergence of such a community. This implies that not only do we need methods for documenting collaborative interactions, but we also need ways to understand the environment (e.g. the classroom) in which the CSCL tool was used. A better understanding of these issues is critical to assess the fruitfulness of collaborative learning and to inform the design of CSCL environments. This workshop will therefore provide an opportunity for researchers to discuss answers to questions such as

- What are the characteristics of successful collaborative interactions?
- How do students learn in a collaborative environment? What do we document in order to understand how they learn?
- What are the data gathering and analysis tools that can we use? Examples include thread lengths, log files, videos, dialogues, etc.
- What factors affect collaborative interactions and under what conditions?
- How can we document that collaborative interactions have helped create communities of learners?
- What defines a successful community of learners?
- The aim of the workshop is to look at the different approaches used to document collaborative interactions, factors that affect collaboration as well as their effect on learning outcomes, and the development of a community of learners. The results of the workshop will help in a more rigorous understanding of the ways to document collaborative learning and inform the design of the next generation of CSCL tools. Possible outcomes include an edited volume or a special issue of a journal, and a web site to continue the dialogue initiated in the workshop.

INTENDED AUDIENCE

The workshop is intended for researchers as well as practitioners who have or are developing or using collaborative environments and are exploring ways to document and analyze collaborative learning. We are interested in submissions from individuals who present 1. novel methods of documenting collaborative learning 2. data indicating how the method worked 3. implications for understanding collaboration and its effect on learning outcomes and 4. implications for design. We are especially interested in an interdisciplinary focus and encourage researchers from such fields as Cognitive Science, Educational Psychology, Artificial Intelligence and Human-Computer interaction to participate.

ORGANIZATION

Depending on the number of presenters, the workshop will be structured around key themes. Some themes that we are envisioning are 1. documenting the social aspects of collaborative interactions; 2. the number and patterns of the interactions; 3. the quality of interactions; 4. novel methods to understand collaboration such as the use of representations, etc. All papers will be categorized into the themes and the workshop will be structured around the themes. Within each theme, we will have interactive activities for participants to try different methods of analysis. For example, participants might watch videos of collaborative interactions and evaluate them in different ways, leading to a discussion of the methods and approaches. After presentations and activities in each theme, there will be reflection and discussion of the key issues raised. Finally, there will be an overall discussion of the issues raised, concluding with a summary of the implications for designers.

WORKSHOP ORGANIZERS

Sadhana Puntambekar
Assistant Professor,
Department of Educational Psychology
Neag School of Education
University of Connecticut
Storrs, CT 06279
Email: sadhana@uconnvm.uconn.edu

Rosemary Luckin
Lecturer,
School of Cognitive and Computing Sciences
University of Sussex
Falmer, Brighton BN1 9QH
UK.
Email: rosel@cogs.susx.ac.uk

Learning Environments for Inquiry Skills

Tom Murray, Wouter van Joolingen

Computer based learning environments have been designed with the intent of facilitating higher order thinking skills for some time, but recent research in cognition, learning theory, and instructional systems have begun to clarify the nature of these skills. Progress has been made in particular in the area of learning scientific inquiry skills---their component skills, the role of collaboration and knowledge sharing, and instructional methods that support them. This workshop will bring together researchers working on projects that involve both learning environments and scientific inquiry skills, to share current results and dialog about key issues at the research forefront.

CO-CHAIRS:

Tom Murray - tmurray@hampshire.edu

Wouter van Joolingen - Wouter@ilo.uva.nl

TUTORIAL PROGRAM

Using P2P e-Learning Technology to Turbocharge Learning Environments

Richard Yelle et al.

INSTRUCTORS

Richard Wilfred Yelle, Professor Product Design

Parsons School of Design At New School University

yeller@newschool.edu

Chuck Dornbush, Founder and CEO, dornbush@athenium.com

Lynn Heffron, Vice President Business Development, heffron@athenium.com

www.athenium.com

GOALS AND OBJECTIVES:

Education and commerce in the 21st century is very different from the industrial age and is characterized by rapid changes in student diversity and expectations, educational content, and in products, markets, and competitors. Educational content, problems and opportunities often are complex, and the expertise needed to address them may be distributed among several people. More and more teams perform most learning/work in order to aggregate the required talent, skills and experience. There may not be any acknowledged experts to learn from, but only a set of colleagues with varying talents and experiences.

The expert/student model of learning no longer adequately fits the needs of an increasing number of organizations and institutions. Much of what knowledge workers or students need to know at any time is already resident within the organization/institution. The challenge is how to harvest the knowledge assets, and then how to do something useful with them. A new approach to learning, which leverages the knowledge, collective skills and experience of all faculty or workers, is needed. This tutorial will provide a perspective on using Collaborative e-Learning Technology to address these learning needs in the new millennium.

TUTORIAL CONTENT

What is peer-to-peer learning? By peer-to-peer learning we mean any form of collaboration among three or more people with the explicit intent of fostering the learning or skill development of the participants. Peer-to-peer e-Learning extends that definition to embrace computer-mediated collaboration as the primary means of collaboration.P2P learning may complement other means of learning, or it may exist as a separate form of learning. Peer-to-peer learning has two principal attributes.

1.) The learners create much of the learning content.

2.) Peer-generated content is amplified through interaction and feedback from the learners.

Why is peer-to-peer learning important? The rapid changes in technologies, products, markets, and organizations makes new content delivery systems, continues training and learning a strategic imperative. The same factors also make it increasingly difficult for any central group of experts to stay abreast of all developments. The traditional top-down model of learning cannot keep pace and must be augmented or replaced with a more flexible, decentralized approach.

There is also strong evidence that P2P learning is more effective than expert-centered learning. We have known for many years that learning retention and skill development is strongly influenced by the degree of involvement of learners. The following graphic depicts a simplified view of learning retention as a function of the type of communication mode employed with the learner. While individual learning styles vary quite a bit, the general pattern represented by this graphic provides useful insight. Peer-to-peer learning leverages the learning pyramid by relying heavily on direct discussion, knowledge sharing, and teaching modes of communication. As P2P learners, we are all teachers, critics, and students at the same time. Performing in these multiple roles facilitates the learning process.

The TEAMThink approach to delivering effective P2P e-Learning

In this tutorial we will first demonstrate the TEAMThink (TT) application, and then have the attendees actively engage in using TT online, and finally, present 4 case studies for more detailed analysis. The four case studies will be presented by describing the collaborative course processes, illustrate the use of peer-to-peer collaboration technology, and examine the impact of peer-to-peer collaboration technologies on learning and the development of strategic partnerships.

Case Studies:

Parsons is a recognized leader in the teaching of design, and it's students and faculty members partner with industry to tackle business-constrained issues and technology applications. Our Mission: To shape the design agenda for the 21st century by bringing together design, technology and business to collaborate on innovations in technology, materials, process or teamwork. Cases: Part 1.) The Design and Marketing of French Luxury Products in the Digital Age: A unique collaborative effort between Parsons School of Design and Columbia Business School - focused on design and marketing. The Colbert Foundation, whose primary aim is to promote an exchange of business, design and management ideals, sponsors the course. 2.) Environmentally Conscious Re-design of a Cellular Telephone Housing: A distance Collaboration between the University of Michigan Colleges of Engineering and School of Art and Design, and Parsons School of Design 3.) Techno Culture, a Parsons Liberal Arts Senior Seminar. Part II: 4.) Duke University's Graduate School of Engineering uses the TEAMThink model to foster student in-depth critical thinking and analysis skills. Case: Wireless Technology Course.

Latent Semantic Analysis: Theory, Method and Application

Tom Landauer et al.

INSTRUCTORS

Tom Landauer, University of Colorado and Knowledge Analysis Technologies,

landauer@knowledge-technologies.com

Scott Dooley, Knowledge Analysis Technologies,

dooley@knowledge-technologies.com

OBJECTIVES

Latent Semantic Analysis (LSA) is a powerful tool for use in the support of learning in collaborative environments. We will provide participants with a basic understanding of LSA theory and methods and demonstrate applications of its use in support of collaboration and learning.

CONTENT

Latent Semantic Analysis (LSA) is a computational method for simulating the degree of similarity of meaning of words and passages of text (Landauer and Dumais, 1997; Landauer, Foltz and Laham, 1998.). The potential uses in Computer Supported Collaborative Learning environments include:

- recognizing which participants are and are not making on-topic contributions,
- relating the content of one person's verbal contributions to another's,
- providing meaning-based retrieval of notes and archival materials,
- automatically scoring and diagnosing essay tests,
- continuously and cumulatively assessing discussion contributions of individuals and the group as a whole.

In the first half of this tutorial, the underlying cognitive theory and computational basis of LSA will be described, then the manner in which it is applied. We will try to introduce the mathematics in a generally accessible way, while giving enough detail for those with knowledge of linear and matrix algebra to appreciate the techniques. LSA can be applied either through web-based user-level facilities maintained by the Institute of Cognitive Science at the University of Colorado, , through specific application packages offered commercially by Knowledge Analysis Technologies, , and others, in roll-your-own mode by obtaining patent and/or software licenses from Telcordia, or--in academic research--by re-implementation.

The second half of the tutorial will review and demonstrate several existing applications and engage attendees in discussion of new potential uses in CSCL. Some existing applications include prototypes of applications listed above, and some that are not in CSCL as such, but in closely related areas of distributed tools for information finding, assessment, and individualized interactive and dialog-based tutors.

About the Instructors

Tom Landauer is a professor of Psychology at the University of Colorado and President of Knowledge Analysis Technologies, LLC. Scott Dooley is a Senior Developer of educational technology and groupware at Knowledge Analysis Technologies.

Presentation

Lecture, demonstration and discussion. The demonstration will be interactive for participants who bring computers ready for network connectivity via DHCP.

SELECTED BIBLIOGRAPHY

Berry, M. W. (1992). "Large scale singular value computations." International Journal of Supercomputer Application 6(1): 13-49.

Berry, M. W., Dumais, S. T. and O'Brien, G. W. (1995). "Using linear algebra for intelligent information retrieval." SIAM: Review 37(4): 573-595.

Deerwester, S., Dumais, S. T., Furnas, G. W., Landauer, T. K. and Harshman, R. A. (1990). "Indexing By Latent Semantic Analysis." Journal of the American Society for Information Science 41(6): 391-407.

Kintsch, E., Steinhart, D., Stahl, G., Mathews, C., Lamb, R. and Group, L. R. (2000). "Developing summarization skills through the use of LSA-based feedback." Interactive Learning Environments 8: 87-109.

Landauer, T.K. (1998) "Learning and representing meaning: The Latent Semantic Analysis theory." Current directions in Psychological Science, 7, 161-164.

Landauer, T. K., & Dumais, S. T. (1996). "How come you know so much? From practical problem to theory." In D. Hermann, C. McEvoy, M. Johnson, & P. Hertel (Eds.), Memory in context. Hillsdale, N.J.: Lawrence Erlbaum Associates.

Landauer, T. K. & Dumais, S. T. (1997). "A solution to Plato's problem: The Latent Semantic Analysis theory of the acquisition, induction, and representation of knowledge." Psychological Review, 104, 11-140

Landauer, T. K., Laham, D. and Foltz, P. W. (2000). "Automated essay scoring." IEEE Intelligent Systems and Applications.

Landauer, T.K. and Psotka, J. (2000). "Simulating text understanding for educational applications with Latent Semantic Analysis: Introduction to LSA." Interactive Learning Environments,8(1),1-14.

Steinhart, D. (2000). Summary Street: An LSA-based Intelligent Tutoring System for Writing and Revising Summaries. Doctoral Dissertation, University of Colorado.

Scandinavian Perspectives on CSCL

Annita Fjuk et al.

INSTRUCTORS

Lone Dirckinck-Holmfeld (Professor), University of Aalborg (Denmark)

Annita Fjuk (Associate Professor), University of Oslo/ Telenor Research and Development (Norway)

Elsebeth Korsgaard Sorensen (Associate Professor), Aalborg University (Denmark)

Håkon Tolsby (M. Sci.), University of Aalborg (Denmark)

Barbara Wasson (Professor), University of Bergen (Norway)

BENEFITS

The tutorial focuses on the specific conditions that are manifested in distributed collaborative learning environments. These new environments designate new forms of learning where the distance is not only distance in space or time as in traditional distance education, but includes the mediation of learning activities by a variety of technological solutions. The new conditions are approached by discussing two Scandinavian traditions as powerful approaches for understanding and exploring a complexity that characterise many distributed collaborative learning environments. The traditions are found within academic systems development and the pedagogical philosophy of problem oriented project pedagogy. The traditions are both based on democratic ideals that emphasise participant involvement, participant control as well as the fact that that learning problems originates in the participant and is owned by the participant.

ORIGINS

The applications of the perspectives during several years of practice, design and development

FEATURES

What issues should be focused in designing for change and innovation with respect to new learning environments and based on a Scandinavian approach.

What challenges do processes such as giving explanations, arguing a position, or negotiating meaning, impose on distributed learning environments.

What do the discussed issues mean for CSCL research?

Audience

Designers, facilitators, researchers and developers of distributed learning environments. The focus of the tutorial is in the conceptual, pedagogical and organisational issues related to design of new and innovative learning environments.

PRESENTATION

Lectures and participants discussions

INSTRUCTOR BACKGROUND

Dr. Lone Dirckinck-Holmfeld is research professor at Humanistic Informatics at Aalborg University, Department of Communication. She is the coordinator of several research groups on distributed learning in Denmark and has co-authored several books and articles in this topic. Her main field of research is computer-supported (distance) collaborative learning (CSdCL), participatory design and implementation.

Dr. Annita Fjuk is considered as one of the gründers on netbased learning in Norway. Her research focus is on flexibility in terms of social interactions and collaboration patterns as well as in terms of the individual learner`s access to services and solutions .These problem areas are addressed through the use of social-cultural theories, with particular attention on activity theory.

Dr. Elsebeth Korsgaard Sorensen is one of the initiators behind the web-based MS in ICT and Learning, offered on the basis of collaboration between five Danish Universities. Her research comprises pedagogical/instructional design and implementation of technology in relation to design of distributed learning processes. The perspective of her research is found within the establishment of dialogue, reflection and collaboration.

Håkon Tolsby is a Ph.d student at Aalborg University. His research focus is on design and implementation of digital learning environments based on an experiential and social learning epistemology.

Dr. Barbara Wasson is Scientific Leader of InterMedia, University of Bergen, Norway a Professor in Information Science at the University of Bergen. Current research interests are focused on collaborative telelearning, sociocultural learning theories, research methodologies for studying virtual environments and pedagogical agents. She is conference chair for EuroCSCL 2003.

The Inquiry Page: A Collaboratory for Curricular Innovation

Bertram C. Bruce et al.

INSTRUCTORS

Bertram C. Bruce, Ann P. Bishop, Jennifer Robins (all in the Graduate School of Library and Information Science, University of Illinois at Urbana-Champaign, USA)

BENEFITS

Learn about participatory design by engaging in an examination of the Inquiry Page; learn how to use it and related tools to support teaching and learning in diverse communities--schools, universities, libraries, museums, workplaces, and community settings; participants will come away with Inquiry Units they can use in applications of interest to them.

ORIGINS

Based on development and implementation work the presenters have been doing over the last three years, and use of the Inquiry Page in diverse communities.

FEATURES

Developing a tool to support inquiry-based teaching and learning

Understanding local knowledge

Developing curricula through inquiry

Inquiry-based process for designing/evaluating computer-supported cooperative learning tools

Demos/critiques of units created in various K-12, university, community, or workplace learning settings

Participants explore the Inquiry Page; create an inquiry unit valuable in their own work

Presentation of inquiry units created by participants

Discussion/reflection on settings, use of the tools, fit

Discussion of tutorial as a design/evaluation process

Audience

Anyone with interests in curriculum development in K-12, university, community, or workplace settings, or interests in participatory design

PRESENTATION

Some formal presentation; active discussion; creation of web-based inquiry units; participation in the Inquiry Page design process

INSTRUCTOR BACKGROUND

Ann Bishop has extensive experience building community information systems and conducting user studies of digital libraries. She is widely known for her work to bridge the digital divide. Bertram Bruce has worked on a variety of educational resources to support student learning in science, mathematics, reading, and writing. He has published extensively on new literacies and community-based learning. Both Bishop and Bruce are on the faculty in Library and Information Science. Jennifer Robins is a PhD student in Library and Information Science studying collaboratories and information structures.

Teaching Computer Classes Using Mind Mapping Techniques

Belinda Moses

INSTRUCTOR

Belinda Moses, ABD

University of Phoenix

Bake College - Clinton Township, MI

Wayne County Community College

Family Empowerment Institute/Faith

Based Initiative - Technology Director

Detroit, Michigan

mosesm@ameritech.net

BENEFIT:

Participates will learn how to use the student's prior knowledge (experience) a long with images to teach computer skills.

ORIGIN:

Mind Mapping has been proven very effective in helping students retain a higher level of the material presented. It is a powerful technique that allows the learner to fully utilize brainpower by enhancing cortical and creative skills. It helps convert random thoughts generated through creativity into linear thoughts needed for communication. Mind Mapping uses color, images, and sounds to bring the learning process expressed in words to life. It is an effective graphics-based method of taking notes, brainstorming, and organizing thoughts that helps you relate and arrange random ideas into memorable tree-like diagrams. Unlike outlining methods, you are not constrained in your creative inclinations by requiring you to think sequentially.

IT HAS FOUR IMPORTANT CHARACTERISTICS:

(1) The subject is represented by a central image.

(2) The main themes of the subject radiate from the central image as main branches.

(3) Minor themes are linked to the main themes.

(4) All the branches are connected forming a nodal structure.

AUDIENCE:

Teachers/instructors at all academia levels.

FEATURE:

Participants will learn basic Mind Mapping techniques. They will develop simple lesson plans, activities, and projects to enhance students learning experience. Information will be evaluated and shared among participants.

PRESENTATION:

Workshop will be a hand on interactive workshop. Participants will leave with a portfolio of resources to immediately implement in the classrooms, along with a list of recommended reading, software and other resources.

BACKGROUND:

I have taken several Mind Mapping classes and for the past two years, I have done extensive research to perfect these skills. The result of my research has been incorporated into my Dissertation work (Ph.D. program in Education with a specialization Technology). I am interested in improving teaching techniques for all students but in particular, young children and senior citizen that require similar visual teaching styles. Computer Instructor at the University of Phoenix, Baker College and Wayne College Community College.

Installing and Using Collaborative Websites

Mark Guzdial et al.

INSTRUCTORS

Mark Guzdial, Jochen "Je77" Rick

College of Computing / GVU Center

Georgia Institute of Technology

Atlanta, Georgia 30332-0280

guzdial@cc.gatech.edu, jochen.rick@cc.gatech.edu

GOALS AND OBJECTIVES

CoWeb (short for Collaborative Web-site) is a simple freely-available hypermedia space that has been used in a variety of settings, including over 100 courses at Georgia Tech and dozens of institutions around the world. CoWeb is simple to use and flexible enough to be used for many activities; even non-technical teachers are inventing educational activities using the tool. CoWeb is easy to install on any common computer (MacOS, Windows, Linux, etc.). In this tutorial, we lead participants through installing and administering CoWeb on their laptop machine, and we lead participants through design and implementation of their own collaborative learning activities in the CoWeb. The presentation will include a tour of real classroom sites. By the end of the tutorial, participants will be able to administer CoWeb and know how to use CoWeb to support various activities.

TUTORIAL CONTENT

CoWeb is conceptually based on WikiWikiWeb (or Wiki) by Ward Cunningham (Leuf & Cunningham, 2001). Wiki is a web-site that invites all users to edit any page within the site and add new pages using only a common web browser; the text is edited in an HTML text area without special applets or plug-ins. Wiki is an unusual collaboration space in its total freedom, ease of access and use, and lack of structure. Wiki is inherently democratic–every user has exactly the same capabilities as any other user.

Like Wiki, CoWeb looks like a traditional web-site, except that every page has a set of buttons at the top that allow the user to do various things such as edit the page, (un)lock the page, or view the history of the page over time. Links between pages are created by referencing pages within the same site by name, e.g., *Page Name*. If a page with the given name doesn't already exist, a create link shows up next to the name upon save; clicking on this creates the new page.

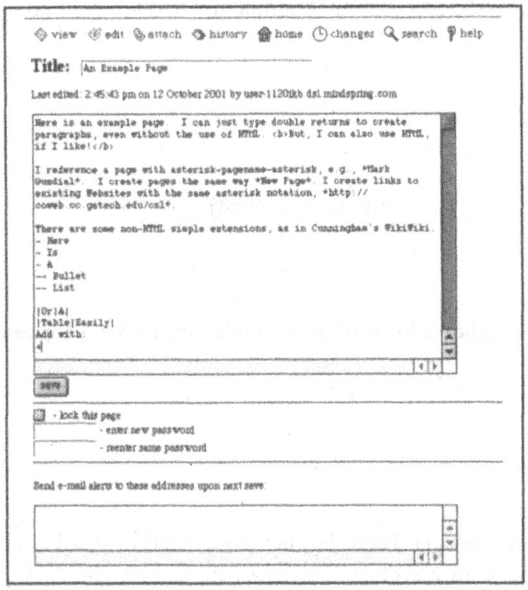

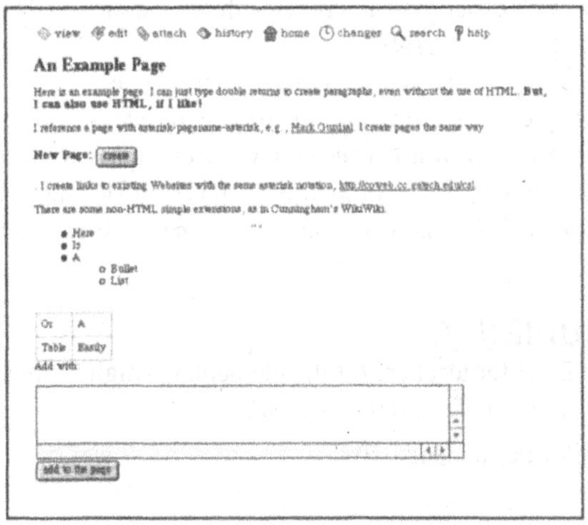

CoWeb (or Squeak Wiki, Swiki) has been tuned to meet the needs of students and teachers in higher education, through an open source development effort spawning over a dozen iterations in three years (Guzdial, Rick, & Kerimbaev, 2000). The most intriguing thing about CoWeb is the way that it has been adopted and adapted by teachers at Georgia Tech (Guzdial, Rick, & Kehoe, 2001b). We have catalogued over two dozen activities that have been invented by teachers for their own classrooms (Collaborative Software Lab (Guzdial, 2000). These range from fairly domain-specific activities (such as "close reading" in English composition courses where students collaboratively annotate a text) to general activities (such as design reviews, used in Architecture, Computer Science, and Media Design). The role of CoWeb is to provide a simple and open space that teachers can use in a flexible manner to create the kinds of a collaborative learning activities that they desire. It is an open source project which is being used at several institutions, from higher-ed (e.g., U. North Carolina at Chapel Hill) to business (Boeing and Disney).

>From a technical perspective, CoWeb is interesting because it is implemented in the cross-platform programming language, Squeak. This allows us to provide binary downloads of CoWeb for several different operating systems (Macintosh, Windows, and Linux) as well as instructions for how to get it set up on any of the other 22 platforms that Squeak runs on.

Over the last year, we have been carefully collecting cost data on CoWeb; we find that it is low-cost to install and maintain (Guzdial et al., 2001a). The time cost to the teacher is typically equivalent to one office hour period per week. The cost to maintain and administer the system is less than an hour per semester.

GOALS FOR THE TUTORIAL

Participants will understand how to use and administer a CoWeb.

Participants will learn to design and implement collaborative learning activities using the CoWeb.

Participants will review several activities in real use in classrooms, as sources for their own use ideas.

CONTENT OF THE TUTORIAL

- Our plan for the tutorial is to have three stages in a half-day setting.
- Participants will install CoWeb on their own laptop computer (pre-configured for DHCP, to connect to provided Internet drops.)
- We will review several of the CoWeb activities that have been used in classes, including:
- External (with experts) or internal (with peer students) design reviews, as used in Architecture and CS Human-Computer Interface classes.
- "Close-reading" activities, as used in Writing classes.
- Case library construction, used in Architecture and CS classes.
- Group progress portfolio, as used in CS video classes.
- Shared construction of multimedia, as in CS music classes.
- Participants will setup, design, and implement one of these activities (per individual interest).

INTENDED AUDIENCE

This tutorial is intended for teachers (at the elementary, high school, and higher-education levels) who are looking for tools and techniques to support collaborative learning.

Maximum Number of Participants: 20

INSTRUCTOR BACKGROUND

Mark Guzdial is an associate professor in the College of Computing at Georgia Tech. He developed the original Swiki based on Cunningham's WikiWikiWeb in Fall 1997 and has been using it in his classes since then. Jochen "Je77" Rick created the current version of the Swiki software and is developing it as part of his Ph.D. research in the College of Computing.

SELECTED BIBLIOGRAPHY

Collaborative Software Lab (Guzdial, K., Realff, Morley, Ludovice, et al.). (2000). A Catalog of CoWeb Uses (Georgia Tech GVU Center Technical Report GIT-GVU-00-19). Atlanta, Georgia: Georgia Tech GVU Center.

Guzdial, M., Ludovice, P., Realff, M., Morley, T., Carroll, K., & Ladak, A. (October, 2001a). The challenge of collaborative learning in engineering and math, Proceedings of IEEE/ASEE Frontiers in Education (FIE) 2001 Conference Reno, NV: IEEE.

Guzdial, M., J. Rick & C. Kehoe (2001). "Beyond adoption to invention: Teacher-created collaborative activities in higher education." Journal of the Learning Sciences, 10(3), (pp. 265-279).

Guzdial, M., Rick, J., & Kerimbaev, B. (2000). Recognizing and Supporting Roles in CSCW, Proceedings of CSCW'2000 (pp. 261-268).

Leuf, B., Cunningham, W. (2001). The Wiki Way: Quick Collaboration on the Web. Addison Wesley.

DOCTORAL CONSORTIUM PROGRAM

Scaffolding the Development of Critical Standards of Design with a Computer-Based Critique Tool

Denise Conanan
University of Michigan, USA

Understanding Algorithms through Shared Representations

Teresa Hübscher-Younger
Auburn University, USA

Disengaging from Intrinsically Transient Social Worlds: The Case of a Distance Learning Community

Michelle Kazmer
University of Illinois at Urbana-Champaign, USA

Elaborated Group Feedback in Virtual Learning Environments

Ulrike-Marie Krause
Ludwig-Maximilians-Universität Munchen, Germany

Examining the Range and Benefits of High School Students' Membership in a Political Community of Learners

Todd Reimer
Northwestern University, USA

Learning Environments for Learning Object-Oriented Thinking

Jakob Tholander
Stockholm University, Sweden

Collaborative and Multi-Paradigm Programming for Children

Tim Wright
University of Canterbury, New Zealand

INDEX OF AUTHORS

IDEA CATCHING PAGE